LEGACIES

FICTION · POETRY · DRAMA · NONFICTION

LEGACIES

FICTION • POETRY • DRAMA • NONFICTION

CARLEY REES BOGARAD
SUNY New Paltz

JAN ZLOTNIK SCHMIDT
SUNY New Paltz

Harcourt Brace College Publishers

Fort Worth   Philadelphia   San Diego
New York   Orlando   Austin   San Antonio
Toronto   Montreal   London   Sydney   Tokyo

Editor-in-Chief	Ted Buchholz
Senior Acquisitions Editor	Michael Rosenberg
Development Editor	Karl Yambert
Production Manager	Jane Tyndall Ponceti
Book Designer	Jim Dodson
Permissions Editor	Sheila Shutter
Project Editor	Nancy Marcus Land
Composition	Publications Development Co.

ISBN 0-15-500213-9

Library of Congress Card Number 94-076817

Literary credits begin on page 1366.

Printed in the United States of America

0 1 2 3   0 6 7   9 8 7 6 5 4

PREFACE

Legacies challenges students to enter the world of the late twentieth century, a culturally diverse place in which peoples' fates are crucially interconnected. It also introduces students to analysis of literature and to critical thinking. The readings—fiction, poetry, drama, and nonfiction—represent complex and exciting traditions from 500 B.C. to the final decade of the twentieth century. They include both global masterpieces and contemporary works from Lao-tzu to Rigoberta Menchú, from Sophocles to Rita Dove, from Seami to Ernest Hemingway. As a thematic exploration of the individual in social, political, and cultural contexts, *Legacies* engages us in intellectual inquiry and provides personal pleasures offered only in the arts, particularly in literature.

By reading and responding to fiction, poetry, drama, and nonfiction, we discover more about ourselves and others; we expand our thinking as conscious human beings. We develop moral imagination so that we can envision the views, experiences, and beliefs of others. Reading and writing about literature involves us in a process of critical analysis no different from the faculties we use in our everyday lives, but the process becomes directed, focused, and intensified. Interpretation of literary works encourages us to question, to observe keenly, to probe, and to critique—habits of mind central to liberal education.

Because we agree with Wittgenstein's statement that "the limits of [our] language mean the limits of [our] world," we have written and edited this textbook with excellence and expansiveness as guiding principles. We have divided the book into three major sections and extensive appendixes. In Part One, Acts of Interpretation, the first chapter defines types of critical thinking, then connects these ideas to the analysis of literature. Chapter 2 contains a discussion of critical reading and of reader response. Chapter 3 presents the process of writing about literary works and the forms of the essay. Part Two, the Thematic Anthology, features readings organized by genre around five themes that progress from exploration of the self to larger issues: Initiation and Identity, Family, Love, War and Injustice, and The Global Village. We hope that each work will open and illuminate the others in order to inspire dynamic and complex inquiry and insight in every reader. Part Three, Reading and Writing About the Genres, introduces forms and elements of the four genres of fiction, poetry, drama, and nonfiction. The appendixes include a research casebook of readings about D. H. Lawrence's "The Rocking-Horse Winner," a full description of the research process and MLA documentation, and an overview of contemporary approaches to literary criticism.

In each anthology chapter of Part Two, an introduction articulates provocative ideas about the theme, selections, and connections among the texts. We intend our comments not as definitive interpretations but as starting points for discussion. The Thematic Previews in the chapters combine works from different genres to offer various possibilities for analysis. Biographical headnotes precede all selections; and exploratory questions, suggestions for journal entries, and ideas for writing follow the texts. Extensive, process-oriented writing assignments appear at the end of each chapter.

Legacies engages students in the indivisible activities of reading and writing and enlarges their capacities to develop ideas and to appreciate the richness and depth of responding to literature through the following important features:

- **Emphasis on Critical Thinking and on the Reading and Writing Processes.** Chapters 1 to 3 present numerous examples of student responses, formal writing, and a profile of one student's writing process: cluster, outline, and initial and final drafts of an essay on Jamaica Kincaid's "Girl."

- **A Wide Variety of Readings from Traditional and Nontraditional Canons.** Selections represent the best of new voices and of classic writers. These diverse readings, which prompt us to consider issues of gender, ethnicity, class, and sexual orientation, embody our heritage, our literary legacies.

- **Juxtapositions of Readings within Themes.** In each chapter, readings are organized by genre, but they can also be studied by juxtaposing a number of works, according to subtopics of the major theme, gender, new and traditional voices, or regions of the world, to name only a few possibilities. This process leads naturally to contrastive analysis, to questioning, and to examination of issues from multiple perspectives.

- **Thematic Previews: Combining the Genres.** These sets of suggested readings from each genre introduce each anthology chapter and exemplify the principle of juxtaposition. In each preview, the poem may serve, for example, as motivation for discussion, the essay may provide a framework for analysis, and the fiction and/or drama may play against or complement each other. Together, these works can stimulate a dynamic process of critical inquiry.

- **Extensive Questions for Exploration of the Text.** These questions may be used for individual study, for guided class discussion, for lesson plans, or for collaborative (group) work. The questions begin with issues intrinsic to a given work (both textual and interpretive), then consider thematic connections with other works. Questions have been field-tested: the number and nature of the exploratory questions represent the suggestions of students in classes.

- **Variety of Writing Activities.** Possibilities for journal entries and ideas for writing follow each reading. They provide opportunities for personal reaction, creative expression, practice in various modes of exposition and argument, analysis and interpretation of literature, and consideration of formal elements of the genres.

- **Sample Student Essays.** Each anthology chapter offers a model student writing, illustrating a different form of the essay about literature, such as thematic analysis, comparison/contrast, critical analysis, explication, and argument.

- **Interesting and Ample Writing Assignments.** At the end of each anthology chapter, many of the assignments require a number of stages which encourage thorough exploration of topics; many others are traditional, and some contain directed research topics.

- **Extensive Treatment of the Forms and Features of Each Genre.** Chapters 9 to 12 feature comprehensive discussions of the genres with lively examples. The models of student writing in each chapter offer a wide range of approaches to all aspects of the reading and writing processes: reader response, explication, critical analysis—character, and evaluation.

- **Casebook of D. H. Lawrence's "The Rocking-Horse Winner" (Appendix A).** This casebook includes eight primary and secondary sources about the short story and the writer. The critics' views represent different approaches to literary criticism. We have provided ample selections for a documented essay about the story.

- **Research, MLA Documentation, and Student Essay with Editorial Comments (Appendix B).** This appendix introduces a complete study of the research process and documentation, all major forms of MLA citation, and an example of a student paper with comments. No handbook should be necessary for the research process.

- **Critical Theory (Appendix C).** *Legacies* presents a concise explanation of current approaches to literature and demonstrates these theories through multiple interpretations of Kate Chopin's "The Story of an Hour."

- **Extensive Definitions of Literary Terms.** Definitions for terms appear in the text as well as in the Glossary. Terms are printed in boldface type when they first appear in the text.

- **Comprehensive Instructor's Manual.** Our Instructor's Manual, based on materials tested and developed in the classroom, includes sample syllabi (with readings organized by theme or genre), answers to the "Explorations of the Text" for each selection, suggested further works and films to complement the readings in each chapter, an additional casebook organized around Luisa Valenzuela's short story "I'm Your Horse in the Night," lesson plans, and a brief bibliography of books helpful to teachers of writing.

Eduardo Galeano suggests that "one writes out of a need to communicate and to commune with others. . . . One assumes that literature transmits knowledge and affects the behavior and language of those who read, thus helping us to know ourselves better and to save ourselves collectively." We hope that this book will prompt readers to "communicate and to commune." In large measure, we have based this volume on what our students have told us that they want to "know." It reflects their choices of texts and presents examples of their thoughts and writing. It is their book, their legacy.

ACKNOWLEDGMENTS

We wish to thank everyone who contributed to *Legacies*. First, we thank our students for their cooperation and contributions to this project. For their valuable research and writing, we offer our gratitude to our collegues, Dorrit Berg, Kathleen Bienvenue, Sharon Kahn, Elizabeth Laskoski, Amanda Merritt, Michelle Morano, Fiona Paton, Candice Piaget, Martha Robinson, Ann Toner, and Kappa Waugh. For her editing, we want to note Sharon Kahn's special assistance in the development of this book. Harold A. Zlotnik edited the chapters on genre with great intelligence and clarity. For both of us, he has proved to be a wonderful mentor.

We also acknowledge colleagues, family, and friends who contributed their insights, suggestions, and proofreading skills: Barbara and Michael Adams, John Alphonso-Karkala, Catherine Banks, Kathleen and Gordon Bienvenue, Arthur Cash, Karen Chaffee, Pam Chergotis, Janet DeSimone, Mary Fakler, Joanne Ferreira, Mary Gordon, Richard Hathaway, Daniel Kempton, Eleanor H. Kuykendall, Carrie Landi, Elizabeth Megarr, Sandra Miller, Christina Nelson, Joan Perisse, Ann Marie Phillips, Deborah Roth, Marleigh Grayer Ryan, Philip Schmidt, Sheila Schwartz, Fran Seaholm, H. R. Stoneback, Sara Wenk, John Wiggins, Pam Wiggins, Margaret Winters, and Mae and Harold Zlotnik.

For their strong support of this project through grants sponsored by the Research Foundation at New Paltz, we thank President Alice Chandler, Vice

President William Wood Vasse, and Dean A. David Kline. In addition, we wish to acknowledge Maria Helena Price and Carol Schneider of the Association of American Colleges for their enthusiastic responses to this book.

For her work on all areas of *Legacies,* we want to recognize the untiring efforts of Pamela Wiggins. Without her, this volume could not have been written. For their advice, patience, and emotional support, we also want to thank Philip and Reed Schmidt and Mae and Harold Zlotnik.

We thank Marie Gabriel, Sandra Gildersleeve, and Claudia Johnston for word-processing and preparation of the manuscript. Sandra Gildersleeve deserves special recognition for her extraordinary dedication to the project.

We are grateful for the many productive suggestions and comments from the following reviewers, though, of course, any remaining shortcomings of the book are our responsibility alone: Martha Ackmann (Mount Holyoke College), Larry Beason (Eastern Washington University), Kathleen Bell (University of Central Florida), Marsha Bryant (University of Florida-Gainesville), Shireen Carroll (Davidson College), Robert Colbert (Louisiana State University-Shreveport), Pamela Collins (SUNY-Cobleskil), John L. Davis (University of Texas-Austin), James Dyer (Mohawk Valley Community College), Judith Funston (SUNY-Potsdam), Julia Hamilton (Inver Hills Community College), Alan Kaufman (Bergen Community College), Martha Kendall (San Jose City College), Elisabeth Leyson (Fullerton College), Meritt W. Stark, Jr. (Henderson State University), Harriett Williams (University of South Carolina-Columbia), and Gary Zacharias (Palomar College).

Above all, we want to acknowledge the value of collaboration; our work together has enriched our lives. We thank Michael Rosenberg, senior acquisitions editor at Harcourt Brace, for believing in the book and in our collaboration. We especially recognize his guidance and his assistance in shaping the text. We also owe much to the efforts of Jane Ponceti, Kathy Ferguson, Jim Dodson, Shana Lum, Tina Winslow, Van Strength, and Sheila Shutter. For their superb production of this manuscript, we offer our gratitude to Nancy Marcus Land, a project editor beyond our wildest dreams, and her staff at Publications Development Company. Karl Yambert has been an extraordinary developmental editor; our highest praise we reserve for him and for Michael.

To our families—Pam Wiggins, Leonard and Cynthia Bogarad, Catherine and Julie Banks, Philip and Reed Schmidt, Marilyn Zlotnik and Peter Hultberg, Mae and Harold Zlotnik—for their unending encouragement, we are deeply grateful. They have been our best readers. We dedicate this book to them and to our students.

BRIEF CONTENTS

CONTENTS

Part Three   Reading and Writing About the Genres

ALTERNATE CONTENTS

Poetry

Drama

LEGACIES

FICTION • POETRY • DRAMA • NONFICTION

Part One

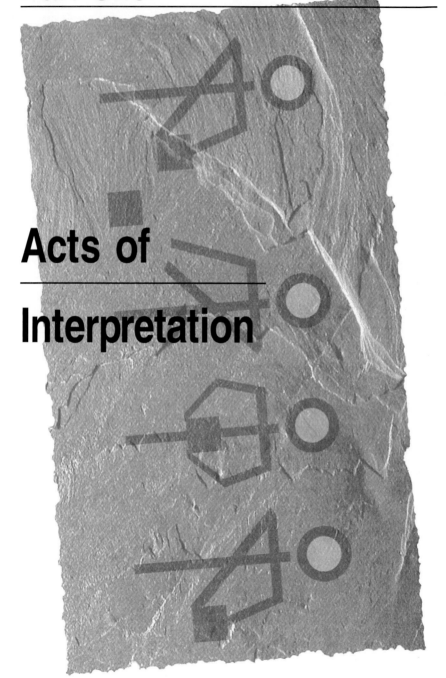

Acts of

Interpretation

CRITICAL THINKING AND CRITICAL ANALYSIS OF LITERATURE

The challenge for me has first been to see things as they are, whether a portrait, a city street, or a bouncing ball. In a word I have tried to be objective. What I mean by objectivity is not the objectivity of a machine, but of a sensible human being with the mystery of personal selection at the heart of it. The second challenge has been to impose order onto the things seen and to supply the visual context and the intellectual framework—that to me is the art of photography.

Berenice Abbott

Human beings constantly seek meaning from and impose meaning on experience. Berenice Abbott, a photographer, articulates the constructive acts of mind "at the heart of" human nature. Like Abbott, we observe, "see things as they are," absorb, and react. In our desire to comprehend, we "impose order onto . . . things"; and we establish meaning and "context," in other words, interpretations of our world. Only humans can think about their thinking; only humans can understand and reflect on their perceptions, feelings, events, ideas, languages, and questions. We consider critical thinking to be these capacities to "see," react, select, order, interpret, and create "intellectual framework[s]" and significance.

CRITICAL THINKING

The multiplicity of forms involved in critical thinking requires some definitions and explanations. One mode of critical thinking is emotional reaction. **Affective** (emotional) responses include *feeling, remembering,* and *associating* events and memories. We may believe that emotions have no place in thinking critically, but they continuously affect perception, observation, and our use of language. As we discover the influence of emotion on our reasoning processes and seek to elicit feelings from others, we become aware of their power and of our responsibility to use this type of reaction judiciously.

1

Memory, too, plays an important part in almost all forms of thinking as we seek and create meaning from the past to attempt to explain the present. A more complex activity occurs when we associate feelings or memories with current experiences, ideas, or events. The simple, pleasant memory of a first kiss, for example, may create wild anticipation of a lover's meeting when we associate our initial feelings with the desire to kiss again.

We also may distinguish between elementary and complex levels of thinking. Elementary forms are perception, observation, and simple inferences derived from these observations. *Perception* includes an awareness of objects and consciousness, direct knowledge of anything known through the senses. Perception involves three activities: selection of important sensations, organization of these sensations into a design, and interpretation of the meaning of the design. As we perceive, we speedily and automatically perform these three functions—often unaware of our actions. In order to think about our perceptions, we must become actively conscious of the meanings of the patterns that we create, and we must check the accuracy of our information. We must compare our perceptions with those of others and seek external methods of independent confirmation or proof of our interpretations.

Observation means taking notice and watching in order to give first-hand reports of data or events. This act, seemingly uncomplicated, requires accuracy, attentiveness, and clarity of mind. Observations—reports useful in science—must meet these criteria. We arrive at *simple inferences* from acts of observation. When we infer, we develop assumptions about our observations; and we discover implied patterns of meaning that have not been stated. We look beneath the surface to find hidden messages. Then we form *conclusions* about our inferences. In this process, we need to ask ourselves the following questions:

1. What is stated?
2. What exists beyond the surface level?
3. What information do we need to make inferences?
4. What is implied?
5. What are our biases?

Think again about the kiss and the anticipated meeting of the lover. Let us assume that he or she arrives late and seems inattentive, that the expected kiss becomes a light brush on the cheek. From these observations, we perceive a change in attitude. We may infer that desire has cooled or that the lover has reasons to be distracted.

More complex acts of critical thinking include forming complicated inferences and conclusions, interpreting, and classifying information. Many of the inferences and conclusions that we make are not simple. Much of our understanding of the world depends on our capacity to infer in a logical, intricate, and organized manner. Through complicated *inferential reasoning,* we develop abstractions, general ideas based on data, through which we order and comprehend experience, phenomena, and knowledge. We call this process, the creation of general ideas from particulars, *generalizing;* and we focus on properties shared by a group in order to derive **generalizations** that explain the properties. As we find patterns of meaning through these activities, we create *interpretations.* Returning to our example of the lover, we examine particulars—the late arrival, inattentiveness, the brush on the cheek—and we notice that the lover's desire to touch and talk has changed. We begin to infer and create a pattern of meaning. We compare these actions to other relationships and conclude that the lover may have become dissatisfied, that the first blush of love may be gone. We may even generalize about the inevitability of loss in love.

As an important activity in generalization, *classifying* is crucial in our efforts to organize and understand the world. **Classification** is the process by which we group things according to their similarities. Our capacity to discover similarity in difference (separate things are not alike) and to make groups by classes enables us to make sense of experience. We classify by properties and place objects, ideas, and events into categories according to these properties.

Analysis and *synthesis,* two other types of higher order reasoning, depend, to some degree, on classification. Analysis means to take things apart to understand them. We separate a process or situation into components and offer explanations of the relationship of the parts to the whole. We classify the separate pieces, identify and describe the organizing principles, and then ponder anew the relation of the parts to the whole. Unlike analysis, synthesis requires tying or joining things together, seeing them in relation to each other, and forming conclusions about these connections in order to gain further understanding. We connect experiences, ideas, concepts, belief systems, forms of knowledge, or events.

One other important process is *evaluation* and *judgment.* We not only experience the world, but we also assess our reactions, observations, and encounters. We critique phenomena and our experiences with others and with works of art. These exchanges may cause us to test our own beliefs and to alter our values. We may discard false impressions and biases; we then may formulate new attitudes and ideas. Through evaluation, we learn to question, to broaden our perspectives, and to discover and to create other intellectual frameworks.

In discussing these capacities for critical thinking, we have treated them as if they were separate processes. In actuality, we perform many of these functions simultaneously. As we observe, we conclude; as we categorize, we evaluate and judge—and our categories and judgments, in turn, shape our observations. Even though the acts of critical thinking are closely intertwined, to understand them more fully, we must discuss them separately.

How do these processes take shape in us? Let us analyze one moment after we get up in the morning. We open our eyes, gaze out the window, observe, and perceive a winter day. We decide that the color of the sky is gray-black and that we feel discouraged because it will be another cloudy, winter day. Or we may stay in bed and reminisce about the weather: last summer's picnics, a movie with a rainy scene, Gene Kelly in *Singing in the Rain,* a horror movie with a storm scene, or memories of a walk in a rain shower with a friend. Based on our observations of the sky, we may infer that the weather looks windy and chilly and then classify the day as another bleak mid-winter moment. We also may analyze—take the moment apart— to comprehend it more fully. We may assess the storm clouds, the gray sky, and the shade of light. We may observe the roof of a neighboring home to determine if it has rained or has snowed during the night. After examining this data, we conclude that rain or snow is imminent and that it would be best to wear jeans, a sweater, and to take a raincoat or an umbrella to work. We also may synthesize—make connections among this scene and other phenomena. The scene may remind us of a painting or a group of paintings, or we may imagine it as the opening of a certain kind of drama—with ominous beginnings. Finally, we may evaluate and assess. The day promises not to be spectacular or pleasing because our standards of judgment require a winter morning, crisp, clear, snowy—a dazzling blue sky and bright sun. The prospect of the day, then, surely will be judged disappointing. In an instant, we react to our environment, observe, feel, remember past experiences, think of images, infer from data, come to conclusions, generalize, analyze, synthesize, evaluate, and judge. Through these processes, we create meaning.

Critical Analysis of Literature

The acts by which we create meaning in daily life and the acts by which we read, write, and analyze literature and nonfiction are similar, although they take different forms. We perform the same meaning-making activities in our experiences and in our interactions with others as we do in our analyses of literary works. However, in critical analysis of literature, certain aspects of the thinking process are heightened and intensified—interpretation, judgment, and evaluation. We observe and ask ourselves about the effect of the words on the page. We consider the ideas that are implicit in the words. We read to interpret and to ask if the ideas are of value. We also evaluate the language. We may examine these words for evidence of a writer's bias and assumptions, and we draw conclusions about the writer's attitude toward his or her subject and his or her beliefs. We may compare the author's stance with our own beliefs. We may criticize, argue with, and debate the meanings and views of a text—accept or reject its ideas and embrace or disdain its author's point of view.

We may judge the language to determine effectiveness. If the text is an argument, we may ask if the writer is persuasive. If it is a descriptive piece, we may examine our involvement in the world of the reading. If it is a political speech, we may ask how the politician wants us to feel. We may wonder if we are being manipulated by the words of the speech and try to discover the slant of the speaker.

We may focus intensively on a study of language and explore the effects of words: the **denotations** (dictionary definitions) and **connotations** (associations) of the words; the author's tone (attitude) toward his or her subject; the structure (organization) of the work; style (detail, imagery, word choice); the use of evidence; the soundness of the writer's reasoning and logic. Finally, we may ask ourselves if the work seems effective and worthwhile. We may determine its merits according to our standards of judgment.

Let us examine part of a short essay, "Toys," by Roland Barthes and focus on his pattern of critical thinking. Barthes' process is mirrored in this work: reaction, observation, conclusion, and critical judgment.

Toys

1 French toys: one could not find a better illustration of the fact that the adult Frenchman sees the child as another self. All the toys one commonly sees are essentially a microcosm of the adult world; they are all reduced copies of human objects, as if in the eyes of the public the child was, all told, nothing but a smaller man, a homunculus to whom must be supplied objects of his own size.

2   Invented forms are very rare: a few sets of blocks, which appeal to the spirit of do-it-yourself, are the only ones which offer dynamic forms. As for the others, French toys *always mean something,* and this something is always entirely socialized, constituted by the myths or the techniques of modern adult life: the Army, Broadcasting, the Post Office, Medicine (miniature instrument-cases, operating theatres for dolls), School, Hair-Styling (driers for permanent-waving), the Air Force (Parachutists), Transport (trains, Citroëns, Vedettes, Vespas, petrol-stations), Science (Martian toys).

3   The fact that French toys *literally* prefigure the world of adult functions obviously cannot but prepare the child to accept them all, by constituting for him, even before he can think about it, the alibi of a Nature which has at all times created soldiers, postmen, and Vespas.

Barthes observes children playing with many toys, infers, finds patterns of meaning, and concludes that these objects are tools that indoctrinate children into the values of French culture and prepare them to be responsible adults. As a result of his analysis, Barthes critiques and evaluates this cultural phenomenon. He longs for toys like blocks, toys that engage children's imaginations and encourage creativity rather than objects that insure the preservation of the status quo.

How do we analyze this work? We may read Barthes' essay and react to the vision of toys and then compare Barthes' ideas with our observations of toys in North American culture or with our childhood memories of playthings; we may come to conclusions about the social meaning of toys.

We also may question or disagree with Barthes' interpretations. We may agree with his theory that playthings indoctrinate children into gender roles. We may work to discover the ideas behind Barthes' words. What is his view of French culture? Clearly he disapproves of strictly defined social roles. How does he view convention and conformity? We may want to learn more historical information about men's and women's roles in contemporary France. Or maybe we wish to question Barthes' attitudes toward capitalism. Behind the words—behind the choice of details—are judgments concerning material goods, replication of people's functions in a capitalist economy, and the perpetuation of a particular economic and social world. We may ask about Barthes' political bias and be prompted to study his biography. Does he value a society that produces "soldiers, postmen, and Vespas"?

Barthes' argument may impel us to consider our values and attitudes toward childhood roles, the games that children play ("house," "doctor," NBA Jam, "fireman," Barbie dolls), and social roles. We may examine North American society's gender or social roles and their relationships to children's play. We even may question our beliefs, attitudes, and views toward parenting. Our encounter with Barthes' essay stirs in us ideas that may move us beyond our initial responses to the work, may prompt us to evaluate our attitudes, beliefs, and values, and may spur us to form new conceptions of ourselves and our world. The process of critical analysis enlarges our capacities for abstract reasoning and leads us to analyze and often to change our behavior.

In addition, we may judge the language and prose style of the essay. We may find worthy its opening short phrase, "French toys," because it immediately captures our attention as readers. We may deem strong the image of toys as a "microcosm" and the idea that the child is a "homunculus" (a little man) because it suggests the ways in which childhood is a miniature adult world and not separate from adult experience. The contrasts in size emphasize the power of indoctrination since in the embryonic world of childhood the germs of dominant adult roles already are prevalent. The power of social conditioning is apparent in the images. We may continue to admire the essay and single out for praise the progression of topics and list of illustrations of the "socialized" roles of "modern adult life." We may find refreshing the compactness of the argument: the statement of problem in paragraph 1; the illustrations in paragraph 2; the statement of conclusion in paragraph 3. We may puzzle over and then praise the metaphor, "the alibi of . . . Nature," for its clever depiction of social conditioning as the excuse for a belief that gender roles are determined by "Nature."

One of the major ways, then, that we exercise critical thinking is interpretation of language: reading and analysis of written texts. What follows is a catalogue of students' comments that emerged from a class discussion of Theodore Roethke's "My Papa's Waltz." The teacher asked the students to react to the poem; she listed their responses in categories on the board; and then the class developed and expanded their comments. The exercise demonstrates both the simultaneity of the processes of critical thinking and critical analysis and the multifaceted and complex nature of the response to literature.

My Papa's Waltz

The whiskey on your breath
Could make a small boy dizzy;
But I hung on like death:
Such waltzing was not easy.

We romped until the pans
Slid from the kitchen shelf;
My mother's countenance
Could not unfrown itself.

The hand that held my wrist
Was battered on one knuckle;
At every step you missed
My right ear scraped a buckle.

You beat time on my head
With a palm caked hard by dirt,
Then waltzed me off to bed
Still clinging to your shirt.

■ Emotional Responses (Feelings)

I'm angry.

I feel the movement, but I also feel the father "beat[ing] time" on the boy's head.

I am glad that the boy loves his father, but he must experience mixed emotions.

I have mixed emotions about the situation.

I am sad that the mother is passive and angry.

I worry about the boy.

I do not like the father because he seems to be a bully.

I fear that the boy never quite recovered.

The end of the poem makes me feel relieved since the boy is "clinging" to his father's shirt and the father is waltzing him off to bed.

■ Associations with the Work (Memories)

The scene reminds me of moments as a child when I could feel my parents' rage.

It reminds me of child abuse cases.

And I remember a social worker saying that children will stay with abusive parents because the abusers are their only source of security.

I remember dancing with my father as a child and standing on his shoes. He was alcoholic like the father in the poem. The smell of whiskey was strong on his breath. The memory brings pleasure as well as regret.

■ Observations of Information

The basic facts: drunken father, a dance between father and child, an angry mother.

The scene is in the kitchen. The dance creates a mess—the pans fall down.

Father is a worker. He has "battered" knuckles and dirt under his palms.

The child is as tall as the father's belt buckle. The buckle is scraping the child.

The father carries the boy to bed.

The boy is "clinging."

The anger between the parents remains unresolved.

Title: "My Papa's Waltz"—It is the father's dance.

■ Inferences and Conclusions Drawn from the Information

"Such waltzing was not easy." Is it not easy because the boy is struggling to hold on, to cling to security? Or is it not easy to keep up with his father? Or is it not easy because the boy is afraid?

Father "beat time on [his] head." The "battered knuckles" mean that the father might work with his hands, might do manual labor. Is the father angry with his son? Is he happy dancing with his son? Is he deliberately hurting his son? Or is he carried away with the movement of the waltzing itself?

Is he too drunk to notice that he is wounding his child?

Is the dance a moment of closeness between father and son?

How much love is there?

What is the reason for the mother's anger? Does the division between mother and father come from alcohol? Or is the mother simply angry because they are dancing, causing a ruckus, and disturbing the order of her kitchen?

Title—The father is in a position of control.

■ Interpretations

A memory of a confusing moment between father and son.

There is abuse, but there also is love.

The son needs his father's love.

The father seems oblivious to the boy's pain.

The mother is passive and angry.

The poem poses a question: Does the father mean well?

Life is the waltz: this dance represents everyone's movements.

■ Evaluations and Judgments

Subtle and powerful evocation of a common experience—the parent and child dancing.

Spare and excellent choice of words ("We romped until the pans/Slid from the kitchen shelf. . .").

Impressive, but unobtrusive form and rhyme reinforce movement of the dance. The four line pattern and the three beat rhythm create a simulation of ¾ waltz time. The poem becomes a waltz.

Effective use of sound ("dizzy"; "knuckle"; "buckle").

An important theme made concrete by vivid details ("clinging to your shirt")—A child's desire to love and be loved by his parents.

As the students categorized their ideas about "My Papa's Waltz," they began to understand the various processes required by each mode of feeling and thinking. They realized that some kinds of reasoning demand more complicated responses than others. They identified initial emotions evoked by the waltzing in the poem more easily than inferences about the speaker and his parents. They concluded that evaluation of the meaning and judgments concerning the value of the themes involved knowledge of poetic form and understanding of certain complexities of language, abstract conceptualizations acquired and created by learning and by intricate processes of thinking. They reached some common agreements concerning the interpretation of Roethke's poem through examination of many levels of critical analysis, levels that finally led to assessment and a heightened appreciation of language.

In reading any text, we do not separate modes of feeling and of thinking; but we simultaneously engage in many critical acts of interpretation. We react, remember, associate, observe, infer from information, form conclusions, analyze, synthesize, evaluate, and judge. These processes constitute our desire and capacity to think and act in ways that fulfill our human potential. They constitute photographer Berenice Abbott's "mystery of personal selection at the heart" of human understanding.

THE READING PROCESS

Refugee Ship

like wet cornstarch
I slide past mi abuelita's[1] eyes
bible placed by her side
she removes her glasses
the pudding thickens

mama raised me with no language
I am an orphan to my spanish name
the words are foreign, stumbling on my tongue
I stare at my reflection in the mirror
brown skin, black hair

I feel I am a captive
aboard the refugee ship
a ship that will never dock
a ship that will never dock

Lorna Dee Cervantes

What are the connections between critical thinking and critical reading? Consider students' responses during a class discussion of Cervantes' "Refugee Ship" as an illustration of the relationship between these two processes. First the students reacted to the title and stated that the poem made them feel sad and that it invoked comparisons with the plight of the Vietnamese, with the predicament of other immigrant groups who came earlier to the United States, and with the tragedy of the Haitian and Chinese boat people. As they pondered the significance of the title in relation to the story of a grandmother and a granddaughter, they expressed feelings, discovered associations, and asked questions. They also gathered information from the poem and focused on understanding the grandmother's character through analyzing the objects associated with her, "glasses," "the bible," and her gesture of taking off her spectacles. Some descriptive details (the images of "cornstarch" and the

---

[1] *mi abuelita's* eyes: my grandmother's eyes.

"pudding [that] thickens") puzzled them. They wondered, "What is 'like wet cornstarch'?" "Who is the speaker?" "Why is she described as an 'orphan' and as a 'captive'?" They began by making observations; and then they discovered patterns of meaning: context and interpretation.

The students concluded that the grandmother and granddaughter exist in separate worlds, alienated from each other. The granddaughter, the speaker, cannot communicate with her grandmother because the latter cannot speak or understand English. The **persona** (the speaker in the poem) has learned "no language"; she has not learned Spanish; and, therefore, she finds herself with "words [that] are foreign, stumbling on [her] tongue," her Spanish heritage lost. The granddaughter yearns to know Spanish, to communicate with her grandmother, and to learn more about her people. As the students formed conclusions about the meaning of the work, they realized that the speaker feels as if she lives like a "captive" on a "refugee ship/a ship that will never dock." At this point, one student exclaimed, "Oh, the movement of the ship—anxiety—oh, never to be able to dock, to find stability, home, roots, never to be able to feel rooted"; and another reflected, "The repetition of the last line adds emphasis and sadness."

The class discussion dynamically progressed from observation to selection of details, to analysis, to interpretation, and to judgment. The students moved beyond their first impressions of the work and discovered multiple layers of meaning. They also evaluated and judged the work and realized that each word, phrase, and image evoked vivid and significant ideas. A deceptively simple poem became a compelling vision of loss of heritage and of language.

READER RESPONSE

The class discussion of the poem illustrates a complex process of thinking and reading. To be frank, not every reading experience becomes a full, rich, interpretation of a text. Many times we read simply to garner information, as when we survey road signs, food labels, or sets of instructions. We may read newspapers, letters, and textbooks in our college classes; and the main aim may be solely to summarize information. At other times, we may wish to read a book on a level approaching pure emotional response and appreciation. Often, while we read, our minds are wandering, not concentrating on the work. However, the process of critical reading that we wish to emphasize is one in which the reader is fully involved, responding on many levels of feeling and thinking. We do not simply scan words on a page; we form emotional reactions, gather information, construct patterns of meaning, analyze, interpret, and evaluate a work to determine its effectiveness and its worth.

Writing helps to develop the reading process and keeps it active and critical. The following are some procedures for reading and reacting to a text, called *reader response strategies,* all of which involve writing. These procedures include *glossing* and *annotating, brainstorming, listing, freewriting,* and *journal writing.*

Glossing and Annotating

Examine a series of reader responses written by students about Gloria Anzaldúa's poem, "horse," from her autobiography, *Borderlands: La Frontera— The New Mestiza.* You may react to this poem in many ways. Reading theorists suggest that you first preview the work by looking at the title and scan the poem to gain an overview of it. Then read the passage again to learn content and to write notes about your reactions to the text. This process is called *glossing* and *annotating.* When you gloss a work, you read it to understand content; and you take notes, called *annotations,* as you read. You may make comments in the margins, underline the title and key words, and record reactions or questions. You create a map of the reading so that you know its structure and key points. You also discover your own questions, reactions, and initial responses. After you have completed your marginal annotations, you might make *end comments* that include the key ideas and describe the impact of the work on you. Analyze this annotation and end comment for "horse":

Why the title?
Why small letters?

horse

(para la gente de Hargill, Texas [1])

Is this a true story? What does the dedication mean?

Horse is free, powerful.

Great horse running in the fields
come thundering toward
the outstretched hands
nostrils flaring at the corn
only it was knives in the hidden hands
can a horse smell tempered steel? *✱ Shift to death and destruction*

Look at ing verbs : power — action

Anoche [2] some kids cut up a horse
it was night and the pueblo [3] slept
the Mexicans mutter among themselves:
they hobbled the two front legs
the two hind legs, kids aged sixteen
but they're gringos
and the sheriff won't do a thing
he's just say boys will be boys
just following their instincts.

Contrast Spanish words vs. anglos Spanish gringo Mexican World

Key: hobbled crippled horse

Narrative form Build up of story

Horse — Soul of people ← But it's the mind that kills
the animal the mexicanos murmur
killing it would have been a mercy
black horse running in the dark

---

[1] *para la gente de Hargill, Texas:* for the people of Hargill, Texas.
[2] Anoche: last night.
[3] pueblo: town or village.

[Handwritten annotation, left]: Horse—symbol of Mexican identity

Mexican people?

came thundering toward
the outstretched hands
nostrils flaring at the smell
only it was knives in the hidden hands
did it pray all night for morning?

[Handwritten, right]: } Repetition—Contrast Power of horse vs. crippling

It was the owner came running
30.30 in his hand
put the caballo[4] out of its pain
the Chicanos shake their heads
turn away some rich father
fished out his wallet
held out the folds of green
as if green could staunch red
pools dripping from the ribbons
on the horse's flanks
could cast up testicles
grow back the ears on the horse's head
no ears of corn but sheaths
hiding blades of steel
earth drinking blood sun rusting it
in that small Texas town
the mexicanos shuffle their feet
shut their faces stare at the ground.

[Handwritten, right]: A Mexican must put horse out of pain. Mexican people go home to die.

[Handwritten, left]: Strong images of blood. Graphic. Is the horse castrated?

What does the corn symbolize?

[Handwritten, right]: Boys "get off." Money is power.

Corn—symbol of sustenance, replaced by knives, death. Oppositions.

Dead horse neighing in the night
come thundering toward the open faces
hooves iron-shod hurling lightning
Repetition of color
only it is red red in the moonlight
in their sleep the gringos cry out
the mexicanos mumble if you're Mexican
you are born old.

[Handwritten]: Why are hooves hurling lightning? Is it anger at racism?

Gringos cry out—why?

Cycle of racism?

[Handwritten]: Key lines: "mind that kills"/..."if you're Mexican you are born old."

End Comment: Does this poem use a true story of boys crippling and mutilating a horse to suggest the pain and suffering of Mexicans in Texas facing prejudice and racism?

Brainstorming

Another notetaking process is *brainstorming,* a process in which you write down ideas and comments in any order without attention to sequence, logic, or sentence structure. Register as many of your reactions as you can as your mind "storms" through a work. Jot single words or phrases without worrying

[4] caballo: horse

about creating coherent, grammatical sentences and without worrying about organization and development. This technique allows you to sketch the range of your responses; later you can select certain ideas to compose your essay. Examine Mark Greenberg's brainstorming exercise for "horse":

Who is the "great horse"? Symbol?

Who is the speaker?

Who has the knives?

Why are they hidden?

A story breaks the silence of night. They "cut up a horse."

The horse is hobbled—gruesome like Stephen King's *Misery*.

Distinction between Mexicans and Gringos. Revolting.

Why did they do it?

The sheriff is hateful.

How can he use such lame excuses—"boys will be boys?" I'm a man, and I would never participate in such a terrible act.

These men are pigs.

Why does the father cover for the son? My dad would kill me.

"The red/pools dripping from the ribbons"

Strong images—sad, martyred horse.

The dead horse can thunder, can hurl lightning.

Is this the poet's retelling of the story? Autobiographical?

The horse, in many images, has many meanings.

Social tensions—inequalities between gringos and Mexicans.

I hate this poem's cruelty.

Finally something about race relations.

A true story?

In his exercise, Greenberg focuses on the events of the poem, on the cruelty, and on his reactions to the sheriff and to the father who excuses the barbaric actions of the "boys." His responses direct Greenberg to the beginning of an interpretation: a poem about "inequalities between gringos and Mexicans" and "race relations."

Listing

A more focused form of brainstorming is *listing*, making lists of related ideas that may form topics and subtopics, becoming the kernel of an outline for an essay. The ideas that you categorize may come directly from your reading notes, or they may be borrowed from your brainstorming notes. Here is Greenberg's list, developed from his notes.

```
Main Idea:    Inequalities between Gringos and Mexicans.
Subtopics:    Symbols of the hobbled horse = Mexicans, and the
              knives symbolize the power of the Gringos.

              Sheriff and the father vs. the silence of the
              Mexicans.

              The father and money vs. the "red/pools
              dripping. . ."

              Retribution—"dead horse" and "lightning." What
              do they mean? Is there retribution?

              Why are the Mexicans "born old"?
```

Note the difference between Greenberg's initial brainstorming and the concentrated attention in the list to the main idea that he wants to pursue—inequality—and his focus on aspects of the poem that support his view (the symbols of the hobbled horse and knives, the behavior of the sheriff and Mexicans, for example). He also begins to expand his understanding of the meaning of the work through exploring questions of retribution.

Freewriting

Another method to express your responses, reactions, questions, associations, and analysis of the work is to freewrite immediately after you finish reading. *Freewriting* is a process in which you give yourself a certain amount of time, say, five minutes, to compose sentences without stopping and without censoring your thoughts. Just as with brainstorming, write without stopping, without worrying, and without rereading—just keep going. Do not worry about grammar, spelling, punctuation, or meaning. Freewriting is a way to unleash ideas, to discover your own responses and ideas. It is a way to bypass the part of the writer's self who is the editor and critic, that part of the self that blocks and censors the process of discovery. Often it is helpful not only to freewrite immediately after a first reading, but also to freewrite after several readings. You can compose a first sample, then isolate one idea from that work, and draft another version based on that idea. This second activity is called *focused freewriting*. You may create a series of freewritings that prompt you to discover your full reactions and to develop your thoughts into an essay.

Here are two examples of freewriting about "horse":

horse
Frances Gonzalez

> The poem presents a powerful set of contrasts between the soul of the Mexican people and what happens to people when there is racism. The horse is powerful, black, free. The "thundering" gives a feeling of strength and force. Then the horse is "hobbled"; racism cripples. The black horse "running" "thundering" is contrasted with the impotence of the powerlessness of the Mexicans who "mumble" "shake their

heads" "shuffle" "stare at the ground" and "mumble." They seem
weak, yet there is some hope. For the "dead horse" in the night
"comes thundering" "hurling lightning"—that "lightning" is
"red red." Does that mean that the Mexicans will rebel against
injustice—that eventually justice will be done? Is the poet
"hurling lightning" hoping to cry out—hoping her words will be
heard that people will learn and speak "from the mind" in a
different way? Not a way that kills?

horse
Julie Miller

I love the feeling of freedom at the beginning of the
poem. There are such powerful images of the horse—running,
"thundering"—"nostrils flaring." The horse is powerful and
alive—then I knew danger was coming in the image of the
knives. Why did the boys cut up the horse? Why would anyone do
anything that senseless? I thought that it was so brutal and
cruel that the horse was mutilated. It was hard to read. What
did the horse symbolize? Did it symbolize the Mexicans? The
"gringos" just think nothing of cutting up the horse. In the
same way the white world in Texas is stopping Mexicans from
having opportunities. The poem is asking people to feel the
way the Mexicans are treated unfairly. The way they are being
oppressed. The white world wins—The "rich father" pays off
the owner. The boys aren't punished. The gringos have power.
I understand the lines "if you're Mexican/you are born old."
You are born with the knowledge of prejudice. This poem makes
a powerful plea for understanding injustice.

Journal Writing

You may chart your reading responses by keeping a journal: an informal
record of your thoughts and impressions. Your instructor already may have
asked you to write a personal journal. A *reader response journal* provides an
opportunity for you to write informally about the works that you read and
encourages an expansion of the process of personal writing. The methods
previously discussed are appropriate for a reader response journal in which
you may include glosses and annotations (if you include the works), brainstorming and notes, freewrites, and responses to texts. In your reader response journal, you may write significant ideas and quotations. You may
focus on any one of the following subjects:

Explication, analyses (explanations of the works)

Personal response (feelings-reactions to the works)

Likes/dislikes

Associations with other characters, other works, other readings,
   themes, issues, current events, materials in other classes

Associations with events in your life

Responses to character

Responses to key events

Responses to key passages

Responses to issues presented (social, political)

Judgments of character

Arguments with the writer, with key ideas, with characters' views

Arguments with positions presented in class discussion

Creative Writing (stories, poems, plays)

Imitations of style

Again, as in freewriting, you need not worry about grammar, punctuation, spelling, or logical presentation of subject matter. Follow your own responses, ideas, and questions; and let them take over. A journal entry, however, may be more developed and more structured than a freewrite. You may be asked to revise your reactions as developed paragraphs. Your journal may become the source of ideas for essays. In your journal, you may have a record not only of your reading responses, but also of your emotional and intellectual development.

In this entry about "horse," Mark Greenberg summarizes information, reacts to descriptive language, begins to respond to details in the poem, and ends with his feelings about the message of the work.

horse

    The black horse "thundered" toward the boys because they
    beckoned it. How could they summon a "great horse," the
    Mexican, only to cut it to pieces with knives, knives hidden
    in their hands? They tortured the animal because they
    believed that they had a right to do so. The "red red" blood,
    the flaying, excited them. They expected their fathers to
    pay for their cruelty and the owner of the horse to kill it—to
    finish their game. They exercised rights which they believed
    came with the color of their skin, with their social and
    economic positions. Little did they know that the dark horse
    would invade their dreams and make them "cry out," the dead
    horse—"red red"—"hurling lightning" through their dreams
    forever.

Another method of becoming an active reader is to keep a *double-entry notebook,* a form of journal writing adapted from theorist Ann Berthoff, who contends that writing and reading processes involve us in continually "interpreting our interpretations." Berthoff suggests that readers sometimes recognize only one level of reaction to a text—summary of main information—and neglect other levels of thinking provoked by the words: reactions, associations, questionings, analysis, synthesis, and theorizing. The double-entry notebook, or *dialectical notebook* as Berthoff calls it, prompts readers to be aware of all acts of interpretation and creates what Berthoff calls "the continuing audit of meaning." The journal entries provide readers with records of their thinking about their own thinking.

For a double-entry notebook, we recommend that you write on the left-hand page of a notebook the facts, key points, and main information from a work. On the right-hand page, write all of your other responses, feelings, associations, questions, comparisons with other ideas, and interpretations. The notes need to be recorded as the reading takes place so that you capture your mind in action. Alternate from the left-hand page to the right-hand page. Keep writing back and forth from fact to reaction, analysis, questions, and comments. The double-entry notebook results in a more complete response to a work. You are, therefore, much better prepared to write an essay about the text.

Examine the beginning and the conclusion of Mark Greenberg's double-entry notebook concerning "horse":

horse
Gloria Anzaldúa

Title "horse"	Symbolic. Why no caps?
para la gente de Hargill	I don't know Spanish, but I can guess that the words mean—"For the people of Hargill." Why does she dedicate the poem? Is it a true story?

Great horse
    running
    thundering
    nostrils flaring
	The horse is powerful, beautiful, expectant. Progressives add power and action. Good parallel constructions.

Knives in hidden hands	Why offer corn and hide knives? Who?
Question about smelling steel	Rhetorical? Good sounds. Does steel have a smell?
"Anoche"	"Night"? "Last night"? "The night before"? "At night"?
The Mexicans slept, and boys cut up a horse	The straight story. Incredible cruelty. A narrative poem.
The Mexicans "mutter"	They cannot protest aloud.

The "gringos" hobbled the legs	How did they conceive of such cruelty? The horse is like the Mexicans—hobbled.
Sheriff "boys will be boys" following instincts	The law does not apply to gringos. What is wrong with us? This racism is blatant.
It's the mind that kills the animal	This statement is like a thesis sentence. It clearly emphasizes the situation of the Mexicans.
Mexicans "murmur"	Again, they cannot speak loudly.
Killing would have been mercy	These boys feel no sadness, have no mercy. The suffering seems unbearable. The writer must want me to feel this pain.

Repetition of images and event
    black horse thundering
    outstretched hands
    flaring nostrils
    corn–knives
	Now that I know about the knives, the repetition is incredibly effective. The horse represents everything and everyone who was ever destroyed by promises of kindness and who was nurtured only to be conquered, tortured, or killed. This poem is difficult to read, to face, and to accept. The horse symbolizes the Mexicans.

*   *   *   *   *

Dead horse neighing in night
    thundering hooves
    "iron-shod"
    hurling lightning
	Paradox—unravels in dreams Retribution for the knives.

"red red in moonlight"	The horse has turned red, transformation. Blood, anger, revenge?
"gringos" "cry out"	The horse enters their dreams; they are not

| | absolved; they have not triumphed. They have received a life sentence of nightmares. |
| The Mexicanos "mumble" "If you're Mexican/you are born old." | They do not speak. They are not empowered by the horse which hurls lightning. They are born old in a corrupt and oppressive environment. I want racism to disappear. I want a world which includes everyone. I want it now. |

Note the writer's questions, analysis of the portrait and the symbolism of the horse, and inferences about the knife and the central action of the poem. Notice also the judgments about the boy's behavior and about the effectiveness of the verbs and images. The double-entry exercise prompted the writer to engage in all aspects of critical thinking and analysis.

Critical analysis requires your active involvement in the process. These forms of reader response—glossing, annotating, brainstorming, listing, freewriting, journal writing, and keeping a double-entry notebook—will help you to become a more involved reader and lead to richer, fuller, more complex interpretations and judgments of literary works.

Some Final Considerations about the Reading Process

These methods of reader response enable us to discover ideas and to unpeel the layers of our reactions to a work. They also validate our approaches to literature. They remind us that the reading process is both objective and subjective—objective, because we interpret verifiable texts; subjective, because we are unique in our reactions to those texts. We create meanings as a result of our own perspectives, backgrounds, cultural contexts, and values. The process of reading is interactive. The writer, who has a particular perspective, personality, and background and who is part of a particular culture at a specific time in history, creates a work and invests it with a set of meanings. The reader, who, likewise, is a product of individual traits and cultural influences at a particular point in history, brings ideas and values to the work and derives meaning from the work. The text acts on the reader; the reader creates the text.

Certain aspects of literature, however, may be more widely comprehended. *Hamlet's famous soliloquy* generally may be understood as an exploration of questions concerning suicide. "Do Not Go Gentle Into That Good

Night" by Dylan Thomas generally will be considered a meditation on mortality. Yet each period's writers, each culture's writers, reinterpret these objective judgments, guided by emotional, personal, and social concerns. Each literary work, then, represents both a moment in history and in culture and a moment in an individual reader's and writer's life.

Would Harriet Beecher Stowe have written her antislavery novel, *Uncle Tom's Cabin,* if she had not been the daughter of an abolitionist minister, if she had not been driven by moral outrage and financial need, if she had not known the patterns of slave narratives, if she had not herself seen a place where runaway slaves had crossed the Ohio River to freedom? In each century, readers interpret Stowe's fiction differently. During her lifetime, readers in New England were moved by her novel to struggle to abolish slavery; her book was a bestseller. Some contemporary readers criticize her sentimentality and her depiction of the black slave.

Interpretations will vary, but some analyses of a work seem more valid than others. To verify our interpretations, we return continually to the work as the primary source, and we share our views with others in a community of readers in order to discuss and to compare ideas. In dialogue with others, we may critique; and we may change our ideas and impressions. We may agree with an interpretation which differs from our original conclusion. We can enlarge our understanding of a work as we engage in the cyclic activities required by thinking, reading, and writing. Through these processes, which are *recursive,* to which we continuously return, we develop new perspectives on a work. For example, we may reread "Refugee Ship" and suddenly decide to study the poem from the point of view of the grandmother who cannot understand her granddaughter. The "glasses," the "bible," and the "pudding" assume new connotations as we shift attention from the speaker to the situation of another character in the work. Like the students who discovered many patterns of meaning in Cervantes' "Refugee Ship," we recognize that critical reading activities lead to a more comprehensive understanding of literature.

THE WRITING PROCESS

When you approach the task of writing about literature, you may worry that you will not understand the text, that you will miss its hidden messages, and that you will not give the responses the instructor expects. You might believe that you have nothing to say. Such anxieties are natural—and groundless. Keep in mind that writing essays about literature evolves from the processes of critical thinking and reader response described in Chapters 1 and 2. These multifaceted activities provide no right or wrong answers.

You will not be asked to write compositions that pose correct answers, although you will be expected to provide thoughtful interpretations supported by careful reading of a work. As you learn to trust your own thinking, you also will learn to trust your own acts of interpretation. Remember that you have valuable insights to contribute and that you will have opportunities to question, to test ideas with your peers and instructor, and to construct more developed interpretations that confirm, deny, or expand your initial views of a work.

INTERRELATED STAGES OF WRITING

Writing essays about literature follows directly from procedures for reader response. You should realize, however, that an essay is not composed in a short burst of reader reaction or in moments of brilliant creative insights. Rather, the best essays result from many, many hours of thinking; and they take shape on paper in interrelated stages that include the following:

1. **Prewriting:** Discovering and planning ideas for writing.
2. **Shaping:** Organizing, outlining, and structuring ideas with an audience in mind.
3. **Drafting:** Composing and concentrating on organization, development, and fluency.
4. **Revising and Editing:** Sharpening wording, sentence structure, and style; rearranging, deleting, and clarifying; checking for sentence variety and correct usage.
5. **Proofreading:** Correcting grammar, spelling, and punctuation.

These stages do not always occur in this sequential order; they vary from person to person and from writing task to writing task. Some people draft, edit, and proofread as they work. Others quickly write a first draft and check spelling, grammar, and punctuation later. Different writing situations dictate different processes: a laboratory report, a research paper, a meditative essay, a journal, and a research paper all require distinct approaches to writing. Whatever your task, you will probably engage in many of these activities before you submit the final version of your essay. Consider each of these stages in detail.

Prewriting

Prewriting, the first stage of the process, takes place even before beginning a first draft and involves finding ideas for composing. As you prewrite, you discover subject matter, approach, and **point of view** (attitude to the subject matter). Various prewriting strategies include these techniques—annotating, brainstorming, taking notes, listing, freewriting, clustering, mapping, and journal writing—and talking with others. You also will select the form of your essay: think about the requirements of your assignment (page length and designated rhetorical mode—exposition, argument, research—for example). Then consider the purpose of your assignment, your main goal in writing. Some central purposes for writing are the following: to express yourself; to inform; to argue; or to create a literary work. You will begin to define your audience. In writing about literary subjects, you may assume that your audience is your instructor and your classmates—people who are familiar with the works that you discuss. Your instructor may designate such different audiences for your material as the campus newspaper or some group interested in the subject. Considerations of point of view, purpose, and audience constitute the **rhetorical situation** of a writing.

Shaping

The second stage of the writing process involves clear definition of focus, point of view, tone, tentative thesis, main idea, and topics for discussion. In terms of point of view and tone, you need to decide how you want your essay to sound to the reader. Will you write formally or informally? Will you sound sympathetic, involved, or angry? Will you be lyrical, meditative, or persuasive? These decisions fall into place as you determine your thesis, topics, method of organization, and relationship to audience. At this point, you assess your audience, determine the direction of thesis and topics, and develop and shape supporting evidence with your audience in mind. Then you map ideas, plan your writing, and create informal or formal outlines.

Drafting

The third stage of the writing process is drafting. In creating versions of essays, you still consider not only purpose, requirements of the assignment, and audience, but also development and organization. You may recast your thesis, alter points, delete and add supporting information, and sharpen language.

Revising and Editing

The fourth stage of the writing process involves revising and editing your essay. Consider your relationship with your audience, and ask yourself if you have organized and developed points with a particular audience in mind. Ask yourself if your tone and point of view are appropriate, if they are likely to interest your readers, and if they are convincing and strong. Examine your introduction to determine if it will capture your readers' attention and establish your purpose and thesis. Evaluate your conclusion and decide if it conveys the proper emphasis. Rewriting sometimes necessitates a reconceptualization of ideas and clarification of points—perhaps, even rethinking the entire piece—but it also involves fine tuning through editing, through changes in word choice, and through small alterations of order and structure.

Proofreading

Proofreading is the final stage of the writing process. Check your final draft for grammatical, punctuation, spelling, and typographical errors. For example, if you have trouble with sentence fragments, review sentence structure. If you tend to confuse "it's" and "its," reread your paper with this problem in mind. Examine the manuscript to assure that it still follows the original requirements of the assignment.

Summary

There are as many composing processes as there are students and writing situations. You need to work through the process in *your* own way; the omission of the stages of composing can lead to weaknesses in your final draft. For example, if you do not spend enough time planning your writing, your essay may be disorganized and unconvincing. If you do not spend enough time prewriting and exploring ideas, you may submit a final draft that is lifeless and undeveloped. If you do not spend enough time editing and proofreading, you may create a work so riddled with distracting, grammatical errors and spelling mistakes that your essay will fail to convince your readers of the merit of your ideas. Each stage of the writing process is necessary to the development of a strong essay.

TYPES OF WRITERS

If you find that your writing process does not work, it may help if you become more aware of the kind of writer whose methods characterize your style. Once you have recognized your own approach, you may be able to identify the aspects that do not work and revise them. If you have models for alternatives, you may feel free to experiment and to devise new strategies that will be successful for you. From our discussions about the writing process with many students, we have compiled these general portraits of four kinds of writers:

1. *The Breakneck Writer.* This writer fears losing ideas and, therefore, writes a first draft at "breakneck" speed, without stopping to assess ideas or to check organization, spelling, or grammar. Once the first draft is written, the writer reviews the work and begins to develop ideas within paragraphs and to shape an introduction and a conclusion. The next phase is the development of a thesis and addition of evidence to support the central ideas. The breakneck writer works through several versions and focuses first on drafting, then on the organization and development of ideas, and finally on grammar and style.

2. *The Methodical Writer.* This writer moves slowly through a draft from a carefully developed outline. Each paragraph and each sentence are closely assessed for development of a main idea, use of evidence, effective style, and correct grammar. For the methodical writer, the outline and first draft often suffice as precursors to a final draft.

3. *The Skeletal Writer.* This writer composes a sketchy first draft to create the skeleton of the essay—the main ideas, topics, and subtopics. The writer then reviews the draft and assesses its presentation of ideas, its organization, its logic, and its argument. In successive versions, the writer adds evidence to support points and also progresses from concerns of organization to some assessment of style, wording, and grammar. The skeletal writer tends to be a multiple-draft writer who continues to prewrite and to generate ideas while she or he moves from revision to revision until the essay eventually is fully developed.

4. *The Collage Writer.* This writer prewrites and drafts at the same time. Each paragraph may be a different idea or approach that may be based on initial freewriting. Composing, then, consists of a number of small, disjointed sets of ideas like the bits and pieces pasted on a collage. The writer must examine the collage to discover both a main idea and an approach to that idea. Gradually, she or he finds the form, topics, evidence, and organization that connect the different paragraphs. The writer may cut and paste and incorporate the paragraphs directly into the next draft of an essay. Alternatively, the writer may rearrange them to create a scratch outline for the next version.

These are only some of the many models for the writing process. You may want to experiment with different alternatives to find an approach to composing that works well for you.

THE WRITING PROCESS: AN EXAMPLE

Girl

Wash the white clothes on Monday and put them on the stone heap; wash the color clothes on Tuesday and put them on the clothes-line to dry; don't walk barehead in the hot sun; cook pumpkin fritters in very hot sweet oil; soak your little cloths right after you take them off; when buying cotton to make yourself a nice blouse, be sure that it doesn't have gum on it, because that way it won't hold up well after a wash; soak salt fish overnight before you cook it; is it true that you sing benna[1] in Sunday school?; always eat your food in such a way that it won't turn someone else's stomach; on Sundays try to walk like a lady and not like the slut you are so bent on becoming; don't sing benna in Sunday school; you mustn't speak to wharf-rat boys, not even to give directions; don't eat fruits on the street—flies will follow you; *but I don't sing benna on Sundays at all and never in Sunday school;* this is how to sew on a button; this is how to make a buttonhole for the button you have just sewed on; this is how to hem a dress when you see the hem coming down and so to prevent yourself from looking like the slut I know you are so bent on becoming; this is how you iron your father's khaki shirt so that it doesn't have a crease; this is how you iron your father's khaki pants so that they don't have a crease; this is how you grow okra—far from the house, because okra tree harbors red ants; when you are growing dasheen[2], make sure it gets plenty of water or else it makes your throat itch when you are eating it; this is how you sweep a corner; this is how you sweep a whole house; this is how you sweep a yard; this is how you smile to someone you don't like too much; this is how you smile to someone you don't like at all; this is how you smile to someone you like completely; this is how you set a table for tea; this is how you set a table for dinner; this is how you set a table for dinner with an important guest; this is how you set a table for lunch; this is how you set a table for breakfast; this is how to behave in the presence of men who don't know you very well, and this way they won't recognize immediately the slut I have warned you against becoming; be sure to wash every day, even if it is with your

---

[1] *benna:* calypso music.
[2] *dasheen:* a kind of potato.

own spit; don't squat down to play marbles—you are not a boy, you
know; don't pick people's flowers—you might catch something;
don't throw stones at blackbirds, because it might not be a blackbird
at all; this is how to make a bread pudding; this is how to make
doukona[3]; this is how to make pepper pot[4]; this is how to make a
good medicine for a cold; this is how to make a good medicine to
throw away a child before it even becomes a child; this is how to
catch a fish; this is how to throw back a fish you don't like, and that
way something bad won't fall on you; this is how to bully a man; this
is how a man bullies you; this is how to love a man, and if this
doesn't work there are other ways, and if they don't work don't feel
too bad about giving up; this is how to spit up in the air if you feel
like it, and this is how to move quick so that it doesn't fall on you;
this is how to make ends meet; always squeeze bread to make sure
it's fresh; *but what if the baker won't let me feel the bread?;* you
mean to say that after all you are really going to be the kind of
woman who the baker won't let near the bread?

As an exercise in reading, responding, and writing, assume that your instructor has asked you to create a short essay, a reaction to any aspect of "Girl"
by Jamaica Kincaid. She has assigned you an open topic. Here is an example of
one student's process of writing a response essay about "Girl." This example
may give you concrete ideas concerning the assignment and concerning the
process of writing about a literary work. Jane Anderson began her paper by
prewriting: by brainstorming and by composing a journal entry. Next she discovered a focus for her paper by trying another form of brainstorming: *clustering.* She placed a topic word in the center of the page as a starting point, and
then she wrote her associations with the topic word and indicated her reactions to other words as well. She drew arrows to connect the associated concepts, and she jotted down everything that came to her mind. Look at her
clustering for "Girl" on page 28.

Anderson tried to organize her ideas through this method. Note that she
has categorized the kinds of advice that the mother has given her daughter,
for example, domestic responsibilities, acceptable manners, and social and
sexual behavior. She has attempted to explore both the mother's and the
daughter's voices in the story. The clustering also prompted her to conclude,
"The work examines a girl's duties, a mother's teaching her daughter about
her role as a woman, and the daughter's rebellion against her mother's authoritarian commands."

This initial work encouraged Anderson to develop a possible thesis and
topics, a rough outline for her essay as shown at the bottom of page 28.

---

[3] *doukona:* a spicy pudding containing plantain.
[4] *pepper pot:* a kind of stew.

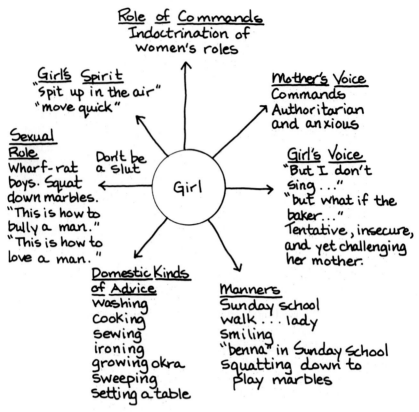

Closing — moves duties to arrival at being a woman to daughter's rebellion.

Outline

Thesis: "Girl" presents a mother's advice to her daughter and the mother's way of educating and indoctrinating her daughter both into duties, responsibilities, and the role of women in Antigua. The story gains tension because the mother gives her daughter advice in a very authoritarian manner, in a very urgent manner as if she's scared that her daughter will go astray. The daughter pricks at her mother's secure position by asking questions and by rebelling through her comments.

Topics: Mother's Voice—Commands and Dictates

       Mother's Advice—Duties and Responsibilities

       Mother's Advice—Manners

       Mother's Advice—Sexual Roles—"Lady" not "Slut"

       Ironic—Mother's Advice—Be strong-Willed

       Have Spirit

Style—Commands

Single Sentences—Use of Semicolon

Relay Power of Mother

Single Sentence—Tie of Mother and Daughter

"But what if. . . ." Insecure Yet Questioning

Presence of Daughter

Concrete Details—Very Specific Picture of Growing Up as a Woman in Antigua

Conclusion: "Girl" gives the reader a striking picture of the relationship between a mother and daughter, of the mother's desire to direct the development of her daughter's identity as a woman and of the daughter's desire to rebel and to strike out on her own. Interestingly, in this portrait that focuses on closeness and breaking away, the reader also sees the undeniable connection of the mother and daughter. They are two parts of one whole, two parts of one being.

After completing prewriting and outlining, Anderson wrote a draft of her essay and then revised it. Study carefully the first and final versions with the writer's personal evaluations and with the instructor's comments and suggestions.

Rough Draft
Girls Will Be Girls

In "Girl" Jamaica Kincaid presents a very convincing portrayal of a mother-daughter relationship. The mother is trying to indoctrinate her daughter into the ways of her society so that the "girl" will grow up to be a responsible woman in that world, and the girl on her side comments and resists her social indoctrination. Interestingly, it is a story for all women in all cultures, it is a true story, this fact is emphasized in the word choice, "Girl," for the title.

Is it indoctrination? How does the girl resist? Does she?

Solid Thesis

Comma splices

Tangent? Use later?

The mother is giving her daughter instructions on being a girl and her duties in all areas of life. The advice concerns keeping house, serving food, setting a table, and being a lady. The mother covers all the areas of a girl's life.

Vague. Be more precise here.

But the mother doesn't stop there. She not only wants to teach her daughter not to do things, but behaving like a lady is important to her. For example, she tells her daughter not to play or speak with "wharf-rat boys," not to play

Parallelism not only— but also.

—good fine use of example

marbles, not to sing "benna" in Sunday school.
She clearly is teaching her to be proper.

In addition, she is concerned with having a
daughter properly fulfill a woman's sexual role.

Word choice A lot of the comments have to do with the
restraining of sexuality. The "wharf-boys" are
associated with the life of the street;
unrestrained life. She is told not to play marbles
and squat down. Squatting down would show too much
of her body. Finally, the mother teaches her
daughter how to control her smile, to set the
proper relationship with a man. She constantly
warns her daughter against being a "slut."

Again good use of example but be careful not to repeat details.

She moves back and forth in her advice
between handling aspects of daily life and then
aspects of women's roles. Her daughter, the
silent figure in the work, does not seem to
respond. But she does resist and rebel. She
clearly is the kind of girl who does sing
Repetition? "benna" in Sunday school. She clearly is the
kind of girl who would talk to "wharf-rat boys"
and play marbles (Is the mother trying to tame a
wild child?). The daughter rebels by protesting
that she is not the kind of girl to sing "*benna.*"
And she relates her insecurities by saying "but
what if the baker won't let me feel the bread?"
The daughter both must be independent, and
always still tied to her mother and tied to
pleasing her. Her rebellion comes in telling
her mother she isn't a "slut." *Word choice*

How does the girl respond? Expand.

Good point.

Kincaid suggests the urgency of her mother's
desire to shape her daughter's self-image and
values by having the piece be a single sentence
with semicolons. This stresses the pounding flow
of the message. She always stresses that there is
only one right way by saying, "This is how . . . "
The mother is an authority figure determined to
teach her daughter the right way of behaving. She
conveys her disapproval of her daughter by
repeating, "You mean. . . . "

Add example.

To what does "This" refer? Clarify.

Be more exact in your inclusion of quotations. The mother says, "You mean to say..." once.

Weak closing— revise. "Girl" offers the reader a striking picture
of the relationship of mother and daughter, of
the mother's desire to direct the development of
her daughter's character, and the daughter's
desire to break away.

I am most satisfied with . . .
My division of the mother's advice, the
discussion of duties and responsibilities and of
cultural roles.

I am least satisfied with . . .

    My portrayal of the daughter's sexual role and of the daughter's reaction—her voice in the piece—and the relationship of mother and daughter. I need more in my introduction to interest a reader. My discussion of style is weak and choppy. I have to be careful of comma splices and repetitions.

Teacher's Comments:

You have an excellent analysis of the desire of mothers to teach their daughters about society—of their desire to teach them to be women. Your essay presents a very good analysis of the kinds of advice given. I agree with your evaluation of your essay. You have treated that topic very well. I note you have created an excellent division into categories! You need more examples. I suggest that you extend the interpretation of the mother's view of her daughter and their relationship. Why is the mother so insistent? Develop your section on style. Be careful to avoid tangents and to check your logic, paragraph structure, and word choice. Incidentally, is "indoctrination" the right word? You have interesting material in your journal on *Annie John*. You could use that insight in your opening or closing paragraphs.

Revised Essay
Girls Will Be Girls

Improved introduction.

    In "Girl," Jamaica Kincaid presents a very convincing portrayal of a mother-daughter relationship. The mother attempts to mold her daughter's identity and sense of self so that she will be able to assume the roles and responsibilities of a woman in Antiguan society. She wants her to become a proper West Indian lady. The daughter subtly resists her mother's control. The mother-daughter struggle is a universal one. The mother sees the daughter as a reflection of herself and her values, and the daughter must resist and rebel to create a sense of self.

Excellent thesis

Can you support this assertion?

Good point.

    The mother gives her daughter instructions about the duties of being a woman in Antigua. She offers not only advice, but also rather detailed orders that cover all areas of life and are presented as the only correct way to behave. The daughter is told to "wash. . .clothes"; to cook "pumpkin fritters in very hot sweet oil"; to "make a bread pudding"; and a "pepper pot"; to sweep and

I like the parallel construction.

Good use of example and of quotation from the text

to set a table. The mother very carefully distinguishes between right and wrong ways of doing things. Her daughter must learn the right way. For example, the girl must learn to buy cotton that will last and not to buy cotton with "gum" on it; to iron so that the clothes "don't crease"; or to plant okra "far from the house," so that the "red ants" don't come into the house. Clearly her mother intends to give her daughter the "right" advice. The mother also is sure that she is right.

word choice

You have mastered the correct form for integration of quotations into your analysis. Excellent.

(She wants to teach her daughter to behave like a young lady.) She must not sing "benna" in Sunday school. She must not "speak to wharf-rat boys." She must eat her food daintily so that it doesn't "turn someone else's stomach."

Repetition omit?

Besides duties and manners, the mother is teaching her daughter how to fulfill her sexual role. The mother is afraid that her daughter will be a "slut," will throw herself away for a man. Her daughter must not "become a slut"—"the slut that [she is] bent on becoming." She must not act on her sexual urges. She must not talk to "wharf-rat boys," she must not sing "benna," and she must not squat. These actions suggest yielding to instinct and impulse. She wants to teach her daughter not to succumb to sexual urges, but to control them and use her sexuality for her own benefit. For example, she teaches her daughter several different ways to smile based on what she wants. She tells her "to spit" so that it doesn't land on her. Most important, she teaches her "how to throw away a child." Interestingly she wants her daughter to use her sexuality as a weapon, as a tool for power—ultimate control rests in handling reproductive functions. She warns her daughter against being a "slut," which means giving in to her sexual impulses, giving herself away, giving control away.

Move this sentence? If you wish to include a discussion of manners, you will need a more developed paragraph and better examples.

The central concern.

Very well done.

word choice—clarify

Good analysis.

In her advice, the mother moves back and forth between duties and sexual roles; the daughter in her responses also weaves back and forth in her attitude toward her role as a woman. She responds to her mother, *but I don't sing benna on Sundays or at all and never in Sunday school.* She angrily retorts that she hasn't misbehaved, and then she quietly expresses her insecurity, her fear that she cannot fulfill her mother's commands, that she cannot "feel the bread" properly. In both cases, her responses and questions are silent

word order— change.

You need to expand this section. Concentrate on the daughter's character.

forms of resistance. In addition, the mother is concerned that the daughter will rebel, for she keeps repeating the phrase, "The slut. . .you are so bent on becoming." Why is the mother so concerned? Is she afraid that her daughter is as strong-willed as she is?

Important question.

The style of the story also demonstrates the mother's fierce urge to make her daughter conform. Her commands suggest order and obedience. The phrases which begin "this is how" suggest that there is only one right way and that the mother knows it. The mother states, for example, "This is how to bully a man. . ." The use of semicolons and the fact that the story is a single sentence present the commands as one fierce yell—a rush of emotion. She is "hitting" her child over the head with this advice. The repetition of the sentence stresses urgency and power.

This paragraph provides an outline of good points. Develop.

How?

This story (is) the common struggle of a mother and a daughter who are part of one whole, the mother trying to make the daughter a replica of herself. The daughter, dependent on her mother, insecure, is trying to create her own self and destiny, separate from her mother. In *Annie John*, another of Kincaid's books, this vision is expressed in the dream in which the main character swims with her mother in a an ocean. The child swims on her mother's back; and when the mother leaves her on the shore and then swims alone and disappears, the child is terrified. But she too must swim alone. She both needs and rebels against her mother's overpowering presence. In this way "Girl" tells the same story. It is the story of most girls (hence the reason for the title), who must grow up, leave their mothers, and maybe, in some ways, become like their mothers. It is a story of growing up.

Use a stronger verb.

comma here

Excellent inclusion of your journal entry.

Good conclusion

Strengthen this statement. Fine revision.

I am most satisfied with . . .
Expanded treatment of sexuality and mother-daughter relationship and the closing.

I am least satisfied with . . .
The discussion of style. That discussion still is sketchy.

Teacher's Comments:

You have explored the mother-daughter relationships and all aspects of social mores well. You have strengthened your

discussion by adding and developing examples. I commend your
excellent work in the expansion of the discussion of sexual
roles. You still could provide a more extensive analysis of
the daughter's character. You also could expand the section
on style. How do the commands progress? The introduction and
conclusion are much improved. I like the inclusion of the
information from the journal. Congratulations.

Be aware that you may exchange early drafts of your essays with a peer
for feedback if your instructor so desires, or your instructor may read and
comment on drafts of your writing. Three levels of peer critique are helpful:

1. *Provide Initial Reaction.* A peer may give you an initial emotional
   response and react to specific sections of the work in terms of his or
   her feelings and thoughts about the work.

2. *Indicate Organizational Strengths and Weaknesses.* A peer reader
   can outline the work—pinpointing thesis, key points, and
   details—to check the progression and development of the writer's
   arguments. A peer editor also may single out examples that are most
   convincing and vivid and note areas that are confusing and/or need
   further development.

3. *Provide an Evaluative Response.* Your instructor or your peer
   reviewers can provide a detailed evaluation of your essay's focus,
   thesis, organization, paragraph development, logic, transitions,
   style, and sentence structure.

It is helpful to evaluate a draft with a set of questions in mind so that the
critical responses might provide pointed, productive feedback. Here is a
checklist for evaluating a draft of writing:

■ **Reader Responses**
   1. Have I used some form of reader response first to gain ideas?
   2. What is the focus of my response? What is my purpose?

■ **Content**
   3. What is my main idea? My thesis? Who is my audience? Have I
      structured my thesis and topics with my audience in mind?
   4. Do my major points follow from the thesis? Are they appropriate for
      the audience?

■ **Organization**
   5. Are my major points arranged in a logical order? Do they build? Do
      I emphasize my most convincing point?
   6. Does my essay have an introduction, middle paragraphs, and
      conclusion?
   7. Will my introduction interest a reader and give the reader a sense of
      the direction of my essay?

8. Does my conclusion end emphatically and reinforce my main idea and points? Do I leave the reader with something to consider?

■ **Development**

9. Have I included enough evidence (reasons, details, and examples) from the work to explain my points? Have I explained the examples sufficiently?

10. Have I included this evidence properly? Have I used proper quoting techniques and proper techniques for paraphrasing?

■ **Grammar, Style, Sentence Sense**

11. Have I written about the work in the present tense?

12. Have I maintained a consistent tone? (e.g., objective? personal? persuasive? meditative?)

13. Am I satisfied with wording, sentence structure, patterns of sentences (emphasis, variety)? Have I avoided repetitive wording and phrasing?

14. Have I created coherence by repeating key words, by creating transitions from point to point, and by using parallelism?

15. Have I shifted levels of diction?

16. Is my word choice specific, pointed, not vague?

17. Have I checked the final draft for grammar, for punctuation, and for spelling errors?

SPECIAL REQUIREMENTS FOR WRITING ABOUT LITERATURE

Several special requirements for writing about literature are important to note. First, compose primarily in the present tense. Use the past tense to refer only to events in a text that clearly took place in the past. For example, in "Girl" you would use the present tense to describe the mother's commands, but you would use the past tense to describe the girl's birth because that event happened before the narrator begins her story.

Another important feature of writing about literature is the inclusion of quotations from the work. When you quote, be careful to cite the exact quotation and to insert ellipses (. . .) for any information that you delete within a quotation; use four periods (. . . .) for any part of a sentence that you delete at the end of the quotation. Block and indent quotations of more than four lines of prose or three lines of poetry. You also must make the quotation consistent with the preceding discussion. Use brackets to insert any changes in wording so that the quotation fits content and presentation of ideas and so that it makes sense. For example, consider this sentence from Anderson's essay, "Her daughter must not become a 'slut'—'the slut that [she is] bent on becoming.'" The writer changed the "you" to "she" and "are" to "is" so that the pronoun agreed with the noun in the earlier part of the sentence and so that the verb agreed with the subject.

Select sufficient quotations from the work as evidence. Your writing will be more persuasive if you include specifics from the work. Remember the student's weaving of quotations into her discussion of "Girl." Be aware, however, that it is disastrous to overload your analysis with unexplained or extensive quotations. This technique could lead a reader to assume that you have not understood the work fully.

Another important aspect of using evidence from a text is to **paraphrase** correctly. Where you do not use quotations, you still might want to support your points with descriptions, examples, or events in the text by phrasing them in your own words—that is, by paraphrasing the original work. Be careful to choose only your own words in such cases; any of the original language must be placed within quotation marks. Consider this additional example from Anderson's essay, "She angrily reports that she hasn't misbehaved, and then she quietly expresses her insecurity, her fear that she cannot fulfill her mother's commands, that she cannot 'feel the bread' properly." First Anderson paraphrases the girl's reactions to her mother—"she hasn't misbehaved"—and then quotes the daughter's response.

Forms of the Essay about Literature

In critical analysis of literature, you experience a complicated process of response. In writing about literature, you focus your energies on one aspect, one strand of your reading experience. Depending on your particular reading and on your goals in writing, you may then compose an essay in response to literature that may assume any of several different forms: response, explication, comparison-contrast, argumentation, critical analysis, review, and research.

Response Essay

A response essay is an analysis of a reader's emotional response to a work. In this kind of paper, you explain both your reading experience and the parts of the work that evoke your reaction. For example, you might respond to Luisa Valenzuela's story "I'm Your Horse in the Night" (Chapter 7) by discussing your mounting horror and disgust as the characters suffer torture and death at the hands of the government police in Argentina. You may want to proceed sequentially through the story to discuss the stages and aspects of your response. Or you may focus on one main emotional reaction and explore its components: the elements of the story that provoke your reaction.

Explication Essay

Another form of response, explication, is a careful analysis of the work to examine its meaning. In this type of essay, the writer proceeds through the text methodically and analyzes those aspects of the work and the writer's technique that create the themes. Usually explications of meaning are done on short texts so that the work can be analyzed in depth and treated fully. For example, a student may explore a theme of Emily Dickinson's "I'm Nobody! Who are you?" (Chapter 7) by carefully examining each line, each image, and each stanza and by finding the strands of connection revealed by this process. Such analysis demonstrates aspects of the poem (wording, imagery, figurative language, point of view, tone, rhythm, and rhyme) that develop Dickinson's message.

Comparison/Contrast Essay

In this form of essay, you may compare and/or contrast two works to find similarities and differences. Then you may have to decide to concentrate on treatment of theme, character, style, or technique. Instructors often specify the subject of the comparison and ask students to compare two characters in two different stories, to evaluate two poems with similar themes, or to assess two plays to determine which treatment of character or theme seems more effective.

There are two major organizational patterns for a comparison/contrast essay. You may treat one text first and then the other in successive paragraphs: this format is labeled *block* or *side-by-side* organization. For example, you might devote several paragraphs to a given theme, such as coming of age in "A White Heron," followed immediately by several paragraphs on the same theme in "Barn Burning" (Chapter 4). This type of pattern is sometimes not effective because it separates the discussion of the two works and confuses or loses the reader. The other pattern relies on *point-by-point* organization. In this form of the essay, each of the middle (body) paragraphs presents the treatment of a key topic (point) in both of the works. For example, in a discussion of coming of age in "A White Heron" and in "Barn Burning," one middle paragraph might focus on the innocence of the main protagonist. The next paragraph might explain each protagonist's capability for moral decision making as a prerequisite for growing beyond childhood. In every paragraph, the writer would consider first "A White Heron" and then "Barn Burning." This method keeps the topics for comparison foremost in the reader's mind and allows the reader to weigh and compare the evidence from each story.

BLOCK OR SIDE-BY-SIDE		POINT-BY-POINT	
Introduction—Thesis		Introduction—Thesis	
Middle Paragraphs		Middle Paragraphs	
Work A	"A White Heron"	Topic 1	Innocence of Protagonist
Topic 1	Innocence of Protagonist	Work A	"A White Heron"
Topic 2	Capacity for moral decisions	Work B	"Barn Burning"
Work B	"Barn Burning"	Topic 2	Capacity for moral decisions
Topic 1	Innocence of Protagonist	Work A	"A White Heron"
Topic 2	Capacity for moral decisions	Work B	"Barn Burning"
Conclusion		Conclusion	

Argumentation Essay

An argument presents your point of view, your opinion (position), reasons, and supporting evidence. For an argumentative paper on literature, you take a particular position regarding the text; and then you defend your position by providing reasons and supporting evidence from the text. As in other forms of argument, you will need to create a sound thesis, defend your thesis with logical reasoning, and provide sufficient evidence to prove your points and to convince the reader. In addition, you need to consider the opposing point of view: to evaluate and to analyze arguments in opposition to yours. An example of an argumentative question follows:

Do you agree that Oedipus creates his destiny? (See Chapter 7.) To write about this query, you would take a position and compose an argumentative essay in response to the assignment.

You can structure your response in any of several ways. You might consider one classical pattern of argument:

Opening paragraph:	Presentation of argumentative thesis
Second paragraph:	Acknowledgment of opposition—rebuttal
Subsequent paragraphs:	Reasons and proof
Closing paragraph:	Reinforcement of your position. The rebuttal of the opposition may also be placed in the next to last or closing paragraph.

Two major types of reasoning processes, *deduction* and *induction,* facilitate thinking and problem solving in your daily life and provide a basis for constructing formal written arguments. *Deduction* requires reasoning from premises (supporting statements) that are assumed to be true and that lead to a *conclusion* which follows logically from the premises. This form is called a syllogism. Deduction begins with a *general* claim and ends with a *specific* statement. Here is the most famous syllogism:

All men are mortal.   (major premise)

Socrates is a man.   (minor premise)

Therefore, Socrates is mortal.   (conclusion)

If the form of the argument follows the prescribed structure and if the conclusion follows logically from the premise, then the argument is *valid.* However, the validity of the structure does not necessarily guarantee that the argument reveals the truth. A deductive conclusion may be true or false. Only if both premises are true, is the conclusion *true.* A good deduction must be both valid and true. The example concerning the mortality of Socrates provides a **syllogism** that meets both criteria.

Inductive reasoning is a form of argument which begins with *specific* instances or events and ends with a *general* conclusion supported by the specific premises. You will consider the conclusion to be reliable or unreliable, an indication of the probability of its truth. Since induction is a process based on a sample of the facts, certainty is not possible. Instead, you will seek to make inductive arguments reliable through the quality and quantity of supporting evidence. All types of induction—scientific inquiry, for instance—seek to discover new truths. *Causal reasoning* is a form of induction in which an event is claimed to be the result of another event. Another type of induction is an **empirical** (founded upon experiment or experience) generalization, a general statement about a whole group based on observation of some members of the group. For example, you might claim: In a recent poll, most people in the United States do not want the Congress to raise taxes. The conclusion is derived from premises that offer evidence that is probably, but not certainly, true.

In critical analysis of literature, these two forms of reasoning become essential. For example, a common conclusion about the character of Oedipus results from a deduction represented by this syllogism:

> **Heroes must possess a tragic flaw.   (major premise)**
>
> **Oedipus is a hero.   (minor premise)**
>
> **Oedipus must possess a tragic flaw.   (conclusion)**

An inductive analysis of the character of Oedipus, based on an examination of evidence in the play, might lead to a similar conclusion. A careful reading of his actions and words might confirm that he exhibits excessive pride (**hubris**) and anger. Therefore, he has a tragic flaw (**hamartia**) that causes his downfall. (There is a discussion of Greek drama in Chapter 11.)

Critical Analysis Essay

In a *critical analysis,* you are asked to analyze a literary work according to a single principle: theme, character, style, or a particular technique of fiction, poetry, drama, or nonfiction. For example, you may be asked to explore one theme of "Hills Like White Elephants" (Chapter 6); or you might be asked to analyze the character of the woman in that story; your instructor may ask you to analyze Hemingway's style; or you might be asked to focus on the imagery of the hills or the symbolism of the title. In each case, you isolate one level of a work and explore its function and its impact. Critical analysis often leads to judgments of effectiveness. Is the theme treated compellingly? Is the character portrayal moving? believable? Is the imagery powerful? Is Hemingway's style effective?

Evaluation and Review Essay

Evaluation and *review* are forms of critical analysis that focus on determining the effectiveness of a work. When you are asked to evaluate a text, you compare the text with chosen standards and come to conclusions about its worth and effectiveness. You might evaluate Athol Fugard's *"Master Harold" . . . and the Boys* (Chapter 8), for example, and conclude that its characters, dialogue, conflict, and themes create a drama of great power.

A *review* is a particular form of evaluative response that often follows this set pattern:

Paragraph One:	General assessment of a work.
Paragraph Two:	Summary of key features of the work.
	(The reviewer assumes that the reader has not yet seen or read the work.)
Paragraph Three:	Strengths
Paragraph Four:	Weaknesses
Conclusion:	A general recommendation

Reviews are a common form of both academic and journalistic prose. Many instructors in college courses require book, magazine, or film reviews. Consequently, this form is a valuable one to learn.

THE RESEARCH ESSAY

The *research paper* is a writing assignment that involves searching beyond the text to find information that expands your understanding of the work. Research opens the text to different interpretations and enriches the reading experience. Research may move in different directions. You may explore any one of the following areas:

- *Biographical research:* Research on the writer's life. Exploration of the connections between the writer's life and art.
- *Research on the historical, cultural, political, philosophical, or sociological background of the work.*
- *Reading of criticism that treats the work.* This reading of another's exploration of the text will help you understand it and, perhaps, explain aspects that are puzzling. Critics provide you with alternative interpretations.
- *Reading of specific forms of literary criticism.* Historical, cultural, social, formalist, feminist, deconstructive. (See Appendix C.) These particular schools of literary criticism will provide you with frameworks and theories that will help you read the work in particular ways and place it in new intellectual contexts.

In each instance, once you write about secondary sources, you must cite the sources of the information and give adequate documentation for the works that you quote or paraphrase. One accepted method of documenting information in essays about literature is MLA (Modern Language Association of America) citation form as recommended in the *MLA Handbook for Writers of Research Papers.* The MLA citation form involves two steps: citations of references in the work itself and a "Works Cited" page that contains all of your primary and secondary sources in alphabetical order by author's last name. The MLA citations within the discussion sections of your paper include two parts: author, page. If the author's name is presented in your essay, you only indicate page number. If an author has written two books, you should include an abbreviated title in the citation. Note the following excerpt from a rough draft of a student research essay on Sylvia Plath's theme of transcendence. The writer, Kevin Stoffel, contends that an examination of the drafts of Plath's poems reveals a transformation of suffering into images of power, autonomy, and purity. Note the correct form of MLA citation. You can find a complete discussion of MLA documentation and of this research paper in Appendix B.

> Plath's poems were an outlet for her constant pain. From her swings and fits of mania and depression, she drew on the theme of transcendence. The transformation of this theme, from its early stages to its final state, can be seen in the drafts of the poems, "Fever 103°," "Ariel," and "Edge."
>
> In a statement prepared by a BBC reading, Plath wrote of "Fever 103°":
>
> > This poem is about two kinds of fire—the fires of hell, which merely agonize, and the fires of heaven which purify. During the poem, the first sort of fire suffers into the second. (Newman 62)
>
> "Fever 103°" is one of several poems in which fire serves to bring about a sense of purity equivalent to a type of transcendence, a movement to a higher plane.

SUMMARY

The recursive processes of critical thinking, reader response, and composing the essay about literature develop new capacities for understanding texts in different genres—fiction, poetry, drama, and nonfiction. As you read, analyze, and write about selections in the thematic anthology that follows, you not only will find yourself more interested in characters like Jamaica Kincaid's "Girl" from Antigua, but you also will find your life enriched by the insights and ideas provided by the study of these works.

Part Two

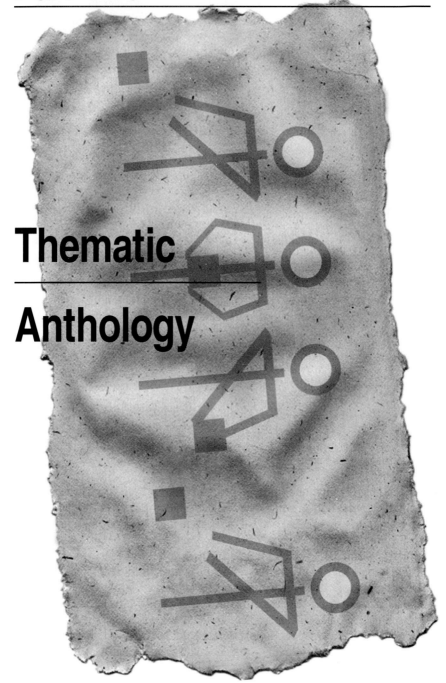

Thematic

Anthology

INITIATION AND IDENTITY

I came to explore the wreck.
The words are purposes.
The words are maps.
I came to see the damage that was done
and the treasures that prevail.

Adrienne Rich, "Diving into the Wreck"

It is not possible to define the self without acts of consciousness, without surveying "the damage that was done/and the treasures that prevail"; similarly, it
is not possible to grow without being challenged by experience and by cultural mores. When we are young, we live in a seemingly idyllic world. As we
mature, we face the experiences that affect our innocence, that complicate
our lives, and that provide the basis for growth and for the development of
identity.

For characters in literary works, loss of innocence often comes in facing
the transitory nature of life, the facts of birth and death, as in Sarah Orne
Jewett's "A White Heron" and Walt Whitman's "Out of the Cradle Endlessly
Rocking." Or the protagonist learns the limits of moral responsibility, as in
William Faulkner's "Barn Burning." Part of the inevitable process of matur-
ing becomes facing disappointment, learning that adults are not always wise
or correct in their views of the world, and gaining an understanding, often
painful, of the discrepancy between the ideal and the real, between the dream
and the reality. Such struggle and disillusionment are portrayed in Countee
Cullen's "Incident," Liliana Heker's "The Stolen Party," and Lorna Dee Cervantes's "Uncle's First Rabbit."

Literary rites of passage include knowledge of sexuality, of violence, of
discrimination, and of disillusionment with the adult world. In the Thematic
Preview, Luisa Valenzuela's "The Verb to Kill," Joyce Carol Oates' "Where Are
You Going, Where Have You Been?," and Margaret Atwood's "The Game After
Supper" depict characters grappling with the emergence of their sexuality
and questioning their sexual roles. In these works, sexuality has a violent
edge and destructive consequences. William Kowinski's "Kids in the Mall"
warns us about the negative effects that malls and other aspects of mass culture have upon the development of selfhood.

Adolescence is not necessarily a dangerous phase of life; it may be a time of
great growth, challenge, and joy. Many works affirmatively portray the physical

energy and vitality of adolescence. Witness the exuberance of the teenage boys in Gary Soto's "Oranges" or in Victor Hernandez Cruz's "Energy." The expression of selfhood in Nikki Giovanni's "Ego-Tripping" is equally positive. Margaret Mead's "Adolescents" confirms this view.

In some cases, the vitality of adolescence emerges from the drive to rebel. Members of ethnic groups who experience alienation in North American culture often use rebellion to gain an understanding of prejudice and a rejection of societal mores. Richard Wright's protagonist in "The Man Who Was Almost a Man" and Louise Erdrich's runaways from the "Indian Boarding School" experience disillusionment with the adult world.

Experiencing discrimination can lead to an awareness of difference and to confusion about cultural heritage. Should we aspire to assimilate, to embrace our cultural legacies, or are we caught between worlds? These alternatives plague the speakers in Cathy Song's "Lost Sister," Sandra Cisneros' "My Name," and James Reiss' "¿Habla Usted Español?"

The process of coming of age differs for men and for women and from culture to culture. Many times literary characters decide to reject the mores, the cultural norms of their societies; they deem them corrupt and destructive. In Louise Erdrich's "Jacklight," the young couple's venture into the woods represents a rejection of the world of the hunters and a longing for freedom. The African-American persona in Rita Dove's "Adolescence I, II, III" experiences phases of her emerging womanhood. "Black Hair," Gary Soto's partially autobiographical poem of growing up in the barrio, presents a struggle to attain manhood, a struggle that reflects the realities of his Chicano background; yet his need "To become a man," to please his father, becomes mythic in its proportions.

One outcome of these challenges is the consolidation of identity—"the treasures that prevail": the movement from confusion to a surer, albeit not necessarily static, sense of the adult self. Confusion and development persist into adulthood (the twenties, thirties, forties). We continue to face experiences like Raymond Carver's narrator in "Cathedral," ones that challenge us to define and to redefine self. We separate from and align ourselves with others as Lewis Thomas metaphorically suggests in "The Medusa and the Snail." In both Oscar Hijuelos' "When I Called the Number" and in William Shakespeare's *Hamlet,* the ghosts of the fathers appear to haunt the sons; the profound loss of the father serves as a symbol for the continual insistence and intrusion of the past into the present. The sons must try to resolve such conflicts in order to live as adults. In Hijuelos' novel, the son embraces the ghost and comes to terms with the music of his family and of his culture. Hamlet, however, must seek revenge, a revenge that leads to tragic consequences.

As readers we are cognizant that acts of writing, acts of communication, are revelatory. Like Adrienne Rich, we know that words are the "purposes," the "maps," by which we come to know ourselves and to find our ways into the world.

The Verb to Kill

Luisa Valenzuela   Translated by Helen Lane

Born in Buenos Aires, Argentina, Luisa Valenzuela (1938–   ) grew up in a literary atmosphere in which writing was considered a high calling. After graduation from the University of Buenos Aires, Valenzuela worked for a number of magazines and newspapers and travelled widely in Europe, North America, and Latin America. Hay Que Sonreír *(1966), her first short story collection, was published as* Clara *in the United States in 1979, followed by* Strange Things Happen Here *(1976, 1979). In 1979, Valenzuela moved to New York City where she now resides. She has published a novel,* The Lizard's Tale *(1963), and three collections of stories,* Other Weapons *(1985),* He Who Searches *(1987), and* Open Door *(1989).*

In "The Verb to Kill," two sisters believe that an adolescent boy is a murderer. Their strong reaction to him creates astonishment in readers.

1   He kills—he killed—he will kill—he has killed—he had killed—he will have killed—he would have killed—he is killing—he was killing—he has been killing—he would have been killing—he will have been killing—he will be killing—he would be killing—he may kill.

2   We decided that none of these tenses or moods suited him. Did he kill, will he kill, will he have killed? We think he *is* killing, with every step, with every breath, with every . . . We don't like him to get close to us but we come across him when we go clam-digging on the beach. We walk from north to south, and he comes from south to north, closer to the dunes, as if looking for pebbles. He looks at us and we look at him—did he kill, will he kill, would he have killed, is he killing? We put down the sack with the clams and hold each other's hand till he passes. He doesn't throw so much as one little pebble at us, he doesn't even look at us, but afterward we're too weak in the knees to go on digging clams.

3   The other day he walked by us and right afterward we found an injured sea gull on the beach. We took the poor thing home and on the way we told it that we were good, not like him, that it didn't have to be afraid of us, and we even covered it up with my jacket so the cold wind wouldn't hurt its broken wing. Later we ate it in a stew. A little tough, but tasty.

4   The next day we went back to run on the beach. We didn't see him and we didn't find a single injured sea gull. He may be bad, but he's got something that attracts animals. For example, when we were fishing: hours without a bite until he suddenly showed up and then we caught a splendid sea bass. He didn't look at our catch or smile, and it's good he didn't because he looked more like a murderer than ever with his long bushy hair and gleaming eyes. He just went on gathering his pebbles as though nothing were wrong, thinking about the girls that he has killed, will kill, kills.

5   When he passes by we're petrified—will it be our turn someday? In school we conjugate the verb *to kill* and the shiver that goes up our spine isn't the same as when we see him passing on the beach, all puffed up with pride and gathering his pebbles. The shiver on the beach is lower down in our bodies and more stimulating, like sea air. He gathers all those pebbles to cover up the graves of his victims—very small, transparent pebbles that he holds up to the sun and looks through from time to time so as to make certain that the sun exists. Mama says that if he spends all day looking for pebbles, it's because he *eats* them. Mama can't think about anything but food, but I'm sure he eats something else. The last breath of his victims, for example. There's nothing more nourishing than the last sigh, the one that brings with it everything that a person has gathered over the years. He must have some secret for trapping this essence that escapes his victims, and that's why he doesn't need vitamins. My sister and I are afraid he'll catch us some night and kill us to absorb everything that we've been eating over the last few years. We're terribly afraid because we're well nourished, Mama has always seen to it that we eat balanced meals and we've never lacked for fruit or vegetables even though they're very expensive in this part of the country. And clams have lots of iodine, Mama says, and fish are the healthiest food there is even though the taste of it bores us but why should he be bored because while he kills his victims (always girls, of course) he must do those terrible things to them that my sister and I keep imagining, just for fun. We spend hours talking about the things that he does to his victims before killing them just for fun. The papers often talk about degenerates like him but he's one of the worst because that's all he eats. The other day we spied on him while he was talking to the lettuce he has growing in his garden (he's crazy as well as degenerate). He was saying affectionate things to it and we were certain it was poisoned lettuce. For our part we don't say anything to lettuce, we have to eat it with oil and lemon even though it's disgusting, all because Mama says it has lots of vitamins. And now we have to swallow vitamins for him, what a bother, because the better fed we are the happier we'll make him and the more he'll like doing those terrible things the papers talk about and we imagine, just before killing us so as to gulp down our last breath full of vitamins in one big mouthful. He's going to do a whole bunch of things so repulsive we'll be ashamed to tell anybody, and we only say them in a whisper when we're on the beach and there's nobody within miles. He's going to take our last breath and then he'll be as strong as a bull to go kill other little girls like us. I hope he catches Pocha. But I hope he doesn't do any of those repulsive

things to her before killing her because she might like it, the dirty thing. I hope he kills her straightaway by plunging a knife in her belly. But he'll have his fun with us for a long time because we're pretty and he'll like our bodies and our voices when we scream. And we will scream and scream but nobody will hear us because he's going to take us to a place very far away and then he will put in our mouths that terrible thing we know he has. Pocha already told us about it—he must have an enormous thing that he uses to kill his victims.

6   An enormous one, even though we've never seen it. To show how brave we are, we tried to watch him while he made peepee, but he saw us and chased us away. I wonder why he didn't want to show it to us. Maybe it's because he wants to surprise us on our last day here and catch us while we're pure so's to get more pleasure. That must be it. He's saving himself for our last day and that's why he doesn't try to get close to us.

7 Not anymore.

8 Papa finally lent us the rifle after we asked and asked for it to hunt rabbits. He told us we were big girls now, that we can go out alone with the rifle if we want to, but to be careful, and he said it was a reward for doing so well in school. It's true we're doing well in school. It isn't hard at all to learn to conjugate verbs:

9   He will be killed—he is killed—he has been killed.

■ EXPLORATIONS OF THE TEXT ■

1. Notice the verb tenses and moods at the beginning. The narrator says "We decided that none of these tenses or moods suited him." Why?
2. Characterize the boy. What are his alleged actions?
3. What is the relationship between eating and violence?
4. What is the relationship between sexuality and death?
5. Explain the emphasis on "breath."
6. Explore the significance of the images of the beach, of birds and fish, and of vegetables?
7. Trace the verb "to kill" through the story. What do you conclude?
8. What does the ending mean? What has really happened to the boy? Will there be consequences for the girls?

■■ JOURNAL ENTRIES ■■

1. What is fantastic and what is real in this story?
2. Look at the sentence structure. How does Valenzuela establish the voice of the speaker? What impact does the voice have?

---

1. What is the meaning of violence in this work?
2. Compare the experience of adolescent fear and fantasy in this story
    with the situations in other works such as "Where Are You Going,
    Where Have You Been?" or "Game after Supper."

Where Are You Going, Where Have You Been?

Joyce Carol Oates

*Born in Lockport, New York, Joyce Carol Oates (1938–   ) majored
in English at Syracuse University and received her M.A. from the
University of Wisconsin in 1961. With the publication of* A Garden of
Earthly Delights *(1967) and* Expensive People *(1968), she became
famous. In 1969, her novel,* them, *won the National Book Award.
Known for her prolific and varied writing, Oates, Professor of Hu-
manities at Princeton University, has published almost forty
books—novels, short fiction, poetry, essays, and literary criticism.
Recent works include* On Boxing *(1987) (nonfiction),* American
Appetite *(1989), and* Black Water *(1992).*

*Oates based "Where Are You Going, Where Have You Been?" on
an article in* Life *magazine about a murderer, Charles Schmid, of
Tucson, Arizona. She describes Connie as "struggling heroically to
define personal identity in the face of incredible opposition, even in
the face of death itself."*

To Bob Dylan

1   Her name was Connie. She was fifteen and she had a quick nervous gig-
ling habit of craning her neck to glance into mirrors or checking other
people's faces to make sure her own was all right. Her mother, who noticed
everything and knew everything and who hadn't much reason any longer to
look at her own face, always scolded Connie about it. "Stop gawking at yourself, who are you? You think you're so pretty?" she would say. Connie would
raise her eyebrows at these familiar complaints and look right through her
mother, into a shadowy vision of herself as she was right at that moment: she
knew she was pretty and that was everything. Her mother had been pretty

once too, if you could believe those old snapshots in the album, but now her looks were gone and that was why she was always after Connie.

"Why don't you keep your room clean like your sister? How've you got your hair fixed—what the hell stinks? Hair spray? You don't see your sister using that junk."

Her sister June was twenty-four and still lived at home. She was a secretary in the high school Connie attended, and if that wasn't bad enough—with her in the same building—she was so plain and chunky and steady that Connie had to hear her praised all the time by her mother and her mother's sisters. June did this, June did that, she saved money and helped clean the house and cooked and Connie couldn't do a thing, her mind was all filled with trashy daydreams. Their father was away at work most of the time and when he came home he wanted supper and he read the newspaper at supper and after supper he went to bed. He didn't bother talking much to them, but around his bent head Connie's mother kept picking at her until Connie wished her mother were dead and she herself were dead and it were all over. "She makes me want to throw up sometimes," she complained to her friends. She had a high, breathless, amused voice which made everything she said sound a little forced, whether it was sincere or not.

There was one good thing: June went places with girlfriends of hers, girls who were just as plain and steady as she, and so when Connie wanted to do that her mother had no objections. The father of Connie's best girlfriend drove the girls the three miles to town and left them off at a shopping plaza, so that they could walk through the stores or go to a movie, and when he came to pick them up again at eleven he never bothered to ask what they had done.

5   They must have been familiar sights, walking around that shopping plaza in their shorts and flat ballerina slippers that always scuffed the sidewalk, with charm bracelets jingling on their thin wrists; they would lean together to whisper and laugh secretly if someone passed by who amused or interested them. Connie had long dark blond hair that drew anyone's eye to it, and she wore part of it pulled up on her head and puffed out and the rest of it she let fall down her back. She wore a pullover jersey blouse that looked one way when she was at home and another way when she was away from home. Everything about her had two sides to it, one for home and one for anywhere that was not home: her walk that could be childlike and bobbing, or languid enough to make anyone think she was hearing music in her head, her mouth which was pale and smirking most of the time, but bright and pink on these evenings out, her laugh which was cynical and drawling at home—"Ha, ha, very funny"—but high-pitched and nervous anywhere else, like the jingling of the charms on her bracelet.

Sometimes they did go shopping or to a movie, but sometimes they went across the highway, ducking fast across the busy road, to a drive-in restaurant where older kids hung out. The restaurant was shaped like a big bottle, though squatter than a real bottle, and on its cap was a revolving figure of a grinning boy who held a hamburger aloft. One night in midsummer they ran across, breathless with daring, and right away someone leaned out a car window and invited them over, but it was just a boy from high school they didn't like. It made them feel good to be able to ignore him. They went up through the maze of parked and cruising cars to the bright-lit, fly-infested restaurant, their faces pleased and expectant as if they were entering a sacred building that loomed out of the night to give them what haven and what blessing they yearned for. They sat at the counter and crossed their legs at the ankles, their thin shoulders rigid with excitement, and listened to the music that made everything so good: the music was always in the background like music at a church service, it was something to depend upon.

A boy named Eddie came in to talk with them. He sat backward on his stool, turning himself jerkily around in semicircles and then stopping and turning again, and after a while he asked Connie if she would like something to eat. She said she did and so she tapped her friend's arm on her way out— her friend pulled her face up into a brave droll look—and Connie said she would meet her at eleven, across the way. "I just hate to leave her like that," Connie said earnestly, but the boy said that she wouldn't be alone for long. So they went out to his car and on the way Connie couldn't help but let her eyes wander over the windshields and faces all around her, her face gleaming with a joy that had nothing to do with Eddie or even this place; it might have been the music. She drew her shoulders up and sucked in her breath with the pure pleasure of being alive, and just at that moment she happened to glance at a face just a few feet from hers. It was a boy with shaggy black hair, in a convertible jalopy painted gold. He stared at her and then his lips widened into a grin. Connie slit her eyes at him and turned away, but she couldn't help glancing back and there he was still watching her. He wagged a finger and laughed and said, "Gonna get you, baby," and Connie turned away again without Eddie noticing anything.

She spent three hours with him, at the restaurant where they ate hamburgers and drank Cokes in wax cups that were always sweating, and then down an alley a mile or so away, and when he left her off at five to eleven only the movie house was still open at the plaza. Her girlfriend was there, talking with a boy. When Connie came up and the two girls smiled at each other and Connie said, "How was the movie?" and the girl said, "*You* should know." They rode off with the girl's father, sleepy and pleased, and Connie couldn't help but look at the darkened shopping plaza with its big empty parking lot and its signs that were faded and ghostly now, and over at the drive-in restaurant where cars were still circling tirelessly. She couldn't hear the music at this distance.

Next morning June asked her how the movie was and Connie said, "So-so."

10   She and that girl and occasionally another girl went out several times a week that way, and the rest of the time Connie spent around the house—it was summer vacation—getting in her mother's way and thinking, dreaming, about the boys she met. But all the boys fell back and dissolved into a single face that was not even a face, but an idea, a feeling, mixed up with the urgent

insistent pounding of the music and the humid night air of July. Connie's mother kept dragging her back to the daylight by finding things for her to do or saying, suddenly, "What's this about the Pettinger girl?"

And Connie would say nervously, "Oh, her. That dope." She always drew thick clear lines between herself and such girls, and her mother was simple and kindly enough to believe her. Her mother was so simple, Connie thought, that it was maybe cruel to fool her so much. Her mother went scuffling around the house in old bedroom slippers and complained over the telephone to one sister about the other, then the other called up and the two of them complained about the third one. If June's name was mentioned her mother's tone was approving, and if Connie's name was mentioned it was disapproving. This did not really mean she disliked Connie and actually Connie thought that her mother preferred her to June because she was prettier, but the two of them kept up a pretense of exasperation, a sense that they were tugging and struggling over something of little value to either of them. Sometimes, over coffee, they were almost friends, but something would come up—some vexation that was like a fly buzzing suddenly around their heads—and their faces went hard with contempt.

One Sunday Connie got up at eleven—none of them bothered with church—and washed her hair so that it could dry all day long, in the sun. Her parents and sisters were going to a barbecue at an aunt's house and Connie said no, she wasn't interested, rolling her eyes to let her mother know just what she thought of it. "Stay home alone then," her mother said sharply. Connie sat out back in a lawn chair and watched them drive away, her father quiet and bald, hunched around so that he could back the car out, her mother with a look that was still angry and not at all softened through the windshield, and in the back seat poor old June all dressed up as if she didn't know what a barbecue was, with all the running yelling kids and the flies. Connie sat with her eyes closed in the sun, dreaming and dazed with the warmth about her as if this were a kind of love, the caresses of love, and her mind slipped over onto thoughts of the boy she had been with the night before and how nice he had been, how sweet it always was, not the way someone like June would suppose but sweet, gentle, the way it was in movies and promised in songs; and when she opened her eyes she hardly knew where she was, the back yard ran off into weeds and a fence line of trees and behind it the sky was perfectly blue and still. The asbestos "ranch house" that was now three years old startled her—it looked small. She shook her head as if to get awake.

It was too hot. She went inside the house and turned on the radio to drown out the quiet. She sat on the edge of her bed, barefoot, and listened for an hour and a half to a program called XYZ Sunday Jamboree, record after record of hard, fast, shrieking songs she sang along with, interspersed by exclamations from "Bobby King": "An' look here you girls at Napoleon's—Son and Charley want you to pay real close attention to this song coming up!"

And Connie paid close attention herself, bathed in a glow of slow-pulsed joy that seemed to rise mysteriously out of the music itself and lay languidly about the airless little room, breathed in and breathed out with each gentle rise and fall of her chest.

15   After a while she heard a car coming up the drive. She sat up at once, startled, because it couldn't be her father so soon. The gravel kept crunching all the way in from the road—the driveway was long—and Connie ran to the window. It was a car she didn't know. It was an open jalopy, painted a bright gold that caught the sunlight opaquely. Her heart began to pound and her fingers snatched at her hair, checking it, and she whispered "Christ, Christ," wondering how bad she looked. The car came to a stop at the side door and the horn sounded four short taps as if this were a signal Connie knew.

She went into the kitchen and approached the door slowly, then hung out the screen door, her bare toes curling down off the step. There were two boys in the car and now she recognized the driver: he had shaggy, shabby black hair that looked crazy as a wig and he was grinning at her.

"I ain't late, am I?" he said.

"Who the hell do you think you are?" Connie said.

"Toldja I'd be out, didn't I?"

20   "I don't even know who you are."

She spoke sullenly, careful to show no interest or pleasure, and he spoke in a fast bright monotone. Connie looked past him to the other boy, taking her time. He had fair brown hair, with a lock that fell onto his forehead. His sideburns gave him a fierce, embarrassed look, but so far he hadn't even bothered to glance at her. Both boys wore sunglasses. The driver's glasses were metallic and mirrored everything in miniature.

"You wanta come for a ride?" he said.

Connie smirked and let her hair fall loose over one shoulder.

"Don'tcha like my car? New paint job," he said. "Hey."

25   "What?"

"You're cute."

She pretended to fidget, chasing flies away from the door.

"Don'tcha believe me, or what?" he said.

"Look, I don't even know who you are," Connie said in disgust.

30   "Hey, Ellie's got a radio, see. Mine's broke down." He lifted his friend's arm and showed her the little transistor the boy was holding, and now Connie began to hear the music. It was the same program that was playing inside the house.

"Bobby King?" she said.

"I listen to him all the time. I think he's great."

"He's kind of great," Connie said reluctantly.

"Listen, that guy's *great*. He knows where the action is."

35   Connie blushed a little, because the glasses made it impossible for her to see just what this boy was looking at. She couldn't decide if she liked him or if he was just a jerk, and so she dawdled in the doorway and wouldn't come down or go back inside. She said, "What's all that stuff painted on your car?"

"Can'tcha read it?" He opened the door very carefully, as if he was afraid it might fall off. He slid out just as carefully, planting his feet firmly on the ground, the tiny metallic world in his glasses slowing down like gelatine hardening and in the midst of it Connie's bright green blouse. "This here is my name, to begin with," he said. ARNOLD FRIEND was written in tarlike black letters on the side, with a drawing of a round grinning face that reminded Connie of a pumpkin, except it wore sunglasses. "I wanta introduce myself, I'm Arnold Friend and that's my real name and I'm gonna be your friend, honey, and inside the car's Ellie Oscar, he's kinda shy." Ellie brought his transistor radio up to his shoulder and balanced it there. "Now these numbers are a secret code, honey," Arnold Friend explained. He read off the numbers 33, 19, 17 and raised his eyebrows at her to see what she thought of that, but she didn't think much of it. The left rear fender had been smashed and around it was written, on the gleaming gold background: DONE BY CRAZY WOMAN DRIVER. Connie had to laugh at that. Arnold Friend was pleased at her laughter and looked up at her. "Around the other side's a lot more—you wanta come and see them?"

"No."

"Why not?"

"Why should I?"

40   "Don'tcha wanta see what's on the car? Don'tcha wanta go for a ride?"

"I don't know."

"Why not?"

"I got things to do."

"Like what?"

45   "Things."

He laughed as if she had said something funny. He slapped his thighs. He was standing in a strange way, leaning back against the car as if he were balancing himself. He wasn't tall, only an inch or so taller than she would be if she came down to him. Connie liked the way he was dressed, which was the way all of them dressed: tight faded jeans stuffed into black, scuffed boots, a belt that pulled his waist in and showed how lean he was, and a white pullover shirt that was a little soiled and showed the hard small muscles of his arms and shoulders. He looked as if he probably did hard work, lifting and carrying things. Even his neck looked muscular. And his face was a familiar face, somehow: the jaw and chin and cheeks slightly darkened, because he hadn't shaved for a day or two, and the nose long and hawklike, sniffing as if she were a treat he was going to gobble up and it was all a joke.

"Connie, you ain't telling the truth. This is your day set aside for a ride with me and you know it," he said, still laughing. The way he straightened and recovered from his fit of laughing showed that it had been all fake.

"How do you know what my name is?" she said suspiciously.

"It's Connie."

50   "Maybe and maybe not."

"I know my Connie," he said, wagging his finger. Now she remembered him even better, back at the restaurant, and her cheeks warmed at the thought of how she sucked in her breath just at the moment she passed him—how she must have looked at him. And he had remembered her. "Ellie and I come out here especially for you," he said. "Ellie can sit in back. How about it?"

"Where?"

"Where what?"

"Where're we going?"

55   He looked at her. He took off the sunglasses and she saw how pale the skin around his eyes was, like holes that were not in shadow but instead in light. His eyes were like chips of broken glass that catch the light in an amiable way. He smiled. It was as if the idea of going for a ride somewhere, to some place, was a new idea to him.

"Just for a ride, Connie sweetheart."

"I never said my name was Connie," she said.

"But I know what it is. I know your name and all about you, lots of things," Arnold Friend said. He had not moved yet but stood still leaning back against the side of his jalopy. "I took a special interest in you, such a pretty girl, and found out all about you like I know your parents and sister are gone somewheres and I know where and how long they're going to be gone, and I know who you were with last night, and your best girlfriend's name is Betty. Right?"

He spoke in a simple lilting voice, exactly as if he were reciting the words to a song. His smile assured her that everything was fine. In the car Ellie turned up the volume on his radio and did not bother to look around at them.

60   "Ellie can sit in the back seat," Arnold Friend said. He indicated his friend with a casual jerk of his chin, as if Ellie did not count and she should not bother with him.

"How'd you find out all that stuff?" Connie said.

"Listen: Betty Schultz and Tony Fitch and Jimmy Pettinger and Nancy Pettinger," he said, in a chant. "Raymond Stanley and Bob Hutter—"

"Do you know all those kids?"

"I know everybody."

65   "Look, you're kidding. You're not from around here."

"Sure."

"But—how come we never saw you before?"

"Sure you saw me before," he said. He looked down at his boots, as if he were a little offended. "You just don't remember."

"I guess I'd remember you," Connie said.

70   "Yeah?" He looked up at this, beaming. He was pleased. He began to mark time with the music from Ellie's radio, tapping his fists lightly together. Connie looked away from his smile to the car, which was painted so bright it almost hurt her eyes to look at it. She looked at that name, ARNOLD FRIEND. And up at the front fender was an expression that was familiar—MAN THE FLYING SAUCERS. It was an expression kids had used the year before, but didn't use this year. She looked at it for a while as if the words meant something to her that she did not yet know.

"What're you thinking about? Huh?" Arnold Friend demanded. "Not worried about your hair blowing around in the car, are you?"

"No."

"Think I maybe can't drive good?"

"How do I know?"

75   "You're a hard girl to handle. How come?" he said. "Don't you know I'm your friend? Didn't you see me put my sign in the air when you walked by?"

"What sign?"

"My sign." And he drew an X in the air, leaning out toward her. They were maybe ten feet apart. After his hand fell back to his side the X was still in the air, almost visible. Connie let the screen door close and stood perfectly still inside it, listening to the music from her radio and the boy's blend together. She stared at Arnold Friend. He stood there so stiffly relaxed, pretending to be relaxed, with one hand idly on the door handle as if he were keeping himself up that way and had no intention of ever moving again. She recognized most things about him, the tight jeans that showed his thighs and buttocks and the greasy leather boots and the tight shirt, and even that slippery friendly smile of his, that sleepy dreamy smile that all the boys used to get across ideas they didn't want to put into words. She recognized all this and also the singsong way he talked, slightly mocking, kidding, but serious and a little melancholy, and she recognized the way he tapped one fist against the other in homage of the perpetual music behind him. But all these things did not come together.

She said suddenly, "Hey, how old are you?"

His smile faded. She could see then that he wasn't a kid, he was much older—thirty, maybe more. At this knowledge her heart began to pound faster.

80   "That's a crazy thing to ask. Can'tcha see I'm your own age?"

"Like hell you are."

"Or maybe a coupla years older, I'm eighteen."

"Eighteen?" she said doubtfully.

He grinned to reassure her and lines appeared at the corners of his mouth. His teeth were big and white. He grinned so broadly his eyes became slits and she saw how thick the lashes were, thick and black as if painted with a black tarlike material. Then he seemed to become embarrassed, abruptly, and looked over his shoulder at Ellie. "*Him,* he's crazy," he said. "Ain't he a riot, he's a nut, a real character." Ellie was still listening to the music. His sunglasses told nothing about what he was thinking. He wore a bright orange shirt unbuttoned halfway to show his chest, which was a pale, bluish chest and not muscular like Arnold Friend's. His shirt collar was turned up all around and the very tips of the collar pointed out past his chin as if they were protecting him. He was pressing the transistor radio up against his ear and sat there in a kind of daze, right in the sun.

85   "He's kinda strange," Connie said.

"Hey, she says you're kinda strange! Kinda strange!" Arnold Friend cried. He pounded on the car to get Ellie's attention. Ellie turned for the first time and Connie saw with shock that he wasn't a kid either—he had a fair, hairless face, cheeks reddened slightly as if the veins grew too close to the surface of his skin, the face of a forty-year-old baby. Connie felt a wave of dizziness rise in her at this sight and she stared at him as if waiting for something to change the shock of the moment, make it all right again. Ellie's lips kept shaping words, mumbling along with the words blasting in his ear.

"Maybe you two better go away," Connie said faintly.

"What? How come?" Arnold Friend cried. "We come out here to take you for a ride. It's Sunday." He had the voice of the man on the radio now. It was the same voice, Connie thought. "Don'tcha know it's Sunday all day and honey, no matter who you were with last night today you're with Arnold Friend and don't you forget it!—Maybe you better step out here," he said, and this last was in a different voice. It was a little flatter, as if the heat was finally getting to him.

"No. I got things to do."

90   "Hey."

"You two better leave."

"We ain't leaving until you come with us."

"Like hell I am—"

"Connie, don't fool around with me. I mean, I mean, don't fool *around,*" he said, shaking his head. He laughed incredulously. He placed his sunglasses on top of his head, carefully, as if he were indeed wearing a wig, and brought the stems down behind his ears. Connie stared at him, another wave of dizziness and fear rising in her so that for a moment he wasn't even in focus but was just a blur, standing there against his gold car, and she had the idea that he had driven up the driveway all right but had come from nowhere before that and belonged nowhere and that everything about him and even about the music that was so familiar to her was only half real.

95   "If my father comes and sees you—"

"He ain't coming. He's at a barbecue."

"How do you know that?"

"Aunt Tillie's. Right now they're—uh—they're drinking. Sitting around," he said vaguely, squinting as if he were staring all the way to town and over to Aunt Tillie's back yard. Then the vision seemed to get clear and he nodded energetically. "Yeah. Sitting around. There's your sister in a blue dress, huh? And high heels, the poor sad bitch—nothing like you, sweetheart! And your mother's helping some fat woman with the corn, they're cleaning the corn—husking the corn—"

"What fat woman?" Connie cried.

100   "How do I know what fat woman, I don't know every goddam fat woman in the world!" Arnold laughed.

"Oh, that's Mrs. Hornby . . . Who invited her?" Connie said. She felt a little light-headed. Her breath was coming quickly.

"She's too fat. I don't like them fat. I like them the way you are, honey," he said, smiling sleepily at her. They stared at each other for a while, through the screen door. He said softly, "Now what you're going to do is this: you're going to come out that door. You're going to sit up front with me and Ellie's going to sit in the back, the hell with Ellie, right? This isn't Ellie's date. You're my date. I'm your lover, honey."

"What? You're crazy—"

"Yes, I'm your lover. You don't know what that is, but you will," he said. "I know that too. I know all about you. But look: it's real nice and you couldn't ask for nobody better than me, or more polite. I always keep my word. I'll tell you how it is, I'm always nice at first, the first time. I'll hold you so tight you won't think you have to try to get away or pretend anything because you'll know you can't. And I'll come inside you where it's all secret and you'll give in to me and you'll love me—"

105   "Shut up! You're crazy!" Connie said. She backed away from the door. She put her hands against her ears as if she'd heard something terrible, something not meant for her. "People don't talk like that, you're crazy," she muttered. Her heart was almost too big now for her chest and its pumping made sweat break out all over her. She looked out to see Arnold Friend pause and then take a step toward the porch lurching. He almost fell. But, like a clever drunken man, he managed to catch his balance. He wobbled in his high boots and grabbed hold of one of the porch posts.

"Honey?" he said. "You still listening?"

"Get the hell out of here!"

"Be nice, honey. Listen."

"I'm going to call the police—"

110   He wobbled again and out of the side of his mouth came a fast spat curse, an aside not meant for her to hear. But even this "Christ!" sounded forced. Then he began to smile again. She watched this smile come, awkward as if he were smiling from inside a mask. His whole face was a mask, she thought wildly, tanned down onto his throat but then running out as if he had plastered makeup on his face but had forgotten about his throat.

"Honey—? Listen, here's how it is. I always tell the truth and I promise you this: I ain't coming in that house after you."

"You better not! I'm going to call the police if you—if you don't—"

"Honey," he said, talking right through her voice, "honey, I'm not coming in there but you are coming out here. You know why?"

She was panting. The kitchen looked like a place she had never seen before, some rooms she had run inside but which wasn't good enough, wasn't going to help her. The kitchen window had never had a curtain, after three years, and there were dishes in the sink for her to do—probably—and if you ran your hand across the table you'd probably feel something sticky there.

115   "You listening, honey? Hey?"

"—going to call the police—"

"Soon as you touch the phone I don't need to keep my promise and can come inside. You won't want that."

She rushed forward and tried to lock the door. Her fingers were shaking. "But why lock it," Arnold Friend said gently, talking right into her face. "It's just a screen door. It's just nothing." One of his boots was at a strange angle, as if his foot wasn't in it. It pointed out to the left, bent at the ankle. "I mean, anybody can break through a screen door and glass and wood and iron or anything else if he needs to, anybody at all and specially Arnold Friend. If the place got lit up with a fire honey you'd come runnin' out into my arms, right into my arms an' safe at home—like you knew I was your lover and'd stopped fooling around. I don't mind a nice shy girl but I don't like no fooling around." Part of those words were spoken with a slight rhythmic lilt, and Connie somehow recognized them—the echo of a song from last year, about a girl rushing into her boyfriend's arms and coming home again—

Connie stood barefoot on the linoleum floor, staring at him. "What do you want?" she whispered.

120   "I want you," he said.

"What?"

"Seen you that night and thought, that's the one, yes sir. I never needed to look any more."

"But my father's coming back. He's coming to get me. I had to wash my hair first—" She spoke in a dry, rapid voice, hardly raising it for him to hear.

"No, your Daddy is not coming and yes, you had to wash your hair and you washed it for me. It's nice and shining and all for me, I thank you, sweetheart," he said, with a mock bow, but again he almost lost his balance. He had to bend and adjust his boots. Evidently his feet did not go all the way down; the boots must have been stuffed with something so that he would seem taller. Connie stared out at him and behind him Ellie in the car, who seemed to be looking off toward Connie's right into nothing. This Ellie said, pulling the words out of the air one after another as if he were just discovering them, "You want me to pull out the phone?"

125   "Shut your mouth and keep it shut," Arnold Friend said, his face red from bending over or maybe from embarrassment because Connie had seen his boots. "This ain't none of your business."

"What—what are you doing? What do you want?" Connie said. "If I call the police they'll get you, they'll arrest you—"

"Promise was not to come in unless you touch the phone, and I'll keep that promise," he said. He resumed his erect position and tried to force his shoulders back. He sounded like a hero in a movie, declaring something important. He spoke too loudly and it was as if he were speaking to someone behind Connie. "I ain't made plans for coming in that house where I don't belong but just for you to come out to me, the way you should. Don't you know who I am?"

"You're crazy," she whispered. She backed away from the door but did not want to go into another part of the house, as if this would give him permission to come through the door. "What do you . . . You're crazy, you . . ."

"Huh? What're you saying, honey?"

130   Her eyes darted everywhere in the kitchen. She could not remember what it was, this room.

"This is how it is, honey; you come out and we'll drive away, have a nice ride. But if you don't come out we're gonna wait till your people come home and then they're all going to get it."

"You want that telephone pulled out?" Ellie said. He held the radio away from his ear and grimaced, as if without the radio the air was too much for him.

"I toldja shut up, Ellie," Arnold Friend said, "you're deaf, get a hearing aid, right? Fix yourself up. This little girl's no trouble and's gonna be nice to me, so Ellie keep to yourself, this ain't your date—right? Don't hem in on me. Don't hog. Don't crush. Don't bird dog. Don't trail me," he said in a rapid meaningless voice, as if he were running through all the expressions he'd learned but was no longer sure which one of them was in style, then rushing on to new ones, making them up with his eyes closed, "Don't crawl under my fence, don't squeeze in my chipmunk hole, don't sniff my glue, suck my popsicle, keep your own greasy fingers on yourself!" He shaded his eyes and peered in at Connie, who was backed against the kitchen table. "Don't mind him honey he's just a creep. He's a dope. Right? I'm the boy for you and like I said you come out here nice like a lady and give me your hand, and nobody else gets hurt, I mean, your nice old bald-headed daddy and your mummy and your sister in her high heels. Because listen: why bring them in this?"

"Leave me alone," Connie whispered.

135   "Hey, you know that old woman down the road, the one with the chickens and stuff—you know her?"

"She's dead!"

"Dead? What? You know her?" Arnold Friend said.

"She's dead—"

"Don't you like her?"

140   "She dead—she's—she isn't there any more—"

"But don't you like her, I mean, you got something against her? Some grudge or something?" Then his voice dipped as if he were conscious of a rudeness. He touched the sunglasses perched on top of his head as if to make sure they were still there. "Now you be a good girl."

"What are you going to do?"

"Just two things, or maybe three," Arnold Friend said. "But I promise it won't last long and you'll like me the way you get to like people you're close to. You will. It's all over for you here, so come on out. You don't want your people in any trouble, do you?"

She turned and bumped against a chair or something, hurting her leg, but she ran into the back room and picked up the telephone. Something roared in her ear, a tiny roaring, and she was so sick with fear that she could do nothing but listen to it—the telephone was clammy and very heavy and her fingers groped down to the dial but were too weak to touch it. She began to scream into the phone, into the roaring. She cried out, she cried for her mother, she felt her breath start jerking back and forth in her lungs as if it were something Arnold Friend were stabbing her with again and again with no tenderness. A noisy sorrowful wailing rose all about her and she was locked inside it the way she was locked inside this house.

145   After a while she could hear again. She was sitting on the floor with her wet back against the wall.

Arnold Friend was saying from the door, "That's a good girl. Put the phone back."

She kicked the phone away from her.

"No, honey. Pick it up. Put it back right."

She picked it up and put it back. The dial tone stopped.

150   "That's a good girl. Now you come outside."

She was hollow with what had been fear, but what was now just an emptiness. All that screaming had blasted it out of her. She sat, one leg cramped under her, and deep inside her brain was something like a pinpoint of light that kept going and would not let her relax. She thought, I'm not going to see my mother again. She thought, I'm not going to sleep in my bed again. Her bright green blouse was all wet.

Arnold Friend said, in a gentle-loud voice that was like a stage voice. "The place where you came from ain't there any more, and where you had in mind to go is canceled out. This place you are now—inside your daddy's house—is nothing but a cardboard box I can knock down any time. You know that and always did know it. You hear me?"

She thought, I have got to think. I have to know what to do.

"We'll go out to a nice field, out in the country here where it smells so nice and it's sunny," Arnold Friend said. "I'll have my arms tight around you so you won't need to try to get away and I'll show you what love is like, what it does. The hell with this house! It looks solid all right," he said. He ran a fingernail down the screen and the noise did not make Connie shiver, as it would have the day before. "Now put you hand on your heart, honey. Feel that? That feels solid too, but we know better, be nice to me, be sweet like you can because what else is there for a girl like you but to be sweet and pretty and give in?—and get away before her people come back?"

155   She felt her pounding heart. Her hand seemed to enclose it. She thought for the first time in her life that it was nothing that was hers, that belonged to her, but just a pounding, living thing inside this body that wasn't really hers either.

"You don't want them to get hurt," Arnold Friend went on. "Now get up, honey. Get up all by yourself."

She stood.

"Now turn this way. That's right. Come over here to me—Ellie, put that away, didn't I tell you? You dope. You miserable creepy dope," Arnold Friend said. His words were not angry but only part of an incantation. The incantation was kindly. "Now come out through the kitchen to me honey, and let's see a smile, try it, you're a brave sweet little girl and now they're eating corn and hot dogs cooked to bursting over an outdoor fire, and they don't know one thing about you and never did and honey you're better than them because not a one of them would have done this for you."

Connie felt the linoleum under her feet; it was cool. She brushed her hair back out of her eyes. Arnold Friend let go of the post tentatively and opened his arms for her, his elbows pointing in toward each other and his wrists limp, to show that this was an embarrassed embrace and a little mocking, he didn't want to make her self-conscious.

160   She put out her hand against the screen. She watched herself push the door slowly open as if she were safe back somewhere in the other doorway, watching this body and this head of long hair moving out into the sunlight were Arnold Friend waited.

"My sweet little blue-eyed girl," he said, in a half-sung sigh that had nothing to do with her brown eyes but was taken up just the same by the vast sunlit reaches of the land behind him and on all sides of him, so much land that Connie had never seen before and did not recognize except to know that she was going to it.

■   **EXPLORATIONS OF THE TEXT**   ■

1. Joyce Carol Oates wrote this story after listening to Bob Dylan's "It's All Over Now, Baby Blue." What are the roles of music, sex, restaurants, malls, and cars in this work?
2. Characterize Connie. Why is her sense of her own identity so vague?
3. Why does the narrator say of Connie that "everything about her had two sides to it"?
4. How do Arnold's car and clothes reflect his character?
5. What is Ellie's role in the story?
6. What does the religious imagery suggest? Explore the references to fairy tales in the story.
7. Interpret the ending. Does Arnold commit rape and murder?
8. Compare this story with Luisa Valenzuela's "The Verb to Kill." What does each writer suggest about adolescent sexuality?

■■   **JOURNAL ENTRIES**   ■■

1. Gothic literature is characterized by gloomy settings, mysterious and violent events, and an atmosphere of death and decay. What are the gothic elements in this story?
2. Does Connie lack inner resources?

■■■   **IDEAS FOR WRITING**   ■■■

1. Is this story still relevant to contemporary teenage culture? Using Kowinski's "Kids in the Mall" as a resource, construct an argument which addresses this question.
2. Why would this story win a prize? Evaluate the work. Consider such elements of fiction as point of view, conflict, character development, language, and tone (see Chapter 9).

Game After Supper

Margaret Atwood

Margaret Atwood (1939–   ) was born in Ottawa, Ontario, Canada and grew up in northern Ontario, Quebec, and Toronto. She was educated at the University of Toronto, Radcliffe College, and Harvard University. She has written more than twenty books of fiction, poetry, and nonfiction. Her works include Surfacing *(1972),* Lady Oracle *(1976),* Bodily Harm *(1981),* The Handmaid's Tale *(1985),* Cat's Eye *(1988), and* The Robber Bride *(1993). Her collections of short fiction are* Dancing Girls *(1977),* Bluebeard's Egg *(1983), and* Wilderness Tips *(1991). A characteristic tension in Atwood's work is expressed in violent images and opposites, destructive relationships, loneliness, and the need for genuine human communication.*

In "Game After Supper," the speaker creates a childhood scene from memory, a scene which involves fear and death.

This is before electricity,
it is when there were porches.

On the sagging porch an old man
is rocking. The porch is wooden,

5 the house is wooden and grey;
in the living room which smells of
smoke and mildew, soon
the woman will light the kerosene lamp.

There is a barn but I am not in the barn;
10 there is an orchard too, gone bad,
its apples like soft cork
but I am not there either.

I am hiding in the long grass
with my two dead cousins,
15 the membrane grown already
across their throats.

We hear crickets and our own hearts
close to our ears;
though we giggle, we are afraid.

20 From the shadows around
the corner of the house
a tall man is coming to find us:

He will be an uncle,
if we are lucky.

■ **EXPLORATIONS OF THE TEXT** ■

1. What does the locale (the porch, the house, barn, orchard) signify in relation to the rest of the poem?
2. What is the "game after supper"? Why are they hiding? What do they fear?
3. Who is the "tall man"? What does he symbolize?
4. What is the significance of the lines: "He will be an uncle if we are lucky"?

■■ **JOURNAL ENTRIES** ■■

1. Respond to the settings in the poem.
2. Write about the associations this poem evokes in you.

■■■ **IDEAS FOR WRITING** ■■■

1. Compare this initiation experience with incidents in "The Verb to Kill"; in "Where Are You Going . . ."; and in "Adolescence I, II, III."
2. Isolate and list those words and phrases that create the mood of the poem. Write a short paragraph about Atwood's method of establishing the mood.

Kids in the Mall

William S. Kowinski

A poet, fiction writer, and critic, William Severini Kowinski studied at Knox College and has been a writer and editor for the Boston Phoenix *and Washington* Newsworks. *He has published in numerous magazines, among them* Esquire, New Times, *and* The New York Times Magazine. *His book,* The Malling of America: An Inside Look at the Great Consumer Paradise *(1985), is an investigation of the effects of shopping malls on the lives of adolescents.*

In this selection from his volume, Kowinski argues that malls play an important role in the lives of teenagers, one that he and others might not choose.

1   **B**utch heaved himself up and loomed over the group. "Like it was different for me," he piped. "My folks used to drop me off at the shopping mall every morning and leave me all day. It was like a big free baby-sitter, you know? One night they never came back for

me. Maybe they moved away. Maybe there's some kind of a Bureau of Missing Parents I could check with."

—*Richard Peek*
Secrets of the Shopping Mall
a novel for teenagers

2   From his sister at Swarthmore, I'd heard about a kid in Florida whose mother picked him up after school every day, drove him straight to the mall, and left him there until it closed—all at his insistence. I'd heard about a boy in Washington who, when his family moved from one suburb to another, pedaled his bicycle five miles every day to get back to his old mall, where he once belonged.

3   These stories aren't unusual. The mall is a common experience for the majority of American youth; they have probably been going there all their lives. Some ran within their first large open space, saw their first fountain, bought their first toy, and read their first book in a mall. They may have smoked their first cigarette or first joint or turned them down, had their first kiss or lost their virginity in the mall parking lot. Teenagers in America now spend more time in the mall than anywhere else but home and school. Mostly it is their choice, but some of that mall time is put in as the result of two-paycheck and single-parent households, and the lack of other viable alternatives. But are these kids being harmed by the mall?

4   I wondered first of all what difference it makes for adolescents to experience so many important moments in the mall. They are, after all, at play in the fields of its little world and they learn its ways; they adapt to it and make it adapt to them. It's here that these kids get their street sense, only it's mall sense. They are learning the ways of a large-scale artificial environment: its subtleties and flexibilities, its particular pleasures and resonances, and the attitudes it fosters.

5   The presence of so many teenagers for so much time was not something mall developers planned on. In fact, it came as a big surprise. But kids became a fact of mall life very early, and the International Council of Shopping Centers found it necessary to commission a study, which they published along with a guide to mall managers on how to handle the teenage incursion.

6   The study found that "teenagers in suburban centers are bored and come to the shopping centers mainly as a place to go. Teenagers in suburban centers spent more time fighting, drinking, littering and walking than did their urban counterparts, but presented fewer overall problems." The report observed that "adolescents congregated in groups of two to four and predominantly at locations selected by them rather than management." This probably had something to do with the decision to install game arcades, which allow management to channel these restless adolescents into naturally contained areas away from major traffic points of adult shoppers.

7   The guide concluded that mall management should tolerate and even encourage the teenage presence because, in the words of the report, "The vast majority support the same set of values as does shopping center management."

The same set of values means simply that mall kids are already prepro-grammed to be consumers and that the mall can put the finishing touches to them as hard-core, lifelong shoppers just like everybody else. That, after all, is what the mall is about. So it shouldn't be surprising that in spending a lot of time there, adolescents find little that challenges the assumption that the goal of life is to make money and buy products, or that just about everything else in life is to be used to serve those ends.

8   Growing up in a high-consumption society already adds inestimable pressure to kids' lives. Clothes consciousness has invaded the grade schools, and popularity is linked with having the best, newest clothes in the currently acceptable styles. Even what they read has been affected. "Miss [Nancy] Drew wasn't obsessed with her wardrobe," noted *The Wall Street Journal,* "but to-day the mystery in teen fiction for girls is what outfit the heroine will wear next." Shopping has become a survival skill and there is certainly no better place to learn it than the mall, where its importance is powerfully reinforced and certainly never questioned.

9   The mall as a university of suburban materialism, where Valley Girls and Boys from coast to coast are educated in consumption, has its other lessons in this era of change in family life and sexual mores and their economic and social ramifications. The plethora of products in the mall, plus the pressure on teens to buy them, may contribute to the phenomenon that psychologist David Elkind calls "the hurried child": kids who are exposed to too much of the adult world too quickly, and must respond with a sophistication that be-lies their still-tender emotional development. Certainly the adult products marketed for children—form-fitting designer jeans, sexy tops for preteen girls—add to the social pressure to look like an adult, along with the home-grown need to understand adult finances (why mothers must work) and adult emotions (when parents divorce).

10   Kids spend so much time at the mall partly because their parents allow it and even encourage it. The mall is safe, it doesn't seem to harbor any unsa-vory activities, and there is adult supervision; it is, after all, a controlled envi-ronment. So the temptation, especially for working parents, is to let the mall be their babysitter. At least the kids aren't watching TV. But the mall's role as a surrogate mother may be more extensive and more profound.

11   Karen Lansky, a writer living in Los Angeles, has looked into the subject and she told me some of her conclusions about the effects on its teenaged denizens of the mall's controlled and controlling environment. "Structure is the dominant idea, since true 'mall rats' lack just that in their home lives," she said, "and adolescents about to make the big leap into growing up crave more structure than our modern society cares to acknowledge." Karen pointed out some of the elements malls supply that kids used to get from their families, like warmth (Strawberry Shortcake dolls and similar cute and cuddly mer-chandise), old-fashioned mothering ("We do it all for you," the fast-food slo-gan), and even home cooking (the "homemade" treats at the food court).

12   The problem in all this, as Karen Lansky sees it, is that while families nur-ture children by encouraging growth through the assumption of responsibility

and then by letting them rest in the bosom of the family from the rigors of growing up, the mall as a structural mother encourages passivity and consumption, as long as the kid doesn't make trouble. Therefore all they learn about becoming adults is how to act and how to consume.

13   Kids are in the mall not only in the passive role of shoppers—they also work there, especially as fast-food outlets infiltrate the mall's enclosure. There they learn how to hold a job and take responsibility, but still within the same value context. When *CBS Reports* went to Oak Park Mall in suburban Kansas City, Kansas, to tape part of their hour-long consideration of malls, "After the Dream Comes True," they interviewed a teenaged girl who worked in a fast-food outlet there. In a sequence that didn't make the final program, she described the major goal of her present life, which was to perfect the curl on top of the ice-cream cones that were her store's speciality. If she could do that, she would be moved from the lowly soft-drink dispenser to the more prestigious ice-cream division, the curl on top of the status ladder at her restaurant. These are the achievements that are important at the mall.

14   Other benefits of such jobs may also be overrated, according to Laurence D. Steinberg of the University of California at Irvine's social ecology department, who did a study on teenage employment. Their jobs, he found, are generally simple, mindlessly repetitive and boring. They don't really learn anything, and the jobs don't head anywhere. Teenagers also work primarily with other teenagers; even their supervisors are often just a little older than they are. "Kids need to spend time with adults," Steinberg told me. "Although they get benefits from peer relationships, without parents and other adults it's a one-sided socialization. They hang out with each other, have age-segregated jobs, and watch TV."

15   Perhaps much of this is not so terrible or even so terribly different. Now that they have so much more to contend with in their lives, adolescents probably need more time to spend with other adolescents without adult impositions, just to sort things out. Though it is more concentrated in the mall (and therefore perhaps a clearer target), the value system there is really the dominant one of the whole society. Attitudes about curiosity, initiative, self-expression, empathy, and disinterested learning aren't necessarily made in the mall; they are mirrored there, perhaps a bit more intensely—as through a glass brightly.

16   Besides, the mall is not without its educational opportunities. There are bookstores, where there is at least a short shelf of classics at great prices, and other books from which it is possible to learn more than how to do sit-ups. There are tools, from hammers to VCRs, and products, from clothes to records, that can help the young find and express themselves. There are older people with stories, and places to be alone or to talk one-on-one with a kindred spirit. And there is always the passing show.

17   The mall itself may very well be an education about the future. I was struck with the realization, as early as my first forays into Greengate, that the mall is only one of a number of enclosed and controlled environments that are part of the lives of today's young. The mall is just an extension, say, of those large suburban schools—only there's Karmelkorn instead of chem lab,

the ice rink instead of the gym: It's high school without the impertinence of classes.

18   Growing up, moving from home to school to the mall—from enclosure to enclosure, transported in cars—is a curiously continuous process, without much in the way of contrast or contact with unenclosed reality. Places must tend to blur into one another. But whatever differences and dangers there are in this, the skills these adolescents are learning may turn out to be useful in their later lives. For we seem to be moving inexorably into an age of pre-planned and regulated environments, and this is the world they will inherit.

19   Still, it might be better if they had more of a choice. One teenaged girl confessed to *CBS Reports* that she sometimes felt she was missing something by hanging out at the mall so much. "But I'm here," she said, "and this is what I have."

■ EXPLORATIONS OF THE TEXT ■

1. How does the opening quotation from Richard Peck's *Secrets of the Shopping Mall* establish the point of view, tone, and concerns of the essay?
2. Why does Kowinski include several personal anecdotes in the opening paragraph?
3. What negative effects does Kowinski attribute to teenagers' "hanging out"? Is he persuasive?
4. In what ways does Kowinski suggest that teenagers benefit at all from the experience? Do you agree with his conclusions?
5. Agree or disagree with Karen Lansky's statement that the mall is a surrogate mother figure that "encourages passivity and consumption."
6. How is Connie in "Where Are You Going, Where Have You Been?" similar to the adolescents presented in this essay? How is Connie a product of mall culture?

■■ JOURNAL ENTRIES ■■

1. Did you "hang out" as a teenager? Describe your "hang out" and your friends. You may want to write a dialogue.

■■■ IDEAS FOR WRITING ■■■

1. Go to a mall and observe; write about your impressions. Or interview people in a shopping mall about their reactions to mall culture.
2. Write an argument: refute or agree with Kowinski's position or the position of one of the experts quoted in his essay.

FICTION

A White Heron

Sarah Orne Jewett

*Born in South Berwick, Maine, Theodora Sarah Orne Jewett (1849–
1909) graduated from Berwick Academy (1865). She often said,
however, that she received her true education making rounds to local farms with her father, a physician. She began writing stories
under the pseudonym A. C. Eliot for the* Atlantic. *In 1877, she published her first collection,* Deephaven. *Other volumes followed:* A
White Heron, and Other Stories *(1886) and* The King of Folly Island
(1888), and the novels, The Country Doctor *and* The Country of
Pointed Firs *(1896).*

*Jewett stated that she wrote about those "country characters
and landscapes to which [she herself] belonged, and which [she] had
been taught to love with all [her] heart." In "A White Heron"
Sylvia's conflict between her admiration for the young ornithologist
and her love for a wild bird provokes a hint of tragedy.*

I

1   The woods were already filled with shadows one June evening, just before
eight o'clock, though a bright sunset still glimmered faintly among the
trunks of the trees. A little girl was driving home her cow, a plodding, dila-
tory, provoking creature in her behavior, but a valued companion for all that.
They were going away from the western light, and striking deep into the dark
woods, but their feet were familiar with the path, and it was no matter
whether their eyes could see it or not.

There was hardly a night the summer through when the old cow could be
found waiting at the pasture bars; on the contrary, it was her greatest pleasure to hide herself away among the high huckleberry bushes, and though she
wore a loud bell she had made the discovery that if one stood perfectly still it
would not ring. So Sylvia had to hunt for her until she found her, and call
Co'! Co'! with never an answering Moo, until her childish patience was quite
spent. If the creature had not given good milk and plenty of it, the case would
have seemed very different to her owners. Besides, Sylvia had all the time
there was, and very little use to make of it. Sometimes in pleasant weather it
was a consolation to look upon the cow's pranks as an intelligent attempt to
play hide and seek, and as the child had no playmates she lent herself to this

amusement with a good deal of zest. Though this chase had been so long that the wary animal herself had given an unusual signal of her whereabouts, Sylvia had only laughed when she came upon Mistress Moolly at the swamp-side, and urged her affectionately homeward with a twig of birch leaves. The old cow was not inclined to wander farther, she even turned in the right direction for once as they left the pasture, and stepped along the road at a good pace. She was quite ready to be milked now, and seldom stopped to browse. Sylvia wondered what her grandmother would say because they were so late. It was a great while since she had left home at half past five o'clock, but everybody knew the difficulty of making this errand a short one. Mrs. Tilley had chased the horned torment too many summer evenings herself to blame any one else for lingering, and was only thankful as she waited that she had Sylvia, nowadays, to give such valuable assistance. The good woman suspected that Sylvia loitered occasionally on her own account; there never was such a child for straying about out-of-doors since the world was made! Everybody said that it was a good change for a little maid who had tried to grow for eight years in a crowded manufacturing town, but, as for Sylvia herself, it seemed as if she never had been alive at all before she came to live at the farm. She thought often with wistful compassion of a wretched dry geranium that belonged to a town neighbor.

"'Afraid of folks,'" old Mrs. Tilley said to herself, with a smile, after she had made the unlikely choice of Sylvia from her daughter's houseful of children, and was returning to the farm. "'Afraid of folks,' they said! I guess she won't be troubled no great with 'em up to the old place!" When they reached the door of the lonely house and stopped to unlock it, and the cat came to purr loudly, and rub against them, a deserted pussy, indeed, but fat with young robins, Sylvia whispered that this was a beautiful place to live in, and she never should wish to go home.

The companions followed the shady wood-road, the cow taking slow steps, and the child very fast ones. The cow stopped long at the brook to drink, as if the pasture were not half a swamp, and Sylvia stood still and waited, letting her bare feet cool themselves in the shoal water, while the great twilight moths struck softly against her. She waded on through the brook as the cow moved away, and listened to the thrushes with a heart that beat fast with pleasure. There was a stirring in the great boughs overhead. They were full of little birds and beasts that seemed to be wide-awake, and going about their world, or else saying good-night to each other in sleepy twitters. Sylvia herself felt sleepy as she walked along. However, it was not much farther to the house, and the air was soft and sweet. She was not often in the woods so late as this, and it made her feel as if she were a part of the gray shadows and the moving leaves. She was just thinking how long it seemed since she first came to the farm a year ago, and wondering if everything went on in the noisy town just the same as when she was there; the thought of the great red-faced boy who used to chase and frighten her made her hurry along the path to escape from the shadow of the trees.

5   Suddenly this little woods-girl is horror-stricken to hear a clear whistle not very far away. Not a bird's whistle, which would have a sort of friendliness, but a boy's whistle, determined, and somewhat aggressive. Sylvia left the cow to whatever sad fate might await her, and stepped discreetly aside into the bushes, but she was just too late. The enemy had discovered her, and called out in a very cheerful and persuasive tone. "Halloa, little girl, how far is it to the road?" and trembling Sylvia answered almost inaudibly, "A good ways."

She did not dare to look boldly at the tall young man, who carried a gun over his shoulder, but she came out of her bush and again followed the cow, while he walked alongside.

"I have been hunting for some birds," the stranger said kindly, "and I have lost my way, and need a friend very much. Don't be afraid," he added gallantly. "Speak up and tell me what your name is, and whether you think I can spend the night at your house, and go out gunning early in the morning."

Sylvia was more alarmed than before. Would not her grandmother consider her much to blame? But who could have foreseen such an accident as this? It did not appear to be her fault, and she hung her head as if the stem of it were broken, but managed to answer, "Sylvy," with much effort when her companion again asked her name.

Mrs. Tilley was standing in the doorway when the trio came into view. The cow gave a loud moo by way of explanation.

10   "Yes, you'd better speak up for yourself, you old trial! Where'd she tucked herself away this time. Sylvy?" Sylvia kept an awed silence; she knew by instinct that her grandmother did not comprehend the gravity of the situation. She must be mistaking the stranger for one of the farmer-lads of the region.

The young man stood his gun beside the door, and dropped a heavy game-bag beside it; then he bade Mrs. Tilley good evening, and repeated his wayfarer's story, and asked if he could have a night's lodging.

"Put we anywhere you like," he said. "I must be off early in the morning, before day; but I am very hungry, indeed. You can give me some milk at any rate, that's plain."

"Dear sakes, yes," responded the hostess, whose long slumbering hospitality seemed to be easily awakened. "You might fare better if you went out on the main road a mile or so, but you're welcome to what we've got. I'll milk right off, and you make yourself at home. You can sleep on husks or feathers," she proffered graciously. "I raised them all myself. There's good pasturing for geese just below here towards the ma'sh. Now step round and set a plate for the gentleman, Sylvy!" And Sylvia promptly stepped. She was glad to have something to do, and she was hungry herself.

It was a surprise to find so clean and comfortable a little dwelling in this New England wilderness. The young man had known the horrors of its most primitive housekeeping, and the dreary squalor of that level of society which does not rebel at the companionship of hens. This was the best thrift of an old-fashioned farmstead, though on such a small scale that it seemed like a hermitage. He listened eagerly to the old woman's quaint talk, he watched Sylvia's pale face and shining gray eyes with ever growing enthusiasm, and insisted that this was the best supper he had eaten for a month; then, afterward, the new-made friends sat down in the doorway together while the moon came up.

15   Soon it would be berry time, and Sylvia was a great help at picking. The cow was a good milker, though a plaguy thing to keep track of, the hostess gossiped frankly, adding presently that she had buried four children, so that Sylvia's mother, and a son (who might be dead) in California were all the children she had left. "Dan, my boy, was a great hand to go gunning," she explained sadly. "I never wanted for pa'tridges or gray squer'ls while he was to home. He's been a great wand'rer, I expect, and he's no hand to write letters. There, I don't blame him, I'd ha' seen the world myself if it had been so I could."

"Sylvia takes after him," the grandmother continued affectionately, after a minute's pause. "There ain't a foot o' ground she don't know her way over, and the wild creatur's counts her one o' themselves. Squer'ls she'll tame to come an' feed right out o' her hands, and all sorts o' birds. Last winter she got the jay-birds to bangeing here, and I believe she'd 'a' scanted herself of her own meals to have plenty to throw out amongst 'em, if I hadn't kep' watch. Anything but crows, I tell her, I'm willin' to help support,—though Dan he went an' tamed one o' them that did seem to have reason same as folks. It was round here a good spell after he went away. Dan an' his father they didn't hitch,—but he never held up his head ag'in after Dan had dared him an' gone off."

The guest did not notice this hint of family sorrows in his eager interest in something else.

"So Sylvy knows all about birds, does she?" he exclaimed, as he looked round at the little girl who sat, very demure but increasingly sleepy, in the moonlight. "I am making a collection of birds myself. I have been at it ever since I was a boy." (Mrs. Tilley smiled.) "There are two or three very rare ones I have been hunting for these five years. I mean to get them on my own ground if they can be found."

"Do you cage 'em up?" asked Mrs. Tilley doubtfully, in response to this enthusiastic announcement.

20   "Oh, no, they're stuffed and preserved, dozens and dozens of them," said the ornithologist, "and I have shot or snared every one myself. I caught a glimpse of a white heron three miles from here on Saturday, and I have followed it in this direction. They have never been found in this district at all. The little white heron, it is," and he turned again to look at Sylvia with the hope of discovering that the rare bird was one of her acquaintances.

But Sylvia was watching a hop toad in the narrow footpath.

"You would know the heron if you saw it," the stranger continued eagerly. "A queer tall white bird with soft feathers and long thin legs. And it would have a nest perhaps in the top of a high tree, made of sticks, something like a hawk's nest."

Sylvia's heart gave a wild beat; she knew that strange white bird, and had once stolen softly near where it stood in some bright green swamp grass, away over at the other side of the woods. There was an open place where the sunshine always seemed strangely yellow and hot, where tall, nodding rushes grew, and her grandmother had warned her that she might sink in the soft black mud underneath and never be heard of more. Not far beyond were the salt marshes and beyond those was the sea, the sea which Sylvia wondered and dreamed about, but never had looked upon, though its great voice could often be heard above the noise of the woods on stormy nights.

"I can't think of anything I should like so much as to find that heron's nest," the handsome stranger was saying. "I would give ten dollars to anybody who could show it to me," he added desperately, "and I mean to spend my whole vacation hunting for it if need be. Perhaps it was only migrating, or had been chased out of its region by some bird of prey."

25   Mrs. Tilley gave amazed attention to all this, but Sylvia still watched the toad, not divining, as she might have done at some calmer time, that the creature wished to get to its hole under the doorstep, and was much hindered by the unusual spectators at that hour of the evening. No amount of thought, that night, could decide how many wished-for treasures the ten dollars, so lightly spoken of, would buy.

The next day the young sportsman hovered about the woods, and Sylvia kept him company, having lost her first fear of the friendly lad, who proved to be most kind and sympathetic. He told her many things about the birds and what they knew and where they lived and what they did with themselves. And he gave her a jackknife, which she thought as great a treasure as if she were a desert-islander. All day long he did not once make her troubled or afraid except when he brought down some unsuspecting singing creature from its bough. Sylvia would have liked him vastly better without his gun; she could not understand why he killed the very birds he seemed to like so much. But as the day waned, Sylvia still watched the young man with loving admiration. She had never seen anybody so charming and delightful: the woman's heart, asleep in the child, was vaguely thrilled by a dream of love. Some premonition of that great power stirred and swayed these young foresters who traversed the solemn woodlands with soft-footed silent care. They stopped to listen to a bird's song; they pressed forward again eagerly, parting the branches—speaking to each other rarely and in whispers; the young man going first and Sylvia following, fascinated, a few steps behind, with her gray eyes dark with excitement.

She grieved because the longed-for white heron was elusive, but she did not lead the guest, she only followed, and there was no such thing as speaking first. The sound of her own unquestioned voice would have terrified her—it was hard enough to answer yes or no when there was need of that. At last evening began to fall, and they drove the cow home together, and Sylvia smiled with pleasure when they came to the place where she heard the whistle and was afraid only the night before.

II

Half a mile from home, at the farther edge of the woods, where the land was highest, a great pine-tree stood, the last of its generation. Whether it was left for a boundary mark, or for what reason, no one could say; the woodchoppers who had felled its mates were dead and gone long ago, and a whole forest of sturdy trees, pines and oaks and maples, had grown again. But the stately head of this old pine towered above them all and made a landmark for sea and shore miles and miles away. Sylvia knew it well. She had always believed that whoever climbed to the top of it could see the ocean; and the little girl had often laid her hand on the great rough trunk and looked up wistfully at those dark boughs that the wind always stirred, no matter how hot and still the air might be below. Now she thought of the tree with a new excitement, for why, if one climbed it at break of day, could not one see all the world, and easily discover whence the white heron flew, and mark the place, and find the hidden nest?

What a spirit of adventure, what wild ambition! What fancied triumph and delight and glory for the later morning when she could make known the secret! It was almost too real and too great for the childish heart to bear.

30 All night the door of the little house stood open, and the whippoorwills came and sang upon the very step. The young sportsman and his old hostess were sound asleep, but Sylvia's great design kept her broad awake and watching. She forgot to think of sleep. The short summer night seemed as long as the winter darkness, and at last when the whippoorwills ceased, and she was afraid the morning would after all come too soon, she stole out of the house and followed the pasture path through the woods, hastening toward the open ground beyond, listening with a sense of comfort and companionship to the drowsy twitter of a half-awakened bird, whose perch she had jarred in passing. Alas, if the great wave of human interest which flooded for the first time this dull little life should sweep away the satisfactions of an existence heart to heart with nature and the dumb life of the forest!

There was the huge tree asleep yet in the paling moonlight, and small and hopeful Sylvia began with utmost bravery to mount to the top of it, with tingling, eager blood coursing the channels of her whole frame, with her bare feet and fingers, that pinched and held like bird's claws to the monstrous ladder reaching up, up, almost to the sky itself. First she must mount the white oak tree that grew alongside, where she was almost lost among the dark branches and the green leaves heavy and wet with dew; a bird fluttered off its nest, and a red squirrel ran to and fro and scolded pettishly at the harmless housebreaker. Sylvia felt her way easily. She had often climbed there, and knew that higher still one of the oak's upper branches chafed against the pine trunk, just where its lower boughs were set close together. There, when she made the dangerous pass from one tree to the other, the great enterprise would really begin.

She crept out along the swaying oak limb at last, and took the daring step across into the old pine-tree. The way was harder than she thought; she must reach far and hold fast, the sharp dry twigs caught and held her and scratched her like angry talons, the pitch made her thin little fingers clumsy and stiff as she went round and round the tree's great stem, higher and higher upward. The sparrows and robins in the woods below were beginning to wake and twitter to the dawn, yet it seemed much lighter there aloft in the pine-tree, and the child knew that she must hurry if her project were to be of any use.

The tree seemed to lengthen itself out as she went up, and to reach farther and farther upward. It was like a great main-mast to the voyaging earth; it must truly have been amazed that morning through all its ponderous frame as it felt this determined spark of human spirit creeping and climbing from higher branch to branch. Who knows how steadily the least twigs held themselves to advantage this light, weak creature on her way! The old pine must have loved his new dependent. More than all the hawks, and bats, and moths, and even the sweet-voiced thrushes, was the brave, beating heart of the solitary gray-eyed child. And the tree stood still and held away the winds that June morning while the dawn grew bright in the east.

Sylvia's face was like a pale star, if one had seen it from the ground, when the last thorny bough was past, and she stood trembling and tired but wholly triumphant, high in the tree-top. Yes, there was the sea with the dawning sun making a golden dazzle over it, and toward that glorious east flew two hawks with slow-moving pinions.[1] How low they looked in the air from that height when before one had only seen them far up, and dark against the blue sky. Their gray feathers were as soft as moths; they seemed only a little way from the tree, and Sylvia felt as if she too could go flying away among the clouds. Westward, the woodlands and farms reached miles and miles into the distance; here and there were church steeples, and white villages; truly it was a vast and awesome world.

35   The birds sang louder and louder. At last the sun came up bewilderingly bright. Sylvia could see the white sails of ships out at sea, and the clouds that were purple and rose-colored and yellow at first began to fade away. Where was the white heron's nest in the sea of green branches, and was this wonderful sight and pageant of the world the only reward for having climbed to such a giddy height? Now look down again, Sylvia, where the green marsh is set among the shining birches and dark hemlocks; there where you saw the white heron once you will see him again; look, look! a white spot of him like a single floating feather comes up from the dead hemlock and grows larger, and rises, and comes close at last, and goes by the landmark pine with steady sweep of wing and outstretched slender neck and crested head. And wait! wait! do not move a foot or a finger, little girl, do not send an arrow of light and consciousness from your two eager eyes, for the heron has perched on a pine bough not far beyond yours, and cries back to his mate on the nest, and plumes his feathers for the new day!

The child gives a long sigh a minute later when a company of shouting cat-birds comes also to the tree, and vexed by their fluttering and lawlessness

---

[1] Parts of a bird's wing; wings or feathers.

the solemn heron goes away. She knows his secret now, the wild, light, slender bird that floats and wavers, and goes back like an arrow presently to his home in the green world beneath. Then Sylvia, well satisfied, makes her perilous way down again, not daring to look far below the branch she stands on, ready to cry sometimes because her fingers ache and her lamed feet slip. Wondering over and over again what the stranger would say to her, and what he would think when she told him how to find his way straight to the heron's nest.

"Sylvy, Sylvy!" called the busy old grandmother again and again, but nobody answered, and the small husk bed was empty, and Sylvia had disappeared.

The guest waked from a dream, and remembering his day's pleasure hurried to dress himself that it might sooner begin. He was sure from the way the shy little girl looked once or twice yesterday that she had at least seen the white heron, and now she must really be persuaded to tell. Here she comes now, paler than ever, and her worn old frock is torn and tattered, and smeared with pine pitch. The grandmother and the sportsman stand in the door together and question her, and the splendid moment has come to speak of the dead hemlock-tree by the green marsh.

But Sylvia does not speak after all, though the old grandmother fretfully rebukes her, and the young man's kind appealing eyes are looking straight in her own. He can make them rich with money; he has promised it, and they are poor now. He is so well worth making happy, and he waits to hear the story she can tell.

40   No, she must keep silence! What is it that suddenly forbids her and makes her dumb? Has she been nine years growing, and now, when the great world for the first time puts out a hand to her, must she thrust it aside for a bird's sake? The murmur of the pine's green branches is in her ears, she remembers how the white heron came flying through the golden air and how they watched the sea and the morning together, and Sylvia cannot speak; she cannot tell the heron's secret and give its life away.

Dear loyalty, that suffered a sharp pang as the guest went away disappointed later in the day, that could have served and followed him and loved him as a dog loves! Many a night Sylvia heard the echo of his whistle haunting the pasture path as she came home with the loitering cow. She forgot even her sorrow at the sharp report of his gun and the piteous sight of thrushes and sparrows dropping silent to the ground, their songs hushed and their pretty feathers stained and wet with blood. Were the birds better friends than their hunter might have been,—who can tell? Whatever treasures were lost to her, woodlands and summer-time, remember! Bring your gifts and graces and tell your secrets to this lonely country child!

■ EXPLORATIONS OF THE TEXT ■

1. What is the relationship of landscapes to character? What is the significance of the girl's name?
2. Characterize the ornithologist. Why does Sylvia want to please the young man? What are the complications?
3. What is the relationship between the grandmother and Sylvia?
4. Why does Sylvia save the bird? How does she decide?
5. How does this story differ in theme and style from Wright's "The Man Who Was Almost a Man" or Faulkner's "Barn Burning"? What elements are the same?

■■ JOURNAL ENTRIES ■■

1. Describe female initiation in Jewett's story. What does Sylvia learn?
2. React to the depiction of nature in this work.
3. Write a monologue in the voice of the ornithologist.

■■■ IDEAS FOR WRITING ■■■

1. Write about the conflict between love and principle in "A White Heron."
2. Compare the depiction of hunting and violence in "A White Heron" and in "Uncle's First Rabbit."

Barn Burning

William Faulkner

William Faulkner (1897–1962) lived most of his life in Oxford, Mississippi. His literary career began in New Orleans where he wrote newspaper stories for the Times—Picayune. *With the assistance of the writer Sherwood Anderson, whom he met in New Orleans, Faulkner published his first novel,* Soldiers' Pay *(1926). In his major novels, he created an imaginary region near Oxford called Yoknapatawpha County. He chronicled a new Southern history in* The Sound and the Fury *(1929),* As I Lay Dying *(1930),* Sanctuary *(1931),* Light in August *(1932),* Absalom, Absalom! *(1936), and* The Hamlet *(1940). His short fiction can be found in* The Short Stories of William Faulkner *(1950). Faulkner received the Nobel Prize for Literature in 1949.*

In "Barn Burning" the boy loses his home again and again because of his father. Gradually he develops his own sense of values.

1　The store in which the Justice of the Peace's court was sitting smelled of cheese. The boy, crouched on his nail keg at the back of the crowded room, knew he smelled cheese, and more; from where he sat he could see the ranked shelves close-packed with the solid, squat, dynamic shapes of tin cans whose labels his stomach read, not from the lettering which meant nothing to his mind but from the scarlet devils and the silver curve of fish—this, the cheese which he knew he smelled and the hermetic meat[1] which his intestines believed he smelled coming in intermittent gusts momentary and brief between the other constant one, the smell and sense just a little of fear because mostly of despair and grief, the old fierce pull of blood. He could not see the table where the Justice sat and before which his father and his father's enemy (*our enemy* he thought in that despair; *ourn! mine and his both! He's my father!*) stood, but he could hear them, the two of them that is, because his father had said no word yet:

"But what proof have you, Mr. Harris?"

"I told you. The hog got into my corn. I caught it up and sent it back to him. He had no fence that would hold it. I told him so, warned him. The next time I put the hog in my pen. When he came to get it I gave him enough wire to patch up his pen. The next time I put the hog up and kept it. I rode down to his house and saw the wire I gave him still rolled on to the spool in his yard. I told him he could have the hog when he paid me a dollar pound fee. That evening a nigger came with the dollar and got the hog. He was a strange nigger. He said, 'He say to tell you wood and hay kin burn.' I said, 'What?' 'That what he say to tell you,' the nigger said. 'Wood and hay kin burn.' That night my barn burned. I got the stock out but I lost the barn."

"Where is the nigger? Have you got him?"

5　"He was a strange nigger, I tell you. I don't know what became of him."

"But that's not proof. Don't you see that's not proof?"

"Get that boy up here. He knows." For a moment the boy thought too that the man meant his older brother until Harris said. "Not him. The little one. The boy," and, crouching, small for his age, small and wiry like his father, in patched and faded jeans even too small for him, with straight, uncombed, brown hair and eyes gray and wild as storm scud, he saw the men between himself and the table part and become a lane of grim faces, at the end of which he saw the Justice, a shabby, collarless, graying man in spectacles, beckoning him. He felt no floor under his bare feet; he seemed to walk beneath the palpable weight of the grim turning faces. His father, stiff in his black Sunday coat donned not for the trial but for the moving, did not even

---

[1] Canned meat.

look at him. *He aims for me to lie,* he thought, again with that frantic grief and despair. *And I will have to do hit.*

"What's your name, boy?" the Justice said.

"Colonel Sartoris Snopes," the boy whispered.

10   "Hey?" the Justice said. "Talk louder. Colonel Sartoris? I reckon anybody named for Colonel Sartoris in this country can't help but tell the truth, can they?" The boy said nothing. *Enemy! Enemy!* he thought; for a moment he could not even see, could not see that the Justice's face was kindly nor discern that his voice was troubled when he spoke to the man named Harris: "Do you want me to question this boy?" But he could hear, and during those subsequent long seconds there was absolutely no sound in the crowded little room save that of quiet and intent breathing it was as if he had swung outward at the end of a grape vine, over a ravine, and at the top of the swing had been caught in a prolonged instant of mesmerized gravity, weightless in time.

"No!" Harris said violently, explosively. "Damnation! Send him out of here!" Now time, the fluid world, rushed beneath him again, the voices coming to him again through the smell of cheese and sealed meat, the fear and despair and the old grief of blood:

"This case is closed. I can't find against you, Snopes, but I can give you advice. Leave this country and don't come back to it."

His father spoke for the first time, his voice cold and harsh, level, without emphasis: "I aim to. I don't figure to stay in a country among people who . . ." he said something unprintable and vile, addressed to no one.

"That'll do," the Justice said, "Take your wagon and get out of this country before dark. Case dismissed."

15   His father turned, and he followed the stiff black coat, the wiry figure walking a little stiffly, from where a Confederate provost's man's musket ball had taken him in the heel on a stolen horse thirty years ago, followed the two backs now, since his older brother had appeared from somewhere in the crowd, no taller than the father but thicker, chewing tobacco steadily, between the two lines of grim-faced men and out of the store and across the worn gallery and down the sagging steps and among the dogs and half-grown boys in the mild May dust, where as he passed a voice hissed:

"Barn burner!"

Again he could not see, whirling; there was a face in a red haze, moonlike, bigger than the full moon, the owner of it half again his size, he leaping in the red haze toward the face, feeling no blow, feeling no shock when his head struck the earth, scrabbling up and leaping again, feeling no blow this time either and tasting no blood, scrabbling up to see the other boy in full flight and himself already leaping into pursuit as his father's hand jerked him back, the harsh, cold voice speaking above him: "Go get in the wagon."

It stood in a grove of locusts and mulberries across the road. His two hulking sisters in their Sunday dresses and his mother and her sister in calico and sunbonnets were already in it, sitting on and among the sorry residue of the dozen and more movings which even the boy could remember—the battered stove, the broken beds and chairs, the clock inlaid with mother-of-pearl, which would not run, stopped at some fourteen minutes past two o'clock of a dead and forgotten day and time, which had been his mother's dowry. She was crying, though when she saw him she drew her sleeve across her face and began to descend from the wagon. "Get back," the father said.

"He's hurt, I got to get some water and wash his . . ."

20   "Get back in the wagon," his father said. He got in too, over the tail-gate. His father mounted to the seat where the older brother already sat and struck the gaunt mules two savage blows with the peeled willow, but without heat. It was not even sadistic; it was exactly that same quality which in later years would cause his descendants to over-run the engine before putting a motor car into motion, striking and reining back in the same movement. The wagon went on, the store with its quiet crowd of grimly watching men dropped behind; a curve in the road hid it. *Forever* he thought. *Maybe he's done satisfied now, now that he has* . . . stopping himself, not to say it aloud even to himself. His mother's hand touched his shoulder.

"Does hit hurt?" she said.

"Naw," he said. "Hit don't hurt. Lemme be."

"Can't you wipe some of the blood off before hit dries?"

"I'll wash tonight," he said. "Lemme be, I tell you."

25   The wagon went on. He did not know where they were going. None of them ever did or ever asked, because it was always somewhere, always a house of sorts waiting for them a day or two days or even three days away. Likely his father had already arranged to make a crop on another farm before he . . . Again he had to stop himself. He (the father) always did. There was something about his wolf-like independence and even courage when the advantage was at least neutral which impressed strangers, as if they got from his latent ravening ferocity not so much a sense of dependability as a feeling that his ferocious conviction in the rightness of his own actions would be of advantage to all whose interest lay with his.

That night they camped, in a grove of oaks and beeches where a spring ran. The nights were still cool and they had a fire against it, of a rail lifted from a nearby fence and cut into lengths—a small fire, neat, niggard almost, a shrewd fire; such fires were his father's habit and custom always, even in freezing weather. Older, the boy might have remarked this and wondered why not a big one; why should not a man who had not only seen the waste and extravagance of war, but who had in his blood an inherent prodigality with material not his own, have burned everything in sight? Then he might have gone a step farther and thought that that was the reason; that niggard blaze was the living fruits of nights passed during those four years in the woods hiding from all men, blue or grey, with his strings of horses (captured horses, he called them). And older still, he might have divined the true reason: that the element of fire spoke to some deep mainspring of his father's being, as the element of steel or of powder spoke to other men, as the one weapon for the preservation of integrity, else breath were not worth the breathing, and hence to be regarded with respect and used with discretion.

But he did not think this now and he had seen those same niggard blazes all his life. He merely ate his supper beside it and was already half asleep over his iron plate when his father called him, and once more he followed the stiff back, the stiff and ruthless limp, up the slope and on to the starlit road where, turning, he could see his father against the stars but without face or depth— a shape black, flat, and bloodless as though cut from tin in the iron folds of the frockcoat which had not been made for him, the voice harsh like tin and without heat like tin:

"You were fixing to tell them. You would have told him." He didn't answer. His father struck him with the flat of his hand on the side of the head, hard but without heat, exactly as he had struck the two mules at the store, exactly as he would strike either of them with any stick in order to kill a horse fly, his voice still without heat or anger: "You're getting to be a man. You got to learn. You got to learn to stick to your own blood or you ain't going to have any blood to stick to you. Do you think either of them, any man there this morning, would? Don't you know all they wanted was a chance to get at me because they knew I had them beat? Eh?" Later, twenty years later, he was to tell himself, "If I had said they wanted only truth, justice, he would have hit me again." But now he said nothing. He was not crying. He just stood there. "Answer me," his father said.

"Yes," he whispered. His father turned.

30 "Get on to bed. We'll be there tomorrow."

Tomorrow they were there. In the early afternoon the wagon stopped before a paintless two-room house identical almost with the dozen others it had stopped before even in the boy's ten years, and again, as on the other dozen occasions, his mother and aunt got down and began to unload the wagon, although his two sisters and his father and brother had not moved.

"Likely hit ain't fitten for hawgs," one of the sisters said.

"Nevertheless, fit it will and you'll hog it and like it," his father said. "Get out of them chairs and help your Ma unload."

The two sisters got down, big, bovine, in a flutter of cheap ribbons; one of them drew from the jumbled wagon bed a battered lantern, the other a worn broom. His father handed the reins to the older son and began to climb stiffly over the wheel. "Whey they get unloaded, take the team to the barn and feed them." Then he said, and at first the boy thought he was still speaking to his brother: "Come with me."

35 "Me?" he said.

"Yes," his father said. "You."

"Abner," his mother said. His father paused and looked back—the harsh level stare beneath the shaggy, graying, irascible brows.

"I reckon I'll have a word with the man that aims to begin tomorrow owning me body and soul for the next eight months."

They went back up the road. A week ago—or before last night, that is— he would have asked where they were going, but not now. His father had struck him before last night but never before had he paused afterward to explain why; it was as if the blow and the following calm, outrageous voice still rang, repercussed, divulging nothing to him save the terrible handicap of being young, the light weight of his few years, just heavy enough to prevent his soaring free of the world as it seemed to be ordered but not heavy enough to keep footed solid in it, to resist it and try to change the course of its events.

40   Presently he could see the grove of oaks and cedars and the other flowering trees and shrubs where the house would be, though not the house yet. They walked beside a fence massed with honeysuckle and Cherokee roses and came to a gate swinging open between two brick pillars, and now, beyond a sweep of drive, he saw the house for the first time and at that instant he forgot his father and the terror and despair both, and even when he remembered his father again (who had stopped) the terror and despair did not return. Because, for all the twelve movings, they had sojourned until now in a poor country, a land of small farms and fields and houses, and he had never seen a house like this before. *Hit's big as a courthouse* he thought quietly, with a surge of peace and joy whose reason he could not have thought into words, being too young for that: *They are safe from him. People whose lives are a part of this peace and dignity are beyond his touch, he no more to them than a buzzing wasp: capable of stinging for a little moment but that's all; the spell of this peace and dignity rendering even the barns and stable and cribs which belong to it impervious to the puny flames he might contrive . . .* this, the peace and joy, ebbing for an instant as he looked again at the stiff black back, the stiff and implacable limp of the figure which was not dwarfed by the house, for the reason that it had never looked big anywhere and which now, against the serene columned backdrop, had more than ever that impervious quality of something cut ruthlessly from tin, depthless, as though, sidewise to the sun, it would cast no shadow. Watching him, the boy remarked the absolutely undeviating course which his father held and saw the stiff foot come squarely down in a pile of fresh droppings where a horse had stood in the drive and which his father could have avoided by a simple change of stride. But it ebbed only for a moment, though he could not have thought this into words either, walking on in the spell of the house, which he could even want but without envy, without sorrow, certainly never with that ravening and jealous rage which unknown to him walked in the ironlike black coat before him: *Maybe he will feel it too. Maybe it will even change him now from what maybe he couldn't help but be.*

They crossed the portico. Now he could hear his father's stiff foot as it came down on the boards with clocklike finality, a sound out of all proportion to the displacement of the body it bore and which was not dwarfed either by the white door before it, as though it had attained to a sort of vicious and ravening minimum not to be dwarfed by anything—the flat, wide, black hat, the formal coat of broadcloth which had once been black but which had now that friction-glazed greenish cast of the bodies of old house flies, the lifted sleeve which was too large, the lifted hand like a curled claw. The door opened so promptly that the boy knew the Negro must have been watching them all the time, an old man with neat grizzled hair, in a linen jacket, who stood barring the door with his body, saying "Wipe yo foots, white man, fo you come in here. Major ain't home nohow."

"Get out of my way, nigger," his father said, without heat too, flinging the door back and the Negro also and entering, his hat still on his head. And now the boy saw the prints of the stiff foot on the doorsill and saw them appear on the pale rug behind the machinelike deliberation of the foot which seemed to bear (or transmit) twice the weight which the body compassed. The Negro was shouting "Miss Lula! Miss Lula!" somewhere behind them, then the boy, deluged as though by a warm wave by a suave turn of carpeted stair and a pendant glitter of chandeliers and a mute gleam of gold frames, heard the swift feet and saw her too, a lady—perhaps he had never seen her like before either—in a gray, smooth gown with lace at the throat and an apron tied at the waist and the sleeves turned back, wiping cake or biscuit dough from her hands with a towel as she came up the hall, looking not at his father at all but at the tracks on the blond rug with an expression of incredulous amazement.

"I tried," the Negro cried. "I tole him to . . ."

"Will you please go away?" she said in a shaking voice. "Major de Spain is not at home. Will you please go away?"

45   His father had not spoken again. He did not speak again. He did not even look at her. He just stood stiff in the center of the rug, in his hat, the shaggy iron-gray brows twitching slightly above the pebble-colored eyes as he appeared to examine the house with brief deliberation. Then with the same deliberation he turned; the boy watched him pivot on the good leg and saw the stiff foot drag round the arc of the turning, leaving a final long and fading smear. His father never looked at it, he never once looked down at the rug. The Negro held the door. It closed behind them, upon the hysteric and indistinguishable woman-wail. His father stopped at the top of the steps and scraped his boot clean on the edge of it. At the gate he stopped again. He stood for a moment, planted stiffly on the stiff foot, looking back at the house. "Pretty and white, ain't it?" he said. "That's sweat. Nigger sweat. Maybe it ain't white enough yet to suit him. Maybe he wants to mix some white sweat with it."

Two hours later the boy was chopping wood behind the house within which his mother and aunt and the two sisters (the mother and aunt, not the two girls, he knew that; even at this distance and muffled by walls the flat loud voices of the two girls emanated an incorrigible idle inertia) were setting up the stove to prepare a meal, when he heard the hooves and saw the linen-clad man on a fine sorrel mare, whom he recognized even before he saw the rolled rug in front of the Negro youth following on a fat bay carriage horse—a suffused, angry face vanishing, still at full gallop, beyond the corner of the house where his father and brother were sitting in the two tilted chairs; and a moment later, almost before he could have put the axe down, he heard the hooves again and watched the sorrel mare go back out of the yard, already galloping again. Then his father began to shout one of the sisters' names, who presently emerged backward from the kitchen door dragging the rolled rug along the ground by one end while the other sister walked behind it.

"If you ain't going to tote, go on and set up the wash pot," the first said.

"You, Sarty!" the second shouted. "Set up the wash pot!" His father appeared at the door, framed against that shabbiness, as he had been against that other bland perfection, impervious to either, the mother's anxious face at his shoulder.

"Go on," the father said. "Pick it up." The two sisters stooped, broad, lethargic; stooping, they presented an incredible expanse of pale cloth and a flutter of tawdry ribbons.

50 "If I thought enough of a rug to have to git hit all the way from France I wouldn't keep hit where folks coming in would have to tromp on hit," the first said. They raised the rug.

"Abner," the mother said. "Let me do it."

"You go back and git dinner," his father said. "I'll tend to this."

From the woodpile through the rest of the afternoon the boy watched them, the rug spread flat in the dust beside the bubbling wash pot, the two sisters stooping over it with that profound and lethargic reluctance, while the father stood over them in turn, implacable and grim, driving them though never raising his voice again. He could smell the harsh homemade lye they were using; he saw his mother come to the door once and look toward them with an expression not anxious now but very like despair; he saw his father turn, and he fell to with the axe and saw from the corner of his eye his father raise from the ground a flattish fragment of field stone and examine it and return to the pot, and this time his mother actually spoke: "Abner. Abner. Please don't. Please, Abner."

Then he was done too. It was dusk; the whippoorwills had already begun. He could smell coffee from the room where they would presently eat the cold food remaining from the mid-afternoon meal, though when he entered the house he realized they were having coffee again because there was a fire on the hearth, before which the rug now lay spread over the backs of the two chairs. The tracks of his father's foot were gone. Where they had been were now long, water-cloudy scoriations resembling the sporadic course of a Lilliputian[2] mowing machine.

55 It still hung there while they ate the cold food and then went to bed, scattered without order or claim up and down the two rooms, his mother in one bed, where his father would later lie, the older brother in the other, himself, the aunt, and the two sisters on pallets on the floor. But his father was not in bed yet. The last thing the boy remembered was the depthless, harsh silhouette of the hat and coat bending over the rug and it seemed to him that he had not even closed his eyes when the silhouette was standing over him, the fire almost dead behind it, the stiff foot prodding him awake. "Catch up the mule," his father said.

When he returned with the mule his father was standing in the black door, the rolled rug over his shoulder. "Ain't you going to ride?" he said.

"No. Give me your foot."

---

[2] Referring to Lilliput, an imaginary island in Jonathan Swift's *Gulliver's Travels,* the inhabitants of which were six inches tall; diminutive.

He bent his knee into his father's hand, the wiry, surprising power flowed smoothly, rising, he rising with it, on to the mule's bare back (they had owned a saddle once; the boy could remember it though not when or where) and with the same effortlessness his father swung the rug up in front of him. Now in the starlight they retraced the afternoon's path, up the dusty road rife with honeysuckle, through the gate and up the black tunnel of the drive to the lightless house, where he sat on the mule and felt the rough warp of the rug drag across his thighs and vanish.

"Don't you want me to help?" he whispered. His father did not answer and now he heard again that stiff foot striking the hollow portico with that wooden and clocklike deliberation, that outrageous overstatement of the weight it carried. The rug, hunched, not flung (the boy could tell that even in the darkness) from his father's shoulder, struck the angle of wall and floor with a sound unbelievably loud, thunderous, then the foot again, unhurried and enormous; a light came on in the house and the boy sat, tense, breathing steadily and quietly and just a little fast, though the foot itself did not increase its beat at all, descending the steps now; now the boy could see him.

60   "Don't you want to ride now?" he whispered. "We kin both ride now," the light within the house altering now, flaring up and sinking. *He's coming down the stairs now,* he thought. He had already ridden the mule up beside the horse block; presently his father was up behind him and he doubled the reins over and slashed the mule across the neck, but before the animal could begin to trot the hard, thin arm came round him, the hard, knotted hand jerking the mule back to a walk.

In the first red rays of the sun they were in the lot, putting plow gear on the mules. This time the sorrel mare was in the lot before he heard it at all, the rider collarless and even bareheaded, trembling, speaking in a shaking voice as the woman in the house had done, his father merely looking up once before stooping again to the hame he was buckling, so that the man on the mare spoke to his stooping back:

"You must realize you have ruined that rug. Wasn't there anybody here, any of your women . . ." He ceased, shaking, the boy watching him, the older brother leaning now in the stable door, chewing, blinking slowly and steadily at nothing apparently. "It cost a hundred dollars. But you never had a hundred dollars. You never will. So I'm going to charge you twenty bushels of corn against your crop. I'll add it in your contract and when you come to the commissary you can sign it. That won't keep Mrs. de Spain quite but maybe it will teach you to wipe your feet off before you enter her house again."

Then he was gone. The boy looked at his father, who still had not spoken or even looked up again, who was now adjusting the logger-head in the hame.

"Pap," he said. His father looked at him—the inscrutable face, the shaggy brows beneath which the gray eyes glinted coldly. Suddenly the boy went toward him, fast, stopping as suddenly. "You done the best you could!" he cried. "If he wanted hit done different why didn't he wait and tell you how? He won't git no twenty bushels! He won't git none! We'll get hit and hide hit! I kin watch . . ."

65   "Did you put the cutter back in that straight stock like I told you?"

"No, sir," he said.

"Then go do it."

That was Wednesday. During the rest of that week he worked steadily, at what was within his scope and some which was beyond it, with an industry that did not need to be driven nor even commanded twice; he had this from his mother, with the difference that some at least of what he did he liked to do, such as splitting wood with the half-size axe which his mother and aunt had earned, or saved money somehow, to present him with at Christmas. In company with the two older women (and on one afternoon even one of the sisters), he built pens for the shoat and the cow which were a part of his father's contract with the landlord, and one afternoon, his father being absent, gone somewhere on one of the mules, he went to the field.

They were running a middle buster now, his brother holding the plow straight while he handled the reins, and walking beside the straining mule, the rich black soil shearing cool and damp against his bare ankles, he thought *Maybe this is the end of it. Maybe even that twenty bushels that seems hard to have to pay for just a rug will be a cheap price for him to stop forever and always from being what he used to be;* thinking, dreaming now, so that his brother had to speak sharply to him to mind the mule: *Maybe he even won't collect the twenty bushels. Maybe it will all add up and balance and vanish— corn, rug, fire; the terror and grief, the being pulled two ways like between two teams of horses—gone, done with forever and ever.*

70   Then it was Saturday; he looked up from beneath the mule he was harnessing and saw his father in the black coat and hat. "Not that," his father said. "The wagon gear." And then, two hours later, sitting in the wagon bed behind his father and brother on the seat, the wagon accomplished a final curve, and he saw the weathered paintless store with its tattered tobacco- and patent-medicine posters and the tethered wagons and saddle animals below the gallery. He mounted the gnawed steps behind father and brother, and there again was the lane of quiet, watching faces for the three of them to walk through. He saw the man in spectacles sitting at the plank table and he did not need to be told this was Justice of the Peace; he sent one glare of fierce, exultant, partisan defiance at the man in collar and cravat now, whom he had seen but twice in his life, and that on a galloping horse, who now wore on his face an expression not of rage but of amazed unbelief which the boy could not have known was at the incredible circumstance of being sued by one of his own tenants, and came and stood against his father and cried at the Justice: "He ain't done it! He ain't burnt . . ."

"Go back to the wagon," his father said.

"Burnt?" the Justice said. "Do I understand this rug was burned too?"

"Does anybody here claim it was?" his father said. "Go back to the wagon." But he did not, he merely retreated to the rear of the room, crowded as that other had been, but not to sit down this time, instead, to stand pressing among the motionless bodies, listening to the voices:

"And you claim twenty bushels of corn is too high for the damage you did to the rug?"

75   "He brought the rug to me and said he wanted the tracks washed out of it. I washed the tracks out and took the rug back to him."

"But you didn't carry the rug back to him in the same condition it was in before you made the tracks on it."

His father did not answer, and now for perhaps half a minute there was no sound at all save that of breathing, the faint, steady suspiration of complete and intent listening.

"You decline to answer that, Mr. Snopes?" Again his father did not answer. "I'm going to find against you, Mr. Snopes. I'm going to find that you were responsible for the injury to Major de Spain's rug and hold you liable for it. But twenty bushels of corn seems a little high for a man in your circumstances to have to pay. Major de Spain claims it cost a hundred dollars. October corn will be worth about fifty cents. I figure that if Major de Spain can stand a ninety-five-dollar loss on something he paid cash for, you can stand a five-dollar loss you haven't earned yet. I hold you in damages to Major de Spain to the amount of ten bushels of corn over and above your contract with him, to be paid to him out of your crop at gathering time. Court adjourned."

It had taken no time hardly, the morning was but half begun. He thought they would return home and perhaps back to the field, since they were late, far behind all other farmers. But instead his father passed on behind the wagon, merely indicating with his hand for the older brother to follow with it, and crossed the road toward the blacksmith shop opposite, pressing on after his father, overtaking him, speaking, whispering up at the harsh, calm face beneath the weathered hat: "He won't git no ten bushels neither. He won't git one. We'll . . ." until his father glanced for an instant down on him, the face absolutely calm, the grizzled eyebrows tangled above the cold eyes, the voice almost pleasant, almost gentle:

80   "You think so? Well, we'll wait till October anyway."

The matter of the wagon—the setting of a spoke or two and the tightening of the tires—did not take long either, the business of the tires accomplished by driving the wagon into the spring branch behind the shop and letting it stand there, the mules nuzzling into the water from time to time, and the boy on the seat with the idle reins, looking up the slope and through the sooty tunnel of the shed where the slow hammer rang and where his father sat on an upended cypress bolt, easily, either talking or listening, still sitting there when the boy brought the dripping wagon up out of the branch and halted it before the door.

"Take them on to the shade and hitch," his father said. He did so and returned. His father and the smith and a third man squatting on his heels inside the door were talking, about crops and animals; the boy, squatting too in the ammoniac dust and hoof-parings and scales of rust, heard his father tell a long and unhurried story out of the time before the birth of the older brother even when he had been a professional horsetrader. And then his father came up beside him where he stood before a tattered last year's circus poster on the other side of the store, gazing rapt and quiet at the scarlet horses, the incredible poisings and convolutions of tulle and tights and the painted leers of comedians, and said, "It's time to eat."

But not at home. Squatting beside his brother against the front wall, he watched his father emerge from the store and produce from a paper sack a segment of cheese and divided it carefully and deliberately into three with his pocket knife and produce crackers from the same sack. They all three squatted on the gallery and ate slowly, without talking; then in the store again, they drank from a tin dipper tepid water smelling of the cedar bucket and of living beech trees. And still they did not go home. It was a horse lot this time, a tall rail fence upon and along which men stood and sat and out of which one by one horses were led, to be walked and trotted and then cantered back and forth along the road while the slow swapping and buying went on and the sun began to slant westward, they—the three of them—watching and listening, the older brother with his muddy eyes and his steady inevitable tobacco, the father commenting now and then on certain of the animals, to no one in particular.

It was after sundown when they reached home. They ate supper by lamplight, then, sitting on the doorstep, the boy watched the night fully accomplish, listening to the whippoorwills and the frogs, when he heard his mother's voice: "Abner! No! No! Oh, God, Oh, God, Abner!" and he rose, whirled, and saw the altered light through the door where a candle stub now burned in a bottle neck on the table and his father, still in the hat and coat, at once formal and burlesque as though dressed carefully for some shabby and ceremonial violence, emptying the reservoir of the lamp back into the five-gallon kerosene can from which it had been filled, while the mother tugged at his arm until he shifted the lamp to the other hand and flung her back, not savagely or viciously, just hard, into the wall, her hands flung out against the wall for balance, her mouth open and in her face the same quality of hopeless despair as had been in her voice. Then his father saw him standing in the door.

85   "Go to the barn and get that can of oil we were oiling the wagon with," he said. The boy did not move. Then he could speak.

"What . . ." he cried. "What are you . . ."

"Go get that oil," his father said. "Go."

Then he was moving, running, outside the house, toward the stable: this the old habit, the old blood which he had not been permitted to choose for himself, which had been bequeathed him willy nilly and which had run for so long (and who knew where, battening on what of outrage and savagery and lust) before it came to him. *I could keep on,* he thought, *I could run on and on and never look back, never need to see his face again. Only I can't. I can't,* the rusted can in his hand now, the liquid sloshing in it as he ran back to the house and into it, into the sound of his mother's weeping in the next room, and handed the can to his father.

"Ain't you going to even send a nigger?" he cried. "At least you sent a nigger before!"

90   This time his father didn't strike him. The hand came even faster than the blow had, the same hand which had set the can on the table with almost excruciating care flashing from the can toward him too quick for him to follow it, gripping him by the back of his shirt and on to tiptoe before he had seen it quit the can, the face stooping at him in breathless and frozen ferocity, the cold, dead voice speaking over him to the older brother who leaned against the table, chewing with that steady, curious, sidewise motion of cows:

"Empty the can into the big one and go on. I'll catch up with you."

"Better tie him up to the bedpost," the brother said.

"Do like I told you," the father said. Then the boy was moving, his bunched shirt and the hard, bony hand between his shoulder-blades, his toes just touching the floor, across the room and into the other one, past the sisters sitting with spread heavy thighs in the two chairs over the cold hearth, and to where his mother and aunt sat side by side on the bed, the aunt's arms about the mother's shoulders.

"Hold him," the father said. The aunt made a startled movement. "Not you," the father said. "Lennie. Take hold of him. I want to see you do it." His mother took him by the wrist. "You'll hold him better than that. If he gets loose don't you know what he is going to do? He will go up yonder." He jerked his head toward the road. "Maybe I'd better tie him."

95   "I'll hold him," his mother whispered.

"See you do then." Then his father was gone, the stiff foot heavy and measured upon the boards, ceasing at last.

Then he began to struggle. His mother caught him in both arms, he jerking and wrenching at them. He would be stronger in the end, he knew that. But he had not time to wait for it. "Lemme go!" he cried. "I don't want to have to hit you!"

"Let him go!" the aunt said. "If he don't go, before God, I am going up there myself!"

"Don't you see I can't?" his mother cried. "Sarty! Sarty! No! No! Help me, Lizzie!"

100   Then he was free. His aunt grasped at him but it was too late. He whirled, running, his mother stumbled forward on to her knees behind him, crying to the nearer sister: "Catch him, Net! Catch him!" But that was too late too, the sister (the sisters were twins, born at the same time, yet either of them now gave the impression of being, encompassing as much living meat and volume and weight as any other two of the family) not yet having begun to rise from the chair, her head, face, alone merely turned, presenting to him in the flying instant an astonishing expanse of young female features untroubled by any surprise even, wearing only an expression of bovine interest. Then he was out of the room, out of the house, in the mild dust of the starlit road and the heavy rifeness of honeysuckle, the pale ribbon unspooling with terrific slowness under his running feet, reaching the gate at last and turning in, running, his

heart and lungs drumming, on up the drive toward the lighted house, the lighted door. He did not knock, he burst in, sobbing for breath, incapable for the moment of speech; he saw the astonished face of the Negro in the line jacket without knowing when the Negro had appeared.

"De Spain!" he cried, panted. "Where's . . ." then he saw the white man too emerging from a white door down the hall. "Barn!" he cried. "Barn!"

"What?" the white man said. "Barn?"

"Yes!" the boy cried. "Barn!"

"Catch him!" the white man shouted.

105 But it was too late this time too. The Negro grasped his shirt, but the entire sleeve, rotten with washing, carried away, and he was out that door too and in the drive again, and had actually never ceased to run even while he was screaming into the white man's face.

Behind him the white man was shouting. "My horse! Fetch my horse!" and he thought for an instant of cutting across the park and climbing the fence into the road, but he did not know the park nor how high the vine-massed fence might be and he dared not risk it. So he ran on down the drive, blood and breath roaring; presently he was in the road again though he could not see it. He could not hear either: the galloping mare was almost upon him before he heard her, and even then he held his course, as if the very urgency of his wild grief and need must in a moment more find him wings, waiting until the ultimate instant to hurl himself aside and into the weed-choked roadside ditch as the horse thundered past and on, for an instant in furious silhouette against the stars, the tranquil early summer night sky which, even before the shape of the horse and rider vanished, strained abruptly and violently upward: a long, swirling roar incredible and soundless, blotting the stars, and he springing up and into the road again, running again, knowing it was too late yet still running even after he heard the shot and, an instant later, two shots, pausing now without knowing he had ceased to run, crying "Pap! Pap!," running again before he knew he had begun to run, stumbling, tripping over something and scrabbling up again without ceasing to run, looking backward over his shoulder at the glare as he got up, running on among the invisible trees, panting, sobbing, "Father! Father!"

At midnight he was sitting on the crest of a hill. He did not know it was midnight and he did not know how far he had come. But there was no glare behind him now and he sat now, his back toward what he had called home for four days anyhow, his face toward the dark woods which he would enter when breath was strong again, small, shaking steadily in the chill darkness, hugging himself into the remainder of his thin, rotten shirt, the grief and despair now no longer terror and fear but just grief and despair. *Father. My father,* he thought. "He was brave!" he cried suddenly, aloud but not loud, no more than a whisper: "He was! He was in the war! He was in Colonel Sartoris' cav'ry!" not knowing that his father had gone to that war a private in the fine old European sense, wearing no uniform, admitting the authority of and giving fidelity to no man or army or flag, going to war as Malbrouck[3] himself did: for booty—it meant nothing and less than nothing to him if it were enemy booty or his own.

The slow constellations wheeled on. It would be dawn and then sun-up after a while and he would be hungry. But that would be tomorrow and now he was only cold, and walking would cure that. His breathing was easier now and he decided to get up and go on, and then he found that he had been asleep because he knew it was almost dawn, the night almost over. He could tell that from the whippoorwills. They were everywhere now among the dark trees below him, constant and inflectioned and ceaseless, so that, as the instant for giving over to the day birds drew nearer and nearer, there was no interval at all between them. He got up. He was a little stiff, but walking would cure that too as it would the cold, and soon there would be the sun. He went on down the hill, toward the dark woods within which the liquid silver voices of the birds called unceasing—the rapid and urgent beating of the urgent and quiring heart of the late spring night. He did not look back.

■ EXPLORATIONS OF THE TEXT ■

1. Describe the courtroom scene at the beginning of the story. How does Sarty feel and react?
2. Why does the boy feel "peace and joy" when he sees Major de Spain's house?
3. What are the father's values? Does the boy renounce them? Does the boy really betray the father?
4. What image characterizes the women in the story? What do you conclude?
5. What concepts of justice emerge in "Barn Burning"? What is implied about the evolution of justice from rudimentary to more civilized ideas?
6. Trace the changes in Sarty's character. Be specific.
7. Read the last two paragraphs carefully. Is the ending pessimistic or optimistic? Which words give evidence for a conclusion?
8. Faulkner is noted for his complex style. Is the style appropriate in this story?

■■ JOURNAL ENTRIES ■■

1. Discuss the logic of each participant in the courtroom scene.
2. Evaluate Faulkner's technique in the opening of the story.

---

[3] Hero of an old French ballad ("Malbrouck s'en va-t-en guerre"); the original Malbrouck was the English Duke of Marborough (1650–1722), accused of profiteering during wartime (1702-13).

■■■ IDEAS FOR WRITING ■■■

1. Describe the father's past and explain his actions in the story. Does the reader have any sympathy for him?
2. How does Faulkner portray women in "Barn Burning"?
3. Write on one of the following themes: betrayal, guilt and redemption, or sins of the father.

The Stolen Party

Liliana Heker

Born in Argentina, Liliana Heker published her first volume of short stories, Those Who Beheld the Burning Bush, *when she was still a teenager. Later she served as editor of a literary journal,* El Ornitorrinco, *(The Platypus) during the years of Argentina's dictatorships, a time when many writers "disappeared," a time when many who objected to oppression were tortured and killed by death squads.*

In "The Stolen Party," Rosaura believes that her invitation to the celebration symbolizes friendship; her mother believes that the child remains simply "the maid's daughter."

1   As soon as she arrived she went straight to the kitchen to see if the monkey was there. It was: what a relief! She wouldn't have liked to admit that her mother had been right. *Monkeys at a birthday?* her mother had sneered. *Get away with you, believing any nonsense you're told!* She was cross, but not because of the monkey, the girl thought; it's just because of the party.

"I don't like you going," she told her. "It's a rich people's party."

"Rich people go to Heaven too," said the girl, who studied religion at school.

"Get away with Heaven," said the mother. "The problem with you, young lady, is that you like to fart higher than your ass."

5   The girl didn't approve of the way her mother spoke. She was barely nine, and one of the best in her class.

"I'm going because I've been invited," she said. "And I've been invited because Luciana is my friend. So there."

"Ah yes, your friend," her mother grumbled. She paused. "Listen, Rosaura," she said at last. "That one's not your friend. You know what you are to them? The maid's daughter, that's what."

Rosaura blinked hard: she wasn't going to cry. Then she yelled: "Shut up! You know nothing about being friends!"

Every afternoon she used to go to Luciana's house and they would both finish their homework while Rosaura's mother did the cleaning. They had their tea in the kitchen and they told each other secrets. Rosaura loved everything in the big house, and she also loved the people who lived there.

10   "I'm going because it will be the most lovely party in the whole world, Luciana told me it would. There will be a magician, and he will bring a monkey and everything."

The mother swung around to take a good look at her child, and pompously put her hands on her hips.

"Monkeys at a birthday?" she said. "Get away with you, believing any nonsense you're told!"

Rosaura was deeply offended. She thought it unfair of her mother to accuse other people of being liars simply because they were rich. Rosaura too wanted to be rich, of course. If one day she managed to live in a beautiful palace, would her mother stop loving her? She felt very sad. She wanted to go to that party more than anything else in the world.

"I'll die if I don't go," she whispered, almost without moving her lips.

15   And she wasn't sure whether she had been heard, but on the morning of the party she discovered that her mother had starched her Christmas dress. And in the afternoon, after washing her hair, her mother rinsed it in apple vinegar so that it would be all nice and shiny. Before going out, Rosaura admired herself in the mirror, with her white dress and glossy hair, and thought she looked terribly pretty.

Señora Ines seemed to notice. As soon as she saw her, she said:

"How lovely you look today, Rosaura."

Rosaura gave her starched skirt a slight toss with her hands and walked into the party with a firm step. She said hello to Luciana and asked about the monkey. Luciana put on a secretive look and whispered into Rosaura's ear: "He's in the kitchen. But don't tell anyone, because it's a surprise."

Rosaura wanted to make sure. Carefully she entered the kitchen and there she saw it: deep in thought, inside its cage. It looked so funny that the girl stood there for while, watching it, and later, every so often, she would slip out of the party unseen and go and admire it. Rosaura was the only one allowed into the kitchen. Señora Ines had said: "You yes, but not the others, they're much too boisterous, they might break something." Rosaura had never broken anything. She even managed the jug of orange juice, carrying it from the kitchen into the dining room. She held it carefully and didn't spill a single drop. And Señora Ines had said: "Are you sure you can manage a jug as big as that?" Of course she could manage. She wasn't a butterfingers, like the others. Like that blonde girl with the bow in her hair. As soon as she saw Rosaura, the girl with the bow had said:

20   "And you? Who are you?"

"I'm a friend of Luciana," said Rosaura.

"No," said the girl with the bow, "you are not a friend of Luciana because I'm her cousin and I know all her friends. And I don't know you."

"So what," said Rosaura. "I come here every afternoon with my mother and we do our homework together."

"You and your mother do your homework together?" asked the girl, laughing.

25 "I and Luciana do our homework together," said Rosaura, very seriously.

The girl with the bow shrugged her shoulders.

"That's not being friends," she said. "Do you go to school together?"

"No."

"So where do you know her from?" said the girl, getting impatient.

30 Rosaura remembered her mothers's words perfectly. She took a deep breath.

"I'm the daughter of the employee," she said.

Her mother had said very clearly: "If someone asks, you say you're the daughter of the employee; that's all." She also told her to add: "And proud of it." But Rosaura thought that never in her life would she dare say something of the sort.

"What employee?" said the girl with the bow. "Employee in a shop?"

"No," said Rosaura angrily. "My mother doesn't sell anything in any shop, so there."

35 "So how come she's an employee?" said the girl with the bow.

Just then Señora Ines arrived saying *shh shh*, and asked Rosaura if she wouldn't mind helping serve out the hotdogs, as she knew the house so much better than the others.

"See?" said Rosaura to the girl with the bow, and when no one was looking she kicked her in the shin.

Apart from the girl with the bow, all the others were delightful. The one she liked best was Luciana, with her golden birthday crown; and then the boys. Rosaura won the sack race, and nobody managed to catch her when they played tag. When they split into two teams to play charades, all the boys wanted her for their side. Rosaura felt she had never been so happy in all her life.

But the best was still to come. The best came after Luciana blew out the candles. First the cake. Señora Ines had asked her to help pass the cake around, and Rosaura had enjoyed the task immensely, because everyone called out to her, shouting "Me, me!" Rosaura remembered a story in which there was a queen who had the power of life or death over her subjects. She had always loved that, having the power of life or death. To Luciana and the boys she gave the largest pieces, and to the girl with the bow she gave a slice so thin one could see through it.

40 After the cake came the magician, tall and bony, with a fine red cape. A true magician: he could untie handkerchiefs by blowing on them and make a chain with links that had no openings. He could guess what cards were pulled out from a pack, and the monkey was his assistant. He called the monkey "partner."

"Let's see here, partner," he would say, "turn over a card." And, "Don't run away, partner: time to work now."

"The final trick was wonderful. One of the children had to hold the monkey in his arms and the magician said he would make him disappear.

"What, the boy?" they all shouted.

"No, the monkey!" shouted back the magician.

Rosaura thought that this was truly the most amusing party in the whole world.

45   The magician asked a small fat boy to come and help, but the small fat boy got frightened almost at once and dropped the monkey on the floor. The magician picked him up carefully, whispered something in his ear, and the monkey nodded almost as if he understood.

"You mustn't be so unmanly, my friend," the magician said to the fat boy.

"What's unmanly?" said the fat boy.

The magician turned around as if to look for spies.

"A sissy," said the magician. "Go sit down."

50   Then he stared at all the faces, one by one. Rosaura felt her heart tremble.

"You, with the Spanish eyes," said the magician. And everyone saw that he was pointing at her.

She wasn't afraid. Neither holding the monkey, nor when the magician made him vanish; not even when, at the end, the magician flung his red cape over Rosaura's head and uttered a few magic words . . . and the monkey reappeared, chattering happily, in her arms. The children clapped furiously. And before Rosaura returned to her seat, the magician said:

"Thank you very much, my little countess."

She was so pleased with the compliment that a while later, when her mother came to fetch her, that was the first thing she told her.

55   "I helped the magician and he said to me, 'Thank you very much, my little countess.'"

It was strange because up to then Rosaura had thought that she was angry with her mother. All along Rosaura had imagined that she would say to her: "See that the monkey wasn't a lie?" But instead she was so thrilled that she told her mother all about the wonderful magician.

Her mother tapped her on the head and said: "So now we're a countess!"

But one could see that she was beaming.

And now they both stood in the entrance, because a moment ago Señora Ines, smiling, had said: "Please wait here a second."

60   Her mother suddenly seemed worried.

"What is it?" she asked Rosaura.

"What is what?" said Rosaura. "It's nothing; she just wants to get the presents for those who are leaving, see?"

She pointed at the fat boy and at a girl with pigtails who were also waiting there, next to their mothers. And she explained about the presents. She knew, because she had been watching those who left before her. When one of the girls was about to leave, Señora Ines would give her a bracelet. When a boy left, Señora Ines gave him a yo-yo. Rosaura preferred the yo-yo because it sparkled, but she didn't mention that to her mother. Her mother might have said: "So why don't you ask for one, you blockhead?" That's what her mother was like. Rosaura didn't feel like explaining that she'd be horribly ashamed to be the odd one out. Instead she said:

"I was the best-behaved at the party."

65   And she said no more because Señora Ines came out into the hall with two bags, one pink and one blue.

First she went up to the fat boy, gave him a yo-yo out of the blue bag, and the fat boy left with his mother. Then she went up to the girl and gave her a bracelet out of the pink bag, and the girl with the pigtails left as well.

Finally she came up to Rosaura and her mother. She had a big smile on her face and Rosaura liked that. Señora Ines looked down at her, then looked up at her mother, and then said something that made Rosaura proud:

"What a marvelous daughter you have, Herminia."

For an instant, Rosaura thought that she'd give her two presents: the bracelet and the yo-yo. Señora Ines bent down as if about to look for something. Rosaura also leaned forward, stretching out her arm. But she never completed the movement.

70   Señora Ines didn't look in the pink bag. Nor did she look in the blue bag. Instead she rummaged in her purse. In her hand appeared two bills.

"You really and truly earned this," she said handing them over. "Thank you for all your help, my pet."

Rosaura felt her arms stiffen, stick close to her body, and then she noticed her mother's hand on her shoulder. Instinctively she pressed herself against her mother's body. That was all. Except her eyes. Rosaura's eyes had a cold, clear look that fixed itself on Señora Ines's face.

Señora Ines, motionless, stood there with her hand outstretched. As if she didn't dare draw it back. As if the slightest change might shatter an infinitely delicate balance.

■ EXPLORATIONS OF THE TEXT ■

1. What is the central conflict between the mother and Rosaura?
2. What fantasies does Rosaura invent about herself and about her life?
3. How does Heker weave a subtle pattern of servitude into Rosaura's participation in the party?
4. In the episode with the monkey, what is the role of the fat boy? What does the incident symbolize?
5. Why does Señora Ines offer Rosaura money? What does Rosaura's "cold, clear look" suggest? What is "the infinitely delicate balance" at the end?
6. Two pairs of mothers and daughters appear in this story. What do you learn about the social status and world views of these characters?
7. How would you characterize the tone of this story? Why?
8. How do details contribute to the theme of the story? What can you learn about subtlety, about irony, and about organization from Liliana Heker?

■■ JOURNAL ENTRIES ■■

1. How is the party "stolen"?
2. Continue the story.
3. What characterizes children's perceptions of prejudice or stereotyping in the works by Heker and by Countee Cullen?

■■■ IDEAS FOR WRITING ■■■

1. How does point of view contribute to the development of the themes in this work?
2. Write about a "stolen party" from your childhood or adolescence. What did you realize? Or compare a party that you attended as a child with Rosaura's experience.

The Man Who Was Almost a Man

Richard Wright

Richard Wright (1908–1960) was born on a plantation near Natchez, Mississippi. As a young adult, he moved to Chicago where he became a member of the Communist Party in 1932. (He resigned from the party in 1944.) In 1937, he moved to New York where he was a reporter for The Daily Worker *in Harlem. Influenced by Hemingway's style, he wrote novellas which appeared in* Uncle Tom's Children *(1938), a volume which won the Federal Writers' Project first prize. His first novel,* Native Son *(1940), became an American classic. In 1945, he wrote* Black Boy, *his compelling autobiography, after which he left the United States to live permanently in Paris. He attributed his commitment to literature to reading books: "It had been my accidental reading of fiction . . . that had evoked in me vague glimpses of life's possibilities." His second book of short fiction,* Eight Men, *published posthumously in 1961, included "The Man Who Was Almost a Man."*

In the story, Dave yearns to be treated like a man; and he believes that a gun can earn him the respect he desires.

1   Dave struck out across the fields, looking homeward through paling light. Whut's the use talking wid em niggers in the field? Anyhow, his mother was putting supper on the table. Them niggers can't understan nothing. One of these days he was he was going to get a gun and practice shooting, then

they couldn't talk to him as though he were a little boy. He slowed, looking at the ground. Shucks, Ah ain scareda them even ef they are biggern me! Aw, Ah know whut Ahma do. Ahm going by ol Joe's sto n git that Sears Roebuck catlog n look at them guns. Mebbe Ma will lemme buy one when she gits mah pay from ol man Hawkins. Ahma beg her t gimme some money. Ahm ol ernough to hava gun. Ahm seventeen. Almos a man. He strode, feeling his long loose-jointed limbs. Shucks, a man oughta hava little gun aftah he done worked hard all day.

He came in sight of Joe's store. A yellow lantern glowed on the front porch. He mounted steps and went through the screen door, hearing it bang behind him. There was a strong smell of coal oil and mackerel fish. He felt very confident until he saw fat Joe walk in through the rear door, then his courage began to ooze.

"Howdy, Dave! Whutcha want?"

"How yuh, Mistah Joe? Aw, Ah don wanna buy nothing. Ah jus wanted t see ef yuhd lemme look at tha catlog erwhile."

5   "Sure! You wanna see it here?"

"Nawsuh. Ah wants t take it home wid me. Ah'll bring it back termorrow when Ah come in from the fiels."

"You plannin on buying something?"

"Yessuh."

"Your ma lettin you have your own money now?"

10   "Shucks. Mistah Joe, Ahm gittin t be a man like anybody else!"

Joe laughed and wiped his greasy white face with a red bandanna.

"What you plannin on buyin?"

Dave looked at the floor, scratched his head, scratched his thigh, and smiled. Then he looked up shyly.

"Ah'll tell yuh, Mistah Joe, ef yuh promise yuh won't tell."

15   "I promise."

"Waal, Ahma buy a gun."

"A gun? What you want with a gun?"

"Ah wanna keep it."

"You ain't nothing but a boy. You don't need a gun."

20   "Aw, lemme have the catlog, Mistah Joe. Ah'll bring it back."

Joe walked through the rear door. Dave was elated. He looked around at barrels of sugar and flour. He heard Joe coming back. He craned his neck to see if he were bringing the book. Yeah, he's got it. Gawddog, he's got it!

"Here, but be sure you bring it back. It's the only one I got."

"Sho, Mistah Joe."

"Say, if you wanna buy a gun, why don't you buy one from me? I gotta gun to sell."

25   "Will it shoot?"

"Sure it'll shoot."

"What kind is it?"

"Oh, it's kinda old . . . a left-hand Wheeler. A pistol. A big one."

"Is it got bullets in it?"

30   "It's loaded."

"Kin Ah see it?"

"Where's your money?"

"What yuh wan fer it?"

"I'll let you have it for two dollars."

35   "Just two dollahs? Shucks, Ah could buy tha when Ah git mah pay."

"I'll have it here when you want it."

"Awright, suh. Ah be in fer it."

He went through the door, hearing it slam again behind him. Ahma git some money from Ma n buy me a gun! Only two dollahs! He tucked the thick catalogue under his arm and hurried.

"Where yuh been, boy?" His mother held a steaming dish of black-eyed peas.

40   "Aw, Ma, Ah jus stopped down the road t talk wid the boys."

"Yuh know bettah t keep suppah waiting."

He sat down, resting the catalogue on the edge of the table.

"Yuh git up from there and git to the well n wash yosef! Ah ain feedin no hogs in mah house!"

She grabbed his shoulder and pushed him. He stumbled out of the room, then came back to get the catalogue.

45   "Whut this?"

"Aw, Ma, it's jusa catlog."

"Who yuh git it from?"

"From Joe, down at the sto."

"Waal, thas good. We kin use it in the outhouse."

50   "Naw, Ma." He grabbed for it. "Gimme ma catlog, Ma."

She held onto it and glared at him.

"Quit hollerin at me! Whut's wrong wid yuh? Yuh crazy?"

"But Ma, please. It ain mine! It's Joe's! He tol me t bring it back t im termorrow."

She gave up the book. He stumbled down the back steps, hugging the thick book under his arm. When he had splashed water on his face and hands, he groped back to the kitchen and fumbled in a corner for the towel. He bumped into a chair; it clattered to the floor. The catalogue sprawled at his feet. When he had dried his eyes he snatched up the book and held it again under his arm. His mother stood watching him.

55   "Now, ef yuh gonna act a fool over that ol book, Ah'll take it n burn it up."

"Naw, Ma, please."

"Waal, set down n be still!"

He sat down and drew the oil lamp close. He thumbed page after page, unaware of the food his mother set on the table. His father came in. Then his small brother.

"Whutcha got there, Dave?" his father asked.

60   "Jusa catlog," he answered, not looking up.

"Yeah, here they is!" His eyes glowed at blue-and-black revolvers. He glanced up, feeling sudden guilt. His father was watching him. He eased the book under the table and rested it on his knees. After the blessing was asked, he ate. He scooped up peas and swallowed fat meat without chewing. Buttermilk helped to wash it down. He did not want to mention money before his father. He would do much better by cornering his mother when she was alone. He looked at his father uneasily out of the edge of his eye.

"Boy, how come yuh don quit foolin wid tha book n eat yo suppah?"

"Yessuh."

"How you n ol man Hawkins gitten erlong?"

65   "Suh?"

"Can't yuh hear? Why don yuh lissen? Ah ast yu how wuz yuh n ol man Hawkins gittin erlong?"

"Oh, swell, Pa. Ah plows mo lan than anybody over there."

"Waal, yuh oughta keep you mind on whut yuh doin."

"Yessuh."

70   He poured his plate full of molasses and sopped it up slowly with a chunk of cornbread. When his father and brother had left the kitchen, he still sat and looked again at the guns in the catalogue, longing to muster courage enough to present his case to his mother. Lawd, ef Ah only had tha pretty one! He could almost feel the slickness of the weapon with his fingers. If he had a gun like that he would polish it and keep it shining so it would never rust. N Ah'd keep it loaded, by Gawd!

"Ma?" His voice was hesitant.

"Hunh?"

"Ol man Hawkins give yuh mah money yit?"

"Yeah, but ain no usa yuh thinking bout throwin nona it erway. Ahm keeping tha money sos yuh kin have cloes to go to school this winter."

75   He rose and went to her side with the open catalogue in his palms. She was washing dishes, her head bent low over a pan. Shyly he raised the book. When he spoke, his voice was husky, faint.

"Ma, Gawd knows Ah wans one of these."

"One of whut?" she asked, not raising her eyes.

"One of these," he said again, not daring even to point. She glanced up at the page, then at him with wide eyes.

"Nigger, is yuh gone plumb crazy?"

80   "Aw, Ma—"

"Git outta here! Don yuh talk t me bout no gun! Yuh a fool!"

"Ma, Ah kin buy one fer two dollahs."

"Not ef Ah knows it, yuh ain!"

"But yuh promised me one—"

85   "Ah don care what Ah promised! Yuh ain nothing but a boy yit!"

"Ma, ef yuh lemme buy one Ah'll *never* ast yuh fer nothing no mo."

"Ah tol yuh t git outta here! Yuh ain gonna toucha penny of tha money fer no gun! Thas how come Ah has Mistah Hawkins t pay yo wages to me, cause Ah knows yuh ain got no sense."

"But, Ma, we needa gun. Pa ain got no gun. We needa gun in the house. Yuh kin never tell whut might happen."

"Now don yuh try to maka fool outta me, boy! Ef we did hava gun, yuh wouldn't have it!"

90   He laid the catalogue down and slipped his arm around her waist.

"Aw, Ma, Ah done worked hard alla summer n ain ast yuh fer nothing, is Ah, now?"

"Thas whut yuh spose t do!"

"But Ma, Ah wans a gun. Yuh kin lemme have two dollahs outta mah money. Please, Ma. I kin give it to Pa. . . . Please, Ma! Ah loves yuh, Ma."

When she spoke her voice came soft and low.

95   "What yu wan wida gun, Dave? Yuh don need no gun. Yuh'll git in trouble. N ef yo pa jus thought Ah let yuh have money t buy a gun he'd hava fit."

"Ah'll hide it, Ma. It ain but two dollahs."

"Lawd, chil, whut's wrong wid yuh?"

"Ain nothin wrong, Ma. Ahm almos a man now. Ah wans a gun."

"Who gonna sell yuh a gun?"

100   "Ol Joe at the sto."

"N it don cos but two dollahs?"

"Thas all, Ma. Jus two dollahs. Please, Ma."

She was stacking the plates away; her hands moved slowly, reflectively. Dave kept an anxious silence. Finally, she turned to him.

"Ah'll let yuh git tha gun ef yuh promise me one thing."

105   "What's tha, Ma?"

"Yuh bring it straight back t me, yuh hear? It be fer Pa."

"Yessum! Lemme go now, Ma."

She stooped, turned slightly to one side, raised the hem of her dress, rolled down the top of her stocking, and came up with a slender wad of bills.

"Here," she said. "Lawd knows yuh don need no gun. But yer pa does. Yuh bring it right back t me, yuh hear? Ahma put it up. Now ef yuh don, Ahma have yuh pa lick yuh so hard yuh won fergit it."

110   "Yessum."

He took the money, ran down the steps, and across the yard.

"Dave! Yuuuuuh Daaaaave!"

He heard, but he was not going to stop now. "Naw, Lawd!"

The first movement he made the following morning was to reach under his pillow for the gun. In the gray light of dawn he held it loosely, feeling a sense of power. Could kill a man with a gun like this. Kill anybody, black or white. And if he were holding his gun in his hand, nobody could run over him; they would have to respect him. It was a big gun, with a long barrel and a heavy handle. He raised and lowered it in his hand, marveling at its weight.

115   He had not come straight home with it as his mother had asked; instead he had stayed out in the fields, holding the weapon in his hand, aiming it now and then at some imaginary foe. But he had not fired it; he had been afraid that his father might hear. Also he was not sure he knew how to fire it.

To avoid surrendering the pistol he had not come into the house until he knew that they were all asleep. When his mother had tiptoed to his bedside late that night and demanded the gun, he had first played possum; then he had told her that the gun was hidden outdoors, that he would bring it to her in the morning. Now he lay turning it slowly in his hands. He broke it, took out the cartridges, felt them, and then put them back.

He slid out of bed, got a long strip of old flannel from a trunk, wrapped the gun in it, and tied it to his naked thigh while it was still loaded. He did not go in to breakfast. Even though it was not yet daylight, he started for Jim Hawkins' plantation. Just as the sun was rising he reached the barns where the mules and plows were kept.

"Hey! That you, Dave?"

He turned. Jim Hawkins stood eying him suspiciously.

120 "What're yuh doing here so early?"

"Ah didn't know Ah wuz gettin up so early, Mistah Hawkins. Ah was fixin t hitch up ol Jenny n take her t the fiels."

"Good. Since you're so early, how about plowing that stretch down by the woods?"

"Suits me, Mistah Hawkins."

"O.K. Go to it!"

125 He hitched Jenny to a plow and started across the fields. Hot dog! This was just what he wanted. If he could get down by the woods, he could shoot his gun and nobody would hear. He walked behind the plow, hearing the traces creaking, feeling the gun tied tight to his thigh.

When he reached the woods, he plowed two whole rows before he decided to take out the gun. Finally, he stopped, looked in all directions, then untied the gun and held it in his hand. He turned to the mule and smiled.

"Know whut this is, Jenny? Naw, yuh wouldn know! Yuhs jusa ol mule! Anyhow, this is a gun, n it kin shoot, by Gawd!"

He held the gun at arm's length. Whut t hell, Ahma shoot this thing! He looked at Jenny again.

"Lissen here, Jenny! When Ah pull this ol trigger, Ah don wan yuh t run n acka fool now!"

130 Jenny stood with head down, her short ears pricked straight. Dave walked off about twenty feet, held the gun far out from him at arm's length, and turned his head. Hell, he told himself, Ah ain afraid. The gun felt loose in his fingers; he waved it wildly for a moment. Then he shut his eyes and tightened his forefinger. Bloom! A report half deafened him and he thought his right hand was torn from his arm. He heard Jenny whinnying and galloping over the field, and he found himself on his knees, sqeezing his fingers hard between his legs. His hand was numb; he jammed it into his mouth, trying to warm it, trying to stop the pain. The gun lay at his feet. He did not quite know what had happened. He stood up and stared at the gun as though it were a living thing. He gritted his teeth and kicked the gun. Yuh almos broke mah arm! He turned to look for Jenny; she was far over the fields, tossing her head and kicking wildly.

"Hol on there, ol mule!"

When he caught up with her she stood trembling, walling her big white eyes at him. The plow was far away; the traces had broken. Then Dave stopped short, looking, not believing. Jenny was bleeding. Her left side was red and wet with blood. He went closer. Lawd, have mercy! Wondah did Ah shoot this mule? He grabbed for Jenny's mane. She flinched, snorted, whirled, tossing her head.

"Hol on now! Hol on."

Then he saw the hole in Jenny's side, right between the ribs. It was round, wet, red. A crimson stream streaked down the front leg, flowing fast. Good Gawd! Ay wuzn't shootin at tha mule. He felt panic. He knew he had to stop that blood, or Jenny would bleed to death. He had never seen so much blood in all his life. He chased the mule for half a mile, trying to catch her. Finally she stopped, breathing hard, stumpy tail half arched. He caught her mane and led her back to where the plow and gun lay. Then he stopped and grabbed handfuls of damp black earth and tried to plug the bullet hole. Jenny shuddered, whinnied, and broke from him.

135   "Hol on! Hol on now!"

He tried to plug it again, but blood came anyhow. His fingers were hot and sticky. He rubbed dirt into his palms, trying to dry them. Then again he attempted to plug the bullet hole, but Jenny shied away, kicking her heels high. He stood helpless. He had to do something. He ran at Jenny; she dodged him. He watched a red stream of blood flow down Jenny's leg and form a bright pool at her feet.

"Jenny . . . Jenny," he called weakly.

His lips trembled. She's bleeding t death! He looked in the direction of home, wanting to go back, wanting to get help. But he saw the pistol lying in the damp black clay. He had a queer feeling that if he only did something, this would not be; Jenny would not be there bleeding to death.

When he went to her this time, she did not move. She stood with sleepy, dreamy eyes; and when he touched her she gave a low-pitched whinny and knelt to the ground, her front knees slopping in blood.

140   "Jenny . . . Jenny . . ." he whispered.

For a long time she held her neck erect. He picked up the gun and held it gingerly between his thumb and forefinger. He buried it at the foot of a tree. He took a stick and tried to cover the pool of blood with dirt—but what was the use? There was Jenny lying with her mouth open and her eyes walled and glassy. He could not tell Jim Hawkins he had shot his mule. But he had to tell something. Yeah, Ah'll tell em Jenny started gittin wil n fell on the joint of the plow. . . . But that would hardly happen to a mule. He walked across the field slowly, head down.

It was sunset. Two of Jim Hawkins' men were over near the edge of the woods digging a hole in which to bury Jenny. Dave was surrounded by a knot of people, all of whom were looking down at the dead mule.

"I don't see how in the world it happened," said Jim Hawkins for the tenth time.

The crowd parted and Dave's mother, father, and small brother pushed into the center.

145   "Where Dave?" his mother called.

"There he is," said Jim Hawkins.

His mother grabbed him.

"Whut happened, Dave? Whut yuh done?"

"Nothin."

150   "C'mon, boy, talk," his father said.

Dave took a deep breath and told the story he knew nobody believed.

"Waal," he drawled. "Ah brung ol Jenny down here sos Ah could do mah plowin. Ah plowed bout two rows, just like yuh see." He stopped and pointed at the long rows of upturned earth. "Then somethin musta been wrong wid ol Jenny. She wouldn ack right a-tall. She started snortin n kickin her heels. Ah tried t hol her, but she pulled erway, rearin n going on. Then when the point of the plow was stickin up in the air, she swung erroun n twisted herself back on it. . . . She stuck herself n started t bleed. N fo Ah could do anything, she wuz dead."

"Did you ever hear of anything like that in all your life?" asked Jim Hawkins.

There were white and black standing in the crowd. They murmured. Dave's mother came close to him and looked hard into his face. "Tell the truth, Dave," she said.

155   "Looks like a bullet hole to me," said one man.

"Dave, whut yuh do wid the gun?" his mother asked.

The crowd surged in, looking at him. He jammed his hands into his pockets, shook his head slowly from left to right, and backed away. His eyes were wide and painful.

"Did he hava gun?" asked Jim Hawkins.

"By Gawd, Ah tol yuh tha wuz a gun wound," said a man, slapping his thigh.

160   His father caught his shoulders and shook him till his teeth rattled.

"Tell whut happened, yuh rascal! Tell whut. . . ."

Dave looked at Jenny's stiff legs and began to cry.

"Whut yuh do wid tha gun?" his mother asked.

"What wuz he doin wida gun?" his father asked.

165   "Come on and tell the truth," said Hawkins. "Ain' nobody going to hurt you. . . ."

His mother crowded close to him.

"Did yuh shoot tha mule, Dave?"

Dave cried, seeing blurred white and black faces.

"Ahh ddinn gggo tt sshooot hher. . . . Ah ssswear ffo Gawd Ahh ddin. . . . Ah wuz a-tryin t sssee ef the old gggun would sshoot—"

170   "Where yuh git the gun from?" his father asked.

"Ah got it from Joe, at the sto."

"Where yuh git the money?"

"Ma give it t me."

"He kept worryin me, Bob. Ah had t. Ah tol im t bring the gun right back t me. . . . It was fer yuh, the gun."

175   "But how yuh happen to shoot that mule?" asked Jim Hawkins.

"Ah wuzn shootin at the mule, Mistah Hawkins. The gun jumped when Ah pulled the trigger. . . . N fo Ah knowed anythin Jenny was there a-bleedin."

Somebody in the crowd laughed. Jim Hawkins walked close to Dave and looked into his face.

"Well, looks like you have bought you a mule, Dave."

"Ah swear fo Gawd, Ah didn go t kill the mule, Mistah Hawkins!"

180   "But you killed her!"

All the crowd was laughing now. They stood on tiptoe and poked heads over one another's shoulders.

"Well, boy, looks like yuh done bought a dead mule! Hahaha!"

"Ain tha ershame."

"Hohohohoho."

185   Dave stood, head down, twisting his feet in the dirt.

"Well, you needn't worry about it, Bob," said Jim Hawkins to Dave's father. "Just let the boy keep on working and pay me two dollars a month."

"Whut yuh wan fer yo mule, Mistah Hawkins?"

Jim Hawkins screwed up his eyes.

"Fifty dollars."

190   "Whut yuh do wid tha gun?" Dave's father demanded.

Dave said nothing.

"Yuh wan me t take a tree n beat yuh till yuh talk!"

"Nawsuh!"

"Whut yuh do wid it?"

195   "Ah throwed it erway."

"Where?"

"Ah . . . Ah throwed it in the creek."

"Waal, c mon home. N firs thing in the mawnin git to tha creek n fin tha gun."

"Yessuh."

200   "Whut yuh pay fer it?"

"Two dollahs."

"Take tha gun n git yo money back n carry it to Mistah Hawkins, yuh hear? N don fergit Ahma lam you black bottom good fer this! Now march yosef on hom, suh!"

Dave turned and walked slowly. He heard people laughing. Dave glared, his eyes welling with tears. Hot anger bubbled in him. Then he swallowed and stumbled on.

That night Dave did not sleep. He was glad that he had gotten out of killing the mule so easily, but he was hurt. Something hot seemed to turn over inside him each time he remembered how they had laughed. He tossed on his bed, feeling his hard pillow. *N Pa says he's gonna beat me. . . .* He remembered other beatings, and his back quivered. *Naw, naw, Ah sho don wan im t beat me tha way no mo. Dam em all! Nobody ever gave him anything. All he did was work. They treat me like a mule, n then they beat me.* He gritted his teeth. *N Ma had t tell on me.*

205 Well, if he had to, he would take old man Hawkins that two dollars. But that meant selling the gun. And he wanted to keep that gun. Fifty dollars for a dead mule.

He turned over, thinking how he had fired the gun. He had an itch to fire it again. *Ef other men kin shoota gun, by Gawd, Ah kin!* He was still, listening. *Mebbe they all sleeping now.* The house was still. He heard the soft breathing of his brother. *Yes, now!* He would go down and get that gun and see if he could fire it! He eased out of bed and slipped into overalls.

The moon was bright. He ran almost all the way to the edge of the woods. He stumbled over the ground, looking for the spot where he had buried the gun. *Yeah, here it is.* Like a hungry dog scratching for a bone, he pawed it up. He puffed his black cheeks and blew dirt from the trigger and barrel. He broke it and found four cartridges unshot. He looked around; the fields were filled with silence and moonlight. He clutched the gun stiff and hard in his fingers. But, as soon as he wanted to pull the trigger, he shut his eyes and turned his head. *Naw, Ah can't shoot wid mah eyes closed n mah head turned.* With effort he held his eyes open; then he squeezed. *Blooooom!* He was stiff, not breathing. The gun was still in his hands. *Dammit, he'd done it!* He fired again. *Blooooom!* He smiled. *Blooooom! Blooooom! Click, click.* There! It was empty. If anybody could shoot a gun, he could. He put the gun into his hip pocket and started across the fields.

When he reached the top of a ridge he stood straight and proud in the moonlight, looking at Jim Hawkins' big white house, feeling the gun sagging in his pocket. *Lawd, ef Ah had just one mo bullet Ah'd taka shot at tha house. Ah'd like t scare ol man Hawkins jusa little. . . . Jusa enough t let im know Dave Saunders is a man.*

To his left the road curved, running to the tracks of the Illinois Central. He jerked his head, listening. From far off came a faint *hoooof-hoooof; hoooof-hoooof.* . . . He stood rigid. *Two dollahs a mont. Les see now. . . . Tha means it'll take bout two years. Shucks! Ah'll be dam!*

210 He started down the road, toward the tracks. *Yeah, here she comes!* He stood beside the track and held himself stiffly. *Here she comes, erroun the ben. . . C mon, yuh slow poke! C mon!* He had his hand on his gun; something quivered in his stomach. Then the train thundered past, the gray and brown box cars rumbling and clinking. He gripped the gun tightly; then he jerked his hand out of his pocket. *Ah betcha Bill wouldn't do it! Ah betcha. . . .* The cars slid past, steel grinding upon steel. *Ahm ridin yuh ter night, so hep me Gawd!* He was hot all over. He hesitated just a moment; then he grabbed, pulled atop of a car, and lay flat. He felt his pocket; the gun was still there. Ahead the long rails were glinting in the moonlight, stretching away, away to somewhere, somewhere where he could be a man. . . .

■ EXPLORATIONS OF THE TEXT ■

---

1. Why does Dave want a gun? Why does his mother give him the money to purchase the gun?
2. Is the shooting of the mule deliberate? What is Dave's motivation, if any, for the killing? Is the shooting symbolic?
3. Why does everyone deny Dave's manhood? What is the role of the father?
4. In the punishment scene, is the penalty just?
5. Why does Dave leave home in the end? What are negative and positive consequences of this choice?
6. What is the effect of the use of dialect in this story?
7. Examine the imagery of the last paragraph. What does the language reveal? Is it hopeful?
8. What do you learn about persuasion from Dave? What do you learn about persuasion from Wright?
9. How does the rite of passage in this work differ from initiations in the stories by Faulkner, Heker, and Oates in this chapter?

■■ JOURNAL ENTRIES ■■

---

1. What do you conclude from the scene about the death of the mule?
2. What does the gun represent for Dave? Why does he not throw it away?

■■■ IDEAS FOR WRITING ■■■

---

1. Using Journal Entry 2 as a basis for discussion, draw some conclusions about the North American fascination with guns.
2. Compare and contrast the endings of this story and of "Barn Burning." Focus on the imagery of these endings.

When I Called the Number
from **The Mambo Kings Play Songs of Love**

Oscar Hijuelos

Born in New York City, Oscar Hijuelos (1951–   ) received both his B.A. (1975) and his M.A. (1976) from City College of the City University of New York. He worked for several years in advertising before devoting himself to writing. His novels include Our House in the Last World *(1983),* The Mambo Kings Play Songs of Love *(1989), which won the Pulitzer Prize for Fiction, and* The Fourteen Sisters of Emilio Montez O'Brien *(1993).*

Critic Joseph Coates observed that Mambo Kings, *like Gabriel García Márquez's* One Hundred Years of Solitude *(1967), presents "a new way of looking at the hemisphere's experiences of uprootedness, migration and attempts at community." "When I Called the Number" appears as part of the last section of* The Mambo Kings. *In this selection, the narrator presents records made by his father and by his uncle to Desi Arnaz who symbolizes the importance of Cuban culture and music in North America.*

1   When I called the number that had been listed on Desi Arnaz's letterhead, I expected to speak with a secretary, but it was Mr. Arnaz himself who answered the phone.

"Mr. Arnaz?"

"Yes."

"I'm Eugenio Castillo."

5   "Ah, Eugenio Castillo, Nestor's son?"

"Yes."

"Nice to hear from you, and where are you calling from?"

"From Los Angeles."

"Los Angeles? What brings you out here?"

10   "Just a vacation."

"Well then, if you are so close by, you must come to visit me."

"Yes?"

"Of course. Can you come out tomorrow?"

"Yes."

15   "Then come. In the late afternoon. I'll be waiting to see you."

It had taken me a long time to finally work up the nerve to call Desi Arnaz. About a year ago, when I had written to him about my uncle, he was kind enough to send his condolences and ended that letter with an invitation to his home. When I finally decided to take him up on his offer and flew to Los Angeles, where I stayed in a motel near the airport, I had wanted to call him every day for two weeks. But I was afraid that his kindness would turn into air, like so many other things in this life, or that, he would be different from what I had imagined. Or he would be cruel or disinterested, or simply not really concerned about visitors like me. Instead, I drank beer by the motel swimming pool and passed my days watching jet planes crossing the sky. Then I made the acquaintance of one of the blondes by the pool, and she seemed to have a soft spot for guys like me, and we fell desperately in love for a week. Then ended things badly. But one afternoon, a few days later, while I was resting in bed and looking through my father's old book, *Forward America!,* just the contact of my thumb touching the very pages that he—and my uncle—had once turned (the spaces in all the little letters were looking at me like sad eyes) motivated me to pick up the telephone. Once I'd arranged the visit, my next problem was to get out to Belmont. On the map, it was about thirty miles north of San Diego along the coast, but I didn't drive. So I ended up on a bus that got me into Belmont around three in the afternoon. Then I took a cab and soon found myself standing before the entranceway to Desi Arnaz's estate.

A stone wall covered with bougainvillea, like the flower-covered walls of Cuba, and flowers everywhere. Inside the gate, a walkway to the large pink ranch-style house with a tin roof, a garden, a patio, and a swimming pool. Arched doorways and shuttered windows. Iron balconies on the second floor. And there was a front garden where hibiscus, chrysanthemums, and roses grew. Somehow I had expected to hear the *I Love Lucy* theme, but that place, outside of birdsong, the rustling of trees, and the sound of water running in a fountain, was utterly tranquil. Birds chirping everywhere, and a gardener in blue coveralls standing in the entranceway of the house, looking over the mail spread out on a table. He was a white-haired, slightly stooped man, thick around the middle, with a jowly face, a bundle of letters in one hand, a cigar in the other.

As I approached him, saying, "Hello?" he turned around, extended his hand, and said, "Desi Arnaz."

When I shook his hand, I could feel his callused palms. His hands were mottled with age spots, his fingers nicotine-stained, and the face that had charmed millions looked much older, but when he smiled, the young Arnaz's face revealed itself.

20   Immediately he said, "Ah, but you must be hungry. Would you like a sandwich? Or a steak?" Then: "Come with me."

I followed Desi Arnaz down his hallway. On the walls, framed photographs of Arnaz with just about every major movie star and musician, from John Wayne to Xavier Cugat.[1] And then there was a nice hand-colored glamour-girl photograph of Lucille Ball from when she was a model in the 1930s. Above a cabinet filled with old books, a framed map of Cuba, circa 1952, with more photographs. Among them that photograph of Cesar, Desi, and Nestor.

Then this, in a frame: *I come here because I do not know when the Master will return. I pray because I do not know when the Master will want me to*

---

[1] Cuban band leader.

pray. I look into the light of heaven because I do not know when the Master will take the light away.

"I'm retired these days," Mr. Arnaz said, leading me through the house. "Sometimes I'll do a little television show, like Merv Griffin, but I mainly like to spend my time with my children or in my garden."

When he had passed out of the house through another arched doorway, we reached a patio that looked out over Arnaz's trees and terraced gardens. There were pear, apricot, and orange trees everywhere, a pond in which floated water lilies. Pinks and yellows and brilliant reds coming out of the ground and clustered in bushes. And beyond all this, the Pacific Ocean.

25 ". . . But I can't complain. I love my flowers and little plants."

He rang a bell and a Mexican woman came out of the house.

"Make some sandwiches and bring us some beer. Dos Equis, huh?"

Bowing, the maid backed out through a doorway.

"So, what can I do for you, my boy? What is it that you have there?"

30 "I brought something for you."

They were just some of my uncle's and father's records from back when, Mambo King recordings. There were five of them, just some old 78s and a 33, "The Mambo Kings Play Songs of Love." Looking over the first of the records, he sucked in air through his teeth fiercely. On the cover of that record my father and uncle were posed together, playing a drum and blowing a trumpet for a pretty woman in a tight dress. Putting that aside, and nodding, he looked at the others.

"Your father and uncle. They were good fellows." And: "Good songwriters."

And he started to sing "Beautiful María of My Soul," and although he couldn't remember all the words, he filled in the missing phrases with humming.

"A good song filled with emotion and affection."

35 Then he looked over the others. "Are you selling these?"

"No, because I want to give them to you."

"Why, thank you, my boy."

The maid brought in our sandwiches, nice thick roast beef, lettuce, and tomato, and mustard, on rye bread, and the beers. We ate quietly. Every now and then, Arnaz would look up at me through heavy-lidded eyes and smile.

"You know, *hombre,* "[2] Arnaz said, chewing. "I wish there was something I could do for you." Then: "The saddest thing in life is when someone dies, don't you think, *chico?* "[3]

40 "What did you say?"

"I said, do you like California?"

"Yes."

"It's beautiful. I chose this climate here because it reminds me of Cuba. Here grow many of the same plants and flowers. You know, me and your father and uncle came from the same province, Oriente. I haven't been back there in

---

[2] Man.

[3] Lad or boy.

over twenty years. Could you have imagined what Fidel[4] would have made of Desi Arnaz going back to Cuba? Have you ever been there?"

"No."

45   "Well, that's a shame. It's a little like this." He stretched and yawned.

"Tell you what we'll do, boy. We'll set you up in the guest room, and then I'll show you around. Do you ride horses?"

"No."

"A shame." He winced, straightening up his back. "Do me a favor, boy, and give me a hand up."

Arnaz reached out and I pulled him to his feet.

50   "Come on, I'll show you my different gardens."

Beyond the patio, down a few steps, was another stairway, and that led to another patio, bounded by a wall. A thick scent of flowers in the air.

"This garden is modeled after one of my favorite little plazas in Santiago. You came across it on your way to the harbor. I used to take my girls there." And he winked. "Those days are long gone.

"And from this *placita* you could see all of Santiago Bay. At sunset the sky burned red, and that's when, if you were lucky, you might steal a kiss. Or make like Cuban Pete. That's one of the songs that made me famous."

Nostalgically, Arnaz sang, "My name is Cuban Pete, I'm the King of the Rumba Beat!"

55   Then we both stood for a moment looking at how the Pacific seemed to go on forever and forever.

"One day, all this will either be gone or it will last forever. Which do you think?"

"About what?"

"The afterlife. I believe in it. You?"

I shrugged.

60   "Maybe there's nothing. But I can remember when life felt like it would last forever. You're a young man, you wouldn't understand. You know what was beautiful, boy? When I was little and my mother would hold me in her arms."

I wanted to fall on my knees and beg him to save me. I wanted to hold him tight and hear him say, "I love you," just so I could show Arnaz that I really did appreciate love and just didn't throw it back into people's faces. Instead, I followed him back into the house.

"Now I have to take care of some telephone calls. But make yourself at home. The bar's over there."

Arnaz disappeared, and I walked over to the bar and fixed myself a drink. Through the big window, the brilliant blue California sky and the ocean.

Sitting in Desi Arnaz's living room, I remember the episode of the *I Love Lucy* show in which my father and uncle had once appeared, except it now seemed to be playing itself out right before me. I blinked my eyes and my father and uncle were sitting on the couch opposite me. Then I heard the

---

[4] Cuban leader Fidel Castro.

rattle of coffee cups and utensils and Lucille Ball walked into the living room. She then served the brothers their coffee.

65   When I thought, Poppy, my father looked up at me and smiled sadly.

"I'm so happy to see you again."

"And, son, I'm happy to see you."

My uncle smiled, too.

That's when Arnaz came in, but he wasn't the white-haired gentleman with the jowlish face and kind, weary eyes who had led me around the grounds. It was the cocky, handsome Arnaz of youth.

70   "Gee, fellows," he said. "It's nice to see you again. How are things down in Cuba?"

And I couldn't help myself. I walked over and sat on the couch and wrapped my arms around my father. Expected to find air, but hit on solid flesh. And his neck was warm. His expression pained and timid, like a hick off the boat. He was alive!

"Poppy, but I'm glad to see you."

"It is the same for me, son. It will always be the same."

Embracing him, I started to feel myself falling through an endless space, my father's heart. Not the heart of flesh and blood that had stopped beating, but this other heart filled with light and music, and I felt myself being pulled back into a world of pure affection, before torment, before loss, before awareness.

■ EXPLORATIONS OF THE TEXT ■

1. What does the writer gain by including real such persons as Desi Arnaz and Lucille Ball? What does Arnaz symbolize?
2. Why does the narrator hesitate to call the number?
3. Discuss the scene in which the narrator meets Desi Arnaz. Why is the setting given in such detail?
4. What does music mean to Arnaz, to the Mambo Kings, to the narrator? What does Cuba symbolize?
5. Why does the narrator give Arnaz the records?
6. What does the appearance of the ghosts of the father and of the uncle signify? Why does Arnaz become a youth again?
7. Examine the last paragraph and the symbolism of the "father's heart." What is lost and what is gained?
8. Compare the narrative to "Energy" and to the sections from *The House on Mango Street*.

■■ JOURNAL ENTRIES ■■

1. Watch a rerun of "I Love Lucy," and write a response that connects the program with "When I Called the Number."
2. Write about the title.

■■■ Ideas for Writing ■■■

---

1. What is the role of the ghosts of the fathers in "When I Called the Number" and in *Hamlet*?
2. Write about the loss of innocence in this piece and in "Out of the Cradle Endlessly Rocking."
3. Discuss the revelations experienced by the adult narrators in "When I Called the Number" and "Cathedral." Will these insights lead to change?

Cathedral

Raymond Carver

Raymond Carver (1938–1989) grew up in Oregon, and in 1958 he enrolled at Chico State College in California where he studied creative writing with John Gardner. He earned a B.A. (1963) from Humboldt State College in California, and he was admitted to the writing program at the University of Iowa (1963–1964). He taught at a number of colleges, principally at Syracuse University. His first collection of short stories, Will You Please Be Quiet, Please?, *received a nomination for the National Book Award in 1976. He later wrote ten more collections of short stories and poetry, which include* What We Talk About When We Talk About Love *(1981),* Cathedral *(1984), and* Where I'm Calling From *(1988). His last book of poems,* A New Path to the Waterfall *(1989), reveals the influence of Chekhov on his work.*

This story is the title piece of Carver's collection, Cathedral. *The speaker at first resists connection to the blind man and to the meaning of the visions of the cathedral, but his feelings change in a dramatic way.*

1 This blind man, an old friend of my wife's, he was on his way to spend the night. His wife had died. So he was visiting the dead wife's relatives in Connecticut. He called my wife from his in-laws'. Arrangements were made. He would come by train, a five-hour trip, and my wife would meet him at the station. She hadn't seen him since she worked for him one summer in Seattle ten years ago. But she and the blind man had kept in touch. They made tapes and mailed them back and forth. I wasn't enthusiastic about his visit. He was no one I knew. And his being blind bothered me. My idea of blindness came from the movies. In the movies, the blind moved slowly and never laughed. Sometimes they were led by seeing-eye dogs. A blind man in my house was not something I looked forward to.

That summer in Seattle she had needed a job. She didn't have any money. The man she was going to marry at the end of the summer was in officers' training school. He didn't have any money, either. But she was in love with the guy, and he was in love with her, etc. She'd seen something in the paper: HELP WANTED—*Reading to Blind Man,* and a telephone number. She phoned and went over, was hired on the spot. She'd worked with this blind man all summer. She read stuff to him, case studies, reports, that sort of thing. She helped him organize his little office in the county social-service department. They'd become good friends, my wife and the blind man. How do I know these things? She told me. And she told me something else. On her last day in the office, the blind man asked if he could touch her face. She agreed to this. She told me he touched his fingers to every part of her face, her nose—even her neck! She never forgot it. She even tried to write a poem about it. She was always trying to write a poem. She wrote a poem or two every year, usually after something really important had happened to her.

When we first started going out together, she showed me the poem. In the poem, she recalled his fingers and the way they had moved around over her face. In the poem, she talked about what she had felt at the time, about what went through her mind when the blind man touched her nose and lips. I can remember I didn't think much of the poem. Of course, I didn't tell her that. Maybe I just don't understand poetry. I admit it's not the first thing I reach for when I pick up something to read.

Anyway, this man who'd first enjoyed her favors, the officer-to-be, he'd been her childhood sweetheart. So okay. I'm saying that at the end of the summer she let the blind man run his hands over her face, said goodbye to him, married her childhood etc., who was now a commissioned officer, and she moved away from Seattle. But they'd kept in touch, she and the blind man. She made the first contact after a year or so. She called him up one night from an Air Force base in Alabama. She wanted to talk. They talked. He asked her to send him a tape and tell him about her life. She did this. She sent the tape. On the tape, she told the blind man about her husband and about their life together in the military. She told the blind man she loved her husband but she didn't like it where they lived and she didn't like it that he was a part of the military-industrial thing. She told the blind man she'd written a poem and he was in it. She told him that she was writing a poem about what it was like to be an Air Force officer's wife. The poem wasn't finished yet. She was still writing it. The blind man made a tape. He sent her the tape. She made a tape. This went on for years. My wife's officer was posted to one base and then another. She sent tapes from Moody AFB, McGuire, McConnell, and finally Travis, near Sacramento, where one night she got to feeling lonely and cut off from people she kept losing in that moving-around life. She got to feeling she couldn't go it another step. She went in and swallowed all the pills and capsules in the medicine chest and washed them down with a bottle of gin. Then she got into a hot bath and passed out.

5   But instead of dying, she got sick. She threw up. Her officer—why should he have a name? he was the childhood sweetheart, and what more does he

want?—came home from somewhere, found her, and called the ambulance. In time, she put it all on a tape and sent the tape to the blind man. Over the years, she put all kinds of stuff on tapes and sent the tapes off lickety-split. Next to writing a poem every year, I think it was her chief means of recreation. On one tape, she told the blind man she'd decided to live away from her officer for a time. On another tape, she told him about her divorce. She and I began going out, and of course she told her blind man about it. She told him everything, or so it seemed to me. Once she asked me if I'd like to hear the latest tape from the blind man. This was a year ago. I was on the tape, she said. So I said okay, I'd listen to it. I got us drinks and we settled down in the living room. We made ready to listen. First she inserted the tape into the player and adjusted a couple of dials. Then she pushed a lever. The tape squeaked and someone began to talk in this loud voice. She lowered the volume. After a few minutes of harmless chitchat, I heard my own name in the mouth of this stranger, this blind man I didn't even know! And then this: "From all you've said about him, I can only conclude—" But we were interrupted, a knock at the door, something, and we didn't ever get back to the tape. Maybe it was just as well. I'd heard all I wanted to.

Now this same blind man was coming to sleep in my house.

"Maybe I could take him bowling," I said to my wife. She was at the draining board doing scalloped potatoes. She put down the knife she was using and turned around.

"If you love me," she said, "you can do this for me. If you don't love me, okay. But if you had a friend, any friend, and the friend came to visit, I'd make him feel comfortable." She wiped her hands with the dish towel.

"I don't have any blind friends," I said.

10   "You don't have *any* friends," she said. "Period. Besides," she said, "goddamn it, his wife's just died! Don't you understand that? The man's lost his wife!"

I didn't answer. She'd told me a little about the blind man's wife. Her name was Beulah. Beulah! That's a name for a colored woman.

"Was his wife a Negro?" I asked.

"Are you crazy?" my wife said. "Have you just flipped or something?" She picked up a potato. I saw it hit the floor, then roll under the stove. "What's wrong with you?" she said. "Are you drunk?"

"I'm just asking," I said.

15   Right then my wife filled me in with more detail than I cared to know. I made a drink and sat at the kitchen table to listen. Pieces of the story began to fall into place.

Beulah had gone to work for the blind man the summer after my wife had stopped working for him. Pretty soon Beulah and the blind man had themselves a church wedding. It was a little wedding—who'd want to go to such a wedding in the first place?—just the two of them, plus the minister and the minister's wife. But it was a church wedding just the same. It was what Beulah had wanted, he's said. But even then Beulah must have been carrying the cancer in her glands. After they had been inseparable for eight years—my wife's word, *inseparable*—Beulah's health went into a rapid decline. She died in a Seattle hospital room, the blind man sitting beside the bed and holding on to her hand. They'd married, lived and worked together, slept together—had sex, sure—and then the blind man had to bury her. All this without his having ever seen what the goddamned woman looked like. It was beyond my understanding. Hearing this, I felt sorry for the blind man for a little bit. And then I found myself thinking what a pitiful life this woman must have led. Imagine a woman who could never see herself as she was seen in the eyes of her loved one. A woman who could go on day after day and never receive the smallest compliment from her beloved. A woman whose husband could never read the expression on her face, be it misery or something better. Someone who could wear makeup or not—what difference to him? She could, if she wanted, wear green eye-shadow around one eye, a straight pin in her nostril, yellow slacks and purple shoes, no matter. And then to slip off into death, the blind man's hand on her hand, his blind eyes streaming tears—I'm imagining now—her last thought maybe this: that he never even knew what she looked like, and she on an express to the grave. Robert was left with a small insurance policy and half of a twenty-peso Mexican coin. The other half of the coin went into the box with her. Pathetic.

So when the time rolled around, my wife went to the depot to pick him up. With nothing to do but wait—sure, I blamed him for that—I was having a drink and watching the TV when I heard the car pull into the drive. I got up from the sofa with my drink and went to the window to have a look.

I saw my wife laughing as she parked the car. I saw her get out of the car and shut the door. She was still wearing a smile. Just amazing. She went around to the other side of the car to where the blind man was already starting to get out. This blind man, feature this, he was wearing a full beard! A beard on a blind man! Too much, I say. The blind man reached into the back seat and dragged out a suitcase. My wife took his arm, shut the car door, and, talking all the way, moved him down the drive and then up the steps to the front porch. I turned off the TV. I finished my drink, rinsed the glass, dried my hands. Then I went to the door.

My wife said, "I want you to meet Robert. Robert, this is my husband. I've told you all about him." She was beaming. She had this blind may by his coat sleeve.

20 The blind man let go of his suitcase and up came his hand.

I took it. He squeezed hard, held my hand, and then he let it go.

"I feel like we've already met," he boomed.

"Likewise," I said. I didn't know what else to say. Then I said, "Welcome. I've heard a lot about you." We began to move then, a little group, from the porch into the living room, my wife guiding him by the arm. The blind man was carrying his suitcase in his other hand. My wife said things like, "To your left here, Robert. That's right. Now watch it, there's a chair. That's it. Sit down right here. This is the sofa. We just bought this sofa two weeks ago."

I started to say something about the old sofa. I'd liked that old sofa. But I didn't say anything. Then I wanted to say something else, small-talk, about the scenic ride along the Hudson. How going *to* New York, you should sit on the right-hand side of the train, and coming *from* New York, the left-hand side.

25   "Did you have a good train ride?" I said. "Which side of the train did you sit on, by the way?"

"What a question, which side!" my wife said. "What's it matter which side?" she said.

"I just asked," I said.

"Right side," the blind man said. "I hadn't been on a train in nearly forty years. Not since I was a kid. With my folks. That's been a long time. I'd nearly forgotten the sensation. I have winter in my beard now," he said. "So I've been told, anyway. Do I look distinguished, my dear?" the blind man said to my wife.

"You look distinguished, Robert," she said. "Robert," she said. "Robert, it's just so good to see you."

30   My wife finally took her eyes off the blind man and looked at me. I had the feeling she didn't like what she saw. I shrugged.

I've never met, or personally known, anyone who was blind. This blind man was late forties, a heavy-set, balding man with stooped shoulders, as if he carried a great weight there. He wore brown slacks, brown shoes, a light-brown shirt, a tie, a sports coat. Spiffy. He also had this full beard. But he didn't use a cane and he didn't wear dark glasses. I'd always thought dark glasses were a must for the blind. Fact was, I wished he had a pair. At first glance, his eyes looked like anyone else's eyes. But if you looked close, there was something different about them. Too much white in the iris, for one thing, and the pupils seemed to move around in the sockets without his knowing it or being able to stop it. Creepy. As I stared at his face, I saw the left pupil turn in toward his nose while the other made an effort to keep in one place. But it was only an effort, for that eye was on the roam without his knowing it or wanting it to be.

I said, "Let me get you a drink. What's your pleasure? We have a little of everything. It's one of our pastimes."

"Bub, I'm a Scotch man myself," he said fast enough in this big voice.

"Right," I said. Bub! "Sure you are. I knew it."

35   He let his fingers touch his suitcase, which was sitting alongside the sofa. He was taking his bearings. I didn't blame him for that.

"I'll move that up to your room," my wife said.

"No, that's fine," the blind man said loudly. "It can go up when I go up."

"A little water with the Scotch?" I said.

"Very little," he said.

40   "I knew it," I said.

He said, "Just a tad. The Irish actor, Barry Fitzgerald? I'm like that fellow. When I drink water, Fitzgerald said, I drink water. When I drink whiskey, I drink whiskey." My wife laughed. The blind man brought his hand up under his beard. He lifted his beard slowly and let it drop.

I did the drinks, three big glasses of Scotch with a splash of water in each. Then we made ourselves comfortable and talked about Robert's travels. First the long flight from the West Coast to Connecticut, we covered that. Then from Connecticut up here by train. We had another drink concerning that leg of the trip.

I remembered having read somewhere that the blind didn't smoke because, as speculation had it, they couldn't see the smoke they exhaled. I thought I knew that much and that much only about blind people. But this blind man smoked his cigarette down to the nubbin and then lit another one. This blind man filled his ashtray and my wife emptied it.

When we sat down at the table for dinner, we had another drink. My wife heaped Robert's plate with cube steak, scalloped potatoes, green beans. I buttered him up two slices of bread. I said, "Here's bread and butter for you." I swallowed some of my drink. "Now let us pray," I said, and the blind man lowered his head. My wife looked at me, her mouth agape. "Pray the phone won't ring and the food doesn't get cold," I said.

45   We dug in. We ate everything there was to eat on the table. We ate like there was no tomorrow. We didn't talk. We ate. We scarfed. We grazed that table. We were into serious eating. The blind man had right away located his foods, he knew just where everything was on his plate. I watched with admiration as he used his knife and fork on the meat. He'd cut two pieces of meat, fork the meat into his mouth, and then go all out for the scalloped potatoes, the beans next, and then he'd tear off a hunk of buttered bread and eat that. He'd follow this up with a big drink of milk. It didn't seem to bother him to use his fingers once in a while, either.

We finished everything, including half a strawberry pie. For a few moments, we sat as if stunned. Sweat beaded on our faces. Finally, we got up from the table and left the dirty plates. We didn't look back. We took ourselves into the living room and sank into our places again. Robert and my wife sat on the sofa. I took the big chair. We had us two or three more drinks while they talked about the major things that had come to pass for them in the past ten years. For the most part, I just listened. Now and then I joined in. I didn't want him to think I'd left the room, and I didn't want her to think I was feeling left out. They talked of things that had happened to them—to them!—these past ten years. I waited in vain to hear my name on my wife's sweet lips: "And then my dear husband came into my life"—something like that. But I heard nothing of the sort. More talk of Robert. Robert had done a little of everything, it seemed, a regular blind jack-of-all-trades. But most recently he and his wife had had an Amway distributorship, from which, I gathered, they'd earned their living, such as it was. The blind man was also a ham radio operator. He talked in his loud voice about conversations he'd had with fellow operators in Guam, in the Philippines, in Alaska, and even in Tahiti. He said he'd have a lot of friends there if he ever wanted to go visit those places. From time to time, he'd turn his blind face toward me, put his hand under his beard, ask me something. How long had I been in my present position? (Three years.) Did I like my work? (I didn't.) Was I going to stay with it? (What were the options?) Finally, when I thought he was beginning to run down, I got up and turned on the TV.

My wife looked at me with irritation. She was heading toward a boil. Then she looked at the blind man and said, "Robert, do you have a TV?"

The blind man said, "My dear, I have two TVs. I have a color set and a black-and-white thing, an old relic. It's funny, but if I turn the TV on, and I'm always turning it on, I turn on the color set. It's funny, don't you think?"

I didn't know what to say to that. I had absolutely nothing to say to that. No opinion. So I watched the news program and tried to listen to what the announcer was saying.

50   "This is a color TV," the blind man said. "Don't ask me how, but I can tell."

"We traded up a while ago," I said.

The blind man had another taste of his drink. He lifted his beard, sniffed it, and let it fall. He leaned forward on the sofa. He positioned his ashtray on the coffee table, then put the lighter to his cigarette. He leaned back on the sofa and crossed his legs at the ankles.

My wife covered her mouth, and then she yawned. She stretched. She said, "I think I'll go upstairs and put on my robe. I think I'll change into something else. Robert, you make yourself comfortable," she said.

"I'm comfortable," the blind man said.

55   "I want you to feel comfortable in this house," she said.

"I am comfortable," the blind man said.

After she'd left the room, he and I listened to the weather report and then to the sports roundup. By that time, she'd been gone so long I didn't know if she was going to come back. I thought she might have gone to bed. I wished she'd come back downstairs. I didn't want to be left alone with a blind man. I asked him if he wanted another drink, and he said sure. Then I asked if he wanted to smoke some dope with me. I said I'd just rolled a number. I hadn't, but I planned to do so in about two shakes.

"I'll try some with you," he said.

"Damn right," I said. "That's the stuff."

60   "I got our drinks and sat down on the sofa with him. Then I rolled us two fat numbers. I lit one and passed it. I brought it to his fingers. He took it and inhaled.

"Hold it as long as you can," I said. I could tell he didn't know the first thing.

My wife came back downstairs wearing her pink robe and her pink slippers.

"What do I smell?" she said.

"We thought we'd have us some cannabis," I said.

65   My wife gave me a savage look. Then she looked at the blind man and said, "Robert, I didn't know you smoked."

He said, "I do now, my dear. There's a first time for everything. But I don't feel anything yet."

"This stuff is pretty mellow," I said. "This stuff is mild. It's dope you can reason with," I said. "It doesn't mess you up."

"Not much it doesn't, bub," he said, and laughed.

My wife sat on the sofa between the blind man and me. I passed her the number. She took it and toked and then passed it back to me. "Which way is this going?" she said. Then she said, "I shouldn't be smoking this. I can hardly keep my eyes open as it is. That dinner did me in. I shouldn't have eaten so much."

70   "It was the strawberry pie," the blind man said. "That's what did it," he said, and he laughed his big laugh. Then he shook his head.

"There's more strawberry pie," I said.

"Do you want some more, Robert?" my wife said.

"Maybe in a little while," he said.

We gave our attention to the TV. My wife yawned again. She said, "Your bed is made up when you feel like going to bed, Robert. I know you must have had a long day. When you're ready to go to bed, say so." She pulled his arm. "Robert?"

75   He came to and said, "I've had a real nice time. This beats tapes, doesn't it?"

I said, "Coming at you," and I put the number between his fingers. He inhaled, held the smoke, and then let it go. It was like he'd been doing it since he was nine years old.

"Thanks, bub," he said. "But I think this is all for me. I think I'm beginning to feel it," he said. He held the burning roach out for my wife.

"Same here," she said. "Ditto. Me, too." She took the roach and passed it to me. "I may just sit here for a while between you two guys with my eyes closed. But don't let me bother you, okay? Either one of you. If it bothers you, say so. Otherwise, I may just sit here with my eyes closed until you're ready to go to bed," she said. "Your bed's made up, Robert, when you're ready. It's right next to our room at the top of the stairs. We'll show you up when you're ready. You wake me up now, you guys, if I fall asleep." She said that and then she closed her eyes and went to sleep.

The news program ended. I got up and changed the channel. I sat back down on the sofa. I wished my wife hadn't pooped out. Her head lay across the back of the sofa, her mouth open. She'd turned so that her robe had slipped away from her legs, exposing a juicy thigh. I reached to draw her robe back over her, and it was then that I glanced at the blind man. What the hell! I flipped the robe open again.

80   "You say when you want some strawberry pie," I said.

"I will," he said.

I said, "Are you tired? Do you want me to take you up to your bed? Are you ready to hit the hay?"

"Not yet," he said. "No, I'll stay up with you, bub. If that's all right. I'll stay up until you're ready to turn in. We haven't had a chance to talk. Know what I mean? I feel like me and her monopolized the evening." He lifted his beard and he let it fall. He picked up his cigarettes and his lighter.

"That's all right," I said. Then I said, "I'm glad for the company."

85   And I guess I was. Every night I smoked dope and stayed up as long as I could before I fell asleep. My wife and I hardly ever went to bed at the same time. When I did go to sleep, I had these dreams. Sometimes I'd wake up from one of them, my heart going crazy.

Something about the church and the Middle Ages was on the TV. Not your run-of-the-mill TV fare. I wanted to watch something else. I turned to the other channels. But there was nothing on them, either. So I turned back to the first channel and apologized.

"Bub, it's all right," the blind man said. "It's fine with me. Whatever you want to watch is okay. I'm always learning something. Learning never ends. It won't hurt me to learn something tonight. I got ears," he said.

We didn't say anything for a time. He was leaning forward with his head turned at me, his right ear aimed in the direction of the set. Very disconcerting. Now and then his eyelids drooped and then they snapped open again. Now and then he put his fingers into his beard and tugged, like he was thinking about something he was hearing on the television.

On the screen, a group of men wearing cowls was being set upon and tormented by men dressed in skeleton costumes and men dressed as devils. The men dressed as devils wore devil masks, horns, and long tails. This pageant was part of a procession. The Englishman who was narrating the thing said it took place in Spain once a year. I tried to explain to the blind man what was happening.

90   "Skeletons," he said. "I know about skeletons," he said, and he nodded.

The TV showed this one cathedral. Then there was a long, slow look at another one. Finally, the picture switched to the famous one in Paris, with its flying buttresses and its spires reaching up to the clouds. The camera pulled away to show the whole of the cathedral rising above the skyline.

There were times when the Englishman who was telling the thing would shut up, would simply let the camera move around over the cathedrals. Or else the camera would tour the countryside, men in fields walking behind oxen. I waited as long as I could. Then I felt I had to say something. I said, "They're showing the outside of this cathedral now. Gargoyles. Little statues carved to look like monsters. Now I guess they're in Italy. Yeah, they're in Italy. There's paintings on the walls of this one church."

"Are those fresco paintings, bub?" he asked, and he sipped from his drink.

I reached for my glass. But it was empty. I tried to remember what I could remember. "You're asking me are those frescoes?" I said. "That's a good question. I don't know."

95   The camera moved to a cathedral outside Lisbon. The differences in the Portuguese cathedral compared with the French and Italian were not that great. But they were there. Mostly the interior stuff. Then something occurred to me, and I said, "Something has occurred to me. Do you have any idea what a cathedral is? What they look like, that is? Do you follow me? If

somebody says cathedral to you, do you have any notion what they're talking about? Do you know the difference between that and a Baptist church, say?"

He let the smoke dribble from his mouth. "I know they took hundreds of workers fifty or a hundred years to build," he said. "I just heard the man say that, of course. I know generations of the same families worked on a cathedral. I heard him say that, too. The men who began their life's work on them, they never lived to see the completion of their work. In that wise, bub, they're no different from the rest of us, right?" He laughed. Then his eyelids drooped again. His head nodded. He seemed to be snoozing. Maybe he was imagining himself in Portugal. The TV was showing another cathedral now. This one was in Germany. The Englishman's voice droned on. "Cathedrals," the blind man said. He sat up and rolled his head back and forth. "If you want the truth, bub, that's about all I know. What I just said. What I heard him say. But maybe you could describe one to me? I wish you'd do it. I'd like that. If you want to know, I really don't have a good idea."

I stared hard at the shot of the cathedral on the TV. How could I even begin to describe it? But say my life depended on it. Say my life was being threatened by an insane guy who said I had to do it or else.

I stared some more at the cathedral before the picture flipped off into the countryside. There was no use. I turned to the blind man and said, "To begin with, they're very tall." I was looking around the room for clues. "They reach way up. Up and up. Toward the sky. They're so big, some of them, they have to have these supports. To help hold them up, so to speak. These supports are called buttresses. They remind me of viaducts, for some reason. But maybe you don't know viaducts, either? Sometimes the cathedrals have devils and such carved into the front. Sometimes lords and ladies. Don't ask me why this is," I said.

He was nodding. The whole upper part of his body seemed to be moving back and forth.

100   "I'm not doing so good, am I?" I said.

He stopped nodding and leaned forward on the edge of the sofa. As he listened to me, he was running his fingers through his beard. I wasn't getting through to him, I could see that. But he waited for me to go on just the same. He nodded, like he was trying to encourage me. I tried to think what else to say. "They're really big," I said. "They're massive. They're built of stone. Marble, too, sometimes. In those olden days, when they built cathedrals, men wanted to be close to God. In those olden days, God was an important part of everyone's life. You could tell this from their cathedral-building. I'm sorry," I said, "but it looks like that's the best I can do for you. I'm just no good at it."

"That's all right, bub," the blind man said. "Hey, listen. I hope you don't mind my asking you. Can I ask you something? Let me ask you a simple question, yes or no. I'm just curious and there's no offense. You're my host. But let me ask if you are in any way religious? You don't mind my asking?"

I shook my head. He couldn't see that, though. A wink is the same as a nod to a blind man. "I guess I don't believe in it. In anything. Sometimes it's hard. You know what I'm saying?"

"Sure, I do," he said.

105 "Right," I said.

The Englishman was still holding forth. My wife sighed in her sleep. She drew a long breath and went on with her sleeping.

"You'll have to forgive me," I said. "But I can't tell you what a cathedral looks like. It just isn't in me to do it. I can't do any more than I've done."

The blind man sat very still, his head down, as he listened to me.

I said, "The truth is, cathedrals don't mean anything special to me. Nothing. Cathedrals. They're something to look at on late-night TV. That's all they are."

110 It was then that the blind man cleared his throat. He brought something up. He took a handkerchief from his back pocket. Then he said, "I get it, bub. It's okay. It happens. Don't worry about it," he said. "Hey, listen to me. Will you do me a favor? I got an idea. Why don't you find us some heavy paper? And a pen. We'll do something. We'll draw one together. Get us a pen and some heavy paper. Go on, bub, get the stuff," he said.

So I went upstairs. My legs felt like they didn't have any strength in them. They felt like they did after I'd done some running. In my wife's room, I looked around. I found some ballpoints in a little basket on her table. And then I tried to think where to look for the kind of paper he was talking about.

Downstairs, in the kitchen, I found a shopping bag with onion skins in the bottom of the bag. I emptied the bag and shook it. I brought it into the living room and sat down with it near his legs. I moved some things, smoothed the wrinkles from the bag, spread it out on the coffee table.

The blind man got down from the sofa and sat next to me on the carpet.

He ran his fingers over the paper. He went up and down the sides of the paper. The edges, even the edges. He fingered the corners.

115 "All right," he said. "All right, let's do her."

He found my hand, the hand with the pen. He closed his hand over my hand. "Go ahead, bub, draw," he said. "Draw. You'll see. I'll follow along with you. It'll be okay. Just begin now like I'm telling you. You'll see. Draw," the blind man said.

So I began. First I drew a box that looked like a house. It could have been the house I lived in. Then I put a roof on it. At either end of the roof, I drew spires. Crazy.

"Swell," he said. "Terrific. You're doing fine," he said. "Never thought anything like this could happen in your lifetime, did you, bub? Well, it's a strange life, we all know that. Go on now. Keep it up."

I put in windows with arches. I drew flying buttresses.[1] I hung great doors. I couldn't stop. The TV station went off the air. I put down the pen and closed and opened my fingers. The blind man felt around over the paper. He

---

[1]A crucial part of the architecture of Gothic cathedrals; an external support arch that carries an outward and downward thrust to a solid buttress, thereby creating a vertical thrust against a masonry wall to help hold the structure.

moved the tips of his fingers over the paper, all over what I had drawn, and he nodded.

120   "Doing fine," the blind man said.

I took up the pen again, and he found my hand. I kept at it. I'm no artist. But I kept drawing just the same.

My wife opened up her eyes and gazed at us. She sat up on the sofa, her robe hanging open. She said, "What are you doing? Tell me, I want to know."

I didn't answer her.

The blind man said, "We're drawing a cathedral. Me and him are working on it. Press hard," he said to me. "That's right. That's good," he said. "Sure. You got it, bub. I can tell. You didn't think you could. But you can, can't you? You're cooking with gas now. You know what I'm saying? We're going to really have us something here in a minute. How's the old arm?" he said. "Put some people in there now. What's a cathedral without people?"

125   My wife said, "What's going on? Robert, what are you doing? What's going on?"

"It's all right," he said to her. "Close your eyes now," the blind man said to me.

I did it. I closed them just like he said.

"Are they closed?" he said. "Don't fudge."

"They're closed," I said.

130   "Keep them that way," he said. He said, "Don't stop now. Draw."

So we kept on with it. His fingers rode my fingers as my hand went over the paper. It was like nothing else in my life up to now.

Then he said, "I think that's it. I think you got it," he said. "Take a look. What do you think?"

But I had my eyes closed. I thought I'd keep them that way for a little longer. I thought it was something I ought to do.

"Well?" he said. "Are you looking?"

135   My eyes were still closed. I was in my house. I knew that. But I didn't feel like I was inside anything.

"It's really something," I said.

■   **EXPLORATIONS OF THE TEXT**   ■

---

1. Examine the character of the speaker: his attitudes, values, actions, speech.
2. Why does only the blind man have a name? Describe his attitudes, his physical characteristics, and his capacity for friendship.
3. What is the nature of the relationship between the wife and Robert? Between the wife and the narrator?
4. Why does the woman leave Robert and the narrator together? Is her action deliberate?

5. Does the incident concerning the cathedral have religious meaning? What is the symbolism of the title? In what way does the narrator change at the end of the story?
6. Compare and contrast the themes concerning blindness in *Oedipus Rex* (Chapter 7) and in "Cathedral."

■■ JOURNAL ENTRIES ■■

1. What does the narrator mean when he says, "I didn't feel like I was inside anything"?
2. Extend the narrative: write about possible changes in the narrator when the blind man leaves.

■■■ IDEAS FOR WRITING ■■■

1. Write a character analysis of the wife that takes into account her first marriage, her suicide attempt, her friendship with Robert, and her present life.
2. Explore the symbolism of the cathedral.
3. Carver mentions television numerous times in the opening paragraphs of the story. Why? Use evidence from the story to support your thesis.

POETRY

Incident

Countee Cullen

Born in New York City, Countee Cullen (1903–1946) was a central figure of the Harlem Renaissance. A formalist and romantic poet, Cullen acknowledged Keats as his greatest influence. He published his first collection of poems, Color, *in 1925 while he was a student at New York University. He received a Guggenheim Fellowship and published* Black Christ and Other Poems *in France in 1929. Cullen also wrote a novel, children's stories, and poems. He collaborated with his friend Arna Bontemps on a play,* St. Louis Woman, *which became a popular Broadway musical in 1946.*

"Incident" shows the insidious power of prejudice to destroy a child's innocent view of the world. It also demonstrates that negative presuppositions about others are learned early.

Once riding in old Baltimore,
    Heart-filled, head-filled with glee,
I saw a Baltimorean
    Keep looking straight at me.

5 Now I was eight and very small,
    And he was no whit bigger,
And so I smiled, but he poked out
    His tongue and called me, "Nigger."

I saw the whole of Baltimore
10   From May until December:
Of all the things that happened there
    That's all that I remember.

■   **EXPLORATIONS OF THE TEXT**   ■

1. What is the nature of the interaction between the two boys?
2. Why does the speaker remember nothing more than the incident, even though he stayed in Baltimore from "May until December"?

3. See how much Cullen conveys in few and simple words. How can you transfer this power of compression in poetry to forms of nonfiction?
4. What aspects of this poem are similar to the story by Heker?

■■ JOURNAL ENTRIES ■■

1. Compare your experience of prejudice with the persona in the poem.
2. Compare the reactions of the persona with those in the works by Heker, Cruz, and Erdrich.

■■■ IDEAS FOR WRITING ■■■

1. What do its form and rhyme add to this poem?
2. What is the power of language? What are the effects of the use of the term *nigger?*

Uncle's First Rabbit

Lorna Dee Cervantes

Born in San Francisco and educated in California, Lorna Dee Cervantes (1954–) is active in the Chicana community and in literary affairs. In 1976, she founded Mango Publications, a small press that publishes a literary journal and both Mexican-American and multicultural books. Her volume of poetry, Emplumada *(1981), received high praise from critics.*

In this poem, Cervantes writes of an early event in the uncle's life, the killing of a rabbit, which becomes a symbol for both violence and violation.

> He was a good boy
> making his way through
> the Santa Barbara[1] pines,
> sighting the blast of fluff
> 5 as he leveled the rifle,
> and the terrible singing began.
> He was ten years old,
> hunting my grandpa's supper.

---

[1] A city in California.

He had dreamed of running,
10 shouldering the rifle to town,
selling it, and taking the next
train out.
     Fifty years
have passed and he still hears
15 that rabbit "just like a baby."
He remembers how the rabbit
stopped keening under the butt
of his rifle, how he brought
it home with tears streaming
20 down his blood soaked jacket.
"That bastard. That bastard."
He cried all night and the week
after, remembering that voice
like his dead baby sister's,
25 remembering his father's drunken
kicking that had pushed her
into birth. She had a voice
like that, growing faint
at its end; his mother rocking,
30 softly, keening. He dreamed
of running, running
the bastard out of his life.
He would forget them, run down
the hill, leave his mother's
35 silent waters, and the sounds
of beating night after night,
     When war came,
he took the man's vow. He was
finally leaving and taking
40 the bastard's last bloodline
with him. At war's end, he could
still hear her, her soft
body stiffening under water
like a shark's. The color
45 of the water, darkening, soaking,
as he clung to what was left
of a ship's gun. Ten long hours
off the coast of Okinawa,[2] he sang
so he wouldn't hear them.
50 He pounded their voices out
of his head, and awakened

---

[2] One of the islands of the Ryukyu group, part of Japan, occupied by the United States from 1945–1972 when it was returned to Japan.

to find himself slugging the bloodied
face of his wife.
     Fifty years
55 have passed and he has not run
the way he dreamed. The Paradise
pines shadow the bleak hills
to his home. His hunting hounds,
dead now. His father, long dead.
60 His wife, dying, hacking in the bed
she has not let him enter for the last
thirty years. He stands looking,
he mouths the words, "Die you bitch.
I'll live to watch you die." He turns,
65 entering their moss-soft livingroom.
He watches out the picture window
and remembers running: how he'll
take the new pickup to town, sell it,
and get the next train out.

■ EXPLORATIONS OF THE TEXT ■

1. What events relate to the killing of the rabbit? Why is it compared to a baby?
2. What is the narrator's point of view?
3. How has the uncle changed in fifty years?
4. Why does the uncle not leave? Will he ever leave?
5. What connections can you find between this poem and "Barn Burning" or "The Man Who Was Almost a Man"?

■■ JOURNAL ENTRIES ■■

1. Paraphrase this poem in a paragraph.
2. Respond to the actions of the uncle.

■■■ IDEAS FOR WRITING ■■■

1. What is the poet's attitude toward killing the rabbit? Which words provide clues or evidence for your position?
2. Analyze the uncle's character.
3. Compare this presentation of hunting with the hunting scene in Alberto Moravia's "The Chase" (in Chapter 6) or with David Higgins' essay, "The Earnestness of Life" in this chapter.

Out of the Cradle Endlessly Rocking

Walt Whitman

Walt Whitman (1819–1892) was born on Long Island. Until the early 1850s, he alternated among printing, writing, and teaching jobs in New York. The first edition of Whitman's Leaves of Grass *was published in 1855 and consisted of twelve untitled poems, including the work eventually titled "Song of Myself." The spacious, unconventional verse patterns in* Leaves of Grass *have had a profound, lasting effect on North American poetry.*

In addition to the following selection, other major poems in Leaves of Grass *include "Crossing Brooklyn Ferry," "O Captain! My Captain!," "When Lilacs Last in the Dooryard Bloom'd," and "Democratic Vista."*

In "Out of the Cradle Endlessly Rocking," Whitman creates songs within a song to reflect on the connections among art, memory, life, and death. The setting for the poem is Long Island, which he calls "Paumanok," its Native-American name.

Out of the cradle endlessly rocking,
Out of the mocking-bird's throat, the musical shuttle,
Out of the Ninth-month[1] midnight,
Over the sterile sands and the fields beyond, where the child leaving his
    bed wander'd alone, bareheaded, barefoot,
5 Down from the shower'd halo,
Up from the mystic play of shadows twining and twisting as if they were
    alive,
Out from the patches of briers and blackberries,
From the memories of the bird that chanted to me,
From your memories sad brother, from the fitful risings and fallings I
    heard,
10 From under that yellow half-moon late-risen and swollen as if with tears,
From those beginning notes of yearning and love there in the mist,
From the thousand responses of my heart never to cease,
From the myriad thence-arous'd words,
From the word stronger and more delicious than any,
15 For such as now they start the scene revisiting,
As a flock, twittering, rising, or overhead passing,
Borne hither, ere all eludes me, hurriedly,
A man, yet by these tears a little boy again,

---

[1] Quaker name for September.

Throwing myself on the sand, confronting the waves,
20 I, chanter of pains and joys, uniter of here and hereafter,
Taking all hints to use them, but swiftly leaping beyond them,
A reminiscence sing.

Once Paumanok,
When the lilac-scent was in the air and Fifth-month grass was growing,
25 Up this seashore in some briers,
Two feather'd guests from Alabama, two together,
And their nest, and four light-green eggs spotted with brown,
And every day the he-bird to and fro near at hand,
And every day the she-bird crouch'd on her nest, silent, with bright eyes,
30 And every day I, a curious boy, never too close, never disturbing them,
Cautiously peering, absorbing, translating.

Shine! shine! shine!
Pour down your warmth, great sun!
While we bask, we two together.
35 *Two together!*
Winds blow south, or winds blow north,
Day come white, or night come black,
Home, or rivers and mountains from home,
Singing all time, minding no time,
40 *While we two keep together.*

Till of a sudden,
May-be kill'd, unknown to her mate,
One forenoon the she-bird crouch'd not on the nest,
Nor return'd that afternoon, nor the next,
45 Nor ever appear'd again.

And thenceforward all summer in the sound of the sea,
And at night under the full of the moon in calmer weather,
Over the hoarse surging of the sea,
Or flitting from brier to brier by day,
50 I saw, I heard at intervals the remaining one, the he-bird,
The solitary guest from Alabama.

Blow! blow! blow!
Blow up sea-winds along Paumanok's shore;
I wait and I wait till you blow my mate to me.

55 Yes, when the stars glisten'd,
All night long on the prong of a moss-scallop'd stake,
Down almost amid the slapping waves,
Sat the lone singer wonderful causing tears.

He call'd on his mate,
60 He pour'd forth the meanings which I of all men know.

Yes my brother I know,
The rest might not, but I have treasur'd every note,
For more than once dimly down to the beach gliding,
Silent, avoiding the moonbeams, blending myself with the shadows,
65 Recalling now the obscure shapes, the echoes, the sounds and sights after
    their sorts,
The white arms out in the breakers tirelessly tossing,
I, with bare feet, a child, the wind wafting my hair,
Listen'd long and long.

Listen'd to keep, to sing, now translating the notes,
70 Following you my brother.

Soothe! soothe! soothe!
Close on its wave soothes the wave behind,
And again another behind embracing and lapping, every one close,
But my love soothes not me, not me.

75 *Low hangs the moon, it rose late,*
It is lagging—O I think it is heavy with love, with love.

O madly the sea pushes upon the land,
With love, with love.

O night! do I not see my love fluttering out among the breakers?
80 *What is that little black thing I see there in the white?*

Loud! loud! loud!
Loud I call to you, my love!

High and clear I shoot my voice over the waves,
Surely you must know who is here, is here,
85 *You must know whom I am, my love.*

Low-hanging moon!
What is that dusky spot in your brown yellow?
O it is the shape, the shape of my mate!
O moon do not keep her from me any longer.

90 *Land! land! O land!*
Whichever way I turn, O I think you could give me my mate back again if
    you only would,
For I am almost sure I see her dimly whichever way I look.

O rising stars!
Perhaps the one I want so much will rise, will rise with some of you.

95 *O throat! O trembling throat!*
Sound clearer through the atmosphere!
Pierce the woods, the earth,
Somewhere listening to catch you must be the one I want.

Shake out carols!
100 *Solitary here, the night's carols!*
Carols of lonesome love! death's carols!
Carols under that lagging, yellow, waning moon!
O under that moon where she droops down into the sea!
O reckless despairing carols.

105 *But soft! sink low!*
Soft! let me just murmur,
And do you wait a moment you husky-nois'd sea,
For somewhere I believe I heard my mate responding to me,
So faint, I must be still, be still to listen,
110 *But not altogether still, for then she might not come immediately to me.*

Hither my love!
Here I am! here!
With this just-sustain'd note I announce myself to you,
This gentle call is for you my love, for you.

115 *Do not be decoy'd elsewhere,*
That is the whistle of the wind, it is not my voice,
That is the fluttering, the fluttering of the spray,
Those are the shadows of leaves.

O darkness! O in vain!
120 *O I am very sick and sorrowful.*
O brown halo in the sky near the moon, drooping upon the sea!
O troubled reflection in the sea!

O throat! O throbbing heart!
And I singing uselessly, uselessly all the night.

125 *O past! O happy life! O songs of joy!*
In the air, in the woods, over fields,
Loved! loved! loved! loved! loved!
But my mate no more, no more with me!
We two together no more.

130 The aria[2] sinking,
All else continuing, the stars shining,
The winds blowing, the notes of the bird continuous echoing,
With angry moans the fierce old mother incessantly moaning,
On the sands of Paumanok's shore gray and rustling,
135 The yellow half-moon enlarged, sagging down, drooping, the face of the sea almost touching
The boy ecstatic, with his bare feet the waves, with his hair the atmosphere dallying,
The love in the heart long pent, now loose, now at last tumultuously bursting,
The aria's meaning, the ears, the soul, swiftly depositing,
The strange tears down the cheeks coursing,
140 The colloquy there, the trio, each uttering,
The undertone, the savage old mother incessantly crying,
To the boy's soul's questions sullenly timing, some drown'd secret hissing,
To the outsetting bard.[3]

Demon or bird! (said the boy's soul,)
145 Is it indeed toward your mate you sing? or is it really to me?
For I, that was a child, my tongue's use sleeping, now I have heard you,
Now in a moment I know what I am for, I awake,
And already a thousand singers, a thousand songs, clearer, louder and more sorrowful than yours,
A thousand warbling echoes have started to live within me, never to die.

150 O you singer solitary, singing by yourself, projecting me,
O solitary me listening, never more shall I cease perpetuating you,
Never more shall I escape, never more the reverberations,
Never more the cries of unsatisfied love be absent from me,
Never again leave me to be the peaceful child I was before what there in the night,
155 By the sea under the yellow and sagging moon,
The messenger there arous'd, the fire, the sweet hell within,
The unknown want, the destiny of me.

O give me the clew! (it lurks in the night here somewhere,)
O if I am to have so much, let me have more!

160 A word then, (for I will conquer it,)
The word final, superior to all,
Subtle, sent up—what is it?—I listen;

---

[2] A song performed by a single voice in opera.
[3] A poet.

Are you whispering it, and have been all the time, you sea waves?
Is that it from your liquid rims and wet sands?

165 Whereto answering, the sea,
Delaying not, hurrying not,
Whisper'd me through the night, and very plainly before daybreak,
Lisp'd to me the low and delicious word death,
And again death, death, death, death,
170 Hissing melodious, neither like the bird nor like my arous'd child's heart,
But edging near as privately for me rustling at my feet,
Creeping thence steadily up to my ears and laving me softly all over,
Death, death, death, death, death.

Which I do not forget,
175 But fuse the song of my dusky demon and brother,
That he sang to me in the moonlight on Paumanok's gray beach,
With the thousand responsive songs at random,
My own songs awaked from that hour,
And with them the key, the word up from the waves,
180 The word of the sweetest song and all songs,
The strong and delicious word which, creeping to my feet,
(Or like some old crone rocking the cradle, swathed in sweet garments,
  bending aside,)
The sea whisper'd me.

■ EXPLORATIONS OF THE TEXT ■

1. About what does the speaker reminisce? What is the speaker's motivation for this "reminiscence" song?
2. What is the mood of the prologue?
3. What is the message of the he-bird's lament? Is the personification effective?
4. What does the boy learn of life through the "reminiscence" song? What does the adult speaker learn?
5. Explore the connections of birth, love, and death expressed in this poem.
6. Whitman is known for his organic free verse (poetry that has music, form, and rhythm, but not a standard metric or rhythmic pattern. (See the Glossary and Chapter 10.) How does Whitman's free verse work in this poem?
7. How does Whitman make use of musical form?

■■   JOURNAL ENTRIES   ■■

1. Freewrite about one of the following symbols: star, bird, or sea.
2. Study the he-bird's song. Create a free verse monologue spoken by a bird or other creature. In a concrete manner, convey an abstract idea, such as loss, betrayal, death, or love.

■■■   IDEAS FOR WRITING   ■■■

1. Analyze the **persona**. (See lines 1–21 and 130–182.)
2. What do the repeated symbols of the star, bird, and sea suggest?

Black Hair

Gary Soto

Born in Fresno, California, Gary Soto (1952–   ) won the American Book Award for his volume of autobiographical essays, Living Up the Street *(1984). He has written three volumes of poetry,* The Element of San Joaquin *(1977),* The Tale of Sunlight *(1978), and* Black Hair *(1985), and has edited* Pieces of the Heart: New Chicano Fiction *(1993). Gary Soto teaches Chicano Studies and English at the University of California in Berkeley. He has received a Guggenheim Fellowship, the Academy of American Poets Award, and other honors.*

In "Black Hair," a child embraces his heritage through baseball and hero worship.

> At eight I was brilliant with my body.
> In July, that ring of heat
> We all jumped through, I sat in the bleachers
> Of Romain Playground, in the lengthening
> 5 Shade that rose from our dirty feet.
> The game before us was more than baseball.
> It was a figure—Hector Moreno
> Quick and hard with turned muscles,
> His crouch the one I assumed before an altar
> 10 Of worn baseball cards, in my room.
>
> I came here because I was Mexican, a stick
> Of brown light in love with those
> Who could do it—the triple and hard slide,

The gloves eating balls into double plays.
15 What could I do with 50 pounds, my shyness,
My black torch of hair, about to go out?
Father was dead, his face no longer
Hanging over the table or our sleep,
And mother was the terror of mouths
20 Twisting hurt by butter knives.

In the bleachers I was brilliant with my body,
Waving players in and stomping my feet,
I chewed sunflower seeds. I drank water
And bit my arm through the late innings.
25 When Hector lined balls into deep
Center, in my mind I rounded the bases
With him, my face flared, my hair lifting
Beautifully, because we were coming home
To the arms of brown people.

■ EXPLORATIONS OF THE TEXT ■

1. What is the speaker's view of Hector Moreno? What does Hector Moreno represent?
2. How are the speaker's attitudes toward being Mexican and toward baseball intertwined?
3. What is the nature of the narrator's relationship with his father and his mother?
4. What is the significance of the image of "black hair"?
5. Contrast the speaker's position in this poem with the experience of the teenagers in "Indian Boarding School: The Runaways."

■■ JOURNAL ENTRIES ■■

1. Why are sports important to teenagers?
2. What are ways that ethnic groups have found to break cultural barriers in the United States? How has North American culture changed as a result?

■■■ IDEAS FOR WRITING ■■■

1. Write about the possible meanings and connotations of the word *brilliant* in "Black Hair."
2. Hector Moreno is the speaker's hero. Write about a hero in your own life.

Oranges

Gary Soto

In this poem, Soto explores a young male's sexual awakening. This work offers both a wry and serious view of adolescence.

The first time I walked
With a girl, I was twelve,
Cold, and weighted down
With two oranges in my jacket.
5 December. Frost cracking
Beneath my steps, my breath
Before me, then gone,
As I walked toward
Her house, the one whose
10 Porch light burned yellow
Night and day, in any weather.
A dog barked at me, until
She came out pulling
At her gloves, face bright
15 With rouge. I smiled,
Toucher her shoulder, and led
Her down the street, across
A used car lot and a line
Of newly planted trees,
20 Until we were breathing
Before a drugstore. We
Entered, the tiny bell
Bringing a saleslady
Down a narrow aisle of goods.
25 I turned to the candies
Tiered like bleachers,
And asked what she wanted—
Light in her eyes, a smile
Starting at the corners
30 Of her mouth. I fingered
A nickel in my pocket,
And when she lifted a chocolate
That cost a dime,
I didn't say anything.
35 I took the nickel from
My pocket, then an orange,
And set them quietly on
The counter. When I looked up,

The lady's eyes met mine,
40 And held them, knowing
Very well what it was all
About.

Outside,
A few cars hissing past,
45 Fog hanging like old
Coats between the trees.
I took my girl's hand
In mine for two blocks,
Then released it to let
50 Her unwrap the chocolate.
I peeled my orange
That was so bright against
The gray of December
That, from some distance,
55 Someone might have thought
I was making a fire in my hands.

■ EXPLORATIONS OF THE TEXT ■

1. What is the significance of the purchase at the drugstore?
2. Explore the symbolism of peeling the paper from the chocolate, peeling the orange, and the last line. What do these images suggest?
3. Examine the images associated with weather. How does the time of year enhance the mood of the poem?

■■ JOURNAL ENTRIES ■■

1. Write a monologue in the voice of the young girl.
2. How does the outside world, the environment, influence the speaker's experience? Are there clues in the poem?

■■■ IDEAS FOR WRITING ■■■

1. What do the last two lines of the poem mean? Do they present a satisfying conclusion?
2. Write about your first date.

Adolescence—I
Adolescence—II
Adolescence—III

Rita Dove

Rita Dove (1952–   ) was born in Akron, Ohio. She began teaching at Arizona State University in Tempe in 1981 and is currently a professor at the University of Virginia. In 1987, she was awarded the Pulitzer Prize in poetry for Thomas and Beulah, *poems based loosely on the lives of Dove's maternal grandparents. In 1993, she was appointed Poet Laureate of the United States, not only the first African-American, but also the youngest person ever to receive this honor.*

Major works include Yellow House on the Corner *(1980),* Museum *(1983),* Grace Notes *(1989), and* Selected Poems *(1993). Dove also has written a play, a volume of short stories,* Fifth Sunday *(1985), and a novel,* Through the Ivory Gates *(1992).*

In Adolescence I, II, *and* III, *the stages of emerging female sexuality appear in dramatic and tense recollections.*

Adolescence—I

In water-heavy nights behind grandmother's porch
We knelt in the tickling grasses and whispered:
Linda's face hung before us, pale as a pecan,
And it grew wise as she said:
5   "A boy's lips are soft,
        As soft as baby's skin."
The air closed over her words.
A firefly whirred near my ear, and in the distance
I could hear streetlamps ping
10 Into miniature suns
Against a feathery sky.

Adolescence—II

Although it is night, I sit in the bathroom, waiting.
Sweat prickles behind my knees, the baby-breasts are alert.
Venetian blinds slice up the moon; the tiles quiver in pale strips.

Then they come, the three seal men with eyes as round
5 As dinner plates and eyelashes like sharpened tines.
They bring the scent of licorice. One sits in the washbowl,

One on the bathtub edge; one leans against the door.
"Can you feel it yet?" they whisper.
I don't know what to say, again. They chuckle,

10 Patting their sleek bodies with their hands.
"Well, maybe next time." And they rise,
Glittering like pools of ink under moonlight,

And vanish. I clutch at the ragged holes
They leave behind, here at the edge of darkness.
15 Night rests like a ball of fur on my tongue.

Adolescence—III

With Dad gone, Mom and I worked
The dusky rows of tomatoes.
As they glowed orange in sunlight
And rotted in shadow, I too
5 Grew orange and softer, swelling out
Starched cotton slips.

The texture of twilight made me think of
Lengths of Dotted Swiss.[1] In my room
I wrapped scarred knees in dresses
10 That once went to big-band dances;
I baptized my earlobes with rosewater.
Along the window-sill, the lipstick stubs
Glittered in their steel shells.

Looking out at the rows of clay
15 And chicken manure, I dreamed how it would happen:
He would meet me by the blue spruce,
A carnation over his heart, saying,
"I have come for you, Madam;
I have loved you in my dreams."
20 At his touch, the scabs would fall away.
Over his shoulder, I see my father coming toward us:
He carries his tears in a bowl,
And blood hangs in the pine-soaked air.

---

[1] A muslin material with raised dots.

■ EXPLORATIONS OF THE TEXT ■

I.

1. What is the focus of the girls' gatherings?
2. What are the mood and tone of the poem? What images create the mood and tone?
3. What is the meaning of the images of "suns," "firefly," and "feathers"?

II.

1. Who are the "seal men"? Explore their symbolic significance.
2. For what does she wait?
3. How does the mood change in this section?
4. Explain the line, "Night rests like a ball of fur on my tongue."

III.

1. What are the roles of the mother and the father?
2. Explore the symbolism of "tomatoes," "sunlight," and "twilight."
3. What is the meaning of the closing lines concerning the father: "He carries his tears in a bowl," and "blood hangs in the pine-soaked air"? What are the consequences of sexual awakening?

■■ JOURNAL ENTRIES ■■

1. How do the views of female sexuality change in these three poems?

■■■ IDEAS FOR WRITING ■■■

1. Characterize the stages of adolescence in the three poems.
2. Compare Dove's view of coming of age as a female with Soto's view of coming in age in "Oranges" and in "Black Hair" or Reiss's view in "¿Habla Usted Español?"

Ego Tripping

Nikki Giovanni

Born and educated in Tennessee, Nikki Giovanni (1943–   ) has taught creative writing at Rutgers University and other colleges. Her volumes of poetry include Ego Tripping and Other Poems *(1973),* Cotton Candy on a Rainy Day *(1978),* Spin a Soft Black Song *(1985), and* Sacred Cows and Other Edibles *(1988). She wrote an autobiography,* Gemini, *in 1971 (reprinted 1980).*

Nikki Giovanni seldom comments on her work, but she wrote about "Ego Tripping": "i wanted to write a sassy, hands-on-the-hips poem. . . . i think it works because the more you know about anthropology and history the more you can follow what i am saying; on the other hand you can be a little child . . . and catch the joy of the poem."

(there may be a reason why)

I was born in the congo
I walked to the fertile crescent and built
    the sphinx[1]
I designed a pyramid so tough that a star
5   that only glows every one hundred years falls
    into the center giving divine perfect light
I am bad

I sat on the throne
    drinking nectar with allah[2]
10 I got hot and sent an ice age to europe
    to cool my thirst
My oldest daughter is nefertiti[3]
    the tears from my birth pains
    created the nile[4]
15 I am a beautiful woman

I gazed on the forest and burned
    out the sahara desert

---

[1] A mythical creature with the head of a human or animal, the body of a lion, and the wings of an eagle. One of the famous monuments in ancient Egypt, near the pyramids. In Greek mythology, the Sphinx proposed a riddle to Oedipus; and when he answered it, she killed herself.
[2] In Islam, the name of God; Supreme Being.
[3] An Egyptian queen (fourteenth century B.C.), known for her beauty.
[4] Longest river in Africa, flowing north from Lake Victoria to the Mediterranean.

with a packet of goat's meat
and a change of clothes
20 I crossed it in two hours
I am a gazelle so swift
      so swift you can't catch me

For a birthday present when he was three
I gave my son hannibal[5] an elephant
25   He gave me rome for mother's day
My strength flows ever on

My son noah built new/ark and
I stood proudly at the helm
      as we sailed on a soft summer day
30 I turned myself into myself and was
     jesus
     men intone my loving name

All praises All praises
I am the one who would save

35 I sowed diamonds in my back yard
My bowels deliver uranium
     the filings from my fingernails are
     semi-precious jewels
     On a trip north
40 I caught a cold and blew
My nose giving oil to the arab world
I am so hip even my errors are correct
I sailed west to reach east and had to round off
     the earth as I went
45   The hair from my head thinned and gold was laid
     across three continents

I am so perfect so divine so ethereal so surreal
I cannot be comprehended
     except by my permission

50 I mean . . . I . . . can fly
     like a bird in the sky . . .

---

[5] A Carthaginian general who crossed the Mediterranean and the Alps and attacked Italy.
Carthage—a country in North Africa.

■ **EXPLORATIONS OF THE TEXT** ■

1. What is the speaker's view of herself? What character traits does she attribute to herself?
2. How is the title a clue to the meaning of the poem? In what ways does the poem extend its themes beyond the ego?
3. How does the poet use such devices from oral tradition as exaggeration and repetition to create an impact?
4. How does humor contribute to the poem's effect?
5. Identify the historical and anthropological references in the poem. How do these allusions enrich this work?
6. Contrast the speaker's sense of self with the persona's identity in "Energy," "Oranges," or "My Name."

■■ **JOURNAL ENTRIES** ■■

1. Write a prose version of this poem.
2. What are the advantages and disadvantages of hyperbole (exaggeration)? Use details from this poem to support your position.

■■■ **IDEAS FOR WRITING** ■■■

1. Analyze the voice of the speaker of this poem.
2. How does the tone contribute to the meaning of the poem?
3. Write a short essay that explicates one of the allusions in the poem.

Energy

Victor Hernandez Cruz

Victor Hernandez Cruz (1949–   ) was born in Puerto Rico. He has taught at San Francisco State University since 1973. His volumes of poems include By Lingual Wholes *(1982) and* Rhythm, Content and Flavor: New and Selected Poems *(1989).*

Cruz says that he writes "from the center of a culture which is not on its native soil, a culture in flight . . . becoming something totally new and unique." In his poem, "Energy," metaphors of food and of music represent the sources of vitality in Latin culture.

```
   is
   red beans
   ray barretto¹
   banging away
 5 steam out the
   radio
   the five-stair
   steps
   is mofongo²
10 chuchifrito stand³
   outside down
   the avenue
   that long hill
   of a block
15 before the train
   is pacheco⁴
   playing with
   bleeding
   blue lips
```

■   **EXPLORATIONS OF THE TEXT**   ■

1. Cruz's poem can be considered an extended metaphor for "energy." Paraphrase the metaphors into literal prose statements. What does this translation reveal about the meanings of the poem?
2. How does the use of specific words, the naming of things, add to the impact of the metaphors?
3. What is the significance of the closing image of "bleeding/blue lips."
4. What is his view of Latin identity?
5. How do the form and line arrangement of the poem contribute to its message?

■■   **JOURNAL ENTRIES**   ■■

1. Write a character portrait of the speaker of the poem. Describe him. Describe his actions. Where is he standing? Where is he going?
2. Write a short opening to a short story with the speaker of the poem as the main character. Create scene, point of view, and other characters.

---

¹ A Puerto Rican musician.
² A kind of stew.
³ A place to buy fried foods (Puerto Rican).
⁴ A last name.

■■■ IDEAS FOR WRITING ■■■

---

1. Write about the power and meaning of music and food in Latin culture or in another culture with which you are familiar.
2. Interview someone about customs in his or her culture. Write about your interview.

¿Habla Usted Español?

James Reiss

James Reiss (1941–   ) was born in New York City and educated at the University of Chicago. He has taught at Miami University in Ohio since 1965. He is the co-editor of Self-Interviews *by James Dickey and is a regular poetry critic for the Cleveland* Plain Dealer.

"¿Habla Usted Español?" is selected from Reiss's first collection of poems, The Breathers *(1974). Reiss contrasts the beauty and power of the Spanish language with cultural presuppositions about Mexican-Americans.*

> The Spanish expression *Cuando yo era muchacho*
> may be translated: when I was a boy,
> as, for example, "When I was a boy I wanted to be
> a train driver," or "When I was a boy I was completely
> unaware of the flimsy orchid of life."
> 5 It is the kind of expression found in textbooks of the blue breeze
> and is more useful, really, than expressions like "Please put
> the bananas on the table, Maria,"
> or "Take it easy is the motto of the happy-go-lucky Mexican."
> When I was a boy the sun was a horse.
> When I was a boy I sang "Rum and Coca-Cola."
> 10 When I was a boy my father told me the mountains were the
> earth's sombreros.

■ EXPLORATIONS OF THE TEXT ■

---

1. What does the speaker mean by the phrase, "Cuando yo era muchacho"? (Look particularly at line 6 for clues.)
2. What is the impact of using "may be translated" rather than "is translated"?

3. What contrast of meaning is established by the last four lines of the poem?
4. How does the boy view his childhood?
5. Discuss the irony of the title.
6. Compare the persona in this poem with the speakers in Soto's "Oranges" and "Black Hair."

■■ JOURNAL ENTRIES ■■

1. Respond to one of the images in the last four lines.
2. Wittgenstein wrote, "The limits of your language are the limits of your world." Connect this statement with Reiss's poem.

■■■ IDEAS FOR WRITING ■■■

1. Contrast the views of cultural identity implied in the lines in the poem which begin "When I was . . . ."
2. Compare the view of cultural identity and male roles in "¿Habla Usted Español?," "Energy," and "When I Called the Number."

My Name, A House of My Own, and Mango Says Goodbye Sometimes
from The House on Mango Street

Sandra Cisneros

Sandra Cisneros (1954–   ) was born in Chicago to a Mexican-American mother and a Mexican father. She has worked as an arts administrator and college recruiter and has taught both high school drop-outs and university students. Her publications include Bad Boys *(1980),* The House on Mango Street *(1984),* My Wicked Wicked Ways *(1987),* Woman Hollering Creek and Other Stories *(1991), and* Loose Woman *(1994).*

Many of Cisneros's poems affirm the importance of female roles and relationships among later women. In The House on Mango Street, *the restless voice of young Esperanza Cordero resonates with longing, determination, and humor above the desolate tenement landscape.*

My Name

1   In English my name means hope. In Spanish it means too many letters. It means sadness, it means waiting. It is like the number nine. A muddy color. It is the Mexican records my father plays on Sunday mornings when he is shaving, songs like sobbing.

It was my great-grandmother's name and now it is mine. She was a horse woman too, born like me in the Chinese year of the horse—which is supposed to be bad luck if you're born female—but I think this is a Chinese lie because the Chinese, like the Mexicans, don't like their women strong.

My great-grandmother. I would've liked to have known her, a wild horse of a woman, so wild she wouldn't marry. Until my great-grandfather threw a sack over her head and carried her off. Just like that, as if she were a fancy chandelier. That's the way he did it.

And the story goes she never forgave him. She looked out the window her whole life, the way so many women sit their sadness on an elbow. I wonder if she made the best with what she got or was she sorry because she couldn't be all the things she wanted to be. Esperanza. I have inherited her name, but I don't want to inherit her place by the window.

5   At school they say my name funny as if the syllables were made out of tin and hurt the roof of your mouth. But in Spanish my name is made out of a softer something, like silver, not quite as thick as sister's name—Magdalena— which is uglier than mine. Magdalena who at least can come home and become Nenny. But I am always Esperanza.

I would like to baptize myself under a new name, a name more like the real me, the one nobody sees. Esperanza as Lisandra or Maritza or Zeze the X. Yes. Something like Zeze the X will do.

■ **EXPLORATIONS OF THE TEXT** ■

1.   How does the narrator view her name?
2.   Discuss the character of the great-grandmother.
3.   Why does the narrator want to rename herself?

■■ **JOURNAL ENTRIES** ■■

1.   Explore the significance of your name as Cisneros does. Do you think your name fits your personality?
2.   Choose a new name for yourself. Why did you choose the name?

■■■ **IDEAS FOR WRITING** ■■■

1. What does the story of the great-grandmother symbolize to Esperanza?
2. What does the imagery of language and names signify in this work?

A House of My Own

1   Not a flat. Not an apartment in back. Not a man's house. Not a daddy's. A house all my own. With my porch and my pillow, my pretty purple petunias. My books and my stories. My two shoes waiting beside the bed. Nobody to shake a stick at. Nobody's garbage to pick up after.

Only a house quiet as snow, a space for myself to go, clean as paper before the poem.

Mango Says Goodbye Sometimes

1   I like to tell stories. I tell them inside my head. I tell them after the mailman says, Here's your mail. Here's your mail he said.

I make a story for my life, for each step my brown shoe takes. I say, "And so she trudged up the wooden stairs, her sad brown shoes taking her to the house she never liked."

I like to tell stories. I am going to tell you a story about a girl who didn't want to belong.

We didn't always live on Mango Street. Before that we lived on Loomis on the third floor, and before that we lived on Keeler. Before Keeler it was Paulina, but what I remember most is Mango Street, sad red house, the house I belong but do not belong to.

5   I put it down on paper and then the ghost does not ache so much. I write it down and Mango says goodbye sometimes. She does not hold me with both arms. She sets me free.

One day I will pack my bags of books and paper. One day I will say goodbye to Mango. I am too strong for her to keep me here forever. One day I will go away.

Friends and neighbors will say, What happened to that Esperanza? Where did she go with all those books and paper? Why did she march so far away?

They will not know I have gone away to come back. For the ones I left behind. For the ones who cannot out.

■ EXPLORATIONS OF THE TEXT ■

1. What are the connections between the house and the self?
2. Why does she want "a room of [her] own"?
3. Explore the significance of the metaphors in the statement: "Only a house quiet as snow, a space for myself to go, clean as paper before the poem."
4. What do you notice about sentence structure in "A House of My Own"? What is the impact of this choice of form?
5. What do you see as innovative in Cisneros' narrative style and form?
6. Will the narrator be able to leave Mango Street?

■■ JOURNAL ENTRIES ■■

1. Create some experiences that you think Cisneros might have depicted in her novel, *The House on Mango Street.*
2. What do you think will happen to Esperanza?

■■■ IDEAS FOR WRITING ■■■

1. "Mango Says Goodbye Sometimes" is the last excerpt in the novel. "My Name" is one of the first vignettes. Compare the two. You may want to read the novel for this assignment.

Lost Sister

Cathy Song

Cathy Song (1955–) won the Yale Younger Poets Award for her first book, Picture Bride *(1983), in which she wrote about her Korean grandmother, who was purchased as a mail-order bride on the basis of her photograph. In her second volume of poetry,* Frameless Windows, Squares of Light *(1988), Song expanded her analysis of family, of heritage, and of the past.*

"Lost Sister" explores the changes in identity in three generations of Chinese women: those who lived in China, those who emigrated to the United States, and the daughters of the émigrés.

1

In China,
even the peasants
named their first daughters
Jade—
5 the stone that in the far fields
could moisten the dry season,
could make men move mountains
for the healing green of the inner hills
glistening like slices of winter melon.

10 And the daughters were grateful:
They never left home.
To move freely was a luxury
stolen from them at birth.
Instead, they gathered patience,
15 learning to walk in shoes
the size of teacups,
without breaking—
the arc of their movements
as dormant as the rooted willow,
20 as redundant as the farmyard hens.
But they traveled far
in surviving,
learning to stretch the family rice,
to quiet the demons,
25 the noisy stomachs.

2

There is a sister
across the ocean,
who relinquished her name,
diluting jade green
30 with the blue of the Pacific.
Rising with a tide of locusts,
she swarmed with others
to inundate another shore.
In America,
35 there are many roads
and women can stride along with men.

But in another wilderness,
the possibilities,
the loneliness,

40 can strangulate like jungle vines.
The meager provisions and sentiments
of once belonging—
fermented roots, Mah-Jong[1] tiles and firecrackers—set but
a flimsy household
45 in a forest of nightless cities.
A giant snake rattles above,
spewing black clouds into your kitchen.
Dough-faced landlords
slip in and out of your keyholes,
50 making claims you don't understand,
tapping into your communication systems
of laundry lines and restaurant chains.

You find you need China:
your one fragile identification,
55 a jade link
handcuffed to your wrist.
You remember your mother
who walked for centuries,
footless—
60 and like her,
you have left no footprints,
but only because
there is an ocean in between,
the unremitting space of your rebellion.

■ EXPLORATIONS OF THE TEXT ■

1. What view emerges in Part 1 of women's roles in China?
2. Why does the speaker state that "even the peasants/named their first daughters/Jade"?
3. What is the conflict for first-generation Chinese-American women presented in the poem?
4. How are the "daughter" and "mother" similar in the end?

■■ JOURNAL ENTRIES ■■

1. In Part 2, the poet depicts the "lost sister" in America. What are the consequences of rebellion?

---

[1] Chinese game, similar to dominoes.

■■■ **IDEAS FOR WRITING** ■■■

1. Why do the Chinese women who have immigrated to the United States still need China?
2. Discuss the symbolism of jade.

Indian Boarding School: The Runaways

Louise Erdrich

Louise Erdrich (1954–   ) was born in Minnesota to a French-Chippewa mother and a German father. She received her B.A. from Dartmouth and her M.A. from the Writing Seminars of Johns Hopkins University. Her first volume of poems, Jacklight *(1984), and her first novel,* Love Medicine *(1984), both won major awards. Her other novels include* The Beet Queen *(1986),* Tracks *(1988), and* The Bingo Palace *(1994).*

In "Indian Boarding School: The Runaways," which appeared in Jacklight, *the nameless children in the poem suffer "worn-down welts/of ancient punishments."*

Home's the place we head for in our sleep.
Boxcars stumbling north in dreams
don't wait for us. We catch them on the run.
The rails, old lacerations that we love,
5   shoot parallel across the face and break
just under Turtle Mountains.[1] Riding scars
you can't get lost. Home is the place they cross.

The lame guard strikes a match and makes the dark
less tolerant. We watch through cracks in boards
10   as the land starts rolling, rolling till it hurts
to be here, cold in regulation clothes.
We know the sheriff's waiting at midrun
to take us back. His car is dumb and warm.
The highway doesn't rock, it only hums
15   like a wing of long insults. The worn-down welts
of ancient punishments lead back and forth.

---

[1] The location of a Chippewa Indian reservation in North Dakota.

All runaways wear dresses, long green ones,
the color you would think shame was. We scrub
the sidewalks down because it's shameful work.
20 Our brushes cut the stone in watered arcs
and in the soak frail outlines shiver clear
a moment, things us kids pressed on the dark
face before it hardened, place, remembering
delicate old injuries, the spines of names and leaves.

■ EXPLORATIONS OF THE TEXT ■

1. Who are the runaways?
2. What has the school done to or for the children? What is the root of their fear?
3. What does home mean to them? Discuss locations and landscape in the poem.
4. In what sense is the poem realistic? fantastic? In what sense does it recreate a recurring experience?
5. Who is the enemy? Is it the school? the sheriff? the guard?
6. How are "insults" to the land and the punishments of the children connected? Why are the welts "worn-down"?
7. Follow the order of the narrative in each stanza. How is the poem organized?

■■ JOURNAL ENTRIES ■■

1. Choose the most powerful lines in this poem. What makes them strong?
2. Does running away help or hinder rites of passage into the adult world?

■■■ IDEAS FOR WRITING ■■■

1. Analyze Erdrich's depiction of nature in "Jacklight" and in "Indian Boarding School: The Runaways."
2. Explore the imagery concerning punishment and pain in this poem.
3. Compare the portrayal of running away in this poem, in "Barn Burning," and/or in "The Man Who Was Almost a Man."

Jacklight[1]

Louise Erdrich

In this poem, a couple's rendezvous in the woods conflicts with the habits of hunters and leads to revelation.

The same Chippewa word is used both for flirting and hunting game, while another Chippewa word connotes both using force in intercourse and also killing a bear with one's bare hands.
—DUNNING 1959

We have come to the edge of the woods,
out of brown grass where we slept, unseen,
out of knotted twigs, out of leaves creaked shut,
out of hiding.

5 At first the light wavered, glancing over us.
Then it clenched to a fist of light that pointed,
searched out, divided us.
Each took the beams like direct blows the heart answers.
Each of us moved forward alone.

10 We have come to the edge of the woods,
drawn out of ourselves by this night sun,
this battery of polarized acids,
that outshines the moon.

We smell them behind it
15 but they are faceless, invisible.
We smell the raw steel of their gun barrels,
mink oil on leather, their tongues of sour barley.
We smell their mother buried chin-deep in wet dirt.

We smell their fathers with scoured knuckles,
20 teeth cracked from hot marrow.
We smell their sisters of crushed dogwood, bruised apples,
of fractured cups and concussions of burnt hooks.

We smell their breath steaming lightly behind the jacklight.
We smell the itch underneath the caked guts on their clothes.
25 We smell their minds like silver hammers
cocked back, held in readiness
for the first of us to step into the open.

---

[1]A torch or flashlight used for night hunting.

We have come to the edge of the woods,
out of brown grass where we slept, unseen,
30 out of leaves creaked shut, out of our hiding.
We have come here too long.

It is their turn now,
their turn to follow us. Listen,
they put down their equipment.
35 It is useless in the tall brush.
And now they take the first steps, not knowing
how deep the woods are and lightless.
How deep the woods are.

■ **EXPLORATIONS OF THE TEXT** ■

1. What is "jacklight"? What context is established by the title?
2. Who are "we"? Who are "they"?
3. What do the "woods" signify to the speaker and to her friend? Explore the images of the woods: "grass," "twigs," and "leaves."
4. Discuss the symbolism of the light. What power does the light have?
5. What vision emerges of the nameless "they"? Can they harm the speaker and her friend?
6. Discuss the revelation in the closing stanza. Why are the woods "lightless" and "deep"? Why is it "their turn to follow"?
7. Examine the initiation into sexuality and into the adult world in this poem and in "The Verb to Kill," "Where Are You Going, Where Have You Been?," "Adolescence I, II, III," and/or "Oranges."

■■ **JOURNAL ENTRIES** ■■

1. Use one of these lines as a beginning for an entry: "We have come to the edge of the woods," "We have come here too long," or "How deep the woods are."
2. Imagine the voice of one of the "they." Write a monologue in that voice.
3. Discuss the repetition of the phrase "We smell" or of the line "We have come to the edge of the woods."

■■■ **IDEAS FOR WRITING** ■■■

1. Why do you think that the couple has been in the woods? Construct reasons for their "hiding."
2. Examine the relevance of the epigraph to the themes of the poem.
3. Is there a critique of North American society presented in the poem?

Poems for Further Reading

When I consider how my light is spent
John Milton (1608–1674)

When I consider how my light is spent
 Ere half my days, in this dark world and wide,
 And that one talent which is death to hide[1]
 Lodged with me useless, though my soul more bent
5 To serve therewith my Maker, and present
 My true account, lest he returning chide;
 "Doth God exact day-labor, light denied?"
 I fondly[2] ask; but Patience to prevent[3]
That murmur, soon replies, "God doth not need
10 Either man's work or his own gifts; who best
 Bear his mild yoke, they serve him best. His state
Is kingly. Thousands at his bidding speed
 And post o'er land and ocean without rest:
 They also serve who only stand and wait."

[Alone I sat; the summer day]
Emily Brontë (1818–1848)

Alone I sat; the summer day
Had died in smiling light away;
I saw it die, I watched it fade
From misty hill and breezeless glade:

5 And thoughts in my soul were gushing,
And my heart bowed beneath their power;
And tears within my eyes were rushing

---

[1] Reference to Christ's "Parable of the Talents" (Matthew 25:14ff) in which a servant is chastised for not using his talent (a monetary unit): an intended pun. Note also play on words in "use," meaning using or interest.
[2] Foolishly.
[3] To forestall.

Because I could not speak the feeling,
The solemn joy around me stealing
10 In that divine, untroubled hour.

I asked myself, "O why has heaven
Denied the precious gift to me,
The glorious gift to many given
To speak their thoughts in poetry?

15 "Dreams have encircled me," I said,
"From careless childhood's sunny time;
Visions by ardent fancy fed
Since life was in its morning prime."[1]

But now, when I had hoped to sing,
20 My fingers strike a tuneless string;
And still the burden[2] of the strain
Is "Strive no more; 'tis all in vain."

There Was a Child Went Forth

Walt Whitman (1819–1892)

There was a child went forth every day,
And the first object he look'd upon, that object he became,
And that object became part of him for the day or a certain part
  of the day,
Or for many years or stretching cycles of years.

5 The early lilacs became part of this child,
And grass and white and red morning-glories, and white and red
  clover, and the song of the phoebe-bird,
And the Third-month lambs and the sow's pink-faint litter, and
  the mare's foal and the cow's calf,
And the noisy brood of the barnyard or by the mire of the pond-
  side,
And the fish suspending themselves so curiously below there, and
  the beautiful curious liquid,
And the water-plants with their graceful flat heads, all became part
10   of him.

---

[1] Beginning of the day.
[2] Bass or section of music; a strain—a song, melody, passage of music.

The field-sprouts of Fourth-month and Fifth-month became part
of him,
Winter-grain sprouts and those of the light-yellow corn, and the
esculent roots of the garden,
And the apple-trees cover'd with blossoms and the fruit afterward,
and wood-berries, and the commonest weeds by the road,
And the old drunkard staggering home from the outhouse of the
tavern whence he had lately risen,
15 And the schoolmistress that pass'd on her way to the school,
And the friendly boys that pass'd, and the quarrelsome boys,
And the tidy and fresh-cheek'd girls, and the barefoot negro boy
and girl,
And all the changes of city and country wherever he went.

His own parents, he that had father'd him and she that had con-
ceiv'd him in her womb and birth'd him,
20 They gave this child more of themselves than that,
They gave him afterward every day, they became part of him.

The mother at home quietly placing the dishes on the supper-
table,
The mother with mild words, clean her cap and gown, a wholesome odor falling off her person and clothes as she walks by,
The father, strong, self-sufficient, manly, mean, anger'd, unjust,
25 The blow, the quick loud word, the tight bargain, the crafty lure,
The family usages, the language, the company, the furniture, the
yearning and swelling heart,
Affection that will not be gainsay'd, the sense of what is real, the
thought if after all it should prove unreal,
The doubts of day-time and the doubts of night-time, the curious
whether and how,
Whether that which appears so is so, or is it all flashes and specks?
Men and women crowding fast in the streets, if they are not flashes
30   and specks what are they?
The streets themselves and the façades of houses, and goods in
the windows,
Vehicles, teams, the heavy-plank'd wharves, the huge crossing at
the ferries,
The village on the highland seen from afar at sunset, the river
between,
Shadows, aureola and mist, the light falling on roofs and gables of
white or brown two miles off,
The schooner near by sleepily dropping down the tide, the little
35   boat slack-tow'd astern,
The hurrying tumbling waves, quick-broken crests, slapping,

The strata of color'd clouds, the long bar of maroon-tint away
   solitary by itself, the spread of purity it lies motionless in,
The horizon's edge, the flying sea-crow, the fragrance of salt
   marsh and shore mud,
These became part of that child who went forth every day, and
   who now goes, and will always go forth every day.

My Life Had Stood—

Emily Dickinson (1830–1886)

My Life had stood—a Loaded Gun—
In Corners—till a Day
The Owner passed—identified—
And carried Me away—

5 And now We roam in Sovereign Woods—
And now We hunt the Doe—
And every time I speak for Him—
The Mountains straight reply—

And do I smile, such cordial light
10 Upon the Valley glow—
It is as a Vesuvian[1] face
Had let its pleasure through—

And when at Night—Our good Day done—
I guard My Master's Head—
15 'Tis better than the Eider-Duck's
Deep Pillow[2]—to have shared—

To foe of His—I'm deadly foe—
None stir the second time—
On whom I lay a Yellow Eye—
20 Or an emphatic Thumb—

Though I than He—may longer live
He longer must—than I—
For I have but the power to kill,
Without—the power to die—

---

[1] Resembling Mount Vesuvius, a volcano in Italy.
[2] Eider down; referring to soft feathers from the female Eider-Duck.

Spring and Fall: To a Young Child

Gerard Manley Hopkins (1844–1889)

Márgarét, are you gríeving
Over Goldengrove unleaving?
Léaves, líke things of man, you
With your fresh thoughts care for, can you?
5 Áh! ás the heart grows older
It will come to such sights colder
By and by, nor spare a sigh
Though worlds of wanwood[1] leafmeal[2] lie;
And yet you will weep and know why.
10 Now no matter, child, the name:
Sórrow's spríngs áre the same.
Nor mouth had, no nor mind, expressed
What heart heard of, ghost[3] guessed:
It ís the blight man was born for,
15 It ís Margaret you mourn for.

---

[1] Melancholy woods.
[2] Leaves broken up piecemeal.
[3] Spirit.

DRAMA

Hamlet

William Shakespeare

William Shakespeare (1564–1616), the most widely known writer of English literature, was born in Stratford-on-Avon, England. By 1592, Shakespeare had become an accomplished actor and playwright in London. With several other actors, Shakespeare formed a syndicate to build a new playhouse, The Globe, one of the most famous theaters of its time. Shakespeare wrote thirty-seven plays and is believed to have played such supporting roles as the ghost of Hamlet's father.

The dramas in the accepted canon—works authentically Shakespeare's—are generally arranged into four categories: comedies, histories, tragedies, and romances. Of the tragedies, Hamlet *remains the most frequently staged and analyzed.*

Written during the height of Shakespeare's powers, Hamlet *was actually the reworking of an old play with even older themes, principally revenge and the pursuit of truth. Shakespeare's recasting of character and dramatic structure and his addition of poetic images and Elizabethan psychology have rendered a work of art as viable and complex today as it was then. Even after four centuries,* Hamlet *remains a profound, ultimately elusive, and mysterious exploration of the human spirit.*

Dramatis Personae

Claudius, King of Denmark
Hamlet, son to the late, and
    nephew to the present King
Polonius, Lord Chamberlain
Horatio, friend to Hamlet
Laertes, son to Polonius
Voltimand ⎫
Cornelius ⎪
Rosencrantz ⎬ courtiers
Guildenstern ⎪
Osric ⎪
A Gentleman ⎭
A Priest
Marcellus ⎫ officers
Bernardo ⎭

Francisco, a soldier
Reynaldo, servant to Polonius
Players
Two Clowns, gravediggers
Fortinbras, Prince of Norway
A Captain
English Ambassadors
Gertrude, Queen of Denmark, and mother to
    Hamlet
Ophelia, daughter to Polonius
Lords, Ladies, Officers, Soldiers, Sailors,
    Messengers, and other Attendants
Ghost of Hamlet's father
Scene—Denmark.

Act I

Scene I. Elsinore. A platform[1] before the castle.

[Francisco at his post. Enter to him Bernardo.]

Bernardo: Who's there?
Francisco: Nay, answer me. Stand, and unfold yourself.[2]
Bernardo: Long live the King![3]
Francisco: Bernardo?
5 **Bernardo:** He.
Francisco: You come most carefully upon your hour.
Bernardo: 'Tis now struck twelve. Get thee to bed, Francisco.
Francisco: For this relief much thanks. 'Tis bitter cold,
    And I am sick at heart.
10 **Bernardo:** Have you had quiet guard?
Francisco: Not a mouse stirring.
Bernardo: Well, good night.
    If you do meet Horatio and Marcellus,
    The rivals[4] of my watch, bid them make haste.
Francisco: I think I hear them. Stand, ho! Who is there!

[Enter Horatio and Marcellus.]

15 **Horatio:** Friends to this ground.
Marcellus: And liegemen[5] to the Dane.
Francisco: Give you good night.
Marcellus: Oh, farewell, honest soldier.
    Who hath relieved you?
Francisco: Bernardo hath my place.
    Give you good night.   *[Exit.]*
Marcellus: Holloa! Bernardo!
Bernardo: Say,
    What, is Horatio there?
Horatio: A piece of him.
20 **Bernardo:** Welcome, Horatio. Welcome, good Marcellus.
Marcellus: What, has this thing appeared again tonight?
Bernardo: I have seen nothing.
Marcellus: Horatio says 'tis but our fantasy,[6]
    And will not let belief take hold of him
25   Touching this dreaded sight twice seen of us.
    Therefore I have entreated him along
    With us to watch the minutes of this night,

---

[1] **platform:** the level space on the ramparts where the cannon were mounted.   [2] **unfold yourself:** reveal who you are.   [3] **Long . . . King:** probably the password for the night.   [4] **rivals:** partners.   [5] **liegemen:** loyal subjects.   [6] **fantasy:** imagination.

That if again this apparition come,
He may approve our eyes[7] and speak to it.

30 **Horatio:** Tush, tush, 'twill not appear.
Bernardo: Sit down awhile,
And let us once again assail your ears,
That are so fortified against our story,
What we have two nights seen.
Horatio: Well, sit we down,
And let us hear Bernardo speak of this.

35 **Bernardo:** Last night of all,
When yond same star that's westward from the pole[8]
Had made his course to illume[9] that part of heaven
Where now it burns, Marcellus and myself,
The bell then beating one—

[Enter Ghost.]

40 **Marcellus:** Peace, break thee off. Look where it comes again!
Bernardo: In the same figure, like the King that's dead.
Marcellus: Thou art a scholar.[10] Speak to it, Horatio.
Bernardo: Looks it not like the King? Mark it, Horatio.
Horatio: Most like. It harrows[11] me with fear and wonder.
45 **Bernardo:** It would be spoken to.
Marcellus: Question it, Horatio.
Horatio: What art thou that usurp'st this time of night,
Together with[12] that fair and warlike form
In which the majesty of buried Denmark[13]
Did sometimes march? By Heaven I charge thee, speak!
50 **Marcellus:** It is offended.
Bernardo: See, it stalks away!
Horatio: Stay! Speak, speak! I charge thee, speak!

[Exit Ghost.]

Marcellus: 'Tis gone, and will not answer.
Bernardo: How now, Horatio! You tremble and look pale.
Is not this something more than fantasy?
55   What think you on 't?
Horatio: Before my God, I might not this believe
Without the sensible and true avouch
Of mine own eyes.[14]
Marcellus: Is it not like the King?

---

[7] approve our eyes: verify what we have seen.   [8] pole: Polestar.   [9] illume: light.
[10] scholar: As Latin was the proper language in which to address and exorcise evil spirits, a
scholar was necessary.   [11] harrows: distresses; lit., plows up.   [12] Together with: i.e.,
appearing in.   [13] majesty . . . Denmark: the dead King.   [14] Without . . . eyes: unless
my own eyes had vouched for it. sensible: perceived by my senses.

Horatio: As thou art to thyself.
60   Such was the very armor he had on
      When he the ambitious Norway combated.
      So frowned he once when, in an angry parle,[15]
      He smote the sledded Polacks[16] on the ice.
      'Tis strange.
65 **Marcellus:** Thus twice before, and jump at this dead hour,[17]
      With martial stalk hath he gone by our watch.
   Horatio: In what particular thought to work I know not,
      But in the gross and scope[18] of my opinion
      This bodes some strange eruption[19] to our state.
70 **Marcellus:** Good now, sit down and tell me, he that knows,
      Why this same strict and most observant watch
      So nightly toils[20] the subject[21] of the land;
      And why such daily cast of brazen cannon
      And foreign mart[22] for implements of war;
75   Why[23] such impress[24] of shipwrights, whose sore task
      Does not divide the Sunday from the week;
      What might be toward,[25] that this sweaty haste
      Doth make the night joint laborer with the day.
      Who is 't that can inform me?
   Horatio: That can I,
80   At least the whisper goes so. Our last King,
      Whose image even but now appeared to us,
      Was, as you know, by Fortinbras of Norway,
      Thereto pricked[26] on by a most emulate[27] pride,
      Dared to the combat, in which our valiant Hamlet—
85   For so this side of our known world esteemed him—
      Did slay this Fortinbras. Who[28] by a sealed compact,[29]
      Well ratified by law and heraldry,[30]
      Did forfeit, with his life, all those his lands
      Which he stood seized of[31] to the conqueror.
90   Against the which, a moiety competent[32]
      Was gagèd[33] by our King, which had returned

---

[15] parle: parley.   [16] sledded Polacks: There has been much controversy about this phrase. Q_1 and Q_2 read "sleaded Pollax." F_1 reads "sledded Pollax." Either the late King smote his heavy (leaded) poleax on the ice, or else he attacked the Poles in their sledges. There is no further reference to this incident.   [17] jump . . . hour: just at deep midnight.
[18] gross . . . scope: general conclusion.   [19] eruption: violent disturbance.
[20] toils: wearies.   [21] subject: subjects.   [22] foreign mart: purchase abroad.
[23] Why . . . day: i.e., workers in shipyards and munition factories are working night shifts and Sundays.   [24] impress: conscription.   [25] toward: in preparation.   [26] pricked: spurred.   [27] emulate: jealous.   [28] Who . . . Hamlet: i.e., before the combat it was agreed that the victor should win the land of the vanquished.   [29] sealed compact: formal agreement.   [30] heraldry: The heralds were responsible for arranging formal combats. See App. 9.   [31] seized of: possessed of, a legal term.   [32] moiety competent: adequate portion.   [33] gaged: pledged.

To the inheritance of Fortinbras
Had he been vanquisher, as by the same covenant
And carriage of the article designed[34]
95   His fell to Hamlet. Now, sir, young Fortinbras,
Of unimprovèd mettle[35] hot and full,
Hath in the skirts[36] of Norway here and there
Sharked[37] up a list of lawless resolutes,[38]
For food and diet,[39] to some enterprise
100   That hath a stomach[40] in 't. Which is no other—
As it doth well appear unto our state—
But to recover of us, by strong hand
And terms compulsatory,[41] those foresaid lands
So by his father lost. And this, I take it,
105   Is the main motive of our preparations,
The source of this our watch and the chief head[42]
Of this posthaste and romage[43] in the land.
Bernardo: I think it be no other but e'en so.
Well may it sort[44] that this portentous figure
110   Comes armèd through our watch, so like the King
That was and is the question of these wars.
Horatio: A mote[45] it is to trouble the mind's eye.
In the most high and palmy[46] state of Rome,
A little ere the mightiest Julius fell,
115   The graves stood tenantless, and the sheeted[47] dead
Did squeak and gibber[48] in the Roman streets.
As stars[49] with trains of fire and dews of blood,
Disasters[50] in the sun, and the moist star[51]
Upon whose influence Neptune's empire stands
120   Was sick almost to doomsday with eclipse.
And even the like precurse[52] of fierce events,
As harbingers[53] preceding still the fates
And prologue to the omen[54] coming on,
Have Heaven and earth together demonstrated
125   Unto our climatures[55] and countrymen.

---

[34] carriage . . . designed: fulfillment of the clause in the agreement.   [35] unimproved mettle: untutored, wild material, nature.   [36] skirts: outlying parts.   [37] Sharked: collected indiscriminately, as a shark bolts its prey.   [38] lawless resolutes: gangsters. [39] diet: maintenance.   [40] stomach: resolution.   [41] terms compulsatory: force. [42] chief head: main purpose.   [43] posthaste . . . romage: urgency and bustle. [44] Well . . . sort: it would be a natural reason.   [45] mote: speck of dust.   [46] palmy: flourishing.   [47] sheeted: in their shrouds.   [48] gibber: utter strange sounds. [49] As stars: The sense of the passage is here broken; possibly a line has been omitted after l. 116.   [50] Disasters: unlucky signs.   [51] moist star: the moon, which influences the tides.   [52] precurse: forewarning.   [53] harbingers: forerunners. The harbinger was an officer of the Court who was sent ahead to make the arrangements when the Court went on progress.   [54] omen: disaster.   [55] climatures: regions.

[Re-enter Ghost.] But soft, behold! Lo where it comes again!
I'll cross it,[56] though it blast me. Stay, illusion!
If thou hast any sound, or use of voice,
Speak to me.
130 If[57] there be any good thing to be done
That may to thee do ease and grace to me,[58]
Speak to me.
If thou art privy to[59] thy country's fate,
Which, happily,[60] foreknowing may avoid,
135 Oh, speak!
Or if thou hast uphoarded in thy life
Extorted[61] treasure in the womb of earth,
For which, they say, you spirits oft walk in death,
Speak of it. Stay, and speak! *[The cock crows.* [62]*]* Stop it, Marcellus.
140 **Marcellus:** Shall I strike at it with my partisan?[63]
Horatio: Do, if it will not stand.
Bernardo: 'Tis here!
Horatio: 'Tis here!
Marcellus: 'Tis gone!   *[Exit Ghost.]*
We do it wrong, being so majestical,
To offer it the show of violence,
145 For it is as the air invulnerable,
And our vain blows malicious mockery.
Bernardo: It was about to speak when the cock crew.
Horatio: And then it started like a guilty thing
Upon a fearful[64] summons. I have heard
150 The cock, that is the trumpet to the morn,
Doth with his lofty and shrill-sounding throat
Awake the god of day, and at his warning,
Whether in sea or fire, in earth or air,
The extravagant and erring[65] spirit hies
155 To his confíne.[66] And of the truth herein
This present object made probation.[67]
Marcellus: It faded on the crowing of the cock.
Some say that ever 'gainst[68] that season comes
Wherein Our Saviour's birth is celebrated,
160 The bird of dawning singeth all night long.

---

[56] **cross it:** stand in its way.   [57] **If . . . speak:** In popular belief there were four reasons why
the spirit of a dead man should *walk:* (a) to reveal a secret, (b) to utter a warning, (c) to
reveal concealed treasure, (d) to reveal the manner of its death. Horatio thus adjures the
ghost by three potent reasons, but before he can utter the fourth the cock crows.   [58] **grace
to me:** bring me into a state of spiritual grace.   [59] **privy to:** have secret knowledge
of.   [60] **happily:** by good luck.   [61] **Extorted:** evilly acquired.   [62] **s.d., cock crows:** i.e.,
a sign that dawn is at hand. See ll. 147–64.   [63] **partisan:** spear-like weapon.
[64] **fearful:** causing fear.   [65] **extravagant . . . erring:** both words mean "wandering."
[66] **confine:** place of confinement.   [67] **probation:** proof.   [68] **'gainst:** in anticipation of.

And then, they say, no spirit dare stir abroad,
The nights are wholesome, then no planets[69] strike,
No fairy takes[70] nor witch hath power to charm,
So hallowed and so gracious is the time.
165 **Horatio:** So have I heard and do in part believe it.
But look, the morn, in russet mantle clad,
Walks o'er the dew of yon high eastward hill.
Break we our watch up, and by my advice
Let us impart what we have seen tonight
170 Unto young Hamlet, for upon my life,
This spirit, dumb to us, will speak to him.
Do you consent we shall acquaint him with it,
As needful in our loves, fitting our duty?
Marcellus: Let's do 't, I pray. And I this morning know
175 Where we shall find him most conveniently.

[Exeunt.]

Scene II. A room of state in the castle.

*[Flourish.[1] Enter the King, Queen, Hamlet, Polonius, Laertes, Volti-
mand, Cornelius, Lords, and Attendants.]*

King: Though yet of Hamlet our dear brother's death
The memory be green,[2] and that it us befitted
To bear our hearts in grief and our whole kingdom
To be contracted in one brow of woe,[3]
5 Yet so far hath discretion[4] fought with nature[5]
That we with wisest sorrow think of him,
Together with remembrance of ourselves.
Therefore our sometime sister,[6] now our Queen,
The imperial jointress[7] to this warlike state,
10 Have we, as 'twere with a defeated joy—
With an auspicious and a dropping eye,[8]
With mirth in funeral and with dirge in marriage,
In equal scale weighing delight and dole[9]—
Taken to wife. Nor have we herein barred
15 Your better wisdoms,[10] which have freely gone

---

[69] planets: Planets were supposed to bring disaster.   [70] takes: bewitches.
[1] Flourish: fanfare of trumpets.   [2] green: fresh.   [3] contracted . . . woe: i.e., every
subject's forehead should be puckered with grief.   [4] discretion: common sense.
[5] nature: natural sorrow.   [6] sister: sister-in-law.   [7] jointress: partner by
marriage.   [8] auspicious . . . eye: an eye at the same time full of joy and tears.
[9] dole: grief.   [10] barred . . . wisdoms: i.e., in taking this step we have not shut out your
advice. As is obvious throughout the play, the Danes chose their King by election and not by
right of birth.

　　　　With this affair along. For all, our thanks.
　　　　Now follows that you know. Young Fortinbras,
　　　　Holding a weak supposal[11] of our worth,
　　　　Or thinking by our late dear brother's death
20　　　Our state to be disjoint and out of frame,
　　　　Colleagued with the dream of his advantage,[12]
　　　　He hath not failed to pester us with message
　　　　Importing the surrender of those lands
　　　　Lost by his father, with all bonds of law,[13]
25　　　To our most valiant brother. So much for him.
　　　　Now for ourself, and for this time of meeting.
　　　　Thus much the business is: We have here writ
　　　　To Norway, uncle of young Fortinbras—
　　　　Who, impotent and bedrid, scarcely hears
30　　　Of this his nephew's purpose—to suppress
　　　　His further gait[14] herein, in that the levies,
　　　　The lists[15] and full proportions,[16] are all made
　　　　Out of his subject.[17] And we here dispatch
　　　　You, good Cornelius, and you, Voltimand,
35　　　For bearers of this greeting to old Norway,
　　　　Giving to you no further personal power
　　　　To business with the King more than the scope[18]
　　　　Of these delated articles[19] allow.
　　　　Farewell, and let your haste commend[20] your duty.
40　**Cornelius & Voltimand:** In that and all things will we show our duty.
　　　King: We doubt it nothing. Heartily farewell.
　　　　　　　　　　　　　　　　　[Exeunt Voltimand and Cornelius.]
　　　　And now, Laertes, what's the news with you?
　　　　You told us of some suit[21]—what is 't, Laertes?
　　　　You cannot speak of reason to the Dane
45　　　And lose your voice. What wouldst thou beg, Laertes,
　　　　That shall not be my offer, not thy asking?
　　　　The head is not more native[22] to the heart,
　　　　The hand more instrumental[23] to the mouth,
　　　　Than is the throne of Denmark to thy father.
50　　　What wouldst thou have, Laertes?

---

[11] weak supposal: poor opinion.　　[12] Colleagued . . . advantage: uniting himself with this dream that here was a good opportunity.　　[13] with . . . law: legally binding.
[14] gait: progress.　　[15] lists: rosters.　　[16] proportions: military establishments.
[17] subject: subjects.　　[18] scope: limit.　　[19] delated articles: detailed instructions. Claudius is following usual diplomatic procedure. Ambassadors sent on a special mission carried with them a letter of introduction and greeting to the King of the foreign Court and detailed instructions to guide them in the negotiations.　　[20] commend: display; lit., recommend.　　[21] suit: petition.　　[22] native: closely related.
[23] instrumental: serviceable.

Laertes: My dread[24] lord,
　　Your leave and favor to return to France,
　　From whence though willingly I came to Denmark
　　To show my duty in your coronation,
　　Yet now, I must confess, that duty done,
55　　My thoughts and wishes bend again toward France
　　And bow them to your gracious leave and pardon.
King: Have you your father's leave? What says Polonius?
Polonius: He hath, my lord, wrung from me my slow leave
　　By laborsome petition, and at last
60　　Upon his will[25] I sealed my hard consent.[26]
　　I do beseech you give him leave to go.
King: Take thy fair hour, Laertes, time be thine,
　　And thy best graces spend[27] it at thy will!
　　But now, my cousin[28] Hamlet, and my son—
65 Hamlet: *[Aside]* A little more than kin and less than kind.[29]
King: How is it that the clouds still hang on you?
Hamlet: Not so, my lord. I am too much i' the sun.
Queen: Good Hamlet, cast thy nighted color[30] off.
　　And let thine eye look like a friend on Denmark.
70　　Do not forever with thy vailèd lids[31]
　　Seek for thy noble father in the dust.
　　Thou know'st 'tis common—all that lives must die,
　　Passing through nature to eternity.
Hamlet: Aye, madam, it is common.
Queen: If it be,
75　　Why seems it so particular with thee?
Hamlet: Seems, madam! Nay, it is. I know not "seems."
　　'Tis not alone my inky cloak, good Mother,
　　Nor customary suits of solemn black,
　　Nor windy suspiration of forced breath—
80　　No, nor the fruitful river[32] in the eye,
　　Nor the dejected havior of the visage,[33]
　　Together with all forms, moods, shapes of grief—
　　That can denote me truly. These indeed seem,
　　For they are actions that a man might play.[34]
85　　But I have that within which passeth show,

---

[24] dread: dreaded, much respected.   [25] will: desire.   [26] sealed . . . consent: agreed to,
but with great reluctance.   [27] best . . . spend: i.e., use your time well.   [28] cousin:
kinsman. The word was used for any near relation.   [29] A . . . kind: too near a relation
(uncle-father) and too little natural affection. kind: affectionate.   [30] nighted color: black.
Hamlet alone is in deep mourning; the rest of the Court wear gay clothes.   [31] vailed
lids: lowered eyelids.   [32] fruitful river: stream of tears.   [33] dejected . . . visage:
downcast countenance.   [34] play: act, as in a play.

These but the trappings[35] and the suits of woe.
King: 'Tis sweet and commendable in your nature, Hamlet,
    To give these mourning duties to your father.
    But you must know your father lost a father,
90 That father lost, lost his, and the survivor bound
    In filial obligation for some term
    To do obsequious sorrow.[36] But to persévér
    In obstinate condolement[37] is a course
    Of impious stubbornness, 'tis unmanly grief.
95 It shows a will most incorrect to Heaven,
    A heart unfortified,[38] a mind impatient,
    An understanding simple and unschooled.
    For what we know must be and is as common
    As any the most vulgar[39] thing to sense,
100 Why should we in our peevish opposition
    Take it to heart? Fie! 'Tis a fault to Heaven,
    A fault against the dead, a fault to nature,
    To reason most absurd, whose common theme
    Is death of fathers, and who still hath cried,
105 From the first corse[40] till he that died today,
    "This must be so." We pray you throw to earth
    This unprevailing[41] woe, and think of us
    As of a father. For let the world take note,
    You are the most immediate[42] to our throne,
110 And with no less nobility of love
    Than that which dearest father bears his son
    Do I impart toward you. For your intent
    In going back to school[43] in Wittenberg,
    It is most retrograde[44] to our desire.
115 And we beseech you bend you[45] to remain
    Here in the cheer and comfort of our eye,
    Our chiefest courtier, cousin, and our son.
Queen: Let not thy mother lose her prayers, Hamlet.
    I pray thee, stay with us, go not to Wittenberg.
120 **Hamlet:** I shall in all my best obey you, Madam.
King: Why, 'tis a loving and a fair reply.
    Be as ourself in Denmark. Madam, come,
    This gentle and unforced accord of Hamlet
    Sits smiling to my heart. In grace whereof,

---

[35] trappings: ornaments.   [36] obsequious sorrow: the sorrow usual at funerals.
[37] obstinate condolement: lamentation disregarding the will of God.   [38] unfortified: not
strengthened with the consolation of religion.   [39] vulgar: common.   [40] corse: corpse.
There is unconscious irony in this remark, for the first corpse was that of Abel, also slain by
his brother.   [41] unprevailing: futile.   [42] most immediate: next heir.   [43] school:
university.   [44] retrograde: contrary.   [45] bend you: incline.

125   No jocund health that Denmark drinks today
       But the great cannon[46] to the clouds shall tell,
       And the King's rouse[47] the Heaven shall bruit[48] again,
       Respeaking earthly thunder. Come away.

[Flourish. Exeunt all but Hamlet.]

Hamlet: Oh, that this too too solid flesh would melt,
130   Thaw, and resolve itself into a dew!
       Or that the Everlasting had not fixed
       His canon[49] 'gainst self-slaughter! Oh, God! God!
       How weary, stale, flat, and unprofitable
       Seem to me all the uses[50] of this world!
135   Fie on 't, ah, fie! 'Tis an unweeded garden,
       That grows to seed, things rank[51] and gross in nature
       Possess it merely.[52] That it should come to this!
       But two months dead! Nay, not so much, not two.
       So excellent a King, that was, to this,
140   Hyperion[53] to a satyr.[54] So loving to my mother
       That he might not beteem[55] the winds of heaven
       Visit her face too roughly. Heaven and earth!
       Must I remember? Why, she would hang on him
       As if increase of appetite had grown
145   By what it fed on. And yet within a month—
       Let me not think on 't.—Frailty, thy name is woman!—
       A little month, or ere those shoes were old
       With which she followed my poor father's body,
       Like Niobe[56] all tears.—Why she, even she—
150   Oh, God! A beast that wants discourse of reason[57]
       Would have mourned longer—married with my uncle,
       My father's brother, but no more like my father
       Than I to Hercules. Within a month,
       Ere yet the salt of most unrighteous tears
155   Had left the flushing in her gallèd[58] eyes,
       She married. Oh, most wicked speed, to post[59]
       With such dexterity[60] to incestuous sheets!
       It is not, nor it cannot, come to good.
       But break, my heart, for I must hold my tongue!

---

[46] **great cannon:** This Danish custom of discharging cannon when the King proposed a toast was much noted by Englishmen.   [47] **rouse:** deep drink.   [48] **bruit:** sound loudly, echo.
[49] **canon:** rule, law.   [50] **uses:** ways.   [51] **rank:** coarse.   [52] **merely:** entirely.
[53] **Hyperion:** the sun god.   [54] **satyr:** a creature half man, half goat—ugly and lecherous.
[55] **beteem:** allow.   [56] **Niobe:** She boasted of her children, to the annoyance of the goddess Artemis, who slew them all. Thereafter Niobe became so sorrowful that she changed into a rock everlastingly dripping water.   [57] **wants . . . reason:** is without ability to reason.
[58] **galled:** sore.   [59] **post:** hasten.   [60] **dexterity:** nimbleness.

[Enter Horatio, Marcellus, and Bernardo.]

160 **Horatio:** Hail to your lordship!
Hamlet: I am glad to see you well.
    Horatio—or I do forget myself.
Horatio: The same, my lord, and your poor servant ever.
Hamlet: Sir, my good friend—I'll change that name[61] with you.
    And what make you from Wittenberg, Horatio?
165   Marcellus?
Marcellus: My good lord?
Hamlet: I am very glad to see you. *[To Bernardo]* Good even, sir.
    But what, in faith, make you from Wittenberg?
Horatio: A truant disposition, good my lord.
170 **Hamlet:** I would not hear your enemy say so,
    Nor shall you do my ear that violence
    To make it truster of your own report
    Against yourself. I know you are no truant.
    But what is your affair in Elsinore?
175   We'll teach you to drink deep[62] ere you depart.
Horatio: My lord, I came to see your father's funeral.
Hamlet: I pray thee do not mock me, fellow student.
    I think it was to see my mother's wedding.
Horatio: Indeed, my lord, it followed hard upon.
180 **Hamlet:** Thrift, thrift, Horatio! The funeral baked meats
    Did coldly furnish forth the marriage tables.[63]
    Would I had met my dearest[64] foe in Heaven
    Or ever I had seen that day, Horatio!
    My father!—Methinks I see my father.
185 **Horatio:** Oh, where, my lord?
Hamlet: In my mind's eye, Horatio.
Horatio: I saw him once. He was a goodly King.
Hamlet: He was a man, take him for all in all.
    I shall not look upon his like again.
Horatio: My lord, I think I saw him yesternight.
190 **Hamlet:** Saw? Who?
Horatio: My lord, the King your father.
Hamlet: The King my father!
Horatio: Season your admiration[65] for a while
    With an attent[66] ear till I may deliver,
    Upon the witness of these gentlemen,
195   This marvel to you.

---

[61] that name: i.e., friend.   [62] drink deep: For more on the drunken habits of the Danes, see
I.iv. 8–38.   [63] Thrift . . . tables: they hurried on the wedding for economy's sake, so that
the remains of food served at the funeral might be used cold for the wedding. **baked
meats:** feast.   [64] dearest: best-hated.   [65] Season . . . admiration: moderate your
wonder.   [66] attent: attentive.

Hamlet: For God's love, let me hear.
Horatio: Two nights together had these gentlemen,
    Marcellus and Bernardo, on their watch
    In the dead vast and middle of the night,[67]
    Been thus encountered. A figure like your father,
200   Armed at point exactly, cap-a-pie,[68]
    Appears before them and with solemn march
    Goes slow and stately by them. Thrice he walked
    By their oppressed and fear-surprisèd eyes
    Within his truncheon's[69] length, whilst they, distilled[70]
205   Almost to jelly with the act of fear,
    Stand dumb, and speak not to him. This to me
    In dreadful secrecy impart they did,
    And I with them the third night kept the watch.
    Where, as they had delivered, both in time,
210   Form of the thing, each word made true and good,
    The apparition comes. I knew your father.
    These hands are not more like.
Hamlet: But where was this?
Marcellus: My lord, upon the platform where we watched.
Hamlet: Did you not speak to it?
Horatio: My lord, I did,
215   But answer made it none. Yet once methought
    It lifted up it[71] head and did address
    Itself to motion, like as it would speak.
    But even then the morning cock crew loud,
    And at the sound it shrunk in haste away
220   And vanished from our sight.
Hamlet: 'Tis very strange.
Horatio: As I do live, my honored lord, 'tis true,
    And we did think it writ down in our duty
    To let you know of it.
Hamlet: Indeed, indeed, sirs, but this troubles me.
225   Hold you the watch tonight?
Marcellus & Bernardo: We do, my lord.
Hamlet: Armed, say you?
Marcellus & Bernardo: Armed, my lord.
Hamlet: From top to toe?
Marcellus & Bernardo: My lord, from head to foot.
Hamlet: Then saw you not his face?
Horatio: Oh yes, my lord, he wore his beaver[72] up.
230 Hamlet: What, looked he frowningly?

---

[67] dead . . . night: deep, silent midnight.   [68] at . . . cap-a-pie: complete in every detail,
head to foot.   [69] truncheon: a general's staff.   [70] distilled: melted.   [71] it: its.
[72] beaver: front part of the helmet, which could be raised.

Horatio: A countenance more in sorrow than in anger.
Hamlet: Pale, or red?
Horatio: Nay, very pale.
Hamlet: And fixed his eyes upon you?
235 **Horatio:** Most constantly.
Hamlet: I would I had been there.
Horatio: It would have much amazed you.
Hamlet: Very like, very like. Stayed it long?
Horatio: While one with moderate haste might tell[73] a hundred.
Marcellus & Bernardo: Longer, longer.
240 **Horatio:** Not when I saw 't.
Hamlet: His beard was grizzled?[74] No?
Horatio: It was as I have seen it in his life,
    A sable silvered.[75]
Hamlet: I will watch tonight.
    Perchance 'twill walk again.
Horatio: I warrant it will.
Hamlet: If it assume my noble father's person,
245   I'll speak to it though Hell itself should gape
    And bid me hold my peace. I pray you all,
    If you have hitherto concealed this sight,
    Let it be tenable[76] in your silence still,
    And whatsoever else shall hap tonight,
250   Give it an understanding, but no tongue.
    I will requite[77] your loves. So fare you well.
    Upon the platform, 'twixt eleven and twelve,
    I'll visit you.
All: Our duty to your Honor.
Hamlet: Your loves, as mine to you. Farewell.

[Exeunt all but Hamlet.]

255   My father's spirit in arms! All is not well.
    I doubt[78] some foul play. Would the night were come!
    Till then sit still, my soul. Foul deeds will rise.
    Though all the earth o'erwhelm them, to men's eyes.   *[Exit.]*

Scene III. A room in Polonius's house.

[Enter Laertes and Ophelia.]

Laertes: My necessaries[1] are embarked. Farewell.
    And, Sister, as the winds give benefit

---

[73] tell: count.   [74] grizzled: gray.   [75] sable silvered: black mingled with white.
[76] tenable: held fast.   [77] requite: repay.   [78] doubt: suspect.
[1] necessaries: baggage.

And convoy is assistant,[2] do not sleep,
But let me hear from you.
Ophelia: Do you doubt that?
5 Laertes: For Hamlet, and the trifling of his favor,[3]
Hold it a fashion and a toy in blood,[4]
A violet in the youth of primy[5] nature,
Forward, not permanent, sweet, not lasting,
The perfume and suppliance of a minute[6]—
No more.
10 Ophelia: No more but so?
Laertes: Think it no more.
For Nature crescent does not grow alone
In thews and bulk,[7] but as this temple[8] waxes
The inward service of the mind and soul
Grows wide withal. Perhaps he loves you now,
15   And now no soil nor cautel[9] doth besmirch
The virtue of his will.[10] But you must fear,
His greatness weighed,[11] his will is not his own.
For he himself is subject to his birth.
He may not, as unvalued persons do,
20   Carve[12] for himself, for on his choice depends
The safety and health of this whole state,
And therefore must his choice be circumscribed[13]
Unto the voice and yielding of that body
Whereof he is the head. Then if he says he loves you,
25   It fits your wisdom so far to believe it
As he in his particular act and place
May give his saying deed, which is no further
Than the main voice of Denmark goes withal.
Then weigh what loss your honor may sustain
30   If with too credent[14] ear you list his songs,
Or lose your heart, or your chaste treasure[15] open
To his unmastered importunity.
Fear it, Ophelia, fear it, my dear sister,
And keep you in the rear[16] of your affection,
35   Out of the shot and danger of desire.
The chariest maid is prodigal enough
If she unmask her beauty to the moon.

---

[2]convoy . . . assistant: means of conveyance is available.   [3]favor: i.e., toward you.
[4]toy in blood: trifling impulse.   [5]primy: springtime; i.e., youthful.   [6]perfume . . .
minute: perfume which lasts only for a minute.   [7]For . . . bulk: for natural growth is
not only in bodily bulk.   [8]temple: i.e., the body.   [9]cautel: deceit.   [10]will: desire.
[11]His . . . weighed: when you consider his high position.   [12]Carve: choose.
[13]circumscribed: restricted.   [14]credent: credulous.   [15]chaste treasure: the treasure of
your chastity.   [16]in . . . rear: i.e., farthest from danger.

Virtue itself 'scapes not calumnious strokes.
The canker galls the infants[17] of the spring
40   Too oft before their buttons[18] be disclosed,
And in the morn and liquid dew of youth
Contagious blastments[19] are most imminent.
Be wary, then, best safety lies in fear.
Youth to itself rebels, though none else near.[20]
45 Ophelia: I shall the effect of this good lesson keep
As watchman to my heart. But, good my brother,
Do not, as some ungracious pastors do,
Show me the steep and thorny way to Heaven
Whilst, like a puffed[21] and reckless libertine,
50   Himself the primrose path of dalliance[22] treads
And recks not his own rede.[23]
Laertes: Oh, fear me not.
I stay too long. But here my father comes.
[Enter Polonius.] A double blessing is a double grace,
Occasion smiles[24] upon a second leave.
55 Polonius: Yet here, Laertes! Aboard, aboard, for shame!
The wind sits in the shoulder of your sail
And you are stayed[25] for. There, my blessing with thee!
And these few precepts in thy memory
Look thou charácter.[26] Give thy thoughts no tongue,
60   Nor any unproportioned[27] thought his act.
Be thou familiar, but by no means vulgar.
Those friends thou hast, and their adoption tried,[28]
Grapple them to thy soul with hoops of steel,
But do not dull thy palm with entertainment[29]
65   Of each new-hatched unfledged[30] comrade. Beware
Of entrance to a quarrel, but being in,
Bear 't that the opposèd may beware of thee.
Give every man thy ear, but few thy voice.[31]
Take each man's censure,[32] but reserve thy judgment.
70   Costly thy habit[33] as thy purse can buy,
But not expressed in fancy[34]—rich, not gaudy.
For the apparel oft proclaims the man,

---

[17] canker . . . infants: maggot harms the unopened buds.   [18] buttons: buds.
[19] Contagious blastments: infectious blasts.   [20] though . . . near: without anyone else to
encourage it.   [21] puffed: panting.   [22] primrose . . . dalliance: i.e., the pleasant way of
love-making.   [23] recks . . . rede: takes no heed of his own advice.   [24] Occasion
smiles: i.e., here is a happy chance.   [25] stayed: waited.   [26] character: inscribe.
[27] unproportioned: unsuitable.   [28] adoption tried: friendship tested by experience.
[29] dull . . . entertainment: let your hand grow callous with welcome.   [30] unfledged: lit.,
newly out of the egg, immature.   [31] Give . . . voice: listen to everyone but commit
yourself to few.   [32] censure: opinion.   [33] habit: dress.   [34] expressed in fancy:
fantastic.

And they in France of the best rank and station
Are of a most select and generous chief in that.[35]

75   Neither a borrower nor a lender be,
For loan oft loses both itself and friend
And borrowing dulls the edge of husbandry.[36]
This above all: To thine own self be true,
And it must follow, as the night the day,

80   Thou canst not then be false to any man.
Farewell. My blessing season[37] this in thee!

Laertes: Most humbly do I take my leave, my lord.

Polonius: The time invites you. Go, your servants tend.[38]

Laertes: Farewell, Ophelia, and remember well

85   What I have said to you.

Ophelia: 'Tis in my memory locked,
And you yourself shall keep the key of it.

Laertes: Farewell.   *[Exit.]*

Polonius: What is 't, Ophelia, he hath said to you?

Ophelia: So please you, something touching the Lord Hamlet.

90 **Polonius:** Marry,[39] well bethought.[40]
'Tis told me he hath very oft of late
Given private time to you, and you yourself
Have of your audience been most free and bounteous.
If it be so—as so 'tis put on me,

95   And that in way of caution—I must tell you
You do not understand yourself so clearly
As it behooves[41] my daughter and your honor.
What is between you? Give me up the truth.

Ophelia: He hath, my lord, of late made many tenders[42]

100   Of his affection to me.

Polonius: Affection! Pooh! You speak like a green girl,
Unsifted[43] in such perilous circumstance.
Do you believe his tenders, as you call them?

Ophelia: I do not know, my lord, what I should think.

105 **Polonius:** Marry, I'll teach you. Think yourself a baby
That you have ta'en these tenders[44] for true pay,
Which are not sterling.[45] Tender yourself more dearly,
Or—not to crack the wind of[46] the poor phrase,
Running it thus—you'll tender me a fool.

---

[35] **Are . . . that:** A disputed line; this is the F reading. Q_2 reads "Or of the most select and generous, chief in that"; i.e., the best noble and gentle families are very particular in their dress. **generous:** of gentle birth.   [36] **husbandry:** economy.   [37] **season:** bring to fruit. [38] **tend:** attend.   [39] **Marry:** Mary, by the Virgin Mary.   [40] **well bethought:** well remembered.   [41] **behooves:** is the duty of.   [42] **tenders:** offers.   [43] **Unsifted:** untried. [44] **tenders . . . tender:** Polonius puns on "tenders," counters (used for money in games); "tender," value; "tender," show.   [45] **sterling:** true currency.   [46] **crack . . . of:** i.e., ride to death.

110 Ophelia: My lord, he hath importuned me with love
      In honorable fashion.
    Polonius: Aye, fashion[47] you may call it. Go to, go to.
    Ophelia: And hath given countenance to his speech,[48] my lord,
      With almost all the holy vows of Heaven.
115 Polonius: Aye, springes[49] to catch woodcocks.[50] I do know,
      When the blood burns, how prodigal[51] the soul
      Lends the tongue vows. These blazes,[52] daughter,
      Giving more light than heat, extinct in both,
      Even in their promise as it is a-making,
120   You must not take for fire. From this time
      Be something scanter of your maiden presence,
      Set your entreatments at a higher rate
      Than a command to parley.[53] For Lord Hamlet,
      Believe so much in him, that he is young,
125   And with a larger tether[54] may he walk
      Than may be given you. In few,[55] Ophelia,
      Do not believe his vows, for they are brokers,[56]
      Not of that dye which their investments[57] show,
      But mere implorators[58] of unholy suits,
130   Breathing like sanctified and pious bawds[59]
      The better to beguile. This is for all.
      I would not, in plain terms, from this time forth
      Have you so slander any moment leisure[60]
      As to give words or talk with the Lord Hamlet.
135   Look to 't, I charge you. Come your ways.
    Ophelia: I shall obey, my lord.   *[Exeunt.]*

Scene IV. The platform

[Enter Hamlet, Horatio, and Marcellus.]

Hamlet: The air bites shrewdly.[1] It is very cold.
Horatio: It is a nipping and an eager[2] air.
Hamlet: What hour now?
Horatio: I think it lacks of twelve.

---

[47] fashion: mere show.   [48] given . . . speech: confirmed his words.   [49] springes: snares.
[50] woodcocks: foolish birds.   [51] prodigal: extravagantly.   [52] blazes: flashes, quickly
extinguished *(extinct).*   [53] Set . . . parley: when you are asked to see him do not regard it
as a command to negotiate. parley: meeting to discuss terms.   [54] tether: rope by which a
grazing animal is fastened to its peg.   [55] In few: in short.   [56] brokers: traveling
salesmen.   [57] investments: garments.   [58] implorators: men who solicit.   [59] bawds:
keepers of brothels. F₁ and Q₂ read "bond," an easy misprint for "baud"—the Elizabethan
spelling of "bawd."   [60] slander . . . leisure: misuse any moment of leisure.
[1] shrewdly: bitterly.   [2] eager: sharp.

Marcellus: No, it is struck.

5 **Horatio:** Indeed? I heard it not. It then draws near the season
Wherein the spirit held his wont to walk.

[A flourish of trumpets, and ordnance
shot off within. [3]*]*

What doth this mean, my lord?

Hamlet: The King doth wake[4] tonight and takes his rouse,[5]
Keeps wassail,[6] and the swaggering upspring reels.[7]

10 And as he drains his draughts of Rhenish[8] down,
The kettledrum and trumpet thus bray out
The triumph of his pledge.

Horatio: Is it a custom?

Hamlet: Aye, marry, is 't.
But to my mind, though I am native here

15 And to the manner born, it is a custom
More honored in the breach than the observance.
This heavy-headed revel[9] east and west
Makes us traduced and taxed of[10] other nations.
They clepe[11] us drunkards, and with swinish phrase

20 Soil our addition,[12] and indeed it takes
From our achievements, though performed at height,[13]
The pith and marrow of our attribute.[14]
So oft it chances in particular men,
That for some vicious mole[15] of nature in them,

25 As in their birth—wherein they are not guilty,
Since nature cannot choose his origin—
By the o'ergrowth of some complexion,[16]
Oft breaking down the pales[17] and forts of reason,
Or by some habit that too much o'erleavens[18]

30 The form of plausive[19] manners, that these men—
Carrying, I say, the stamp of one defect,
Being Nature's livery,[20] or Fortune's star[21]—
Their virtues else—be they as pure as grace,
As infinite as man may undergo—

35 Shall in the general censure take corruption

---

[3] within: off stage.   [4] wake: "makes a night of it."   [5] rouse: See I.ii. 127,n.   [6] wassail: revelry.   [7] swaggering . . . reels: reel in a riotous dance.   [8] Rhenish: Rhine wine. [9] heavy-headed revel: drinking which produces a thick head.   [10] traduced . . . of: disgraced and censured by.   [11] clepe: call.   [12] soil . . . addition: smirch our honor. addition: lit., title of honor added to a man's name.   [13] though . . . height: though of the highest merit.   [14] pith . . . attribute: essential part of our honor; i.e., we lose the honor due to our achievements because of our reputation for drunkenness.   [15] mole: blemish.   [16] o'ergrowth . . . complexion: some quality allowed to overbalance the rest. [17] pales: defenses.   [18] o'erleavens: mixes with.   [19] plausive: agreeable.   [20] Nature's livery: i.e., inborn.   [21] Fortune's star: the result of ill luck.

From that particular fault. The dram of eale
Doth all the noble substance of a doubt
To his own scandal.[22]

[Enter Ghost.]

Horatio: Look, my lord, it comes!
Hamlet: Angels and ministers of grace defend us!
40   Be thou a spirit of health or goblin damned,[23]
Bring with thee airs from Heaven or blasts from Hell,
Be thy intents wicked or charitable,
Thou comest in such a questionable[24] shape
That I will speak to thee. I'll call thee Hamlet,
45   King, Father, royal Dane. Oh, answer me!
Let me not burst in ignorance, but tell
Why thy canónized[25] bones, hearsèd[26] in death,
Have burst their cerements,[27] why the sepulcher
Wherein we saw thee quietly inurned[28]
50   Hath oped his ponderous and marble jaws
To cast thee up again. What may this mean,
That thou, dead corse, again, in complete steel,[29]
Revisit'st thus the glimpses of the moon,
Making night hideous, and we fools[30] of nature
55   So horridly to shake our disposition[31]
With thoughts beyond the reaches of our souls?
Say, why is this? Wherefore? What should we do?

[Ghost beckons Hamlet.]

Horatio: It beckons you to go away with it,
As if it some impartment[32] did desire
60   To you alone.

---

[22] The . . . scandal: This is the most famous of all disputed passages in Shakespeare's plays. The general meaning is clear: "a small portion of evil brings scandal on the whole substance, however noble." "Eale" is an Elizabethan spelling and pronunciation of "evil," as later in Q_2; "deale" is the spelling and pronunciation of "Devil." The difficulty lies in "of a doubt," which is obviously a misprint for some such word as "corrupt"; but to be satisfactory it must fit the meter and be a plausible misprint. So far, although many guesses have been made, none is wholly convincing. The best is perhaps "often dout"—often put out.   [23] spirit . . . damned: a holy spirit or damned fiend. Hamlet, until convinced at the end of the play scene (III.ii.), is perpetually in doubt whether the ghost which he sees is a good spirit sent to warn him, a devil sent to tempt him into some damnable action, or a hallucination created by his own diseased imagination.   [24] questionable: inviting question.
[25] canonized: buried with full rites according to the canon of the Church.
[26] hearsed: buried.   [27] cerements: waxen shroud, used to wrap the bodies of the illustrious dead.   [28] inurned: buried.   [29] complete steel: full armor.   [30] fools: dupes.
[31] disposition: nature.   [32] impartment: communication.

Marcellus: Look with what courteous action
    It waves you to a more removèd ground.
    But do not go with it.
Horatio: No, by no means.
Hamlet: It will not speak. Then I will follow it.
Horatio: Do not, my lord.
Hamlet: Why, what should be the fear?
65   I do not set my life as a pin's fee,[33]
    And for my soul, what can it do to that,
    Being a thing immortal as itself?
    It waves me forth again. I'll follow it.
Horatio: What if it tempt you toward the flood, my lord,
70   Or to the dreadful summit of the cliff
    That beetles o'er[34] his base into the sea,
    And there assume some other horrible form
    Which might deprive your sovereignty of reason[35]
    And draw you into madness? Think of it.
75   The very place puts toys of desperation,[36]
    Without more motive, into every brain
    That looks so many fathoms to the sea
    And hears it roar beneath.
Hamlet: It waves me still.
    Go on. I'll follow thee.
80 Marcellus: You shall not go, my lord.
Hamlet: Hold off your hands.
Horatio: Be ruled. You shall not go.
Hamlet: My fate cries out,
    And makes each petty artery in this body
    As hardy as the Nemean lion's nerve.[37]
    Still am I called. Unhand me, gentlemen.
85   By Heaven, I'll make a ghost of him that lets[38] me!
    I say, away! Go on. I'll follow thee.

[Exeunt Ghost and Hamlet.]

Horatio: He waxes desperate with imagination.
Marcellus: Let's follow. 'Tis not fit thus to obey him.
Horatio: Have after. To what issue will this come?
90 Marcellus: Something is rotten in the state of Denmark.
Horatio: Heaven will direct it.
Marcellus: Nay, let's follow him.   *[Exeunt.]*

---

[33] fee: value.   [34] beetles o'er: juts out over.   [35] sovereignty of reason: control of your reason over your actions.   [36] toys of desperation: desperate fancies.   [37] Nemean . . . nerve: sinew of a fierce beast slain by Hercules.   [38] lets: hinders.

Scene V. Another part of the platform.

[Enter Ghost and Hamlet.]

Hamlet: Whither wilt thou lead me? Speak. I'll go no further.
Ghost: Mark me.
Hamlet: I will.
Ghost: My hour is almost come
 When I to sulphurous and tormenting flames
 Must render up myself.
Hamlet: Alas, poor ghost!
5 Ghost: Pity me not, but lend thy serious hearing
 To what I shall unfold.
Hamlet: Speak. I am bound to hear.
Ghost: So art thou to revenge, when thou shalt hear.
Hamlet: What?
Ghost: I am thy father's spirit,
10 Doomed for a certain term to walk the night
 And for the day confined to fast in fires
 Till the foul crimes done in my days of nature
 Are burnt and purged away. But that I am forbid
 To tell the secrets of my prison house,
15 I could a tale unfold whose lightest word
 Would harrow up thy soul, freeze thy young blood,
 Make thy two eyes, like stars, start from their spheres,[1]
 Thy knotted and combinèd[2] locks to part
 And each particular[3] hair to stand an[4] end
20 Like quills upon the fretful porpentine.[5]
 But this eternal blazon[6] must not be
 To ears of flesh and blood. List, list, oh, list!
 If thou didst ever thy dear father love—
Hamlet: Oh, God!
25 Ghost: Revenge his foul and most unnatural murder.
Hamlet: Murder!
Ghost: Murder most foul, as in the best[7] it is,
 But this most foul, strange, and unnatural.
Hamlet: Haste me to know 't, that I, with wings as swift
30 As meditation or the thoughts of love,
 May sweep to my revenge.
Ghost: I find thee apt,
 And duller shouldst thou be than the fat[8] weed

---

[1] spheres: the circles in which the planets and stars were supposed to move.   [2] knotted
. . . combined: the hair that lies together in a mass.   [3] particular: individual.
[4] an: on.   [5] porpentine: porcupine.   [6] eternal blazon: description of eternity.   [7] in . . .
best: i.e., murder is foul even when there is a good excuse.   [8] fat: thick, slimy, motionless.

That roots itself in ease[9] of Lethe wharf[10]
Wouldst thou not stir in this. Now, Hamlet, hear.
35   'Tis given out that, sleeping in my orchard,
A serpent stung me—so the whole ear of Denmark
Is by a forgèd process[11] of my death
Rankly abused. But know, thou noble youth,
The serpent that did sting thy father's life
40   Now wears his crown.
Hamlet: Oh, my prophetic soul!
My uncle!
Ghost: Aye, that incestuous, that adulterate beast,
With witchcraft of his wit, with traitorous gifts—
O wicked wit and gifts, that have the power
45   So to seduce!—won to his shameful lust
The will of my most seeming-virtuous Queen.
O Hamlet, what a falling-off was there!
From me, whose love was of that dignity
That it went hand in hand even with the vow
50   I made to her in marriage, and to decline
Upon a wretch whose natural gifts were poor
To those of mine!
But virtue, as it never will be moved
Though lewdness court it in a shape of Heaven,[12]
55   So Lust, though to a radiant angel linked,
Will sate itself[13] in a celestial bed
And prey on garbage.
But soft! Methinks I scent the morning air.
Brief let me be. Sleeping within my orchard,
60   My custom always of the afternoon,
Upon my secure hour[14] thy uncle stole
With juice of cursèd hebenon[15] in a vial,
And in the porches[16] of my ears did pour
The leperous distillment,[17] whose effect
65   Holds such an enmity with blood of man
That swift as quicksilver it courses through
The natural gates and alleys of the body,
And with a sudden vigor it doth posset[18]
And curd, like eager[19] droppings into milk,
70   The thin and wholesome blood. So did it mine,

---

[9] in ease: undisturbed.   [10] Lethe wharf: the bank of Lethe, the river of forgetfulness in the underworld.   [11] forged process: false account.   [12] lewdness . . . Heaven: though wooed by Lust disguised as an angel.   [13] state itself: gorge.   [14] secure hour: time of relaxation.   [15] hebenon: probably henbane, a poisonous plant.   [16] porches: entrances.
[17] leperous distillment: distillation causing leprosy.   [18] posset: curdle.   [19] eager: acid.

And a most instant tetter barked[20] about,
Most lazarlike,[21] with vile and loathsome crust,
All my smooth body.
Thus was I, sleeping, by a brother's hand
75   Of life, of crown, of Queen, at once dispatched—
Cut off even in the blossoms of my sin,[22]
Unhouseled, disappointed, unaneled,[23]
No reckoning made, but sent to my account
With all my imperfections on my head.
80   Oh, horrible! Oh, horrible, most horrible!
If thou hast nature[24] in thee, bear it not.
Let not the royal bed of Denmark be
A couch for luxury[25] and damned incest.
But, howsoever thou pursuest this act,
85   Taint not thy mind, nor let thy soul contrive
Against thy mother aught. Leave her to Heaven
And to those thorns that in her bosom lodge
To prick and sting her. Fare thee well at once!
Thy glowworm shows the matin[26] to be near,
90   And 'gins to pale his uneffectual[27] fire.
Adieu, adieu, adieu! Remember me.   *[Exit.]*
Hamlet: O all you host of Heaven! O earth! What else?
And shall I couple Hell? Oh, fie! Hold, hold, my heart,
And you, my sinews, grow not instant old
95   But bear me stiffly up. Remember thee!
Aye, thou poor ghost, while memory holds a seat
In this distracted globe.[28] Remember thee!
Yea, from the table[29] of my memory
I'll wipe away all trivial fond[30] recórds,
100   All saws[31] of books, all forms,[32] all pressures[33] past,
That youth and observation copied there,
And thy commandment all alone shall live
Within the book and volume of my brain,
Unmixed with baser matter. Yes, by Heaven!
105   O most pernicious woman!
O villain, villain, smiling, damnèd villain!
My tables—meet it is I set it down

---

[20] **tetter barked:** eruption formed a bark.   [21] **lazarlike:** like leprosy.   [22] **Cut . . . sin:** cut off in a state of sin and so in danger of damnation.   [23] **Unhouseled . . . unaneled:** without receiving the sacrament, not properly prepared, unanointed—without extreme unction.
[24] **nature:** natural feelings.   [25] **luxury:** lust.   [26] **matin:** morning.   [27] **uneffectual:** made ineffectual by daylight.   [28] **globe:** i.e., head.   [29] **table:** notebook. Intellectual young men carried notebooks in which they recorded good sayings and notable observations.
[30] **fond:** trifling.   [31] **saws:** wise sayings.   [32] **forms:** images in the mind.
[33] **pressures:** impressions.

[Writing] That one may smile, and smile, and be a villain.
At least I'm sure it may be so in Denmark.
110 So, Uncle, there you are. Now to my word.[34]
It is "Adieu, adieu! Remember me."
I have sworn 't.
Horatio & Marcellus: *[Within]* My lord, my lord!

[Enter Horatio and Marcellus.]

Marcellus: Lord Hamlet!
Horatio: Heaven secure him!
Hamlet: So be it!
115 Marcellus: Illo, ho, ho,[35] my lord!
Hamlet: Hillo, ho, ho, boy! Come, bird, come.
Marcellus: How is 't, my noble lord?
Horatio: What news, my lord?
Hamlet: Oh, wonderful!
Horatio: Good my lord, tell it.
Hamlet: No, you will reveal it.
120 Horatio: Not I, my lord, by Heaven.
Marcellus: Nor I, my lord.
Hamlet: How say you, then, would heart of man once think it?
     But you'll be secret?
Horatio & Marcellus: Aye, by Heaven, my lord.
Hamlet: There's ne'er a villain dwelling in all Denmark
     But he's an arrant[36] knave.
125 Horatio: There needs no ghost, my lord, come from the grave
     To tell us this.
Hamlet: Why, right, you are i' the right.
     And so, without more circumstance[37] at all,
     I hold it fit that we shake hands and part—
     You as your business and desire shall point you,
130 For every man hath business and desire,
     Such as it is. And for my own poor part,
     Look you, I'll go pray.
Horatio: These are but wild and whirling[38] words, my lord.
Hamlet: I'm sorry they offend you, heartily,
135 Yes, faith, heartily.
Horatio: There's no offense, my lord.
Hamlet: Yes, by Saint Patrick, but there is, Horatio,
     And much offense too. Touching this vision here,
     It is an honest[39] ghost, that let me tell you.
     For your desire to know what is between us,

---

[34] word: cue.   [35] Illo . . . ho: the falconer's cry to recall the hawk.   [36] arrant:
out-and-out.   [37] circumstance: ceremony.   [38] whirling: violent.   [39] honest: true.

140   O'ermaster 't as you may. And now, good friends,
       As you are friends, scholars, and soldiers,
       Give me one poor request.
       Horatio: What is 't, my lord? We will.
       Hamlet: Never make known what you have seen tonight.
145   **Horatio & Marcellus:** My lord, we will not.
       Hamlet: Nay, but swear 't.
       Horatio: In faith,
       My lord, not I.
       Marcellus: Nor I, my lord, in faith.
       Hamlet: Upon my sword.
       Marcellus: We have sworn, my lord, already.
       Hamlet: Indeed, upon my sword,[40] indeed.
       Ghost: *[Beneath]* Swear.
150   **Hamlet:** Ah, ha, boy! Say'st thou so? Art thou there, truepenny?[41]
       Come on. You hear this fellow in the cellarage.
       Consent to swear.
       Horatio: Propose the oath, my lord.
       Hamlet: Never to speak of this that you have seen,
       Swear by my sword.
155   **Ghost:** *[Beneath]* Swear.
       Hamlet: *Hic et ubique?*[42] Then we'll shift our ground.
       Come hither, gentlemen,
       And lay your hands again upon my sword.
       Never to speak of this that you have heard,
160   Swear by my sword.
       Ghost: *[Beneath]* Swear.
       Hamlet: Well said, old mole! Canst work i' the earth so fast?
       A worthy pioner![43] Once more remove,[44] good friends.
       Horatio: Oh, day and night, but this is wondrous strange!
165   **Hamlet:** And therefore as a stranger give it welcome.
       There are more things in Heaven and earth, Horatio,
       Than are dreamt of in your philosophy.
       But come,
       Here, as before, never, so help you mercy,
170   How strange or odd soe'er I bear myself,
       As I perchance hereafter shall think meet
       To put an antic disposition[45] on,
       That you, at such times seeing me, never shall,
       With arms encumbered[46] thus, or this headshake,
175   Or by pronouncing of some doubtful phrase,

---

[40] upon . . . sword: on the cross made by the hilt of the sword; but for soldiers the sword itself was a sacred object.   [41] truepenny: old boy.   [42] Hic et ubique: here and everywhere.   [43] pioner: miner.   [44] remove: move.   [45] antic disposition: mad behavior.   [46] encumbered: folded.

As "Well, well, we know," or "We could an if we would,"
Or "If we list to speak," or "There be, an if they might,"
Or such ambiguous giving out, to note
That you know aught of me. This not to do,
180   So grace and mercy at your most need help you,
Swear.
Ghost: *[Beneath]* Swear.
Hamlet: Rest, rest, perturbèd spirit! *[They swear.]* So, gentlemen,
With all my love I do commend me to you.
185   And what so poor a man as Hamlet is
May do to express his love and friending[47] to you,
God willing, shall not lack. Let us go in together.
And still your fingers on your lips, I pray.
The time is out of joint. Oh, cursèd spite
190   That ever I was born to set it right!
Nay, come, let's go together.   *[Exeunt.]*

Act II

Scene I. A room in Polonius's house.

[Enter Polonius and Reynaldo.]

Polonius: Give him this money and these notes, Reynaldo.
Reynaldo: I will, my lord.
Polonius: You shall do marvelous wisely, good Reynaldo.
Before you visit him, to make inquire
5   Of his behavior.
Reynaldo: My lord, I did intend it.
Polonius: Marry, well said, very well said. Look you, sir,
Inquire me first what Danskers[1] are in Paris,
And how, and who, what means,[2] and where they keep,[3]
What company, at what expense, and finding
10   By this encompassment and drift of question[4]
That they do know my son, come you more nearer
Than your particular demands will touch it.[5]
Take you, as 'twere, some distant knowledge of him,
As thus, "I know his father and his friends,
15   And in part him." Do you mark this, Reynaldo?
Reynaldo: Aye, very well, my lord.
Polonius: "And in part him, but," you may say, "not well.
But if 't be he I mean, he's very wild,

---

[47] friending: friendship.
[1] Danskers: Danes.   [2] what means: what their income is.   [3] keep: live.
[4] encompassment . . . question: roundabout method of questioning.   [5] your . . . it:
i.e., you won't get at the truth by straight questions.

Addicted so and so"—and there put on him
20   What forgeries[6] you please. Marry, none so rank[7]
As may dishonor him, take heed of that,
But, sir, such wanton, wild, and usual slips
As are companions noted and most known
To youth and liberty.
Reynaldo: As gaming, my lord.
25 Polonius: Aye, or drinking, fencing,[8] swearing, quarreling,
Drabbing.[9] You may go so far.
Reynaldo: My lord, that would dishonor him.
Polonius: Faith, no, as you may season[10] it in the charge.
You must not put another scandal on him,
30   That he is open to incontinency.[11]
That's not my meaning. But breathe his faults so quaintly[12]
That they may seem the taints of liberty,
The flash and outbreak of a fiery mind,
A savageness in unreclaimèd[13] blood,
Of general assault.[14]
35 Reynaldo: But, my good lord—
Polonius: Wherefore should you do this?
Reynaldo: Aye, my lord,
I would know that.
Polonius: Marry, sir, here's my drift,[15]
And I believe it is a fetch of warrant.[16]
You laying these slight sullies[17] on my son,
40   As 'twere a thing a little soiled i' the working,
Mark you,
Your party in converse, him you would sound,
Having ever seen[18] in the prenominate[19] crimes
The youth you breathe of guilty, be assured
45   He closes with you in this consequence[20]—
"Good sir," or so, or "friend," or "gentleman,"
According to the phrase or the addition[21]
Of man and country.
Reynaldo: Very good, my lord.
50 Polonius: And then, sir, does he this—he does—What was I about to say? By
the mass, I was about to say something. Where did I leave?

---

[6] forgeries: inventions.   [7] rank: gross.   [8] fencing: A young man who haunted fencing
schools would be regarded as quarrelsome and likely to belong to the sporting
set.   [9] Drabbing: whoring.   [10] season: qualify.   [11] open . . . incontinency: So long as
Laertes does his drabbing inconspicuously Polonius would not be disturbed.
[12] quaintly: skillfully.   [13] unreclaimed: naturally wild.   [14] Of . . . assault: common to
all men.   [15] drift: intention.   [16] fetch . . . warrant: trick warranted to work.
[17] sullies: blemishes.   [18] Having . . . seen: if ever he has seen.   [19] prenominate:
aforementioned.   [20] closes . . . consequence: follows up with this reply.
[21] addition: title.

Reynaldo: At "closes in the consequence," or "friend or
    so," and "gentleman."
Polonius: At "closes in the consequence," aye, marry,
55   He closes with you thus: "I know the gentleman.
      I saw him yesterday, or t'other day,
      Or then, or then, with such, or such, and, as you say,
      There was a' gaming, there o'ertook in 's rouse,
      There falling out at tennis."[22] Or perchance,
60   "I saw him enter such a house of sale,"
      Videlicet,[23] a brothel, or so forth.
      See you now,
      Your bait of falsehood takes this carp of truth.
      And thus do we of wisdom and of reach,[24]
65   With windlasses[25] and with assays of bias,[26]
      By indirections find directions out.[27]
      So, by my former lecture and advice,
      Shall you my son. You have me, have you not?
Reynaldo: My lord, I have.
Polonius: God be wi' ye, fare ye well.
70 Reynaldo: Good my lord!
Polonius: Observe his inclination in[28] yourself.
Reynaldo: I shall, my lord.
Polonius: And let him ply his music.
Reynaldo: Well, my lord.
Polonius: Farewell!   *[Exit Reynaldo.]*
75   *[Enter Ophelia.]* How now, Ophelia! What's the matter?
Ophelia: Oh, my lord, my lord, I have been so affrighted!
Polonius: With what, i' the name of God?
Ophelia: My lord, as I was sewing in my closet,[29]
      Lord Hamlet, with his doublet[30] all unbraced,
80   No hat upon his head, his stockings fouled,
      Ungartered and down-gyved[31] to his ankle,
      Pale as his shirt, his knees knocking each other,
      And with a look so piteous in purport
      As if he had been loosèd out of Hell
85   To speak of horrors, he comes before me.

---

[22] **tennis:** Visitors to France were much impressed by the enthusiasm of all classes of Frenchmen for tennis, which in England was mainly a courtier's game.   [23] **Videlicet:** namely, "viz."   [24] **wisdom . . . reach:** of far-reaching wisdom.   [25] **windlasses:** roundabout methods.   [26] **assays of bias:** making our bowl take a curved course.   [27] **indirections . . . out:** by indirect means come at the direct truth.   [28] **in:** for.   [29] **closet:** private room.   [30] **doublet:** the short close-fitting coat which was braced to the hose by laces. When a man was relaxing or careless of appearance, he *unbraced,* as a modern man takes off his coat or unbuttons his waistcoat.   [31] **down-gyved:** hanging around his ankles like fetters.

Polonius: Mad for thy love?
Ophelia: My lord, I do not know,
    But truly I do fear it.
Polonius: What said he?
Ophelia: He took me by the wrist and held me hard.
    Then goes he to the length of all his arm,
90   And with his other hand thus o'er his brow,
    He falls to such perusal of my face
    As he would draw it. Long stayed he so.
    At last, a little shaking of mine arm,
    And thrice his head thus waving up and down,
95   He raised a sigh so piteous and profound
    As it did seem to shatter all his bulk
    And end his being. That done, he lets me go.
    And with his head over his shoulder turned,
    He seemed to find his way without his eyes;
100 For out o' doors he went without their helps,
    And to the last bended their light on me.
Polonius: Come, go with me. I will go seek the King.
    This is the very ecstasy[32] of love,
    Whose violent property fordoes[33] itself
105 And leads the will to desperate undertakings
    As oft as any passion under heaven
    That does afflict our natures. I am sorry.
    What, have you given him any hard words of late?
Ophelia: No, my good lord, but, as you did command,
110 I did repel his letters and denied
    His access to me.
Polonius: That hath made him mad.
    I am sorry that with better heed and judgment
    I had not quoted[34] him. I feared he did but trifle
    And meant to wreck thee, but beshrew[35] my jealousy!
115 By Heaven, it is as proper[36] to our age
    To cast beyond ourselves[37] in our opinions
    As it is common for the younger sort
    To lack discretion. Come, go we to the King.
    This must be known, which, being kept close, might move
120 More grief to hide than hate to utter love.[38]
    Come.   *[Exeunt.]*

---

[32] ecstasy: frenzy.   [33] property fordoes: natural quality destroys.   [34] quoted: observed carefully.   [35] beshrew: a plague on.   [36] proper: natural.   [37] cast . . . ourselves: be too clever.   [38] which . . . love: by being kept secret it may cause more sorrow than it will cause anger by being revealed; i.e., the King and Queen may be angry at the thought of the Prince's marrying beneath his proper rank.

Scene II. A room in the castle.

[Flourish. Enter King, Queen, Rosencrantz, Guildenstern, and Attendants.]

King: Welcome, dear Rosencrantz and Guildenstern!
    Moreover[1] that we much did long to see you,
    The need we have to use you did provoke
    Our hasty sending. Something have you heard
5   Of Hamlet's transformation—so call it,
    Sith[2] nor the exterior nor the inward man
    Resembles that it was. What it should be,
    More than his father's death, that thus hath put him
    So much from the understanding of himself
10   I cannot dream of. I entreat you both
    That, being of so young days brought up with him
    And sith so neighbored to his youth and havior[3]
    That you vouchsafe your rest[4] here in our Court
    Some little time, so by your companies
15   To draw him on to pleasures, and to gather
    So much as from occasion you may glean,
    Whether aught to us unknown afflicts him thus
    That opened lies within our remedy.[5]
Queen: Good gentlemen, he hath much talked of you,
20   And sure I am two men there art not living
    To whom he more adheres.[6] If it will please you
    To show us so much gentry[7] and goodwill
    As to expend your time with us a while
    For the supply and profit of our hope,[8]
25   Your visitation shall receive such thanks
    As fits a king's remembrance.
Rosencrantz: Both your Majesties
    Might, by the sovereign power you have of us,
    Put your dread pleasures more into command
    Than to entreaty.
Guildenstern: But we both obey,
30   And here give up ourselves, in the full bent[9]
    To lay our service freely at your feet,
    To be commanded.
King: Thanks, Rosencrantz and gentle Guildenstern.
Queen: Thanks, Guildenstern and gentle Rosencrantz.

---

[1] Moreover: in addition to the fact that.   [2] Sith: since.   [3] neighbored . . . havior: so near to his youthful manner of living.   [4] vouchsafe . . . rest: consent to stay.
[5] opened . . . remedy: if revealed, might be put right by us.   [6] To . . . adheres: whom he regards more highly.   [7] gentry: courtesy.   [8] supply . . . hope: to bring a profitable conclusion to our hope.   [9] in . . . bent: stretched to our uttermost.

35   And I beseech you instantly to visit
     My too-much-changèd son. Go, some of you,
     And bring these gentlemen where Hamlet is.
Guildenstern: Heavens make our presence and our practices
     Pleasant and helpful to him!
Queen: Aye, amen!   *[Exeunt Rosencrantz,*
                                            Guildenstern, and some Attendants.]

        [Enter Polonius.]

40 **Polonius:** The ambassadors from Norway, my good lord,
     Are joyfully returned.
King: Thou still[10] hast been the father of good news.
Polonius: Have I, my lord? I assure my good liege
     I hold my duty as I hold my soul,
45   Both to my God and to my gracious King.
     And I do think, or else this brain of mine
     Hunts not the trail of policy so sure
     As it hath used to do,[11] that I have found
     The very cause of Hamlet's lunacy.
50 **King:** Oh, speak of that. That do I long to hear.
Polonius: Give first admittance to the ambassadors.
     My news shall be the fruit[12] to that great feast.
King: Thyself do grace[13] to them and bring them in.   *[Exit Polonius.]*
     He tells me, my dear Gertrude, he hath found
55   The head and source of all your son's distemper.[14]
Queen: I doubt it is no other but the main,[15]
     His father's death and our o'erhasty marriage.
King: Well, we shall sift him.
                                        [Re-enter Polonius, with Voltimand
                                            and Cornelius.]
                              Welcome, my good friends!
           Say, Voltimand, what from our brother Norway?
60 **Voltimand:** Most fair return of greetings and desires.
     Upon our first,[16] he sent out to suppress
     His nephew's levies, which to him appeared
     To be a preparation 'gainst the Polack,
     But better looked into, he truly found
65   It was against your Highness, whereat, grieved
     That so his sickness, age, and impotence

---

[10] still: always.   [11] Hunts . . . do: is not so good at following the scent of political events
as it used to be.   [12] fruit: the dessert, which comes at the end of the feast.   [13] do grace:
honor; i.e., by escorting them into the royal presence.   [14] distemper: mental
disturbance.   [15] main: principal cause.   [16] first: i.e., audience.

Was falsely borne in hand,[17] sends out arrests
On Fortinbras; which he, in brief, obeys,
Receives rebuke from Norway, and in fine[18]
70 Makes vow before his uncle never more
To give the assay of arms[19] against your Majesty.
Whereon old Norway, overcome with joy,
Gives him three thousand crowns in annual fee
And his commission to employ those soldiers,
75 So levied as before, against the Polack.
With an entreaty, herein further shown,

[Giving a paper]

That it might please you to give quiet pass[20]
Through your dominions for this enterprise,
On such regards of safety and allowance[21]
As therein are set down.
80 **King:** It likes[22] us well,
And at our more considered time we'll read,
Answer, and think upon this business.
Meantime we thank you for your well-took labor.
Go to your rest. At night we'll feast together.
Most welcome home!

[Exeunt Voltimand and Cornelius.]

85 **Polonius:** This business is well ended.
My liege, and madam, to expostulate[23]
What majesty should be, what duty is,
Why day is day, night night, and time is time,
Were nothing but to waste night, day, and time.
90 Therefore, since brevity is the soul of wit
And tediousness the limbs and outward flourishes,[24]
I will be brief. Your noble son is mad.
Mad call I it, for to define true madness,
What is 't but to be nothing else but mad?
But let that go.
95 **Queen:** More matter, with less art.[25]
Polonius: Madam, I swear I use no art at all.
That he is mad, 'tis true. 'Tis true 'tis pity,
And pity 'tis 'tis true—a foolish figure,[26]
But farewell it, for I will use no art.
100 Mad let us grant him, then. And now remains

---

[17] borne in hand: imposed upon.   [18] in fine: in the end.   [19] give . . . arms: make an attack.   [20] quiet pass: unmolested passage.   [21] regards . . . allowance: safeguard and conditions.   [22] likes: pleases.   [23] expostulate: indulge in an academic discussion.   [24] flourishes: ornaments.   [25] art: ornament.   [26] figure: i.e., a figure of speech.

That we find out the cause of this effect,
Or rather say the cause of this defect,
For this effect defective comes by cause.
Thus it remains and the remainder thus.
105   Perpend.[27]
I have a daughter—have while she is mine—
Who in her duty and obedience, mark,
Hath given me this. Now gather and surmise.[28]
[Reads.]
"To the celestial, and my soul's idol, the most beautified[29] Ophelia—"
110   That's an ill phrase, a vile phrase, "beautified" is a
vile phrase. But you shall hear. Thus: *[Reads.]*
"In her excellent white bosom, these," and so forth.
Queen: Came this from Hamlet to her?
115 Polonius: Good madam, stay awhile, I will be faithful.
[Reads.] "Doubt thou the stars are fire,
Doubt that the sun doth move,
Doubt truth to be a liar,
But never doubt I love.
120   "O dear Ophelia, I am ill at these numbers,[30] I
have not art to reckon my groans, but that I love thee
best, O most best, believe it. Adieu.
"Thine evermore, most dear lady, whilst this
machine[31] is to him, Hamlet."
125   This in obedience hath my daughter shown me,
And more above, hath his solicitings,
As they fell out by time, by means and place,
All given to mine ear.
King: But how hath she
Received his love?
Polonius: What do you think of me?
130 King: As of a man faithful and honorable.
Polonius: I would fain prove so. But what might you think,
When I had seen this hot love on the wing—
As I perceived it, I must tell you that,
Before my daughter told me—what might you
135   Or my dear Majesty your Queen here think
If I had played the desk or table book,[32]
Or given my heart awinking, mute and dumb,
Or looked upon this love with idle sight—

---

[27] Perpend: note carefully.   [28] surmise: guess the meaning.   [29] beautified: beautiful.
[30] numbers: verses.   [31] machine: i.e., body, an affected phrase.   [32] desk . . . book: i.e.,
acted as silent go-between (desks and books being natural post offices for a love letter), or
been a recipient of secrets but took no action (as desks and notebooks are the natural but
inanimate place for keeping secrets).

What might you think? No, I went round[33] to work,
140 And my young mistress thus I did bespeak:[34]
"Lord Hamlet is a Prince, out of thy star.[35]
This must not be." And then I prescripts[36] gave her
That she should lock herself from his resort,
Admit no messengers, receive no tokens.
145 Which done, she took the fruits of my advice.
And he, repulsèd, a short tale to make,
Fell into a sadness, then into a fast,
Thence to a watch, thence into a weakness,
Thence to a lightness,[37] and by this declension[38]
150 Into the madness wherein now he raves
And all we mourn for.
King: Do you think this?
Queen: It may be, very like.
Polonius: Hath there been such a time, I'd fain know that,
That I have positively said "'Tis so"
155 When it proved otherwise?
King: Not that I know.
Polonius: *[Pointing to his head and shoulder.]* Take this from this, if this be
    otherwise.
If circumstances lead me, I will find
Where truth is hid, though it were hid indeed
Within the center.[39]
King: How may we try it further?
160 Polonius: You know sometimes he walks four hours together.
Here in the lobby.
Queen: So he does indeed.
Polonius: At such a time I'll loose[40] my daughter to him.
Be you and I behind an arras[41] then.
Mark the encounter. If he love her not,
165 And be not from his reason fall'n thereon,
Let me be no assistant for a state,
But keep a farm and carters.[42]
King: We will try it.
Queen: But look where sadly the poor wretch comes reading.
Polonius: Away, I do beseech you, both away.
170 I'll board[43] him presently.   *[Exeunt King, Queen,*
                                           and Attendants.]

---

[33] round: straight.   [34] bespeak: address.   [35] out . . . star: above your destiny.
[36] prescripts: instructions.   [37] Fell . . . lightness: Hamlet's case history, according to
Polonius, develops by stages—melancholy, loss of appetite, physical weakness,
mental instability, and finally madness.   [38] declension: decline.   [39] center: the very
center of the earth.   [40] loose: turn loose.   [41] arras: tapestry hanging.
[42] keep . . . carters: i.e., turn country squire—like Justice Shallow.   [43] board: accost.

[Enter Hamlet, reading.] Oh, give me leave, How does my good Lord Hamlet?

Hamlet: Well, God-a-mercy.

Polonius: Do you know me, my lord?

Hamlet: Excellent well. You are a fishmonger.[44]

Polonius: Not I, my lord.

175 Hamlet: Then I would you were so honest a man.

Polonius: Honest, my lord!

Hamlet: Aye, sir, to be honest, as this world goes, is to be one man picked out of ten thousand.

Polonius: That's very true, my lord.

180 Hamlet: For if the sun breed maggots[45] in a dead dog, being a god[46] kissing carrion[47]—Have you a daughter?

Polonius: I have, my lord.

Hamlet: Let her not walk i' the sun. Conception is a blessing, but not as your daughter may conceive—friend, look to 't.

185 Polonius: *[Aside]* How say you by that? Still harping on my daughter. Yet he knew me not at first, he said I was a fishmonger. He is far gone, far gone. And truly in my youth I suffered much extremity for love, very near this. I'll speak to him again.—What do you read, my lord?

Hamlet: Words, words, words.

190 Polonius: What is the matter, my lord?

Hamlet: Between who?

Polonius: I mean the matter that you read, my lord.

Hamlet: Slanders, sir. For the satirical rogue says here that old men have gray beards, that their faces are wrinkled, their eyes purging thick amber and

195 plum-tree gum, and that they have a plentiful lack of wit, together with most weak hams.[48] All which, sir, though I most powerfully and potently believe, yet I hold it not honesty to have it thus set down; for yourself, sir, should be old as I am if like a crab you could go backward.

Polonius: *[Aside]* Though this be madness, yet there is method[49] in 't.—Will

200 you walk out of the air, my lord?

Hamlet: Into my grave.

Polonius: Indeed, that's out of the air. *[Aside]* How pregnant[50] sometimes his replies are! A happiness[51] that often madness hits on, which reason and sanity could not so prosperously be delivered of. I will leave him, and

205 suddenly contrive the means of meeting between him and my daughter.— My honorable lord, I will most humbly take my leave of you.

Hamlet: You cannot, sir, take from me anything that I will more willingly part withal—except my life, except my life, except my life.

Polonius: Fare you well, my lord.

---

[44] fishmonger: Hamlet is now in his "antic disposition," enjoying himself by fooling Polonius.   [45] sun . . . maggots: a general belief.   [46] god: Q_2 and F_1 read "good."   [47] carrion: flesh.   [48] hams: knee joints.   [49] method: order, sense.   [50] pregnant: apt, meaningful.   [51] happiness: good turn of phrase.

210   Hamlet: These tedious old fools!

[Enter Rosencrantz and Guildenstern.]

Polonius: You go to seek the Lord Hamlet. There he is.
Rosencrantz: *[To Polonius]* God save you, sir!

[Exit Polonius.]

Guildenstern: My honored lord!
Rosencrantz: My most dear lord!
215   Hamlet: My excellent good friends![52] How dost thou, Guildenstern? Ah,
      Rosencrantz! Good lads, how do you both?
Rosencrantz: As the indifferent[53] children of the earth.
Guildenstern: Happy in that we are not overhappy. On Fortune's cap we are
      not the very button.[54]
220   Hamlet: Nor the soles of her shoe?
Rosencrantz: Neither, my lord.
Hamlet: Then you live about her waist, or in the middle of her favors?
Guildenstern: Faith, her privates[55] we.
Hamlet: In the secret parts of Fortune? Oh, most true, she is a strumpet.
225   What's the news?
Rosencrantz: None, my lord, but that the world's grown honest.
Hamlet: Then is Doomsday near. But your news is not true. Let me question
      more in particular. What have you, my good friends, deserved at the
      hands of Fortune, that she sends you to prison hither?
230   Guildenstern: Prison, my lord!
Hamlet: Denmark's a prison.
Rosencrantz: Then is the world one.
Hamlet: A goodly one, in which there are many confines,[56] wards,[57] and dun-
      geons, Denmark being one o' the worst.
235   Rosencrantz: We think not so, my lord.
Hamlet: Why, then 'tis none to you, for there is nothing either good or bad
      but thinking makes it so. To me it is a prison.
Rosencrantz: Why, then your ambition[58] makes it one. 'Tis too narrow for
      your mind.
Hamlet: Oh, God, I could be bounded in a nutshell and count myself a king of
240   infinite space were it not that I have bad dreams.
Guildenstern: Which dreams indeed are ambition, for the very substance of
      the ambitious[59] is merely the shadow of a dream.
Hamlet: A dream itself is but a shadow.

---

[52] My . . . friends: As soon as Polonius has gone, Hamlet drops his assumed madness and
greets Rosencrantz and Guildenstern naturally.   [53] indifferent: neither too great nor too
little.   [54] button: i.e., at the top.   [55] privates: with a pun on "private parts" and "private,"
not concerned with politics.   [56] confines: places of confinement.   [57] wards:
cells.   [58] your ambition: Rosencrantz is feeling after one possible cause of Hamlet's
melancholy—thwarted ambition.   [59] substance . . . ambitious: that on which an
ambitious man feeds his fancies.

Rosencrantz: Truly, and I hold ambition of so airy and light a quality that it
245   is but a shadow's shadow.

Hamlet: Then are our beggars bodies, and our monarchs and outstretched
heroes the beggars' shadows.[60] Shall we to the Court? For, by my fay,[61] I
cannot reason.[62]

Rosencrantz & Guildenstern: We'll wait upon you.[63]

250 **Hamlet:** No such matter. I will not sort[64] you with the rest of my servants,
for, to speak to you like an honest man, I am most dreadfully attended.[65]
But in the beaten way of friendship, what make you at Elsinore?

Rosencrantz: To visit you, my lord, no other occasion.

Hamlet: Beggar that I am, I am even poor in thanks, but I thank you. And
255   sure, dear friends, my thanks are too dear a halfpenny.[66] Were you not
sent for? Is it your own inclining? Is it a free visitation?[67] Come, deal
justly with me. Come, come. Nay, speak.

Guildenstern: What should we say, my lord?

Hamlet: Why, anything, but to the purpose.[68] You were sent for, and there is
260   a kind of confession in your looks which your modesties have not craft
enough to color.[69] I know the good King and Queen have sent for you.

Rosencrantz: To what end, my lord?

Hamlet: That you must teach me. But let me conjure[70] you, by the rights of
our fellowship,[71] by the consonancy[72] of our youth, by the obligation of
265   our ever preserved love, and by what more dear a better proposer could
charge you withal, be even[73] and direct with me, whether you were sent
for, or no.

Rosencrantz: *[Aside to Guildenstern]* What say you?

Hamlet: *[Aside]* Nay, then, I have an eye of you.—
270   If you love me, hold not off.

Guildenstern: My lord, we were sent for.

Hamlet: I will tell you why. So shall my anticipation prevent your discovery,
and your secrecy to the King and Queen molt no feather.[74] I have of
late—but wherefore I know not—lost all my mirth, forgone all custom of
275   exercises, and indeed it goes so heavily with my disposition that this
goodly frame the earth seems to me a sterile promontory. This most excellent canopy,[75] the air, look you, this brave o'erhanging firmament,[76]
this majestical roof fretted[77] with golden fire—why, it appears no other

---

[60] Then . . . shadows: i.e., by your reasoning beggars are the only men of substance, for kings and heroes are by nature ambitious and therefore "the shadows of a dream." outstretched: of exaggerated reputation.   [61] fay: faith.   [62] reason: argue.   [63] wait . . . you: be your servants.   [64] sort: class.   [65] dreadfully attended: my attendants are a poor crowd.   [66] too . . . halfpenny: not worth a halfpenny.   [67] free visitation: voluntary visit.   [68] anything . . . purpose: anything so long as it is not true.   [69] color: conceal.   [70] conjure: make solemn appeal to.   [71] fellowship: comradeship. [72] consonancy: concord.   [73] even: straight.   [74] So . . . feather: i.e., so by my telling you first you will not be obliged to betray the secrets of the King. prevent: forestall. molt no feather: be undisturbed.   [75] canopy: covering.   [76] firmament: sky.   [77] fretted: ornamented.

thing to me than a foul and pestilent congregation of vapors. What a
280   piece of work is a man! How noble in reason! How infinite in faculty![78] In
form and moving[79] how express[80] and admirable! In action how like an
angel! In apprehension how like a god! The beauty of the world! The
paragon of animals! And yet, to me, what is this quintessence[81] of dust?
Man delights not me—no, nor woman neither, though by your smiling
285   you seem to say so.

Rosencrantz: My lord, there was no such stuff in my thoughts.

Hamlet: Why did you laugh, then, when I said "Man delights not me"?

Rosencrantz: To think, my lord, if you delight not in man, what lenten entertainment[82] the players shall receive from you. We coted[83] them on the way,
290   and hither are they coming to offer you service.

Hamlet: He that plays the King shall be welcome, His Majesty shall have
tribute of me. The adventurous knight shall use his foil and target,[84] the
lover shall not sigh gratis, the humorous man[85] shall end his part in
peace, the clown shall make those laugh whose lungs are tickle o' the
295   sere,[86] and the lady shall say her mind freely or the blank verse shall
halt[87] for 't. What players are they?

Rosencrantz: Even those you were wont to take such delight in, the tragedians
of the city.

Hamlet: How chances it they travel? Their residence, both in reputation and
300   profit, was better both ways.[88]

Rosencrantz: I[89] think their inhibition[90] comes by the means of the late innovation.[91]

Hamlet: Do they hold the same estimation they did when I was in the city?
Are they so followed?

Rosencrantz: No, indeed are they not.

305 Hamlet: How comes it? Do they grow rusty?

Rosencrantz: Nay, their endeavor keeps in the wonted pace.[92] But there is, sir,
an eyrie[93] of children, little eyases,[94] that cry out on the top of question[95]
and are most tyrannically[96] clapped for 't. These are now the fashion, and

---

[78] faculty: power of the mind.   [79] moving: movement.   [80] express: exact.
[81] quintessence: perfection; the fifth essence, which would be left if the four elements were
taken away.   [82] lenten entertainment: meager welcome.   [83] coted: overtook.
[84] foil . . . target: rapier and small shield.   [85] humorous man: the man who specializes in
character parts.   [86] are . . . sere: explode at a touch. The *sere* is part of the trigger
mechanism of a gun which if "ticklish" will go off at a touch.   [87] halt: limp.
[88] Their . . . ways: i.e., if they stayed in the city, it would bring them more profit and
fame.   [89] I . . . too (ll. 301–323): This reference to the stage war between the Children's
Companies is one of the several topical references in *Hamlet*.   [90] inhibition: formal
prohibition.   [91] innovation: riot.   [92] endeavor . . . pace: they try as hard as
ever.   [93] eyrie: nest.   [94] eyases: young hawks.   [95] cry . . . question: either "cry in a
shrill voice" or perhaps "cry out the latest detail of the dispute."   [96] tyrannically:
outrageously.

so berattle[97] the common stages[98]—so they call them—that many wear-
310   ing rapiers are afraid of goose quills[99] and dare scarce come thither.
Hamlet: What, are they children? Who maintains 'em? How are they escoted?[100] Will they pursue the quality[101] no longer than they can sing?
Will they not say afterward, if they should grow themselves to common
players—as it is most like if their means are no better—their writers do
315   them wrong to make them exclaim against their own succession?[102]
Rosencrantz: Faith, there has been much to-do on both sides, and the nation
holds it no sin to tarre[103] them to controversy. There was for a while no
money bid for argument[104] unless the poet and the player went to cuffs[105]
in the question.
320 **Hamlet:** Is 't possible?
Guildenstern: Oh, there has been much throwing-about of brains.
Hamlet: Do the boys carry it away?
Rosencrantz: Aye, that they do, my lord, Hercules and his load[106] too.
Hamlet: It is not very strange, for my uncle is King of Denmark, and those
325   that would make mows[107] at him while my father lived give twenty, forty,
fifty, a hundred ducats apiece for his picture in little. 'Sblood,[108] there is
something in this more than natural, if philosophy could find it out.

[Flourish of trumpets within.]

Guildenstern: There are the players.
Hamlet: Gentlemen, you are welcome to Elsinore. Your hands. Come then.
330   The appurtenance of welcome is fashion and ceremony.[109] Let me comply[110] with you in this garb,[111] lest my extent[112] to the players—which, I
tell you, must show fairly outward—should more appear like entertainment[113] than yours. You are welcome. But my uncle-father and aunt-
mother are deceived.
335 **Guildenstern:** In what, my dear lord?
Hamlet: I am but mad north-northwest.[114] When the wind is southerly,[115] I
know a hawk from a handsaw.[116]

[Re-enter Polonius.]

---

[97] **berattle:** abuse.   [98] **common stages:** the professional players. The boys acted in "private"
playhouses.   [99] **goose quills:** pens; i.e., of such as Ben Jonson.   [100] **escoted:** paid.
[101] **quality:** acting profession.   [102] **exclaim . . . succession:** abuse the profession to which
they will afterward belong.   [103] **tarre:** urge on to fight; generally used of encouraging a
dog.   [104] **argument:** plot of a play.   [105] **went to cuffs:** boxed each other's
ears.   [106] **Hercules . . . load:** Hercules carrying the globe on his shoulders was the sign of
the Globe Playhouse.   [107] **mows:** grimaces.   [108] **'Sblood:** by God's blood.
[109] **appurtenance . . . ceremony:** that which pertains to welcome is formal ceremony.
[110] **comply:** use the formality of welcome; i.e., shake hands with you.   [111] **garb:** fashion.
[112] **extent:** outward behavior.   [113] **entertainment:** welcome.   [114] **north-northwest:** i.e.,
327° (out of 360°) of the compass.   [115] **wind is southerly:** The south wind was considered
unhealthy.   [116] **hawk . . . handsaw:** Either "handsaw" is a corruption of "heronshaw,"
heron, or a hawk is a tool like a pickax. The phrase means "I'm not so mad as you think."

Polonius: Well be with you, gentlemen!

Hamlet: Hark you, Guildenstern, and you too—at each ear a hearer. That
340   great baby you see there is not yet out of his swaddling clouts.[117]

Rosencrantz: Happily he's the second time come to them, for they say an old
man is twice a child.

Hamlet: I will prophesy he comes to tell me of the players, mark it. You say
right, sir. O' Monday morning, 'twas so indeed.

345 Polonius: My lord, I have news to tell you.

Hamlet: My lord, I have news to tell you. When Roscius[118] was an actor in
Rome—

Polonius: The actors are come hither, my lord.

Hamlet: Buzz, buzz![119]

350 Polonius: Upon my honor—

Hamlet: Then came each actor on his ass—

Polonius: The[120] best actors in the world, either for tragedy, comedy, history,
pastoral, pastoral-comical, historical-pastoral, tragical-historical, tragical-
comical-historical-pastoral, scene individable[121] or poem unlimited.[122]

355   Seneca cannot be too heavy, nor Plautus[123] too light. For the law of writ[124]
and the liberty,[125] these are the only men.

Hamlet: O Jephthah,[126] judge of Israel, what a treasure hadst thou!

Polonius: What a treasure had he, my lord?

Hamlet: Why,

> "One[127] fair daughter, and no more,
> The which he lovèd passing well."

360 Polonius: *[Aside]* Still[128] on my daughter.

Hamlet: Am I not i' the right, old Jephthah?

Polonius: If you call me Jephthah, my lord, I have a daughter that I love
passing well.

Hamlet: Nay, that follows not.

365 Polonius: What follows, then, my lord?

Hamlet: Why,

> "As by lot, God wot,"[129]

and then you know,

---

[117] clouts: clothes.   [118] Roscius: the most famous of Roman actors.   [119] Buzz, buzz:
slang for "stale news."   [120] The . . . men: Polonius reads out the accomplishments of the
actors from the license which they have presented him.   [121] **scene individable:** i.e., a play
preserving the unities.   [122] **poem unlimited:** i.e., a play which disregards the rules.
[123] Seneca . . . Plautus: the Roman writers of tragedy and comedy with whose plays every
educated man was familiar.   [124] law of writ: the critical rules; i.e., classical plays.
[125] liberty: plays freely written; i.e., "modern" drama.   [126] Jephthah: The story of Jephthah
is told in Judges, Chapter II. He vowed that if successful against the Ammonites he would
sacrifice the first creature to meet him on his return, which was his daughter.
[127] One . . . was: Quotations from a ballad of Jephthah.   [128] Still: always.   [129] wot: knows.

"It came to pass, as most like it was—"
the first row[130] of the pious chanson[131] will show you more, for look
370   where my abridgement[132] comes. *[Enter four or five Players.]* You are
welcome, masters, welcome all. I am glad to see thee well. Welcome,
good friends. Oh, my old friend![133] Why, thy face is valanced[134] since I saw
thee last. Comest thou to beard[135] me in Denmark? What, my young
lady[136] and mistress! By 'r Lady, your ladyship is nearer to Heaven than
375   when I saw you last, by the altitude of a chopine.[137] Pray God your voice,
like a piece of uncurrent gold, be not cracked within the ring.[138] Masters,
you are all welcome. We'll e'en to 't like French falconers,[139] fly at anything we see. We'll have a speech straight. Come, give us a taste of your
quality[140]—come, a passionate speech.
380 **I. Player:** What speech, my good lord?
Hamlet: I heard thee speak me a speech once, but it was never acted, or if it
was, not above once; for the play, I remember, pleased not the million,
'twas caviar[141] to the general.[142] But it was—as I received it, and others,
whose judgments in such matters cried in the top of mine[143]—an excel-
385   lent play, well digested[144] in the scenes, set down with as much modesty[145] as cunning. I remember one said there were no sallets[146] in the
lines to make the matter savory, nor no matter in the phrase that might
indict the author of affection,[147] but called it an honest method, as
wholesome as sweet, and by very much more handsome than fine.[148] One
390   speech in it I chiefly loved. 'Twas Aeneas' tale to Dido,[149] and thereabout
of it especially where he speaks of Priam's[150] slaughter. If it lives in your
memory, begin at this line—let me see, let me see—

"The rugged Pyrrhus,[151] like th' Hyrcanian beast,[152]—"
It is not so. It begins with "Pyrrhus."

---

[130] **row:** line.   [131] **pious chanson:** godly poem.   [132] **abridgement:** entertainment.
[133] **old friend:** i.e., the leading player.   [134] **valanced:** bearded. A valance is a fringe hung
round the sides and bottom of a bed.   [135] **beard:** dare, with a pun on "valanced."
[136] **young lady:** i.e., the boy who takes the woman's parts.   [137] **chopine:**
lady's shoe with thick cork sole.   [138] **cracked . . . ring:** Before coins were milled on the
rim they were liable to crack. When the crack reached the ring surrounding the device,
the coin was no longer valid.   [139] **French falconers:** They were famous for their skill in
hawking.   [140] **quality:** skill as an actor.   [141] **caviar:** sturgeon's roe, a Russian delicacy not
then appreciated (or known) by any but gourmets.   [142] **general:** common herd.
[143] **cried . . . mine:** surpassed mine.   [144] **digested:** composed.   [145] **modesty:**
moderation.   [146] **sallets:** tasty bits.   [147] **phrase . . . affection:** nothing in the language
which could charge the author with affectation.   [148] **fine:** subtle.   [149] **Aeneas' . . . Dido:**
the story of the sack of Troy as told by Aeneas to Dido, Queen of Carthage. The original is in
Virgil's *Aeneid*. A similar speech occurs in Marlowe's play *Dido, Queen of Carthage*.
[150] **Priam:** the old King of Troy.   [151] **Pyrrhus:** the son of Achilles, one of the Greeks
concealed in the Wooden Horse.   [152] **Hyrcanian beast:** the tiger.

395   "The[153] rugged Pyrrhus, he whose sable[154] arms,
Black as his purpose, did the night resemble
When he lay couchèd in the ominous[155] horse,[156]
Hath now this dread and black complexion smeared
With heraldry[157] more dismal. Head to foot
400   Now is he total gules, horridly tricked
With blood of fathers, mothers, daughters, sons,
Baked and impasted[158] with the parching streets
That lend a tyrannous and a damnèd light
To their lord's murder. Roasted in wrath and fire,
405   And thus o'ersized with coagulate gore,[159]
With eyes like carbuncles, the hellish Pyrrhus
Old grandsire Priam seeks."
So, proceed you.
Polonius: 'Fore God, my lord, well spoken, with good accent and good discretion.
I. Player: "Anon he finds him
410   Striking too short at Greeks. His antique sword,
Rebellious to his arm, lies where it falls,
Repugnant to command.[160] Unequal matched,
415   Pyrrhus at Priam drives, in rage strikes wide,
But with the whiff and wind of his fell sword
The unnerved father falls. Then senseless Ilium,[161]
Seeming to feel this blow, with flaming top
Stoops to his base,[162] and with a hideous crash
420   Takes prisoner Pyrrhus' ear. For, lo! his sword,
Which was declining[163] on the milky[164] head
Of reverend Priam, seemed i' the air to stick.
So as a painted tyrant[165] Pyrrhus stood,
And like a neutral to his will and matter,[166]
425   Did nothing.
But as we often see, against[167] some storm
A silence in the heavens, the rack[168] stand still,
The bold winds speechless and the orb[169] below

---

[153] **The . . . gods:** The speech may be from some lost play of *Dido and Aeneas,* but more likely it is Shakespeare's own invention. It is written in the heavy elaborate style still popular in the dramas of the Admiral's Men. The first player delivers it with excessive gesture and emotion.   [154] **sable:** black.   [155] **ominous:** fateful.   [156] **horse:** the Wooden Horse by which a small Greek force was enabled to make a secret entry into Troy.
[157] **heraldry:** painting. The image of heraldic painting is kept up in *gules* (the heraldic term for red) and *tricked* (painted).   [158] **impasted:** turned into a crust by the heat of the burning city.   [159] **o'ersized . . . gore:** covered over with congealed blood.   [160] **Repugnant to command:** refusing to be used.   [161] **Ilium:** the citadel of Troy.   [162] **stoops . . . base:** collapses.   [163] **declining:** bending toward.   [164] **milky:** milk-white.   [165] **painted tyrant:** as in the painting of a tyrant.   [166] **neutral . . . matter:** one midway (*neutral*) between his desire (*will*) and action (*matter*).   [167] **against:** just before.   [168] **rack:** the clouds in the upper air.   [169] **orb:** world.

As hush as death, anon the dreadful thunder
430   Doth rend the region[170]—so after Pyrrhus' pause
Arousèd vengeance sets him new awork.
And never did the Cyclops'[171] hammers fall
On Mars's armor, forged for proof eterne,[172]
With less remorse[173] than Pyrrhus' bleeding sword
435   Now falls on Priam.
Out, out, thou strumpet, Fortune! All you gods,
In general synod[174] take away her power,
Break all the spokes and fellies[175] from her wheel,
And bowl the round nave[176] down the hill of Heaven
440   As low as to the fiends!"

Polonius: This is too long.

Hamlet: It shall to the barber's, with your beard. Prithee, say on. He's for a
     jig[177] or a tale of bawdry, or he sleeps. Say on. Come to Hecuba.

I. Player: "But who, oh, who had seen the mobled[178] Queen—"

445 **Hamlet:** "The mobled Queen"?

Polonius: That's good, "mobled Queen" is good.

I. Player: "Run barefoot up and down, threatening the flames
With bisson rheum,[179] a clout[180] upon that head
Where late the diadem stood, and for a robe,
450   About her lank and all o'erteemed[181] loins
A blanket, in the alarm of fear caught up.
Who this had seen, with tongue in venom steeped
'Gainst Fortune's state would treason have pronounced.[182]
But if the gods themselves did see her then,
455   When she saw Pyrrhus make malicious sport
In mincing with his sword her husband's limbs,
The instant burst of clamor that she made,
Unless things mortal move them not at all,
Would have made milch[183] the burning eyes of Heaven
460   And passion in the gods."

Polonius: Look whether he has not turned his color and has tears in 's
     Prithee, no more.

Hamlet: 'Tis well; I'll have thee speak out the rest of this soon. Good my lord,
     will you see the players well bestowed?[184] Do you hear, let them be well

---

[170] region: the country round.   [171] Cyclops': of Titans, giants who aided Vulcan, the
blacksmith god, to make armor for Mars, the war god.   [172] proof eterne: everlasting
protection.   [173] remorse: pity.   [174] synod: council.   [175] fellies: the pieces forming the
circumference of a wooden wheel.   [176] nave: center of the wheel.   [177] jig: bawdy dance.
[178] mobled: muffled.   [179] bisson rheum: blinding moisture.   [180] clout: rag.
[181] o'erteemed: exhausted by bearing children; she had borne fifty-two.   [182] Who
. . . pronounced: anyone who had seen this sight would with bitter words have uttered
treason against the tyranny of Fortune.   [183] milch: milky, i.e., dripping moisture.
[184] bestowed: housed.

465   used, for they are the abstract and brief chronicles of the time.[185] After
      your death you were better have a bad epitaph than their ill report while
      you live.

Polonius: My lord, I will use them according to their desert.[186]

Hamlet: God's bodykins,[187] man, much better. Use every man after his desert
470   and who shall 'scape whipping? Use them after your own honor and dig-
      nity. The less they deserve, the more merit is in your bounty. Take them in.

Polonius: Come, sirs.

Hamlet: Follow him, friends. We'll hear a play tomorrow. *[Exit Polonius with
      all the Players but the First.]* Dost thou hear me, old friend? Can you
475   play *The Murder of Gonzago?*

I. Player: Aye, my lord.

Hamlet: We'll ha 't tomorrow night. You could, for a need, study a speech of
      some dozen or sixteen lines which I would set down and insert in 't, could
      you not?

480 I. Player: Aye, my lord.

Hamlet: Very well. Follow that lord, and look you mock him not. *[Exit First
      Player.]* My good friends, I'll leave you till night. You are welcome to
      Elsinore.

Rosencrantz: Good my lord!

485 Hamlet: Aye, so, God be wi' ye! *[Exeunt Rosencrantz and Guildenstern.]*
      Now I am alone.

      Oh, what a rogue and peasant slave am I!
      Is it not monstrous that this player here,
      But in a fiction, in a dream of passion,[188]
490   Could force his soul so to his own conceit[189]
      That from her working[190] all his visage wanned,[191]
      Tears in his eyes, distraction[192] in 's aspect,[193]
      A broken voice, and his whole function[194] suiting
      With forms to his conceit? And all for nothing!
495   For Hecuba!
      What's Hecuba to him or he to Hecuba,
      That he should weep for her? What would he do
      Had he the motive and the cue for passion
      That I have? He would drown the stage with tears
500   And cleave the general ear[195] with horrid speech,
      Make mad the guilty and appal the free,[196]

---

[185] abstract . . . time: they summarize and record the events of our time. Elizabethan players
were often in trouble for too saucily commenting on their betters in plays dealing with history
or contemporary events and persons.   [186] desert: rank.   [187] God's bodykins: by God's little
body.   [188] dream of passion: imaginary emotion.   [189] conceit: imagination.   [190] her
working: i.e., the effect of imagination.   [191] wanned: went pale.   [192] distraction: frenzy.
[193] aspect: countenance.   [194] function: behavior.   [195] general ear: ears of the audience.
[196] free: innocent.

Confound the ignorant, and amaze indeed
The very faculties of eyes and ears.
Yet I,
505   A dull and muddy-mettled[197] rascal, peak,[198]
Like John-a-dreams,[199] unpregnant of my cause,[200]
And can say nothing—no, not for a King
Upon whose property[201] and most dear life
A damned defeat[202] was made. Am I a coward?
510   Who[203] calls me villain? Breaks my pate across?
Plucks off my beard and blows it in my face?
Tweaks me by the nose? Gives me the lie i' the throat
As deep as to the lungs? Who does me this?
Ha!
515   'Swounds,[204] I should take it. For it cannot be
But I am pigeon-livered[205] and lack gall[206]
To make oppression bitter, or ere this
I should have fatted all the region kites
With this slave's offal.[207] Bloody, bawdy villain!
520   Remorseless, treacherous, lecherous, kindless[208] villain!
Oh, vengeance!
Why, what an ass am I! This is most brave,
That I, the son of a dear father murdered,
Prompted to my revenge by Heaven and Hell,
525   Must, like a whore, unpack my heart with words
And fall a-cursing like a very drab,[209]
A scullion![210]
Fie upon 't! Foh! About, my brain! Hum, I have heard
That guilty creatures sitting at a play
530   Have by the very cunning of the scene
Been struck so to the soul that presently[211]
They have proclaimed their malefactions;[212]
For murder, though it have no tongue, will speak
With most miraculous organ. I'll have these players
535   Play something like the murder of my father
Before mine uncle. I'll observe his looks,
I'll tent[213] him to the quick. If he but blench,[214]

---

[197]muddy-mettled: made of mud, not iron.   [198]peak: mope.   [199]John-a-dreams: "Sleepy Sam."   [200]unpregnant . . . cause: barren of plans for vengeance.   [201]property: personality, life.   [202]defeat: ruin.   [203]Who . . . this: Hamlet runs through all the insults which provoked a resolute man to mortal combat. pate: head. lie . . . throat: the bitterest of insults.   [204]'Swounds: by God's wounds.   [205]pigeon-livered: "as gentle as a dove."   [206]gall: spirit.   [207]I . . . offal: before this I would have fed this slave's (i.e., the King's) guts to the kites. fatted: made fat.   [208]kindless: unnatural.   [209]drab: "moll."   [210]scullion: the lowest of the kitchen servants.   [211]presently: immediately.   [212]proclaimed . . . malefactions: shouted out their crimes.   [213]tent: probe.   [214]blench: flinch.

I know my course. The spirit that I have seen
May be the Devil, and the Devil hath power
540   To assume a pleasing shape. Yea, and perhaps
Out of my weakness and my melancholy,
As he is very potent with such spirits,
Abuses me to damn me.[215] I'll have grounds[216]
More relative than this.[217] The play's the thing
545   Wherein I'll catch the conscience of the King.

[Exit.]

Act III

Scene I. A room in the castle.

[Enter King, Queen, Polonius, Ophelia, Rosencrantz, and Guildenstern.]

King: And can you, by no drift of circumstance,[1]
Get from him why he puts on this confusion,
Grating[2] so harshly all his days of quiet
With turbulent and dangerous lunacy?
5 **Rosencrantz:** He does confess he feels himself distracted,
But from what cause he will by no means speak.
Guildenstern: Nor do we find him forward to be sounded,[3]
But, with a crafty madness, keeps aloof
When we would bring him on to some confession
Of his true state.
10 **Queen:**   Did he receive you well?
Rosencrantz: Most like a gentleman.
Guildenstern: But with much forcing of his disposition.[4]
Rosencrantz: Niggard of question,[5] but of our demands
Most free in his reply.
Queen: Did you assay him
15   To any pastime?[6]
Rosencrantz: Madam, it so fell out that certain players
We o'erraught[7] on the way. Of these we told him,
And there did seem in him a kind of joy
To hear of it. They are about the Court,

---

[215] **Abuses . . . me:** i.e., deceives me so that I may commit the sin of murder which will bring me to damnation.   [216] **grounds:** reasons for action.   [217] **relative . . . this:** i.e., more convincing than the appearance of a ghost.
[1] **drift of circumstance:** circumstantial evidence, hint.   [2] **grating:** disturbing.
[3] **forward . . . sounded:** eager to be questioned.   [4] **much . . . disposition:** making a great effort to be civil to us.   [5] **Niggard of question:** not asking many questions.
[6] **Did . . . pastime:** did you try to interest him in any amusement.   [7] **o'erraught:** overtook.

20   And, as I think, they have already order
        This night to play before him.
Polonius: 'Tis most true.
        And he beseeched me to entreat your Majesties
        To hear and see the matter.
King: With all my heart, and it doth much content me
25   To hear him so inclined.
        Good gentlemen, give him a further edge,[8]
        And drive his purpose on to these delights.
Rosencrantz: We shall, my lord.
                              [Exeunt Rosencrantz and Guildenstern.]

King: Sweet Gertrude, leave us too,
        For we have closely[9] sent for Hamlet hither,
30   That he, as 'twere by accident, may here
        Affront[10] Ophelia.
        Her father and myself, lawful espials,[11]
        Will so bestow ourselves that, seeing unseen,
        We may of their encounter frankly judge
35   And gather by him, as he is behaved,[12]
        If 't be the affliction of his love or no
        That thus he suffers for.
Queen: I shall obey you.
        And for your part, Ophelia, I do wish
        That your good beauties be the happy cause
40   Of Hamlet's wildness. So shall I hope your virtues
        Will bring him to his wonted way[13] again,
        To both your honors.
Ophelia: Madam, I wish it may.   *[Exit Queen]*
Polonius: Ophelia, walk you here. Gracious,[14] so please you,
        We will bestow outselves. *[To Ophelia]* Read on this book,[15]
45   That show of such an exercise may color
        Your loneliness. We are oft to blame in this—
        'Tis too much proved—that with devotion's visage[16]
        And pious action we do sugar o'er
        The Devil himself.
King: *[Aside]* Oh, 'tis too true!
50   How smart a lash that speech doth give my conscience!
        The harlot's cheek, beautied with plastering art,
        Is not more ugly to the thing that helps it[17]

---

[8] edge: encouragement.   [9] closely: secretly.   [10] Affront: encounter.   [11] lawful espials:
who are justified in spying on him.   [12] by . . . behaved: from him, from his behavior.
[13] wonted way: normal state.   [14] Gracious: your Majesty—addressed to the King.
[15] book: i.e., of devotions.   [16] devotion's visage: an outward appearance of religion.
[17] ugly . . . it: i.e., lust, which is the cause of its artificial beauty.

Than is my deed to my most painted[18] word.
Oh, heavy burden!

55 **Polonius:** I hear him coming. Let's withdraw, my lord.

[Exeunt King and Polonius.]
[Enter Hamlet. [19]]

Hamlet: To be, or not to be—that is the question.
Whether 'tis nobler in the mind to suffer
The slings and arrows of outrageous[20] fortune,
Or to take arms against a sea[21] of troubles
60 And by opposing end them. To die, to sleep—
No more, and by a sleep to say we end
The heartache and the thousand natural shocks
That flesh is heir to. 'Tis a consummation[22]
Devoutly to be wished. To die, to sleep,
65 To sleep—perchance to dream. Aye, there's the rub,[23]
For in that sleep of death what dreams may come
When we have shuffled off this mortal coil[24]
Must give us pause. There's the respect[25]
That makes calamity of so long life.[26]
70 For who would bear the whips and scorns of time,
The oppressor's wrong, the proud man's contumely[27]
The pangs of déspised love, the law's delay,
The insolence of office[28] and the spurns
That patient merit of the unworthy takes,[29]
75 When he himself might his quietus[30] make
With a bare bodkin?[31] Who would fardels[32] bear,
To grunt and sweat under a weary life,
But that the dread of something after death,
The undiscovered country from whose bourn[33]
80 No traveler returns, puzzles the will,[34]
And makes us rather bear those ills we have
Than fly to others that we know not of?
Thus[35] conscience does make cowards of us all,

---

[18] painted: i.e., false.   [19] Enter Hamlet: In Q_1 the King draws attention to Hamlet's approach with the words "See where he comes poring upon a book." Hamlet is again reading, and is too much absorbed to notice Ophelia.   [20] outrageous: cruel.   [21] sea: i.e., an endless turmoil.   [22] consummation: completion.   [23] rub: impediment. See App. 13.
[24] shuffled . . . coil: cast off this fuss of life.   [25] respect: reason.   [26] makes . . . life: makes it a calamity to have to live so long.   [27] contumely: insulting behavior.
[28] insolence of office: insolent behavior of government officials.   [29] spurns . . . takes: insults which men of merit have patiently to endure from the unworthy.   [30] quietus: discharge.   [31] bodkin: dagger.   [32] fardels: burdens, the coolie pack.
[33] bourn: boundary.   [34] will: resolution, ability to act.   [35] Thus . . . action: the religious fear that death may not be the end makes men shrink from heroic actions.

And thus the native hue[36] of resolution
85   Is sicklied o'er with the pale cast[37] of thought,
And enterprises of great pitch[38] and moment
With this regard their currents turn awry
And lose the name of action.[39]—Soft you now!
The fair Ophelia! Nymph, in thy orisons[40]
90   Be all my sins remembered.

Ophelia: Good my lord,
How does your Honor for this many a day?
Hamlet: I humbly thank you—well, well, well.
Ophelia: My lord, I have remembrances of yours
That I have longed long to redeliver.
95   I pray you now receive them.
Hamlet: No, not I.
I never gave you aught.
Ophelia: My honored lord, you know right well you did,
And with them words of so sweet breath composed
As made the things more rich. Their perfume lost,
100   Take these again, for to the noble mind
Rich gifts wax poor when givers prove unkind.
There, my lord.
Hamlet: Ha, ha! Are you honest?[41]
Ophelia: My lord?
105 Hamlet: Are you fair?
Ophelia: What means your lordship?
Hamlet: That if you be honest and fair, your honesty should admit no discourse to your beauty.[42]
Ophelia: Could beauty, my lord, have better commerce than with honesty?
110 Hamlet: Aye, truly, for the power of beauty will sooner transform honesty from what it is to a bawd[43] than the force of honesty can translate beauty into his likeness. This was sometime a paradox,[44] but now the time gives it proof. I did love you once.
Ophelia: Indeed, my lord, you made me believe so.
115 Hamlet: You should not have believed me, for virtue cannot so inoculate our old stock but we shall relish[45] of it. I loved you not.
Ophelia: I was the more deceived.
Hamlet: Get thee to a nunnery. Why wouldst thou be a breeder of sinners? I am myself indifferent honest,[46] but yet I could accuse me of such things

---

[36] native hue: natural color.   [37] cast: color.   [38] pitch: height; used of the soaring flight of a hawk.   [39] With . . . action: by brooding on this thought great enterprises are diverted from their course and fade away.   [40] orisons: prayers.   [41] honest: chaste.
[42] That . . . beauty: if you are chaste and beautiful your chastity should have nothing to do with your beauty—because (so Hamlet thinks in his bitterness) beautiful women are seldom chaste.   [43] bawd: brothel-keeper.   [44] paradox: statement contrary to accepted opinion.
[45] relish: have some trace.   [46] indifferent honest: moderately honorable.

120   that it were better my mother had not borne me. I am very proud, re-
vengeful, ambitious, with more offenses at my beck[47] than I have
thoughts to put them in, imagination to give them shape, or time to act
them in. What should such fellows as I do crawling between heaven and
earth? We are arrant knaves all. Believe none of us. Go thy ways to a nun-
125   nery.[48] Where's your father?

Ophelia: At home, my lord.

Hamlet: Let the doors be shut upon him, that he may play the fool nowhere
but in 's own house. Farewell.

Ophelia: Oh, help him, you sweet Heavens!

130   Hamlet: I thou dost marry, I'll give thee this plague for thy dowry: Be thou as
chaste as ice, as pure as snow—thou shalt not escape calumny.[49] Get thee
to a nunnery, go. Farewell. Or if thou wilt needs marry, marry a fool, for
wise men know well enough what monsters[50] you make of them. To a
nunnery, go, and quickly too. Farewell.

135   Ophelia: O heavenly powers, restore him!

Hamlet: I have heard of your paintings[51] too, well enough. God hath given you
one face and you make yourselves another. You jig,[52] you amble,[53] and
you lisp,[54] and nickname God's creatures, and make your wantonness
your ignorance.[55] Go to, I'll no more on 't—it hath made me mad. I say

140   we will have no more marriages. Those that are married already, all but
one, shall live; the rest shall keep as they are. To a nunnery, go.   *[Exit.]*

Ophelia: Oh, what a noble mind is here o'erthrown!
The courtier's, soldier's, scholar's, eye, tongue, sword—
The expectancy and rose[56] of the fair state,

145   The glass[57] of fashion and the mold of form,[58]
The observed of all observers—quite, quite down!
And I, of ladies most deject and wretched,
That sucked the honey of his music vows,
Now see that noble and most sovereign reason,

150   Like sweet bells jangled, out of tune and harsh,
That unmatched[59] form and feature of blown[60] youth
Blasted with ecstasy.[61] Oh, woe is me,
To have seen what I have seen, see what I see!

[Re-enter King and Polonius.]

---

[47] at . . . beck: waiting to come when I beckon.   [48] nunnery: i.e., a place where she will
be removed from temptation.   [49] calumny: slander.   [50] monsters: horned beasts,
cuckolds.   [51] paintings: using make-up.   [52] jig: dance lecherously.
[53] amble: walk artificially.   [54] lisp: talk affectedly.   [55] nickname . . . ignorance: give
things indecent names and pretend to be too simple to understand their meanings.
[56] expectancy . . . rose: bright hope. The rose is used as a symbol for beauty and perfection.
[57] glass: mirror.   [58] mold of form: perfect pattern of manly beauty.
[59] unmatched: unmatchable.   [60] blown: perfect, like an open flower at its best.
[61] Blasted . . . ecstasy: ruined by madness.

King: Love! His affections[62] do not that way tend,
155   Nor what he spake, though it lacked form a little,
      Was not like madness. There's something in his soul
      O'er which his melancholy sits on brood,[63]
      And I do doubt the hatch and the disclose[64]
      Will be some danger. Which for to prevent,
160   I have in quick determination
      Thus set it down: He shall with speed to England,
      For the demand of our neglected tribute.
      Haply[65] the seas and countries different
      With variable objects[66] shall expel
165   This something-settled[67] matter in his heart
      Whereon his brains still beating puts him thus
      From fashion of himself.[68] What think you on 't?
Polonius: It shall do well. But yet do I believe
      The origin and commencement of his grief
170   Sprung from neglected love. How now, Ophelia!
      You need not tell us what Lord Hamlet said,
      We heard it all. My lord, do as you please,
      But, if you hold it fit, after the play
      Let his Queen mother all alone entreat him
175   To show his grief. Let her be round[69] with him,
      And I'll be placed, so please you, in the ear
      Of all their conference. If she find him not,
      To England send him, or confine him where
      Your wisdom best shall think.
King: It shall be so.
180   Madness in great ones must not unwatched go.

[Exeunt.]

Scene II. A hall in the castle.

[Enter Hamlet and Players.]

Hamlet: Speak the speech,[1] I pray you, as I pronounced it to you, trippingly[2] on the tongue. But if you mouth[3] it, as many of your players do, I had as

---

[62] affections: state of mind.   [63] sits . . . brood: sits hatching.   [64] doubt . . . disclose: suspect the brood which will result.   [65] Haply: perhaps.   [66] variable objects: novel sights.   [67] something-settled: somewhat settled; i.e., not yet incurable.   [68] puts . . . himself: i.e., separates him from his normal self.   [69] round: direct.
[1] the speech: which he has written. The whole passage which follows is Shakespeare's own comment on the actor's art and states the creed and practice of his company as contrasted with the more violent methods of Edward Alleyn and his fellows.   [2] trippingly: smoothly, easily.   [3] mouth: "ham" it.

lief[4] the town crier spoke my lines. Nor do not saw the air too much with your hand, thus, but use all gently. For in the very torrent, tempest, and,
5   as I may say, whirlwind of passion, you must acquire and beget a temperance that may give it smoothness. Oh, it offends me to the soul to hear a robustious[5] peri-wig-pated[6] fellow tear a passion to tatters, to very rags, to split the ears of the groundlings,[7] who for the most part are capable of nothing but inexplicable dumb shows[8] and noise. I would have such a
10   fellow whipped for o'erdoing Termagant[9]—it out-Herods Herod. Pray you, avoid it.

I. Player: I warrant your Honor.

Hamlet: Be not too tame neither, but let your own discretion be your tutor. Suit the action to the word, the word to the action, with this special ob-
15   servance, that you o'erstep not the modesty of nature. For anything so overdone is from[10] the purpose of playing, whose end, both at the first and now, was and is to hold as 'twere the mirror up to Nature—to show Virtue her own feature, scorn her own image, and the very age and body of the time his form and pressure.[11] Now this overdone or come tardy off,
20   thought it make the unskillful laugh, cannot but make the judicious grieve, the censure of the which one[12] must in your allowance o'erweigh a whole theater of others. Oh, there be players[13] that I have seen play, and heard others praise—and that highly, not to speak it profanely—that neither having the accent of Christians nor the gait of Christian, pagan, nor
25   man, have so strutted and bellowed that I have thought some of Nature's journeymen[14] had made men, and not made them well, they imitated humanity so abominably.

I. Player: I hope we have reformed that indifferently[15] with us, sir.

Hamlet: Oh, reform it altogether. And let those that play your clowns[16] speak
30   no more than is set down for them. For there be of them that will themselves laugh, to set on some quantity of barren spectators to laugh too, though in the meantime some necessary question of the play be then

---

[4] lief: soon.   [5] robustious: ranting.   [6] periwig-pated: wearing a wig.   [7] groundings: the poorer spectators, who stood in the yard of the playhouse.   [8] dumb shows: an old-fashioned dramatic device, still being used by the Admiral's Men: before a tragedy, and sometimes before each act, the characters mimed the action which was to follow.
[9] Termagant: God of the Saracens, who, like Herod, was presented in early stage plays as a roaring tyrant.   [10] from: contrary to.   [11] very . . . pressure: an exact reproduction of the age. form: shape. pressure: imprint (of a seal).   [12] the . . . one: i.e., the judicious spectator.   [13] there . . . players: An obvious attack on Alleyn.   [14] journeymen: hired workmen, not masters of the trade.   [15] indifferently: moderately.   [16] those . . . clowns: A hit at Will Kempe, the former clown of Shakespeare's company. Q₁ adds the passage "And then you have some again that keep one suit of jests, as a man is known by one suit of apparel, and gentlemen quote his jests down in their tables before they come to the play, as thus: 'Cannot you stay till I eat my porridge?' and 'You owe me a quarter's wages,' and 'My coat wants a cullison,' and 'Your beer is sour,' and blabbering with his lips, and thus keeping in his cinquepace of jests, when God knows the warm clown cannot make a jest unless by chance, as the blind man catcheth a hare. Masters tell him of it."

to be considered. That's villainous, and shows a most pitiful[17] ambition
in the fool that uses it. Go, make you ready. *[Exeunt Players. Enter*
35   *Polonius, Rosencrantz, and Guildenstern.]* How now, my lord! Will the
King hear this piece of work?

Polonius: And the Queen too, and that presently.

Hamlet: Bid the players make haste. *[Exit Polonius.]* Will you two help to hasten them?

40   **Rosencrantz & Guildenstern:** We will, my lord.

[Exeunt Rosencrantz and Guildenstern.]

Hamlet: What ho! Horatio!

[Enter Horatio.]

Horatio: Here, sweet lord, at your service.

Hamlet: Horatio, thou art e'en as just a man
As e'er my conversation coped[18] withal.

45   Horatio: Oh, my dear lord—

Hamlet: Nay, do not think I flatter,
For what advancement[19] may I hope from thee,
That no revénue hast but thy good spirits
To feed and clothe thee? Why should the poor be flattered?
No, let the candied[20] tongue lick absurd pomp
50   And crook the pregnant hinges of the knee
Where thrift may follow fawning.[21] Dost thou hear?
Since my dear soul was mistress of her choice
And could of men distinguish, her election
Hath sealed[22] thee for herself. For thou hast been
55   As one in suffering all that suffers nothing,
A man that fortune's buffets and rewards
Hast ta'en with equal thanks. And blest are those
Whose blood and judgment are so well commingled
That they are not a pipe[23] for fortune's finger
60   To sound what stop she please. Give me that man
That is not passion's slave, and I will wear him
In my heart's core—aye, in my heart of heart,
As I do thee. Something too much of this.
There is a play tonight before the King.
65   One scene of it comes near the circumstance
Which I have told thee of my father's death.
I prithee when thou seest that act afoot,

---

[17] pitiful: contemptible.   [18] coped: met.   [19] advancement: promotion.   [20] candied:
sugared over with hypocrisy.   [21] crook . . . fawning: bend the ready knees whenever gain
will follow flattery.   [22] sealed: set a mark on.   [23] pipe: an instrument that varies its
notes.

Even with the very comment[24] of thy soul
Observe my uncle. If his occulted[25] guilt
70   Do not itself unkennel[26] in one speech
It is a damnèd ghost[27] that we have seen
And my imaginations are as foul
As Vulcan's[28] stithy.[29] Give him heedful note,[30]
For I mine eyes will rivet to his face,
75   And after we will both our judgments join
In censure of his seeming.[31]
Horatio: Well, my lord.
If he steal aught the whilst this play is playing,
And 'scape detecting, I will pay the theft.
Hamlet: They are coming to the play. I must be idle.[32]
80   Get you a place.

*[Danish march. A flourish. Enter King, Queen, Polonius, Ophelia,
Rosencrantz, Guildenstern, and other Lords attendant, with the Guard
carrying torches.]*

King: How fares our cousin Hamlet?
Hamlet: Excellent, i' faith, of the chameleon's dish. I eat the air, promise-
crammed. You cannot feed capons so.[33]
King: I have nothing with this answer,[34] Hamlet. These words are not mine.
85   **Hamlet:** No, nor mine now.[35] *[To Polonius]* My lord, you played once i' the
university, you say?
Polonius: That did I, my lord, and was accounted a good actor.
Hamlet: What did you enact?
Polonius: I did enact Julius Caesar. I was killed i' the Capitol. Brutus killed
me.
90   **Hamlet:** It was a brute part of him to kill so capital a calf there. Be the play-
ers ready?
Rosencrantz: Aye, my lord, they stay upon your patience.[36]
Queen: Come hither, my dear Hamlet, sit by me.
Hamlet: No, good Mother, here's metal more attractive.
95   **Polonius:** *[To the King]* Oh ho! Do you mark that?
Hamlet: Lady, shall I lie in your lap?

[Lying down at Ophelia's feet]

---

[24] **comment:** close observation.   [25] **occulted:** concealed.   [26] **unkennel:** come to light;
lit., force a fox from his hole.   [27] **damned ghost:** evil spirit.   [28] **Vulcan:** the blacksmith
god.   [29] **stithy:** smithy.   [30] **heedful note:** careful observation.   [31] **censure . . .
seeming:** judgment on his looks.   [32] **be idle:** seem crazy.   [33] **Excellent . . . so:** Hamlet
takes "fare" literally as "what food are you eating." The chameleon was supposed to feed on
air. **promise-crammed:** stuffed, like a fattened chicken (*capon*)—but with empty promises.
[34] **I . . . answer:** I cannot make any sense of your answer.   [35] **nor . . . now:** i.e., once
words have left the lips they cease to belong to the speaker.   [36] **stay . . . patience:** wait for
you to be ready.

Ophelia: No, my lord.

Hamlet: I mean, my head upon your lap?

Ophelia: Aye, my lord.

100 **Hamlet:** Do you think I meant country matters?[37]

Ophelia: I think nothing, my lord.

Hamlet: That's a fair thought to lie between maids' legs.

Ophelia: What is, my lord?

Hamlet: Nothing.

105 **Ophelia:** You are merry, my lord.

Hamlet: Who, I?

Ophelia: Aye, my lord.

Hamlet: Oh God, your only jig-maker.[38] What should a man do but be merry? For look you how cheerfully my mother looks, and my father died within

110   's two hours.

Ophelia: Nay, 'tis twice two months, my lord.

Hamlet: So long? Nay, then, let the Devil wear black, for I'll have a suit of sables.[39] Oh heavens! Die two months ago, and not forgotten yet? Then there's hope a great man's memory may outlive his life half a year. But,

215   by 'r Lady, he must build churches then, or else shall he suffer not thinking on, with the hobbyhorse,[40] whose epitaph is "For, oh, for oh, the hobbyhorse is forgot."

[Hautboys[41] play. The dumb show enters.[42] Enter a King and a Queen very lovingly, the Queen embracing him and he her. She kneels, and makes show of protestation unto him. He takes her up, and declines his head upon her neck, lays him down upon a bank of flowers. She, seeing him asleep, leaves him. Anon comes in a fellow, takes off his crown, kisses it, and pours poison in the King's ears, and exit. The Queen returns, finds the King dead, and makes passionate action. The Poisoner, with some two or three Mutes, comes in again, seeming to lament with her. The dead body is carried away. The Poisoner woos the Queen with gifts. She seems loath and unwilling awhile, but in the end accepts his love.   Exeunt.]

Ophelia: What means this, my lord?

Hamlet: Marry, this is miching mallecho.[43] It means mischief.

220 **Ophelia:** Belike this show imports the argument[44] of the play.

---

[37] **country matters:** something indecent.   [38] **jig-maker:** composer of jigs.   [39] **suit of sables:** a quibble on "sable," black, and "sable," gown trimmed with sable fur, worn by wealthy old gentlemen.   [40] **hobbyhorse:** imitation horse worn by performers in a morris dance, an amusement much disapproved of by the godly.   [41] **Hautboys:** oboes.   [42] **The dumb show enters:** Critics have been disturbed because this dumb show cannot be exactly paralleled in any other Elizabethan play, and because the King is apparently not disturbed by it. Shakespeare's intention, however, in presenting a play within a play is to produce something stagy and artificial compared with the play proper. Moreover, as Hamlet has already complained, dumb shows were often inexplicable.   [43] **miching mallecho:** slinking mischief.   [44] **argument:** plot. She too is puzzled by the dumb show.

[Enter Prologue.]

Hamlet: We shall know by this fellow. The players cannot keep counsel, they'll tell all.

Ophelia: Will he tell us what this show meant?

Hamlet: Aye, or any show that you'll show him. Be not you ashamed to show,
225   he'll not shame to tell you what it means.

Ophelia: You are naught,[45] you are naught. I'll mark the play.

Prologue: For us, and for our tragedy,
            Here stooping to your clemency,
            We beg your hearing patiently.
230 Hamlet: Is this a prologue, or the posy of a ring?[46]

Ophelia: 'Tis brief, my lord.

Hamlet: As woman's love.

[Enter two Players, King and Queen]

Player King: Full[47] thirty times hath Phoebus' cart[48] gone round
            Neptune's[49] salt wash and Tellus'[50] orbèd ground,
235   And thirty dozen moons with borrowed sheen[51]
            About the world have times twelve thirties been,
            Since love our hearts and Hymen[52] did our hands
            Unite commutual[53] in most sacred bands.

Player Queen: So many journeys may the sun and moon
240   Make us again count o'er ere love be done!
            But, woe is me, you are so sick of late,
            So far from cheer and from your former state,
            That I distrust[54] you. Yet, though I distrust,
            Discomfort you, my lord, it nothing must.
245   For women's fear and love holds quantity[55]
            In neither aught or in extremity.[56]
            Now what my love is, proof hath made you know,
            And as my love is sized, my fear is so.
            Where love is great, the littlest doubts are fear,
250   Where little fears grow great, great love grows there.

Player King: Faith, I must leave thee,[57] love, and shortly too,
            My operant powers[58] their functions leave to do.
            And thou shalt live in this fair world behind,

---

[45] naught: i.e., disgusting.   [46] posy . . . ring: It was a pretty custom to inscribe rings with little mottoes or messages, which were necessarily brief.   [47] Full . . . twain: The play is deliberately written in crude rhyming verse, full of ridiculous and bombastic phrases. [48] Phoebus' cart: the chariot of the sun.   [49] Neptune: the sea god.   [50] Tellus: the earth goddess.   [51] borrowed sheen: light borrowed from the sun.   [52] Hymen: god of marriage.   [53] commutual: mutually.   [54] distrust: am anxious about.   [55] quantity: proportion.   [56] In . . . extremity: either nothing or too much.   [57] leave thee: i.e., die. [58] operant powers: bodily strength.

Honored, beloved, and haply one as kind
255   For husband shalt thou—
Player Queen: Oh, confound the rest!
Such love must needs be treason in my breast.
In second husband let me be accurst!
None wed the second but who killed the first.
Hamlet: *[Aside]* Wormwood,[59] wormwood.
260 **Player Queen:** The instances[60] that second marriage move
Are base respects of thrift,[61] but none of love.
A second time I kill my husband dead
When second husband kisses me in bed.
Player King: I do believe you think what now you speak,
265   But what we do determine oft we break.
Purpose is but the slave to memory,
Of violent birth but poor validity,
Which now, like fruit unripe, sticks on the tree
But fall unshaken when they mellow be.
270   Most necessary 'tis that we forget
To pay ourselves what to ourselves is debt.
What to ourselves in passion we propose,
That passion ending, doth the purpose lose.
The violence of either grief or joy
275   Their own enactures[62] with themselves destroy.
Where joy most revels, grief doth most lament,
Grief joys, joy grieves, on slender accident.
This world is not for aye,[63] nor 'tis not strange
That even our loves should with our fortunes change,
280   For 'tis a question left us yet to prove
Whether love lead fortune or else fortune love.
The great man down, you mark his favorite flies,
The poor advanced makes friends of enemies.
And hitherto doth love on fortune tend,
285   For who not needs shall never lack a friend,
And who in want a hollow friend doth try
Directly seasons[64] him his enemy.
But, orderly to end where I begun,
Our wills and fates do so contráry run
290   That our devices still are overthrown,
Our thoughts are ours, their ends none of our own.
So think thou wilt no second husband wed,
But die thy thoughts when thy first lord is dead.
Player Queen: Nor earth to me give food nor Heaven light!
295   Sport and repose lock from me day and night!

---

[59] **Wormwood:** bitterness.   [60] **instances:** arguments.   [61] **respects of thrift:** considerations of gain.   [62] **enactures:** performance.   [63] **aye:** ever.   [64] **seasons:** ripens into.

To desperation turn my trust and hope!
An anchor's[65] cheer in prison be my scope!
Each opposite that blanks[66] the face of joy
Meet what I would have well and it destroy!
300   Both here and hence pursue me lasting strife
If, once a widow, ever I be wife!
Hamlet: If she should break it now!
Player King: 'Tis deeply sworn. Sweet, leave me here a while.
My spirits grow dull, and fain I would beguile
305   The tedious day with sleep.   *[Sleeps.]*
Player Queen: Sleep rock thy brain,
And never come mischance betwéen us twain!

                                                                                          [Exit.]

Hamlet: Madam, how like you this play?
Queen: The lady doth protest too much, methinks.
Hamlet: Oh, but she'll keep her word.
310   King: Have you heard the argument?[67] Is there no offense in 't?
Hamlet: No, no, they do but jest, poison in jest—no offense i' the world.
King: What do you call the play?
Hamlet: *The Mousetrap.* [68] Marry, how? Tropically.[69] This play is the image of
        a murder done in Vienna. Gonzago is the Duke's name, his wife. Baptista.
315   You shall see anon. 'Tis a knavish piece of work, but what o' that? Your
        Majesty, and we that have free[70] souls, it touches us not. Let the galled
        jade wince, our withers are unwrung.[71]
[Enter Lucianus.] This is one Lucianus, nephew to the King.
Ophelia: You are as good as a chorus,[72] my lord.
320   Hamlet: I could interpret between you and your love, if I could see the pup-
        pets dallying.[73]
Ophelia: You are keen, my lord, you are keen.
Hamlet: I would cost you a groaning to take off my edge.
Ophelia: Still better, and worse.
325   Hamlet: So you must take your husbands.[74] Begin, murderer. Pox, leave
        thy damnable faces and begin. Come, the croaking raven doth bellow
        for revenge.

---

[65] anchor: anchorite, hermit.   [66] blanks: makes pale.   [67] argument: plot. When
performances were given at Court it was sometimes customary to provide a written or printed
synopsis of the story for the distinguished spectators.   [68] Mousetrap: The phrase was
used of a device to entice a person to his own destruction (OED).   [69] Tropically:
figuratively, with a pun on "trap."   [70] free: innocent.   [71] galled . . . unwrung: let a
nag with a sore back flinch when the saddle is put on; our shoulders (being ungalled) feel no
pain.   [72] chorus: the chorus sometimes introduced the characters and commented on what
was to follow.   [73] puppets dallying: Elizabethan puppets were crude marionettes, popular at
fairs. While the figures were put through their motions, the puppet master explained what
was happening.   [74] So . . . husbands: i.e., as the marriage service expresses it, "for better,
for worse."

Lucianus: Thoughts black, hands apt, drugs fit, and time agreeing,
    Confederate season, else no creature[75] seeing,
330   Thou mixture rank of midnight weeds collected,
    With Hecate's ban[76] thrice blasted, thrice infected,
    Thy natural magic and dire property[77]
    On wholesome life usurp immediately.

[Pours the poison into the sleeper's ear.]

Hamlet: He poisons him i' the garden for his estate.[78] His name's Gonzago.
335   The story is extant, and written in very choice Italian. You shall see anon
    how the murderer gets the love of Gonzago's wife.
Ophelia: The King rises.
Hamlet: What, frighted with false fire![79]
Queen: How fares my lord?
340 **Polonius:** Give o'er the play.
King: Give me some light. Away!
Polonius: Lights, lights, lights!

[Exeunt all but Hamlet and Horatio.]

Hamlet: "Why, let the stricken deer go weep,
    The hart ungallèd play,
345   For some must watch while some must sleep.
    Thus runs the world away."
    Would not this, sir, and a forest of feathers[80]—if the rest of my fortunes
    turn Turk[81] with me—with two Provincial roses[82] on my razed[83]
    shoes, get me a fellowship[84] in a cry[85] of players, sir?
350 **Horatio:** Half a share.
Hamlet: A whole one, I.
        "For thou dost know, O Damon[86] dear,
        This realm dismantled[87] was
        Of Jove himself, and now reigns here
355   A very, very—pajock."[88]
Horatio: You might have rhymed.
Hamlet: O good Horatio, I'll take the ghost's word for a thousand pound.
    Didst perceive?
Horatio: Very well, my lord.
360 **Hamlet:** Upon the talk of the poisoning?

---

[75] confederate . . . creature: the opportunity conspiring with me, no other creature.
[76] Hecate's ban: the curse of Hecate, goddess of witchcraft.   [77] property: nature.
[78] estate: kingdom.   [79] false fire: a mere show.   [80] forest of feathers: set of plumes, much
worn by players.   [81] turn Turk: turn heathen, and treat me cruelly.   [82] Provincial
roses: rosettes, worn on the shoes.   [83] razed: slashed, ornamented with cuts.
[84] fellowship: partnership.   [85] cry: pack.   [86] Damon: Damon and Pythias were types of
perfect friends.   [87] dismantled: robbed.   [88] pajock: peacock, a strutting, lecherous bird.
These verses, and the lines above, may have come from some ballad, otherwise lost.

Horatio: I did very well note him.
Hamlet: Ah, ha! Come, some music! Come, the recorders![89]
    "For if the King like not the comedy,
    Why then, belike, he likes it not, perdy."[90]
365   Come, some music!

[Re-enter Rosencrantz and Guildenstern.]

Guildenstern: Good my lord, vouchsafe me a word with you.
Hamlet: Sir, a whole history.
Guildenstern: The King, sir—
Hamlet: Aye, sir, what of him?
370 Guildenstern: Is in his retirement marvelous distempered.[91]
Hamlet: With drink, sir?
Guildenstern: No, my lord, rather with choler.[92]
Hamlet: Your wisdom should show itself more richer to signify this to the
    doctor, for me to put him to his purgation[93] would perhaps plunge him
375   into far more choler.
Guildenstern: Good my lord, put your discourse into some frame,[94] and start
    not so wildly from my affair.
Hamlet: I am tame, sir. Pronounce.
Guildenstern: The Queen your mother, in most great affliction of spirit, hath
380   sent me to you.
Hamlet: You are welcome.
Guildenstern: Nay, good my lord, this courtesy is not of the right breed. If it
    shall please you to make me a wholesome answer, I will do your mother's
    commandment. If not, your pardon and my return shall be the end of my
385   business.
Hamlet: Sir, I cannot.
Guildenstern: What, my lord?
Hamlet: Make you a wholesome answer, my wit's diseased. But, sir, such an-
    swer as I can make you shall command, or rather, as you say, my mother.
390   Therefore no more, but to the matter. My mother, you say—
Rosencrantz: Then thus she says. Your behavior hath struck her into amaze-
    ment and admiration.[95]
Hamlet: Oh, wonderful son that can so astonish a mother! But is there no
    sequel at the heels of this mother's admiration? Impart.
395 Rosencrantz: She desires to speak with you in her closet ere you go to bed.
Hamlet: We shall obey, were she ten times our mother. Have you any further
    trade with us?

---

[89] recorders: wooden pipes.   [90] perdy: by God.   [91] distempered: disturbed: but Hamlet
takes the word in its other sense of "drunk."   [92] choler: anger, which Hamlet again
pretends to understand as meaning "biliousness."   [93] put . . . purgation: "give him a dose
of salts."   [94] frame: shape; i.e., "please talk sense."   [95] admiration: wonder.

Rosencrantz: My lord, you once did love me.

Hamlet: So I do still, by these pickers and stealers.[96]

400 **Rosencrantz:** Good my lord, what is your cause of distemper? You do surely bar the door upon your own liberty if you deny your griefs[97] to your friend.

Hamlet: Sir, I lack advancement.[98]

Rosencrantz: How can that be when you have the voice of the King himself for your succession in Denmark?

405 **Hamlet:** Aye, sir, but "While the grass grows"[99]—the proverb is something musty. *[Re-enter Players with recorders.]* Oh, the recorders![100] Let me see one. To withdraw[101] with you—why do you go about to recover the wind[102] of me, as if you would drive me into a toil?[103]

Guildenstern: O my lord, if my duty be too bold, my love is too unmannerly.[104]

410 **Hamlet:** I do not well understand that. Will you play upon this pipe?

Guildenstern: My lord, I cannot.

Hamlet: I pray you.

Guildenstern: Believe me, I cannot.

Hamlet: I do beseech you.

415 **Guildenstern:** I know no touch of it, my lord.

Hamlet: It is as easy as lying. Govern these ventages[105] with your fingers and thumb, give it breath with your mouth, and it will discourse most eloquent music. Look you, these are the stops.

Guildenstern: But these cannot I command to any utterance of harmony, I 420 have not the skill.

Hamlet: Why, look you now, how unworthy a thing you make of me! You would play upon me, you would seem to know my stops, you would pluck out the heart of my mystery, you would sound me from my lowest note to the top of my compass—and there is much music, excellent voice, in 425 this little organ—yet cannot you make it speak. 'Sblood, do you think I am easier to be played on than a pipe? Call me what instrument you will, though you can fret[106] me, you cannot play upon me. *[Re-enter Polonius.]* God bless you, sir!

Polonius: My lord, the Queen would speak with you, and presently.

430 **Hamlet:** Do you see yonder cloud that's almost in shape of a camel?

Polonius: By the mass, and 'tis like a camel indeed.

Hamlet: Methinks it is like a weasel.

---

[96] pickers . . . stealers: i.e., hands—an echo from the Christian's duty in the catechism to keep his hands "from picking and stealing." [97] deny . . . griefs: refuse to tell your troubles. [98] advancement: promotion. Hamlet harks back to his previous interview with Rosencrantz and Guildenstern. [99] While . . . grows: the proverb ends "the steed starves." [100] recorders: wooden pipes. [101] withdraw: go aside. Hamlet leads Guildenstern to one side of the stage. [102] recover . . . wind: a hunting metaphor; approach me with the wind against you. [103] toil: net. [104] if . . . unmannerly: if I exceed my duty by asking these questions, then my affection for you shows lack of manners; i.e., forgive me if I have been impertinent. [105] ventages: holes, stops. [106] fret: annoy, with a pun on the frets or bars on stringed instruments by which the fingering is regulated.

Polonius: It is backed like a weasel.

Hamlet: Or like a whale?

435 Polonius: Very like a whale.

Hamlet: Then I will come to my mother by and by. They fool me to the top of
my bent.[107] I will come by and by.

Polonius: I will say so.   *[Exit Polonius.]*

Hamlet: "By and by" is easily said. Leave me, friends. *[Exeunt all but Hamlet.]*

440   'Tis now the very witching time[108] of night,
           When churchyards yawn and Hell itself breathes out
           Contagion[109] to this world. Now could I drink hot blood,
           And do such bitter business as the day
           Would quake to look on. Soft! Now to my mother.
445   O heart, lose not thy nature, let not ever
           The soul of Nero[110] enter this firm bosom.
           Let me be cruel, not unnatural.
           I will speak daggers to her, but use none.
           My tongue and soul in this be hypocrites,
450   How in my words soever she be shent,[111]
           To give them seals[112] never, my soul, consent!

                                                                  [Exit.]

Scene III. A room in the castle.

[Enter King, Rosencrantz, and Guildenstern.]

King: I like him not, nor stands it safe with us
      To let his madness range.[1] Therefore prepare you.
      I your commission will forthwith dispatch,
      And he to England shall along with you.
5   The terms of our estate[2] may not endure
      Hazard so near us as doth hourly grow
      Out of his lunacies.

Guildenstern: We will ourselves provide.[3]
      Most holy and religious fear[4] it is
      To keep those many many bodies safe
10   That live and feed upon your Majesty.

Rosencrantz: The single and peculiar[5] life is bound
      With all the strength and armor of the mind

---

[107] top . . . bent: to the utmost.   [108] witching time: when witches perform their foul rites.
[109] Contagion: infection.   [110] Nero: Nero killed his own mother. Hamlet is afraid that in the
interview to come he will lose all self-control.   [111] shent: rebuked.
[112] give . . . seals: ratify words by actions.
[1] range: roam freely.   [2] terms . . . estate: i.e., one in my position.   [3] ourselves
provide: make our preparations.   [4] fear: anxiety.   [5] peculiar: individual.

To keep itself from noyance,[6] but much more
That spirit upon whose weal[7] depends and rests
15   The lives of many. The cease of majesty[8]
Dies not alone, but like a gulf[9] doth draw
What's near it with it. It is a massy[10] wheel
Fixed on the summit of the highest mount,
To whose huge spokes ten thousand lesser things
20   Are mortised[11] and adjoined; which, when it falls,
Each small annexment, petty consequence,[12]
Attends[13] the boisterous ruin. Never alone
Did the King sigh but with a general groan.
King: Arm you, I pray you, to this speedy voyage,
25   For we will fetters put upon this fear,
Which now goes too free-footed.
Rosencrantz & Guildenstern: We will haste us.

[Exeunt Rosencrantz and Guildenstern.]
[Enter Polonius.]

Polonius: My lord, he's going to his mother's closet.
Behind the arras I'll convey myself
To hear the process.[14] I'll warrant she'll tax[15] him home.
30   And, as you said,[16] and wisely was it said,
'Tis meet that some more audience than a mother,
Since nature makes them partial, should o'erhear
The speech, of vantage.[17] Fare you well, my liege.
I'll call upon you ere you go to bed
And tell you what I know.
35 **King:** Thanks, dear my lord.   *[Exit Polonius.]*
Oh, my offense is rank,[18] it smells to Heaven.
It hath the primal eldest curse[19] upon 't,
A brother's murder. Pray can I not,
Though inclination be as sharp as will.[20]
40   My stronger guilt defeats my strong intent,
And like a man to double business bound,
I stand in pause where I shall first begin,
And both neglect. What if this cursèd hand
Were thicker than itself with brother's blood,
45   Is there not rain enough in the sweet heavens
To wash it white as snow? Whereto serves mercy

---

[6] noyance: injury.   [7] weal: welfare.   [8] cease of majesty: death of a king.   [9] gulf: whirlpool.   [10] massy: massive.   [11] mortised: firmly   [12] annexment . . . consequence: attachment, smallest thing connected with it.   [13] Attends: waits on, is involved in. [14] process: proceeding.   [15] tax: censure.   [16] as . . . said: Actually Polonius himself had said it.   [17] of vantage: from a place of vantage; i.e., concealment.   [18] rank: foul. [19] primal . . . curse: the curse laid upon Cain, the first murderer, who also slew his brother.   [20] will: desire.

But to confront the visage of offense?[21]
And what's in prayer but this twofold force,
To be forestalled[22] ere we come to fall

50   Or pardoned being down? Then I'll look up,
My fault is past. But oh, what form of prayer
Can serve my turn? "Forgive me my foul murder"?
That cannot be, since I am still possessed
Of those effects[23] for which I did the murder—

55   My crown, mine own ambition, and my Queen.
May one be pardoned and retain the offense?[24]
In the corrupted currents[25] of this world
Offense's gilded hand may shove by justice,
And oft 'tis seen the wicked prize[26] itself

60   Buys out the law. But 'tis not so above.
There is no shuffling, there the action lies
In his true nature,[27] and we ourselves compelled
Even to the teeth and forehead[28] of our faults
To give in evidence. What then? What rests?

65   Try what repentance can. What can it not?
Yet what can it when one cannot repent?
Oh, wretched state! Oh, bosom black as death!
Oh, limèd[29] soul, that struggling to be free
Art more engaged![30] Help, angels! Make assay![31]

70   Bow, stubborn knees, and heart with strings of steel,
Be soft as sinews of the newborn babe!
All may be well.   *[Retires and kneels.]*

[Enter Hamlet.]

Hamlet: Now might I do it pat, now he is praying,
And now I'll do 't. And so he goes to Heaven,[32]

75   And so am I revenged. That would be scanned:
A villain kills my father, and for that
I, his sole son, do this same villain send
To Heaven.
Oh, this is hire and salary,[33] not revenge.

80   He took my father grossly,[34] full of bread,
With all his crimes broad blown, as flush[35] as May,
And how his audit[36] stands who knows save Heaven?

---

[21] confront . . . offense: look crime in the face.   [22] forestalled: prevented.   [23] effects:
advantages.   [24] offense: i.e., that for which he has offended.   [25] currents: courses, ways.
[26] wicked prize: the proceeds of the crime.   [27] there . . . nature: in Heaven the case is
tried on its own merits.   [28] teeth . . . forehead: i.e., face to face.   [29] limed: caught as in
birdlime.   [30] engaged: stuck fast.   [31] assay: attempt.   [32] And . . . Heaven: Praying,
Claudius is in a state of grace.   [33] hire . . . salary: i.e., a kind of action deserving pay.
[34] grossly: i.e., when he was in a state of sin.   [35] broad . . . flush: in full blossom, as
luxuriant.   [36] audit: account.

But in our circumstance and course of thought,[37]
'Tis heavy with him. And am I then revenged,
85   To take him in the purging of his soul,
When he is fit and seasoned,[38] for his passage?
No.
Up, sword, and know thou a more horrid hent.[39]
When he is drunk asleep, or in his rage,
90   Or in the incestuous pleasure of his bed—
At gaming, swearing, or about some act
That has no relish of salvation in 't—
Then trip him, that his heels may kick at Heaven
And that his soul may be as damned and black
95   As Hell, whereto it goes. My mother stays.
This physic but prolongs thy sickly days.   *[Exit.]*
King: *[Rising]* My words fly up, my thoughts remain below.
Words without thoughts never to Heaven go.

                                                             [Exit.]

Scene IV. The Queen's closet.

[Enter Queen and Polonius.]

Polonius: He will come straight. Look you lay home to[1] him.
Tell him his pranks have been too broad[2] to bear with,
And that your grace hath screened and stood between
Much heat and him. I'll sconce me[3] even here.
5   Pray you, be round with him.
Hamlet: *[Within]* Mother, Mother, Mother!
Queen: I'll warrant you,
Fear me not. Withdraw, I hear him coming.

                        [Polonius hides behind the arras.]
                                      [Enter Hamlet.]

Hamlet: Now, Mother, what's the matter?
Queen: Hamlet, thou hast thy father much offended.
10 Hamlet: Mother, you have my father much offended.
Queen: Come, come, you answer with an idle[4] tongue.
Hamlet: Go, go, you question with a wicked tongue.
Queen: Why, how now, Hamlet!
Hamlet: What's the matter now?

---

[37] circumstance . . . thought: as it appears to my mind.   [38] seasoned: ripe.
[39] hent: opportunity.
[1] lay . . . to: be strict with.   [2] broad: unrestrained. Polonius is thinking of the obvious
insolence of the remarks about second marriage in the play scene.   [3] sconce me: hide
myself.   [4] idle: foolish.

Queen: Have you forgot me?

Hamlet: No, by the rood,[5] not so.

15   You are the Queen, your husband's brother's wife,
       And—would it were not so!—you are my mother.

Queen: Nay, then, I'll set those to you that can speak.

Hamlet: Come, come, and sit you down. You shall not budge,
       You go not till I set you up a glass[6]

20   Where you may see the inmost part of you.

Queen: What wilt thou do? Thou wilt not murder me?
       Help, help, ho!

Polonius: *[Behind]* What ho! Help, help, help!

Hamlet: *[Drawing]* How now! A rat? Dead, for a ducat, dead! *[Makes a pass*

25   *through the arras.]*

Polonius: *[Behind]* Oh, I am slain!   *[Falls and dies.]*

Queen: Oh me, what hast thou done?

Hamlet: Nay, I know not. Is it the King?

Queen: Oh, what a rash and bloody deed is this!

Hamlet: A bloody deed! Almost as bad, good Mother,

30   As kill a king and marry with his brother.

Queen: As kill a king!

Hamlet: Aye, lady, 'twas my word.
                    [Lifts up the arras and discovers Polonius.]
       Thou wretched, rash, intruding fool, farewell!
       I took thee for thy better. Take thy fortune.
       Thou find 'st to be too busy is some danger.

35   Leave wringing of your hands. Peace! Sit you down,
       And let me wring your heart. For so I shall
       If it be made of penetrable stuff,
       If damnèd custom have not brassed[7] it so
       That it be proof and bulwark against sense.

40 Queen: What have I done that thou darest wag thy tongue
       In noise so rude against me?

Hamlet: Such an act
       That blurs the grace and blush of modesty,
       Calls virtue hypocrite, takes off the rose
       From the fair forehead of an innocent love,

45   And sets a blister[8] there—makes marriage vows
       As false as dicers' oaths. Oh, such a deed
       As from the body of contraction[9] plucks
       The very soul, and sweet religion makes
       A rhapsody of words.[10] Heaven's face doth glow,

50   Yea, this solidity and compound mass,[11]

---

[5] rood: crucifix.   [6] glass: looking-glass.   [7] brassed: made brazen; i.e., impenetrable.
[8] sets a blister: brands as a harlot.   [9] contraction: the marriage contract.   [10] rhapsody of
words: string of meaningless words.   [11] solidity . . . mass: i.e., solid earth.

With tristful visage, as against the doom,[12]
Is thought-sick at the act.
Queen: Aye me, what act
That roars so loud and thunders in the index?[13]
Hamlet: Look here upon this picture,[14] and on this,
55   The counterfeit presentment[15] of two brothers.
See what a grace was seated on this brow—
Hyperion's curls, the front[16] of Jove himself,
An eye like Mars, to threaten and command,
A station[17] like the herald Mercury[18]
60   New-lighted[19] on a heaven-kissing hill,
A combination[20] and a form indeed
Where every god did seem to set his seal[21]
To give the world assurance of a man.
This was your husband. Look you now what follows.
65   Here is your husband, like a mildewed ear,
Blasting his wholesome brother. Have you eyes?
Could you on this fair mountain leave to feed
And batten[22] on this moor? Ha! Have you eyes?
You cannot call it love, for at your age
70   The heyday[23] in the blood is tame, it's humble,
And waits upon the judgment. And what judgment
Would step from this to this? Sense[24] sure you have,
Else could you not have motion.[25] But sure that sense
Is apoplexed;[26] for madness would not err,
75   Nor sense to ecstasy[27] was ne'er so thralled[28]
But it reserved some quantity of choice
To serve in such a difference.[29] What devil was 't
That thus hath cozened[30] you at hoodman-blind?[31]
Eyes without feeling, feeling without sight,
80   Ears without hands or eyes, smelling sans[32] all,
Or but a sickly part of one true sense
Could not so mope.[33]

---

[12] tristful . . . doom: sorrowful face, as in anticipation of Doomsday.   [13] in . . . index:
i.e., if the beginning (*index*, i.e., table of contents) is so noisy, what will follow?
[14] picture: Modern producers usually interpret the pictures as miniatures, Hamlet wearing
one of his father, Gertrude one of Claudius. In the eighteenth century, wall portraits were
used.   [15] counterfeit presentment: portrait.   [16] front: forehead.   [17] station: figure; lit.,
standing.   [18] Mercury: messenger of the gods, and one of the most
beautiful.   [19] New-lighted: newly alighted.   [20] combination: i.e., of physical qualities.
[21] set . . . seal: guarantee as a perfect man.   [22] batten: glut yourself.   [23] heyday:
excitement.   [24] Sense: feeling.   [25] Motion: desire.   [26] apoplexed: paralyzed.
[27] ecstasy: excitement, passion.   [28] thralled: enslaved.   [29] serve . . . difference: to
enable you to see the difference between your former and your present husband.
[30] cozened: cheated.   [31] hoodman-blind: blind-man's-buff.   [32] sans: without.
[33] mope: be dull.

Oh, shame! Where is thy blush? Rebellious[34] Hell,
If thou canst mutine[35] in a matron's bones,
85   To flaming youth let virtue be as wax
And melt in her own fire. Proclaim no shame
When the compulsive ardor[36] gives the charge,
Since frost itself as actively doth burn,
And reason panders[37] will.
Queen: O Hamlet, speak no more.
90   Thou turn'st mine eyes into my very soul,
And there I see such black and grainèd[38] spots
As will not leave their tinct.[39]
Hamlet: Nay, but to live
In the rank sweat of an enseamèd[40] bed,
Stewed in corruption, honeying and making love
95   Over the nasty sty—
Queen: Oh, speak to me no more,
These words like daggers enter in my ears.
No more, sweet Hamlet!
Hamlet: A murderer and a villain,
A slave that is not twentieth part the tithe[41]
Of your precedent[42] lord, a vice of kings,[43]
100   A cutpurse[44] of the empire and the rule,
That from a shelf the precious diadem stole
And put it in his pocket!
Queen: No more!
Hamlet: A king of shreds and patches—
[Enter Ghost] Save me, and hover o'er me with your wings,
105   You heavenly guards! What would your gracious figure?
Queen: Alas, he's mad!
Hamlet: Do you not come your tardy son to chide
That, lapsed in time and passion, lets go by
The important acting of your dread command?[45]
110   Oh, say!
Ghost: Do not forget. This visitation
Is but to whet thy almost blunted purpose.
But look, amazement on thy mother sits.
Oh, step between her and her fighting soul.
115   Conceit[46] in weakest bodies strongest works.

---

[34] Rebellious . . . will: i.e., if the passion *(Hell)* of a woman of your age is uncontrollable *(rebellious)*, youth can have no restraints; there is no shame in a young man's lust when the elderly are just as eager and their reason (which should control desire) encourages them.
[35] mutine: mutiny.   [36] compulsive ardor: compelling lust.   [37] panders: acts as go-between.   [38] grained: dyed in the grain.   [39] tinct: color.   [40] enseamed: greasy.
[41] tithe: tenth part.   [42] precedent: former.   [43] vice of kings: caricature of a king.
[44] cutpurse: thief.   [45] That . . . command: who has allowed time to pass and passion to cool and neglects the urgent duty of obeying your dread command.   [46] Conceit: imagination.

        Speak to her, Hamlet.
Hamlet: How is it with you, lady?
Queen: Alas, how is 't with you
        That you do bend your eye on vacancy[47]
        And with the incorporal[48] air do hold discourse?
120   Forth at your eyes your spirits wildly peep,
        And as the sleeping soldiers in the alarm,
        Your bedded[49] hairs, like life in excrements,[50]
        Start up and stand an[51] end. O gentle son,
        Upon the heat and flame of thy distemper[52]
125   Sprinkle cool patience. Whereon do you look?
Hamlet: On him, on him! Look you how pale he glares!
        His form and cause conjoined,[53] preaching to stones,
        Would make them capable.[54] Do not look upon me,
        Lest with this piteous action you convert
130   My stern effects.[55] Then what I have to do
        Will want true color—tears perchance for blood.
Queen: To whom to you speak this?
Hamlet: Do you see nothing there?
Queen: Nothing at all, yet all that is I see.
Hamlet: Nor did you nothing hear?
Queen: No, nothing but ourselves.
135 **Hamlet:** Why, look you there! Look how it steals away!
        My father, in his habit as he lived!
        Look where he goes, even now, out at the portal!

                                        [Exit Ghost.]

Queen: This is the very coinage of your brain.
        This bodiless creation ecstasy[56]
140   Is very cunning in.
Hamlet: Ecstasy!
        My pulse, as yours, doth temperately keep time,
        And makes as healthful music. It is not madness
        That I have uttered. Bring me to the test
        And I the matter will reword, which madness
145   Would gambol[57] from. Mother, for love of grace,
        Lay not that flattering unction[58] to your soul,
        That not your trespass but my madness speaks.
        It will but skin and film the ulcerous place,
        Whiles rank corruption, mining[59] all within,

---

[47] vacancy: empty space.   [48] incorporal: bodiless.   [49] bedded: evenly laid.
[50] excrements: anything that grows out of the body, such as hair or fingernails: here hair.   [51] an: on.   [52] distemper: mental disturbance.   [53] form . . . conjoined: his appearance and the reason for his appearance joined.   [54] capable: i.e., of feeling.
[55] convert . . . effects: change the stern action which should follow.   [56] ecstasy: madness.   [57] gambol: start away.   [58] unction: healing ointment.   [59] mining: undermining.

150 Infects unseen. Confess yourself to Heaven,
 Repent what's past, avoid what is to come,
 And do not spread the compost[60] on the weeds
 To make them ranker. Forgive me this my virtue,
 For in the fatness[61] of these pursy[62] times
155 Virtue itself of vice must pardon beg—
 Yea, curb[63] and woo for leave to do him good.
Queen: O Hamlet, thou hast cleft my heart in twain.
Hamlet: Oh, throw away the worser part of it,
 And live the purer with the other half.
160 Good night. But go not to my uncle's bed.
 Assume a virtue if you have it not.
 That[64] monster, custom, who all sense doth eat,
 Of habits devil,[65] is angel yet in this,
 That to the use[66] of actions fair and good
165 He likewise gives a frock or livery
 That aptly[67] is put on. Refrain tonight,
 And that shall lend a kind of easiness
 To the next abstinence, the next more easy.
 For use almost can change the stamp[68] of nature,
170 And either the Devil,[69] or throw him out
 With wondrous potency. Once more, good night.
 And when you are desirous to be blest,
 I'll blessing beg of you. For this same lord,

[Pointing to Polonius]

 I do repent; but Heaven hath pleased it so,
175 To punish me with this, and this with me,
 That I must be their scourge and minister.
 I will bestow[70] him, and will answer well
 The death I gave him. So again good night.
 I must be cruel only to be kind.
180 Thus bad begins, and worse remains behind.
 One word more, good lady.
Queen: What shall I do?
Hamlet: Not this, by no means, that I bid you do.
 Let the bloat[71] king tempt you again to bed,
 Pinch wanton[72] on your cheek, call you his mouse,

---

[60] compost: manure. [61] fatness: grossness. [62] pursy: bloated. [63] curb: bow low.
[64] That . . . on: i.e., custom (bad habits) like an evil monster destroys all sense of good and evil, but yet can become an angel (good habits) when it makes us perform good actions as mechanically as we put on our clothes. [65] devil: This is the Q2 reading; the passage is omitted in F1. Probably the word should be "evil." [66] use: practice. [67] aptly: readily.
[68] stamp: impression. [69] either the Devil: some verb such as "shame" or "curb" has been omitted. [70] bestow: get rid of. [71] bloat: bloated. [72] wanton: lewdly.

185   And let him, for a pair of reechy[73] kisses
        Or paddling in your neck with his damned fingers,
        Make you to ravel[74] all this matter out,
        That I essentially am not in madness,
        But mad in craft. 'Twere good you let him know.
190   For who that's but a Queen, fair, sober, wise,
        Would from a paddock,[75] from a bat, a gib,[76]
        Such dear concernings[77] hide? Who would do so?
        No, in despite[78] of sense and secrecy,
        Unpeg the basket on the house's top,
195   Let the birds fly, and like the famous ape,[79]
        To try conclusions,[80] in the basket creep
        And break your own neck down.
Queen: Be thou assured if words be made of breath
        And breath of life, I have no life to breathe
200   What thou hast said to me.
Hamlet: I must to England. You know that?
Queen: Alack,
        I had forgot. 'Tis so concluded on.
Hamlet: There's letters sealed, and my two school fellows,
        Whom I will trust as I will adders fanged,
205   They bear the mandate.[81] They must sweep my way,
        And marshal me to knavery. Let it work,
        For 'tis the sport to have the enginer[82]
        Hoist with his own petar.[83] And 't shall go hard
        But I will delve one yard below their mines
210   And blow them at the moon: Oh, 'tis most sweet
        When in one line two crafts[84] directly meet.
        This man shall set me packing.
        I'll lug the guts into the neighbor room.
        Mother, good night. Indeed this counselor
215   Is now most still, most secret, and most grave
        Who was in life a foolish prating knave.
        Come, sir, to draw toward an end with you.
        Good night, Mother.
                                        [Exeunt severally,[85]
                                        Hamlet dragging in Polonius.]

---

[73] reechy: foul.   [74] ravel: unravel, reveal.   [75] paddock: toad.   [76] gib: tomcat.   [77] dear
concernings: important matters.   [78] despite: spite.   [79] famous ape: The story is not
known, but evidently told of an ape that let the birds out of their cage and, seeing them fly,
crept into the cage himself and jumped out, breaking his own neck.   [80] try conclusions:
repeat the experiment.   [81] mandate: command.   [82] enginer: engineer.   [83] petar:
petard, land mine.   [84] crafts: devices.   [85] Exeunt severally: i.e., by separate exits. In FI
there is no break here. The King enters as soon as Hamlet has dragged the body away. Q₂
marks the break. The act division was first inserted in a quarto of 1676.

Act IV

Scene I. A room in the castle.

[Enter King, Queen, Rosencrantz, and Guildenstern.]

King: There's matter[1] in these sighs, these profound heaves,
You must translate. 'Tis fit we understand them.
Where is your son?
Queen: Bestow this place[2] on us a little while.
                         [Exeunt Rosencrantz and Guildenstern.]
5   Ah, mine own lord, what have I seen tonight!
King: What, Gertrude? How does Hamlet?
Queen: Mad as the sea and wind when both contend
Which is the mightier. In his lawless fit,
Behind the arras hearing something stir,
10   Whips out his rapier, cries "A rat, a rat!"
And in this brainish apprehension[3] kills
The unseen good old man.
King: Oh, heavy deed!
It had been so with us had we been there.
His liberty is full of threats to all,
15   To you yourself, to us, to everyone.
Alas, how shall this bloody deed be answered?
It will be laid to us, whose providence[4]
Should have kept short,[5] restrained and out of haunt,[6]
This mad young man. But so much was our love
20   We would not understand what was most fit,
But, like the owner of a foul disease,
To keep it from divulging[7] let it feed
Even on the pith[8] of life. Where is he gone?
Queen: To draw apart the body he hath killed,
25   O'er whom his very madness, like some ore
Among a mineral of metals base,
Shows itself pure. He weeps for what is done.
King: O Gertrude, come away!
The sun no sooner shall the mountains touch
30   But we will ship him hence. And this vile deed
We must, with all our majesty and skill,
Both countenance[9] and excuse. Ho, Guildenstern!
                         [Re-enter Rosencrantz and Guildenstern.]
Friends both, go join you with some further aid.

---

[1] matter: something serious.   [2] Bestow . . . place: give place, leave us.   [3] brainish
apprehension: mad imagination.   [4] providence: foresight.   [5] short: confined.   [6] out of
haunt: away from others.   [7] divulging: becoming known.   [8] pith: marrow.
[9] counteance: take responsibility for.

Hamlet in madness hath Polonius slain,
35   And from his mother's closet hath he dragged him.
Go seek him out, speak fair, and bring the body
Into the chapel. I pray you, haste in this.
                              [Exeunt Rosencrantz and Guildenstern.]
Come, Gertrude, we'll call up our wisest friends,
And let them know both what we mean to do
40   And what's untimely done,[10]
Whose whisper o'er the world's diameter
As level as the cannon to his blank[11]
Transports his poisoned shot, may miss our name
And hit the woundless air. Oh, come away!
My soul is full of discord and dismay.   *[Exeunt.]*

Scene II. Another room in the castle.

[Enter Hamlet.]

Hamlet: Safely stowed.
Rosencrantz & Guildenstern: *[Within]* Hamlet! Lord Hamlet!
Hamlet: But soft, what noise? Who calls on Hamlet?
    Oh, here they come.

[Enter Rosencrantz and Guildenstern.]

5 **Rosencrantz:** What have you done, my lord, with the dead body?
Hamlet: Compounded it with dust, whereto 'tis kin.
Rosencrantz: Tell us where 'tis, that we may take it thence
    And bear it to the chapel.
Hamlet: Do not believe it.
10 **Rosencrantz:** Believe what?
Hamlet: That I can keep your counsel and not mine own. Besides, to be de-
    manded of a sponge! What replication[1] should be made by the son of a king?
Rosencrantz: Take you me for a sponge, my lord?
Hamlet: Aye, sir, that soaks up the King's countenance,[2] his rewards, his au-
    thorities. But such officers do the King best service in the end. He keeps
    them, like an ape, in the corner of his jaw, first mouthed, to be last swal-
    lowed. When he needs what you have gleaned, it is but squeezing you
    and, sponge, you shall be dry again.
Rosencrantz: I understand you not, my lord.
Hamlet: I am glad of it. A knavish speech sleeps in a foolish ear.[3]

---

[10] done: A half-line has been omitted. Some editors fill the gap with "So, haply slander."
[11] blank: target.
[1] replication: answer.   [2] countenance: favor.   [3] A . . . ear: a fool never understands the
point of a sinister speech.

Rosencrantz: My lord, you must tell us where the body is; and go with us to
the King.

Hamlet: The body is with the King, but the King is not with the body.[4] The
King is a thing—

Guildenstern: A thing, my lord?

Hamlet: Of nothing. Bring me to him. Hide fox, and all after.[5]   *[Exeunt.]*

Scene III. Another room in the castle.

[Enter King, attended.]

King: I have sent to seek him, and to find the body.
How dangerous is it that this man goes loose!
Yet must not we put the strong law on him.
He's loved of the distracted[1] multitude,
5 Who like not in their judgment but their eyes;[2]
And where 'tis so, the offender's scourge[3] is weighed,
But never the offense. To bear[4] all smooth and even,
This sudden sending him away must seem
Deliberate pause.[5] Diseases desperate grown
10 By desperate appliance are relieved,
Or not at all.
[Enter Rosencrantz.] How now! What hath befall'n?

Rosencrantz: Where the dead body is bestowed, my lord,
We cannot get from him.

King: But where is he?

Rosencrantz: Without, my lord, guarded, to know your pleasure.

15 King: Bring him before us.

Rosencrantz: Ho, Guildenstern! Bring in my lord.

[Enter Hamlet and Guildenstern.]

King: Now, Hamlet, where's Polonius?

Hamlet: At supper.

King: At supper! Where?

20 Hamlet: Not where he eats, but where he is eaten. A certain convocation of
politic worms[6] are e'en at him. Your worm is your only emperor for diet.
We fat all creatures else to fat us, and we fat ourselves for maggots. Your
fat king and your lean beggar is but variable service,[7] two dishes, but to
one table. That's the end.

---

[4] The . . . body: Hamlet deliberately bewilders his companions.   [5] Hide . . . after:
a form of the game of hide-and-seek. With these words Hamlet runs away from them.
[1] distracted: bewildered.   [2] like . . . eyes: whose likings are swayed not by judgment but
by looks.   [3] scourge: punishment.   [4] bear: make.   [5] Deliberate pause: the result of
careful planning.   [6] convocation . . . worms: an assembly of political-minded worms.
[7] variable service: choice of alternatives.

25 **King:** Alas, alas!

Hamlet: A man may fish with the worm that hath eat of a king, and eat of the fish that hath fed of that worm.

King: What dost thou mean by this?

Hamlet: Nothing but to show you how a king may go a progress[8] through the
30   guts of a beggar.

King: Where is Polonius?

Hamlet: In Heaven—send thither to see. If your messenger find him not there, seek him i' the other place yourself. But indeed if you find him not within this month, you shall nose him as you go up the stairs into the lobby.

35 **King:** *[To some Attendants]* Go seek him there.

Hamlet: He will stay till you come.

[Exeunt Attendants.]

King: Hamlet, this deed, for thine especial safety,
        Which we do tender,[9] as we dearly grieve
        For that which thou hast done, must send thee hence
40   With fiery quickness. Therefore prepare thyself.
        The bark is ready and the wind at help,[10]
        The associates tend,[11] and every thing is bent[12]
        For England.

Hamlet: For England?

King: Aye, Hamlet.

Hamlet: Good.

King: So is it if thou knew'st our purposes.

45 **Hamlet:** I see a cherub that sees them. But, come, for England! Farewell, dear Mother.

King: Thy loving father, Hamlet.

Hamlet: My mother. Father and mother is man and wife, man and wife is one flesh, and so, my mother. Come, for England!   *[Exit.]*

50 **King:** Follow him at foot,[13] tempt[14] him with speed aboard.
        Delay it not, I'll have him hence tonight.
        Away! For everything is sealed and done
        That else leans on the affair. Pray you make haste.

[Exeunt Rosencrantz and Guildenstern.]

        And, England, if my love thou hold'st at aught—
55   As my great power thereof may give thee sense,
        Since yet thy cicatrice[15] looks raw and red
        After the Danish sword, and thy free awe[16]
        Pays homage to us—thou mayst not coldly set
        Our sovereign process,[17] which imports at full,

---

[8] go a progress: make a state journey.   [9] tender: regard highly.   [10] at help: favorable.
[11] associates tend: your companions are waiting.   [12] bent: ready.   [13] at foot: at his
heels.   [14] tempt: entice.   [15] cicatrice: scar. There is nothing in the play to explain this
incident.   [16] free awe: voluntary submission.   [17] coldly . . . process: hesitate to carry
out our royal command.

60 By letters congruing[18] to that effect,
The present[19] death of Hamlet. Do it, England,
For like the hectic[20] in my blood he rages,
And thou must cure me. Till I know 'tis done,
Howe'er my haps,[21] my joys were ne'er begun.

[Exit.]

Scene IV. A plain in Denmark.

[Enter Fortinbras, a Captain and Soldiers, marching.]

Fortinbras: Go, Captain, from me greet the Danish King.
Tell him that by his license Fortinbras
Craves the conveyance of a promised march[1]
Over his kingdom. You know the rendezvous.
5 If that His Majesty would aught with us,
We shall express our duty in his eye,[2]
And let him know so.
Captain: I will do 't, my lord.
Fortinbras: Go softly on.

[Exeunt Fortinbras, and Soldiers.]
[Enter Hamlet, Rosencrantz, Guildenstern, and others.]
Hamlet: Good sir, whose powers[3] are these?
10 Captain: They are of Norway, sir.
Hamlet: How purposed, sir, I pray you?
Captain: Against some part of Poland.
Hamlet: Who commands them, sir?
Captain: The nephew to old Norway, Fortinbras.
15 Hamlet: Goes it against the main[4] of Poland, sir,
   Or for some frontier?
Captain: Truly to speak, and with no addition,[5]
   We go to gain a little patch of ground
   That hath in it no profit but the name.
20 To pay five ducats, five, I would not farm it,
   Nor will it yield to Norway or the Pole
   A ranker[6] rate should it be sold in fee.[7]
Hamlet: Why, then the Polack never will defend it.
Captain: Yes, it is already garrisoned.

---

[18] congruing: agreeing.   [19] present: immediate.   [20] hectic: fever.   [21] Howe'er my haps: whatever may happen to me.
[1] Craves . . . march: asks for permission to transport his army, as had already been promised.   [2] in . . . eye: before his eyes; i.e., in person.
[3] powers: forces.   [4] main: mainland.   [5] addition: exaggeration.   [6] ranker: richer.
[7] in fee: with possession as freehold.

25 **Hamlet:** Two thousand souls and twenty thousand ducats
          Will not debate the question of this straw.
          This is the imposthume of[8] much wealth and peace,
          That inward breaks, and shows no cause without
          Why the man dies. I humbly thank you, sir.
30 **Captain:** God be wi' you, sir.   *[Exit.]*
    Rosencrantz: Will 't please you go, my lord?
    Hamlet: I'll be with you straight. Go a little before.

                                      [Exeunt all but Hamlet.]

          How[9] all occasions do inform against[10] me
          And spur my dull revenge! What is a man
          If his chief good and market[11] of his time
35   Be but to sleep and feed? A beast, no more.
          Sure. He that made us with such large discourse,
          Looking before and after,[12] gave us not
          That capability and godlike reason
          To fust[13] in us unused. Now whether it be
40   Bestial oblivion, or some craven scruple
          Of thinking too precisely on the event—
          A thought which, quartered, hath but one part wisdom
          And ever three parts coward—I do not know
          Why yet I live to say "This thing's to do,"
45   Sith I have cause, and will, and strength, and means
          To do 't. Examples gross[14] as earth exhort me.
          Witness this army, of such mass and charge,[15]
          Led by a delicate and tender Prince
          Whose spirit with divine ambition puffed
50   Makes mouths at the invisible event,[16]
          Exposing what is mortal and unsure
          To all that fortune, death, and danger dare,
          Even for an eggshell.[17] Rightly to be great
          Is not to stir without great argument,
55   But greatly to find quarrel in a straw
          When honor's at the stake.[18] How stand I then,
          That have a father killed, a mother stained,
          Excitements of my reason and my blood,
          And let all sleep while to my shame I see
60   The imminent death of twenty thousand men

---

[8] imposthume of: inward swelling caused by.   [9] How . . . worth: The soliloquy and all the
dialogue after the exit of Fortinbras are omitted in FI.   [10] inform against: accuse.
[11] market: profit.   [12] such . . . after: intelligence that enables us to consider the future
and the past.   [13] fust: grow musty.   [14] gross: large.   [15] charge: expense.
[16] Makes . . . event: mocks at the unseen risk.   [17] eggshell: i.e., worthless trifle.
[18] Rightly . . . stake: true greatness is a matter of fighting not for a mighty cause but for the
merest trifle when honor is concerned.

That for a fantasy and trick[19] of fame
Go to their graves like beds, fight for a plot
Whereon the numbers cannot try the cause,[20]
Which is not tomb enough and continent[21]
65   To hide the slain? Oh, from this time forth,
My thoughts be bloody or be nothing worth!

[Exit.]

Scene V. Elsinore. A room in the castle.

[Enter Queen, Horatio, and a Gentleman.]

Queen: I will not speak with her.
Gentleman: She is importunate, indeed distract.[1]
Her mood will needs be pitied.
Queen: What would she have?
Gentleman: She speaks much of her father, says she hears
5   There's tricks[2] i' the world, and hems[3] and beats her heart,
Spurns enviously[4] at straws, speaks things in doubt
That carry but half-sense. Her speech is nothing,
Yet the unshaped use[5] of it doth move
The hearers to collection.[6] They aim[7] at it,
10   And botch[8] the words up fit to their own thoughts,
Which, as her winks and nods and gestures yield them,
Indeed would make one think there might be thought,
Though nothing sure, yet much unhappily.
Horatio: 'Twere good she were spoken with, for she may strew
15   Dangerous conjectures in ill-breeding minds.
Queen: Let her come in.   *[Exit Gentleman.]*
[Aside] To my sick soul, as sin's true nature is,
Each toy[9] seems prologue to some great amiss.[10]
So full of artless jealousy[11] is guilt,
20   It spills itself in fearing to be spilt.[12]

[Re-enter Gentleman, with Ophelia.[13]]

---

[19] fantasy . . . trick: illusion and whim.   [20] Whereon . . . cause: a piece of ground so small that it would not hold the combatants.   [21] continent: large enough to contain.
[1] distract: out of her mind.   [2] tricks: trickery.   [3] hems: makes significant noises.
[4] Spurns enviously: kicks spitefully.   [5] unshaped use: disorder.   [6] collection: i.e., attempts to find a sinister meaning.   [7] aim: guess.   [8] botch: patch.   [9] toy: trifle.
[10] amiss: calamity.   [11] artless jealousy: clumsy suspicion.   [12] It . . . spilt: guilt reveals itself by its efforts at concealment.   [13] Re-enter . . . Ophelia: QI notes "Enter Ophelia playing on a lute, and her hair down, singing."

Ophelia: Where is the beauteous Majesty of Denmark?

Queen: How now, Ophelia!

Ophelia: *[Sings.]*

25
"How should I your truelove know
            From another one?
            By his cockle hat[14] and staff
            And his sandal shoon."[15]

Queen: Alas, sweet lady, what imports this song?

Ophelia: Say you? nay, pray you, mark. *[Sings.]*

30
"He is dead and gone, lady,
            He is dead and gone,
            At his head a grass-green turf,
            At his heels a stone."
            Oh, oh!

35 **Queen:** Nay, but, Ophelia—

Ophelia: Pray you, mark. *[Sings.]*
"White his shroud as the mountain snow—"

[Enter King.]

Queen: Alas, look here, my lord.

Ophelia: *[Sings.]*

"Larded[16] with sweet flowers,
40
            Which bewept to the grave did go
            With truelove showers."[17]

King: How do you, pretty lady?

Ophelia: Well, God 'ild[18] you! They say the owl was a baker's daughter.[19] Lord, we know what we are but know not what we may be. God be at your table!

45 **King:** Conceit upon her father.

Ophelia: Pray you let's have no words of this, but when they ask you what it means, say you this
[Sings]:

"Tomorrow is Saint Valentine's day,[20]
            All in the morning betime,
50
And I a maid at your window,
            To be your Valentine.
"Then up he rose, and donned his clothes,
            And dupped[21] the chamber door,

---

[14] **cockle hat:** a hat adorned with a cockleshell worn by pilgrims.   [15] **sandal shoon:** sandals, the proper footwear of pilgrims.   [16] **Larded:** garnished.   [17] **truelove showers:** the tears of his faithful love.   [18] **'ild (yield):** reward.   [19] **owl . . . daughter:** An allusion to a legend that Christ once went into a baker's shop and asked for bread. The baker's wife gave him a piece but was rebuked by her daughter for giving him too much. Thereupon the daughter was turned into an owl.   [20] **Saint . . . day:** February 14, the day when birds are supposed to mate. According to the old belief the first single man then seen by a maid is destined to be her husband.   [21] **dupped:** opened.

Let in the maid, that out a maid
55   Never departed more."

King: Pretty Ophelia!

Ophelia: Indeed, la, without an oath, I'll make an end on 't. *[Sings.]*
             "By Gis[22] and by Saint Charity,
                 Alack, and fie for shame!
60   Young men will do 't, if they come to 't,
                 By cock, they are to blame.
             Quoth she, before you tumbled me,
                 You promised me to wed."

       He answers:

65   "So would I ha' done, by yonder sun,
                 An thou hadst not come to my bed."

King: How long hath she been thus?

Ophelia: I hope all will be well. We must be patient. But I cannot choose but weep to think they should lay him i' the cold ground. My brother shall know
70 of it. And so I thank you for your good counsel. Come, my coach! Good night, ladies, good night, sweet ladies, good night, good night.   *[Exit.]*

King: Follow her close,[23] give her good watch, I pray you.   *[Exit Horatio.]*
Oh, this is the poison of deep grief. It springs
All from her father's death. O Gertrude, Gertrude.
75 When sorrows come, they come not single spies,[24]
But in battalions! First, her father slain.
Next, your son gone, and he most violent author[25]
Of his own just remove. The people muddied,
Thick and unwholesome in their thoughts and whispers,
80 For good Polonius' death. And we have done but greenly[26]
In huggermugger[27] to inter him. Poor Ophelia
Divided from herself and her fair judgment,[28]
Without the which we are pictures,[29] or mere beasts.
Last, and as much containing as all these,
85 Her brother is in secret come from France,
Feeds on his wonder, keeps himself in clouds,
And wants not buzzers[30] to infect his ear
With pestilent speeches of his father's death,
Wherein necessity, of matter beggared,
90 Will nothing stick our person to arraign[31]
In ear and ear. O my dear Gertrude, this,

---

[22] Gis . . . cock: for "Jesus" and "God," both words being used instead of the sacred names, like the modern "Jeez" and "Gee."   [23] close: closely.   [24] spies: scouts.   [25] author: cause.   [26] done . . . greenly: shown immature judgment.   [27] huggermugger: secret haste, "any which way."   [28] Divided . . . judgment: no longer able to use her judgment. [29] pictures: lifeless imitations.   [30] buzzers: scandalmongers.   [31] Wherein . . . arraign: in which, knowing nothing of the true facts, he may necessarily accuse us.

Like to a murdering piece,[32] in many places
Gives me superfluous death.   *[A noise within.]*
Queen: Alack, what noise is this?
King: Where are my Switzers?[33] Let them guard the door.
95   *[Enter another Gentleman.]* What is the matter?
Gentleman: Save yourself, my lord!
The ocean, overpeering of his list,[34]
Eats not the flats[35] with more impetuous haste
Than young Laertes, in a riotous head,[36]
O'erbears your officers. The rabble call him lord.
100   And as the world were now but to begin,
Antiquity forgot, custom not known,
The ratifiers and props of every word,[37]
They cry "Choose we—Laertes shall be King!"
Caps, hands, and tongues applaud it to the clouds—
105   "Laertes shall be King, Laertes King!"
Queen: How cheerfully on the false trail they cry!
Oh, this is counter,[38] you false Danish dogs!

                                        [Noise within]

King: The doors are broke.

[Enter Laertes, armed, Danes following.]

Laertes: Where is this King? Sirs, stand you all without.
110 Danes: No, let's come in.
Laertes: I pray you, give me leave.
Danes: We will, we will.

                              [They retire without the door.]

Laertes: I thank you. Keep the door. O thou vile King,
Give me my father!
Queen: Calmly, good Laertes.
Laertes: That drop of blood that's calm proclaims me bastard,
115   Cries cuckold[39] to my father, brands the harlot[40]
Even here, between the chaste unsmirchèd brows
Of my true mother.
King: What is the cause, Laertes,
That thy rebellion looks so giantlike?
Let him go, Gertrude. Do not fear[41] our person.

---

[32] murdering piece: cannon loaded with grapeshot.   [33] Switzers: Swiss bodyguard.
[34] overpeering . . . list: looking over its boundary; i.e., flooding the mainland.   [35] Eats
. . . flats: floods not the flat country.   [36] in . . . head: with a force of rioters.
[37] Antiquity . . . word: forgetting ancient rule and ignoring old custom, by which all
promises must be maintained.   [38] counter: in the wrong direction of the scent.
[39] cuckold: a husband deceived by his wife.   [40] brands . . . harlot: Convicted harlots were
branded with a hot iron.   [41] fear: fear for.

120   There's such divinity doth hedge a king[42]
      That treason can but peep[43] to what it would,
      Acts little of his will. Tell me, Laertes,
      Why thou art thus incensed. Let him go, Gertrude.
      Speak, man.
125 Laertes: Where is my father?
    King: Dead.
    Queen: But not by him.
    King: Let him demand his fill.
    Laertes: How came he dead? I'll not be juggled with.
      To Hell, allegiance! Vows, to the blackest devil!
      Conscience and grace, to the profoundest pit!
130   I dare damnation. To this point I stand,
      That both the worlds I give to negligence.[44]
      Let come what comes, only I'll be revenged
      Most throughly[45] for my father.
    King: Who shall stay you?
    Laertes: My will, not all the world.
135   And for my means, I'll husband[46] them so well
      They shall go far with little.
    King: Good Laertes,
      If you desire to know the certainty
      Of your dear father's death, is 't writ in your revenge
      That, swoopstake,[47] you will draw both friend and foe,
140   Winner and loser?
    Laertes: None but his enemies.
    King: Will you know them, then?
    Laertes: To his good friends thus wide I'll ope my arms,
      And like the kind life-rendering pelican,[48]
      Repast[49] them with my blood.
    King: Why, now you speak
145   Like a good child and a true gentleman.
      That I am guiltless of your father's death,
      And am most sensibly[50] in grief for it,
      It shall as level[51] to your judgment pierce
      As day does to your eye.
    Danes: *[Within]* Let her come in.
150 Laertes: How now! What noise is that?
      [Re-enter Ophelia.] O heat, dry up my brains! Tears seven times salt
      Burn out the sense and virtue of mine eye!

---

[42] divinity . . . king: divine protection surrounds a king as with a hedge.   [43] peep: look over, not break through.   [44] That . . . negligence: I do not care what happens to me in this world or the next.   [45] throughly: thoroughly.   [46] husband: use economically.
[47] swoopstake: "sweeping the board."   [48] life-rendering pelican: The mother pelican was supposed to feed her young with blood from her own breast.   [49] Repast: feed.
[50] sensibly: feelingly.   [51] level: clearly.

By Heaven, thy madness shall be paid with weight
        Till our scale turn the beam.[52] O rose of May![53]
155   Dear maid, kind sister, sweet Ophelia!
        Oh heavens! Is 't possible a young maid's wits
        Should be as mortal as an old man's life?
        Nature is fine in love, and where 'tis fine
        It sends some precious instance of itself
160   After the thing it loves.[54]
Ophelia: *[Sings.]*
                "They bore him barefaced on the bier,
                    Hey non nonny, nonny, hey nonny,
                And in his grave rained many a tear—"
165   Fare you well, my dove!
Laertes: Hadst thou thy wits and didst persuade revenge,
        It could not move thus.
Ophelia: *[Sings.]*
                "You must sing down a-down
170   An you call him a-down-a."
        Oh, how the wheel[55] becomes it! It is the false steward, that stole his
            master's daughter.
Laertes: This nothing's more than matter.[56]
Ophelia: There's[57] rosemary, that's for remembrance—pray you, love, remem-
175   ber. And there is pansies, that is for thoughts.
Laertes: A document[58] in madness, thoughts and remembrance fitted.
Ophelia: There's fennel for you, and columbines. There's rue for you, and
            here's some for me—we may call it herb of grace o' Sundays. Oh, you must
            wear your rue with a difference. There's a daisy. I would give you some
180   violets, but they withered all when my father died. They say a' made a good
            end. *[Sings.]*
                "For bonny sweet Robin is all my joy."
Laertes: Thought and affliction, passion, Hell itself,
        She turns to favor[59] and to prettiness.
185 Ophelia: *[Sings.]*
                "And will a' not come again?"

---

[52] turn . . . beam: weigh down the beam of the scale.   [53] rose of May: perfection of young
beauty.   [54] Nature . . . loves: i.e., her love for her father was so exquisite that she has sent
her sanity after him. Laertes, especially in moments of emotion, is prone to use highly
exaggerated speech.   [55] wheel: explained variously as the spinning wheel, Fortune's wheel,
or the refrain. The likeliest explanation is that she breaks into a little dance at the words "You
must sing," and that the *wheel* is the turn as she circles round.
[56] This . . . matter: this nonsense means more than sense.   [57] There's . . . died: In the
language of flowers, each has its peculiar meaning, and Ophelia distributes them
appropriately: for her brother rosemary (remembrance) and pansies (thoughts); for the King
fennel (flattery) and columbine (thanklessness); for the Queen rue, called also herb o' grace
(sorrow), and daisy (light of love). Neither is worthy of violets (faithfulness).
[58] document: instruction.   [59] favor: charm.

And will a' not come again?
No, no, he is dead,
Go to thy deathbed,
190   He never will come again.

"His beard was as white as snow,
All flaxen was his poll.[60]
He is gone, he is gone,
And we cast away moan.
195   God ha' mercy on his soul!"
And of all Christian souls, I pray God. God be wi' you.   *[Exit.]*

Laertes: Do you see this, O God?

King: Laertes, I must commune with your grief,
Or you deny me right. Go but apart,
200   Make choice of whom your wisest friends you will,
And they shall hear and judge 'twixt you and me.
If by direct or by collateral[61] hand
They find us touched,[62] we will our kingdom give,
Our crown, our life, and all that we call ours,
205   To you in satisfaction. But if not,
Be you content to lend your patience to us
And we shall jointly labor with your soul
To give it due content.

Laertes: Let this be so.
His means of death, his obscure funeral,[63]
210   No trophy, sword, nor hatchment[64] o'er his bones,
No noble rite nor formal ostentation,[65]
Cry to be heard, as 'twere from Heaven to earth,
That I must call 't in question.

King: So you shall,
And where the offense is let the great ax fall.
215   I pray you, go with me.   *[Exeunt.]*

Scene VI. Another room in the castle.

[Enter Horatio and a Servant.]

Horatio: What are they that would speak with me?

Servant: Seafaring men, sir. They say they have letters for you.

Horatio: Let them come in.   *[Exit Servant.]*

---

[60] flaxen . . . poll: white as flax was his head.   [61] collateral: i.e., as an accessory.
[62] touched: implicated.   [63] obscure funeral: Men of rank were buried with much ostentation. To bury Polonius "huggermugger" was thus an insult to his memory and to his family.   [64] hatchment: device of the coat of arms carried in a funeral and hung up over the tomb.   [65] formal ostentation: ceremony properly ordered.

I do not know from what part of the world
5   I should be greeted, if not from Lord Hamlet.

[Enter Sailors.]

I. Sailor: God bless you, sir.
Horatio: Let Him bless thee too.
I. Sailor: He shall, sir, an 't please Him. There's a letter for you, sir. It comes
       from the ambassador that was bound for England—if your name be
10   Horatio, as I am let to know it is.
Horatio: *[Reads.]* "Horatio, when thou shalt have overlooked[1] this, give these
       fellows[2] some means to the King. They have letters for him. Ere we were
       two days old at sea, a pirate of very warlike appointment[3] gave us chase.
       Finding ourselves too slow of sail, we put on a compelled valor, and in the
15   grapple I boarded them. On the instant they got clear of our ship, so I
       alone became their prisoner. They have dealt with me like thieves of
       mercy; but they knew what they did—I am to do a good turn for them. Let
       the King have the letters I have sent, and repair thou to me with as much
       speed as thou wouldest fly death. I have words to speak in thine ear
20   will make thee dumb, yet are they much too light for the bore of the mat-
       ter.[4] These good fellows will bring thee where I am. Rosencrantz and
       Guildenstern hold their course for England. Of them I have much to tell
       thee. Farewell.
              "He that thou knowest thine.
                            "Hamlet"
       Come, I will make you way for these your letters,
25   And do 't the speedier that you may direct me
       To him from whom you brought them.   *[Exeunt.]*

Scene VII. Another room in the castle.

[Enter King and Laertes.]

King: Now must your conscience my acquittance seal,[1]
       And you must put me in your heart for friend,
       Sith you have heard, and with a knowing ear,
       That he which hath your noble father slain
5   Pursued my life.
Laertes: It well appears. But tell me
       Why you proceeded not against these feats,[2]
       So crimeful and so capital[3] in nature,

---

[1] overlooked: read.   [2] means: access.   [3] appointment: equipment.   [4] too . . . matter:
i.e., words fall short, like a small shot fired from a cannon with too wide a bore.
[1] my . . . seal: acquit me.   [2] feats: acts.   [3] capital: deserving death.

As by your safety, wisdom, all things else,
You mainly were stirred up.

King: Oh, for two special reasons,

10   Which may to you perhaps seem much unsinewed,[4]
        But yet to me they're strong. The Queen his mother
        Lives almost by his looks, and for myself—
        My virtue or my plague, be it either which—
        She's so conjunctive[5] to my life and soul

15   That as the star moves not but[6] in his sphere,
        I could not but by her. The other motive
        Why to a public count[7] I might not go
        Is the great love the general gender[8] bear him,
        Who, dipping all his faults in their affection,[9]

20   Would, like the spring that turneth wood to stone,[10]
        Convert his gyves to graces.[11] So that my arrows,
        Too slightly timbered[12] for so loud a wind,
        Would have reverted to my bow again
        And not where I had aimed them.

25 Laertes: And so have I a noble father lost,
        A sister driven into desperate terms,[13]
        Whose worth, if praises may go back again,[14]
        Stood challenger on mount of all the age
        For her perfections.[15] But my revenge will come.

30 King: Break not your sleeps for that. You must not think
        That we are made of stuff so flat and dull
        That we can let our beard be shook with danger
        And think it pastime. You shortly shall hear more.[16]
        I loved your father, and we love ourself,

35   And that, I hope, will teach you to imagine—
        [Enter a Messenger, with letters.] How now! What news!

Messenger: Letters, my lord, from Hamlet.
        This to your Majesty, this to the Queen.

King: From Hamlet! Who brought them?

40 Messenger: Sailors, my lord, they say—I saw them not.
        They were given me by Claudio, he received them
        Of him that brought them.

King: Laertes, you shall hear them.

---

[4] **unsinewed:** weak, flabby.   [5] **conjunctive:** joined inseparably.   [6] **moves . . . but:** moves only in.   [7] **count:** trial.   [8] **general gender:** common people.   [9] **dipping . . . affection:** gilding his faults with their love.   [10] **like . . . stone:** In several places in England there are springs of water so strongly impregnated with lime that they will quickly cover with stone anything placed under them.   [11] **Convert . . . graces:** regard his fetters as honorable ornaments.   [12] **timbered:** shafted. A light arrow is caught by the wind and blown back.   [13] **terms:** condition.   [14] **if . . . again:** if one may praise her for what she used to be.   [15] **Stood . . . perfections:** i.e., her worth challenged the whole world to find one as perfect.   [16] **hear more:** i.e., when news comes from England that Hamlet is dead.

Leave us.　　　　　　　　　　　　　　*[Exit Messenger.]*

45　*[Reads.]* "High and Mighty, you shall know I am set naked[17] on your
　　　kingdom. Tomorrow shall I beg leave to see your kingly eyes, when I
　　　shall, first asking your pardon thereunto, recount the occasion of my
　　　sudden and more strange return.

　　　　　　　　　　　　　　　　　"Hamlet"

　　　What should this mean? Are all the rest come back?

50　　Or is it some abuse,[18] and no such thing?

Laertes: Know you the hand?

King: 'Tis Hamlet's character.[19] "Naked!"
　　　And in a postscript here, he says "alone."
　　　Can you advise me?

55 Laertes: I'm lost in it, my lord. But let him come.
　　　It warms the very sickness in my heart
　　　That I shall live and tell him to his teeth
　　　"Thus didest thou."

King:　　　　　　　　If it be so, Laertes—
　　　As how should it be so, how otherwise?—

60　　Will you be ruled by me?

Laertes:　　　　　　　　　Aye, my lord,
　　　So you will not o'errule[20] me to a peace.

King: To thine own peace. If he be now returned,
　　　As checking at[21] his voyage, and that he means
　　　No more to undertake it, I will work him

65　　To an exploit now ripe in my device,
　　　Under the which he shall not choose but fall.
　　　And for his death no wind of blame shall breathe,
　　　But even his mother shall uncharge the practice[22]
　　　And call it accident.

Laertes:　　　　　　　　My lord, I will be ruled,

70　　The rather if you could devise it so
　　　That I might be the organ.[23]

King:　　　　　　　　　It falls right.
　　　You have been talked of since your travel much,
　　　And that in Hamlet's hearing, for a quality
　　　Wherein they say you shine. Your sum of parts[24]

75　　Did not together pluck such envy from him
　　　As did that one, and that in my regard
　　　Of the unworthiest siege.[25]

---

[17] naked: destitute.　　[18] abuse: attempt to deceive.　　[19] character: handwriting.
[20] o'errule: command.　　[21] checking at: swerving aside from, like a hawk that leaves the
pursuit of his prey.　　[22] uncharge . . . practice: not suspect that his death was the result of
the plot.　　[23] organ: instrument.　　[24] sum of parts: accomplishments as a whole.
[25] siege: seat, place.

Laertes: What part is that, my lord?
King: A very ribbon in the cap of youth,
        Yet needful too; for youth no less becomes
80   The light and careless livery that it wears
        Than settled age his sables and his weeds,[26]
        Importing health and graveness. Two months since,
        Here was a gentleman of Normandy.
        I've seen myself, and served against, the French,
85   And they can well[27] on horseback; but this gallant
        Had witchcraft in 't, he grew unto his seat,
        And to such wondrous doing brought his horse
        As had he been incorpsed and deminatured[28]
        With the brave beast. So far he topped my thought[29]
90   That I, in forgery of shapes and tricks,[30]
        Come short of what he did.
Laertes: A Norman was 't?
King: A Norman.
Laertes: Upon my life, Lamond.
King: The very same.
Laertes: I know him well. He is the brooch[31] indeed
95   And gem of all the nation.
King: He made confession[32] of you,
        And gave you such a masterly report
        For art and exercise in your defense,
        And for your rapier most especial,
100   That he cried out 'twould be a sight indeed
        If one could match you. The scrimers[33] of their nation,
        He swore, had neither motion, guard, nor eye
        If you opposed them. Sir, this report of his
        Did Hamlet so envenom[34] with his envy
105   That he could nothing do but wish and beg
        Your sudden coming o'er, to play with him.
        Now, out of this—
Laertes: What out of this, my lord?
King: Laertes, was your father dear to you?
        Or are you like the painting[35] of a sorrow,
110   A face without a heart?
Laertes: Why ask you this?
King: Not that I think you did not love your father,
        But that I know love is begun by time,

---

[26] sables . . . weeds: dignified roles.   [27] can well: can do well.
[28] incorpsed . . . deminatured: of one body.   [29] topped my thoughts: surpassed what
I could imagine.   [30] forgery . . . tricks: imagination of all kinds of fancy tricks.
shapes: fancies.   [31] brooch: ornament.   [32] confession: report.   [33] scrimers: fencers.
[34] envenom: poison.   [35] painting: i.e., imitation.

And that I see, in passages of proof,[36]
Time qualifies[37] the spark and fire of it.
115　There lives within the very flame of love
A kind of wick or snuff[38] that will abate it.
And nothing is at a like goodness still,[39]
For goodness, growing to a pleurisy,[40]
Dies in his own too much. That we would do
120　We should do when we would; for this "would" changes
And hath abatements and delays as many
As there are tongues, are hands, are accidents,
And then this "should" is like a spendthrift[41] sigh
That hurts by easing. But to the quick o' the ulcer.[42]
125　Hamlet comes back. What would you undertake
To show yourself your father's son in deed
More than in words?
Laertes:　　　　　　　To cut his throat i' the church.[43]
King: No place indeed should murder sanctuarize,[44]
Revenge should have no bounds. But, good Laertes,
130　Will you do this, keep close within your chamber.
Hamlet returned shall know you are come home.
We'll put on those[45] shall praise your excellence
And set a double varnish on the fame
The Frenchman gave you, bring you in fine[46] together
135　And wager on your heads. He, being remiss,[47]
Most generous[48] and free from all contriving,[49]
Will not peruse the foils, so that with ease,
Or with a little shuffling, you may choose
A sword unbated,[50] and in a pass of practice[51]
140　Requite him for your father.
Laertes:　　　　　　　I will do 't,
And for that purpose I'll anoint my sword.
I bought an unction[52] of a mountebank[53]
So mortal that but dip a knife in it,
Where it draws blood no cataplasm[54] so rare,

---

[36] **passages of proof:** experiences which prove.　[37] **qualifies:** diminishes.　[38] **snuff:** Before the invention of self-consuming wicks for candles, the wick smoldered and formed a ball of soot which dimmed the light and gave out a foul smoke.　[39] **still:** always.　[40] **pleurisy:** fullness.　[41] **spendthrift:** wasteful, because sighing was supposed to be bad for the blood.　[42] **quick . . . ulcer:** i.e., to come to the real issue. **quick:** flesh, sensitive part.
[43] **cut . . . church:** i.e., to commit murder in a holy place, which would bring Laertes in danger of everlasting damnation; no crime could be worse.　[44] **sanctuarize:** give sanctuary to.　[45] **put . . . those:** set on some.　[46] **fine:** short.　[47] **remiss:** careless.
[48] **generous:** noble.　[49] **contriving:** plotting.　[50] **unbated:** not blunted, with a sharp point.　[51] **pass of practice:** treacherous thrust.　[52] **unction:** poison.　[53] **mountebank:** quack doctor.　[54] **cataplasm:** poultice.

145   Collected from all simples[55] that have virtue
         Under the moon,[56] can save the thing from death
         That is but scratched withal. I'il touch my point
         With this contagion, that if I gall[57] him slightly,
         It may be death.
     King: Let's further think of this,
150   Weigh what convenience both of time and means
         May fit us to our shape.[58] If this should fail,
         And that our drift look through our bad performance,[59]
         'Twere better not assayed. Therefore this project
         Should have a back or second, that might hold
155   If this did blast in proof.[60] Soft! Let me see—
         We'll make a solemn wager on your cunnings.
         I ha 't.
         When in your motion you are hot and dry—
         As make your bouts[61] more violent to that end—
160   And that he calls for drink, I'll have prepared him
         A chalice[62] for the nonce,[63] whereon but sipping,
         If he by chance escape your venomed stuck,[64]
         Our purpose may hold there. But stay, what noise?
         [Enter Queen.] How now, Sweet Queen!
165 Queen: One woe doth tread upon another's heel.
         So fast they follow. Your sister's drowned, Laertes.
     Laertes: Drowned! Oh, where?
     Queen: There is a willow grows aslant a brook
         That shows his hoar[65] leaves in the glassy stream.
170   There with fantastic garlands did she come
         Of crowflowers, nettles, daises, and long purples
         That liberal[66] shepherds give a grosser name,
         But our cold maids do dead-men's-fingers call them.
         There on the pendent[67] boughs her coronet weeds[68]
175   Clambering to hang, an envious sliver[69] broke,
         When down her weedy trophies and herself
         Fell in the weeping brook. Her clothes spread wide,
         And mermaidlike awhile they bore her up—
         Which time she chanted snatches of old tunes,

---

[55] simples: herbs.   [56] Under . . . moon: herbs collected by moonlight were regarded as
particularly potent.   [57] gall: break the skin.   [58] Weigh . . . shape: consider the best
time and method of carrying out a plan.   [59] drift . . . performance: intention be revealed
through bungling.   [60] blast in proof: break in trial, like a cannon which bursts when being
tested.   [61] bouts: attacks, in the fencing match.   [62] chalice: cup.   [63] nonce:
occasion.   [64] stuck: thrust.   [65] hoar: gray. The underside of the leaves of the willow are
silver-gray.   [66] liberal: coarse-mouthed.   [67] pendent: hanging over the water.
[68] coronet weeds: wild flowers woven into a crown.   [69] envious sliver: malicious branch.

180   As one incapable[70] of her own distress,
       Or like a creature native and indued[71]
       Unto that element. But long it could not be
       Till that her garments, heavy with their drink,
       Pulled the poor wretch from her melodious lay[72]
185   To muddy death.
  Laertes: Alas, then, she is drowned!
  Queen: Drowned, drowned.
  Laertes: Too much of water hast thou, poor Ophelia,
       And therefore I forbid my tears. But yet
       It is our trick[73]—Nature her custom holds,
190   Let shame say what it will. When these[74] are gone,
       The woman will be out.[75] Adieu, my lord.
       I have a speech of fire that fain[76] would blaze
       But that this folly douts[77] it.   *[Exit.]*
  King: Let's follow, Gertrude.
       How much I had to do to calm his rage!
195   Now fear I this will give it start again,
       Therefore let's follow.   *[Exeunt.]*

Act V

Scene I. A churchyard.

[Enter two Clowns,[1] with spades, etc.]

1. **Clown:** Is she to be buried in Christian burial[2] that willfully seeks her own
   salvation?
2. **Clown:** I tell thee she is, and therefore make her grave straight.[3] The
   crowner[4] hath sat on her, and finds it Christian burial.
5 1. **Clown:** How can that be, unless she drowned herself in her own defense?
2. **Clown:** Why, 'tis found so.
1. **Clown:** It must be "se offendendo,"[5] it cannot be else. For here lies the
   point. If I drown myself wittingly,[6] it argues an act, and an act hath three
   branches—it is to act, to do, and to perform. Argal,[7] she drowned herself
10   wittingly.

---

[70] incapable: not realizing.   [71] indued: endowed; i.e., a creature whose natural home is the
water *(element)*.   [72] lay: song.   [73] But . . . trick: it is our habit; i.e., to break into tears
of great sorrow.   [74] these: i.e., my tears.   [75] woman . . . out: I shall be a man
again.   [76] fain: willingly.   [77] douts: puts out.
[1] Clowns: countrymen.   [2] Christian burial: Suicides were not allowed burial in consecrated
ground, but were buried at crossroads. The gravediggers and the priest are professionally
scandalized that Ophelia should be allowed Christian burial solely because she is a lady of the
Court.   [3] straight: straightway.   [4] crowner: coroner.   [5] se offendendo: for *defendendo*,
in self-defense.   [6] wittingly: with full knowledge.   [7] Argal: for the Latin *ergo*, therefore.

2. Clown: Nay, but hear you, goodman delver.[8]

I. Clown: Give me leave. Here lies the water, good. Here stands the man, good. If the man go to this water and drown himself, it is will he, nill he[9] he goes, mark you that; but if the water come to him and drown him, he
15 drowns not himself. Argal, he that is not guilty of his own death shortens not his own life.

2. Clown: But is this law?

I. Clown: Aye, marry, is 't, crowner's quest[10] law.

2. Clown: Will you ha' the truth on 't? If this had not been a gentlewoman, she
20 should have been buried out o' Christian burial.

I. Clown: Why, there thou say'st. And the more pity that great folks should have countenance[11] in this world to drown or hang themselves more than their even[12] Christian. Come, my spade. There is no ancient gentlemen but gardeners, ditchers, and gravemakers. They hold up[13] Adam's profession.
25 **2. Clown:** Was he a gentleman?

I. Clown: A' was the first that ever bore arms.[14]

2. Clown: Why, he had none.

I. Clown: What, art a heathen? How dost thou understand the Scripture? The Scripture says Adam digged. Could he dig without arms? I'll put another
30 question to thee. If thou answerest me not to the purpose, confess thyself—

2. Clown: Go to.

I. Clown: What is he that builds stronger than either the mason, the shipwright, or the carpenter?

2. Clown: The gallows-maker, for that frame outlives a thousand tenants.
35 **I. Clown:** I like thy wit well, in good faith. The gallows does well, but how does it well? It does well to those that do ill. Now thou dost ill to say the gallows is built stronger than the church; argal, the gallows may do well to thee. To 't again, come.

2. Clown: Who builds stronger than a mason, a shipwright, or a carpenter?
40 **I. Clown:** Aye, tell me that, and unyoke.[15]

2. Clown: Marry, now I can tell.

I. Clo: To 't.

2. Clown: Mass,[16] I cannot tell.

[Enter Hamlet and Horatio, afar off.]

I. Clown: Cudgel thy brains no more about it, for your dull ass will not mend
45 his pace with beating, and when you are asked this question next, say "A gravemaker." The houses that he makes last till Doomsday. Go, get thee to Yaughan,[17] fetch me a stoup[18] of liquor.   *[Exit Second Clown.]*
[First Clown digs, and sings.]

---

[8] delver: digger.   [9] will he, nill he: willy-nilly, whether he wishes or not.   [10] quest: inquest.   [11] countenance: favor.   [12] even: fellow.   [13] hold up: support.   [14] bore arms: had a coat of arms—the outward sign of a gentleman. See App. 9.   [15] unyoke: finish the job, unyoking the plow oxen being the end of the day's work.   [16] Mass: by the mass.   [17] Yaughan: apparently an innkeeper near the Globe Theatre.   [18] stoup: large pot.

"In youth,[19] when I did love, did love,
Methought it was very sweet,

50   To contract; oh, the time, for-a my behoove,[20]
Oh, methought, there-a was nothing-a meet."

Hamlet: Has this fellow no feeling for his business, that he sings at grave-making?

Horatio: Custom hath made it in him a property of easiness.[21]

55 **Hamlet:** 'Tis e'en so. The hand of little employment hath the daintier sense.[22]

I. Clown: *[Sings.]* "But age, with his stealing steps,
Hath clawed me in his clutch,
And hath shipped me intil the land[23]
As if I had never been such."

[Throws up a skull.]

60 **Hamlet:** That skull had a tongue in it, and could sing once. How the knave jowls[24] it to the ground, as if it were Cain's jawbone, that did the first murder! It might be the pate of a politician which this ass now o'erreaches[25]—one that would circumvent[26] God, might it not?

Horatio: It might, my lord.

65 **Hamlet:** Or of a courtier, which could say "Good morrow, sweet lord! How dost thou, good lord?" This might be my lord Such-a-one that praised my lord Such-a-one's horse when he meant to beg it, might it not?

Horatio: Aye, my lord.

Hamlet: Why, e'en so. And now my Lady Worm's chapless,[27] and knocked

70   about the mazzard[28] with a sexton's spade. Here's fine revolution, an we had the trick to see 't. Did these bones cost no more the breeding but to play at loggats[29] with 'em? Mine ache to think on 't.

I. Clown: *[Sings.]* "A pickax and a spade, a spade,
For and a shrouding sheet—

75   Oh, a pit of clay for to be made
For such a guest is meet."

[Throws up another skull.]

Hamlet: There's another. Why may not that be the skull of a lawyer?[30] Where be his quiddities now, his quillets, his cases, his tenures, and his tricks? Why does he suffer this rude knave now to knock him about the sconce[31]

80   with a dirty shovel, and will not tell him of his action of battery? Hum!

---

[19] **In youth . . . meet:** The song which the gravedigger sings without much care for accuracy or sense was first printed in *Tottel's Miscellany,* 1558.   [20] **behoove:** benefit.   [21] **property of easiness:** careless habits.   [22] **hand . . . sense:** those who have little to do are the most sensitive.   [23] **shipped . . . land:** shoved me into the ground.   [24] **jowls:** dashes.
[25] **o'erreaches:** gets the better of.   [26] **circumvent:** get around.   [27] **chapless:** without jaws.
[28] **mazzard:** head, a slang word; lit., drinking-bowl.   [29] **loggats:** a game in which billets of wood or bones were stuck in the ground and knocked over by throwing at them.
[30] **lawyer . . . indentures:** Hamlet strings out a number of the legal phrases loved by lawyers: *quiddities:* subtle arguments; *quillets:* quibbles; *tenures:* titles to property; *tricks:* knavery; *statutes:* bonds; *recognizances:* obligation; *fines:* conveyances; *vouchers:* guarantors; *recoveries:* transfers; *indentures:* agreements.   [31] **sconce:** head; lit., blockhouse.

This fellow might be in 's time a great buyer of land, with his statutes, his recognizances, his fines, his double vouchers, his recoveries. Is this the fine[32] of his fines and the recovery of his recoveries, to have his fine pate full of fine dirt? Will his vouchers vouch him no more of his purchase,

85   and double ones too, than the length and breadth of a pair of indentures? The very conveyances of his lands will hardly lie in this box,[33] and must the interior himself have no more, ha?

Horatio: Not a jot more, my lord.

Hamlet: Is not parchment made of sheepskins?

90   Horatio: Aye, my lord, and of calfskins too.

Hamlet: They are sheep and calves which seek out assurance in that. I will speak to this fellow. Whose grave's this, sirrah?

I. Clown: Mine, sir. *[Sings.]*

> "Oh, a pit of clay for to be made
95   For such a guest is meet."

Hamlet: I think it be thine indeed, for thou liest in 't.

I. Clown: You lie out on 't, sir, and therefore 'tis not yours. For my part, I do not lie in 't, and yet it is mine.

Hamlet: Thou does lie in 't, be in 't and say it is thine. 'Tis for the dead, not

100   for the quick, therefore thou liest.

I. Clown: 'Tis a quick lie, sir, 'twill away again, from me to you.

Hamlet: What man dost thou dig it for?

I. Clown: For no man, sir.

Hamlet: What woman, then?

105   I. Clown: For none, neither.

Hamlet: Who is to be buried in 't?

I. Clown: One that was a woman, sir, but, rest her soul, she's dead.

Hamlet: How absolute[34] the knave is! We must speak by the card,[35] or equivocation[36] will undo us. By the Lord, Horatio, this three years I have taken

110   note of it—the age is grown so picked[37] that the toe of the peasant comes so near the heel of the courtier, he galls his kibe.[38] How long hast thou been a gravemaker?

I. Clown: Of all the days i' the year, I came to 't that day that our last King Hamlet o'ercame Fortinbras.

115   Hamlet: How long is that since?

I. Clown: Cannot you tell that? Every fool can tell that. It was that very day that young Hamlet was born, he that is mad, and sent into England.

---

[32] fine: ending.   [33] box: coffin.   [34] absolute: exact.   [35] by . . . card: exactly. The card is the mariner's compass.   [36] equivocation: speaking with a double sense. The word was much discussed when *Hamlet* was written.   [37] picked: refined.   [38] toe . . . kibe: i.e., the peasant follows the courtier so closely that he rubs the courtier's heel into a blister. From about 1598 onward, writers, especially dramatists, often satirized the practice of yeoman farmers grown rich from war profits in sending their awkward sons to London to learn gentlemanly manners. Ben Jonson portrays two specimens in Stephen in *Every Man in His Humour* and Sogliardo in *Every Man out of His Humour.*

Hamlet: Aye, marry, why was he sent into England?

I. Clown: Why, because a' was mad. A' shall recover his wits there, or, if a' do
120   not, 'tis no great matter there.

Hamlet: Why?

I. Clown: 'Twill not be seen in him there—there the men are as mad as he.

Hamlet: How came he mad?

I. Clown: Very strangely, they say.

125 **Hamlet:** How "strangely"?

I. Clown: Faith, e'en with losing his wits.

Hamlet: Upon what ground?

I. Clown: Why, here in Denmark. I have been sexton here, man and boy,
        thirty years.[39]

130 **Hamlet:** How long will a man lie i' the earth ere he rot?

I. Clown: I' faith, if a' be not rotten before a' die—as we have many pocky[40]
        corses nowadays that will scarce hold the laying in—a' will last you some
        eight year or nine year. A tanner will last you nine year.

Hamlet: Why he more than another?

135 **I. Clown:** Why, sir, his hide is so tanned with his trade that a' will keep out
        water a great while, and your water is a sore decayer of your whoreson[41]
        dead body. Here's a skull now. This skull has lain in the earth three and
        twenty years.

Hamlet: Whose was it?

140 **I. Clown:** A whoreson mad fellow's it was. Whose do you think it was?

Hamlet: Nay, I know not.

I. Clown: A pestilence on him for a mad rogue! A' poured a flagon of Rhenish
        on my head once. This same skull, sir, was Yorick's skull, the King's jester.

Hamlet: This?

145 **I. Clown:** E'en that.

Hamlet: Let me see. *[Takes the skull.]* Alas, poor Yorick! I knew him, Horatio—
        a fellow of infinite jest, of most excellent fancy. He hath borne me on his
        back a thousand times, and now how abhorred in my imagination it is! My
        gorge rises[42] at it. Here hung those lips that I have kissed I know not how
150   oft. Where be your gibes now? Your gambols? Your songs? Your flashes of
        merriment that were wont to set the table on a roar? Not one now, to mock
        your own grinning? Quite chop-fallen?[43] Now get you to my lady's chamber
        and tell her, let her paint an inch thick, to this favor[44] she must come—
        make her laugh at that. Prithee, Horatio, tell me one thing.

155 **Horatio:** What's that, my lord?

Hamlet: Dost thou think Alexander looked o' this fashion i' the earth?

---

[39] **thirty years:** The Clown's chronology has puzzled critics, for the general impression is that
Hamlet was much younger.   [40] **pocky:** suffering from the pox (venereal disease).
[41] **whoreson:** bastard, "son of a bitch."   [42] **My . . . rises:** I feel sick. **gorge:** throat.
[43] **chop-fallen:** downcast, with a pun on "chapless."   [44] **favor:** appearance, especially in
the face.

Horatio: E'en so.

Hamlet: And smelt so? Pah!

[Puts down the skull.]

Horatio: E'en so, my lord.

160 Hamlet: To what base uses we may return, Horatio! Why may not imagination
trace the noble dust of Alexander till he find it stopping a bunghole?[45]

Horatio: 'Twere to consider too curiously[46] to consider so.

Hamlet: No, faith, not a jot, but to follow him thither with modesty[47] enough
and likelihood to lead it. As thus: Alexander died, Alexander was buried,
165 Alexander returneth into dust; the dust is earth; of earth we make loam;[48]
and why of that loam, whereto he was converted, might they not stop a
beer barrel?

"Imperious Caesar, dead and turned to clay,
Might stop a hole to keep the wind away.
170 Oh, that that earth which kept the world in awe
Should patch a wall to expel the winter's flaw!"[49]
But soft! But soft! Aside—here comes the King.

[Enter Priests,[50] *etc., in procession; the corpse of Ophelia, Laertes and
Mourners following; King, Queen, their trains, etc.]*

The Queen, the courtiers—who is this they follow?
And with such maimèd[51] rites? This doth betoken[52]
175 The corse they follow did with desperate hand
Fordo[53] its own life. 'Twas of some estate.[54]
Couch[55] we awhile, and mark.

[Retiring with Horatio.]

Laertes: What ceremony else?

Hamlet: That is Laertes, a very noble youth. Mark.

180 Laertes: What ceremony else?

I. Priest: Her obsequies have been as far enlarged
As we have warranty.[56] Her death was doubtful,
And but that great command o'ersways the order,[57]
She should in ground unsanctified have lodged
185 Till the last trumpet; for[58] charitable prayers,

---

[45] bunghole: the hole in a beer barrel.   [46] curiously: precisely.   [47] with modesty: without
exaggeration.   [48] loam: mixture of clay and sand, used in plastering walls.   [49] flaw:
blast.   [50] Enter Priests: The stage directions in early texts are less elaborate. Q2 notes,
curtly, *Enter K.Q. Laertes and the corse.* FI has *Enter King, Queen, Laertes, and a coffin,
with Lords attendant.* QI prints *Enter King and Queen, Laertes and other lords, with a Priest
after the coffin.* This probably was how the scene was originally staged. The modern
directions ignore the whole significance of the "maimed rites"—Ophelia's funeral is
insultingly simple.   [51] maimed: curtailed.   [52] betoken: indicate.   [53] Fordo: destroy.
[54] estate: high rank.   [55] Couch: lie down.   [56] Her . . . warranty: the funeral rites have
been as complete as may be allowed.   [57] but . . . order: if the King's command had not
overruled the proper procedure.   [58] for: instead of.

Shards,[59] flints, and pebbles should be thrown on her.
Yet here she is 'loweed her virgin crants,[60]
Her maiden strewments[61] and the bringing home
Of bell and burial.
190 **Laertes:** Must there no more be done?
I. Priest: No more be done.
We should profane the service of the dead
To sing a requiem and such rest to her
As to peace-parted souls.[62]
Laertes: Lay her i' the earth.
And from her fair and unpolluted flesh
195 May violets spring! I tell thee, churlish priest,
A ministering angel shall my sister be
When thou liest howling.
Hamlet: What, the fair Ophelia!
Queen: *[Scattering flowers]* Sweets to the sweet. Farewell!
I hoped thou shouldst have been my Hamlet's wife,
200 I thought thy bride bed to have decked, sweet maid,
And not have strewed thy grave.
Laertes: Oh, treble woe
Fall ten times treble on that cursèd head
Whose wicked deed thy most ingenious sense[63]
Deprived thee of! Hold off the earth a while
205 Till I have caught her once more in mine arms.
                                       [Leaps into the grave.]
Now pile your dust upon the quick[64] and dead
Till of this flat a mountain you have made
To o'ertop old Pelion[65] on the skyish[66] head
Of blue Olympus.
210 **Hamlet:** *[Advancing]* What is he whose grief
Bears such an emphasis? Whose phrase of sorrow
Conjures the wandering stars and makes them stand[67]
Like wonder-wounded hearers? This is I,
Hamlet the Dane.   *[Leaps into the grave.]*
215 **Laertes:** The Devil take thy soul!
                                       [Grappling with him]
Hamlet: Thou pray'st not well.
I prithee, take thy fingers from my throat,
For though I am not splenitive[68] and rash,

---

[59] **Shards:** pieces of broken crockery.   [60] **crants:** wreaths of flowers—a sign that she had
died unwed.   [61] **maiden strewments:** the flowers strewn on the corpse of a maiden.
[62] **peace-parted souls:** souls which departed in peace, fortified with the rites of the
Church.   [63] **most . . . sense:** lively intelligence.   [64] **quick:** living.   [65] **Pelion:** When
the giants fought against the gods in order to reach Heaven, they tried to pile Mount Pelion
and Mount Ossa on Mount Olympus, the highest mountain in Greece.   [66] **skyish:** reaching
the sky.   [67] **stand:** stand still.   [68] **splenitive:** hot-tempered.

Yet have I in me something dangerous,
Which let thy wisdom fear. Hold off thy hand.

220 **King:** Pluck them asunder.

Queen: Hamlet, Hamlet!

All: Gentlemen—

Horatio: Good my lord, be quiet.

*[The Attendants part them,
and they come out of the grave.]*

Hamlet: Why, I will fight with him upon this theme
Until my eyelids will no longer wag.

Queen: O my son, what theme?

225 **Hamlet:** I loved Ophelia. Forty thousand brothers
Could not, with all their quantity of love,
Make up my sum. What wilt thou do for her?

King: Oh, he is mad, Laertes.

Queen: For love of God, forbear him.[69]

230 **Hamlet:** 'Swounds,[70] show me that thou'lt do.
Woo 't weep? Woo 't fight? Woo 't fast? Woo 't tear thyself?
Woo 't drink up eisel?[71] Eat a crocodile?
I'll do 't. Dost thou come here to whine?
To outface[72] me with leaping in her grave?
235 Be buried quick with her, and so will I.
And if thou prate of mountains, let them throw
Millions of acres on us, till our ground,
Singeing his pate against the burning zone,
Make Ossa[73] like a wart! Nay, an thou 'lt mouth,
240 I'll rant as well as thou.

Queen: This is mere madness.
And thus awhile the fit will work on him.
Anon, as patient as the female dove
When that her golden couplets[74] are disclosed,[75]
His silence will sit drooping.

Hamlet: Hear you, sir.
245 What is the reason that you use me thus?
I loved you ever. But it is no matter,
Let Hercules himself do what he may,
The cat will mew and dog will have his day.[76]   *[Exit.]*

---

[69] forbear him: leave him alone.   [70] 'Swounds . . . thou: Hamlet in his excitement cries out that if Laertes wishes to make extravagant boasts of what he will do to show his sorrow, he will be even more extravagant.   [71] eisel: vinegar.   [72] outface: brow beat.   [73] Ossa: See l. 208, n.   [74] couplets: eggs, of which the dove lays two only.   [75] disclosed: hatched.   [76] Let . . . day: i.e., let this ranting hero have his turn; mine will come sometime.

King: I pray thee, good Horatio, wait upon him.

[Exit Horatio.]

250 *[To Laertes]* Strengthen your patience in our last night's speech.
We'll put the matter to the present push.[77]
Good Gertrude, set some watch over your son.
This grave shall have a living monument.[78]
An hour of quiet shortly shall we see,

255 Till then, in patience our proceeding be.   *[Exeunt.]*

Scene II. A hall in the castle.

[Enter Hamlet and Horatio.]

Hamlet: So much for this, sir. Now shall you see the other.
You do remember all the circumstance?
Horatio: Remember it, my lord!
Hamlet: Sir, in my heart there was a kind of fighting

5   That would not let me sleep. Methought I lay
Worse than the mutines in the bilboes.[1] Rashly,
And praised be rashness for it, let us know,
Our indiscretion sometime serves us well
When our deep plots do pall.[2] And that should learn[3] us

10   There's a divinity that shapes our ends,
Roughhew them how we will.[4]
Horatio: That is most certain.
Hamlet: Up from my cabin,
My sea gown[5] scarfed[6] about me, in the dark
Groped I to find out them,[7] had my desire,

15   Fingered their packet, and in fine withdrew
To mine own room again, making so bold,
My fears forgetting manners, to unseal
Their grand commission where I found, Horatio—
Oh royal knavery!—an exact command,

20   Larded[8] with many several sorts of reasons,
Importing Denmark's health and England's too,
With, ho! such bugs[9] and goblins in my life[10]
That, on the supervise,[11] no leisure bated,[12]

---

[77] push: test; lit., thrust of a pike.   [78] living monument: with the double meaning of "lifelike memorial" and "the death of Hamlet."
[1] mutines . . . bilboes: mutineers in the shackles used on board ship.   [2] pall: fail.
[3] learn: teach.   [4] There's . . . will: though we may make the rough beginning, God finishes our designs.   [5] sea gown: a thick coat with a high collar worn by seamen.
[6] scarfed: wrapped.   [7] them: i.e., Rosencrantz and Guildenstern.   [8] Larded: garnished.
[9] bugs: bugbears.   [10] in my life: so long as I was alive.   [11] supervise: reading.
[12] bated: allowed.

No, not to stay the grinding of the ax,
25   My head should be struck off.
Horatio: Is 't possible?
Hamlet: Here's the commission. Read it at more leisure
        But wilt thou hear me how I did proceed?
Horatio: I beseech you.
Hamlet: Being thus benetted round with villainies—
30   Ere I could make a prologue to my brains,
        They had begun the play—I sat me down,
        Devised a new commission, wrote it fair.
        I once did hold it, as our statists[13] do,
        A baseness to write fair, and labored much
35   How to forget that learning, but, sir, now
        It did me yeoman's service.[14] Wilt thou know
        The effect of what I wrote?
Horatio: Aye, good my lord.
Hamlet: An earnest conjuration from the King,
        As England was his faithful tributary,
40   As love between them like the palm might flourish,
        As peace should still her wheaten garland wear
        And stand a comma 'tween their amities,[15]
        And many suchlike "Ases"[16] of great charge,[17]
        That, on the view and knowing of these contents,
45   Without debatement[18] further, more or less,
        He should the bearers put to sudden death,
        Not shriving time allowed.[19]
Horatio: How was this sealed?
Hamlet: Why, even in that was Heaven ordinant.[20]
        I had my father's signet in my purse,
50   Which was the model[21] of that Danish seal—
        Folded the writ[22] up in the form of the other,
        Subscribed[23] it, gave 't the impression,[24] placed it safely,
        The changeling[25] never known. Now the next day

---

[13] statists: statesmen. As scholars who have had to read Elizabethan documents know, the more exalted the writer, the worse his handwriting. As a girl Queen Elizabeth wrote a beautiful script; as Queen her letters are as illegible as any. All but the most confidential documents were copied out in a fair hand by a secretary.   [14] yeoman's service: faithful service. The most reliable English soldiers were yeomen—farmers and their men.
[15] stand . . . amities: be a connecting link of their friendship.   [16] "Ases": Official documents were written in flowery language full of metaphorical clauses beginning with "As." Hamlet puns on "asses."   [17] great charge: "great weight" and "heavy burden."
[18] debatement: argument.   [19] Not . . . allowed: without giving them time even to confess their sins.   [20] ordinant: directing, in control.   [21] model: copy.   [22] writ: writing.
[23] Subscribed: signed.   [24] impression: of the seal.   [25] changeling: lit., an ugly child exchanged by the fairies for a fair one.

Was our sea fight, and what to this was sequent[26]
55   Thou know'st already.
Horatio: So Guildenstern and Rosencrantz go to 't.
Hamlet: Why, man, they did make love to this employment.
      They are not near my conscience, their defeat[27]
      Does by their own insinuation[28] grow.
60   'Tis dangerous when the baser nature comes
      Between the pass and fell incensèd points
      Of mighty opposites.[29]
Horatio: Why, what a King is this!
Hamlet: Does it not, think'st thee, stand me now upon—
      He that hath killed my King and whored my mother,
65   Popped in between the election and my hopes,[30]
      Thrown out his angle[31] for my proper[32] life,
      And with such cozenage[33]—is 't not perfect conscience,
      To quit[34] him with this arm? And is 't not to be damned,
      To let this canker[35] of our nature come
70   In further evil?
Horatio: It must be shortly known to him from England
      What is the issue of the business there.
Hamlet: It will be short. The interim[36] is mine,
      And a man's life's no more than to say "One."
75   But I am very sorry, good Horatio,
      That to Laertes I forgot myself,
      For by the image of my cause I see
      The portraiture of his. I'll court his favors.
      But, sure, the bravery[37] of his grief did put me
80   Into a towering passion.
Horatio: Peace! Who comes here?

      [Enter Osric.[38]]

Osric: Your lordship is right welcome back to Denmark.
Hamlet: I humbly thank you, sir. Dost know this water fly?[39]
Horatio: No, my good lord.

---

[26] sequent: following.   [27] defeat: destruction.   [28] by . . . insinuation: because they insinuated themselves into this business.   [29] 'Tis . . . opposites: it is dangerous for inferior men to interfere in a duel between mighty enemies. pass: thrust. fell: fierce. [30] Popped . . . hopes: As is from time to time shown in the play, the Danes chose their King by election.   [31] angle: fishing rod and line.   [32] proper: own.   [33] cozenage: cheating. [34] quit: pay back.   [35] canker: maggot.   [36] interim: interval; between now and the news from England.   [37] bravery: excessive show.   [38] Osric: Osric is a specimen of the fashionable, effeminate courtier. He dresses prettily and talks the jargon of his class, which at this time affected elaborate and allusive metaphors and at all costs avoided saying plain things plainly.   [39] water fly: a useless little creature that flits about.

Hamlet: Thy state is the more gracious,[40] for 'tis a vice to know him. He hath
85   much land, and fertile. Let a beast be lord of beasts and his crib shall
stand at the King's mess.[41] 'Tis a chough,[42] but, as I say, spacious[43] in the
possession of dirt.

Osric: Sweet lord, if your lordship were at leisure, I should impart a thing to
you from His Majesty.

90 Hamlet: I will receive it, sir, with all diligence of spirit. Put your bonnet to
his right use,[44] 'tis for the head.

Osric: I thank your lordship, it is very hot.

Hamlet: No, believe me, 'tis very cold. The wind is northerly.

Osric: It is indifferent[45] cold, my lord, indeed.

95 Hamlet: But yet methinks it is very sultry and hot, for my complexion—

Osric: Exceedingly, my lord. It is very sultry, as 'twere—I cannot tell how.
But, my lord, His Majesty bade me signify to you that he has laid a great
wager on your head. Sir, this is the matter—

Hamlet: I beseech you, remember—

[Hamlet moves him to put on his hat.]

100 Osric: Nay, good my lord, for mine ease, in good faith. Sir, here is newly come
to Court Laertes—believe me, an absolute[46] gentleman, full of most excellent differences,[47] of very soft society[48] and great showing.[49] Indeed, to
speak feelingly[50] of him, he is the card or calendar of gentry,[51] for you shall
find in him the continent of what part a gentleman would see.[52]

105 Hamlet: Sir,[53] his definement suffers no perdition in you, though I know to
divide him inventorially would dizzy the arithmetic of memory, and yet
but yaw neither, in respect of his quick sail. But in the verity of extolment, I take him to be a soul of great article, and his infusion of such

---

[40] Thy . . . gracious: you are in the better state.   [41] Let . . . mess: i.e., any man,
however low, who has wealth enough will find a good place at Court. **crib:** manger.
mess: table.   [42] chough: jackdaw.   [43] spacious: wealthy.   [44] Put . . . use: i.e., put
your hat on your head. Osric is so nice-mannered that he cannot bring himself to wear his
hat in the presence of the Prince.   [45] indifferent: moderately.   [46] absolute: perfect.
[47] differences: qualities peculiar to himself.   [48] soft society: gentle breeding.   [49] great
showing: distinguished appearance.   [50] feelingly: with proper appreciation.
[51] card . . . gentry: the very fashion plate of what a gentleman should be.   [52] continent
. . . see: all the parts that should be in a perfect gentleman.   [53] Sir . . . more: Hamlet
retorts in similar but even more extravagant language. This is too much for Osric (and for
most modern readers). Hamlet's words may be paraphrased: "Sir, the description of this
perfect gentleman loses nothing in your account of him; though I realize that if one were to
try to enumerate his excellences, it would exhaust our arithmetic, and yet"—here he changes
the image to one of sailing—"we should still lag behind him as he outsails us. But in the
true vocabulary of praise, I take him to be a soul of the greatest worth, and his
perfume"—i.e., his personal essence—"so scarce and rare that to speak truly of him, the only
thing like him is his own reflection in his mirror, and everyone else who tries to follow him
merely his shadow." **yaw:** fall off from the course laid. **verity . . . extolment:** in true praise.
infusion: essence. **semblable:** resemblance. **trace:** follow. **umbrage:** shadow.

dearth and rareness as, to make true diction of him, his semblable is his
110   mirror, and who else would trace him, him umbrage—nothing more.

Osric: Your lordship speaks most infallibly of him.

Hamlet: The concernancy,[54] sir? Why do we wrap the gentleman in our more
rawer breath?[55]

Osric: Sir?[56]

115 **Horatio:** Is 't not possible to understand in another tongue? You will do 't,
sir, really.

Hamlet: What imports the nomination[57] of this gentleman?

Osric: Of Laertes?

Horatio: His purse is empty already, all's golden words are spent.

120 **Hamlet:** Of him, sir.

Osric: I know you are not ignorant—

Hamlet: I would you did, sir. Yet, in faith, if you did, it would not much approve[58] me. Well, sir?

Osric: You are not ignorant of what excellence Laertes is—

125 **Hamlet:** I dare not confess that, lest I should compare with him in excellence, but to know a man well were to know himself.

Osric: I mean, sir, for his weapon,[59] but in the imputation[60] laid on him by
them, in his meed[61] he's unfellowed.[62]

Hamlet: What's his weapon?

130 **Osric:** Rapier and dagger.

Hamlet: That's two of his weapons, but, well.

Osric: The King, sir, hath wagered with him six Barbary horses, against the
which he has imponed,[63] as I take it, six French rapiers and poniards,
with their assigns,[64] as girdle, hanger,[65] and so—three of the carriages, in
135   faith, are very dear to fancy,[66] very responsive to[67] the hilts, most delicate
carriages, and of very liberal conceit.[68]

Hamlet: What call you the carriages?

Horatio: I knew you must be edified by the margent[69] ere you had done.

Osric: The carriages, sir, are the hangers.

140 **Hamlet:** The phrase would be more germane[70] to the matter if we could
carry a cannon by our sides. I would it might be hangers till then. But,
on—six Barbary horses against six French swords, their assigns, and
three liberal-conceited carriages. That's the French bet against the Danish. Why is this "imponed," as you call it?

---

[54] concernancy: i.e., what is all this talk about?   [55] Why . . . breath: why do we discuss the
gentleman with our inadequate voices?   [56] Sir: Osric is completely baffled.
[57] nomination: naming.   [58] approve: commend.   [59] his weapon: i.e., skill with his
weapon.   [60] imputation: reputation.   [61] meed: merit.   [62] unfellowed: without an
equal.   [63] imponed: laid down as a stake.   [64] assigns: that which goes with them.
[65] hanger: straps by which the scabbard was hung from the belt, for specimens.   [66] dear
to fancy: of beautiful design.   [67] responsive to: matching.   [68] liberal conceit: elaborately
artistic.   [69] edified . . . margent: informed by the notes. In Shakespeare's time the notes
were often printed in the margin.   [70] germane: related.

145 Osric: The King, sir, hath laid, sir, that in a dozen passes between yourself and him, he shall not exceed you three hits. He hath laid on twelve for nine,[71] and it would come to immediate trial if your lordship would vouchsafe the answer.

Hamlet: How if I answer no?

150 Osric: I mean, my lord, the opposition of your person in trial.

Hamlet: Sir, I will walk here in the hall. If it please His Majesty, it is the breathing-time of day with me.[72] Let the foils be brought, the gentleman willing, and the King hold his purpose, I will win for him an I can. If not, I will gain nothing but my shame and the odd hits.

155 Osric: Shall I redeliver you e'en so?

Hamlet: To this effect, sir, after what flourish[73] your nature will.

Osric: I commend my duty to your lordship.

Hamlet: Yours, yours. *[Exit Osric.]* He does well to commend it himself, there are no tongues else for 's turn.

160 Horatio: This lapwing[74] runs away with the shell on his head.

Hamlet: He did comply with his dug[75] before he sucked it. Thus has he—and many more of the same breed that I know the drossy[76] age dotes on— only got the tune of the time and outward habit of encounter,[77] a kind of yesty collection[78] which carries them through and through the most
165 fond[79] and winnowed[80] opinions—and do but blow them to their trial, the bubbles are out.[81]

[Enter a Lord.]

Lord: My lord, His Majesty commended him to you by young Osric, who brings back to him that you attend him in the hall. He sends to know if your pleasure hold to play with Laertes, or that you will take longer time.

170 Hamlet: I am constant to my purpose, they follow the King's pleasure. If his fitness speaks, mine is ready, now or whensoever, provided I be so able as now.

Lord: The King and Queen and all are coming down.

Hamlet: In happy time.[82]

175 Lord: The Queen desires you to use some gentle entertainment[83] to Laertes before you fall to play.

Hamlet: She well instructs me.   *[Exit Lord.]*

---

[71] twelve . . . mine: Laertes has bet the King he will hit Hamlet twelve times before Hamlet hits him nine.   [72] breathing-time . . . me: time when I take exercise.
[73] flourish: fanfare, elaborate phrasing.   [74] lapwing: a pretty, lively little bird. It is so lively that it can run about the moment it is hatched.   [75] did . . . dug: was ceremonious with the nipple; i.e., behaved in this fantastic way from his infancy.   [76] drossy: scummy, frivolous.   [77] tune . . . encounter: i.e., they sing the same tune as everyone else and have the same society manners.   [78] yesty collection: frothy catchwords.   [79] fond: foolish.
[80] winnowed: light as chaff. Winnowing is the process of fanning the chaff from the grain.   [81] do . . . out: force them to make sense of their words and they are deflated, as Hamlet has just deflated Osric.   [82] In . . . time: at a good moment.   [83] gentle entertainment: kindly treatment; i.e., be reconciled after the brawl in the churchyard.

Horatio: You will lose this wager, my lord.

Hamlet: I do not think so. Since he went into France I have been in continual
180 practice, I shall win at the odds. But thou wouldst not think how ill all's
here about my heart—but it is no matter.

Horatio: Nay, good my lord—

Hamlet: It is but foolery, but it is such a kind of gaingiving[84] as would perhaps trouble a woman.

185 **Horatio:** If your mind dislike anything, obey it. I will forestall their repair
hither and say you are not fit.

Hamlet: Not a whit, we defy augury.[85] There's special providence in the fall of
a sparrow.[86] If it be now, 'tis not to come; if it be not to come, it will be
now; if it be not now, yet it will come. The readiness is all. Since no man
190 has aught of what he leaves, what is 't to leave betimes? Let be.

*[Enter King, Queen, Laertes, and Lords, Osric and other Attendants with
foils; a table and flagons of wine on it.]*

King: Come, Hamlet, come, and take this hand from me.

[The King puts Laertes' hand into Hamlet's.]

Hamlet: Give me your pardon, sir. I've done you wrong,
But pardon 't, as you are a gentleman.
This presence[87] knows,
195 And you must needs have heard, how I am punished
With sore distraction. What I have done
That might your nature, honor, and exception[88]
Roughly awake, I here proclaim was madness.
Was 't Hamlet wronged Laertes? Never Hamlet.
200 If Hamlet from himself be ta'en away,[89]
And when he's not himself does wrong Laertes,
Then Hamlet does it not, Hamlet denies it.
Who does it, then? His madness. If 't be so,
Hamlet is of the faction that is wronged,
205 His madness is poor Hamlet's enemy.
Sir, in this audience
Let my disclaiming from a purposed evil[90]
Free me so far in your most generous thoughts
That I have shot mine arrow o'er the house,
210 And hurt my brother.

Laertes: I am satisfied in nature,
Whose motive, in this case, should stir me most

---

[84] gaingiving: misgiving.   [85] augury: omens.   [86] special . . . sparrow. The idea comes
from Matthew 10:25, "Are not two sparrows sold for a farthing? and one of them shall not fall
to the ground without your Father."   [87] presence: the whole Court.   [88] exception:
resentment.   [89] If . . . away: i.e., Hamlet mad is not Hamlet.   [90] Let . . . evil: let my
declaration that I did not intend any harm.

To my revenge. But in my terms of honor
I stand aloof, and will no reconcilement
Till by some elder masters of known honor

215 I have a voice and precedent of peace
To keep my name ungored.[91] But till that time
I do receive your offered love like love
And will not wrong it.

Hamlet: I embrace it freely,
And will this brother's wager frankly play.

220 Give us the foils. Come on.

Laertes: Come, one for me.

Hamlet: I'll be your foil,[92] Laertes. In mine ignorance
Your skill shall, like a star i' the darkest night,
Stick[93] fiery off indeed.

Laertes: You mock me, sir.

Hamlet: No, by this hand.

225 King: Give them the foils, young Osric. Cousin Hamlet,
You know the wager?

Hamlet: Very well, my lord.
Your Grace has laid the odds o' the weaker side.

King: I do not fear it, I have seen you both.
But since he is bettered,[94]

230 we have therefore odds.

Laertes: This is too heavy, let me see another.

Hamlet: This likes[95] me well. These foils have all a length?[96] *[They prepare
to play.]*

Osric: Aye, my good lord.

235 King: Set me the stoups[97] of wine upon that table.
If Hamlet give the first or second hit,
Or quit[98] in answer of the third exchange,
Let all the battlements their ordnance fire.
The King shall drink to Hamlet's better breath,

240 And in the cup a union[99] shall he throw
Richer than that which four successive kings
In Denmark's crown have worn. Give me the cups,
And let the kettle[100] to the trumpet speak,
The trumpet to the cannoneer without,

---

[91] I . . . ungored: I bear you no grudge so far as concerns my personal feelings, which would most readily move me to vengeance; but as this matter touches my honor, I cannot accept your apology until I have been assured by those expert in matters of honor that I may so do without loss of reputation.   [92] foil: Hamlet puns on the other meaning of foil—tin foil set behind a gem to give it luster.   [93] Stick . . . off: Shine out.   [94] bettered: considered your superior.   [95] likes: pleases.   [96] have . . . length: are all of equal length.
[97] stoups: drinking vessels.   [98] quit: strike back.   [99] union: a large pearl.
[100] kettle: kettledrum.

245　　The cannon to the Heavens, the Heaven to earth,
　　　　"Now the King drinks to Hamlet." Come, begin,
　　　　And you, the judge, bear a wary eye.
Hamlet: Come on, sir.
Laertes:　　　　　　　Come, my lord.　　　　　　　　*[They play.]*
Hamlet:　　　　　　　　　　　One.
Laertes:　　　　　　　　　　　　No.
Hamlet:　　　　　　　　　　　　　　Judgment.
Osric: A hit, a very palpable[101] hit.
Laertes:　　　　　　　　　　　Well, again.
250　King: Stay, give me drink. Hamlet, this pearl is thine[102]—
　　　　Here's to thy health.
　　　　[Trumpets sound, and cannon shot off within.]
　　　　　　　　　　　Give him the cup.
Hamlet: I'll play this bout first. Set it by a while.
　　　　Come. *[They play.]*
　　　　Another hit, what say you?
255　Laertes: A touch, a touch, I do confess.
King: Our son shall win.
Queen:　　　　　　　He's fat[103] and scant of breath.
　　　　Here, Hamlet, take my napkin, rub thy brows.
　　　　The Queen carouses to thy fortune, Hamlet.
Hamlet: Good madam!
260　King: Gertrude, do not drink.
Queen: I will, my lord, I pray you pardon me.

　　　　　　　　　　　　　　　　　　　　[She drinks.]

King: *[Aside]* It is the poisoned cup, it is too late.
Hamlet: I dare not drink yet, madam—by and by.
Queen: Come, let me wipe thy face.
265　Laertes: My lord, I'll hit him now.
King:　　　　　　　　　　　I do not think 't.
Laertes: *[Aside]* And yet 'tis almost against my conscience.
Hamlet: Come, for the third, Laertes. You but dally.[104]
　　　　I pray you pass with your best violence,
　　　　I am afeard you make a wanton of me.[105]
270　Laertes: Say you so? Come on.　　　　　　　*[They play.]*
Osric: Nothing, neither way.
Laertes: Have at you now!

　　　　*[Laertes wounds Hamlet; then, in scuffling, they change rapiers,[106] and
　　　　Hamlet wounds Laertes.]*

---

[101] palpable: clear.　　[102] this . . . thine: With these words the King drops the poisoned pearl into the cup intended for Hamlet.　　[103] fat: out of condition.　　[104] dally: play.　　[105] make . . . me: treat me like a child by letting me win.　　[106] they . . . rapiers: With the exchange of rapiers, Hamlet wounds Laertes with the pointed and poisoned weapon.

King: Part them, they are incensed.

Hamlet: Nay, come, again.   *[The Queen falls.]*

Osric: Look to the Queen there, ho!

Horatio: They bleed on both sides. How is it, my lord?

275 Osric: How is 't, Laertes?

Laertes: Why, as a woodcock to mine own springe,[107] Osric,
    I am justly killed with mine own treachery.

Hamlet: How does the Queen?

King: She swounds to see them bleed.

Queen: No, no, the drink, the drink!—O my dear Hamlet—

280   The drink, the drink! I am poisoned.   *[Dies.]*

Hamlet: Oh, villainy! Ho! Let the door be locked.
    Treachery! Seek it out.   *[Laertes falls.]*

Laertes: It is here, Hamlet. Hamlet, thou art slain.
    No medicine in the world can do thee good,

285   In thee there is not half an hour of life.
    The treacherous instrument is in thy hand,
    Unbated and envenomed. The foul practice
    Hath turned itself on me. Lo, here I lie
    Never to rise again. Thy mother's poisoned.

290   I can no more. The King, the King's to blame.

Hamlet: The point envenomed too!
    Then, venom, to thy work.   *[Stabs the King.]*

All: Treason! Treason!

King: Oh, yet defend me, friends, I am but hurt.

295 Hamlet: Here, thou incestuous, murderous, damnèd Dane,
    Drink off this potion. Is thy union[108] here?
    Follow my mother.   *[King dies.]*

Laertes: He is justly served.
    It is a poison tempered[109] by himself.
    Exchange forgiveness with me, noble Hamlet.

300   Mine and my father's death come not upon thee,[110]
    Nor thine on me!   *[Dies.]*

Hamlet: Heaven make thee free of it![111] I follow thee,
    I am dead, Horatio. Wretched Queen, adieu!
    You that look pale and tremble at this chance,

305   That are but mutes or audience to this act,
    Had I but time—as this fell[112] sergeant,[113] Death,
    Is strict in his arrest—oh, I could tell you—
    But let it be. Horatio, I am dead,

---

[107] springe: snare.   [108] union: pearl.   [109] tempered: mixed.   [110] come . . . thee: are not on your head.   [111] Heaven . . . it: God forgives you.   [112] fell: dread.
[113] sergeant: the officer of the Court who made arrests.

Thou livest. Report me and my cause aright
310   To the unsatisfied.[114]
Horatio: Never believe it.
I am more an antique Roman[115] than a Dane.
Here's yet some liquor left.
Hamlet: As thou 'rt a man,
Give me the cup. Let go—by Heaven, I'll have 't.
O good Horatio, what a wounded name,
315   Things standing thus unknown, shall live behind me!
If thou didst ever hold me in thy heart,
Absent thee from felicity a while,
And in this harsh world draw thy breath in pain
To tell my story. *[March afar off, and shot within]*
What warlike noise is this?
320 Osric: Young Fortinbras, with conquest come from Poland,
To the ambassadors of England gives
This warlike volley.
Hamlet: Oh, I die, Horatio,
The potent poison quite o'ercrows[116] my spirit.
I cannot live to hear the news from England,
325   But I do prophesy the election[117] lights
On Fortinbras. He has my dying voice.[118]
So tell him, with the occurrents, more and less,
Which have solicited.[119] The rest is silence.   *[Dies.]*
Horatio: Now cracks a noble heart. Good night, sweet Prince,
330   And flights of angels sing thee to thy rest!

[March within.]

Why does the drum come hither?

[Enter Fortinbras, and the English Ambassadors, with drum, colors, and Attendants.]

Fortinbras: Where is this sight?
Horatio: What is it you would see?
If aught of woe or wonder, cease your search.
Fortinbras: This quarry cries on havoc.[120] O proud Death,
335   What feast is toward[121] in thine eternal cell
That thou so many princes at a shot
So bloodily hast struck?

---

[114] unsatisfied: who do not know the truth.   [115] antique Roman: like Cato and Brutus, who
killed themselves rather than survive in a world which was unpleasing to them.
[116] o'ercrows: overpowers.   [117] election: as King of Denmark.   [118] voice: support.
[119] occurrents . . . solicited: events great and small which have caused me to
act.   [120] quarry . . . havoc: heap of slain denotes a pitiless slaughter.   [121] toward:
being prepared.

I. Ambassador: The sight is dismal,
    And our affairs from England come too late.
    The ears are senseless that should give us hearing,
340   To tell him his commandment is fulfilled,
    That Rosencrantz and Guildenstern are dead.
    Where should we have our thanks?
Horatio: Not from his mouth
    Had it the ability of life to thank you.
    He never gave commandment for their death.
345   But since, so jump[122] upon this bloody question,[123]
    You from the Polack wars, and you from England,
    Are here arrived, give order that these bodies
    High on a stage be placèd to the view,
    And let me speak to the yet unknowing world
350   How these things came about. So shall you hear
    Of carnal, bloody, and unnatural acts,
    Of accidental judgments, casual slaughters,
    Of deaths put on by cunning and forced cause,
    And, in this upshot, purposes mistook
355   Fall'n on the investors' heads.[124] All this can I
    Truly deliver.
Fortinbras: Let us haste to hear it,
    And call the noblest to the audience.
    For me, with sorrow I embrace my fortune.
    I have some rights of memory[125] in this kingdom,
360   Which now to claim my vantage[126] doth invite me.
Horatio: Of that I shall have also cause to speak,
    And from his mouth whose voice will draw on more.[127]
    But let this same be presently performed,
    Even while men's minds are wild, lest more mischance
365   On plots and errors happen.
Fortinbras: Let four captains
    Bear Hamlet, like a soldier, to the stage.
    For he was likely, had he been put on,[128]
    To have proved most royally. And for his passage

---

[122] jump: exactly.   [123] question: matter.   [124] carnal . . . heads: These lines sum up the whole tragedy: Claudius' adultery with Gertrude, his murder of his brother, the death of Ophelia due to an accident, that of Polonius by casual chance, Hamlet's device which caused the deaths of Rosencrantz and Guildenstern, the plan which went awry and caused the deaths of Claudius and Laertes.   [125] rights of memory: rights which will be remembered; i.e., with the disappearance of all the family of the original King Hamlet the situation reverts to what it was before the death of Fortinbras' father.   [126] vantage: i.e., my advantage, there being none to dispute my claim.   [127] voice . . . more: i.e., Hamlet's dying voice will strengthen your claim.   [128] had . . . on: had he become King.

The soldiers' music and the rites of war
370   Speak loudly for him.
Take up the bodies. Such a sight as this
Becomes the field, but here shows much amiss.
Go, bid the soldiers shoot.

[A dead march. Exeunt, bearing off the bodies;
after which a peal of ordnance is shot off.]

■ EXPLORATIONS OF THE TEXT ■

Act I

1. Discuss the first scene in *Hamlet*. What is wrong in the State of Denmark?
2. Why does Claudius ask Hamlet to abandon his "impious stubbornness"?
3. In Act I, Scene II, what does Hamlet reveal about himself in his first **soliloquy** (a speech directed to the audience recreating thoughts not known to other characters)?
4. What do Laertes and Polonius believe about Ophelia's love for Hamlet? What do they want her to do?
5. What does Polonius' advice (Act I, Scene III) reveal of life at court?
6. What does the ghost tell Hamlet? What is his request?

Act II

1. How is Hamlet changed by his father's death and by his mother's remarriage? Is he mad, or is he pretending to be mad (II, i)?
2. What do you learn about Polonius through his diagnosis of and reaction to Hamlet's madness (II, ii)?

Act III

1. Why does Hamlet find it difficult to avenge his father? Explain his famous soliloquy which begins "To be or not to be."
2. Consider Hamlet's treatment of Ophelia in Act III, Scene I. Find evidence that Hamlet knows that Claudius and Polonius listen to this conversation.
3. Why does Ophelia become insane?
4. How does "The Murder of Gonzago," the play-within-the-play, relate to *Hamlet?* What does Hamlet learn from Claudius' reaction?
5. Is Claudius a good ruler, a loving husband and father, and a reasonable man?
6. Why does Hamlet not kill Claudius at prayer?
7. Interpret Hamlet's treatment of Gertrude in Act III. What crimes does Hamlet believe that Gertrude has committed?
8. Is Polonius a wise counselor, sycophant, hypocrite, and/or fool?

9. Is Laertes' desire to avenge the death of Polonius less or more justified than Hamlet's mandate for revenge?

Act IV

1. How does Claudius manipulate Laertes? To what extent does Laertes comply?
2. Identify the conflicts in *Hamlet*. Which is the central conflict?

Act V

1. In the scene with the gravediggers, how does the comedy function in relation to the themes of the play?
2. What does Hamlet tell Horatio about life? How has Hamlet changed (V, i)?
3. Polonius, Rosencrantz, Guildenstern, Ophelia, Laertes, Gertrude, Claudius, and Hamlet all die in *Hamlet*. Who is responsible for these deaths—Claudius and/or Hamlet?
4. Explain the appearance of Fortinbras (V, i). Is this a tragedy of state as well as a personal tragedy?

■■   JOURNAL ENTRIES   ■■

1. Select a famous or intriguing line or passage from this play, and write about it. Consider language, tone, character, conflict, or theme. Add personal reflections.
2. Choose a character from the play, and write a description of appearance, voice, personality, habits, motives, conflicts, virtues, and/or flaws.

■■■   IDEAS FOR WRITING   ■■■

1. Write an analysis of Hamlet's character. Refer to literary criticism if you wish.
2. Discuss a relationship in *Hamlet*. (Suggestions: Hamlet and Ophelia, Hamlet and Gertrude, Claudius and Gertrude, Hamlet and Laertes, or Hamlet and Horatio)
3. Using Journal Entry 1, consider a famous quotation from *Hamlet* in relation to two other works in this chapter.
4. Compose an essay on the theme of betrayal, revenge, or love in this play.
5. Read about the Globe Theater and about the staging and production of *Hamlet*. Write a paper on a topic which emerges from this research.

NONFICTION

Adolescents
from Family

Margaret Mead

Born in Philadelphia, Margaret Mead (1901–1978) was the eldest daughter in a family of educators. Mead was educated at home by her grandmother, who proved to be an important influence in her life. As an undergraduate student at Barnard College, Mead was taught by anthropologist Frank Boas, from whom she acquired her interest in cultural anthropology.

As a graduate student at Columbia, Mead pursued field work in the South Pacific in a small village in Samoa. Mead's dissertation, Coming of Age in Samoa *(1928), demonstrated that adolescence is not a time of turmoil in all cultures and provided a model for the study of the impact of culture on human development. Her books include* Growing Up in New Guinea *(1930),* Sex and Temperament in Three Primitive Societies *(1935), and* Culture and Commitment *(1970). She later used her observations of South Pacific cultures to examine contemporary life in the United States, specifically gender roles.*

Mead was a curator at the Museum of Natural History in New York City and taught at Columbia and at many other universities. In 1979, she was posthumously awarded the Presidential Medal of Freedom. As she suggests in her autobiography, Blackberry Winter *(1972), she "spent most of [her] life studying the lives of other peoples, far away peoples, so that Americans might better understand themselves." In this selection from* Family, *Mead theorizes about the nature and functions of adolescence, both for the individual and for society in agrarian and in urban cultures.*

1   At adolescence children begin to move toward an unknown future. The translucent walls of childhood no longer close them in, for suddenly they discover the wide gateways and the gates ready to swing open at a touch of the hand. The way is open for them to move away from the family, away from the familiar gardens and ponds and woods where they came to know the natural world, away from the fireside stories told them by their grandmothers, away from the brothers and sisters who will always be older and younger than they, and away from the playmates who shared their earliest games.

2   Up to adolescence the child lived in a circumscribed world. However individual and gifted, lively and intelligent he seemed to his parents, he was still a child for whom others had to plan, who had to be admonished, hedged about with protective rules, and kept within bounds. But with adolescence the old rules lose their meaning, and children begin to look beyond the old boundaries with new farseeing eyes. The adolescent boy gives up the dream of competition with his father in which he sometimes triumphed and sometimes despaired of ever accomplishing as much as his father had. Instead, he now looks forward to what he actually may become. The adolescent girl who once held her doll as her mother held her baby now looks forward in earnest, picturing the woman she will become and the living child she may rock in her arms. At adolescence, children stand at the gates, vividly seeing—and yet not seeing—the pathways of their own lives. For better or worse, each family has accomplished the task of caring for its sons and daughters, and they have learned, well or badly, the essential lessons their parents could teach them.

3   For the adolescent the paths leading out from the swinging gates are both entrancing and frightening. Even for the youth who has been an intrepid child traveler, the first journeys away from home may seem too difficult to accomplish. Girls who ranged the streams and mountains beside their brothers become shy and timid, their hands hot and cold, their smiles precarious. One day they want to dress as children, the next as women of the world. Each adolescent in his own way hesitates at the threshold. One sallies out and then, frightened by his own temerity, hurries back; but safely inside he looks out longingly, ready to be off again. Another hangs back, willing and unwilling, until at some sign known only to himself he moves ahead boldly, once and for all.

4   Everywhere in the world people mark the moment when a girl passes from childhood to physical maturity and the time when the boy's voice cracks and deepens and his beard, slight as it may be for some racial stocks, begins to grow. For the elders these changes signal the end of one kind of responsibility and the beginning of another more onerous one. Little children must be ceaselessly guarded and cared for, but adolescents, who still are in need of protection, are creatures whom it is almost impossible to protect. Their safety now depends on their earlier learning in childhood and on the way the other adolescents around them are growing toward adulthood.

5   In a society in which boys go out on dangerous raids, a mother may make magic to protect her adolescent son's life, but any attempt to keep him at home when others go out will also endanger him. Where adolescent girls have a special house to which boys come with flutes to court them, a father may tremble for his daughter's safety and fear that the wooing may go wrong, but by interfering he will only create new difficulties. In every society adolescents take over the world's ways and parents must yield their assent.

6   Sometimes parents are permitted to lock up their daughters, and girls can only whisper to their lovers through barred windows. Sometimes boys are shut up in schools were older boys teach and harry them and men wearing the masks of frightening authority give them a last set of admonitions

about manliness. Sometimes, at the beginning of adolescence, boys are sent as war scouts on dangerous missions and on long night errands through the enemy-infested bush. And sometimes each boy must go out alone and wait, fasting and vigilant, in the hope of winning the protection of a guardian spirit. Whatever the customary ways are for children to emerge into youth, these indicate the kinds of paths adolescents must take. Individual families can neither shield their children nor safely direct them along different paths. Individual parents who set themselves against custom become involved in a much greater struggle than those who watch with bated breath as their children set out on their first adventures.

7   The world over, adolescence is the period of greatest differentiation between boys and girls, not only in the anxieties felt by their parents but also in the dreams that animate them. Yet the boy and the girl, each in a different way, are equally preoccupied by the task of becoming, physically, a man and a woman—no longer someone's child, but potentially the parent of a child. Within their own bodies changes are taking place that they cannot ignore, and in the world outside they are confronted by alterations in treatment that match their visible growth and approaching maturity.

8   In some societies adolescents are left to realize change at their own pace. No one records their age. No one complains about the slow pace of this boy or the fast pace of that girl in growing up. Children are safe in their childhood as long as they are unready; and each chooses when to begin courtship and the first tentative search for a mate. One by one, the boys drift away from the boys' gang, take on the stance of young men, and move toward the girls who also, one by one, grow into readiness to receive them. No one will hurry them.

9   But in most societies adults express old fears and new fears, old hopes and new hopes as they urge on and hold back adolescent boys and girls, guard them and leave them to fend for themselves. All the girls may be betrothed early in childhood and sent to their prospective husbands' homes before they reach puberty. In this the girls have no choice. They must accept their new families as unquestioningly as they accepted the families into which they were born. And the boys, given their wives, have as little choice and yet are expected to be grateful to those who have made this provision for their future.

10   At the other extreme are the adolescents who are trapped in the neglect and poverty of great cities. Growing up in families whose kinship ties are disrupted and whose links to a more stable past are broken, they can expect no help from parents who do not understand their new urban life. Unschooled, unprotected, and unguided, each adolescent is left to follow the initiative of other adolescents. In a society that makes no coherent plan for them and coming from families who do not know what plans to make, they turn to radio and television, mass magazines and comic strips in search of guidance. Children of the mass media, they learn from headlines how other adolescents, equally at sea, dress and talk, think and act. In a simpler society, adolescents share the channeled dreams of all young people, and their parents, whose adolescence differed hardly at all from their own, can set up guideposts that will lead a new generation safely into adulthood. In contrast,

modern adolescents are exposed to the fads and extreme actions of hundreds of thousands of young people who drift on a chartless course between a narrower, traditional world and a world whose dimensions are still unclear. All they have to follow are the published statistics of how many of them are now—this year, this month, this week—turning in questing masses first in one direction and then in another. For these adolescents, as in no other generation, the end of the journey in adulthood is unknown.

11   An unbridgeable gulf seems to separate the life of the five boys who are growing up in a shepherd hamlet, each of whom will choose a wife from among the six girls in that hamlet or the twenty girls living in nearby villages, from the life of young people who crowd, ten thousand strong, to welcome a television star at an airport. Yet the tasks confronting the shepherd boy are no different from those facing the teen-age city boy who moves so lightly to the rhythm set last week by a new hit record. For now, at adolescence, both boys must give up the dependence of childhood and move toward the autonomy and interdependence of adulthood.

12   Wherever a boy grows up, he must learn to leave home without fear, leaving behind him the old battles of childhood, and learn to return home from school or work or an assignment in a far city or overseas ready to treat his parents differently. Where he is permitted choice, he must be prepared to make a choice. Where no choice is open to him, the decision to go another way means that he must be prepared to blaze a new and lonely path. If he succeeds, he may open that path to others. If he fails, others coming after him may have a harder time.

13   For the young boy who rebels against the choices that have been made for him—refuses the wife who has been chosen in his name, deserts the craft to which he has been apprenticed, leaves the school or college to which he has been sent—the battle is a lonely one. At the moment of rebellion the battle is joined not with his whole society—for if it is, he becomes a criminal—but with his own parents whose demands he cannot meet. Such a battle generates an almost unbearable tension, as his old childish love and dependence must be opposed both to a desire for independence which his parents approve and to a course which they disapprove. In some societies, it is not only the rebel who suffers, but also the boy struggling to meet the demands made on him—to show bravery in battle, seek a vision on a mountainside, endure a period of poverty and self-discipline in a monastery, work as an ill-fed and much-abused apprentice, last out the hard grind before he can enter a profession, practice every day the difficult skills that will make him an athlete, a mountain guide, or a pilot. If he fails, or even thinks he has failed, he has been taught to feel he will betray his parents, and he may be tempted to revenge himself on them by killing the child they failed to rear in their image of what their child should be. In still other societies grandfathers stand behind the springing young boys, guarding their inexperience. But elsewhere there are no such safeguards. Fathers relinquish their authority early, and boys of thirteen or fourteen, long before they can break away in rebellion, are

pushed into manhood and have the cares and responsibilities of manhood thrust on their shoulders.

14   The problems girls face, the world over, are not those that confront their brothers, but very different ones. For the adolescent girl may still feel like a child or she may still long to roam the hills with her brothers as she did when she was a child, but now, unlike a child, she can conceive. And long before she has the discretion or the judgment to choose among suitors or to weigh the temptation of the moment against her hopes for the future, her body, outstripping her imagination, or her imagination, outstripping her physical readiness, may involve her in an irrevocable act. The boy who breaks his bow string, turns tail in battle, hesitates before an order, or fails in school can still retrieve his losses by stringing the bow better, returning to school, learning to obey and to command. But for the girl herself and for society, the change is irreversible. It does not matter whether the child she has conceived is lost immediately after conception, whether it is born in wedlock or out of wedlock, whether it lives or dies. The event cannot be set aside. One more child, if it lives, will have started life in one way and not in another, and the girl herself can go on, but she cannot begin afresh.

15   Because parenthood for the girl and parenthood for the boy are fundamentally different, it has taken a very long time to develop contexts in which girls can be allowed to become persons before they become mothers. And because, in the end, the education of boys depends partly on the mothers who rear them, and the sisters with whom they play and compete or whom they cherish and protect, it also took a long time before boys were permitted to become full persons. Throughout human history, most peoples have been intent, most of the time, on turning most young boys and girls into parents whose primary task it has been to rear children who, in their turn, would become parents also. With rare exceptions, girls have always been reared to become parents, and persons only incidentally, and boys, too, have been reared to become parents, and persons only if they have belonged to some specially privileged elite.

16   But very slowly the burden has been lifting. Each small savage society had to lay on every able member the responsibility of reproduction first and then for continual, unremitting daily concern for food and for protection against cold and danger. The burden was lifted first from the sons of those of high rank and, occasionally, the youth of high promise, and later from a few daughters who shared, almost accidentally, in their brothers' privileges. Gradually it has been lifted also from larger and larger numbers of young people in those countries that have conquered the relentless problems of hunger and cold. In the past, most boys, as soon as they left childhood, had no choice but to hunt, herd sheep, fish, toil in the fields, or work at a craft, or, in more recent times, work as unskilled laborers who never earned more than was enough to buy tomorrow's food and pay next week's rent. But in modern societies, it has been possible to keep an ever larger number of adolescents in school and to give them an opportunity to think further than

their fathers thought, explore the life of other periods and other cultures, and to become both civilized men, inheritors of the past, and modern men, ready to make a different future. And as our capacity to free more adolescents has increased, our willingness also has grown to permit them to become what they have the potentiality to be as persons.

17   This change has coincided with a tremendous increase in the world's population. In the past, men struggled desperately to preserve the small tribes or nations to which they owed their sense of identity. Today we are engaged in a common enterprise in the attempt to preserve mankind, as all men are endangered by the weapons of destruction they have now—and will always have—the knowledge to build. In the past people counted the children who were born, wept for the many who died, and wondered whether the living were enough to do the work, guard the group from danger, and reproduce the group in the next generation. Now we know we must stem the uncontrolled growth of the earth's population. When almost all children live, fewer children need be born. When almost no mothers die, fewer women need bear children. When as many children grow up in small families as once survived only in very large families, so many of whose children died, men and women need not marry so early or devote so large a part of their lives to parenthood. Now, when our task is to balance the world's population at a level at which every child who is born anywhere, in the most remote valley and on the highest plateau, will have an opportunity to become a person, we do not need to organize the world in such a way that the relentless, unremitting needs of parenthood and poverty weigh down adolescents as soon as they leave childhood behind, making them old before their time. Our new command of nature, which makes it possible for the first time in human history to organize a world without war, save the children who are born, and feed and clothe every child, also allows us to offer to all adolescents, not only the chosen and privileged few, a chance to grow further.

18   Man's history has been one of longer and longer periods of growth. In the very distant past, before men as we know them had evolved, the period of growth must have been even shorter and boys must have been ready for the tasks of procreation and parenthood very young. Later, when members of our own species were living under extremely primitive conditions, boys had learned all they needed to know in order to survive by the time they were six or seven years of age, but they matured more slowly. At adolescence they were ready to assume the responsibilities of manhood, and so it has remained for primitive men, for peasants, and for the poor in industrial cities. The demands made on them permitted them to grow no more. Even when the years of education lengthened a little in the more fortunate modern countries, the idea survived that growth stopped somewhere in mid-adolescence. There was, as there still is, a general expectation that most young people would give up learning and growing when they left school. Set in a mold, they were ready to work day in and day out, because otherwise they and their children would not eat. They stepped from childhood to adolescence and from early adolescence immediately into maturity, and then aged early.

19   But in the last ten thousand years—and possibly for a longer time—some societies began to benefit from the accumulated knowledge that made it possible for men to plan ahead—to raise more food than they immediately needed, to store food, and to feed a larger number of people—so that some men were freed to study, to think, and to build a larger tradition. In time, in some societies, men watched the stars and measured the phases of the sun and the moon, designed great buildings, carved, painted, created systems of notation, built cities and organized nations, and dreamed of including all men, not merely the members of their own tribe, their own city, or their own race, within one system of values, cherishing common goals.

20   With leisure and the freedom given to some young men to pursue the new arts and sciences of civilization, a new human capacity was discovered: the idealism of adolescence. Among a primitive people, as each new generation lives much the same life the parent generation also lived, adolescents do not reveal their capacity to dream soaring dreams, make mighty plans, leap in thought to new formulations of the relations of mind and matter, and visualize the place of man on earth, in the solar system, in the galaxy, in an expanding universe. Until men lived in the kinds of societies in which leisure was a possibility, and a few adolescents had time to grow further away from childhood, youth was untouched by idealism. Indeed, in many societies, young people were more cowed, more submissive, and less rebellious than their aging and less responsible elders.

21   With the development of civilization, as knowledge accumulated and systems of writing made it possible to preserve and communicate to others, as yet unborn, what was known, new processes of development were also revealed in adolescents. Moving away from childhood, boys and young men were no longer exposed only to the drudgery and the small excitements of the daily round. Some of them, at least, heard and saw and read about the things earlier great men had dreamed of and sung of, written about, and built. The spacious vision of the exceptional man did not die with him, but became the property of young men who came after him. In each generation there were young men, and occasionally young women, who could match the unsatisfactory present against the prophecies of a better future or the dream of a golden past, and these young people, in their turn, were led to prophesy, strike out in bold adventure, break the bonds of tradition, discover new fields, and plunge forward into some new understanding of the universe and man.

22   In any growing civilization, some young men have been allowed to live out and prolong their adolescence, free from the pressure to marry and from the necessity of working for their bread. This leisure not only has given them time to grow, but also time for friendship before parenthood. It is essentially in the continuation of companionship outside the family, in relationships other than those concerned with courtship, marriage, and parenthood, that adolescents can seek and find the strength and the vision to carry one step farther the civilization into which they were born and of which they are the heirs. The urgent desire, everywhere in the world, to give children more schooling and more time to learn has at its base a very profound need. The rationale of educational

plans in the contemporary world is the necessity of having a more literate population, able to do the work of a more literate and complicated society. But the underlying need goes far beyond this. Giving children time to prolong their growing is intrinsic to the very creation of that literate and complicated society. Without vision the people perish, and the power of seeing visions must be fostered in adolescents if we are to have the visionaries the world needs.

23   For many centuries civilizations have struggled with the problem of how to give men—and sometimes women—the freedom in which inspiration, knowledge, and art can flower. One solution has been to create a dichotomy in which the life of sex and parenthood has been set apart from a life of celibacy, asceticism, and thought or prayer. In a society that accepted this solution, the parent was never so specialized or developed a person as were those who carried on the spiritual, intellectual, and artistic work of the world. Moreover, every child was presented with two conflicting life paths, as he had to choose between the pursuit of knowledge, on the one hand, and the life of the family, on the other. Only in the next generation, if he chose to have children, might a son realize his other dreams and, turning away from parenthood, devote himself entirely to religion, the arts, scholarship, or science. In other societies, all boys have lived for a period apart from the secular world, as a way of giving them access to traditional knowledge and insight into the spiritual resources of a great religion, as one aspect of their on-going lives. In still other societies, childhood and old age were equated in the sense that the intensive learning of childhood, practiced throughout life, came to flower only when men retired from everyday responsibilities and could devote themselves wholly to thought, poetry, painting, and music. But all these have been essentially conservative solutions, the solutions worked out by societies among whom only a few were the chosen carriers of a great tradition, and only a few had the freedom to become creative individuals.

24   In most modern societies this selection and segregation of the few from the many is breaking down. Those who dedicate themselves wholly to important work now live in the world. Even though they may not marry, they do not live a life apart. However, where once the population was divided into the many who bore and reared children and the few who had time all their lives to think and to grow, there is now developing in many parts of the modern world a new dichotomy based on sex. For increasingly, adolescent boys are being educated, while girls, like the vast majority of men and women in medieval Europe who chose parenthood, are asked to set aside their dreams of what they might become in favor of immediate marriage and parenthood.

25   In creating this new dichotomy we resemble the primitive peoples who did not understand paternity. For we do not take into account fatherhood or realize that in establishing a kind of society in which girls must become mothers as adolescents, before they have had time to become individuals, we also are forcing boys to become fathers before they have become individuals. In our civilization we are the beneficiaries of poor societies in which only a few had leisure, but we are not yet fully conscious of the power our new affluence gives us to make all men the beneficiaries of that past and to open the

way for every adolescent to grow slowly through a long youth into mature individuality.

26   All around the world, youth is stirring. Often that stirring is the blind movement of disorganized mobs. There is a restlessness that is widely expressed in demands for privilege, for power, for change, for marriage as a right rather than as a responsibility, and for parenthood as a pleasure rather than as a vocation. That blind movement and those demands express the deep contradictions characteristic of our time—a time of transition.

27   Perhaps even more important than the revolution in the lives of peoples who for centuries have been subjected to tyranny and alien authority is the surging revolution of young people who are seeking a new place in a new kind of world. The more rapidly the world changes, the greater is the contrast between older people, who have had to learn so many new things during their lifetime, and younger people, who take the same things for granted. Young people who all their lives have been familiar with cars and how they are driven, who know how a jet plane is operated and how a computer is built, have an appearance of startling precocity as they move among adults for whom this knowledge and these skills are still new and strange. How can parents feel that their adolescent children are, in fact, adolescents, when these children know so much that they, the parents, learned only yesterday and with great difficulty? The authority in adult voices flickers, hesitates, grows shrill, and young people, sensing adult uncertainty and weakness, press harder against the barriers that hold them back from full participation in life. From their viewpoint they are asking for full citizenship and the right to be men and women at once, because they are already more skilled and knowledgeable than their parents. But the fulfillment of their demands would have the effect of putting the clock back, rather than moving it forward, and of reinstating a kind of world in which all young people were set to work at sober, confining tasks as soon as they were able to undertake them. At the threshold of a new age, it is as if a generation was turning in blind flight from its vast possibilities.

28   For all over the world a new age is struggling to be born, an age in which all children can grow up in families and all adolescents can have time to become individuals who are able to meet the demands of a fully adult life. In this new age, in which adolescents need not be forced to become mothers and fathers and grow old before their time, we can set a new value on adolescence of the mind and the spirit. In a society in which no one will be forced into premature adulthood, many people will remain adolescents all their lives, following a vision that is not yet clear, puzzling over a theory that is not yet fully formulated, attempting to create in sound or in color, in meditation or in prayer, in the laboratory or in the library, in the halls of government or in the councils of the nations something as yet unknown.

29   For long ages the prospect opening out from childhood closed in almost at once. Only a few were free long enough to glimpse a wider horizon, a visionary gleam. With the knowledge gained through their labor and their imagination, still more could be set free. When childhood stretched only a few years ahead, early man was set free to learn a little; when adolescence was prolonged, the

men of earlier civilizations were able to leap ahead. In the future we may hope to meet the magnificent responsibilities of our knowledge through the visions of boys and girls who will remain all their lives, not only as adolescents but as adults, open to the widest prospects, "moving about in worlds not realized."

■ EXPLORATIONS OF THE TEXT ■

1. What is Mead's view of the period of adolescence?
2. According to Mead, does adolescence differ for boys and for girls in a culture?
3. How do rites of passage in adolescence contribute to the development of society? How do they affect adolescents?
4. What factors are changing rites of passage in modern society? What results does Mead predict? (Look carefully at the last four paragraphs.)
5. Does Mead conceive of adolescence as a time of confusion, ambivalence, and turmoil?

■■ JOURNAL ENTRIES ■■

1. Compare one aspect of Mead's pattern of adolescence with a similar stage in one work in this chapter.
2. Compare her view of adolescence with your own ideas about the subject.
3. When does an adolescent become an adult?

■■■ IDEAS FOR WRITING ■■■

1. Agree or disagree with any of Mead's points.
2. Select one of the characters in a work in this chapter, such as Connie in "Where Are You Going, Where Have You Been?," Dave in "The Man Who Was Almost a Man," or Hamlet. Create the character's response to one of Mead's arguments.

The Medusa and the Snail

Lewis Thomas

Born in New York City, Lewis Thomas (1913–1993) graduated from Princeton and from the Harvard Medical School. He was president of the Memorial Sloan-Kettering Cancer Center in New York. He also taught at the University of Minnesota, New York University - Bellevue, and the Yale Medical School. The Lives of a Cell *(1974), his first book of essays, won the National Book Award for Arts and Letters in 1975. Other volumes written by Dr. Thomas include* Late Night Thoughts on Listening to Mahler's Ninth Symphony *(1985) and* The Fragile Species *(1992).*

In the title essay from his second book, The Medusa and the Snail *(1979), Thomas discusses our preoccupation with self and the value of symbiosis in nature. Through this work, the reader can appreciate the style and the extension of scientific knowledge into inquiries about central human ideas and concerns.*

1 We've never been so self-conscious about our selves as we seem to be these days. The popular magazines are filled with advice on things to do with a self: how to find it, identify it, nurture it, protect it, even, for special occasions, weekends, how to lose it transiently. There are instructive books, best sellers on self-realization, self-help, self-development. Groups of self-respecting people pay large fees for three-day sessions together, learning self-awareness. Self-enlightenment can be taught in college electives.

2 You'd think, to read about it, that we'd only just now discovered selves. Having long suspected that there was *something alive* in there, running the place, separate from everything else, absolutely individual and independent, we've celebrated by giving it a real name. My self.

3 It is an interesting word, formed long ago in much more social ambiguity than you'd expect. The original root was *se* or *seu,* simply the pronoun of the third person, and most of the descendant words, except "self" itself, were constructed to allude to other, somehow connected people; "sibs" and "gossips," relatives and close acquaintances, came from *seu. Se* was also used to indicate something outside or apart, hence words like "separate," "secret," and "segregate." From an extended root *swedh* it moved into Greek as *ethnos,* meaning people of one's own sort, and *ethos,* meaning the customs of such people. "Ethics" means the behavior of people like one's self, one's own ethnics.

4 We tend to think of our selves as the only wholly unique creations in nature, but it is not so. Uniqueness is so commonplace a property of living things that there is really nothing at all unique about it. A phenomenon can't be unique and universal at the same time. Even individual, free-swimming bacteria can be viewed as unique entities, distinguishable from each other

even when they are the progeny of a single clone. Spudich and Koshland have recently reported that motile microorganisms of the same species are like solitary eccentrics in their swimming behavior. When they are searching for food, some tumble in one direction for precisely so many seconds before quitting, while others tumble differently and for different, but characteristic, periods of time. If you watch them closely, tethered by their flagellae to the surface of an antibody-coated slide, you can tell them from each other by the way they twirl, as accurately as though they had different names.

5   Beans carry self-labels, and are marked by these as distinctly as a mouse by his special smell. The labels are glycoproteins, the lectins, and may have something to do with negotiating the intimate and essential attachment between the bean and the nitrogen-fixing bacteria which live as part of the plant's flesh, embedded in root nodules. The lectin from one line of legume has a special affinity for the surfaces of the particular bacteria which colonize that line, but not for bacteria from other types of bean. The system seems designed for the maintenance of exclusive partnerships. Nature is pieced together by little snobberies like this.

6   Coral polyps are biologically self-conscious. If you place polyps of the same genetic line together, touching each other, they will fuse and become a single polyp, but if the lines are different, one will reject the other.

7   Fish can tell each other apart as individuals, by the smell of self. So can mice, and here the olfactory discrimination is governed by the same H_2 locus which contains the genes for immunologic self-marking.

8   The only living units that seem to have no sense of privacy at all are the nucleated cells that have been detached from the parent organism and isolated in a laboratory dish. Given the opportunity, under the right conditions, two cells from wildly different sources, a yeast cell, say, and a chicken erythrocyte, will touch, fuse, and the two nuclei will then fuse as well, and the new hybrid cell will now divide into monstrous progeny. Naked cells, lacking self-respect, do not seem to have any sense of self.

9   The markers of self, and the sensing mechanisms responsible for detecting such markers, are conventionally regarded as mechanisms for maintaining individuality for its own sake, enabling one kind of creature to defend and protect itself against all the rest. Selfness, seen thus, is for self-preservation.

10   In real life, though, it doesn't seem to work this way. The self-marking of invertebrate animals in the sea, who must have perfected the business long before evolution got around to us, was set up in order to permit creatures of one kind to locate others, not for predation but to set up symbiotic households. The anemones who live on the shells of crabs are precisely finicky; so are the crabs. Only a single species of anemone will find its way to only a single species of crab. They sense each other exquisitely, and live together as though made for each other.

11   Sometimes there is such a mix-up about selfness that two creatures, each attracted by the molecular configuration of the other, incorporate the two selves to make a single organism. The best story I've ever heard about this is

the tale told of the nudibranch and medusa living in the Bay of Naples. When first observed, the nudibranch, a common sea slug, was found to have a tiny vestigial parasite, in the form of a jellyfish, permanently affixed to the ventral surface near the mouth. In curiosity to learn how the medusa got there, some marine biologists began searching the local waters for earlier developmental forms, and discovered something amazing. The attached parasite, although apparently so specialized as to have given up living for itself, can still produce offspring, for they are found in abundance at certain seasons of the year. They drift through the upper waters, grow up nicely and astonishingly, and finally become full-grown, handsome, normal jellyfish. Meanwhile, the snail produces snail larvae, and these too begin to grow normally, but not for long. While still extremely small, they become entrapped in the tenacles of the medusa and then engulfed within the umbrella-shaped body. At first glance, you'd believe the medusae are now the predators, paying back for earlier humiliations, and the snails the prey. But no. Soon the snails, undigested and insatiable, begin to eat, browsing away first at the radial canals, then the borders of the rim, finally the tentacles, until the jellyfish becomes reduced in substance by being eaten while the snail grows correspondingly in size. At the end, the arrangement is back to the first scene, with the full-grown nudibranch basking, and nothing left of the jellyfish except the round, successfully edited parasite, safely affixed to the skin near the mouth.

12   It is a confusing tale to sort out, and even more confusing to think about. Both creatures are designed for this encounter, marked as selves as that they can find each other in the waters of the Bay of Naples. The collaboration, if you want to call it that, is entirely specific; it is only this species of medusa and only this kind of nudibranch that can come together and live this way. And, more surprising, they cannot live in any other way; they depend for their survival on each other. They are not really selves, they are specific *others*.

13   The thought of these creatures gives me an odd feeling. They do not remind me of anything, really. I've never heard of such a cycle before. They are bizarre, that's it, unique. And at the same time, like a vaguely remembered dream, they remind me of the whole earth at once. I cannot get my mind to stay still and think it through.

■ **EXPLORATIONS OF THE TEXT** ■

1.   Why does Thomas give the definition and etymology of "self"? How can a writer use definitions without being predictable or trite?
2.   What are the examples of "unique entities" in the essay? How do they add to the conception of self?
3.   What is symbiosis? How do the medusa and the snail differ from other symbiotic relationships in nature?
4.   What is disturbing about the medusa and the snail?

5. Why does Thomas end the essay with uncertainties and state, "I cannot get my mind to stay still and think it through"?
6. What analogy does Thomas imply in "The Medusa and the Snail"? What can a writer learn about the use and rhetorical power of analogy from this work?

■■ JOURNAL ENTRIES ■■

1. Do you agree with Thomas's first statement: "We've never been so self-conscious about our selves as we seem to be these days"?
2. Consider interdependence as a prerequisite for selfhood. How much privacy does an individual need?

■■■ IDEAS FOR WRITING ■■■

1. Use Thomas's ideas as the beginning of an inquiry into the nature of identity. Compare your views with Thomas's essay or Margaret Mead's "Adolescents."
2. Construct your own analogy for identity and relationships, and use Thomas's work as a model.

Student Essay: Exposition

The Earnestness of Life

David Higgins

This essay corresponds to writing assignment 6 in this chapter. The narrator reflects on a rite of passage and its consequences: his first encounter with hunting and death. Higgins' work may be read in conjunction with "A White Heron" by Sarah Orne Jewett, "The Man Who Was Almost a Man" by Richard Wright, and "Uncle's First Rabbit" by Lorna Dee Cervantes. Currently Higgins is employed as a Stationary Engineer. He attends the State University of New York at New Paltz and has recently completed his first novel. With his wife, MaryJane, he resides in a growing household not far from the scenes described in "The Earnestness of Life."

1   My career as a huntsman began and ended on a summer day when I was twelve years old. In the years since, I have had to shoot animals for reasons ranging from adolescent bravado to acts of mercy. Yet I have never approached the task with the same light-hearted anticipation I felt that day.

2   I was born in Sundown, a hamlet nestled in a valley of the Catskills and straddling the headwaters of the Rondout. This was before the social landscape of the region had been transformed by infusions of people from urban areas. When I was a youngster, most of the people I knew were basically rural in habit and outlook. Hunting and fishing loomed large in the imaginations of the boys I knew. As a native of the area, it was only natural that I should want to join the chase.

3   Eunice Terwilliger was an elderly spinster who lived next door to my family. As it happened, her old dog, Queenie, had died that spring. Without Queenie around, pests were getting into Eunice's garden and devouring the greens as fast as they grew. Although I had never shot anything but innumerable tin cans and tree stumps, I volunteered to do something about the problem. Eunice was pleased with my offer, but before I could put my plan into action, I had to obtain permission from my parents. This was forthcoming only after a stern lecture on gun safety and responsibility.

4   It was late morning when I sallied out, even though I knew that the best time of day for the work at hand was twilight. In my pocket, I had fifty rounds of "long rifle" cartridges, a somewhat heavier load than regular .22 ammunition. My rifle, a hand-me-down from my eldest brother, John, was a single shot, bolt-action target piece. Its open sight were rudimentary but

surprisingly accurate. Being light and easy to wield, it was an ideal weapon for a beginning marksman. For a novice hunter, the cumbersome safety mechanism and bolt-action were drawbacks, as they make for a slow reload.

5   As I approached the garden, I carried the rifle loosely, with a cartridge in the chamber and the bolt open. At that time of day, I did not expect to find any game there. A narrow arm of the hay field that separated our house and Eunice's stretched behind the garden. Along the edge of the field, there was a low blind of brush, beyond which rose a thicket of pine and sumac. This seemed the most likely place to find quarry. A right of way, which led to a summer cabin by the creek, skirted the southern edge of the thicket. I circled around on this, since it would afford me a quieter approach than crashing about in the bushes.

6   When I reached a clearing by the creek, I stopped. The air was absolutely still and oppressively hot. The birds were silent, nothing moved. The only sound was the barely audible rustle of the Rondout. Even here, so close to the water, the heat was enervating. I doubted that anything would be afoot. Debating whether to carry on or come back and try again at dusk, I stood for a time. I had almost decided to leave when I detected a slight movement in the high grass at the edge of the clearing. A moment later, a large rabbit, the color of burlap, moved into the open, a scant thirty feet away.

7   It was unaware of my presence. I closed the bolt and carefully pulled back the safety, fearing that the sharp 'click' it made would spook the rabbit. Facing away from me, it still did not register the presence of danger. It even turned slightly, presenting me with a clean, easy shot at its neck. I held my breath and lifted the rifle to my shoulder. That was when things began to go wrong.

8   I was surprised to find that my hands were shaking so much that I could hardly take aim. The rifle kept jouncing from side to side, as if it had become animated. In my excitement, I fired, regardless of aim. A spray of gravel showed where the slug buried itself a foot or two short of the target. The rabbit, startled by the noise, darted forward a dozen paces, then stopped to listen. Eternity seemed to elapse while I fumbled another round into the .22. I was a little steadier when I let fly again. This time I found the mark. The rabbit was bowled over by the impact. Reloading as I sprang forward, anxious lest my quarry get away, I was too busy to savor any thrill of the chase. Had I felt anything, my elation would have been short-lived. When I next spied the rabbit, a greyness clouded my senses that still colors my recollection of the event. The shot had not been fatal, but had broken the rabbit's back. Its hind legs were paralyzed and it was desperately dragging itself away from me with its forepaws. It was one of the saddest spectacles I have ever witnessed. The next shot struck home, putting it out of its misery. But I was already sick at heart, ashamed at what I had done, and ashamed of being ashamed.

9   When I got close to the rabbit, it was lying on its side. The eyes were open, although I thought it was dead. Then oddly, its jaw moved, as if it were nibbling

clover. I shot it again. The unmistakable glaze of death came over its eyes and it lay still. Then I carried it back to Eunice's and buried it in the garden.

10   I put on a bold front, but somehow never got around to stalking any more prey that year. For a long time, the affair bothered and baffled me. Like so many passages of life, this episode seems of trifling significance at first glance. A boy shoots his first rabbit and is repelled by the grisly reality of death. It is not so simple as that. To this day, I cannot take an animal's life without feeling a sharp pang of remorse, akin to the sadness I felt when I killed the rabbit. Yet, once the animal is dead, I can wade into the business of dressing and butchering the carcass with bloody-minded gusto. In a dim, distant way, I discerned more wisdom than I knew, on that summer morning in 1971. What I learned had nothing to do with the ugliness of death. For the first time, I had caught a glimpse of the terrible earnestness of life.

WRITING ASSIGNMENTS

1. a. What makes you proud of your background? Freewrite.
   b. Compare your view of cultural pride and identity with the views in two of the following poems: "Energy," "Ego Tripping," "¿Habla Usted Español?," "Indian Boarding School: The Runaways," and "Lost Sister."
2. a. Compare the view of gaining sexual awareness and identity for men and for women in any of the works in this chapter.
   b. Interview several people about their experiences in gaining sexual awareness.
   c. Based on the works in this chapter and/or your interviews, write an essay which classifies ways in which adolescents acquire sexual knowledge.
3. Rites of passage may be characterized as those which involve loss, those which entail facing death, those which include isolation, and those which involve gaining new knowledge. Analyze two or three of the works in the chapter according to one of these categories.
4. Compare Mead's view of adolescence with that in one of the works in this chapter.
5. Coming of age and initiation experiences prompt adolescents either to accept or to reject adult responsibilities. Analyze the conflicts of a character in one of the works in this chapter in light of this idea.
6. Use one of these topic areas as the basis for an essay on a rite of passage: driving, flying, running, being caged, facing the self, hunting, lying.
7. a. Freewrite on a coming-of-age ritual you have experienced, for example, a Bar Mitzvah.
   b. Read about coming-of-age rituals in a particular culture. Take notes. Examine the origins, the evolution, and the current practice of the ritual (for example, Bar Mitzvah in Jewish culture). Write an outline, draft, revision, and final version of a research paper concerning one such ritual.
8. Contrast views of cultural identity in this chapter.
9. a. List the ways in which you have assimilated and the ways in which you have asserted your identity.
   b. Write about a single event which symbolizes the conflict between assimilation and assertion of identity.
   c. Coming of age involves coming to terms with one's culture. Discuss the struggle between acceptance and rejection of cultural roots as it is presented in several works in the chapter.
10. Discuss how a scene or vignette from a story or play functions in the development of a particular character.
11. Many of the works in this chapter depend on **irony**. Choose two or three selections, and discuss the function and effects of irony.

(Suggestions: "The Verb to Kill," "Barn Burning," "The Stolen Party," and/or *Hamlet*.)

12. a. Write a journal entry on your search for selfhood.
    b. Compare your process of individuation with the struggles of a character in a work in this chapter.
    c. Discuss the themes concerning the search for self in two works in this chapter in relation to concepts of individuation and symbiosis in Lewis Thomas' "The Medusa and the Snail."

13. a. Write a journal entry on a coming-of-age experience.
    b. Compare your experience with the conflict concerning the coming of age of a character in one of the works in this chapter.

14. Discuss the connection between "Kids in the Mall" and "Where Are You Going, Where Have You Been?"

15. Initiation stories often involve the spilling of blood. Using examples from the works in this chapter, argue in support or refutation of such an assertion.

16. Choose two or three works which exemplify the theme of initiation at different ages. What similarities and differences are apparent?

17. a. Interview your parents or other adults about conflicts between parents and children in adolescence.
    b. Interview several teenagers about their perspectives concerning conflicts between parents and adolescents.
    c. Write a summary of these responses.
    d. Write an essay which compares these perspectives.

18. Explore the connection between sexuality and violence in the works in the Thematic Preview: Valenzuela's "The Verb to Kill," Oates' "Where Are You Going, Where Have You Been?," Atwood's "Game After Supper," and Kowinski's "Kids in the Mall."

FAMILY

"We live our lives like chips in a kaleidoscope always part of patterns that are larger than ourselves and somehow more than the sum of their parts."

Salvador Minuchin, *Family Kaleidoscope*

We live as part of a kaleidoscope that is "larger than ourselves." The chips of the patterns are variegated, beautiful, and complex. The first movers of the pattern are family members. They provide the initial forms of bonding; they provide the crucial experiences of security and insecurity, of love and hate. These early relationships of intimacy, connection, and conflict with parents and siblings influence our responses to the world and to others.

Our memories of those relationships and experiences change. As children, we become conscious of our parents' power over us, the ways in which their needs and values have shaped ours; and conversely, as adults, we recognize the ways in which we have emerged as distinct individuals. As we grow, we understand the family—its benefits, its disadvantages, and its enduring importance in our lives.

The Thematic Preview presents visions of complicated relationships between parents and children. In D. H. Lawrence's "The Rocking-Horse Winner," a mother's inability to love shapes the life of her child, a child who desperately seeks her affection. In "Those Winter Sundays" by Robert Hayden, the adult speaker remembers his childhood and finally understands his father's silences that created a gulf between them. *Riders to the Sea* portrays a mother's fierce struggle to prevent her son from breaking away—to avoid inevitable separation. His desire to wander, to flee, has tragic consequences. In Franz Kafka's letter, he sends a rebellious message to an authoritarian father.

Literature is replete with images of the father as the authority figure, as the protector, and as the provider. What happens when fathers fail in these obligations, when fathers do not provide and protect? This failure is treated in different ways by T. C. Boyle in "If the River Was Whiskey" and by João Guimarães Rosa in "The Third Bank of the River." Authority and absence become swords—damaging a child's individuality and sense of integrity. Theodore Roethke's "My Papa's Waltz" depicts a father's thoughtless behavior which wounds the son. Sometimes children perceive fathers as unapproachable and silent. The absence of the father becomes as formative and critical as the authoritarian presence. Witness Sylvia Plath's speaker's inability to talk to "Daddy": "the tongue stuck in [her] jaw." Witness the boy in Rosa's story who silently waits by the bank of the river for his father to leave his boat on the water and to return home.

Relationships with fathers are also life-giving and nurturing. Fathers demonstrate their values and teach their children to live in the world. In Simon Ortiz's "My Father's Song," the father gives his son a philosophy of existing in accord with and not dominant over nature. In "Visions and Interpretations," Li-Young Lee's speaker visits his father's grave and explores the traditions, "the old book" that his father left as a legacy. In "My Father Moved Through Dooms of Love," E. E. Cummings focuses on his father's capacity for love, tenderness, and moral empathy—gifts that he shares with his son.

Like fathers' bonds with their children, mothers' relationships with their sons and daughters are life-giving and nurturing and fraught with anxiety and danger. Amy Tan's "Scar" presents a daughter who primally bonds with her mother whereas Jamaica Kincaid's "Girl" humorously portrays a mother who attempts to direct her daughter's life and a "girl" who both conforms and desires to be free. Positive images of mothers and daughters emerge in Anne Sexton's "Little Girl, My Stringbean, My Lovely Woman" and in Maxine Kumin's "Making the Jam Without You." Other poets create voices of daughters who assert their selfhood in different keys. In Lyn Lifshin's "My Mother and the Bed" and in Audre Lorde's "From the House of Yemanjá," the daughters struggle to break free, threatened by the physical and emotional energy of enormous and powerful mother figures. In Kumin's "Making the Jam Without You," the speaker recognizes the intense bond between mothers and daughters and the inevitable need for the mother to be only a "sliver" in the daughter's adult life. She recognizes the obligation of parents to release their children.

These works concerning parents and children, then, are stories of love and nurture as well as of loss and recognition of loss—the parents' recognition of overwhelming spiritual, physical, and emotional ties with their children. Ben Jonson in "On My First Son," Amiri Baraka in "Preface to a Twenty Volume Suicide Note," and W. D. Snodgrass in "Heart's Needle" cope with their understanding that these ties are fragile.

The works also emphasize the difficulties of parenting; they acknowledge that fate, circumstance, economic conditions, and culture influence parenting. In Tillie Olsen's "I Stand Here Ironing," the mother's perceived failures are shaped by social and economic circumstances, and she mourns not only her lost connection with her daughter, but also her own powerlessness. Like the mother and son in *Riders to the Sea,* this portrait evokes enormous sympathy for both characters.

Some stories demonstrate the mistakes of parents, and they record the anger of the children who perceive that parents have failed them—failed them because of their own limits, failed them because of desires for their children to be perfect, to be like them, and to compensate for their deficiencies. In "Ruth's Song," Gloria Steinem portrays her mother as a woman defeated by marriage. The mother's weaknesses determined the course of her child's life. As an adult, Steinem comes to terms with her mother's madness and with the limits of love and of understanding.

The same kaleidoscope of relationships exists among siblings. In Durango Mendoza's "Summer Water and Shirley," we discover a brother who so loves his sister that he attempts to save her life; and because of her intrepid personality, she, in turn, inadvertently gives him strength of character. In James Baldwin's "Sonny's Blues," we find two brothers, opposites, unable to communicate, who begin to discover a common ground because of tragedies in their lives. In Lonne Elder's *Ceremonies in Dark Old Men,* two brothers and a sister seek to define their identities in a threatening urban landscape while the old men enact the rituals which preserve their culture.

Parent substitutes also give children rich gifts of love, of spirit, of joy, and of endurance. From his cousin, his companion as a child in "A Christmas Memory," Truman Capote learns to appreciate the simple pleasures in life and to find "magic" and "wonder" in the things of this world. "In Search of Our Mothers' Gardens" presents Alice Walker's appreciation of her mother and grandmothers for the rich heritage of beauty, an artistry of mind and spirit, that they offer her: spiritual and creative gifts that shape her artistic temperament.

Several stories and poems affirm kinship ties, those bonds with others that become sources of strength. In "The Idea of Ancestry," Etheridge Knight gains spiritual sustenance in his jail cell from the forty-seven pictures of his relatives. As he says, "I am all of them,/they are all of me, I am me, they are they, and I have no children/to float in the space between." An appreciation of ancestry provides identity, continuity, and a way of facing one's present and of shaping one's future. Storytelling keeps kinship bonds strong. Words renew ancestral ties, our senses of self, and our sense of community. These bonds exist as our "lineage," our roots, as Margaret Walker suggests.

THEMATIC PREVIEW: COMBINING THE GENRES

The Rocking-Horse Winner

D. H. Lawrence

D. H. (David Herbert) Lawrence (1885–1930) was born in Notting-
ham, England, the son of a coalminer and a former schoolteacher.
He became a major literary figure with the publication of Sons and
Lovers *in 1913. Some of Lawrence's best known works are* The Rain-
bow *(1915),* Women in Love *(1920), and* Lady Chatterley's Lover
(1928). His shorter works and poems are most easily found in The
Complete Stories *(1961),* Four Short Novels *(1965), and* Complete
Poems *(1964).*

Lawrence's life was often as controversial as his writing. He
eloped with a woman who was married and the mother of three chil-
dren. He was suspected of disloyalty during World War I because of
his pacifism and his wife's German origin. He was harassed
throughout his life by efforts to censor his books and paintings. Suf-
fering from tuberculosis and disgusted with his country's industrial-
ism and commercialism, Lawrence spent much of his life traveling
through Italy, France, Australia, the United States, and Mexico.

In this story, Paul, the young protagonist, attempts to win his
mother's affection by giving her money. As he feverishly rides his
rocking horse and gambles on horse races, his search for luck and
love results in disaster.

1 There was a woman who was beautiful, who started with all the advantages, yet she had no luck. She married for love, and the love turned to
dust. She had bonny children, yet she felt they had been thrust upon her, and
she could not love them. They looked at her coldly, as if they were finding
fault with her. And hurriedly she felt she must cover up some fault in herself.
Yet what it was that she must cover up she never knew. Nevertheless, when
her children were present, she always felt the centre of her heart go hard.
This troubled her, and in her manner she was all the more gentle and anxious
for her children, as if she loved them very much. Only she herself knew that
at the centre of her heart was a hard little place that could not feel love, no,
not for anybody. Everybody else said of her: "She is such a good mother. She
adores her children." Only she herself, and her children themselves, knew it
was not so. They read it in each other's eyes.

There were a boy and two little girls. They lived in a pleasant house, with a garden, and they had discreet servants, and felt themselves superior to anyone in the neighborhood.

Although they lived in style, they felt always an anxiety in the house. There was never enough money. The mother had a small income, and the father had a small income, but not nearly enough for the social position which they had to keep up. The father went into town to some office. But though he had good prospects, these prospects never materialized. There was always the grinding sense of the shortage of money, though the style was always kept up.

At last the mother said: "I will see if *I* can't make something." But she did not know where to begin. She racked her brains, and tried this thing and the other, but could not find anything successful. The failure made deep lines come into her face. Her children were growing up, they would have to go to school. There must be more money, there must be more money. The father, who was always very handsome and expensive in his tastes, seemed as if he never *would* be able to do anything worth doing. And the mother, who had a great belief in herself, did not succeed any better, and her tastes were just as expensive.

5   And so the house came to be haunted by the unspoken phrase: *There must be more money! There must be more money!* The children could hear it all the time though nobody said it aloud. They heard it at Christmas, when the expensive and splendid toys filled the nursery. Behind the shining modern rocking horse, behind the smart doll's house, a voice would start whispering: "There *must* be more money! There *must* be more money!" And the children would stop playing, to listen for a moment. They would look into each other's eyes, to see if they had all heard. And each one saw in the eyes of the other two that they too had heard. "There *must* be more money! There *must* be more money!"

It came whispering from the springs of the still-swaying rocking horse, and even the horse, bending his wooden, champing head, heard it. The big doll, sitting so pink and smirking in her new pram,[1] could hear it quite plainly, and seemed to be smirking all the more self-consciously because of it. The foolish puppy, too, that took the place of the teddy bear, he was looking so extraordinarily foolish for no other reason but that he heard the secret whisper all over the house: "There *must* be more money!"

Yet nobody ever said it aloud. The whisper was everywhere, and therefore no one spoke it. Just as no one ever says: "We are breathing!" in spite of the fact that breath is coming and going all the time.

"Mother," said the boy Paul one day, "why don't we keep a car of our own? Why do we always use Uncle's, or else a taxi?"

"Because we're the poor members of the family," said the mother.

10   "But why *are* we, Mother?"

"Well—I suppose," she said slowly and bitterly, "it's because your father has no luck."

---

[1] Baby carriage.

The boy was silent for some time.

"Is luck money, Mother?" he asked rather timidly.

"No, Paul. Not quite. It's what causes you to have money."

15 "Oh!" said Paul vaguely. "I thought when Uncle Oscar said *filthy lucker,* it meant money."

"*Filthy lucre* does mean money," said the mother. "But it's lucre, not luck."

"Oh!" said the boy. "Then what *is* luck, Mother?"

"It's what causes you to have money. If you're lucky you have money. That's why it's better to be born lucky than rich. If you're rich, you may lose your money. But if you're lucky, you will always get more money."

"Oh! Will you? And is Father not lucky?"

20 "Very unlucky, I should say," she said bitterly.

The boy watched her with unsure eyes.

"Why?" he asked.

"I don't know. Nobody ever knows why one person is lucky and another unlucky."

"Don't they? Nobody at all? Does *nobody* know?"

25 "Perhaps God. But He never tells."

"He ought to, then. And aren't you lucky either, Mother?"

"I can't be, if I married an unlucky husband."

"But by yourself, aren't you?"

"I used to think I was, before I married. Now I think I am very unlucky indeed."

30 "Why?"

"Well—never mind! Perhaps I'm not really," she said.

The child looked at her, to see if she meant it. But he saw, by the lines of her mouth, that she was only trying to hide something from him.

"Well, anyhow," he said stoutly, "I'm a lucky person."

"Why?" said his mother, with a sudden laugh.

35 He stared at her. He didn't even know why he had said it.

"God told me," he asserted, brazening it out.

"I hope He did, dear!" she said, again with a laugh, but rather bitter.

"He did, Mother!"

"Excellent!" said the mother.

40 The boy saw she did not believe him; or, rather, that she paid no attention to his assertion. This angered him somewhere, and made him want to compel her attention.

He went off by himself, vaguely, in a childish way, seeking for the clue to "luck." Absorbed, taking no heed of other people, he went about with a sort of stealth, seeking inwardly for luck. He wanted luck, he wanted it, he wanted it. When the two girls were playing dolls in the nursery, he would sit on his big rocking horse, charging madly into space, with a frenzy that made the little girls peer at him uneasily. Wildly the horse careered, the waving dark hair of the boy tossed, his eyes had a strange glare in them. The little girls dared not speak to him.

When he had ridden to the end of his mad little journey, he climbed down and stood in front of his rocking horse, staring fixedly into its lowered face. Its red mouth was slightly open, its big eye was wide and glassy-bright.

Now! he could silently command the snorting steed. Now, take me to where there is luck! Now take me!

And he would slash the horse on the neck with the little whip he had asked Uncle Oscar for. He *knew* the horse could take him to where there was luck, if only he forced it. So he would mount again, and start on his furious ride, hoping at last to get there. He knew he could get there.

45   "You'll break your horse, Paul!" said the nurse.

"He's always riding like that! I wish he'd leave off!" said his elder sister Joan.

But he only glared down on them in silence. Nurse gave him up. She could make nothing of him. Anyhow he was growing beyond her.

One day his mother and his uncle Oscar came in when he was on one of his furious rides. He did not speak to them.

"Hallo, you young jockey! Riding a winner?" said his uncle.

50   "Aren't you growing too big for a rocking horse? You're not a very little boy any longer, you know," said his mother.

But Paul only gave a blue glare from his big, rather close-set eyes. He would speak to nobody when he was in full tilt. His mother watched him with an anxious expression on her face.

At last he suddenly stopped forcing his horse into the mechanical gallop and slid down.

"Well, I got there!" he announced fiercely, his blue eyes still flaring, and his sturdy long legs straddling apart.

"Where did you get to?" asked his mother.

55   "Where I wanted to go," he flared back at her.

"That's right, son!" said Uncle Oscar. "Don't you stop till you get there. What's the horse's name?"

"He doesn't have a name," said the boy.

"Gets on without all right?" asked the uncle.

"Well, he has different names. He was called Sansovino last week."

60   "Sansovino, eh? Won the Ascot.[2] How did you know his name?"

"He always talks about horse races with Bassett," said Joan.

The uncle was delighted to find that his small nephew was posted with all the racing news. Bassett, the young gardener, who had been wounded in the left foot in the war and had got his present job through Oscar Cresswell, whose batman[3] he had been, was a perfect blade of the "turf."[4] He lived in the racing events, and the small boy lived with him.

Oscar Cresswell got it all from Bassett.

---

[2] Major annual horse race. The Lincoln, the Grand National, Derby, and Lincolnshire also are
mentioned in the story.
[3] Orderly.
[4] Horse racing fan.

"Master Paul comes and asks me, so I can't do more than tell him, sir," said Bassett, his face terribly serious, as if he were speaking of religious matters.

65 "And does he ever put anything on a horse he fancies?"

"Well—I don't want to give him away—he's a young sport, a fine sport, sir. Would you mind asking him himself? He sort of takes a pleasure in it, and perhaps he'd feel I was giving him away, sir, if you don't mind."

Bassett was serious as a church.

The uncle went back to his nephew and took him off for a ride in the car.

"Say, Paul, old man, do you ever put anything on a horse?" the uncle asked.

70 The boy watched the handsome man closely.

"Why, do you think I oughtn't to?" he parried.

"Not a bit of it! I thought perhaps you might give me a tip for the Lincoln."

The car sped on into the country, going down to Uncle Oscar's place in Hampshire.[5]

"Honor bright?" said the nephew.

75 "Honor bright, son!" said the uncle.

"Well, then, Daffodil."

"Daffodil! I doubt it, sonny. What about Mirza?"

"I only know the winner," said the boy. "That's Daffodil."

"Daffodil, eh?"

80 There was a pause. Daffodil was an obscure horse comparatively.

"Uncle!"

"Yes, son?"

"You won't let it go any further, will you? I promised Bassett."

"Bassett be damned, old man! What's he got to do with it?"

85 "We're partners. We've been partners from the first. Uncle, he lent me my first five shillings, which I lost. I promised him, honor bright, it was only between me and him; only you gave me that ten-shilling note I started winning with, so I thought you were lucky. You won't let it go any further, will you?"

The boy gazed at his uncle from those big, hot, blue eyes, set rather close together. The uncle stirred and laughed uneasily.

"Right you are, son! I'll keep your tip private. Daffodil, eh? How much are you putting on him?"

"All except twenty pounds," said the boy. "I keep that in reserve."

The uncle thought it a good joke.

90 "You keep twenty pounds in reserve, do you, you young romancer? What are you betting, then?"

"I'm betting three hundred," said the boy gravely. "But its between you and me, Uncle Oscar! Honor bright?"

The uncle burst into a roar of laughter.

---

[5] County in southern England.

"It's between you and me all right, you young Nat Gould,"[6] he said, laughing. "But where's your three hundred?"

"Bassett keeps it for me. We're partners."

95   "You are, are you! And what is Bassett putting on Daffodil?"

"He won't go quite as high as I do, I expect. Perhaps he'll go a hundred and fifty."

"What, pennies?" laughed the uncle.

"Pounds," said the child, with a surprised look at his uncle. "Bassett keeps a bigger reserve than I do."

Between wonder and amusement Uncle Oscar was silent. He pursued the matter no further, but he determined to take his nephew with him to the Lincoln races.

100   "Now, son," he said, "I'm putting twenty on Mirza, and I'll put five for you on any horse you fancy. What's your pick?"

"Daffodil, Uncle."

"No, not the fiver for Daffodil!"

"I should if it was my own fiver," said the child.

"Good! Good! Right you are! A fiver for me and a fiver for you on Daffodil."

105   The child had never been to a race meeting before, and his eyes were blue fire. He pursed his mouth tight, and watched. A Frenchman just in front had put his money on Lancelot. Wild with excitement, he flailed his arms up and down, yelling *Lancelot! Lancelot!* in his French accent.

Daffodil came in first, Lancelot second, Mirza third. The child, flushed and with eyes blazing, was curiously serene. His uncle brought him four five-pound notes, four to one.

"What am I to do with these?" he cried, waving them before the boy's eyes.

"I suppose we'll talk to Bassett," said the boy. "I expect I have fifteen hundred now; and twenty in reserve; and this twenty."

His uncle studied him for some moments.

110   "Look here, son!" he said. "You're not serious about Bassett and that fifteen hundred, are you?"

"Yes, I am. But it's between you and me, Uncle. Honor bright!"

"Honor bright all right, son! But I must talk to Bassett."

"If you'd like to be a partner, Uncle, with Bassett and me, we could all be partners. Only, you'd have to promise, honor bright, Uncle, not to let it go beyond us three. Bassett and I are lucky, and you must be lucky, because it was your ten shillings I started winning with. . . ."

Uncle Oscar took both Bassett and Paul into Richmond Park for an afternoon, and there they talked.

115   "It's like this, you see, sir," Bassett said. "Master Paul would get me talking about racing events, spinning yarns, you know, sir. And he was always keen on knowing if I'd made or if I'd lost. It's about a year since, now, that I put five shillings on Blush of Dawn for him—and we lost. Then the luck

---

[6] Nathaniel Gould (1857–1919), British novelist and sports columnist best known for fiction about horse racing.

turned, with that ten shillings he had from you, that we put on Singhalese. And since that time, it's been pretty steady, all things considering. What do you say, Master Paul?"

"We're all right when we're sure," said Paul. "It's when we're not quite sure that we go down."

"Oh, but we're careful then," said Bassett.

"But when are you *sure?*" Uncle Oscar smiled.

"It's Master Paul, sir," said Bassett, in a secret, religious voice. "It's as if he had it from heaven. Like Daffodil, now, for the Lincoln. That was as sure as eggs."

120   "Did you put anything on Daffodil?" asked Oscar Cresswell.

"Yes, sir. I made my bit."

"And my nephew?"

Bassett was obstinately silent, looking at Paul.

"I made twelve hundred, didn't I, Bassett? I told Uncle I was putting three hundred on Daffodil."

125   "That's right," said Bassett, nodding.

"But where's the money?" asked the uncle.

"I keep it safe locked up, sir. Master Paul he can have it any minute he likes to ask for it."

"What, fifteen hundred pounds?"

"And twenty! And *forty,* that is, with the twenty he made on the course."

130   "It's amazing!" said the uncle.

"If Master Paul offers you to be partners, sir, I would, if I were you; if you'll excuse me," said Bassett.

Oscar Cresswell thought about it.

"I'll see the money," he said.

They drove home again, and sure enough, Bassett came round to the garden house with fifteen hundred pounds in notes. The twenty pounds reserve was left with Joe Glee, in the Turf Commission deposit.

135   "You see, it's all right, Uncle, when I'm *sure!* Then we go strong, for all we're worth. Don't we, Bassett?"

"We do that, Master Paul."

"And when are you sure?" said the uncle, laughing.

"Oh, well, sometimes I'm *absolutely* sure, like about Daffodil," said the boy; "and sometimes I have an idea; and sometimes I haven't even an idea, have I, Bassett? Then we're careful, because we mostly go down."

"You do, do you! And when you're sure, like about Daffodil, what makes you sure, sonny?"

140   "Oh, well, I don't know," said the boy uneasily. "I'm sure, you know, Uncle; that's all."

"It's as if he had it from heaven, sir," Bassett reiterated.

"I should say so!" said the uncle.

But he became a partner. And when the Leger was coming on, Paul was "sure" about Lively Spark, which was a quite inconsiderable horse. The boy insisted on putting a thousand on the horse, Bassett went for five hundred, and Oscar Cresswell two hundred. Lively Spark came in first, and the betting had been ten to one against him. Paul had made ten thousand.

"You see," he said, "I was absolutely sure of him."

145   Even Oscar Cresswell had cleared two thousand.

"Look here, son," he said, "this sort of thing makes me nervous."

"It needn't, Uncle! Perhaps I shan't be sure again for a long time."

"But what are you going to do with your money?" asked the uncle.

"Of course," said the boy, "I started it for Mother. She said she had no luck, because Father is unlucky, so I thought if *I* was lucky, it might stop whispering."

150   "What might stop whispering?"

"Our house. I *hate* our house for whispering."

"What does it whisper?"

"Why—why"—the boy fidgeted—"why, I don't know. But it's always short of money, you know, Uncle."

"I know it, son, I know it."

155   "You know people send Mother writs,[7] don't you, Uncle?"

"I'm afraid I do," said the uncle.

"And then the house whispers, like people laughing at you behind your back. It's awful, that is! I thought if I was lucky. . . ."

"You might stop it," added the uncle.

The boy watched him with big blue eyes, that had an uncanny cold fire in them, and he said never a word.

160   "Well, then!" said the uncle. "What are we doing?"

"I shouldn't like Mother to know I was lucky," said the boy.

"Why not, son?"

"She'd stop me."

"I don't think she would."

165   "Oh!"—and the boy writhed in an odd way—"I *don't* want her to know, Uncle."

"All right, son! We'll manage it without her knowing."

They managed it very easily. Paul, at the other's suggestion, handed over five thousand pounds to his uncle, who deposited it with the family lawyer, who was then to inform Paul's mother that a relative had put five thousand pounds into his hands, which sum was to be paid out a thousand pounds at a time, on the mother's birthday, for the next five years.

"So she'll have a birthday present of a thousand pounds for five successive years," said Uncle Oscar. "I hope it won't make it all the harder for her later."

Paul's mother had her birthday in November. The house had been "whispering" worse than ever lately, and, even in spite of his luck, Paul could not bear up against it. He was very anxious to see the effect of the birthday letter, telling his mother about the thousand pounds.

170   When there were no visitors, Paul now took his meals with his parents, as he was beyond the nursery control. His mother went into town nearly

---

[7] Legal notices concerning payment of debts.

every day. She had discovered that she had an odd knack of sketching furs and dress materials, so she worked secretly in the studio of a friend who was the chief artist for the leading drapers. She drew the figures of ladies in furs and ladies in silk and sequins for the newspaper advertisements. This young woman artist earned several thousand pounds a year, but Paul's mother only made several hundred, and she was again dissatisfied. She so wanted to be first in something, and she did not succeed, even in making sketches for drapery advertisements.

She was down to breakfast on the morning of her birthday. Paul watched her face as she read her letters. He knew the lawyer's letter. As his mother read it, her face hardened and became more expressionless. Then a cold, determined look came on her mouth. She hid the letter under the pile of others, and said not a word about it.

"Didn't you have anything nice in the post for your birthday, Mother?" said Paul.

"Quite moderately nice," she said, her voice cold and absent.

She went away to town without saying more.

175   But in the afternoon Uncle Oscar appeared. He said Paul's mother had had a long interview with the lawyer, asking if the whole five thousand could not be advanced at once, as she was in debt.

"What do you think, Uncle?" asked the boy.

"I leave it to you, son."

"Oh, let her have it, then! We can get some more with the other," said the boy.

"A bird in the hand is worth two in the bush, laddie!" said Uncle Oscar.

180   "But I'm sure to *know* for the Grand National; or the Lincolnshire; or else the Derby. I'm sure to know for *one* of them," said Paul.

So Uncle Oscar signed the agreement, and Paul's mother touched the whole five thousand. Then something very curious happened. The voices in the house suddenly went mad, like a chorus of frogs on a spring evening. There was certain new furnishings, and Paul had a tutor. He was *really* going to Eton, his father's school, in the following autumn. There were flowers in the winter, and a blossoming of the luxury Paul's mother had been used to. And yet the voices in the house, behind the sprays of mimosa and almond blossom, and from under the piles of iridescent cushions, simply trilled and screamed in a sort of ecstasy: "There *must* be more money! Oh-h-h; there *must* be more money. Oh, now, now-w! Now-w-w—there *must* be more money!—more than ever! More than ever!"

It frightened Paul terribly. He studied away at his Latin and Greek. But his intense hours were spent with Bassett. The Grand National had gone by; he had not "known," and had lost a hundred pounds. Summer was at hand. He was in agony for the Lincoln. But even for the Lincoln he didn't "know," and he lost fifty pounds. He became wild-eyed and strange, as if something were going to explode in him.

"Let it alone, son! Don't you bother about it!" urged Uncle Oscar. But it was as if the boy couldn't really hear what his uncle was saying.

"I've got to know for the Derby! I've got to know for the Derby!" the child reiterated, his big blue eyes blazing with a sort of madness.

185 His mother noticed how overwrought he was.

"You'd better go to the seaside. Wouldn't you like to go now to the seaside, instead of waiting? I think you'd better," she said, looking down at him anxiously, her heart curiously heavy because of him.

But the child lifted his uncanny blue eyes. "I couldn't possibly go before the Derby, Mother!" he said. "I couldn't possibly!"

"Why not?" she said, her voice becoming heavy when she was opposed. "Why not? You can still go from the seaside to see the Derby with your uncle Oscar, if that's what you wish. No need for you to wait here. Besides, I think you care too much about these races. It's a bad sign. My family has been a gambling family, and you won't know till you grow up how much damage it has done. But it has done damage. I shall have to send Bassett away, and ask Uncle Oscar not to talk racing to you, unless you promise to be reasonable about it; go away to the seaside and forget it. You're all nerves!"

"I'll do what you like, Mother, so long as you don't send me away till after the Derby," the boy said.

190 "Send you away from where? Just from this house?"

"Yes," he said, gazing at her.

"Why, you curious child, what makes you care about this house so much, suddenly? I never knew you loved it."

He gazed at her without speaking. He had a secret within a secret, something he had not divulged, even to Bassett or to his uncle Oscar.

But his mother, after standing undecided and a little bit sullen for some moments, said:

195 "Very well, then! Don't go to the seaside till after the Derby, if you don't wish it. But promise me you won't let your nerves go to pieces. Promise you won't think so much about horse racing and *events,* as you call them!"

"Oh no," said the boy casually. "I won't think much about them, Mother. You needn't worry. I wouldn't worry, Mother, if I were you."

"If you were me and I were you," said his mother, "I wonder what we *should* do!"

"But you know you needn't worry, Mother, don't you?" the boy repeated.

"I should be awfully glad to know it," she said wearily.

200 "Oh, well you *can,* you know. I mean, you *ought* to know you needn't worry," he insisted.

"Ought I? Then I'll see about it," she said.

Paul's secret of secrets was his wooden horse, that which had no name. Since he was emancipated from a nurse and a nursery governess, he had had his rocking horse removed to his own bedroom at the top of the house.

"Surely, you're too big for a rocking horse!" his mother had remonstrated.

"Well, you see, Mother, till I can have a *real* horse, I like to have *some* sort of animal about," had been his quaint answer.

205 "Do you feel he keeps you company?" she laughed.

"Oh yes! He's very good, he always keeps me company, when I'm there," said Paul.

So the horse, rather shabby, stood in an arrested prance in the boy's bedroom.

The Derby was drawing near, and the boy grew more and more tense. He hardly heard what was spoken to him, he was very frail, and his eyes were really uncanny. His mother had sudden strange seizures of uneasiness about him. Sometimes, for half an hour, she would feel a sudden anxiety about him that was almost anguish. She wanted to rush to him at once, and know he was safe.

Two nights before the Derby, she was at a big party in town, when one of her rushes of anxiety about her boy, her firstborn, gripped her heart till she could hardly speak. She fought with the feeling, might and main, for she believed in common sense. But it was too strong. She had to leave the dance and go downstairs to telephone to the country. The children's nursery governess was terribly surprised and startled at being rung up in the night.

210 "Are the children all right, Miss Wilmot?"

"Oh, yes, they are quite all right."

"Master Paul? Is he all right?"

"He went to bed as right as a trivet. Shall I run up and look at him?"

"No," said Paul's mother reluctantly. "No! Don't trouble. It's all right. Don't sit up. We shall be home fairly soon." She did not want her son's privacy intruded upon.

215 "Very good," said the governess.

It was about one o'clock when Paul's mother and father drove up to their house. All was still. Paul's mother went to her room and slipped off her white fur cloak. She had told her maid not to wait up for her. She heard her husband downstairs, mixing a whisky and soda.

And then, because of the strange anxiety at her heart, she stole upstairs to her son's room. Noiselessly she went along the upper corridor. Was there a faint noise? What was it?

She stood, with arrested muscles, outside his door, listening. There was a strange, heavy, and yet not loud noise. Her heart stood still. It was a soundless noise, yet rushing and powerful. Something huge, in violent, hushed motion. What was it? What in God's name was it? She ought to know. She felt that she knew the noise. She knew what it was.

Yet she could not place it. She couldn't say what it was. And on and on it went, like a madness.

220 Softly, frozen with anxiety and fear, she turned the door handle.

The room was dark. Yet in the space near the window, she heard and saw something plunging to and fro. She gazed in fear and amazement.

Then suddenly she switched on the light, and saw her son, in his green pajamas, madly surging on the rocking horse. The blaze of light suddenly lit him up, as he urged the wooden horse, and lit her up, as she stood, blonde, in her dress of pale green and crystal, in the doorway.

"Paul!" she cried. "Whatever are you doing?"

"It's Malabar!" he screamed, in a powerful, strange voice. "It's Malabar!"

225   His eyes blazed at her for one strange and senseless second, as he ceased urging his wooden horse. Then he fell with a crash to the ground, and she, all her tormented motherhood flooding upon her, rushed to gather him up.

But he was unconscious, and unconscious he remained, with some brain fever. He talked and tossed, and his mother sat stonily by his side.

"Malabar! It's Malabar! Bassett, Bassett, I *know!* It's Malabar!"

So the child cried, trying to get up and urge the rocking horse that gave him his inspiration.

"What does he mean by Malabar?" asked the heart-frozen mother.

230   "I don't know," said the father stonily.

"What does he mean by Malabar?" she asked her brother Oscar.

"It's one of the horses running for the Derby," was the answer.

And, in spite of himself, Oscar Cresswell spoke to Bassett, and himself put a thousand on Malabar: at fourteen to one.

The third day of the illness was critical: they were waiting for a change. The boy, with his rather long, curly hair, was tossing ceaselessly on the pillow. He neither slept nor regained consciousness, and his eyes were like blue stones. His mother sat, feeling her heart had gone, turned actually into a stone.

235   In the evening, Oscar Cresswell did not come, but Bassett sent a message, saying could he come up for one moment, just one moment? Paul's mother was very angry at the intrusion, but on second thought she agreed. The boy was the same. Perhaps Bassett might bring him to consciousness.

The gardener, a shortish fellow with a little brown mustache and sharp little brown eyes, tiptoed into the room, touched his imaginary cap to Paul's mother, and stole to the bedside, staring with glittering, smallish eyes at the tossing, dying child.

"Master Paul!" he whispered. "Master Paul! Malabar came in first all right, a clean win. I did as you told me. You've made over seventy thousand pounds, you have; you've got over eighty thousand. Malabar came in all right, Master Paul."

"Malabar! Malabar! Did I say Malabar, Mother? Did I say Malabar? Do you think I'm lucky, Mother? I knew Malabar, didn't I? Over eighty thousand pounds! I call that lucky, don't you, Mother? Over eighty thousand pounds! I knew, didn't I know I knew? Malabar came in all right. If I ride my horse till I'm sure, then I tell you, Bassett, you can go as high as you like. Did you go for all you were worth, Bassett?"

"I went a thousand on it, Master Paul."

240   "I never told you, Mother, that if I can ride my horse, and *get there,* then I'm absolutely sure—oh, absolutely! Mother, did I ever tell you? I *am* lucky!"

"No, you never did," said his mother.

But the boy died in the night.

And even as he lay dead, his mother heard her brother's voice saying to her: "My God, Hester, you're eighty-odd thousand to the good, and a poor devil of a son to the bad. But, poor devil, poor devil, he's best gone out of a life where he rides his rocking horse to find a winner." [1926]

■ EXPLORATIONS OF THE TEXT ■

1. Why is the mother's heart "hard"? Does she love her children?
2. What is the nature of her relationship with her husband?
3. Why is the house "haunted"? Why is it "whispering"? Why does Paul want luck? Why do the voices go "mad" and intensify after Paul gives his mother 5,000 pounds?
4. Examine the connotations of "luck" in the story. How are "luck" and "filthy lucre" related?
5. Explain the significance of the symbol of the rocking horse and of Paul's riding. What does he need and want?
6. Examine the images of "eyes" in the text. How do the images change? What do these images suggest about Paul's character?
7. Why does Paul die? Does the mother love Paul in the end?
8. There are fairy tale and fantasy elements in the story. What effect do they have? Look particularly at the first six paragraphs.

■■ JOURNAL ENTRIES ■■

1. Write a personal response to Paul or to his mother.
2. Is money the root of all evil?

■■■ IDEAS FOR WRITING ■■■

1. Compare and contrast the eye imagery and symbolism in this story with Sophocles' *Oedipus Rex,* (Chapter 7) or Raymond Carver's "Cathedral" (Chapter 4).
2. Critics have interpreted this story as an indictment of modern materialism, as a critique of class structure, as a psychoanalytic exploration of Oedipal attachment, and as a spiritual examination of evil. Which interpretation do you favor? Why? Defend your choice. (You might wish to refer to the casebook in Appendix A for this assignment.)

Those Winter Sundays

Robert Hayden

Robert E. Hayden (1913–1980) was born in Detroit, Michigan. He attended Detroit City College (now Wayne State University) and received his M.A. at the University of Michigan. He taught at various universities before returning to the University of Michigan in 1969, where he taught until his death. He garnered many honors and fellowships, including two Hopwood awards. In 1976, he became the first African-American poet to be chosen as Consultant in Poetry to the Library of Congress.

Hayden's works include Heart-Shape in the Dust *(1940),* A Ballad of Remembrance *(1962),* Words in Mourning Time *(1970),* American Journal *(1978), and* Collected Prose *(1984). The present selection is from* Robert Hayden: Collected Poems, *published in 1982. In "Those Winter Sundays," a mature narrator expresses anger, understanding, and love for his father whom he failed to appreciate when he was young.*

> Sundays too my father got up early
> and put his clothes on in the blueblack cold,
> then with cracked hands that ached
> from labor in the weekday weather made
> 5 banked fires blaze. No one ever thanked him.
>
> I'd wake and hear the cold splintering, breaking.
> When the rooms were warm, he'd call,
> and slowly I would rise and dress,
> fearing the chronic angers of that house,
>
> 10 Speaking indifferently to him,
> who had driven out the cold
> and polished my good shoes as well.
> What did I know, what did I know
> of love's austere and lonely offices?

■ **EXPLORATIONS OF THE TEXT** ■

1. What hints about the father's work does Hayden provide?
2. Which details define the family's economic condition?
3. What do the images of cold and warmth suggest about the life of the family?
4. Discuss the "chronic angers" of the house.

5. What meanings are suggested by the speaker's question: "What did I know/of love's austere and lonely offices?"
6. In what ways has the speaker's attitude toward his father changed now that he is an adult?

■■ JOURNAL ENTRIES ■■

1. Remember an incident from childhood, a Saturday or Sunday morning at home with a parent. You might begin with: "Sunday mornings, I . . . ."
2. Interpret the quotation from Paul Simon's song, "The Sound of Silence": "Silence like a cancer grows." Connect it with the conflict of the speaker in this poem.

■■■ IDEAS FOR WRITING ■■■

1. Compare the barriers between fathers and sons in Hayden's poem and in other works in this chapter. Cite your personal experience and observation, too.
2. **Explicate** (examine line by line) this poem. Concentrate on point of view, imagery, theme.

Riders to the Sea

John Millington Synge

John Millington Synge (1871–1909), the youngest of five children, was born to Protestant, English parents in Rathfarnham, near Dublin, Ireland. Synge graduated from Trinity College, Dublin, in 1892; and for the ten years following his graduation, he travelled on the Continent. In Paris, he met W. B. Yeats, who suggested that Synge visit the Aran Islands off the west coast of Ireland in response to the latter's interest in Celtic language and lore. Yeats later concluded in A Vision *that this 1899 trip "formed the basis for [Synge's] artistic awakening."*

Synge's first play, In The Shadow of the Glen, *was produced at the Abbey Theatre in Dublin in 1903;* Riders to the Sea, *in 1904;* Playboy of the Western World, *his masterpiece, in 1907; and* The Tinker's Wedding *was produced in London in 1909. With Yeats and other playwrights and artists, Synge created a legendary Irish theatre at the Abbey and was responsible for the renaissance of Irish literature at the turn of the century. Noted for his realistic view of the Irish, his tragicomic and ironic visions, his poetic style and dialogue, and his compressed and lyrical visions, he is acknowledged to be one of Ireland's great playwrights.*

The germ of Riders to the Sea, *the beloved son, the sailor, lost at sea, may be traced to Synge's visit to the Aran Islands.*

Characters

Maurya, an old woman
Bartley, her son
Cathleen, her daughter
Nora, a younger daughter
Men and Women

An Island off the west of Ireland.

Cottage kitchen, with nets, oil-skins, spinning-wheel, some new boards standing by the wall, etc. Cathleen, a girl of about twenty finishes kneading cake, and puts it down on the pot-oven by the fire; then wipes her hands, and begins to spin at the wheel. Nora, a young girl, puts her head in at the door.

Nora *(In a low voice):* Where is she?
Cathleen: She's lying down, God help her, and may be sleeping, if she's able.

(Nora comes in softly, and takes a bundle from under her shawl)

Cathleen *(Spinning the wheel rapidly):* What is it you have?
Nora: The young priest is after bringing them. It's a shirt and a plain stocking were got off a drowned man in Donegal.[1]

(Cathleen stops her wheel with a sudden movement, and leans out to listen)

5 Nora: We're to find out if it's Michael's they are, some time herself will be down looking by the sea.
Cathleen: How would they be Michael's, Nora? How would he go the length of that way to the Far North?
Nora: The young priest says he's known the like of it. "If it's Michael's they are," says he, "you can tell herself he's got a clean burial by the grace of God, and if they're not his, let no one say a word about them, for she'll be getting her death," says he, "with crying and lamenting."

(The door which Nora half closed is blown open by a gust of wind)

Cathleen *(Looking out anxiously):* Did you ask him would he stop Bartley going this day with the horses to the Galway[2] fair?

---

[1] County in Northwestern Ireland; in Ulster.
[2] City in West Central Ireland.

Nora: "I won't stop him," says he, "but let you not be afraid. Herself does be saying prayers half through the night, and the Almighty God won't leave her destitute." says he, "with no son living."

10 **Cathleen:** Is the sea bad by the white rocks, Nora?

Nora: Middling bad, God help us. There's a great roaring in the west, and it's worse it'll be getting when the tide's turned to the wind. *(She goes over to the table with the bundle)* Shall I open it now?

Cathleen: Maybe she'd wake up on us, and come in before we'd done. *(Coming to the table)* It's a long time we'll be, and the two of us crying.

Nora *(Goes to the inner door and listens):* She's moving about on the bed. She'll be coming in a minute.

Cathleen: Give me the ladder, and I'll put them up in the turf-loft, the way she won't know of them at all, and maybe when the tide turns she'll be going down to see would he be floating from the east.

(They put the ladder against the gable of the chimney; Cathleen goes up a few steps and hides the bundle in the turf-loft. Maurya comes from the inner room)

15 **Maurya** *(Looking up at Cathleen and speaking querulously):* Isn't it turf enough you have for this day and evening?

Cathleen: There's a cake baking at the fire for a short space *(Throwing down the turf)* and Bartley will want it when the tide turns if he goes to Connemara.[3]

(Nora picks up the turf and puts it round the pot-oven)

Maurya *(Sitting down on a stool at the fire):* He won't go this day with the wind rising from the south and west. He won't go this day, for the young priest will stop him surely.

Nora: He'll not stop him, Mother, and I heard Eamon Simon and Stephen Pheety and Colum Shawn saying he would go.

Maurya: Where is he itself?

20 **Nora:** He went down to see would there be another boat sailing in the week, and I'm thinking it won't be long till he's here now, for the tide's turning at the green head, and the hooker's[4] tacking from the east.

Cathleen: I hear some one passing the big stones.

Nora *(Looking out):* He's coming now, and he in a hurry.

Bartley *(Comes in and looks round the room; speaking sadly and quietly):* Where is the bit of new rope, Cathleen, was bought in Connemara?

Cathleen *(Coming down):* Give it to him, Nora; it's on a nail by the white boards. I hung it up this morning, for the pig with the black feet was eating it.

25 **Nora** *(Giving him a rope):* Is that it, Bartley?

---

[3] Region of West Ireland.
[4] One-masted fishing boat used on the English and Irish coast.

Maurya: You'd do right to leave that rope, Bartley, hanging by the boards. *(Bartley takes the rope)* It will be wanting in this place, I'm telling you, if Michael is washed up tomorrow morning, or the next morning, or any morning in the week, for it's a deep grave we'll make him by the grace of God.

Bartley *(Beginning to work with the rope):* I've no halter the way I can ride down on the mare, and I must go now quickly. This is the one boat going for two weeks or beyond it, and the fair will be a good fair for horses I heard them saying below.

Maurya: It's a hard thing they'll be saying below if the body is washed up and there's no man in it to make the coffin, and I after giving a big price for the finest white boards you'd find in Connemara. *(She looks round at the boards)*

Bartley: How would it be washed up, and we after looking each day for nine days, and a strong wind blowing a while back from the west and south?

30 Maurya: If it wasn't found itself, that wind is raising the sea, and there was a star up against the moon, and it rising in the night. If it was a hundred horses, or a thousand horses you had itself, what is the price of a thousand horses against a son where there is one son only?

Bartley *(Working at the halter, to Cathleen):* Let you go down each day, and see the sheep aren't jumping in on the rye, and if the jobber[5] comes you can sell the pig with the black feet if there is a good price going.

Maurya: How would the like of her get a good price for a pig?

Bartley *(To Cathleen):* If the west wind holds with the last bit of the moon let you and Nora get up weed enough for another cock[6] for the kelp. It's hard set we'll be from this day with no one in it but one man to work.

Maurya: It's hard set we'll be surely the day you're drowned'd with the rest. What way will I live and the girls with me, and I an old woman looking for the grave?

(Bartley lays down the halter, takes off his old coat, and puts on a newer one of the same flannel)

35 Bartley *(To Nora):* Is she coming to the pier?

Nora *(Looking out):* She's passing the green head and letting fall her sails.

Bartley *(Getting his purse and tobacco):* I'll have half an hour to go down, and you'll see my coming again in two days, or in three days, or maybe in four days if the wind is bad.

Maurya *(Turning round to the fire, and putting her shawl over her head):* Isn't it a hard and cruel man won't hear a word from an old woman, and she holding him from the sea?

Cathleen: It's the life of a young man to be going on the sea, and who would listen to an old woman with one thing and she saying it over?

---

[5] Wholesaler.
[6] A small pile for burning seaweed into kelp (used as fertilizer).

40 Bartley *(Taking the halter):* I must go now quickly. I'll ride down on the red mare, and the gray pony'll run behind me. . . . The blessing of God on you. *(He goes out)*

Maurya *(Crying out as he is in the door):* He's gone now, God spare us, and we'll not see him again. He's gone now, and when the black night is falling I'll have no son left me in the world.

Cathleen: Why wouldn't you give him your blessing and he looking round in the door? Isn't it sorrow enough is on every one in this house without your sending him out with an unlucky word behind him and a hard word in his ear?

(Maurya takes up the tongs and begins raking the fire aimlessly without looking round)

Nora *(Turning toward her):* You're taking away the turf from the cake.

Cathleen *(Crying out):* The Son of God forgive us, Nora, we're after forgetting his bit of bread. *(She comes over to the fire)*

45 Nora: And it's destroyed he'll be going till dark night, and he after eating nothing since the sun went up.

Cathleen *(Turning the cake out of the oven):* It's destroyed he'll be, surely. There's no sense left on any person in a house where an old woman will be talking forever.

(Maurya sways herself on her stool)

Cathleen *(Cutting off some of the bread and rolling it in a cloth; to Maurya):* Let you go down now to the spring well and give him this and he passing. You'll see him then and the dark word will be broken, and you can say "God speed you," the way he'll be easy in his mind.

Maurya *(Taking the bread):* Will I be in it as soon as himself?

Cathleen: If you go now quickly.

50 Maurya *(Standing up unsteadily):* It's hard set I am to walk.

Cathleen *(Looking at her anxiously):* Give her the stick, Nora, or maybe she'll slip on the big stones.

Nora: What stick?

Cathleen: The stick Michael brought from Connemara.

Maurya *(Taking a stick Nora gives her):* In the big world the old people do be leaving things after them for their sons and children, but in this place it is the young men do be leaving things behind for them that do be old.

(She goes out slowly. Nora goes over to the ladder)

55 Cathleen: Wait, Nora, maybe she'd turn back quickly. She's that sorry, God help her, you wouldn't know the thing she'd do.

Nora: Is she gone round by the bush?

Cathleen *(Looking out):* She's gone now. Throw it down quickly, for the Lord knows when she'll be out of it again.

Nora *(Getting the bundle from the loft):* The young priest said he'd be passing tomorrow, and we might go down and speak to him below if it's Michael's they are surely.

Cathleen *(Taking the bundle):* Did he say what way they were found?

60 Nora *(Coming down):* "There were two men," says he, "and they rowing round with poteen[7] before the cocks crowed, and the oar of one of them caught the body, and they passing the black cliffs of the north."

Cathleen *(Trying to open the bundle):* Give me a knife, Nora, the string's perished with the salt water, and there's a black knot on it you wouldn't loosen in a week.

Nora *(Giving her a knife):* I've heard tell it was a long way to Donegal.

Cathleen *(Cutting the string):* It is surely. There was a man in here a while ago—the man sold us that knife—and he said if you set off walking from the rocks beyond, it would be seven days you'd be in Donegal.

Nora: And what time would a man take, and he floating?

(Cathleen opens the bundle and takes out a bit of a stocking. They look at them eagerly)

65 Cathleen *(In a low voice):* The Lord spare us, Nora! isn't it a queer hard thing to say if it's his they are surely?

Nora: I'll get his shirt off the hook the way we can put the one flannel on the other. *(She looks through some clothes hanging in the corner)* It's not with them, Cathleen, and where will it be?

Cathleen: I'm thinking Bartley put it on him in the morning, for his own shirt was heavy with the salt in it. *(Pointing to the corner)* There's a bit of a sleeve was of the same stuff. Give me that and it will do.

(Nora brings it to her and they compare the flannel)

Cathleen: It's the same stuff, Nora; but if it is itself aren't there great rolls of it in the shops of Galway, and isn't it many another man may have a shirt of it as well as Michael himself?

Nora *(Who has taken up the stocking and counted the stitches, crying out):* It's Michael, Cathleen, it's Michael; God spare his soul, and what will herself say when she hears this story, and Bartley on the sea?

70 Cathleen *(Taking the stocking):* It's a plain stocking.

Nora: It's the second one of the third pair I knitted, and I put up threescore stitches, and I dropped four of them.

Cathleen *(Counts the stitches):* It's that number is in it. *(Crying out)* Ah, Nora, isn't it a bitter thing to think of him floating that way to the Far North, and no one to keen[8] him but the black hags that do be flying on the sea?

Nora *(Swinging herself round, and throwing out her arms on the clothes):* And isn't it a pitiful thing when there is nothing left of a man who was a great rower and fisher, but a bit of an old shirt and a plain stocking?

Cathleen *(After an instant):* Tell me is herself coming, Nora? I hear a little sound on the path.

---

[7] Illegally distilled whiskey.
[8] Ritualized lamentation for the dead; wailing with deep sorrow about the dead.

75 Nora *(Looking out):* She is, Cathleen. She's coming up to the door.

Cathleen: Put these things away before she'll come in. Maybe it's easier she'll be after giving her blessing to Bartley, and we won't let on we've heard anything the time he's on the sea.

Nora *(Helping Cathleen to close the bundle):* We'll put them here in the corner.

(They put them into a hole in the chimney corner. Cathleen goes back to the spinning-wheel)

Nora: Will she see it was crying I was?

Cathleen: Keep your back to the door the way the light'll not be on you.

(Nora sits down at the chimney corner, with her back to the door. Maurya comes in very slowly, without looking at the girls, and goes over to her stool at the other side of the fire. The cloth with the bread is still in her hand. The girls look at each other, and Nora points to the bundle of bread)

80 Cathleen *(After spinning for a moment):* You didn't give him his bit of bread? *(Maurya begins to keen softly, without turning round)*

Cathleen: Did you see him riding down?

(Maurya goes on keening)

Cathleen *(A little impatiently):* God forgive you; isn't it a better thing to raise your voice and tell what you seen, than to be making lamentation for a thing that's done? Did you see Bartley, I'm saying to you.

Maurya *(With a weak voice):* My heart's broken from this day.

Cathleen *(As before):* Did you see Bartley?

85 Maurya: I seen the fearfulest thing.

Cathleen *(Leaves her wheel and looks out):* God forgive you; he's riding the mare now over the green head, and the gray pony behind him.

Maurya *(Starts, so that her shawl falls back from her head and shows her white tossed hair. With a frightened voice):* The gray pony behind him.

Cathleen *(Coming to the fire):* What is it ails you, at all?

Maurya *(Speaking very slowly):* I've seen the fearfulest thing any person has seen, since the day Bride Dara seen the dead man with a child in his arms.

90 Cathleen and Nora: Uah.

(They crouch down in front of the old woman at the fire)

Nora: Tell us what it is you seen.

Maurya: I went down to the spring well, and I stood there saying a prayer to myself. Then Bartley came along, and he riding on the red mare with the gray pony behind him. *(She puts up her hands, as if to hide something from her eyes)* The Son of God spare us, Nora!

Cathleen: What is it you seen?

Maurya: I seen Michael himself.

95 **Cathleen** *(Speaking softly):* You did not, Mother; it wasn't Michael you seen
for his body is after being found in the Far North, and he's got a clean
burial by the grace of God.

Maurya *(A little defiantly):* I'm after seeing him this day, and he riding and
galloping. Bartley came first on the red mare; and I tried to say, "God
speed you," but something choked the words in my throat. He went by
quickly; and "the blessing of God on you," says he, and I could say nothing. I looked up then, and I crying, at the gray pony, and there was
Michael upon it—with fine clothes on him, and new shoes on his feet.

Cathleen *(Begins to keen):* It's destroyed we are from this day. It's destroyed,
surely.

Nora: Didn't the young priest say the Almighty God wouldn't leave her destitute with no son living?

Maurya *(In a low voice, but clearly):* It's little the like of him knows of the
sea. . . . Bartley will be lost now, and let you call in Eamon and make
me a good coffin out of the white boards, for I won't live after them. I've
had a husband, and a husband's father, and six sons in this house—six
fine men, though it was a hard birth I had with every one of them and
they coming to the world—and some of them were found and some of
them were not found, but they're gone now the lot of them. . . . There
was Stephen, and Shawn, were lost in the great wind, and found after in
the Bay of Gregory of the Golden Mouth, and carried up the two of them
on the one plank, and in by that door.

*(She pauses for a moment, the girls start as if they heard something
through the door that is half open behind them)*

100 **Nora** *(In a whisper):* Did you hear that, Cathleen? Did you hear a noise in the
northeast?

Cathleen *(In a whisper):* There's some one after crying out by the seashore.

Maurya *(Continues without hearing anything):* There was Sheamus and his
father, and his own father again, were lost in a dark night, and not a stick
or sign was seen of them when the sun went up. There was Patch after was
drowned out of a curagh that turned over. I was sitting here with Bartley,
and he a baby, lying on my two knees, and I seen two women, and three
women, and four women coming in, and they crossing themselves, and
not saying a word. I looked out then, and there were men coming after
them, and they holding a thing in the half of a red sail, and water dripping
out of it—it was a dry day, Nora—and leaving a track to the door.

*(She pauses again with her hand stretched out toward the door. It opens
softly and old women begin to come in, crossing themselves on the
threshold, and kneeling down in front of the stage with red petticoats
over their heads)*

Maurya *(Half in a dream, to Cathleen):* Is it Patch, or Michael, or what is it
at all?

Cathleen: Michael is after being found in the Far North, and when he is found there how could he be here in this place?

105 Maurya: There does be a power of young men floating round in the sea, and what way would they know if it was Michael they had, or another man like him, for when a man is nine days in the sea, and the wind blowing, it's hard set his own mother would be to say what man was it.

Cathleen: It's Michael, God spare him, for they're after sending us a bit of his clothes from the Far North.

(She reaches out and hands Maurya the clothes that belonged to Michael. Maurya stands up slowly, and takes them in her hands. Nora looks out)

Nora: They're carrying a thing among them and there's water dripping out of it and leaving a track by the big stones.

Cathleen *(In a whisper to the women who have come in):* Is it Bartley it is?

One of the Women: It is surely, God rest his soul.

(Two younger women come in and pull out the table. Then men carry in the body of Bartley, laid on a plank, with a bit of a sail over it, and lay it on the table)

110 Cathleen *(To the women, as they are doing so):* What way was he drowned?

One of the Women: The gray pony knocked him into the sea, and he was washed out where there is a great surf on the white rocks.

(Maurya has gone over and knelt down at the head of the table. The women are keening softly and swaying themselves with a slow movement. Cathleen and Nora kneel at the other end of the table. The men kneel near the door)

Maurya *(Raising her head and speaking as if she did not see the people around her):* They're all gone now, and there isn't anything more the sea can do to me. . . . I'll have no call now to be up crying and praying when the wind breaks from the south, and you can hear the surf is in the east, and the surf is in the west, making a great stir with the two noises, and they hitting one on the other. I'll have no call now to be going down and getting Holy Water in the dark nights after Sambain,[9] and I won't care what way the sea is when the other women will be keening. *(To Nora)* Give me the Holy Water, Nora, there's a small sup still on the dresser.

(Nora gives it to her)

Maurya *(Drops Michael's clothes across Bartley's feet, and sprinkles the Holy Water over him):* It isn't that I haven't prayed for you, Bartley, to

---

[9] Similar to all hallows, a holiday which falls on November 1 and marks the beginning of winter; it is celebrated with harvest rites and a Feast of the Dead.

the Almighty God. It isn't that I haven't said prayers in the dark night till you wouldn't know what I'd be saying; but it's a great rest I'll have now, and it's time surely. It's a great rest I'll have now, and great sleeping in the long nights after Samhain, if it's only a bit of wet flour we do have to eat, and maybe a fish that would be stinking.

(She kneels down again, crossing herself, and saying prayers under her breath)

Cathleen *(To an old man):* Maybe yourself and Eamon would make a coffin when the sun rises. We have fine white boards herself bought. God help her, thinking Michael would be found, and I have a new cake you can eat while you'll be working.

115 The Old Man *(Looking at the boards):* Are there nails with them?

Cathleen: There are not, Colum; we didn't think of the nails.

Another Man: It's a great wonder she wouldn't think of the nails, and all the coffins she's seen made already.

Cathleen: It's getting old she is, and broken.

(Maurya stands up again very slowly and spreads out the pieces of Michael's clothes beside the body, sprinkling them with the last of the Holy Water)

Nora *(In a whisper to Cathleen):* She's quiet now and easy; but the day Michael was drowned you could hear her crying out from this to the spring well. It's fonder she was of Michael, and would any one have thought that?

120 Cathleen *(Slowly and clearly):* An old woman will be soon tired with anything she will do, and isn't it nine days herself is after crying and keening, and making great sorrow in the house?

Maurya *(Puts the empty cup mouth downwards on the table, and lays her hands together on Bartley's feet):* They're all together this time, and the end is come. May the Almighty God have mercy on Bartley's soul, and on Michael's soul, and on the souls of Sheamus and Patch, and Stephen and Shawn; *(Bending her head)* and may He have mercy on my soul, Nora, and on the soul of every one is left living in the world.

(She pauses, and the keen rises a little more loudly from the women, then sinks away)

Maurya *(Continuing):* Michael has a clean burial in the Far North, by the grace of the Almighty God. Bartley will have a fine coffin out of the white boards, and a deep grave surely. What more can we want than that? No man at all can be living forever, and we must be satisfied.

(She kneels down again and the curtain falls slowly)

■ EXPLORATIONS OF THE TEXT ■

1. What does the initial dialogue between Nora and Cathleen reveal about the protagonists' world? What do they fear?
2. Discuss the characters of Nora, Cathleen, and Bartley as individuals and as family members. How are they different from each other?
3. How do the sisters realize their brother is dead? Interpret the symbolism of Michael's clothes.
4. What is the meaning of Maurya's vision of Michael "on the red mare with the gray pony behind him"? Why is Maurya so concerned with a proper burial and coffin?
5. Consider Maurya's character. What has been her role as a mother? How does she handle the deaths of her sons?
6. Why does Maurya claim: "They're all gone now, and there isn't anything more the sea can do to me"? Do you believe her when she claims, "No man at all can be living forever, and we must be sacrificed"?
7. Do the images of sea, surf, and wind change in the play? Are they negative or positive?
8. Compare the view of fate in this work with similar ideas in the "The Rocking-Horse Winner."

■■ JOURNAL ENTRIES ■■

1. Synge's play is about people living on a small island off the coast of Ireland in the early 1900s. Does the fate of these people have relevance for us today? Why?
2. Discuss rituals of mourning and experiences of grief. (You may wish to refer to your own experience.)

■■■ IDEAS FOR WRITING ■■■

1. Choose a detail of the play—a stage direction, a gesture, an aspect of scene, a prop, an image—and analyze its relationship to theme.
2. Distinguish between the roles and concerns of men and of women in the play.
3. What does Synge believe about the power of the sea?
4. Synge has been quoted as saying, "the drama, like the symphony, does not teach or prove anything." After reading Riders to the Sea, do you agree with him?

Letter to His Father

Franz Kafka
Translated by Ernest Kaiser and Eithene Wilkins

*Franz Kafka (1883–1924) was born in Prague, Czechoslovakia to Jewish parents with whom he lived most of his life. Kafka was plagued by emotional and physical infirmities, and he completed and published very few of his works. Before he died of tuberculosis at the age of forty-one, he instructed his friend Max Brod to destroy his remaining manuscripts, but fortunately Brod did not do so. Three unfinished novels—*The Trial *(1925),* The Castle *(1926), and* Amerika *(1927)—brought Kafka international recognition, albeit posthumously. His stories, translated from German into English, can be found in* The Great Wall of China *(1933),* The Penal Colony *(1948), and* The Complete Stories *(1976).*

In the long missive later published as "Letter to His Father," Kafka, at age thirty-six, reproaches his father for his cruel, intimidating, and boorish behavior.

1   Dearest Father:
You asked me recently why I maintain that I am afraid of you. As usual I was unable to think of any answer to your question, partly for the very reason that I am afraid of you, and partly because an explanation of the grounds for this fear would mean going into far more details than I could even approximately keep in mind while talking. And if I now try to give you an answer in writing, it will still be very incomplete, because even in writing this fear and its consequences hamper me in relation to you and because [anyway] the magnitude of the subject goes far beyond the scope of my memory and power of reasoning. . . .

2   Compare the two of us: I, to put it in a very much abbreviated form, a Löwy with a certain basis of Kafka, which, however, is not set in motion by the Kafka will to life, business, and conquest, but by a Löwyish spur that urges more secretly, more diffidently, and in another direction, and which often fails to work entirely. You, on the other hand, a true Kafka in strength, health, appetite, loudness of voice, eloquence, self-satisfaction, worldly dominance, endurance, presence of mind, knowledge of human nature, a certain way of doing things on a grand scale, of course with all the defects and weaknesses that go with all these advantages and into which your temperament and sometimes your hot temper drive you. . . .

3   However it was, we were so different and in our difference so dangerous to each other that, if anyone had tried to calculate in advance how I, the slowly developing child, and you, the full-grown man, would stand to each other, he could have assumed that you would simply trample me underfoot so that nothing was left of me. Well, that didn't happen. Nothing alive can be calculated. But perhaps something worse happened. And in saying this I

would all the time beg of you not to forget that I never, and not even for a single moment, believe any guilt to be on your side. The effect you had on me was the effect you could not help having. But you should stop considering it some particular malice on my part that I succumbed to that effect.

4   I was a timid child. For all that, I am sure I was also obstinate, as children are. I am sure that Mother spoilt me too, but I cannot believe I was particularly difficult to manage; I cannot believe that a kindly word, a quiet taking of me by the hand, a friendly look, could not have got me to do anything that was wanted of me. Now you are after all at bottom a kindly and softhearted person (what follows will not be in contradiction to this, I am speaking only of the impression you made on the child), but not every child has the endurance and fearlessness to go on searching until it comes to the kindliness that lies beneath the surface. You can only treat a child in the way you yourself are constituted, with vigor, noise, and hot temper, and in this case this seemed to you, into the bargain, extremely suitable, because you wanted to bring me up to be a strong brave boy. . . .

5   There is only one episode in the early years of which I have a direct memory. You may remember it, too. Once in the night I kept on whimpering for water, not, I am certain, because I was thirsty, but probably partly to be annoying, partly to amuse myself. After several vigorous threats had failed to have any effect, you took me out of bed, carried me out onto the *pavlatche* and left me there alone for a while in my nightshirt, outside the shut door. I am not going to say that this was wrong—perhaps at that time there was really no other way of getting peace and quiet that night—but I mention it as typical of your methods of bringing up a child and their effect on me. I dare say I was quite obedient afterwards at that period, but it did me inner harm. What was for me a matter of course, that senseless asking for water, and the extraordinary terror of being carried outside were two things that I, my nature being what it was, could never properly connect with each other. Even years afterwards I suffered from the tormenting fancy that the huge man, my father, the ultimate authority, would come almost for no reason at all and take me out of bed in the night and carry me out onto the *pavlatche,* and that therefore I was such a mere nothing for him.

6   That then was only a small beginning, but this sense of nothingness that often dominates me (a feeling that is in another respect, admittedly, also a noble and fruitful one) comes largely from your influence. What I would have needed was a little encouragement, a little friendliness, and little keeping open of my road, instead of which you blocked it for me, though of course with the good intention of making me go another road. But I was not fit for that. You encouraged me, for instance, when I saluted and marched smartly, but I was no future soldier, or you encouraged me when I was able to eat heartily or even drink beer with my meals, or when I was able to repeat songs, singing what I had not understood, or prattle to you using your own favorite expressions, imitating you, but nothing of this had anything to do with my future. And it is characteristic that even today you really only encourage me in anything when you yourself are involved in it, when what is at stake is your sense of self-importance.

7   At that time, and at that time everywhere, I would have needed encouragement. I was, after all, depressed even by your mere physical presence. I remember, for instance, how we often undressed together in the same bathing hut. There was I, skinny, weakly, slight; you strong, tall, broad. Even inside the hut I felt myself a miserable specimen, and what's more, not only in your eyes but in the eyes of the whole world, for you were for me the measure of all things. But then when we went out of the bathing hut before the people, I with you holding my hand, a little skeleton, unsteady, barefoot on the boards, frightened of the water, incapable of copying your swimming strokes, which you, with the best of intentions, but actually to my profound humiliation, always kept on showing me, then I was frantic with desperation and all my bad experiences in all spheres at such moments fitted magnificently together. . . .

8   In keeping with that, furthermore, was your intellectual domination. You had worked your way up so far alone, by your own energies, and as a result you had unbounded confidence in your opinion. For me as a child that was not yet so dazzling as later for the boy growing up. From your armchair you ruled the world. Your opinion was correct, every other was mad, wild, *meshugge,* not normal. With all this your self-confidence was so great that you had no need to be consistent at all and yet never ceased to be in the right. It did sometimes happen that you had no opinion whatsoever about a matter and as a result all opinions that were at all possible with respect to the matter were necessarily wrong without exception. You were capable, for instance, of running down the Czechs, and then the Germans, and then the Jews, and what is more, not only selectively but in every respect, and finally nobody was left except yourself. For me you took on the enigmatic quality that all tyrants have whose rights are based on their person and not on reason. At least so it seemed to me.

9   Now where I was concerned you were in fact astonishingly often in the right, which was a matter of course in talk, for there was hardly ever any talk between us, but also in reality. Yet this too was nothing particularly incomprehensible; in all my thinking I was, after all, under the heavy pressure of your personality, even in that part of it—and particularly in that—which was not in accord with yours. All these thoughts, seemingly independent of you, were from the beginning loaded with the burden of your harsh and dogmatic judgments; it was almost impossible to endure this, and yet to work out one's thoughts with any measure of completeness and permanence. I am not here speaking of any sublime thoughts, but of every little enterprise in childhood. It was only necessary to be happy about something or other, to be filled with the thought of it, to come home and speak of it, and the answer was an ironical sigh, a shaking of the head, a tapping of the table with one finger: "Is that all you're so worked up about?" or "I wish I had your worries!" or "The things some people have time to think about!" or "What can you buy yourself with that?" or "What a song and dance about nothing!" Of course, you couldn't be expected to be enthusiastic about every childish triviality, toiling and moiling as you used to. But that wasn't the point. The point was, rather, that you could

not help always and on principle causing the child such disappointments, by virtue of your antagonistic nature, and further that this antagonism was ceaselessly intensified through accumulation of its material, that it finally became a matter of established habit even when for once you were of the same opinion as myself, and that finally these disappointments of the child's were not disappointments in ordinary life but, since what it concerned was your person, which was the measure of all things, struck to the very core. Courage, resolution, confidence, delight in this and that, did not endure to the end when you were against whatever it was or even if your opposition was merely to be assumed; and it was to be assumed in almost everything I did. . . .

10   You have, I think, a gift for bringing up children: you could, I am sure, have been of use to a human being of your own kind with your methods; such a person would have seen the reasonableness of what you told him, would not have troubled about anything else, and would quietly have done things the way he was told. But for me a child everything you shouted at me was positively a heavenly commandment, I never forgot it, it remained for me the most important means of forming a judgment of the world, above all of forming a judgment of you yourself, and there you failed entirely. Since as a child I was together with you chiefly at meals, your teaching was to a large extent teaching about proper behavior at table. What was brought to the table had to be eaten up, there could be no discussion of the goodness of the food—but you yourself often found the food uneatable, called it "this swill," said "that brute" (the cook) had ruined it. Because in accordance with your strong appetite and your particular habit you ate everything fast, hot and in big mouthfuls, the child had to hurry, there was a somber silence at table, interrupted by admonitions: "Eat first, talk afterwards," or "faster, faster, faster," or "there you are, you see, I finished ages ago." Bones mustn't be cracked with the teeth, but you could. Vinegar must not be sipped noisily, but you could. The main thing was that the bread should be cut straight. But it didn't matter that you did it with a knife dripping with gravy. One had to take care that no scraps fell on the floor. In the end it was under your chair that there were most scraps. At table one wasn't allowed to do anything but eat, but you cleaned and cut your fingernails, sharpened pencils, cleaned your ears with the toothpick. Please, Father, understand me rightly: these would in themselves have been utterly insignificant details, they only became depressing for me because you, the man who was so tremendously the measure of all things for me, yourself did not keep the commandments you imposed on me. Hence the world was for me divided into three parts: into one in which I, the slave, lived under laws that had been invented only for me and which I could, I did not know why, never completely comply with; then into a second world, which was infinitely remote from mine, in which you lived, concerned with government, with the issuing of orders and with annoyance about their not being obeyed; and finally into a third world where everybody else lived happily and free from orders and from having to obey. I was continually in disgrace, either I obeyed your orders, and that was a disgrace, for they applied, after all, only to me, or I was defiant, and that was a disgrace too, for how

could I presume to defy you, or I could not obey because, for instance, I had not your strength, your appetite, your skill, in spite of which you expected it of me as a matter of course; this was the greatest disgrace of all. What moved in this way was not the child's reflections, but his feelings. . . .

11   It was true that Mother was illimitably good to me, but all that was for me in relation to you, that is to say, is no good relation. Mother unconsciously played the part of a beater during a hunt. Even if your method of upbringing might in some unlikely case have set me on my own feet by means of producing defiance, dislike, or even hate in me, Mother canceled that out again by kindness, by talking sensibly (in the maze and chaos of my childhood she was the very pattern of good sense and reasonableness), by pleading for me, and I was again driven back into your orbit, which I might perhaps otherwise have broken out of, to your advantage and to my own. Or it was so that no real reconciliation ever came about, that Mother merely shielded me from you in secret, secretly gave me something, or allowed me to do something, and then where you were concerned I was again the furtive creature, the cheat, the guilty one, who in his worthlessness could only pursue backstairs methods even to get the things he regarded as his right. Of course, I then became used to taking such courses also in quest of things to which, even in my own view, I had no right. This again meant an increase in the sense of guilt.

12   It is also true that you hardly ever really gave me a whipping. But the shouting, the way your face got red, the hasty undoing of the braces and the laying of them ready over the back of the chair, all that was almost worse for me. It is like when someone is going to be hanged. If he is really hanged, then he's dead and it's all over. But if he has to go through all the preliminaries to being hanged and only when the noose is dangling before his face is told of his reprieve, then he may suffer from it all his life long. Besides, from so many occasions when I had, as you clearly showed you thought, deserved to be beaten, when you were however gracious enough to let me off at the last moment, here again what accumulated was only a huge sense of guilt. On every side I was to blame, I was in debt to you.

13   You have always reproached me (and what is more either alone or in front of others, you having no feeling for the humiliation of this latter, your children's affairs always being public affairs) for living in peace and quiet, warmth, and abundance, lack for nothing, thanks to your hard work. I think here of remarks that must positively have worn grooves in my brain, like: "When I was only seven I had to push the barrow from village to village." "We all had to sleep in one room." "We were glad when we got potatoes." "For years I had open sores on my legs from not having enough clothes to wear in winter." "I was only a little boy when I was sent away to Pisek to go into business." "I got nothing from home, not even when I was in the army, even then I was sending money home." "But for all that, for all that—Father was always Father to me. Ah, nobody knows what that means these days! What do these children know of things? Nobody's been through that! Is there any child that understands such things today?" Under other conditions such stories might have been very educational, they might have been a way of encouraging one and strengthening

one to endure similar torments and deprivations to those one's father had undergone. But that wasn't what you wanted at all; the situation had, after all, become quite different as a result of all your efforts, and there was no opportunity to distinguish oneself in the world as you had done. Such an opportunity would first of all have had to be created by violence and revolution, it would have meant breaking away from home (assuming one had had the resolution and strength to do so and that Mother wouldn't have worked against it, for her part, with other means). But all that was not what you wanted at all, that you termed ingratitude, extravagance, disobedience, treachery, madness. And so, while on the one hand you tempted me to it by means of example, story, and humiliation, on the other hand you forbade it with the utmost severity. . . .

14   (Up to this point there is in this letter relatively little I have intentionally passed over in silence, but now and later I shall have to be silent on certain matters that it is still too hard for me to confess—to you and to myself. I say this in order that, if the picture as a whole should be somewhat blurred here and there, you should not believe that what is to blame is any lack of evidence; on the contrary, there is evidence that might well make the picture unbearably stark. It is not easy to strike a median position.) Here, it's enough to remind you of early days. I had lost my self-confidence where you were concerned, and in its place had developed a boundless sense of guilt. (In recollection of this boundlessness I once wrote of someone accurately: "He is afraid the shame will outlive him, even.") I could not suddenly undergo a transformation when I came into the company of other people; on the contrary, with them I came to feel an even deeper sense of guilt, for, as I have already said, in their case I had to make good the wrongs done them by you in the business, wrongs in which I too had my share of responsibility. Besides, you always, of course, had some objection to make, frankly or covertly, to everyone I associated with, and for this too I had to beg his pardon. The mistrust that you tried to instill into me, at business and at home, towards most people (tell me of any single person who was of importance to me in my childhood whom you didn't at least once tear to shreds with your criticism), this mistrust, which oddly enough was no particular burden to you (the fact was that you were strong enough to bear it, and besides it was in reality perhaps only a token of the autocrat), this mistrust, which for me as a little boy was nowhere confirmed in my own eyes, since I everywhere saw only people excellent beyond all hope of emulation, in me turned into mistrust of myself and into perpetual anxiety in relation to everything else. There, then, I was in general certain of not being able to escape from you.

■ EXPLORATIONS OF THE TEXT ■

1. Why is Kafka "afraid" to talk to his father? Why does he write a letter instead?
2. What are the differences between the Löwys and Kafkas? How do these differences manifest themselves in the tension between Kafka and his father?
3. What is Kafka's perception of himself as a child? How does he think that his father should have treated him?
4. Which examples of the father's mistreatment of his son have the most impact on you? Why?
5. How did the father's character and actions affect the development of his son's personality?
6. What is the mother's role in the family?
7. The essay balances complex sentences with short simple ones. What does the sentence structure in the last paragraph accomplish? Is the last sentence powerful? Why or why not?
8. How does Kafka's argument progress? How does it follow the classic structure of an argument?
9. Compare the portrait of Kafka's father with the portrayal of Plath's "Daddy."

■■ JOURNAL ENTRIES ■■

1. Write a letter to one of your parents expressing your feeling concerning an issue or experience about which you have kept silent. *OR*
   Say something that you have always wanted to express to them (positive or negative).
2. Does the writer's argument convince you? Why? Why not?

■■■ IDEAS FOR WRITING ■■■

1. Create an argument from the point of view of the father concerning his behavior toward his son.
2. Write a monologue in the voice of the father.
3. Why does Kafka write in a legalistic tone and point of view? What do these techniques accomplish?

I Stand Here Ironing

Tillie Olsen

Born in Omaha, Nebraska, Tillie Olsen (1913–   ) is the daughter of blue-collar workers who fled Czarist Russia after the 1905 revolution. She grew up in poverty and at age fifteen quit high school to help support her family during the Depression. Celebrated as a crusader of the feminist movement and other causes, Olsen was presented the O. Henry Award in 1961 for Tell Me a Riddle, *from which the present piece is selected. Her first novel,* Yonnondio, *started in 1934, finally was published in 1974;* Silences, *a study exploring circumstances that interfere with women's creativity, appeared in 1978.*

In "I Stand Here Ironing," Olsen presents a mother's dilemma as a parent of a daughter, a mother who faces difficult circumstances. The selection clearly reflects Olsen's experiences as a private and as a political person.

1   I stand here ironing, and what you asked me moves tormented back and forth with the iron.

"I wish you would manage the time to come and talk with me about your daughter. I'm sure you can help me understand her. She's a youngster who needs help and whom I'm deeply interested in helping."

"Who needs help." . . . Even if I came, what good would it do? You think because I am her mother I have a key, or that in some way you could use me as a key? She has lived for nineteen years. There is all that life that has happened outside of me, beyond me.

And when is there time to remember, to sift, to weigh, to estimate, to total? I will start and there will be an interruption and I will have to gather it all together again. Or I will become engulfed with all I did or did not do, with what should have been and what cannot be helped.

5   She was a beautiful baby. The first and only one of our five that was beautiful at birth. You do not guess how new and uneasy her tenancy in her now-loveliness. You did not know her all those years she was thought homely, or see her poring over her baby pictures, making me tell her over and over how beautiful she had been—and would be, I would tell her—and was now, to the seeing eye. But the seeing eyes were few or nonexistent. Including mine.

I nursed her. They feel that's important nowadays. I nursed all the children, but with her, with all the fierce rigidity of first motherhood, I did like the books then said. Though her cries battered me to trembling and my breasts ached with swollenness, I waited till the clock decreed.

Why do I put that first? I do not even know if it matters, or if it explains anything.

She was a beautiful baby. She blew shining bubbles of sound. She loved motion, loved light, loved color and music and textures. She would lie on the floor in her blue overalls patting the surface so hard in ecstasy her hands and feet would blur. She was a miracle to me, but when she was eight months old I had to leave her daytimes with the woman downstairs to whom she was no miracle at all, for I worked or looked for work and for Emily's father, who "could no longer endure" (he wrote in his good-bye note) "sharing want with us."

I was nineteen. It was the pre-relief, pre-WPA[1] world of the depression. I would start running as soon as I got off the streetcar, running up the stairs, the place smelling sour, and awake or asleep to startle awake, when she saw me she would break into a clogged weeping that could not be comforted, a weeping I can hear yet.

10   After a while I found a job hashing at night so I could be with her days, and it was better. But it came to where I had to bring her to this family and leave her.

It took a long time to raise the money for her fare back. Then she got chicken pox and I had to wait longer. When she finally came, I hardly knew her, walking quick and nervous like her father, looking like her father, thin, and dressed in a shoddy red that yellowed her skin and glared at the pockmarks. All the baby loveliness gone.

She was two. Old enough for nursery school they said, and I did not know then what I know now—the fatigue of the long day, and the lacerations of group life in the kinds of nurseries that are only parking places for children.

Except that it would have made no difference if I had known. It was the only place there was. It was the only way we could be together, the only way I could hold a job.

And even without knowing, I knew. I knew the teacher that was evil because all these years it has curdled into my memory, the little boy hunched in the corner, her rasp, "why aren't you outside, because Alvin hits you? that's no reason, go out, scaredy." I knew Emily hated it even if she did not clutch and implore "don't go Mommy" like the other children, mornings.

15   She always had a reason why we should stay home. Momma, you look sick. Momma, I feel sick. Momma, the teachers aren't there today, they're sick. Momma, we can't go, there was a fire there last night. Momma, it's a holiday today, no school, they told me.

But never a direct protest, never rebellion. I think of our others in their three-, four-year-oldness—the explosions, the tempers, the denunciations, the demands—and I feel suddenly ill. I put the iron down. What in me demanded that goodness in her? And what was the cost, the cost to her of such goodness?

---

[1] Work Projects Administration: a federal agency which administered public works to relieve unemployment from 1935–1943.

The old man living in the back once said in his gentle way: "You should smile at Emily more when you look at her." What *was* in my face when I looked at her? I loved her. There were all the acts of love.

It was only with the others I remembered what he said, and it was the face of joy, and not of care or tightness or worry I turned to them—too late for Emily. She does not smile easily, let alone almost always as her brothers and sisters do. Her face is closed and sombre, but when she wants, how fluid. You must have seen it in her pantomimes, you spoke of her rare gift for comedy on the stage that rouses a laughter out of the audience so dear they applaud and applaud and do not want to let her go.

Where does it come from, that comedy? There was none of it in her when she came back to me that second time, after I had had to send her away again. She had a new daddy now to learn to love, and I think perhaps it was a better time.

20   Except when we left her alone nights, telling ourselves she was old enough.

"Can't you go some other time, Mommy, like tomorrow?" she would ask. "Will it be just a little while you'll be gone? Do you promise?"

The time we came back, the front door open, the clock on the floor in the hall. She rigid awake. "It wasn't just a little while. I didn't cry. Three times I called you, just three times, and then I ran downstairs to open the door so you could come faster. The clock talked loud. I threw it away, it scared me what it talked."

She said the clock talked loud again that night I went to the hospital to have Susan. She was delirious with the fever that comes before red measles, but she was fully conscious all the week I was gone and the week after we were home when she could not come near the new baby or me.

She did not get well. She stayed skeleton thin, not wanting to eat, and night after night she had nightmares. She would call for me, and I would rouse from exhaustion to sleepily call back: "You're all right, darling, go to sleep, it's just a dream," and if she still called, in a sterner voice, "now go to sleep, Emily, there's nothing to hurt you." Twice, only twice, when I had to get up for Susan anyhow, I went in to sit with her.

25   Now when it is too late (as if she would let me hold and comfort her like I do the others) I get up and go to her at once at her moan or restless stirring. "Are you awake, Emily? Can I get you something?" And the answer is always the same: "No, I'm all right, go back to sleep, Mother."

They persuaded me at the clinic to send her away to a convalescent home in the country where "she can have the kind of food and care you can't manage for her, and you'll be free to concentrate on the new baby." They still send children to that place. I see pictures on the society page of sleek young women planning affairs to raise money for it, or dancing at the affairs, or decorating Easter eggs or filling Christmas stockings for the children.

They never have a picture of the children so I do not know if the girls still wear those gigantic red bows and the ravaged looks on the every other Sunday when parents can come to visit "unless otherwise notified"—as we were notified the first six weeks.

Oh it is a handsome place, green lawns and tall trees and fluted flower beds. High up on the balconies of each cottage the children stand, the girls in their red bows and white dresses, the boys in white suits and giant red ties. The parents stand below shrieking up to be heard and the children shriek down to be heard, and between them the invisible wall "Not to Be Contaminated by Parental Germs or Physical Affection."

There was a tiny girl who always stood hand in hand with Emily. Her parents never came. One visit she was gone. "They moved her to Rose Cottage," Emily shouted in explanation. "They don't like you to love anybody here."

30 She wrote once a week, the labored writing of a seven-year-old. "I am fine. How is the baby. If I write my leter nicly I will have a star. Love" There never was a star. We wrote every other day, letters she could never hold or keep but only hear read—once. "We simply do not have room for children to keep any personal possessions," they patiently explained when we pieced one Sunday's shrieking together to plead how much it would mean to Emily, who loved so to keep things, to be allowed to keep her letters and cards.

Each visit she looked frailer. "She isn't eating," they told us.

(They had runny eggs for breakfast or mush with lumps, Emily said later, I'd hold it in my mouth and not swallow. Nothing ever tasted good, just when they had chicken.)

It took us eight months to get her released home, and only the fact that she gained back so little of her seven lost pounds convinced the social worker.

I used to try to hold and love her after she came back, but her body would stay stiff, and after a while she'd push away. She ate little. Food sickened her, and I think much of life too. Oh she had physical lightness and brightness, twinkling by on skates, bouncing like a ball up and down up and down over the jump rope, skimming over the hill; but these were momentary.

35 She fretted about her appearance, thin and dark and foreign-looking at a time when every little girl was supposed to look or thought she should look a chubby blonde replica of Shirley Temple. The doorbell sometimes rang for her, but no one seemed to come and play in the house or be a best friend. Maybe because we moved so much.

There was a boy she loved painfully through two school semesters. Months later she told me how she had taken pennies from my purse to buy him candy. "Licorice was his favorite and I brought him some every day, but he still liked Jennifer better'n me. Why, Mommy?" The kind of question for which there is no answer.

School was a worry to her. She was not glib or quick in a world where glibness and quickness were easily confused with ability to learn. To her overworked and exasperated teachers she was an overconscientious "slow learner" who kept trying to catch up and was absent entirely too often.

I let her be absent, though sometimes the illness was imaginary. How different from my now-strictness about attendance with the others. I wasn't working. We had a new baby, I was home anyhow. Sometimes, after Susan grew old enough, I would keep her home from school, too, to have them all together.

Mostly Emily had asthma, and her breathing, harsh and labored, would fill the house with a curiously tranquil sound. I would bring the two old dresser mirrors and her boxes of collections to her bed. She would select beads and single earrings, bottle tops and shells, dried flowers and pebbles, old postcards and scraps, all sorts of oddments; then she and Susan would play Kingdom, setting up landscapes and furniture, peopling them with action.

40   Those were the only times of peaceful companionship between her and Susan. I have edged away from it, that poisonous feeling between them, that terrible balancing of hurts and needs I had to do between the two, and did so badly, those earlier years.

41   Oh there are conflicts between the others too, each one human, needing, demanding, hurting, taking—but only between Emily and Susan, no, Emily toward Susan that corroding resentment. It seems so obvious on the surface, yet it is not obvious. Susan, the second child, Susan, golden- and curly-haired and chubby, quick and articulate and assured, everything in appearance and manner Emily was not; Susan, not able to resist Emily's precious things, losing or sometimes clumsily breaking them; Susan telling jokes and riddles to company for applause while Emily sat silent (to say to me later: that was *my* riddle, Mother, I told it to Susan); Susan, who for all the five years' difference in age was just a year behind Emily in developing physically.

42   I am glad for that slow physical development that widened the difference between her and her contemporaries, though she suffered over it. She was too vulnerable for that terrible world of youthful competition, of preening and parading, of constant measuring of yourself against every other, of envy, "If I had that copper hair," "If I had that skin. . . ." She tormented herself enough about not looking like the others, there was enough of the unsureness, the having to be conscious of words before you speak, the constant caring—what are they thinking of me? without having it all magnified by the merciless physical drives.

43   Ronnie is calling. He is wet and I change him. It is rare there is such a cry now. That time of motherhood is almost behind me when the ear is not one's own but must always be racked and listening for the child cry, the child call. We sit for a while and I hold him, looking out over the city spread in charcoal with its soft aisles of light. "*Shoogily,*" he breathes and curls closer. I carry him back to bed, asleep. *Shoogily.* A funny word, a family word, inherited from Emily, invented by her to say: *comfort.*

44   In this and other ways she leaves her seal, I say aloud. And startle at my saying it. What do I mean? What did I start to gather together, to try and make coherent? I was at the terrible, growing years. War years. I do not remember them well. I was working, there were four smaller ones now, there was not time for her. She had to help be a mother, and housekeeper, and shopper. She had to set her seal. Mornings of crisis and near hysteria trying to get lunches packed, hair combed, coats and shoes found, everyone to school or Child Care on time, the baby ready for transportation. And always the paper scribbled on by a smaller one, the book looked at by Susan then mislaid, the homework not done. Running out to that huge school where she was one,

she was lost, she was a drop; suffering over the unpreparedness, stammering and unsure in her classes.

45   There was so little time left at night after the kids were bedded down. She would struggle over books, always eating (it was in those years she developed her enormous appetite that is legendary in our family) and I would be ironing, or preparing food for the next day, or writing V-mail to Bill, or tending the baby. Sometimes, to make me laugh, or out of her despair, she would imitate happenings or types at school.

I think I said once: "Why don't you do something like this in the school amateur show?" One morning she phoned me at work, hardly understandable through the weeping: "Mother, I did it. I won, I won; they gave me first prize; they clapped and clapped and wouldn't let me go."

Now suddenly she was Somebody, and as imprisoned in her difference as she had been in anonymity.

She began to be asked to perform at other high schools, even in colleges, then at city and statewide affairs. The first one we went to, I only recognized her that first moment when thin, shy, she almost drowned herself into the curtains. Then: Was this Emily? The control, the command, the convulsing and deadly clowning, the spell, then the roaring, stamping audience, unwilling to let this rare and precious laughter out of their lives.

Afterwards: You ought to do something about her with a gift like that— but without money or knowing how, what does one do? We have left it all to her, and the gift has as often eddied inside, clogged and clotted, as been used and growing.

50   She is coming. She runs up the stairs two at a time with her light graceful step, and I know she is happy tonight. Whatever it was that occasioned your call did not happen today.

"Aren't you ever going to finish the ironing, Mother? Whistler[2] painted his mother in a rocker. I'd have to paint mine standing over an ironing board." This is one of her communicative nights and she tells me everything and nothing as she fixes herself a plate of food out of the icebox.

She is so lovely. Why did you want me to come in at all? Why were you concerned? She will find her way.

She starts up the stairs to bed. "Don't get me up with the rest in the morning." "But I thought you were having midterms." "Oh, those," she comes back in, kisses me, and says quite lightly, "in a couple of years when we'll all be atom-dead they won't matter a bit."

She has said it before. She *believes* it. But because I have been dredging the past, and all that compounds a human being is so heavy and meaningful in me, I cannot endure it tonight.

55   I will never total it all. I will never come in to say: She was a child seldom smiled at. Her father left me before she was a year old. I had to work her first six years when there was work, or I sent her home and to his relatives. There

---

[2] James (Abbott) Mc-Neill Whistler (1834–1908), United States painter and etcher.

were years she had care she hated. She was dark and thin and foreign-looking in a world where the prestige went to blondeness and curly hair and dimples, she was slow where glibness was prized. She was a child of anxious, not proud, love. We were poor and could not afford for her the soil of easy growth. I was a young mother, I was a distracted mother. There were other children pushing up, demanding. Her younger sister seemed all that she was not. There were years she did not want me to touch her. She kept too much in herself, her life was such she had to keep too much in herself. My wisdom came too late. She has much to her and probably little will come of it. She is a child of her age, of depression, of war, of fear.

Let her be. So all that is in her will not bloom—but in how many does it? There is still enough left to live by. Only help her to know—help make it so there is cause for her to know—that she is more than this dress on the ironing board, helpless before the iron.

■ EXPLORATIONS OF THE TEXT ■

1. How does the mother view her daughter Emily as a baby?
2. How do economic and social circumstances affect the mother's ability to take care of Emily?
3. Characterize Emily as a baby and at different stages in her life. According to the narrator, what needs, yearnings, and conflicts shape the daughter's view of herself?
4. Analyze the images describing Emily's body. How do societal conceptions of beauty figure in Emily's development?
5. What are reasons for the conflict between Emily and Susan?
6. How does the mother feel about herself as a parent? Is she a "good mother"? Is she to blame for what has happened to Emily?
7. Explore the significance of the title and the symbol of ironing. Does Tillie Olsen present a critique of woman's position in society?
8. How does the opening, the interchange between the unnamed social worker and the mother, develop the story?
9. What vision of parenting is presented in the story? How much control do parents possess? How much depends on fate or circumstance?

■■ JOURNAL ENTRIES ■■

1. What effect does the first-person point of view have on the story? Rewrite several passages in third person. How does the perspective change?
2. Write a monologue in the voice of Emily, and present her version of her upbringing.

■■■ **IDEAS FOR WRITING** ■■■

1. Compare this story with "The Rocking-Horse Winner" and with "Scar."
2. Some psychologists suggest that "wounds" in childhood may later become sources of creativity. Is there support for this theory in the story?

If the River Was Whiskey

T. Coraghessan Boyle

T. (for Tom) Coraghessan Boyle (1948–   ) was born in Peekskill, New York, to Irish immigrant parents. He received his M.F.A. and Ph.D at the Iowa University's Writers' Workshop. He currently teaches writing at the University of California in Los Angeles.

Boyle's writing career began when Esquire *published "Heart of a Champion," the story of television's Lassie and her amorous coyote friend. His first novel,* Water Music, *a raucous, account of two British men's adventures in Africa, assured Boyle's reputation as an American fiction humorist. His most recent novel,* The Road to Wellville, *is a satire about food fadism set in 1907 in Battle Creek, Michigan.*

The present selection, "If the River Was Whiskey," is taken from a collection of the same title published in 1989. In this story, uncharacteristically lyrical and sad, Boyle creates a vision of an estranged father and son.

1   The water was a heartbeat, a pulse, it stole the heat from his body and pumped it to his brain. Beneath the surface, magnified through the shimmering lens of his face mask, were silver shoals of fish, forests of weed, a silence broken only by the distant throbbing hum of an outboard. Above, there was the sun, the white flash of a faraway sailboat, the weatherbeaten dock with its weatherbeaten rowboat, his mother in her deck chair, and the vast depthless green of the world beyond.

He surfaced like a dolphin, spewing water from the vent of his snorkel, and sliced back to the dock. The lake came with him, two bony arms and the wedge of a foot, the great heaving splash of himself flat out on the dock like something thrown up in a storm. And then, without pausing even to snatch up a towel, he had the spinning rod in hand and the silver lure was sizzling out over the water, breaking the surface just above the shadowy arena he'd fixed in his mind. He mother looked up at the splash. "Tiller," she called, "come get a towel."

His shoulders quaked. He huddled and stamped his feet, but he never took his eyes off the tip of the rod. Twitching it suggestively, he reeled with the jerky, hesitant motion that would drive lunker fish to a frenzy. Or so he'd read, anyway.

"Tilden, do you hear me?"

5 "I saw a Northern," he said. "A big one. Two feet maybe." The lure was in. A flick of his wrist sent it back. Still reeling, he ducked his head to wipe his nose on his wet shoulder. He could feel the sun on his back now and he envisioned the skirted lure in the water, sinuous, sensual, irresistible, and he waited for the line to quicken with the strike.

* * *

The porch smelled of pine—old pine, dried up and dead—and it depressed him. In fact, everything depressed him—especially this vacation. Vacation. It was a joke. Vacation from what?

He poured himself a drink—vodka and soda, tall, from the plastic half-gallon jug. It wasn't noon yet, the breakfast dishes were in the sink, and Tiller and Caroline were down at the lake. He couldn't see them through the screen of trees, but he heard the murmur of their voices against the soughing of the branches and the sadness of the birds. He sat heavily in the creaking wicker chair and looked out on nothing. He didn't feel too hot. In fact, he felt as if he'd been cored and dried, as if somebody had taken a pipe cleaner and run it through his veins. His head ached too, but the vodka would take care of that. When he finished it, he'd have another, and then maybe a grilled swiss on rye. Then he'd start to feel good again.

* * *

His father was talking to the man and his mother was talking to the woman. They'd met at the bar about twenty drinks ago and his father was into his could-have-been, should-have-been, way-back-when mode, and the man, bald on top and with a ratty beard and long greasy hair like his father's, was trying to steer the conversation back to building supplies. The woman had whole galaxies of freckles on her chest, and she leaned forward in her sundress and told his mother scandalous stories about people she'd never heard of. Tiller had drunk all the Coke and eaten all the beer nuts he could hold. He watched the Pabst Blue Ribbon sign flash on and off above the bar and he watched the woman's freckles move in and out of the gap between her breasts. Outside it was dark and a cool clean scent came in off the lake.

"Un huh, yeah," his father was saying, "the To the Bone Band. I played rhythm and switched off vocals with Dillie Richards. . . ."

10 The man had never heard of Dillie Richards.

"Black dude, used to play with Taj Mahal?"[1]

The man had never heard of Taj Mahal.

"Anyway," his father said, "we used to do all this really outrageous stuff by people like Muddy, Howlin' Wolf, Luther Allison—"

"She didn't," his mother said.

---

[1] A 1970s rock group.

15   The woman threw down her drink and nodded and the front of her dress went crazy. Tiller watched her and felt the skin go tight across his shoulders and the back of his neck, where he'd been burned the first day. He wasn't wearing any underwear, just shorts. He looked away. "Three abortions, two kids," the woman said. "And she never knew who the father of the second one was."

"Drywall isn't worth a damn," the man said. "But what're you going to do?"

"Paneling?" his father offered.

The man cut the air with the flat of his hand. He looked angry. "Don't talk to me about paneling," he said.

*   *   *

Mornings, when his parents were asleep and the lake was still, he would take the rowboat to the reedy cove on the far side of the lake where the big pike lurked. He didn't actually know if they lurked there, but if they lurked anywhere, this would be the place. It looked fishy, mysterious, sunken logs looming up dark from the shadows beneath the boat, mist rising like steam, as if the bottom were boiling with ravenous, cold-eyed, killer pike that could slice through monofilament with a snap of their jaws and bolt ducklings in a gulp. Besides, Joe Matochik, the old man who lived in the cabin next door and could charm frogs by stroking their bellies, had told him that this was where he'd find them.

20   It was cold at dawn and he'd wear a thick homeknit sweater over his T-shirt and shorts, sometimes pulling the stretched-out hem of it down like a skirt to warm his thighs. He'd take an apple with him or a slice of brown bread and peanut butter. And of course the orange lifejacket his mother insisted on.

When he left the dock he was always wearing the lifejacket—for form's sake and for the extra warmth it gave him against the raw morning air. But when he got there, when he stood in the swaying basin of the boat to cast his Hula Popper[2] or Abu Relfex,[3] it got in the way and he took it off. Later, when the sun ran through him and he didn't need the sweater, he balled it up on the seat beside him, and sometimes, if it was good and hot, he shrugged out of his T-shirt and shorts too. No one could see him in the cove, and it made his breath come quick to be naked like that under the morning sun.

*   *   *

"I heard you," he shouted, and he could feel the veins stand out in his neck, the rage come up in him like something killed and dead and brought back to life. "What kind of thing is that to tell a kid, huh? About his own father?"

She wasn't answering. She'd backed up in a corner of the kitchen and she wasn't answering. And what could she say, the bitch? He'd heard her. Dozing on the trundle bed under the stairs, wanting a drink but too weak to get up

---

[2] Kind of fishing lure.
[3] Kind of reel.

and make one, he'd heard voices from the kitchen, her voice and Tiller's. "Get used to it," she said, "he's a drunk, your father's a drunk," and then he was up off the bed as if something had exploded inside of him and he had her by the shoulders—always the shoulders and never the face, that much she'd taught him—and Tiller was gone, out the door and gone. Now, her voice low in her throat, a sick and guilty little smile on her lips, she whispered, "It's true."

"Who are you to talk?—you're shit-faced yourself." She shrank away from him, that sick smile on her lips, her shoulders hunched. He wanted to smash things, kick in the damn stove, make her hurt.

25 "At least I have a job," she said.

"I'll get another one, don't you worry."

"And what about Tiller? We've been here two weeks and you haven't done one damn thing with him, nothing, zero. You haven't even been down to the lake. Two hundred feet and you haven't even been down there once." She came up out of the corner now, feinting like a boxer, vicious, her sharp little fists balled up to drum on him. She spoke in a snarl. "What kind of father are you?"

He brushed past her, slammed open the cabinet, and grabbed the first bottle he found. It was whiskey, cheap whiskey, Four Roses, the shit she drank. He poured out half a water glass full and drank it down to spite her. "I hate the beach, boats, water, trees. I hate you."

She had her purse and she was halfway out the screen door. She hung there a second, looking as if she'd bitten into something rotten. "The feeling's mutual," she said, and the door banged shut behind her.

*   *   *

30 There were too many complications, too many things to get between him and the moment, and he tried not to think about them. He tried not to think about his father—or his mother either—in the same way that he tried not to think about the pictures of the bald-headed stick people in Africa or meat in its plastic wrapper and how it got there. But when he did think about his father he thought about the river-was-whiskey day.

It was a Tuesday or Wednesday, middle of the week, and when he came home from school the curtains were drawn and his father's car was in the driveway. At the door, he could hear him, the chunk-chunk of the chords and the rasping nasal whine that seemed as if it belonged to someone else. His father was sitting in the dark, hair in his face, bent low over the guitar. There was an open bottle of liquor on the coffee table and a clutter of beer bottles. The room stank of smoke.

It was strange, because his father hardly ever played his guitar anymore—he mainly just talked about it. In the past tense. And it was strange too—and bad—because his father wasn't at work. Tiller dropped his bookbag on the telephone stand. "Hi, Dad," he said.

His father didn't answer. Just bent over the guitar and played the same song, over and over, as if it were the only song he knew. Tiller sat on the sofa and listened. There was a verse—one verse—and his father repeated it three or four times before he broke off and slurred the words into a sort of chant or hum, and then he went back to the words again. After the fourth repetition, Tiller heard it:

> *If the river was whiskey,*
> *And I was a divin' duck,*
> *I'd swim to the bottom,*
> *Drink myself back up.*

For half an hour his father played that song, played it till anything else would have sounded strange. He reached for the bottle when he finally stopped, and that was when he noticed Tiller. He looked surprised. Looked as if he'd just woke up. "Hey, ladykiller Tiller," he said, and took a drink from the mouth of the bottle.

35   Tiller blushed. There'd been a Sadie Hawkins dance[4] at school and Janet Rumery had picked him for her partner. Ever since, his father had called him ladykiller, and though he wasn't exactly sure what it meant, it made him blush anyway, just from the tone of it. Secretly, it pleased him. "I really liked the song, Dad," he said.

"Yeah?" His father lifted his eyebrows and made a face. "Well, come home to Mama, doggie-o. Here," he said, and he held out an open beer. "You ever have one of these, ladykiller Tiller?" He was grinning. The sleeve of his shirt was torn and his elbow was raw and there was a hard little clot of blood over his shirt pocket. "With your sixth-grade buddies out behind the handball court, maybe? No?"

Tiller shook his head.

"You want one? Go ahead, take a hit."

Tiller took the bottle and sipped tentatively. The taste wasn't much. He looked up at his father. "What does it mean?" he said. "The song, I mean—the one you were singing. About the whiskey and all."

40   His father gave him a long slow grin and took a drink from the big bottle of clear liquor. "I don't know," he said finally, grinning wider to show his tobacco-stained teeth. "I guess he just liked whiskey, that's all." He picked up a cigarette, made as if to light it, and then put it down again. "Hey," he said, "you want to sing it with me?"

* * *

All right, she'd hounded him and she'd threatened him and she was going to leave him, he could see that clear as day. But he was going to show her. And the kid too. He wasn't drinking. Not today. Not a drop.

He stood on the dock with his hands in his pockets while Tiller scrambled around with the fishing poles and oars and the rest of it. Birds were

---

[4] Traditional dance from the comic strip, "L'il Abner" in which women or girls choose their partners.

screeching in the trees and there was a smell of diesel fuel on the air. The sun cut into his head like a knife. He was sick already.

"I'm giving you a big pole, Dad, and you can row if you want."

He eased himself into the boat and it fell away beneath him like the mouth of a bottomless pit.

45 "I made us egg salad, Dad, your favorite, and I brought some birch beer."

He was rowing. The lake was churning underneath him, the wind was up and reeking of things washed up on the shore, and the damn oars kept slipping out of the oarlocks, and he was rowing. At the last minute he'd wanted to go back for a quick drink, but he didn't and now he was rowing.

"We're going to catch a pike," Tiller said, hunched like a spider in the stern.

There was spray off the water. He was rowing. He felt sick. Sick and depressed.

"We're going to catch a pike, I can feel it. I know we are," Tiller said, "I know it. I just know it."

* * *

50 It was too much for him all at once—the sun, the breeze that was so sweet he could taste it, the novelty of his father rowing, pale arms and a dead cigarette clenched between his teeth, the boat rocking, and the birds whispering—and he closed his eyes a minute, just to keep from going dizzy with the joy of it. They were in deep water already. Tiller was trolling[5] with a plastic worm and spinner,[6] just in case, but he didn't have much faith in catching anything out here. He was taking his father to the cove with the submerged logs and beds of weed—that's where they'd connect, that's where they'd catch pike.

"Jesus," his father said when Tiller spelled him at the oars. Hands shaking, he crouched in the stern and tried to light a cigarette. His face was gray and his hair beat crazily around his face. He went through half a book of matches and then threw the cigarette in the water. "Where are you taking us, anyway," he said, "—the Indian Ocean?"

"The pike place," Tiller told him. "You'll like it, you'll see."

The sun was dropping behind the hills when they got there, and the water went from blue to gray. There was no wind in the cove. Tiller let the boat glide out across the still surface while his father finally got a cigarette lit, and then he dropped anchor. He was excited. Swallows dove at the surface, bullfrogs burped from the reeds. It was the perfect time to fish, the hour when the big lunker pike would cruise among the sunken logs, hunting.

"All right," his father said, "I'm going to catch the biggest damn fish in the lake," and he jerked back his arm and let fly with the heaviest sinker in the tackle box dangling from the end of the rod. The line hissed through the guys and there was a thunderous splash that probably terrified every pike within half a mile. Tiller looked over his shoulder as he reeled in his silver spoon. His father winked at him, but he looked grim.

---

[5] Moving the line or bait in fishing.
[6] Kind of lure.

55   It was getting dark, his father was out of cigarettes, and Tiller had cast the spoon so many times his arm was sore, when suddenly the big rod began to buck. "Dad! Dad!" Tiller shouted, and his father lurched up as if he'd been stabbed. He'd been dozing, the rod propped against the gunwale,[7] and Tiller had been studying the long suffering-lines in his father's face, the grooves in his forehead, and the puffy discolored flesh beneath his eyes. With his beard and long hair and with the crumpled suffering look on his face, he was the picture of the crucified Christ Tiller had contemplated a hundred times at church. But now the rod was bucking and his father had hold of it and he was playing a fish, a big fish, the tip of the rod dipping all the way down to the surface.

"It's a pike, Dad, it's a pike!"

His father strained at the pole. His only response was a grunt, but Tiller saw something in his eyes he hardly recognized anymore, a connection, a charge, as if the fish were sending a current up the line, through the pole, and into his hands and body and brain. For a full three minutes he played the fish, his slack biceps gone rigid, the cigarette clamped in his mouth, while Tiller hovered over him with the landing net. There was a surge, a splash, and the thing was in the net, and Tiller had it over the side and into the boat. "It's a pike," his father said, "goddamnit, look at the thing, look at the size of it."

It wasn't a pike. Tiller had watched Joe Matochik catch one off the dock one night. Joe's pike had been dangerous, full of teeth; a long, lean, tapering strip of muscle and pounding life. This was no pike. It was a carp. A fat, pouty, stinking, ugly mud carp. Trash fish. They shot them with arrows and threw them up on the shore to rot. Tiller looked at his father and felt like crying.

"It's a pike," his father said, and already the thing in his eyes was gone, already it was over, "it's a pike. Isn't it?"

* * *

60   It was late—past two, anyway—and he was drunk. Or no, he was beyond drunk. He'd been drinking since morning, one tall vodka and soda after another, and he didn't feel a thing. He sat on the porch in the dark and he couldn't see the lake, couldn't hear it, couldn't even smell it. Caroline and Tiller were asleep. The house was dead silent.

Caroline was leaving him, which meant that Tiller was leaving him. He knew it. He could see it in her eyes and he heard it in her voice. She was soft once, his soft-eyed lover, and now she was hard, unyielding, now she was his worst enemy. They'd had the couple from the roadhouse in for drinks and burgers earlier that night and he'd leaned over the table to tell the guy something—Ed, his name was—joking really, nothing serious, just making conversation. "Vodka and soda," he said "that's my drink. I used to drink vodka and grapefruit juice, but it tore the lining out of my stomach." And then Caroline, who wasn't even listening, stepped in and said, "Yeah, and that"—

---

[7] The upper edge of the side of a boat.

pointing to the glass—"tore the lining out of your brain." He looked up at her. She wasn't smiling.

All right. That was how it was. What did he care? He hadn't wanted to come up here anyway—it was her father's idea. Take the cabin for a month, the old man had said, pushing, pushing in that way he had, and get yourself turned around. Well, he wasn't turning around, and they could all go to hell.

After a while the chill got to him and he pushed himself up from the chair and went to bed. Caroline said something in her sleep and pulled away from him as he lifted the covers and slid in. He was awake for a minute or two, feeling depressed, so depressed he wished somebody would come in and shoot him, and then he was asleep.

In his dream, he was out in the boat with Tiller. The wind was blowing, his hands were shaking, he couldn't light a cigarette. Tiller was watching him. He pulled at the oars and nothing happened. Then all of a sudden they were going down, the boat sucked out from under them, the water icy and black, beating in on them as if it were alive. Tiller called out to him. He saw his son's face, saw him going down, and there was nothing he could do.

■ **EXPLORATIONS OF THE TEXT** ■

1. What does the water mean to the boy, Tiller? Why does the boy love fishing? Does his relationship with the river change?
2. The story is told from two points of view. Whose? What does this shift in perspective accomplish as the story progresses?
3. Why is the father "cored and dried"? What does the metaphor suggest about his character? What do the father's singing and love of music suggest about him?
4. What is the significance of the song, "If the River Was Whiskey"? Why does Tiller remember "the river-was-whiskey day"?
5. Describe Tiller. What kind of child is he?
6. What is the mother's role in the story? What is the conflict between Tiller and Caroline?
7. What is the significance of his father's mistaken notion that the carp he catches is a pike? What does this episode suggest about the father and about his relationship with his son?
8. What does the father's dream foreshadow about the father's character? about the intertwined fates of father and son?
9. Explain the significance of the title and the images of the river. Compare the river imagery with "The Third Bank of the River."
10. The story starts in the middle of the breakdown of the parents' marriage and then moves backward and forward in time. What is the impact of this narrative structure?

■■ JOURNAL ENTRIES ■■

1. Discuss the shifting images of the river.
2. Write a memory piece about a song or story which reminds you of a parent, a member of your family, or a friend.
3. How do you react to the final paragraph or to the central episode about the carp?

■■■ IDEAS FOR WRITING ■■■

1. Compare the fathers in "The Third Bank of the River," "Sonny's Blues," and this story. What are the sources of their anger? disappointment?
2. What do this story, "Those Winter Sundays," and "My Papa's Waltz" reveal about children caught in the conflict between parents *or* about the relationships between fathers and sons?
3. Compare the mother in "I Stand Here Ironing" with the father in this story.

The Third Bank of the River

João Guimarães Rosa
Translated by William L. Grossman

Born in Minas Gerais, Brazil, João Guimarães Rosa (1908–1967) was a doctor who practiced medicine in the military and in the mountain regions of Brazil. The subject matter of his novels and short stories is complex, mysterious, and enigmatic. His volume of short fiction, Sagarana, *was translated into English in 1966; and his novel,* The Devil To Pay in the Backlands, *was published in Brazil in 1956.*

The speaker in "The Third Bank of the River" spends his life in an attempt to reach his father who has inexplicably chosen to live in a boat on a river and never to return home. This provocative piece raises more questions than it answers.

1 My father was a dutiful, orderly, straightforward man. And according to several reliable people of whom I inquired, he had had these qualities since adolescence or even childhood. By my own recollection, he was neither jollier nor more melancholy than the other men we knew. Maybe a little quieter. It was Mother, not Father, who ruled the house. She scolded us daily— my sister, my brother, and me. But it happened one day that Father ordered a boat.

He was very serious about it. It was to be made specially for him, of mimosa wood. It was to be sturdy enough to last twenty or thirty years and just large enough for one person. Mother carried on plenty about it. Was her husband going to become a fisherman all of a sudden? Or a hunter? Father said nothing. Our house was less than a mile from the river, which around there was deep, quiet, and so wide you couldn't see across it.

I can never forget the day the rowboat was delivered. Father showed no joy or other emotion. He just put on his hat as he always did and said good-by to us. He took along no food or bundle of any sort. We expected Mother to rant and rave, but she didn't. She looked very pale and bit her lip, but all she said was: "If you go away, stay away. Don't ever come back!"

Father made no reply. He looked gently at me and motioned me to walk along with him. I feared Mother's wrath, yet I eagerly obeyed. We headed toward the river together. I felt bold and exhilarated, so much so that I said: "Father, will you take me with you in your boat?"

5　　He just looked at me, gave me his blessing, and by a gesture, told me to go back. I made as if to do so but, when his back was turned, I ducked behind some bushes to watch him. Father got into the boat and rowed away. Its shadow slid across the water like a crocodile, long and quiet.

Father did not come back. Nor did he go anywhere, really. He just rowed and floated across and around, out there in the river. Everyone was appalled. What had never happened, what could not possibly happen, was happening. Our relatives, neighbors, and friends came over to discuss the phenomenon.

Mother was ashamed. She said little and conducted herself with great composure. As a consequence, almost everyone thought (though no one said it) that Father had gone insane. A few, however, suggested that Father might be fulfilling a promise he had made to God or to a saint, or that he might have some horrible disease, maybe leprosy, and that he left for the sake of the family, at the same time wishing to remain fairly near them.

Travelers along the river and people living near the bank on one side or the other reported that Father never put foot on land, by day or night. He just moved about on the river, solitary, aimless, like a derelict. Mother and our relatives agreed that the food which he had doubtless hidden in the boat would soon give out and that then he would either leave the river and travel off somewhere (which would be at least a little more respectable) or he would repent and come home.

How far from the truth they were! Father had a secret source of provisions: me. Every day I stole food and brought it to him. The first night after he left, we all lit fires on the shore and prayed and called to him. I was deeply distressed and felt a need to do something more. The following day I went down to the river with a loaf of corn bread, a bunch of bananas, and some bricks of raw brown sugar. I waited impatiently a long, long hour. Then I saw the boat, far off, alone, gliding almost imperceptibly on the smoothness of the river. Father was sitting in the bottom of the boat. He saw me but he did not row toward me or make any gesture. I showed him the food and then I placed it in a hollow rock on the river bank; it was safe there from animals, rain, and dew. I did this day after day, on and on and on. Later I learned to my surprise, that Mother knew what I was doing and left food around where I could easily steal it. She had a lot of feelings she didn't show.

10   Mother sent for her brother to come and help on the farm and in business matters. She had the schoolteacher come and tutor us children at home because of the time we had lost. One day, at her request, the priest put on his vestments, went down to the shore, and tried to exorcise the devils that had got into my father. He shouted that Father had a duty to cease his unholy obstinacy. Another day she arranged to have two soldiers come and try to frighten him. All to no avail. My father went by in the distance, sometimes so far away he could barely be seen. He never replied to anyone and no one ever got close to him. When some newspapermen came in a launch to take his picture, Father headed his boat to the other side of the river and into the marshes, which he knew like the palm of his hand but in which other people quickly got lost. There in his private maze, which extended for miles, with heavy foliage overhead and rushes on all sides, he was safe.

We had to get accustomed to the idea of Father's being out on the river. We had to but we couldn't, we never could. I think I was the only one who understood to some degree what our father wanted and what he did not want. The thing I could not understand at all was how he stood the hardship. Day and night, in sun and rain, in heat and in the terrible midyear cold spells, with his old hat on his head and very little other clothing, week after week, month after month, year after year, unheedful of the waste and emptiness in which his life was slipping by. He never set foot on earth or grass, on isle or mainland shore. No doubt he sometimes tied up the boat at a secret place, perhaps at the tip of some island, to get a little sleep. He never lit a fire or even struck a match and he had no flashlight. He took only a small part of the food that I left in the hollow rock—not enough, it seemed to me, for survival. What could his state of health have been? How about the continual drain on his energy, pulling and pushing the oars to control the boat? And how did he survive the annual floods, when the river rose and swept along with it all sorts of dangerous objects—branches of trees, dead bodies of animals—that might suddenly crash against his little boat?

He never talked to a living soul. And we never talked about him. We just thought. No, we could never put our father out of mind. If for a short time we seemed to, it was just a lull from which we would be sharply awakened by the realization of his frightening situation.

My sister got married, but Mother didn't want a wedding party. It would have been a sad affair, for we thought of him every time we ate some especially tasty food. Just as we thought of him in our cozy beds on a cold, stormy night—out there, alone and unprotected, trying to bail out the boat with only his hands and a gourd. Now and then someone would say that I was getting to look more and more like my father. But I knew that by then his hair and beard must have been shaggy and his nails long. I pictured him thin and sickly, black with hair and sunburn, and almost naked despite the articles of clothing I occasionally left for him.

He didn't seem to care about us at all. But I felt affection and respect for him, and, whenever they praised me because I had done something good, I said: "My father taught me to act that way."

15   It wasn't exactly accurate but it was a truthful sort of lie. As I said, Father didn't seem to care about us. But then why did he stay around there? Why didn't he go up the river or down the river, beyond the possibility of seeing us or being seen by us? He alone knew the answer.

My sister had a baby boy. She insisted on showing Father his grandson. One beautiful day we all went down to the riverbank, my sister in her white wedding dress, and she lifted the baby high. Her husband held a parasol above them. We shouted to Father and waited. He did not appear. My sister cried; we all cried in each other's arms.

My sister and her husband moved far away. My brother went to live in a city. Times changed, with their usual imperceptible rapidity. Mother finally moved too; she was old and went to live with her daughter. I remained behind, a leftover. I could never think of marrying. I just stayed there with the impediments of my life. Father, wandering alone and forlorn on the river, needed me. I knew he needed me, although he never even told me why he was doing it. When I put the question to people bluntly and insistently, all they told me was that they heard that Father had explained it to the man who made the boat. But now this man was dead and nobody knew or remembered anything. There was just some foolish talk, when the rains were especially severe and persistent, that my father was wise like Noah and had the boat built in anticipation of a new flood; I dimly remember people saying this. In any case, I would not condemn my father for what he was doing. My hair was beginning to turn gray.

I have only sad things to say. What bad had I done, what was my great guilt? My father always away and his absence always with me. And the river, always the river, perpetually renewing itself. The river, always. I was beginning to suffer from old age, in which life is just a sort of lingering. I had attacks of illness and of anxiety. I had a nagging rheumatism. And he? Why, why was he doing it? He must have been suffering terribly. He was so old. One day, in his failing strength, he might let the boat capsize; or he might let the current carry it downstream, on and on, until it plunged over the waterfall to the boiling turmoil below. It pressed upon my heart. He was out there and I was forever robbed of my peace. I am guilty of I know not what, and my pain is an open wound inside me. Perhaps I would know—if things were different. I began to guess what was wrong.

Out with it! Had I gone crazy? No, in our house that word was never spoken, never through all the years. No one called anybody crazy, for nobody is crazy. Or maybe everybody. All I did was go there and wave a handkerchief so he would be more likely to see me. I was in complete command of myself. I waited. Finally he appeared in the distance, there, then over there, a vague shape sitting in the back of the boat. I called to him several times. And I said what I was so eager to say, to state formally and under oath. I said it as loud as I could:

20   "Father, you have been out there long enough. You are old. . . . Come
back, you don't have to do it anymore. . . . Come back and I'll go instead.
Right now, if you want. Any time. I'll get into the boat. I'll take your place."

And when I had said this my heart beat more firmly.

He heard me. He stood up. He maneuvered with his oars and headed the
boat toward me. He had accepted my offer. And suddenly I trembled, down
deep. For he had raised his arm and waved—the first time in so many, so
many years. And I couldn't . . . In terror, my hair on end, I ran, I fled madly.
For he seemed to come from another world. And I'm begging forgiveness,
begging, begging.

I experienced the dreadful sense of cold that comes from deadly fear, and I
became ill. Nobody ever saw or heard about him again. Am I a man, after such
a failure? I am what never should have been. I am what must be silent. I know
it is too late. I must stay in the deserts and unmarked plains of my life, and I
fear I shall shorten it. But when death comes I want them to take me and put
me in a little boat in this perpetual water between the long shores; and I, down
the river, lost in the river, inside the river . . . the river . . .

■   **EXPLORATIONS OF THE TEXT**   ■

---

1.   What can you predict about the story from the opening paragraph and
     from its description of the narrator's father?
2.   What does the father's life on the river signify? What is the symbolism
     of the father's voyage on the river and of the river itself?
3.   Why does the narrator stay and not abandon his father? Why do other
     family members move away or decide to leave?
4.   Explain the narrator's decision not to take his father's place in the
     boat.
5.   How have the father's life and failures shaped his son's decisions? Will
     the narrator's inner conflict ever be resolved?
6.   What is the impact of narrating this story as a remembrance?
7.   What is the significance of the title? Can there be a third bank of a
     river?

■■   **JOURNAL ENTRIES**   ■■

---

1.   Have you ever felt "absent" or felt someone else's "absence"? OR
     Discuss an experience in which you longed for something.
2.   List and discuss aspects of the story that you find most puzzling.
3.   List questions about the story. Then answer them.

■■■ IDEAS FOR WRITING ■■■

1. Like "The Rocking-Horse Winner," this story is an example of magical realism. In both cases, the action is fantastic, yet realistic portraits of characters emerge. Compare the magical and realistic elements of both stories.
2. How does Rosa present the themes of absence and longing in this story?
3. Is what ways is this story an allegory of life and death?
4. Take one of your questions and answers, and write an essay about the subject.

Sonny's Blues

James Baldwin

James Baldwin (1924–1987) was born and raised in Harlem. He grew up in a large family, and his stepfather was an evangelical preacher. Baldwin was an excellent student who enjoyed reading, writing, theater-going, and the movies. In 1942, after graduation from high school, Baldwin took a defense industry job in Belle Meade, New Jersey, to help support his family and ailing stepfather. The combination of on-the-job discrimination and the death of his stepfather precipitated Baldwin's move to Greenwich Village where he vowed to make writing his life's work.

Although several well-known publications accepted his essays and short stories and although Richard Wright helped him to win a fellowship, it was not until he moved to Europe in 1948 that Baldwin's creative powers emerged. His first novel, Go Tell It on the Mountain *(1953), is about a Harlem teenager's conflicts with a repressive father; and his first play,* The Amen Corner *(1955), which deals with the pentecostal faith, represents Baldwin's search for his racial heritage. These were followed by* Notes of a Native Son *(1955), the 1956 novel* Giovanni's Room, Nobody Knows My Name: More Notes of a Native Son *(1961), and* The Fire Next Time *(1963).*

At the time of his death from cancer in 1987, Baldwin was at work on a biography of Martin Luther King. Even though he spent most of his life in France, he retained his United States citizenship and preferred to call himself a commuter rather than an expatriate.

A study of two brothers, "Sonny's Blues" evokes the danger and the glory of being African-American and male. The characters change and grow in their efforts to know each other as brothers and as adults.

1   I read about it in the paper, in the subway, on my way to work. I read it, and
       I couldn't believe it, and I read it again. Then perhaps I just stared at it, at
the newsprint spelling out his name, spelling out the story. I stared at it
in the swinging lights of the subway car, and in the faces and bodies of the
people, and in my own face, trapped in the darkness which roared outside.

       It was not to be believed and I kept telling myself that, as I walked from
the subway station to the high school. And at the same time I couldn't doubt
it. I was scared, scared for Sonny. He became real to me again. A great block
of ice got settled in my belly and kept melting there slowly all day long, while
I taught my classes algebra. It was a special kind of ice. It kept melting, sending trickles of ice water all up and down my veins, but it never got less. Sometimes it hardened and seemed to expand until I felt my guts were going to
come spilling out or that I was going to choke or scream. This would always
be at a moment when I was remembering some specific thing Sonny had
once said or done.

       When he was about as old as the boys in my classes his face had been
bright and open, there was a lot of copper in it; and he'd had wonderfully direct
brown eyes, and great gentleness and privacy. I wondered what he looked like
now. He had been picked up, the evening before, in a raid on an apartment
downtown, for peddling and using heroin.

       I couldn't believe it: but what I mean by that is that I couldn't find any
room for it anywhere inside me. I had kept it outside me for a long time. I
hadn't wanted to know. I had had suspicions, but I didn't name them, I kept
putting them away. I told myself that Sonny was wild, but he wasn't crazy.
And he'd always been a good boy, he hadn't ever turned hard or evil or disrespectful, the way kids can, so quick, so quick, especially in Harlem. I didn't
want to believe that I'd ever see my brother going down, coming to nothing,
all that light in his face gone out, in the condition I'd already seen so many
others. Yet it had happened and here I was, talking about algebra to a lot
of boys who might, every one of them for all I knew, be popping off needles
every time they went to the head. Maybe it did more for them than algebra
could.

5   I was sure that the first time Sonny had ever had horse, he couldn't have
been much older than these boys were now. These boys, now, were living as
we'd been living then, they were growing up with a rush and their heads
bumped abruptly against the low ceiling of their actual possibilities. They
were filled with rage. All they really knew were two darknesses, the darkness
of their lives, which was now closing in on them, and the darkness of the
movies, which had blinded them to that other darkness, and in which they
now, vindictively, dreamed, at once more together than they were at any
other time, and more alone.

       When the last bell rang, the last class ended, I let out my breath. It
seemed I'd been holding it for all that time. My clothes were wet—I may have
looked as though I'd been sitting in a steam bath, all dressed up, all afternoon. I sat alone in the classroom a long time. I listened to the boys outside,

downstairs, shouting and cursing and laughing. Their laughter struck me for perhaps the first time. It was not the joyous laughter which—God knows why—one associates with children. It was mocking and insular, its intent was to denigrate. It was disenchanted, and in this, also, lay the authority of their curses. Perhaps I was listening to them because I was thinking about my brother and in them I heard my brother. And myself.

One boy was whistling a tune, at once very complicated and very simple, it seemed to be pouring out of him as though he were a bird, and it sounded very cool and moving through all that harsh, bright air, only just holding its own through all those other sounds.

I stood up and walked over to the window and looked down into the courtyard. It was the beginning of the spring and the sap was rising in the boys. A teacher passed through them every now and again, quickly, as though he or she couldn't wait to get out of that courtyard, to get those boys out of their sight and off their minds. I started collecting my stuff. I thought I'd better get home and talk to Isabel.

The courtyard was almost deserted by the time I got downstairs. I saw this boy standing in the shadow of a doorway, looking just like Sonny. I almost called his name. Then I saw that it wasn't Sonny, but somebody we used to know, a boy from around our block. He'd been Sonny's friend. He'd never been mine, having been too young for me, and, anyway, I'd never liked him. And now, even though he was a grown-up man, he still hung around that block, still spent hours on the street corners, was always high and raggy. I used to run into him from time to time and he'd often work around to asking me for a quarter or fifty cents. He always had some real good excuse, too, and I always gave it to him, I don't know why.

10 But now, abruptly, I hated him. I couldn't stand the way he looked at me, partly like a dog, partly like a cunning child. I wanted to ask him what the hell he was doing in the school courtyard.

He sort of shuffled over to me, and he said, "I see you got the papers. So you already know about it."

"You mean about Sonny? Yes, I already know about it. How come they didn't get you?"

He grinned. It made him repulsive and it also brought to mind what he'd looked like as a kid. "I wasn't there. I stay away from them people."

"Good for you." I offered him a cigarette and I watched him through the smoke. "You come all the way down here just to tell me about Sonny?"

15 "That's right." He was sort of shaking his head and his eyes looked strange, as though they were about to cross. The bright sun deadened his damp dark brown skin and it made his eyes look yellow and showed up the dirt in his kinked hair. He smelled funky. I moved a little away from him and I said, "Well, thanks. But I already know about it and I got to get home."

"I'll walk you a little ways," he said. We started walking. There were a couple of kids still loitering in the courtyard and one of them said goodnight to me and looked strangely at the boy beside me.

"What're you going to do?" he asked me. "I mean, about Sonny?"

"Look. I haven't seen Sonny for over a year, I'm not sure I'm going to do anything. Anyway, what the hell *can* I do?"

"That's right," he said quickly, "ain't nothing you can do. Can't much help old Sonny no more, I guess."

20   It was what I was thinking and so it seemed to me he had no right to say it.

"I'm surprised at Sonny, though," he went on—he had a funny way of talking, he looked straight ahead as though he were talking to himself—"I thought Sonny was a smart boy, I thought he was too smart to get hung."

"I guess he thought so too," I said sharply, "and that's how he got hung. And now about you? You're pretty goddamn smart, I bet."

Then he looked directly at me, just for a minute. "I ain't smart," he said. "If I was smart, I'd have reached for a pistol a long time ago."

"Look. Don't tell *me* your sad story, if it was up to me, I'd give you one." Then I felt guilty—guilty, probably, for never having supposed that the poor bastard *had* a story of his own, much less a sad one, and I asked, quickly, "What's going to happen to him now?"

25   He didn't answer this. He was off by himself some place. "Funny thing," he said, and from his tone we might have been discussing the quickest way to get to Brooklyn, "when I saw the papers this morning, the first thing I asked myself was if I had anything to do with it. I felt sort of responsible."

I began to listen more carefully. The subway station was on the corner, just before us, and I stopped. He stopped, too. We were in front of a bar and he ducked slightly, peering in, but whoever he was looking for didn't seem to be there. The juke box was blasting away with something black and bouncy and I half watched the barmaid as she danced her way from the juke box to her place behind the bar. And I watched her face as she laughingly responded to something someone said to her, still keeping time to the music. When she smiled one saw the little girl, one sensed the doomed, still-struggling woman beneath the battered face of the semi-whore.

"I never give Sonny nothing," the boy said finally, "but a long time ago I come to school high and Sonny asked me how it felt." He paused, I couldn't bear to watch him, I watched the barmaid, and I listened to the music which seemed to be causing the pavement to shake. "I told him it felt great." The music stopped, the barmaid paused and watched the juke box until the music began again. "It did."

All this way carrying me some place I didn't want to go. I certainly didn't want to know how it felt. It filled everything, the people, the houses, the music, the dark, quick-silver barmaid, with menace: and this menace was their reality.

"What's going to happen to him now?" I asked again.

30   "They'll send him away some place and they'll try to cure him." He shook his head. "Maybe he'll even think he's kicked the habit. Then they'll let him loose"—he gestured, throwing his cigarette into the gutter. "That's all."

"What do you mean, that's *all?*"

But I knew what he meant.

"I mean, that's *all.*" He turned his head and looked at me, pulling down the corners of his mouth. "Don't you know what I mean?" he asked, softly.

"How the hell would I know what you mean?" I almost whispered it. I don't know why.

35   "That's right," he said to the air, "how would he know what I mean?" He turned toward me again, patient and calm, and yet I somehow felt him shaking, shaking as though he were going to fall apart. I felt that ice in my guts again, the dread I'd felt all afternoon; and again I watched the barmaid, moving about the bar, washing glasses, and singing. "Listen. They'll let him out and then it'll just start all over again. That's what I mean."

"You mean—they'll let him out. And then he'll just start working his way back in again. You mean he'll never kick the habit. Is that what you mean?"

"That's right," he said, cheerfully. "You see what I mean."

"Tell me," I said at last, "why does he want to die? He must want to die, he's killing himself, why does he want to die?"

He looked at me in surprise. He licked his lips. "He don't want to die. He wants to live. Don't nobody want to die, ever."

40   Then I wanted to ask him—too many things. He could not have answered, or if he had, I could not have borne the answers. I started walking. "Well, I guess it's none of my business."

"It's going to be rough on old Sonny," he said. We reached the subway station. "This is your station?" he asked. I nodded. I took one step down. "Damn!" he said, suddenly. I looked up at him. He grinned again. "Damn it if I didn't leave all my money home. You ain't got a dollar on you, have you? Just for a couple of days, is all."

All at once something inside gave and threatened to come pouring out of me. I didn't hate him any more, I felt that in another moment I'd start crying like a child.

"Sure," I said. "Don't swear." I looked in my wallet and didn't have a dollar, I only had a five. "Here," I said. "That hold you?"

He didn't look at it—he didn't want to look at it. A terrible, closed look came over his face, as though he were keeping the number on the bill a secret from him and me. "Thanks," he said, and now he was dying to see me go. "Don't worry about Sonny. Maybe I'll write him or something."

45   "Sure," I said. "You do that. So long."

"Be seeing you," he said. I went down the steps.

And I didn't write Sonny or send him anything for a long time. When I finally did, it was just after my little girl died, he wrote me back a letter which made me feel like a bastard.

Here's what he said:

Dear Brother,

You don't know how much I needed to hear from you. I wanted to write you many a time but I dug how much I must have hurt you and so I didn't write. But now I feel like a man who's been trying to climb up out of some deep, real deep and funky hole and just saw the sun up there, outside. I got to get outside.

I can't tell you much about how I got here. I mean I don't know how to tell you. I guess I was afraid of something or I was trying to escape from something and you know I have never been very strong in the head (smile). I'm glad Mama and Daddy are dead and can't see what's happened to their son and I swear if I'd known what I was doing I would never have hurt you so, you and a lot of other fine people who were nice to me and who believed in me.

I don't want you to think it had anything to do with me being a musician. It's more than that. Or maybe less than that. I can't get anything straight in my head down here and I try not to think about what's going to happen to me when I get outside again. Sometime I think I'm going to flip and never get outside and sometime I think I'll come straight back, I tell you one thing, though. I'd rather blow my brains out than go through this again. But that's what they all say, so they tell me. If I tell you when I'm coming to New York and if you could meet me, I sure would appreciate it. Give my love to Isabel and the kids and I was sure sorry to hear about little Gracie. I wish I could be like Mama and say the Lord's will be done, but I don't know it seems to me that trouble is the one thing that never does get stopped and I don't know what good it does to blame it on the Lord. But maybe it does some good if you believe it.

Your brother,
Sonny

Then I kept in constant touch with him and I sent him whatever I could and I went to meet him when he came back to New York. When I saw him many things I thought I had forgotten came flooding back to me. This was because I had begun, finally, to wonder about Sonny, about the life that Sonny lived inside. This life, whatever it was, had made him older and thinner and it had deepened the distant stillness in which he had always moved. He looked very unlike my baby brother. Yet, when he smiled, when we shook hands, the baby brother I'd never known looked out from the depths of his private life, like an animal waiting to be coaxed into the light.

50   "How you been keeping?" he asked me.

"All right. And you?"

"Just fine." He was smiling all over his face. "It's good to see you again."

"It's good to see you."

The seven years' difference in our ages lay between us like a chasm: I wondered if these years would ever operate between us as a bridge. I was remembering, and it made it hard to catch my breath, that I had been there when he was born; and I had heard the first words he had ever spoken. When he started to walk, he walked from our mother straight to me. I caught him just before he fell when he took the first steps he ever took in this world.

55   "How's Isabel?"

"Just fine. She's dying to see you."

"And the boys?"

"They're fine, too. They're anxious to see their uncle."

"Oh, come on. You know they don't remember me."

60   "Are you kidding? Of course they remember you."

He grinned again. We got into a taxi. We had a lot to say to each other, far too much to know how to begin.

As the taxi began to move, I asked, "You still want to go to India?"

He laughed. "You still remember that. Hell, no. This place is Indian enough for me."

"It used to belong to them," I said.

65   And he laughed again. "They damn sure knew what they were doing when they got rid of it."

Years ago, when he was around fourteen, he'd been all hipped on the idea of going to India. He read books about people sitting on rocks, naked, in all kinds of weather, but mostly bad, naturally, and walking barefoot through hot coals and arriving at wisdom. I used to say that it sounded to me as though they were getting away from wisdom as fast as they could. I think he sort of looked down on me for that.

"Do you mind," he asked, "if we have the driver drive alongside the park? On the west side—I haven't seen the city in so long."

"Of course not," I said. I was afraid that I might sound as though I were humoring him, but I hoped he wouldn't take it that way.

So we drove along, between the green of the park and the stony, lifeless elegance of hotels and apartment buildings, toward the vivid, killing streets of our childhood. These streets hadn't changed, though housing projects jutted up out of them now like rocks in the middle of a boiling sea. Most of the houses in which we had grown up had vanished, as had the stores from which we had stolen, the basements in which we had first tried sex, the rooftops from which we had hurled tin cans and bricks. But houses exactly like the houses of our past yet dominated the landscape, boys exactly like the boys we once had been found themselves smothering in these houses, came down into the streets for light and air and found themselves encircled by disaster. Some escaped the trap, most didn't. Those who got out always left something of themselves behind, as some animals amputate a leg and leave it in the trap. It might be said, perhaps, that I had escaped, after all, I was a school teacher; or that Sonny had, he hadn't lived in Harlem for years. Yet, as the cab moved uptown through streets which seemed, with a rush, to darken with dark people, and as I covertly studied Sonny's face, it came to me that what we both were seeking through our separate cab windows was that part of ourselves which had been left behind. It's always at the hour of trouble and confrontation that the missing member aches.

70   We hit 110th Street and started rolling up Lenox Avenue. And I'd known this avenue all my life, but it seemed to me again, as it had seemed on the day I'd first heard about Sonny's trouble, filled with a hidden menace which was its very breath of life.

"We almost there," said Sonny.

"Almost." We were both too nervous to say anything more.

We live in a housing project. It hasn't been up long. A few days after it was up it seemed uninhabitably new, now, of course, it's already rundown. It looks like a parody of the good, clean, faceless life—God knows the people who live in it do their best to make it a parody. The beat-looking grass lying around isn't enough to make their lives green, the hedges will never hold out the streets, and they know it. The big windows fool no one, they aren't big enough to make space out of no space. They don't bother with the windows, they watch the TV screen instead. The playground is most popular with the children who don't play at jacks, or skip rope, or roller skate, or swing, and they can be found in it after dark. We moved in partly because it's not too far from where I teach, and partly for the kids; but it's really just like the houses in which Sonny and I grew up. The same things happen, they'll have the same things to remember. The moment Sonny and I started into the house I had the feeling that I was simply bringing him back into the danger he had almost died trying to escape.

Sonny has never been talkative. So I don't know why I was sure he'd be dying to talk to me when supper was over the first night. Everything went fine, the oldest boy remembered him, and the youngest boy liked him, and Sonny had remembered to bring something for each of them; and Isabel, who is really much nicer than I am, more open and giving, had gone to a lot of trouble about dinner and was genuinely glad to see him. And she's always been able to tease Sonny in a way that I haven't. It was nice to see her face so vivid again and to hear her laugh and watch her make Sonny laugh. She wasn't, or, anyway, she didn't seem to be, at all uneasy or embarrassed. She chatted as though there were no subject which had to be avoided and she got Sonny past his first, faint stiffness. And thank God she was there, for I was filled with that icy dread again. Everything I did seemed awkward to me, and everything I said sounded freighted with hidden meaning. I was trying to remember everything I'd heard about dope addiction and I couldn't help watching Sonny for signs. I wasn't doing it out of malice. I was trying to find out something about my brother. I was dying to hear him tell he was safe.

75   "Safe!" my father grunted, whenever Mama suggested trying to move to a neighborhood which might be safer for children. "Safe, hell! Ain't no place safe for kids, nor nobody."

He always went on like this, but he wasn't, ever, really as bad as he sounded, not even on weekends, when he got drunk. As a matter of fact, he was always on the lookout for "something a little better," but he died before he found it. He died suddenly, during a drunken weekend in the middle of the war, when Sonny was fifteen. He and Sonny hadn't ever got on too well. And this was partly because Sonny was the apple of his father's eye. It was because he loved Sonny so much and was frightened for him, that he was always fighting with him. It doesn't do any good to fight with Sonny. Sonny just moves back, inside himself, where he can't be reached. But the principal reason that they never hit it off is that they were so much alike. Daddy was big and rough and loud-talking, just the opposite of Sonny, but they both had—that same privacy.

Mama tried to tell me something about this, just after Daddy died. I was home on leave from the army.

This was the last time I ever saw my mother alive. Just the same, this picture gets all mixed up in my mind with pictures I had of her when she was younger. The way I always see her is the way she used to be on a Sunday afternoon, say, when the old folks were talking after the big Sunday dinner. I always see her wearing pale blue. She'd be sitting on the sofa. And my father would be sitting in the easy chair, not far from her. And the living room would be full of church folks and relatives. There they sit, in chairs all around the living room, and the night is creeping up outside, but nobody knows it yet. You can see the darkness growing against the windowpanes and you hear the street noises every now and again, or maybe the jangling beat of a tambourine from one of the churches close by, but it's real quiet in the room. For a moment nobody's talking, but every face looks darkening, like the sky outside. And my mother rocks a little from the waist, and my father's eyes are closed. Everyone is looking at something a child can't see. For a minute they've forgotten the children. Maybe a kid is lying on the rug, half asleep. Maybe somebody's got a kid in his lap and is absent-mindedly stroking the kid's head. Maybe there's a kid, quiet and big-eyed, curled up on a big chair in the corner. The silence, the darkness coming, and the darkness in the faces frightens the child obscurely. He hopes that the hand which strokes his forehead will never stop—will never die. He hopes that there will never come a time when the old folks won't be sitting around the living room, talking about where they've come from, and what they've seen, and what's happened to them and their kinfolk.

But something deep and watchful in the child knows that this is bound to end, is already ending. In a moment someone will get up and turn on the light. Then the old folks will remember the children and they won't talk any more that day. And when light fills the room, the child is filled with darkness. He knows that every time this happens he's moved just a little closer to that darkness outside. The darkness outside is what the old folks have been talking about. It's what they've come from. It's what they endure. The child knows that they won't talk any more because if he knows too much about what's happened to *them,* he'll know too much too soon, about what's going to happen to *him.*

80   The last time I talked to my mother, I remember I was restless. I wanted to get out and see Isabel. We weren't married then and we had a lot to straighten out between us.

There Mama sat, in black, by the window. She was humming an old church song, *Lord, you brought me from a long ways off.* Sonny was out somewhere. Mama kept watching the streets.

"I don't know," she said, "if I'll ever see you again, after you go off from here. But I hope you'll remember the things I tried to teach you."

"Don't talk like that," I said, and smiled. "You'll be here a long time yet."

She smiled, too, but she said nothing. She was quiet for a long time. And I said, "Mama, don't you worry about nothing. I'll be writing all the time, and you be getting the checks. . . ."

85   "I want to talk to you about your brother," she said, suddenly. "If anything happens to me he ain't going to have nobody to look out for him."

"Mama," I said, "ain't nothing going to happen to you *or* Sonny. Sonny's all right. He's a good boy and he's got good sense."

"It ain't a question of his being a good boy," Mama said, "nor of his having good sense. It ain't only the bad ones, nor yet the dumb ones that gets sucked under." She stopped, looking at me. "Your Daddy once had a brother," she said, and she smiled in a way that made me feel she was in pain. "You didn't never know that, did you?"

"No," I said, "I never knew that," and I watched her face.

"Oh, yes," she said, "your Daddy had a brother." She looked out of the window again. "I know you never saw your Daddy cry. But *I* did—many a time, through all these years."

90   I asked her, "What happened to his brother? How come nobody's ever talked about him?"

This was the first time I ever saw my mother look old.

"His brother got killed," she said, "when he was just a little younger than you are now. I knew him. He was a fine boy. He was maybe a little full of the devil, but he didn't mean nobody no harm."

Then she stopped and the room was silent, exactly as it had sometimes been on those Sunday afternoons. Mama kept looking out into the streets.

"He used to have a job in the mill," she said, "and, like all young folks, he just liked to perform on Saturday nights. Saturday nights, him and your father would drift around to different places, go to dances and things like that, or just sit around with people they knew, and your father's brother would sing, he had a fine voice, and play along with himself on his guitar. Well, this particular Saturday night, him and your father was coming home from some place, and they were both a little drunk and there was a moon that night, it was bright like day. Your father's brother was feeling kind of good, and he was whistling to himself, and he had his guitar slung over this shoulder. They was coming down a hill and beneath them was a road that turned off from the highway. Well, your father's brother, being always kind of frisky, decided to run down this hill, and he did, with that guitar banging and clanging behind him, and he ran across the road, and he was making water behind a tree. And your father was sort of amused at him and he was still coming down the hill, kind of slow. Then he heard a car motor and that same minute his brother stepped from behind the tree, into the road, in the moonlight. And he started to cross the road. And your father started to run down the hill, he says he don't know why. This car was full of white men. They was all drunk, and when they seen your father's brother they let out a great whoop and holler and they aimed the car straight at him. They was having fun, they just wanted to scare him, the way they do sometimes, you know. But they was drunk. And I guess the boy, being drunk, too, and scared, kind of lost his head. By the time he jumped it was too late. Your father says he heard his brother scream when the car rolled over him, and he heard the wood of that guitar when it give, and he heard them strings go flying, and he heard them white men shouting, and the car kept on a-going and it ain't stopped till this day. And, time your father got down the hill, his brother weren't nothing but blood and pulp."

95   Tears were gleaming on my mother's face. There wasn't anything I could say.

"He never mentioned it," she said, "because I never let him mention it before you children. Your Daddy was like a crazy man that night and for many a night thereafter. He says he never in his life seen anything as dark as that road after the lights of that car had gone away. Weren't nothing, weren't nobody on that road, just your Daddy and his brother and that busted guitar. Oh, yes. Your Daddy never did really get right again. Till the day he died he weren't sure but that every white man he saw was the man that killed his brother."

She stopped and took out her handkerchief and dried her eyes and looked at me.

"I ain't telling you all this," she said, "to make you scared or bitter or to make you hate nobody. I'm telling you this because you got a brother. And the world ain't changed."

I guess I didn't want to believe this. I guess she saw this in my face. She turned away from me, toward the window again, searching those streets.

100   "But I praise my Redeemer," she said at last, "that He called your Daddy home before me. I ain't saying it to throw no flowers at myself, but, I declare, it keeps me from feeling too cast down to know I helped your father get safely through this world. Your father always acted like he was the roughest, strongest man on earth. And everybody took him to be like that. But if he hadn't had *me* there—to see his tears!"

She was crying again. Still, I couldn't move. I said, "Lord, Lord, Mama, I didn't know it was like that."

"Oh, honey," she said, "there's a lot that you don't know. But you are going to find it out." She stood up from the window and came over to me. "You got to hold on to your brother," she said, "and don't let him fall, no matter what it looks like is happening to him and no matter how evil you gets with him. You going to be evil with him many a time. But don't you forget what I told you, you hear?"

"I won't forget," I said. "Don't you worry, I won't forget. I won't let nothing happen to Sonny."

My mother smiled as though she were amused at something she saw in my face. Then, "You may not be able to stop nothing from happening. But you got to let him know you's *there.*"

105   Two days later I was married, and then I was gone. And I had a lot of things on my mind and I pretty well forgot my promise to Mama until I got shipped home on a special furlough for her funeral.

And after the funeral, with just Sonny and me alone in the empty kitchen, I tried to find out something about him.

"What do you want to do?" I asked him.

"I'm going to be a musician," he said.

For he had graduated, in the time I had been away, from dancing to the juke box to finding out who was playing what, and what they were doing with it, and he had bought himself a set of drums.

110 "You mean, you want to be a drummer?" I somehow had the feeling that being a drummer might be all right for other people but not for my brother Sonny.

"I don't think," he said, looking at me very gravely, "that I'll ever be a good drummer. But I think I can play a piano."

I frowned. I'd never played the role of the older brother quite so seriously before, had scarcely ever, in fact, *asked* Sonny a damn thing. I sensed myself in the presence of something I didn't really know how to handle, didn't understand. So I made my frown a little deeper as I asked: "What kind of musician do you want to be?"

He grinned, "How many kinds do you think there are?"

"Be *serious,*" I said.

115 He laughed, throwing his head back, and then looked at me. "I *am* serious."

"Well, then, for Christ's sake, stop kidding around and answer a serious question. I mean, do you want to be a concert pianist, you want to play classical music and all that, or—or what?" Long before I finished he was laughing again. "For Christ's *sake,* Sonny!"

He sobered, but with difficulty. "I'm sorry, But you sound so—*scared!*" and he was off again.

"Well, you may think it's funny now, baby, but it's not going to be so funny when you have to make your living at it, let me tell you *that.*" I was furious because I knew he was laughing at me and I didn't know why.

"No," he said, very sober now, and afraid, perhaps, that he'd hurt me. "I don't want to be a classical pianist. That isn't what interests me. I mean"—he paused, looking hard at me, as though his eyes would help me to understand, and then gestured helplessly, as though perhaps his hand would help—"I mean, I'll have a lot of studying to do, and I'll have to study *everything,* but, I mean, I want to play *with*—jazz musicians." He stopped, "I want to play jazz," he said.

120 Well, the word had never before sounded as heavy, as real, as it sounded that afternoon in Sonny's mouth. I just looked at him and I was probably frowning a real frown by this time. I simply couldn't see why on earth he'd want to spend his time hanging around nightclubs, clowning around on bandstands, while people pushed each other around a dance floor. It seemed—beneath him, somehow. I had never thought about it before, had never been forced to, but I suppose I had always put jazz musicians in a class with what Daddy called "good-time people."

"Are you *serious?*"

"Hell, *yes,* I'm serious."

He looked more helpless than ever, and annoyed, and deeply hurt.

I suggested, helpfully: "You mean—like Louis Armstrong?"[1]

---

[1] Famous jazz trumpet player.

125   His face closed as though I'd struck him. "No. I'm not talking about none of that old-time, down home crap."

"Well, look, Sonny, I'm sorry, don't get mad. I just don't altogether get it, that's all. Name somebody—you know, a jazz musician you admire."

"Bird."

"Who?"

"Bird! Charlie Parker![2] Don't they teach you nothing in the goddamn army?"

130   I lit a cigarette. I was surprised and then a little amused to discover that I was trembling. "I've been out of touch," I said. "You'll have to be patient with me. Now. Who's this Parker character?"

"He's just one of the greatest jazz musicians alive," said Sonny, sullenly, his hands in his pockets, his back to me. "Maybe *the* greatest," he added, bitterly, "that's probably why *you* never heard of him."

"All right," I said, "I'm ignorant. I'm sorry. I'll go out and buy all the cat's records right away, all right?"

"It don't," said Sonny, with dignity, "make any difference to me. I don't care what you listen to. Don't do me no favors."

I was beginning to realize that I'd never seen him so upset before. With another part of my mind I was thinking that this would probably turn out to be one of those things kids go through and that I shouldn't make it seem important by pushing it too hard. Still, I didn't think it would do any harm to ask: "Doesn't all this take a lot of time? Can you make a living at it?"

135   He turned back to me and half leaned, half sat, on the kitchen table. "Everything takes time," he said, "and—well, yes, sure, I can make a living at it. But what I don't seem to be able to make you understand is that it's the only thing I want to do."

"Well, Sonny," I said, gently, "you know people can't always do exactly what they *want* to do—"

"*No,* I don't know that," said Sonny, surprising me. "I think people *ought* to do what they want to do, what else are they alive for?"

"You getting to be a big boy," I said desperately, "it's time you started thinking about your future."

"I'm thinking about my future," said Sonny, grimly. "I think about it all the time."

140   I gave up. I decided, if he didn't change his mind, that we could always talk about it later. "In the meantime," I said, "you got to finish school." We had already decided that he'd have to move in with Isabel and her folks. I knew this wasn't the ideal arrangement because Isabel's folks are inclined to be dicty[3] and they hadn't especially wanted Isabel to marry me. But I didn't know what else to do. "And we have to get you fixed up at Isabel's."

There was a long silence. He moved from the kitchen table to the window. "That's a terrible idea. You know it yourself."

"Do you have a *better* idea?"

---

[2] Famous jazz musician, nicknamed Bird.
[3] Putting on fine airs.

He just walked up and down the kitchen for a minute. He was as tall as I was. He had started to shave. I suddenly had the feeling that I didn't know him at all.

He stopped at the kitchen table and picked up my cigarettes. Looking at me with a kind of mocking, amused defiance, he put one between his lips. "You mind?"

145   "You smoking already?"

He lit the cigarette and nodded, watching me through the smoke. "I just wanted to see if I'd have the courage to smoke in front of you." He grinned and blew a great cloud of smoke to the ceiling. "It was easy." He looked at my face. "Come on, now. I bet you was smoking at my age, tell the truth."

I didn't say anything but the truth was on my face, and he laughed. But now there was something very strained in his laugh. "Sure. And I bet that ain't all you was doing."

He was frightening me a little. "Cut the crap," I said. "We already decided that you was going to go and live at Isabel's. Now what's got into you all of a sudden?"

"*You* decided it," he pointed out. "*I* didn't decide nothing." He stopped in front of me, leaning against the stove, arms loosely folded. "Look, brother. I don't want to stay in Harlem no more, I really don't." He was very earnest. He looked at me, then over toward the kitchen window. There was something in his eyes I'd never seen before, some thoughtfulness, some worry all his own. He rubbed the muscle of one arm. "It's time I was getting out of here."

150   "Where do you want to *go,* Sonny?"

"I want to join the army. Or the navy, I don't care. If I say I'm old enough, they'll believe me."

Then I got mad. It was because I was so scared. "You must be crazy. You goddamn fool, what the hell do you want to go and join the *army* for?"

"I just told you. To get out of Harlem."

"Sonny, you haven't even finished *school.* And if you really want to be a musician, how do you expect to study if you're in the *army?*"

155   He looked at me, trapped, and in anguish. "There's ways. I might be able to work out some kind of deal. Anyway, I'll have the G.I. Bill when I come out."

"*If* you come out." We stared at each other. "Sonny, please. Be reasonable. I know the setup is far from perfect. But we got to do the best we can."

"I ain't learning nothing in school," he said. "Even when I go." He turned away from me and opened the window and threw his cigarette out into the narrow alley. I watched his back. "At least, I ain't learning nothing you'd want me to learn." He slammed the window so hard I thought the glass would fly out, and turned back to me. "And I'm sick of the stink of these garbage cans!"

"Sonny," I said, "I know how you feel. But if you don't finish school now, you're going to be sorry later that you didn't." I grabbed him by the shoulders. "And you only got another year. It ain't so bad. And I'll come back and I swear I'll help you do *whatever* you want to do. Just try to put up with it till I come back. Will you please do that? For me?"

He didn't answer and he wouldn't look at me.

160   "Sonny. You hear me?"

He pulled away. "I hear you. But you never hear anything *I* say."

I didn't know what to say to that. He looked out of the window and then back at me. "OK," he said, and sighed. "I'll try."

Then I said, trying to cheer him up a little, "They got a piano at Isabel's. You can practice on it."

And as a matter of fact, it did cheer him up for a minute. "That's right," he said to himself. "I forgot that." His face relaxed a little. But the worry, the thoughtfulness, played on it still, the way shadows play on a face which is staring into the fire.

165   But I thought I'd never hear the end of that piano. At first, Isabel, would write me, saying how nice it was that Sonny was so serious about his music and how, as soon as he came in from school, or wherever he had been when he was supposed to be at school, he went straight to that piano and stayed there until suppertime. And, after supper, he went back to that piano and stayed there until everybody went to bed. He was at the piano all day Saturday and all day Sunday. Then he bought a record player and started playing records. He'd play one record over and over again, all day long sometimes, and he'd improvise along with it on the piano. Or he'd play one section of the record, one chord, one change, one progression, then he'd do it on the piano. Then back to the record. Then back to the piano.

Well, I really don't know how they stood it. Isabel finally confessed that it wasn't like living with a person at all, it was like living with sound. And the sound didn't make any sense to her, didn't make any sense to any of them— naturally. They began, in a way, to be afflicted by this presence that was living in their home. It was as though Sonny were some sort of god, or monster. He moved in an atmosphere which wasn't like theirs at all. They fed him and he ate, he washed himself, he walked in and out of their door; he certainly wasn't nasty or unpleasant or rude, Sonny isn't any of those things; but it was as though he were all wrapped up in some cloud, some fire, some vision all his own; and there wasn't any way to reach him.

At the same time, he wasn't really a man yet, he was still a child, and they had to watch out for him in all kinds of ways. They certainly couldn't throw him out. Neither did they dare to make a great scene about that piano be-cause even they dimly sensed, as I sensed, from so many thousands of miles away, that Sonny was at that piano playing for his life.

But he hadn't been going to school. One day a letter came from the school board and Isabel's mother got it—there had, apparently, been other letters but Sonny had torn them up. This day, when Sonny came in, Isabel's mother showed him the letter and asked where he'd been spending his time. And she finally got it out of him that he'd been down in Greenwich Village, with musicians and other characters, in a white girl's apartment. And this scared her and she started to scream at him and what came up, once she be-gan—though she denies it to this day—was what sacrifices they were making to give Sonny a decent home and how little he appreciated it.

Sonny didn't play the piano that day. By evening, Isabel's mother had calmed down but then there was the old man to deal with, and Isabel herself. Isabel says she did her best to be calm but she broke down and started crying. She says she just watched Sonny's face. She could tell, by watching him, what was happening with him. And what was happening was that they penetrated his cloud, they had reached him. Even if their fingers had been a thousand times more gentle than human fingers ever are, he could hardly help feeling that they had stripped him naked and were spitting on that nakedness. For he also had to see that his presence, that music, which was life or death to him, had been torture for them and that they had endured it, not at all for his sake, but only for mine. And Sonny couldn't take that. He can take it a little better today than he could then but he's still not very good at it and, frankly, I don't know anybody who is.

170   The silence of the next few days must have been louder than the sound of all the music ever played since time began. One morning, before she went to work, Isabel was in his room for something and she suddenly realized that all of his records were gone. And she knew for certain that he was gone. And he was. He went as far as the navy would carry him. He finally sent me a postcard from some place in Greece and that was the first I knew that Sonny was still alive. I didn't see him any more until we were both back in New York and the war had long been over.

He was a man by then, of course, but I wasn't willing to see it. He came by the house from time to time, but we fought almost every time we met. I didn't like the way he carried himself, loose and dreamlike all the time, and I didn't like his friends, and his music seemed to be merely an excuse for the life he led. It sounded just that weird and disordered.

Then we had a fight, a pretty awful fight, and I didn't see him for months. By and by I looked him up, where he was living, in a furnished room in the Village, and I tried to make it up. But there were lots of other people in the room and Sonny just lay on his bed, and he wouldn't come downstairs with me, and he treated these other people as though they were his family and I weren't. So I got mad and then he got mad, and then I told him that he might just as well be dead as live the way he was living. Then he stood up and he told me not to worry about him any more in life, that he *was* dead as far as I was concerned. Then he pushed me to the door and the other people looked on as though nothing were happening, and he slammed the door behind me. I stood in the hallway, staring at the door. I heard somebody laugh in the room and then the tears came to my eyes. I started down the steps, whistling to keep from crying. I kept whistling to myself, *You going to need me, baby, one of these cold, rainy days.*

I read about Sonny's trouble in the spring. Little Grace died in the fall. She was a beautiful little girl. But she only lived a little over two years. She died of polio and she suffered. She had a slight fever for a couple of days, but it didn't seem like anything and we just kept her in bed. And we would certainly have called the doctor, but the fever dropped, and she seemed to be all right. So we thought it had just been a cold. Then, one day, she was up, playing, Isabel was in the kitchen fixing lunch for the two boys when they'd come in from school, and she heard Grace fall down in the living room. When you have a lot of children you don't always start running when one of them falls, unless they start screaming or something. And, this time, Grace was quiet. Yet, Isabel says that when she heard that *thump* and then that silence, something happened in her to make her afraid. And she ran to the living room and there was little Grace on the floor, all twisted up, and the reason she hadn't screamed was that she couldn't get her breath. And when she did scream, it was the worst sound, Isabel says, that she'd ever heard in all her life, and she still hears it sometimes in her dreams. Isabel will sometimes wake me up with a low, moaning, strangled sound and I have to be quick to awaken her and hold her to me and where Isabel is weeping against me seems a mortal wound.

I think I may have written Sonny the very day that little Grace was buried. I was sitting in the living room in the dark, by myself, and I suddenly thought of Sonny. My trouble made his real.

175   One Saturday afternoon, when Sonny had been living with us, or, anyway, been in our house, for nearly two weeks, I found myself wandering aimlessly about the living room, drinking from a can of beer, and trying to work up the courage to search Sonny's room. He was out, he was usually out whenever I was home, and Isabel had taken the children to see their grandparents. Suddenly I was standing still in front of the living room window, watching Seventh Avenue. The idea of searching Sonny's room made me still. I scarcely dared to admit to myself what I'd be searching for. I didn't know what I'd do if I found it. Or if I didn't.

On the sidewalk across from me, near the entrance to a barbecue joint, some people were holding an old-fashioned revival meeting. The barbecue cook, wearing a dirty white apron, his conked hair reddish and metallic in the pale sun, and a cigarette between his lips, stood in the doorway, watching them. Kids and older people paused in their errands and stood there, along with some older men and a couple of very tough-looking women who watched everything that happened on the avenue, as though they owned it, or were maybe owned by it. Well, they were watching this, too. The revival was being carried on by three sisters in black, and a brother. All they had were their voices and their Bibles and a tambourine. The brother was testifying and while he testified two of the sisters stood together, seeming to say, amen, and the third sister walked around with the tambourine outstretched and a couple of people dropped coins into it. Then the brother's testimony ended and the sister who had been taking up the collection dumped the coins into her palm and transferred them to the pocket of her long black robe. Then she raised both hands, striking the tambourine against the air, and then against one hand, and she started to sing. And the two other sisters and the brother joined in.

It was strange, suddenly, to watch, though I had been seeing these street meetings all my life. So, of course, had everybody else down there. Yet, they paused and watched and listened and I stood still at the window. *"Tis the old ship of Zion,"* they sang, and the sister with the tambourine kept a steady, jangling beat, *"it has rescued many a thousand!"* Not a soul under the sound of their voices was hearing this song for the first time, not one of them had been rescued. Nor had they seen much in the way of rescue work being done around them. Neither did they especially believe in the holiness of the three sisters and the brother, they knew too much about them, knew where they lived, and how. The woman with the tambourine, whose voice dominated the air, whose face was bright with joy, was divided by very little from the woman who stood watching her, a cigarette between her heavy, chapped lips, her hair a cuckoo's nest, her face scarred and swollen from many beatings, and her black eyes glittering like coal. Perhaps they both knew this, which was why, when, as rarely, they addressed each other, they addressed each other as Sister. As the singing filled the air the watching, listening faces underwent a change, and eyes focusing on something within; the music seemed to soothe a poison out of them; and time seemed, nearly, to fall away from the sullen, belligerent, battered faces, as though they were fleeing back to their first condition, while dreaming of their last. The barbecue cook half shook his head and smiled, and dropped his cigarette and disappeared into his joint. A man fumbled in his pockets for change and stood holding it in his hand impatiently, as though he had just remembered a pressing appointment further up the avenue. He looked furious. Then I saw Sonny, standing on the edge of the crowd. He was carrying a wide, flat notebook with a green cover, and it made him look, from where I was standing, almost like a schoolboy. The coppery sun brought out the copper in his skin, he was very faintly smiling, standing very still. Then the singing stopped, the tambourine turned into a collection plate again. The furious man dropped in his coins and vanished, so did a couple of the women, and Sonny dropped some change in the plate, looking directly at the woman with a little smile. He started across the avenue, toward the house. He has a slow, loping walk, something like the way Harlem hipsters walk, only he's imposed on this his own half-beat. I had never really noticed it before.

I stayed at the window, both relieved and apprehensive. As Sonny disappeared from my sight, they began singing again. And they were still singing when his key turned in the lock.

"Hey," he said.

180   "Hey, yourself. You want some beer?"

"No. Well, maybe." But he came up to the window and stood beside me, looking out. "What a warm voice," he said.

They were singing *If I could only hear my mother pray again!*

"Yes," I said, "and she can sure beat that tambourine."

"But what a terrible song," he said, and laughed. He dropped his notebook on the sofa and disappeared into the kitchen. "Where's Isabel and the kids?"

185   "I think they went to see their grandparents. You hungry?"

"No." He came back into the living room with his can of beer. "You want to come some place with me tonight?"

I sensed, I don't know how, that I couldn't possibly say no. "Sure. Where?"

He sat down on the sofa and picked up his notebook and started leafing through it. "I'm going to sit in with some fellows in a joint in the Village."

"You mean, you're going to play, tonight?"

190 "That's right." He took a swallow of his beer and moved back to the window. He gave me a sidelong look. "If you can stand it."

"I'll try," I said.

He smiled to himself and we both watched as the meeting across the way broke up. The three sisters and the brother, heads bowed, were singing *God be with you till we meet again.* The faces around them were very quiet. Then the song ended. The small crowd dispersed. We watched the three women and the lone man walk slowly up the avenue.

"When she was singing before," said Sonny, abruptly, "her voice reminded me for a minute of what heroin feels like sometimes—when it's in your veins. It makes you feel sort of warm and cool at the same time. And distant. And—and sure." He sipped his beer, very deliberately not looking at me. I watched his face. "It makes you feel—in control. Sometimes you've got to have that feeling."

"Do you?" I sat down slowly in the easy chair.

195 "Sometimes." He went to the sofa and picked up his notebook again. "Some people do."

"In order," I asked, "to play?" And my voice was very ugly, full of contempt and anger.

"Well"—he looked at me with great, troubled eyes, as though, in fact, he hoped his eyes would tell me things he could never otherwise say— "they *think* so. And *if* they think so—!"

"And what do *you* think?" I asked.

He sat on the sofa and put his can of beer on the floor. "I don't know," he said, and I couldn't be sure if he were answering my question or pursuing his thoughts. He face didn't tell me. "It's not so much to *play.* It's to *stand* it, to be able to make it at all. On any level." He frowned and smiled: "In order to keep from shaking to pieces."

200 "But these friends of yours," I said, "they seem to shake themselves to pieces pretty goddamn fast."

"Maybe." He played with the notebook. And something told me that I should curb my tongue, that Sonny was doing his best to talk, that I should listen. "But of course you only know the ones that've gone to pieces. Some don't—or at least they haven't *yet* and that's just about all *any* of us can say." He paused. "And then there are some who just live, really, in hell, and they know it and they see what's happening and they go right on. I don't know." He sighed, dropped the notebook, folded his arms. "Some guys, you can tell from the way they play, they on something *all* the time. And you can see that, well, it makes something real for them. But of course," he picked up his beer from the floor and sipped it and put the can down again, "they *want* to, too, you've got to see that. Even some of them that say they don't—*some,* not all."

"And what about you?" I asked—I couldn't help it. "What about you? Do *you* want to?"

He stood up and walked to the window and remained silent for a long time. Then he sighed. "Me," he said. Then: "While I was downstairs before, on my way here, listening to that woman sing, it struck me all of a sudden how much suffering she must have had to go through—to sing like that. It's *repulsive* to think you have to suffer that much."

I said: "But there's no way not to suffer—is there, Sonny?"

205 "I believe not," he said and smiled, "but that's never stopped anyone from trying." He looked at me. "Has it?" I realized, with this mocking look, that there stood between us, forever, beyond the power of time or forgiveness, the fact that I had held silence—so long!—when he had needed human speech to help him. He turned back to the window. "No, there's no way not to suffer. But you try all kinds of ways to keep from drowning in it, to keep on top of it, and to make it seem—well, like *you*. Like you did something, all right, and now you're suffering for it. You know?" I said nothing. "Well you know," he said, impatiently, "why *do* people suffer? Maybe it's better to do something to give it a reason, *any* reason."

"But we just agreed," I said, "that there's no way not to suffer. Isn't it better, then, just to—take it?"

"But nobody just takes it," Sonny cried, "that's what I'm telling you! *Everybody* tries not to. You're just hung up on the *way* some people try—it's not *your* way!"

The hair on my face began to itch, my face felt wet. "That's not true," I said, "that's not true. I don't give a damn what other people do, I don't even care how they suffer. I just care how *you* suffer." And he looked at me. "Please believe me," I said, "I don't want to see you—die—trying not to suffer."

"I won't," he said, flatly, "die trying not to suffer. At least, not any faster than anybody else."

210 "But there's no need," I said, trying to laugh, "is there? in killing yourself."

I wanted to say more, but I couldn't. I wanted to talk about will power and how life could be—well, beautiful. I wanted to say that it was all within; but was it? or, rather, wasn't that exactly the trouble? And I wanted to promise that I would never fail him again. But it would all have sounded—empty words and lies.

So I made the promise to myself and prayed that I would keep it.

"It's terrible sometimes, inside," he said, "that's what's the trouble. You walk these streets, black and funky and cold, and there's not really a living ass to talk to, and there's nothing shaking, and there's no way of getting it out—that storm inside. You can't talk it and you can't make love with it, and when you finally try to get with it and play it, you realize *nobody's* listening. So *you've* got to listen. You got to find a way to listen."

And then he walked away from the window and sat on the sofa again, as though all the wind had suddenly been knocked out of him. "Sometimes you'll do *anything* to play, even cut your mother's throat." He laughed and looked at me. "Or your brother's." Then he sobered. "Or your own." Then:

"Don't worry. I'm all right now and I think I'll *be* all right. But I can't forget—where I've been. I don't mean just the physical place I've been, I mean where I've *been.* And *what* I've been."

215   "What have you been, Sonny?" I asked.

He smiled—but sat sideways on the sofa, his elbow resting on the back, his fingers playing with his mouth and chin, not looking at me. "I've been something I didn't recognize, didn't know I could be. Didn't know anybody could be." He stopped, looking inward, looking helplessly young, looking old. "I'm not talking about it now because I feel *guilty* or anything like that—maybe it would be better if I did, I don't know. Anyway, I can't really talk about it. Not to you, not to anybody," and now he turned and faced me. "Sometimes, you know, and it was actually when I was most *out* of the world, I felt that I was in it, that I was *with* it, really, and I could play or I didn't really have to *play,* it just came out of me, it was there. And I don't know how I played, thinking about it now, but I know I did awful things, those times, sometimes, to people. Or it wasn't that I *did* anything to them—it was that they weren't real." He picked up the beer can; it was empty; he rolled it between his palms: "And other times—well, I needed a fix, I needed to find a place to lean, I needed to clear a space to *listen*—and I couldn't find it, and I—went crazy, I did terrible things to *me,* I was terrible *for* me." He began pressing the beer can between his hands, I watched the metal begin to give. It glittered, as he played with it, like a knife, and I was afraid he would cut himself, but I said nothing. "Oh well, I can never tell you. I was all by myself at the bottom of something, stinking and sweating and crying and shaking, and I smelled it, you know? *my* stink, and I thought I'd die if I couldn't get away from it and yet, all the same, I knew that everything I was doing was just locking me in with it. And I didn't know," he paused, still flattening the beer can, "I didn't know, I still *don't* know, something kept telling me that maybe it was good to smell your own stink, but I didn't think that *that* was what I'd been trying to do—and—who can stand it?" and he abruptly dropped the ruined beer can, looking at me with a small, still smile, and then rose, walking to the window as though it were the lodestone rock. I watched his face, he watched the avenue. "I couldn't tell you when Mama died—but the reason I wanted to leave Harlem so bad was to get away from drugs. And then, when I ran away, that's what I was running from—really. When I came back, nothing had changed, *I* hadn't changed, I was just—older." And he stopped, drumming with his fingers on the windowpane. The sun had vanished, soon darkness would fall. I watched his face. "It can come again," he said, almost as though speaking to himself. Then he turned to me. "It can come again," he repeated. "I just want you to know that."

"All right," I said, at last. "So it can come again, All right."

He smiled, but the smile was sorrowful. "I had to try to tell you," he said.

"Yes," I said. "I understand that."

220   "You're my brother," he said, looking straight at me, and not smiling at all.

"Yes," I repeated, "yes. I understand that."

He turned back to the window, looking out. "All that hatred down there," he said, "all that hatred and misery and love. It's a wonder it doesn't blow the avenue apart."

We went to the only nightclub on a short, dark street, downtown. We squeezed through the narrow, chattering, jampacked bar to the entrance of the big room, where the bandstand was. And we stood there for a moment, for the lights were very dim in this room and we couldn't see. Then, "Hello, boy," said a voice and an enormous black man, much older than Sonny or myself, erupted out of all that atmospheric lighting and put an arm around Sonny's shoulder. "I been sitting right here," he said, "waiting for you."

He had a big voice, too, and heads in the darkness turned toward us.

225   Sonny grinned and pulled a little away, and said, "Creole, this is my brother. I told you about him."

Creole shook my hand. "I'm glad to meet you, son," he said, and it was clear that he was glad to meet me *there,* for Sonny's sake. And he smiled, "You got a real musician in *your* family," and he took his arm from Sonny's shoulder and slapped him, lightly, affectionately, with the back of his hand.

"Well. Now I've heard it all," said a voice behind us. This was another musician, and a friend of Sonny's, a coal-black, cheerful-looking man, built close to the ground. He immediately began confiding to me, at the top of his lungs, the most terrible things about Sonny, his teeth gleaming like a lighthouse and his laugh coming up out of him like the beginning of an earthquake. And it turned out that everyone at the bar knew Sonny, or almost everyone; some were musicians, working there, or nearby, or not working, some were simply hangers-on, and some were there to hear Sonny play. I was introduced to all of them and they were all very polite to me. Yet it was clear that, for them, I was only Sonny's brother. Here, I was in Sonny's world. Or, rather: his kingdom. Here, it was not even a question that his veins bore royal blood.

They were going to play soon and Creole installed me, by myself, at a table in a dark corner. Then I watched them, Creole, and the little black man, and Sonny, and the others, while they horsed around, standing just below the bandstand. The light from the bandstand spilled just a little short of them and, watching them laughing and gesturing and moving about, I had the feeling that they, nevertheless, were being most careful not to step into that circle of light too suddenly: that if they moved into the light too suddenly, without thinking, they would perish in flame. Then, while I watched, one of them, the small, black man, moved into the light and crossed the bandstand and started fooling around with his drums. Then—being funny and being, also, extremely ceremonious—Creole took Sonny by the arm and led him to the piano. A woman's voice called Sonny's name and a few hands started clapping. And Sonny, also being funny and being ceremonious, and so touched, I think, that he could have cried, but neither hiding it nor showing it, riding it like a man, grinned, and put both hands to his heart and bowed from the waist.

Creole then went to the bass fiddle and a lean, very bright-skinned brown man jumped up on the bandstand and picked up his horn. So there they were, and the atmosphere on the bandstand and in the room began to change and tighten. Someone stepped up to the microphone and announced them. Then there were all kinds of murmurs. Some people at the bar shushed others. The waitress ran around, frantically getting in the last orders, guys and chicks got closer to each other, and the lights on the bandstand, on the quartet, turned to a kind of indigo. Then they all looked different there. Creole looked about him for the last time, as though he were making certain that all his chickens were in the coop, and then he—jumped and struck the fiddle. And there they were.

230   All I know about music is that not many people ever really hear it. And even then, on the rare occasions when something opens within, and the music enters, what we mainly hear, or hear corroborated, are personal, private, vanishing evocations. But the man who creates the music is hearing something else, is dealing with the roar rising from the void and imposing order on it as it hits the air. What is evoked in him, then, is of another order, more terrible because it has no words, and triumphant, too, for that same reason. And his triumph, when he triumphs, is ours. I just watched Sonny's face. His face was troubled, he was working hard, but he wasn't with it. And I had the feeling that, in a way, everyone on the bandstand was waiting for him, both waiting for him and pushing him along. But as I began to watch Creole, I realized that it was Creole who held them all back. He had them on a short rein. Up there, keeping the beat with his whole body, wailing on the fiddle, with his eyes half closed, he was listening to everything, but he was listening to Sonny. He was having a dialogue with Sonny. He wanted Sonny to leave the shoreline and strike out for the deep water. He was Sonny's witness that deep water and drowning were not the same thing—he had been there, and he knew. And he wanted Sonny to know. He was waiting for Sonny to do the things on the keys which would let Creole know that Sonny was in the water.

And, while Creole listened, Sonny moved, deep within, exactly like someone in torment. I had never before thought of how awful the relationship must be between the musician and his instrument. He has to fill it, this instrument, with the breath of life, his own. He has to make it do what he wants it to do. And a piano is just a piano. It's made out of so much wood and wires and little hammers and big ones, and ivory. While there's only so much you can do with it, the only way to find this out is to try; to try and make it do everything.

And Sonny hadn't been near a piano for over a year. And he wasn't on much better terms with his life, not the life that stretched before him now. He and the piano stammered, started one way, got scared, stopped; started another way, panicked, marked time, started again; then seemed to have found a direction, panicked again, got stuck. And the face I saw on Sonny I'd never seen before. Everything had been burned out of it, and, at the same time, things usually hidden were being burned in, by the fire and fury of the battle which was occurring in him up there.

Yet, watching Creole's face as they neared the end of the first set, I had the feeling that something had happened, something I hadn't heard. Then they finished, there was scattered applause, and then, without an instant's warning, Creole started into something else, it was almost sardonic, it was *Am I Blue*. And, as though he commanded, Sonny began to play. Something began to happen. And Creole let out the reins. The dry, low, black man said something awful on the drums, Creole answered, and the drums talked back. Then the horn insisted, sweet and high, slightly detached perhaps, and Creole listened, commenting now and then, dry, and driving, beautiful and calm and old. Then they all came together again, and Sonny was part of the family again. I could tell this from his face. He seemed to have found, right there beneath his fingers, a damn brand-new piano. It seemed that he couldn't get over it. Then, for awhile, just being happy with Sonny, they seemed to be agreeing with him that brand-new pianos certainly were a gas.

Then Creole stepped forward to remind them that what they were playing was the blues. He hit something in all of them, he hit something in me, myself, and the music tightened and deepened, apprehension began to beat the air. Creole began to tell us what the blues were all about. They were not about anything very new. He and his boys up there were keeping it new, at the risk of ruin, destruction, madness, and death, in order to find new ways to make us listen. For, while the tale of how we suffer, and how we are delighted, and how we may triumph is never new, it always must be heard. There isn't any other tale to tell, it's the only light we've got in all this darkness.

235   And this tale, according to that face, that body, those strong hands on those strings, has another aspect in every country, and a new depth in every generation. Listen, Creole seemed to be saying, listen. Now these are Sonny's blues. He made the little black man on the drums know it, and the bright, brown man on the horn. Creole wasn't trying any longer to get Sonny in the water. He was wishing him Godspeed. Then he stepped back, very slowly, filling the air with the immense suggestion that Sonny speak for himself.

Then they all gathered around Sonny and Sonny played. Every now and again one of them seemed to say, amen. Sonny's fingers filled the air with life, his life. But that life contained so many others. And Sonny went all the way back, he really began with the spare, flat statement of the opening phrase of the song. Then he began to make it his. It was very beautiful because it wasn't hurried and it was no longer a lament. I seemed to hear with what burning he had made it his, with what burning we had yet to make it ours, how we could cease lamenting. Freedom lurked around us and I understood, at last, that he could help us to be free if we would listen, that he would never be free until we did. Yet, there was no battle in his face now. I heard what he had gone through, and would continue to go through until he came to rest in earth. He had made it his: that long line, of which we knew only Mama and Daddy. And he was giving it back, as everything must be given back, so that, passing through death, it can live forever. I saw my mother's face again, and felt, for the first time, how the stones of the road she had walked on must have bruised her feet. I saw the moonlit road where my father's brother died. And it brought something else back to me, and carried me past it, I saw my little girl again and felt Isabel's tears again, and I felt my own tears begin to rise. And I was yet aware that this was only a moment, that the world waited outside, as hungry as a tiger, and that trouble stretched above us, longer than the sky.

Then it was over. Creole and Sonny let out their breath, both soaking wet, and grinning. There was a lot of applause and some of it was real. In the dark, the girl came by and I asked her to take drinks to the bandstand. There was a long pause, while they talked up there in the indigo light and after awhile I saw a girl put a Scotch and milk on top of the piano for Sonny. He didn't seem to notice it, but just before they started playing again, he sipped from it and looked toward me, and nodded. Then he put it back on top of the piano. For me, then, as they began to play again, it glowed and shook above my brother's head like the very cup of trembling.[4]

■ EXPLORATIONS OF THE TEXT ■

1. After reading the first paragraph, what do you predict about the **narrator** and about the **plot** of the story? Why is the narrator's face "trapped in the darkness which roared outside"?
2. Explore the metaphor of "the block of ice." What does the metaphor reveal about the narrator's feelings for Sonny?
3. What characterizes the narrator's relationship with his brother at the beginning of the story?
4. Characterize the narrator. What is revealed about his personality in his constant position as an onlooker (at the window in the schoolroom, at the window in his apartment, at the jazz club)?
5. Compare and contrast the narrator and Sonny. Why have they grown up differently?
6. Why does Sonny turn to the life of the streets? drugs? What importance does music play in his life?
7. Why does the relationship between the narrator and Sonny change? What are the narrator's feelings for his brother at the end of the story?
8. What is the meaning of the scene in the club at the end? What does the narrator realize?
9. The story is told through a series of **flashbacks**. What would the story lose if it were structured chronologically?

■■ JOURNAL ENTRIES ■■

1. Baldwin wrote this story in 1957 about life in Harlem. Does this vision of life still seem real? What might Baldwin write about today?
2. Respond to a nonverbal art form (a photograph, a painting, a piece of music) so that someone unfamiliar with the work can share your feelings.
3. Can Sonny be saved by music?

---

[4] An allusion to the *Bible,* Isaiah 51:22; "I have taken out of thine hand the cup of trembling . . . thou shalt no more drink it again. . . ."

■■■ IDEAS FOR WRITING ■■■

1. Is violence part of the life of the nuclear family? Explore this **theme** in the works of Rosa, Hayden, Roethke, Boyle, and/or Baldwin.
2. How do the images of light and darkness function in this story? What do they suggest about growing up in Harlem?
3. Imagine Sonny's future.
4. What are the causes of Sonny's problems? Propose possible solutions. (Use Journal Entry 1 as a beginning.)

Summer Water and Shirley

Durango Mendoza

Born in Oklahoma to a Mexican-American father and a Creek mother, Durango Mendoza (1946–) is in many ways a participant in, and outsider to, Native-American, Chicano, and white cultures. His work has been widely published in literary journals, including Prairie Schooner.

In "Summer Water and Shirley," Mendoza combines folk tales with modern, realistic setting and characters. In this story, love between a brother and a sister overcomes everything, even death. Although Shirley provides the focus for the action, her unnamed brother becomes an unlikely hero.

1   It was in the summer that had burned every stalk of corn and every blade of grass and dried up the creek until it only flowed in trickles across the ford below the house where in the pools the boy could scoop up fish in a dishpan.

The boy lived with his mother and his sister, Shirley, and the three smaller children eleven miles from Weleetka, and near Lthwathlee Indian church where it was Eighth Sunday meeting and everyone was there. The boy and his family stayed at the camp house of his dead father's people.

Shirley and her brother, who was two years older and twelve, had just escaped the deacon and were lying on the brown, sun-scorched grass behind the last camp house. They were out of breath and giggled as they peeped above the slope and saw the figure of the deacon, Hardy Eagle, walking slowly toward the church house.

"Boy, we sure out-fooled him, huh?" Shirley laughed lightly and jabbed her elbow in her brother's shaking side. "Whew!" She ran her slim hand over her eyes and squinted at the sky. They both lay back and watched the cloudless sky until the heat in their blood went down and their breath slowed to normal. They lay there on the hot grass until the sun became too much for them.

5   "Hey, let's go down to the branch and find a pool to wade in, okay?" She had rolled over suddenly and spoke directly into the boy's ear.

"I don't think we better. Mama said to stay around the church grounds."

"Aw, you're just afraid."

"No, it's just that—"

"'Mama said to stay around the church grounds!' Fraidy-cat, I'll go by myself then." She sat up and looked at him. He didn't move and she sighed. Then she nudged him. "Hey." She nudged him again and assumed a stage whisper. "Looky there! See that old man coming out of the woods?"

10   The boy looked and saw the old man shuffling slowly through the high Johnson grass between the woods and the clearing for the church grounds. He was very old and still wore his hair in the old way.

"Who is he?" Shirley whispered. "Who is he?"

"I can't tell yet. The heat makes everything blurry." The boy was looking intently at the old man who was moving slowly in the sweltering heat through the swaying grass that moved with the sound of light tinsel in the dry wind.

"Let's go sneak through the grass and scare him," Shirley suggested. "I bet that'd make him even run." She moved her arms as if she were galloping and broke down into giggles. "Come on," she said, getting to one knee.

"Wait!" He pulled her back.

15   "What do you mean, 'wait'? He'll be out of the grass pretty soon and we won't—" She broke off. "What's the matter? What're you doing?"

The boy had started to crawl away on his hands and knees and was motioning for her to follow. "Come on, Shirley," he whispered. "That's old Ansul Middlecreek!"

"Who's *he?*"

"Don't you remember? Mama said he's the one that killed Haskell Day— with witchcraft. He's a *stiginnee!*"

"A *stiginnee?* Aw, you don't believe that, do you? Mama says you can tell them by the way they never have to go to the toilet, and that's where he's been. Look down there." She pointed to the little unpainted house that stood among the trees.

20   "I don't care *where* he's been! Come on, Shirley! Look! Oh my gosh! He saw you pointing!"

"I'm coming," she said and followed him quickly around the corner of the camp house.

They sat on the porch. Almost everyone was in for the afternoon service and they felt alone. The wind was hot and it blew from the southwest. It blew past them across the dry fields of yellow weeds that spread before them up to the low hills that wavered in the heat and distance. They could smell the dry harshness of the grass and they felt the porch boards hot underneath them. Shirley bent over and wiped her face with the skirt of her dress.

"Come on," she said. "Let's go down to the creek branch before that deacon comes back." She pulled at his sleeve and they stood up.

"Okay," he said and they skirted the outer camp houses and followed the dusty road to the bridge, stepping from tuft to tuft of scorched grass.

25 Toward evening and suppertime they climbed out of the dry bed of the branch, over the huge boulders to the road and started for the camp grounds. The sun was in their eyes as they trudged up the steep road from the bridge. They had found no water in the branch so they had gone on down to the creek. For the most part it was too dry.

Suddenly they saw a shadow move into the dust before them. They looked up and saw old Ansul Middlecreek shuffling toward them. His cracked shoes raised little clouds of dust that rose around his ankles and made whispering sounds as he moved along.

"Don't look when you go by," the boy whispered intently, and he pushed her behind him. But as they passed by, Shirley looked up.

"Hey, Ansul Middlecreek," she said cheerfully. *"Henkschay!"* [1] Then with a swish of her skirt she grabbed her brother and they ran. The old man stopped and the puffs of dust around his feet moved ahead as he grumbled, his face still in shadow because he did not turn around. The two didn't stop until they had reached the first gate. Then they slowed down and the boy scolded his sister all the way to their camp. And all through supper he looked at the dark opening of the door and then at Shirley who sat beside him, helping herself with childish appetite to the heavy, greasy food that was set before her.

"You better eat some," she told her brother. "Next meetin's not 'til next month."

30 Soon after they had left the table she began to complain that her head hurt and their mother got them ready to go home. They took the two little girls and the baby boy from where they were playing under the arbor and cleaned them up before they started out. Their uncle, George Hulegy, would go with them and carry the biggest girl. The mother carried the other one while the boy struggled in the rear with the baby. Shirley followed morosely behind them all as they started down the road that lay white and pale under the rising moon.

She began to fall further behind and shuffled her bare feet into the warm underlayer of dust. The boy gave to his uncle the sleeping child he carried and took Shirley by the hand, surprised that it was so hot and limp.

"Come on, Shirley, come on. Mama, Shirley's got a fever. Don't walk so fast—we can't keep up. Come on, Shirley," he coaxed. "Hurry."

They turned into their lane and followed it until they were on the little hill above the last stretch of road and started down its rocky slope to the sandy road below. Ahead, the house sat wanly under the stars, and Rey, the dog, came out to greet them, sniffing and wriggling his black body and tail.

George Hulegy and the mother were already on the porch as the boy led his sister into the yard. As they reached the porch they saw the lamp begin to glow

---

[1] Hello.

orange in the window. Then Shirley took hold of the boy's arm and pointed weakly toward the back yard and the form of the storehouse.

35   "Look, Sonny! Over there, by the storehouse:" The boy froze with fear but he saw nothing. "They were three little men," she said vaguely and then she collapsed.

"Mama!" But as he screamed he saw a great yellow dog with large brown spots jump off the other end of the porch with a click of its heavy nails and disappear into the shadows that led to the creek. The boy could hear the brush rustle and a few pebbles scatter as it went. Rey only whined uneasily and did not even look to where the creature had gone.

"What is it? What's wrong?" The two older persons had come quickly onto the porch and the mother bent immediately to help her daughter.

"Oh, Shirley! George! Help me. Oh gosh! She's burning up. Sonny, put back the covers of the big bed. Quick now!"

They were inside now and the boy spoke.

40   "She saw dwarfs," he said solemnly and the mother looked at George Hulegy. "And there was a big yellow dog that Rey didn't even see."

"Oh, no, no," the mother wailed and leaned over Shirley who had begun to writhe and moan. "Hush, baby, hush. Mama's here. Hush, baby, your Mama's here." She began to sing softly a very old song while George Hulegy took a lantern from behind the stove.

"I'm going to the creek and get some pebbles where the water still runs," he said. "I have to hurry." He closed the screen quietly behind him and the boy watched him as he disappeared with the swinging lantern through the brush and trees, down into the darkness to the ford. Behind him the mother still sang softly as Shirley's voice began to rise, high and thin like a very small child's. The boy shivered in the heat and sat down in the corner to wait helplessly as he tried not to look at the dark space of the window. He grew stiff and tired trying to control his trembling muscles as they began to jump.

Then George Hulegy came in with some pebbles that still were dripping and they left little wet spots of dark on the floor as he placed them above all the doors and windows throughout the house. Finally he placed three round ones at the foot of the bed where Shirley lay twisting and crying with pain and fever.

The mother had managed to start a small fire in the kitchen stove and told the boy to go out and bring in a few pieces of cook wood from the woodpile. He looked at her and couldn't move. He stood stiff and alert and heard George Hulegy, who was bending close over Shirley, muttering some words that he could not understand. He looked at the door but the sagging screen only reflected the yellow lamplight so that he couldn't see through into the darkness; he froze even tighter.

45   "Hurry, son!"

He looked at Shirley lying on the bed and moving from side to side.

"Sonny, I have to make Shirley some medicine!" His body shook from a spasm. The mother saw and turned to the door.

"I'll get them," she said.

"Mama!"

50   She stopped and he barged through the door and found the darkness envelop him. As he fixed his wide-open gaze on the woodpile that faintly reflected the starlight and that of the moon which had risen above the trees, he couldn't look to either side nor could he run. When he reached for the first piece of wood, the hysteria that was building inside him hardened into an aching bitter core. He squeezed the rough cool wood to his chest and felt the fibers press into his bare arms as he staggered toward the house and the two rectangles of light. The closer he came the higher the tension inside him stretched until he could scarcely breathe. Then he was inside again and he sat limply in the corner, light and drained of any support. He could feel nothing except that Shirley was lying in the big feather bed across the room, wailing with hurt and a scalding fever.

His mother was hurrying from the kitchen with a tin cup of grass tea when Shirley began to scream, louder and louder until the boy thought that he would never hear another sound as he stood straight and hard, not leaning at all.

She stopped.

In the silence he saw his mother standing above and behind the lamp, casting a shadow on the ceiling, stopped with fear as they heard the other sound. The little girls had come into the room from their bedroom and were standing whimpering in their nightgowns by the door. The mother signaled and they became still and quiet, their mouths slightly open and their eyes wide. They heard nothing.

Then like a great, beating heart the sound rose steadily until they could smell the heat of a monstrous flesh, raw and hot. Steadily it grew to a gagging, stifling crescendo—then stopped. They heard the click of dog's nails on the porch's wooden planks, and afterwards, nothing. In the complete silence the air became cold for an instant and Shirley was quiet.

55 It was three days now since Shirley had begun to die and everyone knew now and had given up any hope. Even the white doctor could find nothing wrong and all the old Indians nodded their solemn heads when he went away saying that Shirley would be up in a few days, for now, to them, her manner of death was confirmed. He said to send for him if there was any "real" change. No need to move her—there was nothing wrong—nothing physically wrong, he had said. He could not even feel her raging fever. To him Shirley was only sleeping.

Everyone had accepted that Shirley was going to die and they were all afraid to go near her. "There is evil around her," they said. They even convinced the mother to put her in the back room and close off all light and only open it after three days. She would not die until the third day's night, nor would she live to see the fourth day's dawn. This they could know. A very old woman spoke these words to the mother and she could not disbelieve.

On this third day the boy sat and watched the flies as they crawled over the dirty floor, over the specks and splotches, the dust and crumbs. They buzzed and droned about some drops of water, rubbing their legs against themselves, nibbling, strutting, until the drops dried into meaningless little

rings while the hot wind blew softly through the open window, stirring particles of dust from the torn screen. A droplet of sweat broke away from above
his eyebrow and ran a crooked rivulet down his temple until he wiped it away.
In his emptiness the boy did not want his sister to die.

"Mama?"

"What is it, son?"

60   "Is Shirley going to die?"

"Yes, son."

He watched her as she stood with her back to him. She moved the heavy
skillet away from the direct heat and turned the damper so that the flames
would begin to die. She moved automatically, as if faster movement would
cause her to breathe in too much of the stifling heat. And as she moved the
floor groaned under the shift in weight and her feet made whispering sounds
against the sagging boards. The flies still flitted about, mindless and nasty, as
the boy looked away from them to his mother.

"Does she have to, Mama?"

"Shirley is dying, son."

65   Again he saw how the flies went about, unaware of the heat, himself, his
mother across the room or that Shirley lay in her silence in the back room.
He splashed some more water from his glass and they knew he was there but
immediately forgot and settled back to their patternless walking about. And
even though the table was clean they walked jerkily among the dishes and
inspected his tableware. The boy had lived all his life among these creatures,
but now he could not stand their nature.

"Darn flies!"

"Well, we won't have to worry when cold weather gets here," she said.
"Now go call the kids and eat. I want to get some sewing done this afternoon."

He said nothing and watched her as she went into the other room. He
went to the door and leaned out to call the small children. Then he slipped
quietly into the back room and closed the door behind him, fastening the
latch in the dark. The heat was almost choking and he blinked away the salti-
ness that stung his eyes. He stood by the door until he could see a little better. High above his head a crack in the shingles filtered down a star of
daylight and he stepped to the bed that stood low against the rough planks of
the wall. There were no flies in this room and there was no sound.

The boy sat down on a crate and watched the face of his sister emerge
from the gloom where she lay. Straining his eyes, he finally saw the rough
army blanket rise and fall, but so slight was the movement that when his eyes
lost their focus he could not see it and he quickly put out his hand, but
stopped. Air caught in his throat and he stifled a cough, still letting his hand
hover over the motionless face. Then he touched the smooth forehead and
jerked his hand away as if he had been burned.

70   He sat and watched his sister's well-formed profile and saw how the skin
of the nose and forehead had become taut and dry and now gleamed pale and
smooth like old ivory in the semi-darkness. A smell like that of hot wood
filled the room, but underneath it the boy could smell the odor of something
raw, something evil—something that was making Shirley die.

The boy sat on the empty crate in the darkness through the late afternoon and did not answer when his mother called him. He knew that she would not even try the door to this room. He waited patiently for his thoughts to come together, not moving in the lifeless heat, and let the sweat flow from his body. He smelled the raw smell, and when it became too strong he touched the smooth, round pebbles that had come from the creek where it still flowed, and the smell receded.

For many hours he sat, and then he got up and took down the heavy blanket that had covered the single window and let the moonlight fall across the face of his sister through the opening. He began to force his thoughts to remember, to relive every living moment of his life and every part that Shirley had lived in it with him. And then he spoke softly, saying what they had done, and how they would do again what they had done because he had not given up, for he was alive, and she was alive, and they had lived and would *still* live. And so he prayed to his will and forced his will out through his thoughts and spoke softly his words and was not afraid to look out through the window into the darkness through which came the coolness of the summer night. He smelled its scents and let them touch his flesh and come to rest around the "only sleeping" face of his sister. He stood, watching, listening, living.

Then they came, silently, dark-bellied clouds drifting up from the south, and the wind, increasing, swept in the heavy scent of the approaching storm. Lightning flashed over the low, distant hills and the clouds closed quietly around the moon as the thunder rumbled and the heavy drops began to fall, slowly at first, then irregularly, then increasing to a rhythmic rush of noise as the gusts of wind forced the rain in vertical waves across the shingled roof.

Much later, when the rain had moved ahead and the room became chilly when the water began to drip from the roof and the countless leaves, the boy slipped out of his worn denim pants and took off his shirt and lay down beside his sister. She felt him and woke up.

75   "You just not gettin' to bed?" she asked. "It's pretty late for that, ain't it?"

"No, Shirley," he said. "Go on back to sleep. It'll be morning pretty soon, and when it gets light again we'll go see how high the water's risen in the creek."

He pulled the cover over him and drew his bare arms beneath the blanket and pulled it over their shoulders as he turned onto his side. Lying thus, he could see in the darkness the even darker shapes of the trees and the storehouse his father had built.

■ EXPLORATIONS OF THE TEXT ■

1. What is the role of the opening paragraph? What can you predict about the story from the opening?
2. How are Shirley and her brother characterized? Consider their interchange at the beginning of the story.

3. What role do Native-American beliefs—specifically the relation to nature—play in the story?
4. What is the role of Ansul Middlecreek?
5. How do the images of drought, water, wind, and rain create the message of the story?
6. What is the nature of Shirley's illness?
7. How and why is the boy able to cure his sister? Why are the adults not able to heal Shirley?
8. How does the brother's character change? What moves him to action?
9. What does the story teach us about love and about relationships?

■■ JOURNAL ENTRIES ■■

1. What Native-American traditions appear in this story?
2. How does your relationship with an older/younger sibling compare with either "Sonny's Blues," *Ceremonies in Dark Old Men,* or this story?

■■■ IDEAS FOR WRITING ■■■

1. Do you think Americans have a strong sense of the mythic or spiritual? What has replaced spiritual values?
2. Compare this story with Native-American visions by Erdrich (in Chapter 4) or Ortiz (in this chapter).

Scar
from The Joy Luck Club

Amy Tan

Amy Tan (1952–   ) was born in Oakland, California, shortly after her parents immigrated to the United States from China. Her father, an electrical engineer and Baptist minister who died when Tan was fifteen, shared his knowledge of Chinese and Western literature with his daughter. Her mother had been born into a well-to-do Shanghai family and left China after a disastrous first marriage. Tan recalls her mother's life in China in her second book, The Kitchen God's Wife *(1991).*

Tan received a B.A. from San Francisco State University and an M.A. from San Jose University. After graduation, Tan concentrated on technical and business writing. Not until she read Louise Er-drich's novel Love Medicine—*stories about successive generations of Native-Americans—did Tan decide to write about her own culture's painful and often humorous experiences.*

The Joy Luck Club (1989), excerpted here, contains sixteen stories related by a group of Chinese immigrant women and their four American-born daughters. The stories reveal the poignant, often comical circumstances of the characters as they struggle to identify themselves as women, mothers, daughters, wives, Americans, and, of course, Chinese.

In "Scar," An-Mei Hsu, one of the mothers, relates her recollection of a central episode in her relationship with her mother, a scorned and shamed fourth wife of a wealthy businessman.

1 When I was a young girl in China, my grandmother told me my mother was a ghost. This did not mean my mother was dead. In those days, a ghost was anything we were forbidden to talk about. So I knew Popo wanted me to forget my mother on purpose, and this is how I came to remember nothing of her. The life that I knew began in the large house in Ningpo with the cold hallways and tall stairs. This was my uncle and auntie's family house, where I lived with Popo and my little brother.

But I often heard stories of a ghost who tried to take children away, especially strong-willed little girls who were disobedient. Many times Popo said aloud to all who could hear that my brother and I had fallen out of the bowels of a stupid goose, two eggs that nobody wanted, not even good enough to crack over rice porridge. She said this so that the ghosts would not steal us away. So you see, to Popo we were also very precious.

All my life, Popo scared me. I became even more scared when she grew sick. This was in 1923, when I was nine years old. Popo had swollen up like an overripe squash, so full her flesh had gone soft and rotten with a bad smell. She would call me into her room with the terrible stink and tell me stories. "An-mei," she said, calling me by my school name. "Listen carefully." She told me stories I could not understand.

One was about a greedy girl whose belly grew fatter and fatter. This girl poisoned herself after refusing to say whose child she carried. When the monks cut open her body, they found inside a large white winter melon.

5 "If you are greedy, what is inside you is what makes you always hungry," said Popo.

Another time, Popo told me about a girl who refused to listen to her elders. One day this bad girl shook her head so vigorously to refuse her auntie's simple request that a little white ball fell from her ear and out poured all her brains, as clear as chicken broth.

"Your own thoughts are so busy swimming inside that everything else gets pushed out," Popo told me.

Right before Popo became so sick she could no longer speak, she pulled me close and talked to me about my mother. "Never say her name," she warned. "To say her name is to spit on your father's grave."

The only father I knew was a big painting that hung in the main hall. He was a large, unsmiling man, unhappy to be so still on the wall. His restless eyes followed me around the house. Even from my room at the end of the hall, I could see my father's watching eyes. Popo said he watched me for any signs of disrespect. So sometimes, when I had thrown pebbles at other children at school, or had lost a book through carelessness, I would quickly walk by my father with a know-nothing look and hide in a corner of my room where he could not see my face.

10   I felt our house was so unhappy, but my little brother did not seem to think so. He rode his bicycle through the courtyard, chasing chickens and other children, laughing over which ones shrieked the loudest. Inside the quiet house, he jumped up and down on Uncle and Auntie's best feather sofas when they were away visiting village friends.

But even my brother's happiness went away. One hot summer day when Popo was already very sick, we stood outside watching a village funeral procession marching by our courtyard. Just as it passed our gate, the heavy framed picture of the dead man toppled from its stand and fell to the dusty ground. An old lady screamed and fainted. My brother laughed and Auntie slapped him.

My auntie, who had a very bad temper with children, told him he had no *shou*, no respect for ancestors or family, just like our mother. Auntie had a tongue like hungry scissors eating silk cloth. So when my brother gave her a sour look, Auntie said our mother was so thoughtless she had fled north in a big hurry, without taking the dowry furniture from her marriage to my father, without bringing her ten pairs of silver chopsticks, without paying respect to my father's grave and those of our ancestors. When my brother accused Auntie of frightening our mother away, Auntie shouted that our mother had married a man named Wu Tsing who already had a wife, two concubines, and other bad children.

And when my brother shouted that Auntie was a talking chicken without a head, she pushed my brother against the gate and spat on his face.

"You throw strong words at me, but you are nothing," Auntie said. "You are the son of a mother who has so little respect she has become *ni*, a traitor to our ancestors. She is so beneath others that even the devil must look down to see her."

15   That is when I began to understand the stories Popo taught me, the lessons I had to learn for my mother. "When you lose your face, An-mei," Popo often said, "it is like dropping your necklace down a well. The only way you can get it back is to fall in after it."

Now I could imagine my mother, a thoughtless woman who laughed and shook her head, who dipped her chopsticks many times to eat another piece of sweet fruit, happy to be free of Popo, her unhappy husband on the wall, and

her two disobedient children. I felt unlucky that she was my mother and unlucky that she had left us. These were the thoughts I had while hiding in the
corner of my room where my father could not watch me.

I was sitting at the top of the stairs when she arrived. I knew it was my
mother even though I had not seen her in all my memory. She stood just
inside the doorway so that her face became a dark shadow. She was much
taller than my auntie, almost as tall as my uncle. She looked strange, too, like
the missionary ladies at our school who were insolent and bossy in their too-
tall shoes, foreign clothes, and short hair.

My auntie quickly looked away and did not call her by name or offer her
tea. An old servant hurried away with a displeased look. I tried to keep very
still, but my heart felt like crickets scratching to get out of a cage. My mother
must have heard, because she looked up. And when she did, I saw my own
face looking back at me. Eyes that stayed wide open and saw too much.

In Popo's room my auntie protested, "Too late, too late," as my mother
approached the bed. But this did not stop my mother.

20   "Come back, stay here," murmured my mother to Popo. "*Nuyer* is here.
You daughter is back." Popo's eyes were open, but now her mind ran in many
different directions, not staying long enough to see anything. If Popo's mind
had been clear she would have raised her two arms and flung my mother out
of the room.

I watched my mother, seeing her for the first time, this pretty woman
with her white skin and oval face, not too round like Auntie's or sharp like
Popo's. I saw that she had a long white neck, just like the goose that had laid
me. That she seemed to float back and forth like a ghost, dipping cool cloths
to lay on Popo's bloated face. As she peered into Popo's eyes, she clucked soft
worried sounds. I watched her carefully, yet it was her voice that confused
me, a familiar sound from a forgotten dream.

When I returned to my room later that afternoon, she was there, standing tall. And because I remember Popo told me not to speak her name, I stood
there, mute. She took my hand and led me to the settee. And then she also sat
down as though we had done this every day.

My mother began to loosen my braids and brush my hair with long
sweeping strokes.

"An-mei, you have been a good daughter?" she asked, smiling a secret
look.

25   I looked at her with my know-nothing face, but inside I was trembling. I
was the girl whose belly held a colorless winter melon.

"An-mei, you know who I am," she said with a small scold in her voice.
This time I did not look for fear my head would burst and my brains would
dribble out of my ears.

She stopped brushing. And then I could feel her long smooth fingers rubbing and searching under my chin, finding the spot that was my smooth-neck
scar. As she rubbed this spot, I became very still. It was as though she were
rubbing the memory back into my skin. And then her hand dropped and she

began to cry, wrapping her hands around her own neck. She cried with a wailing voice that was so sad. And then I remembered the dream with my mother's voice.

I was four years old. My chin was just above the dinner table, and I could see my baby brother sitting on Popo's lap, crying with an angry face. I could hear voices praising a steaming dark soup brought to the table, voices murmuring politely, *"Ching! Ching!"*—Please, eat!

And then the talking stopped. My uncle rose from his chair. Everyone turned to look at the door, where a tall woman stood. I was the only one who spoke.

30   "Ma," I had cried, rushing off my chair, but my auntie slapped my face and pushed me back down. Now everyone was standing up and shouting, and I heard my mother's voice crying, "An-mei! An-mei!" Above this noise, Popo's shrill voice spoke.

"Who is this ghost? Not an honored widow. Just a number-three concubine. If you take your daughter, she will become like you. No face. Never able to lift up her head."

Still my mother shouted for me to come. I remember her voice so clearly now. An-mei! An-mei! I could see my mother's face across the table. Between us stood the soup pot on its heavy chimney-pot stand—rocking slowly, back and forth. And then with one shout this dark boiling soup spilled forward and fell all over my neck. It was as though everyone's anger were pouring all over me.

This was the kind of pain so terrible that a little child should never remember it. But it is still in my skin's memory. I cried out loud only a little, because soon my flesh began to burst inside and out and cut off my breathing air.

I could not speak because of this terrible choking feeling. I could not see because of all the tears that poured out to wash away the pain. But I could hear my mother's crying voice. Popo and Auntie were shouting. And then my mother's voice went away.

35   Later that night Popo's voice came to me.

"An-mei, listen carefully." Her voice had the same scolding tone she used when I ran up and down the hallway. "An-mei, we have made your dying clothes and shoes for you. They are all white cotton."

I listened, scared.

"An-mei," she murmured, now more gently. "Your dying clothes are very plain. They are not fancy, because you are still a child. If you die, you will have a short life and you will still owe your family a debt. Your funeral will be very small. Our mourning time for you will be very short."

And then Popo said something that was worse than the burning on my neck.

40   "Even your mother has used up her tears and left. If you do not get well soon, she will forget you."

Popo was very smart. I came hurrying back from the other world to find my mother.

Every night I cried so that both my eyes and my neck burned. Next to my bed sat Popo. She would pour cool water over my neck from the hollowed cup of a large grapefruit. She would pour and pour until my breathing became soft and I could fall asleep. In the morning, Popo would use her sharp fingernails like tweezers and peel off the dead membranes.

In two years' time, my scar became pale and shiny and I had no memory of my mother. That is the way it is with a wound. The wound begins to close in on itself, to protect what is hurting so much. And once it is closed, you no longer see what is underneath, what started the pain.

I worshipped this mother from my dream. But the woman standing by Popo's bed was not the mother of my memory. Yet I came to love this mother as well. Not because she came to me and begged me to forgive her. She did not. She did not need to explain that Popo chased her out of the house when I was dying. This I knew. She did not need to tell me she married Wu Tsing to exchange one unhappiness for another. I knew this as well.

45   Here is how I came to love my mother. How I saw in her my own true nature. What was beneath my skin. Inside my bones.

It was late at night when I went to Popo's room. My auntie said it was Popo's dying time and I must show respect. I put on a clean dress and stood between my auntie and uncle at the foot of Popo's bed. I cried a little, not too loud.

I saw my mother on the other side of the room. Quiet and sad. She was cooking a soup, pouring herbs and medicines into the steaming pot. And then I saw her pull up her sleeve and pull out a sharp knife. She put this knife on the softest part of her arm. I tried to close my eyes, but could not.

And then my mother cut a piece of meat from her arm. Tears poured from her face and blood spilled to the floor.

My mother took her flesh and put it in the soup. She cooked magic in the ancient tradition to try to cure her mother this one last time. She opened Popo's mouth, already too tight from trying to keep her spirit in. She fed her this soup, but that night Popo flew away with her illness.

50   Even though I was young, I could see the pain of the flesh and the worth of the pain.

This is how a daughter honors her mother. It is *shou* so deep it is in your bones. The pain of the flesh is nothing. The pain you must forget. Because sometimes that is the only way to remember what is in your bones. You must peel off your skin, and that of your mother, and her mother before her. Until there is nothing. No scar, no skin, no flesh.

■ **EXPLORATIONS OF THE TEXT** ■

1.   Why is An-Mei Hsu's mother considered a "ghost" by the family? Why is she a "ghost" to the little girl?
2.   Why does Popo tell the child scary stories?

3. What are An-Mei's feelings about her father? Explain the symbolism of the portrait.
4. What motivates Auntie's behavior? What effect do her actions have on An-Mei and on her brother?
5. What are the connotations of "luck" in this story?
6. Does An-Mei feel that her mother loves her when her mother returns?
7. What are the symbolic implications of the scenes in which An-Mei becomes sick because the soup spilled and in which An-Mei's mother cut her own flesh and put it into the soup for her mother, Popo?

■■ JOURNAL ENTRIES ■■

1. What is the importance of the scar? Discuss the meaning of this passage: "In two years' time, my scar became pale and shiny and I had no memory of my mother. That is the way it is with a wound. The wound begins to close in on itself, to protect what is hurting so much. And once it is closed, you no longer see what is underneath, what started the pain."
2. What does the closing paragraph reveal? What is meant by "You must peel off your skin, and that of your mother, and her mother before her. Until there is nothing. No scar, no skin, no flesh."?

■■■ IDEAS FOR WRITING ■■■

1. What does "Scar" imply about the relationships of parents and children in Chinese society? How are children supposed to behave? What values are important?
2. Explore the theme of intense connectedness between mothers and their daughters and sons in "The Rocking-Horse Winner," "Girl," "From the House of Yemanjá," and/or "Scar."
3. Explore the theme of loss between parents and children in "Scar," "The Rocking-Horse Winner," "Daddy," and/or "Ruth's Song."
4. What do images or dreams suggest about the hold of the past in "Scar," "The Third Bank of the River," "The Rocking-Horse Winner," "Making the Jam Without You," and/or "Ruth's Song"?

On My First Son [1]

Ben Jonson

Ben Jonson (1572(?)–1637) was born in London shortly after the death of his father, a Scottish minister. He attended Westminster School and then became apprenticed as a bricklayer, his stepfather's trade. Although his formal education was limited to those years at Westminster, he is considered the most learned of the Elizabethan dramatists.

For a short time he served as a soldier in the Netherlands, then returned to England, married, and worked as an actor and as a playwright. Jonson's first original play, Every Man in His Humour, *was performed in 1598, the same year that he was imprisoned for killing a fellow actor in a duel. The play also featured Shakespeare as a cast member. Jonson narrowly escaped execution by citing an ancient law which forbade hanging literate people. Jonson continued to write satirical plays that assailed Elizabethan morals and his fellow playwrights.*

After the death of Queen Elizabeth and the accession of James I in 1603, Jonson wrote a few classical tragedies before turning his attention to writing twenty-four masques for the new court. Between 1605 and 1616, he also wrote five comedies which were the jewels of his dramatic career: Volpone, or the Fox *(1605),* Epicene, or the Silent Woman *(1609),* The Alchemist *(1610),* Bartholomew Fair *(1614), and* The Devil is an Ass *(1616). All satirized greed, hypocrisy, and other foibles of the age.*

Jonson's nondramatic verse, while not as famous as his plays, inspired an entourage of seventeenth century Cavalier poets, the "Sons of Ben," to compose verses reminiscent of Jonson's style and subject matter. Jonson's balanced and controlled lyrics often celebrate courtly manners, the good life, the power of friendship, the psychology of love, and the desire to minimize the ravages of time.

Among the Epigrams *is a poem mourning the death of his seven-year-old son, Benjamin, who died of the plague in 1603 when Jonson was away.*

---

[1] Jonson's oldest son, Benjamin, died in 1603 on his seventh birthday.

Farewell, thou child of my right hand,[2] and joy;
My sin was too much hope of thee, loved boy;
Seven years thou wert lent to me, and I thee pay,
Exacted by thy fate, on the just day.
5 Oh, could I lose all father, now! For why
Will man lament the state he should envy?
To have so soon scaped world's, and flesh's rage,
And, if no other misery, yet age?
Rest in soft peace, and, asked, say here doth lie
10 Ben Jonson his best piece of poetry,
For whose sake, henceforth, all his vows be such,
As what he loves may never like too much.

■ EXPLORATIONS OF THE TEXT ■

1. How does the **allusion** to the Hebrew source of the child's name create an effect in the opening?
2. What **metaphoric reference** does Jonson make in lines 3 and 4? How does the metaphor strengthen the lament?
3. Explain the lines: "Oh, could I lose all father, now! For why/Will man lament the state he should envy?/To have so soon scaped world's and flesh's rage."
4. What poetic device is evident in "soft peace"? What is its effect upon a reader?
5. Why does the speaker call his son, "his best piece of poetry"?
6. What is revealed in the closing couplet?
7. What is the rhyme scheme? How does rhyme reinforce meaning?

■■ JOURNAL ENTRIES ■■

1. How does a parent feel who has lost a child?

■■■ IDEAS FOR WRITING ■■■

1. **Explicate** this poem.
2. Discuss the grief of the loss of children in "Heart's Needle" and "On My First Son."

---

[2] Translated literally from the Hebrew, the name means Ben—"son of"—and Jamin—"my right hand."

Preface to a Twenty Volume Suicide Note

Amiri Baraka

*Born Everett LeRoi Jones in Newark, New Jersey, Baraka (1934–   )
changed his name in 1967 to the Muslim appellation Imamu Ameer
Baraka (later modified to Amiri Baraka). A precocious child, Baraka
wrote science fiction, designed comic strips, and graduated two
years early from high school. He attended Rutgers and Howard Universities before serving two and a half years in the Air Force. During
the early 1960s, Baraka lived in Greenwich Village, obtained an
M.A. in Philosophy and one in German and socialized with bohemian, beat generation writers. He published the small but important magazines* Yugen *and* Bear *with his first wife. His first book of
poetry,* Preface to a Twenty Volume Suicide Note *(1961), was published prior to Baraka's trip to Cuba. While there, Baraka underwent radical political and artistic changes.*

Fame arrived with the 1964 publication of his play, Dutchman,
*about a murderous encounter between a young black man and a
white woman. Baraka won the* Village Voice *Obie Award. He founded
the Black Arts Repertory Theater in Harlem, then in 1966 relocated
to the slums of Newark where he organized a community called
Spirit House.*

*In 1974, Baraka became a socialist. A controversial, prolific
writer whose works span the literary spectrum, Baraka has brought
radical politics into mainstream North American literature. In addition to the Obie, Baraka has received fellowships from the Guggenheim, Rockefeller, and John Whitney foundations, an American
Book Award, and prizes from the International Art Festival, the National Endowment for the Arts, and the New Jersey Council for
the Arts.*

*This poem, the title work from Baraka's first volume, presents a
father's fears and hopes for his young daughter whose "clasped
hands" symbolize a tender and fragile movement against all of the
forces that seem to eradicate the will to live.*

(For Kellie Jones, born 16 May 1959)

Lately, I've become accustomed to the way
The ground opens up and envelops me
Each time I go out to walk the dog.
Or the broad-edged silly music the wind
5 Makes when I run for a bus . . .

Things have come to that.

And now, each night I count the stars,
And each night I get the same number.
And when they will not come to be counted,
10 I count the holes they leave.

Nobody sings anymore.

And then last night, I tiptoed up
To my daughter's room and heard her
Talking to someone, and when I opened
15 The door, there was no one there . . .
Only she on her knees, peeking into

Her own clasped hands.

■ EXPLORATIONS OF THE TEXT ■

1. What is the mood of the speaker in the opening lines? What images suggest his feelings?
2. What is the significance of music—the absence of song—in this poem?
3. What is the significance of the daughter's gesture of peeking into her own clasped hands?
4. What does the title mean? How does it explain the closing line?
5. Why does Baraka have three short lines, separated as stanzas? How do they convey the message of the poem?
6. Why does Baraka begin stanzas with "Lately," "And now," and "And then"? What do these transition words accomplish?
7. How does the speaker feel about his daughter? What does she represent to him?

■■ JOURNAL ENTRIES ■■

1. Is the experience of parenting different for mothers and for fathers? Refer to two works which you have read.

2. Describe a moment when you watched someone who was not aware of your presence.

1. How does Baraka use figurative language in this poem? Is the figurative language effective?
2. What do children represent and give to their parents in two of the following poems: "Preface to a Twenty Volume Suicide Note," "Heart's Needle," "Making the Jam Without You," "My Little Girl, My Stringbean, My Lovely Woman"?

Heart's Needle

W. D. Snodgrass

William Dewitt Snodgrass (1926–) was born in Wilkinsburg, Pennsylvania, and grew up near the West Virginia border. Snodgrass attended Geneva College, interrupting his undergraduate work with military service at the end of World War II. Snodgrass received his B.A., M.A., and M.F.A. in Creative Writing from the University of Iowa. He has taught at several universities and colleges and has led a number of poetry workshops.

Although credited as a co-founder of the "confessional" school of poetry, Snodgrass eschews the term and association with it. Even so, the self-analytic style which distinguishes his Pulitzer Prize winning first collection, Heart's Needle *(1959), was widely imitated by students of the confessional mode. The title, selected from an old Irish saying that "An only daughter is the needle in the heart," refers to a series of poems inspired by the sense of losing his daughter because of his divorce.*

Snodgrass's second volume, After Experience, *published eleven years later in 1967, attempts in its concern with social and philosophical subjects to transcend the poetry of personal confession. The* Führer Bunker: A Cycle of Poems in Progress *(1977) is a collection of dramatic monologues spoken by men and women who shared Hitler's bunker in the last days of the Second World War. Snodgrass was accused of trying to arouse sympathy for people who do not warrant such consideration, but, rather than excusing such individuals, Snodgrass forces us to examine our common humanity.*

1.

Child of my winter, born
When the new fallen soldiers froze
In Asia's steep ravines and fouled the snows,[1]
When I was torn

5 By love I could not still,
By fear that silenced my cramped mind
To that cold war[2] where, lost, I could not find
My peace in my will,

All those days we could keep
10 Your mind a landscape of new snow
Where the chilled tenant-farmer finds, below,
His fields asleep

In their smooth covering, white
As quilts to warm the resting bed
15 Of birth or pain, spotless as paper spread
For me to write,

And thinks: Here lies my land
Unmarked by agony, the lean foot
Of the weasel tracking, the thick trapper's boot;
20 And I have planned

My chances to restrain
The torments of demented summer or
Increase the deepening harvest here before
It snows again.

■ EXPLORATIONS OF THE TEXT ■

1. Why does Snodgrass address his daughter as "child of my winter"?
2. What is the speaker's crisis? Why is he "torn" by love and fear?
3. How do the images of "landscape of new snow" and "fields asleep" characterize a father's relationship with a daughter?
4. Why does the poet use images of war? How do these images relate to the love the speaker "could not still"?
5. What is the significance of the seasonal imagery in the poem? How do the images of snow change?

---

[1] Reference to the Korean War.
[2] Another reference to the Korean War.

6.   What is his final wish for his daughter in the closing stanzas?
7.   Where does Snodgrass use **personification**? What does the technique accomplish?

■■   **JOURNAL ENTRIES**   ■■

1.   Compare Baraka's and Snodgrass's states of mind, their relationships with their daughters, and their wishes for their children.
2.   Compare your mood, state of mind, or the state of a relationship to a landscape. Try this approach: "When I am . . . . (Fill in with a mood), my mind becomes like . . . . (fill in with descriptive detail). Expand the simile, and extend it.

■■■   **IDEAS FOR WRITING**   ■■■

1.   What common pain of divorce does this poem portray? Which images support your analysis?
2.   Is this poem or Baraka's "Preface to a Twenty Volume Suicide Note" more powerful? Why?

My Papa's Waltz

Theodore Roethke

Theodore Roethke (1908–1963) was born in Saginaw, Michigan. His father, a horticulturist and greenhouse owner who died when Roethke was fourteen, had a profound effect on Roethke's life and imagination. Greenhouse imagery and recollections of a lost childhood figure prominently in Roethke's poetry.

After graduating magna cum laude from the University of Michigan in 1929, Roethke attended graduate school for a year at Harvard, then returned to the University of Michigan to complete his M.A. Roethke taught English at numerous colleges before settling at the University of Washington. Roethke's full-throttle teaching and writing styles led to exhaustion and were, in part, responsible for his well-publicized breakdowns.

Roethke spent the first fifteen years of his career cultivating his craft through, in his own words, "conscious imitation" of established poetic tradition. He borrowed from his contemporaries, W. H. Auden, Louise Bogan, and William Carlos Williams, as well as from earlier poets. His first published volume, Open House *(1941), reflected these influences; and critical reviews were favorable. He established himself immediately as an "introspective" poet, inclined to focus on the self rather than on social or political concerns. His second volume,* The Lost Son *(1948), is dominated by one of Roethke's central themes: a child's search for identity. The following poem reflects Roethke's memory of a dance with his father.*

The whiskey on your breath
Could make a small boy dizzy;
But I hung on like death:
Such waltzing was not easy.

5 We romped until the pans
Slid from the kitchen shelf;
My mother's countenance
Could not unfrown itself.

The hand that held my wrist
10 Was battered on one knuckle;
At every step you missed
My right ear scraped a buckle.

You beat time on my head
With a palm caked hard by dirt,
15 Then waltzed me off to bed
Still clinging to your shirt.

■ **EXPLORATIONS OF THE TEXT** ■

1. What first impression of the father emerges from the first three lines?
2. Both positive and negative words describe the dance. Which predominate?
3. What is the boy's reaction to the "waltzing"?
4. What is the mother's response to the dance?
5. What is the boy's relationship with his father? Does the father love his son? Does the son love his father?

■■ **JOURNAL ENTRIES** ■■

1. How do you react to this poem?
2. Rewrite this poem from the father's or mother's point of view.

■■■ IDEAS FOR WRITING ■■■

1. Use this poem as an idea for a short story.
2. Is the father well-meaning, or is he abusive?
3. Write about how the form of the poem corresponds to its subject and meaning (for example, the waltzing).

Daddy

Sylvia Plath

Sylvia Plath (1932–1963) was born in Boston, Massachusetts, the daughter of German immigrants who both taught at Boston University. She went to Smith College where Plath won a contest that sent her to work on a national magazine in New York, much like the protagonist of her novel, The Bell Jar *(1963).*

Plath won a Fulbright scholarship to Cambridge University in England where she met the poet Ted Hughes. They were married in 1956 and returned to Smith College where Plath taught for a short time. The couple returned to England where they had two children before separating. Her first volume of poems, The Colossus, *appeared in 1960. Plath committed suicide in 1963 at the age of thirty and left the manuscript containing the highly acclaimed posthumous collection of poems,* Ariel *(1965). Like Anne Sexton and Robert Lowell, she is considered a confessional poet.*

When Plath was eight years old, her father died, an event from which she never seemed to recover. Biographical accounts show some connection between the man in her famous elegy, "Daddy," the present selection, and her father. Plath herself acknowledged, however, that the two should not be confused. When she read the poem for the BBC, she suggested that the narrator, who sees her father first as a god, then as a Nazi, suffered from an Electra complex.

You do not do, you do not do
Any more, black shoe
In which I have lived like a foot
For thirty years, poor and white,
5 Barely daring to breathe or Achoo.

Daddy, I have had to kill you.
You died before I had time—

Marble-heavy, a bag full of God,
Ghastly statue[1] with one grey toe
10   Big as a Frisco seal

And a head in the freakish Atlantic
Where it pours bean green over blue
In the waters off beautiful Nauset.[2]
I used to pray to recover you.
15   Ach, du.[3]

In the German tongue, in the Polish town
Scraped flat by the roller
Of wars, wars, wars.
But the name of the town is common.
20   My Polack friend

Says there are a dozen or two.
So I never could tell where you
Put your foot, your root,
I never could talk to you.
25   The tongue stuck in my jaw.

It stuck in a barb wire snare.
Ich, ich, ich, ich,[4]
I could hardly speak.
I thought every German was you.
30   And the language obscene

An engine, an engine
Chuffing me off like a Jew.
A Jew to Dachau, Auschwitz, Belsen.[5]
I began to talk like a Jew.
35   I think I may well be a Jew.

The snows of the Tyrol,[6] the clear beer of Vienna
Are not very pure or true.
With my gypsy ancestress and my weird luck
And my Taroc pack and my Taroc pack
40   I may be a bit of a Jew.

---

[1] The Colossus at Rhodes, a gigantic statue of Apollo protecting the harbor at Rhodes; the Colossus was known as one of the seven wonders of the world.
[2] A place on the shore on Cape Cod in Massachusetts.
[3] "Oh, you" (translation from German).
[4] "I, I, I, I" (translation from German).
[5] Locations of concentration camps.
[6] Region of the Alps in West Austria and Northern Italy.

I have always been scared of *you,*
With your Luftwaffe,[7] your gobbledygoo.
And your neat moustache
And your Aryan[8] eye, bright blue.
45 Panzer-man,[9] panzer-man, O You—

Not God but a swastika
So black no sky could squeak through.
Every woman adores a Fascist,
The boot in the face, the brute
50 Brute heart of a brute like you.

You stand at the blackboard, daddy,
In the picture I have of you,
A cleft in your chin instead of your foot
But no less a devil for that, no not
55 Any less the black man who

Bit my pretty red heart in two.
I was ten when they buried you.
At twenty I tried to die
And get back, back, back to you.
60 I thought even the bones would do.

But they pulled me out of the sack,
And they stuck me together with glue.
And then I knew what to do.
I made a model of you,
65 A man in black with a Meinkampf[10] look

And a love of the rack and the screw.[11]
And I said I do, I do.
So daddy, I'm finally through.
The black telephone's off at the root,
70 The voices just can't worm through.

If I've killed one man, I've killed two—
The vampire who said he was you
And drank my blood for a year,

---

[7] The German air force.
[8] Of or pertaining to a presumed ethnic type descended from early speakers of Indo-European languages; a term used by the Nazi party in World War II to denote racial purity.
[9] A *panzer* is a "tank" (translation from German).
[10] Book written by Hitler; *My Struggle* (translation from German).
[11] Instruments of torture.

Seven years, if you want to know.
75 Daddy, you can lie back now.

There's a stake in your fat black heart
And the villagers never liked you.
They are dancing and stamping on you.
They always *knew* it was you.
80 Daddy, daddy, you bastard, I'm through.

■ EXPLORATIONS OF THE TEXT ■

1. What is the significance of the "black shoe"?
2. To what nursery rhyme does the poet allude? How does the allusion dictate the rhyme scheme? What is the emotional effect of the dominant sounds of the rhyme scheme?
3. How does the speaker first present her father? Why does she envision him as "Marble-heavy, a bag full of God"?
4. Why does she compare her father to a German? a Nazi? Why does she compare herself to a Jew?
5. Why does she compare her father to a "devil"?
6. Why does the speaker try to kill herself at twenty?
7. Why does the speaker state: "If I've killed one man, I've killed two"?
8. To what does the movie imagery in the last stanza refer? What is the effect of Plath's use of black humor.
9. Compare Plath's vision with Kafka's view of his father.

■■ JOURNAL ENTRIES ■■

1. Plath described the persona as a girl with an Electra complex. What is an Electra complex? Is this an adequate explanation for the behavior of the persona in the poem?
2. "Every woman adores a Fascist." Respond.

■■■ IDEAS FOR WRITING ■■■

1. How does Plath use sound and rhyme in "Daddy"? How do these techniques develop themes of the poem?
2. Why is the persona so angry at "Daddy"? Is the conflict resolved? Is she "through"?

My Father's Song

Simon Ortiz

Simon Ortiz (1941–   ), an Acoma Pueblo Indian, was born in Albuquerque, New Mexico. Between 1961 and 1969, Ortiz attended college. He served in the U.S. Army in Vietnam from 1963 to 1966.

Ortiz has taught in colleges on the West Coast and in the Southwest since 1974. In 1969, he won a Discovery Award from the National Endowment for the Arts. Although he published poetry earlier, Going for the Rain *(1976) is considered his first major collection. These poems follow a cyclical structure similar to a Pueblo rain song, moving from creation to death to rebirth and demonstrate that modern human beings are disturbed and sick because they have forgotten their origins. By recounting ancient Native-American folklore, they can begin to heal and to understand the world. Ortiz's next book of poems,* A Good Journey *(1977), portrays elements of the Acoma people's world view and lifestyle that Ortiz believes are common to all. Two more volumes,* Fight Back: For the Sake of the People, For the Sake of the Land *(1980) and* From Sand Creek: Rising in This Heart Which Is Our America *(1981), focus on the intertwined destinies of Native-Americans and others, alienation of human beings from their roots, and his dream for productive harmony between humans and nature. Ortiz's stories echo themes of his poetry, especially his conviction that Indians and all Americans share critical life experiences.*

In this poem, the speaker celebrates his love for his father and grandfather and the sacred role of storytelling in Native-American tradition.

> Wanting to say things,
> I miss my father tonight.
> His voice, the slight catch,
> the depth from his thin chest,
> 5 the tremble of emotion
> in something he has just said
> to his son, his song:
>
> We planted corn one Spring at Acu—
> we planted several times
> 10 but this one particular time
> I remember the soft damp sand
> in my hand.
>
> My father had stopped at one point
> to show me an overturned furrow;

15 the plowshare had unearthed
the burrow nest of a mouse
in the soft moist sand.

Very gently, he scooped tiny pink animals
into the palm of his hand
20 and told me to touch them.
We took them to the edge
of the field and put them in the shade
of a sand moist clod.

I remember the very softness
25 of cool and warm sand and tiny alive mice
and my father saying things.

■ EXPLORATIONS OF THE TEXT ■

1. Who is the speaker in the first stanza of the poem? Who is the speaker
    in the last four stanzas?
2. What picture emerges of the father in the first stanza? What images
    give you clues?
3. What does "his song" suggest about the speaker, his father, and his
    grandfather?
4. Why does the poet repeat the image of "damp sand"? How do the
    associations of "sand" change or build?
5. What is the significance of the central images of "cool and warm sand"
    and "tiny alive mice"? What do the furrows and the ploughing suggest?
6. What inheritance does the grandfather want to give to his son? What
    does the father want to leave to the speaker?

■■ JOURNAL ENTRIES ■■

1. Contrast the inability to communicate in "Daddy" with the memory of
    voice in "My Father's Song."

■■■ IDEAS FOR WRITING ■■■

1. Explicate and evaluate this poem. (See Chapter 10.)
2. What is the relation of human beings to the earth in "My Father's
    Song"?

Visions and Interpretations

Li-Young Lee

Li-Young Lee (1957–   ) was born in Indonesia to Chinese parents. In 1957, his father was jailed by then dictator Sukarno for nineteen months, sixteen of which were spent in a leper colony. After his father escaped, the family fled the country, settling in western Pennsylvania. Lee's culturally diverse background is evident in his love of both the Chinese poetry and Bible verses recited to him by his classically educated parents.

Lee's first volume of poetry, Rose, *was issued in 1986. His second volume,* The City in Which I Love You, *won the coveted Lamont Prize for poetry in 1990.*

In "Visions and Interpretations," the speaker visits his father's grave and learns that the truths of his life and of his heritage are elusive.

Because this graveyard is a hill,
I must climb up to see my dead,
stopping once midway to rest
beside this tree.

5 It was here, between the anticipation
of exhaustion, and exhaustion,
between vale and peak,
my father came down to me

and we climbed arm in arm to the top.
10 He cradled the bouquet I'd brought,
and I, a good son, never mentioned his grave,
erect like a door behind him.

And it was here, one summer day, I sat down
to read an old book. When I looked up
15 from the noon-lit page, I saw a vision
of a world about to come, and a world about to go.

Truth is, I've not seen my father
since he died, and, no, the dead
do not walk arm in arm with me.

20 If I carry flowers to them, I do so without their help,
the blossoms not always bright, torch-like,
but often heavy as sodden newspaper.

Truth is, I came here with my son one day,
and we rested against this tree,
25 and I fell asleep, and dreamed

a dream which, upon my boy waking me, I told.
Neither of us understood.
Then we went up.

Even this is not accurate.
30 Let me begin again:

Between two griefs, a tree.
Between my hands, white chrysanthemums, yellow
    chrysanthemums.

The old book I finished reading
I've since read again and again.

35 And what was far grows near,
and what is near grows more dear,

and all of my visions and interpretations
depend on what I see,

and between my eyes is always
40 the rain, the migrant rain.

■ **EXPLORATIONS OF THE TEXT** ■

1. Why does the speaker declare that his father has greeted him as a ghost?
2. Why does he use the preposition "between" so often?
3. What is the significance of his position "midway" to the top of the hill?
4. What is the symbolism of "the flowers," of "the old book," and of the "tree"?
5. Why does the speaker feel caught between generations when he takes his son to the grave? Is the conflict resolved?
6. What does the title mean? What is the "migrant rain"?
7. Why does Lee begin with **quatrains** (four-line stanzas), then shift to **triplets** (three-line stanzas), and to **couplets** (two-line stanzas)? What effects are achieved?

■■   **JOURNAL ENTRIES**   ■■

---

1. Choose a quote from the poem as the first line of a journal entry.
2. Discuss the distinctions between vision and interpretation and between truth and understanding.

■■■   **IDEAS FOR WRITING**   ■■■

---

1. How is the speaker caught between two cultures? Find evidence of this conflict in the text.
2. How does the process of denial function as both theme and structure in this poem?
3. What is the symbolism of "the old book"?

My Father Moved Through Dooms of Love

e. e. cummings

e[dward] e[stlin] cummings (1894–1962) was born in Cambridge, Massachusetts, the son of a Unitarian minister who also taught sociology at Harvard. Cummings received both B.A. and M.A. degrees from Harvard and then volunteered to serve as an ambulance driver in France during World War I. He mistakenly was imprisoned for three months in a French concentration camp, an experience he commemorated in his novel, The Enormous Room *(1922).*

For several years after the war, Cummings lived, wrote, and painted in Paris. His first book of poems, Tulips and Chimneys *(1923), typifies his lifelong battle between positive, organic life and sterile, mechanized manunkind [Cummings' term]. Despite his disregard to typographical convention, syntax, and the establishment, in general, Cummings' innovative style is often used to express fairly uncomplicated, conventional feelings.*

In a letter to a good friend, Cummings lovingly described his father as "a New Hampshire man, 6 foot 2, a crack shot & a famous fly-fisherman & a firstrate sailor . . . a preacher who . . . one beautiful Sunday in Spring remarked from the pulpit that he couldn't understand why anyone had come to hear him on such a day & horribly shocked his pewholders by crying 'the Kingdom of Heaven is no spiritual roofgarden: it's inside you.'" Cummings' innovative and experimental poem presents a compelling portrait of the father and of the relationship of father and son.

my father moved through dooms of love
through sames of am through haves of give,
singing each morning out of each night
my father moved through depths of height

5 this motionless forgetful where
turned at his glance to shining here;
that if (so timid air is firm)
under his eyes would stir and squirm

newly as from unburied which
10 floats the first who, his april touch
drove sleeping selves to swarm their fates
woke dreamers to their ghostly roots

and should some why completely weep
my father's fingers brought her sleep:
15 vainly no smallest voice might cry
for he could feel the mountains grow.

Lifting the valleys of the sea
my father moved through griefs of joy:
praising a forehead called the moon
20 singing desire into begin

joy was his song and joy so pure
a heart of star by him could steer
and pure so now and now so yes
the wrists of twilight would rejoice

25 keen as midsummer's keen beyond
conceiving mind of sun will stand,
so strictly (over utmost him
so hugely) stood my father's dream

his flesh was flesh his blood was blood:
30 no hungry man but wished him food;
no cripple wouldn't creep one mile
uphill to only see him smile.

Scorning the pomp of must and shall
my father moved through dooms of feel;
35 his anger was as right as rain
his pity was as green as grain

septembering arms of year extend
less humbly wealth to foe and friend
than he to foolish and to wise
40 offered immeasurable is

proudly and (by octobering flame
beckoned) as earth will downward climb,
so naked for immortal work
his shoulders marched against the dark

45 his sorrow was as true as bread:
no liar looked him in the head;
if every friend became his foe
he'd laugh and build a world with snow.

My father moved through theys of we,
50 singing each new leaf out of each tree
(and every child was sure that spring
danced when she heard my father sing)

then let men kill which cannot share,
let blood and flesh be mud and mire,
55 scheming imagine, passion willed,
freedom a drug that's bought and sold

giving to steal and cruel kind,
a heart to fear, to doubt a mind,
to differ a disease of same,
60 conform the pinnacle of am

though dull were all we taste as bright,
bitter all utterly things sweet,
maggoty minus and dumb death
all we inherit, all bequeath

65 and nothing quite so least as truth
—i say though hate were why men breathe—
because my father lived his soul
love is the whole and more than all

■ EXPLORATIONS OF THE TEXT ■

1. What is the significance of the **paradoxes** "dooms of love," "haves of give," "depths of height"? How does the poet use paradox throughout the poem?
2. What is the father's power? (Look at stanzas 3–4.)
3. What is the father's philosophy of life? What is the speaker's view of his father's moral code, values, and ethics?
4. Does the speaker see his father as different from other men? What is the significance of the closing, particularly the last line?
5. What is the effect of the form, the rhythm, and the rhyme scheme in this poem? How do they enhance the meaning of the poem?
6. How effective is Cummings' technique of transforming verbs into abstractions and abstractions into particulars?

■■ JOURNAL ENTRIES ■■

1. What seems most characteristic of Cummings' poetic technique? His imagery? novel word choices? lack of punctuation or capitalization?
2. Why do you think he chose to write in this manner?
3. Create an imitation if you wish.

■■■ IDEAS FOR WRITING ■■■

1. Write a character portrait of the father.
2. Do you like this poem? Why? Why not?

The House of Yemanjá[1]

Audre Lorde

Audre Lorde (1934–1993) was born in New York City of West Indian parents. She attended National University of Mexico, Hunter College, and Columbia University where she received her M.L.S. in 1961. She subsequently worked as a librarian and taught school, and she spent a year at Tougaloo College, Mississippi, as poet-in-residence. Lorde taught writing and English at several colleges, before becoming a professor of English at Hunter College in 1980.

Lorde's work includes many volumes of poetry, fiction, and nonfiction. Her romantic poetry is sprinkled throughout her published volumes, including The New York Head Shop and Museum *(1974),* Coal *(1976), and* The Black Unicorn *(1978). Lorde's poetry of anger, perhaps her best-known work, is prevalent in* Cables to Rage *(1970) where she protests injustice toward African-Americans. Lorde also wrote an account of her courageous struggle with breast cancer and mastectomy in* The Cancer Journals *(1980). Her 1982 prose autobiography,* Zami: A New Spelling of My Name, *combines elements of West Indian mythology and history with Lorde's personal experiences.*

Lorde explains: ". . . I write for myself and my children and for as many people as possible who can read me. When I say myself, I mean not only the Audre who inhabits my body but all those feisty, incorrigible black women who insist on standing up and saying I am, and you can't wipe me out, no matter how irritating I am."

In her own note for this poem, Lorde explains that Yemanjá is the mother of the all other Yoruban deities.

> My mother had two faces and a frying pot
> where she cooked up her daughters
> into girls
> before she fixed our dinner.
> 5 My mother had two faces
> and a broken pot
> where she hid out a perfect daughter
> who was not me
> I am the sun and moon and forever hungry
> 10 for her eyes.

---

[1]"Mother of the other *Orisha* [Yoruban deities], Yemanjá is also the goddess of oceans. Rivers are said to flow from her breasts. One legend has it that a son tried to rape her. She fled until she collapsed, and from her breasts, the rivers flowed. Another legend says that a husband insulted Yemanjá's long breasts, and when she fled with her pots he knocked her down. From her breasts flowed the rivers, and from her body then sprang forth all the other *Orisha*. River-smooth stones are Yemanjá's symbol, and the sea is sacred to her followers. Those who please her are blessed with many children" [Lorde's note].

I bear two women upon my back
one dark and rich and hidden
in the ivory hungers of the other
mother
15 pale as a witch
yet steady and familiar

brings me bread and terror
in my sleep
her breasts are huge exciting anchors
20 in the midnight storm.

All this has been
before
in my mother's bed
time has no sense
25 I have no brothers
and my sisters are cruel.

Mother I need
mother I need
mother I need your blackness now
30 as the august earth needs rain.
I am
the sun and moon and forever hungry
the sharpened edge
where day and night shall meet
35 and not be
one.

■   **EXPLORATIONS OF THE TEXT**   ■

1. Why does the speaker insist that her mother "had two faces"? What do the "two faces" represent for the speaker?
2. What was the speaker's relationship as a child with her mother? as an adult? What does the adult "need" from her mother?
3. What is the significance of the broken pot (line 6)? Why is the pot "broken"?
4. What is the meaning of the repetition of the line in the last stanza?
5. What is the symbolism of "the sharpened edge/where day and night shall meet/and not be/one"? Why shall "day and night" "not be/one"?
6. Explain the title: "From the House of Yemanjá." What is the role of the mythological **allusion** to Yemanjá in the poem?

---

1. Create a **monologue** in the voice of the mother or a **dialogue** between the mother and daughter.
2. The poem presents primarily metaphors, with few specific examples of the mother's behavior. Create a catalogue of specific actions for the mother which would exemplify her "two faces."
3. Create a metaphor for your upbringing. You may begin with "My mother or father was. . . ."

---

1. Write a dialogue between the persona in this poem and her mother.
2. Do the allusions to mythology and to fairy tale strengthen the poem? Explain.

My Mother and the Bed

Lyn Lifshin

Lyn Lifshin (1944–   ), born in Burlington, Vermont, has become one of America's most prolific, widely recognized contemporary poets. During her career, she has taught writing and poetry at universities and colleges throughout the United States and has received numerous awards for her poetry.

Lifshin's first collection, Why Is the House Dissolving?, *appeared in 1968, although she had been writing poetry since age three. Many critics consider her finest work to be about historical subjects. In the* Shaker House Poems *(1976), Lifshin captures the essence of early American Shaker religious communities. Her poetic reflections on early Eskimo culture of the Arctic are contained in* Leaning South *(1977). One critic explained that in her historical poems Lifshin formulates "a psycho-historical large canvas that traces the evolution of woman within the Occident."*

Lifshin has also written a series of energetic, humorous, often satirical "Madonna" poems which feature modern female archetypes.

In "My Mother and the Bed," Lifshin writes about a mother and daughter who share a motel room; she considers the parent's desire, even compulsion, to design the daughter's life.

No, not that way she'd
say when I was 7, pulling
the bottom sheet smooth,
you've got to   saying
5 hospital corners

I wet the bed much later
than I should, until
just writing this I
hadn't thought of
10 the connection

My mother would never
sleep on sheets someone
else had   I never
saw any stains on hers
15 tho her bedroom was

a maze of powder   hair
pins   black dresses
Sometimes she brings her
own sheets to my house,
20 carries toilet seat covers

Did anybody sleep
in my   she always asks
Her sheets   her hair
she says the rooms here
25 smell funny

We drive at 3 am
slowly into Boston and
strip what looks like
two clean beds as the
30 sky gets light   I

smooth on the form
fitted flower bottom,
she redoes it

She thinks of my life
35 as a bed only she
can make right

■ **EXPLORATIONS OF THE TEXT** ■

---

1. What does the symbol of the bed reveal about each stage of the speaker's life? What does it suggest about the relationship of the speaker and her mother?
2. What conclusions do you draw about the character of the mother?
3. What is the significance of the closing stanza of the poem?
4. Does the humor in the poem add to or detract from the message?
5. Do you think the lack of punctuation enhances the poem? Why? In what ways?

■■ **JOURNAL ENTRIES** ■■

---

1. Based on your own experience and observations, what truths about the mother-daughter relationship does the poem suggest? Is the poem realistic? Why? Why not?
2. What role does humor play in this poem?

■■■ **IDEAS FOR WRITING** ■■■

---

1. Write a humorous portrayal of your relationship with a family member.
2. Analyze your essay. Is the humor effective?

Girl

Jamaica Kincaid

Jamaica Kincaid (1949–) was born in Antigua in the West Indies. Kincaid immigrated to the United States to attend college which she found "a dismal failure." She is now a naturalized citizen, living in New York City and in Bennington, Vermont. Her first collection of short stories, At the Bottom of the River *(1983), won the Morton Dauwen Zabel Award of the American Academy and Institute of Arts and Letters. In 1985, she published* Annie John, *a cycle of interrelated stories about growing up in Antigua.*

Kincaid's fiction centers on the powerful, emotional ties between mothers and daughters and the daughters' conflicting, often ambiguous needs for independence. Although the source and settings of her stories are the British West Indies, Kincaid credits the United States as the place where she discovered herself and her voice.

"Girl" was her first published piece of fiction (in The New Yorker*), written in 1977 after reading Elizabeth Bishop's "In the Waiting Room." She drafted it in one rush of energy, and it is one long sentence. The tensions that emerge suggest the mother's powerful concern for the daugher and the girl's desire both for stability and for independence from parents. This theme is prevalent in the autobiographical novels,* Annie John *and* Lucy.

1   Wash the white clothes on Monday and put them on the stone heap; wash the color clothes on Tuesday and put them on the clothesline to dry; don't walk barehead in the hot sun; cook pumpkin fritters in very hot sweet oil; soak your little cloths right after you take them off; when buying cotton to make yourself a nice blouse, be sure that it doesn't have gum on it, because that way it won't hold up well after a wash; soak salt fish overnight before you cook it; is it true that you sing benna[1] in Sunday school?; always eat your food in such a way that it won't turn someone else's stomach; on Sundays try to walk like a lady and not like the slut you are so bent on becoming; don't sing benna in Sunday school; you mustn't speak to wharf-rat boys, not even to give directions; don't eat fruits on the street—flies will follow you; *but I don't sing benna on Sundays at all and never in Sunday school;* this is how to sew on a button; this is how to make a button-hole for the button you have just sewed on; this is how to hem a dress when you see the hem coming down and so to prevent yourself from looking like the slut I know you are so bent on becoming; this is how you iron your father's khaki shirt so that it doesn't have a crease; this is how you iron your father's khaki pants so that they don't have a crease, this is how you grow okra—far from the house, because okra tree harbors red ants: when you are growing dasheen,[2] make sure it gets plenty of water or else it makes your throat itch when you are eating it; this is how you sweep a corner; this is how you sweep a whole house; this is how you sweep a yard; this is how you smile to someone you don't like too much; this is how you smile to someone you don't like at all; this is how you smile to someone you like completely; this is how you set a table for tea; this is how you set a table for dinner; this is how you set a table for dinner with an important guest; this is how you set a table for lunch; this is how you set a table for breakfast; this is how to behave in the presence of men who don't know you very well, and this way they won't recognize immediately the slut I have warned you against becoming; be sure to wash every day, even if it is with your own spit; don't squat down to play marbles—you are not a boy, you know; don't pick people's flowers—you might catch something; don't throw stones at blackbirds, because it might not be a blackbird at all; this is how to make a bread pudding; this is how to make doukona,[3] this is how to make pepper pot;[4] this is how to make a good medicine for a cold;

---

[1] Calypso music.
[2] A kind of potato.
[3] A spicy pudding made of plantains.
[4] A kind of stew.

this is how to make a good medicine to throw away a child before it even becomes a child; this is how to catch a fish; this is how to throw back a fish you don't like, and that way something bad won't fall on you; this is how to bully a man; this is how a man bullies you; this is how to love a man, and if this doesn't work there are other ways, and if they don't work don't feel too bad about giving up; this is how to spit up in the air if you feel like it, and this is how to move quick so that it doesn't fall on you; this is how to make ends meet; always squeeze bread to make sure it's fresh; *but what if the baker won't let me feel the bread?;* you mean to say that after all you are really going to be the kind of woman who the baker won't let near the bread? [1984]

■ EXPLORATIONS OF THE TEXT ■

1. Who speaks which lines in the poem?
2. The speech is a single sentence filled with commands. What do they suggest about the main speaker's intentions?
3. What is the main speaker's tone? What is the significance of the variations of the phrase, "not like the slut you are so bent on becoming"?
4. What do the girl's lines reveal about her character? about her relationship with the speaker?
5. Why does the speaker say, "You mean to say that after all you are really going to be the kind of woman who the baker won't let near the bread?"
6. What vision of female roles emerges in this piece?
7. What is the impact of the repeated phrasing, of the parallel structure, and of its form as a single sentence?

■■ JOURNAL ENTRIES ■■

1. Create an imitation of this speech as a mother/father giving advice to a child in North America. You may create the voice of your parent talking to you.
2. Become a representative figure and give advice (e.g., a teenager giving advice about how to be a "teen" in North America to a foreign student; a senior giving advice to a college freshman).

■■■ IDEAS FOR WRITING ■■■

1. What motivates the mother's speech? Is her approach effective? Why? Why not?

My Little Girl, My Stringbean, My Lovely Woman

Anne Sexton

Anne (Harvey) Sexton (1928–1974) was born in Newton, Massachu-
setts. She attended Garland Junior College, taught in high school, at
Boston University (1970–71), and at Colgate University (1971–72).
After suffering one of many nervous breakdowns, Sexton was urged
by a psychiatrist to try writing poetry. She did so with immediate
success. Among her mentors was the poet, Robert Lowell.

Anne Sexton is associated with the "confessional" school. She
drew on intensely personal subject matter for her poems, including
her immediate family, her sexuality, and experiences as a woman, her
collapse and recovery from various breakdowns, and her preoccupa-
tion with death. Anne Sexton committed suicide in 1974.

In "My Little Girl, My Stringbean, My Lovely Woman," the
speaker both celebrates her daughter's youth and sexuality and pro-
vides counsel about "growing up female."

My daughter, at eleven
(almost twelve), is like a garden.

Oh, darling! Born in that sweet birthday suit
and having owned it and known it for so long,
5 now you must watch high noon enter—
noon, that ghost hour.
Oh, funny little girl—this one under a blueberry sky,
this one! How can I say that I've known
just what you know and just where you are?

10 It's not a strange place, this odd home
where your face sits in my hand
so full of distance,
so full of its immediate fever.
The summer has seized you,
15 as when, last month in Amalfi,[1] I saw
lemons as large as your desk-side globe—
that miniature map of the world—
and I could mention, too,
the market stalls of mushrooms
20 and garlic buds all engorged.

---

[1] Town in Italy.

Or I think even of the orchard next door,
where the berries are done
and the apples are beginning to swell.
And once, with our first backyard,
25 I remember I planted an acre of yellow beans
we couldn't eat.

Oh, little girl,
my stringbean,
how do you grow?
30 *You grow this way.*
You are too many to eat.

I hear
as in a dream
the conversation of the old wives
35 speaking of *womanhood.*
I remember that I heard nothing myself.
I was alone.
I waited like a target.

Let high noon enter—
40 the hour of the ghosts.
Once the Romans believed
that noon was the ghost hour,
and I can believe it, too,
under that startling sun,
45 and someday they will come to you,
someday, men bare to the waist, young Romans
at noon where they belong,
with ladders and hammers
while no one sleeps.

50 But before they enter
I will have said,
Your bones are lovely,
and before their strange hands
there was always this hand that formed.

55 Oh, darling, let your body in,
let it tie you in,
in comfort.
What I want to say, Linda,
is that women are born twice.

60 If I could have watched you grow
as a magical mother might,
if I could have seen through my magical transparent belly,
there would have been such ripening within:
your embryo,
65 the seed taking on its own,
life clapping the bedpost,
bones from the pond,
thumbs and two mysterious eyes,
the awfully human head,
70 the heart jumping like a puppy,
the important lungs,
the becoming—
while it becomes!
as it does now,
75 a world of its own,
a delicate place.

I say hello
to such shakes and knockings and high jinks,
such music, such sprouts,
80 such dancing-mad-bears of music,
such necessary sugar,
such goings-on!

Oh, little girl,
my stringbean,
85 *how do you grow?*
You grow this way.
You are too many to eat.

What I want to say, Linda,
is that there is nothing in your body that lies.
90 All that is new is telling the truth.
I'm here, that somebody else,
an old tree in the background.

Darling,
stand still at your door,
95 sure of yourself, a white stone, a good stone—
as exceptional as laughter
you will strike fire,
that new thing!

■ EXPLORATIONS OF THE TEXT ■

1. What is the significance of the garden imagery? What is the meaning of the refrain?
2. The poem shifts from garden imagery to birth imagery. What do "birth" and "womb" images suggest about the speaker's view of her daughter's imminent adolescence?
3. What does "high noon" signify?
4. What does the speaker envision as her role in her daughter's life?
5. Explore the significance of the statement that "women are born twice."
6. What are the speaker's final wishes for her daughter expressed in the last two stanzas? How will she help her daughter in adolescence?
7. Contrast the image of the mother who "waited like a target" with the image of the daughter who "will strike fire."
8. Compare the speaker's relationship with her daughter with relationships in poems by Baraka, Snodgrass, and Kumin.

■■ JOURNAL ENTRIES ■■

1. How does Sexton use nursery and children's rhymes? How do the rhymes develop the poem's themes?
2. Based on your experience, offer advice about growing up and about sexuality to an adolescent.

■■■ IDEAS FOR WRITING ■■■

1. What are the speaker's feelings toward her daughter? How does the tone of the poem reveal her attitude? Which specific words and phrases create the tone?
2. Sexton's, Lifshin's, Lorde's, and Kincaid's works portray intense bonds between mothers and daughters. What differences appear in these writers' treatments of mother-daughter relationships?

Making the Jam Without You
for Judy

Maxine Kumin

Maxine Kumin (1925–   ) was born in Philadelphia, Pennsylvania. Although raised in a major metropolitan area, Kumin is known as a pastoral, New England poet and concedes that most of her poems "come out of this geography and state of mind." She makes her home on a farm in Warner, New Hampshire.

Kumin received her B.A. and M.A. from Radcliffe College. She has lectured at several universities across the country. A former poetry consultant to the Library of Congress, Kumin traveled with the U.S. Information Agency's Arts America Tour and served on the staff of the Bread Loaf Writers' Conference.

As a freshman at Radcliffe, she asked a professor to critique a collection of her poems. His written comments were, "Say it with flowers, but for God's sake don't try to write poems." Kumin stopped writing poetry for six years, got married, had three children, and then enrolled in writing workshops at the Boston Center for Adult Education.

Kumin's celebrated friendship with Anne Sexton began at the writing workshops. They collaborated on four children's books and generally influenced one another's artistic development by telephone and letter, although each denied interfering with the other's voice.

In 1973, Kumin received a Pulitzer Prize for her fourth volume of poetry, Up Country: Poems of New England *(1972). Along with five other poetry collections, Kumin has published several novels, twenty-two children's books, a collection of short stories, and two volumes of essays.*

Kumin's themes encompass human fragility and mortality, nature's cyclical patterns, human beings' place in the natural world, and relationships between parents and their children—what Kumin herself calls "loss of the parent, relinquishment of the child." One critic notes that "children, especially daughters, keep cropping up, growing as they go . . . no poet writes more richly and more subtly of mother–daughter relations."

> Old daughter, small traveler
> asleep in a German featherbed
> under the eaves in a postcard town
> of turrets and towers,
> 5 I am putting a dream in your head.

Listen! Here it is afternoon.
The rain comes down like bullets.
I stand in the kitchen,
that harem of good smells
10 where we have bumped hips and
cracked the cupboards with our talk
while the stove top danced with pots
and it was not clear who did
the mothering. Now I am
15 crushing blackberries
to make the annual jam
in a white cocoon of steam.

Take it, my sleeper. Redo it
in any of your three
20 languages and nineteen years.
Change the geography.
Let there be a mountain,
the fat cows on it belled
like a cathedral. Let

25 there be someone beside you
as you come upon the ruins
of a schloss,[1] all overgrown
with a glorious thicket,
its brambles soft as wool.
30 Let him bring the buckets
crooked on his angel arms
and may the berries, vaster
than any forage in
the mild hills of New Hampshire,
35 drop in your pail, plum size,
heavy as the eyes
of any honest dog
and may you bear them
home together to a square
40 white unreconstructed kitchen
not unlike this one.
Now may your two heads
touch over the kettle,
over the blood of the berries
45 that drink up sugar and sun,
over that tar-thick boil
love cannot stir down.

---

[1] Castle.

More plainly than
the bric-a-brac of shelves
50 filling with jelly glasses,
more surely than
the light driving through them
trite as rubies, I see him
as pale as paraffin beside you.
55 I see you cutting
fresh baked bread to spread it
with the bright royal fur.

At this time
I lift the flap of your dream
60 and slip out thinner than a sliver
as your two mouths open
for the sweet stain of purple.

■ EXPLORATIONS OF THE TEXT ■

1. What mood and tone are established by the speaker's imagined scene of the girl asleep "under the eaves in a postcard town"?
2. What is the mother's dream? What is the effect of the dream images (fanciful, mysterious)?
3. What is the significance of the **simile**, "the rain comes down like bullets"?
4. How does the poet develop the symbol of the berries? In what ways do the meanings of the berries change and build?
5. What is the speaker's position in the last stanza? Why does she "slip out thinner than a sliver"?
6. What is the speaker's final wish for her daughter?

■■ JOURNAL ENTRIES ■■

1. Write a monologue in the speaker's voice, and make explicit her dreams for her daughter. As a parent, would you have similar hopes?
2. How does Kumin use the imagery of the berries?

■■■ IDEAS FOR WRITING ■■■

1. What images indicate a symbiotic relationship between mother and daughter? Which images evoke the mother's letting go of the daughter?
2. Compare this poem with Lifshin's, Synge's, and Lorde's visions.

Lineage

Margaret Walker

Margaret Walker (1915–) was born in Birmingham, Alabama. Walker, whose father was a Methodist preacher and whose mother was a musician, grew up in a home dominated by oratory and the doctrine of salvation. After graduating from Northwestern University and receiving her M.A. from the University of Iowa, she worked as a magazine editor, social worker, and college lecturer in English.

Walker became the first African-American woman in American literary history to win the Yale Younger Poets Award for her first volume of poetry, For My People *(1942). The book, a collection of ballads, sonnets, and free verse, reveals the spirit, language, and perseverance of African-Americans.*

Her second book, Jubilee *(1965), an historical novel about a slave family during and after the Civil War, took Walker thirty years to complete. She was awarded a Houghton-Mifflin fellowship for this accomplishment. During these years, Walker married a disabled veteran, raised four children, taught full-time, and earned a Ph.D. Walker's next volume of poems, the highly acclaimed* Prophets for a New Day *(1970), parallels people and happenings of the 1960s with Biblical figures and events.*

"Lineage" celebrates the idea of kinship and the strengths of African-American grandmothers.

My grandmothers were strong.
They followed plows and bent to toil.
They moved through fields sowing seed.
They touched earth and grain grew.
5 They were full of sturdiness and singing.
My grandmothers were strong.

My grandmothers are full of memories
Smelling of soap and onions and wet clay
With veins rolling roughly over quick hands
10 They have many clean words to say.
My grandmothers were strong.
Why am I not as they?

■ **EXPLORATIONS OF THE TEXT** ■

1. What portrait of the grandmothers emerges from the specific details and concrete, physical images Walker uses to describe them?
2. What is the significance of "They touched earth and grain grew" and "They have many clean words to say"?
3. What is the meaning of the closing question? How does the speaker view herself in relation to her grandmothers?
4. How do repetition and parallel structure work in the poem? What is their impact?
5. What does the title mean?
6. Why are kin and the memories of kin important?

■■ **JOURNAL ENTRIES** ■■

1. Create a one-paragraph character portrait or poem about someone whom you admire through using specific details and physical, concrete images.

■■■ **IDEAS FOR WRITING** ■■■

1. Compare or contrast Alice Walker's, Margaret Walker's, and Etheridge Knight's views of the role of the artist in the preservation of cultural legacies.

The Idea of Ancestry

Etheridge Knight

Etheridge Knight (1931–   ) grew up in Indianapolis and was sentenced to prison for twenty years in 1960. He began writing poetry and short stories during this period. Eight years later, when he was released on parole, he published a remarkable volume, Poems from Prison *(1968). Knight declared, "I died in Korea from a shrapnel wound and narcotics resurrected me. I died in 1960 from a prison sentence and poetry brought me back to life."*

In 1968, Black Voices from Prison *also appeared. In her introduction to the volume, Gwendolyn Brooks wrote, "This poetry is a major announcement." "The Idea of Ancestry," chosen from this book, centers on the power of family ties to enable the speaker not only to survive, but also to prevail. Even though gray prison walls dam his stream, he feels the "stir" to swim in the cool waters like salmon, the "stir [of his] genes." Each fall he experiences reminders of his lineage, of the yearning to be part of that lineage, and of the deep desire to melt into it and beyond it.*

1

*Taped to the wall of my cell are 47 pictures: 47 black
faces: my father, mother, grandmothers (1 dead), grandfathers (both dead), brothers, sisters, uncles, aunts,
cousins (1st & 2nd), nieces, and nephews. They stare*
5 *across the space at me sprawling on my bunk. I know
their dark eyes, they know mine. I know their style,
they know mine. I am all of them, they are all of me;
they are farmers, I am a thief, I am me, they are thee.*

I have at one time or another been in love with my mother,
10 *1 grandmother, 2 sisters, 2 aunts (1 went to the asylum),
and 5 cousins. I am now in love with a 7 yr old niece
(she sends me letters written in large block print, and
her picture is the only one that smiles at me).*

I have the same name as 1 grandfather, 3 cousins, 3 nephews,
15 *and 1 uncle. The uncle disappeared when he was 15, just took
off and caught a freight (they say). He's discussed each year
when the family has a reunion, he causes uneasiness in
the clan, he is an empty space. My father's mother, who is 93
and who keeps the Family Bible with everybody's birth dates*
20 *(and death dates) in it, always mentions him. There is no
place in her Bible for "whereabouts unknown."*

*Each fall the graves of my grandfathers call me, the brown
hills and red gullies of mississippi send out their electric
messages, galvanizing my genes. Last yr / like a salmon quitting*
25 *the cold ocean-leaping and bucking up his birthstream / I
hitchhiked my way from L.A. with 16 caps[1] in my pocket and a
monkey on my back.[2] And I almost kicked it with the kinfolks.
I walked barefooted in my grandmother's backyard / I smelled the old
land and the woods / I sipped cornwhiskey from fruit jars with the
        men /*

---

[1] Capsules or vials of drugs.
[2] Being high; having a drug habit.

30 *I flirted with the women / I had a ball till the caps ran out*
and my habit came down. That night I looked at my grandmother
and split / my guts were screaming for junk[3] / but I was almost
contented / I had almost caught up with me.
(The next day in Memphis I cracked a croaker's crib for a fix.)

35 *This yr there is a gray stone wall damming my stream, and when*
the falling leaves stir my genes, I pace my cell or flop on my bunk
and stare at 47 black faces across the space. I am all of them,
they are all of me, I am me, they are thee, and I have no children
to float in the space between.

■ EXPLORATIONS OF THE TEXT ■

1. What is the importance of the setting?
2. What does the refrain "I am all of them, they are all of me" suggest?
3. Discuss the concept of the extended family in each stanza. What is the progression?
4. What is the meaning of the line, "I cracked a croaker's crib for a fix"?
5. How do the speaker's ancestors help him to survive? Do the closing lines of the poem offer clues?
6. How do the levels of style (e.g., slang, Biblical language) add to the effect of the poem?
7. Find lines which state a thesis of the poem.

■■ JOURNAL ENTRIES ■■

1. What is one "Idea of Ancestry" in this poem and in "Lineage"?
2. Assume that you are confined in a room or in a space for a prolonged period. How would you choose to decorate the walls? *OR* Select one character from this chapter, and create a room for him or her.

■■■ IDEAS FOR WRITING ■■■

1. What consequences of incarceration are expressed in this poem?
2. Write about the African-American concept of extended family. Use this poem and other works in this chapter to support your analysis.

---

[3] Heroin.

Poems for Further Reading

Lord Randal

Anonymous

"O where hae[1] ye been, Lord Randal, my son?
O where hae ye been, my handsome young man?"
"I hae been to the wild wood; mother, make my bed soon,
For I'm weary wi' hunting, and fain wald[2] lie down."

5 "Where gat[3] ye your dinner, Lord Randal, my son?
Where gat ye your dinner, my handsome young man?"
"I din'd wi' my true-love; mother, make my bed soon,
For I'm weary wi' hunting, and fain wald lie down."

"What gat ye to your dinner, Lord Randal, my son?
10 What gat ye to your dinner, my handsome young man?"
"I gat eels boil'd in broo;[4] mother, make my bed soon,
For I'm weary wi' hunting, and fain wald lie down."

"What became of your bloodhounds, Lord Randal, my son?
What became of your bloodhounds, my handsome young man?"
15 "O they swell'd and they died; mother, make my bed soon,
For I'm weary wi' hunting, and fain wald lie down."

"O I fear ye are poison'd, Lord Randal, my son!
I fear ye are poison'd, my handsome young man!"
"O yes! I am poison'd; mother, make my bed soon,
20 For I'm sick at the heart, and I fain wald lie down."

[1] Have.
[2] Would like to.
[3] Got.
[4] Broth.

On My First Daughter

Ben Jonson (1572–1637)

Here lies, to each her parents' ruth,[1]
Mary, the daughter of their youth;
Yet all heaven's gifts being heaven's due,
It makes the father less to rue.
5 At six months' end she parted hence
With safety of her innocence;
Whose soul heaven's queen, whose name she bears,
In comfort of her mother's tears,
Hath placed amongst her virgin-train:
10 Where, while that severed doth remain,
This grave partakes the fleshly birth;
Which cover lightly, gentle earth!

To My Dear and Loving Husband

Anne Bradstreet (1612?–1672)

If ever two were one, then surely we.
If ever man were loved by wife, then thee;
If ever wife was happy in a man,
Compare with me, ye women, if you can.
5 I prize thy love more than whole mines of gold
Or all the riches that the East doth hold.
My love is such that rivers cannot quench,
Nor ought but love from thee, give recompense.
Thy love is such I can no way repay,
10 The heavens reward thee manifold, I pray.
Then while we live, in love let's so persevere
That when we live no more, we may live ever.

---

[1] Grief.

The Sailor's Mother

William Wordsworth (1770–1850)

One morning (raw it was and wet—
A foggy day in winter time)
A Woman on the road I met,
Not old, though something past her prime:
5   Majestic in her person, tall and straight;
And like a Roman matron's was her mien and gait.

The ancient spirit is not dead;
Old times, thought I, are breathing there;
Proud was I that my country bred
10   Such strength, a dignity so fair:
She begged an alms, like one in poor estate;
I looked at her again, nor did my pride abate.

When from these lofty thoughts I woke,
"What is it," said I, "that you bear,
15   Beneath the covert of your Cloak,
Protected from this cold damp air?"
She answered, soon as she the question heard,
"A simple burthen, Sir, a little Singing-bird."

And, thus continuing, she said,
20   "I had a Son, who many a day
Sailed on the seas, but he is dead;
In Denmark he was cast away:
And I have travelled weary miles to see
If aught which he had owned might still remain for me.

25   "The bird and cage they both were his:
'Twas my Son's bird; and neat and trim
He kept it: many voyages
The singing-bird had gone with him;
When last he sailed, he left the bird behind;
30 From bodings, as might be, that hung upon his mind.

"He to a fellow-lodger's care
Had left it, to be watched and fed,
And pipe its song in safety;—there
I found it when my Son was dead;
35   And now, God help me for my little wit!
I bear it with me, Sir;—he took so much delight
    in it."

The Slave Mother

Frances Ellen Watkins Harper (1825–1911)

Heard you that shriek? It rose
    So wildly on the air.
It seemed as if a burden'd heart
    Was breaking in despair.

5 Saw you those hands so sadly clasped—
    The bowed the feeble head—
The shuddering of that fragile form—
    That look of grief and dread?

Saw you the sad, imploring eye?
10   Its every glance was pain,
As if a storm of agony
    Were sweeping through the brain.

She is a mother, pale with fear,
    Her boy clings to her side,
15 And in her kirtle[1] vainly tries
    His trembling form to hide.

He is not hers, although she bore
    For him a mother's pains;
He is not hers, although her blood
20   Is coursing through his veins!

He is not hers, for cruel hands
    May rudely tear apart
The only wreath of household love
    That binds her breaking heart.

25 His love has been a joyous light
    That o'er her pathway smiled,
A fountain gushing ever new,
    Amid life's desert wild.

His lightest word has been a tone
30   Of music round her heart,
Their lives a streamlet blent in one—
    Oh, Father! must they part?

[1] Loose-fitting gown.

They tear him from her circling arms,
  Her last and fond embrace.
35 Oh! never more may her sad eyes
   Gaze on his mournful face.

No marvel, then, these bitter shrieks
  Disturb the listening air:
She is a mother, and her heart
40   Is breaking in despair.

Piano

D. H. Lawrence (1885–1930)

Softly, in the dusk, a woman is singing to me;
Taking me back down the vista of years, till I see
A child sitting under the piano, in the boom of the tingling strings
And pressing the small, poised feet of a mother who smiles as she sings.

5 In spite of myself, the insidious mastery of song
Betrays me back, till the heart of me weeps to belong
To the old Sunday evenings at home, with winter outside
And hymns in the cozy parlour, the tinkling piano our guide.

So now it is vain for the singer to burst into clamour
10 With the great black piano appassionato. The glamour
Of childish days is upon me, my manhood is cast
Down in the flood of remembrance, I weep like a child for the past.

Ceremonies in Dark Old Men

Lonne Elder III

*Born in Americus, Georgia and orphaned in adolescence, Lonne El-
der III (1931–   ) is a successful playwright, screenwriter, and freelance writer. He is or has been a political activist, phone clerk, dock
worker, professional gambler, military serviceman, and actor. While
serving in the army, he met poet and teacher Robert Hayden who
read his work and urged him to continue writing. Later, he shared
an apartment with Douglas Turner Ward who, during that time,
wrote his first play. This prompted Elder to turn to the creation of
drama. His acting from 1959–1961 in* A Raisin in the Sun *and in
1965 in* A Day of Absence *gave him useful background in the theatre. His plays include* A Hysterical Turtle in a Rabbit Race *(1961),
for which he received a Christopher Award and a Pulitzer Prize
nomination,* Kissing Rattlesnakes Can Be Fun *(1966), and* Splendid
Mummer *(1988). His screenplays include* The Terrible Veil, *which
was produced on NBC television (1964); William Armstrong's*
Sounder, *which was produced and won several awards; and an adaptation of a Richard Pryor story,* Bustin' Loose *(1981).*

*About the play that follows, Elder has claimed, "Often I used to
ask myself: How did we as black Americans survive for so many years
the constant psychological and physical brutality perpetrated by
American racism and yet remain a people, a glorious and beautiful
lot? I would say that our most fervent desire was to survive and that
desire out of necessity was colored with style, ceremony, and ritual."*

Cast of Characters (In Order of Their Appearance)

Mr. Russell B. Parker
Mr. William Jenkins
Theopolis Parker
Adele Eloise Parker
Bobby Parker
Blue Haven
Young Girl

TIME: Early spring, about four-thirty in the afternoon, the present time.

PLACE: A small, poverty-stricken barber shop on 126th Street between Seventh and Lenox avenues, Harlem, U.S.A.

    There is only one barber's throne in this barber shop. There is a not too lengthy mirror running along the wall and a high, broad shelf in the immediate, reachable area of the throne. There are two decks of shelves of equal width projecting just below the main shelf. These shelves are covered by small sliding panels. To the far left corner of the shop is the street door, and to the far right corner of the shop is a door leading to a back room. Just to the right of this door, flush against the wall, is a card table with two chairs. Even farther right of this area is a clothes rack. Against the wall to the far left of the shop, near the door, are four chairs lined in uniformity.

    The back room is as all back rooms are in poverty-stricken barber shops. It has an old refrigerator, an even older antique desk, and a medium-size bed. To the far right section of the room is a short group of stairs, in sight, suggesting that they lead upwards to a first-floor apartment.

    The entire action of the play takes place in the two areas referred to in the above notes. There are no suggested lighting cues, other than those directly related to the intent and meaning of a given scene. There are sinks in both areas.

ACT I

Scene 1

As the curtain rises, Mr. Russell B. Parker is seated in the single barber's throne, reading a book. He is a man in his early or middle fifties. He rises nervously, moves to the window and peers outward with his right hand over the brows of his eyes. He returns to the throne and continues to read his book. He checks his watch, rises, and once again moves to the window to take a look-see. It appears that he recognizes the party he has been waiting for nearing him. He moves to the door and opens it. A man enters. Mr. William Jenkins: In his early fifties, dressed well in a complete suit, and carrying a newspaper under his arm.

Mr. Parker *(moves away from Mr. Jenkins toward the center of the barber shop and turns):* Where have you been?

Mr. Jenkins: Whatcha mean? You know where I was . . .

Mr. Parker: I thought you said you was gon get up here as quick as you could?

Mr. Jenkins: I'm here . . .

5 Mr. Parker: I talked to you at three o'clock . . . *(Checks his watch)*—it's now four-thirty.

Mr. Jenkins: That's as quick as I could . . .

Mr. Parker: Now I *told* you Adele would be getting home *soon* . . .

Mr. Jenkins: That's too bad, I just can't walk off and leave my job the moment you call me.

Mr. Parker: You want to play the game or not?

10 Mr. Jenkins: That's what I came here for . . .

Mr. Parker: I wanted to get in at least three games, but this way, we'll be lucky if we get in one . . . *(Bends down by the barber's chair and opens up one of the sliding panels.)*

Mr. Jenkins: Stop complaining and get the board out. I'll beat you, and that will be that.

Mr. Parker *(pulls out a checkerboard, and a small can. He moves and places the items on the table to the rear of the shop):* I can do without your bragging . . . *(Shakes up the can)* Close your eyes and take a man . . .

Mr. Jenkins *(closing his eyes):* You never learn . . . *(Reaches into the can and pulls out a checker)* It's red . . .

15 Mr. Parker: All right, I get the black . . . *(Sits at the table and rushes to place his men down in their respective spots)* Get your men down, Jenkins!

Mr. Jenkins *(sitting at the table):* Aw man, take it easy, the checkers ain't gon run away! *Setting up his men)* If you could play the game, I wouldn't mind it—but you can't play! *(His men are in order now.)* Your move . . .

Mr. Parker: I'll start here . . . *(Makes his move)* Ever since Doris died, Adele's been giving me a fit about getting a job, and I know she's gon start messing with me again tonight about it . . .

Mr. Jenkins: Don't you think it's about time? In the five years I've been knowing you, I can count the heads of hair you done cut in this shop on one hand . . . I'll do this . . .

Mr. Parker: This shop is gon work yet—I know it can—just give me one more year, and you'll see . . . Going out to get a job ain't gon solve nothing—all it's gon do is create a lot of bad feelings with everybody . . . I can't work! I don't know how to! . . . I'll go there . . .

20 Mr. Jenkins: And I'll go there . . . I bet if you had take care of yourself and live alone like I do, you'd know how to. That's one thing I don't understand about you, Parker. How can you expect your daughter to go on supporting you and those two boys?

Mr. Parker: I don't expect that, man! I'll give you this man . . . I just want some time until I can straighten things out. My dear Doris understood that . . . She understood me like a book . . .

Mr. Jenkins: You mean to tell me your wife enjoyed working for you?

Mr. Parker: Of course she didn't—but she never worried me. You been married, Jenkins—you know what happens to a man when a woman worries him all the time, and that's what Adele's been doing—worrying my head off!

Mr. Jenkins: Whatcha gon do about it?

25 Mr. Parker: I'm gon get tough—that's the only sign a woman gets from a man . . . Get tough and evil, that's what you do—and you know me,

Jenkins, when I get evil, I get greasy, rusty, dusty evil! *(Makes a move and rises)* You're trapped, Jenkins!

Mr. Jenkins *(pondering):* Hmmmmmmmm . . . It looks that way, don't it?

Mr. Parker *(moves for the door):* While you're moaning over the board, I'll just make a little check to see if Adele is coming—don't cheat now! *(He moves backwards towards the window to make certain that his adversary does not cheat on him. He gets to the window and quickly takes a look out.)* Uh uh! It's Adele! She's in the middle of the block talking to Miss Thomas! *(Rushes back to the table)* We got to quit now! *(Rushes to the shelf, takes a towel, returns to the table and spreads it over the checkerboard)* Come on man! *(Grabbing Mr. Jenkins by the arm and forcibly leading him to the barber's throne.)*

Mr. Jenkins: *What are you doing, Parker?*

Mr. Parker *(forcing him into the throne):* You need a shave!

30 **Mr. Jenkins** *(jumping out of the throne and onto the floor):* I don't need no shave!

Mr. Parker: Then you gon have to hide out in the back room, cause if Adele comes in here and sees you, she'll think that you and me have been playing checkers all day!

(The lights come up full on the back room where Theopolis Parker is descending the stairs, carrying a square bundle wrapped in an army blanket. He is in his twenties, of medium height, and has a lean solid physique. He places the bundle on the old desk. He is followed by his younger brother, Bobby Parker, carrying a jug of liquid. He places the jug under the desk. Bobby is a well-built boy in his early twenties.)

Mr. Jenkins: I don't care about that!

(The two boys hear the fuss with the two men and tiptoe to the door to listen in.)

Mr. Parker: You wan't to finish the game, don't you?

Mr. Jenkins: Yeah, but—

35 **Mr. Parker:** All you have to do, Jenks, is just lay low for a minute. One minute and that's all—She'll stop in like she always do—she'll ask me what I want for supper, and then she'll go on upstairs. There won't be nobody . . . left here, but you and me, and maybe the boys, but them two lazy bums don't count for nothing. Whatcha say, Jenks?

Mr. Jenkins *(pause):* All right I'll do it—I don't like it, but I'll do it, and you better not mention this to nobody—you hear?

Mr. Parker: Not a single soul in this world will know but you and me.

(They move for the back room. Theopolis and Bobby rip away from the door and scamper under the bed.)

Mr. Jenkins *(moves just inside the room and stands to the side of the door against the wall):* This is the most ridiculous thing I ever heard—of hiding in somebody's back room just to finish up a checker game . . .

Mr. Parker: Stop fighting it man!

40 **Mr. Jenkins:** All right, I'm not—now get away from this door.

Mr. Parker: Not there!

Mr. Jenkins (*moving briskly back into the shop*): What in the hell is it, now?

Mr. Parker: *You've got to get under the bed!*

Mr. Jenkins: I'm not gettin' under *nobody's* bed!

45 **Mr. Parker** (*rushes to the window, takes a quick look, and turns back to Mr. Jenkins*): Sometimes when Adele comes in, she goes through the back room, and up the basement stairs to the apartment. Now you want her to catch you standing behind that door, looking like a fool?

Mr. Jenkins: No—I can take myself out of here, and go home!

(*Starts towards the door.*)

Mr. Parker (*grabbing him by the arms*): No you don't!

Mr. Jenkins: Are you crazy, Parker?

Mr. Parker (*pushes his friend over to the table and lifts the towel from the checkerboard*): Look at this! Now you just take a good look at this board! (*Releases him.*)

50 **Mr. Jenkins:** I'm looking, so what?

Mr. Parker: So what? I got you and you know it! There ain't no way in the world you'll ever get out of that little trap I got you in. *And it's your move.* How many years we been playing against each other?

Mr. Jenkins: Three . . .

Mr. Parker: Never won a game from you in all that time, have I?

Mr. Jenkins: That ain't the half of it—you ain't gon win one either.

55 **Mr. Parker:** Now that I finally got you, that's easy talk comin' from a running man . . . All right, go on—run . . . (*Moves away from him.*)

Mr. Jenkins: Go to hell! All I gotta do is put my king here, give you this jump here, move this man over there, and you're dead!

Mr. Parker (*turns to him*): Try me then—try me or are you scared at last I'm gon beat you!

Mr. Jenkins: I can't do it now—there ain't enough time!

Mr. Parker (*moves away from him, strutting like a sport*): Run rabbit, run . . .

60 **Mr. Jenkins:** All right, I'll hide under your bed, but I swear, I'm gon beat you, Parker!

Mr. Parker: Under the bed then . . .

Mr. Jenkins (*moves to the door and stops*): It's got to be under?

(*It is at this precise moment that the two boys are scrambling to get out from under the bed. They make their way to the stairs and stop about three or four steps up.*)

Mr. Parker: All the way under . . .

Mr. Jenkins: You'll have to help me—I'm not used to crawling under people's beds . . .

65 **Mr. Parker:** I'll help you . . .

(*The two boys' heads can be seen projecting out slowly, peeping on the old men as they foolishly struggle on the floor near the bed. After a short while, they make it, and Mr. Parker hurriedly moves back out into the barber shop. He takes out a notebook and pencil. He sits in the throne as if he's working out some astronomical plan or idea.)*

Adele *(Enters. She is in her late twenties, well dressed in the conventional New York female office worker's garb. She is carrying a smart-looking purse, and a brown office envelope in her right hand):* Hello, Father . . .

Mr. Parker: Oh—Hi honey . . .

Adele *(moves to him and kisses him on the forehead):* How's business?

Mr. Parker *(answers her as if he is deeply involved):* Slow . . .

70 Adele: In other words, as usual . . .

Mr. Parker: As usual, but I've been sitting here for the past two hours, working out some new ideas.

Adele: Good! We could use some new ideas—in fact, we could use a few old ones. *(Sits at the table where the checkerboard is.)*

Mr. Parker *(cringes for a moment):* My birthday comes up on the tenth of next month, and I plan to celebrate it with that one big idea to capture the attention of everybody within twenty blocks of this neighborhood, and then, I'm gon really go to the country.

Adele: Don't go to the country—just cut a few hairs, huh . . . Oh God, I'm tired!

75 Mr. Parker *(jumps down from the chair and pulls her up in his arms):* Come on and let me take you upstairs so you can get yourself some rest—I know you must've had yourself a real rough day at the office . . . *(Leading her away from the table)* And you can forget about cooking supper and all that stuff . . .

Adele *(breaks away from him and moves to the window and stops):* Thank you, Father, but I've already given myself the privilege of not cooking your supper tonight.

Mr. Parker: You did?

Adele: There are a few matters you and I are going to take time out for—now.

Mr. Parker: Oh yeah—like what, honey?

(Theopolis and Bobby step down into the room and listen in on their conversation momentarily, then move out into the shop and stand next to the door, side by side. They have surreptitious grins on their faces.)

80 Adele: Mother's insurance policy, and—*(Catches sight of the two boys)* Well! From what cave did you fellows crawl out of? I had no idea you hung around barbershops—Want a haircut, boys.

Theo: For your information, this is the first time we been in this barbershop today. We been upstairs, thinking . . .

Adele: With what?

Theo: With our *minds*, baby!

Adele: If the two of you found that house upstairs so attractive to keep you in it all day, then I can think of only three things: the telephone, the bed, and the kitchen.

85 Bobby: The kitchen, that's it—we been washing dishes all day!

Adele: I don't like that, Bobby!

Theo: And I don't like your attitude!

Adele: Do you like it when I go out of here every morning to work!?

Theo *(pause):* Mama understood—I don't know why you gotta give everybody a hard time . . .

90 Adele: That was one of Mama's troubles: understanding everybody. *(Pause)* Bless her . . .

Theo: Now don't start that!

Adele: I have got to start *that,* MR. THEOPOLIS PARKER!

Mr. Parker: Hold on now—there's no need for all this!

Adele: There is a need for something—Mama's been dead for three months . . . *(She opens the envelope and goes through the papers.)* and you fellows have gone on as if nothing happened—the only difference being, that there is one woman working instead of two—but I want to tell you: I am tired, and I have made it up in my mind, that some quick and pretty changes are going to be made if we're going to live together in this place . . .

95 Theo: And who gives you the right to say that?

Adele: Me, Adele Eloise Parker, black, over twenty-one, and the only working *person in this house! (Fingers through the bills)* Every one of these bills here are in the name of *Doris Alice Parker,* and since I am the only one that's working who else was she going to leave them to—Here's your policy Daddy . . . *(Hands him the policy.)*

Mr. Parker *(taking the policy from her):* I've been looking all over for this policy, where—

Adele: Let's talk about these bills! *(Pause)* Now something's got to be done about this situation, Daddy. It was enough of a hard time with just me and Mama working, but with Mama gone, it will simply be impossible for me to carry all this weight alone—and I am not going to let the three of you drive me into the graveyard the way Mama was . . . And if you really want to know how I feel about that, I'll tell you. Mama killed herself because there was no kind of order in this house—there was nothing but her old fashion love for a bum like you, Theo . . . and this one . . . *(points to Bobby)* who's got nothing better to do with his time but to idolize you . . . And you, Daddy—you and those fanciful stories you're always ready to tell, and all the talk of the good old days when you were the big vaudeville star, of hitting the numbers. How? How Daddy? The money you spent on the numbers, you got from Mama. In a way, you let Mama make a bum out of you—You let her kill herself!

Mr. Parker: That's a terrible thing to say, Adele, and I'm not going to let you put that off on me!

100 Adele: But the fact remains that in the seven years you have been in this barbershop, you haven't earned enough money to buy seven hot dogs! *(She moves abruptly to the table and snatches the towel from the checkerboard.)* Most of your time is spent with *this!*

(Mr. Parker indignantly moves to the table and gazes down sadly on the board.)

Theo: I hope you know what you're doing . . .

Adele *(turns on him):* You object? *(Theo turns his back on her.)* Bobby?

Bobby: It's okay with me . . .

Adele: Theo?

105 **Theo:** Theo, what?

Adele: You just go right on and be a clown if you want to!

Theo: I don't need you, Adele . . . Why don't you get married or something, and stop using me and Bobby to make yourself feel important. We don't need you—Pop is here—it's *his house! (Turns to his father)* We're your sons, ain't that right, Pop?

Adele: You're lucky I don't get married and—

Theo: Nobody wants you, baby!

110 **Adele** *(Theo's remark stabs and stops her for a moment. She resettles herself):* All right—or you just let someone ask me, and I'll leave you here with *Pop,* to starve with *Pop* —but that wouldn't be right, soon you'd have him in his grave . . . Or there's another way—why don't you just leave and try making it on your own? Why don't we try that, Theo? *(Everyone looks to Theo.)* Well?

Theo *(pause):* I'll stay . . .

Adele: Under whose conditions?

Theo *(pause):* Yours . . .

Adele: And those conditions have to do with getting a job for the three of you, starting with you, Daddy . . .

115 **Mr. Parker:** Work?

Adele: That's right, Daddy, work . . .

Mr. Parker: What's goin' to happen to my shop?

Adele: There's going to be no more shop—it was a bad investment and the whole of Harlem knows it!

Mr. Parker *(grabbing her by the arm desperately):* I'm an old man!

120 **Adele** *(pulling away from him):* Don't touch me!

Mr. Parker *(waving the policy in his hand):* I have this!

Adele: Hush, Daddy, please hush—the money Mama left you on that policy couldn't feed you for six months—

Mr. Parker: You go ahead and do what you want, but I'm not leaving this shop!

Adele: Can't you understand, Father! *I'm a woman,* I can't go on supporting three grown men! *That ain't right!*

125 **Mr. Parker** *(her remark shakes him up a bit):* No, it's not right—it's not right at all . . .

Adele: Something has to be done, Father—you should realize that . . . *(Theo and Bobby start for the exit. Catching sight of them)* Come back here you two!

Theo: Now what?

Adele: Jobs boys, jobs . . . The two of you, out of here tomorrow morning. I'll give you two weeks, and if you haven't found anything by that time, out you go!

Theo: That ain't fair!

130 **Adele:** I don't want to hear it—it's going to be *me* or *you.*

Bobby: I'll do what I can, Adele . . .

Adele: You'll do more than you can . . .

Bobby: I'll do more than I can . . .

Adele: Is that all right by you, Mr. Theopolis?

135 **Theo:** Yes!

Adele: That's fine . . . Out of this house tomorrow morning, before I leave here or with me—suit your choice. And don't look so mournful boys . . . *(Gathers up her belongings at the shelf)* Smile—you're going to be happier than you think, earning a living for a change . . . *(Moves through the back room and on up the stairs.)*

Bobby: You do look pretty bad, Theo . . . A job might be just the thing for you . . .

Theo: Who the hell do she think she's kidding—nobody's happy in Harlem.

(Mr. Jenkins scrambles out from under the bed in the back room and rushes into the shop.)

Mr. Jenkins: I heard every word she said, and I'm getting out of here!

140 **Bobby** *(kidding):* Mr. Jenkins! When did you get here?

Mr. Jenkins: I let you make a fool out of me, Parker!

Mr. Parker: We can still play!

Mr. Jenkins: We can't play nothing, I'm going home where I belong!

Mr. Parker: Okay, okay, I'll come over to your place tonight . . .

145 **Mr. Jenkins:** That's the only way—I ain't gon have my feelings hurt by that girl of yours.

Mr. Parker: I'll see you tonight—about eight . . .

Mr. Jenkins *(at the door):* Parker, tell me something.

Mr. Parker: Yeah, Jenks?

Mr. Jenkins: You sure Adele is your daughter?

150 **Mr. Parker:** Get out of here! *(Mr. Jenkins rushes out.)* Now what made him ask such a silly question like that?

Theo: I think he was trying to tell you that you ain't supposed to be taking all that stuff from Adele.

Bobby: Yeah Pop—he's right . . .

(Mr. Parker starts to put his checkerboard together.)

Theo: Why don't you be quiet. You had your chance a few minutes ago, but all you did was poke your eyes at me, and nod your head like a fool; mumbling, "Yes, yes Miss Adele!"

Bobby: I don't have anything against Adele. I don't see why you gotta make a big thing out of her taking charge . . . Somebody's gotta do it—I think she's right!

155 Theo: But she wants us to go out and get jobs! We ain't hit a lick at a snake in years! Now how she gon ask somebody to just up and switch their lives around like that, and go out and work on some job?

Bobby: She's not right!

Theo: She's crazy! I've got other things to do with my life . . . I'm a painter, an artist! That's what I am. I ain't got time for no job—I've got artistry to think about.

Bobby: You don't say!

(Mr. Parker is standing at the throne fingering a pair of scissors. He motions to Bobby to get into the chair, Bobby sits in the chair as his father starts setting him up for a trim.)

Theo *(sits in one of the chairs):* I know what she's up to . . . She wants us to get jobs so she can fix the house up like she always wanted it, and then it's gon happen . . .

160 Bobby: What's that?

Theo: She gon get married to some konk head[1] out on the Avenue, and then she gon throw us out the door.

Bobby: She wouldn't do that . . .

Theo: She wouldn't huh? Put yourself in her place—she's busting thirty wide open . . . *Thirty years old*—that's a lot of years for a broad that's not married.

Bobby: I never thought of it that way . . .

165 Theo *(in half-confidence):* You know what? I peeped her bank book one day, and you know what she's got stashed away?

Mr. Parker and Bobby *(both turning their heads in his direction at the same time):* How much?

Theo: Four thousand, two hundred and sixty five dollars!

Bobby: WHAT!

Mr. Parker: I don't believe it!

170 Theo: You better—and don't let her hand you that business about how she been sacrificing all these years for the house . . . The only way she could've saved up that kind of money was by staying right here! She better watch out is all I gotta say, cause I know some birds out there on that Avenue, who practice and practice every day of their lives on how to run through working girls and their savings accounts.

Mr. Parker: You oughta know, cause you're one of them yourself. Adele can take care of herself.

Theo: I wouldn't bet on it . . .

Mr. Parker: The way I figure it, Theo—anybody that can handle you, the way she did, can very well take care of themselves.

Theo: That's mighty big talk coming from you, after the way she treated you a few minutes ago. But he don't care, Bobby, he's not like you and me. We heard you tell Mr. Jenkins we weren't nothing but a couple of bums. He

---

[1] An African-American who straightens his/her hair.

can talk that way, he's got his—got himself a big ol' fat policy in his hand . . . How much is it, Pop?

175 **Mr. Parker:** None of your damn business . . .

Theo: You got all that money and you goin' out to look for a job?

Mr. Parker: I'm giving it some serious thought . . .

Theo: Well, I'm not . . .

Bobby: You lied when you said you would look for a job?

180 **Theo:** Didn't you?

Bobby: Yeah, I guess I was lying . . .

Theo: She ain't using me for something as low and dirty as a job. I got my paintings to think about.

Bobby: Do you really think you're some kind of painter or something?

Theo: You've seen them . . .

185 **Bobby:** Yeah, but how would I know?

Theo: Yeah, how would you . . .

Mr. Parker: You're going to get a job or Adele's gon throw you out.

Theo: I can get by that—there are plenty of ways to fool her. And remember, I can always tell her I was discriminated against . . . That one always gets 'em . . .

Bobby: You'll have to get up in the morning . . .

190 **Theo:** And I won't like it—but you can't win 'em all . . . I'll get up, like the good guy I am—leave the house, walk across 126th till I hit Fifth Avenue, make a right to 125th, back across to Lenox, make another right on Seventh, then another right on 126th, and by that time, she should be downtown, slaving away for the man.

Bobby: That sounds more like work than getting a job . . . After all that, then what?

Theo: Back to bed—maybe get on the phone and call up one of my little girls . . .

Bobby *(His father has finished with his hair. He hops down out of the chair):* I thought you said you wanted to do something with them pictures. You just jiving—you ain't no painter!

Theo *(heads for the back room):* I see you've got to be convinced . . . *(Theo rushes into the back room and unwraps his bundle on the old desk, takes out a painting, and hurriedly returns to the outer area of the shop. He holds the painting up before the eyes of Bobby. It is an abstract conglomeration of many colors. Surprisingly, the painting is well done, and denotes a sense of style. Mr. Parker is at the other end of the shop, sweeping the floor.)* Now tell me what you see . . .

195 **Bobby:** Nothing . . .

Theo: You've got to see something—even an idiot has impressions.

Bobby: I ain't no idiot . . .

Theo: All right—sub-idiot.

Bobby: Now look, you better stop throwing them words "fool" and "idiot" at me any time you feel like it. I'm gonna be one more "fool," and then my fist is gonna land right upside your head!

200 **Theo:** Take it easy now—look, Bobby, you must see something . . . I tell
you what: try to see something . . .

Bobby: Try?

Theo: Yeah, close your eyes and really try . . .

Bobby *(closing his eyes):* Okay, I'm trying, but I don't know how I'm gon see
anything with my eyes closed.

Theo: Well open them!

205 **Bobby:** They opened . . .

Theo: Now tell me what you see . . .

Bobby: I see paint . . .

Theo: I know you see paint, stupid!

Bobby *(slaps him ferociously across the face):* Now I told you to stop it!

210 **Theo:** That hurts!

Bobby: You ain't begun to hurt yet, if you keep calling me out of my name.

Theo: Can I call you *Robert* or *Bob?*

Bobby: Just call me Bobby—that's what I'm used to . . .

Theo: *Bobby,* tell me about the paint you see . . .

215 **Bobby:** There's red, yellow, and—

Theo: *Colors?*

Bobby: That's right—colors . . .

Theo: Do the colors remind you of anything or anybody?

Bobby: Russians and cowards!

220 **Theo:** Oh no! You will never understand!

Bobby: All I know is that a picture is supposed to be pretty, but I'm sorry,
that picture is ugly!

Theo: You're hopeless . . . You understand this, don't you, Pop? *(Moving
towards his father to exhibit the painting.)*

Mr. Parker *(ignoring him in not looking at the painting):* Don't ask me—I
don't know nothing about no painting.

Theo: You were an artist once . . .

225 **Mr. Parker:** That was a different kind . . .

Theo: Didn't you ever go out on the stage with a new thing inside of you?
One of them nights when you just didn't want to do that ol' "Uncle Tom"[2]
soft shoe routine. You knew you had you gave it a little bite here, a little
acid there, and still with all of that, they laughed at you anyway. Didn't
that ever happen to you?

Mr. Parker: More than once . . .

Theo: Well, it's the same way with me . . . I want you and Bobby to look at
this painting and see what's behind it. Not just colors that are pretty or
ugly, but life!

Mr. Parker: Then you better stop beating around the bush about it, and stop
trying to make me think to see . . . I got eyes—let me see first, let me

---

[2] A character from Harriet Beecher Stowe's *Uncle Tom's Cabin;* a negative term for a black
person who is considered to be too deferential to whites.

have no doubts about what I'm seeing, Then I'll tell you what I'm thinking about.

230 **Bobby:** Me too . . .

Theo: You! *(Pause)* Maybe you got something . . .

Mr. Parker: I think you're BS'n boy . . . You been something every year since you quit school . . . First you was going to be a writer, then a airplane pilot, then a office big shot. Now it's a painter. As smart a boy as you is, you should stick to one thing, and maybe you'll be it. But who do you think you're fooling—it all boils down to one thing—you don't want to work—but I'll tell you something, Theo—time done run out on you . . . Adele's not playing, so you just might as well put them pictures away.

Theo: Aw no, Pop, I believe in these paintings. I put a lot of my time, and myself, into this.

Mr. Parker: Don't tell it to me—tell it to Adele . . .

235 **Theo:** Who the hell is Adele . . . you're my father, you're the man of the house . . .

Mr. Parker: True, and that's what I intend to be, but until I get a job, I'm gon play it cool . . .

Theo: You're going to let her push you out into the streets to hussle up a job. You're an old man, Pop. You ain't used to working—it might kill you . . .

Mr. Parker: Yeah, but what kind of leg do I have to stand on if she tells me to get out?

Theo: She's bluffing!

240 **Mr. Parker:** The last fellow I knew who was in this kind of fix told me exactly what you just said. Well, the last time I saw him, he was standing on the corner of Eighth Avenue and 125th Street, at four o'clock in the morning—twenty degree weather! In nothing but his drawers! Mumbling to himself, "I could've sworn she was bluffing!"

Theo: Let me put it to you this way. If none of us come up with anything in that two-week deadline she gave us . . . None of us, you hear me?

Mr. Parker: I hear you, and that's about all . . .

Theo: Don't you get the point? That's three of us—you, me, and Bobby. What she gon do? Throw the three of us out? I tell you, Pop, she ain't gon do that!

Mr. Parker: If you want to take that chance, that's your business, but don't try to make me take it with you. Anyway, it ain't right, she has to work for three grown rusty men—it just ain't right . . .

245 **Theo:** Mama did it for you . . .

Mr. Parker: That was different . . . She was my wife . . . She knew things about me you will never know. We oughtn' talk about her at all . . .

Theo: I'm sorry Pop, but ever since Mama's funeral, I've been thinking. Mama was the hardest working person I have ever known, and it killed her! Is that what I'm supposed to do? No, that's not it—I know that's not it . . . So, I went to talk to some people—some people right here in Harlem. I told them about this big idea of mine—

Mr. Parker: You are loaded with ideas, boy—*bad ideas!*

Theo: WHY DON'T YOU LISTEN TO WHAT I HAVE TO SAY?

250 Mr. Parker *(pause):* Let me see those paintings.

> *(Theo gives him the one painting he has been holding in his hand and moves into the back room to get the others. He rushes back out with two other paintings and holds them up before Mr. Parker's eyes.)*

Theo: How am I doing?

Mr. Parker *(scanning):* Bobby was right, they're ugly . . .

Theo *(moves back into the back room to put the paintings away):* I haven't seen many pretty things in my life, Pop.

Mr. Parker *(talking to him from out in the shop):* Whatever it was you had in mind when you painted these colors, it was all your own—you weren't lying!

255 Theo *(stands in the doorway of the back room):* Naw, I wasn't lying—*this is something I really want to do*—I can feel it worrying me when I don't think I know what I'm doing—when I think, maybe I wasn't cut out to be anything but what I am. I need my own time to find that out—I swear to God I do, Pop . . .

Mr. Parker: You're a smart boy—in a strange sort of way though. I call it uneducated smart, and that's the best kinda smart there is. That's the way I am. I think I'm gon let you help me with the writing of my book of old time stories.

Theo *(turns into the back room, drops to his knees, and opens up a trap door on the floor):* When you get ready for me to help you, I'll be right here, but first I got something here I want you to taste . . . *(Takes out a jug from under the floor, rises, moves out into the shop, holding it up in his right hand.)*

Mr. Parker: What is it?

Theo: Whiskey—corn whiskey . . . You want some?

> *(Bobby fetches three glasses and places them on the table.)*

260 Mr. Parker: Well I'll try a little bit of it out. But we better not let Adele see it . . .

Theo *(sits at the table):* You could let that girl put a scare in you Pop—and I remember you when you wouldn't take no stuff off Mama, Adele or nobody. You used to get so mean and bad, you'd get scared of yourself . . .

Mr. Parker: God is the only person I fear . . . *(Sits.)*

Theo *(starts to unscrew the top):* You're all alike!

Mr. Parker: Who're you talking about?

265 Theo: You, the way Mama was—ask you a question—any question you can't answer, and you throw that Bible stuff at us.

Mr. Parker: I don't get you . . .

Theo *(having trouble unscrewing the cork):* For instance, let me ask you about the black man's oppression; and you'll tell me about some small nation in the East rising one day to rule the world . . . Ask you about pain and dying; and you say, God wills it . . . Fear?—and you'll tell me about Daniel, and how Daniel wasn't scared of them lions[3] . . . Am I right or wrong?

Mr. Parker: It's in the book and you can't dispute it.

Theo *(finally opens the jug):* You wanta bet? If that nation in the East ever do rise, I don't think I'm gon be around that long to see it, and if by some chance I am, how can I be sure they won't be worse than the jokers we got already . . . Nobody, but nobody wills me to pain and dying—not if I can do something about it—that goes for John, Peter, Mary, J. C., the whole bunch of 'em! And as for ol' Daniel—Sure, Daniel didn't care nothing about them lions—*but them lions didn't give a damn about him, either! They tore him up!*

270 **Mr. Parker** *(rises from the table indignantly):* That's an ungodly, unholy lie! *(Takes his Bible from the shelf)* And I'll prove it!

Theo: What lie?

Mr. Parker *(moving to the table thumbing through his Bible):* You and those bastard ideas of yours . . . Here, here it is! *(Reading from the Bible)*

> *And when he came near unto the den to Daniel, he cried with a pained voice; the King spoke and said to Daniel: "O Daniel, servant of the living God, is thy God, Whom thou servest continually, able to deliver thee from the lions?" Then said Daniel unto the King: "O King, live forever! My God hath sent His angels, and hath shut the lions' mouths, and they have not hurt me; forasmuch as before Him innocency was found in me, and also before thee, O King, have I done no hurt." Then was the King exceeding glad, and commanded that they should take Daniel up out of the den. So Daniel was taken up out of the den, and no manner of hurt was found upon him, because he trusted in his God!*

(Slams the book closed, triumphantly.)

Theo: Hollywood, Pop, Hollywood!

Mr. Parker: Damn you! Have I ever brought somethin' like you into this world, I will never know! You are no damn good! Sin! That's who your belief is! Sin and corruption! With you, it's noting but women! Whiskey! Women! Whiskey! *(While he is carrying on in this ranting fashion, Theo pours out a glass of his corn and slides the glass just under Mr. Parker's hand at the table. Reaches for the glass)* Whisk—*(Takes a taste)* Where did you get this from!?

275 **Theo** *(slapping Bobby's hand):* I knew you'd get the message, Pop—I just knew it!

Mr. Parker: This is great corn, boy!

---

[3] A reference to the prophet Daniel and the lion's den, from the Book of Daniel in the Old Testament. During the Babylonian captivity of the Jews, he became adviser to the King and emerged unharmed when he was cast into the lion's den.

Bobby: And Theo makes it like he was born to make it!

Mr. Parker: Where did you learn to make corn like this?

Theo: Don't you remember?—you taught me.

280 Mr. Parker: By George, I did . . . Why, you weren't no morn' nine years old . . .

Theo: Eight—let's have another one . . . *(He pours another round for the three of them.)* Drink up . . . Here's to ol' Daniel . . . You got to admit one thing—he had a whole lot of heart!

Mr. Parker *(drinks up and puts his hand out again):* Another one, please . . .

Theo *(pouring):* Anything you say, Pop! *You're the boss of this place!*

Mr. Parker *(drinks up):* Now that's the truth if you ever spoke it . . . *(Puts his glass out again)* Whew! This is good! *(Getting tipsy now.)*

285 Theo *(pouring):* About this idea I had, Pop . . . Well, it's got something to do with this corn . . .

Mr. Parker *(drinks up):* Yeah! *(Puts his glass out again.)*

Theo: Well, I tested some of it out the other day, and I was told this corn liquor here could start a revolution—that is, if I wanted to start one. I let a preacher taste some, and he asked me to make him a whole keg for his communion next month.

Mr. Parker *(drinks up):* God dammit! *(Throws his glass on the floor.)*

Bobby: What's wrong, Pop?

290 Mr. Parker: I miss her, boy, I tell you, I miss her!

Bobby: Pop—Pop, don't, don't you cry like that—don't you cry.

Mr. Parker: Was it really God's will?

Theo: Don't you believe that—don't you ever believe that!

Mr. Parker: But I think, boy—I think hard!

295 Theo: That's all right . . . We think hard too. We got it from you, ain't that right, Bobby?

Bobby: Yeah . . .

Mr. Parker *(pause):* You know something? That woman was the first woman I ever kissed . . . Your Mama . . .

Bobby: How old were you?

Mr. Parker: Twenty . . .

300 Bobby: Aw come on, Pop!

Mr. Parker: May God wipe me away from this earth . . .

Theo: Twenty years old—damn, you must've been in bad shape!

Mr. Parker: I'll tell you about it . . .

Theo: I knew it! Here he goes with another one of his famous stories!

305 Mr. Parker: I can always go on upstairs, you know . . .

Theo: All right, let us hear it . . .

Mr. Parker: Well, I was working in this circus in Tampa, Florida—your mother's home town. You remember Bob Shepard—well, we had this little dance routine of ours we used to do a sample of outside the tent. One day, we was out there doing one of our numbers, when right in the middle of the number, I spied this fine, foxy looking thing, blinking her eyes at me. Course ol' Bob kept telling me it was him she was looking at, but I knew it was *me*—cause if there was one thing that was my specialty, it was a fine-looking woman.

Theo: Twenty years, and *your specialty?*

Mr. Parker: Yeah, being that—

310 **Theo:** —that you had never had a woman for all them terrible years, naturally, it was on your mind all the time . . .

Mr. Parker: That's right . . .

Theo: —and it being on your mind so much, you sorta became a specialist on women.

Mr. Parker: Right again . . .

Theo *(laughs):* I don't know, but I guess you got a point there! *(Continues to laugh.)*

315 **Mr. Parker:** You want to hear this or not!

Bobby: You go on, Pop . . .

Mr. Parker: Well, while I was standing on the back of the platform, I motions to her with my hand to kinda move around to the side of the stand, so I could talk to 'er. She strolled round to the side, stood there for a while, and you know what? Ol' Bob wouldn't let me get a word in edgewise. But you know what she told him; she said, "Mister, you talk like a fool!" *(Laughs.)*

Bobby: That was Mama . . .

Mr. Parker: So, I asked her if she would like to meet me after the circus closed down, and I would take her for a walk. When I got off that night, sure enough, she was waiting for me. We walked up to the main section of town, off to the side of the road, cause we had a hard rain that day, and the road was full of muddy little ponds. I got to talking to her and telling her funny little stories, and she would laugh—boy I'm telling you, that woman could laugh!

320 **Theo:** That was your technique, huh? Keep 'em laughing . . .

Mr. Parker: Believe it or not, it worked—cause she let me kiss her. I kissed her under this big ol' pecan tree. She could kiss too. When that woman kissed me, somethin' grabbed me so hard, and shook me so, I fell flat on my back into a big puddle of water! *And that woman killed herself laughing! (pause)* I married her two weeks later . . .

Theo: And then you started making up for lost time. I'm glad you did, Pop—cause if you hadn't, I wouldn't he here today.

Mr. Parker: If I know you, you'd have made some kind of arrangement.

Bobby: What happened after that?

325 **Mr. Parker:** We just lived and had fun—and children too, that part you know about. We lived bad and we lived good—and then my legs got wobbly, and my feet got heavy, and nothing seemed to change any more. I lost my feeling, and everything just stayed as it was. *(Pause)* I only wish I had been as good a haircutter as I was a dancer. Maybe she wouldn't have had to work so hard. She might be living today.

Theo: Forget it Pop—it's all in the gone by . . . Come on, you need another drink . . . *(Pouring.)*

Mr. Parker *(taking the drink):* Get me talking about them old days—it hurts, I tell you it—

Theo: Pop, you have got to stop thinking about those things. We've got work to do!

Mr. Parker: You said you had an idea . . .

330 Theo: Yes—you see, Pop, this idea has to do with Harlem. It has to do with the preservation of Harlem. That's what it's all about. So, I went to see this leader, and I spoke to him about it. He thought it was great and said he would pay me to use it!

Mr. Parker: Who the hell wants to preserve this dump? Tear it down is what I say!

Theo: But this is a different kind of preserving . . . Preserve it for black men—that's my idea—preserve it for men like you, me and Bobby.

Mr. Parker: That sounds good . . .

Theo: Well, I told this leader, I would never promise to do anything until I had spoken to my father. So, I said, after I had straightened out everything with you, I would make arrangements for the two of you to meet.

335 Mr. Parker: Meet him for what?

Theo: For making money! For business! *This man knows how to put people in business!*

Mr. Parker: All right, I'll meet this man, what his name—

Theo: But you're gonna have to have a showdown with Adele, and put her in her place, once and for all . . .

Mr. Parker: I don't know how I'm gon do that now . . .

340 Theo: This man can't be dealing with no men who let women rule them. Pop, you've got to show that girl a thing or two, or we cannot call ourselves men!

Mr. Parker: And if I don't—what do we call us?

Theo: What do they call men who wear pink and silk bloomers?

Mr. Parker: All right! If Adele don't like it that's too bad! That's one thing I ain't never been accused of!

Theo: Now, that's the way I like to hear my old man talk! Take a drink, Pop! *(Theo starts popping his fingers and moving dancingly about the floor.)*

> We're gonna show 'em now
> We're gonna show 'em how
> All over
> This ol' Harlem Town!

(Theo and Bobby start making rhythmic scat sounds with their lips as they move about dancing on the floor.) Come on, Pop—show us how you used to cut one of them things!

345 Bobby *(trying his hand at the dance):* This is the way he did it!

Theo: Nawwww, that's not it—he did it like this! *(Makes an attempt.)*

Mr. Parker: No, no! Neither one of you got it! Speed that riff up a little bit . . . *(The two boys speed up the riff a bit, singing, stomping their feet, and clapping their hands. Humped over, looking on the floor with pointed concentration)* Faster! *(They speed it up more.)*

Theo: Come on now, Pop—let 'er loose!

Mr. Parker: Give me time . . .

350 Bobby: Let that man have some time!

(Mr. Parker breaks into his dance.)

Theo: Come on Pop, take it with you!

Bobby: Work, Pop!

Theo: Downtown!

(Mr. Parker does a coasting "camel walk.")

Bobby: Now bring it on back uptown!

(He really breaks loose into a rapid series of complicated dance steps.)

355 Theo: Yeah!

Bobby: That's what I'm talking about!

(Adele enters and quickly moves out into the shop. Bobby, in one motion, grabs the broom and starts sweeping; Theo, in one motion, picks up the waste basket and is heading for the door. Mr. Parker reaches for his razor and starts sharpening on his throne's belt.)

Adele: Fellows! *(They all stop in their motions.)* You can come upstairs now—dinner is served!

CURTAIN

ACT I

Scene 2

Two weeks later . . . late afternoon.

Bobby is seated in the barber's throne, eating away on a sandwich. Theo enters from the front of the shop.

Theo: At it again, dammit!

Bobby: Hi . . .

Theo: This is a miserable world we live in . . .

Bobby: Uh huh . . .

5 Theo: Don't you think so?

Bobby: Naw . . .

Theo *(snatching the sandwich out of his mouth):* Because you eat too damn much!

Bobby: Why did you do that?

Theo *(handing the sandwich back to him):* Because I can never talk to you . . . I can never talk to you like brother to brother—cause you always got a mouth full of peanut butter and jelly!

10 **Bobby:** I'm hungry! And let me tell you something—don't you *ever* snatch
    any food from my mouth again.

    Theo: You'll hit me—that's because you're violent . . . You don't care noth-
    ing about your brother—that's why you're always hitting me. One of these
    days, I'm gon hit back.

    Bobby: The day you swing your hand on me, you'll draw back a nub!

    Theo: You see! That's exactly what I mean. Now when Blue gets here tonight
    I don't want you talking like that or else you gon blow the whole deal.

    Bobby: I know how to act, and I don't need no lessons from you.

15 **Theo:** Good—cause I got a job for you.

    Bobby: A job! *(Jumps out of the chair.)*

    Theo: Don't get knocked out—it ain't no real job. I just want you to jump
    over to Smith's on 125th, and pick me up a portable typewriter.

    Bobby: Typewriter—for what?

    Theo: Don't ask questions, just go and get it . . .

20 **Bobby:** Them typewriters cost a lotta money . . .

    Theo: You ain't gon use money . . .

    Bobby: You mean—

    Theo: I mean you walk in there and take one . . .

    Bobby: Naw, you don't mean I walk into nowhere and take nothing!

25 **Theo:** Now, Bobby—

    Bobby: No!

    Theo: Aw, come on baby Bobby, you the one been bragging about how good
    you are, and how you can walk into any store and *buy* anything you
    wanted, provided it was not too heavy to carry out.

    Bobby: I ain't gon do it!

    Theo: You know what day it is?

30 **Bobby:** Thursday . . .

    Theo: That's right, Thursday, October 10th . . .

    Bobby: What's that suppose to mean; thieves' convention at the furniture
    stores on 125th?

    Theo: You know? For a brother of mine, you sure don't have much faith in
    me . . . *It's Pop's birthday!*

    Bobby: I didn't know he was still having them . . .

35 **Theo:** Oh yes, and you wanta know who remembered it before we did? Adele,
    and she's planning on busting into this shop tonight with a birthday cake
    to surprise him—all she gon have is a cake and a box of cigars—but with
    a typewriter, we'll be giving him something different!

    Bobby: Nope . . .

    Theo: Okay, I'll go get it myself . . .

    Bobby: That I'd like to see . . . TYPEWRITER! *(Laughs.)*

    Theo: Have all the fun you want . . .

40 **Bobby:** What's he gon type?

    Theo: Them lies he's always telling—like the one about how he met Momma.
    Pop can tell some of the greatest lies you ever heard of . . . You heard
    him say he was writing them down.

Bobby: Pop don't know nothing about writing—specially no typewriting!

Theo *(takes out his father's notebook):* Oh no—take a look at this . . . *(Hands the notebook to his brother)* All he has to do is put it down on paper the way he tells it. Who knows, somebody might get interested in it, and we can make ourselves some money, and besides, I kinda think he would get a real charge out of you thinking about him that way—don't you.

Bobby: Well, ain't no use in lettin' you go over there with your old clumsy fingers . . .

45 Theo: Good boy, baby Bobby . . . *(Mr. Parker enters the shop from the front entrance.)* Hey, Pop!

Mr. Parker: Hi son . . .

Theo: Did you get that thing straighten out with Adele, yet?

Mr. Parker: What?

Theo: *Adele?*

50 Mr. Parker: Oh yeah, I'm gon do that as soon as I get time . . .

Theo: Where you been all day?

Mr. Parker: Downtown, seeing about some jobs . . .

Theo: You sure don't care much about yourself . . .

Mr. Parker: I can agree with you, because looking for a job can really hurt a man . . .

55 Theo: Didn't I tell you . . .

Mr. Parker: I was interviewed five times today, and I could've shot every last one of them interviewers—the white ones, and the colored ones too. I don't know if I can take any more of this.

Theo: Yeah, looking for a job can be very low grading to a man, even more so after you get one. Anyway, I'm glad you got back here on time or you would've missed your appointment.

Mr. Parker: What appointment?

Theo: Now don't tell me you don't remember! The man, the man that's suppose to come here and tell you how life in Harlem can be profitable.

60 Mr. Parker: Oh, that . . .

Theo: Oh, that my foot! Today is the day we're suppose to come up with those jobs, and you ain't said one word to Adele about it—not one single word! All you do is waste your time, looking for work! Now that don't make no sense at all, Pop, and you know it . . .

Mr. Parker: Look, son—let me go upstairs now and tell her about all the disappointments I suffered today—that'll soften her up a bit, and then I'll come on back down here to meet your man. I promise, you won't have to worry about me going downtown anymore—not after what I went through today, and I certainly ain't giving up my shop, for nobody!

Theo: Now that's the way to talk!

(Mr. Parker moves through the back room and on up the stairway. A jet black-complexioned young man, dressed in all black, wearing large dark sun glasses, and holding a gold-top cane in his right hand, enters. He is

carrying a large salesman's valise in his left hand. He stops just inside the door.) Blue baby! *(Extending his hand for a shake.)*

Blue: Am I late?

65 Theo: No, my father just walked into the door—he's upstairs now, but he'll be right back down in two minutes . . . Let me take your things . . . *(Relieves Blue of his cane and valise)* Sit down man and I'll serve you a drink . . . *(Moves into the back room and places Blue's things on the bed.)*

Blue: Hey, Bobby, how's the stores been treating you? *(Sits.)*

Bobby: I'm planning on retiring next year . . . *(Laughs.)*

Theo *(Returning with his jug and three glasses. Moves to the table and starts pouring):* I was thinking, Blue—I don't think we oughta tell Pop about our "Piano Brigade" . . . That's the one thing he will not buy. Let's just keep that to ourselves, and we can play it where he will never never know.

Blue: You know your father . . . *(Takes a drink.)*

70 Bobby *(taking his drink):* What's the "Piano Brigade"?

Theo: Blue here has some of the best thieves in this part of town, and we plan to work on those stores over on 125th until they run the insurance companies out of business . . .

Bobby: You mean breaking into people's stores at night, and taking their stuff?

Theo: That's right, but not the way you do it. We'll be organized, and on top of it, we'll be revolutionary.

Bobby: If the police catch you, he ain't gon care what you is, and if Pop ever finds out, the police gon seem like church girls! *(Moves hurriedly out of the front door.)*

75 Theo: You just remember that the only crime is the one you get caught at!

Blue: How's your sister, Theo?

Theo: You mean Adele?

Blue: You got a sister named Mary or something?

Theo: What's this business with Adele?

80 Blue: I want to know how are you going to get along with her, selling bootleg whiskey in this place?

Theo: This is not her place—it's my father's, and once he puts his okay on the deal, that's it . . . What kind of house do you think we're living in, where we gon let some woman tell us what to do . . . Come here, let me show you something . . . *(Moves into the back room as Blue follows)* How you like it? Ain't it something?

Blue *(standing in the doorway):* It's a back room . . .

Theo: Yeah, I know, but I have some great plans for reshaping it by knocking this wall down, and putting—

Blue: Like I said, it's a back room—all I wanta know is will it do the job . . . It's a good room and you'll do great with that good-tasting corn liquor of yours. You're going to be so busy here, you're going to grow to hate this place—you might not have any time for your love life, Theopolis!

85 Theo *(laughing):* Don't you worry about that—I can manage my sex life!

Blue: Sex? Who's talking about sex? You surprise me, Theo . . . Everyone's been telling me about how you got so much heart, how you so deep. I sit and talk to you about life, and you don't know the difference between sex and love.

Theo: Is it that important?

Blue: Yes it is ol' buddy if you want to hang out with me, and you do want to hang out with me, don't you?

Theo: That depends . . .

90 Blue: It depends on you knowing that sex's got nothing to do with anything but you and some woman laying up in some funky bed, pumping and sweating your life away all for one glad moment—you hear that, *one moment!*

Theo: I'll take that moment!

Blue: With every woman you've had?

Theo: One out of a hundred!

Blue *(laughing):* One out of a hundred! All that sweat! All that pumping and grinding for the sake of one little dead minute out of a hundred hours!

(Mr. Parker enters the shop from upstairs briskly, but stops in his tracks upon seeing Blue. He stares bewilderedly at the man.)

95 Theo: Pop, you know who this is?

Mr. Parker *(moves near the young man, bends, straining his eyes to get a good look):* I can't see him . . .

Theo: This is Blue!

Mr. Parker: Blue who?

Theo: The man I was telling you about . . . *Mr. Blue Haven.*

100 Mr. Parker: Oh yeah . . . *(Extends his hand for a shake)* Glad to make your acquaintance, Mr. Haven . . .

Blue *(shaking Mr. Parker's hand):* Same to you, Mr. Parker . . .

Mr. Parker: I'm sorry to keep you waiting, but my daughter and me, we had to talk over some important matters . . .

Theo: You sure you don't know who Blue Haven is, Pop?

Mr. Parker: I'm sorry, but I truly don't know you, Mr. Haven . . . If you're a celebrity, you must accept my apology. You see, since I got out of the business, I don't read *Variety*[4] anymore.

105 Theo: I'm not talking about a celebrity.

Mr. Parker: Oh, no?

Theo: He's the leader!

Mr. Parker: OH!

Theo: Right here in Harlem . . .

110 Mr. Parker: Where else he gon be but in Harlem—we got more leaders within ten square blocks of this barbershop than they got liars in City Hall—that's why you dressed up that way, huh boy? So they can pick you out of a crowded room!

---

[4] Entertainment periodical.

Theo: Pop, this is serious!

Mr. Parker: All right, go on. There are some things I don't catch on to right away, Mr. Blue . . .

Theo: Get to this. I got to thinking the other day when Adele busted in here shoving everybody around—I was thinking about this barbershop, and I said to myself: Pop's gon lose this shop if he don't start making himself some money.

Mr. Parker: Now tell me something I don't know . . .

115 Theo: Here, I go . . . What would you say, if I were to tell you, that Blue here can make it possible for you to have a thriving business going on, right here in this shop, for twenty-four hours a day?

Mr. Parker: What is he? Some kind of hair-grower!

Theo: Even if you don't cut but one head of hair a week!

Mr. Parker: Do I look like a fool to you?

Theo *(holds up his jug):* Selling this!

120 Mr. Parker *(pause):* Well, well, well. I knew it was something like that. I didn't exactly know what it was, but I knew it was something, and I don't want to hear it!

Theo: Pop, you've always been a man to listen . . . Even when you didn't agree, even when I was wrong, you listened! You are charitable that way, that's the kind of man you are! You—

Mr. Parker: I'm listening!

Theo *(pause):* Tell him who you are, Blue . . .

Blue: I am the Prime Minister of the Harlem De-Colonization Association.

125 Mr. Parker *(pause):* Some kind of organization?

Blue: Yes . . .

Mr. Parker *(as an aside, almost under his breath):* They got all kinds of committees in Harlem. What was that name again, "De"?

Theo: De-colo-ni-zation! Which means that Harlem is owned and operated by *"Mr. You Know Who."* Come on here in the back, and we will show you something. *(Mr. Parker follows the young men into the back room where they get busy immediately, pinning charts on the wall.)* Take a look at these charts if you think we're fooling.

Mr. Parker *(reading from the center chart):* The Harlem De-Colonization Association, with future perspectives for Bedford Stuyvesant. *(Turns to Blue)* All right, so you got an organization. What do you do? I've never heard of you.

130 Blue: The only reason you've never head of us is because we don't believe in picketing, demonstrating, rioting, and all that stuff. We're different . . . We're nonviolent. I wouldn't ask you to do anything that was violent. You might get yourself hurt that way. I have a sworn affidavit, signed personally by myself, that none of my members will ever get hurt. We stand firm as nonviolents. Of course, that don't mean we're passive. To the contrary—we believe in direct action. We are doers, enterprisers, thinkers, and most important of all, we're businessmen! Our aim is to drive "Mr. You Know Who" out of Harlem.

Mr. Parker: Who's this "Mr. You Know Who"?

Theo: Damn, Pop! *The white man!*

Mr. Parker: OH, himmm!

Blue: We like to use that name for our members, in order to get away from the bad feelings we have whenever we use the word "white." We want our members to always be objective. And in this way, we'll drive forward, and before we get through, there won't be a single "Mr. You Know Who" left in this part of town. We're going to capture the imagination of the people of Harlem. That's never been done before, you know.

135 Mr. Parker: Now tell me how.

Blue *(standing before the charts with his cane pointed on the wall):* You see this here . . . This is what we call a "Brigade." And you see this yellow circle here?

Mr. Parker: Uh huh . . .

Blue: That's what we call the "Circle Brigade."

Mr. Parker: What's that for?

140 Blue: That is part of my dream to create here in Harlem a symbolic life force in the heart of the people . . .

Mr. Parker: I see . . .

Blue: Pin up that target, Theo . . .

(Theo takes a large sheet of paper from Blue's bag and pins it on the wall. It is a dart target with the face of a beefy-faced Southern-looking white man right in the bull's-eye area of the target.)

Mr. Parker: Why that's that ol' dirty sheriff from that little town in Mississippi!

Blue *(taking one of the darts from Theo):* That's right—we got a face on a target for every need. We got governors, mayors, backwoods crackers,[5] city crackers, Southern crackers, and Northern crackers. We got all kinds of faces on these targets, that any good Harlemite would be willing to buy one for the sake of slinging one of these darts right in this bastard's throat!

(Blue throws the dart and it punctures the face on the board.)

145 Mr. Parker: Let me try it one time . . . *(He takes dart from board, moves back, and slings it into the target's face.)* Got him! *(A big laugh.)*

Blue: It's like I said, Mr. Parker, the idea is to capture the imagination of the people of Harlem!

Mr. Parker: You got more? Let me see more!

Blue: Now over here where you see this red circle. That's Theo and his corn liquor. This corn liquor of Theo's can make an everlasting contribution to this life force I've been talking about. I've tested this whiskey out in every neighborhood in Harlem, and everybody claimed it was the best they ever

---

[5] Negative term for poor white person.

tasted this side of Washington, D. C. We plan to supply every after-hour joint in this area.

Theo: You see, Pop, this can only be unless the barbershop is opened night and day, so the people can come and go as they please, to pick up their play for the day, to get a bottle of corn, and to take one of the targets home to the kiddies. They can walk in just as if they were getting a haircut. In fact, I told Blue that we can give a haircut as a bonus for anyone who buys two quarts at a time, and later on we can give out "Triple S Stamps" for gifts. *(Pause.)*

150 **Mr. Parker:** What am I suppose to say now?

Theo: You're suppose to be daring. You're suppose to wake up to the times, Pop . . . These are urgent days—a man has to stand up and be counted!

Mr. Parker: The police might have some counting of their own to do . . .

Theo: Do you think I would bring you into something that was going to get us in trouble? Blue has an organization! Just like "Mr. You Know Who." He's got members on the police force! In the city government, the state government, and we're working on the White House!

Mr. Parker: Boy, there is no end to you. You're just like that old man in that song about a river. You just go on and on and on!

155 **Blue:** Mr. Parker, if you have any reservations concerning the legitimacy of my association, I'd be only too happy to have you come to my summer home, and I'll let you in on everything—especially our protective system against being caught doing this thing.

Theo: You hear that, Pop, *he's got a summer home!*

Mr. Parker: Aw shut up boy! Let me think! *(Pause)* So you want to use my place as a headquarters for Theo's corn, and them targets?

Blue: Servicing the area of 125th to 145th, from East to West rivers.

Mr. Parker *(pause):* I'm sorry fellows, but I can't do it . . .

160 **Theo:** Why, Pop?

Mr. Parker: It's not right . . .

Theo: Not right! What are you talking about? Is it right, that all that's out there for me is to go downtown and push one of them carts? I have done that, and I ain't gon do it no more! You hear me, Pop? No more!

Mr. Parker: That still don't make it right . . .

Theo: I don't buy it! I'm going into this thing with Blue, with or without you!

165 **Mr. Parker:** Go on, I don't care! You quit school, I couldn't stop you from that! I asked you to get a job, you wouldn't work! You have never paid any attention to any of my advice, and I don't expect you to start heeding me now!

Theo: Pop, please—it'll work, I know it'll work . . . Give me this one chance, and I swear to do something with my life! Please!

Mr. Parker: Stop begging, Theo! *(To Blue)* Why?

Blue: I don't get you . . .

Mr. Parker: Why have you gone to so much pain to dream up this cockeyed ridiculous plan of yours?

170 **Blue:** It is not ridiculous! It works! It grooves! It moves! It soothes the soul! It upends! It transcends! It deliberates! It copulates!

Mr. Parker: Hold it! Hold it! I believe you!

Blue: Mr. Parker, I was born and raised about six blocks from here, and before I was ten, I had the feeling I had been living for a hundred years. I got so old and tired, I didn't know how to cry. Now you just think about that—a ten-year-old boy who couldn't cry. But about two years ago, I woke up one morning, bawling and wailing like a baby—what a reverse that was—and I've been crying like a man that was out of his mind ever since! *(Reaches into his pocket, pulls out a stack of bills, and places it on the table)* I'm ready to put you in business, *man!*

(Mr. Parker takes the money from the table and sifts through the stack.)

Theo: That's to get us started—and if we can make a dent into "Mr. You Know Who's" going-ons in Harlem, nobody's gon think of us as crooks. We'll be heroes from 110th Street to Sugar Hill.[6] And just think, Pop, you won't have to worry about jobs and all that. You'll have so much time for you and Mr. Jenkins to play checkers, your arms will drop off. You'll be able to sit as long as you want, and tell enough stories and lies to fit between the covers of a five-hundred-page book. That's right! Remember you said you wanted to write all them stories down! Now you'll have the time for it! You can dress up the way you used to in the old days—and the girls . . . Remember how you used to be so tough with the girls before you got married? All that can come back to you, Pop! And some of that you never had. It's so easy! All you have to do is call Adele down those stairs, and let her know that you're going into business, and if she don't like it, she can move out, because you're not going to let her drive you down, you've got too much at stake, you're a man, and—

Mr. Parker: All right! All right! *(Pause)* I'd do it under one condition. . . .

175 **Blue:** Yes . . .

Mr. Parker: That is if my buddy Jenkins wanta buy into this deal, you'll let him . . .

Blue: Theo . . . ?

Theo: Why not . . .

Mr. Parker *(extending his hand to Blue):* Then you got yourself some partners, Mr. Haven!

180 **Blue:** Welcome into the Association, Mr. Parker . . .

Mr. Parker: Welcome into my barbershop!

Theo *(jumps up into the air):* Yeah!

Blue *(checks his watch, and immediately starts gathering his materials and putting them into his large valise):* Well I have to check out now, but I'll stop over tomorrow and we'll set the whole thing up just as you want it, Mr. Parker . . . See you later Theo . . . *(Starts out the door.)*

---

[6] Section of Harlem in New York City.

Mr. Parker *(To Blue as he is moving out of the door):* You should stick around awhile and watch my polish!

185 **Theo:** Pop, don't you think it would be better if you would let me give the word to Adele?

Mr. Parker: No. If I'm going to run a crooked house, *I'm* going to run it, and that goes for you as well as her.

Theo: But Pop, sometimes she kinda gets by you.

Mr. Parker: Boy, I have never done anything like this in my life, but since I have made up my mind to do it, you have nothing to say! Not a word! *(Moves to the base of the stairs in the back room)* Well, here goes nothing . . . ADELE! *(Moves back out into the shop.)*

Bobby *(stopping just inside the door):* Hi . . .

190 **Mr. Parker:** Hi son, what you got there?

Bobby: Uh, uh—fish!

Mr. Parker: Well, you better get them in the refrigerator before they stink on you . . .

Bobby: Refrigerator?

Mr. Parker: Where else you gon put them?

195 **Bobby:** That's right, Pa—you sure is right . . . *(Heads for the back room.)*

(The lights suddenly go out, and then come back up. Adele is standing in the shop with a birthday cake in her hands, smiling gleefully.)

Adele: Happy birthday, Daddy!

Mr. Parker: What is this?

Adele: Surprise!

Mr. Parker: Now hold on!

200 **Adele:** What's wrong, Daddy?

Mr. Parker: Well, it's—it's . . . *(Pause)* Nothing . . .

Adele *(placing the cake on the table and handing him a knife):* Here . . .

Mr. Parker *(takes the knife):* I, er . . . This just knocks me out . . . I swear, it just completely knocks me out! *(Cutting the cake.)*

Adele: Something else for you! *(Hands him a gift-wrapped package.)*

205 **Mr. Parker** *(takes the package):* Now what—*(Unwraps the package)* Cigars! The same brand I used to smoke when I was on the stage! Look at this fellows!

Theo: Me an' Bobby got something for you too, Pop . . .

Mr. Parker: What's going on here?

Theo: Give it to him, Bobby . . .

Bobby *(hands him the package wrapped in newspaper wrappings):* Here, Pop . . .

210 **Mr. Parker:** The fish! *(Hurriedly unwraps the package)* Well, I'll be damn, a typewriter!

Theo: That's right . . .

Mr. Parker *(laughing):* Now what am I going to do with a typewriter? Son, I don't know nothing about typing!

Theo: You know what you told me about writing down your stories. You can write them down, three times as quick!

Mr. Parker: But I don't know how to type!

215 **Theo:** With the money we're gonna be having, I can hire a somebody to teach you!

Adele: What money you're going to have?

Theo: We're going into business, baby—right here in this barbershop!

Mr. Parker *(tapping the boy on the shoulder):* Theo . . .

Theo *(paying no attention to his father):* We're going to sell bootleg whiskey!

220 **Adele:** You're what?

Mr. Parker: Theo . . .

Theo: You heard me, and if you don't like it, you can pack your bags and leave . . .

Adele: Leave? I pay the rent here!

Theo: No more! I pay it now!

225 **Mr. Parker:** Shut up, Theo!

Theo: We're going to show you something, girl, we'll—

Mr. Parker: *I said shut up!*

Adele: Is he speaking the truth?

Mr. Parker: Yes he is . . .

230 **Adele:** You're going to turn this shop into a bootleg joint?

Mr. Parker: I'll turn it into anything I want to!

Adele: Not while I'm still here!

Mr. Parker: The lease on this house has my signature, not yours!

Adele: And I pay for it!

235 **Mr. Parker:** And that's what I'm goin' to put a stop to—you pay no more!

Adele: I'm not going to let you do this!

Mr. Parker: You got no choice, Adele—you hear me—you don't have a single thing to say!

Adele *(turns on Theo):* You put him up to this!

Mr. Parker: Nobody puts me up to anything I don't want to do! These two boys have made it up in their minds that they're not going to work for nobody but themselves, and the thought in my mind is, *why should they?* I did like you said, I went downtown, and it's been a long time since I did that, but you're down there every day, and you oughta know by now that I'm too old a man to ever dream I could overcome the dirt and filth they got waiting for me down there. I'm surprised at you, that you would have so little care in you to shove me into the middle of that mob.

240 **Adele:** You can talk about caring? What about Mama? *She was old!* She *died* working for you! Did you ever stop to think about that? In fact, DID YOU EVER LOVE HER? NO!

Mr. Parker: That's a lie!

Adele: I hope that one day you'll be able to do one good thing to drive that doubt out of my mind . . . *But this is not it!* You've let this hoodlum sell you his twisted dream of getting through life without caring that there are other people about him—who have feelings—who hurt the same as he does. Don't let this boy ruin you, Daddy—don't let him do it!

Theo *(into her face):* Start packing, baby!

Adele *(strikes him across the face):* Don't you talk like that to me!

(Theo draws his hand back in retaliation.)

245 **Mr. Parker:** Drop your hand, boy! *(Theo does not respond to his father's command. He still has his hand held up as if to strike.) Drop your god damn hand!*

Theo *(backing away from his father):* She hit me!

Mr. Parker: I don't care if she had broken your jaw—if you ever draw your hand back to hit this girl again—*as long as you live!*—you better not be in my hand's reach when you do—*I'll split your back in two! (To Adele)* We're going into business, Adele. I have come to that conclusion, and I have come to it on my own. I am going to stop worrying once and for all whether I live naked in the cold or whether I die like an animal, unless I can live the best way I know how to. I am getting old and I oughta have some fun. I'm going to get me some money, and I am going to spend it! I'm going to get drunk! I'm going to dance some more! *I am getting old! I am going to fall in love one more time before I die!* So get to that, girl, and if it's too much for you to take, I wouldn't hold it against you if you walked away from here this very minute . . . *(He moves through the back room.)*

Adele *(moves swiftly to the door leading to the back room):* I am not leaving . . . I am not moving one step . . . *Happy birthday!*

Mr. Parker *(stops in his tracks and turns sharply):* That's another thing! I fooled all of you! *Today is not my birthday!*

(Turns, moves through the room and up the stairs to the apartment.)

250 **Adele:** It's not going to work! You're going to cut your throat! You hear that? You're going to rip yourself into little pieces! *(Turns on Theo)* Now, boy, the world's going to spin itself all around just for you—is that what it's going to do? *(Theo does not respond to her.)* I am talking to you!

Theo *(pause):* It might . . . Me and Bobby—we're men. . . If we lived the way you wanted us to, we wouldn't have nothing but big fat veins popping out of our heads.

Adele: Are you sure that won't happen anyway? That this whole damn house won't crumble down into your face one day?

Theo: No, I am not sure!

Adele: Then you think about that every time a cop walks through that door—every time a stranger steps into this back room, and you can't be so sure that you can trust him—you think about your father sitting alone in a jail man's cell one day . . .

255 **Theo:** What else am I going to do? You tell me when and where I can go to spin the world round before it gets too late—like Mama living fifty whole years just to die on a 126th Street! *You tell me of a place to go where there are no old crippled vaudeville men!*

Adele: THERE IS NO SUCH PLACE! *(Turns and moves slowly for the entrance upstairs)* but the one you make for yourself—even where you are sick—where you are alone in some cold dark place—*where everything in you wants to erupt into joy!*—and there is no joy—there is nothing but the cold boundaries of trying to keep alive so that you don't lose the most precious thing that's yours, and that is your wonder, boy—your everlasting gift to WONDER!

Theo: I wonder all the time, Adele—I wonder how you ever got to be such a damn fool . . .

CURTAIN

ACT II

Scene 1

Two months later . . . It is about 9:00 P.M. in the evening. As the curtain rises, the lights come up on the back room where Theo is busy at the desk going over a set of books with a pen in his hand. He puts the pen down hurriedly and rushes to the latest addition to the room, a stove, where there are two huge pots steaming with his recipe of corn liquor. He moves away from the stove and looks on an uncompleted painting of his, resting on a canvas near the stairs. He moves back to the desk and continues to work on the books.

Bobby descends the stairs and moves right past Theo out into the outer part of the shop, carrying a target rolled up in his hand and two darts. He is wearing a fancy sport shirt, new trousers, new keen-toed shoes, and a stingy-brimmed, diddy-bop hat. He pins the target up on the wall of the shop. The face at the center of the target is that of a well-known American racist.

Bobby *(moves away from the target, aims a dart, and throws it):* That's for Pop! Hunh! *(Throws another dart)* And that's for me! Hunh! *(He moves to the target to pull the darts out. The doorbell rings.)*

Theo *(calling out to Bobby from the back room):* Lock that door!

Bobby: Lock it yourself!

Theo *(with definite, hurried steps, he moves out of the back room for the front door):* I'm not selling another bottle, target or anything til' I get some help! *(Locks the door to the persistence of the ringing)* We're closed!

5 Bobby: I don't think Blue is gonna like you turning away customers.

Theo: You can tell Blue I don't like standing over that stove all day—that I don't like him promising me helpers that don't ever show up. There are a lot of things I don't go for, like Pop taking off and not showing up for two days. I don't like having to make whiskey—to sell it, keeping books, and peddling those damn targets! *And I don't like you standing around here all day not lifting a finger to help me!*

Bobby *(sits in the throne, takes out a cigar and lights it up):* I don't hear you . . .

Theo: I know what your bag is—you're a stealer . . .

Bobby *(jumps down out of the throne):* I don't wanta hear nothing! You do what you wanta do, and leave me alone!

10 **Theo:** What am I suppose to be, a work mule or something?

Bobby: You're the one that's so smart—you can't answer your own stupid questions?

Theo: You done let Blue turn you against me, huh?

Bobby: You ask the questions, and you gon answer them—but for now, stop blowing your breath in my face!

Theo *(moves away from Bobby and steps into the back room and looks on his painting):* At the rate I'm going, I will never finish this painting!

(Adele steps down immediately from the stairs and looks on the painting with amazement. She is dressed in a very smart outfit.)

15 **Adele:** What is this?

Theo *(moves to the stove and proceeds to stir his mixture with a long ladle):* Somebody I know!

Adele *(she turns the easel, making the painting visible downstage):* This, you call somebody? *(The painting is an abstraction of something or other, but it is definitely not representative of a human person.)*

Theo: Yeah, Johnny!

Adele: Johnny?

20 **Theo:** Johnny All American—everybody knows Johnny All American but you . . .

Adele *(moves from the painting):* It's terrible!

Theo: Don't you ever have anything good to say?

Adele: I'm honest . . .

Theo: Honest? You're just hot because Pop decided to do something my way for a change . . .

25 **Adele:** That's a joke, when you haven't seen him in two whole days. Or do you know where he has gone to practically every night since you opened up this little store?

Theo: He's out having a little sport for himself. What's wrong with that? He hasn't had any fun in a long time . . .

Adele: Is fun all you can think of? When *my* father doesn't show up for two days, I worry . . .

Theo: Don't—when Blue comes tonight with that money, he'll be here!

Adele: I hope so . . . *(Starts out.)*

30 **Theo:** Where are you going?

Adele *(stops and turns abruptly):* I'm going out! Do you mind?

Theo: That's all you ever do!

Adele: Yes, you're right . . .

Theo: What are you doing, girl? You got a man or something out there on that Avenue?

35 **Adele:** What I have or don't have is none of your damn business! *(Moves out of the door sharply.)*

Theo *(stands in the back room doorway with a long, deep look in his eyes):* I'm beginning to have a thought about that girl—a thought I don't particularly want to think about . . .

(He closes the door behind him. Blackout on the back room. Mr. Parker steps into the shop, all dapper, dressed in a light beige suit, black shirt, brown tie, tan and white shoes, large dark sunglasses, holding a gold-top cane in one hand and a book in the other. Bobby is staring on him with bewildered eyes.)

Bobby: What's that you got on?

Mr. Parker: What does it look like?

Bobby: Nothing . . .

40 **Mr. Parker:** You call this nothing!

Bobby: Nothing—I mean, I didn't mean nothing when I asked you that question . . .

Mr. Parker: Where's Theo?

Bobby: In the back, working . . .

Mr. Parker: Good! Shows he's got his mind stretched out for good and great things . . .

45 **Bobby:** He's been stretching his mind out to find out where you been . . .

Mr. Parker: Where I been is none of his business—Blue is the man to think about—it's pay day, and I wanta know where the hell is he! *(Checks his watch, taps Bobby on the hip, indicating that he should step down from the throne.)*

Bobby *(hopping down from the chair):* Whatcha reading?

Mr. Parker: A book I picked up yesterday. I figured since I'm in business, I might as well read a businessman's book. *(Sits in the chair.)*

Bobby: Let me see it . . . *(Takes the book in his hand) A Thief's Journal* by Jean Gin-net[7] . . . *(Fingering through the book)* Is it a good story?

50 **Mr. Parker:** So far . . .

Bobby *(hands it back to him):* What's it all about?

Mr. Parker: A Frenchman who was a thief . . .

Bobby: Steal things?

Mr. Parker: Uh huh . . .

55 **Bobby:** Where did he get all that time to write a book?

Mr. Parker: Oh, he had the time all right, cause he spent most of it in jail . . .

Bobby: Some thief!

Mr. Parker: The trouble with this bird is that he became a thief, and then he became a thinker.

Bobby: No shucking?

60 **Mr. Parker:** No shucking—but it is my logicalism that you've got to become a thinker, and then you become a crook! Or else, why is it when you read

---

[7] Jean Genet (1910–1986). French writer and poet, whose work reflects his experiences as a criminal and as a prisoner.

up on some of these politicians' backgrounds, you find they all went to one of them big law colleges—that's where you get your start!

Bobby: Well, I be damn!

Mr. Parker: You see, son, stealing done got educational as well as political . . . You have to study it out, get yourself a plan the way me and Blue did, and then you get into operation. If this fellow had been thinking before he started stealing, he wouldn't have been a failure . . . *(Jumps down out of the chair and moves briskly for the door)* Now where is Blue! He said he would be here nine-thirty on the nose! *(Opens the door)* Hey, Jenkins! What's up?

Mr. Jenkins: That Blue fellow show up yet?

Mr. Parker: No, he didn't and I'm gon call him down about that too—

65 **Mr. Jenkins:** It don't matter—I just want whatever money I got coming, and then I'm getting out of this racket . . .

Mr. Parker: This is not a racket, it's a committee!

Mr. Jenkins: This committee is no committee—it ain't nothing but a racket, and I'm getting out of it!

Mr. Parker: You put your money into this thing, man—it ain't good business to walk out on an investment like that . . .

Mr. Jenkins: I can, and that's what I'm doing before I find myself in jail!

70 **Mr. Parker:** There ain't nothing for you to be scared of, Jenkins—Blue guaranteed me against ever being caught by the police. Now that's all right by me, but I've got some plans of my own. Tonight, I'm gon force him to make me one of the leaders in this group, and if he don't watch out, I just might take the whole operation over from him—I'll make you my right-hand man, and not only will you be getting more money, and I just won't guarantee you against getting caught, but I'll guarantee you against being scared!

Mr. Jenkins: There's nothing you can say to make me change my mind. I shouldn't've let you talk me into this mess from the start. I'm getting out, and that's it . . . *(Starts for the door)* And if he gets back before I do, you hold my money for me! *(Exits.)*

Mr. Parker: Suit yourself, but you're cutting your own throat—this little setup is the biggest thing to hit this neighborhood since the day I started dancing! *(Goes to the mirror to primp)* Fool . . .

Bobby: Going somewhere again?

Mr. Parker: Got myself a little date to get to, if Blue ever gets here with our money—*and he better get here with our money!*

75 **Bobby:** You been dating a lot lately—nighttime dates, and day ones too, and Theo's not happy about it. He says you don't stay here long enough to cut Yul Brynner's head[8] . . .

Mr. Parker: He can complain all he wants to—I'm the boss here, and he better not forget it . . . He's the one that's got some explaining to do—don't

---

[8] Actor, well-known for his role as the King in the musical comedy, *The King and I;* an allusion to his baldness.

talk to nobody no more—don't go nowhere, looking like he's mad all the time. I've also noticed that he don't get along with you anymore . . .

Bobby: Well, Pop, that's another story . . .

Mr. Parker: Come on boy, there's something on his mind, and you know what it is . . .

Bobby: Nothing, except he wants to tell what to do all the time—but I've got some ideas of my own. I ain't no dumbbell—I just don't talk as much as he do . . . If I did, the people that I talk to would know as much as I do. I just want him to go his way, and I'll go mine . . .

80 **Mr. Parker:** There's more to it than that, and I wanta know what it is.

Bobby: There's nothing . . .

Mr. Parker: Come on now, boy . . .

Bobby: That's all, Pop!

Mr. Parker *(grabs him by the collar):* It's not and you better say something!

85 **Bobby** *(pause):* He—he found out Blue killed a man one time . . .

Mr. Parker: Where did he hear this?

Bobby: Somebody on the Avenue told him—said Blue killed this man for saying something about his woman, and this woman got a child by Blue, but Blue never married her, and this man started signifying about it . . . Blue hit him, the man reached for a gun in his pocket, Blue took the gun from him, and the man started running, but by that time, Blue had fire in his eyes, and he shot the man three times.

Mr. Parker: Well . . .

Bobby: Blue got only two years for it!

90 **Mr. Parker:** Two years, huh? That's another thing I'm gon throw in his face tonight, if he tries to get smart with me. Ain't that something! Going around bumping people off, and getting away with it too! What do he think he is, white or something! *(Checks his watch)* I'm getting tired of this! *(Moves and snatches the back room door open to the surprise of Theo sitting at the desk)* Where's that friend of yours? I don't have to wait around this barbershop all night for him. It's been two months now, and I want my money! When I say be here at nine-thirty, I mean be here!

Theo *(rising from the chair at the desk):* Where have you been, Pop?

Mr. Parker: That's none of your business! Now where is that man with my money?

Theo: Money is not your problem—you've been spending it all over town!

Mr. Parker: What do you know?

95 **Theo:** It's in the books and the books don't lie!

Mr. Parker: So what—I borrowed a little from the box . . .

Theo: You call seven hundred dollars a little?

Mr. Parker: Never mind what I do! It's been two months now, and he ain't shown me a dime!

Theo: What are you doing with all that money, Pop?

100 **Mr. Parker:** I don't have to answer to you! I'm the boss here! And another thing, there's a lot about Blue and this association I want to know about!

I want a position! I don't have to sit around here every month or so, waiting for somebody to bring me *my* money.

Theo: Why don't you think about us once in a while? I didn't go into this thing just for myself—I wasn't out to prove how wrong Adele was . . . I wanted to make up for all them years we laid around here, letting Mama break into pieces! *(Pause)* And Pop, do you know about that girl?

Mr. Parker: What about her?

Theo: She's out of this house every night, and you know how strict she is about saving money—well let me tell you something—half of her savings are gone . . .

Mr. Parker: What?

105 Theo: And I am not talking about the money—*I'm talking about what's happening to her!*

Mr. Parker: I didn't know all of this was going on . . .

Theo: If you stayed in the shop more, you'd know what's going on.

Mr. Parker: That's too bad—I have things to do. I don't worry about where you're going when you leave here . . .

Theo: I don't go anywhere and you know it . . . If I did, we wouldn't do an hour's business. *But we have been doing great business!* And you wanta know why? They love it! *Everybody* loves the way ol' Theo brews corn! Every after-hours joint is burning with it! And for us to do that kind of business, I've had to sweat myself down in this hole for something like sixteen hours a day for two *whole* months!

110 Mr. Parker: What do you want from me? I don't know how to boil that stuff!

Theo: You can get Blue to move his stuff out and rent another place! A cop walked in that door this afternoon while I had three customers in here, and I had to put one of them in that chair, and cut his hair!

Mr. Parker: How did you make out?

Theo: What do you think?

Mr. Parker: All right, I'll talk to him—

115 Theo: And make him guarantee me three helpers.

Mr. Parker: You'll get that too . . . But you've got to admit one thing, though, you've always been a lazy boy. I didn't expect you to jump up and all of a sudden act like John Henry!

Theo: I have never been lazy—I just didn't wanta break my back for the man!

Mr. Parker *(puts his arm around his son's shoulders):* I can't blame you for that. I know because I've done it. I did it when they didn't pay me a single dime!

Bobby: When was that, Pop?

120 Mr. Parker: When I was on the chain gang!

Theo *(breaks way from him):* Now you know you ain't never been on no chain gang!

Mr. Parker *(holds up two fingers):* Two months, that's all it was—just two months . . .

Theo: Two months, my foot!

Mr. Parker: I swear to heaven I was—It was in nineteen-o-something, I was living in Jersey City, New Jersey . . .

125 **Theo:** Here we go with another story!

Mr. Parker *(snaps his fingers):* And I'm gon put this one down! Get the pencil and paper out, Theo!

Theo *(takes a pencil and pad from the shelf and moves for the throne):* Now where did you say this place was? *(Sits in the chair.)*

Mr. Parker: Jersey City . . .

Theo *(writing):* In "19 'o' something" the man said . . .

130 **Mr. Parker:** That was just before I started working as a vaudeville man, and there was this ol' cousin of mine we used to call "Dub," and he had this job driving a trailer truck from Jersey City to Jacksonville, Florida. One day he asked me to come along with him for company—I weren't doing nothing at the time, and—

Theo: Say that again . . .

Mr. Parker: I said I weren't doing nothing at the time!

Theo: As usual . . .

Mr. Parker: I didn't say that! What you trying to do, make out like I didn't wanta work? I was unemployed! I was oppressed! So, I went along with him . . .

135 **Theo:** Go on . . .

Mr. Parker: Anyway, we drove along, everything was fine til' we hit Macon, Georgia. We weren't doing a thing, but before we knew it, this cracker police stopped us, claiming we'd ran through a red light. He was yelling and holling, and boyyy did I get mad—I was ready to get a hold of that cracker, and work on his head, until—

Theo: I know, but what happened?

Mr. Parker: Oh, they put us on the chain gang, and the chain gang they put us on was a chain gang and a half! I busted some rocks John Wayne couldn't've busted. I was a rock-busting fool! *(Gives a demonstration as to how he swung the hammer)* I would do it like this! I would hit the rock, and the hammer would bounce—bounce so hard it would take my hand up in the air with it, but I'd grab it with my other hand, and bring it down like this, "Hunh!" *(He gets carried away by the rhythm of his story, and he starts twisting his whole body to the swing of it.)* It would get so good to me, I'd say, "Hunh! Yeah! Hunh!" I'd say, "Oooooooo weeee!" I'm wide open now! *(Swinging and twisting)* Yeah baby, I say, "Hunh!" Sooner or later, that rock would crack! Old "Dub" one day ran into a rock that was hard as Theo's head. He couldn't bust that rock for nothing. He pumped and swung, but that rock would not move. So, finally he said to the captain, "I'm sorry, Cap, but a elephant couldn't break this rock." Cap didn't wanna hear nothing—he said, "Well 'Dub,' I wanna tell you something—your lunch and your supper is in the middle of that rock." On the next swing of the hammer, "Dub" busted that rock into a thousand pieces! *(Laughs)* I'm telling you, them crackers is mean—don't let nobody tell you about no communists, Chinese or anything—there ain't nothing on this earth meaner and dirtier than an American-born cracker! We used to sleep in them long squad tents on the ground, and we was all hooked up to this one big long chain—the guards had orders to shoot at random in the dark if ever one of them chains would rattle. You couldn't even turn over in your sleep!

Theo: A man can't help but turn over in his sleep!

140 Mr. Parker: Not on this chain gang you didn't. You turn over on this chain gang in your sleep, and your behind was shot! But if you had to; you would have to wake up, announce that you was turning over, and then you go back to sleep!

Theo: What?

Mr. Parker: Just like this: Number four turning over! But that made all the other chains on the other convicts rattle, and they had to turn over and say: Number five turning over! Number six! Number seven turning over!

Theo: Why don't you stop it!

Mr. Parker: I ain't lying!

145 Theo: Is that all?

Mr. Parker: Yeah, and I'm gon get Adele to type that up for me on my type-writer! *(Goes to the window)* Now where the hell is that Blue Haven? *(He sees Mr. Jenkins coming and he opens up the door. Mr. Jenkins enters.)* I see you're back—well, he didn't show up yet, but if you've got a moment, I'll beat you a game one time . . . *(Takes out the checkerboard.)*

Bobby: Tear him up, Pop!

(Mr. Parker is at the table setting up the board.)

Mr. Jenkins *(joining him):* It's hopeless—I been playing your father for three solid years, and he has yet to beat me one solid game!

Mr. Parker: Yeah, but his luck done come to past!

150 Mr. Jenkins: My luck ain't come to past, cause my luck is skill . . . *(Spells the word out)* S-K-I-L-L . . .

Mr. Parker: And I say if you call your playing any kind of skill, I say you're lying like a thief . . .

Mr. Jenkins: You better be careful how you call me a liar, Parker . . .

Mr. Parker: I say you're lucky, you say you ain't, and I say you're lying . . .

Mr. Jenkins: That's calling me a liar!

155 Mr. Parker: I said you was lying—I didn't say you were a liar.

Mr. Jenkins: You did!

Mr. Parker: Now when did I say that?

Mr. Jenkins: You said, cause I said I got the greatest skill, you said I was lying . . . Now tell me you didn't say that . . .

Mr. Parker: I did . . .

160 Mr. Jenkins: That's calling me a liar!

Mr. Parker: Spell it . . .

Mr. Jenkins *(spelling):* L-I-A-R . . .

Mr. Parker: Now spell lying . . .

Mr. Jenkins *(spelling):* L-Y-I-N-G . . .

165   **Mr. Parker:** You see the difference?

Mr. Jenkins: There ain't no difference!

Mr. Parker *(shakes up the can):* Come on now Jenkins, let's play the game . . . Take one . . . *(Mr. Jenkins pulls a man)* You see there, you get the first move . . .

Mr. Jenkins: You take me for a fool, and just for that, I ain't gon let you get a king . . .

Mr. Parker: Put your money where your lips is . . . I say, I'm gon win this game!

170   **Mr. Jenkins:** I don't want your money—I'm just gon beat you!

Mr. Parker: I got twenty dollars here to make a liar out of you! *(Slams down a twenty-dollar bill on the table.)*

Mr. Jenkins: You see, you see, he said it!

Mr. Parker: Said what?

Mr. Jenkins: You called me a liar!

175   **Mr. Parker:** Sit down, Jenkins! *(Pause)* Now you doing all the bragging about how I never beat you, but I'm valiant enough to say that from here on in, you can't win air, and I got twenty dollars up on the table to back it up.

Mr. Jenkins *(pause):* Oh well, he ain't satisfied with me beating him all the time for sport—he wants me to take his money too . . .

Mr. Parker: But that's the difference . . .

Mr. Jenkins: What kind of difference?

Mr. Parker: We're playing for money, and I don't think you can play under that kind of pressure. You do have twenty dollars, don't you? *(Looks back at Theo and Bobby, breaking out with a big laugh.)*

180   **Mr. Jenkins:** I don't know what you're laughing about—I always keep some money on me.

Mr. Parker: Put it on the table where I can see it.

Mr. Jenkins: You don't trust me?

Mr. Parker: I trust you all right, but to see it gives me inspiration!

Mr. Jenkins *(puts twenty dollars on the table):* You get a little money in your pocket, and you get carried away.

185   **Mr. Parker:** Your move . . .

Mr. Jenkins: Start you off over here in this corner.

Mr. Parker: Give you that little ol' fellow there . . .

Mr. Jenkins: I'll take him . . .

Mr. Parker: I'll take him, so you can take that . . .

190   **Mr. Jenkins** *(thinks for a while):* I'll jump him . . .

Mr. Parker: And I'll take these three . . . Boom! Boom! Boom! *(Jumping Mr. Jenkins' men and laughing loud. There are a series of grunts and groans as they exchange men. The game is now in definite favor of Mr. Parker. Mr. Jenkins is pondering over his situation. Relishing Mr. Jenkins' predicament)* Study long, you study wrong . . . *(Pause)* I'm afraid that's you, ol' buddy . . . *(Pause)* I knew it, I knew it all the time—I used to ask myself, I used to say: I wonder how ol' Jenks would play if he really had some pressure on him? You remember how the Dodgers used to raise hell every year until they met the Yankees in the World Series,[9] and how under all that pressure they used to crack up? *(Laughs)* That pressure got him!

Mr. Jenkins: Hush up man, I'm thinking!

Mr. Parker: I don't know what you thinking about—cause the rooster done came and wrote, skiddy biddy!

Mr. Jenkins *(finally makes a move)*: There . . .

195 Mr. Parker *(singsong)*: That's all . . . That's all . . . *(Makes another jump)* Boom! Just like you say, Bobby, "tear him up!" *(Rears his head back in laughter.)*

Mr. Jenkins *(makes a move)*: It's your move . . .

Mr. Parker *(brings his head back down, and the laughing trails off sickly upon the realization that the game is now in his opponent's favor)*: Well, I see . . . I guess this kinda changes the color of things . . . Let me see . . .

Mr. Jenkins *(getting revenge)*: Why don't you laugh some more . . . I like the way you laugh, Parker . . .

Mr. Parker: Shut up Jenkins, I'm thinking!

200 Mr. Jenkins: I don't know what you could be thinking about . . . *(Rises, moves away from the table fanning his hand)* When I get up from the table that's it! *(Laughs heavily. Mr. Parker sorrily makes his move. Rushing back to the table)* Uh huh! Lights out! *(Still laughing and making his move)* Game time and you know it! Take your jump! *(Mr. Parker is forced to take his jump; Mr. Jenkins takes his last three men)* I told you about laughing and bragging in my game! Boom! Boom! Boom!

Mr. Parker *(rising abruptly from the table)*: Dammit! *(Rushes into the back room.)*

Mr. Jenkins: Where you going, ain't we gon play some more?

Mr. Parker: I don't wanta play you no more, you too lucky!

Mr. Jenkins: Aw come on, Parker . . . I don't want your money, I just want to play!

205 Mr. Parker: You won it, you keep it—I can afford it! But one of these days, you're going to leave that voodoo root of yours home, and that's gonna be the day . . . You hear me, you sonofabitch!

Theo: Pop!

Mr. Parker: I don't want to hear nothing from you!

Mr. Jenkins *(realizing that his friend is honestly upset over the affair)*: It's only a game . . .

(*Mr. Parker is standing in the center of the back room, with his back towards them. Mr. Jenkins steps out into the center of the outer area, and addresses his remarks to Mr. Parker's back.*) and it don't have

---

[9] Reference to the Brooklyn Dodgers and to the New York Yankees, both New York City teams in the 1950s; and to their famous rivalry which culminated in the 1955 World Series (called the "Subway Series").

nothing to do with luck . . . But you keep trying, Parker, and one of these days you're going to beat me—and when you do, it won't have nothing to do with luck—it just might be the unluckiest and worst day of your life. You'll be champion checker player in all this world. Meanwhile, I'm the champ, *and you're gonna have to live with it!*

Mr. Parker *(smiling, moves out toward him with his hand extended):* Jenkins! All right, Champ! *(They shake.)* But I'm going to beat you! I'm going to whip your behind until it turns white!

210 **Bobby:** That's gon be some strong whipping! *(There is a tap at the door.)* That must be Blue . . . *(Goes to the door and opens it.)*

Mr. Parker: About time . . . *(Reaches for his coat on the rack and puts it on. Blue enters.)* Hey boy, where have you been?

Blue *(moving in carrying a regular attaché bag):* You'll have to forgive me, Mr. Parker, but I got stuck with an emergency council meeting . . .

Mr. Parker: What kind of council?

Blue: *The council of the Association*—I see you're sporting a new piece of cloth there, "Mr. P" . . .

215 **Mr. Parker:** Just a little something I picked up the other day . . .

Blue: The next time you want to dress up, you come to me, and I'll get you the best for the least cost . . .

Mr. Parker: You can do that?

Blue: That's right . . . Blue Haven, mastermind, evil genius, racketeer, hijacker, bootlegger, pirate on the high seas of the Harlem River, hipper like a long-tongued fox, crouched in the alleys and hallways for the great siege upon all the young cherries of the world. A house possessor of young black-brown-high yellow girls of classic beauty, strong-long-short agile legs, smooth healthy bodies with breasts so full—with so much life in 'em to cause a hundred-year-old buzzard to have visions of living forever!

Mr. Parker: Where is this house, Blue? *(Theo and Bobby burst out laughing. Blue just smiles surreptitiously.)* Cut it! There's too much that's funny when I'm talking, and I want you to put a stop to it! *(Pause)* Where's the money, Blue?

220 **Blue:** You'll get your money, but first I want to see those books. *(They move into the back room. Blue sits at the desk, pulling out pencil, pad, and a group of papers.)* Well, look at this, that corn whiskey of yours is flying, Theo!

Theo: I've tried . . .

Blue *(closing one book and opening up another one):* And I see the targets are doing well . . .

Mr. Parker: Come on man, give me my money!

Blue: Take it easy, Mr. Parker . . . *(He takes a white envelope from his inside pocket and passes it on to Mr. Parker.)* Here's your money . . .

225 **Mr. Parker:** Now this is what I like to see! *(Starts counting the money.)*

Blue *(passes a group of bills on to Mr. Jenkins):* And you too, Mr. Jenkins . . .

Mr. Jenkins: Thank you young man, and from here on in, you can count me out of your operation . . .

Blue: What's the trouble?

Mr. Jenkins: No trouble at all—I just want to be out of it . . .

230 Blue: People and headaches—that's all I ever get from all the *Mr. Jenkinses* in this world!

Mr. Parker: Why don't you be quiet sometime, boy . . .

Blue *(pause):* I got a call the other day from one of them committees here in Harlem . . .

Theo: What did they want?

Blue: They wanted to know what we did—they said they had *heard* of us, but they never see us—meaning, they never see us picketing, demonstrating, and demanding something all the time . . .

235 Theo: So . . . ?

Blue: They want us to demonstrate with them next Saturday, and I have decided to set up a demonstrating committee, with you in charge, Mr. Parker . . .

Mr. Parker: You what!

Blue: You'd be looking good!

Mr. Parker *(cynical laughter):* You hear that! *I'd be looking good!* Count me out! When I demonstrate, it's for real!

240 Blue: You demonstrate in front of any store out on that street, and you'll have a good sound reason for being there!

Mr. Parker: Aren't we doing enough? Two stores already done put up "going out of business" signs . . .

Blue: That's what we started this whole thing for—to drive the man back to where he came from, and that's what we're doing.

Mr. Parker: Well then you tell me—you tell me what we're doing that's so hot, that would cause a liquor store, a clothing store, and a radio store to just all of a sudden close down like that. Unless we've been raiding them at night or something like that . . .

(Bobby moves out of the shop and up the back room stairs.)

Blue: It's the psychological thing that's doing it, man!

245 Mr. Parker: Psychological? Boy, you ain't telling me everything, and anyway, I wanna know who made this decision about picketing . . .

Blue: The council!

Mr. Parker: Who is on this council?

Blue: You know we don't throw names around like that!

Mr. Parker: I don't get all the mystery, Blue. This is my house, and you know everything about it from top to bottom. I got my whole family in this racket!

250 Blue: You're getting a good share of the money—ain't that enough?

Mr. Parker: Not when I'm dealing with you in the dark . . .

Blue: You're asking for something, now what is it?

Mr. Parker: You been promising my boy some help for two months now, and he's still waiting . . . Now I want you to give him that help starting tomorrow . . . and from here on in, I want to know everything that's to be known about this "decolonization committee"—how it works, who's in it, who's running it, *and I want to be on that council you was talking about!*

Blue: That can't be, Mr. Parker!

255   Mr. Parker: Then I can't cooperate with you anymore!

Blue: What does that mean?

Mr. Parker: It means we can call our little deal off, and you can take your equipment out of here . . .

Blue: Just like that?

Mr. Parker *(starts getting his cane, coat, etc.):* Just any ol' way you want it . . . I take too many risks in this place, not to know where I stand . . . *(Starts out)* Good night!

260   Blue: Mr. Parker . . .

Mr. Parker *(stops and turns):* All right, let me hear it and let me hear it quick!

Blue: There is an opening on our council—it's a—

Mr. Parker: Just tell me what position is it!

Blue: President . . .

265   Mr. Parker: President?

Blue: The highest office on our council . . .

Mr. Parker: Boy, you're gonna have to get up real early to get an old fox like me. A few minutes ago you offered me nothing, and now you say I can be president—that should even sound strange to *you!*

Blue: There's nothing strange—a few minutes ago you weren't ready to throw me out of your place, but now *I've got no other choice!*

Mr. Parker *(pointing his finger at him and laughing):* That's true! You don't! . . . All right, I'll give you a break—I accept! But I want it in writing by tomorrow night! *(Puts on his coat, sunglasses, etc.)* Come, Jenkins, let's get out of here! *(Starts out with Mr. Jenkins.)*

270   Theo: Hey Pop, you're going out there with all that money in your pocket . . .

Mr. Parker: I'm a grown man, I can take care of myself . . .

Theo: But what about our part of it . . .

Mr. Parker: You'll get it when I get back . . .

Theo: But Pop—

275   Mr. Parker: Look son, he held me up—I'm late already—good night, Theo! *(He bolts out of the door with Mr. Jenkins following.)*

Theo *(rushes to the door):* Pop, you better be careful! I'll be waiting for you! I don't care if it's dawn!

Blue: You're becoming a worrier, Theo! *(Pause)* But that's the nature of all things . . . I'm forever soothing and pacifying someone—sometimes, even myself. Now you don't think that that president stuff is going to mean anything, do you? He'll know less, and I'll have more control over him . . . And over you too . . .

Theo: What do you mean by that?

Blue: I mean that I know he's been spending money out of the box, and I'm not being told about it . . .

280 Theo: Why should I? I trust your intelligence . . .

Blue: But whether I know or not, I don't want it to happen again!

Theo: Then hire yourself a bookkeeper!

Blue: What about Adele? That was a thought in my mind, but I put that away real quick—seems she's took to the Avenue—and with the good-time company she's keeping, I'd probably have more trouble with her than I'm having with you . . .

Theo: She's got nothing to do with anything . . .

285 Blue: But she does—when a girl like your sister takes to the Avenue, it means that she's got some trouble in her, and that trouble can break us up!

Theo: What do you want me to do? Knock her over her head?

Blue: You told me you were going to get her out of here!

Theo: You want her out—you talk to the old man about that—

Blue: Look, man—we're into something . . . To be honest with you, I didn't really think this thing was going to work—but Theo, *it is working!* I've got three places, just like this one, and another one is on the way—a man has to care about what he does—don't you want to get out of this place?

290 Theo: Yes, but lately, I've been getting the feeling that I'm gonna have to hurt somebody to do that—I've been working like a dog here every day, trying to get out of here—and if you were to ask me where would I go, if I did, I couldn't answer you, because everybody around me is breaking down!

Blue: I see . . .

Theo: For instance—you think the old man was asking you those questions about stores closing down as a joke or something?

Blue: He asked because he's in the dark!

Theo: He was playing with you! And when my father holds something inside of him, and plays with a man, he's getting meaner and more dangerous by the minute . . .

295 Blue: Then that's something else you better get straight—now it's your time to soothe and pacify!

Theo: Why should I, when you've been sending my brother out every night with that band of thieves of yours . . .

Blue: He wanted to go—he said he needed the money, and he's a better man than anybody I got . . .

Theo: And I told you, I didn't want that!

Blue: Well, let's face it, baby! Bobby's been prancing around stores and stealing all of his life!

300 Theo: I don't care if he was born at midnight in Gimbel's basement, I want a stop put to it!

Blue: I have enough trouble as it is, man . . . Bobby loves to steal, and I think that's something to bow down to—your old man is smart, and I respect him, but they're both black, and they're in trouble just like you and me! So, don't ride so hard, Theo! Get off the talk! the walk! the balk! the stalk! cause the monkey is dead and in his grave, no more signifying will he crave, on his tombstone, these words are writ, he died as he lived, with his signifying shit!

Theo: Blue, that kind of talk don't sell to me—not with all that I feel tonight . . .

(Bobby descends the stairs and moves out into the shop.)

Blue: Your brother is getting scared, Bobby . . . *(Moves to Theo and places his hand on his face)* He's cold too . . . *(Moves away from him)* I'm scared too, and as for my hands, they stay cold all the time—not to mention the rest of me . . . *(Moves to the room in the back, opens up one of the books, and starts running his fingers across one of the pages)* I went up to the hill the other day to see my little boy . . . I took the little fellow out for a ride, and as we were riding along the streets, he asked me where all the people were coming from. I said, from work, going home, going to the store, and coming back from the store . . . *(Closes the book and turns towards Theo)* Then we went out to watch the river, and he asked me about the water, the ships, the weeds—everything . . . That kid asked me so many questions, I got dizzy—I wanted to hit him to shut him up. He was just a little dark boy, discovering for the first time that there are things in the world, like stones and trees. *(He starts putting his papers away in his attaché bag.)* It got late and dark, so I took him home, and watched him fall asleep. Then I grabbed his mother, and put her into bed, and I laid there for a while, listening to her call me all kinds of dirty motherfuckers . . . *(Closes the bag and puts it down on the desk, and moves for the rack to get his coat)* and after she got that out of her system, I put my hands on her, and before long, our arms were locked at each others' shoulders, and then my thighs moved down between her thighs . . . and then my honeycomb rolled with her sweetbread until the both of us were screaming as if the last piece of love was dying forever. *(Moves back into the back room and picks up his attaché bag from the desk)* After that, we just laid there, talking soft. I would tell her she was the loveliest bitch that ever lived, and all of a sudden, she was no longer calling me a dirty motherfucker, she was calling me a sweet motherfucker! It got quiet, I sat up on the edge of the bed, with my head hanging long and deep, trying to push myself out of the room, and back into it at one and the same time. She looked up at me, and I got that same question all over again—will you marry me? Will you be the father of your son? I tried to move away from her, but she dug her fingernails into my shoulders—I struck her once, twice, and again, and again—with this hand! And her face was a bloody mess! I put my clothes on and I walked out into the streets, trembling because I knew, for the last time, I was gonna have to go back and save that little boy from being a bastard all the days of his life. So, now I have a tender little boy to walk in the park every Sunday, who may one day blow my head off—and an abiding wife, who on a given evening may get herself caught in the bed of some other man, and I could be sealed in a dungeon until dead! I was found lying in a well of blood on the day I was born! I have been kind! I have kissed babies for the simple reason they were babies! I'm going to get married, and that gets me to shaking all over! The last time I trembled this way, *I killed a man!* I can't ever let that happen again. Yes, I'm scared too, Theo—but my head is not hanging! *(Starts to leave)* I'm leaving it up to you for now—but if your father gets too sporty—you get sporty with him, and don't let him spend all that money in one city . . . *(Exits. Theo moves into the back room and sits on the bed. Bobby moves to the door and stands there for a while.)*

Theo: Bobby, I want you to stay away from those store raids . . .

305 Bobby: Not as long as I can get myself some extra money.

Theo: Extra money or no, I don't want you doing it!

Bobby: You don't tell me what to do!

Theo: What are you, some kind of idiot?

Bobby *(strikes him across the face):* Every time you call me that, you get hit! You didn't say nothing to me before, when I was stealing every other day, and I was giving you half of everything I stole! You didn't think nothing that day you sent me for that typewriter!

310 Theo: No, I didn't, stupid! Idiot! Fool! *(Bobby draws back to hit him.)* Hit me! Go on, hit me!

Bobby *(pause):* I don't want to hit you . . . You don't hit back, unless it's a woman . . .

Theo: I don't know what you're going to do from here on in—because I'm telling Pop it's time to call the whole thing off with Blue . . .

Theo: That won't stop me, and you know it!

Theo: What is it Bobby? We used to be so close, and I—

315 Bobby: You know what they called me when we was so tight? Faggot. They said you was slapping me on my naked behind.

Theo: You didn't go for that!

Bobby: Hell, no, I didn't . . . Anybody said something like that to me, got stomped in the ground!

Theo: Bobby, don't get too far away from me!

Bobby: What do you want me to do? Stick around you all the time? *I'm tired of you!*

320 Theo: You can get hurt!

Bobby: Nobody's gonna put their hands on me! *(Pause)* I stick by you, and I don't know what to do! I steal, and that puts clothes on my back, and money in my pockets! *That's something to do!* But I sit up here with you all day, just thinking about the next word I'm gonna say . . . *I'm not stupid! I sit here all day thinking about what I'm going to say to you.* But all I can think about is knowing that that is not enough! I stuck by you, and I hoped for you, because whatever you became, I was gonna become . . . I thought about that too, and that ain't shit! I don't want to talk like that to you, Theo—I swear to that, Theo—I swear to that! I don't want to hurt nobody! *(Pause)* Can we let it be what Pop always say—can we throw it away—can we throw it into the river, Theo?

Theo: Yeah—let's do that . . . *(He hears approaching sounds.)* Shhhh! *(Rising from the bed quickly)* That's Pop, with somebody!

(They dash out into the outer area of the shop. Theo quickly turns the lights out, and they hide in the far right corner of the shop, against the wall, next to the back room.)

Mr. Parker *(stepping down into the room):* Come on girl!

(A very beautiful, well-dressed young girl in her early twenties steps down into the room behind him.)

Girl *(looking about the place):* So this is where you do all your business . . .

325 **Mr. Parker:** You like it—ever been in a place like this before?

Girl: Now what would I be doing in a place like this?

Mr. Parker *(opens the door to the shop and takes a look about in the dark):* I'll fix us a drink . . . *(Heads for the refrigerator)* Sit down, sweetheart . . . *(The Girl sits on the bed as Mr. Parker opens the refrigerator and takes out a jug of corn.)* I'm going to give you a special drink, made from my own hands.

Girl: That should be exciting . . .

Mr. Parker: Here . . . *(Hands her the drink.)*

330 **Girl** *(taking the drink):* Thank you . . .

Mr. Parker *(sits next to her on the bed):* Toujours L'amour![10]

Girl: Same to you! *(She drinks.)* Hmmmmmmm . . . it's delicious!

Mr. Parker: I told you, didn't I . . . I only make that for the family here . . . Private stock—never let a drop of it out of the house . . . *(Kisses her on the cheek.)*

Girl: Did you give any thought to what I said to you last night?

335 **Mr. Parker:** I certainly did, but I'll have to wait a little while before we can go ahead . . .

Girl: You said you loved me . . .

Mr. Parker: Like a flower—like singing a song in the rain . . . *(Kisses her on the cheek.)*

Girl: Sometimes, you make me feel as if you don't trust me, but I thought that love and trust went together.

Mr. Parker: I'm not so sure about that . . . My son, Theo—I'm wild about him, but I wouldn't trust him no farther than I could throw him.

340 **Girl:** I'm not your son! *(Pause)* Well, what can I say if you don't trust me?

Mr. Parker: I didn't say that at all, honey . . . What I said, was that I still don't know if I can get married right now. My wife ain't been dead a year yet, I just can't up and get married, like that. It would break the children's hearts.

Girl: But where does that leave me? I'm a woman, and I've got feelings . . . I'm alive. It's not every day I fall in love with someone, and as for

---

[10] Love always.

marriage, I've never given it a thought, for anyone! Now you think about that!

Mr. Parker *(starts to fondle her thighs):* I think all the time, sweetheart . . .

Girl *(breaks away from him):* No!

345 **Mr. Parker:** What's wrong?

Girl: You've got to say you'll marry me!

Mr. Parker: All right, I'll say it . . .

Girl: And you've got to mean it!

Mr. Parker *(pause):* I mean it—I'll take you down to the courthouse on Monday . . .

350 **Girl:** I don't want to push you into anything, Russell, but all men ever want to do is put you into bed.

Mr. Parker: You don't say! I'm not like that . . . I'm a man of many worlds, many things, and I've been taking care of you, and I'm gon continue to take care of you . . . *(Takes out the envelope from his pocket and exhibits a stack of bills)* You see this . . . I'm gon take you downtown tomorrow, and let you spend til' the store runs out. *(Peels off a few hundred)* Here's some pocket money for you . . .

Girl *(taking the money quickly and putting it away):* Russell, you're always giving me money, and you've got to stop it!

Mr. Parker: Now, I don't want to hear you talking about money to me, baby. I've got plenty of it! *(Rises quickly, moves to the desk, and takes out his notebook)* You've got to understand—I'm the most different man you ever met . . . I've been around this world—I danced before the King and Queen of England . . . I've seen and heard a whole lot of things in my lifetime. And you know what—I'm putting it all down on paper. My story!

Girl: Your story?

355 **Mr. Parker:** Here it is, right here . . . *(Sits back down next to her on the bed and opens up the notebook.)*

Girl: You write too?

Mr. Parker: I certainly do . . .

Girl *(opens up the book):* All this you wrote . . . A whole page!

Mr. Parker: Every word of it, and I been thinking about writing a poem about you . . .

360 **Girl:** What? Write a poem about me?

Mr. Parker: I'm gon do it tonight before I go to sleep.

Girl: You're so kind to me, Russell . . . I guess that's why I'm so impatient . . . I just can't wait to get all of you for myself. I do love you, Russell . . . *(He embraces and kisses her.)* You hold a woman so much like a man . . .

Mr. Parker *(kissing her on the neck and reaching for the tip of her dress at the knees):* Uh huh . . .

Girl *(breaks away from him):* No, Russell, not here!

365 **Mr. Parker:** Why not, we're on a bed!

Girl: Just because there's a bed wherever we go don't mean that we have to jump into it.

Mr. Parker: I have heard of people doing it on the floor—that's not my style, but if the floor is all right by you, I'm willing to go along with the program, so long as we—

Girl: You don't understand, Russell!

(Blackout on back room, and spots come up on Bobby and Theo in the outer part of the shop.)

Bobby: What's going on in there?

370 **Theo:** Didn't you hear them?

Bobby: Let's peep!

Theo: We can't do that! If he catches us here, he'll kill us. *(Pause)* Come on, let's ease our way out of the door before the action starts.

(Spots off Bobby and Theo. Lights come up full on the back room.)

Girl: You've got to start treating me the same as if I was your wife!

Mr. Parker: That's exactly what I'm trying to do!

375 **Girl:** You keep yelling at me, I'm going to cry!

Mr. Parker: All right, whatever you do, don't cry . . . I tell you what, let's just lie down for a while and talk . . . I ain't gon try nothing . . .

Girl: Russell . . .

Mr. Parker: May the Lord smack me down this minute into hell . . . I swear I won't do nothing.

Girl: What are the three biggest lies men tell to women, Russell?

380 **Mr. Parker:** I ain't just any man—you already said that yourself!

Girl: Okay, Russell, we'll lie down but you've got to keep your word. If I'm the girl you want to marry, you've got to learn to keep your word. *(Sits on the bed.)*

Mr. Parker *(jumps on the bed and lands on his back):* Ahhhhh—that feels good! *(Pause)* Baby, you are as cute as a button, the way you say things, when you ain't too sure of yourself . . .

Girl *(still sitting, looking down on him):* Am I?

Mr. Parker *(stroking her back):* Yeah, and you're soft like a kitten . . . *(Pulls her by the shoulders)* Come here . . . *(He pulls her down to the bed, takes her in his arms, and kisses her. Immediately, he is again reaching for the tip of her dress.)*

385 **Girl** *(struggling):* Russell, you said you wouldn't do anything!

Mr. Parker: I ain't! I just want to get a little closer to you!

Girl: Russell, not here!

Mr. Parker: Just let me feel it a little bit!

Girl: You swore to God, Russell!

390 **Mr. Parker:** I ain't gon do nothing! *(A big noise lets out in the shop. One of the boys has knocked down the clothes rack. Mr. Parker rises quickly, goes to the door, opens it, and turns the lights on. There are Bobby and Theo, on their knees, crawling frantically to get to the door leading to the street.)* What are you doing here?

(Bobby jumps up and dashes out of the front door.)

Theo *(rising slowly):* Er—er . . .

Mr. Parker: Er, what?

Theo: We, we were just trying to er—it was so dark in here, we were trying to feel our way to the door, and we didn't want to disturb you . . .

Mr. Parker: Disturb what?

395   Theo: Well, you was er, you was er—

Mr. Parker: You waser! You waser! I have been having a private talk with a good friend of mine . . . Now get out of here!

(The Girl, still on the bed, rises sharply as Adele staggers down from the stairs. She leans on the wall at the base of the stairs. She is obviously drunk.)

Adele: Who are you?

(The Girl does not answer, and rushes out of the room into the outer part of the shop, closing the door behind her.)

Mr. Parker: Where are you going?

Girl: I'm going home!

400   Mr. Parker: Hold it now, honey . . .

Girl: If you want me, I'll be home . . . I never should have come to this barbershop in the first place!

Mr. Parker: I'll be right over there as soon as I get things straight here. Will you be waiting for me?

Girl: Yes, but don't you keep me waiting for you all night . . .

Mr. Parker *(kisses her on the cheek):* You run along now, I'll be right over there . . . *(The Girl exits out of the front door. To Theo)* I thought I told you to move!

405   Theo: I'm not going anywhere until I get my money . . .

Mr. Parker: You'll get your part tomorrow, I told you that!

Theo: I want it now, before you give it all to that girl! . . . Cut that broad loose, Pop!

Mr. Parker *(turns back toward Theo sharply):* What did you say?

Theo: Give me my money . . . I worked hard for that money! *You are my father!* I don't have to be treated like this! *(Tears are welling in his eyes.)*

410   Mr. Parker: You heard me—*what did you say?*

Theo: I said, cut her loose! That bitch is a hustler!

Mr. Parker *(strikes him across the face with the back of his hand):* Bite your tongue!

Theo *(pause):* Just be careful, Pop . . . please be careful . . .

Mr. Parker: If there's anybody I got to be careful of, it's you! You lying, selfish sonofabitch! You think I don't know about you and Blue running that gang of thieves?

415   Theo: You know why I didn't tell you?

Mr. Parker: I don't give a damn about those stories! But you sent your own brother out there!

Theo: I didn't do that!

Mr. Parker: If Bobby gets hurt on them streets out there, I'm gonna kill you, boy! I'm gonna kill you!

Theo: You're not worried about Bobby! All you can think about is the money you're rolling in! The clothes! And that stupid outfit you've got on—and now you're the great lover!

(Adele staggers to the doorway leading out into the shop.)

420 Adele: He loves the way she walks, he loves the way she talks. *He is the apple of her orchard grove; He is her master!* He is a fool . . .

Mr. Parker: Adele . . . *(Goes to her and puts his arm around her shoulders.)*

Adele: Take your hands off me!

Theo: Did you think that everything would stop and stand still while you were being reborn again?

Mr. Parker: What do you want from me? Call this whole thing off? This was your idea, not mine! I've got myself something, and I'm not going to throw it away for nobody!

425 Theo: But can't you see what's happening here?

Mr. Parker: If she wants to be a drunken wench out in that street—let her do it! But I'm not going to take the blame for it! That's not me out there throwing myself in the arms of a bunch of rattlesnakes! And as for you . . . *(Goes into his pocket)* If you want this money, you can take it from me—I can throw every dollar of it into the ocean if I want to! *I'm burning!* I'm going to marry that girl! She is not a whore! She is a woman! And I'm going to marry her! And if you don't like it, you can kiss my ass! *(Bolts out of the door and into the streets.)*

Adele *(staggers to the door hurriedly and stops there):* You're going to kill yourself, old man! You're nothing but a stupid old man that's about to die!

Theo *(goes to her and puts his arms around her):* What are you doing to yourself?

Adele *(breaks away from him, mocks):* "I'm black—I've been violated by my environment," so anything goes! Isn't that the damnable excuse we always give?

430 Theo: I see a boy dying in the streets from an overload of cocaine—I don't pity him, I don't put him down, and I don't feel guilty because I'm too chicken shit to go near him. He's gon die anyway—this whole place was built for him to die in, but I'm not going to die, Adele—I'll do anything to keep alive, even if I have to live in this hole forever!

Adele: If you wanta live, Theo, and if you think you've got anything to spread across that canvas, then you should take that brush and stroke that canvas until your hands bleed, until you get so tired you want to cry.

Theo: It's not that simple!

Adele: Nothing is!

Theo: Why don't you leave me alone, woman!

435 Adele: If I did, all of you would be on the streets tomorrow!

Theo: And don't hand me all that business about sacrificing your life away for the house—taking care of everybody. You stayed here because you had no other place to go. You got scared too soon and too young, and you're still shaking in your bones, baby!

Adele *(pause):* Yes, that's true, and I suppose I did know the difference between what was happening to me here, and what could have happened any place—that somehow, Mother would have died whether I was with her or not, that life was just as dangerous on a countryside in California as it was here, because what I did was to merely wait for her to die, and still she took too long for that, and when life did pass on for her—*I wanted to celebrate!* I thought then I was going to build a huge bright palace only suited for the living, but all I could feel was the trouble of having someone to die in order that I might finally wake up and live—I began to know what was nailing Father against all these walls, and I wanted to rip him loose—I thought it would be my duty to free all of us, but who the hell ever told every black woman she was some kind of damn saviour! *(Pause)* That can cause your body to grow cold until pain becomes a pleasure—till you have no sense for the sweetness of water, because you're already drenched in it—till you live everyday as if it was a desperate task or duty—Sure, this place was built for us to die in, but if we're not very, very careful, Theo—that can actually happen . . . *(Pause.)*

Theo *(rushes into the back room):* Dammit! *(Takes out the targets and starts tearing them up.)* Get away from me, Blue! Get away man! Get out of here! *(Takes out some of his bottles. There is a loud banging on the front door.)* Get out of there! We're closed! Forever! *(The banging persists with a voice calling out to Theo.)*

Adele *(rushes to the door and peeps from behind the shade):* It's Mr. Jenkins . . . *(She opens the door and allows him to enter. Mr. Jenkins enters.)*

440 Adele: Something wrong, Mr. Jenkins . . . ? *(He does not respond.)* Mr. Jenkins, I asked if there was something wrong. *(He still does not respond.)*

Theo: God dammit man, what's wrong with you?

Mr. Jenkins *(pause):* I . . . *(Looks long at her, then turns his back to walk away)* No . . .

Adele *(grabs him by the arm and spins him around):* Mr. Jenkins!

Mr. Jenkins *(searching for a word to begin what he has to say):* They . . . I was having a drink at Lou's, and they broke into this store, right next door—three of 'em . . . Two got caught, and the other one ran . . . They shot him two times!

445 Adele: Oh no . . . *(Moves away from him briskly and stops at the door to the back room with her back on them.)*

Theo: What is it, Mr. Jenkins?

Mr. Jenkins: Your brother Bobby is dead . . .

Theo *(pause):* It's a crime, Mr. Jenkins . . . It's a crime—that's all it is . . .

Mr. Jenkins: If there's something I can do to—

450 Theo: There is nothing, Mr. Jenkins . . .

Mr. Jenkins: Good night, Theo . . . Good night, Adele . . . *(He moves out of the front door.)*

Theo *(looks in on Adele, still with her back to him in the back room doorway, with her head buried in her hands):* Let's go see him, and then we'll try to find the old man . . .

CURTAIN

ACT II

Scene 2

About two hours later, in the shop.

Mr. Parker and Mr. Jenkins enter the front part of the shop. Mr. Parker is drunk, and Mr. Jenkins is assisting him to move on his feet. He finally seats him on the barber's throne.

Mr. Parker: Thank you, Jenkins—you are the greatest friend a man can have. They don't make 'em like you anymore. You are one of the last of the great friends, Jenkins . . . Pardon me—Mr. Jenkins. No more will I ever call you Jenks or Jenkins . . . From now on, it's Mr. Jenkins!

Mr. Jenkins: Thank you, but when I ran into Theo and Adele tonight, they said they had something important to say to you, and I thing you oughta see them . . .

Mr. Parker: I know what they want . . . They wanta tell me what an old fool I am . . .

Mr. Jenkins: I don't think that's it, and you should go on upstairs and—

5 **Mr. Parker:** Never! Upstairs is for the people upstairs!

Mr. Jenkins: Russell, I—

Mr. Parker: I am downstairs people! You ever hear of downstairs people?

Mr. Jenkins *(pause):* No . . .

Mr. Parker: Well, they're the people to watch in this world . . .

10 **Mr. Jenkins:** If you say so . . .

Mr. Parker: *Put your money on 'em!*

Mr. Jenkins: Come on, Mr. Parker, why don't you at least lie down in the back room . . .

Mr. Parker: Oh no—you don't think I'd have you come all the way over here just for me to go to bed, do you? I wouldn't do a thing like that to you, Jenkins—I'm sorry—"Mr. Jenkins" . . .

Mr. Jenkins: Well, for one thing, I could use some sleep myself.

15 **Mr. Parker:** Just stay with me for a little while, Mr. Jenkins . . .

Mr. Jenkins: For a little while . . .

Mr. Parker: Why did that girl lock me out? She said she would be waiting for me but she locked me out. Why did she do a thing like that? I give her everything—money, clothes, pay her rent—I even love her!

Mr. Jenkins: Please, Mr. Parker, you have got to get yourself some sleep.

Mr. Parker: Tell me something, Mr. Jenkins—since you are my friend—why do you think she locked me out?

20 **Mr. Jenkins:** I don't know what to tell you . . .

Mr. Parker: I am an old man and all I've got is a few dollars in my pocket—ain't that it?

Mr. Jenkins: I don't know, Parker!

Mr. Parker: Come on man, the truth!

Mr. Jenkins *(pause):* Well that's the way it is with these young girls . . .

25 **Mr. Parker:** How would you know?

Mr. Jenkins *(pause):* I had a young girl myself about a year ago—that was enough for me, and now I've got to—*(Starts for the door.)*

Mr. Parker *(stumbles down from the chair and blocks him at the door):* You never told me about that . . .

Mr. Jenkins: Let me out of here, Parker—please let me out of here!

Mr. Parker: Something happened to you, man, I need to know!

30 **Mr. Jenkins:** It's not that important!

Mr. Parker: I am your friend—you talk to a friend about things like that . . .

Mr. Jenkins: I was ashamed!

Mr. Parker: Before me? Russell B. Parker?

Mr. Jenkins: I just didn't want to talk about it! It happened so fast, I wanted to forget it!

35 **Mr. Parker** *(pause):* Please stay and tell me what happened, Mr. Jenkins . . . *(He moves away from him, takes up a jug of whiskey from the table, and moves back to him, pouring a drink.)*

Mr. Jenkins *(takes the glass of whiskey from him):* She left me, but what hurted me was that she didn't leave me for another man, she left me for *another woman* . . .

Mr. Parker: Took your love and your materials, and left you for *another woman?*

Mr. Jenkins: Yes . . .

Mr. Parker: That's a dirty way to lose a woman . . .

40 **Mr. Jenkins** *(puts his glass out for another drink):* I didn't tell anybody about it . . . I just wanted to forget it as quick as *I could.*

Mr. Parker *(pours him a big drink):* I can't blame you for that—It ain't every day a man loses his *woman* to a *woman.*

Mr. Jenkins *(drinks up):* Good night, Parker . . .

Mr. Parker *(immediately taking the glass from his hand and pouring him another large drink):* You think a man was in that room with my girl?

Mr. Jenkins *(taking the glass back into his hand with his patience just about gone):* YES!

45 **Mr. Parker:** God dammit! God dammit!

Mr. Jenkins: Russell . . .

Mr. Parker: I don't believe it! When I love 'em, they stay loved!

Mr. Jenkins: Nobody's got that much love, man!

Mr. Parker *(pause):* No, no . . . You're wrong . . . My wife—my dear Doris—had more love in her than life should've allowed . . . A hundred men couldn't have taken all that love . . .

50 **Mr. Jenkins:** We're not talking about Doris, Russell—We're talking about these young girls—either they're not built to take what we can give them, or we're just old men with nothing much to give them anyway . . .

Mr. Parker: Aw forget it! *(Moves into the back room, and takes out a bottle from the refrigerator)* It just can't be! *(Pours a drink for himself and passes the bottle on to his friend)* A long time before my wife died, I stopped loving her, and for a long time, I spent all of my days and nights feeling sick about it, because not a day passed I didn't look out of that window to see some woman I wanted to at least try to love . . . I tried to push the feeling back . . . I had it in me! Why can't I live and love until the day I die?

Mr. Jenkins *(pours himself a drink):* When you live as long as we have, you begin to think that everything is possible. I mean, that's all we've got, Parker. You go downtown, looking and believing you can get a job as an elevator operator in one of those high buildings, and when they send you to the basement with a broom, you still don't believe it, because when you go to work, you wear a better suit of clothes than the man who runs the place. You change over into overalls, but you don't give a damn about them overalls. You go home in your suit, you conquer the saloons, the pool halls, the numbers, and the checker games. You lie like all hell. You smile at them young girls, and tell them you're the supervisor of the place where you work—you dine 'em, dance 'em, and you take 'em to bed—you're a moon messiah, a desert God! But everything you do is nothing more than what you do from *memory!*

Mr. Parker *(after a moment of complete silence, standing before Mr. Jenkins with his hands in his pockets, does a little dance):* All from memory? *(Stops.)*

Mr. Jenkins: All . . .

55 **Mr. Parker:** Dammit! You die in your heart not to forget!

Mr. Jenkins: You stumble about like an old black cow!

Mr. Parker *(does another little dance):* You fall down one day! *(Deliberately lets himself fall to the floor.)*

Mr. Jenkins: And you never get up again!

Mr. Parker *(lying on the floor in a relaxed position, singing):*

> I have had my fun!
> If I don't get well no more!
> I have had my fun!
> If I—

Get up old bastard! Get up! *(Rises to his feet)* Get up and fall back down again . . . Come on, Mr. Jenkins, let's play a game of checkers!

60 **Mr. Jenkins:** Man, why don't you go to bed!

Mr. Parker *(starts setting up the board):* Playing checkers Mr. Jenkins is all right—you have nothing to remember but how you beat me all the time . . .

Mr. Jenkins: *I want to get out of this damn place!*

Mr. Parker *(pause):* Why do you curse my home, Mr. Jenkins?

Mr. Jenkins *(pause):* I apologize for that . . .

65 Mr. Parker: Come on, have a game of checkers with your good friend . . .

Mr. Jenkins *(moves to the table):* All right, one game and then I'm going home.

Mr. Parker: One game. *(He shakes up the can, and Mr. Jenkins takes a man. They start their exchange of moves and jumps.)*

Mr. Parker *(pause):* I said a lot of dirty things to my children tonight. The kind of things you have to live a long time to overcome.

Mr. Jenkins: I know what you mean—That's why I'm glad none of mine are living anywhere close to me.

70 Mr. Parker: Theo is a good boy, and a smart one too, but he lets people push him around. I guess that's because he's always trying to con somebody out of something—you know the kind, can't see for looking . . . And Bobby? You should've seen him . . . take off from here, when I caught him and Theo peeping on me tonight . . . *(Laughs)* Bobby wouldn't hurt a flea . . . A lot of people think that boy is dumb, but just let somebody try to trick or fool him if they dare! *(Pause)* Got a story for you . . .

Mr. Jenkins: No stories tonight, Parker . . .

Mr. Parker: Call me Mr. Parker . . .

Mr. Jenkins: Mr. Parker . . .

(The last move is made. The game is over, and Mr. Parker is, at long last, the victor.)

Mr. Parker *(rises from the table):* Call me champ!

(Theo and Adele enter from the front entrance. Theo remains at the door, and Adele moves down the aisle of the shop and stops just at the doorway of the back room.)

75 Mr. Parker *(laughing):* You're beat! I beat you! I beat you! *(Mr. Jenkins starts out, but Mr. Parker throws his arms around his waist and holds him from the rear.)* You fall down, and you never get up! *(Laughing)* Fall down, old man! Fall down! *(He releases Mr. Jenkins.)* You hear that, children, I beat him! I beat him! *(He realizes that they are not responding to him. He looks about, groping, then reaches into his inside coat pocket, and pulls out the money.)* Here, Theo—here's your money . . . *(Goes to him)* . . . Take it, it's yours—go out and try to get happy, boy. *(Theo does not move, nor does he speak. Mr. Parker then turns to Adele; her face is almost a blank.)* Why don't somebody say something? *(With still no reaction from them, he moves for the back room.)* I know, you have some trouble with me . . . *(He takes his notebook from the old desk in the back room, moves back out into the shop, and stands before Adele.)*

You have a woman—you love her—you stop loving her, and sooner or later, she ups and dies, and you sit around behaving like you was a killer. I didn't have no more in me. *I just didn't have no more in me! (pause)* I know you don't believe I *ever* loved her, but it's here in this book . . . Read it . . . *(She does not respond, but he turns sharply to Theo.)* You wanta read something, boy? *(Theo just stands there with his hands in his pockets. Mr. Parker moves to the throne and sits. He hands the notebook out to Mr. Jenkins.)* Please say something to me children! *(Almost in a whisper)* I just didn't have no more in me . . . *(He moves down out of the chair and addresses his remarks to Mr. Jenkins.)* I got sour the day my legs got so trembly sore on the stage of the Strand Theatre—I couldn't even move out to take a proper bow. That was a long hard day for me, and it took me three weeks to talk to my Doris about it. And you know something? She didn't say a word—she just went out and got a job—she did it as if it was her duty. And as for me, I didn't know what I was supposed to do—I just couldn't run downtown to meet the man the way she did—not after all those years of shuffling round like I was a dumb clown, with my feet hurting and aching the way they did, having my head patted as if I was some little pet animal, back of the bus, front of the train, yassah, nosuh, grinning when I was bleeding to death! After all of that I was going to ask for more by throwing myself into the low drag of some dusty old factory in Brooklyn? Sure, I felt sick for having to depend so much on my wife, and my daughter here—but if I had done the right thing—just think about that now, the right thing!—it would have blinded my eyes forever, ruptured my heart, and broken every bone in my soul. All I could do was to stay here in this shop with you, my good friend, and we played a game. I just couldn't move! An old man pays his dues, and a time comes when all he can do is to act out the ceremony of a game, and hope to lie down easily one day, and die quietly . . . That's all we could afford, Mr. Jenkins . . . And you, boy . . . *(Turns to Theo)* you and Blue with your ideas of overcoming the evil of white men—to an old man like me, it was nothing more than an ounce of time to end my dragging about this shop—it sent me sailing out into those streets to live a time—and I did live myself a time. I did it amongst a bunch of murderers, all kinds of 'em—where at times it gets so bad, til' it seems that the only thing that's left for you is to go out there and kill somebody before they kill you. To eat out your own gizzards, just so's you don't get to become a killer. *That's all that's out there!* And if at my age, I was stupid enough to think that I could have stepped out of here and won that little girl, loved her, and moved through the rest of my days without killing anybody, *that was a victory! (He moves to the center of the floor, stands silently for awhile, and then does a little dance.)* Be a dancer—any kind of dancer you wanta be—but whatever you do, dance it! *(Tries out a difficult step, but can't quite make it)* Uh uhhh! Can't make that one no more . . . *(Continues to dance)* Be a singer—sing any song you wanta sing—but sing! *(Stops in his tracks) And you've got*

enough trouble to take you to the graveyard! But think of all that life
you had before they buried you! (He breaks into a frantic dance, at-
tempting steps that are crossing him up. He stumbles about until he
falls. Theo, Mr. Jenkins, and Adele rush to pick him up from the floor.)
I'm okay—I'm okay . . . *(He rises from the floor quickly on his own.*
They stop in their tracks.) I'm tired, I'm going to bed, and by the time
tomorrow comes around, children, let's see if we can't throw it all into
the river. *(Moves into the back room, singing)*

> I have had my fun
> If I don't get well no more
> I have had my fun
> If I don't get well no more

(Stops in the center of the room, turns looking over Adele's shoulder
through the door out into the shop) Jenkins, you said the day I beat you
playing checkers, you said it could be the unluckiest day of my
life . . . But after all that's happened today—I'm straight—I feel just
great! *(Moves sharply to the stairs, stops and turns)* Say, where's Bobby?

CURTAIN

■ EXPLORATIONS OF THE TEXT ■

Act I

1. What associations does the setting of the barber shop evoke? What
   connotations and **ironies** does the term *barber throne* suggest?
2. What are your first impressions of Mr. Parker? Of Mr. Jenkins? What
   are the two men's positions regarding work?
3. Examine Theo's and Bobby's characters. How are Theo and Bobby their
   father's sons? How do they differ from each other?
4. Analyze Mr. Parker's character. Why does he remain in the barber shop
   although the enterprise is a failure?
5. What is the nature of the conflict between Adele and her father and
   brothers? Why does she deliver the ultimatum about their finding jobs?
6. Why is Mister Blue able to entice Mr. Parker, Bobby, and Theo?
   Describe and assess Blue's character. What does he symbolize?
7. What does the Harlem De-Colonization Association signify? What is its
   function? What political critique is implied?
8. What are the relationships of the main protagonists at the end of Act I?
   How has the balance of power shifted in the family? Analyze each
   family member's last speech.

Act II

9. How does having money change the central protagonists?
10. Analyze Blue's monologue in Act II, Scene 1. Contrast his character and Theo's.
11. How does Theo's and Bobby's relationship change in Act II?
12. What are the tragedies of Mr. Parker's and Mr. Jenkins's lives? How did love fail them? How did "work" fail them?
    What does Mr. Parker mean when he implores: "Be a dancer—any kind of dancer you wanta be—but whatever you do, dance it!"?
13. What is the symbolism of the checker game?
14. Explore the **dramatic irony** of the closing line: "Say, where's Bobby?" What is the significance of Bobby's death?
15. Examine the relationship of African-American men, the white world of work, and the American dream; of black women and that world.
16. How does the North American political and economic system fail all of these characters?
17. Discuss the theme of aging in the play. What is the significance of the title?
18. What are the "ceremonies of dark old men"? Be specific.

■■ JOURNAL ENTRIES ■■

1. Mr. Parker calls Theo "uneducated smart." Write a reaction to this statement. Is "uneducated smart" the best form of education?
2. React to the portrayal of the women in this drama.
3. Respond to Mr. Parker's last long monologue.
4. What is Mr. Jenkins' role in the drama?
5. React to the title.

■■■ IDEAS FOR WRITING ■■■

1. Compare Bobby and Theo.
2. What perversions of the dream of "getting rich quick," of the Horatio Alger myth of success, does the playwright depict? What are the consequences of believing in this twisted fantasy?
3. How are love and work interrelated? the personal and the political entwined?
4. Contrast the lives of the men and women in the play.
5. What problems of urban life, of street life, of life in the inner city does the drama portray? You also may refer to "Sonny's Blues."

NONFICTION

A Christmas Memory

Truman Capote

Born Truman Streckfus Persons (1924–1984) in New Orleans, Louisiana, Truman Capote lived a difficult and lonely childhood. Even before his parents were divorced and he had turned four, Capote's mother, a former Miss Alabama who later committed suicide, sent him away to live with relatives in Alabama. At nine, Capote was adopted by his stepfather, Joe Capote. Despite unusually high scores on intelligence tests, Capote performed poorly in school. After high school, vowing never to set foot in a college classroom, he accepted a clerical job with The New Yorker *and began a long relationship with the magazine that eventually serialized his most famous work,* In Cold Blood *(1966).*

Capote's first novel, Other Voices, Other Rooms *(1948) was a partially autobiographical, highly provocative story of a young man's search for love with another man. Capote wrote short stories (*A Tree of Night *in 1949), nonfiction travel essays and portraits (*Local Color *in 1950 and a commentary for Richard Avedon's* Observations *in 1959), original film scripts for* Beat the Devil *(1954) and* The Innocents *(1961), and adaptations of his earlier novel,* The Grass Harp *(1951), and short story, "House of Flowers," into Broadway plays.*

After Breakfast at Tiffany's *(1958), a novel in which he drew fictionalized accounts of real life incidents and which was adapted into a popular film, Capote began his search for an innovative genre that would bring "the art of the novelist together with the technique of journalism." The result,* In Cold Blood *(1966), was not only a critical and commercial success, but also a significant contribution to a new experimental genre, the nonfiction novel.*

His awards include an O. Henry Award, a National Institute of Arts and Letters Award, an Edgar Award from Mystery Writers of America, and an Emmy Award for a television adaptation of "A Christmas Memory."

This essay is Capote's partially autobiographical account of his childhood relationship with his distant cousin.

1   Imagine a morning in late November. A coming of winter morning more than twenty years ago. Consider the kitchen of a spreading old house in a country town. A great black stove is its main feature; but there is also a big round table and a fireplace with two rocking chairs placed in front of it. Just today the fireplace commenced its seasonal roar.

    A woman with shorn white hair is standing at the kitchen window. She is wearing tennis shoes and a shapeless gray sweater over a summery calico dress. She is small and sprightly, like a bantam hen; but, due to a long youthful illness, her shoulders are pitifully hunched. Her face is remarkable—not unlike Lincoln's, craggy like that, and tinted by sun and wind; but it is delicate too, finely boned, and her eyes are sherry-colored and timid. "Oh my," she exclaims, her breath smoking the windowpane, "it's fruitcake weather!"

    The person to whom she is speaking is myself. I am seven; she is sixty-something. We are cousins, very distant ones, and we have lived together—well, as long as I can remember. Other people inhabit the house, relatives; and though they have power over us, and frequently make us cry, we are not, on the whole, too much aware of them. We are each other's best friend. She calls me Buddy, in memory of a boy who was formerly her best friend. The other Buddy died in the 1880s, when she was still a child. She is still a child.

    "I knew it before I got out of bed," she says, turning away from the window with a purposeful excitement in her eyes. "The courthouse bell sounded so cold and clear. And there were no birds singing; they've gone to warmer country, yes indeed. Oh, Buddy, stop stuffing biscuit and fetch our buggy. Help me find my hat. We've thirty cakes to bake."

5   It's always the same: a morning arrives in November, and my friend, as though officially inaugurating the Christmas time of year that exhilarates her imagination and fuels the blaze of her heart, announces: "It's fruitcake weather! Fetch our buggy. Help me find my hat."

    The hat is found, a straw cartwheel corsaged with velvet roses out-of-doors has faded: it once belonged to a more fashionable relative. Together, we guide our buggy, a dilapidated baby carriage, out to the garden and into a grove of pecan trees. The buggy is mine; that is, it was bought for me when I was born. It is made of wicker, rather unraveled, and the wheels wobble like a drunkard's legs. But it a faithful object; springtimes, we take it to the woods and fill it with flowers, herbs, wild fern for our porch pots; in the summer, we pile it with picnic paraphernalia and sugar-cane fishing poles and roll it down to the edge of a creek; it has its winter uses, too: as a truck for hauling firewood from the yard to the kitchen, as a warm bed for Queenie, our tough little orange and white rat terrier who has survived distemper and two rattlesnake bites. Queenie is trotting beside it now.

    Three hours later we are back in the kitchen hulling a heaping buggyload of windfall pecans. Our backs hurt from gathering them: how hard they were to find (the main crop having been shaken off the trees and sold by the orchard's owners, who are not us) among the concealing leaves, the frosted, deceiving grass. Caarackle! A cheery crunch, scraps of miniature thunder sound as the shells collapse and the golden mound of sweet oily ivory meat mounts in the milk-glass bowl. Queenie begs to taste, and now and again my friend sneaks her a mite, though insisting we deprive ourselves. "We mustn't, Buddy. If we start, we won't stop. And there's scarcely enough as there is. For thirty cakes." The kitchen is growing dark. Dusk turns the window into a mirror: our reflections mingle with the rising moon as we work by the fireside in the firelight. At last, when the moon is quite high, we toss the final hull into the fire and, with joined sighs, watch it catch flame. The buggy is empty, the bowl is brimful.

We eat our supper (cold biscuits, bacon, blackberry jam) and discuss tomorrow. Tomorrow the kind of work I like best begins: buying Cherries and citron, ginger and vanilla and canned Hawaiian pineapple, rinds and raisins and walnuts and whiskey and oh, so much flour, butter, so many eggs, spices, flavorings: why, we'll need a pony to pull the buggy home.

But before these purchases can be made, there is the question of money. Neither of us has any. Except for skinflint sums persons in the house occasionally provide (a dime is considered very big money); or what we earn ourselves from various activities: holding rummage sales, selling buckets of hand-picked blackberries, jars of homemade jam and apple jelly and peach preserves, rounding up flowers for funerals and weddings. Once we won seventy-ninth prize, five dollars, in a national football contest. Not that we know a fool thing about football. It's just that we enter any contest we hear about: at the moment our hopes are centered on the fifty-thousand-dollar Grand Prize being offered to name a new brand of coffee (we suggested "A.M."; and, after some hesitation, for my friend thought it perhaps sacrilegious, the slogan "A.M.! Amen!"). To tell the truth, our only *really* profitable enterprise was the Fun and Freak Museum we conducted on a back-yard woodshed two summers ago. The Fun was a stereopticon with slide views of Washington and New York lent us by a relative who had been to those places (she was furious when she discovered why we'd borrowed it); the Freak was a three-legged biddy chicken hatched by one of our own hens. Everybody hereabouts wanted to see that biddy: we charged grownups a nickel, kids two cents. And took in a good twenty dollars before the museum shut down due to the decease of the main attraction.

10   But one way and another we do each year accumulate Christmas savings, a Fruitcake Fund. These moneys we keep hidden in an ancient bead purse under a loose board under the floor under a chamber pot under my friend's bed. The purse is seldom removed from this safe location except to make a deposit, or, as happens every Saturday, a withdrawal; for on Saturdays I am allowed ten cents to go to the picture show. My friend has never been to a picture show, nor does she intend to: "I'd rather hear you tell the story, Buddy. That way I can imagine it more. Besides, a person my age shouldn't squander their eyes. When the Lord comes, let me see him clear." In addition to never having seen a movie, she has never: eaten in a restaurant, traveled more than five miles from home, received or sent a telegram, read anything except funny papers and the Bible, worn cosmetics, cursed, wished someone harm, told a lie on purpose, let a hungry dog go hungry. Here are a few things

she has done, does do: killed with a hoe the biggest rattlesnake ever seen in this county (sixteen rattles), dip snuff (secretly), tame hummingbirds (just try it) till they balance on her finger, tell ghost stories (we both believe in ghosts) so tingling they chill you in July, talk to herself, take walks in the rain, grow the prettiest japonicas in town, know the recipe for every sort of old-time Indian cure, including a magical wart-remover.

Now, with supper finished, we retire to the room in a faraway part of the house where my friend sleeps in a scrap-quilt-covered iron bed painted rose pink, her favorite color. Silently, wallowing in the pleasures of conspiracy, we take the bead purse from its secret place and spill its contents on the scrap quilt. Dollar bills, tightly rolled and green as May buds. Somber fifty-cent pieces, heavy enough to weight a dead man's eyes. Lovely dimes, the liveliest coin, the one that really jingles. Nickels and quarters, worn smooth as creek pebbles. But mostly a hateful heap of bitter-odored pennies. Last summer others in the house contracted to pay us a penny for every twenty-five flies we killed. Oh, the carnage of August: the flies that flew to heaven! Yet it was not work in which we took pride. And, as we sit counting pennies, it is as though we were back tabulating dead flies. Neither of us has a head for figures; we count slowly, lose track, start again. According to her calculations, we have $12.73. According to mine, exactly $13. "I do hope you're wrong, Buddy. We can't mess around with thirteen. The cakes will fall. Or put somebody in the cemetery. Why, I wouldn't dream of getting out of bed on the thirteenth." This is true: she always spends thirteenths in bed. So, to be on the safe side, we subtract a penny and toss it out the window. Of the ingredients that go into our fruitcakes, whiskey is the most expensive, as well as the hardest to obtain: State laws forbid its sale. But everybody knows you can buy a bottle from Mr. Haha Jones. And the next day, having completed our more prosaic shopping, we set out for Mr. Haha's business address, a "sinful" (to quote public opinion) fish-fry and dancing café down by the river. We've been there before, and on the same errand; but in previous years our dealings have been with Haha's wife, an iodine-dark Indian woman with brassy per-oxided hair and a dead-tired disposition. Actually, we've never laid eyes on her husband, though we've heard that he's an Indian too. A giant with razor scars across his cheeks. They call him Haha because he's so gloomy, a man who never laughs. As we approach his café (a large log cabin festooned in-side and out with chains of garish-gay naked light bulbs and standing by the river's muddy edge under the shade of river trees where moss drifts through the branches like gray mist) our steps slow down. Even Queenie stops prancing and sticks close by. People have been murdered in Haha's café. Cut to pieces. Hit on the head. There's a case coming up in court next month. Naturally these goings-on happen at night when the colored lights cast crazy patterns and the victrola wails. In the daytime Haha's is shabby and deserted. I knock at the door, Queenie barks, my friend calls. "Mrs. Haha, ma'am? Anyone to home?"

Footsteps. The door opens. Our hearts overturn. It's Mr. Haha Jones him-self! And he *is* a giant; he *does* have scars; he *doesn't* smile. No, he glowers at us through Satan-tilted eyes and demands to know: "What you want with Haha?"

For a moment we are too paralyzed to tell. Presently my friend half-finds her voice, a whispery voice at best: "If you please, Mr. Haha, we'd like a quart of your finest whiskey."

His eyes tilt more. Would you believe it? Haha is smiling! Laughing, too. "Which one of you is a drinkin' man?"

15   "It's for making fruitcakes, Mr. Haha. Cooking."

This sobers him, He frowns. "That's no way to waste good whiskey." Nevertheless, he retreats into the shadowed café and seconds later appears carrying a bottle of daisy yellow unlabeled liquor. He demonstrates its sparkle in the sunlight and says: "Two dollars."

We pay him with nickels and dimes and pennies. Suddenly, jangling the coins in his hand like a fistful of dice, his face softens. "Tell you what," he proposes, pouring the money back into the purse, "just send me one of them fruitcakes instead."

"Well," my friend remarks on our way home, "there's a lovely man. We'll put an extra cup of raisins in *his* cake."

The black stove, stoked with coal and firewood, glows like a lighted pumpkin. Eggbeaters whirl, spoons spin round in bowls of butter and sugar, vanilla sweetens the air, ginger spices it; melting, nose-tingling odors saturate the kitchen, suffuse the house, drift out to the world on puffs of chimney smoke. In four days our work is done. Thirty-one cakes, dampened with whiskey, bask on window sills and shelves.

20   Who are they for?

Friends. Not necessarily neighbor friends: indeed, the larger share are intended for persons we've met maybe once, perhaps not at all. People who've struck our fancy. Like President Roosevelt.[1] Like the Reverend and Mrs. J. C. Lucey, Baptist missionaries to Borneo[2] who lectured here last winter. Or the little knife grinder who comes through town twice a year. Or Abner Packer, the driver of the six o'clock bus from Mobile, who exchanges waves with us every day as he passes in a dust-cloud whoosh. Or the young Wistons, a California couple whose car one afternoon broke down outside the house and who spent a pleasant hour chatting with us on the porch (young Mr. Wiston snapped our picture, the only one we've ever had taken). Is it because my friend is shy with everyone except strangers that these strangers, and merest acquaintances, seem to us our truest friends? I think yes. Also, the scrapbooks we keep of thank-you's on White House stationery, time-to-time communications from California and Borneo, the knife grinder's penny post cards, make us feel connected to eventful worlds beyond the kitchen with its view of a sky that stops.

Now a nude December fig branch grates against the window. The kitchen is empty, the cakes are gone; yesterday we carted the last of them to the post

---

[1] Reference to Franklin Delano Roosevelt (1882–1945), President from 1933–1945.
[2] Island in the Pacific, southwest of the Philippines.

office, where the cost of stamps turned our purse inside out. We're broke. That rather depresses me, but my friend insists on celebrating—with two inches of whiskey left in Haha's bottle. Queenie has a spoonful in a bowl of coffee (she likes her coffee chicory-flavored and strong). The rest we divide between a pair of jelly glasses. We're both quite awed at the prospect of drinking straight whiskey; the taste of it brings screwed-up expressions and sour shudders. But by and by we begin to sing, the two of us singing different songs simultaneously. I don't know the words to mine, just: *Come on along, come on along, to the dark-town strutters' ball.* But I can dance: that's what I mean to be, a tap dancer in the movies. My dancing shadow rollicks on the walls; our voices rock the chinaware; we giggle: as if unseen hands were tickling us. Queenie rolls on her back, her paws plow the air, something like a grin stretches her black lips. Inside myself, I feel warm and sparky as those crumbling logs, carefree as the wind in the chimney. My friend waltzes round the stove, the hem of her poor calico skirt pinched between her fingers as though it were a party dress: *Show me the way to go home,* she sings, her tennis shoes squeaking on the floor. *Show me the way to go home.*

Enter: two relatives. Very angry. Potent with eyes that scold, tongues that scald. Listen to what they have to say, the words tumbling together into a wrathful tune: "A child of seven! whiskey on his breath! are you out of your mind? feeding a child of seven! must be loony! road to ruination! remember Cousin Kate? Uncle Charlie? Uncle Charlie's brother-in-law? shame! scandal! humiliation! kneel, pray, beg the Lord!"

Queenie sneaks under the stove. My friend gazes at her shoes, her chin quivers, she lifts her skirt and blows her nose and runs to her room. Long after the town has gone to sleep and the house is silent except for the chimings of clocks and the sputter of fading fires, she is weeping into a pillow already as wet as a widow's handkerchief.

25   "Don't cry," I say, sitting at the bottom of her bed and shivering despite my flannel nightgown that smells of last winter's cough syrup, "don't cry," I beg, teasing her toes, tickling her feet "you're too old for that."

"It's because," she hiccups, "I *am* too old. Old and funny."

"Not funny. Fun. More fun than anybody. Listen. If you don't stop crying you'll be so tired tomorrow we can't go cut a tree."

She straightens up. Queenie jumps on the bed (where Queenie is not allowed) to lick her cheeks. "I know where we'll find real pretty trees, Buddy. And holly, too. With berries big as your eyes. It's way off in the woods. Farther than we've ever been. Papa used to bring us Christmas trees from there: carry them on his shoulder. That's fifty years ago. Well, now: I can't wait for morning."

Morning. Frozen rime lusters the grass; the sun, round as orange and orange as hot-weather moons, balances on the horizon, burnishes the silvered winter woods. A wild turkey calls. A renegade hog grunts in the undergrowth. Soon, by the edge of knee-deep, rapid-running water, we have to abandon the buggy. Queenie wades the stream first, paddles across barking complaints at the swiftness of the current, the pneumonia-making coldness of it. We follow, holding our shoes and equipment (a hatchet, a burlap sack) above our heads. A mile more: of chastising thorns, burs and briars that catch at our clothes; of rusty pine needles brilliant with gaudy fungus and molted feathers. Here, there, a flash, a flutter, an ecstasy of shrillings remind us that not all the birds have flown south. Always, the path unwinds through lemony sun pools and pitch vine tunnels. Another creek to cross: a disturbed armada of speckled trout froths the water round us, and frogs the size of plates practice belly flops; beaver workmen are building a dam. On the farther shore, Queenie shakes herself and trembles. My friend shivers, too: not with cold but enthusiasm. One of her hat's ragged roses sheds a petal as she lifts her head and inhales the pine-heavy air. "We're almost there; you can smell it, Buddy?" she says, as though we were approaching an ocean.

30   And, indeed, it is a kind of ocean. Scented acres of holiday trees, prickly-leafed holly. Red berries shiny as Chinese bells; black crows swoop upon them screaming. Having stuffed our burlap sacks with enough greenery and crimson to garland a dozen windows, we set about choosing a tree. "It should be," muses my friend, "twice as tall as a boy. So a boy can't steal the star." The one we pick is twice as tall as me. A brave handsome brute that survives thirty hatchet strokes before it keels with a creaking rending cry. Lugging it like a kill, we commence the long trek out. Every few yards we abandon the struggle, sit down and pant. But we have the strength of triumphant huntsmen; that and the tree's virile, icy perfume revive us, goad us on. Many compliments accompany our sunset return along the red clay road to town; but my friend is sly and noncommittal when passers-by praise the treasure perched in our buggy: what a fine tree and where did it come from? "Yonderways," she murmurs vaguely. Once a car stops and the rich mill owner's lazy wife leans out and whines: "Giveya two-bits cash for that ol tree." Ordinarily my friend is afraid of saying no; but on this occasion she promptly shakes her head: "We wouldn't take a dollar." The mill owner's wife persists. "A dollar, my foot! Fifty cents. That's my last offer. Goodness, woman, you can get another one." In answer, my friend gently reflects: "I doubt it. There's never two of anything."

Home: Queenie slumps by the fire and sleeps till tomorrow, snoring loud as a human.

A trunk in the attic contains: a shoebox of ermine tails (off the opera cape of a curious lady who once rented a room in the house), coils of frazzled tinsel gone gold with age, one silver star, a brief rope of dilapidated, undoubtedly dangerous candy-like light bulbs. Excellent decorations, as far as they go, which isn't far enough: my friend wants our tree to blaze "like a Baptist window," droop with weighty snows of ornament. But we can't afford the made-in-Japan splendors at the five-and-dime. So we do what we've always done: sit for days at the kitchen table with scissors and crayons and stacks of colored paper. I make sketches and my friend cuts them out: lots of cats, fish too (because they're easy to draw), some apples, some watermelons, a few winged angels devised from saved-up sheets of Hershey-bar tin foil. We use safety pins to attach these creations to the tree; as a final touch, we sprinkle the branches with shredded cotton (picked in August for this purpose). My friend, surveying the effect, clasps her hands together. "Now honest, Buddy. Doesn't it look good enough to eat?" Queenie tries to eat an angel.

After weaving and ribboning holly wreaths for all the front windows, our next project is the fashioning of family gifts. Tie-dye scarves for the ladies, for the men a home-brewed lemon and licorice and aspirin syrup to be taken "at the first Symptoms of a Cold and after Hunting." But when it comes time for making each other's gift, my friend and I separate to work secretly. I would like to buy her a pearl-handled knife, a radio, a whole pound of chocolate-covered cherries (we tasted some once, and she always swears: "I could live on them, Buddy, Lord yes I could—and that's not taking His name in vain"). Instead, I am building her a kite. She would like to give me a bicycle (she's said so on several million occasions: "If only I could, Buddy. It's bad enough in life to do without something *you* want; but confound it, what gets my goat is not being able to give somebody something you want *them* to have. Only one of these days I will, Buddy. Locate you a bike. Don't ask how. Steal it, maybe"). Instead, I'm fairly certain that she is building me a kite—the same as last year, and the year before: the year before that we exchanged slingshots. All of which is fine by me. For we are champion kite-fliers who study the wind like sailors; my friend, more accomplished than I, can get a kite aloft when there isn't enough breeze to carry clouds.

Christmas Eve afternoon as we scrape together a nickel and go to the butcher's to buy Queenie's traditional gift, a good gnawable beef bone. The bone, wrapped in funny paper, is placed high in the tree near the silver star. Queenie knows it's there. She squats at the foot of the tree staring up in a trance of greed: when bedtime arrives she refuses to budge. Her excitement is equaled by my own. I kick the covers and turn my pillow as though it were a scorching summer's night. Somewhere a rooster crows: falsely, for the sun is still on the other side of the world.

35 "Buddy, are you awake?" It is my friend, calling from her room, which is next to mine; and an instant later she is sitting on my bed holding a candle. "Well, I can't sleep a hoot," she declares. "My mind's jumping like a jack rabbit. Buddy, do you think Mrs. Roosevelt will serve our cake at dinner?" We huddle in the bed, and she squeezes my hand I-love-you. "Seems like your hand used to be so much smaller. I guess I hate to see you grow up. When you're grown up, will we still be friends?" I say always. "But I feel so bad, Buddy. I wanted so bad to give you a bike. I tried to sell my cameo Papa gave me, Buddy—" she hesitates, as though embarrassed—"I made you another kite." Then I confess that I made her one, too; and we laugh. The candle burns too short to hold. Out it goes, exposing the starlight, the stars spinning at the window like a visible caroling that slowly, slowly daybreak silences. Possibly we doze; but the beginnings of dawn splash us like cold water: we're up, wide-eyed and wandering while we wait for others to waken. Quite deliberately my friend drops a kettle on the kitchen floor. I tap-dance in front of closed doors. One by one the household emerges, looking as though they'd like to kill us both; but it's Christmas, so they can't. First, a gorgeous breakfast: just everything you can imagine—from flapjacks and fried squirrel to

hominy grits[3] and honey-in-the-comb. Which puts everyone in a good humor except my friend and I. Frankly, we're so impatient to get at the presents we can't eat a mouthful.

Well, I'm disappointed. Who wouldn't be? With socks, a Sunday school shirt, some handkerchiefs, a hand-me-down sweater and a year's subscription to a religious magazine for children. *The Little Shepherd.* It makes me boil. It really does.

My friend has a better haul. A sack of Satsumas,[4] that's her best present. She is proudest, however, of a white wool shawl knitted by her married sister. But she *says* her favorite gift is the kite I built her. And it *is* very beautiful; though not as beautiful as the one she made me, which is blue and scattered with gold and green Good Conduct stars; moreover, my name is painted on it, "Buddy."

"Buddy, the wind is blowing."

The wind is blowing, and nothing will do till we've run to a pasture below the house where Queenie has scooted to bury her bone (and where, a winter hence, Queenie will be buried, too.) There, plunging through the healthy waist-high grass, we unreel our kites, feel them twitching at the string like sly fish as they swim into the wind. Satisfied, sun-warmed, we sprawl in the grass and peel Satsumas and watch our kites cavort. Soon I forget the socks and hand-me-down sweater. I'm as happy as if we'd already won the fifty-thousand-dollar Grand Prize in that coffee-naming contest.

40 "My, how foolish I am!" my friend cries, suddenly alert, like a woman remembering too late she has biscuits in the oven. "You know what I've always thought?" she asks in a tone of discovery, and not smiling at me but a point beyond. "I've always thought a body would have to be sick and dying before they saw the Lord. And I imagined that when He came it would be like looking at the Baptist window; pretty as colored glass with the sun pouring through, such a shine you don't know it's getting dark. And it's been a comfort: to think of that shine taking away all the spooky feeling. But I'll wager it never happens. I'll wager at the very end a body realizes the Lord has already shown Himself. That things as they are"—her hand circles in a gesture that gathers clouds and kites and grass and Queenie pawing earth over her bone— "just what they've always been, was seeing Him. As for me, I could leave the world with today in my eyes."

This is our last Christmas together.

Life separates us. Those who Know Best decide that I belong in a military school. And so follows a miserable succession of bugle-blowing prisons, grim reveille-ridden summer camps. I have a new home too. But it doesn't count. Home is where my friend is, and there I never go.

And there she remains, puttering around the kitchen. Alone with Queenie. Then alone. ("Buddy dear," she writes in her wild hard-to-read script, "yesterday Jim Macy's horse kicked Queenie bad. Be thankful she didn't feel much.

---

[3] A form of corn, coarsely ground into a white meal, cooked like a cereal.
[4] A hard, fine-grained buff Japanese pottery.

I wrapped her in a Fine Linen sheet and rode her in the buggy down to Simpson's pasture where she can be with all her Bones . . ."). For a few Novembers she continues to bake her fruitcakes single-handed; not as many, but some: and, of course, she always sends me "the best of the batch." Also, in every letter she encloses a dime wadded in toilet paper: "See a picture show and write me the story." But gradually in her letters she tends to confuse me with her other friend, the Buddy who died in the 1880's; more and more thirteenths are not the only days she stays in bed: a morning arrives in November, a leafless birdless coming of winter morning, when she cannot rouse herself to exclaim: "Oh my, it's fruitcake weather!"

And when that happens, I know it. A message saying so merely confirms a piece of news some secret vein had already received, severing from me an irreplaceable part of myself, letting it loose like a kite on a broken string. That is why, walking across a school campus on this particular December morning, I keep searching the sky. As, if I expected to see, rather like hearts, a lost pair of kites hurrying toward heaven.

■ EXPLORATIONS OF THE TEXT ■

1. What feeling and mood emerge from the opening scene? What does the fireplace symbolize?
2. What qualities characterize Capote's distant cousin? What can you tell about her from her appearance? clothes? dialogue? actions?
3. Is Capote writing from the point of view of an adult or a child? What is his attitude toward his cousin? Why does he call her his "friend"?
4. What is the nature of their relationship with each other? with others in the house?
5. Examine the following scenes: "the buggy" and the pecan search; the visit with Haha Jones: the cooking of the fruitcakes; dancing after the fruitcakes are sent out; the search for a tree; and kite flying. What do these episodes suggest about the characters of the cousins?
6. Explore the significance of Capote's cousin's statement in paragraph 40.
7. What is the meaning of the ending? What does the kite represent?
8. Effective writing rests in sharp, vivid, sensory details. Isolate several examples of this kind of detail, and analyze their impact on the narrative.

■■ JOURNAL ENTRIES ■■

1. Think of a particular holiday memory. Why does it stand out in your mind? Describe the moment. Include at least one color and several sensory details in your description.
2. Do you have a "cousin" in your life? Respond.

■■■ IDEAS FOR WRITING ■■■

1. Truman Capote's essay, partially autobiographical, depicts a central figure from his childhood. Is the piece sentimental? How does Capote control his material?
2. In this essay, the artistic impulse is nourished by people other than immediate family members. How does this theme function in this work?

Ruth's Song

Gloria Steinem

Gloria Steinem (1934–) was born in Toledo, Ohio. Her parents divorced when she was very young; and at ten, she had to care for her mentally ill mother, Ruth. Steinem attended Smith College on a scholarship and graduated, magna cum laude, in 1956. Between 1957 and 1958, she attended the Universities of Delhi and Calcutta in India on a fellowship and worked as a member of a peacekeeping team. She returned to the United States and worked for the civil rights and peace movements throughout the 1960s. She also participated in the political campaigns of Adlai Stevenson, Robert F. Kennedy, Eugene McCarthy, Shirley Chisholm, and George McGovern.

Steinem's best-known article from her early career, "I Was a Playboy Bunny," resulted from an undercover assignment for the 1963 opening of New York City's Playboy Club. In 1968, she was a co-founder of New York *magazine. She gradually began writing more articles about women's issues and in January 1972 co-founded* Ms. *magazine. She became a spokesperson for the burgeoning women's movement.*

Among Steinem's many awards and fellowships are nine citations from the World Almanac as one of twenty-five most influential American women, the Ceres Medal from the United Nations, and a Woodrow Wilson International Center for Scholars award. Her writings include The Thousand Indias *(1957),* The Beach Book *(1963),* Outrageous Acts and Everyday Rebellions *(1983),* Marilyn: Norma Jean *(1986),* The Bedside Book of Self Esteem *(1989), and* Revolution From Within *(1991). She continues to work for social change through her writing, fund-raising, and speaking engagements.*

Gloria Steinem's essay presents a complex and compassionate portrait of her mother, Ruth, and of their relationship.

1   Happy or unhappy, families are all mysterious. We have only to imagine how differently we would be described—and will be, after our deaths—by each of the family members who believe they know us. The only question is, Why are some mysteries more important than others?

The fate of my Uncle Ed was a mystery of importance in our family. We lavished years of speculation on his transformation from a brilliant young electrical engineer to the town handyman. What could have changed this elegant, Lincolnesque student voted "Best Dressed" by his classmates to the gaunt, unshaven man I remember? Why did he leave a young son and a first wife of the "proper" class and religion, marry a much less educated woman of the "wrong" religion, and raise a second family in a house near an abandoned airstrip; a house whose walls were patched with metal signs to stop the wind? Why did he never talk about his transformation?

For years, I assumed that some secret and dramatic events of a year he spent in Alaska had made the difference. Then I discovered that the trip had come after his change and probably been made because of it. Strangers he worked for as a much-loved handyman talked about him as one more tragedy of the Depression, and it was true that Uncle Ed's father, my paternal grandfather, had lost his money in the stockmarket Crash and died of (depending on who was telling the story) pneumonia or a broken heart. But the Crash of 1929 also had come long after Uncle Ed's transformation. Another theory was that he was afflicted with a mental problem that lasted most of his life, yet he was supremely competent at his work, led an independent life, and asked for help from no one.

Perhaps he had fallen under the spell of a radical professor in the early days of the century, the height of this country's romance with socialism and anarchism. That was the theory of another uncle on my mother's side. I do remember that no matter how much Uncle Ed needed money, he would charge no more for his work than materials plus 10 percent, and I never saw him in anything other than ancient boots and overalls held up with strategic safety pins. Was he really trying to replace socialism-in-one-country with socialism-in-one-man? If so, why did my grandmother, a woman who herself had run for the school board in coalition with anarchists and socialists, mistrust his judgment so much that she left his share of her estate in trust, even though he was over fifty when she died? And why did Uncle Ed seem uninterested in all other political words and acts? Was it true instead that, as another relative insisted, Uncle Ed had chosen poverty to disprove the myths of Jews and money?

5   Years after my uncle's death, I asked a son in his second family if he had the key to his family mystery. No, he said. He had never known his father any other way. For that cousin, there had been no question. For the rest of us, there was to be no answer.

For many years I also never imagined my mother any way other than the person she had become before I was born. She was just a fact of life when I was growing up; someone to be worried about and cared for; an invalid who lay in bed with eyes closed and lips moving in occasional response to voices only she could hear; a woman to whom I brought an endless stream of toast and coffee, bologna sandwiches and dime pies, in a child's version of what meals should be. She was a loving, intelligent, terrorized woman who tried hard to clean our littered house whenever she emerged from her private world, but who could rarely be counted on to finish one task. In many ways, our roles were reversed: I was the mother and she was the child. Yet that didn't help her, for she still worried about me with all the intensity of a frightened mother, plus the special fears of her own world full of threats and hostile voices.

Even then I suppose I must have known that, years before she was thirty-five and I was born, she had been a spirited adventurous young woman who struggled out of a working-class family and into college, who found work she loved and continued to do, even after she was married and my older sister was there to be cared for. Certainly, our immediate family and nearby relatives, of whom I was by far the youngest, must have remembered her life as a whole and functioning person. She was thirty before she gave up her own career to help my father run the Michigan summer resort that was the most practical of his many dreams, and she worked hard there as everything from book-keeper to bar manager. The family must have watched this energetic, fun-loving, book-loving woman turn into someone who was afraid to be alone, who could not hang on to reality long enough to hold a job, and who could rarely concentrate enough to read a book.

Yet I don't remember any family speculation about the mystery of my mother's transformation. To the kind ones and those who liked her, this new Ruth was simply a sad event, perhaps a mental case, a family problem to be accepted and cared for until some natural process made her better. To the less kind or those who had resented her earlier independence, she was a willful failure, someone who lived in a filthy house, a woman who simply would not pull herself together.

Unlike the case of my Uncle Ed, exterior events were never suggested as reason enough for her problems. Giving up her own career was never cited as her personal parallel of the Depression. (Nor was there discussion of the Depression itself, though my mother, like millions of others, had made potato soup and cut up blankets to make my sister's winter clothes.) Her fears of dependence and poverty were no match for my uncle's possible political beliefs. The real influence of newspaper editors who had praised her reporting was not taken as seriously as the possible influence of one radical professor.

10   Even the explanation of mental illness seemed to contain more personal fault when applied to my mother. She had suffered her first "nervous break-down," as she and everyone else called it, before I was born and when my sister was about five. It followed years of trying to take care of a baby, be the wife of a kind but financially irresponsible man with show business dreams, and still keep her much-loved job as reporter and newspaper editor. After many months in a sanatorium, she was pronounced recovered. That is, she was able to take care of my sister again, to move away from the city and the

job she loved, and to work with my father at the isolated rural lake in Michigan he was trying to transform into a resort worthy of the big dance bands of the 1930s.

But she was never again completely without the spells of depression, anxiety, and visions into some other world that eventually were to turn her into the nonperson I remember. And she was never again without a bottle of dark, acrid-smelling liquid she called "Doc Howard's medicine": a solution of chloral hydrate that I later learned was the main ingredient of "Mickey Finns" or "knockout drops," and that probably made my mother and her doctor the pioneers of modern tranquilizers. Though friends and relatives saw this medicine as one more evidence of weakness and indulgence, to me it always seemed an embarrassing but necessary evil. It slurred her speech and slowed her coordination, making our neighbors and my school friends believe she was a drunk. But without it, she would not sleep for days, even a week at a time, and her feverish eyes began to see only that private world in which wars and hostile voices threatened the people she loved.

Because my parents had divorced and my sister was working in a far-away city, my mother and I were alone together then, living off the meager fixed income that my mother got from leasing her share of the remaining land in Michigan. I remember a long thanksgiving weekend spent hanging on to her with one hand and holding my eighth-grade assignment of *Tale of Two Cities*[1] in the other, because the war outside our house was so real to my mother that she had plunged her hand through a window, badly cutting her arm in an effort to help us escape. Only when she finally agreed to swallow the medicine could she sleep, and only then could I end the terrible calm that comes with crisis and admit to myself how afraid I had been.

No wonder that no relative in my memory challenged the doctor who prescribed this medicine, asked if some of her suffering and hallucinating might be due to overdose or withdrawal, or even consulted another doctor about its use. It was our relief as well as hers.

But why was she never returned even to that first sanatorium? Or to help that might come from other doctors? It's hard to say. Partly, it was her own fear of returning. Partly, it was too little money, and a family's not-unusual assumption that mental illness is an inevitable part of someone's personality. Or perhaps other family members had feared something like my experience when, one hot and desperate summer between the sixth and seventh grade, I finally persuaded her to let me take her to the only doctor from those sanatorium days whom she remembered without fear.

15   Yes, this brusque old man told me after talking to my abstracted, timid mother for twenty minutes: She definitely belongs in a state hospital. I should put her there right away. But even at that age, *Life* magazine and newspaper exposés had told me what horrors went on inside those hospitals. Assuming there to be no other alternative, I took her home and never tried again.

---

[1] Novel by Charles Dickens, a nineteenth-century English writer.

In retrospect, perhaps the biggest reason my mother was cared for but not helped for twenty years was the simplest: her functioning was not that necessary to the world. Like women alcoholics who drink in their kitchens while costly programs are constructed for executives who drink, or like the homemakers subdued with tranquilizers while male patients get therapy and personal attention instead, my mother was not an important worker. She was not even the caretaker of a very young child, as she had been when she was hospitalized the first time. My father had patiently brought home the groceries and kept our odd household going until I was eight or so and my sister went away to college. Two years later when wartime gas rationing closed his summer resort and he had to travel to buy and sell in summer as well as winter, he said: How can I travel and take care of your mother? How can I make a living? He was right. It was impossible to do both. I did not blame him for leaving once I was old enough to be the bringer of meals and answerer of my mother's questions. ("Has your sister been killed in a car crash?" "Are there German soldiers outside?") I replaced my father, my mother was left with one more way of maintaining a sad status quo, and the world went on undisturbed.

That's why our lives, my mother's from forty-six to fifty-three, and my own from ten to seventeen, were spent alone together. There was one sane winter in a house we rented to be near my sister's college in Massachusetts, then one bad summer spent house-sitting in suburbia while my mother hallucinated and my sister struggled to hold down a summer job in New York. But the rest of those years were lived in Toledo where both my mother and father had been born, and on whose city newspapers an earlier Ruth had worked.

First we moved into a basement apartment in a good neighborhood. In those rooms behind a furnace, I made one last stab at being a child. By pretending to be much sicker with a cold than I really was, I hoped my mother would suddenly turn into a sane and cheerful woman bringing me chicken soup à la Hollywood. Of course, she could not. It only made her feel worse that she could not. I stopped pretending.

But for most of those years, we lived in the upstairs of the house my mother had grown up in and her parents left her—a deteriorating farm house engulfed by the city, with poor but newer houses stacked against it and a major highway a few feet from its sagging front porch. For a while, we could rent the two downstairs apartments to a newlywed factory worker and a local butcher's family. Then the health department condemned our ancient furnace for the final time, sealing it so tight that even my resourceful Uncle Ed couldn't produce illegal heat.

20   In that house, I remember:

 . . . lying in the bed my mother and I shared for warmth, listening on the early morning radio to the royal wedding of Princess Elizabeth and Prince Philip being broadcast live, while we tried to ignore and thus protect each other from the unmistakable sounds of the factory worker downstairs beating up and locking up his pregnant wife.

 . . . hanging paper drapes I had bought in the dime store; stacking books and papers in the shape of two armchairs and covering them with blankets;

evolving my own dishwashing system (I waited until all the dishes were dirty, then put them in the bathtub); and listening to my mother's high praise for these housekeeping efforts to bring order from chaos, though in retrospect I think they probably depressed her further.

. . . coming back from one of the Eagles' Club shows where I and other veterans of a local tap-dancing school made ten dollars a night for two shows, and finding my mother waiting with a flashlight and no coat in the dark cold of the bus stop, worried about my safety walking home.

. . . in a good period, when my mother's native adventurousness came through, answering a classified ad together for an amateur acting troupe that performed Biblical dramas in churches, and doing several very corny performances of *Noah's Ark* while my proud mother shook metal sheets backstage to make thunder.

25   . . . on a hot summer night, being bitten by one of the rats that shared our house and its back alley. It was a terrifying night that turned into a touching one when my mother, summoning courage from some unknown reservoir of love, became a calm, comforting parent who took me to a hospital emergency room despite her terror at leaving home.

. . . coming home from a local library with the three books a week into which I regularly escaped, and discovering that for once there was no need to escape. My mother was calmly planting hollyhocks in the vacant lot next door.

But there were also times when she woke in the early winter dark, too frightened and disoriented to remember that I was at my usual after-school job, and so called the police to find me. Humiliated in front of my friends by sirens and policemen, I would yell at her—and she would bow her head in fear and say "I'm sorry, I'm sorry, I'm sorry," just as she had done so often when my otherwise-kindhearted father had yelled at her in frustration. Perhaps the worst thing about suffering is that it finally hardens the hearts of those around it.

And there were many, many times when I badgered her until her shaking hands had written a small check to cash at the corner grocery and I could leave her alone while I escaped to the comfort of well-heated dime stores that smelled of fresh doughnuts, or to air-conditioned Saturday-afternoon movies that were windows on a very different world.

But my ultimate protection was this: I was just passing through, a guest in the house; perhaps this wasn't my mother at all. Though I knew very well that I was her daughter, I sometimes imagined that I had been adopted and that my real parents would find me, a fantasy I've since discovered is common. (If children wrote more and grownups less, being adopted might be seen not only as a fear but also as a hope.) Certainly, I didn't mourn the wasted life of this woman who was scarcely older than I am now. I worried only about the times when she got worse.

30   Pity takes distance and a certainty of surviving. It was only after our house was bought for demolition by the church next door, and after my sister had performed the miracle of persuading my father to give me a carefree time before college by taking my mother with him to California for a year, that I could afford to think about the sadness of her life. Suddenly, I was far away in

Washington, living with my sister and sharing a house with several of her friends. While I finished high school and discovered to my surprise that my classmates felt sorry for me because my mother *wasn't* there, I also realized that my sister, at least in her early childhood, had known a very different person who lived inside our mother, an earlier Ruth.

She was a woman I met for the first time in a mental hospital near Baltimore, a humane place with gardens and trees where I visited her each weekend of the summer after my first year away in college. Fortunately, my sister hadn't been able to work and be our mother's caretaker, too. After my father's year was up, my sister had carefully researched hospitals and found the courage to break the family chain.

At first, this Ruth was the same abstracted, frightened woman I had lived with all those years, though now all the sadder for being approached through long hospital corridors and many locked doors. But gradually she began to talk about her past life, memories that doctors there must have been awakening. I began to meet a Ruth I had never known.

. . . A tall, spirited, auburn-haired high-school girl who loved basketball and reading; who tried to drive her uncle's Stanley Steamer when it was the first car in the neighborhood; who had a gift for gardening and who sometimes, in defiance of convention, wore her father's overalls; a girl with the courage to go to dances even though her church told her that music itself was sinful, and whose sense of adventure almost made up for feeling gawky and unpretty next to her daintier, dark-haired sister.

. . . A very little girl, just learning to walk, discovering the body places where touching was pleasurable, and being punished by her mother who slapped her hard across the kitchen floor.

35 . . . A daughter of a handsome railroad-engineer and a schoolteacher who felt she had married "beneath her"; the mother who took her two daughters on Christmas trips to faraway New York on an engineer's free railroad pass and showed them the restaurants and theaters they should aspire to— even though they could only stand outside them in the snow.

. . . A good student at Oberlin College, whose freethinking traditions she loved, where friends nicknamed her "Billy"; a student with a talent for both mathematics and poetry, who was not above putting an invisible film of Karo syrup on all the john seats in her dormitory the night of a big prom; a daughter who had to return to Toledo, live with her family, and go to a local university when her ambitious mother—who had scrimped and saved, ghostwritten a minister's sermons, and made her daughters' clothes in order to get them to college at all—ran out of money. At home, this Ruth became a parttime bookkeeper in a lingerie shop for the very rich, commuting to classes and listening to her mother's harsh lectures on the security of becoming a teacher; but also a young woman who was still rebellious enough to fall in love with my father, the editor of her university newspaper, a funny and charming young man who was a terrible student, had no intention of graduating, put on all the campus dances, and was unacceptably Jewish.

I knew from family lore that my mother had married my father twice: once secretly, after he invited her to become the literary editor of his campus newspaper, and once a year later in a public ceremony, which some members of both families refused to attend as the "mixed marriage" of its day.

And I knew that my mother had gone on to earn a teaching certificate. She had used it to scare away truant officers during the winters when, after my father closed the summer resort for the season, we lived in a house trailer and worked our way to Florida or California and back by buying and selling antiques.

But only during those increasingly adventurous weekend outings from the hospital—going shopping, to lunch, to the movies—did I realize that she had taught college calculus for a year in deference to her mother's insistence that she have teaching "to fall back on." And only then did I realize she had fallen in love with newspapers along with my father. After graduating from the university paper, she wrote a gossip column for a local tabloid, under the name "Duncan MacKenzie," since women weren't supposed to do such things, and soon had earned a job as society reporter on one of Toledo's two big dailies. By the time my sister was four or so, she had worked her way up to the coveted position of Sunday editor.

40 It was a strange experience to look into those brown eyes I had seen so often and realize suddenly how much they were like my own. For the first time, I realized that she might really by my mother.

I began to think about the many pressures that might have led up to that first nervous breakdown: leaving my sister who she loved very much with a grandmother whose values my mother didn't share; trying to hold on to a job she loved but was being asked to leave by her husband; wanting very much to go with a woman friend to pursue their own dreams in New York; falling in love with a co-worker at the newspaper who frightened her by being more sexually attractive, more supportive of her work than my father, and perhaps the man she should have married; and finally, nearly bleeding to death with a miscarriage because her own mother had little faith in doctors and refused to get help.

Did those months in the sanatorium brainwash her in some Freudian or very traditional way into making what were, for her, probably the wrong choices? I don't know. It almost doesn't matter. Without extraordinary support to the contrary, she was already convinced that divorce was unthinkable. A husband could not be left for another man, and certainly not for a reason as selfish as a career. A daughter could not be deprived of her father and certainly not be uprooted and taken off to an uncertain future in New York. A bride was supposed to be virginal (not "shop-worn," as my euphemistic mother would have said), and if your husband turned out to be kind, but innocent of the possibility of a woman's pleasure, then just be thankful for kindness.

Of course, other women have torn themselves away from work and love and still survived. But a story my mother told me years later has always symbolized for me the formidable forces arrayed against her.

It was early spring, nothing was open yet. There was nobody for miles around. We had stayed at the late that winter, so I was alone a lot while your father took the car and traveled around on business. You were a baby. Your sister was in school, and there was no phone. The last straw was that the radio broke. Suddenly it seemed like forever since I'd been able to talk with anyone—or even hear the sound of another voice.

45 *I bundled you up, took the dog, and walked out to the Brooklyn road. I thought I'd walk the four or five miles to the grocery store, talk to some people, and find somebody to drive me back. I was walking along with Fritzie running up ahead in the empty road—when suddenly a car came out of nowhere and down the hill. It hit Fritzie head on and threw him over to the side of the road. I yelled and screamed at the driver, but he never slowed down. He never looked at us. He never even turned his head.*

Poor Fritzie was all broken and bleeding, but he was still alive. I carried him and sat down in the middle of the road, with his head cradled in my arms. I was going to make the next car stop and help.

But no car ever came. I sat there for hours, I don't know how long, with you in my lap and holding Fritzie, who was whimpering and looking up at me for help. It was dark by the time he finally died. I pulled him over to the side of the road and walked back home with you and washed the blood out of my clothes.

I don't know what it was about that one day—it was like a breaking point. When your father came home, I said: "From now on, I'm going with you. I won't bother you. I'll just sit in the car. But I can't bear to be alone again."

I think she told me that story to show she had tried to save herself, or perhaps she wanted to exorcise a painful memory by saying it out loud. But hearing it made me understand what could have turned her into the woman I remember: a solitary figure sitting in the car, perspiring through the summer, bundled up in winter, waiting for my father to come out of this or that antique shop, grateful just not to be alone. I was there, too, because I was too young to be left at home, and I loved helping my father wrap and unwrap the newspaper around the china and small objects he had bought at auctions and was selling to dealers. It made me feel necessary and grown-up. But sometimes it was hours before we came back to the car again and to my mother who was always patiently, silently waiting.

50   At the hospital and later when Ruth told me stories of her past, I used to say, "But why didn't you leave? Why didn't you take the job? Why didn't you marry the other man?" She would always insist it didn't matter, she was lucky

to have my sister and me. If I pressed hard enough, she would add, "If I'd left you never would have been born."

I always thought but never had the courage to say: *But you might have been born instead.*

I'd like to tell you that this story has a happy ending. The best I can do is one that is happier than its beginning.

After many months in that Baltimore hospital, my mother lived on her own in a small apartment for two years while I was in college and my sister married and lived nearby. When she felt the old terrors coming back, she returned to the hospital at her own request. She was approaching sixty by the time she emerged from there and from a Quaker farm that served as a halfway house, but she confounded her psychiatrists' predictions that she would be able to live outside for shorter and shorter periods. In fact, she never returned. She lived more than another twenty years, and for six of them, she was well enough to stay in a rooming house that provided both privacy and company. Even after my sister and her husband moved to a larger house and generously made two rooms into an apartment for her, she continued to have some independent life and many friends. She worked part-time as a "salesgirl" in a china shop; went away with me on yearly vacations and took one trip to Europe with relatives; went to women's club meetings; found a multiracial church that she loved; took meditation courses; and enjoyed many books. She still could not bear to see a sad movie, to stay alone with any of her six grandchildren while they were babies, to live without many tranquilizers, or to talk about those bad years in Toledo. The old terrors were still in the back of her mind, and each day was a fight to keep them down.

It was the length of her illness that had made doctors pessimistic. In fact, they could not identify any serious mental problem and diagnosed her only as having "an anxiety neurosis": low self-esteem, a fear of being dependent, a terror of being alone, a constant worry about money. She also had spells of what now would be called agoraphobia, a problem almost entirely confined to dependent women: fear of going outside the house, and incapacitating anxiety attacks in unfamiliar or public places.

55 Would you say, I asked one of her doctors, that her spirit had been broken? "I guess that's as good a diagnosis as any," he said. "And it's hard to mend anything that's been broken for twenty years."

But once out of the hospital for good, she continued to show flashes of the different woman inside; one with a wry kind of humor, a sense of adventure, and a love of learning. Books on math, physics, and mysticism occupied a lot of her time. ("Religion," she used to say firmly, "begins in the laboratory.") When she visited me in New York during her sixties and seventies, she always told taxi drivers that she was eighty years old ("so they will tell me how young I look"), and convinced theater ticket sellers that she was deaf long before she really was ("so they'll give us seats in the front row"). She made friends easily, with the vulnerability and charm of a person who feels entirely dependent on the approval of others. After one of her visits, every shopkeeper within blocks of my apartment would say, "Oh yes, I know your mother!" At home, she complained that people her own age were too old and stodgy for her. Many of her friends were far younger than she. It was as if she were making up for her own lost years.

She was also overly appreciative of any presents given to her—and that made giving them irresistible. I loved to send her clothes, jewelry, exotic soaps, and additions to her collection of tarot cards. She loved receiving them, though we both knew they would end up stored in boxes and drawers. She carried on a correspondence in German with our European relatives, and exchanges with many other friends, all written in her painfully slow, shaky handwriting. She also loved giving gifts. Even as she worried about money and figured out how to save pennies, she would buy or make carefully chosen presents for grandchildren and friends.

Part of the price she paid for this much health was forgetting. A single reminder of those bad years in Toledo was enough to plunge her into days of depression. There were times when this fact created loneliness for me, too. Only two of us had lived most of my childhood. Now, only one of us remembered. But there were also times in later years when, no matter how much I pled with reporters *not* to interview our friends and neighbors in Toledo, *not* to say that my mother had been hospitalized, they published things that hurt her very much and sent her into a downhill slide.

One the other hand, she was also her mother's daughter, a person with a certain amount of social pride and pretension, and some of her objections had less to do with depression than false pride. She complained bitterly about one report that we had lived in a house trailer. She finally asked angrily: "Couldn't they at least say 'vacation mobile home'?" Divorce was still a shame to her. She might cheerfully tell friends, "I don't know *why* Gloria says her father and I were divorced—we never were." I think she justified this to herself with the idea that they had gone through two marriage ceremonies, one in secret and one in public, but been divorced only once. In fact, they were definitely divorced, and my father had briefly married someone else.

60 She was very proud of my being a published writer, and we generally shared the same values. After her death, I found a mother-daughter morals quiz I once had written for a women's magazine. In her unmistakably shaky writing, she had recorded her own answers, her entirely accurate imagination of what my answers would be, and a score that concluded our differences were less than those "normal for women separated by twenty-odd years." Nonetheless, she was quite capable of putting a made-up name on her name tag when going to a conservative women's club where she feared our shared identity would bring controversy or even just questions. When I finally got up the nerve to tell her I was signing a 1972 petition of women who publicly said we had had abortions and were demanding the repeal of laws that made them illegal and dangerous, her only reply was sharp and aimed to hurt back. "Every starlet says she's had an abortion," she said. "It's just a way of getting publicity." I knew she agreed that abortion should be a legal choice, but I also knew she would never forgive me for embarrassing her in public.

In fact, her anger and a fairly imaginative ability to wound with words increased in her last years when she was most dependent, most focused on herself, and most likely to need the total attention of others. When my sister made a courageous decision to go to law school at the age of fifty, leaving my mother in a house that not only had many loving teenage grandchildren in it but a kindly older woman as a paid companion besides, my mother reduced her to frequent tears by insisting that this was a family with no love in it, no home-cooked food in the refrigerator; not a real family at all. Since arguments about home cooking wouldn't work on me, my punishment was creative and different. She was going to call up *The New York Times,* she said, and tell them that this was what feminism did: it left old sick women all alone.

Some of this bitterness brought on by failing faculties was eventually solved by a nursing home near my sister's house where my mother not only got the twenty-four-hour help her weakening body demanded, but the attention of affectionate nurses besides. She charmed them, they loved her, and she could still get out for an occasional family wedding. If I ever had any doubts about the debt we owe to nurses, those last months laid them to rest.

When my mother died just before her eighty-second birthday in a hospital room where my sister and I were alternating the hours in which her heart wound slowly down to its last sounds, we were alone together for a few hours while my sister slept. My mother seemed bewildered by her surroundings and the tubes that invaded her body, but her consciousness cleared long enough for her to say: "I want to go home. Please take me home." Lying to her one last time, I said I would. "Okay, honey," she said. "I trust you." Those were her last understandable words.

The nurses let my sister and me stay in the room long after there was no more breath. She had asked us to do that. One of her many fears came from a story she had been told as a child about a man whose coma was mistaken for death. She also had made out a living will requesting that no extraordinary measures be used to keep her alive, and that her ashes be sprinkled in the same stream as my father's.

65 Her memorial service was in the Episcopalian church that she loved because it fed the poor, let the homeless sleep in its pews, had members of almost every race, and had been sued by the Episcopalian hierarchy for having a woman priest. Most of all, she loved the affection with which its members had welcomed her, visited her at home, and driven her to services. I think she would have liked the Quaker-style informality with which people rose to tell their memories of her. I know she would have loved the presence of many friends. It was to this church that she had donated some of her remaining Michigan property in the hope that it could be used as a multiracial camp, thus getting even with those people in the tiny nearby town who had snubbed my father for being Jewish.

I think she also would have been pleased with her obituary. It emphasized her brief career as one of the early women journalists and asked for donations to Oberlin's scholarship fund so others could go to this college she loved so much but had to leave.

I know I will spend the next years figuring out what her life has left in me.

I realize that I've always been more touched by old people than by children. It's the talent and hopes locked up in a failing body that gets to me; a poignant contrast that reminds me of my mother, even when she was strong.

I've always been drawn to any story of a mother and a daughter on their own in the world. I saw *A Taste of Honey* several times as both a play and a film, and never stopped feeling it. Even *Gypsy* I saw over and over again, sneaking in backstage for the musical and going to the movies as well. I told myself that I was learning the tap-dance routines, but actually my eyes were full of tears.

70   I once fell in love with a man only because we both belonged to that large and secret club of children who had "crazy mothers." We traded stories of the shameful houses to which we could never invite our friends. Before he was born, his mother had gone to jail for her pacifist convictions. Then she married the politically ambitious young lawyer who had defended her, stayed home and raised many sons. I fell out of love when he confessed that he wished I wouldn't smoke or swear, and he hoped I wouldn't go on working. His mother's plight had taught him self-pity—nothing else.

I'm no longer obsessed, as I was for many years, with the fear that I would end up in a house like that one in Toledo. Now, I'm obsessed instead with the things I could have done for my mother while she was alive, or the things I should have said.

I still don't understand why so many, many years passed before I saw my mother as a person and before I understood that many of the forces in her life are patterns women share. Like a lot of daughters, I suppose I couldn't afford to admit that what had happened to my mother was not all personal or accidental, and therefore could happen to me.

One mystery has finally cleared. I could never understand why my mother hadn't been helped by Pauline, her mother-in-law; a woman she seemed to love more than her own mother. This paternal grandmother had died when I was five, before my mother's real problems began but long after that "nervous breakdown," and I knew Pauline was once a suffragist who addressed Congress, marched for the vote, and was the first woman member of a school board in Ohio. She must have been a courageous and independent woman, yet I could find no evidence in my mother's reminiscences that Pauline had encouraged or helped my mother toward a life of her own.

I finally realized that my grandmother never changed the politics of her own life, either. She was a feminist who kept a neat house for a husband and four antifeminist sons, a vegetarian among five male meat eaters, and a woman who felt so strongly about the dangers of alcohol that she used only paste vanilla; yet she served both meat and wine to the men of the house and made sure their lives and comforts were continued undisturbed. After the vote was won, Pauline seems to have stopped all feminist activity. My mother greatly admired the fact that her mother-in-law kept a spotless house and prepared a week's meals at a time. Whatever her own internal torments, Pauline was to my mother a woman who seemed able to "do it all." "Whither thou goest, I shall go," my mother used to say to her much-loved mother-in-law, quoting the Ruth of the Bible. In the end, her mother-in-law may have added to my mother's burdens of guilt.

75   Perhaps like many later suffragists, my grandmother was a public feminist and a private isolationist. That may have been heroic in itself, the most she could be expected to do, but the vote and a legal right to work were not the only kind of help my mother needed.

The world still missed a unique person named Ruth. Though she longed to live in New York and in Europe, she became a woman who was afraid to take a bus across town. Though she drove the first Stanley Steamer, she married a man who never let her drive.

I can only guess what she might have become. The clues are in moments of spirit or humor.

After all the years of fear, she still came to Oberlin with me when I was giving a speech there. She remembered everything about its history as the first college to admit blacks and the first to admit women, and responded to students with the dignity of a professor, the accuracy of a journalist, and a charm that was all her own.

When she could still make trips to Washington's wealth of libraries, she became an expert genealogist, delighting especially in finding the rogues and rebels in our family tree.

80   Just before I was born, when she had cooked one more enormous meal for all the members of some famous dance band at my father's resort and they failed to clean their plates, she had taken a shotgun down from the kitchen wall and held it over their frightened heads until they had finished the last crumb of strawberry shortcake. Only then did she tell them the gun wasn't loaded. It was a story she told with great satisfaction.

Though sex was a subject she couldn't discuss directly, she had a great appreciation of sensuous men. When a friend I brought home tried to talk to her about cooking, she was furious. ("He came out in the kitchen and talked to me about *stew!*") But she forgave him when we went swimming. She whispered, "He has wonderful legs!"

On her seventy-fifth birthday, she played softball with her grandsons on the beach, and took pride in hitting home runs into the ocean.

Even in the last year of her life, when my sister took her to visit a neighbor's new and luxurious house, she looked at the vertical stripes of a very abstract painting in the hallway and said, tartly, "Is that the price code?"

She worried terribly about being socially accepted herself, but she never withheld her own approval for the wrong reasons. Poverty or style or lack of education couldn't stand between her and a new friend. Though she lived in a mostly white society and worried if I went out with a man of the "wrong" race, just as she had once married a man of the "wrong" religion, she always accepted each person as an individual.

85   "Is he *very* dark?" she once asked worriedly about a friend. But when she met this very dark person, she only said afterward, "What a kind and nice man!"

My father was the Jewish half of the family, yet it was my mother who taught me to have pride in that tradition. It was she who encouraged me to listen to a radio play about a concentration camp when I was little. "You should know that this can happen," she said. Yet she did it just enough to teach, never enough to frighten.

It was she who introduced me to books and a respect for them, to poetry that she knew by heart, and to the idea that you could never criticize someone unless you "walked miles in their shoes."

It was she who sold that Toledo house, the only home she had, with the determination that the money be used to start me in college. She gave both her daughters the encouragement to leave home for four years of independence that she herself had never had.

After her death, my sister and I found a journal she had kept of her one cherished and belated trip to Europe. It was a trip she had described very little when she came home: she always deplored people who talked boringly about their personal travels and showed slides. Nonetheless, she had written a descriptive essay called "Grandma Goes to Europe." She still must have thought of herself as a writer. Yet she showed this long journal to no one.

90   I miss her, but perhaps no more in death than I did in life. Dying seems less sad then having lived too little. But at least we're now asking questions about all the Ruths and all our family mysteries.

If her song inspires that, I think she would be the first to say: It was worth the singing.

■   **EXPLORATIONS OF THE TEXT**   ■

---

1. "Happy or unhappy, families are all mysterious." Does this opening statement provide clues about Steinem's possible purposes in writing?
2. How does Steinem's discussion of her Uncle Ed provide the framework for the portrait of her mother?
3. What are some of the "mysteries" in the life of Steinem's mother?
4. What role must Steinem assume? How does she react to it? What do her short anecdotes reveal about her childhood with her mother?
5. To what possible causes does Steinem trace her mother's breakdown?
6. How has Steinem's life as a child and as an adult been shaped by her mother's life? by her relationship with her mother?
7. Steinem states: "But at least we're now asking questions about all the Ruths and all our family mysteries." How does her mother become a representative figure? What does she represent?
8. Steinem gains control of her material through explicit and implicit comparisons. Examine this structural device. What comparisons guide this essay?
9. The essay begins in "mystery." Does it end in "mystery"?

■■ JOURNAL ENTRIES ■■

1. Explore how the story of Steinem's mother on the road represents (as Steinem suggests) "the formidable forces arrayed against" her mother.
2. Does Steinem's process of remembering and writing lead to discovery? Does it lead to a happier ending?

■■■ IDEAS FOR WRITING ■■■

1. Compare the mothers in "Rocking-Horse Winner," "From The House of Yemanjá," "Riders to the Sea," and this essay.
2. How does Steinem characterize her mother?
3. What revelations about family do you learn from Steinem's essay?
4. Using this work as a model, write about a mysterious relationship in your life.

In Search of Our Mothers' Gardens

Alice Walker

Alice Walker (1944–   ), born in Georgia where her father was a tenant farmer, is one of eight children. The youngest daughter, she learned early from her mother to be strong. In her essay, "In Search of Our Mothers' Gardens," she describes this influence, "We were not really allowed to be discouraged. Discouragement could not hold out against her faith." After college, influenced by her involvement in voter registration in Georgia and in welfare programs in Mississippi, Walker began to write.

Her first volume of poetry, Once: Poems *(1968), contains accounts of this work and of her travels to Africa. In 1982, she won the National Book Award and the Pulitzer Prize for* The Color Purple, *an exploration in letters of the African-American experience. As editor of the writings of Zora Neale Hurston,* I Love Myself When I Am Laughing *(1979), Alice Walker assumed primary responsibility for new interest and appreciation of Hurston's work. Walker's recent work,* Warrior Marks, *appeared in 1993.*

In her essay "In Search of Our Mothers' Gardens," Walker envisions the legacies left by her African-American mothers—the "crazy Saints"—whose gardens and quilts are artistic achievements.

I described her own nature and temperament. Told how they needed a larger life for their expression . . . I pointed out that in lieu of proper channels, her emotions had overflowed into paths that dissipated them. I talked, beautifully I thought, about an art that would be born, an art that would open the way for women the likes of her. I asked her to hope, and build up an inner life against the coming of that day. . . . I sang, with a strange quiver in my voice, a promise song.
—*Jean Toomer, "Avey," Cane*[1]

The poet speaking to a prostitute who falls asleep while he's talking—

1   When the poet Jean Toomer walked through the South in the early twenties, he discovered a curious thing: black women whose spirituality was so intense, so deep, so *unconscious,* that they were themselves unaware of the richness they held. They stumbled blindly through their lives: creatures so abused and mutilated in body, so dimmed and confused by pain, that they considered themselves unworthy even of hope. In the selfless abstractions their bodies became to the men who used them, they became more than "sexual objects," more even than mere women: they became "Saints." Instead of being perceived as whole persons, their bodies became shrines: what was thought to be their minds became temples suitable for worship. These crazy Saints stared out at the world, wildly, like lunatics—or quietly, like suicides; and the "God" that was in their gaze was as mute as a great stone.

Who were these Saints? These crazy, loony, pitiful women?

Some of them, without a doubt, were our mothers and grandmothers.

In the still heat of the post-Reconstruction South,[2] this is how they seemed to Jean Toomer: exquisite butterflies trapped in an evil honey, toiling away their lives in an era, a century, that did not acknowledge them, except as "the *mule* of the world." They dreamed dreams that no one knew—not even themselves, in any coherent fashion—and saw visions no one could understand. They wandered or sat about the countryside crooning lullabies to ghosts, and drawing the mother of Christ in charcoal on courthouse walls.

5   They forced their minds to desert their bodies and their striving spirits sought to rise, like frail whirlwinds from the hard red clay. And when those frail whirlwinds fell, in scattered particles, upon the ground, no one mourned. Instead, men lit candles to celebrate the emptiness that remained, as people do who enter a beautiful but vacant space to resurrect a God.

Our mothers and grandmothers, some of them: moving to music not yet written. And they waited.

---

[1] Exerpt from *Cane* by Jean Toomer (1894–1967), a major writer of the Harlem Renaissance.
[2] The South after efforts during the period of "Reconstruction" following the Civil War.

They waited for a day when the unknown thing that was in them would be made known; but guessed, somehow in their darkness, that on the day of their revelation they would be long dead. Therefore to Toomer they walked, and even ran, in slow motion. For they were going nowhere immediate, and the future was not yet within their grasp. And men took our mothers and grandmothers, "but got no pleasure from it." So complex was their passion and their calm.

To Toomer, they lay vacant and fallow as autumn fields, with harvest time never in sight: and he saw them enter loveless marriages, without joy; and become prostitutes, without resistance; and become mothers of children, without fulfillment.

For these grandmothers and mothers of ours were not Saints, but Artists; driven to a numb and bleeding madness by the springs of creativity in them for which there was no release. They were Creators, who lived lives of spiritual waste, because they were so rich in spirituality—which is the basis of Art—that the strain of enduring their unused and unwanted talent drove them insane. Throwing away this spirituality was their pathetic attempt to lighten the soul to a weight their work-worn, sexually abused bodies could bear.

10   What did it mean for a black woman to be an artist in our grandmothers' time? In our great-grandmothers' day? It is a question with an answer cruel enough to stop the blood.

Did you have a genius of a great-great-grandmother who died under some ignorant and depraved white overseer's lash? Or was she required to bake biscuits for a lazy backwater tramp, when she cried out in her soul to paint watercolors of sunsets, or the rain falling on the green and peaceful pasturelands? Or was her body broken and forced to bear children (who were more often than not sold away from her)—eight, ten, fifteen, twenty children—when her one joy was the thought of modeling heroic figures of rebellion, in stone or clay?

How was the creativity of the black woman kept alive, year after year and century after century, when for most of the years black people have been in America, it was a punishable crime for a black person to read or write? And the freedom to paint, to sculpt, to expand the mind with action did not exist. Consider, if you can bear to imagine it, what might have been the result if singing, too, had been forbidden by law. Listen to the voices of Bessie Smith, Billie Holiday, Nina Simone, Roberta Flack, and Aretha Franklin,[3] among others, and imagine those voices muzzled for life. Then you may begin to comprehend the lives of our "crazy," "Sainted" mothers and grandmothers. The agony of the lives of women who might have been Poets, Novelists, Essayists, and Short-Story Writers (over a period of centuries), who died with their real gifts stifled within them.

---

[3] African-American female singers.

And, if this were the end of the story, we would have cause to cry out in my paraphrase of Okot p'Bitek's[4] great poem:

> O, my clanswomen
> Let us all cry together!
> Come,
> Let us mourn the death of our mother,
> The death of a Queen
> The ash that was produced
> By a great fire!
> O, this homestead is utterly dead
> Close the gates
> With *lacari* thorns,
> For our mother
> The creator of the Stool is lost!
> And all the young women
> Have perished in the wilderness!

But this is not the end of the story, for all the young women—our mothers and grandmothers, *ourselves*—have not perished in the wilderness. And if we ask ourselves why, and search for and find the answer, we will know beyond all efforts to erase it from our minds, just exactly who, and of what, we black American women are.

15   One example, perhaps the most pathetic, most misunderstood one, can provide a backdrop for our mothers' work: Phillis Wheatley,[5] a slave in the 1700s.

Virginia Woolf,[6] in her book *A Room of One's Own,* wrote that in order for a woman to write fiction she must have two things, certainly: a room of her own (with key and lock) and enough money to support herself.

What then are we to make of Phillis Wheatley, a slave, who owned not even herself? This sickly, frail black girl who required a servant of her own at times—her health was so precarious—and who, had she been white, would have been easily considered the intellectual superior of all the women and most of the men in the society of her day.

Virginia Woolf wrote further, speaking of course not of our Phillis, that "any woman born with a great gift in the sixteenth century [insert "eighteenth century," insert "black woman," insert "born or made a slave"] would certainly have gone crazed, shot herself, or ended her days in some lonely cottage outside the village, half witch, half wizard [insert "Saint"], feared and mocked at. For it needs little skill and psychology to be sure that a highly gifted girl who had tried to use her gift for poetry would have been so thwarted and hindered by contrary instincts [add "chains, guns, the lash, the ownership of one's body by someone else,

---

[4] African poet.
[5] Slave who wrote poetry (1753–1784).
[6] Major British novelist (1884–1941).

submission to an alien religion"], that she must have lost her health and sanity to a certainty."

The key words, as they relate to Phillis, are "contrary instincts." For when we read the poetry of Phillis Wheatley—as when we read the novels of Nella Larsen or the oddly false-sounding autobiography of that freest of all black women writers, Zora Hurston[7]—evidence of "contrary instincts" is everywhere. Her loyalties were completely divided, as was, without question, her mind.

20   But how could this be otherwise? Captured at seven, a slave of wealthy, doting whites who instilled in her the "savagery" of the Africa they "rescued" her from . . . one wonders if she was even able to remember her homeland as she had known it, or as it really was.

Yes, because she did try to use her gift for poetry in a world that made her a slave, she was "so thwarted and hindered by . . . contrary instincts, that she . . . lost her health. . . ." In the last years of her brief life, burdened not only with the need to express her gift but also with a penniless, friendless "freedom" and several small children for whom she was forced to do strenuous work to feed, she lost her health, certainly. Suffering from malnutrition and neglect and who knows what mental agonies, Phillis Wheatley died.

So torn by "contrary instincts" was black, kidnapped, enslaved Phillis that her description of "the Goddess"—as he poetically called the Liberty she did not have—is ironically, cruelly humorous. And, in fact, has held Phillis up to ridicule for more than a century. It is usually read prior to hanging Phillis's memory as that of a fool. She wrote:

> *The Goddess comes, she moves divinely fair,*
> *Olive and laurel binds her golden hair.*
> *Wherever shines this native of the skies,*
> *Unnumber'd charms and recent graces rise. [My italics]*

It is obvious that Phillis, the slave, combed the "Goddess's" hair every morning; prior, perhaps, to bringing in the milk, or fixing her mistress's lunch. She took her imagery from the one thing she saw elevated above all others.

With the benefit of hindsight we ask, "How could she?"

25   But at last, Phillis, we understand. No more snickering when your stiff, struggling, ambivalent lines are forced on us. We know now that you were not an idiot or a traitor; only a sickly little black girl, snatched from your home and country and made a slave; a woman who still struggled to sing the song that was your gift, although in a land of barbarians who praised you for your bewildered tongue. It is not so much what you sang, as that you kept alive, in so many of our ancestors, *the notion of song.*

---

[7] African-American novelist (1901–1960).

Black women are called, in the folklore that so aptly identifies one's status in society, "the *mule* of the world," because we have been handed the burdens that everyone else—*everyone* else—refused to carry. We have also been called "Matriarchs," "Superwomen," and "Mean and Evil Bitches." Not to mention "Castraters" and "Sapphire's Mama."[8] When we have pleaded for understanding, our character has been distorted; when we have asked for simple caring, we have been handed empty inspirational appellations, then stuck in the farthest corner. When we have asked for love, we have been given children. In short, even our plainer gifts, our labors of fidelity and love, have been knocked down our throats. To be an artist and a black woman, even today, lowers our status in many respects, rather than raises it: and yet, artists we will be.

Therefore we must fearlessly pull out of ourselves and look at and identify with our lives the living creativity some of our great-grandmothers were not allowed to know. I stress *some* of them because it is well known that the majority of our great-grandmothers knew, even without "knowing" it, the reality of their spirituality, even if they didn't recognize it beyond what happened in the singing at church—and they never had any intention of giving it up.

How they did it—those millions of black women who were not Phillis Wheatley, or Lucy Terry or Frances Harper or Zora Hurston or Nella Larsen[9] or Bessie Smith;[10] or Elizabeth Catlett,[11] or Katherine Dunham,[12] either—brings me to the title of this essay, "In Search of Our Mothers' Gardens," which is a personal account that is yet shared, in its theme and its meaning, by all of us. I found, while thinking about the far-reaching world of the creative black woman, that often the truest answer to a question that really matters can be found very close.

In the late 1920s my mother ran away from home to marry my father. Marriage, if not running away, was expected of seventeen-year-old girls. By the time she was twenty, she had two children and was pregnant with a third. Five children later, I was born. And this is how I came to know my mother: she seemed a large, soft, loving-eyed woman who was rarely impatient in our home. Her quick, violent temper was on view only a few times a year, when she battled with the white landlord who had the misfortune to suggest to her that her children did not need to go to school.

30   She made all the clothes we wore, even my brothers' overalls. She made all the towels and sheets we used. She spent the summers canning vegetables and fruits. She spent the winter evenings making quilts enough to cover all our beds.

---

[8] Wife of "the Kingfish" in Amos and Andy, radio and television show.

[9] African-American female writers.

[10] African-American blues singer (1898–1937).

[11] African-American artist, sculptor, and educator (1915 ?–).

[12] African-American dancer and choreographer (1910–).

During the "working" day, she labored beside—not behind—my father in the fields. Her day began before sunup, and did not end until late at night. There was never a moment for her to sit down, undisturbed, to unravel her own private thoughts; never a time free from interruption—by work or the noisy inquiries of her many children. And yet, it is to my mother—and all our mothers who were not famous—that I went in search of the secret of what has fed that muzzled and often mutilated, but vibrant, creative spirit that the black woman has inherited, and that pops out in wild and unlikely places to this day.

But when, you will ask, did my overworked mother have time to know or care about feeding the creative spirit?

The answer is so simple that many of us have spent years discovering it. We have constantly looked high, when we should have looked high—and low.

For example: in the Smithsonian Institution in Washington, D.C., there hangs a quilt unlike any other in the world. In fanciful, inspired, and yet simple and identifiable figures, it portrays the story of the Crucifixion. It is considered rare, beyond price. Though it follows no known pattern of quilt-making, and though it is made of bits and pieces of worthless rags, it is obviously the work of a person of powerful imagination and deep spiritual feeling. Below this quilt I saw a note that says it was made by "an anonymous Black woman in Alabama, a hundred years ago."

35   If we could locate this "anonymous" black woman from Alabama, she would turn out to be one of our grandmothers—an artist who left her mark in the only materials she could afford, and in the only medium her position in society allowed her to use.

As Virginia Woolf wrote further, in *A Room of One's Own:*

> *yet genius of a sort must have existed among women as it must have existed among the working class. [Change this to "slaves" and "the wives and daughters of sharecroppers."] Now and again an Emily Brontë*[13] *or a Robert Burns*[14] *[change this to "a Zora Hurston or a Richard Wright"]*[15] *blazes out and proves its presence. But certainly it never got itself on to paper. When, however, one reads of a witch being ducked, or a woman possessed by devils [or "Sainthood"], of a wise woman selling herbs [our root workers], or even a very remarkable man who had a mother, then I think we are on the track of a lost novelist, a suppressed poet, of some mute and inglorious Jane Austen.*[16] *Indeed, I would venture to guess that Anon, who wrote so many poems without signing them, was often a woman. . . .*

---

[13] English novelist and poet (1819–1848).
[14] Scottish poet (1759–1796).
[15] African-American autobiographer, novelist, poet (1908–1960).
[16] English novelist (1775–1817).

And so our mothers and grandmothers have, more often than not anonymously, handed on the creative spark, the seed of the flower they themselves never hoped to see: or like a sealed letter they could not plainly read.

And so it is, certainly, with my own mother. Unlike "Ma" Rainey's[17] songs, which retained their creator's name even while blasting forth from Bessie Smith's mouth, no song or poem will bear my mother's name. Yet so many of the stories that I write, that we all write, are my mother's stories. Only recently did I fully realize this: that through years of listening to my mother's stories of her life, I have absorbed not only the stories themselves, but something of the manner in which she spoke, something of the urgency that involves the knowledge that her stories—like her life—must be recorded. It is probably for this reason that so much of what I have written is about characters whose counterparts in real life are so much older than I am.

40   But the telling of these stories, which came from my mother's lips as naturally as breathing, was not the only way my mother showed herself as an artist. For stories, too, were subject to being distracted, to dying without conclusion. Dinners must be started, and cotton must be gathered before the big rains. The artist that was and is my mother showed itself to me only after many years. This is what I finally noticed:

Like Men, a character in *The Third Life of Grange Copeland*,[18] my mother adorned with flowers whatever shabby house we were forced to live in. And not just your typical straggly country stand of zinnias, either. She planted ambitious gardens—and still does—with over fifty different varieties of plants that bloom profusely from early March until late November. Before she left home for the fields, she watered her flowers, chopped up the grass, and laid out new beds. When she returned from the fields she might divide clumps of bulbs, dig a cold pit, uproot and replant roses, or prune branches from her taller bushes or trees—until night came and it was too dark to see.

Whatever she planted grew as if by magic, and her fame as a grower of flowers spread over three counties. Because of her creativity with her flowers, even my memories of poverty are seen through a screen of blooms—sunflowers, petunias, roses, dahlias, forsythia, spirea, delphiniums, verbena . . . and on and on.

And I remember people coming to my mother's yard to be given cuttings from her flowers; I hear again the praise showered on her because whatever rocky soil she landed on, she turned into a garden. A garden so brilliant with colors, so original in its design, so magnificent with life and creativity, that to this day people drive by our house in Georgia—perfect strangers and imperfect strangers—and ask to stand or walk among my mother's art.

---

[17] Gertrude Pridgett Rainey, African-American blues singer (1886–1939).
[18] Alice Walker's first novel.

I notice that it is only when my mother is working in her flowers that she is radiant, almost to the point of being invisible—except as Creator: hand and eye. She is involved in work her soul must have. Ordering the universe in the image of her personal conception of Beauty.

45   Her face, as she prepared the Art that is her gift, is a legacy of respect she leaves to me, for all that illuminates and cherishes life. She has handed down respect for the possibilities—and the will to grasp them.

For her, so hindered and intruded upon in so many ways, being an artist has still been a daily part of her life. This ability to hold on, even in very simple ways, is work black women have done for a very long time.

This poem is not enough, but it is something, for the woman who literally covered the holes in our walls with sunflowers:

> They were women then
> My mama's generation
> Husky of voice—Stout of
> Step
> With fists as well as
> Hands
> How they battered down
> Doors
> And ironed
> Starched white
> Shirts
> How they led
> Armies
> Headragged Generals
> Across mined
> Fields
> Booby-trapped
> Kitchens
> To discover books
> Desks
> A place for us
> How they knew what we
> Must know
> Without knowing a page
> Of it
> Themselves.

Guided by my heritage of a love of beauty and a respect for strength—in search of my mother's garden, I found my own.

And perhaps in Africa over two hundred years ago, there was just such a mother; perhaps she painted vivid and daring decorations in oranges and yellows and greens on the walls of her hut; perhaps she sang—in a voice like Roberta Flack's—*sweetly* over the compounds of her village; perhaps she wove the most stunning mats or told the most ingenious stories of all the village storytellers. Perhaps she was herself a poet—though only her daughter's name is signed to the poems that we know.

50   Perhaps Phillis Wheatley's mother was also an artist.

Perhaps in more than Phillis Wheatley's biological life is her mother's signature made clear.

■ EXPLORATIONS OF THE TEXT ■

1. What is the problem presented in the first paragraph? Who are the "crazy Saints"?
2. What is Walker's view of her "mothers and grandmothers"? What thesis does she pose? Who is her audience?
3. Why does she include the example of Phillis Wheatley? How does the example support her argument?
4. How does her inclusion of Virginia Woolf develop her argumentative point of view?
5. Why does Walker choose to include so many references to African-American women?
6. Explain the thematic significance of the title and the garden symbolism. What is Walker's inheritance?
7. Walker uses several short sentences in key places in her essay. Why? What impact do these sentences have?
8. Walker uses several metaphors to advance her argument (e.g., honey, garden, quilting). How do they persuade readers?

■■ JOURNAL ENTRIES ■■

1. Whom do you view as an artist, someone not necessarily considered to be an artist by others? Why?
2. Which family legacy is most important to you? Why?
3. Describe a garden.

■■■ IDEAS FOR WRITING ■■■

1. What makes Walker's argument persuasive?
2. Compare and contrast the visions of "creation" presented in this essay, "A Christmas Memory," and "Lineage."

Student Essay: Comparison/Contrast
A Collaborative Writing

Fathers and Sons

Melissa Del Castillo
Michelle Ing

Melissa Del Castillo and Michelle Ing are both students at the State University of New York at New Paltz. They wrote this assignment, a comparison of the father-son relationships in two poems, as an extra credit collaboration in a Freshman Composition course.

I n every society, fathers treat their children differently. In some societies, fathers respect their children and care about them and for them while in other societies, fathers don't believe that the children deserve respect. In the poem, "My Father's Song," a father explains to his son how he looks up to his own father and how he learned to respect the things of this world from his father. In the poem, "My Papa's Waltz," a boy explains that he loves his father despite all of his father's abuse. These poems present different kinds of relationships between fathers and sons.

In "My Father's Song," the father, the main speaker in the poem, relates to his son an experience that he had had with his own father. The father and son were walking in a field "one Spring at Acu" when the father noticed "tiny pink animals" in the furrows of a plough. The speaker states: "The plowshare had unearthed/the burrow nest of a mouse/in the soft moist sand." He began talking to his son, relating his "song" to his son, and teaching him to respect nature. The speaker states: "Very gently, he scooped tiny pink animals/into the palm of his hand/and told me to touch them." His father had enough respect for these animals that he carried them to safety. "We took them to the edge/of the field and put them in the shade/of a sand moist clod." His father, a very gentle man, taught his son love and respect for all creatures, and the speaker hopes that he can do the same for his son. He teaches his son to cherish life, and the son feels his father's love, and learns his grandfather's and father's values. He "miss[es]" a father whom he loves and who loves him. The son hopes that he can do the same thing for his children.

In the poem, "My Papa's Waltz," the father-son relationship appears to be a shaky and uncertain one. Although the father is an abusive alcoholic, the son does indeed love him and clings to him seeking affection. There is evidence of the father's abuse in the speaker's statement: "The whiskey on your breath/ could make a small boy dizzy." But because the boy loves his father, he is not deterred by the alcohol. The father's behavior is revealed in the images of the boy's dance with the father. The dance is wild and then becomes violent: "We romped until the pans/slid from the kitchen shelf." The pans' sliding from the shelves indicates the father's becoming angry and throwing things. "The hand that held [the son's] wrist" which "was battered on one knuckle" became "battered" perhaps because the father was hitting the mother and son. Even after he beat the boy, the son was still attached to the father because he needed his love. The father "beat time on [his] head" and then "waltzed [him] off to bed/still clinging to [the father's] shirt." The boy will take the abuse as long as he can to be close to his father. The boy will hold on and dance with his papa to gain love. The waltz that the son talks about is like the dance of life—the son "clinging" to the father.

In "My Father's Song," the son respected his father, learned about love and caring from the latter, and hoped he could be a good father; meanwhile, in "My Papa's Waltz," the son, the speaker in the poem, remembers a dance with his father, a moment which represented the whole relationship, his father's lack of respect for him. The father didn't care about him, but his son loved him despite the abuse. In both poems, the sons love their fathers, but the difference is that one father cares, and the other doesn't.

WRITING ASSIGNMENTS

1. a. Based on the selections in this chapter, freewrite about what you learned about the experience of parenting or of childhood that was revelatory to you.
   b. Write a journal entry comparing one example of the parent/child relationship presented in the works in this chapter with your own experience.
   c. Make a list of questions which emerge from these explorations of parent/child relationships. Write an answer to one of these questions. Refer to three works in this chapter.
2. a. Diagram a family tree for the central relationships in your life. Include extended family and friends. Draw straight lines for the relationships which represent solidity and broken lines (------) for those which seem fragile or negative.
   b. Write your conclusions in your journal.
   c. Compare the positive and negative aspects of family dynamics in your life with one work in this chapter.
3. a. Think of a moment from your past—a moment of conflict or of closeness. Write a point of view piece, a monologue, for each family member.
   b. After you write these pieces, try several freewrites about characters' conflicts within family settings presented in three works in this chapter. Then create monologues for these characters.
   c. Write an essay about sources of closeness or of conflict between parents and their children. Choose three works from this chapter. Include specific evidence from the texts.
4. Analyze the impact of mothers on their children. What are major issues in mother/daughter relationships evident in works in this chapter? Choose several works for discussion.
5. One important aspect of mothering is the issue of separation from the mother. Is this issue a pattern in the works in this chapter? Are other patterns evident?
6. a. Our views of family change at different stages in our lives. Do a freewrite about several changes in your views of a particular family member. You may begin: "When I was (ten), I thought . . . ."
   b. Find two works by the same writer about the same family member. Compare them.
7. Based on selections in this chapter, compare the relationships of fathers and sons to those of fathers and daughters. What conclusions can you draw about the nature of these relationships?
8. a. Define a good parent. (You may do this as either a freewrite or a journal entry.)
   b. Watch several situation comedies about families. What images of parents appear?

    c. Do any television programs present a realistic view of family life? Your analysis may become an argumentative essay.

    d. Compare a comedy from the fifties or sixties with one which is contemporary.

9. a. Interview several people from different ethnic backgrounds. Concentrate on family life, particularly on the roles and responsibilities of parents and of children. What do you conclude?

    b. Based on your interviews and the selections in this chapter, compare the roles of parents or children in two different cultures. Do parents' roles differ? Are there different cultural expectations for children?

    c. Write an analysis of cultural roles for parents and/or children in Tan's "Scar," Baldwin's "Sonny's Blues," Ortiz's "My Father's Song," or Rosa's "The Third Bank of the River." (Choose three.)

10. a. Using "A Christmas Memory" as a model, write a character sketch about someone who has encouraged the best in you. Make that person come alive.

    b. If you wish, try this inventory for your character: Name, Sex, Age, Height, Weight, Color of Hair and Eyes, Occupation, Mannerisms, Birthplace and Family, Hobbies, Eating Habits, Major Personality Traits, Clothing, Dialogue, Relationships, Key Events Which Reveal Character.

    c. To write this sketch, you may want to organize in one of the following ways: by personality traits, by physical description and key events, by monologue or dialogue.

11. a. Freewrite about which work in this chapter has affected you most intensely.

    b. Which work is the most powerful representation of family life? Why?

    c. Which piece is the least successful? Why?

    d. Write an essay about one of your entries. Direct the essay to the writers of the text.

12. Discuss water imagery in three works.

13. Explore the use of allusions to myth, fable, and fairy tale as literary technique in "The Rocking-Horse Winner," "From the House of Yemanjá," and/or "Sonny's Blues."

14. a. Catalogue the qualities of "the good Mother" and "the bad Mother." What do you conclude?

    b. Compare several works which present visions of good and bad mothers.

    c. Write an essay about a work or works in which the mother's character is stereotypical. Evaluate each portrayal.

    d. You may write about fathers and follow the assignments in a, b, and c above.

15. Explore the idea of kinship and of extended family as it is presented in several works in this chapter.

16. Is the idea of the nuclear family in North America being redefined? Defend your position. You may use evidence from the works you have read or do research on this topic to support your argument.

17. Conceive of a definition of the family in the year 2001. What are its attributes? You may use evidence from the works you have read in this chapter, or you may do research to find information to develop your definition.

18. Choose three characters from works in this chapter, and create a conversation about family life.

19. Explicate one of the poems in this chapter. Concentrate on point of view, tone, imagery, figurative language, and form. How do these aspects of the work develop theme?

20. Several of the essays in this chapter are autobiographical. Reread these works, and determine what creates effective autobiographical writing. (Refer to Chapter 13 for directions for analysis.)

21. Examine a common theme in the readings in the Thematic Preview: "The Rocking-Horse Winner," "Those Winter Sundays," *Riders to the Sea,* and "Letter to His Father." Some suggestions for your consideration are the difficulty of separation, lack of communication, inevitable loss, or the failures of parenting.

LOVE

It is other people who have separated
You and me.
Come, my lord!
Do not dream of listening
To the between-words of people.
My heart, thinking
"How beautiful he is"
Is like a swift river
[Which] though one dams it and dams it,
Will still break through.

"The Lady of Sakanoye," from the Manyō Shū
(compiled A.D. 760)

From the Japanese "Lady of Sakanoye," from the love songs of Sappho, from Kalidasa's *Shakuntala,* from "The Song of Solomon," from William Shakespeare to Anna Akhmatova, artists have written about the longing for love. This yearning represents a need deeper than sexual attraction or survival of the species; it represents the desire for connection that emerges as strongly as the urge for food or drink.

The Thematic Preview asks questions about forms of love: What is romantic love? What constitutes romantic fantasy? passion? These questions are implied in Leslie Silko's "Yellow Woman." The search for love and for fulfillment dominate Shakespeare's "Shall I Compare Thee to a Summer's Day?" and Wakako Yamauchi's *And the Soul Shall Dance.* Julia Kristeva richly depicts the disparities among "words," "letters," and the actual experience of love. The readings in the rest of the chapter present many aspects of love, and they challenge us to understand these dimensions more fully: young love, marriage, illicit relationships, sexuality, gender differences, social conditioning, cultural patterns—the diverse habits of loving.

Love, romance, and passion fascinate writers and readers. In Ernest Hemingway's "Hills Like White Elephants," the lovers, similar to many young people, begin with unrealistic expectations, with a dream of lasting happiness. The dream fades as they journey together. In James Joyce's "The Dead," Gretta's obsession with Michael Furey, her first lover, leaves her with vivid memories of the possibility of grand passion, a desire shared by those who love for the first time.

Disappointment, loss, and sorrow also are aspects of relationships portrayed in literary works. In marriage, the partners discover the complexities of intimacy—the fulfillment and destruction of William Blake's "The Garden of Love," the garden and the graveyard, the blossoms and the weeds. Njabulo Ndebele's "Death of a Son" portrays a couple, unable to relate to each other, torn apart by the random, pointless shooting of their son. Violence, inherent in apartheid, threatens and almost destroys their love. Joyce's "The Dead" presents a classic example of a mature marriage in which wife and husband live in separate worlds and fail to recognize the hollow centers of their relationship and of their lives. Mathew Arnold's "Dover Beach" portrays relationship as the solemn answer to the sorrow and loss at the very heart of the human condition: "Ah, love, let us be true to one another."

Some people are true to one another; both Shakespeare's sonnet "Let Me Not to the Marriage of True Minds" and John Donne's "A Valediction Forbidding Mourning" attest to the beauty of the full closeness of love. Liz Rosenberg writes of elderly couples, still in love, transformed by the lasting bond of marriage in "In the End, We Are All Light."

Illicit love always has tantalized men and women with its promise of the forbidden, of the unknown, of the mysteries, of the unconventional—the promise of fulfillment in contrast to the predictability of daily life. Anton Chekhov's characters escape from their dreary marriages in their moment of passion. In Zhang Jie's "Love Must Not Be Forgotten," the mother holds an ideal of unrealized romantic love that provides sustenance in the midst of an empty, arranged marriage. Like many such relationships, one of the lovers eventually returns to his or her marriage. Anne Sexton's "For My Lover, Returning to His Wife" records a deserted woman's sadness and frustration: "As for me, I am a watercolor/I wash off." Katherine Ann Porter's Granny Weatherall never recovers from disappointment created by being jilted by her beloved on her wedding day.

Desire—of the young and old, of the married and unmarried—remains central to the experience of loving. In "To His Coy Mistress," Andrew Marvell's speaker argues with his beloved and urges her to succumb to his plea. Sexual yearning and communion underlie the actions of lovers. Plato theorizes in "The Sexes" from *The Symposium* that this longing for union emerges from a human sense of incompleteness. Each person seeks his or her other half to become "whole" through love. Is each of us half a person? Olga Broumas clearly does not believe Plato, but her speaker in "Song/For Sanna" still expresses the same yearning, a yearning for someone who always leaves for a safer haven. Sexual fulfillment reaches a spiritual level in Gary Snyder's "The Bath," in Leopold Senghor's "Nuit de Sine," and in Pablo Neruda's "Sweetness, Always." These poems suggest fulfillments that are emotional, sexual, and spiritual. T. S. Eliot's Prufrock both seeks and fears such powerful emotions: he will not "dare."

Conditioned by social mores, men and women have different expectations of roles and behaviors in relationships. Alberto Moravia's "The Chase" and Octavio Paz's "My Life with the Wave" portray male fantasies of love and the disjunction between male dreams and female realities. The men and women in Susan Glaspell's *Trifles* search for clues about motives for murder and create different versions of the crime. Their interpretations reveal the ways in which gender roles shape their views of the world.

Roles for men and for women have been socially constructed. In *The Second Sex,* Simone de Beauvoir contends that women have been objectified and defined as "other." According to de Beauvoir, men have been seen as the dominant presence; women as appendages to men—never subjects, always objects. How does this position shape women's identities and experiences in love relationships? How has the lack of equality affected women's existences? In "The Yellow Wallpaper," Charlotte Perkins Gilman creates a woman driven insane by her role as other. Anna Akhmatova rewrites the story of Lot's Wife and gives the nameless woman a life separate from the Biblical representation of her. May Swenson's "Women" presents a powerful critique of a society that stereotypes women. Even language causes and perpetuates women's position as other. Huda Naamani understands the power of language to imprison women as she mocks the male "word" in "I Take You an Orange." Seizing the lover's word is the ultimate act of defiance.

Finally, culture also shapes the forms of love. The tradition of arranged marriage in China, in "No Name Woman," comes from a contemporary writer, Maxine Hong Kingston, who has witnessed cultural change and the inevitable conflicts that arise among generations when societal mores are challenged. The narrator confronts her mother's conception of woman's place in society by telling her aunt's tragic story and by breaking the imposed silence, a cultural taboo. Through this act, she redefines her identity as a Chinese woman.

In *Tales of Love,* Julia Kristeva calls love "an affliction, a word, a letter" and contends that discourse on love is as difficult as living it. However, saying "I love you" is not as difficult as loving another. Kristeva is not wrong about the joy in all utterances and discussions of love, in all acts of love. Like the Lady of Sakanoye, she understands the power of love which "like a swift river . . . will still break through."

THEMATIC PREVIEW: COMBINING THE GENRES

Yellow Woman

Leslie Marmon Silko

*Born in Albuquerque, New Mexico, Leslie Marmon Silko (1948–   )
grew up on the Laguna Pueblo Reservation. Her heritage—Laguna,
Mexican, and white—provides the material and the inspiration for
her writing. A graduate of the University of New Mexico, she now
teaches at the University of Arizona in Tucson. She first received
critical attention in 1977 for her novel* Ceremony, *the story of a veteran's struggle for sanity.* Storyteller *(1981) is her best known work.
Her most recent novel is* Almanac of the Dead *(1991). Silko's fiction
and poetry have earned her a grant from the National Endowment
for the Arts, a poetry award from* Chicago Review *(1974), the Push-
cart Prize for poetry (1977), and the John D. and Catherine T.
MacArthur Foundation Grant (1983).*

*"Yellow Woman" concerns a Navajo woman who believes that
she has been kidnapped by a man who embodies a spirit. In* Melus,
*A. Ruoff writes, "'Yellow Woman' is based on traditional abduction
tales, [but] it is a more modernized version." The strength of this
story is the interplay of illusion and reality.*

I

1   My thigh clung to his with dampness, and I watched the sun rising up
through the tamaracks and willows. The small brown water birds came
to the river and hopped across the mud, leaving brown scratches in the
alkali-white crust. They bathed in the river silently. I could hear the water,
almost at our feet where the narrow fast channel bubbled and washed green
ragged moss and fern leaves. I looked at him beside me, rolled in the red
blanket on the white river sand. I cleaned the sand out of the cracks between
my toes, squinting because the sun was above the willow trees. I looked at
him for the last time, sleeping on the white river sand.

I felt hungry and followed the river south the way we had come the afternoon before, following our footprints that were already blurred by lizard
tracks and bug trails. The horses were still lying down, and the black one
whinnied when he saw me but he did not get up—maybe it was because the
corral was made out of thick cedar branches and the horses had not yet felt
the sun like I had. I tried to look beyond the pale red mesas to the pueblo. I
knew it was there, even if I could not see it, on the sandrock hill above the

river, the same river that moved past me now and had reflected the moon last night.

The horse felt warm underneath me. He shook his head and pawed the sand. The bay whinnied and leaned against the gate trying to follow, and I remembered him asleep in the red blanket beside the river. I slid off the horse and tied him close to the other horse. I walked north with the river again, and the white sand broke loose in footprints over footprints.

"Wake up."

5   He moved in the blanket and turned his face to me with his eyes still closed. I knelt down to touch him.

"I'm leaving."

He smiled now, eyes still closed. "You are coming with me, remember?" He sat up now with his bare dark chest and belly in the sun.

"Where?"

"To my place."

10   "And will I come back?"

He pulled his pants on. I walked away from him, feeling him behind me and smelling the willows.

"Yellow Woman," he said.

I turned to face him. "Who are you?" I asked.

He laughed and knelt on the low, sandy bank, washing his face in the river. "Last night you guessed my name, and you knew why I had come."

15   I stared past him at the shallow moving water and tried to remember the night, but I could only see the moon in the water and remember his warmth around me.

"But I only said that you were him and that I was Yellow Woman—I'm not really her—I have my own name and I come from the pueblo on the other side of the mesa. Your name is Silva and you are a stranger I met by the river yesterday afternoon."

He laughed softly. "What happened yesterday has nothing to do with what you will do today, Yellow Woman."

"I know—that's what I'm saying—the old stories about the ka'tsina spirit and Yellow Woman can't mean us."

My old grandpa liked to tell those stories best. There is one about Badger and Coyote who went hunting and were gone all day, and when the sun was going down they found a house. There was a girl living there alone, and she had light hair and eyes and she told them that they could sleep with her. Coyote wanted to be with her all night so he sent Badger into a prairie-dog hole, telling him he thought he saw something in it. As soon as Badger crawled in, Coyote blocked up the entrance with rocks and hurried back to Yellow Woman.

20   "Come here," he said gently.

He touched my neck and I moved close to him to feel his breathing and to hear his heart. I was wondering if Yellow Woman had known who she was—if she knew that she would become part of the stories. Maybe she'd had another name that her husband and relatives called her so that only the ka'tsina from the north and the storytellers would know her as Yellow Woman. But I didn't go on; I felt him all around me, pushing me down into the white river sand.

"Yellow Woman went away with the spirit from the north and lived with him and his relatives. She was gone for a long time, but then one day she came back and she brought twin boys.

"Do you know the story?"

"What story?" He smiled and pulled me close to him as he said this. I was afraid lying there on the red blanket. All I could know was the way he felt, warm, damp, his body beside me. This is the way it happens in the stories. I was thinking, with no thought beyond the moment she meets the ka'tsina spirit and they go.

25 "I don't have to go. What they tell in stories was real only then, back in time immemorial, like they say."

He stood up and pointed at my clothes tangled in the blanket. "Let's go," he said.

I walked beside him, breathing hard because he walked fast, his hand around my wrist. I had stopped trying to pull away from him, because his hand felt cool and the sun was high, drying the river bed into alkali. I will see someone, eventually I will see someone, and then I will be certain that he is only a man—some man from nearby—and I will be sure that I am not Yellow Woman. Because she is from out of time past and I live now and I've been to school and there are highways and pickup trucks that Yellow Woman never saw.

It was an easy ride north on horseback. I watched the change from the cottonwood trees along the river to the junipers that brushed past us in the foothills, and finally there were only piñons, and when I looked up at the rim of the mountain plateau I could see pine trees growing on the edge. Once I stopped to look down, but the pale sandstone had disappeared and the river was gone and the dark lava hills were all around. He touched my hand, not speaking, but always singing softly a mountain song and looking into my eyes.

I felt hungry and wondered what they were doing at home now—my mother, my grandmother, my husband, and the baby. Cooking breakfast, saying, "Where did she go?—maybe kidnapped," and Al going to the tribal police with the details: "She went walking along the river."

30 The house was made with black lava rock and red mud. It was high above the spreading miles of arroyos and long mesas. I smelled a mountain smell of pitch and buck brush. I stood there beside the black horse, looking down on the small, dim country we had passed, and I shivered.

"Yellow Woman, come inside where it's warm."

II

He lit a fire in the stove. It was an old stove with a round belly and an enamel coffeepot on top. There was only the stove, some faded Navajo blankets, and a bedroll and cardboard box. The floor was made of smooth adobe plaster, and there was one small window facing east. He pointed at the box.

"There's some potatoes and the frying pan." He sat on the floor with his arms around his knees pulling them close to his chest and he watched me fry the potatoes. I didn't mind him watching me because he was always watching me—he had been watching me since I came upon him sitting on the river bank trimming leaves from a willow twig with his knife. We ate from the pan and he wiped the grease from his fingers on his Levis.

"Have you brought women here before?" He smiled and kept chewing, so I said, "Do you always use the same tricks?"

35   "What tricks?" He looked at me like he didn't understand.

"The story about being a ka'tsina from the mountains. The story about Yellow Woman."

Silva was silent, his face was calm.

"I don't believe it. Those stories couldn't happen now," I said.

He shook his head and said softly, "But someday they will talk about us, and they will say, 'Those two lived long ago when things like that happened.'"

40   He stood up and went out. I ate the rest of the potatoes and thought about things—about the noise the stove was making and the sound of the mountain wind outside. I remembered yesterday and the day before, and then I went outside.

I walked past the corral to the edge where the narrow trail cut through the black rim rock. I was standing in the sky with nothing around me but the wind that came down from the mountain peak behind me. I could see faint mountain images in the distance miles across the vast spread of mesa and valleys and plains. I wondered who was over there to feel the mountain wind on those sheer blue edges—who walks on the pine needles in those blue mountains.

"Can you see the pueblo?" Silva was standing behind me.

I shook my head. "We're too far away."

"From here I can see the world." He stepped out on the edge. "The Navajo reservation begins over there." He pointed to the east. "The Pueblo boundaries are over here." He looked below us to the south, where the narrow trail seemed to come from. "The Texans have their ranches over there, starting with that valley, the Concho Valley. The Mexicans run some cattle over there too."

45   "Do you ever work for them?"

"I steal from them," Silva answered. The sun was dropping behind us and shadows were filling the land below. I turned away from the edge that dropped forever into the valleys below.

"I'm cold," I said; "I'm going inside." I started wondering about this man who could speak the Pueblo language so well but who lived on a mountain and rustled cattle. I decided that this man Silva must be Navajo, because Pueblo men didn't do things like that.

"You must be a Navajo."

Silva shook his head gently. "Little Yellow Woman," he said, "you never give up, do you? I have told you who I am. The Navajo people know me, too." He knelt down and unrolled the bedroll and spread the extra blankets out on a piece of canvas. The sun was down, and the only light in the house came from outside—the dim orange light from sundown.

50　　I stood there and waited for him to crawl under the blankets.

"What are you waiting for?" he said, and I lay down beside him. He undressed me slowly like the night before beside the river—kissing my face gently and running his hands up and down my belly and legs. He took off my pants and then he laughed.

"Why are you laughing?"

"You are breathing so hard."

I pulled away from him and turned my back to him.

55　　He pulled me around and pinned me down with his arms and chest. "You don't understand, do you, little Yellow Woman? You will do what I want."

And again he was all around me with his skin slippery against mine, and I was afraid because I understood that his strength could hurt me. I lay beneath him and I knew that he could destroy me. But later, while he slept beside me, I touched his face and had a feeling—the kind of feeling for him that overcame me that morning along the river. I kissed him on the forehead and he reached out for me.

When I woke up in the morning he was gone. It gave me a strange feeling because for a long time I sat there on the blankets and looked around the little house for some object of his—some proof that he had been there or maybe that he was coming back. Only the blanket and the cardboard box remained. The .30-30 that had been leaning in the corner was gone, and so was the knife I had used the night before. He was gone, and I had my chance to go now. But first I had to eat, because I knew it would be a long walk home.

I found some dried apricots in the cardboard box, and I sat down on a rock at the edge of the plateau rim. There was no wind and the sun warmed me. I was surrounded by silence. I drowsed with apricots in my mouth, and I didn't believe that there were highways or railroads or cattle to steal.

When I woke up, I stared down at my feet in the black mountain dirt. Little black ants were swarming over the pine needles around my foot. They must have smelled the apricots. I thought about my family far below me. They would be wondering about me, because this had never happened to me before. The tribal police would file a report. But if old Grandpa weren't dead he would tell them what happened—he would laugh and say, "Stolen by a ka'tsina, a mountain spirit. She'll come home—they usually do." There are enough of them to handle things. My mother and grandmother will raise the baby like they raised me. Al will find someone else, and they will go on like before, except that there will be a story about the day I disappeared while I was walking along the river. Silva had come for me; he said he had. I did not decide to go. I just went. Moonflowers blossom in the sand hills before dawn just as I followed him. That's what I was thinking as I wandered along the trail through the pine trees.

60　　It was noon when I got back. When I saw the stone house I remembered that I had meant to go home. But that didn't seem important any more, maybe because there were little blue flowers growing in the meadow behind the stone house and the gray squirrels were playing in the pines next to the house. The horses were standing in the corral, and there was a beef carcass hanging on the shady side of a big pine in front of the house. Flies buzzed around the clotted blood that hung from the carcass. Silva was washing his hands in a bucket full of water. He must have heard me coming because he spoke to me without turning to face me.

"I've been waiting for you."

"I went walking in the big pine trees."

I looked into the bucket full of bloody water with brown-and-white animal hairs floating in it. Silva stood there letting his hand drip, examining me intently.

"Are you coming with me?"

65   "Where?" I asked him.

"To sell the meat in Marquez."

"If you're sure it's O.K."

"I wouldn't ask you if it wasn't," he answered.

He sloshed the water around in the bucket before he dumped it out and set the bucket upside down near the door. I followed him to the corral and watched him saddle the horses. Even beside the horses he looked tall, and I asked him again if he wasn't Navajo. He didn't say anything; he just shook his head and kept cinching up the saddle.

70   "But Navajos are tall."

"Get on the horse," he said, "and let's go."

The last thing he did before we started down the steep trail was to grab the .30-30 from the corner. He slid the rifle into the scabbard that hung from his saddle.

"Do they ever try to catch you?" I asked.

"They don't know who I am."

75   "Then why did you bring the rifle?"

"Because we are going to Marquez where the Mexicans live."

III

The trail leveled out on a narrow ridge that was steep on both sides like an animal spine. On one side I could see where the trail went around the rocky gray hills and disappeared into the southeast where the pale sandrock mesas stood in the distance near my home. On the other side was a trail that went west, and as I looked far into the distance I thought I saw the little town. But Silva said no, that I was looking in the wrong place, that I just thought I saw houses. After that I quit looking off into the distance; it was hot and the wildflowers were closing up their deep-yellow petals. Only the waxy cactus flowers bloomed in the bright sun, and I saw every color that a cactus blossom can be: the white ones and the red ones were still buds, but the purple and the yellow were blossoms, open full and the most beautiful of all.

Silva saw him before I did. The white man was riding a big gray horse, coming up the trail toward us. He was traveling fast and the gray horse's feet sent rocks rolling off the trail into the dry tumbleweeds. Silva motioned for me to stop and we watched the white man. He didn't see us right away, but finally his horse whinnied at our horses and he stopped. He looked at us briefly before he loped the gray horse across the three hundred yards that separated us. He stopped his horse in front of Silva, and his young fat face was shadowed by the brim of his hat. He didn't look mad, but his small, pale eyes moved from the blood-soaked gunny sacks hanging from my saddle to Silva's face and then back to my face.

"Where did you get the fresh meat?" the white man asked.

80 "I've been hunting," Silva said, and when he shifted his weight in the saddle the leather creaked.

"The hell you have, Indian. You've been rustling cattle. We've been looking for the thief for a long time."

The rancher was fat, and sweat began to soak through his white cowboy shirt and the wet cloth stuck to the thick rolls of belly fat. He almost seemed to be panting from the exertion of talking, and he smelled rancid, maybe because Silva scared him.

Silva turned to me and smiled. "Go back up the mountain, Yellow Woman."

The white man got angry when he heard Silva speak in a language he couldn't understand. "Don't try anything, Indian. Just keep riding to Marquez. We'll call the state police from there."

85 The rancher must have been unarmed because he was very frightened and if he had a gun he would have pulled it out then. I turned my horse around and the rancher yelled, "Stop!" I looked at Silva for an instant and there was something ancient and dark—something I could feel in my stomach—in his eyes, and when I glanced at his hand I saw his finger on the trigger of the .30-30 that was still in the saddle scabbard. I slapped my horse across the flank and the sacks of raw meat swung against my knees as the horse leaped up the trail. It was hard to keep my balance, and once I thought I felt the saddle slipping backward; it was because of this that I could not look back.

I didn't stop until I reached the ridge where the trail forked. The horse was breathing deep gasps and there was a dark film of sweat on its neck. I looked down in the direction I had come from, but I couldn't see the place. I waited. The wind came up and pushed warm air past me. I looked up at the sky, pale blue and full of thin clouds and fading vapor trails left by jets.

I think four shots were fired—I remember hearing four hollow explosions that reminded me of deer hunting. There could have been more shots after that, but I couldn't have heard them because my horse was running again and the loose rocks were making too much noise as they scattered around his feet.

Horses have a hard time running downhill, but I went that way instead of uphill to the mountain because I thought it was safer. I felt better with the horse running southeast past the round gray hills that were covered with cedar trees and black lava rock. When I got to the plain in the distance I could see the dark green patches of tamaracks that grew along the river; and beyond the river I could see the beginning of the pale sandrock mesas. I stopped the horse and looked back to see if anyone was coming; then I got off the horse and turned the horse around, wondering if it would go back to its corral under the pines on the mountain. It looked back at me for a moment and then plucked a mouthful of green tumbleweeds before it trotted back up the trail with its ears pointed forward, carrying its head daintily to one side to avoid stepping on the dragging reins. When the horse disappeared over the last hill, the gunny sacks full of meat were still swinging and bouncing.

IV

I walked toward the river on a wood-hauler's road that I knew would eventually lead to the paved road. I was thinking about waiting beside the road for someone to drive by, but by the time I got to the pavement I had decided it wasn't very far to walk if I followed the river back the way Silva and I had come.

90   The river water tasted good, and I sat in the shade under a cluster of silvery willows. I thought about Silva, and I felt sad at leaving him; still, there was something strange about him, and I tried to figure it out all the way back home.

I came back to the place on the river bank where he had been sitting the first time I saw him. The green willow leaves that he had trimmed from the branch were still lying there, wilted in the sand. I saw the leaves and I wanted to go back to him—to kiss him and to touch him—but the mountains were too far away now. And I told myself, because I believe it, he will come back sometime and be waiting again by the river.

*   *   *

I followed the path up from the river into the village. The sun was getting low, and I could smell supper cooking when I got to the screen door of my house. I could hear their voices inside—my mother was telling my grandmother how to fix the Jell-o and my husband, Al, was playing with the baby. I decided to tell them that some Navajo had kidnapped me, but I was sorry that old Grandpa wasn't alive to hear my story because it was the Yellow Woman stories he liked to tell best.

■ EXPLORATIONS OF THE TEXT ■

1. How does the story of Yellow Woman and the ka'tsina function in this work?
2. Describe the relationship between the speaker and Silva. How does it change in each section?
3. How do details about the setting and about the horses emphasize the mythic elements of the story? How do the same details emphasize the sexual fascination between the two characters?

4. Discuss Silva's character. Why does he live a solitary life? Why does he steal horses? Why does he have a gun?
5. Why does Yellow Woman agree to help Silva sell the meat? What does the symbolism of the dead animal and of the blood signify?
6. Analyze the encounter between Silva and the rancher. Why does the narrator ride down the mountain? Does she make conscious choices?
7. Is the ending optimistic or pessimistic? What roles do imagination and fantasy play in the narrator's actions? What does the story suggest about the power of sexual fantasy?
8. Discuss the depiction of sexual roles in the story. Compare with Maxine Hong Kingston's "No Name Woman."

■■ JOURNAL ENTRIES ■■

1. Create a **myth** about a ka'tsina. Use Silko's narrative technique as a model.
2. Extend the story to part five. Imitate Silko's style.
3. Freewrite about Silva.

■■■ IDEAS FOR WRITING ■■■

1. Analyze the love relationship in this story. Are the male and female roles stereotypical?
2. Compare this vision of love with Senghor's "Nuit de Sine," Yamauchi's *And The Soul Shall Dance,* or Paz's "My Life with the Wave."

Shall I Compare Thee to a Summer's Day?

William Shakespeare

Shakespeare's sonnets are the most prolific, best loved form of his non-dramatic poetry. Numbering 154 in all, the sonnets, like his plays and Elizabethan poetry in general, incorporate images from everyday life, nature, the fine arts, business, law, and, of course, love. In fact, the characters and situations of Shakespeare's sonnets signaled a departure from the conventional, more restrictive Petrarchan sonnet tradition and enabled Shakespeare to explore themes of time and death, truth and deceit, beauty, decay, permanence, and love in all of its forms.

*In the following sonnet, the three **quatrains** (four-line stanzas) compare the persona's beloved to a "summer's day." The final **couplet** (two-line stanza) confers eternal love and beauty upon the loved one and upon the poem.*

Shall I compare thee to a summer's day?
Thou art more lovely and more temperate.
Rough winds do shake the darling buds of May,
And summer's lease hath all too short a date.
5 Sometimes too hot the eye of heaven shines,
And often is his gold complexion dimmed;
And every fair from fair sometime declines,
By chance, or nature's changing course, untrimmed.
But thy eternal summer shall not fade,
10 Nor lose possession of that fair thou ow'st;[1]
Nor shall death brag thou wand'rest in his shade,
When in eternal lines to time thou grow'st.
So long as men can breathe or eyes can see,
So long lives this, and this gives life to thee.

■ EXPLORATIONS OF THE TEXT ■

1. Why does the speaker consider his loved one more lovely than "a summer's day"? What are the positive qualities of the loved one?
2. List ways in which nature and time change beauty. Interpret lines 3–8.
3. Explain the shift in tone and in subject in line 9. Why does the speaker assure the lover that "eternal summer shall not fade"?
4. What is the relation of art and love? Look carefully at the **couplet** at the end.
5. Which syllables are stressed in the last line? How does this rhythm emphasize the meaning?
6. Identify **metaphors** and **similes** in the sonnet. How do they relate to theme?

■■ JOURNAL ENTRIES ■■

1. Write about the timelessness of art and the fragility of beauty in this sonnet. What do you conclude?
2. Freewrite and create a portrait of a loved one through the use of figurative language (e.g., similes and metaphors).

---

[1] Ownest.

■■■   IDEAS FOR WRITING   ■■■

1. Explicate this sonnet. (Focus on imagery, figurative language, formal elements.)

And the Soul Shall Dance
Wakako Yamauchi

Born in Westmoreland, California, Wakako Yamauchi (1924–   ) is the daughter of Japanese immigrants who worked as farmers. She was interned with her family in a camp for Japanese-Americans during the Second World War (1942). She later became a freelance writer, and her short stories have appeared in numerous anthologies. Her works include "Songs My Mother Taught Me" (1977), "Boatman on Tonch River" (1983), "Surviving the Wasteland Years" (1988), "Makapoo Bay" (1989), and "Maybe" (1990). Her play, And the Soul Shall Dance, *was adapted from a short story with the same title. The dramatic version was first performed in Los Angeles in 1977. Yamauchi also created a screenplay of* And the Soul Shall Dance *for public television.*

The play centers on conflicts between men and women, between generations, and between cultures. Eleven-year-old Masako learns about adult relationships as she watches her parents and as she observes Emiko, who wishes to leave her husband, Oka, and to return to Japan.

Characters

Murata, 40, Issei[1] farmer.
Hana, Issei wife of Murata.
Masako, 11, Nisei[2] daughter of the Muratas.
Oka, 45, Issei farmer.
Emiko, 30, wife of Oka.
Kiyoko, 14, Oka's daughter.

Place and Time

The action of the play takes place on and between two small farms in Southern California's Imperial Valley in the early 1930s.

---

[1] First-generation Japanese-American.
[2] Second-generation Japanese-American.

Act I

Scene 1

Summer 1935, afternoon. Interior of the Murata house. The set is spare. There is a kitchen table, four chairs, a bed, and on the wall, a calendar indicating the year and month: June, 1935. There is a doorway leading to the other room. Props are: a bottle of sake, *two cups, a dish of chiles, a phonograph, and two towels hanging on pegs on the wall. A wide wooden bench sits outside.*

The bathhouse has just burned to the ground due to the carelessness of Masako, Nisei daughter, 11. Off stage there are sounds of Murata, 40, Issei farmer, putting out the fire.

Inside the house Hana Murata, Issei wife, in a drab house dress, confronts Masako (wearing summer dress of the era). Masako is sullen and somewhat defiant. Hana breaks the silence.

Hana: How could you be so careless, Masako? You know you should be extra careful with fire. How often have I told you? Now the whole bathhouse is gone. I told you time and again, when you stoke a fire, you should see that everything is swept into the fireplace.

(Murata enters. He's dressed in old work clothes. He suffers from heat and exhaustion.)

Murata *(Coughing.):* Shack went up like a match box . . . This kind of weather dries everything . . . just takes a spark to make a bonfire out of dry timber.

Hana: Did you save any of it?

Murata: No. Couldn't . . .

5 Hana *(To Masako.):* How many times have I told you . . .

(Masako moves nervously.)

Murata: No use crying about it now. *Shikata ga nai.* It's gone now. No more bathhouse. That's all there is to it.

Hana: But you've got to tell her. Otherwise she'll make the same mistake. You'll be building a bathhouse every year.

(Murata removes his shirt and wipes off his face. He throws his shirt on a chair and sits at the table.)

Murata: *Baka!* Ridiculous!

Masako: I didn't do it on purpose.

(She goes to the bed, opens a book. Hana follows her.)

10 Hana: I know that but you know what this means? It means we bathe in a bucket . . . inside the house. Carry water in from the pond, heat it on the stove . . . We'll use more kerosene.

Murata: Tub's still there. And the fireplace. We can still build a fire under the tub.

Hana *(Shocked.):* But no walls! Everyone in the country can see us!

Murata: Wait 'til dark then. Wait 'til dark.

Hana: We'll be using a lantern. They'll still see us.

15 Murata: Angh! Who? Who'll see us? You think everyone in the country waits
to watch us take a bath? Hunh? You know how stupid you sound? Ridiculous!

Hana *(Defensively.):* It'll be inconvenient.

*(Hana is saved by a rap on the door. Oka, Issei neighbor, 45, enters. He
is short and stout, dressed in faded work clothes.)*

Oka: Hello! Hello! Oi! What's going on here? Hey! Was there some kind of
fire?

*(Hana rushes to the door to let Oka in. He stamps the dust from his
shoes and enters.)*

Hana: Oka-san![3] You just wouldn't believe . . . We had a terrible thing happen.

Oka: Yeah. Saw the smoke from down the road. Thought it was your house.
Came rushing over. Is the fire out?

(Murata half rises and sits back again. He's exhausted.)

20 Murata *(Gesturing.):* Oi, oi. Come in . . . sit down. No big problem. It was
just our bathhouse.

Oka: Just the *furoba,* eh?

Murata: Just the bath.

Hana: Our Masako was careless and the *furoba* caught fire. There's nothing
left of it but the tub.

*(Masako looks up from her book, pained. She makes a very small
sound.)*

Oka: Long as the tub's there, no problem. I'll help you with it. *(He starts to
roll up his sleeves. Murata looks at him.)*

25 Murata: What . . . now? Now?

Oka: Long as I'm here.

Hana: Oh, Papa. Aren't we lucky to have such friends?

Murata *(To Hana.):* Hell, we can't work on it now. The ashes are still hot. I
just now put the damned fire out. Let me rest a while. *(To Oka.)* Oi, how
about a little *sake?*[4] *(Gesturing to Hana.)* Make *sake* for Oka-san. *(Oka
sits at the table. Hana goes to prepare the* sake. *She heats it, gets out the
cups and pours it for the men.)* I'm tired . . . I am *tired.*

Hana: Oka-san has so generously offered his help . . .

*(Oka is uncomfortable. He looks around and sees Masako sitting on
the bed.)*

---

[3] -san: a suffix indicating polite address, similar to Mr., Mrs., or Ms. The suffixes -chan and
-kun, found elsewhere in the text, connote affection and familiarity.

[4] Alcoholic drink, served heated.

30 **Oka:** Hello, there, Masako-chan. You studying?

Masako: No, it's summer vacation.

Murata *(Sucking in his breath.):* Kids nowadays . . . no manners . . .

Hana: She's sulking because I had to scold her.

(Masako makes a small moan.)

Murata: Drink, Oka-san.

35 **Oka** *(Swallowing.):* Ahhh, that's good.

Murata: Eh, you not working today?

Oka: No . . . no . . . I took the afternoon off today. I was driving over to Nagatas' when I saw this big black cloud of smoke coming from your yard.

Hana: It went up so fast . . .

Murata: What's up at Nagatas'? *(To Hana.)* Get the chiles out. Oka-san loves chiles.

(Hana opens a jar of chiles and puts them on a plate. She serves the men and gets her mending basket and walks to Masako. Masako makes room for her on the bed.)

40 **Oka** *(Helping himself.):* Ah, chiles. *(Murata looks at Oka, the question unanswered.)* Well, I want to see him about my horse. I'm thinking of selling my horse.

Murata: Sell your horse!

Oka *(He scratches his head.):* The fact is, I need some money. Nagata-san's the only one around made money this year, and I'm thinking he might want another horse.

Murata: Yeah, he made a little this year. And he's talking big . . . big! Says he's leasing twenty more acres this fall.

Oka: Twenty acres?

45 **Murata:** Yeah. He might want another horse.

Oka: Twenty acres, eh?

Murata: That's what he says. But you know his old woman makes all the decisions. *(Oka scratches his head.)*

Hana: They're doing all right.

Murata: Henh. Nagata-kun's so hen-pecked, it's pathetic. Peko-peko. *(He makes motions of a hen pecking.)*

50 **Oka** *(Feeling the strain.):* I better get over there.

Murata: Why the hell you selling your horse?

Oka: I need cash.

Murata: Oh, yeah. I could use some too. Seems like everyone's getting out of the depression but the poor farmers. Nothing changes for us. We go on and on planting our tomatoes and summer squash and eating them . . . Well, at least it's healthy.

Hana: Papa, do you have lumber?

55 **Murata:** Lumber? For what?

Hana: The bath.

Murata *(Impatiently.):* Don't worry about that. We need more *sake* now.

(Hana rises to serve him.)

Oka: You sure Nagata-kun's working twenty more acres?

Murata: Last I heard. What the hell; if you need a few bucks, I can loan you . . .

60 **Oka:** A few hundred. I need a few hundred dollars.

Murata: Oh, a few hundred. But what the hell you going to do without a horse? Out here a man's horse is as important as his wife.

Oka *(Seriously.):* I don't think Nagata will buy my wife. *(The men laugh, but Hana doesn't find it so funny. Murata glances at her. She fills the cups again. Oka makes a half-hearted gesture to stop her. Masako watches the pantomine carefully. Oka swallows his drink in one gulp.)* I better get moving.

Murata: What's the big hurry?

Oka: Like to get the horse business done.

65 **Murata:** Ehhhh . . . relax. Do it tomorrow. He's not going to die, is he?

Oka *(Laughing.):* Hey he's a good horse. I want to get it settled today. If Nagata-kun won't buy, I got to find someone else. You think maybe Kawaguchi . . . ?

Murata: Not Kawaguchi . . . Maybe Yamamoto.

Hana: What is all the money for, Oka-san? Does Emiko-san need an operation?

Oka: Nothing like that . . .

70 **Hana:** Sounds very mysterious.

Oka: No mystery, Mrs. No mystery. No sale, no money, no story.

Murata *(Laughing.):* That's a good one. "No sale, no money, no . . ." Eh, Mama. *(He points to the empty cups. Hana fills the cups and goes back to Masako.)*

Hana *(Muttering.):* I see we won't be getting any work done today. *(To Masako.)* Are you reading again? Maybe we'd still have a bath if you . . .

Masako: I didn't do it on purpose.

75 **Murata** *(Loudly.):* I sure hope you know what you're doing. Oka-kun. What'd you do without a horse?

Oka: I was hoping you'd lend me yours now and then . . . *(He looks at Hana.)* I'll pay for some of the feed.

Murata *(Emphatically waving his hand.):* Sure! Sure!

Oka: The fact is, I need that money. I got a daughter in Japan and I just got to send for her this year.

(Hana comes to life. She puts down her mending and sits at the table.)

Hana: A daughter? You have a daughter in Japan? Why, I didn't know you had children. Emiko-san and you . . . I thought you were childless.

80 **Oka** *(Scratching his head.):* We are. I was married before.

Murata: You son-of-a-gun!

Hana: Is that so? How old is your daughter?

Oka: Kiyoko must be . . . fifteen now. Yeah, fifteen.

Hana: Fifteen! Oh, that *would* be too old for Emiko-san's child. Is Kiyoko-san living with relatives in Japan?

85 Oka *(Reluctantly.):* Yeah, with grandparents. With Shizue's parents. Well, the fact is, Shizue, that's my first wife, and Emiko were sisters. They come from a family with no sons. I was a boy when I went to work for the family . . . as an apprentice . . . they're blacksmiths. Later I married Shizue and took on the family name—you know, *yoshi*[5]—because they had no sons. My real name is Sakakihara.

Murata: Sakakihara! That's a great name!

Hana: A magnificent name!

Oka: No one knows me by that here.

Murata: Should have kept that . . . Sakakihara.

90 Oka *(Muttering.):* I don't even know myself by that name.

Hana: And Shizue-san passed away and you married Emiko-san?

Oka: Oh, yeah. Shizue and I lived with the family for a while and we had the baby . . . that's, you know, Kiyoko . . . *(The liquor has affected him and he's become less inhibited.)* Well, while I was serving apprentice with the family, they always looked down their noses at me. After I married, it got worse . . . That old man . . . Angh! He was terrible! Always pushing me around, making me look bad in front of my wife and kid. That old man was mean . . . ugly!

Murata: Yeah, I heard about that apprentice work—*detchi-boko* . . . Heard it was damned humiliating.

Oka: That's the God's truth!

95 Murata: Never had to do it myself. I came to America instead. They say *detchi-boko* is bloody hard work.

Oka: The work's all right. I'm not afraid of work. It's the humiliation! I hated them! Pushing me around like I was still a boy . . . Me, a grown man! And married to their daughter! *(Murata groans in sympathy.)* Well, Shizue and I talked it over and we decided the best thing was to get away. We thought if I came to America and made some money . . . you know, send her money until we had enough, I'd go back and we'd leave the family . . . you know, move to another province . . . start a small business, maybe in the city, a noodle shop or something.

Murata: That's everyone's dream. Make money, go home and live like a king.

Oka: I worked like a dog. Sent every penny to Shizue. And then she died. She died on me!

(Hana and Murata observe a moment of silence in respect for Oka's anguish.)

Hana: And you married Emiko-san.

100 Oka: I didn't marry her. They married her to me! Right after Shizue died.

---

[5] Yoshi is a procedure wherein a man married into a family that has no sons is obliged to carry the wife's family name and continue the lineage [Author's note].

Hana: But Oka-san, you were lucky . . .

Oka: Before the body was cold! No respect! By proxy. The old man wrote me they were arranging a marriage by proxy for me and Emiko. They said she'd grown to be a beautiful woman and would serve me well.

Hana: Emiko-san *is* a beautiful woman.

Oka: And they sent her to me. Took care of everything! Immigration, fare, everything.

105 Hana: But she's your sister-in-law—Kiyoko's aunt. It's good to keep the family together.

Oka: That's what I thought. But hear this: Emiko was the favored one. Shizue was not so pretty, not so smart. They were grooming Emiko for a rich man—his name was Yamoto—lived in a grand house in the village. They sent her to schools; you know, the culture thing: tea ceremony, you know, all that. They didn't even like me, and suddenly they married her to me.

Murata: Yeah. You don't need all that formal training to make it over here. Just a strong back.

Hana: And a strong will.

Oka: It was all arranged. I couldn't do anything about it.

110 Hana: It'll be all right. With Kiyoko coming . . .

Oka *(Dubiously.):* I hope so . . . I never knew human beings could be so cruel. You know how they mistreated my daughter? You know after Emiko came over, things got from bad to worse and I *never* had enough money to send to Kiyoko.

Murata: They don't know what it's like here. They think money's picked off the ground here.

Oka: And they treated Kiyoko so bad. They told her I forgot about her. They told her I didn't care—they said I abandoned her. Well, she knew better. She wrote to me all the time and I always told her I'd send for her . . . soon as I got the money. *(He shakes his head.)* I just got to do something this year.

Hana: She'll be happier here. She'll know her father cares.

115 Oka: Kids tormented her for not having parents.

Murata: Kids are cruel.

Hana: Masako will help her. She'll help her get started at school. She'll make friends . . . she'll be all right.

Oka: I hope so. She'll need friends. *(He considers he might be making a mistake after all.)* What could I say to her? Stay there? It's not what you think over here? I can't help her? I just have to do this thing. I just have to do this one thing for her.

Murata: Sure . . .

120 Hana: Don't worry. It'll work out fine.

(Murata gestures to Hana. She fills the cup.)

Murata: You talk about selling your horse, I thought you were pulling out.

Oka: I wish I could. But there's nothing else I can do.

Murata: Without money, yeah . . .

Oka: You can go into some kind of business with money, but a man like me . . . no education . . . there's no kind of job I can do. I'd starve in the city.

125 Murata: Dishwashing, maybe. Janitor . . .

Oka: At least here we can eat. Carrots, maybe, but we can eat.

Murata: All the carrots we been eating 'bout to turn me into a rabbit.

(They laugh. Hana starts to pour more wine for Oka but he stops her.)

Oka: I better not drink any more. Got to drive to Nagata-san's yet. *(He rises and walks over to Masako.)* You study hard, don't you? You'll teach Kiyoko English, eh? When she gets here . . .

Hana: Oh, yes. She will.

130 Murata: Kiyoko-san could probably teach her a thing or two.

Oka: She won't know about American ways . . .

Masako: I'll help her.

Hana: Don't worry, Oka-san. She'll have a good friend in our Masako. *(They move toward the door.)*

Oka: Well, thanks for the *sake.* I guess I talk too much when I drink. *(He scratches his head and laughs.)* Oh. I'm sorry about the fire. By the way, come to my house for your bath . . . until you build yours again.

135 Hana *(Hesitantly.):* Oh, uh . . . thank you. I don't know if . . .

Murata: Good! Good! Thanks a lot. I need a good hot bath tonight.

Oka: Tonight, then.

Murata: We'll be there.

Hana *(Bowing.):* Thank you very much. *Sayonara.*[6]

140 Oka *(Nodding.):* See you tonight.

(Oka leaves. Hana faces her husband as soon as the door closes.)

Hana: Papa, I don't know about going over there.

Murata *(Surprised.):* Why?

Hana: Well, Emiko-san . . .

Murata *(Irritated.):* What's the matter with you? We need a bath and Oka's invited us over.

145 Hana *(To Masako.):* Help me clear the table. *(Masako reluctantly leaves her book and begins to clear the table.)* Papa, you know we've been neighbors already three, four years and Emiko-san's never been very hospitable.

Murata: She's shy, that's all.

Hana: Not just shy . . . she's strange. I feel like she's pushing me off . . . she makes me feel like—I don't know—like I'm prying or something.

Murata: Maybe you are.

Hana: And never put out a cup of tea . . . If she had all that training in the graces . . . why, a cup of tea . . .

---

[6] Farewell; good-bye; until we see each other again.

150 **Murata:** So if you want tea, ask for it.

Hana: I can't do that, Papa. She's strange . . . I don't know . . . *(To Masako.)* When we go there, be very careful not to say anything wrong.

Masako: I never say anything anyway.

Hana *(Thoughtfully.):* Would you believe the story Oka-san just told? Why, I never knew . . .

Murata: There're lot of things you don't know. Just because a man don't . . . talk about them, don't mean he don't feel . . . don't think about . . .

155 **Hana** *(Looking around.):* We'll have to take something . . . There's nothing to take . . . Papa, maybe we can dig up some carrots.

Murata: God, Mama, be sensible. They got carrots. Everybody's got carrots.

Hana: Something . . . maybe I should make something.

Murata: Hell, they're not expecting anything.

Hana: It's not good manners to go empty-handed.

160 **Murata:** We'll take the *sake.*

(Hana grimaces. Masako sees the record player.)

Masako: I know, Mama. We can take the Victrola! We can play records for Mrs. Oka. Then nobody has to talk.

(Murata laughs.)

Fade out.

Scene 2

That evening. We see the exterior wall of the Okas' weathered house. There is a workable screen door and a large screened window. Outside there is a wide wooden bench that can accommodate three or four people. There is one separate chair and a lantern stands against the house.

The last rays of the sun light the area in a soft golden glow. This light grows gray as the scene progresses and it is quite dark at the end of the scene.

Through the screened window, Emiko Oka, Issei woman, 30, can be seen walking erratically back and forth. She wears a drab cotton dress but her grace and femininity come through. Her hair is bunned back in the style of Issei women of the era.

Oka sits cross-legged on the bench. He wears a Japanese summer robe (yukata) and fans himself with a round Japanese fan.

The Muratas enter. Murata carries towels and a bottle of sake. Hana carries the Victrola, and Masako a package containing their yukatas.

Oka *(Standing to receive the Muratas.):* Oh, you've come. Welcome!

Murata: Yah . . . Good of you to ask us.

Hana *(Bowing.):* Yes, thank you very much. *(To Masako.)* Say "hello," Masako.

Masako: Hello.

5 **Hana:** And "thank you."

Masako: Thank you.

(Oka makes motion of protest. Emiko stops her pacing and watches from the window.)

Hana *(Glancing briefly at the window.):* And how is Emiko-san this evening?

Oka *(Turning toward the house.):* Emi! Emiko!

Hana: That's all right. Don't call her out. She must be busy.

10 **Oka** *(Half rising.):* Emiko!

(Emiko comes to the door. Hana starts a deep bow toward the door.)

Murata: *Konbanwa!* *("Good evening!")*

Hana: *Konbanwa,* Emiko-san. I feel so bad about this intrusion. Your husband has told you, our bathhouse was destroyed by fire and he graciously invited us to come use yours.

(Emiko shakes her head.)

Oka: I didn't have a chance to . . .

(Hana recovers and nudges Masako.)

Hana: Say hello to Mrs. Oka.

15 **Masako:** Hello, Mrs. Oka.

(Hana lowers the Victrola on the bench.)

Oka: What's this? You brought a phonograph?

Masako: It's a Victrola.

Hana *(Laughing indulgently.):* Yes. Masako wanted to bring this over and play some records.

Murata *(Extending the wine.):* Brought a little *sake* too.

20 **Oka** *(Taking the bottle.):* Ah, now that I like. Emiko, bring out the cups.

(He waves at his wife, but she doesn't move. He starts to ask again, but decides to get them himself. He enters the house and returns with two cups. Emiko seats herself on the single chair. The Muratas unload their paraphernalia; Oka pours the wine, the men drink, Hana chatters and sorts the records. Masako stands by, helping her.)

Hana: Yes, our Masako loves to play records. I like records too . . . and Papa, he . . .

Murata *(Watching Emiko.):* They take me back home. The only way I can get there . . . in my mind.

Hana: Do you like music, Emiko-san? *(Emiko looks vague but smiles faintly.)* Oka-san, you like them, don't you?

Oka: Yeah. But I don't have a player. No chance to hear them.

25 **Murata:** I had to get this for them. They wouldn't leave me alone until I got it. Well . . . a phonograph . . . what the hell, they got to have *some* fun.

Hana: We don't have to play them, if you'd rather not . . .

Oka: Play. Play them.

Hana: I thought we could listen to them and relax *(She extends some records to Emiko.)* Would you like to look through these, Emiko-san? *(Emiko doesn't respond. She pulls out a sack of Bull Durham and starts to roll a cigarette. Hana pushes Masako to her.)* Take these to her. *(Masako moves toward Emiko with the records. Masako stands watching her as she lights her cigarette.)* Some of these are very old. You might know them, Emiko-san. *(She sees Masako watching Emiko.)* Masako, bring those over here. *(She laughs uncomfortably.)* You might like this one, Emiko-san . . . *(She starts the player.)* Do you know it?

(The record whines out "Kago No Tori."[7] *Emiko listens with her head cocked. She smokes her cigarette. She becomes wrapped in nostalgia and memories of the past. Masako watches her carefully.)*

Masako *(Whispering.):* Mama, she's crying.

(Startled, Hana and Murata look toward Emiko.)

30 **Hana** *(Pinching Masako.):* Shhh. The smoke is in her eyes.

Murata: Did you bring the record I like, Mama?

(Emiko rises abruptly and enters the house.)

Masako: There were tears, Mama.

Hana: From yawning, Masako. *(Regretfully, to Oka.)* I'm afraid we've offended her.

Oka *(Unaware.):* Hunh? Aw . . . no . . . pay no attention . . . no offense . . .

(Masako looks toward the window. Emiko stands forlornly and slowly drifts into a dance.)

35 **Hana:** I'm very sorry. Children, you know . . . they'll say anything, anything that's on their minds.

(Murata notices Masako watching Emiko through the window and tries to divert her attention.)

Murata: The needles. Masako, where're the needles?

Masako *(Still watching.):* I forgot them.

(Hana sees what's going on. Oka is unaware.)

Hana: Masako, go take your bath now. Masako . . .

(Masako reluctantly picks up her towel and leaves.)

---

[7] See lyrics at the end of the play.

Oka: Yeah, yeah . . . take your bath.

40 Murata *(Sees Emiko still dancing.):* Change the record, Mama.

Oka *(Still unaware.):* That's kind of sad.

Murata: No use to get sick over a record. We're supposed to enjoy.

(Hana stops the record. Emiko disappears from the window. Hana selects a lively ondo[8]—"Tokyo Ondo.")

Hana: We'll find something more fun. *(The three begin to tap to the music.)* Can't you just see the festival? The dancers, the bright *kimonos,* the paper lanterns bobbing in the wind, the fireflies . . . How nostalgic . . . Oh, how nostalgic . . .

(From the side of the house Emiko appears. Her hair is down, she wears an old straw hat. She dances in front of the Muratas. They're startled. After the first shock, they watch with frozen smiles. They try to join Emiko's mood but something is missing. Oka is grieved. He finally stands as though he's had enough. Emiko, now close to the door, ducks into the house.)

Hana: That was pretty . . . very nice . . .

(Oka settles down and grunts. Murata clears his throat and Masako returns from her bath.)

45 Murata: You're done already? *(He's glad to see her.)*

Masako: I wasn't very dirty. The water was too hot.

Murata: Good! Just the way I like it.

Hana: Not dirty?

Murata *(Picking up his towel.):* Come on, Mama . . . scrub my back.

50 Hana *(Laughing embarrassedly.):* Oh, oh . . . well . . . *(She stops the player.)* Masako, now don't forget . . . crank the machine and change the needle now and then.

Masako: I didn't bring them.

Hana: Oh. Oh . . . all right. I'll be back soon . . . don't forget . . . crank.

(She leaves with her husband. Oka and Masako are alone. Oka is awkward and falsely hearty.)

Oka: So! So you don't like hot baths, eh?

Masako: Not too hot.

55 Oka *(Laughing.):* I thought you like it real hot. Hot enough to burn the house down. That's a little joke. *(Masako busies herself with the records to conceal her annoyance.)* I hear you're real good in school. Always top of the class.

Masako: It's a small class. Only two of us.

Oka: When Kiyoko comes, you'll help her in school, yeah? You'll take care of her . . . a favor for me, eh?

---

[8] Leading in singing.

Masako: Okay.

Oka: You'll be her friend, eh?

60 Masako: Okay.

Oka: That's good. That's good. You'll like her. She's a nice girl too. *(Oka stands, yawns, and stretches.)* I'll go for a little walk now.

(He touches his crotch to indicate his purpose. Masako turns her attention to the records and selects one, "The Soul Shall Dance,"[9] and begins to sway to the music. The song draws Emiko from the house. She looks out the window, sees Masako is alone and begins to slip into a dance.)

Emiko: Do you like that song, Masa-chan? *(Masako is startled and draws back. She remembers her mother's warning. She doesn't know what to do. She nods.)* That's one of my favorite songs. I remember in Japan I used to sing it so often . . . my favorite song . . . *(She sings along with the record.)*

> Akai kuchibiru
> Kappu ni yosete
> Aoi sake nomya
> Kokoro ga odoru . . .

Do you know what that means, Masa-chan?

Masako: I think so . . . The soul will dance?

Emiko: Yes, yes, that's right.

> The soul shall dance. Red lips against a glass
> Drink the green . . .

65 Masako: Wine?

Emiko *(Nodding.):* Drink the green wine.

Masako: Green? I thought wine is purple.

Emiko *(Nodding.):* Wine is purple . . . but this is a green liqueur. *(Emiko holds up one of the china cups as though it were crystal, and looks at it as though the light were shining through it and she sees the green liquid.)* It's good . . . it warms your heart.

Masako: And the soul dances.

70 Emiko: Yes.

Masako: What does it taste like? The green wine . . .

Emiko: Oh, it's like . . . it's like . . .

(The second verse starts. "Kurai yoru yume, Setsunasa yo, Aoi sake nomya, Yume mo odoru . . .")

Masako: In the dark night . . .

Emiko: Dreams are unbearable . . . insufferable . . . *(She turns sad.)*

75 Masako: Drink the . . .

Emiko *(Nodding.):* Drink the green wine . . .

---

[9] Full lyrics are given on page 584.

Masako: And the dreams will dance.

Emiko *(Softly.):* I'll be going back one day . . .

Masako: To where?

80 Emiko: My home . . . Japan . . . my real home. I'm planning to go back.

Masako: By yourself?

Emiko *(Nodding.):* Oh, yes. It's a secret. You can keep a secret?

Masako: Unhn. I have lots of secrets . . . all my own . . . *(The music stops. Emiko sees Oka approaching and disappears into the house. Masako attends to the record and does not know Emiko is gone.)* Secrets I never tell anyone.

Oka: Secrets? What kind of secrets? What did she say?

85 Masako: Oh. Nothing.

Oka: What did you talk about?

Masako: Nothing . . . Mrs. Oka was talking about the song. She was telling me what it meant . . . about the soul.

Oka *(Scoffing.):* Heh! What does she know about soul? *(Calming down.)* Ehhh . . . some people don't have them . . . souls.

Masako *(Timidly.):* I thought . . . I think everyone has a soul. I read in a book . . .

90 Oka *(Laughing.):* Maybe . . . maybe you're right. I'm not an educated man, you know . . . I don't know too much about books. When Kiyoko comes you can talk to her about it. Kiyoko is very . . . *(From inside the house, we hear Emiko begin to sing loudly at the name Kiyoko as though trying to drown it out. Oka stops talking. Then resumes.)* Kiyoko is very smart. You'll have a good time with her. She'll learn your language fast. How old did you say you are?

Masako: Almost twelve.

(By this time Oka and Masako are shouting, trying to be heard above Emiko's singing.)

Oka: Kiyoko is fifteen . . . Kiyoko . . . *(Oka is exasperated. He rushes into the house seething. Masako hears Oka's muffled rage. "Behave yourself" and "kitchigai" come through. Masako slinks to the window and looks in. Oka slaps Emiko around. Masako reacts to the violence. Oka comes out. Masako returns to the bench in time. He pulls his fingers through his hair and sits next to Masako. She very slightly draws away.)* Want me to light a lantern?

Masako *(Shaken.):* No . . . ye- . . . okay . . .

Oka: We'll get a little light here . . .

(He lights the lantern as the Muratas return from their bath. They are in good spirits.)

95 Murata: Ahhhh . . . Nothing like a good hot bath.

Hana: So refreshing . . .

Murata: A bath should be taken hot and slow. Don't know how Masako gets through so fast.

Hana: She probably doesn't get in the tub.

Masako: I do. *(Everyone laughs.)* Well I do.

> *(Emiko comes out. She has a large purple welt on her face. She sits on the separate chair, hands folded, quietly watching the Muratas. They look at her with alarm. Oka engages himself with his fan.)*

100 Hana: Oh! Emiko-san . . . what . . . ah-ah . . . whaa . . . *(She draws a deep breath.)* What a nice bath we had . . . such a lovely bath. We do appreciate your hos . . . pitality. Thank you so much.

Emiko: Lovely evening, isn't it?

Hana: Very lovely. Very. Ah, a little warm, but nice . . . Did you get a chance to hear the records? *(Turning to Masako.)* Did you play the records for Mrs. Oka?

Masako: Ye- . . . no . . . The needle was . . .

Emiko: Yes, she did. We played the records together.

105 Murata: Oh, you played the songs together?

Emiko: Yes . . . yes . . .

Murata: That's nice . . . Masako can understand pretty good, eh?

Emiko: She understand everything . . . everything I say.

Murata *(Withdrawing.):* Oh, yeah? Eh, Mama, we ought to be going . . . *(He closes the player.)* Hate to bathe and run but . . .

110 Hana: Yes, yes. Tomorrow is a busy day. Come, Masako.

Emiko: Please . . . stay a little longer.

Murata: Eh, well, we got to be going.

Hana: Why, thank you, but . . .

Emiko: It's still quite early.

115 Oka *(Indicating he's ready to say goodbye.):* Enjoyed the music. And the sake.

Emiko: The records are very nice. Makes me remember Japan. I sang those songs . . . those very songs . . . Did you know I used to sing?

Hana *(Politely.):* Why, no . . . no. I didn't know that. You must have a very lovely voice.

Emiko: Yes.

Hana: No, I didn't know that. That's very nice.

120 Emiko: Yes, I sang. My parents were very strict . . . they didn't like it. They said it was frivolous. Imagine?

Hana: Yes, I can imagine. Things were like that . . . in those days singing was not considered proper for nice . . . I mean, only for women in the profess- . . .

Murata: We better get home, Mama.

Hana: Yes, yes. What a shame you couldn't continue with it.

Emiko: In the city I did do some classics: the dance, and the *koto,* and the flower, and, of course, the tea . . . *(She makes the proper gesture for the different disciplines.)* All those. Even some singing . . . classics, of course.

125 Hana *(Politely.):* Of course.

Emiko: All of it is so disciplined . . . so disciplined. I was almost a *natori*. [10]
Hana: Oh! How nice.
Emiko: But everything changed.
Hana: Oh!
130 Emiko: I was sent here to America. *(She glares at Oka.)*
Hana: Oh, too bad . . . I mean, too bad about your *natori*.
Murata *(Loudly to Oka.):* So did you see Nagata today?
Oka: Oh, yeah. Yeah.
Murata: What did he say? Is he interested?
135 Oka: Yeah. Yeah. He's interested.
Murata: He likes the horse, eh?
Oka: Ah . . . yeah.
Murata: I knew he'd like him. I'd buy him myself if I had the money.
Oka: Well, I have to take him over tomorrow. He'll decide then.
140 Murata: He'll buy . . . he'll buy. You'd better go straight over to the ticket
office and get that ticket. Before you—ha-ha—spend the money.
Oka: Ha-ha. Yeah.
Hana: It'll be so nice when Kiyoko-san comes to join you. I know you're
looking forward to it.
Emiko *(Confused.):* Oh . . . oh . . .
Hana: Masako is so happy. It'll be good for her too.
145 Emiko: I had more freedom in the city . . . I lived with an aunt and she let
me . . . She wasn't so strict.

(Murata and Masako have their gear together and stand ready to leave.)

Murata: Good luck on the horse tomorrow.
Oka: Yeah, thanks.
Hana *(Bowing.):* Many, many thanks.
Oka *(Nodding toward the* sake.*):* Thanks for the *sake*.
150 Hana *(Bowing again.):* Goodnight, Emiko-san. We'll see you again soon.
We'll bring the records too.
Emiko *(Softly.):* Those songs . . . those very songs . . .
Murata: Let's go, Mama.

(The Muratas pull away. Light follows them and grows dark on the Okas. The Muratas begin walking home.)

Hana: That was uncomfortable.
Masako: What's the matter with . . .
155 Hana: Shhhh!
Murata: I guess Oka has his problems.
Masako: Is she really *kitchigai*?
Hana: Of course not. She's not crazy. Don't say that word, Masako.
Masako: I heard Mr. Oka call her that.
160 Hana: He called her that?

---

[10] Certified artist.

Masako: I . . . I think so.

Hana: You heard wrong, Masako. Emiko-san isn't crazy. She just likes her drinks. She had too much to drink tonight.

Masako: Oh.

Hana: She can't adjust to this life. She can't get over the good times she had in Japan. Well, it's not easy . . . but one has to know when to bend . . . like the bamboo. When the winds blow, bamboo bends. You bend or crack. Remember that, Masako.

165 **Murata** *(Laughing wryly.):* Bend, eh? Remember that, Mama.

Hana *(Softly.):* You don't know . . . it isn't ever easy.

Masako: Do you want to go back to Japan, Mama?

Hana: Everyone does.

Masako: Do you, Papa?

170 **Murata:** I'll have to make some money first.

Masako: I don't. Not me. Not Kiyoko . . .

Hana: After Kiyoko-san comes, Emiko will have company and things will straighten out. She has nothing to live on but her memories. She doesn't have any friends. At least I have my friends at church . . . at least I have that. She must get awful lonely.

Masako: I know that. She tried to make friends with me.

Hana: She did? What did she say?

175 **Masako:** Well, sort of . . .

Hana: What did she say?

Masako: She didn't say anything. I just felt it. Maybe you should be her friend, Mama.

Murata: Poor woman. We could have stayed longer.

Hana: But you wanted to leave. I tried to be friendly. You saw that. It's not easy to talk to Emiko. She either closes up, you can't pry a word from her, or else she goes on and on . . . all that . . . that . . . about the *koto* and tea and the flower . . . I mean, what am I supposed to say? She's so unpredictable. And the drinking . . .

180 **Murata:** All right, all right, Mama.

Masako: Did you see her black eye?

Hana *(Calming down.):* She probably hurt herself. She wasn't very steady.

Masako: Oh, no. Mr. Oka hit her.

Hana: I don't think so.

185 **Masako:** He hit her. I saw him.

Hana: You saw that? Papa, do you hear that? She saw them. That does it. We're not going there again.

Murata: Aww . . . Oka wouldn't do that. Not in front of a kid.

Masako: Well, they didn't do it in front of me. They were in the house.

Murata: You see . . .

190 **Hana:** That's all right. You just have to fix the bathhouse. Either that or we're going to bathe at home . . . in a bucket. We're not go-ing . . . we'll bathe at home. *(Murata mutters to himself.)* What?

Murata: I said all right, it's the bucket then. I'll get to it when I can.

(Hana passes Murata and walks ahead.)

Fade out.

Scene 3

Same evening. Lights crossfade to the exterior of the Oka house. The Muratas have just left. Emiko sits on the bench. Her back is to Oka. Oka, still standing, looks at her contemptuously as she takes the bottle and one of the cups to pour herself a drink.

Oka: Nothing more disgusting than a drunk woman. *(Emiko ignores him.)* You made a fool of yourself. *Washi baka ni shite!* You made a fool of me! *(Emiko doesn't move.)*

Emiko: One can only make a fool of one's self.

Oka: You learn that in the fancy schools, eh? *(Emiko examines the pattern on her cup.)* Eh? Eh? Answer me! *(Emiko ignores.)* I'm talking to you. Answer me! *(Menacing.)* You don't get away with that. You think you're so fine . . . *(Emiko looks off into the horizon. Oka turns her roughly around.)* When I talk, you listen! *(Emiko turns away again. Oka pulls the cup from her hand.)* Goddamnit! What'd you think my friends think of you? What kind of ass they think I am? *(He grabs her shoulders.)*

Emiko: Don't touch me . . . don't touch me.

5 Oka: Who the hell you think you are? "Don't touch me, don't touch me." Who the hell! High and mighty, eh? Too good for me, eh? Don't put on the act for me . . . I know who you are.

Emiko: Tell me who I am, Mister Smart Peasant.

Oka: Shut your fool mouth, goddamnit! Sure! I'll tell you. I know all about you . . . Shizue told me. The whole village knows.

Emiko: Shizue!

Oka: Yeah! Shizue. Embarrassed the hell out of her, your own sister.

10 Emiko: Embarrassed? I have nothing to be ashamed of. I don't know what you're talking about.

Oka *(Derisively.):* You don't know what I'm talking about. I know. The whole village knows. They're all laughing at you. At me! Stupid Oka got stuck with a second-hand woman. I didn't say anything because . . .

Emiko: I'm not second-hand!

Oka: Who you trying to fool? I know. Knew long time ago . . . Shizue wrote me all about your affairs in Tokyo. The men you were mess- . . .

Emiko: Affairs? Men?

15 Oka: That man you were messing with . . . I knew all along. I didn't say anything because you . . . I . . .

Emiko: I'm not ashamed of it.

Oka: You're not ashamed! What the hell! Your father thought he was pulling a fast one on me . . . thought I didn't know nothing . . . thought I was some kind of dumb ass . . . I didn't say nothing because Shizue's dead . . . Shizue's dead. I was willing to give you a chance.

Emiko *(Laughing.):* A chance?

Oka: Yeah! A chance! Laugh! Give a *joro* another chance. Sure, I'm stupid . . . dumb.

20 Emiko: I'm not a whore. I'm true . . . he knows I'm true.

Oka: True! Ha!

Emiko: You think I'm untrue just because I let . . . let you . . . There's only one man for me.

Oka: Let me *(Obscene gesture.)* you? I can do what I want with you. Your father palmed you off on me—like a dog or cat—an animal . . . couldn't do nothing with you. Even that rich dumb Yamoto wouldn't have you. Your father—greedy father—so proud . . . making big plans for you . . . for himself. Ha! The whole village laughing at him . . . *(Emiko hangs her head.)* Shizue told me. And she was working like a dog . . . trying to keep your goddamn father happy . . . doing my work and yours.

Emiko: My work?

25 Oka: Yeah, your work too! She killed herself working! She killed herself . . . *(He has tender memories of his dull, uncomplaining wife.)* Up in the morning getting the fires started, working the bellows, cleaning the furnace, cooking, and late at night working with the sewing . . . tending the baby . . . *(He mutters.)* The goddamn family killed her. And you . . . you out there in Tokyo with the fancy clothes, doing the *(He sneers.)* dance, the tea, the flower, the *koto,* and the . . . *(Obscene gesture.)*

Emiko *(Hurting.):* Achhhh . . .

Oka: Did you have fun? Did you have fun on your sister's blood? *(Emiko doesn't answer.)* Did you? He must have been a son-of-a-bitch . . . What would make that goddamn greedy old man send his prize mare to a plow horse like me? What kind of bum was he that your father . . .

Emiko: He's not a bum . . . he's not a bum.

Oka: Was he Korean? Was he *Etta?*[11] That's the only thing I could figure.

30 Emiko: I'm true to him. Only him.

Oka: True? You think he's true to you? You think he waits for you? Remembers you? *Aho!* Think he cares?

Emiko *(Nodding quietly.):* He does.

Oka: And waits ten years? *Baka!* Go back to Japan and see. You'll find out. Go back to Japan. *Kaere!*

Emiko: In time.

35 Oka: In time? How about now?

Emiko: I can't now.

Oka: Ha! Now! Go now! Who needs you? Who needs you? You think a man waits ten years for a woman? You think you're some kind of . . . of . . . diamond . . . treasure . . . he's going to wait his life for you?

---

[11] Outcast; social class considered outside the mainstream.

Go to him. He's probably married with ten kids. Go to him. Get out!
Goddamn *joro* . . . Go! Go!

(Oka sweeps Emiko off the bench.)

Emiko *(Hurting.):* Ahhhh! I . . . I don't have the money. Give me money
to . . .

Oka: If I had money I would give it to you ten years ago. You think I been
eating this *kuso* for ten years because I like it?

40 **Emiko:** You're selling the horse . . . Give me the . . .

Oka *(Scoffing.):* That's for Kiyoko. I owe you nothing.

Emiko: Ten years, you owe me.

Oka: Ten years of what? Misery? You gave me nothing. I give you nothing.
You want to go, pack your bag and start walking. Try cross the desert.
When you get dry and hungry, think about me.

Emiko: I'd die out there.

45 **Oka:** Die? You think I didn't die here?

Emiko: I didn't do anything to you.

Oka: No, no you didn't. All I wanted was a little comfort and . . . you . . .
no, you didn't. No. So you die. We all die. Shizue died. If she was here,
she wouldn't treat me like this . . . *(He thinks of his poor dead wife.)*
Ah, I should have brought her with me. She'd be alive now. We'd be
poor but happy . . . like . . . like Murata and his wife . . . and the
kid . . .

Emiko: I wish she were alive too. I'm not to blame for her dying. I didn't
know . . . I was away. I loved her. I didn't want her to die . . . I . . .

Oka *(Softening.):* I know that. I'm not blaming you for that . . . And it's
not my fault what happened to you either . . . *(Emiko is silent and Oka
mistakes that for a change in attitude. He is encouraged.)* You understand that, eh? I didn't ask for you. It's not my fault you're here in this
desert . . . with . . . with me . . . *(Emiko weeps. Oka reaches out.)*
I know I'm too old for you. It's hard for me too . . . but this is the way
it is. I just ask you be kinder . . . understand it wasn't my fault. Try
make it easier for me . . . for yourself too.

(Oka touches her and she shrinks from his touch.)

50 **Emiko:** Ach!

Oka *(Humiliated again.):* Goddamn it! I didn't ask for you! *Aho!* If you was
smart you'd done as your father said . . . cut out that *saru shibai* with
the *Etta* . . . married the rich Yamoto. Then you'd still be in Japan. Not
here to make my life so miserable. *(Emiko is silent.)* And you can have
your *Etta* . . . and anyone else you want. Take them all on . . . *(Oka
is worn out. It's hopeless.)* God, why do we do this all the time? Fighting,
fighting all the time. There must be a better way to live . . . there must
be another way.

*(Oka waits for a response, gives up, and enters the house. Emiko
watches him leave and pours herself another drink. The storm has*

passed, the alcohol takes over. She turns to the door Oka disappeared into.)

Emiko: Because I must keep the dream alive . . . the dream is all I live for. I am only in exile now. Because if I give in, all I've lived before . . . will mean nothing . . . will be for nothing . . . Because if I let you make me believe this is all there is to my life, the dream would die . . . I would die . . . *(She pours another drink and feels warm and good.)*

Fade out.

Act II

Scene 1

Mid-September, afternoon. Muratas' kitchen. The calendar reads September. Masako is at the kitchen table with several books. She thumbs through a Japanese magazine. Hana is with her sewing.

Masako: Do they always wear kimonos in Japan, Mama?

Hana: Most of the time.

Masako: I wonder if Kiyoko will be wearing a kimono like this?

Hana *(Peering into Masako's magazine.):* They don't dress like that . . . not for every day.

5 **Masako:** I wonder what she's like.

Hana: Probably a lot like you. What do you think she's like?

Masako: She's probably taller.

Hana: Mr. Oka isn't tall.

Masako: And pretty . . .

10 **Hana** *(Laughing.):* Mr. Oka . . . Well, I don't suppose she'll look like her father.

Masako: Mrs. Oka is pretty.

Hana: She isn't Kiyoko-san's real mother, remember.

Masako: Oh. That's right.

Hana: But they are related. Well, we'll soon see.

15 **Masako:** I thought she was coming in September. It's already September.

Hana: Papa said Oka-san went to San Pedro a few days ago. He should be back soon with Kiyoko-san.

Masako: Didn't Mrs. Oka go too?

Hana *(Glancing toward the Oka house.):* I don't think so. I see lights in their house at night.

Masako: Will they bring Kiyoko over to see us?

20 **Hana:** Of course. First thing, probably. You'll be very nice to her, won't you?

(Masako leaves the table and finds another book.)

Masako: Sure. I'm glad I'm going to have a friend. I hope she likes me.

Hana: She'll like you. Japanese girls are very polite, you know.

Masako: We have to be or our Mamas get mad at us.

Hana: Then I should be getting mad at you more often.

25 Masako: It's often enough already, Mama. *(She opens a hardback book.)* Look at this, Mama . . . I'm going to show her this book.

Hana: She won't be able to read at first.

Masako: I love this story. Mama, this is about people like us—settlers—it's about the prairie. We live in a prairie, don't we?

Hana: Prairie? Does that mean desert?

Masako: I think so.

30 Hana *(Nodding and looking bleak.):* We live in a prairie.

Masako: It's about the hardships and the floods and droughts and how they have nothing but each other.

Hana *(Nodding.):* We have nothing but each other. But these people— they're white people.

Masako *(Nodding.):* Sure, Mama. They come from the east. Just like you and Papa came from Japan.

Hana: We come from the far far east. That's different. White people are different from us.

35 Masako: I know that.

Hana: White people among white people . . . that's different from Japanese among white people. You know what I'm saying?

Masako: I know that. How come they don't write books about us . . . about Japanese people?

Hana: Because we're nobodies here.

Masako: If I didn't read these, there'd be nothing for me . . .

40 Hana: Some of the things you read, you're never going to know.

Masako: I can dream, though.

Hana *(Sighing.):* Sometimes the dreaming makes the living harder. Better to keep your head out of the clouds.

Masako: That's not much fun.

Hana: You'll have fun when Kiyoko-san comes. You can study together, you can sew, and sometime you can try some of those fancy American recipes.

45 Masako: Mama, you have to have chocolate and cream and things like that.

Hana: We'll get them.

(We hear the putt-putt of Oka's old car. Masako and Hana pause and listen. Masako runs to the window.)

Masako: I think it's them!

Hana: The Okas?

Masako: It's them! It's them!

(Hana stands and looks out. She removes her apron and puts away her sewing.)

50 Hana: Two of them. Emiko-san isn't with them. Let's go outside.

(Oka and Kiyoko, 14, enter. Oka is wearing his going-out clothes: a sweater, white shirt, dark pants, but no tie. Kiyoko walks behind him.

She is short, chunky, broadchested and very self-conscious. Her hair is straight and banded into two shucks. She wears a conservative cotton dress, white socks and two-inch heels. Oka is proud. He struts in, his chest puffed out.)

Oka: Hello, hello . . . We're here. We made it! *(He pushes Kiyoko forward.)* This is my daughter, Kiyoko. *(To Kiyoko.)* Murata-san . . . remember I was talking about? My friends . . .

Kiyoko *(Barely audible, bowing deeply.):* *Hajime mashite yoroshiku onegai shimasu . . .*

Hana *(Also bowing formally.):* I hope your journey was pleasant.

Oka *(While the women are still bowing, he pushes Kiyoko toward Masako.):* This is Masako-chan; I told you about her . . .

(Masako is shocked at Kiyoko's appearance. The girl she expected is already a woman. She stands with her mouth agape and withdraws noticeably. Hana rushes in to fill the awkwardness.)

55 Hana: Say hello, Masako. My goodness, where are your manners? *(She laughs apologetically.)* In this country they don't make much to-do about manners. *(She stands back to examine Kiyoko.)* My, my, I didn't picture you so grown up. My, my . . . Tell me, how was your trip?

Oka *(Proudly.):* We just drove in from Los Angeles just this morning. We spent the night in San Pedro and the next two days we spent in Los Angeles . . . you know, Japanese town.

Hana: How nice!

Oka: Kiyoko was so excited. Twisting her head this way and that—couldn't see enough with her big eyes. *(He imitates her fondly.)* She's from the country, you know . . . just a big country girl. Got all excited about the Chinese dinner—we had a Chinese dinner. She never ate it before.

(Kiyoko covers her mouth and giggles.)

Hana: Chinese dinner!

60 Oka: Oh, yeah. Duck, pakkai, chow mein, seaweed soup . . . the works!

Hana: A feast!

Oka: Oh, yeah. Like a holiday. Two holidays. Two holidays in one.

Hana *(Pushes Masako forward.):* Two holidays in one! Kiyoko-san, our Masako has been looking forward to meeting you.

Kiyoko *(Bowing again.):* *Hajimemashite . . .* [12]

65 Hana: She's been thinking of all sorts of things she can do with you: sewing, cooking . . .

Masako: Oh, Mama.

(Kiyoko covers her mouth and giggles.)

Hana: It's true, Kiyoko-san. She's been looking forward to having a best friend.

---

[12] Polite greeting.

(Kiyoko giggles again and Masako pulls away.)

Oka: Kiyoko, you shouldn't be so shy. The Muratas are my good friends and you should feel free with them. Ask anything, say anything . . . right?

Hana: Of course, of course. *(She is slightly annoyed with Masako.)* Masako, go in and start the tea. *(Masako enters the house.)* I'll call Papa. He's in the yard. Papa! Oka-san is here! *(To Kiyoko.)* Now tell me, how was your trip? Did you get seasick?

70 Kiyoko *(Bowing and nodding.): Eh* ("yes"). A little . . .

Oka: Tell her. Tell her how sick you got.

(Kiyoko covers her mouth and giggles.)

Hana: Oh, I know, I know. I was too. That was a long time ago. I'm sure things are improved now. Tell me about Japan . . . what is it like now? They say it's so changed . . . modern . . .

Oka: Kiyoko comes from the country . . . backwoods. Nothing changes much there from century to century.

Hana: Ah! That's true. That's why I love Japan. And you wanted to leave. It's unbelievable. To come here!

75 Oka: She always dreamed about it.

Hana: Well, it's not really that bad.

Oka: No, it's not that bad. Depends on what you make of it.

Hana: That's right. What you make of it. I was just telling Masako today . . .

(Murata enters. He rubs his hands to take off the soil and comes in grinning. He shakes Oka's hand.)

Murata: Oi, oi . . .

80 Oka: Yah . . . I'm back. This is my daughter.

Murata: No! She's beautiful!

Oka: Finally made it. Finally got her here.

Murata *(To Kiyoko.):* Your father hasn't stopped talking about you all summer.

Hana: And Masako too.

85 Kiyoko *(Bowing.): Hajimemashite . . .*

Murata *(Acknowledging with a short bow.):* Yah. How'd you like the trip?

Oka: I was just telling your wife—had a good time in Los Angeles. Had a couple of great dinners, took in the cinema—Japanese pictures, bought her some American clothes.

Hana: Oh, you bought that in Los Angeles.

Murata: Got a good price for your horse, eh? Lots of money, eh?

90 Oka: Nagata's a shrewd bargainer. Heh. It don't take much money to make her happy. She's a country girl.

Murata: That's all right. Country's all right. Country girl's the best.

Oka: Had trouble on the way back.

Murata: Yeah?

Oka: Fan belt broke.

95 **Murata:** That'll happen.

Oka: Lucky I was near a gasoline station. We were in the mountains. Waited in a restaurant while it was getting fixed.

Hana: Oh, that was good.

Oka: Guess they don't see Japanese much. Stare? Terrible! Took them a long time to wait on us. Dumb waitress practically threw the food at us. Kiyoko felt bad.

Hana: Ah! That's too bad . . . too bad. That's why I always pack a lunch when we take trips.

100 **Murata:** They'll spoil the day for you . . . those barbarians!

Oka: Terrible food too. Kiyoko couldn't swallow the dry bread and bologna.

Hana: That's the food they eat!

Murata: Let's go in . . . have a little wine. Mama, we got wine? This is a celebration.

Hana: I think so . . . a little . . . *(They enter the house talking. Masako has made the tea, and Hana begins to serve the wine.)* How is your mother? Was she happy to see you?

105 **Kiyoko:** Oh, she . . . yes . . .

Hana: I just know she was surprised to see you so grown up. Of course, you remember her from Japan, don't you?

Kiyoko *(Nodding.)*: *Eh* ("yes"). I can barely remember. I was very young . . .

Hana: Of course. But you do, don't you?

Kiyoko: She was gone most of the time . . . at school in Tokyo. She was very pretty, I remember that.

110 **Hana:** She's still very pretty.

Kiyoko: *Eh.* She was always laughing. She was much younger then.

Hana: Oh now, it hasn't been that long ago.

(Masako leaves the room to go outside. The following dialogue continues muted as light goes dim in the house and focuses on Masako. Emiko enters, is drawn to the Murata window and listens.)

Oka: We stayed at an inn on East First Street. *Shizuokaya.* Whole inn filled with Shizuoka people . . . talking the old dialect. Thought I was in Japan again.

Murata: That right?

115 **Oka:** Felt good. Like I was in Japan again.

Hana *(To Kiyoko.)*: Did you enjoy Los Angeles?

Kiyoko *(Nodding.)*: *Eh.*

Oka: That's as close as I'll get to Japan.

Murata: *Mattaku na!* That's for sure.

(Outside Masako becomes aware of Emiko.)

120 **Masako:** Why don't you go in?

Emiko: Oh. Oh. Why don't you?

Masako: They're all grown-ups in there. I'm not grown up.

Emiko *(Softly.):* All grown-ups . . . Maybe I'm not either. *(Her mood changes.)* Masa-chan, do you have a boy friend?

Masako: I don't like boys. They don't like me.

125 Emiko: Oh, that will change. You will change. I was like that too.

Masako: Besides, there're none around here . . . Japanese boys . . . There are some at school, but they don't like girls.

Hana *(Calling from the kitchen.):* Masako . . .

(Masako doesn't answer.)

Emiko: Your mother is calling you.

Masako *(Answering her mother.): Nani?* ("What?")

130 Hana *(From the kitchen.):* Come inside now.

Emiko: You'll have a boy friend one day.

Masako: Not me.

Emiko: You'll fall in love one day. Someone will make the inside of you light up, and you'll know you're in love. *(She relives her own experience.)* Your life will change . . . grow beautiful. It's good, Masa-chan. And this feeling you'll remember the rest of your life . . . will come back to you . . . haunt you . . . keep you alive . . . five, ten years . . . no matter what happens . . . keep you alive.

Hana *(From the kitchen.):* Masako . . . come inside now.

(Masako turns aside to answer and Emiko slips away.)

135 Masako: What, Mama?

(Hana comes out.)

Hana: Come inside. Don't be so unsociable. Kiyoko wants to talk to you.

Masako *(Watching Emiko leave.):* She doesn't want to talk to me. You're only saying that.

Hana: What's the matter with you? Don't you want to make friends with her?

Masako: She's not my friend. She's your friend.

140 Hana: Don't be so silly. She's only fourteen.

Masako: Fifteen. They said fifteen. She's your friend. She's an old lady.

Hana: Don't say that.

Masako: I don't like her.

Hana: Shhh! Don't say that.

145 Masako: She doesn't like me either.

Hana: Ma-chan. Remember your promise to Mr. Oka? You're going to take her to school, teach her the language, teach her the ways of Americans.

Masako: She can do it herself. You did.

Hana: That's not nice, Ma-chan.

Masako: I don't like the way she laughs.

(She imitates Kiyoko holding her hand to her mouth and giggling and bowing.)

150 Hana: Oh, how awful! Stop that. That's the way the girls do in Japan. Maybe she doesn't like your ways either. That's only a difference in manners.

What you're doing now is considered very bad manners. *(She changes tone.)* Ma-chan . . . just wait—when she learns to read and speak, you'll have so much to say to each other. Come on, be a good girl and come inside.

Masako: It's just old people in there, Mama. I don't want to go in.

(Hana calls Kiyoko away from the table and speaks confidentially to her.)

Hana: Kiyoko-san, please come here a minute. Maybe it's better for you to talk to Masako alone. *(Kiyoko leaves the table and walks to Hana outside.)* Masako has a lot of things to tell you about . . . what to expect in school and things . . .

Murata *(Calling from the table.):* Mama, put out something . . . chiles . . . for Oka-san.

(Hana leaves the two girls and enters the house. Kiyoko and Masako stand awkwardly, Kiyoko glancing shyly at Masako.)

Masako: Do you like it here?

155 **Kiyoko** *(Nodding.):* Eh.

(There's an uncomfortable pause.)

Masako: School will be starting next week . . .
Kiyoko *(Nodding.):* Eh.
Masako: Do you want to walk to school with me?
Kiyoko *(Nodding.):* Ah.

(Masako rolls her eyes and tries again.)

160 **Masako:** I leave at 7:30.
Kiyoko: Ah.

(There's a long pause. Masako finally gives up and moves off stage.)

Masako: I have to do something.

(Kiyoko watches her leave and uncertainly moves back to the house. Hana looks up at Kiyoko coming in alone, sighs, and quietly pulls out a chair for her.)

Fade out.

Scene 2

November night. Interior of the Murata house. Lamps are lit. The family is at the kitchen table. Hana sews, Masako does her homework, Murata reads the paper. They're dressed in warm robes and having tea. Outside thunder rolls in the distance and lightning flashes.

Hana: It'll be *ohigan* ("an autumn festival") soon.
Murata: Something to look forward to.
Hana: We will need sweet rice for *omochi* ("rice cakes").

Murata: I'll order it next time I go to town.

5 Hana *(To Masako.):* How is school? Getting a little harder?

Masako: Not that much. Sometimes the arithmetic is hard.

Hana: How is Kiyoko-san doing? Is she getting along all right?

Masako: She's good in arithmetic. She skipped a grade already.

Hana: Already? That's good news. Only November and she skipped a grade! At this rate she'll be through before you.

10 Masako: Well, she's older.

Murata: Sure, she's older, Mama.

Hana: Has she made any friends?

Masako: No. She follows me around all day. She understands okay, but she doesn't talk. She talks like, you know . . . she says "ranchi" for lunch and "ranchi" for ranch too, and like that. Kids laugh and copy behind her back. It's hard to understand her.

Hana: You understand her, don't you?

15 Masako: I'm used to it. *(Murata smiles secretly.)*

Hana: You should tell the kids not to laugh; after all, she's trying. Maybe you should help her practice those words . . . show her what she's doing wrong.

Masako: I already do. Our teacher told me to do that.

Murata *(Looking up from his paper.):* You ought to help her all you can.

Hana: And remember when you started school you couldn't speak English either.

20 Masako: I help her.

(Murata rises and goes to the window. The night is cold. Lightning flashes and the wind whistles.)

Murata: Looks like a storm coming up. Hope we don't have a freeze.

Hana: If it freezes, we'll have another bad year. Maybe we ought to start the smudge pots.

Murata *(Listening.):* It's starting to rain. Nothing to do now but pray.

Hana: If praying is the answer, we'd be in Japan now . . . rich.

25 Murata *(Wryly.):* We're not dead yet. We still have a chance. *(Hana glares at this small joke.)* Guess I'll turn in.

Hana: Go to bed . . . go to bed. I'll sit up and worry.

Murata: If worrying was the answer, we'd be around the world twice and in Japan. Come on, Mama. Let's go to bed. It's too cold tonight to be mad. *(There's an urgent knock on the door. The family react to it.) Dare da!* ("Who is it!") *(Murata goes to the door and pauses.)* Who is it!

Kiyoko *(Weakly.):* It's me . . . help me . . .

(Murata opens the door and Kiyoko enters. She's dressed in a kimono with a shawl thrown over. Her legs are bare except for a pair of straw zori. Her hair is stringy from the rain and she trembles from the cold.)

Murata: My God! Kiyoko-san! What's the matter?

30 Hana: Kiyoko-san! What is it?

Murata: What happened?

Kiyoko *(Gasping.):* They're fighting . . . they're fighting.

Murata: Ah . . . don't worry . . . those things happen. No cause to worry. Mama, make tea for her. Sit down and catch your breath. I'll take you home when you're ready.

Hana: Papa, I'll take care of it.

35　**Murata:** Let me know when you're ready to go home.

Hana: It must be freezing out there. Try to get warm. Try to calm yourself.

Murata: Kiyoko-san . . . don't worry.

(Hana waves Masako and Murata off. Murata leaves. Masako goes to her bed in the kitchen.)

Hana: Papa, I'll take care of it.

Kiyoko *(Looking at Murata's retreating form.):* I came to ask your help.

40　**Hana:** You ran down here without a lantern? You could have fallen and hurt yourself.

Kiyoko: I don't care . . . I don't care.

Hana: You don't know, Kiyoko-san. It's treacherous out there . . . snakes, spiders . . .

Kiyoko: I must go back . . . I . . . I . . . you . . . please come with me.

Hana: First, first, we must get you warm . . . Drink your tea.

45　**Kiyoko:** But they might kill each other. They're fighting like animals. Help me stop them!

(Hana goes to the stove to warm a pot of soup.)

Hana: I cannot interfere in a family quarrel.

Kiyoko: It's not a quarrel . . . it's a . . .

Hana: That's all it is. A family squabble. You'll see. Tomorrow . . .

(Kiyoko rises and puts her hand on Hana's arm.)

Kiyoko: Not just a squabble . . . please! *(She starts toward the door but Hana restrains her.)*

50　**Hana:** Now listen. Listen to me, Kiyoko-san. I've known your father and mother a little while now. I suspect it's been like this for years. Every family has some kind of trouble.

Kiyoko: Not like this . . . not like this.

Hana: Some have it better—some worse. When you get married, you'll understand. Don't worry. Nothing will happen. *(She takes a towel from the wall and dries Kiyoko's hair.)* You're chilled to the bone. You'll catch your death . . .

Kiyoko: I don't care . . . I want to die.

Hana: Don't be silly. It's not that bad.

55　**Kiyoko:** They started drinking early in the afternoon. They make some kind of brew and hide it somewhere in the desert.

Hana: It's illegal to make it. That's why they hide it. That home brew is poison to the body . . . and the mind too.

Kiyoko: It makes them crazy. They drink it all the time and quarrel constantly. I was in the other room studying. I try so hard to keep up with school.

Hana: We were talking about you just this evening. Masako says you're doing so well . . . you skipped a grade?

Kiyoko: It's hard . . . hard . . . I'm too old for the class and the children . . . *(She remembers all her problems and starts to cry again.)*

60 **Hana:** It's always hard in a new country.

Kiyoko: They were bickering and quarreling all afternoon. Then something happened. All of a sudden I saw them on the floor . . . hitting and . . . and . . . He was hitting her in the stomach, the face . . . I tried to stop them, but they were so . . . drunk.

Hana: There, there . . . It's probably all over now.

Kiyoko: Why does it happen like this? Nothing is right. Everywhere I go . . . Masa-chan is so lucky. I wish my life was like hers. I can hardly remember my real mother.

Hana: Emiko-san is almost a real mother to you. She's blood kin.

65 **Kiyoko:** She hates me. She never speaks to me. She's so cold. I want to love her but she won't let me. She hates me.

Hana: I don't think that's true, Kiyoko-san.

Kiyoko: I know it's true.

Hana: No. I don't think you have anything to do with it. It's this place. She hates it. This place is so lonely and alien.

Kiyoko: Then why didn't she go back? Why did they stay here?

70 **Hana:** You don't know. It's not so simple. Sometimes I think . . .

Kiyoko: Then why don't they make the best of it here? Like you?

Hana: That isn't easy either. Believe me. *(She goes to the stove to stir the soup.)* Sometimes . . . sometimes the longing for homeland fills me with despair. Will I never return again? Will I never see my mother, my father, my sisters again? But what can one do? There are responsibilities here . . . children . . . *(She draws a sharp breath.)* And another day passes . . . another month . . . another year. Eventually everything passes. *(She takes the soup to Kiyoko.)* Did you have supper tonight?

Kiyoko *(Bowing gratefully.):* Ah. When my . . . my aunt gets like this, she doesn't cook. No one eats. I don't get hungry anymore.

Hana: Cook for yourself. It's important to keep your health.

75 **Kiyoko:** I left Japan for a better life here . . .

Hana: It isn't easy for you, is it? But you must remember your filial duty.

Kiyoko: It's so hard.

Hana: But you can make the best of it here, Kiyoko-san. And take care of yourself. You owe that to yourself. Eat. Keep well. It'll be better, you'll see. And sometimes it'll seem worse. But you'll survive. We do, you know . . . we do . . . *(She looks around.)* It's getting late.

Kiyoko *(Apprehensively.):* I don't want to go back.

80 **Hana:** You can sleep with Masako tonight. Tomorrow you'll go back. And you'll remember what I told you. *(She puts her arms around Kiyoko,*

who is overcome with self-pity and begins to weep quietly.) Life is never easy, Kiyoko-san. Endure. Endure. Soon you'll be marrying and going away. Things will not always be this way. And you'll look back on this . . . this night and you'll . . .

(There is a rap on the door. Hana exchanges glances with Kiyoko and goes to answer it. She opens it a crack. Oka has come looking for Kiyoko. He's dressed in an overcoat and holds a wet newspaper over his head.)

Oka: Ah! I'm sorry to bother you so late at night . . . the fact is . . .

Hana: Oka-san . . .

Oka *(Jovially.):* Good evening, good evening . . . *(He sees Kiyoko.)* Ah . . . there you are . . . Did you have a nice visit?

Hana *(Irritated.):* Yes, she's here.

85 Oka *(Still cheerful.):* Thought she might be. Ready to come home now?

Hana: She came in the rain.

Oka *(Ignoring Hana's tone.):* That's foolish of you, Kiyoko. You might catch cold.

Hana: She was frightened by your quarreling. She came for help.

Oka *(Laughing with embarrassment.):* Oh! Kiyoko, that's nothing to worry about. It's just we had some disagreement . . .

90 Hana: That's what I told her, but she was frightened all the same.

Oka: Children are . . .

Hana: Not children, Oka-san. Kiyoko. Kiyoko was terrified. I think that was a terrible thing to do to her.

Oka *(Rubbing his head.):* Oh, I . . . I . . .

Hana: If you had seen her a few minutes ago . . . hysterical . . . shaking . . . crying . . . wet and cold to the bone . . . out of her mind with worry.

95 Oka *(Rubbing his head.):* Oh . . . I . . . don't know what she was so worried about.

Hana: You. You and Emiko fighting like you were going to kill each other.

Oka *(There's nothing more to hide. He lowers his head in penitence.):* Aaaaaachhhhhhh . . .

Hana: I know I shouldn't tell you this, but there're one or two things I have to say: You sent for Kiyoko-san and now she's here. You said yourself she had a bad time in Japan, and now she's having a worse time. It isn't easy for her in a strange new country; the least you can do is try to keep her from worrying . . . especially about yourselves. I think it's terrible what you're doing to her . . . terrible!

Oka *(Bowing in deep humility.):* I am ashamed . . .

100 Hana: I think she deserves better. I think you should think about that.

Oka *(Still in his bow.):* I thank you for this reminder. It will never happen again. I promise.

Hana: I don't need that promise. Make it to Kiyoko-san.

Oka *(To Kiyoko.):* Come with Papa now. He did a bad thing. He'll be a good Papa from now. We won't worry his little girl again. All right? All right?

(They move to the door.)

Kiyoko: Thank you so much. *(She takes Murata's robe and tries to return it.)*
105 **Oka:** Madam. I thank you again.
Hana *(To Kiyoko.):* That's all right. You can bring it back tomorrow. *(Aside to Kiyoko.)* Remember . . . remember what we talked about. *(Loudly.)* Goodnight, Oka-san.

(They leave. Hana goes to Masako, who lies on the bed. She covers her. Murata appears from the bedroom. He's heard it all. He and Hana exchange a glance and together they retire to their room.)

Fade out.

Scene 3

The next morning. The Murata house and yard. Hana and Murata have already left the house to examine the rain damage in the fields. Masako prepares to go to school. She puts on a coat and picks up her books and lunch bag. Meanwhile, Kiyoko slips quietly into the yard. She wears a coat and carries Murata's robe and sets it on the outside bench. Masako walks out and is surprised to see Kiyoko.

Masako: Hi. I thought you'd be . . . sick today.
Kiyoko: Oh. I woke up late.
Masako *(Scrutinizing Kiyoko's face.):* Your eyes are red.
Kiyoko *(Averting her eyes.):* Oh. I . . . got . . . sand in it. Yes.
5 **Masako:** Do you want to use eye drops? We have eye drops in the house.
Kiyoko: Oh . . . no. That's all right.
Masako: That's what you call bloodshot.
Kiyoko: Oh.
Masako: My father gets it a lot. When he drinks too much.
10 **Kiyoko:** Oh . . .

(Masako notices Kiyoko doesn't have her lunch.)

Masako: Where's your lunch bag?
Kiyoko: I . . . forgot it.
Masako: Did you make your lunch today?
Kiyoko: Yes. Yes, I did. But I forgot it.
15 **Masako:** Do you want to go back and get it?
Kiyoko: No, that's all right. *(They are silent for a while.)* We'll be late.
Masako: Do you want to practice your words?
Kiyoko *(Thoughtfully.):* Oh . . .
Masako: Say, "My."
20 **Kiyoko:** My?
Masako: Eyes . . .
Kiyoko: Eyes.

Masako: Are . . .
Kiyoko: Are.
25 Masako: Red.
Kiyoko: Red.
Masako: Your eyes are red. *(Kiyoko doesn't repeat it.)* I . . . *(Kiyoko doesn't cooperate.)* Say, "I."
Kiyoko: I.
Masako: Got . . .
30 Kiyoko: Got.
Masako: Sand . . . *(Kiyoko balks.)* Say, "I."
Kiyoko *(Sighing.):* I.
Masako: Reft . . .
Kiyoko: Reft.
35 Masako: My . . .
Kiyoko: My.
Masako: Runch . . .
Kiyoko: Run . . . Lunch. *(She stops.)* Masako-san, you are mean. You are hurting me.
Masako: It's a joke! I was just trying to make you laugh!
40 Kiyoko: I cannot laugh today.
Masako: Sure you can. You can laugh. Laugh! Like this! *(She makes a hearty laugh.)*
Kiyoko: I cannot laugh when you make fun of me.
Masako: Okay, I'm sorry. We'll practice some other words then, okay? *(Kiyoko doesn't answer.)* Say, "Okay."
Kiyoko *(Reluctantly.):* Okay . . .
45 Masako: Okay, then . . . um . . . um . . . *(She still teases and talks rapidly.)* Say . . . um . . . "She sells sea shells on the sea shore." *(Kiyoko turns away indignantly.)* Aw, come on, Kiyoko! It's just a joke. Laugh!
Kiyoko *(Imitating sarcastically.):* Ha-ha-ha! Now you say, *"Kono kyaku wa yoku kaki ku kyaku da!"*
Masako: Sure! I can say it! Kono kyaku waki ku kyoku kaku . . .
Kiyoko: That's not right.
Masako: Koki kuki kya . . .
50 Kiyoko: No.
Masako: Okay, then. You say, "Sea sells she shells . . . shu . . . sss . . ."

(They both laugh, Kiyoko with her hands over her mouth.)

Masako *(Taking Kiyoko's hands from her mouth.):* Not like that! Like this! *(She gives a big belly laugh.)*
Kiyoko: Like this? *(She imitates Masako.)*
Masako: Yeah, that's right! You're not mad anymore?
55 Kiyoko: I'm not mad anymore.
Masako: Okay. You can share my lunch today because we're . . .
Kiyoko: "Flends?"

(Masako looks at Kiyoko, they giggle and move on. Hana and Murata come in from assessing the storm's damage. They are dressed warmly. Hana is depressed. Murata tries hard to be cheerful.)

Murata: It's not so bad, Mama.

Hana: Half the ranch is flooded . . . at least half.

60 Murata: No-no. A quarter, maybe. It's sunny today . . . it'll dry.

Hana: The seedlings will rot.

Murata: No, no. It'll dry. It's all right—better than I expected.

Hana: If we have another bad year, no one will lend us money for the next crop.

Murata: Don't worry. If it doesn't drain by tomorrow, I'll replant the worst places. We still have some seed left. Yeah, I'll replant . . .

65 Hana: More work.

Murata: Don't worry, Mama. It'll be all right.

Hana *(Quietly.):* Papa, where will it end? Will we always be like this—always at the mercy of the weather—prices—always at the mercy of the Gods?

Murata *(Patting Hana's back.):* Things will change. Wait and see. We'll be back in Japan by . . . in two years . . . guarantee . . . Maybe sooner.

Hana *(Dubiously.):* Two years . . .

70 Murata *(Finds the robe on the bench.):* Ah, look, Mama. Kiyoko-san brought back my robe.

Hana *(Sighing.):* Kiyoko-san . . . poor Kiyoko-san . . . and Emiko-san.

Murata: Ah, Mama. We're lucky. We're lucky, Mama.

(Hana smiles sadly at Murata.)

Fade out.

Scene 4

*The following spring, afternoon. Exterior of the Oka house. Oka is dressed to go out. He wears a sweater, long-sleeved white shirt, dark pants, no tie. He puts his foot on the bench to wipe off his shoe with the palm of his hand. He straightens his sleeve, removes a bit of lint and runs his fingers through his hair. He hums under his breath. Kiyoko comes from the house. Her hair is frizzled with a permanent wave, she wears a gaudy new dress and a pair of new shoes. She carries a movie magazine—*Photoplay *or* Modern Screen.

Oka *(Appreciatively.):* Pretty. Pretty.

Kiyoko *(Turning for him.):* It's not too *hadeh?*[13] I feel strange in colors.

Oka: Oh no. Young girls should wear bright colors. There's time enough to wear gray when you get old. Old lady colors. *(Kiyoko giggles.)* Sure you want to go to the picture show? It's such a nice day . . . shame to waste in a dark hall.

---

[13] Gaudy.

Kiyoko: Where else can we go?

5 Oka: We can go to the Muratas.

Kiyoko: All dressed up?

Oka: Or Nagatas. I'll show him what I got for my horse.

Kiyoko *(Laughing.):* Oh, I love the pictures.

Oka: We don't have many nice spring days like this. Here the season is short. Summer comes in like a dragon . . . right behind . . . breathing fire . . . like a dragon. You don't know the summers here. They'll scare you. *(He tousles Kiyoko's hair and pulls a lock of it. It springs back. He shakes his head in wonder.)* Goddamn. Curly hair. Never thought curly hair could make you so happy.

10 Kiyoko *(Giggling.):* All the American girls have curly hair.

Oka: Your friend. Masako like it?

Kiyoko *(Nodding.):* She says her mother will never let her get a permanent wave.

Oka: She said that, eh? Bet she's wanting one.

Kiyoko: I don't know about that.

15 Oka: Bet she's wanting some of your pretty dresses too.

Kiyoko: Her mother makes all her clothes.

Oka: Buying is just as good. Buying is better. No trouble that way.

Kiyoko: Masako's not so interested in clothes. She loves the pictures, but her mother won't let her go. Some day, can we take Masako with us?

Oka: If her mother lets her come. Her mother's got a mind of her own . . . a stiff back.

20 Kiyoko: But she's nice.

Oka *(Dubiously.):* Oh, yeah. Can't be perfect, I guess. Kiyoko, after the harvest I'll have money and I'll buy you the prettiest dress in town. I'm going to be lucky this year. I feel it.

Kiyoko: You're already too good to me . . . dresses, shoes, permanent wave . . . movies . . .

Oka: That's nothing. After the harvest, just wait . . .

Kiyoko: Magazines . . . You do enough. I'm happy already.

25 Oka: You make me happy too, Kiyoko. You make me feel good . . . like a man again . . . *(That statement bothers him.)* One day you're going to make a young man happy. *(Kiyoko giggles.)* Someday we going to move from here.

Kiyoko: But we have good friends here, Papa.

Oka: Next year our lease will be up and we got to move.

Kiyoko: The ranch is not ours?

Oka: No. In America, Japanese cannot own land. We lease and move every two, three years. Next year we going to go someplace where there's young fellows. There's none good enough for you here. *(He watches Kiyoko giggle.)* Yeah. You going to make a good wife. Already a good cook. I like your cooking.

30 Kiyoko *(A little embarrassed.):* Shall we go now?

Oka: Yeah. Put the magazine away.

Kiyoko: I want to take it with me.

Oka: Take it with you?

Kiyoko: Last time, after we came back, I found all my magazines torn in half.

35 Oka *(Looking toward the house.):* Torn?

Kiyoko: This is the only one I have left.

Oka *(Not wanting to deal with it.):* All right. All right.

> *(The two prepare to leave when the door opens. Emiko stands there, her hair is unkempt and she looks wild. She holds an empty can in one hand, the lid in the other.)*

Emiko: Where is it?

> *(Oka tries to make a hasty departure.)*

Kiyoko: Where is what?

> *(Oka pushes Kiyoko ahead of him, still trying to make a getaway.)*

40 Emiko: Where is it? Where is it? What did you do with it? *(Emiko moves toward Oka. He can't ignore her and he stops.)*

Oka *(With false unconcern to Kiyoko.):* Why don't you walk on ahead to the Muratas?

Kiyoko: We're not going to the pictures?

Oka: We'll go. First you walk to the Muratas. Show them your new dress. I'll meet you there.

> *(Kiyoko picks up a small package and exits. Oka sighs and shakes his head.)*

Emiko *(Shaking the can.):* Where is it? What did you do with it?

45 Oka *(Feigning surprise.):* With what?

Emiko: You know what. You stole it. You stole my money.

Oka: *Your* money?

Emiko: I've been saving that money.

Oka: Yeah? Well, where'd you get it? Where'd you get it, eh? You stole it from me! Dollar by dollar . . . You stole it from me! Out of my pocket!

50 Emiko: I saved it!

Oka: From my pocket!

Emiko: It's mine! I saved for a long time . . . Some of it I brought from Japan.

Oka: *Bakayuna!*[14] What'd you bring from Japan? Nothing but some useless kimonos. *(Oka starts to leave but Emiko hangs on to him.)*

Emiko: Give back my money! Thief!

55 Oka *(Swings around and balls his fists but doesn't strike.):* Goddamn! Get off me!

Emiko *(Now pleading.):* Please give it back . . . please . . . please . . . *(She starts to stroke him. Oka pulls her hands away and pushes her from him.)* Oni!

---

[14] Stupid woman.

Oka *(Seething.): Oni?* What does that make you? *Oni baba?* Yeah, that's what
   you are . . . a devil!

Emiko: It's mine! Give it back . . .

Oka: The hell! You think you can live off me and steal my money too? How
   stupid you think I am?

60 Emiko *(Tearfully.):* But I've paid . . . I've paid . . .

Oka: With what?

Emiko: You know I've paid.

Oka *(Scoffing.):* You call that paying?

Emiko: What did you do with it?

65 Oka: I don't have it.

Emiko: It's gone? It's gone?

Oka: Yeah! It's gone. I spent it. The hell! Every last cent.

Emiko: The new clothes . . . the curls . . . restaurants . . . pictures
   . . . shoes . . . My money . . . my going-home money . . .

Oka: You through?

70 Emiko: What will I do? What will . . .

Oka: I don't care what you do. Walk. Use your feet. Swim to Japan. I don't
   care. I give you no more than you gave me. Now I don't want anything. I
   don't care what you do. *(He walks away.)*

*(Emiko still holds the empty can. Off stage we hear Oka's car door slam
and the sound of his old car starting off. Accustomed to crying alone,
she doesn't utter a sound. Her shoulders begin to shake, her dry soundless sobs turn to a silent laugh. She wipes the dust gently from the can
as though comforting a friend. Her movements become sensuous, her
hands move on to her own body, around her throat, over her breasts, to
her hips, caressing, soothing, reminding her of her lover's hands.)*

Fade out.

Scene 5

*Same day, late afternoon. Exterior of the Murata house. The light is
soft. Hana is sweeping the yard; Masako hangs a glass wind chime on
the exposed wall.*

Hana *(Directing Masako.):* There . . . there. That's a good place.

Masako: Here?

Hana *(Nodding.):* It must catch the slightest breeze. *(Sighing and listening.)*
   It brings back so much . . . That's the reason I never hung one before.
   I guess it doesn't matter much any more . . .

Masako: I thought you liked to think about Japan.

5 Hana *(Laughing sadly.):* I didn't want to hear that sound so often . . . get
   too used to it. Sometimes you hear something too often, after a while
   you don't hear it anymore . . . I didn't want that to happen. The same
   thing happens to feelings too, I guess. After a while you don't feel any
   more. You're too young to understand that yet.

Masako: I understand, Mama.

Hana: Wasn't it nice of Kiyoko-san to give us the *furin?*

Masako: I love it. I don't know anything about Japan, but it makes me feel something too.

Hana: Maybe someday when you're grown up, gone away, you'll hear it and remember yourself as this little girl . . . remember this old house, the ranch, and . . . your old mama . . .

10 Masako: That's kind of scary.

(Emiko enters unsteadily. She carries a bundle wrapped in a colorful scarf "furoshiki." In the packages are two beautiful kimonos.)

Hana: Emiko-san! What a pleasant surprise! Please sit down. We were just hanging the *furin.* It was so sweet of Kiyoko-san to give it to Masako. She loves it.

(Emiko looks mildly interested. She acts as normal as she can throughout the scene, but at times drops her facade, revealing her desperation.)

Emiko: Thank you. *(She sets her bundle on the bench but keeps her hand on it.)*

Hana: Your family was here earlier. *(Emiko smiles vaguely.)* On their way to the pictures, I think. *(To Masako.)* Make tea for us, Ma-chan.

Emiko: Please don't . . .

15 Hana: Kiyoko-san was looking so nice—her hair all curly . . . Of course, in our day, straight black hair was desirable. Of course, times change.

Emiko: Yes.

Hana: But she did look fine. My, my, a colorful new dress, new shoes, a permanent wave—looked like a regular American girl. Did you choose her dress?

Emiko: No . . . I didn't go.

Hana: You know, I didn't think so. Very pretty, though. I liked it very much. Of course, I sew all Masako's clothes. It saves money. It'll be nice for you to make things for Kiyoko-san too. She'd be so pleased. I know she'd be pleased . . . *(While Hana talks, Emiko plucks nervously at her package. She waits for Hana to stop talking.)* Emiko-san, is everything all right?

20 Emiko *(Smiling nervously.):* Yes.

Hana: Masako, please go make tea for us. See if there aren't any more of those crackers left. Or did you finish them? *(To Emiko.)* We can't keep anything in this house. She eats everything as soon as Papa brings it home. You'd never know it, she's so skinny. We never have anything left for company.

Masako: We hardly ever have company anyway.

(Hana gives her daughter a strong look, and Masako goes into the house. Emiko is lost in her own thoughts. She strokes her package.)

Hana: Is there something you . . . I can help you with? *(Very gently.)* Emiko-san?

Emiko *(Suddenly frightened.):* Oh no. I was thinking . . . Now that . . . now that . . . Masa-chan is growing up . . . older . . .

25 **Hana** *(Relieved.):* Oh, yes. She's growing fast.

Emiko: I was thinking . . . *(She stops, puts the package on her lap and is lost again.)*

Hana: Yes, she *is* growing. Time goes so fast. I think she'll be taller than me soon. *(She laughs weakly, stops and looks puzzled.)*

Emiko: Yes.

(Emiko's depression pervades the atmosphere. Hana is affected by it. The two women sit in silence. A small breeze moves the wind chimes. At the moment light grows dim on the two lonely figures. Masako comes from the house with a tray of tea. The light returns to normal again.)

Hana *(Gently.):* You're a good girl.

(Masako looks first to Emiko then to her mother. She sets the tray on the bench and stands near Emiko, who seems to notice her for the first time.)

30 **Emiko:** How are you?

(Hana pours the tea and serves her.)

Hana: Emiko-san, is there something I can do for you?

Emiko: There's . . . I was . . . I . . . Masa-chan will be a young lady soon . . .

Hana: Oh, well, now I don't know about "lady."

Emiko: Maybe she would like a nice . . . nice . . . *(She unwaps her package.)* I have kimonos . . . I wore in Japan for dancing . . . maybe she can . . . if you like, I mean. They'll be nice on her . . . she's so slim . . .

(Emiko shakes out a robe. Hana and Masako are impressed.)

35 **Hana:** Ohhhh! Beautiful!

Masako: Oh, Mama! Pretty! *(Hana and Masako finger the material.)* Gold threads, Mama.

Hana: Brocade!

Emiko: Maybe Masa-chan would like them. I mean for her school programs . . . Japanese school . . .

Hana: Oh, no! Too good for country. People will be envious of us . . . wonder where we got them.

40 **Emiko:** I mean for festivals . . . *Obon, Hana Matsuri* . . .

Hana: Oh, but you have Kiyoko-san now. You should give them to her. Has she seen them?

Emiko: Oh . . . no . . .

Hana: She'll love them. You should give them to her . . . not our Masako.

Emiko: I thought . . . I mean I was thinking of . . . if you could give me a little . . . if you could pay . . . manage to give me something for . . .

45 Hana: But these gowns, Emiko-san—they're worth hundreds.

Emiko: I know, but I'm not asking for that. Whatever you can give . . . only as much as you can give.

Masako: Mama?

Hana: Masako, Papa doesn't have that kind of money.

Emiko: Anything you can give . . . anything . . .

50 Masako: Ask Papa.

Hana: There's no use asking. I know he can't afford it.

Emiko *(Looking at Masako.):* A little at a time.

Masako: Mama?

Hana *(Firmly.):* No, Masako. This is a luxury. *(Hana folds the gowns and puts them away. Masako is disappointed. Emiko is devastated. Hana sees this and tries to find some way to help.)* Emiko-san, I hope you understand . . . *(Emiko is silent trying to gather her resources.)* I know you can sell them and get the full price somewhere. Let's see . . . a family with a lot of growing daughters . . . someone who did well last year . . . Nagatas have no girls . . . Umedas have girls but no money . . . Well, let's see . . . Maybe not here in this country town. Ah . . . You can take them to the city, Los Angeles, and sell them to a store . . . or Terminal Island . . . lots of wealthy fishermen there. Yes, that would be the place. Why, it's no problem, Emiko-san. Have your husband take them there. I know you'll get your money. He'll find a buyer. I know he will.

55 Emiko: Yes.

(Emiko finishes folding and ties the scarf. She sits quietly.)

Hana: Please have your tea. I'm sorry . . . I really would like to take them for Masako but it just isn't possible. You understand, don't you? *(Emiko nods.)* Please don't feel so . . . so bad. It's not really a matter of life or death, is it? Emiko-san?

(Emiko nods again. Hana sips her tea.)

Masako: Mama? If you could ask Papa . . .

Hana: Oh, the tea is cold. Masako could you heat the kettle?

Emiko: No more. I must be going. *(She picks up her package and rises slowly.)*

60 Hana *(Looking helpless.):* So soon? Emiko-san, please stay. *(Emiko starts to go.)* Masako will walk with you. *(She pushes Masako forward.)*

Emiko: It's not far.

Hana: Emiko-san? You'll be all right?

Emiko: Yes . . . yes . . . yes . . .

Hana *(Calling as Emiko exits.):* I'm sorry, Emiko-san.

65 Emiko: Yes . . .

(Masako and Hana watch as Emiko leaves. The light grows dim as though a cloud passed over. Emiko exits. Hana strokes Masako's hair.)

Hana: Your hair is so black and straight . . . nice . . .

(They stand close. The wind chimes tinkle; light grows dim. Light returns to normal. Murata enters. He sees this tableau of mother and child and is puzzled.)

Murata: What's going on here?

(The two women part.)

Hana: Oh . . . nothing . . . nothing . . .

Masako: Mrs. Oka was here. She had two kimo- . . .

70 Hana *(Putting her hand on Masako's shoulder.):* It was nothing . . .

Murata: Eh? What'd she want?

Hana: Later, Papa. Right now, I'd better fix supper.

Murata *(Looking at the sky.):* Strange how that sun comes and goes. Maybe I didn't need to irrigate—looks like rain. *(He remembers and is exasperated.)* Ach! I forgot to shut the water.

Masako: I'll do it, Papa.

75 Hana: Masako, that gate's too heavy for you.

Murata: She can handle it. Take out the pin and let the gate fall all the way down. All the way. And put the pin back. Don't forget to put the pin back.

Hana: And be careful. Don't fall in the canal.

(Masako leaves.)

Murata: What's the matter with that girl?

Hana: Nothing. Why?

80 Murata: Usually have to beg her to do . . .

Hana: She's growing up.

Murata: Must be that time of the month.

Hana: Oh, Papa, she's too young for that yet.

Murata *(Genially as they enter the house.):* Got to start some time. Looks like I'll be out-numbered soon. I'm out-numbered already.

(Hana glances at him and quietly sets about preparations for supper. Murata removes his shirt and sits at the table with a paper. Light fades slowly.)

Fade out.

Scene 6

Same evening. Exterior, desert. There is at least one shrub. Masako appears, walking slowly. From a distance we hear Emiko singing the song "And the Soul Shall Dance." Masako looks around, sees the shrub and crouches under it. Emiko appears. She's dressed in her beautiful kimono tied loosely at her waist. She carries a branch of sage. Her hair is loose.

Emiko: *Akai kuchibiru / Kappu ni yosete / Aoi sake nomya / Kokoro ga odoru . . . Kurai yoru no yume / Setsu nasa yo . . .*

(She breaks into a dance, laughs mysteriously, turns round and round, acting out a fantasy. Masako stirs uncomfortably. Emiko senses a presence. She stops, drops her branch and walks off stage singing as she goes.)

Emiko: *Aoi sake nomya / Yume mo odoru . . .*

(Masako watches as Emiko leaves. She rises slowly and picks up the branch Emiko has left. She looks at the branch, moves forward a step and looks off to the point where Emiko disappeared. Light slowly fades until only the image of Masako's face remains etched in the mind.)

Fade out.

KOKORO GA ODORU	**AND THE SOUL SHALL DANCE**
Akai kuchibiru	Red lips
Kappu ni yosete	Press against a glass
Aoi sake nomya	Drink the green wine
Kokoro ga odoru	And the soul shall dance
5 Kurai yoru no yume	5 Dark night dreams
Setsu nasa yo	Are unbearable
Aoi sake nomya	Drink the green wine
Yume mo odoru	And the dreams will dance
Asa no munashisa	Morning's reality
10 Yume wo chirasu	10 Scatter the dreams
Sora to kokoro wa	Sky and soul
Sake shidai	Depend on the wine
Futari wakare no	The loneliness of
Samishisa yo	The two apart
15 Hitori sake nomya	15 Drink the wine alone
Kokoro ga odoru	And the soul shall dance

LYRICS BY WAKAKO YAMAUCHI

KAGO NO TORI	**THE CAGED BIRD**
	(She)
Aitasa, mita sa ni	In the desire to meet her
Kowa sa wo wasure	And the wish to see her
Kurai yomichi wo	He forgets his fear and
Tada hitori	Walks the dark streets alone.

5 Aini kita no ni
Naze dete awan?
Boku no yobu koe
Wasureta ka?

Anata no yobu koe
10 Wasure ma senu ga
Deru ni derareru
Kago no tori

POPULAR SONG

(He)
5 Though I've come to tryst
Why do you not come out?
My voice calling you—
Have you forgotten it?

(She)
Your voice calling me
10 I have not forgotten, but
To leave, to be able to leave—
No choice for the caged bird.

■ EXPLORATIONS OF THE TEXT ■

---

1. Explain the burning of the bathhouse. How does this event function in the play? Does it have multiple meanings?

2. Contrast the two marriages. What strengths do you identify? What difficulties become apparent? Find specific scenes to support your conclusions.

3. Consider the characters' reactions to Japan. Who wishes to assimilate? Who does not?

4. Describe the two girls. What is Kiyoko's relationship to Oka, to Masako? Is Oka's attitude toward Kiyoko incestuous?

5. What are the roles of men and of women in the play? Does anyone break free?

6. What do you learn about the lives of Japanese farmers in the United States in the 1930s? Does anyone experience rootedness or sense of place?

7. Why is alcohol so prominent in the play? What are the consequences?

8. Examine the last scene in *And the Soul Shall Dance*. What has happened to Emiko? Trace the course of her sadness; begin with her lost love and her desire to return to Japan. Why does Oka take her money? Why does Emiko dance at the end? How do you interpret the dance? What is the impact on Masako?

9. Explain the poems at the end and the title. Focus on the themes of the drama.

10. Compare the marriages in this play with the relationships in works by Joyce, Gilman, Glaspell, and Ndebele.

■■ JOURNAL ENTRIES ■■

1. Yamauchi created this play from a short story with the same title. Rewrite some part of this drama in another genre.
2. React to one of the characters in *And the Soul Shall Dance*.
3. Write a monologue in the voice of one of the characters.

■■■ IDEAS FOR WRITING ■■■

1. Choose a central scene in this drama; explore character, conflict, dialogue, theme, language, and/or dramatic effect. Evaluate the success of the scene.
2. What are the responsibilities of men or of women in Japanese-American society?
3. What are the effects of alcoholism on the characters in this play?
4. Write about this drama as an initiation for Masako.

An Affliction, A Word, A Letter
from Tales of Love

Julia Kristeva
Translated by Leon Roudiez

Julia Kristeva (1941–   ) was born in Bulgaria, attended French convent schools, belonged to Communist party children's and youth groups, and worked as a journalist on a Bulgarian paper for Communist youth while studying literature at the university there. Awarded a doctoral fellowship, she emigrated to Paris in 1966 and earned her Doctorat d'État, in 1973 for her essay on literary theory, La Révolution du langue poètique.

Kristeva is presently a professor of linguistics at the University of Paris VII (Jussieu) and regularly visiting professor of French at Columbia University. She also is a psychoanalyst, and, with her husband, the critic and novelist Philippe Sollers, member of the editorial board of the influential literary journal L'Infini.

As Elisabeth Grosz points out in Sexual Subversions, *"Kristeva's conception of her own project has changed. Her critique of individualism and humanism remains powerful, but her desire to establish a scientific methodology and subordinate her analyses to a broader conception of (class) politics is now less obvious." Kristeva is often cited as a feminist by English-speaking critics, as her recent work often examines issues central to women. In "An Affliction, A Word, A Letter," Kristeva discusses the linguistic and emotional complications of love.*

1   L ove at first sight, wild love, immeasurable love, fiery love . . . Trying to talk about it seems to me different from living it, but no less troublesome and delightfully intoxicating. Does this sound ridiculous? It is mad. No doubt the risk of a discourse of love, of a lover's discourse, comes mainly from uncertainty as to its object. Indeed, what are we talking about?

I remember a discussion among several *jeune filles,*[1] of which I was one. A preeminently amorous personage, the *jeune fille*—stereotype of the alluring seductress who mixed pleasure, desire, and ideals in this balefire that she passionately calls "love"—remains nonetheless one of the most intense signs of truth and eternity. We were trying to decide if, when speaking of love, we spoke of the same thing. And of what thing? When we said we were in love, did we reveal to our lovers the true purport of our passions? We weren't sure; for when they in turn declared themselves in love with us we were never sure what that meant exactly, to them.

Perhaps the naiveté of that debate conceals a metaphysical profundity— or at least a linguistic one. Beyond the revelation—yet another one—of the abyss separating the sexes, such questioning hints that love would, in any case, be solitary because incommunicable. As if, at the very moment when the individual discovered himself to be intensely true, powerfully subjective, but violently ethical because he would be generously ready to do anything for the other, he also discovered the confines of his condition and the powerlessness of his language. Are not two loves essentially individual, hence incommensurable, and thus don't they condemn the partners to meet only at a point infinitely remote? Unless they commune through a third party: ideal, god, hallowed group . . . But that is another story, and our lay adolescence unsettled our bodies and skirted ideologies, theologies . . . Finally, to speak of love may be, perhaps, a simple condensation of speech that merely arouses, in the one spoken to, metaphorical capabilities—a whole imaginary, uncontrollable, undecidable flood, of which the loved one alone unknowingly possesses the key . . . what does he understand me to be saying? What do I understand him to be saying? *Everything?*—as *one* tends to believe in those moments of merging apotheoses, as total as they are unspeakable? Or *nothing?*—as *I* think, as *he* may say when the first wound comes and unsettles our vulnerable hall of mirrors . . .

5   Vertigo of identity, vertigo of words: love, for the individual, is that sudden revelation, that irremediable cataclysm, of which one speaks only *after the fact.* Under its sway, one does not speak *of.* One simply has the impression of speaking at last, for the first time, for real. But is it really in order to

---

[1] Young girls.

say something? Not necessarily. If not, what exactly? Even the love letter, that innocently perverse attempt to subdue or revive the game, is too much engulfed in the immediate fire and speaks only of "me" and "you" or even a "we" resulting from the alchemy of identifications, but not of what is really at stake *between*. Not of this state of crisis, collapse, madness capable of sweeping away all the dams of reason, as it is capable, like the dynamics of a living organism in full growth, of transforming an error into a renewal—remodeling, remaking, reviving a body, a mentality, a life. Or even two.

Nevertheless, if one grants—our young unbelieving women lovers notwithstanding, and in spite of the immeasurable amount of affect and meaning set into motion by the protagonists—that one can speak of *a* love, of *Love*, one must also grant that, as bracing as it might be, love never dwells in us without burning us. To speak about it, even after the fact, is probably possible only on the basis of that burning. Following upon the exorbitant, aggrandizement of the loving Self, as extravagant in its pride as in its humility, that exquisite lapse is at the heart of the experience. Narcissistic wound? Ordeal of castration? Death unto oneself?—those are brutal words that give some idea of this state of hardy fragility, serene strength emerging out of love's torrent, or which love's torrent has cast aside, but which still harbors, under the appearance of reconquered sovereignty, a degree of psychic as much as physical pain. That sore spot shows me—through the threat and pleasure it lays in store for me, and before I withdraw into my shell again, temporarily I suppose, in the expectation of another love that I consider impossible for the time being—that in love "I" has been an *other*. That phrase, which leads us to poetry or raving hallucination, suggests a state of instability in which the individual is no longer indivisible and allows himself to become lost in the other, for the other. Within love, a risk that might otherwise be tragic is accepted, normalized, made fully reassuring.

The pain that nevertheless remains bears witness to this experience, which is indeed miraculous—the experience of having been able to exist for, through, with another in mind. When one dreams of a happy, harmonious, utopian society, one imagines it built upon love, since love exalts me at the same time as it exceeds or overtaxes me. Yet, far from amounting to an understanding, passionate love can be equated less with the calm slumber of reconciled civilizations than with their delirium, disengagement, and breach. A fragile crest where death and regeneration vie for dominance.

We have lost the relative strength and security that the old moral codes guaranteed our loves either by forbidding them or determining their limits. Under the crossfire of gynecological surgery rooms and television screens, we have buried love within shame for the benefit of pleasure, desire, if not revolution, evolution, planning, management—hence for the benefit of Politics. Until we discover under the rubble of those ideological structures—which are nevertheless ambitious, often exorbitant, sometimes altruistic—that they were extravagant or shy attempts intended to quench a thirst for love. To recognize this does not amount to a modest withdrawal, it is perhaps to confess to a grandiose pretension. Love is the time and space in which "I" assumes the right to be extraordinary. Sovereign yet not individual. Divisible, lost, annihilated; but also, and through imaginary fusion with the loved one, equal to the infinite space of superhuman psychism. Paranoid? I am, in love, at the zenith of subjectivity.

As a bonus of desire, on the far and near side of pleasure, love skirts or displaces both in order to expand me to the dimensions of the universe. Which one? Ours, his and mine mingled, enlarged. Expanded, infinite space, where, out of my lapses, I utter, through the interpolated loved one, the conjuring up of an ideal vision. Mine? His? Ours? Impossible and yet maintained.

10 Shall I relate its aspects in detail? More skillful stylists have done so. They have opened up a path that one can follow only by changing its place, since every one of those aspects is in the singular . . .

Expectancy makes me painfully sensitive to my incompleteness, of which I was not aware *before*. For now, while waiting, "before" and "after" become merged into a fearsome "never." Love and the loved one erase the reckoning of time . . . The *call*, its call, overwhelms me with a flow in which the upheavals of the body (what people call emotions) are mingled with a whirling thought, as vague, supple, ready to pierce or to wed the other's as it is vigilant, alert, lucid in its impetus . . . toward what? Toward a destiny as relentless and blind as biological programming, as the course of the species . . . A body swept away, present in all its limbs through a delightful absence—shaky voice, dry throat, starry eyes, flushed or clammy skin, throbbing heart . . . Would the symptoms of love be the symptoms of fear? Both a fear and a need of no longer being limited, held back, but going beyond. Dread of transgressing not only proprieties or taboos, but also, and above all, fear of crossing and desire to cross the boundaries of the self . . . The *meeting*, then, mixing pleasure and promise or hopes, remains in a sort of future perfect. It is the nontime of love that, both instant and eternity, past and future, abreacted present, fulfills me, abolishes me, and yet leaves me unsated . . . Till tomorrow, forever, as ever, faithfully, eternally as before, as when it will have been, yours . . . Permanence of desire or of disappointment?

In short, love is an affliction, and by the same token it is a word or a letter.

We invent it each time, with every necessarily unique loved one, at every moment, place, or age . . . Or once and for all.

■ EXPLORATIONS OF THE TEXT ■

1. Is discourse or talking about love as difficult as living it? Discuss the example of the "jeunes filles."
2. Why does the "abyss . . . [between] the sexes" make the individual aware of separateness and of the inability of language to reach the other? Is the language of love simply metaphorical as Kristeva contends?

3. What is the view of love letters in this essay? Do you agree with Kristeva?
4. What does Kristeva mean when she writes: "Within love, a risk that might otherwise be tragic is accepted, normalized, made fully reassuring"?
5. Why does Kristeva believe that passion is an "affliction"?
6. What is "the meeting"? Can it happen?
7. Compare Kristeva's view with Simone de Beauvoir's "Woman as Other" and with Plato's "The Sexes."

■■ JOURNAL ENTRIES ■■

1. Define love. Compare your definition with Kristeva's views.
2. Compose a love letter in an effort to refute Kristeva's argument.

■■■ IDEAS FOR WRITING ■■■

1. Construct an argument which disagrees with one of Kristeva's positions.
2. Discuss love as an "affliction." Refer to works in this chapter to support your ideas.
3. Write about the inability of language, of words to express feelings or ideas. A discussion of the failures of language may focus on love, passion, desire, relationships between lovers, or loss of love.

FICTION

Lady with Lapdog

Anton Chekhov   Translated by David Magarshack

Anton Chekhov (1860–1904) was born in southern Russia. Chekhov's short stories and plays were formative in the development of modern, realistic literature. His popular one-act plays, The Bear *and* The Marriage Proposal, *were produced in 1888. Throughout the 1890s, his major works were staged:* The Sea Gull *(1898);* Uncle Vanya *(1899);* The Three Sisters *(1901); and* The Cherry Orchard *(1904). One central theme dominates these plays: the protagonists' inabilities to change the circumstances of their lives—their imprisonment in the worlds of their failed dreams. During the last phase of his life, he also wrote several volumes of short stories:* Motley Stories *(1886),* Innocent Speeches *(1887),* In The Twilight *(1887), and* Stories *(1889).*

In "Lady with Lapdog," an illicit love relationship, which begins as a superficial liaison, becomes more profound than the two characters could have imagined.

I

1 The appearance on the front of a new arrival—a lady with a lapdog—became the topic of general conversation. Dmitry Dmitrich Gurov, who had been a fortnight in Yalta[1] and got used to its ways, was also interested in new arrivals. One day, sitting on the terrace of Vernet's restaurant, he saw a young woman walking along the promenade; she was fair, not very tall, and wore a toque;[2] behind her trotted a white pomeranian.

Later he came across her in the park and in the square several times a day. She was always alone, always wearing the same toque, followed by the white pomeranian. No one knew who she was, and she became known simply as the lady with the lapdog.

"If she's here without her husband and without any friends," thought Gurov, "it wouldn't be a bad idea to strike up an acquaintance with her."

He was not yet forty, but he had a twelve-year-old daughter and two schoolboy sons. He had been married off when he was still in his second year at the university, and his wife seemed to him now to be almost twice his age. She was a tall, black-browed woman, erect, dignified, austere, and, as she

---

[1] A seaport in the Ukraine on the Black Sea.
[2] A kind of hat.

liked to describe herself, a "thinking person." She was a great reader, preferred the new "advanced" spelling, called her husband by the more formal "Dimitry" and not the familiar "Dmitry"; and though he secretly considered her not particularly intelligent, narrow-minded, and inelegant, he was afraid of her and disliked being at home. He had been unfaithful to her for a long time, he was often unfaithful to her, and that was why, perhaps, he almost always spoke ill of women, and when men discussed women in his presence, he described them as *the lower breed.*

5   He could not help feeling that he had had enough bitter experience to have the right to call them as he pleased, but all the same without *the lower breed* he could not have existed a couple of days. He was bored and ill at ease among men, with whom he was reticent and cold, but when he was among women he felt at ease, he knew what to talk about with them and how to behave, even when he was silent in their company he experienced no feeling of constraint. There was something attractive, something elusive in his appearance, in his character and his whole person that women found interesting and irresistible; he was aware of it, and was himself drawn to them by some irresistible force.

Long and indeed bitter experience had taught him that every new affair, which at first relieved the monotony of life so pleasantly and appeared to be such a charming and light adventure, among decent people and especially among Muscovites, who are so irresolute and so hard to rouse, inevitably developed into an extremely complicated problem and finally the whole situation became rather cumbersome. But at every new meeting with an attractive woman he forgot all about this experience, he wanted to enjoy life so badly and it all seemed so simple and amusing.

And so one afternoon, while he was having dinner at a restaurant in the park, the woman in the toque walked in unhurriedly and took a seat at the table next to him. The way she looked, walked and dressed, wore her hair, told him that she was of good social standing, that she was married, that she was in Yalta for the first time, that she was alone and bored. . . . There was a great deal of exaggeration in the stories about the laxity of morals among the Yalta visitors, and he dismissed them with contempt, for he knew that such stories were mostly made up by people who would gladly have sinned themselves if they had had any idea how to go about it; but when the woman sat down at the table three yards away from him he remembered these stories of easy conquests and excursions to the mountains and the tempting thought of a quiet and fleeting affair, an affair with a strange woman whose very name he did not know, suddenly took possession of him.

He tried to attract the attention of the dog by calling softly to it, and when the pomeranian came up to him he shook a finger at it. The pomeranian growled. Gurov again shook a finger at it.

The woman looked up at him and immediately lowered her eyes.

10   "He doesn't bite," she said and blushed.

"May I give him a bone?" he asked, and when she nodded, he said amiably: "Have you been long in Yalta?"

"About five days."

"And I am just finishing my second week here."

They said nothing for the next few minutes.

15   "Time flies," she said without looking at him, "and yet it's so boring here."

"That's what one usually hears people saying here. A man may be living in Belev and Zhizdra or some other God-forsaken hole and he isn't bored, but the moment he comes here all you hear from him is 'Oh, it's so boring! Oh, the dust!' You'd think he'd come from Granada!"

She laughed. Then both went on eating in silence, like complete strangers; but after dinner they strolled off together, and they embarked on the light playful conversation of free and contented people who do not care where they go or what they talk about. They walked, and talked about the strange light that fell on the sea: the water was of such a soft and warm lilac, and the moon threw a shaft of gold across it. They talked about how close it was after a hot day. Gurov told her that he lived in Moscow, that he was a graduate in philology but worked in a bank, that he had at one time thought of singing in a private opera company but had given up the idea, that he owned two houses in Moscow. . . . From her he learnt that she had grown up in Petersburg, but had got married in the town of S———, where she had been living for the past two years, that she would stay another month in Yalta, and that her husband, who also needed a rest, might join her. She was quite unable to tell him what her husband's job was, whether he served in the offices of the provincial governor or the rural council, and she found this rather amusing herself. Gurov also found out that her name and patronymic were Anna Sergeyevna.

Later, in his hotel room, he thought about her and felt sure that he would meet her again the next day. It had to be. As he went to bed he remembered that she had only recently left her boarding school, that she had been a schoolgirl like his own daughter; he recalled how much diffidence and angularity there was in her laughter and her conversation with a stranger—it was probably the first time in her life she had found herself alone, in a situation when men followed her, looked at her, and spoke to her with only one secret intention, an intention she could hardly fail to guess. He remembered her slender, weak neck, her beautiful grey eyes.

"There's something pathetic about her, all the same," he thought as he fell asleep.

II

20 A week had passed since their first meeting. It was a holiday. It was close indoors, while in the streets a strong wind raised clouds of dust and tore off people's hats. All day long one felt thirsty, and Gurov kept going to the terrace of the restaurant, offering Anna Sergeyevna fruit drinks and ices. There was nowhere to go.

In the evening, when the wind had dropped a little, they went to the pier to watch the arrival of the steamer. There were a great many people taking a walk on the landing pier; some were meeting friends, they had bunches of flowers in their hands. It was there that two peculiarities of the Yalta smart set at once arrested attention: the middle-aged women dressed as if they were still young girls and there was a great number of generals.

Because of the rough sea the steamer arrived late, after the sun had set, and she had to swing backwards and forwards several times before getting alongside the pier. Anna Sergeyevna looked at the steamer and the passengers through her lorgnette, as though trying to make out some friends, and when she turned to Gurov her eyes were sparkling. She talked a lot, asked many abrupt questions, and immediately forgot what it was she had wanted to know; then she lost her lorgnette in the crowd of people.

The smartly dressed crowd dispersed; soon they were all gone, the wind had dropped completely, but Gurov and Anna were still standing there as though waiting to see if someone else would come off the boat. Anna Sergeyevna was no longer talking. She was smelling her flowers without looking at Gurov.

"It's a nice evening," he said. "Where shall we go now? Shall we go for a drive?"

25   She made no answer.

Then he looked keenly at her and suddenly put his arms round her and kissed her on the mouth. He felt the fragrance and dampness of the flowers and immediately looked around him fearfully; had anyone seen them?

"Let's go to your room," he said softly.

And both walked off quickly.

It was very close in her hotel room, which was full of the smell of the scents she had bought in a Japanese shop. Looking at her now, Gurov thought: "Life is full of strange encounters!" From his past he preserved the memory of carefree, good-natured women, whom love had made gay and who were grateful to him for the happiness he gave them, however short-lived; and of women like his wife, who made love without sincerity, with unnecessary talk, affectedly, hysterically, with such an expression, as though it were not love or passion, but something much more significant; and of two or three very beautiful, frigid women, whose faces suddenly lit up with a predatory expression, an obstinate desire to take, to snatch from life more than it could give; these were women no longer in their first youth, capricious, unreasoning, despotic, unintelligent women, and when Gurov lost interest in them, their beauty merely aroused hatred in him and the lace trimmings on their négligés looked to him then like the scales of a snake.

30   But here there was still the same diffidence and angularity of inexperienced youth—an awkward feeling; and there was also the impression of embarrassment, as if someone had just knocked at the door. Anna Sergeyevna, this lady with the lapdog, apparently regarded what had happened in a peculiar sort of way, very seriously, as though she had become a fallen woman—so it seemed to him, and he found it odd and disconcerting. Her features lengthened and drooped, and her long hair hung mournfully on either side of her face; she sank into thought in a despondent pose, like a woman taken in adultery in an old painting.

"It's wrong," she said. "You'll be the first not to respect me now."

There was a water-melon on the table. Gurov cut himself a slice and began to eat it slowly. At least half an hour passed in silence.

Anna Sergeyevna was very touching; there was an air of pure, decent naïve woman about her, a woman who had very little experience of life; the solitary candle burning on the table scarcely lighted up her face, but it was obvious that she was unhappy.

"But, darling, why should I stop respecting you?" Gurov asked. "You don't know yourself what you're saying."

35   "May God forgive me," she said, and her eyes filled with tears. "It's terrible."

"You seem to wish to justify yourself."

"How can I justify myself?" I am a bad, despicable creature. I despise myself and have no thought of justifying myself. I haven't deceived my husband, I've deceived myself. And not only now. I've been deceiving myself for a long time. My husband is, I'm sure, a good and honest man, but, you see, he is a flunkey. I don't know what he does at his office, all I know is that he is a flunkey. I was only twenty when I married him, I was eaten up by curiosity, I wanted something better. There surely must be a different kind of life, I said to myself. I wanted to live. To live, to live! I was burning with curiosity. I don't think you know what I am talking about, but I swear I could no longer control myself, something was happening to me. I could not be held back. I told my husband I was ill, and I came here. . . . Here too I was going about as though in a daze, as though I was mad, and now I've become a vulgar worthless woman whom everyone has a right to despise."

Gurov could not help feeling bored as he listened to her; he was irritated by her naïve tone of voice and her repentance, which was so unexpected and so out of place; but for the tears in her eyes, he might have thought that she was joking or play-acting.

"I don't understand," he said gently, "what it is you want."

40   She buried her face on his chest and clung close to him.

"Please, please believe me," she said. "I love a pure, honest life. I hate immorality. I don't know myself what I am doing. The common people say 'the devil led her astray,' I too can now say about myself that the devil has led me astray."

"There, there . . ." he murmured.

He gazed into her staring, frightened eyes, kissed her, spoke gently and affectionately to her, and gradually she calmed down and her cheerfulness returned; both of them were soon laughing.

Later, when they went out, there was not a soul on the promenade, the town with its cypresses looked quite dead, but the sea was still roaring and dashing itself against the shore; a single launch tossed on the waves, its lamp flickering sleepily.

45   They hailed a cab and drove to Oreanda.

"I've just found out your surname, downstairs in the lobby," said Gurov. "Von Diederitz. Is your husband a German?"

"No. I believe his grandfather was German. He is of the Orthodox faith himself."

In Oreanda they sat on a bench not far from the church, looked down on the sea, and were silent. Yalta could scarcely be seen through the morning mist. White clouds lay motionless on the mountain tops. Not a leaf stirred on the trees, the cicadas chirped, and the monotonous, hollow roar of the sea, coming up from below, spoke of rest, of eternal sleep awaiting us all. The sea had roared like that down below when there was no Yalta or Oreanda, it was roaring now, and it would go on roaring as indifferently and hollowly when we were here no more. And in this constancy, in this complete indifference to life and death of each one of us, there is perhaps hidden the guarantee of our eternal salvation, the neverceasing movement of life on earth, the never-ceasing movement towards perfection. Sitting beside a young woman who looked so beautiful at the break of day, soothed and enchanted by the sight of all that fairy-land scenery—the sea, the mountains, the clouds, the wide sky—Gurov reflected that, when you came to think of it, everything in the world was really really beautiful, everything but our own thoughts and actions when we lose sight of the higher aims of existence and our dignity as human beings.

Someone walked up to them, a watchman probably, looked at them, and went away. And there seemed to be something mysterious and also beautiful in this fact, too. They could see the Theodosia boat coming towards the pier, lit up by the sunrise, and with no lights.

50 "There's dew on the grass," said Anna Sergeyevna, breaking the silence.

"Yes. Time to go home."

They went back to town.

After that they met on the front every day at twelve o'clock, had lunch and dinner together, went for walks, admired the sea. She complained of sleeping badly and of her heart beating uneasily, asked the same questions, alternately worried by feelings of jealousy and by fear that he did not respect her sufficiently. And again and again in the park or in the square, when there was no one in sight, he would draw her to him and kiss her passionately. The complete idleness, these kisses in broad daylight, always having to look round for fear of someone watching them, the heat, the smell of the sea, and the constant looming into sight of idle, well-dressed, and well-fed people seemed to have made a new man of him; he told Anna Sergeyevna that she was beautiful, that she was desirable, made passionate love to her, never left her side, while she was often lost in thought and kept asking him to admit that he did not really respect her, that he was not in the least in love with her and only saw in her a vulgar woman. Almost every night they drove out of town, to Oreanda or to the waterfall; the excursion was always a success, and every time their impressions were invariably grand and beautiful.

They kept expecting her husband to arrive. But a letter came from him in which he wrote that he was having trouble with his eyes and implored his wife to return home as soon as possible. Anna Sergeyevna lost no time in getting ready for her journey home.

55 "It's a good thing I'm going," she said to Gurov. "It's fate."

She took a carriage to the railway station, and he saw her off. The drive took a whole day. When she got into the express train, after the second bell, she said:

"Let me have another look at you. . . . One last look. So."

She did not cry, but looked sad, just as if she were ill, and her face quivered.

"I'll be thinking of you, remembering you," she said. "Good-bye. You're staying, aren't you? Don't think badly of me. We are parting for ever. Yes, it must be so, for we should never have met. Well, good-bye. . . ."

60   The train moved rapidly out of the station; its lights soon disappeared, and a minute later it could not even be heard, just as though everything had conspired to put a quick end to this sweet trance, this madness. And standing alone on the platform gazing into the dark distance, Gurov listened to the chirping of the grasshoppers and the humming of the telegraph wires with a feeling as though he had just woken up. He told himself that this had been just one more affair in his life, just one more adventure, and that it too was over, leaving nothing but a memory. He was moved and sad, and felt a little penitent that the young woman, whom he would never see again, had not been happy with him; he had been amiable and affectionate with her, but all the same in his behavior to her, in the tone of his voice and in his caresses, there was a suspicion of light irony, the somewhat coarse arrogance of the successful male, who was, moreover, almost twice her age. All the time she called him good, wonderful, high-minded; evidently she must have taken him to be quite different from what he really was, which meant that he had involuntarily deceived her.

At the railway station there was already a whiff of autumn in the air; the evening was chilly.

"Time I went north, too," thought Gurov, as he walked off the platform. "High time!"

III

At home in Moscow everything was already like winter: the stoves were heated, and it was still dark in the morning when the children were getting ready to go to school and having breakfast, so that the nurse had to light the lamp for a short time. The frosts had set in. When the first snow falls and the first day one goes out for a ride in a sleigh, one is glad to see the white ground, the white roofs, the air is so soft and wonderful to breathe, and one remembers the days of one's youth. The old lime trees and birches, white with rime, have such a benignant look, they are nearer to one's heart than cypresses and palms, and beside them one no longer wants to think of mountains and the sea.

Gurov had been born and bred in Moscow, and he returned to Moscow on a fine frosty day; and when he put on his fur coat and warm gloves and took a walk down Petrovka Street, and when on Saturday evening he heard the church bells ringing, his recent holiday trip and the places he had visited lost their charm for him. Gradually he became immersed in Moscow life, eagerly reading three newspapers a day and declaring that he never read Moscow papers on principle. Once more, he could not resist the attraction of restaurants, clubs, banquets, and anniversary celebrations, and once more he felt flattered that well-known lawyers and actors came to see him and that in the Medical Club he played cards with a professor as his partner. Once again he was capable of eating a whole portion of the Moscow speciality of sour cabbage and meat served in a frying-pan. . . .

65   Another month and, he thought, nothing but a memory would remain of Anna Sergeyevna; he would remember her as through a haze and only occasionally dream of her with a wistful smile, as he did of the others before her. But over a month passed, winter was at its height, and he remembered her as clearly as though he had only parted from her the day before. His memories haunted him more and more persistently. Every time the voices of his children doing their homework reached him in his study in the stillness of the evening, every time he heard a popular song or some music in a restaurant, every time the wind howled in the chimney—it all came back to him: their walks on the pier, early morning with the mist on the mountains, the Theodosia boat, and the kisses. He kept pacing the room for hours remembering it all and smiling, and then his memories turned into daydreams and the past mingled in his imagination with what was going to happen. He did not dream of Anna Sergeyevna, she accompanied him everywhere like his shadow and followed him wherever he went. Closing his eyes, he saw her as clearly as if she were before him, and she seemed to him lovelier, younger, and tenderer than she had been; and he thought that he too was much better than he had been in Yalta. In the evenings she gazed at him from the bookcase, from the fireplace, from the corner—he heard her breathing, the sweet rustle of her dress. In the street he followed women with his eyes, looking for anyone who resembled her. . . .

He was beginning to be overcome by an overwhelming desire to share his memories with someone. But at home it was impossible to talk of his love, and outside his home there was no one he could talk to. Not the tenants who lived in his house, and certainly not his colleagues in the bank. And what was he to tell them? Had he been in love then? Had there been anything beautiful, poetic, edifying, or even anything interesting about his relations with Anna Sergeyevna? So he had to talk in general terms about love and women, and no one guessed what he was driving at, and his wife merely raised her black eyebrows and said:

"Really, Dimitry, the role of a coxcomb doesn't suit you at all!"

One evening, as he left the Medical Club with his partner, a civil servant, he could not restrain himself, and said:

"If you knew what a fascinating woman I met in Yalta!"

70   The civil servant got into his sleigh and was about to be driven off, but suddenly he turned round and called out:

"I say!"

"Yes?"

"You were quite right; the sturgeon *was* a bit off."

These words, so ordinary in themselves, for some reason hurt Gurov's feelings: they seemed to him humiliating and indecent. What savage manners! What faces! What stupid nights! What uninteresting, wasted days! Crazy gambling at cards, gluttony, drunkenness, endless talk about one and the same thing. Business that was of no use to anyone and talk about one and the same thing absorbed the greater part of one's time and energy, and what was left in the end was a sort of dock-tailed, barren life, a sort of nonsensical existence, and it was impossible to escape from it, just as though you were in a lunatic asylum or a convict chaingang!

75   Gurov lay awake all night, fretting and fuming, and had a splitting headache the whole of the next day. The following nights too he slept badly, sitting up in bed thinking, or walking up and down his room. He was tired of his children, tired of the bank, he did not feel like going out anywhere or talking about anything.

In December, during the Christmas holidays, he packed his things, told his wife that he was going to Petersburg to get a job for a young man he knew, and set off for the town of S———. Why? He had no very clear idea himself. He wanted to see Anna Sergeyevna, to talk to her, to arrange a meeting, if possible.

He arrived in S——— in the morning and took the best room in a hotel, with a fitted carpet of military grey cloth and an inkstand grey with dust on the table, surmounted by a horseman with raised hand and no head. The hall porter supplied him with all the necessary information: Von Diederitz lived in a house of his own in Old Potter's Street, not far from the hotel. He lived well, was rich, kept his own carriage horses, the whole town knew him. The hall-porter pronounced the name: Dridiritz.

Gurov took a leisurely walk down Old Potter's Street and found the house. In front of it was a long grey fence studded with upturned nails.

"A fence like that would make anyone wish to run away," thought Gurov, scanning the windows and the fence.

80   As it was a holiday, he thought, her husband was probably at home. It did not matter either way, though, for he could not very well embarrass her by calling at the house. If he were to send in a note it might fall into the hands of the husband and ruin everything. The best thing was to rely on chance. And he kept walking up and down the street and along the fence, waiting for his chance. He watched a beggar enter the gate and the dogs attack him; then, an hour later, he heard the faint indistinct sounds of a piano. That must have been Anna Sergeyevna playing. Suddenly the front door opened and an old woman came out, followed by the familiar white pomeranian. Gurov was about to call to the dog, but his heart began to beat violently and in his excitement he could not remember its name.

He went on walking up and down the street, hating the grey fence more and more, and he was already saying to himself that Anna Sergeyevna had forgotten him and had perhaps been having a good time with someone else, which was indeed quite natural for a young woman who had to look at that damned fence from morning till night. He went back to his hotel room and sat on the sofa for a long time, not knowing what to do, then he had dinner and after dinner a long sleep.

"How stupid and disturbing it all is," he thought, waking up and staring at the dark windows: it was already evening. "Well, I've had a good sleep, so what now? What am I going to do tonight?"

He sat on a bed covered by a cheap grey blanket looking exactly like a hospital blanket, and taunted himself in vexation:

"A *lady* with a lapdog! Some adventure, I must say! Serves you right!"

85　　At the railway station that morning he had noticed a poster announcing in huge letters the first performance of *The Geisha Girl* at the local theatre. He recalled it now, and decided to go to the theatre.

"Quite possibly she goes to first nights," he thought.

The theatre was full. As in all provincial theatres, there was a mist over the chandeliers and the people in the gallery kept up a noisy and excited conversation; in the first row of the stalls stood the local dandies with their hands crossed behind their backs; here, too, in the front seat of the Governor's box, sat the Governor's daughter, wearing a feather boa, while the Governor himself hid modestly behind the portière so that only his hands were visible; the curtain stirred, the orchestra took a long time tuning up. Gurov scanned the audience eagerly as they filed in and occupied their seats.

Anna Sergeyevna came in too. She took her seat in the third row, and when Gurov glanced at her his heart missed a beat and he realized clearly that there was no one in the world nearer and dearer or more important to him than that little woman with the stupid lorgnette in her hand, who was in no way remarkable. That woman lost in a provincial crowd now filled his whole life, was his misfortune, his joy, and the only happiness that he wished for himself. Listening to the bad orchestra and the wretched violins played by second-rate musicians, he thought how beautiful she was. He thought and dreamed.

A very tall, round-shouldered young man with small whiskers had come in with Anna Sergeyevna and sat down beside her; he nodded at every step he took and seemed to be continually bowing to someone. This was probably her husband, whom in a fit of bitterness at Yalta she had called a flunkey. And indeed there was something of a lackey's obsequiousness in his lank figure, his whiskers, and the little bald spot on the top of his head. He smiled sweetly, and the gleaming insignia of some scientific society which he wore in his buttonhole looked like the number on a waiter's coat.

90　　In the first interval the husband went out to smoke and she was left in her seat. Gurov, who also had a seat in the stalls, went up to her and said in a trembling voice and with a forced smile:

"Good evening!"

She looked up at him and turned pale, then looked at him again in panic, unable to believe her eyes, clenching her fan and lorgnette in her hand and apparently trying hard not to fall into a dead faint. Both were silent. She sat and he stood, frightened by her embarrassment and not daring to sit down beside her. The violinists and the flautist began tuning their instruments, and they suddenly felt terrified, as though they were being watched from all the boxes. But a moment later she got up and walked rapidly towards one of the exits; he followed her, and both of them walked aimlessly along corridors and up and down stairs. Figures in all sorts of uniforms—lawyers, teachers, civil servants, all wearing badges—flashed by them: ladies, fur coats hanging on pegs, the cold draught bringing with it the odour of cigarette-ends. Gurov, whose heart was beating violently, thought:

"Oh, Lord, what are all these people, that orchestra, doing here?"

At that moment, he suddenly remembered how after seeing Anna Sergeyevna off he had told himself that evening at the station that all was over and that they would never meet again. But how far they still were from the end!

95   She stopped on a dark, narrow staircase with a notice over it: "To the Upper Circle."

"How you frightened me!" she said, breathing heavily, still looking pale and stunned. "Oh, dear, how you frightened me! I'm scarcely alive. Why did you come? Why?"

"But, please, try to understand, Anna," he murmured hurriedly. "I beg you, please, try to understand. . . ."

She looked at him with fear, entreaty, love, looked at him intently, so as to fix his features firmly in her mind.

"I've suffered so much," she went on, without listening to him. "I've been thinking of you all the time. The thought of you kept me alive. And yet I tried so hard to forget you—why, oh, why did you come?"

100   On the landing above two schoolboys were smoking and looking down, but Gurov did not care. He drew Anna Sergeyevna towards him and began kissing her face, her lips, her hands.

"What are you doing? What are you doing?" she said in horror, pushing him away. "We've both gone mad. You must go back tonight, this minute. I implore you, by all that's sacred . . . Somebody's coming!"

Somebody was coming up the stairs.

"You must go back," continued Anna Sergeyevna in a whisper. "Do you hear? I'll come to you in Moscow. I've never been happy, I'm unhappy now, and I shall never be happy, never! So please don't make me suffer still more. I swear I'll come to you in Moscow. But now we must part. Oh, my sweet, my darling, we must part!"

She pressed his hand and went quickly down the stairs, looking back at him all the time, and he could see from the expression in her eyes that she really was unhappy. Gurov stood listening for a short time, and when all was quiet he went to look for his coat and left the theatre.

IV

105 Anna Sergeyevna began going to Moscow to see him. Every two or three months she left the town of S_____, telling her husband that she was going to consult a Moscow gynaecologist, and her husband believed and did not

believe her. In Moscow she stayed at the Slav Bazaar and immediately sent a porter in a red cap to inform Gurov of her arrival. Gurov went to her hotel, and no one in Moscow knew about it.

One winter morning he went to her hotel as usual (the porter had called with his message at his house the evening before, but he had not been in). He had his daughter with him, and he was glad of the opportunity of taking her to school, which was on the way to the hotel. Snow was falling in thick wet flakes.

"It's three degrees above zero," Gurov was saying to his daughter, "and yet it's snowing. But then, you see, it's only warm on the earth's surface, in the upper layers of the atmosphere the temperature's quite different."

"Why isn't there any thunder in winter, Daddy?"

He explained that, too. As he was speaking, he kept thinking that he was going to meet his mistress and not a living soul knew about it. He led a double life: one for all who were interested to see, full of conventional truth and conventional deception, exactly like the lives of his friends and acquaintances; and another which went on in secret. And by a kind of strange concatenation of circumstances, possibly quite by accident, everything that was important, interesting, essential, everything about which he was sincere and did not deceive himself, everything that made up the quintessence of his life, went on in secret, while everything that was a lie, everything that was merely the husk in which he hid himself to conceal the truth, like his work at the bank, for instance, his discussions at the club, his ideas of the lower breed, his going to anniversary functions with his wife—all that happened in the sight of all. He judged others by himself, did not believe what he saw, and was always of the opinion that every man's real and most interesting life went on in secret, under cover of night. The personal, private life of an individual was kept a secret, and perhaps that was partly the reason why civilized man was so anxious that his personal secrets should be respected.

110   Having seen his daughter off to her school, Gurov went to the Slav Bazaar. He took off his fur coat in the cloakroom, went upstairs, and knocked softly on the door. Anna Sergeyevna, wearing the grey dress he liked most, tired out by her journey and by the suspense of waiting for him, had been expecting him since the evening before; she was pale, looked at him without smiling, but was in his arms the moment he went into the room. Their kiss was long and lingering, as if they had not seen each other for two years.

"Well," he asked, "how are you getting on there? Anything new?"

"Wait, I'll tell you in a moment. . . . I can't . . ."

She could not speak because she was crying. She turned away from him and pressed her handkerchief to her eyes.

"Well, let her have her cry," he thought, sitting down in an armchair. "I'll wait."

115   Then he rang the bell and ordered tea; while he was having his tea, she was still standing there with her face to the window. She wept because she could not control her emotions, because she was bitterly conscious of the fact that their life was so sad: they could only meet in secret, they had to hide from people, like thieves! Was not their life ruined?

"Please stop crying!" he said.

It was quite clear to him that their love would not come to an end for a long time, if ever. Anna Sergeyevna was getting attached to him more and more strongly, she worshipped him, and it would have been absurd to tell her that all this would have to come to an end one day. She would not have believed it, anyway.

He went up to her and took her by the shoulders, wishing to be nice to her, to make her smile; and at that moment he caught sight of himself in the looking glass.

His hair was already beginning to turn grey. It struck him as strange that he should have aged so much, that he should have lost his good looks in the last few years. The shoulders on which his hands lay were warm and quivering. He felt so sorry for this life, still so warm and beautiful, but probably soon to fade and wilt like his own. Why did she love him so? To women he always seemed different from what he was, and they loved in him not himself, but the man their imagination conjured up and whom they had eagerly been looking for all their lives; and when they discovered their mistake they still loved him. And not one of them had ever been happy with him. Time had passed, he had met women, made love to them, parted from them, but not once had he been in love; there had been everything between them, but no love.

120 It was only now, when his hair was beginning to turn grey, that he had fallen in love properly, in good earnest for the first time in his life.

He and Anna Sergeyevna loved each other as people do who are very dear and near, as man and wife or close friends love each other; they could not help feeling that fate itself had intended them for one another, and they were unable to understand why he should have a wife and she a husband; they were like two migrating birds, male and female, who had been caught and forced to live in separate cages. They had forgiven each other what they had been ashamed of in the past, and forgave each other everything in their present, and felt that this love of theirs had changed them both.

Before, when he felt depressed, he had comforted himself by all sorts of arguments that happened to occur to him on the spur of the moment, but now he had more serious things to think of, he felt profound compassion, he longed to be sincere, tender. . . .

"Don't cry, my sweet," he said. "That'll do, you've had your cry. . . . Let's talk now, let's think of something."

Then they had a long talk. They tried to think how they could get rid of the necessity of hiding, telling lies, living in different towns, not seeing one another for so long. How were they to free themselves from their intolerable chains?

125 "How? How?" he asked himself, clutching at his head. "How?"

And it seemed to them that in only a few more minutes a solution would be found and a new, beautiful life would begin; but both of them knew very well that the end was still a long, long way away and that the most complicated and difficult part was only just beginning.

■ EXPLORATIONS OF THE TEXT ■

1. Analyze Dmitry Gurov's attitude toward women in Part I. Why has he been "unfaithful" to his wife? Why does he describe women as the "lower breed"?
2. Discuss Anna Sergeyevna's character. Why does she have an affair with Gurov?
3. After lovemaking, why does Anna consider herself "a bad, despicable creature"? Is Gurov sympathetic to her?
4. Explain the symbolism of the landscape of Oreanda.
5. After they return to their homes and spouses, do the feelings of Anna and Gurov for each other change?
6. Interpret the ending. Do Anna and Gurov have a deep commitment to each other? Are they deluded?
7. What critique of Russian society and culture is apparent in the story?

■■ JOURNAL ENTRIES ■■

1. With which character do you most sympathize? Why?
2. Explain a love relationship that changed your life or that changed you.

■■■ IDEAS FOR WRITING ■■■

1. Chekhov said about his fictional method that he was not a judge of human character; he simply presented problems. Does this story support his view of his fictional strategy?
2. Chekhov is considered a master of the short story. What are his strengths as a fiction writer? (See the evaluation checklist in Chapter 9.)
3. Explore the theme of delusion in love or of fatal attraction in this story. You also may refer to another work from this chapter.

Death of a Son

Njabulo S. Ndebele

Njabulo S. Ndebele was born and grew up in Charterston Location, a township in South Africa. Educated at Cambridge University where he received an M.A. and at the University of Denver where he earned a Ph.D., he currently teaches African, African-American, and

English literature at the University College of Roma, Lesotho. His volume of short stories, Fools *(1983) is set in a town like Charterston Location and portrays his childhood world. In a 1984 essay, Ndebele urges black writers to create stories that abjure polemic and stereotyping and that represent "lived experience in all its complexities."*

This story exhibits Ndebele's concern both with the "lived experience" of men and women and with the injustice of apartheid. The story also portrays the difference between a man's and a woman's responses to the tragedy of the death of a son.

1   At last we got the body. Wednesday. Just enough time for a Saturday funeral. We were exhausted. Empty. The funeral still ahead of us. We had to find the strength to grieve. There had been no time for grief, really. Only much bewilderment and confusion. Now grief. For isn't grief the awareness of loss?

That is why when we finally got the body, Buntu said: "Do you realize our son is dead?" I realized. Our awareness of the death of our first and only child had been displaced completely by the effort to get his body. Even the horrible events that caused the death: we did not think of them, as such. Instead, the numbing drift of things took over our minds: the pleas, letters to be written, telephone calls to be made, telegrams to be dispatched, lawyers to consult, "influential" people to "get in touch with," undertakers to be contacted, so much walking and driving. That is what suddenly mattered: the irksome details that blur the goal (no matter how terrible it is), each detail becoming a door which, once unlocked, revealed yet another door. Without being aware of it, we were distracted by the smell of the skunk and not by what the skunk had done.

We realized something too, Buntu and I, that during the two-week effort to get our son's body, we had drifted apart. For the first time in our marriage, our presence to each other had become a matter of habit. He was there. He'll be there. And I'll be there. But when Buntu said: "Do you realize our son is dead?" he uttered a thought that suddenly brought us together again. It was as if the return of the body of our son was also our coming together. For it was only at that moment that we really began to grieve; as if our lungs had suddenly begun to take in air when just before, we were beginning to suffocate. Something with meaning began to emerge.

We realized. We realized that something else had been happening to us, adding to the terrible events. Yes, we had drifted apart. Yet, our estrangement, just at that moment when we should have been together, seemed disturbingly comforting to me. I was comforted in a manner I did not quite understand.

5   The problem was that I had known all along that we would have to buy the body anyway. I had known all along. Things would end that way. And when things turned out that way, Buntu could not look me in the eye. For he had said: "Over my dead body! Over my dead body!" as soon as we knew we

would be required to pay the police or the government for the release of the body of our child.

"Over my dead body! Over my dead body!" Buntu kept on saying.

Finally, we bought the body. We have the receipt. The police insisted we take it. That way, they would be "protected." It's the law, they said.

I suppose we could have got the body earlier. At first I was confused, for one is supposed to take comfort in the heroism of one's man. Yet, inwardly, I could draw no comfort from his outburst. It seemed hasty. What sense was there to it when all I wanted was the body of my child? What would happen if, as events unfolded, it became clear that Buntu would not give up his life? What would happen? What would happen to him? To me?

For the greater part of two weeks, all of Buntu's efforts, together with friends, relatives, lawyers and the newspapers, were to secure the release of the child's body without the humiliation of having to pay for it. A "fundamental principle."

10   Why was it difficult for me to see the wisdom of the principle? The worst thing, I suppose, was worrying about what the police may have been doing to the body of my child. How they may have been busy prying it open "to determine the cause of death"?

Would I want to look at the body when we finally got it? To see further mutilations in addition to the "cause of death"? What kind of mother would not want to look at the body of her child? people will ask. Some will say: "It's grief." She is too grief-stricken.

"But still . . . ," they will say. And the elderly among them may say: "Young people are strange."

But how can they know? It was not that I would not want to see the body of my child, but that I was too afraid to confront the horrors of my own imagination. I was haunted by the thought of how useless it had been to have created something. What had been the point of it all? This body filling up with a child. The child steadily growing into something that could be seen and felt. Moving, as it always did, at that time of day when I was all alone at home waiting for it. What had been the point of it all?

How can they know that the mutilation to determine "the cause of death" ripped my own body? Can they think of a womb feeling hunted? Disgorged?

15   And the milk that I still carried. What about it? What had been the point of it all?

Even Buntu did not seem to sense that that principle, the "fundamental principle," was something too intangible for me at that moment, something that I desperately wanted should assume the form of my child's body. He still seemed far from ever knowing.

I remember one Saturday morning early in our courtship, as Buntu and I walked hand-in-hand through town, window-shopping. We cannot even be said to have been window-shopping, for we were aware of very little that was not ourselves. Everything in those windows was merely an excuse for words to pass between us.

We came across three girls sitting on the pavement, sharing a packet of fish and chips after they had just bought it from a nearby Portuguese cafe. Buntu said: "I want fish and chips too." I said: "So seeing is desire." I said: "My man is greedy!" We laughed. I still remember how he tightened his grip on my hand. The strength of it!

Just then, two white boys coming in the opposite direction suddenly rushed at the girls, and, without warning, one of them kicked the packet of fish and chips out of the hands of the girl who was holding it. The second boy kicked away the rest of what remained in the packet. The girl stood up, shaking her hand as if to throw off the pain in it. Then she pressed it under her armpit as if to squeeze the pain out of it. Meanwhile, the two boys went on their way laughing. The fish and chips lay scattered on the pavement and on the street like stranded boats on a river that had gone dry.

20   "Just let them do that to you!" said Buntu, tightening once more his grip on my hand as we passed on like sheep that had seen many of their own in the flock picked out for slaughter. We would note the event and wait for our turn. I remember I looked at Buntu, and saw his face was somewhat glum. There seemed no connection between that face and the words of reassurance just uttered. For a while, we went on quietly. It was then that I noticed his grip had grown somewhat limp. Somewhat reluctant. Having lost its self-assurance, it seemed to have been holding on because it had to, not because of a confident sense of possession.

It was not to be long before his words were tested. How could fate work this way, giving to words meanings and intentions they did not carry when they were uttered? I saw that day, how the language of love could so easily be trampled underfoot, or scattered like fish and chips on the pavement, and left stranded and abandoned like boats in a river that suddenly went dry. Never again was love to be confirmed with words. The world around us was too hostile for vows of love. At any moment, the vows could be subjected to the stress of proof. And love died. For words of love need not be tested.

On that day, Buntu and I began our silence. We talked and laughed, of course, but we stopped short of words that would demand proof of action. Buntu knew. He knew the vulnerability of words. And so he sought to obliterate words with acts that seemed to promise redemption.

On that day, as we continued with our walk in town, that Saturday morning, coming up towards us from the opposite direction, was a burly Boer[1] walking with his wife and two children. They approached Buntu and me with an ominously determined advance. Buntu attempted to pull me out of the way, but I never had a chance. The Boer shoved me out of the way, as if clearing a path for his family. I remember, I almost crashed into a nearby fashion display window. I remember, I glanced at the family walking away, the mother and the father each dragging a child. It was for one of those children that I had been cleared away. I remember, also, that as my tears came out, blurring

---

[1] A South African of Dutch lineage.

the Boer family and everything else, I saw and felt deeply what was inside of me: a desire to be avenged.

But nothing happened. All I heard was Buntu say: "The dog!" At that very moment, I felt my own hurt vanish like a wisp of smoke. And as my hurt vanished, it was replaced, instead, by a tormenting desire to sacrifice myself for Buntu. Was it something about the powerlessness of the curse and the desperation with which it had been made? The filling of stunned silence with an utterance? Surely it ate into him, revealing how incapable he was of meeting the call of his words.

25   And so it was, that that afternoon, back in the township, left to ourselves at Buntu's home, I gave in to him for the first time. Or should I say I offered myself to him? Perhaps from some vague sense of wanting to heal something in him? Anyway, we were never to talk about that event. Never. We buried it alive deep inside of me that afternoon. Would it ever be exhumed? All I vaguely felt and knew was that I had the keys to the vault. That was three years ago, a year before we married.

The cause of death? One evening I returned home from work, particularly tired after I had been covering more shootings by the police in the East Rand. Then I had hurried back to the office in Johannesburg to piece together on my typewriter the violent scenes of the day, and then to file my report to meet the deadline. It was late when I returned home, and when I got there, I found a crowd of people in the yard. They were those who could not get inside. I panicked. What had happened? I did not ask those who were outside, being desperate to get into the house. They gave way easily when they recognized me.

Then I heard my mother's voice. Her cry rose well above the noise. It turned into a scream when she saw me. "What is it, mother?" I asked, embracing her out of a vaguely despairing sense of terror. But she pushed me away with an hysterical violence that astounded me.

"What misery have I brought you, my child?" she cried. At that point, many women in the room began to cry too. Soon, there was much wailing in the room, and then all over the house. The sound of it! The anguish! Understanding, yet eager for knowledge, I became desperate. I had to hold onto something. The desire to embrace my mother no longer had anything to do with comforting her; for whatever she had done, whatever its magnitude, had become inconsequential. I needed to embrace her for all the anguish that tied everyone in the house into a knot. I wanted to be part of that knot, yet I wanted to know what had brought it about.

Eventually, we found each other, my mother and I, and clasped each other tightly. When I finally released her, I looked around at the neighbors and suddenly had a vision of how that anguish had to be turned into a simmering kind of indignation. The kind of indignation that had to be kept at bay only because there was a higher purpose at that moment: the sharing of concern.

30   Slowly and with a calmness that surprised me, I began to gather the details of what had happened. Instinctively, I seemed to have been gathering notes for a news report.

It happened during the day, when the soldiers and the police that had been patrolling the township in their Casspirs[2] began to shoot in the streets at random. Need I describe what I did not see? How did the child come to die just at that moment when the police and the soldiers began to shoot at random, at any house, at any moving thing? That was how one of our windows was shattered by a bullet. And that was when my mother, who looked after her grandchild when we were away at work, panicked. She picked up the child and ran to the neighbors. It was only when she entered the neighbor's house that she noticed the wetness of the blanket that covered the child she held to her chest as she ran for the sanctuary of neighbors. She had looked at her unaccountably bloody hand, then she noted the still bundle in her arms, and began at that moment to blame herself for the death of her grandchild. . .

Later, the police, on yet another round of shooting, found people gathered at our house. They stormed in, saw what had happened. At first, they dragged my mother out, threatening to take her away unless she agreed not to say what had happened. But then they returned and, instead, took the body of the child away. By what freak of logic did they hope that by this act their carnage would never be discovered?

That evening, I looked at Buntu closely. He appeared suddenly to have grown older. We stood alone in an embrace in our bedroom. I noticed, when I kissed his face, how his once lean face had grown suddenly puffy.

At that moment, I felt the familiar impulse come upon me once more, the impulse I always felt when I sensed that Buntu was in some kind of danger, the impulse to yield something of myself to him. He wore the look of someone struggling to gain control of something. Yet, it was clear he was far from controlling anything. I knew that look. Had seen it many times. It came at those times when I sensed that he faced a wave that was infinitely stronger than he, that it would certainly sweep him away, but that he had to seem to be struggling. I pressed myself tightly to him as if to vanish into him; as if only the two of us could stand up to the wave.

35   "Don't worry," he said. "Don't worry. I'll do everything in my power to right this wrong. Everything. Even if it means suing the police!" We went silent.

I knew that silence. But I knew something else at that moment: that I had to find a way of disengaging myself from the embrace.

Suing the police? I listened to Buntu outlining his plans. "Legal counsel. That's what we need," he said. "I know some people in Pretoria,"[3] he said. As he spoke, I felt the warmth of intimacy between us cooling. When he finished, it was cold. I disengaged from his embrace slowly, yet purposefully. Why had Buntu spoken?

Later, he was to speak again, when all his plans had failed to work: "Over my dead body! Over my dead body!"

---

[2] Armored trucks.
[3] The administrative capital of the Republic of South Africa.

He sealed my lips. I would wait for him to feel and yield one day to all the realities of misfortune.

40   Ours was a home, it could be said. It seemed a perfect life for a young couple: I, a reporter; Buntu, a personnel officer at an American factory manufacturing farming implements. He had traveled to the United States and returned with a mind fired with dreams. We dreamed together. Much time we spent, Buntu and I, trying to make a perfect home. The occasions are numerous on which we paged through *Femina, Fair Lady, Cosmopolitan, Home Garden, Car,* as if somehow we were going to surround our lives with the glossiness in the magazines. Indeed, much of our time was spent window-shopping through the magazines. This time, it was different from the window-shopping we did that Saturday when we courted. This time our minds were consumed by the things we saw and dreamed of owning: the furniture, the fridge, TV, videocassette recorders, washing machines, even a vacuum cleaner and every other imaginable thing that would ensure a comfortable modern life.

Especially when I was pregnant. What is it that Buntu did not buy, then? And when the boy was born, Buntu changed the car. A family, he would say, must travel comfortably.

The boy became the center of Buntu's life. Even before he was born, Buntu had already started making inquiries at white private schools. That was where he would send his son, the bearer of his name.

Dreams! It is amazing how the horrible findings of my newspaper reports often vanished before the glossy magazines of our dreams, how I easily forgot that the glossy images were concocted out of the keys of typewriters, made by writers whose business was to sell dreams at the very moment that death pervaded the land. So powerful are words and pictures that even their makers often believe in them.

Buntu's ordeal was long. So it seemed. He would get up early every morning to follow up the previous day's leads regarding the body of our son. I wanted to go with him, but each time I prepared to go he would shake his head.

45   "It's my task," he would say. But every evening he returned, empty-handed, while with each day that passed and we did not know where the body of my child was, I grew restive and hostile in a manner that gave me much pain. Yet Buntu always felt compelled to give a report on each day's events. I never asked for it. I suppose it was his way of dealing with my silence.

One day he would say: "The lawyers have issued a court order that the body be produced. The writ of *habeas corpus.* "[4]

On another day he would say: "We have petitioned the Minister of Justice."

On yet another he would say: "I was supposed to meet the Chief Security Officer. Waited the whole day. At the end of the day they said I would see him tomorrow if he was not going to be too busy. They are stalling."

Then he would say: "The newspapers, especially yours, are raising the hue and cry. The government is bound to be embarrassed. It's a matter of time."

---

[4] Literally translated—to produce the body. Legal jurisdiction to prevent false imprisonment.

50   And so it went on. Every morning he got up and left. Sometimes alone, sometimes with friends. He always left to bear the failure alone.

How much did I care about lawyers, petitions and Chief Security Officers? A lot. The problem was that whenever Buntu spoke about his efforts, I heard only his words. I felt in him the disguised hesitancy of someone who wanted reassurance without asking for it. I saw someone who got up every morning and left not to look for results, but to search for something he could only have found with me.

And each time he returned, I gave my speech to my eyes. And he answered without my having parted my lips. As a result, I sensed, for the first time in my life, a terrible power in me that could make him do anything. And he would never ever be able to deal with that power as long as he did not silence my eyes and call for my voice.

And so, he had to prove himself. And while he left each morning, I learned to be brutally silent. Could he prove himself without me? Could he? Then I got to know, those days, what I'd always wanted from him. I got to know why I have always drawn him into me whenever I sensed his vulnerability.

I wanted him to be free to fear. Wasn't there greater strength that way? Had he ever lived with his own feelings? And the stress of life in this land: didn't it call out for men to be heroes? And should they live up to it even though the details of the war to be fought may often be blurred? They should.

55   Yet it is precisely for that reason that I often found Buntu's thoughts lacking in strength. They lacked the experience of strife that could only come from a humbling acceptance of fear and then, only then, the need to fight it.

Me? In a way, I have always been free to fear. The prerogative of being a girl. It was always expected of me to scream when a spider crawled across the ceiling. It was known I would jump onto a chair whenever a mouse blundered into the room.

Then, once more, the Casspirs came. A few days before we got the body back, I was at home with my mother when we heard the great roar of truck engines. There was much running and shouting in the streets. I saw them, as I've always seen them on my assignments: the Casspirs. On five occasions they ran down our street at great speed, hurling tear-gas canisters at random. On the fourth occasion, they got our house. The canister shattered another window and filled the house with the terrible pungent choking smoke that I had got to know so well. We ran out of the house gasping for fresh air.

So, this was how my child was killed? Could they have been the same soldiers? Now hardened to their tasks? Or were they new ones being hardened to their tasks? Did they drive away laughing? Clearing paths for their families? What paths?

And was this our home? It couldn't be. It had to be a little bird's nest waiting to be plundered by a predator bird. There seemed no sense to the wedding pictures on the walls, the graduation pictures, birthday pictures, pictures of relatives, and paintings of lush landscapes. There seemed no sense anymore to what seemed recognizably human in our house. It took only a random swoop to obliterate personal worth, to blot out any value there may have been to the past. In desperation, we began to live only for the moment. I do feel hunted.

60   It was on the night of the tear gas that Buntu came home, saw what had happened, and broke down in tears. They had long been in the coming. . .

My own tears welled out too. How much did we have to cry to refloat stranded boats? I was sure they would float again.

A few nights later, on the night of the funeral, exhausted, I lay on my bed, listening to the last of the mourners leaving. Slowly, I became conscious of returning to the world. Something came back after it seemed not to have been there for ages. It came as a surprise, as a reminder that we will always live around what will happen. The sun will rise and set, and the ants will do their endless work, until one day the clouds turn gray and rain falls, and even in the township, the ants will fly out into the sky. Come what may.

My moon came, in a heavy surge of blood. And, after such a long time, I remembered the thing Buntu and I had buried in me. I felt it as if it had just entered. I felt it again as it floated away on the surge. I would be ready for another month. Ready as always, each and every month, for new beginnings.

And Buntu? I'll be with him, now. Always. Without our knowing, all the trying events had prepared for us new beginnings. Shall we not prevail?

■ EXPLORATIONS OF THE TEXT ■

1. Why does Buntu not want to pay to have the body returned? Why is the "fundamental principle" so important to him?
2. Why does the narrator not care about this principle? What is her reaction to the death of her child and to the return of the body?
3. What is the purpose of the flashback to the "fish and chips" episode and to the confrontation with the Boers? What do the episodes reveal about the narrator's and Buntu's characters?
4. What is the meaning of the symbolism of the "stranded boats on a river that had gone dry"?
5. In the bedroom on the evening that the child has been killed, how does the narrator respond to the death? How does Buntu respond?
6. Why does Buntu have "to prove himself"?
7. What are the reasons for the rift between Buntu and the narrator? What does the "silence" between them suggest about their relationship and their possibly different ways of dealing with emotions?
8. What does the son represent in their lives?
9. What is the narrator's state of mind at the end of the story? Is the ending believable? falsely optimistic?
10. What do you learn about apartheid in South Africa and its impact on love relationships? family life? development of selfhood?

■■ JOURNAL ENTRIES ■■

1. It is unusual for writers to create first-person narrators of the opposite sex. How successfully does Ndebele convey the state of mind of a female narrator who has lost her child?
2. React to the vision of apartheid in this work.

■■■ IDEAS FOR WRITING ■■■

1. "No one is safe in this world." "No one can protect his/her child." Respond to one of these quotations in light of experience in the United States or in another country with which you are familiar.
2. Contrast the characters of the narrator and Buntu.

Hills Like White Elephants

Ernest Hemingway

Born in Oak Park, Illinois, Ernest Hemingway (1899–1961) served as an ambulance driver during World War I and was severely wounded. After the war, he lived in Paris among many artists and intellectuals who comprised the "Lost Generation."

Encouraged by Ezra Pound, Gertrude Stein, and others, Hemingway published a collection of stories, In Our Time *(1925). His famous novel about the post-war generation,* The Sun Also Rises, *appeared in 1926. After the publication of* A Farewell to Arms *in 1929, many considered him the most influential writer of fiction in the English language in the first half of the twentieth century. To* Have and Have Not *(1937),* For Whom the Bell Tolls *(1940), and* Across the River and into the Trees *(1950) followed. In 1953, he won the Pulitzer Prize for* The Old Man and the Sea, *and he was awarded the Nobel Prize for Literature in 1954. Posthumous publications include* A Movable Feast *(1964) and* The Garden of Eden *(1987).*

Known for his style, Hemingway developed a concise method for evolving conflict through dialogue; his code of "grace under pressure," his heroes, and his insistence on risk have made him legendary. He once compared the power of writing to an iceberg; "there is seven-eighths of it under water for every part that shows. Anything you know you can eliminate, and it only strengthens your iceberg. It is the part that doesn't show."

"Hills Like White Elephants" portrays a young couple caught in a disintegrating relationship.

1 The hills across the valley of the Ebro[1] were long and white. On this side there was no shade and no trees and the station was between two lines of rails in the sun. Close against the side of the station there was the warm shadow of the building and a curtain, made of strings of bamboo beads, hung across the open door into the bar, to keep out flies. The American and the girl with him sat at a table in the shade, outside the building. It was very hot and the express from Barcelona would come in forty minutes. It stopped at this junction for two minutes and went on to Madrid.

"What should we drink?" the girl asked. She had taken off her hat and put it on the table.

"It's pretty hot," the man said.

"Let's drink beer."

5 "Dos cervezas,"[2] the man said into the curtain.

"Big ones?" a woman asked from the doorway.

"Yes. Two big ones."

The woman brought two glasses of beer and two felt pads. She put the felt pads and the beer glasses on the table and looked at the man and the girl. The girl was looking off at the line of hills. They were white in the sun and the country was brown and dry.

"They look like white elephants," she said.

10 "I've never seen one," the man drank his beer.

"No, you wouldn't have."

"I might have," the man said. "Just because you say I wouldn't have doesn't prove anything."

The girl looked at the bead curtain. "They've painted something on it," she said. "What does it say?"

"Anis del Toro. It's a drink."

15 "Could we try it?"

The man called "Listen" through the curtain. The woman came out from the bar.

"Four reales."

"We want two Anis del Toro."

"With water?"

20 "Do you want it with water?"

"I don't know," the girl said. "Is it good with water?"

"It's all right."

"You want them with water?" asked the woman.

"Yes, with water."

25 "It tastes like licorice," the girl said and put the glass down.

"That's the way with everything."

---

[1] River in Spain.
[2] Two beers.

"Yes," said the girl. "Everything tastes of licorice. Especially all the things you've waited so long for, like absinthe."

"Oh, cut it out."

"You started it," the girl said. "I was being amused. I was having a fine time."

30 "Well, let's try and have a fine time."

"All right. I was trying. I said the mountains looked like white elephants. Wasn't that bright?"

"That was bright."

"I wanted to try this new drink. That's all we do, isn't it—look at things and try new drinks?"

"I guess so."

35 The girl looked across the hills.

"They're lovely hills," she said. "They don't really look like white elephants. I just meant the coloring of their skin through the trees."

"Should we have another drink?"

"All right."

The warm wind blew the bead curtain against the table.

40 "The beer's nice and cool," the man said.

"It's lovely," the girl said.

"It's really an awfully simple operation, Jig," the man said. "It's not really an operation at all."

The girl looked at the ground the table legs rested on.

"I know you wouldn't mind it, Jig. It's really not anything. It's just to let the air in."

45 The girl did not say anything.

"I'll go with you and I'll stay with you all the time. They just let the air in and then it's all perfectly natural."

"Then what will we do afterward?"

"We'll be fine afterward. Just like we were before."

"What makes you think so?"

50 "That's the only thing that bothers us. It's the only thing that's made us unhappy."

The girl looked at the bead curtain, put her hand out and took hold of two of the strings of beads.

"And you think then we'll be all right and be happy."

"I know we will. You don't have to be afraid. I've known lots of people that have done it."

"So have I," said the girl. "And afterward they were all happy."

55 "Well," the man said, "if you don't want to you don't have to. I wouldn't have you do it if you didn't want to. But I know it's perfectly simple."

"And you really want to?"

"I think it's the best thing to do. But I don't want you to do it if you don't really want to."

"And if I do it you'll be happy and things will be like they were and you'll love me?"

"I love you now. You know I love you."

60 "I know. But if I do it, then it will be nice again if I say things are like white elephants, and you'll like it?"

"I'll love it. I love it now but I just can't think about it. You know how I get when I worry."

"If I do it you won't every worry?"

"I won't worry about that because it's perfectly simple."

"Then I'll do it. Because I don't care about me."

65 "What do you mean?"

"I don't care about me."

"Well, I care about you."

"Oh, yes. But I don't care about me. And I'll do it and then everything will be fine."

The girl stood up and walked to the end of the station. Across, on the other side, were fields of grain and trees along the banks of the Ebro. Far away, beyond the river, were mountains. The shadow of a cloud moved across the field of grain and she saw the river through the trees.

70 "And we could have all this," she said. "And we could have everything and every day we make it more impossible."

"What did you say?"

"I said we could have everything."

"We can have everything."

"No, we can't."

75 "We can have the whole world."

"No, we can't."

"We can go everywhere."

"No, we can't. It isn't ours any more."

"It's ours."

80 "No, it isn't. And once they take it away, you never get it back."

"But they haven't taken it away."

"We'll wait and see."

"Come on back in the shade," he said. "You mustn't feel that way."

"I don't feel any way," the girl said. "I just know things."

85 "I don't want you to do anything that you don't want to do—"

"No that isn't good for me," she said. "I know. Could we have another beer?"

"All right. But you've got to realize—"

"I realize," the girl said. "Can't we maybe stop talking?"

They sat down at the table and the girl looked across at the hills on the dry side of the valley and the man looked at her and at the table.

90 "You've got to realize," he said, "that I don't want you to do it if you don't want to. I'm perfectly willing to go through with it if it means anything to you."

"Doesn't it mean anything to you? We could get along."

"Of course it does. But I don't want anybody but you. I don't want any one else. And I know it's perfectly simple."

"Yes, you know it's perfectly simple."

"It's all right for you to say that, but I do know it."

95   "Would you do something for me now?"

"I'd do anything for you."

"Would you please please please please please please please stop talking?"

He did not say anything but looked at the bags against the wall of the station. There were labels on them from all the hotels where they had spent nights.

"But I don't want you to," he said, "I don't care anything about it."

100   "I'll scream," the girl said.

The woman came out through the curtains with two glasses of beer and put them down on the damp felt pads. "The train comes in five minutes," she said.

"What did she say?" asked the girl.

"That the train is coming in five minutes."

The girl smiled brightly at the woman, to thank her.

105   "I'd better take the bags over to the other side of the station," the man said. She smiled at him.

"All right. Then come back and we'll finish the beer."

He picked up the two heavy bags and carried them around the station to the other tracks. He looked up the tracks but could not see the train. Coming back, he walked through the barroom, where people waiting for the train were drinking. He drank an Anis at the bar and looked at the people. They were all waiting reasonably for the train. He went out through the bead curtain. She was sitting at the table and smiled at him.

"Do you feel better?" he asked.

"I feel fine," she said. "There's nothing wrong with me. I feel fine."

■   **EXPLORATIONS OF THE TEXT**   ■

---

1.   What mood is created at the beginning of the story?
2.   Examine Jig's and the man's dialogue before the discussion of the operation. What can you infer about the woman's and the man's characters?
3.   What is "it"? "the operation"? How does the symbol of the "white elephant" relate to the operation?
4.   What is the source of the conflict between Jig and the man?
5.   What is Jig's state of mind? What are her concerns? Isolate statements that reveal her feelings.
6.   What are the man's reasons for wanting her to have "the operation"? Discuss his attitudes toward the woman and their relationship.
7.   Why does she want him to "please . . . please stop talking"?
8.   Explain the irony of Jig's last statement: "I feel fine. . . . There's nothing wrong with me. I feel fine."
9.   Evaluate the role of the setting. How does setting develop themes of the story?

■■ JOURNAL ENTRIES ■■

---

1. Imagine the couple after they take the train. What would you say to them if you were a marriage counselor?
2. Does Hemingway sympathize with either character? How can you tell?
3. Create a **monologue** in the voice of Jig or of the man several months or years later.

■■■ IDEAS FOR WRITING ■■■

---

1. Compare Hemingway's view of relationships with Ndebele's portrayal in "Death of a Son."
2. Why does Hemingway choose to present the story almost totally in **dialogue**? Evaluate this technique.
3. Compare Jig's possible feelings about love with the feeling of "the wave" in Paz's "My Life with the Wave."
4. Write about symbolism in the story.

The Dead

James Joyce

Born in Dublin, James Joyce (1882–1941) was the eldest child in a poor, Catholic family. Educated by Jesuits, he learned Latin and the classics and later graduated from University College, Dublin. He moved to Paris where he began writing short lyric poems, the beginnings of his great autobiographical novel, Stephen Hero—*later to become* A Portrait of the Artist as a Young Man—*and plays. Joyce rejected an ardent Irish nationalism, rebelled against Irish politics although he opposed British rule, rejected an orthodox religious stance, and lived in exile for the rest of his life in Europe. He returned only briefly to Ireland in 1903 to stay with his mother during her final illness. Here, he met his future wife, Nora Barnacle, and began to compose the stories that form* The Dubliners. *After his mother's death in 1904, he left Ireland, and returned only twice.*

Throughout his life, Joyce was plagued by inabilities to find publishers. Dubliners, *completed in 1904, did not appear until 1914 because the work was considered too controversial—too realistic for a staid, Victorian audience. This lapse in time allowed him to add "The Dead" to the volume. "The Dead" was the final work in the collection which Joyce intended as a portrayal of twentieth-century middle class life in Dublin. A Portrait of the Artist as a Young Man, published in 1916, focused on the development of the artistic sensibility and the growth of selfhood of its autobiographical central character, Stephen Daedalus. Ulysses, Joyce's masterpiece, was first published in 1922; but it was banned in this country until 1933. Joyce is considered one of the great literary innovators: developing the form of the modern short story and of the novel, experimenting with stream-of-consciousness, with narrative form, with language, with myth, and with symbol.*

Joyce also was keenly aware of the dangers of being immersed in a romance with the past, cut off from the present and from vital living. This tension between past and present informs "The Dead" and the choices that Gabriel, the narrator, and the other characters make.

1 Lily, the caretaker's daughter, was literally run off her feet. Hardly had she brought one gentleman into the little pantry behind the office on the ground floor and helped him off with his overcoat than the wheezy hall-door bell clanged again and she had to scamper along the bare hallway to let in another guest. It was well for her she had not to attend to the ladies also. But Miss Kate and Miss Julia had thought of that and had converted the bathroom upstairs into a ladies' dressing-room. Miss Kate and Miss Julia were there, gossiping and laughing and fussing, walking after each other to the head of the stairs, peering down over the banisters and calling down to Lily to ask her who had come.

It was always a great affair, the Misses Morkan's annual dance. Everybody who knew them came to it, members of the family, old friends of the family, the members of Julia's choir, any of Kate's pupils that were grown up enough and even some of Mary Jane's pupils too. Never once had it fallen flat. For years and years it had gone off in splendid style as long as anyone could remember; ever since Kate and Julia, after the death of their brother Pat, had left the house in Stoney Batter and taken Mary Jane, their only niece, to live with them in the dark gaunt house on Usher's Island,[1] the upper part of which they had rented from Mr Fulham, the corn-factor on the ground floor. That was a good thirty years ago if it was a day. Mary Jane, who was then a little girl in short clothes, was now the main prop of the household for she had the organ in Haddington Road. She had been through the Academy[2] and gave a pupils' concert every year in the upper room of the Antient Concert Rooms.[3] Many of her pupils belonged to better-class families on the Kingstown and Dalkey line. Old as they were, her aunts also did their share. Julia, though she was quite grey, was still the leading soprano in Adam and Eve's,[4] and Kate, being too feeble to go about much, gave music lessons to

---

[1] Broker dealing in grain; commodities broker.
[2] Royal Academy of Music.
[3] Building in which rooms could be rented for concerts.
[4] Church in Dublin.

beginners on the old square piano in the back room. Lily, the caretaker's daughter, did housemaid's work for them. Though their life was modest they believed in eating well; the best of everything: diamond-bone sirloins, three-shilling tea and the best bottled stout. But Lily seldom made a mistake in the orders so that she got on well with her three mistresses. They were fussy, that was all. But the only thing they would not stand was back answers.

Of course they had good reason to be fussy on such a night. And then it was long after ten o'clock and yet there was no sign of Gabriel and his wife. Besides they were dreadfully afraid that Freddy Malins might turn up screwed.[5] They would not wish for worlds that any of Mary Jane's pupils should see him under the influence; and when he was like that it was sometimes very hard to manage him. Freddy Malins always came late but they wondered what could be keeping Gabriel: and that was what brought them every two minutes to the banisters to ask Lily had Gabriel or Freddy come.

—O, Mr Conroy, said Lily to Gabriel when she opened the door for him, Miss Kate and Miss Julia thought you were never coming. Good-night, Mrs Conroy.

5 —I'll engage they did, said Gabriel, but they forget that my wife here takes three mortal hours to dress herself.

He stood on the mat, scraping the snow from his goloshes, while Lily led his wife to the foot of the stairs and called out:

—Miss Kate, here's Mrs Conroy.

Kate and Julia came toddling down the dark stairs at once. Both of them kissed Gabriel's wife, said she must be perished alive and asked was Gabriel with her.

—Here I am as right as the mail, Aunt Kate! Go on up, I'll follow, called out Gabriel from the dark.

10 He continued scraping his feet vigorously while the three women went upstairs, laughing, to the ladies' dressing-room. A light fringe of snow lay like a cape on the shoulders of his overcoat and like toecaps on the toes of his goloshes; and, as the buttons of his overcoat slipped with a squeaking noise through the snow-stiffened frieze, a cold fragrant air from out-of-doors escaped from crevices and folds.

—Is it snowing again, Mr Conroy? asked Lily.

She had preceded him into the pantry to help him off with his overcoat. Gabriel smiled at the three syllables she had given his surname and glanced at her. She was a slim, growing girl, pale in complexion and with hay-coloured hair. The gas in the pantry made her look still paler. Gabriel had known her when she was a child and used to sit on the lowest step nursing a rag doll.

—Yes, Lily, he answered, and I think we're in for a night of it.

He looked up at the pantry ceiling, which was shaking with the stamping and shuffling of feet on the floor above, listened for a moment to the piano

---

[5] Drunk.

and then glanced at the girl, who was folding his overcoat carefully at the end of a shelf.

15 —Tell me, Lily, he said in a friendly tone, do you still go to school?

—O no, sir, she answered. I'm done schooling this year and more.

—O, then, said Gabriel gaily, I suppose we'll be going to your wedding one of these fine days with your young man, eh?

The girl glanced back at him over her shoulder and said with great bitterness:

—The men that is now is only all palaver and what they can get out of you.

20 Gabriel coloured as if he felt he had made a mistake and, without looking at her, kicked off his goloshes and flicked actively with his muffler at his patent-leather shoes.

He was a stout tallish young man. The high colour of his cheeks pushed upwards even to his forehead where it scattered itself in a few formless patches of pale red; and on his hairless face there scintillated restlessly the polished lenses and the bright gilt rims of the glasses which screened his delicate and restless eyes. His glossy black hair was parted in the middle and brushed in a long curve behind his ears where it curled slightly beneath the groove left by his hat.

When he had flicked lustre into his shoes he stood up and pulled his waistcoat down more tightly on his plump body. Then he took a coin rapidly from his pocket.

—O Lily, he said, thrusting it into her hands, it's Christmastime, isn't it? Just . . . here's a little. . . .

He walked rapidly towards the door.

25 —O no, sir! cried the girl, following him. Really sir, I wouldn't take it.

—Christmastime! Christmastime! said Gabriel, almost trotting to the stairs and waving his hand to her in deprecation.

The girl, seeing that he had gained the stairs, called out after him:

—Well, thank you, sir.

He waited outside the drawing-room door until the waltz should finish, listening to the skirts that swept against it and to the shuffling of feet. He was still discomposed by the girl's bitter and sudden retort. It had cast a gloom over him which he tried to dispel by arranging his cuffs and the bows of his tie. Then he took from his waistcoat pocket a little paper and glanced at the headings he had made for his speech. He was undecided about the lines from Robert Browning[6] for he feared they would be above the heads of his hearers. Some quotation that they could recognise from Shakespeare or from the Melodies[7] would be better. The indelicate clacking of the men's heels and the shuffling of their soles reminded him that their grade of culture differed from his. He would only make himself ridiculous by quoting poetry to them which they could not understand. They would think that he was airing his

---

[6] English poet of the nineteenth century.
[7] Irish melodies by poet Thomas Moore (1779–1852).

superior education. He would fail with them just as he had failed with the girl in the pantry. He had taken up a wrong tone. His whole speech was a mistake from first to last, an utter failure.

30   Just then his aunts and his wife came out of the ladies' dressing-room. His aunts were two small plainly dressed old women. Aunt Julia was an inch or so the taller. Her hair, drawn low over the tops of her ears, was grey; and grey also, with darker shadows, was her large flaccid face. Though she was stout in build and stood erect her slow eyes and parted lips gave her the appearance of a woman who did not know where she was or where she was going. Aunt Kate was more vivacious. Her face, healthier than her sister's, was all puckers and creases, like a shrivelled red apple, and her hair, braided in the same old-fashioned way, had not lost its ripe nut colour.

They both kissed Gabriel frankly. He was their favourite nephew, the son of their dead elder sister, Ellen, who had married T. J. Conroy of the Port and Docks.[8]

—Gretta tells me you're not going to take a cab back to Monkstown tonight, Gabriel, said Aunt Kate.

—No, said Gabriel, turning to his wife, we had quite enough of that last year, hadn't we. Don't you remember, Aunt Kate, what a cold Gretta got out of it? Cab windows rattling all the way, and the east wind blowing in after we passed Merrion. Very jolly it was. Gretta caught a dreadful cold.

Aunt Kate frowned severely and nodded her head at every word.

35   —Quite right, Gabriel, quite right, she said. You can't be too careful.

—But as for Gretta there, said Gabriel, she'd walk home in the snow if she were let.

Mrs Conroy laughed.

—Don't mind him, Aunt Kate, she said. He's really an awful bother, what with green shades for Tom's eyes at night and making him do the dumbbells, and forcing Eva to eat the stirabout.[9] The poor child! And she simply hates the sight of it! . . . O, but you'll never guess what he makes me wear now!

She broke out into a peal of laughter and glanced at her husband, whose admiring and happy eyes had been wandering from her dress to her face and hair. The two aunts laughed heartily too, for Gabriel's solicitude was a standing joke with them.

40   —Goloshes! said Mrs Conroy. That's the latest. Whenever it's wet underfoot I must put on my goloshes. To-night even he wanted me to put them on, but I wouldn't. The next thing he'll buy me will be a diving suit.

Gabriel laughed nervously and patted his tie reassuringly while Aunt Kate nearly doubled herself, so heartily did she enjoy the joke. The smile soon faded from Aunt Julia's face and her mirthless eyes were directed towards her nephew's face. After a pause she asked:

—And what are goloshes, Gabriel?

---

[8] Governmental bureau.

[9] A kind of porridge.

—Goloshes, Julia! exclaimed her sister. Goodness me, don't you know what goloshes are? You wear them over your . . . over your boots, Gretta, isn't it?

—Yes, said Mrs Conroy. Guttapercha[10] things. We both have a pair now. Gabriel says everyone wears them on the continent.

45 —O, on the continent, murmured Aunt Julia, nodding her head slowly.

Gabriel knitted his brows and said, as if he were slightly angered:

—It's nothing very wonderful but Gretta thinks it very funny because she says the word reminds her of Christy Minstrels.[11]

—But tell me, Gabriel, said Aunt Kate, with brisk tact. Of course, you've seen about the room. Gretta was saying . . .

—O, the room is all right, replied Gabriel, I've taken one in the Gresham.

50 —To be sure, said Aunt Kate, by far the best thing to do. And the children, Gretta, you're not anxious about them?

—O, for one night, said Mrs Conroy. Besides, Bessie will look after them.

—To be sure, said Aunt Kate again. What a comfort it is to have a girl like that, one you can depend on! There's that Lily, I'm sure I don't know what has come over her lately. She's not the girl she was at all.

Gabriel was about to ask his aunt some questions on this point but she broke off suddenly to gaze after her sister who had wandered down the stairs and was craning her neck over the banisters.

—Now, I ask you, she said, almost testily, where is Julia going? Julia! Julia! Where are you going?

55 Julia, who had gone halfway down one flight, came back and announced blandly:

—Here's Freddy.

At the same moment a clapping of hands and a final flourish of the pianist told that the waltz had ended. The drawing-room door was opened from within and some couples came out. Aunt Kate drew Gabriel aside hurriedly and whispered into his ear:

—Slip down, Gabriel, like a good fellow and see if he's all right, and don't let him up if he's screwed. I'm sure he's screwed. I'm sure he is.

Gabriel went to the stairs and listened over the banisters. He could hear two persons talking in the pantry. Then he recognised Freddy Malins' laugh. He went down the stairs noisily.

60 —It's such a relief, said Aunt Kate to Mrs Conroy, that Gabriel is here. I always feel easier in my mind when he's here. . . . Julia, there's Miss Daly and Miss Power will take some refreshment. Thanks for your beautiful waltz, Miss Daly. It made lovely time.

A tall wizen-faced man, with a stiff grizzled moustache and swarthy skin, who was passing out with his partner said:

—And may we have some refreshment, too, Miss Morkan?

---

[10] Similar to rubber.

[11] Nineteenth-century minstrel show organized by Edwin T. Cristy.

—Julia, said Aunt Kate summarily, and here's Mr Browne and Miss Furlong. Take them in, Julia, with Miss Daly and Miss Power.

—I'm the man for the ladies, said Mr Browne, pursing his lips until his moustache bristled and smiling in all his wrinkles. You know, Miss Morkan, the reason they are so fond of me is—

65   He did not finish his sentence, but, seeing that Aunt Kate was out of earshot, at once led the three young ladies into the back room. The middle of the room was occupied by two square tables placed end to end, and on these Aunt Julia and the caretaker were straightening and smoothing a large cloth. On the sideboard were arrayed dishes and plates, and glasses and bundles of knives and forks and spoons. The top of the closed square piano served also as a sideboard for viands and sweets. At a smaller sideboard in one corner two young men were standing, drinking hop-bitters.

Mr Browne led his charges thither and invited them all, in jest, to some ladies' punch, hot, strong and sweet. As they said they never took anything strong he opened three bottles of lemonade for them. Then he asked one of the young men to move aside, and, taking hold of the decanter, filled out for himself a goodly measure of whisky. The young men eyed him respectfully while he took a trial sip.

—God help me, he said, smiling, it's the doctor's orders.

His wizened face broke into a broader smile, and the three young ladies laughed in musical echo to his pleasantry, swaying their bodies to and fro, with nervous jerks of their shoulders. The boldest said:

—O, now, Mr Browne, I'm sure the doctor never ordered anything of the kind.

70   Mr Browne took another sip of his whisky and said, with sidling mimicry:

—Well, you see, I'm like the famous Mrs Cassidy, who is reported to have said: *Now, Mary Grimes, if I don't take it, make me take it, for I feel I want it.*

His hot face had leaned forward a little too confidentially and he had assumed a very low Dublin accent so that the young ladies, with one instinct, received his speech in silence. Miss Furlong, who was one of Mary Jane's pupils, asked Miss Daly what was the name of the pretty waltz she had played: and Mr Browne, seeing that he was ignored, turned promptly to the two young men who were more appreciative.

A red-faced young woman, dressed in pansy, came into the room, excitedly clapping her hands and crying:

—Quadrilles! Quadrilles![12]

75   Close on her heels came Aunt Kate, crying:

—Two gentlemen and three ladies, Mary Jane!

—O, here's Mr Bergin and Mr Kerrigan, said Mary Jane. Mr Kerrigan, will you take Miss Power? Miss Furlong, may I get you a partner, Mr Bergin. O, that'll just do now.

—Three ladies, Mary Jane, said Aunt Kate.

---

[12] A kind of square dance.

The two young gentlemen asked the ladies if they might have the pleasure, and Mary Jane turned to Miss Daly.

80 —O, Miss Daly, you're really awfully good, after playing for the last two dances, but really we're so short of ladies to-night.

—I don't mind in the least, Miss Morkan.

—But I've a nice partner for you, Mr Bartell D'Arcy, the tenor. I'll get him to sing later on. All Dublin is raving about him.

—Lovely voice, lovely voice! said Aunt Kate.

As the piano had twice begun the prelude to the first figure Mary Jane led her recruits quickly from the room. They had hardly gone when Aunt Julia wandered slowly into the room, looking behind her at something.

85 —What is the matter, Julia? asked Aunt Kate anxiously. Who is it?

Julia, who was carrying a column of table-napkins, turned to her sister and said, simply, as if the question had surprised her:

—It's only Freddy, Kate, and Gabriel with him.

In fact right behind her Gabriel could be seen piloting Freddy Malins across the landing. The latter, a young man of about forty, was of Gabriel's size and build, with very round shoulders. His face was fleshy and pallid, touched with colour only at the thick hanging lobes of his ears and at the wide wings of his nose. He had coarse features, a blunt nose, a convex and receding brow, tumid and protruded lips. His heavy-lidded eyes and the disorder of his scanty hair made him look sleepy. He was laughing heartily in a high key at a story which he had been telling Gabriel on the stairs and at the same time rubbing the knuckles of his left fist backwards and forwards into his left eye.

—Good-evening, Freddy, said Aunt Julia.

90 Freddy Malins bade the Misses Morkan good-evening in what seemed an offhand fashion by reason of the habitual catch in his voice and then, seeing that Mr Browne was grinning at him from the sideboard, crossed the room on rather shaky legs and began to repeat in an undertone the story he had just told to Gabriel.

—He's not so bad, is he? said Aunt Kate to Gabriel.

Gabriel's brows were dark but he raised them quickly and answered:

O no, hardly noticeable.

—Now, isn't he a terrible fellow! she said. And his poor mother made him take the pledge[13] on New Year's Eve. But come on, Gabriel, into the drawing-room.

95 Before leaving the room with Gabriel she signalled to Mr Browne by frowning and shaking her forefinger in warning to and fro. Mr Browne nodded in answer and, when she had gone, said to Freddy Malins:

—Now, then, Teddy, I'm going to fill you out a good glass of lemonade just to buck you up.

Freddy Malins, who was nearing the climax of his story, waved the offer aside impatiently but Mr Browne, having first called Freddy Malins' attention

---

[13] A formal vow not to drink alcoholic beverages.

to a disarray in his dress, filled out and handed him a full glass of lemonade. Freddy Malins' left hand accepted the glass mechanically, his right hand being engaged in the mechanical readjustment of his dress. Mr Browne, whose face was once more wrinkling with mirth, poured out for himself a glass of whisky while Freddy Malins exploded, before he had well reached the climax of his story in a kink of high-pitched bronchitic laughter and, setting down his untasted and overflowing glass, began to rub the knuckles of his left fist backwards and forwards into his left eye, repeating words of his last phrase as well as his fit of laughter would allow him.

*   *   *

Gabriel could not listen while Mary Jane was playing her Academy piece, full of runs and difficult passages, to the hushed drawing-room. He liked music but the piece she was playing had no melody for him and he doubted whether it had any melody for the other listeners, though they had begged Mary Jane to play something. Four young men, who had come from the refreshment-room to stand in the doorway at the sound of the piano, had gone away quietly in couples after a few minutes. The only persons who seemed to follow the music were Mary Jane herself, her hands racing along the key-board or lifted from it at the pauses like those of a priestess in momentary imprecation, and Aunt Kate standing at her elbow to turn the page.

Gabriel's eyes, irritated by the floor, which glittered with beeswax under the heavy chandelier, wandered to the wall above the piano. A picture of the balcony scene in *Romeo and Juliet* hung there and beside it was a picture of the two murdered princes in the Tower[14] which Aunt Julia had worked in red, blue and brown wools when she was a girl. Probably in the school they had gone to as girls that kind of work had been taught, for one year his mother had worked for him as a birthday present a waistcoat of purple tabinet, with little foxes' heads upon it, lined with brown satin and having round mulberry buttons. It was strange that his mother had had no musical talent though Aunt Kate used to call her the brains carrier of the Morkan family. Both she and Julia had always seemed a little proud of their serious and matronly sister. Her photograph stood before the pierglass.[15] She held an open book on her knees and was pointing out something in it to Constantine who, dressed in a man-o'-war[16] suit, lay at her feet. It was she who had chosen the names for her sons for she was very sensible of the dignity of family life. Thanks to her, Constantine was now senior curate in Balbriggan and, thanks to her, Gabriel himself had taken his degree in the Royal University. A shadow passed over his face as he remembered her sullen opposition to his marriage. Some slighting phrases she had used still rankled in his memory;

---

[14] Sons of King Edward IV of England, Edward and Richard, murdered by order of King Richard III.

[15] Tall mirror.

[16] Sailor uniform.

she had once spoken of Gretta as being country cute and that was not true of Gretta at all. It was Gretta who had nursed her during all her last long illness in their house at Monkstown.

100   He knew that Mary Jane must be near the end of her piece for she was playing again the open melody with runs of scales after every bar and while he waited for the end the resentment died down in his heart. The piece ended with a trill of octaves in the treble and a final deep octave in the bass. Great applause greeted Mary Jane as, blushing and rolling up her music nervously, she escaped from the room. The most vigorous clapping came from the four young men in the doorway who had gone away to the refreshment-room at the beginning of the piece but had come back when the piano had stopped.

Lancers[17] were arranged. Gabriel found himself partnered with Miss Ivors. She was a frank-mannered talkative young lady, with a freckled face and prominent brown eyes. She did not wear a low-cut bodice and the large brooch which was fixed in front of her collar bore on it an Irish device.

When they had taken their places she said abruptly:

—I have a crow to pluck with you.[18]

—With me? said Gabriel.

105   She nodded her head gravely.

—What is it? asked Gabriel, smiling at her solemn manner.

—Who is G. C.? answered Miss Ivors, turning her eyes upon him.

Gabriel coloured and was about to knit his brows, as if he did not understand, when she said bluntly:

—O, innocent Amy! I have found out that you write for *The Daily Express.*[19] Now, aren't you ashamed of yourself?

110   —Why should I be ashamed of myself? asked Gabriel, blinking his eyes and trying to smile.

—Well, I'm ashamed of you, said Miss Ivors frankly. To say you'd write for a rag like that. I didn't think you were a West Briton.[20]

A look of perplexity appeared on Gabriel's face. It was true that he wrote a literary column every Wednesday in *The Daily Express,* for which he was paid fifteen shillings. But that did not make him a West Briton surely. The books he received for review were almost more welcome than the paltry cheque. He loved to feel the covers and turn over the pages of newly printed books. Nearly every day when his teaching in the college was ended he used to wander down the quays to the second-hand booksellers, to Hickey's on Bachelor's Walk, to Webb's or Massey's on Aston's Quay, or to O'Clohissey's in the by-street. He did not know how to meet her charge. He wanted to say that literature was above politics. But they were friends of many years' standing and their careers had been parallel, first at the University and then as teachers: he could not risk a grandiose phrase with her. He continued blinking his

---

[17] Set of quadrilles, danced sequentially.
[18] "I have a bone to pick with you."
[19] Newspaper which did not favor Irish liberation from England.
[20] Implication that Gabriel believes himself to be British, not Irish.

eyes and trying to smile and murmured lamely that he saw nothing political in writing reviews of books.

When their turn to cross had come he was still perplexed and inattentive. Miss Ivors promptly took his hand in a warm grasp and said in a soft friendly tone:

—Of course, I was only joking. Come, we cross now.

115   When they were together again she spoke of the University question[21] and Gabriel felt more at ease. A friend of hers had shown her his review of Browning's poems. That was how she had found out the secret: but she liked the review immensely. Then she said suddenly:

—O, Mr Conroy, will you come for an excursion to the Aran Isles[22] this summer? We're going to stay there a whole month. It will be splendid out in the Atlantic. You ought to come. Mr Clancy is coming, and Mr Kilkelly and Kathleen Kearney. It would be splendid for Gretta too if she'd come. She's from Connacht,[23] isn't she?

—Her people are, said Gabriel shortly.

—But you will come, won't you? said Miss Ivors, laying her warm hand eagerly on his arm.

—The fact is, said Gabriel, I have already arranged to go—

120   —Go where? asked Miss Ivors.

—Well, you know, every year I go for a cycling tour with some fellows and so—

—But where? asked Miss Ivors.

—Well, we usually go to France or Belgium or perhaps Germany, said Gabriel awkwardly.

—And why do you go to France and Belgium, said Miss Ivors, instead of visiting your own land?

125   —Well, said Gabriel, it's partly to keep in touch with the languages and partly for a change.

—And haven't you your own language to keep in touch with—Irish? asked Miss Ivors.

—Well, said Gabriel, if it comes to that, you know, Irish is not my language.

Their neighbours had turned to listen to the cross-examination. Gabriel glanced right and left nervously and tried to keep his good humour under the ordeal which was making a blush invade his forehead.

—And haven't you your own land to visit, continued Miss Ivors, that you know nothing of, your own people, and your own country?

130   —O, to tell you the truth, retorted Gabriel suddenly, I'm sick of my own country, sick of it!

—Why? asked Miss Ivors.

Gabriel did not answer for his retort had heated him.

---

[21] Argument concerning the lack of equal educational opportunities for Catholic Trinity College in Dublin.

[22] Islands off the west coast of Ireland, known for the preservation of tradition and language.

[23] Area in northwest Ireland.

—Why? repeated Miss Ivors.

They had to go visiting together and, as he had not answered her, Miss Ivors said warmly:

135 —Of course, you've no answer.

Gabriel tried to cover his agitation by taking part in the dance with great energy. He avoided her eyes for he had seen a sour expression on her face. But when they met in the long chain he was surprised to feel his hand firmly pressed. She looked at him from under her brows for a moment quizzically until he smiled. Then, just as the chain was about to start again, she stood on tiptoe and whispered into his ear:

—West Briton!

When the lancers were over Gabriel went away to a remote corner of the room where Freddy Malins' mother was sitting. She was a stout feeble old woman with white hair. Her voice had a catch in it like her son's and she stuttered slightly. She had been told that Freddy had come and that he was nearly all right. Gabriel asked her whether she had had a good crossing. She lived with her married daughter in Glasgow and came to Dublin on a visit once a year. She answered placidly that she had had a beautiful crossing and that the captain had been most attentive to her. She spoke also of the beautiful house her daughter kept in Glasgow, and of all the nice friends they had there. While her tongue rambled on Gabriel tried to banish from his mind all memory of the unpleasant incident with Miss Ivors. Of course the girl or woman, or whatever she was, was an enthusiast but there was a time for all things. Perhaps he ought not to have answered her like that. But she had no right to call him a West Briton before people, even in joke. She had tried to make him ridiculous before people, heckling him and staring at him with her rabbit's eyes.

He saw his wife making her way towards him through the waltzing couples. When she reached him she said into his ear:

140 —Gabriel, Aunt Kate wants to know won't you carve the goose as usual. Miss Daly will carve the ham and I'll do the pudding.

—All right, said Gabriel.

—She's sending in the younger ones first as soon as this waltz is over so that we'll have the table to ourselves.

—Were you dancing? asked Gabriel.

—Of course I was. Didn't you see me? What words had you with Molly Ivors?

145 —No words. Why? Did she say so?

—Something like that. I'm trying to get that Mr D'Arcy to sing. He's full of conceit, I think.

—There were no words, said Gabriel moodily, only she wanted me to go for a trip to the west of Ireland and I said I wouldn't.

His wife clasped her hands excitedly and gave a little jump.

—O, do go, Gabriel, she cried. I'd love to see Galway[24] again.

---

[24] City in western Ireland, capital of Connaught.

150   —You can go if you like, said Gabriel coldly.

She looked at him for a moment, then turned to Mrs Malins and said:

—There's a nice husband for you, Mrs Malins.

While she was threading her way back across the room Mrs Malins, without adverting to the interruption, went on to tell Gabriel what beautiful places there were in Scotland and beautiful scenery. Her son-in-law brought them every year to the lakes and they used to go fishing. Her son-in-law was a splendid fisher. One day he caught a fish, a beautiful big big fish, and the man in the hotel boiled it for their dinner.

Gabriel hardly heard what she said. Now that supper was coming near he began to think again about his speech and about the quotation. When he saw Freddy Malins coming across the room to visit his mother Gabriel left the chair free for him and retired into the embrasure of the window. The room had already cleared and from the back room came the clatter of plates and knives. Those who still remained in the drawing-room seemed tired of dancing and were conversing quietly in little groups. Gabriel's warm trembling fingers tapped the cold pane of the window. How cool it must be outside! How pleasant it would be to walk out alone, first along by the river and then through the park! The snow would be lying on the branches of the trees and forming a bright cap on the top of the Wellington Monument.[25] How much more pleasant it would be there than at the supper-table!

155   He ran over the headings of his speech: Irish hospitality, sad memories, the Three Graces,[26] Paris,[27] the quotation from Browning. He repeated to himself a phrase he had written in his review: *One feels that one is listening to a thought-tormented music.* Miss Ivors had praised the review. Was she sincere? Had she really any life of her own behind all her propagandism? There had never been any ill-feeling between them until that night. It unnerved him to think that she would be at the supper-table, looking up at him while he spoke with her critical quizzing eyes. Perhaps she would not be sorry to see him fail in his speech. An idea came into his mind and gave him courage. He would say, alluding to Aunt Kate and Aunt Julia: *Ladies and Gentlemen, the generation which is now on the wane among us may have had its faults but for my part I think it had certain qualities of hospitality, of humour, of humanity, which the new and very serious and hypereducated generation that is growing up around us seems to me to lack.* Very good: that was one for Miss Ivors. What did he care that his aunts were only two ignorant old women?

A murmur in the room attracted his attention. Mr Browne was advancing from the door, gallantly escorting Aunt Julia, who leaned upon his arm, smiling and hanging her head. An irregular musketry of applause escorted her

---

[25] Dedicated to the Duke of Wellington (1769–1852), Irish hero.

[26] The goddesses who symbolized the features of beauty—Aglaia (Brilliance), Eurphrosyne (Joy), Thalia (Bloom).

[27] Trojan prince who judged the beauty of the goddesses Athena, Aphrodite, and Hera. Because he selected Aphrodite, she helped him to abduct Helen, wife of Menelaus, an act which precipitated the Trojan War.

also as far as the piano and then, as Mary Jane seated herself on the stool, and Aunt Julia, no longer smiling, half turned so as to pitch her voice fairly into the room, gradually ceased. Gabriel recognised the prelude. It was that of an old song of Aunt Julia's—*Arrayed for the Bridal.* Her voice, strong and clear in tone, attacked with great spirit the runs which embellish the air and though she sang very rapidly she did not miss even the smallest of the grace notes. To follow the voice, without looking at the singer's face, was to feel and share the excitement of swift and secure flight. Gabriel applauded loudly with all the others at the close of the song and loud applause was borne in from the invisible supper-table. It sounded so genuine that a little colour struggled into Aunt Julia's face as she bent to replace in the music-stand the old leather-bound song-book that had her initials on the cover. Freddy Malins, who had listened with his head perched sideways to hear her better, was still applauding when everyone else had ceased and talking animatedly to his mother who nodded her head gravely and slowly in acquiescence. At last, when he could clap no more, he stood up suddenly and hurried across the room to Aunt Julia whose hand he seized and held in both his hands, shaking it when words failed him or the catch in his voice proved too much for him.

—I was just telling my mother, he said, I never heard you sing so well, never. No, I never heard your voice so good as it is to-night. Now! Would you believe that now? That's the truth. Upon my word and honour that's the truth. I never heard your voice sound so fresh and so . . . so clear and fresh, never.

Aunt Julia smiled broadly and murmured something about compliments as she released her hand from his grasp. Mr Browne extended his open hand towards her and said to those who were near him in the manner of a show-man introducing a prodigy to an audience:

—Miss Julia Morkan, my latest discovery!

160   He was laughing very heartily at this himself when Freddy Malins turned to him and said:

—Well, Browne, if you're serious you might make a worse discovery. All I can say is I never heard her sing half so well as long as I am coming here. And that's the honest truth.

—Neither did I, said Mr Browne. I think her voice has greatly improved.

Aunt Julia shrugged her shoulders and said with meek pride:

—Thirty years ago I hadn't a bad voice as voices go.

165   —I often told Julia, said Aunt Kate emphatically, that she was simply thrown away in that choir. But she never would be said by me.

She turned as if to appeal to the good sense of the others against a refractory child while Aunt Julia gazed in front of her, a vague smile of reminiscence playing on her face.

—No, continued Aunt Kate, she wouldn't be said or led by anyone, slaving there in that choir night and day, night and day. Six o'clock on Christmas morning! And all for what?

—Well, isn't it for the honour of God, Aunt Kate? asked Mary Jane, twisting round on the piano-stool and smiling.

Aunt Kate turned fiercely on her niece and said:

170   —I know all about the honour of God, Mary Jane, but I think it's not at all honourable for the pope to turn out the women out of the choirs that have slaved there all their lives and put little whipper-snappers of boys over their heads. I suppose it is for the good of the Church if the pope does it. But it's not just, Mary Jane, and it's not right.

She had worked herself into a passion and would have continued in defence of her sister for it was a sore subject with her but Mary Jane, seeing that all the dancers had come back, intervened pacifically:

—Now, Aunt Kate, you're giving scandal to Mr Browne who is of the other persuasion.

Aunt Kate turned to Mr Browne, who was grinning at this allusion to his religion, and said hastily:

—O, I don't question the pope's being right. I'm only a stupid old woman and I wouldn't presume to do such a thing. But there's such a thing as common everyday politeness and gratitude. And if I were in Julia's place I'd tell that Father Healy straight up to his face . . .

—And besides, Aunt Kate, said Mary Jane, we really are all hungry and when we are hungry we are all very quarrelsome.

—And when we are thirsty we are also quarrelsome, added Mr Browne.

—So that we had better go to supper, said Mary Jane, and finish the discussion afterwards.

On the landing outside the drawing-room Gabriel found his wife and Mary Jane trying to persuade Miss Ivors to stay for supper. But Miss Ivors, who had put on her hat and was buttoning her cloak, would not stay. She did not feel in the least hungry and she had already overstayed her time.

—But only for ten minutes, Molly, said Mrs Conroy. That won't delay you.

180   —To take a pick itself, said Mary Jane, after all your dancing.

—I really couldn't, said Miss Ivors.

—I am afraid you didn't enjoy yourself at all, said Mary Jane hopelessly.

—Ever so much, I assure you, said Miss Ivors, but you really must let me run off now.

—But how can you get home? asked Mrs Conroy.

185   —O, it's only two steps up the quay.

Gabriel hesitated a moment and said:

—If you will allow me, Miss Ivors, I'll see you home if you are really obliged to go.

But Miss Ivors broke away from them.

—I won't hear of it, she cried. For goodness sake go in to your suppers and don't mind me. I'm quite well able to take care of myself.

190   —Well, you're the comical girl, Molly, said Mrs Conroy frankly.

—*Beannacht libh,* [28] cried Miss Ivors, with a laugh, as she ran down the staircase.

---

[28] Gaelic for "Blessing on you."

Mary Jane gazed after her, a moody puzzled expression on her face, while Mrs Conroy leaned over the banisters to listen for the hall-door. Gabriel asked himself was he the cause of her abrupt departure. But she did not seem to be in ill humour: she had gone away laughing. He stared blankly down the staircase.

At that moment Aunt Kate came toddling out of the supper-room, almost wringing her hands in despair.

—Where is Gabriel? she cried. Where on earth is Gabriel? There's everyone waiting in there, stage to let, and nobody to carve the goose!

195 —Here I am, Aunt Kate! cried Gabriel, with sudden animation, ready to carve a flock of geese, if necessary.

A fat brown goose lay at one end of the table and at the other end, on a bed of creased paper strewn with sprigs of parsley, lay a great ham, stripped of its outer skin and peppered over with crust crumbs, a neat paper frill round its shin and beside this was a round of spiced beef. Between these rival ends ran parallel lines of side-dishes: two little minsters of jelly, red and yellow; a shallow dish full of blocks of blancmange and red jam, a large green leaf-shaped dish with a stalk-shaped handle, on which lay bunches of purple raisins and peeled almonds, a companion dish on which lay a solid rectangle of Smyrna figs, a dish of custard topped with grated nutmeg, a small bowl full of chocolates and sweets wrapped in gold and silver papers and a glass vase in which stood some tall celery stalks. In the centre of the table there stood, as sentries to a fruit-stand which upheld a pyramid of oranges and American apples, two squat old-fashioned decanters of cut glass, one containing port and the other dark sherry. On the closed square piano a pudding in a huge yellow dish lay in waiting and behind it were three squads of bottles of stout and ale and minerals, drawn up according to the colours of their uniforms, the first two black, with brown and red labels, the third and smallest squad white, with transverse green sashes.

Gabriel took his seat boldly at the head of the table and, having looked to the edge of the carver, plunged his fork firmly into the goose. He felt quite at ease now for he was an expert carver and liked nothing better than to find himself at the head of a well-laden table.

—Miss Furlong, what shall I send you? A wing or a slice of the breast?

—Just a small slice of the breast.

200 —Miss Higgins, what for you?

—O, anything at all, Mr Conroy.

While Gabriel and Miss Daly exchanged plates of goose and plates of ham and spiced beef Lily went from guest to guest with a dish of hot floury potatoes wrapped in a white napkin. This was Mary Jane's idea and she had also suggested apple sauce for the goose but Aunt Kate had said that plain roast goose without apple sauce had always been good enough for her and she hoped she might never eat worse. Mary Jane waited on her pupils and saw that they got the best slices and Aunt Kate and Aunt Julia opened and carried across from the piano bottles of stout and ale for the gentlemen and bottles of minerals for the ladies. There was a great deal of confusion and laughter and noise, the noise of orders and counter-orders, of knives and forks, of corks and glass-stoppers. Gabriel began to carve second helpings as soon as he had finished the first round without serving himself. Everyone protested loudly so that he compromised by taking a long draught of stout for he had found the carving hot work. Mary Jane settled down quietly to her supper but Aunt Kate and Aunt Julia were still toddling round the table, walking on each other's heels, getting in each other's way and giving each other unheeded orders. Mr Browne begged of them to sit down and eat their suppers and so did Gabriel but they said there was time enough so that, at last, Freddy Malins stood up and, capturing Aunt Kate, plumped her down on her chair amid general laughter.

When everyone had been well served Gabriel said, smiling:

—Now, if anyone wants a little more of what vulgar people call stuffing let him or her speak.

205   A chorus of voices invited him to begin his own supper and Lily came forward with three potatoes which she had reserved for him.

—Very well, said Gabriel amiably, as he took another preparatory draught, kindly forget my existence, ladies and gentlemen, for a few minutes.

He set to his supper and took no part in the conversation with which the table covered Lily's removal of the plates. The subject of talk was the opera company which was then at the Theatre Royal. Mr Bartell D'Arcy, the tenor, a dark-complexioned young man with a smart moustache, praised very highly the leading contralto of the company but Miss Furlong thought she had a rather vulgar style of production. Freddy Malins said there was a negro chieftain singing in the second part of the Gaiety pantomime who had one of the finest tenor voices he had ever heard.

—Have you heard him? he asked Mr Bartell D'Arcy across the table.

—No, answered Mr Bartell D'Arcy carelessly.

210   —Because, Freddy Malins explained, now I'd be curious to hear your opinion of him. I think he has a grand voice.

—It takes Teddy to find out the really good things, said Mr Browne familiarly to the table.

—And why couldn't he have a voice too? asked Freddy Malins sharply. Is it because he's only a black?

Nobody answered this question and Mary Jane led the table back to the legitimate opera. One of her pupils had given her a pass for *Mignon.* [29] Of course it was very fine, she said, but it made her think of poor Georgina Burns. Mr Browne could go back farther still, to the old Italian companies that used to come to Dublin—Tietjens, Ilma de Murzka, Campanini, the great Trebelli, Giuglini, Ravelli, Aramburo. [30] Those were the days, he said, when there was something like singing to be heard in Dublin. He told too of how the top gallery of the old Royal used to be packed night after night, of how one night an Italian tenor had sung five encores to *Let Me Like a Soldier Fall,* [31] introducing a high C every time, and of how the gallery boys would sometimes in their

---

[29] Opera by French composer, Ambroise Thomas (1811–1896).
[30] Nineteenth-century singing stars.
[31] From Maritana by Brunn, Fitzball, and Wallace.

enthusiasm unyoke the horses from the carriage of some great *prima donna* and pull her themselves through the streets to her hotel. Why did they never play the grand old operas now, he asked, *Dinorah, Lucrezia Borgia*?[32] Because they could not get the voices to sing them: that was why.

—O, well, said Mr Bartell D'Arcy, I presume there are as good singers today as there were then.

215 —Where are they? asked Mr Browne defiantly.

—In London, Paris, Milan, said Mr Bartell D'Arcy warmly. I suppose Caruso,[33] for example, is quite as good, if not better than any of the men you have mentioned.

—Maybe so, said Mr Browne. But I may tell you I doubt it strongly.

—O, I'd give anything to hear Caruso sing, said Mary Jane.

—For me, said Aunt Kate, who had been picking a bone, there was only one tenor. To please me, I mean. But I suppose none of you ever heard of him.

220 —Who was he, Miss Morkan? asked Mr Bartell D'Arcy politely.

—His name, said Aunt Kate, was Parkinson. I heard him when he was in his prime and I think he had then the purest tenor voice that was ever put into a man's throat.

—Strange, said Mr Bartell D'Arcy. I never even heard of him.

—Yes, yes, Miss Morkan is right, said Mr Browne. I remember hearing of old Parkinson but he's too far back for me.

—A beautiful pure sweet mellow English tenor, said Aunt Kate with enthusiasm.

225 Gabriel having finished, the huge pudding was transferred to the table. The clatter of forks and spoons began again. Gabriel's wife served out spoonfuls of the pudding and passed the plates down the table. Midway down they were held up by Mary Jane, who replenished them with raspberry or orange jelly or with blancmange and jam. The pudding was of Aunt Julia's making and she received praises for it from all quarters. She herself said that it was not quite brown enough.

—Well, I hope, Miss Morkan, said Mr Browne, that I'm brown enough for you because, you know, I'm all brown.

All the gentlemen, except Gabriel, ate some of the pudding out of compliment to Aunt Julia. As Gabriel never ate sweets the celery had been left for him. Freddy Malins also took a stalk of celery and ate it with his pudding. He had been told that celery was a capital thing for the blood and he was just then under doctor's care. Mrs Malins, who had been silent all through the supper, said that her son was going down to Mount Melleray[34] in a week or so. The table then spoke of Mount Melleray, how bracing the air was down there, how hospitable the monks were and how they never asked for a penny-piece from their guests.

---

[32] Operas by Meyerbeer (1838–1892), German composer, and by Donizetti (1797–1848), Italian composer.

[33] Enrico Caruso, famous operatic tenor (1873–1921).

[34] Monastery in southern Ireland.

—And do you mean to say, asked Mr Browne incredulously, that a chap can go down there and put up there as if it were a hotel and live on the fat of the land and then come away without paying a farthing?

—O, most people give some donation to the monastery when they leave, said Mary Jane.

230 —I wish we had an institution like that in our Church, said Mr Browne candidly.

He was astonished to hear that the monks never spoke, got up at two in the morning and slept in their coffins. He asked what they did it for.

—That's the rule of the order, said Aunt Kate firmly.

—Yes, but why? asked Mr Browne.

Aunt Kate repeated that it was the rule, that was all. Mr Browne still seemed not to understand. Freddy Malins explained to him, as best he could, that the monks were trying to make up for the sins committed by all the sinners in the outside world. The explanation was not very clear for Mr Browne grinned and said:

235 —I like that idea very much but wouldn't a comfortable bed do them as well as a coffin?

—The coffin, said Mary Jane, is to remind them of their last end.

As the subject had grown lugubrious it was buried in a silence of the table during which Mrs Malins could be heard saying to her neighbour in an indistinct undertone:

—They are very good men, the monks, very pious men.

The raisins and almonds and figs and apples and oranges and chocolates and sweets were now passed about the table and Aunt Julia invited all the guests to have either port or sherry. At first Mr Bartell D'Arcy refused to take either but one of his neighbours nudged him and whispered something to him upon which he allowed his glass to be filled. Gradually as the last glasses were being filled the conversation ceased. A pause followed, broken only by the noise of the wine and by unsettlings of chairs. The Misses Morkan, all three, looked down at the tablecloth. Someone coughed once or twice and then a few gentlemen patted the table gently as a signal for silence. The silence came and Gabriel pushed back his chair and stood up.

240 The patting at once grew louder in encouragement and then ceased altogether. Gabriel leaned his ten trembling fingers on the tablecloth and smiled nervously at the company. Meeting a row of upturned faces he raised his eyes to the chandelier. The piano was playing a waltz tune and he could hear the skirts sweeping against the drawing-room door. People, perhaps, were standing in the snow on the quay outside, gazing up at the lighted windows and listening to the waltz music. The air was pure there. In the distance lay the park where the trees were weighted with snow. The Wellington Monument wore a gleaming cap of snow that flashed westward over the white field of Fifteen Acres.[35]

---

[35] Area of the park where the Wellington monument is located.

He began:

—Ladies and Gentlemen.

—It has fallen to my lot this evening as in years past, to perform a very pleasing task but a task for which I am afraid my poor powers as a speaker are all too inadequate.

—No, no! said Mr Browne.

—But, however that may be, I can only ask you to-night to take the will for the deed and to lend me your attention for a few moments while I endeavour to express to you in words what my feelings are on this occasion.

—Ladies and Gentlemen. It is not the first time that we have gathered together under this hospitable roof, around this hospitable board. It is not the first time that we have been the recipients—or perhaps, I had better say, the victims—of the hospitality of certain good ladies.

He made a circle in the air with his arm and paused. Everyone laughed or smiled at Aunt Kate and Aunt Julia and Mary Jane who all turned crimson with pleasure. Gabriel went on more boldly:

—I feel more strongly with every recurring year that our country has no tradition which does it so much honour and which it should guard so jealously as that of its hospitality. It is a tradition that is unique as far as my experience goes (and I have visited not a few places abroad) among the modern nations. Some would say, perhaps, that with us it is rather a failing than anything to be boasted of. But granted even that, it is, to my mind, a princely failing, and one that I trust will long be cultivated among us. Of one thing, at least, I am sure. As long as this one roof shelters the good ladies aforesaid— and I wish from my heart it may do so for many and many a long year to come—the tradition of genuine warm-hearted courteous Irish hospitality, which our forefathers have handed down to us and which we in turn must hand down to our descendants, is still alive among us.A hearty murmur of assent ran round the table. It shot through Gabriel's mind that Miss Ivors was not there and that she had gone away discourteously: and he said with confidence in himself:

250   —Ladies and Gentlemen.

—A new generation is growing up in our midst, a generation actuated by new ideas and new principles. It is serious and enthusiastic for these new ideas and its enthusiasm, even when it is misdirected, is, I believe, in the main sincere. But we are living in a sceptical and, if I may use the phrase, a thought-tormented age: and sometimes I fear that this new generation, educated or hypereducated as it is, will lack those qualities of humanity, of hospitality, of kindly humour which belonged to an older day. Listening tonight to the names of all those great singers of the past it seemed to me, I must confess, that we were living in a less spacious age. Those days might, without exaggeration, be called spacious days: and if they are gone beyond recall let us hope, at least, that in gatherings such as this we shall still speak of them with pride and affection, still cherish in our hearts the memory of those dead and gone great ones whose fame the world will not willingly let die.

—Hear, hear! said Mr Browne loudly.

—But yet, continued Gabriel, his voice falling into a softer inflection, there are always in gatherings such as this sadder thoughts that will recur to our minds: thoughts of the past, of youth, of changes, of absent faces that we miss here to-night. Our path through life is strewn with many such sad memories: and were we to brood upon them always we could not find the heart to go on bravely with our work among the living. We have all of us living duties and living affections which claim, and rightly claim, our strenuous endeavours.

—Therefore, I will not linger on the past. I will not let any gloomy moralising intrude upon us here to-night. Here we are gathered together for a brief moment from the bustle and rush of our everyday routine. We are met here as friends, in the spirit of good-fellowship, as colleagues, also to a certain extent, in the true spirit of *camaraderie,* and as the guests of—what shall I call them?—the Three Graces of the Dublin musical world.

255   The table burst into applause and laughter at this sally. Aunt Julia vainly asked each of her neighbours in turn to tell her what Gabriel had said.

—He says we are the Three Graces, Aunt Julia, said Mary Jane.

Aunt Julia did not understand but she looked up, smiling, at Gabriel, who continued in the same vein:

—Ladies and Gentlemen.

—I will not attempt to play to-night the part that Paris played on another occasion. I will not attempt to choose between them. The task would be an invidious one and one beyond my poor powers. For when I view them in turn, whether it be our chief hostess herself, whose good heart, whose too good heart, has become a byword with all who know her, or her sister, who seems to be gifted with perennial youth and whose singing must have been a surprise and a revelation to us all tonight, or, last but not least, when I consider our youngest hostess, talented, cheerful, hard-working and the best of nieces, I confess, Ladies and Gentlemen, that I do not know to which of them I should award the prize.

260   Gabriel glanced down at his aunts and, seeing the large smile on Aunt Julia's face and the tears which had risen to Aunt Kate's eyes, hastened to his close. He raised his glass of port gallantly, while every member of the company fingered a glass expectantly, and said loudly:

—Let us toast them all three together. Let us drink to their health, wealth, long life, happiness and prosperity and may they continue to hold the proud and self-won position which they hold in their profession and the position of honour and affection which they hold in our hearts.

All the guests stood up, glass in hand, and, turning towards the three seated ladies, sang in unison, with Mr Browne as leader:

> *For they are jolly gay fellows,*
> *For they are jolly gay fellows,*
> *For they are jolly gay fellows,*
> *Which nobody can deny.*

Aunt Kate was making frank use of her handkerchief and even Aunt Julia seemed moved. Freddy Malins beat time with his pudding-fork and the singers turned toward one another, as if in melodious conference, while they sang, with emphasis:

> *Unless he tells a lie,*
> *Unless he tells a lie.*

Then, turning once more towards their hostesses, they sang:

> *For they are jolly gay fellows,*
> *For they are jolly gay fellows,*
> *For they are jolly gay fellows,*
> *Which nobody can deny.*

265   The acclamation which followed was taken up beyond the door of the supper-room by many of the other guests and renewed time after time, Freddy Malins acting as officer with his fork on high.

* * *

The piercing morning air came into the hall where they were standing so that Aunt Kate said:

—Close the door, somebody. Mrs Malins will get her death of cold.

—Browne is out there, Aunt Kate, said Mary Jane.

—Browne is everywhere, said Aunt Kate, lowering her voice.

270   Mary Jane laughed at her tone.

—Really, she said archly, he is very attentive.

—He has been laid on here like the gas, said Aunt Kate in the same tone, all during the Christmas.

She laughed herself this time good-humouredly and then added quickly:

—But tell him to come in, Mary Jane, and close the door. I hope to goodness he didn't hear me.

275   At that moment the hall-door was opened and Mr Browne came in from the doorstep, laughing as if his heart would break. He was dressed in a long green overcoat with mock astrakhan cuffs and collar and wore on his head an oval fur cap. He pointed down the snow-covered quay from where the sound of shrill prolonged whistling was borne in.

—Teddy will have all the cabs in Dublin out, he said.

Gabriel advanced from the little pantry behind the office, struggling into his overcoat and, looking round the hall, said:

—Gretta not down yet?

—She's getting on her things, Gabriel, said Aunt Kate.

280   —Who's playing up there? asked Gabriel.

—Nobody. They're all gone.

—O no, Aunt Kate, said Mary Jane. Bartell D'Arcy and Miss O'Callaghan aren't gone yet.

—Someone is strumming at the piano, anyhow, said Gabriel.

Mary Jane glanced at Gabriel and Mr Browne and said with a shiver:

285   —It makes me feel cold to look at you two gentlemen muffled up like that. I wouldn't like to face your journey home at this hour.

—I'd like nothing better this minute, said Mr Browne stoutly, than a rattling fine walk in the country or a fast drive with a good spanking goer between the shafts.

—We used to have a very good horse and trap[36] at home, said Aunt Julia sadly.

—The never-to-be-forgotten Johnny, said Mary Jane, laughing.

Aunt Kate and Gabriel laughed too.

290   —Why, what was wonderful about Johnny? asked Mr Browne.

—The late lamented Patrick Morkan, our grandfather, that is, explained Gabriel, commonly known in his later years as the old gentleman, was a glue-boiler.

—O, now, Gabriel, said Aunt Kate, laughing, he had a starch mill.

—Well, glue or starch, said Gabriel, the old gentleman had a horse by the name of Johnny. And Johnny used to work in the old gentleman's mill, walking round and round in order to drive the mill. That was all very well; but now comes the tragic part about Johnny. One fine day the old gentleman thought he'd like to drive out with the quality[37] to a military review in the park.

—The Lord have mercy on his soul, said Aunt Kate compassionately.

295   —Amen, said Gabriel. So the old gentleman, as I said, harnessed Johnny and put on his very best tall hat and his very best stock collar and drove out in grand style from his ancestral mansion somewhere near Back Lane, I think.

Everyone laughed, even Mrs Malins, at Gabriel's manner and Aunt Kate said:

—O now, Gabriel, he didn't live in Back Lane, really. Only the mill was there.

—Out from the mansion of his forefathers, continued Gabriel, he drove with Johnny. And everything went on beautifully until Johnny came in sight of King Billy's[38] statue: and whether he fell in love with the horse King Billy sits on or whether he thought he was back again in the mill, anyhow he began to walk round the statue.

Gabriel paced in a circle round the hall in his goloshes amid the laughter of the others.

300   —Round and round he went, said Gabriel, and the old gentleman, who was a very pompous old gentleman, was highly indignant. *Go on, sir! What do you mean, sir? Johnny! Johnny! Most extraordinary conduct! Can't understand the horse!*

The peals of laughter which followed Gabriel's imitation of the incident were interrupted by a resounding knock at the hall-door. Mary Jane ran to open it and let in Freddy Malins. Freddy Malins, with his hat well back on his head and his shoulders humped with cold, was puffing and steaming after his exertions.

---

[36] One horse carriage.

[37] Upper classes.

[38] Statue of King William III of England on horseback. King William was the last conqueror of Ireland in 1690.

—I could only get one cab, he said.

—O, we'll find another along the quay, said Gabriel.

—Yes, said Aunt Kate. Better not keep Mrs Malins standing in the draught.

305 Mrs Malins was helped down the front steps by her son and Mr Browne and, after many manœuvres, hoisted into the cab. Freddy Malins clambered in after her and spent a long time settling her on the seat, Mr Browne helping him with advice. At last she was settled comfortably and Freddy Malins invited Mr Browne into the cab. There was a good deal of confused talk, and then Mr Browne got into the cab. The cabman settled his rug over his knees, and bent down for the address. The confusion grew greater and the cabman was directed differently by Freddy Malins and Mr Browne, each of whom had his head out through a window of the cab. The difficulty was to know where to drop Mr Browne along the route and Aunt Kate, Aunt Julia and Mary Jane helped the discussion from the doorstep with cross-directions and contradictions and abundance of laughter. As for Freddy Malins he was speechless with laughter. He popped his head in and out of the window every moment, to the great danger of his hat, and told his mother how the discussion was progressing till at last Mr Browne shouted to the bewildered cabman above the din of everybody's laughter:

—Do you know Trinity College?

—Yes, sir, said the cabman.

—Well, drive bang up against Trinity College gates, said Mr Browne, and then we'll tell you where to go. You understand now?

—Yes, sir, said the cabman.

310 —Make like a bird for Trinity College.

—Right, sir, cried the cabman.

The horse was whipped up and the cab rattled off along the quay amid a chorus of laughter and adieus.

Gabriel had not gone to the door with the others. He was in the dark part of the hall gazing up the staircase. A woman was standing near the top of the first flight, in the shadow also. He could not see her face but he could see the terracotta and salmonpink panels of her skirt which the shadow made appear black and white. It was his wife. She was leaning on the banisters, listening to something. Gabriel was surprised at her stillness and strained his ear to listen also. But he could hear little save the noise of laughter and dispute on the front steps, a few chords struck on the piano and a few notes of a man's voice singing.

He stood still in the gloom of the hall, trying to catch the air that the voice was singing and gazing up at his wife. There was grace and mystery in her attitude as if she were a symbol of something. He asked himself what is a woman standing on the stairs in the shadow, listening to distant music, a symbol of. If he were a painter he would paint her in that attitude. Her blue felt hat would show off the bronze of her hair against the darkness and the dark panels of her skirt would show off the light ones. *Distant Music* he would call the picture if he were a painter.

315   The hall-door was closed; and Aunt Kate, Aunt Julia and Mary Jane came down the hall, still laughing.

—Well, isn't Freddy terrible? said Mary Jane. He's really terrible.

Gabriel said nothing but pointed up the stairs towards where his wife was standing. Now that the hall-door was closed the voice and the piano could be heard more clearly. Gabriel held up his hand for them to be silent. The song seemed to be in the old Irish tonality and the singer seemed uncertain both of his words and of his voice. The voice, made plaintive by distance and by the singer's hoarseness, faintly illuminated the cadence of the air with words expressing grief:

> *O, the rain falls on my heavy locks*
> *And the dew wets my skin,*
> *My babe lies cold . . .*

—O, exclaimed Mary Jane. It's Bartell D'Arcy singing and he wouldn't sing all the night. O, I'll get him to sing a song before he goes.

—O do, Mary Jane, said Aunt Kate.

320   Mary Jane brushed past the others and ran to the staircase but before she reached it the singing stopped and the piano was closed abruptly.

—O, what a pity! she cried. Is he coming down, Gretta?

Gabriel heard his wife answer yes and saw her come down towards them. A few steps behind her were Mr Bartell D'Arcy and Miss O'Callaghan.

—O, Mr D'Arcy, cried Mary Jane, it's downright mean of you to break off like that when we were all in raptures listening to you.

—I have been at him all the evening, said Miss O'Callaghan, and Mrs Conroy too and he told us he had a dreadful cold and couldn't sing.

325   —O, Mr D'Arcy, said Aunt Kate, now that was a great fib to tell.

—Can't you see that I'm as hoarse as a crow? said Mr D'Arcy roughly.

He went into the pantry hastily and put on his overcoat. The others, taken aback by his rude speech, could find nothing to say. Aunt Kate wrinkled her brows and made signs to the others to drop the subject. Mr D'Arcy stood swathing his neck carefully and frowning.

—It's the weather, said Aunt Julia, after a pause.

—Yes, everybody has colds, said Aunt Kate readily, everybody.

330   —They say, said Mary Jane, we haven't had snow like it for thirty years; and I read this morning in the newspapers that the snow is general all over Ireland.

—I love the look of snow, said Aunt Julia sadly.

—So do I, said Miss O'Callaghan. I think Christmas is never really Christmas unless we have the snow on the ground.

—But poor Mr D'Arcy doesn't like the snow, said Aunt Kate, smiling.

Mr D'Arcy came from the pantry, fully swathed and buttoned, and in a repentant tone told them the history of his cold. Everyone gave him advice and said it was a great pity and urged him to be very careful of his throat in the night air. Gabriel watched his wife who did not join in the conversation. She was standing right under the dusty fanlight and the flame of the gas lit up the rich bronze of her hair which he had seen her drying at the fire a few days before. She was in the same attitude and seemed unaware of the talk about her. At last she turned towards them and Gabriel saw that there was colour on her cheeks and that her eyes were shining. A sudden tide of joy went leaping out of his heart.

335 —Mr D'Arcy, she said, what is the name of that song you were singing?

—It's called *The Lass of Aughrim,* [39] said Mr D'Arcy, but I couldn't remember it properly. Why? Do you know it?

—*The Lass of Aughrim,* she repeated. I couldn't think of the name.

—It's a very nice air, said Mary Jane. I'm sorry you were not in voice tonight.

—Now, Mary Jane, said Aunt Kate, don't annoy Mr D'Arcy. I won't have him annoyed.

340 Seeing that all were ready to start she shepherded them to the door where good-night was said:

—Well, good-night, Aunt Kate, and thanks for the pleasant evening.

—Good-night, Gabriel. Good-night, Gretta!

—Good-night, Aunt Kate, and thanks ever so much. Good-night, Aunt Julia.

—O, good-night, Gretta, I didn't see you.

345 —Good-night, Mr D'Arcy. Good-night, Miss O'Callaghan.

—Good-night, Miss Morkan.

—Good-night, again.

—Good-night, all. Safe home.

—Good-night. Good-night.

350 The morning was still dark. A dull yellow light brooded over the houses and the river; and the sky seemed to be descending. It was slushy underfoot; and only streaks and patches of snow lay on the roofs, on the parapets of the quay and on the arca railings. The lamps were still burning redly in the murky air and, across the river, the palace of the Four Courts stood out menacingly against the heavy sky.

She was walking on before him with Mr Bartell D'Arcy, her shoes in a brown parcel tucked under one arm and her hands holding her skirt up from the slush. She had no longer any grace of attitude but Gabriel's eyes were still bright with happiness. The blood went bounding along his veins; and the thoughts went rioting through his brain, proud, joyful, tender, valorous.

She was walking on before him so lightly and so erect that he longed to run after her noiselessly, catch her by the shoulders and say something foolish and affectionate into her ear. She seemed to him so frail that he longed to defend her against something and then to be alone with her. Moments of their secret life together burst like stars upon his memory. A heliotrope envelope was lying beside his breakfast-cup and he was caressing it with his hand. Birds were twittering in the ivy and the sunny web of the curtain was

---

[39] Version of "The Lass of Loch Royal," child's ballad # 76. In this ballad, the young woman, seduced and abandoned, waits in the rain outside the house of her lover.

shimmering along the floor: he could not eat for happiness. They were standing on the crowded platform and he was placing a ticket inside the warm palm of her glove. He was standing with her in the cold, looking in through a grated window at a man making bottles in a roaring furnace. It was very cold. Her face, fragrant in the cold air, was quite close to his; and suddenly she called out to the man at the furnace:

—Is the fire hot, sir?

But the man could not hear her with the noise of the furnace. It was just as well. He might have answered rudely.

355   A wave of yet more tender joy escaped from his heart and went coursing in warm flood along his arteries. Like the tender fires of stars moments of their life together, that no one knew of or would ever know of, broke upon and illumined his memory. He longed to recall to her those moments, to make her forget the years of their dull existence together and remember only their moments of ecstasy. For the years, he felt, had not quenched his soul or hers. Their children, his writing, her household cares had not quenched all their souls' tender fire. In one letter that he had written to her then he had said: *Why is it that words like these seem to me so dull and cold? Is it because there is no word tender enough to be your name?*

Like distant music these words that he had written years before were borne towards him from the past. He longed to be alone with her. When the others had gone away, when he and she were in their room in the hotel, then they would be alone together. He would call her softly:

—Gretta!

Perhaps she would not hear at once: she would be undressing. Then something in his voice would strike her. She would turn and look at him. . . .

At the corner of Winetavern Street they met a cab. He was glad of its rattling noise as it saved him from conversation. She was looking out of the window and seemed tired. The others spoke only a few words, pointing out some building or street. The horse galloped along wearily under the murky morning sky, dragging his old rattling box after his heels, and Gabriel was again in a cab with her, galloping to catch the boat, galloping to their honeymoon.

360   As the cab drove across O'Connell Bridge Miss O'Callaghan said:

—They say you never cross O'Connell Bridge without seeing a white horse.

—I see a white man this time, said Gabriel.

—Where? asked Mr Bartell D'Arcy.

Gabriel pointed to the statue,[40] on which lay patches of snow. Then he nodded familiarly to it and waved his hand.

365   —Good-night, Dan, he said gaily.

When the cab drew up before the hotel Gabriel jumped out and, in spite of Mr Bartell D'Arcy's protest, paid the driver. He gave the man a shilling over his fare. The man saluted and said:

—A prosperous New Year to you, sir.

—The same to you, said Gabriel cordially.

---

[40] Monument to Daniel O'Connell, Irish hero (1775–1847).

She leaned for a moment on his arm in getting out of the cab and while standing at the curbstone, bidding the others good-night. She leaned lightly on his arm, as lightly as when she had danced with him a few hours before. He had felt proud and happy then, happy that she was his, proud of her grace and wifely carriage. But now, after the kindling again of so many memories, the first touch of her body, musical and strange and perfumed, sent through him a keen pang of lust. Under cover of her silence he pressed her arm closely to his side; and, as they stood at the hotel door, he felt that they had escaped from their lives and duties, escaped from home and friends and run away together with wild and radiant hearts to a new adventure.

370   An old man was dozing in a great hooded chair in the hall. He lit a candle in the office and went before them to the stairs. They followed him in silence, their feet falling in soft thuds on the thickly carpeted stairs. She mounted the stairs behind the porter, her head bowed in the ascent, her frail shoulders curved as with a burden, her skirt girt tightly about her. He could have flung his arms about her hips and held her still for his arms were trembling with desire to seize her and only the stress of his nails against the palms of his hands held the wild impulse of his body in check. The porter halted on the stairs to settle his guttering candle. They halted too on the steps below him. In the silence Gabriel could hear the falling of the molten wax into the tray and the thumping of his own heart against his ribs.

The porter led them along a corridor and opened a door. Then he set his unstable candle down on a toilet-table and asked at what hour they were to be called in the morning.

—Eight, said Gabriel.

The porter pointed to the tap of the electric-light and began a muttered apology but Gabriel cut him short.

—We don't want any light. We have light enough from the street. And I say, he added, pointing to the candle, you might remove that handsome article, like a good man.

375   The porter took up his candle again, but slowly for he was surprised by such a novel idea. Then he mumbled good-night and went out. Gabriel shot the lock to.

A ghostly light from the street lamp lay in a long shaft from one window to the door. Gabriel threw his overcoat and hat on a couch and crossed the room towards the window. He looked down into the street in order that his emotion might calm a little. Then he turned and leaned against a chest of drawers with his back to the light. She had taken off her hat and cloak and was standing before a large swinging mirror, unhooking her waist. Gabriel paused for a few moments, watching her, and then said:

—Gretta!

She turned away from the mirror slowly and walked along the shaft of light towards him. Her face looked so serious and weary that the words would not pass Gabriel's lips. No, it was not the moment yet.

—You looked tired, he said.

380   —I am a little, she answered.

—You don't feel ill or weak?

—No, tired; that's all.

She went on to the window and stood there, looking out. Gabriel waited again and then, fearing that diffidence was about to conquer him, he said abruptly:

—By the way, Gretta!

385   —What is it?

—You know that poor fellow Malins? he said quickly.

—Yes. What about him?

—Well, poor fellow, he's a decent sort of chap after all, continued Gabriel in a false voice. He gave me back that sovereign[41] I lent him and I didn't expect it really. It's a pity he wouldn't keep away from that Browne, because he's not a bad fellow at heart.

He was trembling now with annoyance. Why did she seem so abstracted? He did not know how he could begin. Was she annoyed, too, about something? If she would only turn to him or come to him of her own accord! To take her as she was would be brutal. No, he must see some ardour in her eyes first. He longed to be master of her strange mood.

390   —When did you lend him the pound? she asked, after a pause.

Gabriel strove to restrain himself from breaking out into brutal language about the sottish Malins and his pound. He longed to cry to her from his soul, to crush her body against his, to overmaster her. But he said:

—O, at Christmas, when he opened that little Christmas-card shop in Henry Street.

He was in such a fever of rage and desire that he did not hear her come from the window. She stood before him for an instant, looking at him strangely. Then, suddenly raising herself on tiptoe and resting her hands lightly on his shoulders, she kissed him.

—You are a very generous person, Gabriel, she said.

395   Gabriel, trembling with delight at her sudden kiss and at the quaintness of her phrase, put his hands on her hair and began smoothing it back, scarcely touching it with his fingers. The washing had made it fine and brilliant. His heart was brimming over with happiness. Just when he was wishing for it she had come to him of her own accord. Perhaps her thoughts had been running with his. Perhaps she had felt the impetuous desire that was in him and then the yielding mood had come upon her. Now that she had fallen to him so easily he wondered why he had been so diffident.

He stood, holding her head between his hands. Then, slipping one arm swiftly about her body and drawing her towards him, he said softly:

—Gretta dear, what are you thinking about?

She did not answer nor yield wholly to his arm. He said again, softly:

—Tell me what it is, Gretta, I think I know what is the matter. Do I know?

400   She did not answer at once. Then she said in an outburst of tears:

—O, I am thinking about that song, *The Lass of Aughrim.*

---

[41] Gold coin, worth one English pound.

She broke loose from him and ran to the bed and, throwing her arms across the bed-rail, hid her face. Gabriel stood stockstill for a moment in astonishment and then followed her. As he passed in the way of the cheval-glass he caught sight of himself in full length, his broad, well-filled shirt-front, the face whose expression always puzzled him when he saw it in a mirror and his glimmering gilt-rimmed eyeglasses. He halted a few paces from her and said:

—What about the song? Why does that make you cry?

She raised her head from her arms and dried her eyes with the back of her hand like a child. A kinder note than he had intended went into his voice.

405 —Why, Gretta? he asked.

—I am thinking about a person long ago who used to sing that song.

—And who was the person long ago? asked Gabriel, smiling.

—It was a person I used to know in Galway when I was living with my grandmother, she said.

The smile passed away from Gabriel's face. A dull anger began to gather again at the back of his mind and the dull fires of his lust began to glow angrily in his veins.

410 —Someone you were in love with? he asked ironically.

—It was a young boy I used to know, she answered, named Michael Furey. He used to sing that song, *The Lass of Aughrim.* He was very delicate.

Gabriel was silent. He did not wish her to think that he was interested in this delicate boy.

—I can see him so plainly, she said after a moment. Such eyes as he had: big dark eyes! And such an expression in them—an expression!

—O then, you were in love with him? said Gabriel.

415 —I used to go out walking with him, she said, when I was in Galway.

A thought flew across Gabriel's mind.

—Perhaps that was why you wanted to go to Galway with that Ivors girl? he said coldly.

She looked at him and asked in surprise:

—What for?

420 Her eyes made Gabriel feel awkward. He shrugged his shoulders and said:

—How do I know? To see him perhaps.

She looked away from him along the shaft of light towards the window in silence.

—He is dead, she said at length. He died when he was only seventeen. Isn't it a terrible thing to die so young as that?

—What was he? asked Gabriel, still ironically.

425 —He was in the gasworks, she said.

Gabriel felt humiliated by the failure of his irony and by the evocation of this figure from the dead, a boy in the gasworks. While he had been full of memories of their secret life together, full of tenderness and joy and desire, she had been comparing him in her mind with another. A shameful consciousness of his own person assailed him. He saw himself as a ludicrous figure, acting as a pennyboy[42] for his aunts, a nervous well-meaning sentimentalist, orating to vulgarians and idealising his own clownish lusts, the pitiable fatuous fellow he had caught a glimpse of in the mirror. Instinctively he turned his back more to the light lest she might see the shame that burned upon his forehead.

He tried to keep up his tone of cold interrogation but his voice when he spoke was humble and indifferent.

—I suppose you were in love with this Michael Furey, Gretta, he said.

—I was great with him at that time, she said.

430   Her voice was veiled and sad. Gabriel, feeling now how vain it would be to try to lead her whither he had purposed, caressed one of her hands and said, also sadly:

—And what did he die of so young, Gretta? Consumption, was it?

—I think he died for me, she answered.

A vague terror seized Gabriel at this answer as if, at that hour when he had hoped to triumph, some impalpable and vindictive being was coming against him, gathering forces against him in its vague world. But he shook himself free of it with an effort of reason and continued to caress her hand. He did not question her again for he felt that she would tell him of herself. Her hand was warm and moist; it did not respond to his touch but he continued to caress it just as he had caressed her first letter to him that spring morning.

—It was in the winter, she said, about the beginning of the winter when I was going to leave my grandmother's and come up here to the convent. And he was ill at the time in his lodgings in Galway and wouldn't be let out and his people in Oughterard[43] were written to. He was in decline, they said, or something like that. I never knew rightly.

435   She paused for a moment and sighed.

—Poor fellow, she said. He was very fond of me and he was such a gentle boy. We used to go out together, walking, you know, Gabriel, like the way they do in the country. He was going to study singing only for his health. He had a very good voice, poor Michael Furey.

—Well; and then? asked Gabriel.

—And then when it came to the time for me to leave Galway and come up to the convent he was much worse and I wouldn't be let see him so I wrote a letter saying I was going up to Dublin and would be back in the summer and hoping he would be better then.

She paused for a moment to get her voice under control and then went on:

440   —Then the night before I left I was in my grandmother's house in Nuns' Island, packing up, and I heard gravel thrown up against the window. The window was so wet I couldn't see so I ran downstairs as I was and slipped out the back into the garden and there was the poor fellow at the end of the garden, shivering.

—And did you not tell him to go back? asked Gabriel.

---

[42] Errand boy.

[43] Town near Galway.

—I implored of him to go home at once and told him he would get his death in the rain. But he said he did not want to live. I can see his eyes as well! He was standing at the end of the wall where there was a tree.

—And did he go home? asked Gabriel.

—Yes, he went home. And when I was only a week in the convent he died and he was buried in Oughterard where his people came from. O, the day I heard that, that he was dead!

445 She stopped, choking with sobs, and, overcome by emotion, flung herself face downward on the bed, sobbing in the quilt. Gabriel held her hand for a moment longer, irresolutely, and then, shy of intruding on her grief, let it fall gently and walked quietly to the window.

She was fast asleep.

Gabriel, leaning on his elbow, looked for a few moments unresentfully on her tangled hair and half-open mouth, listening to her deep-drawn breath. So she had had that romance in her life: a man had died for her sake. It hardly pained him now to think how poor a part he, her husband, had played in her life. He watched her while she slept as though he and she had never lived together as man and wife. His curious eyes rested long upon her face and on her hair: and, as he thought of what she must have been then, in that time of her first girlish beauty, a strange friendly pity for her entered his soul. He did not like to say even to himself that her face was no longer beautiful but he knew that it was no longer the face for which Michael Furey had braved death.

Perhaps she had not told him all the story. His eyes moved to the chair over which she had thrown some of her clothes. A petticoat string dangled to the floor. One boot stood upright, its limp upper fallen down: the fellow of it lay upon its side. He wondered at his riot of emotions of an hour before. From what had it proceeded? From his aunt's supper, from his own foolish speech, from the wine and dancing, the merrymaking when saying good-night in the hall, the pleasure of the walk along the river in the snow. Poor Aunt Julia! She, too, would soon be a shade with the shade of Patrick Morkan and his horse. He had caught that haggard look upon her face for a moment when she was singing *Arrayed for the Bridal*. Soon, perhaps, he would be sitting in that same drawing-room, dressed in black, his silk hat on his knees. The blinds would be drawn down and Aunt Kate would be sitting beside him, crying and blowing her nose and telling him how Julia had died. He would cast about in his mind for some words that might console her, and would find only lame and useless ones. Yes, yes: that would happen very soon.

The air of the room chilled his shoulders. He stretched himself cautiously along under the sheets and lay down beside his wife. One by one they were all becoming shades. Better pass boldly into that other world, in the full glory of some passion, than fade and wither dismally with age. He thought of how she who lay beside him had locked in her heart for so many years that image of her lover's eyes when he had told her that he did not wish to live.

450   Generous tears filled Gabriel's eyes. He had never felt like that himself towards any woman but he knew that such a feeling must be love. The tears gathered more thickly in his eyes and in the partial darkness he imagined he saw the form of a young man standing under a dripping tree. Other forms were near. His soul had approached that region where dwell the vast hosts of the dead. He was conscious of, but could not apprehend, their wayward and flickering existence. His own identity was fading out into a grey impalpable world: the solid world itself which these dead had one time reared and lived in was dissolving and dwindling.

A few light taps upon the pane made him turn to the window. It had begun to snow again. He watched sleepily the flakes, silver and dark, falling obliquely against the lamplight. The time had come for him to set out on his journey westward. Yes, the newspapers were right: snow was general all over Ireland. It was falling on every part of the dark central plain, on the treeless hills, falling softly upon the Bog of Allen[44] and, farther westward, softly falling into the dark mutinous Shannon[45] waves. It was falling, too, upon every part of the lonely churchyard on the hill where Michael Furey lay buried. It lay thickly drifted on the crooked crosses and headstones, on the spears of the little gate, on the barren thorns. His soul swooned slowly as he heard the snow falling faintly through the universe and faintly falling, like the descent of their last end, upon all the living and the dead.

■ **EXPLORATIONS OF THE TEXT** ■

1. What is the importance to the story of the "Misses Morkan's annual dance"? How does this Christmas tradition change?
2. What is Gabriel's relationship with Miss Kate and with Miss Julia? What does his conversation with Lily reveal about Gabriel's personality?
3. What is Freddy Malins' role in the story? What do the details of his appearance suggest about his character?
4. What historical Irish conflict does Miss Ivors' dialogue with Gabriel about the "Irish language" present? What position does Gabriel represent? With whom do you think Joyce—the writer—sympathizes?
5. Explain fully the party scene before the dinner. Focus on the symbolic role of the paintings, music, and minor characters.
6. What does Gabriel's dinner table speech signify? Why does he wish to be outside rather than at the dinner table? Consider the entire dinner scene carefully.
7. At the end of the evening, why is Gabriel suddenly drawn to his wife? What do Gabriel's responses reveal about his feelings for his wife?

---

[44] Southwest of Dublin.
[45] River that flows in a western direction through Ireland.

8. What does he hope to recapture at their room in the hotel? Analyze their interaction.
9. What is the significance of the story of Michael Furey? What does the story represent to Gretta? What does Gabriel realize about his relationship with his wife?
10. Explore the significance of this passage: "One by one they were all becoming shades. Better pass boldly into that other world, in the full glory of some passion, than fade and wither dismally with age."
11. Examine and explain the imagery of fire and ice throughout the story and the symbolism of snow in the closing paragraph. How do they elucidate themes of the work?
12. Is the ending of "The Dead" tragic? Why? (See the definition of **tragedy** in the Glossary.) Who are "the dead"?
13. Many critics consider the ending of "The Dead" to be one of the most evocative, powerful closings of a short story ever written. Evaluate the conclusion to determine whether or not you agree. Present your position.

■■ JOURNAL ENTRIES ■■

1. React to the title, "The Dead."
2. React to the world which Joyce creates in this story.
3. Write a first impression and then a later impression of either Gabriel or Gretta.

■■■ IDEAS FOR WRITING ■■■

1. Compare Gabriel's recognition at the end of "The Dead" with the mother's insight in "Love Must Not Be Forgotten" or with Gurov's and Anna's positions in "Lady with Lapdog." What do they suggest about the nature of romantic love? of married love?
2. Analyze the structure of "The Dead" and Joyce's crafting of the work. (Focus on point of view, plot, development of characters, use of dialogue and symbolism.)

Love Must Not Be Forgotten

Zhang Jie

Translated by Gladys Yang

Born in Beijing, China, Zhang Jie (1937–   ), the daughter of a teacher, was educated at People's University in Beijing. During the Cultural Revolution, from 1969–1972, she was sent to a labor camp. Jie began writing fiction at forty and gained renown in China for her novel, Leaden Wings *(1981). A non-conformist, she challenged societal mores by divorcing her first husband and by expressing feminist principles in* Love Must Not Be Forgotten *(1980). Other volumes of her works include* As Long As Nothing Happens, Nothing Will *(1988) and* You Are a Friend of My Soul *(1990).*

"Love Must Not Be Forgotten" caused a furor when it was first published in China because it condoned illicit romantic love, condemned arranged marriage, and presented the possibility of rejecting marriage altogether.

1   I am thirty, the same age as our People's Republic. For a republic thirty is still young. But a girl of thirty is virtually on the shelf.

Actually, I have a bonafide suitor. Have you seen the Greek sculptor Myron's Discobolus? Qiao Lin is the image of that discus thrower. Even the padded clothes he wears in winter fail to hide his fine physique. Bronzed, with clear-cut features, a broad forehead and large eyes, his appearance alone attracts most girls to him.

But I can't make up my mind to marry him. I'm not clear what attracts me to him, or him to me. I know people are gossiping behind my back, "Who does she think she is, to be so choosy?" To them, I'm a nobody playing hard to get. They take offense at such preposterous behavior.

Of course, I shouldn't be captious. In a society where commercial production still exists, marriage like most other transactions is still a form of barter.

5   I have know Qiao Lin for nearly two years, yet still cannot fathom whether he keeps so quiet from aversion to talking or from having nothing to say. When, by way of a small intelligence test, I demand his opinion of this or that, he says "good" or "bad" like a child in kindergarten.

Once I asked, "Qiao Lin, why do you love me?" He thought the question over seriously for what seemed an age. I could see from his normally smooth but now wrinkled forehead that the little grey cells in his handsome head were hard at work cogitating. I felt ashamed to have put him on the spot.

Finally he raised his clear childlike eyes to tell me, "Because you're good!"

Loneliness flooded my heart. "Thank you, Qiao Lin!" I couldn't help wondering, if we were to marry, whether we could discharge our duties to each other as husband and wife. Maybe, because law and morality would have bound us together. But how tragic simply to comply with law and morality! Was there no stronger bond to link us?

When such thoughts cross my mind I have the strange sensation that instead of being a girl contemplating marriage I am an elderly social scientist.

10 Perhaps I worry too much. We can live like most married couples, bringing up children together, strictly true to each other according to the law. . . . Although living in the seventies of the twentieth century, people still consider marriage the way they did millennia ago, as a means of continuing the race, a form of barter or a business transaction in which love and marriage can be separated. Since this is the common practice, why shouldn't we follow suit?

But I still can't make up my mind. As a child, I remember, I often cried all night for no rhyme or reason, unable to sleep and disturbing the whole household. My old nurse, a shrewd though uneducated woman, said an ill wind had blown through my ear. I think this judgment showed prescience, because I still have that old weakness. I upset myself over things which really present no problem, upsetting other people at the same time. One's nature is hard to change.

I think of my mother too. If she were alive, what would she say about my attitude to Qiao Lin and my uncertainty about marrying him? My thoughts constantly turn to her, not because she was such a strict mother that her ghost is still watching over me since her death. No, she was not just my mother but my closest friend. I loved her so much that the thought of her leaving me makes my heart ache.

She never lectured me, just told me quietly in her deep, unwomanly voice about her successes and failures, so that I could learn from her experience. She had evidently not had many successes—her life was full of failures.

During her last days she followed me with her fine, expressive eyes, as if wondering how I would manage on my own and as if she had some important advice for me but hesitated to give it. She must have been worried by my naiveté and sloppy ways. She suddenly blurted out, "Shanshan, if you aren't sure what you want, don't rush into marriage—better live on your own!"

15 Other people might think this strange advice from a mother to her daughter, but to me it embodied her bitter experience. I don't think she underestimated me or my knowledge of life. She loved me and didn't want me to be unhappy.

"I don't want to marry, mother!" I said, not out of bashfulness or a show of coyness. I can't think why a girl should pretend to be coy. She had long since taught me about things not generally mentioned to girls.

"If you meet the right man, then marry him. Only if he's right for you!"

"I'm afraid no such man exists!"

"That's not true. But it's hard. The world is so vast, I'm afraid you may never meet him." Whether married or not was not what concerned her, but the quality of the marriage.

20 "Haven't you managed fine without a husband?"

"Who says so?"

"I think you've done fine."

"I had no choice. . . ." She broke off, lost in thought, her face wistful. Her wistful lined face reminded me of a withered flower I had pressed in a book.

"Why did you have no choice?"

25   "You ask too many questions," she parried, not ashamed to confide in me but afraid that I might reach the wrong conclusion. Besides, everyone treasures a secret to carry to the grave. Feeling a bit put out, I demanded bluntly, "Didn't you love my dad?"

"No, I never loved him."

"Did he love you?"

"No, he didn't."

"Then why get married?"

30   She paused, searching for the right words to explain this mystery, then answered bitterly, "When you're young you don't always know what you're looking for, what you need, and people may talk you into getting married. As you grow older and more experienced you find out your true needs. By then, though, you've done many foolish things for which you could kick yourself. You'd give anything to be able to make a fresh start and live more wisely. Those content with their lot will always be happy, they say, but I shall never enjoy that happiness." She added self-mockingly, "A wretched idealist, that's all I am."

Did I take after her? Did we both have genes which attracted ill winds?

"Why don't you marry again?"

"I'm afraid I'm still not sure what I really want." She was obviously unwilling to tell me the truth.

I cannot remember my father. He and Mother split up when I was very small. I just recall her telling me sheepishly that he was a fine handsome fellow. I could see she was ashamed of having judged by appearances and made a futile choice. She told me, "When I can't sleep at night, I force myself to sober up by recalling all those stupid blunders I made. Of course it's so distasteful that I often hide my face in the sheet for shame, as if there were eyes watching me in the dark. But distasteful as it is, I take some pleasure in this form of atonement."

35   I was really sorry that she hadn't remarried. She was such a fascinating character, if she'd married a man she loved, what a happy household ours would surely have been. Though not beautiful, she had the simple charm of an ink landscape. She was a fine writer too. Another author who knew her well used to say teasingly, "Just reading your works is enough to make anyone love you!"

She would retort, "If he knew that the object of his affection was a white-haired old crone, that would frighten him away." At her age, she must have known what she really wanted, so this was obviously an evasion. I say this because she had quirks which puzzled me.

For instance, whenever she left Beijing on a trip, she always took with her one of the twenty-seven volumes of Chekov's stories[1] published between 1950 and 1955. She also warned me, "Don't touch these books. If you want to read Chekov, read that set I bought you." There was no need to caution me. Having a set of my own why should I touch hers? Besides, she'd told me this

---

[1] Reference to Russian short story writer and dramatist, Anton Chekhov (1860–1904).

over and over again. Still she was on her guard. She seemed bewitched by those books.

So we had two sets of Chekov's stories at home. Not just because we loved Chekov, but to parry other people like me who loved Chekov. Whenever anyone asked to borrow a volume, she would lend one of mine. Once, in her absence, a close friend took a volume from her set. When she found out she was frantic, and at once took a volume of mine to exchange for it.

Ever since I can remember, those books were on her bookcase. Although I admire Chekov as a great writer, I was puzzled by the way she never tired of reading him. Why, for over twenty years, had she had to read him every single day? Sometimes, when tired of writing, she poured herself a cup of strong tea and sat down in front of the bookcase, staring raptly at that set of books. If I went into her room then it flustered her, and she either spilt her tea or blushed like a girl discovered with her lover.

40   I wondered: Has she fallen in love with Chekov? She might have if he'd still been alive.

When her mind was wandering just before her death, her last words to me were: "That set . . ." She hadn't the strength to give it its complete title. But I knew what she meant. "And my diary . . . 'Love Must Not Be Forgotten.' . . . Cremate them with me."

I carried out her last instruction regarding the works of Chekov, but couldn't bring myself to destroy her diary. I thought, if it could be published, it would surely prove the most moving thing she had written. But naturally publication was out of the question.

At first I imagined the entries were raw material she had jotted down. They read neither like stories, essays, a diary or letters. But after reading the whole I formed a hazy impression, helped out by my imperfect memory. Thinking it over, I finally realized that this was no lifeless manuscript I was holding, but an anguished, loving heart. For over twenty years one man had occupied her heart, but he was not for her. She used these diaries as a substitute for him, a means of pouring out her feelings to him, day after day, year after year.

No wonder she had never considered any eligible proposals, had turned a deaf ear to idle talk whether well-meant or malicious. Her heart was already full, to the exclusion of anybody else. "No lake can compare with the ocean, no cloud with those on Mount Wu." Remembering those lines I often reflected sadly that few people in real life could love like this. No one would love me like this.

45   I learned that toward the end of the thirties, when this man was doing underground work for the Party in Shanghai, an old worker had given his life to cover him, leaving behind a helpless wife and daughter. Out of a sense of duty, of gratitude to the dead and deep class feeling, he had unhesitatingly married the daughter. When he saw the endless troubles of couples who had married for "love," he may have thought, "Thank Heaven, though I didn't marry for love, we get on well, able to help each other." For years, as man and wife they lived through hard times.

He must have been my mother's colleague. Had I ever met him? He couldn't have visited our home. Who was he?

In the spring of 1962, Mother took me to a concert. We went on foot, the theater being quite near. On the way a black limousine pulled up silently by the pavement. Out stepped an elderly man with white hair in a black serge tunic-suit. What a striking shock of white hair! Strict, scrupulous, distinguished, transparently honest—that was my impression of him. The cold glint of his flashing eyes reminded me of lightning or swordplay. Only ardent love for a woman really deserving his love could fill cold eyes like those with tenderness.

He walked up to Mother and said, "How are you, Comrade Zhong Yu? It's been a long time."

"How are you!" Mother's hand holding mine suddenly turned icy cold and trembled a little.

50   They stood face to face without looking at each other, each appearing up-set, even stern. Mother fixed her eyes on the trees by the roadside, not yet in leaf. He looked at me. "Such a big girl already. Good, fine—you take after your mother."

Instead of shaking hands with Mother he shook hands with me. His hand was as icy as hers and trembling a little. As if transmitting an electric cur-rent, I felt a sudden shock. Snatching my hand away I cried, "There's nothing good about that!"

"Why not?" he asked with the surprised expression grown-ups always have when children speak out frankly.

I glanced at Mother's face. I did take after her, to my disappointment. "Because she's not beautiful!"

He laughed, then said teasingly, "Too bad that there should be a child who doesn't find her own mother beautiful. Do you remember in '53, when your mother was transferred to Beijing, she came to our ministry to report for duty. She left you outside on the veranda, but like a monkey you climbed all the stairs, peeped through the cracks in doors, and caught your finger in the door of my office. You sobbed so bitterly that I carried you off to find her."

55   "I don't remember that." I was annoyed at his harking back to a time when I was still in open-seat pants.

"Ah, we old people have better memories." He turned abruptly and re-marked to Mother, "I've read that last story of yours. Frankly speaking, there's something not quite right about it. You shouldn't have condemned the heroine. . . . There's nothing wrong with falling in love, as long as you don't spoil someone else's life. . . . In fact, the hero might have loved her too. Only for the sake of a third person's happiness, they had to renounce their love. . . ."

A policeman came over to where the car was parked and ordered the driver to move on. When the driver made some excuse, the old man looked around. After a hasty "Goodbye" he strode back to the car and told the police-man, "Sorry. It's not his fault, it's mine. . . ."

I found it amusing watching this old cadre listening respectfully to the policeman's strictures. When I turned to Mother with a mischievous smile, she looked as upset as a first-form primary schoolchild standing forlornly in front of the stern headmistress. Anyone would have thought she was the one being lectured by the policeman. The car drove off, leaving a puff of smoke. Very soon even this smoke vanished with the wind, as if nothing at all had happened. But the incident stuck in my mind.

Analyzing it now, I realize he must have been the man whose strength of character won Mother's heart. That strength came from his firm political convictions, his narrow escapes from death in the revolution, his active brain, his drive at work, his well-cultivated mind. Besides, strange to say, he and Mother both liked the oboe. Yes, she must have worshipped him. She once told me that unless she worshipped a man, she couldn't love him even for one day.

60   But I could not tell whether he loved her or not. If not, why was there this entry in her diary?

"This is far too fine a present. But how did you know that Chekov's my favorite writer?"
"You said so."
"I don't remember that."
"I remember. I heard you mention it when you were chatting with someone."

So he was the one who had given her the *Selected Stories of Chekhov*. For her that was tantamount to a love letter. Maybe this man, who didn't believe in love, realized by the time his hair was white that in his heart was something which could be called love. By the time he no longer had the right to love, he made the tragic discovery of this love for which he would have given his life. Or did it go deeper even than that?

This is all I remember about him.

How wretched Mother must have been, deprived of the man to whom she was devoted! To catch a glimpse of his car or the back of his head through its rear window, she carefully figured out which roads he would take to work and back. Whenever he made a speech, she sat at the back of the hall watching his face rendered hazy by cigarette smoke and poor lighting. Her eyes would brim with tears, but she swallowed them back. If a fit of coughing made him break off, she wondered anxiously why no one persuaded him to give up smoking. She was afraid he would get bronchitis again. Why was he so near yet so far?

65   He, to catch a glimpse of her, looked out of the car window every day straining his eyes to watch the streams of cyclists, afraid that she might have an accident. On the rare evenings on which he had no meetings, he would walk by a roundabout way to our neighborhood, to pass our compound gate. However busy, he would always make time to look in papers and journals for her work. His duty had always been clear to him, even in the most difficult times. But now confronted by this love he became a weakling, quite helpless. At his age it was laughable. Why should life play this trick on him?

Yet when they happened to meet at work, each tried to avoid the other, hurrying off with a nod. Even so, this would make Mother blind and deaf to everything around her. If she met a colleague named Wang she would call him Guo and mutter something unintelligible.

It was a cruel ordeal for her. She wrote:

> *We agreed to forget each other. But I deceived you, I have never forgotten. I don't think you've forgotten either. We're just deceiving each other, hiding our misery. I haven't deceived you deliberately, though; I did my best to carry out our agreement. I often stay far away from Beijing, hoping time and distance will help me to forget you. But when I return, as the train pulls into the station, my head reels. I stand on the platform looking round intently, as if someone were waiting for me. Of course there is no one. I realize then that I have forgotten nothing. Everything is unchanged. My love is like a tree the roots of which strike deeper year after year—I have no way to uproot it.*
>
> *At the end of every day, I feel as if I've forgotten something important. I may wake with a start from my dreams wondering what has happened. But nothing has happened. Nothing. Then it comes home to me that you are missing! So everything seems lacking, incomplete, and there is nothing to fill up the blank. We are nearing the ends of our lives, why should we be carried away by emotion like children? Why should life submit people to such ordeals, then unfold before you your lifelong dream? Because I started off blindly I took the wrong turning, and now there are insuperable obstacles between me and my dream.*

Yes, Mother never let me go to the station to meet her when she came back from a trip, preferring to stand alone on the platform and imagine that he had met her. Poor mother with her greying hair was as infatuated as a girl.

Not much space in the diary was devoted to their romance. Most entries dealt with trivia: why one of her articles had not come off; her fear that she had no real talent; the excellent play she missed by mistaking the time on the ticket; the drenching she got by going out for a stroll without her umbrella. In spirit they were together day and night, like a devoted married couple. In fact, they spent no more than twenty-four hours together in all. Yet in that time they experienced deeper happiness than some people in a whole lifetime. Shakespeare makes Juliet say, "I cannot sum up half my sum of wealth."[2] And probably that is how Mother felt.

70   He must have been killed in the Cultural Revolution.[3] Perhaps because of the conditions then, that section of the diary is ambiguous and obscure.

---

[2] Reference to William Shakespeare's tragedy, *Romeo and Juliet*.
[3] Period of repression in China after the death of Mao Tse-Tung; a movement led by the so-called Gang of Four.

Mother had been so fiercely attacked for her writing, it amazed me that she went on keeping a diary. From some veiled allusions I gathered that he had questioned the theories advanced by that "theoretician" then at the height of favor, and had told someone, "This is sheer Rightist talk." It was clear from the tear-stained pages of Mother's diary that he had been harshly denounced; but the steadfast old man never knuckled under to the authorities. His last words were, "When I go to meet Marx, I shall go on fighting my case!"

That must have been in the winter of 1969, because that was when Mother's hair turned white overnight, though she was not yet fifty. And she put on a black arm-band. Her position then was extremely difficult. She was criticized for wearing this old style of mourning, and ordered to say for whom she was in mourning.

"For whom are you wearing that, Mother?" I asked anxiously.

"For my lover." Not to frighten me she explained, "Someone you never knew."

"Shall I put one on too?" She patted my cheeks, as she had when I was a child. It was years since she had shown me such affection. I often felt that as she aged, especially during these last years of persecution, all tenderness had left her, or was concealed in her heart, so that she seemed like a man.

75   She smiled sadly and said, "No, you needn't wear one." Her eyes were as dry as if she had no more tears to shed. I longed to comfort her or do something to please her. But she said, "Off you go."

I felt an inexplicable dread, as if dear Mother had already half left me. I blurted out, "Mother!"

Quick to sense my desolation, she said gently, "Don't be afraid. Off you go. Leave me alone for a little."

I was right. She wrote:

> *You have gone. Half my soul seems to have taken flight with you.*
>
> *I had no means of knowing what had become of you, much less of seeing you for the last time. I had no right to ask either, not being your wife or friend. . . . So we are torn apart. If only I could have borne that inhuman treatment for you, so that you could have lived on! You should have lived to see your name cleared and take up your work again, for the sake of those who loved you. I knew you could not be a counter-revolutionary. You were one of the finest men killed. That's why I love you—I am not afraid now to avow it.*
>
> *Snow is whirling down. Heavens, even God is such a hypocrite, he is using this whiteness to cover up your blood and the scandal of your murder.*
>
> *I have never set store by my life. But now I keep wondering whether anything I say or do would make you contract your shaggy eyebrows in a frown. I must live a worthwhile life like you, and do some honest work for our country. Things can't go on like this— those criminals will get what's coming to them.*

> *I used to walk alone along that small asphalt road, the only place where we once walked together, hearing my footsteps in the silent night. . . . I always paced to and fro and lingered there, but never as wretchedly as now. Then, though you were not beside me, I knew you were still in this world and felt that you were keeping me company. Now I can hardly believe that you have gone.*
>
> *At the end of the road I would retrace my steps, then walk along it again. Rounding the fence I always looked back, as if you were still standing there waving goodbye. We smiled faintly, like casual acquaintances, to conceal our undying love. That ordinary evening in early spring a chilly wind was blowing as we walked silently away from each other. You were wheezing a little because of your chronic bronchitis. That upset me. I wanted to beg you to slow down, but somehow I couldn't. We both walked very fast, as if some important business were waiting for us. How we prized that single stroll we had together, but we were afraid we might lose control of ourselves and burst out with "I love you"—those three words which had tormented us for years. Probably no one else could believe that we never once even clasped hands!*

No, Mother, I believe it. I am the only one able to see into your locked heart.

80   Ah, that little asphalt road, so haunted by bitter memories. We shouldn't overlook the most insignificant spots on earth. For who knows how much secret grief and joy they may hide. No wonder that when tired of writing, she would pace slowly along that little road behind our window. Sometimes at dawn after a sleepless night, sometimes on a moonless, windy evening. Even in winter during howling gales which hurled sand and pebbles against the window pane. . . . I thought this was one of her eccentricities, not knowing that she had gone to meet him in spirit.

She liked to stand by the window, too, staring at the small asphalt road. Once I thought from her expression that one of our closest friends must be coming to call. I hurried to the window. It was a late autumn evening. The cold wind was stripping dead leaves from the trees and blowing them down the small empty road.

She went on pouring out her heart to him in her diary as she had when he was alive. Right up to the day when the pen slipped from her fingers. Her last message was:

> *I am a materialist, yet I wish there were a Heaven. For then, I know, I would find you there waiting for me. I am going there to join you, to be together for eternity. We need never be parted again or keep at a distance for fear of spoiling someone else's life. Wait for me, dearest, I am coming—*

I do not know how, on her death bed, Mother could still love so ardently with all her heart. To me it seemed not love but a form of madness, a passion stronger than death. If undying love really exists, she reached its extreme. She obviously died happy, because she had known true love. She had no regrets.

Now these old people's ashes have mingled with the elements. But I know that no matter what form they may take, they still love each other. Though not bound together by earthly laws or morality, though they never once clasped hands, each possessed the other completely. Nothing could part them. Centuries to come, if one white cloud trails another, two grasses grow side by side, one wave splashes another, a breeze follows another . . . believe me, that will be them.

85   Each time I read that diary "Love Must Not Be Forgotten" I cannot hold back my tears. I often weep bitterly, as if I myself experienced their ill-fated love. If not a tragedy it was too laughable. No matter how beautiful or moving I find it, I have no wish to follow suit!

Thomas Hardy[4] wrote that "the call seldom produces the comer, the man to love rarely coincides with the hour for loving." I cannot judge them by conventional moral standards. What I deplore is that they did not wait for a "missing counterpart" to call them. If everyone could wait, instead of rushing into marriage, how many tragedies could be averted!

When we reach communism, will there still be cases of marriage without love? Perhaps . . . since the world is so vast, two kindred spirits may never be able to answer each other's call. But how tragic! Could it be that by then we will have devised ways to escape such tragedies? But this is all conjecture.

Maybe after all we are accountable for these tragedies. Who knows? Should we take the responsibility for the old ideas handed down from the past? Because, if you choose not to marry, your behavior is considered a direct challenge to these ideas. You will be called neurotic, accused of having guilty secrets or having made political mistakes. You may be regarded as an eccentric who looks down on ordinary people, not respecting age-old customs—a heretic. In short they will trump up endless vulgar and futile charges to ruin your reputation. Then you have to succumb to those ideas and marry regardless. But once you put the chains of an indifferent marriage around your neck, you will suffer for it for the rest of your life.

I long to shout: "Mind your own business! Let us wait patiently for our counterparts. Even waiting in vain is better than loveless marriage. To live single is not such a fearful disaster. I believe it may be a sign of a step forward in culture, education and the quality of life."

■   **EXPLORATIONS OF THE TEXT**   ■

1.   What is the narrator's conflict? Why is she dissatisfied with her relationship with her mother?
2.   What issues about romantic love does her mother's story reveal? How are the mother's and daughter's lives intertwined?

---

[4] British novelist and poet (1840–1928).

3. What criticism of Chinese society and marriage customs does the story present?
4. Why does the story shift purpose and tone near the end?
5. What is the effect of the inclusion of letters in the story?

■■ **JOURNAL ENTRIES** ■■

1. Create a monologue for the mother or daughter.
2. Create a monologue in the voice of the man.

■■■ **IDEAS FOR WRITING** ■■■

1. Do research on Chinese marriage customs. How are they changing? Why?
2. Defend a choice never to marry.

The Yellow Wallpaper

Charlotte Perkins Gilman

Born in Hartford, Connecticut, Charlotte Perkins Gilman (1860–1935) was raised by her mother. She was related to the famous Beecher family through her father. In her autobiography, The Living of Charlotte Perkins Gilman *(1935), she records the depression that she suffered after the birth of her only daughter, Katharine, and her treatment by a physician who offered a cure like that prescribed in "The Yellow Wallpaper." Later she moved to California, obtained a divorce, and began to write, to lecture, and to teach. "The Yellow Wallpaper" appeared in 1892 in* New England Magazine. *In* Women and Economics, *published in 1898, Gilman suggested that economic equality was more important than the right to vote. In 1900, she married George Gilman and moved to New York. She wrote books about alternative social structures:* Concerning Children *(1900),* The Home *(1903), and* Human Work *(1904). Her other books,* Man-Made World *(1911) and* His Religion and Hers *(1923), present the female as the primary gender. In 1915, she serialized a feminist utopia,* Herland, *presenting a culture without men and with high ethical values.*

She spoke at national and international women's conferences and moved to California in 1934. She committed suicide in 1935 because she preferred "chloroform to breast cancer" and because she believed in her right to do so. A remarkably productive writer and lecturer, Gilman suffered from her early depression all of her life. In her essay "Why I Wrote The Yellow Wallpaper," she states that the tale "was not intended to drive people crazy, but to save people from being driven crazy, and it worked."

1   It is very seldom that mere ordinary people like John and myself secure ancestral halls for the summer.

A colonial mansion, a hereditary estate, I would say a haunted house and reach the height of romantic felicity—but that would be asking too much of fate!

Still I will proudly declare that there is something queer about it.

Else, why should it be let so cheaply? And why have stood so long untenanted?

5   John laughs at me, of course, but one expects that.

John is practical in the extreme. He has no patience with faith, an intense horror of superstition, and he scoffs openly at any talk of things not to be felt and seen and put down in figures.

John is a physician, and *perhaps*—(I would not say it to a living soul, of course, but this is dead paper and a great relief to my mind)—*perhaps* that is one reason I do not get well faster.

You see he does not believe I am sick! And what can one do?

If a physician of high standing, and one's own husband, assures friends and relatives that there is really nothing the matter with one but temporary nervous depression—a slight hysterical tendency[1]—what is one to do?

10   My brother is also a physician, and also of high standing, and he says the same thing.

So I take phosphates[2] or phosphites—whichever it is—and tonics, and air and exercise, and journeys, and am absolutely forbidden to "work" until I am well again.

Personally, I disagree with their ideas.

Personally, I believe that congenial work, with excitement and change, would do me good.

But what is one to do?

15   I did write for a while in spite of them; but it *does* exhaust me a good deal—having to be so sly about it, or else meet with heavy opposition.

I sometimes fancy that in my condition, if I had less opposition and more society and stimulus—but John says the very worst thing I can do is to think about my condition, and I confess it always makes me feel bad.

---

[1] Hysteria was a general nervous condition, often diagnosed in women in the late nineteenth century. Symptoms included tension, anxiety, nervousness, and depression.

[2] A carbonated beverage made of water, fruit syrup, and phosphoric acid, used for medicinal purposes.

664 Chapter 6 • Love

So I will let it alone and talk about the house.

The most beautiful place! It is quite alone, standing well back from the road, quite three miles from the village. It makes me think of English places that you read about, for there are hedges and walls and gates that lock, and lots of separate little houses for the gardeners and people.

There is a *delicious* garden! I never saw such a garden—large and shady, full of box-bordered paths, and lined with long grape-covered arbors with seats under them.

20 There were greenhouses, but they are all broken now.

There was some legal trouble, I believe, something about the heirs and co-heirs; anyhow, the place has been empty for years.

That spoils my ghostliness, I am afraid, but I don't care—there is something strange about the house—I can feel it.

I even said so to John one moonlight evening, but he said what I felt was a draught, and shut the window.

I get unreasonably angry with John sometimes. I'm sure I never used to be so sensitive. I think it is due to this nervous condition.

25 But John says if I feel so I shall neglect proper self-control; so I take pains to control myself—before him, at least, and that makes me very tired.

I don't like our room a bit. I wanted one downstairs that opened onto the piazza and had roses all over the window, and such pretty old-fashioned chintz hangings! But John would not hear of it.

He said there was only one window and not room for two beds, and no near room for him if he took another.

He is very careful and loving, and hardly lets me stir without special direction.

I have a schedule prescription for each hour in the day; he takes all care from me, and so I feel basely ungrateful not to value it more.

30 He said we came here solely on my account, that I was to have perfect rest and all the air I could get. "Your exercise depends on your strength, my dear," said he, "and your food somewhat on your appetite; but air you can absorb all the time." So we took the nursery at the top of the house.

It is a big, airy room, the whole floor nearly, with windows that look all ways, and air and sunshine galore. It was nursery first, and then playroom and gymnasium, I should judge, for the windows are barred for little children, and there are rings and things in the walls.

The paint and paper look as if a boys' school had used it. It is stripped off—the paper—in great patches all around the head of my bed, about as far as I can reach, and in a great place on the other side of the room low down. I never saw a worse paper in my life. One of those sprawling, flamboyant patterns committing every artistic sin.

It is dull enough to confuse the eye in following, pronounced enough to constantly irritate and provoke study, and when you follow the lame uncertain curves for a little distance they suddenly commit suicide—plunge off at outrageous angles, destroy themselves in unheard-of contradictions.

The color is repellent, almost revolting: a smouldering unclean yellow, strangely faded by the slow-turning sunlight. It is a dull yet lurid orange in some places, a sickly sulphur tint in others.

35 No wonder the children hated it! I should hate it myself if I had to live in this room long.

There comes John, and I must put this away—he hates to have me write a word.

We have been here two weeks, and I haven't felt like writing before, since that first day.

I am sitting by the window now, up in this atrocious nursery, and there is nothing to hinder my writing as much as I please, save lack of strength.

John is away all day, and even some nights when his cases are serious.

40 I am glad my case is not serious!

But these nervous troubles are dreadfully depressing.

John does not know how much I really suffer. He knows there is no reason to suffer, and that satisfies him.

Of course it is only nervousness. It does weigh on me so not to do my duty in any way!

I meant to be such a help to John, such a real rest and comfort, and here I am a comparative burden already!

45 Nobody would believe what an effort it is to do what little I am able—to dress and entertain, and order things.

It is fortunate Mary is so good with the baby. Such a dear baby!

And yet I *cannot* be with him, it makes me so nervous.

I suppose John never was nervous in his life. He laughs at me so about this wallpaper!

At first he meant to repaper the room, but afterward he said that I was letting it get the better of me, and that nothing was worse for a nervous patient than to give way to such fancies.

50 He said that after the wallpaper was changed it would be the heavy bedstead, and then the barred windows, and then that gate at the head of the stairs, and so on.

"You know the place is doing you good," he said, "and really, dear, I don't care to renovate the house just for a three months' rental."

"Then do let us go downstairs," I said. "There are such pretty rooms there."

Then he took me in his arms and called me a blessed little goose, and said he would go down cellar, if I wished, and have it whitewashed into the bargain.

But he is right enough about the beds and windows and things.

55 It is as airy and comfortable room as anyone need wish, and, of course, I would not be so silly as to make him uncomfortable just for a whim.

I'm really getting quite fond of the big room, all but that horrid paper.

Out of one window I can see the garden—those mysterious deep-shaded arbors, the riotous old-fashioned flowers, and bushes and gnarly trees.

Out of another I get a lovely view of the bay and a little private wharf belonging to the estate. There is a beautiful shaded lane that runs down there from the house. I always fancy I see people walking in these numerous paths and arbors, but John has cautioned me not to give way to fancy in the least. He says that with my imaginative power and habit of story-making, a nervous weakness like mine is sure to lead to all manner of excited fancies, and that I ought to use my will and good sense to check the tendency. So I try.

I think sometimes that if I were only well enough to write a little it would relieve the press of ideas and rest me.

60   But I find I get pretty tired when I try.

It is so discouraging not to have any advice and companionship about my work. When I get really well, John says we will ask Cousin Henry and Julia down for a long visit; but he says he would as soon put fireworks in my pillow-case as to let me have those stimulating people about now.

I wish I could get well faster.

But I must not think about that. This paper looks to me as if it *knew* what a vicious influence it had!

There is a recurrent spot where the pattern lolls like a broken neck and two bulbous eyes stare at you upside down.

65   I get positively angry with the impertinence of it and the everlastingness. Up and down and sideways they crawl, and those absurd unblinking eyes are everywhere. There is one place where two breadths didn't match, and the eyes go all up and down the line, one a little higher than the other.

I never saw so much expression in an inanimate thing before, and we all know how much expression they have! I used to lie awake as a child and get more entertainment and terror out of blank walls and plain furniture than most children could find in a toy-store.

I remember what a kindly wink the knobs of our big old bureau used to have, and there was one chair that always seemed like a strong friend.

I used to feel that if any of the other things looked too fierce I could always hop into that chair and be safe.

The furniture in this room is no worse than inharmonious, however, for we had to bring it all from downstairs. I suppose when this was used as a playroom they had to take the nursery things out, and no wonder! I never saw such ravages as the children have made here.

70   The wallpaper, as I said before, is torn off in spots, and it sticketh closer than a brother—they must have had perseverance as well as hatred.

Then the floor is scratched and gouged and splintered, the plaster itself is dug out here and there, and this great heavy bed, which is all we found in the room, looks as if it had been through the wars.

But I don't mind it a bit—only the paper.

There comes John's sister. Such a dear girl as she is, and so careful of me! I must not let her find me writing.

She is a perfect and enthusiastic housekeeper, and hopes for no better profession. I verily believe she thinks it is the writing which made me sick!

75 But I can write when she is out, and see her a long way off from these windows.

There is one that commands the road, a lovely shaded winding road, and one that just looks off over the country. A lovely country, too, full of great elms and velvet meadows.

This wallpaper has a kind of sub-pattern in a different shade, a particularly irritating one, for you can only see it in certain lights, and not clearly then.

But in the places where it isn't faded and where the sun is just so—I can see a strange, provoking, formless sort of figure that seems to skulk about behind that silly and conspicuous front design.

There's sister on the stairs!

80 Well, the Fourth of July is over! The people are all gone, and I am tired out. John thought it might do me good to see a little company, so we just had mother and Nellie and the children down for a week.

Of course I didn't do a thing. Jennie sees to everything now.

But it tired me all the same.

John says if I don't pick up faster he shall send me to Weir Mitchell[3] in the fall.

But I don't want to go there at all. I had a friend who was in his hands once, and she says he is just like John and my brother, only more so!

85 Besides, it is such an undertaking to go so far.

I don't feel as if it was worthwhile to turn my hand over for anything, and I'm getting dreadfully fretful and querulous.

I cry at nothing, and cry most of the time.

Of course I don't when John is here, or anybody else, but when I am alone.

And I am alone a good deal just now. John is kept in town very often by serious cases, and Jennie is good and lets me alone when I want her to.

90 So I walk a little in the garden or down that lovely lane, sit on the porch under the roses, and lie down up here a good deal.

I'm getting really fond of the room in spite of the wallpaper. Perhaps *because* of the wallpaper.

It dwells in my mind so!

I lie here on this great immovable bed—it is nailed down, I believe—and follow that pattern about by the hour. It is as good as gymnastics, I assure you. I start, we'll say, at the bottom, down in the corner over there where it has not been touched, and I determine for the thousandth time that I *will* follow that pointless pattern to some sort of a conclusion.

I know a little of the principle of design, and I know this thing was not arranged on any laws of radiation, or alternation, or repetition, or symmetry, or anything else that I ever heard of.

---

[3] American neurologist who invented the "rest cure" for hysteria and who treated Gilman herself.

95   It is repeated, of course, by the breadths, but not otherwise.

Looked at in one way, each breadth stands alone; the bloated curves and flourishes—a kind of "debased Romanesque"[4] with *delirium tremens*[5]—go waddling up and down in isolated columns of fatuity.

But, on the other hand, they connect diagonally, and the sprawling outlines run off in great slanting waves of optic horror, like a lot of wallowing sea-weeds in full chase.

The whole thing goes horizontally, too, at least it seems so, and I exhaust myself in trying to distinguish the order of its going in that direction.

They have used a horizontal breadth for a frieze,[6] and that adds wonderfully to the confusion.

100   There is one end of the room where it is almost intact, and there, when the crosslights fade and the low sun shines directly upon it, I can almost fancy radiation after all—the interminable grotesque seems to form around a common center and rush off in headlong plunges of equal distraction.

It makes me tired to follow it. I will take a nap, I guess.

I don't know why I should write this.

I don't want to.

I don't feel able.

105   And I know John would think it absurd. But I *must* say what I feel and think in some way—it is such a relief!

But the effort is getting to be greater than the relief.

Half the time now I am awfully lazy, and lie down ever so much. John says I mustn't lose my strength, and has me take cod liver oil and lots of tonics and things, to say nothing of ale and wine and rare meat.

Dear John! He loves me very dearly, and hates to have me sick. I tried to have a real earnest reasonable talk with him the other day, and tell him how I wish he would let me go and make a visit to Cousin Henry and Julia.

But he said I wasn't able to go, nor able to stand it after I got there; and I did not make out a very good case for myself, for I was crying before I had finished.

110   It is getting to be a great effort for me to think straight. Just this nervous weakness, I suppose.

And dear John gathered me up in his arms, and just carried me upstairs and laid me on the bed, and sat by me and read to me till it tired my head.

He said I was his darling and his comfort and all he had, and that I must take care of myself for his sake, and keep well.

He says no one but myself can help me out of it, that I must use my will and self-control and not let any silly fancies run away with me.

---

[4] Style of architecture prevalent from the ninth to twelfth centuries in Europe, characterized by rounded arches and heavy masonry and design.

[5] Condition caused by excessive use of alcohol and characterized by physical trembling and hallucinations.

[6] A decorative band with lettering or sculpture.

There's one comfort—the baby is well and happy, and does not have to occupy this nursery with the horrid wallpaper.

115   If we had not used it, that blessed child would have! What a fortunate escape! Why, I wouldn't have a child of mine, an impressionable little thing, live in such a room for worlds.

I never thought of it before, but it is lucky that John kept me here after all; I can stand it so much easier than a baby, you see.

Of course I never mention it to them any more—I am too wise—but I keep watch for it all the same.

There are things in that wallpaper that nobody knows about but me, or ever will.

Behind that outside pattern the dim shapes get clearer every day.

120   It is always the same shape, only very numerous.

And it is like a woman stooping down and creeping about behind that pattern. I don't like it a bit. I wonder—I begin to think—I wish John would take me away from here!

It is so hard to talk with John about my case, because he is so wise, and because he loves me so.

But I tried it last night.

It was moonlight. The moon shines in all around just as the sun does.

125   I hate to see it sometimes, it creeps so slowly, and always comes in by one window or another.

John was asleep and I hated to waken him, so I kept still and watched the moonlight on that undulating wallpaper till I felt creepy.

The faint figure behind seemed to shake the pattern, just as if she wanted to get out.

I got up softly and went to feel and see if the paper *did* move, and when I came back John was awake.

"What is it, little girl?" he said. "Don't go walking about like that—you'll get cold."

130   I thought it was a good time to talk, so I told him that I really was not gaining here, and that I wished he would take me away.

"Why, darling!" said he. "Our lease will be up in three weeks, and I can't see how to leave before.

"The repairs are not done at home, and I cannot possibly leave town just now. Of course, if you were in any danger, I could and would, but you really are better, dear, whether you can see it or not. I am a doctor, dear, and I know. You are gaining flesh and color, your appetite is better, I feel really much easier about you."

"I don't weigh a bit more," said I, "nor as much; and my appetite may be better in the evening when you are here but it is worse in the morning when you are away!"

"Bless her little heart!" said he with a big hug. "She shall be as sick as she pleases! But now let's improve the shining hours by going to sleep, and talk about it in the morning!"

135   "And you won't go away?" I asked gloomily.

"Why, how can I, dear? It is only three weeks more and then we will take a nice little trip of a few days while Jennie is getting the house ready. Really, dear, you are better!"

"Better in body perhaps—" I began, and stopped short, for he sat up straight and looked at me with such a stern, reproachful look that I could not say another word.

"My darling," said he, "I beg of you, for my sake and for our child's sake, as well as for your own, that you will never for one instant let that idea enter your mind! There is nothing so dangerous, so fascinating, to a temperament like yours. It is a false and foolish fancy. Can you not trust me as a physician when I tell you so?"

So of course I said no more on that score, and we went to sleep before long. He thought I was asleep first, but I wasn't, and lay there for hours trying to decide whether that front pattern and the back pattern really did move together or separately.

140   On a pattern like this, by daylight, there is a lack of sequence, a defiance of law, that is a constant irritant to a normal mind.

The color is hideous enough, and unreliable enough, and infuriating enough, but the pattern is torturing.

You think you have mastered it, but just as you get well under way in following, it turns a back-somersault and there you are. It slaps you in the face, knocks you down, and tramples upon you. It is like a bad dream.

The outside pattern is a florid arabesque, reminding one of a fungus. If you can imagine a toadstool in joints, an interminable string of toadstools, budding and sprouting in endless convolutions—why, that is something like it.

That is, sometimes!

145   There is one marked peculiarity about this paper, a thing nobody seems to notice but myself, and that is that it changes as the light changes.

When the sun shoots in through the east window—I always watch for that first long, straight ray—it changes so quickly that I never can quite believe it.

That is why I watch it always.

By moonlight—the moon shines in all night when there is a moon—I wouldn't know it was the same paper.

At night in any kind of light, in twilight, candlelight, lamplight, and worst of all by moonlight, it becomes bars! The outside pattern, I mean, and the woman behind it is as plain as can be.

150   I didn't realize for a long time what the thing was that showed behind, that dim sub-pattern, but now I am quite sure it is a woman.

By daylight she is subdued, quiet. I fancy it is the pattern that keeps her so still. It is so puzzling. It keeps me quiet by the hour.

I lie down ever so much now. John says it is good for me, and to sleep all I can.

Indeed he started the habit by making me lie down for an hour after each meal.

It is a very bad habit, I am convinced, for you see, I don't sleep.

155   And that cultivates deceit, for I don't tell them I'm awake—oh, no!

The fact is I am getting a little afraid of John.

He seems very queer sometimes, and even Jennie has an inexplicable look.

It strikes me occasionally, just as a scientific hypothesis, that perhaps it is the paper!

I have watched John when he did not know I was looking, and come into the room suddenly on the most innocent excuses, and I've caught him several times *looking at the paper!* And Jennie too. I caught Jennie with her hand on it once.

160 She didn't know I was in the room, and when I asked her in a quiet, a very quiet voice, with the most restrained manner possible, what she was doing with the paper, she turned around as if she had been caught stealing, and looked quite angry—asked me why I should frighten her so!

Then she said that the paper stained everything it touched, that she had found yellow smooches on all my clothes and John's, and she wished we would be more careful!

Did not that sound innocent? But I know she was studying that pattern and I am determined that nobody shall find it out but myself!

Life is very much more exciting now than it used to be. You see, I have something more to expect, to look forward to, to watch. I really do eat better, and am more quiet than I was.

John is so pleased to see me improve! He laughed a little the other day, and said I seemed to be flourishing in spite of my wallpaper.

165 I turned it off with a laugh. I had no intention of telling him it was *because* of the wallpaper—he would make fun of me. He might even want to take me away.

I don't want to leave now until I have found it out. There is a week more, and I think that will be enough.

I'm feeling so much better!

I don't sleep much at night, for it is so interesting to watch developments; but I sleep a good deal during the daytime.

In the daytime it is tiresome and perplexing.

170 There are always new shoots on the fungus, and new shades of yellow all over it. I cannot keep count of them, though I have tried conscientiously. It is the strangest yellow, that wallpaper! It makes me think of all the yellow things I ever saw—not beautiful ones like buttercups, but old, foul, bad yellow things.

But there is something else about that paper—the smell! I noticed it the moment we came into the room, but with so much air and sun it was not bad. Now we have had a week of fog and rain, and whether the windows are open or not, the smell is here.

It creeps all over the house.

I find it hovering in the dining-room, skulking in the parlor, hiding in the hall, lying in wait for me on the stairs.

It gets into my hair.

175   Even when I go to ride, if I turn my head suddenly and surprise it—there is that smell!

Such a peculiar odor, too! I have spent hours in trying to analyze it, to find what it smelled like.

It is not bad—at first—and very gentle, but quite the subtlest, most enduring odor I ever met.

In this damp weather it is awful. I wake up in the night and find it hanging over me.

It used to disturb me at first. I thought seriously of burning the house—to reach the smell.

180   But now I am used to it. The only thing I can think of that it is like is the *color* of the paper! A yellow smell.

There is a very funny mark on this wall, low down, near the mopboard. A streak that runs round the room. It goes behind every piece of furniture, except the bed, a long, straight, even *smooch,* as if it had been rubbed over and over.

I wonder how it was done and who did it, and what they did it for. Round and round and round—round and round and round—it makes me dizzy!

I really have discovered something at last.

Through watching so much at night, when it changes so, I have finally found out.

185   The front pattern *does* move—and no wonder! The woman behind shakes it!

Sometimes I think there are a great many women behind, and sometimes only one, and she crawls around fast, and her crawling shakes it all over.

Then in the very bright spots she keeps still, and in the very shady spots she just takes hold of the bars and shakes them hard.

And she is all the time trying to climb through. But nobody could climb through that pattern—it strangles so; I think that is why it has so many heads.

They get through, and then the pattern strangles them off and turns them upside down, and makes their eyes white!

190   If those heads were covered or taken off it would not be half so bad.

I think that woman gets out in the daytime!

And I'll tell you why—privately—I've seen her!

I can see her out of every one of my windows!

It is the same woman, I know, for she is always creeping, and most women do not creep by daylight.

195   I see her in that long shaded lane, creeping up and down. I see her in those dark grape arbors, creeping all around the garden.

I see her on that long road under the trees, creeping along, and when a carriage comes she hides under the blackberry vines.

I don't blame her a bit. It must be very humiliating to be caught creeping by daylight!

I always lock the door when I creep by daylight. I can't do it at night, for I know John would suspect something at once.

And John is so queer now that I don't want to irritate him. I wish he would take another room! Besides, I don't want anybody to get that woman out at night but myself.

200 I often wonder if I could see her out of all the windows at once.

But, turn as fast as I can, I can only see out of one at one time.

And though I always see her, she *may* be able to creep faster than I can turn! I have watched her sometimes away off in the open country, creeping as fast as a cloud shadow in a wind.

If only that top pattern could be gotten off from the under one! I mean to try it, little by little.

I have found out another funny thing, but I shan't tell it this time! It does not do to trust people too much.

205 There are only two more days to get this paper off, and I believe John is beginning to notice. I don't like the look in his eyes.

And I heard him ask Jennie a lot of professional questions about me. She had a very good report to give.

She said I slept a good deal in the daytime.

John knows I don't sleep very well at night, for all I'm so quiet!

He asked me all sorts of questions, too, and pretended to be very loving and kind.

210 As if I couldn't see through him!

Still, I don't wonder he acts so, sleeping under this paper for three months.

It only interests me, but I feel sure John and Jennie are secretly affected by it. Hurrah! This is the last day, but it is enough. John to stay in town over night, and won't be out until this evening.

Jennie wanted to sleep with me—the sly thing; but I told her I should undoubtedly rest better for a night all alone.

That was clever, for really I wasn't alone a bit! As soon as it was moonlight and that poor thing began to crawl and shake the pattern, I got up and ran to help her.

215 I pulled and she shook. I shook and she pulled, and before morning we had peeled off yards of that paper.

A strip about as high as my head and half around the room.

And then when the sun came and that awful pattern began to laugh at me, I declared I would finish it today!

We go away tomorrow, and they are moving all my furniture down again to leave things as they were before.

Jennie looked at the wall in amazement, but I told her merrily that I did it out of pure spite at the vicious thing.

220 She laughed and said she wouldn't mind doing it herself, but I must not get tired.

How she betrayed herself that time!

But I am here, and no person touches this paper but Me—not *alive!*

She tried to get me out of the room—it was too patent! But I said it was so quiet and empty and clean now that I believed I would lie down again and sleep all I could, and not to wake me even for dinner—I would call when I woke.

So now she is gone, and the servants are gone, and the things are gone, and there is nothing left but that great bedstead nailed down, with the canvas mattress we found on it.

225 We shall sleep downstairs tonight, and take the boat home tomorrow.

I quite enjoy the room, now it is bare again.

How those children did tear about here!

This bedstead is fairly gnawed!

But I must get to work.

230 I have locked the door and thrown the key down into the front path.

I don't want to go out, and I don't want to have anybody come in, till John comes.

I want to astonish him.

I've got a rope up here that even Jennie did not find. If that woman does get out, and tries to get away, I can tie her!

But I forgot I could not reach far without anything to stand on!

235 This bed will *not* move!

I tried to lift and push it until I was lame, and then I got so angry I bit off a little piece at one corner—but it hurt my teeth.

Then I peeled off all the paper I could reach standing on the floor. It sticks horribly and the pattern just enjoys it! All those strangled heads and bulbous eyes and waddling fungus growths just shriek with derision!

I am getting angry enough to do something desperate. To jump out of the window would be admirable exercise, but the bars are too strong even to try.

Besides I wouldn't do it. Of course not. I know well enough that a step like that is improper and might be misconstrued.

240 I don't like to *look* out of the windows even—there are so many of those creeping women, and they creep so fast.

I wonder if they all come out of that wallpaper as I did?

But I am securely fastened now by my well-hidden rope—you don't get *me* out in the road there!

I suppose I shall have to get back behind the pattern when it comes night, and that is hard!

It is so pleasant to be out in this great room and creep around as I please!

245 I don't want to go outside. I won't, even if Jennie asks me to.

For outside you have to creep on the ground, and everything is green instead of yellow.

But here I can creep smoothly on the floor, and my shoulder just fits in that long smooch around the wall, so I cannot lose my way.

Why, there's John at the door!

It is no use, young man, you can't open it!

250 How he does call and pound!

Now he's crying to Jeannie for an axe.

It would be a shame to break down that beautiful door!

"John dear!" said I in the gentlest voice. "The key is down by the front steps, under a plantain leaf!"

That silenced him for a few moments.

255 Then he said, very quietly indeed. "Open the door, my darling!"

"I can't," said I. "The key is down by the front door under a plantain leaf!" And then I said it again, several times, very gently and slowly, and said it so often that he had to go and see, and he got it of course, and came in. He stopped short by the door.

"What is the matter?" he cried. "For God's sake, what are you doing!"

I kept on creeping just the same, but I looked at him over my shoulder.

"I've got out at last," said I, "in spite of you and Jane. And I've pulled off most of the paper, so you can't put me back!"

260 Now why should that man have fainted? But he did, and right across my path by the wall, so that I had to creep over him every time!

■ **EXPLORATIONS OF THE TEXT** ■

1. What attitudes characterize John's treatment of his wife? Do his attitudes contribute to the narrator's situation? Look carefully at terms of endearment.
2. Is the narrator correct in her suspicions about her husband? about her brother? How do her attitudes change in the story?
3. What is the significance of the fact that the narrator's room was originally a nursery?
4. Why does John not want her to write? Why does she want to write?
5. What are the stages in the narrator's psychological breakdown? How are these stages reflected in her obsession with the wallpaper?
6. Who is the "woman" in the wallpaper? Discuss the symbolism of the figure. What does the yellow wallpaper finally symbolize?
7. What does the ending mean? What happens to the narrator? What is the husband's reaction?
8. Explore the point of view and the imagery in this story. How do they contribute to the story's emotional impact?
9. Compare character and theme in this story with those in *And the Soul Shall Dance.*

■■ **JOURNAL ENTRIES** ■■

1. Create a character sketch of the narrator or John. Incorporate specifics from the story.

■■■ IDEAS FOR WRITING ■■■

---

1. Charlotte Perkins Gilman's doctor, treating her for nervous depression, once told her "never to touch pen, brush or pencil again." Why does Gilman imply that the treatment worsens the condition?
2. "The Yellow Wallpaper" was anthologized as a horror or ghost story for many years. Write a defense of "The Yellow Wallpaper" either as a horror story or as more serious fiction.

My Life with the Wave

Octavio Paz

Born in Mexico City, Octavio Paz (1914–   ) was educated in Catholic schools and graduated from the National University of Mexico. At nineteen, he published his first volume of poetry. During the 1920s, he travelled abroad; he fought on the Republican side in the Spanish Civil War and lived in Paris where he encountered many of the Surrealist poets. He returned to Mexico in the 1940s to continue his literary career and also become a diplomat. Paz edited several literary magazines, published many volumes of essays and poetry, and served at the Mexican Embassy in Paris in 1945, then at the Mexican Embassy in Japan in 1951. He became Mexican Ambassador to India from 1962 to 1968, but he resigned in protest over the Mexican government's handling of student radicals in the late 1960s. He then taught at Harvard University and at the University of Texas at Austin. Paz has been an outspoken social critic, a philosopher, an essayist, and a leading figure in the renaissance of Latin American literature.

Paz has published ten volumes of poetry, including Sylvan Moon *(1933);* Salamandra *(1958–1961) (1962); prose poems,* Eagle or Sun *(1976);* Selected Poems *(1967); and* Configurations *(1971). A collected edition of his poems 1957–1987 appeared in 1987. He also has written many volumes of prose. Paz was awarded the Nobel Prize for Literature in 1990.*

In "My Life with the Wave," from Paz's 1949 volume, Arenas Movedizas, *Paz combines elements of parable, of the surreal, and of the fantastic to convey realistic feelings of lovers.*

1   When I left that sea, a wave moved ahead of the others. She was tall and light. In spite of the shouts of the others who grabbed her by her floating clothes, she clutched my arm and went off with me leaping. I didn't want to say anything to her, because it hurt me to shame her in front of her

friends. Besides, the furious stares of the elders paralyzed me. When we got to town, I explained to her that it was impossible, that life in the city was not what she had been able to imagine with the ingenuity of a wave that had never left the sea. She watched me gravely: "No, your decision is made. You can't go back." I tried sweetness, hardness, irony. She cried, screamed, hugged, threatened. I had to apologize.

The next day my troubles began. How could we get on the train without being seen by the conductor, the passengers, the police? Certainly the rules say nothing in respect to the transport of waves on the railroad, but this same reserve was an indication of the severity with which our act would be judged. After much thought I arrived at the station an hour before departure, took my seat, and, when no one was looking, emptied the water tank for the passengers; then, carefully, poured in my friend.

The first incident came about when the children of a nearby couple declared their noisy thirst. I stopped them and promised them refreshments and lemonade. They were at the point of accepting when another thirsty passenger approached. I was about to invite her also, but the stare of her companion stopped me. The lady took a paper cup, approached the tank, and turned the faucet. Her cup was barely half full when I leaped between the woman and my friend. She looked at me astonished. While I apologized, one of the children turned the faucet again. I closed it violently. The lady brought the cup to her lips:

"Agh, this water is salty."

5   The boy echoed her. Various passengers rose. The husband called the conductor:

"This man put salt in the water."

The conductor called the Inspector:

"So you put substances in the water?"

The Inspector in turn called the police:

10   "So you poisoned the water?"

The police in turn called the Captain:

"So you're the poisoner?"

The Captain called three agents. The agents took me to an empty car, amid the stares and whispers of the passengers. At the next station they took me off and pushed and dragged me to the jail. For days no one spoke to me, except during the long interrogations. When I explained my story no one believed me, not even the jailer, who shook his head, saying: "The case is grave, truly grave. You didn't want to poison the children?" One day they brought me before the Magistrate.

"Your case is difficult," he repeated. "I will assign you to the Penal Judge."

15   A year passed. Finally they judged me. As there were no victims, my sentence was light. After a short time, my day of liberty arrived.

The Chief of the Prison called me in:

"Well, now you're free. You were lucky. Lucky there were no victims. But don't do it again, because the next time won't be so short . . ."

And he stared at me with the same grave stare with which everyone watched me.

The same afternoon I took the train and after hours of uncomfortable traveling arrived in Mexico City. I took a cab home. At the door of my apartment I heard laughter and singing. I felt a pain in my chest, like the smack of a wave of surprise when surprise smacks us across the chest: my friend was there, singing and laughing as always.

20   "How did you get back?"

"Simple: in the train. Someone, after making sure that I was only salt water, poured me in the engine. It was a rough trip: soon I was a white plume of vapor, soon I fell in a fine rain on the machine. I thinned out a lot. I lost many drops."

Her presence changed my life. The house of dark corridors and dusty furniture was filled with air, with sun, with sounds and green and blue reflections, a numerous and happy populace of reverberations and echoes. How many waves is one wave, and how it can make a beach or a rock or jetty out of a wall, a chest, a forehead that it crowns with foam! Even the abandoned corners, the abject corners of dust and debris were touched by her light hands. Everything began to laugh and everywhere shined with teeth. The sun entered the old rooms with pleasure and stayed in my house for hours, abandoning the other houses, the district, the city, the country. And some nights, very late, the scandalized stars watched it sneak from my house.

Love was a game, a perpetual creation. All was beach, sand, a bed of sheets that were always fresh. If I embraced her, she swelled with pride, incredibly tall, like the liquid stalk of a poplar; and soon that thinness flowered into a fountain of white feathers, into a plume of smiles that fell over my head and back and covered me with whiteness. Or she stretched out in front of me, infinite as the horizon, until I too became horizon and silence. Full and sinuous, it enveloped me like music or some giant lips. Her presence was a going and coming of caresses, of murmurs, of kisses. Entered in her waters, I was drenched to the socks and in a wink of an eye I found myself up above, at the height of vertigo, mysteriously suspended, to fall like a stone and feel myself gently deposited on the dryness, like a feather. Nothing is comparable to sleeping in those waters, to wake pounded by a thousand happy light lashes, by a thousand assaults that withdrew laughing.

But never did I reach the center of her being. Never did I touch the nakedness of pain and of death. Perhaps it does not exist in waves, that secret site that renders a woman vulnerable and mortal, that electric button where all interlocks, twitches, and straightens out to then swoon. Her sensibility, like that of women, spread in ripples, only they weren't concentric ripples, but rather excentric, spreading each time farther, until they touched other galaxies. To love her was to extend to remote contacts, to vibrate with far-off stars we never suspected. But her center . . . no, she had no center, just an emptiness as in a whirlwind, that sucked me in and smothered me.

25   Stretched out side by side, we exchanged confidences, whispers, smiles. Curled up, she fell on my chest and there unfolded like a vegetation of murmurs. She sang in my ear, a little snail. She became humble and transparent,

clutching my feet like a small animal, calm water. She was so clear I could read all of her thoughts. Certain nights her skin was covered with phosphorescence and to embrace her was to embrace a piece of night tattooed with fire. But she also became black and bitter. At unexpected hours she roared, moaned, twisted. Her groans woke the neighbors. Upon hearing her, the sea wind would scratch at the door of the house or rave in a loud voice on the roof. Cloudy days irritated her; she broke furniture, said bad words, covered me with insults and green and gray foam. She spit, cried, swore, prophesied. Subject to the moon, to the stars, to the influence of the light of other worlds, she changed her moods and appearance in a way that I thought fantastic, but it was as fatal as the tide.

She began to miss solitude. The house was full of snails and conches, of small sailboats that in her fury she had shipwrecked (together with the others, laden with images, that each night left my forehead and sank in her ferocious or pleasant whirlwinds). How many little treasures were lost in that time! But my boats and the silent song of the snails was not enough. I had to install in the house a colony of fish. I confess that it was not without jealousy that I watched them swimming in my friend, caressing her breasts, sleeping between her legs, adorning her hair with light flashes of color.

Among all those fish there were a few particularly repulsive and ferocious ones, little tigers from the aquarium, with large fixed eyes and jagged and bloodthirsty mouths. I don't know by what aberration my friend delighted in playing with them, shamelessly showing them a preference whose significance I preferred to ignore. She passed long hours confined with those horrible creatures. One day I couldn't stand it any more; I threw open the door and launched after them. Agile and ghostly they escaped my hands while she laughed and pounded me until I fell. I thought I was drowning. And when I was at the point of death, and purple, she deposited me on the bank and began to kiss me, saying I don't know what things. I felt very weak, fatigued and humiliated. And at the same time her voluptuousness made me close my eyes, because her voice was sweet and she spoke to me of the delicious death of the drowned. When I recovered, I began to fear and hate her.

I had neglected my affairs. Now I began to visit friends and renew old and dear relations. I met an old girlfriend. Making her swear to keep my secret, I told her of my life with the wave. Nothing moves women so much as the possibility of saving a man. My redeemer employed all of her arts, but what could a woman, master of a limited number of souls and bodies, do in front of my friend who was always changing—and always identical to herself in her incessant metamorphoses.

Winter came. The sky turned gray. Fog fell on the city. Frozen drizzle rained. My friend cried every night. During the day she isolated herself, quiet and sinister, stuttering a single syllable, like an old woman who grumbles in a corner. She became cold; to sleep with her was to shiver all night and to feel freeze, little by little, the blood, the bones, the thoughts. She turned deep, impenetrable, restless. I left frequently and my absences were each time more prolonged. She, in her corner, howled loudly. With teeth like steel and a corrosive tongue she gnawed the walls, crumbled them. She passed the nights in mourning, reproaching me. She had nightmares, deliriums of the sun, of warm beaches. She dreamt of the pole and of changing into a great block of ice, sailing beneath black skies in nights long as months. She insulted me. She cursed and laughed; filled the house with guffaws and phantoms. She called up the monsters of the depths, blind ones, quick ones, blunt. Charged with electricity, she carbonized all she touched; full of acid, she dissolved whatever she brushed against. Her sweet embraces became knotty cords that strangled me. And her body, greenish and elastic, was an implacable whip that lashed, lashed, lashed. I fled. The horrible fish laughed with ferocious smiles.

30   There in the mountains, among the tall pines and precipices, I breathed the cold thin air like a thought of liberty. At the end of a month I returned. I had decided. It had been so cold that over the marble of the chimney, next to the extinct fire, I found a statue of ice. I was unmoved by her weary beauty. I put her in a big canvas sack and went out to the streets with the sleeper on my shoulders. In a restaurant in the outskirts I sold her to a waiter friend who immediately began to chop her into little pieces, which he carefully deposited in the buckets where bottles are chilled.

■ EXPLORATIONS OF THE TEXT ■

1. What merger of the real and the fantastic propels this story? Why does the narrator compare the sea and an elusive lover?
2. How is the wave like a woman? like a man's fantasy of a woman?
3. Explore the incident of the water fountain. Why is the water "salty"? What does the narrator's imprisonment suggest?
4. Once he returns home, how does her presence at first change his life? What stage of love is depicted?
5. What are the implications of these statements: "But never did I reach the center of her being," and "She had no center, just an emptiness as in a whirlwind, that sucked me in and smothered me"?
6. Why does the narrator have to install a colony of fish? Why does she prefer the "little tigers . . . with large fixed eyes and jagged and bloodthirsty mouths"?
7. Explore the sign of the "drowning" episode. Why does he begin "to fear and hate her"?
8. What is the outcome of their relationship? Explore the symbolic dimension of the wave's association with ice.
9. What visions of romantic love, of sexuality, and of relationships does the story present?
10. Why does Paz depict human love through an affair with a wave instead of an affair with a real lover? What is the impact of this metaphor? Is it effective?

1. Write a parable, fable, or story in magical realism for men's and women's relationships. OR Write a feminist fable or fairy tale.
2. Why is the woman characterized as a "wave" rather than as an ocean?

■■■ IDEAS FOR WRITING ■■■

1. Examine the text to determine how Paz created the metamorphosis of the woman as ocean lover. Does it lie in the choice of details? verbs? adjectives? figurative language? Comment on Paz's style.
2. Categorize the stages of romantic love in this story.

The Chase

Alberto Moravia

Alberto Moravia (1907–   ), one of Italy's best known contemporary writers, was born in Rome. Moravia gained early fame for his first novel, The Time of Indifference *(1929). During the 1930s and 1940s, he earned international acclaim for his novels, which include* The Wheel of Fortune *(1937),* Agostino *(1944),* Time of Desecration *(1980). His short-story volumes include* Roman Tales *(1956),* Bitter Honeymoon and Other Stories *(1960),* Command and I Will Obey You *(1969),* Paradise and Other Stories *(1971), and* Erotic Tales *(1985). Moravia is known for his penetrating portraits of men and women in love and their struggle to escape the isolation and sterility symptomatic of a materialistic age.*

"The Chase" critiques social mores—particularly the roles of men and women—and presents the woman's need to find fulfillment and to escape from her futile marriage.

1   I have never been a sportsman—or, rather, I have been a sportsman only once, and that was the first and last time. I was a child, and one day, for some reason or other, I found myself together with my father, who was holding a gun in his hand, behind a bush, watching a bird that had perched on a branch not very far away. It was a large, gray bird—or perhaps it was brown—with a long—or perhaps a short—beak; I don't remember. I only remember what I felt at that moment as I looked at it. It was like watching an animal whose vitality was rendered more intense by the very fact of my watching it and of the animal's not knowing that I was watching it.

At that moment, I say, the notion of wildness entered my mind, never again to leave it: everything is wild which is autonomous and unpredictable and does not depend upon us. Then all of a sudden there was an explosion; I could no longer see the bird and I thought it had flown away. But my father was leading the way, walking in front of me through the undergrowth. Finally he stooped down, picked up something, and put it in my hand. I was aware of something warm and soft and I lowered my eyes: there was the bird in the palm of my hand, its dangling, shattered head crowned with a plume of already-thickening blood. I burst into tears and dropped the corpse on the ground, and that was the end of my shooting experience.

I thought again of this remote episode in my life this very day after watching my wife, for the first and also the last time, as she was walking through the streets of the city. But let us take things in order.

What had my wife been like; what was she like now? She once had been, to put it briefly, "wild"—that is, entirely autonomous and unpredictable; latterly she had become "tame"—that is, predictable and dependent. For a long time she had been like the bird that, on that far-off morning in my childhood, I had seen perching on the bough; latterly, I am sorry to say, she had become like a hen about which one knows everything in advance—how it moves, how it eats, how it lays eggs, how it sleeps, and so on.

5   Nevertheless I would not wish anyone to think that my wife's wildness consisted of an uncouth, rough, rebellious character. Apart from being extremely beautiful, she is the gentlest, politest, most discreet person in the world. Rather her wildness consisted of the air of charming unpredictability, of independence in her way of living, with which during the first years of our marriage she acted in my presence, both at home and abroad. Wildness signified intimacy, privacy, secrecy. Yes, my wife as she sat in front of her dressing table, her eyes fixed on the looking glass, passing the hairbrush with a repeated motion over her long, loose hair, was just as wild as the solitary quail hopping forward along a sun-filled furrow or the furtive fox coming out into a clearing and stopping to look around before running on. She was wild because I, as I looked at her, could never manage to foresee when she would give a last stroke with the hairbrush and rise and come toward me; wild to such a degree that sometimes when I went into our bedroom the smell of her, floating in the air, would have something of the acrid quality of a wild beast's lair.

Gradually she became less wild, tamer. I had had a fox, a quail, in the house, as I have said; then one day I realized that I had a hen. What effect does a hen have on someone who watches it? It has the effect of being, so to speak, an automaton in the form of a bird; automatic are the brief, rapid steps with which it moves about; automatic its hard, terse pecking; automatic the glance of the round eyes in its head that nods and turns; automatic its ready crouching down under the cock; automatic the dropping of the egg wherever it may be and the cry with which it announces that the egg has been laid. Good-by to the fox; good-by to the quail. And her smell—this no longer brought to my mind, in any way, the innocent odor of a wild animal; rather I detected in it the chemical suavity of some ordinary French perfume.

Our flat is on the first floor of a big building in a modern quarter of the town; our windows look out on a square in which there is a small public garden, the haunt of nurses and children and dogs. One day I was standing at the window, looking in a melancholy way at the garden. My wife, shortly before, had dressed to go out; and once again, watching her, I had noticed the irrevocable and, so to speak, invisible character of her gestures and personality; something which gave one the feeling of a thing already seen and already done and which therefore evaded even the most determined observation. And now, as I stood looking at the garden and at the same time wondering why the adorable wildness of former times had so completely disappeared, suddenly my wife came into my range of vision as she walked quickly across the garden in the direction of the bus stop. I watched her and then I almost jumped for joy; in a movement she was making to pull down a fold of her narrow skirt and smooth it over her thigh with the tips of her long, sharp nails, in this movement I recognized the wildness that in the past had made me love her. It was only an instant, but in that instant I said to myself: She's become wild again because she's convinced that I am not there and am not watching her. Then I left the window and rushed out.

But I did not join her at the bus stop; I felt that I must not allow myself to be seen. Instead I hurried to my car, which was standing nearby, got in, and waited. A bus came and she got in together with some other people; the bus started off again and I began following it. Then there came back to me the memory of that one shooting expedition in which I had taken part as a child, and I saw that the bus was the undergrowth with its bushes and trees, my wife the bird perching on the bough while I, unseen, watched it living before my eyes. And the whole town, during this pursuit, became, as though by magic, a fact of nature like the countryside: the houses were hills, the streets valleys, the vehicles hedges and woods, and even the passersby on the pavements had something unpredictable and autonomous—that is, wild—about them. And in my mouth, behind my clenched teeth, there was the acrid, metallic taste of gunfire; and my eyes, usually listless and wandering, had become sharp, watchful, attentive.

These eyes were fixed intently upon the exit door when the bus came to the end of its run. A number of people got out, and then I saw my wife getting out. Once again I recognized, in the manner in which she broke free of the crowd and started off toward a neighboring street, the wildness that pleased me so much. I jumped out of the car and started following her.

10   She was walking in front of me, ignorant of my presence, a tall woman with an elegant figure, long-legged, narrow-hipped, broad-backed, her brown hair falling on her shoulders.

Men turned around as she went past; perhaps they were aware of what I myself was now sensing with an intensity that quickened the beating of my heart and took my breath away: the unrestricted, steadily increasing, irresistible character of her mysterious wildness.

She walked hurriedly, having evidently some purpose in view, and even the fact that she had a purpose of which I was ignorant added to her wildness; I did not know where she was going, just as on that far-off morning I had not known what the bird perching on the bough was about to do. Moreover I thought the gradual, steady increase in this quality of wildness came partly from the fact that as she drew nearer to the object of this mysterious walk there was an increase in her—how shall I express it?—of biological tension, of existential excitement, of vital effervescence. Then, unexpectedly, with the suddenness of a film, her purpose was revealed.

A fair-haired young man in a leather jacket and a pair of corduroy trousers was leaning against the wall of a house in that ancient, narrow street. He was idly smoking as he looked in front of him. But as my wife passed close to him, he threw away his cigarette with a decisive gesture, took a step forward, and seized her arm. I was expecting her to rebuff him, to move away from him, but nothing happened: evidently obeying the rules of some kind of erotic ritual, she went on walking beside the young man. Then after a few steps, with a movement that confirmed her own complicity, she put her arm around her companion's waist and he put his around her.

I understood then that this unknown man who took such liberties with my wife was also attracted by wildness. And so, instead of making a conventional appointment with her, instead of meeting in a café with a handshake, a falsely friendly and respectful welcome, he had preferred, by agreement with her, to take her by surprise—or, rather, to pretend to do so—while she was apparently taking a walk on her own account. All this I perceived by intuition, noticing that at the very moment when he stepped forward and took her arm her wildness had, so to speak, given an upward bound. It was years since I had seen my wife so alive, but alas, the source of this life could not be traced to me.

15   They walked on thus entwined and then, without any preliminaries, just like two wild animals, they did an unexpected thing: they went into one of the dark doorways in order to kiss. I stopped and watched them from a distance, peering into the darkness of the entrance. My wife was turned away from me and was bending back with the pressure of his body, her hair hanging free. I looked at that long, thick mane of brown hair, which as she leaned back fell free of her shoulders, and I felt at that moment her vitality reached its diapason, just as happens with wild animals when the couple and their customary wildness is redoubled by the violence of love. I watched for a long time and then, since the kiss went on and on and in fact seemed to be prolonged beyond the limits of my power of endurance, I saw that I would have to intervene.

I would have to go forward, seize my wife by the arm—or actually by that hair, which hung down and conveyed so well the feeling of feminine passivity—then hurl myself with clenched fists upon the blond young man. After this encounter I would carry off my wife, weeping, mortified, ashamed, while I was raging and brokenhearted, upbraiding her and pouring scorn upon her.

But what else would this intervention amount to but the shot my father fired at that free, unknowing bird as it perched on the bough? The disorder and confusion, the mortification, the shame, that would follow would irreparably destroy the rare and precious moment of wildness that I was witnessing inside the dark doorway. It was true that this wildness was directed against me; but I had to remember that wildness, always and everywhere, is directed against everything and everybody. After the scene of my intervention it might be possible for me to regain control of my wife, but I should find her shattered and lifeless in my arms like the bird that my father placed in my hand so that I might throw it into the shooting bag.

The kiss went on and on: well, it was a kiss of passion—that could not be denied. I waited until they finished, until they came out of the doorway, until they walked on again still linked together. Then I turned back.

■ EXPLORATIONS OF THE TEXT ■

1. Why does the story begin with the incident of the bird? What do you learn about the narrator and his view of his maleness?
2. What does the narrator mean by "wildness"?
3. How has the narrator's wife changed? Explore the significance of the wife's transformation into a "hen about which one knows everything in advance."
4. What is the meaning of "the chase"? the narrator's pursuit of his wife?
5. Why does the narrator decide not to intervene?
6. Consider the narrator's statement in the beginning, when he watches his wife "for the first and also the last time." Why is it the "first" and "the last time"? What will happen after the story ends?
7. How does the hunting anecdote advance the narrative? What does it reveal about the narrator?
8. What critique of marriage, of sexual roles, and of male/female relations emerges in the story?

■■ JOURNAL ENTRIES ■■

1. Compare the narrators in this story and in "My Life with the Wave." Are they reliable narrators? Why or why not?
2. Compare the woman in "The Chase" with the narrator in "Yellow Woman." Who will be happier in her relationship? Why?
3. Create a monologue spoken by the wife in "The Chase."
4. Does romantic love require a sense of intrigue?

▪▪▪ IDEAS FOR WRITING ▪▪▪

1. Rewrite the story with the woman as narrator. Why does the woman have an affair?
2. How is the hunting image central to the development of character, conflict, and theme in "The Chase"?
3. "The one who loves less has the power in a relationship." Use this statement as the basis for a discussion of "The Chase." Cite other stories and/or personal observations and experience if you wish.

The Jilting of Granny Weatherall

Katherine Anne Porter

Katherine Anne Porter (1890–1980) was born in Indian Creek, Texas. She worked for a time as a newspaperwoman in Chicago and Denver and as a freelance writer in New York. Her first book of stories, Flowering Judas *(1930) was followed by other short-story collections and short novels:* Hacienda *(1934),* Noon Wine *(1937),* Pale Horse, Pale Rider *(1939),* The Leaning Tower *(1944), and* Collected Short Stories *(1965). Porter's only novel,* Ship of Fools, *based on the growth of Nazism which she had witnessed in Germany, appeared in 1962. Porter's work brought her many honors including Pulitzer and National Book awards.*

In this story about the final hours of Granny Weatherall, the narrator reminisces and comes to startling revelations about her life.

1   She flicked her wrist neatly out of Doctor Harry's pudgy careful fingers and pulled the sheet up to her chin. The brat ought to be in knee breeches. Doctoring around the country with spectacles on his nose! "Get along now, take your schoolbooks and go. There's nothing wrong with me."

Doctor Harry spread a warm paw like a cushion on her forehead where the forked green vein danced and made her eyelids twitch. "Now, now, be a good girl, and we'll have you up in no time."

"That's no way to speak to a woman nearly eighty years old just because she's down. I'd have you respect your elders, young man."

"Well, Missy, excuse me." Doctor Harry patted her cheek. "But I've got to warn you, haven't I? You're a marvel, but you must be careful or you're going to be good and sorry."

5   "Don't tell me what I'm going to be. I'm on my feet now, morally speaking. It's Cornelia. I had to go to bed to get rid of her."

Her bones felt loose, and floated around in her skin, and Doctor Harry floated like a balloon around the foot of the bed. He floated and pulled down his waistcoat and swung his glasses on a cord. "Well, stay where you are, it certainly can't hurt you."

"Get along and doctor your sick," said Granny Weatherall. "Leave a well woman alone. I'll call for you when I want you. . . . Where were you forty years ago when I pulled through milk-leg[1] and double pneumonia? You weren't even born. Don't let Cornelia lead you on," she shouted, because Doctor Harry appeared to float up to the ceiling and out. "I pay my own bills, and I don't throw my money away on nonsense!"

She meant to wave good-by, but it was too much trouble. Her eyes closed of themselves, it was like a dark curtain drawn around the bed. The pillow rose and floated under her, pleasant as a hammock in a light wind. She listened to the leaves rustling outside the window. No, somebody was swishing newspapers: no, Cornelia and Doctor Harry were whispering together. She leaped broad awake, thinking they whispered in her ear.

"She was never like this, *never* like this!" "Well, what can we expect?" "Yes, eighty years old. . . ."

10   Well, and what if she was? She still had ears. It was like Cornelia to whisper around doors. She always kept things secret in such a public way. She was always being tactful and kind. Cornelia was dutiful; that was the trouble with her. Dutiful and good: "So good and dutiful," said Granny, "that I'd like to spank her." She saw herself spanking Cornelia and making a fine job of it.

"What'd you say, Mother?"

Granny felt her face tying up in hard knots.

"Can't a body think, I'd like to know?"

"I thought you might want something."

15   "I do. I want a lot of things. First off, go away and don't whisper."

She lay and drowsed, hoping in her sleep that the children would keep out and let her rest a minute. It had been a long day. Not that she was tired. It was always pleasant to snatch a minute now and then. There was always so much to be done, let me see: tomorrow.

Tomorrow was far away and there was nothing to trouble about. Things were finished somehow when the time came; thank God there was always a little margin over for peace: then a person could spread out the plan of life and tuck in the edges orderly. It was good to have everything clean and folded away, with the hair brushes and tonic bottles sitting straight on the white embroidered linen: the day started without fuss and the pantry shelves laid out with rows of jelly glasses and brown jugs and white stone-china jars with blue whirligigs and words painted on them: coffee, tea, sugar, ginger, cinnamon, allspice: and the bronze clock with the lion on top nicely dusted off. The dust that lion could collect in twenty-four hours! The box in the attic with all those letters tied up, well she'd have to go through that tomorrow. All those

---

[1] Swelling of the legs, sometimes occurring in women after childbirth.

letters—George's letters and John's letters and her letters to them both— lying around for the children to find afterwards made her uneasy. Yes, that would be tomorrow's business. No use to let them know how silly she had been once.

While she was rummaging around she found death in her mind and it felt clammy and unfamiliar. She had spent so much time preparing for death there was no need for bringing it up again. Let it take care of itself now. When she was sixty she had felt very old, finished, and went around making farewell trips to see her children and grandchildren, with a secret in her mind: This is the very last of your mother, children! Then she made her will and came down with a long fever. That was all just a notion like a lot of other things, but it was lucky too, for she had once for all got over the idea of dying for a long time. Now she couldn't be worried. She hoped she had better sense now. Her father had lived to be one hundred and two years old and had drunk a noggin of strong hot toddy on his last birthday. He told the reporters it was his daily habit, and he owed his long life to that. He had made quite a scandal and was very pleased about it. She believed she'd just plague Cornelia a little.

"Cornelia! Cornelia!" No footsteps, but a sudden hand on her cheek. "Bless you, where have you been?"

20 "Here, mother."

"Well, Cornelia, I want a noggin of hot toddy."

"Are you cold, darling?"

"I'm chilly, Cornelia. Lying in bed stops the circulation. I must have told you that a thousand times."

Well, she could just hear Cornelia telling her husband that Mother was getting childish and they'd have to humor her. The thing that most annoyed her was that Cornelia thought she was deaf, dumb, and blind. Little hasty glances and tiny gestures tossed around her and over her head saying, "Don't cross her, let her have her way, she's eighty years old," and she sitting there as if she lived in a thin glass cage. Sometimes Granny almost made up her mind to pack up and move back to her own house where nobody could remind her every minute that she was old. Wait, wait, Cornelia, till your own children whisper behind your back!

25 In her day she had kept a better house and had got more work done. She wasn't too old yet for Lydia to be driving eighty miles for advice when one of the children jumped the track, and Jimmy still dropped in and talked things over: "Now, Mammy, you've a good business head, I want to know what you think of this? . . ." Old. Cornelia couldn't change the furniture around without asking. Little things, little things! They had been so sweet when they were little. Granny wished the old days were back again with the children young and everything to be done over. It had been a hard pull, but not too much for her. When she thought of all the food she had cooked, and all the clothes she had cut and sewed, and all the gardens she had made—well, the children showed it. There they were, made out of her, and they couldn't get away from that. Sometimes she wanted to see John again and point to them

and say, Well, I didn't do so badly, did I? But that would have to wait. That was for tomorrow. She used to think of him as a man, but now all the children were older than their father, and he would be a child beside her if she saw him now. It seemed strange and there was something wrong in the idea. Why, he couldn't possibly recognize her. She had fenced in a hundred acres once, digging the post holes herself and clamping the wires with just a negro boy to help. That changed a woman. John would be looking for a young woman with the peaked Spanish comb in her hair and the painted fan. Digging post holes changed a woman. Riding country roads in the winter when women had their babies was another thing: sitting up nights with sick horses and sick negroes and sick children and hardly ever losing one. John, I hardly ever lost one of them! John would see that in a minute, that would be something he could understand, she wouldn't have to explain anything!

It made her feel like rolling up her sleeves and putting the whole place to rights again. No matter if Cornelia was determined to be everywhere at once, there were a great many things left undone on this place. She would start tomorrow and do them. It was good to be strong enough for everything, even if all you made melted and changed and slipped under your hands, so that by the time you finished you almost forgot what you were working for. What was it I set out to do? she asked herself intently, but she could not remember. A fog rose over the valley, she saw it marching across the creek swallowing the trees and moving up the hill like an army of ghosts. Soon it would be at the near edge of the orchard, and then it was time to go in and light the lamps. Come in children, don't stay out in the night air.

Lighting the lamps had been beautiful. The children huddled up to her and breathed like little calves waiting at the bars in the twilight. Their eyes followed the match and watched the flame rise and settle in a blue curve, then they moved away from her. The lamp was lit, they didn't have to be scared and hang on to mother any more. Never, never, never more. God, for all my life I thank Thee. Without Thee, my God, I could never have done it. Hail, Mary, full of grace.

I want you to pick all the fruit this year and see that nothing is wasted. There's always someone who can use it. Don't let good things rot for want of using. You waste life when you waste good food. Don't let things get lost. It's bitter to lose things. Now, don't let me get to thinking, not when I am tired and taking a little nap before supper. . . .

The pillow rose about her shoulders and pressed against her heart and the memory was being squeezed out of it: oh, push down the pillow, somebody: it would smother her if she tried to hold it. Such a fresh breeze blowing and such a green day with no threats in it. But he had not come, just the same. What does a woman do when she has put on the white veil and set out the white cake for a man and he doesn't come? She tried to remember. No, I swear he never harmed me but in that. He never harmed me but in that . . . and what if he did? There was the day, the day, but a whirl of dark smoke rose and covered it, crept up and over into the bright field where everything was planted so carefully in orderly rows. That was hell, she knew hell when she saw it. For sixty years she had prayed against remembering him and against losing her soul in the deep pit of hell, and now the two things were mingled in one and the thought of him was a smoky cloud from hell that moved and crept in her head when she had just got rid of Doctor Harry and was trying to rest a minute. Wounded vanity, Ellen, said a sharp voice in the top of her mind. Don't let your wounded vanity get the upper hand of you. Plenty of girls get jilted. You were jilted, weren't you? Then stand up to it. Her eyelids wavered and let in streamers of blue-gray light like tissue paper over her eyes. She must get up and pull the shades down or she'd never sleep. She was in bed again and the shades were not down. How could that happen? Better turn over, hide from the light, sleeping in the light gave you nightmares. "Mother, how do you feel now?" and a stinging wetness on her forehead. But I don't like having my face washed in cold water!

30   Hapsy? George? Lydia? Jimmy? No, Cornelia, and her features were swollen and full of little puddles. "They're coming, darling, they'll all be here soon." Go wash your face, child, you look funny.

Instead of obeying, Cornelia knelt down and put her head on the pillow. She seemed to be talking but there was no sound. "Well, are you tongue-tied? Whose birthday is it? Are you going to give a party?"

Cornelia's mouth moved urgently in strange shapes. "Don't do that, you bother me, daughter."

"Oh, no. Mother, oh, no . . ."

Nonsense. It was strange about children. They disputed your every word. "No what, Cornelia?"

35   "Here's Doctor Harry."

"I won't see that boy again. He just left five minutes ago."

"That was this morning, Mother. It's night now. Here's the nurse."

"This is Doctor Harry, Mrs. Weatherall. I never saw you look so young and happy!"

"Ah, I'll never be young again—but I'd be happy if they'd let me lie in peace and get rested."

40   She thought she spoke up loudly, but no one answered. A warm weight on her forehead, a warm bracelet on her wrist, and a breeze went on whispering, trying to tell her something. A shuffle of leaves in the everlasting hand of God. He blew on them and they danced and rattled. "Mother, don't mind, we're going to give you a little hypodermic." "Look here, daughter, how do ants get in this bed? I saw sugar ants yesterday." Did you send for Hapsy too?

It was Hapsy she really wanted. She had to go a long way back through a great many rooms to find Hapsy standing with a baby on her arm. She seemed to herself to be Hapsy also, and the baby on Hapsy's arm was Hapsy and himself and herself, all at once, and there was no surprise in the meeting. Then Hapsy melted from within and turned flimsy as gray gauze and the baby was a gauzy shadow, and Hapsy came up close and said, "I thought you'd never come," and looked at her very searchingly and said, "You haven't changed a bit!" They leaned forward to kiss, when Cornelia began whispering from a long way off, "Oh, is there anything you want to tell me? Is there anything I can do for you?"

Yes, she had changed her mind after sixty years and she would like to see George. I want you to find George. Find him and be sure to tell him I forgot him. I want him to know I had my husband just the same and my children and my house like any other woman. A good house too and a good husband that I loved and fine children out of him. Better than I hoped for even. Tell him I was given back everything he took away and more. Oh, no, oh, God, no, there was something else besides the house and the man and the children. Oh, surely they were not all? What was it? Something not given back. . . . Her breath crowded down under her ribs and grew into a monstrous frightening shape with cutting edges; it bored up into her head, and the agony was unbelievable: Yes, John, get the Doctor now, no more talk, my time has come.

When this one was born it should be the last. The last. It should have been born first, for it was the one she had truly wanted. Everything came in good time. Nothing left out, left over. She was strong, in three days she would be as well as ever. Better. A woman needed milk in her to have her full health.

"Mother, do you hear me?"

45   "I've been telling you—"

"Mother, Father Connolly's here."

"I went to Holy Communion only last week. Tell him I'm not so sinful as all that."

"Father just wants to speak to you."

He could speak as much as he pleased. It was like him to drop in and inquire about her soul as if it were a teething baby, and then stay on for a cup of tea and a round of cards and gossip. He always had a funny story of some sort, usually about an Irishman who made his little mistakes and confessed them, and the point lay in some absurd thing he would blurt out in the confessional showing his struggles between native piety and original sin. Granny felt easy about her soul. Cornelia, where are your manners? Give Father Connolly a chair. She had her secret comfortable understanding with a few favorite saints who cleared a straight road to God for her. All as surely signed and sealed as the papers for the new Forty Acres. Forever . . . heirs and assigns forever. Since the day the wedding cake was not cut, but thrown out and wasted. The whole bottom dropped out of the world, and there she was blind and sweating with nothing under her feet and the walls falling away. His hand had caught her under the breast, she had not fallen, there was the freshly polished floor with the green rug on it, just as before. He had cursed like a sailor's parrot and said, "I'll kill him for you." Don't lay a hand on him, for my sake leave something to God. "Now, Ellen, you must believe what I tell you. . . ."

50   So there was nothing, nothing to worry about any more, except sometimes in the night one of the children screamed in a nightmare, and they both hustled out shaking and hunting for the matches and calling, "There, wait a

minute, here we are!" John, get the doctor now, Hapsy's time has come. But there was Hapsy standing by the bed in a white cap. "Cornelia, tell Hapsy to take off her cap. I can't see her plain."

Her eyes opened very wide and the room stood out like a picture she had seen somewhere. Dark colors with the shadow rising towards the ceiling in long angles. The tall black dresser gleamed with nothing on it but John's picture, enlarged from a little one, with John's eyes very black when they should have been blue. You never saw him, so how do you know how he looked? But the man insisted the copy was perfect, it was very rich and handsome. For a picture, yes, but it's not my husband. The table by the bed had a linen cover and a candle and a crucifix. The light was blue from Cornelia's silk lamp shades. No sort of light at all, just frippery. You had to live forty years with kerosene lamps to appreciate honest electricity. She felt very strong and she saw Doctor Harry with a rosy nimbus around him.

"You look like a saint, Doctor Harry, and I vow that's as near as you'll ever come to it."

"She's saying something."

"I heard you, Cornelia. What's all this carrying-on?"

55   "Father Connolly's saying—"

Cornelia's voice staggered and bumped like a cart in a bad road. It rounded corners and turned back again and arrived nowhere. Granny stepped up in the cart very lightly and reached for the reins, but a man sat beside her and she knew him by his hands, driving the cart. She did not look in his face, for she knew without seeing, but looked instead down the road where the trees leaned over and bowed to each other and a thousand birds were singing a Mass. She felt like singing too, but she put her hand in the bosom of her dress and pulled out a rosary, and Father Connolly murmured Latin in a very solemn voice and tickled her feet. My God, will you stop that nonsense? I'm a married woman. What if he did run away and leave me to face the priest by myself? I found another a whole world better. I wouldn't have exchanged my husband for anybody except St. Michael himself, and you may tell him that for me with a thank you in the bargain.

Light flashed on her closed eyelids, and a deep roaring shook her. Cornelia, is that lightning? I hear thunder. There's going to be a storm. Close all the windows. Call the children in . . . "Mother, here we are, all of us." "Is that you, Hapsy?" "Oh, no, I'm Lydia. We drove as fast as we could." Their faces drifted above her, drifted away. The rosary fell out of her hands and Lydia put it back. Jimmy tried to help, their hands fumbled together, and Granny closed two fingers around Jimmy's thumb. Beads wouldn't do, it must be something alive. She was so amazed her thoughts ran round and round. So, my dear Lord, this is my death and I wasn't even thinking about it. My children have come to see me die. But I can't, it's not time. Oh, I always hated surprises. I wanted to give Cornelia the amethyst set—Cornelia, you're to have the amethyst set, but Hapsy's to wear it when she wants, and, Doctor Harry, do shut up. Nobody sent for you. Oh, my dear Lord, do wait a minute. I meant to do something about the Forty Acres, Jimmy doesn't need it and

Lydia will later on with that worthless husband of hers. I meant to finish the altar cloth and send six bottles of wine to Sister Borgia for her dyspepsia.[2] I want to send six bottles of wine to Sister Borgia, Father Connolly, now don't let me forget.

Cornelia's voice made short turns and tilted over and crashed. "Oh, Mother, oh, Mother, oh, Mother. . . ."

"I'm not going, Cornelia. I'm taken by surprise. I can't go."

60   You'll see Hapsy again. What about her? "I thought you'd never come." Granny made a long journey outward, looking for Hapsy. What if I don't find her? What then? Her heart sank down and down, there was no bottom to death, she couldn't come to the end of it. The blue light from Cornelia's lampshade drew into a tiny point in the center of her brain, it flickered and winked like an eye, quietly it fluttered and dwindled. Granny lay curled down within herself, amazed and watchful, staring at the point of light that was herself; her body was now only a deeper mass of shadow in an endless darkness and this darkness would curl around the light and swallow it up. God, give a sign!

For the second time there was no sign. Again no bridegroom and the priest in the house. She could not remember any other sorrow because this grief wiped them all away. Oh, no, there's nothing more cruel than this—I'll never forgive it. She stretched herself with a deep breath and blew out the light.

■ EXPLORATIONS OF THE TEXT ■

1. Describe the point of view and voice of Granny Weatherall.
2. What do the interchanges between Granny Weatherall and both Cornelia and the doctor reveal about Granny's nature?
3. Analyze Granny's character as a young wife.
4. On her deathbed, whom does Granny Weatherall remember? What has happened to Hapsy?
5. Examine the symbolism of light, lamplight, shadow, and darkness. How does the symbolism develop themes of the story?
6. Explain the conclusion of the story. Discuss the allusion to the bridegroom. What is the final jilting?

■■ JOURNAL ENTRIES ■■

1. Explore the symbolism of Granny's name.
2. React to the portrayal of Granny Weatherall.
3. Write a letter in the voice of George (a letter taken from the box in the attic).

---

[2] Indigestion.

■■■ IDEAS FOR WRITING ■■■

1. Contrast the external (real) and internal (remembered) worlds in the story. How does Porter create a vision of these two worlds?
2. How does first love affect the rest of Granny Weatherall's life? Gretta's life in "The Dead"? Compare the two women's lives.

POETRY

Let Me Not to the Marriage of True Minds

William Shakespeare

In this poem, Shakespeare refers to "The Order of Solemnization of Matrimony" in the Anglican Book of Common Prayer: *"I require that if either of you know any impediments why ye may not be lawfully joined together in matrimony, ye do now confess it." The persona alludes to the ceremony of marriage, and he defines love by describing its positive qualities and its negative manifestations.*

Let me not to the marriage of true minds
Admit impediments.[1] Love is not love
Which alters when it alteration finds,
Or bends with the remover to remove.
5 O no, it is an ever-fixèd mark
That look on tempests and is never shaken;
It is the star to every wand'ring bark,[2]
Whose worth's unknown, although his height[3] be taken.
Love's not Time's fool,[4] though rosy lips and cheeks
10 Within his bending sickle's compass come;
Love alters not with his brief hours and weeks,
But bears it out[5] even to the edge of doom.[6]
    If this be error and upon me proved,
    I never writ, nor no man every loved.

---

[1] An allusion to "The Order of Solemnization of Matrimony" from the Anglican *Book of Common Prayer:* "I require that if either of you know of any impediment why ye may not be lawfully joined together in matrimony, ye do now confess it."
[2] Small ship.
[3] Altitude.
[4] Slave.
[5] Endures.
[6] The Last Judgment.

■ EXPLORATIONS OF THE TEXT ■

1. Why does the persona speak of a "marriage of true minds"?
2. Paraphrase the first two lines. What does the first statement mean?
3. Why does love not "[alter]" or "[bend]"? Why is it "an ever-fixèd mark"?
4. What do the navigational images mean?
5. Look at personification in this sonnet. What is personified? Why? What is the relationship of love and time? Why is love not "Time's fool"?
6. Discuss the final **couplet**. Solve the **paradox**.
7. Consider the view of love in this sonnet. Is the persona convincing in his contention that true love lasts "even to the edge of doom"?

■■ JOURNAL ENTRIES ■■

1. Define love or another abstract idea by stating what it is not. Begin with: Love is not. . . .
2. Respond to the persona's view of true love.

■■■ IDEAS FOR WRITING ■■■

1. Some critics consider this poem to be Shakespeare's greatest sonnet. Evaluate "Let Me Not to the Marriage of True Minds." (See checklist in Chapter 10.)
2. Contrast this poem with Blake's "Garden of Love."

A Valediction Forbidding Mourning

John Donne

Born into a prominent Catholic family in London during a strongly anti-Catholic time, John Donne (1571–1631) was educated at Oxford and at Cambridge. He participated in several naval expeditions and studied law when he returned to England. He became secretary to Thomas Egerton, Keeper of the Great Seal, from 1598–1602. His secret marriage to Anne More, Egerton's niece, alienated his patron; and Donne was briefly imprisoned for this act. For a number of years, he struggled to earn a living. Having become an Anglican, he took Anglican orders in 1615 at the age of forty-two, and he preached sermons which rank among the greatest speeches of the seventeenth century. From 1621 until his death in 1631, he was Dean of St. Paul's and frequently preached before Charles I.

His verse is distinguished by wit and erudition and by subtlety and emotion. He was considered to be the greatest of the metaphysical poets, whose works combined passion and reason through highly innovative conceits. Among his important poems are: "Progresse of the Souls" (1605), "The Ecstasie," "Hymn to God the Father," "The Flea" and the "Holy Sonnets." Two years after Donne's death, his son published much of his prose work. Imperfect collections of the poems appeared from 1633–1649, and his letters were published in 1651.

In "A Valediction Forbidding Mourning," the major conceit compares the lovers to "twin" geometrical compasses; the one who remains fixed at home nevertheless leans after the moving lover. Donne claims that these lovers enjoy a relationship so "refined" that they can part without "mourning."

> As virtuous men pass mildly away,
>   And whisper to their souls to go,
> Whilst some of their sad friends do say
>   The breath goes now, and some say no:
>
> 5 So let us melt, and make no noise,
>   No tear-floods, nor sigh-tempests move;
> 'Twere profanation[1] of our joys
>   To tell the laity our love.
>
> Moving of th' earth[2] brings harms and fears;
> 10   Men reckon what it did and meant;
> But trepidation of the spheres,[3]
>   Though greater far, is innocent.
>
> Dull sublunary lovers' love
>   (Whose soul is sense)[4] cannot admit
> 15 Absence, because it doth remove
>   Those things which elemented it.
>
> But we, by a love so much refined
>   That ourselves know not what it is,

---

[1] The lovers are like priests, and their love is a mystery.

[2] Earthquakes.

[3] Prior to Newton's explanation of the equinoxes, people assumed that stars and planets had circular positions. The observation of irregularities (the result of the wobbling of the earth's axis) was explained by the theory of trepidation, a trembling which occurred in outer spheres around the earth.

[4] A completely physical attraction.

Inter-assured of the mind,
20   Care less, eyes, lips, and hands to miss.

Our two souls, therefore, which are one,
        Though I must go, endure not yet
A breach, but an expansion,[5]
        Like gold to airy thinness beat.

25 If they be two, they are two so
        As stiff twin compasses are two:[6]
Thy soul, the fixed foot, makes no show
        To move, but doth, if th' other do.

And though it in the center sit,
30   Yet when the other far doth roam,
It leans and harkens after it,
        And grows erect as that comes home.

Such wilt thou be to me, who must,
        Like th' other foot, obliquely run;
35 Thy firmness makes my circle just,[7]
        And makes me end where I begun.

■ EXPLORATIONS OF THE TEXT ■

1. To what event does the speaker compare his separation from his beloved in the first stanza?
2. What does he mean by the "trepidation of the spheres"?
3. Why can "dull" lovers not part easily? Why can they not tolerate "absence"?
4. What does the "refined" love of the speaker require? (See stanza 5.)
5. How does the gold imagery in lines 21–24 expand the vision of the lovers' communion?
6. Examine the metaphysical **conceit** comparing the lovers to "twin compasses." Is this extended figure effective?
7. Is the speaker's argument against "mourning" persuasive?
8. Contrast this poem with Sexton's "For My Lover, Returning to His Wife."

---

[5] Gold is quite malleable.
[6] Compasses used for drawing circles.
[7] Round.

■■ **JOURNAL ENTRIES** ■■

---

1. Many popular songs attest to the difficulty of saying goodbye of separation. Write about one of these themes.
2. Respond to the speaker in the poem.

■■■ **IDEAS FOR WRITING** ■■■

---

1. Both Shakespeare and Donne refer to "the marriage of true minds," a love more refined than ordinary relationship. Take a position on ideal love or on grand passion.
2. Characterize the speaker in the poem; write about his voice, beliefs, attitudes, intelligence, and capacity for love. Use Journal Entry 2 as a beginning.
3. Compare Plato's concept of union with Donne's ideas.

To His Coy Mistress

Andrew Marvell

Andrew Marvell (1621–1678) was born in Winchester near Hull, England, and was educated at Cambridge University. After four years of living in Europe, he became tutor to the daughter of Lord Fairfax in Yorkshire, where he wrote a number of his most famous poems on country life and on gardens; these works include "Appleton House," "The Hill and the Grove at Billborrow," and "The Garden." From 1653 to 1657, he was a tutor to Oliver Cromwell's ward, William Dutton; and he served as John Milton's assistant in the Latin secretaryship in the foreign office in 1657. In 1659, Marvell became a member of Parliament and wrote pamphlets and satires on politics. His lyric poetry speaks of love, nature, and God. A strong defender of Milton, he wrote high praise for Paradise Lost. *Most of Marvell's poems were published posthumously in 1681. His satires did not receive attention until 1689, after the revolution.*

"To His Coy Mistress," Marvell's most well-known poem, represents a common literary motif called carpe diem *which means "seize the day." The poet emphasizes that life is fleeting and urges the person addressed by the speaker—usually a virgin—to enjoy the pleasures of life and of love. Often symbols represent the finality of death and the transitory nature of beauty. Herrick's line, "Gather ye rosebuds while ye may," cites the most frequent symbol, the rose. Marvell's poem presents the speaker's plea with humor and with poignancy.*

Had we but world enough and time,
This coyness, lady, were no crime.
We would sit down and think which way
To walk, and pass our long love's day.
5   Thou by the Indian Ganges'[1] side
Should'st rubies find; I by the tide
Of Humber[2] would complain.[3] I would
Love you ten years before the Flood,
And you should, if you please, refuse
10 Till the conversion of the Jews.
My vegetable love should grow[4]
Vaster than empires, and more slow.
An hundred years should go to praise
Thine eyes, and on thy forehead gaze,
15 Two hundred to adore each breast,
But thirty thousand to the rest.
An age at least to every part,
And the last age should show your heart.
For, lady, you deserve this state,
20 Nor would I love at lower rate.
    But at my back I always hear
Time's wingèd chariot hurrying near,
And yonder all before us lie
Deserts of vast eternity.
25 Thy beauty shall no more be found,
Nor in thy marble vault shall sound
My echoing song; then worms shall try
That long preserved virginity,
And your quaint honor turn to dust,
30 And into ashes all my lust.
The grave's a fine and private place,
But none, I think, do there embrace.
    Now therefore, while the youthful-hue
Sits on thy skin like morning glew[5]
35 And while thy willing soul transpires[6]
At every pore with instant fires,
Now let us sport us while we may;
And now, like amorous birds of prey,
Rather at once our time devour

---

[1] River in India, sacred to Hindus.
[2] Small river that flows through Marvell's hometown of Hull.
[3] Compose love songs.
[4] Slow, unconscious development.
[5] Glow.
[6] Breathes.

40 Than languish in his slow-chapped[7] power.
Let us roll all our strength and all
Our sweetness up into one ball
And tear our pleasures with rough strife
Thorough the iron gates of life.
45 Thus, though we cannot make our sun
Stand still, yet we will make him run.

■ EXPLORATIONS OF THE TEXT ■

1. In what ways does the speaker suggest the lovers might pass their "long love's day" if only they had time?
2. Why is the lady "coy"?
3. Trace the steps in the argument that begin on lines 1, 21, and 33.
4. What concepts of time and of death does the speaker present? What are the consequences to the beloved?
5. What is the speaker's view of "Time's wingèd chariot"?
6. Why does he suggest that "worms" will "try" her "virginity" and her "quaint honor"? Does the image have sexual connotations?
7. In the conclusion, how does his description of proposed acts of love function? How will the lovers make the sun "run"?
8. How does hyperbole add to the humorous and whimsical tone? Contrast the tone of this poem with "Dover Beach" and "The Garden of Love."

■■ JOURNAL ENTRIES ■■

1. Write a feminist critique of this poem.
2. Convince someone to change his or her attitude or behavior about a love relationship. Use **hyperbole** in an effort to be persuasive.

■■■ IDEAS FOR WRITING ■■■

1. Define and critique the argument in "To His Coy Mistress."
2. Write a paper on virginity. Consider such questions as abstinence, social and cultural values, peer pressure, and marriage.

---

[7] Slow-jawed.

Dover Beach

Mathew Arnold

*Born at Laleham, Middlesex, England, Mathew Arnold (1822–1888)
was the son of a famous head master at Rugby. He attended Oxford
where he was awarded the Newdigate Prize for his poem, "Cromwell"
(1843). He was professor of poetry at Oxford from 1857 to 1867; then
an inspector of schools until 1886. His first volume of poetry,* The
Strayed Reveller and Other Poems, *appeared in 1849.* Empedocles and
Other Poems, *including "Tristram and Iseult," was published in 1852.
Both books were withdrawn from circulation shortly afterwards. In
1853, a volume,* Poems, *replaced these collections; this book contained many of his previously published works, and most of his other
famous pieces appeared in* Poems, Second Series *in 1855.*

*Mathew Arnold's prose began to circulate after 1860. The most
significant of these works were* Essays in Criticism *and* Culture and
Anarchy *(1869). He wrote religious criticism as well as social and
political analysis and attempted to improve education, in particular,
secondary education.*

*"Dover Beach," his most famous poem, presents a lover's melan-
choly description of the sea which brings "the eternal note of sadness
in." As the persona speaks to his beloved, he also feels the loss of "the
Sea of Faith," and in this lack of certainty, he pleads for constancy
in love.*

    The sea is calm tonight,
    The tide is full, the moon lies fair
    Upon the straits; on the French coast the light
    Gleams and is gone; the cliffs of England stand,
5 Glimmering and vast, out in the tranquil bay.
    Come to the window, sweet is the night-air!
    Only, from the long line of spray
    Where the sea meets the moon-blanched land,
    Listen! you hear the grating roar
10 Of pebbles which the waves draw back, and fling,
    At their return, up the high strand,
    Begin, and cease, and then again begin,
    With tremulous cadence slow, and bring
    The eternal note of sadness in.[1]

---

[1] A reference to *Antigone* where Sophocles alludes to the tragedies which plague the House of
Oedipus as a "mourning tide."

15 Sophocles long ago
Heard it on the Aegean, and it brought
Into his mind the turbid ebb and flow
Of human misery; we
Find also in the sound a thought,
20 Hearing it by this distant northern sea.

The Sea of Faith
Was once, too, at the full, and round earth's shore
Lay like the folds of a bright girdle[2] furled.
But now I only hear
25 Its melancholy, long, withdrawing roar,
Retreating, to the breath
Of the night-wind, down the vast edges drear
And naked shingles[3] of the world.

Ah, love, let us be true
30 To one another! for the world, which seems
To lie before us like a land of dreams,
So various, so beautiful, so new,
Hath really neither joy, nor love, nor light,
Nor certitude, nor peace, nor help for pain;
35 And we are here as on a darkling plain
Swept with confused alarms of struggle and flight,
Where ignorant armies clash by night.

■ EXPLORATIONS OF THE TEXT ■

1. Compare the initial description with the closing lines (33–37). What is the difference? Are both effective?
2. To whom is the poem addressed? Why?
3. What is "the eternal note of sadness"? What creates the motion and sound of the sea?
4. What is the significance of the "withdrawing roar" of the "Sea of Faith"?
5. What can the lovers do to avoid despair? What can anyone do? Is the speaker hopeful?
6. How would you answer the speaker?
7. Choose the best lines in the poem, and discuss the word choice, sound, and imagery that make them effective.
8. Discuss the title and the setting. Is the sadness a modern attitude, or has it always been central to the human condition?

---

[2] Belt or cord.
[3] Beaches covered with small stones or pebbles.

■■   **JOURNAL ENTRIES**   ■■

---

1. Describe the setting and its effect on the persona and on the themes.
2. Write about the sea. Imitate the tone of "Dover Beach."

■■■   **IDEAS FOR WRITING**   ■■■

---

1. M. H. Abrams has called a poem which uses landscape as a prelude to meditation, "the greater romantic lyric." The first part creates the setting; the second section presents the meditation; the third transforms the landscape according to the persona's insights. Consider "Dover Beach" as a lyric in this mode.
2. Write a meditation in lyric or prose form.
3. Explore the sea as setting, character, and/or theme in Arnold and in Paz.

The Garden of Love

William Blake

Born in London, William Blake (1757–1827) began drawing at an early age; at fourteen, he was apprenticed for seven years to an engraver. Many of the poems he wrote during this period were eventually printed in Poetical Sketches, *his first book of poems, published in 1783.*

In 1789, Blake wrote and engraved his great work, Songs of Innocence, *poems which reveal his tendencies toward mysticism. The* Songs of Experience *(1794) contrasts with* Songs of Innocence *through its exploration of the power of evil, and these poems rank among his best works. Blake's major prose work,* The Marriage of Heaven and Hell *(1790), is revolutionary in its denial of the reality of matter, of hell, of authority.*

In his works, Blake created his own mythology in which Urizen, the giver of moral codes, and Ora, the consummate rebel, represent authority and anarchy in a number of complex, mythic works.

In 1804, he undertook the engravings of his final pieces, Milton, *which was finished around 1808, and* Jerusalem, *finished around 1820. The latter presents Blake's theory of imagination, "the real and eternal world of which the Vegetable Universe is but a faint shadow." He also engraved his own work on copper with the poems surrounded by illustrations which he painted by hand, a process which he called "illuminated printing."*

In "The Garden of Love," Blake's persona returns to the place where he "used to play on the green," and he discovers that the garden has been filled with weeds and graves. He implies that this destruction relates in some central way to the Chapel.

I went to the Garden of Love,
And I saw what I never had seen:
A Chapel was built in the midst,
Where I used to play on the green.

5 And the gates of this Chapel were shut,
And "Thou shalt not" writ over the door:
So I turned to the Garden of Love
That so many sweet flowers bore;

And I saw it was filled with graves,
10 And tomb-stones where flowers should be;
And Priests in black gowns were walking their rounds,
And binding with briars my joys and desires.

■ EXPLORATIONS OF THE TEXT ■

1. What is the speaker's first sense of love?
2. What are the obstacles to the experience of love? What does the Chapel represent?
3. What are the contradictory sides of love suggested in the images of the "green," "the garden," and "graves"?
4. Analyze the rhyme scheme and the form. How do they create meaning?
5. What critique of organized religion appears in this work?

■■ JOURNAL ENTRIES ■■

1. "Love is a time of torment." Comment.
2. "Love is a time of bliss." Comment.
3. Choose a character from one of the short stories in this chapter, and create his/her response to the poem.

■■■ IDEAS FOR WRITING ■■■

1. Compare three views of love presented in three poems in this chapter.
2. Demonstrate the relationship of imagery to theme in this poem.

Sweetness, Always

Pablo Neruda
Translated from the Spanish by Alastair Reid

Born in Chile, Pablo Neruda (1904–1973) received an appointment to the Consular service in his twenties, and he served in India and in other Asian countries. In 1934, he received a post in Spain, where he became deeply involved in the Spanish Civil War. As a result, his poetry, which had presented a romantic view of life, came to express both personal and political concerns. Among his works are Selected Poems of Pablo Neruda *(1961),* The Heights of Macchu Picchu *(1966), and* Pablo Neruda: A New Decade *(1969). His* Collected Poems *have been translated into English and into many other languages. Neruda received the Nobel Prize for Literature in 1971.*

   "Sweetness, Always" defines contemporary poetry as "harsh machinery" and exhorts writers to consider the goodness of life.

Why such harsh machinery?
Why, to write down the stuff
and people of every day,
must poems be dressed up in gold,
5 in old and fearful stone?

I want verses of felt or feather
which scarcely weigh, mild verses
with the intimacy of beds
where people have loved and dreamed.
10 I want poems stained
by hands and everydayness.

Verses of pastry which melt
into milk and sugar in the mouth,
air and water to drink,
15 the bites and kisses of love.
I long for eatable sonnets,
poems of honey and flour.

Vanity keeps prodding us
to lift ourselves skyward
20 or to make deep and useless
tunnels underground.
So we forget the joyous
love-needs of our bodies.
We forget about pastries.
25 We are not feeding the world.

In Madras[1] a long time since,
I saw a sugary pyramid,
a tower of confectionery—
one level after another,
30 and in the construction, rubies,
and other blushing delights,
medieval and yellow.

Someone dirtied his hands
to cook up so much sweetness.

35 Brother poets from here
and there, from earth and sky,
from Medellin,[2] from Veracruz,[3]
Abyssinia,[4] Antofagasta,[5]
do you know the recipe for honeycombs?
40 Let's forget about all that stone.

Let your poetry fill up
the equinoctial pastry shop
our mouths long to devour—
all the children's mouths
45 and the poor adults' also.
Don't go on without seeing,
relishing, understanding
all these hearts of sugar.
Don't be afraid of sweetness.

50 With us or without us,
sweetness will go on living
and is infinitely alive,
forever being revived,
for it's in a man's mouth,
55 whether he's eating or singing,
that sweetness has its place.

---

[1] Industrial city in India.
[2] City in Colombia.
[3] Mexican seaport.
[4] Ethiopia.
[5] Coastal city in Chile.

■ EXPLORATIONS OF THE TEXT ■

1. Whom does the speaker address in the first stanza? Why does he believe that "the stuff/and people of every day" need not be written in "gold" or in "stone"?
2. What kind of poetry does the persona want? Why?
3. Discuss the extended metaphor of "sweetness." What is the connection between love and sweetness?
4. What are the barriers to the poetry of sweetness, to the "eatable sonnets"? What does the speaker mean when he declares, "We are not feeding the world"?
5. Why does he tell about the incident in Madras? Why does he emphasize the cook's dirty hands?
6. Why does he address "brother poets"? Why does he ask the poets to "forget about all that stone"?
7. Why does the speaker say: "Don't be afraid of sweetness"?
8. The speaker contends that sweetness "is infinitely alive," that "it's in a man's mouth." What does he mean?
9. Contrast Neruda's "sweetness" and Arnold's "sadness." What views of life are implied?

■■ JOURNAL ENTRIES ■■

1. Agree or disagree with the speaker's position.
2. Write a short piece in which images of confections represent love. Do *not* be sentimental; control your material.

■■■ IDEAS FOR WRITING ■■■

1. Answer Neruda's "Sweetness, Always." Argue that poetry does not avoid "sweetness" and that poets are not afraid of it.
2. Why does the persona speak only to male poets? Analyze the attitude toward gender presented in the work.
3. Contrast Arnold's vision of "sadness" and Neruda's view of "sweetness." What philosophical stances are suggested?

Nuit de Sine

Léopold-Sédar Senghor   Translated by John Reed and Clive Wake

Léopold-Sédar Senghor (1906–   ) was born in French West Africa, now the republic of Senegal. He fought to gain independence for Senegal and, in 1960, was elected President of the new independent republic. He served in that post until 1981. In addition to being a renowned statesman, he has also written many volumes of poetry and collections of essays, including Ethiopiques *(1956),* Nocturnes *(1961),* Prose and Poetry *(1965),* Selected Poems *(1976), and* Poems of a Black Orpheus *(1981). He has been a chief spokesperson for the literary movement of negritude, promulgating the need for crafting a new African tongue, diction, and form, free of imperialism.*

   Senghor's poetry is characterized by its rhythmic language and its evocative, sensual verse. In "Nuit de Sine," the persona's experience of the body of love is rejuvenating and is connected with the spirit of the "ancients."

Woman, rest on my brow your balsam hands, your hands
      gentler than fur.
The tall palmtrees swinging in the nightwind
Hardly rustle. Not even cradlesongs,
The rhythmic silence rocks us.
5 Listen to its song, listen to the beating of our dark blood, listen
To the beating of the dark pulse of Africa in the mist of lost
      villages.
Now the tired moon sinks towards its bed of slack water,
Now the peals of laughter even fall asleep, and the bards
      themselves
Dandle their heads like children on the banks of their mothers.
10 Now the feet of the dancers grow heavy and heavy grows the
      tongue of the singers.
This is the hour of the stars and of the night that dreams
And reclines on this hill of clouds, draped in her long gown
      of milk.
The roofs of the houses gleam gently. What are they telling
      so confidently to the stars?
Inside the hearth is extinguished in the intimacy of bitter and
      sweet scents.
15 Woman, light the lamp of clear oil, and let the children in bed
      talk about their ancestors, like their parents.
Listen to the voice of the ancients of Elissa.[1] Like we, exiled,

---

[1] A village in Guinea.

They did not want to die, lest their seminal flood be lost in
    the sand.
Let me listen in the smoky hut for the shadowy visit of
    propitious souls,
My head on your breast glowing, like a kuskus[2] ball smoking
    out of the fire,
20 Let me breathe the smell of our dead, let me contemplate and
    repeat their living voice, let me learn
To live before I sink, deeper than the diver, into the lofty depth
    of sleep.

■ EXPLORATIONS OF THE TEXT ■

1. Whom does the speaker address?
2. What mood is created by the setting? How is that mood intrinsic to the development of the vision of love?
3. Why are memories of "the ancestors" invoked? Why does the speaker want to "breathe the smell" of the dead and "repeat their living voices"?
4. Discuss the speaker's final wish, expressed in the last line.
5. Isolate and discuss the effect of the poem's sensory images.
6. Discuss the personification in the poem. What is its impact?
7. What vision of Africa emerges from this poem? Is it solely a poem about love?
8. How is Senghor's vision of passion quite different from the views of Neruda and of Snyder? Why?

■■ JOURNAL ENTRIES ■■

1. Create a scene in which you include details from all of the senses to evoke the mood of love.
2. Contrast this poem with Snyder's "The Bath." What do you conclude about the poets' uses of point of view, tone, and imagery?

■■■ IDEAS FOR WRITING ■■■

1. Determine the mood and tone of the poem. How does the poet create mood and tone?
2. Contrast this poem, written as a dramatic monologue, with "The Love Song of J. Alfred Prufrock." Are they solely about love? How do they differ?

---

[2] A spicy dumpling, cooked in soups.

The Bath

Gary Snyder

Gary (Sherman) Snyder (1930–   ) was born in San Francisco. He attended graduate school in Asian languages at Berkeley and later studied Zen in a monastery in Kyoto. At a very young age, Snyder began to study Native-American cultures, and his devotion to Zen Buddhism provides a complement to his precise and reverent observations of nature. He worked as a seaman, logger, trail crew member, and forester. He first received critical attention as a poet when Riprap *appeared in 1959. Other collections include* Myths and Texts *(1960),* Six Sections from Mountains and Rivers without End *(1965),* Three Worlds, Three Realms, Six Roads *(1966),* The Back Country *(1968),* Songs for Gaia *(1979), and* Left Out in the Rain *(1986). Snyder was awarded the Pulitzer Prize in poetry for 1975 for* Turtle Island, *a Native-American name for North America.*

"The Bath," a partially autobiographical description of a sensuous and spiritual family activity, mentions Snyder's wife, Masa, and his two children. As celebration of human love and as denial of concepts of the duality of body and soul, the poem centers on union. The influences of Buddhism and of Native-American values emerge in rich and concrete detail and in incantations in "The Bath."

Washing Kai in the sauna,
The kerosene lantern set on a box
    outside the ground-level window,
Lights up the edge of the iron stove and the
5   washtub down on the slab
Steaming air and crackle of waterdrops
    brushed by on the pile of rocks on top
He stands in warm water
Soap all over the smooth of his thigh and stomach
10   "Gary don't soap my hair!"
    —his eye-sting fear—
    the soapy hand feeling
    through and around the globes and curves of his body
    up in the crotch,
15 And washing-tickling out the scrotum, little anus,
    his penis curving up and getting hard
    as I pull back skin and try to wash it
Laughing and jumping, flinging arms around,
    I squat all naked too,
20   *is this our body?*

Sweating and panting in the stove-steam hot-stone
    cedar-planking wooden bucket water-splashing

kerosene lantern-flicker wind-in-the-pines-out
sierra forest ridges night—
25 Masa comes in, letting fresh cool air
sweep down from the door
a deep sweet breath
And she tips him over gripping neatly, one knee down
her hair falling hiding one whole side of
30 shoulder, breast, and belly,
Washes deftly Kai's head-hair
as he gets mad and yells—
The body of my lady, the winding valley spine,
the space between the thighs I reach through,
35 cup her curving vulva arch and hold it from behind,
a soapy tickle   a hand of grail
The gates of Awe
That open back a turning double-mirror world of
wombs in wombs, in rings,
40 that start in music,
is this our body?

The hidden place of seed
The veins net flow across the ribs, that gathers
milk and peaks up in a nipple—fits
45 our mouth—
The sucking milk from this our body sends through
jolts of light; the son, the father,
sharing mother's joy
That brings a softness to the flower of the awesome
50 open curling lotus gate I cup and kiss
As Kai laughs at his mother's breast he now is weaned
from, we
wash each other,
this our body

55 Kai's little scrotum up close to his groin,
the seed still tucked away, that moved from us to him
In flows that lifted with the same joys forces
as his nursing Masa later,
playing with her breast,
60 Or me within her,
Or him emerging,
this is our body:

Clean, and rinsed, and sweating more, we stretch
out on the redwood benches hearts all beating
65 Quiet to the simmer of the stove,
the scent of cedar

And then turn over,
>   murmuring gossip of the grasses,
>   talking firewood,
70 Wondering how Gen's napping, how to bring him in
>   soon wash him too—
These boys who love their mother
>   who loves men, who passes on
>   her sons to other women;

75 The cloud across the sky. The windy pines.
>   the trickle gurgle in the swampy meadow

>   *this is our body.*

Fire inside and boiling water on the stove
We sigh and slide ourselves down from the benches
80   wrap the babies, step outside,

black night & all the stars.

Pour cold water on the back and thighs
Go in the house—stand steaming by the center fire
Kai scampers on the sheepskin
85 Gen standing hanging on and shouting,

"Bao! bao! bao! bao! bao!"

This is our body. Drawn up crosslegged by the flames
>   drinking icy water
>   hugging babies, kissing bellies,

90 Laughing on the Great Earth

Come out from the bath.

■   **EXPLORATIONS OF THE TEXT**   ■

---

1. Who is the speaker? Who is Kai? What is the nature of the bath in the first section? Describe the setting.
2. What is the speaker's attitude toward Masa in the second section? What images characterize her?
3. Why does Snyder employ such explicit language about bodies and about love? Are the speaker's values different from other people? from other cultures?
4. How do images of birth and of sexuality function in section four?

5. What does the speaker reveal about himself in the following lines: "These boys who love their mother/who loves men, who passes on/her sons to other women"?
6. Discuss the refrain and its variations.
7. Describe the scene after the bath—the narrative, the setting, and the personae. What do you conclude?
8. What does the speaker mean by the last line: "Come out from the bath"? To whom does he speak?
9. The poem presents a simple action—a family taking a bath in a sauna—but what larger themes does it also evoke?
10. Compare the relationships in this poem with *And the Soul Shall Dance*. What is the role of the bathhouse in each work?

■■ JOURNAL ENTRIES ■■

1. Do you like "The Bath"? Write a reader response journal entry about this poem.
2. Analyze the sexual imagery in the poem.

■■■ IDEAS FOR WRITING ■■■

1. Write an essay that celebrates the body. Refer to Snyder and to Neruda.
2. Discuss the spiritual meaning of "The Bath."
3. Argue against the speaker's attitudes. Are they sexist?
4. How does the setting function in developing narrative, personae, and theme?

In the End, We Are All Light

Liz Rosenberg

Liz Rosenberg (1955–), educated at Bennington College and Johns Hopkins University, is a member of the Creative Writing faculty at the State University of New York at Binghamton where she has taught since 1978. She is a frequent reviewer of poetry, prose, and children's books for the Chicago Tribune, *the* Philadelphia Inquirer, Southwest Review, *and other publications; and her own poems have appeared in a number of journals. She was a Kellog Foundation Fellow (1982–1984) and in 1976 won the Atlantic First Award for her story "Memory."* The Angel Poems *appeared in 1984;*

and her book of poems, The Fire Music *(1986), won the 1985 Agnes Lynch Starrett Award from the University of Pittsburgh Press.*
    In this poem, the title contains a double meaning about enduring love in marriage and in old age: "In The End, We Are All Light."

I love how old men carry purses for their wives,
those stiff light beige or navy wedge-shaped bags
that match the women's pumps,
with small gold clasps that click open and shut.
5 The men drowse off in medical center waiting rooms,
with bags perched in their laps like big tame birds
too worn to flap away. Within, the wives slowly undress,
put on the thin white robes, consult, come out
and wake the husbands dreaming openmouthed.

10 And when they both rise up
to take their constitutional,
walk up and down the block, her arms are free as air,
his right hand dangles down.

So I, desiring to shed this skin
15 for some light silken one,
will tell my husband, "Here, hold this,"
and watch him amble off into the mall among the shining
cans of motor oil, my leather bag
slung over his massive shoulder bone,
20 so prettily slender-waisted, so forgiving of the ways
we hold each other down, that watching him
I see how men love women, and women men,
and how the burden of the other comes to be
light as a feather blown, more quickly vanishing.

■ EXPLORATIONS OF THE TEXT ■

1. Discuss the characters of the "old men" and "their wives." Focus on the simile of the "big tame birds" and on the images of hands.
2. What does the husbands' carrying of their wives' "purses" suggest about their relationships?
3. What is unexpected in this portrayal of marriage and love?
4. What does the speaker conclude from her observations?
5. Characterize the tone of the poem. Does it shift?
   Look carefully at the images of "light." What word play is evident in the use of "light"?

6. Discuss the speaker's revelation at how "the burden of the other comes to be/light as a feather blown, more quickly vanishing."
7. What do you learn about long-lasting marriages? about the state of older people in love?
8. Contrast this marriage with that of the couples in *And The Soul Shall Dance* and in *Trifles*.

■■ JOURNAL ENTRIES ■■

1. Go to a public place. Observe several couples in love. What does their body language reveal about their relationships?
2. Imagine a young couple whom you know. Describe their lives after fifty years of marriage. Write a scene with them in it.

■■■ IDEAS FOR WRITING ■■■

1. Compare and contrast the state of the newly married with that of people who have been married for many years.
2. Use your first journal entry as the basis of portraits of several couples in love. As Rosenberg does, isolate particular details that evoke visions of the people's characters and relationships.
3. Compare the "old men" and Prufrock.

I Take You an Orange

Huda Naamani   Translated from the Arabic by Huda Naamani and Miriam Cooke

Born in Damascus, Syria, Huda Naamani (1930–) earned a law degree from Syrian University and became a court attorney for her uncle's firm. She moved to Beirut in 1968. She writes regularly for Al-Nahar, *the Beirut newspaper, and belongs to the Arab Writers Union. She has published two plays concerning the Lebanese Civil War. Her poetry includes* To You *(1970),* My Fingers . . . No *(1971), and* I Remember I Was a Point I Was a Circle *(1975), a collection of patriotic poems about peace.*

In "I Take You an Orange," Naamani creates a persona who mocks a male lover's "word."

I take you an orange and I squeeze you holding you to my face
Spring you blossom in my eyes

A peacock's tail you gaze at me in the dark
I wear you gipsy garb I fold you a nomad's cloak
5 A flute grass and warmth of sheep flow with you
In the arms of mountains you paint the wreaths of heaven
      And the pains of a goddess

A frame for me I carve you I gild you and
    I fill you with roses
10 A fish I slaughter you, or a sun
    I bake you
    A star
Lightning flashes from your ring
Your eyes hang on my face coffee grounds honeycombs
15 Nigerian songs brush my neck, flocks of geese
Your word is suspended on the back of a door a duck's nose

■ EXPLORATIONS OF THE TEXT ■

1. What images represent the lover and her beloved? Explain the "orange," the "blossom," the "tail," and the "gipsy garb."
2. Why does the beloved "paint the wreaths of heaven/And the pains of a goddess"? What is the meaning of the opposition?
3. What are the changes in the second stanza? Why does the love become increasingly consuming and violent?
4. In the final stanza, the word of the beloved is negated, "a duck's nose." What has happened?
5. Discuss the ironies of the title.
6. Is this poem a declaration of independence or a call to battle? What is the attitude of the speaker?
7. Are the metaphors powerful? effective? Look at word order.

■■ JOURNAL ENTRIES ■■

1. What surprises do you discover in this poem?

■■■ IDEAS FOR WRITING ■■■

1. Why is "the word" of the beloved the most important issue? Explain the power of language in love. Refer to Kristeva's essay.

Song/For Sanna

Olga Broumas

*Born in Greece, Olga Broumas (1949–   ) moved to the United States
with her family at the age of nine. In 1977, she won the Yale Younger
Poets Award for her volume,* Beginning With O. *She is founder and
associate faculty member of Freehand, a community of women writers and photographers in Provincetown, Massachusetts. Her other
publications include* Namaste *(1978),* Pastoral Jazz *(1983),* Black
Holes, Black Stockings *(1985), and* Perpetua *(1989). She also has
translated poems by Odysseas Elytis, Nobel Prize winner, in a collection called* What I Love *(1986).*

*In "Song/For Sanna," the speaker longs for a relationship with
a woman who always returns home to "safer passions" and leaves
the speaker waiting, lonely, and expectant.*

> *. . . in this way the future enters into us,
> in order to transform itself in us before it happens.*
> R. M. Rilke

What hasn't happened
intrudes, so much
hasn't yet happened. In the steamy

kitchens we meet in, kettles
5 are always boiling, water for tea, the steep
infusions we occupy
hands and mouth with, steam
filming our breath, a convenient

subterfuge, a disguise
10 for the now
sharp intake, the measured
outlet of air, the sigh, the gutting
loneliness

of the present where
15 what hasn't happened will
not be ignored, intrudes, separates
from the conversation like milk
from cream, desire

rising between the cups, brimming
20 over our saucers, clouding the minty
air, its own

aroma a pungent
stress, once again, you will get
up, put on your coat, go

25 home to the safer passions, moisture
clinging still to your spoon, as the afternoon
wears on, and I miss, I
miss you.

■ EXPLORATIONS OF THE TEXT ■

1. What is the meaning of the quotation from Rilke, a twentieth-century German poet?
2. The narrator emphasizes "What hasn't happened." To what does she refer?
3. Analyze the kitchen imagery of stanza 2. How does Broumas extend the metaphors throughout the poem?
4. What are the connotations of "disguise," "sharp intake," "measured/outlet of air," "the sigh"?
5. Why is the narrator lonely? What happens to desire?
6. Why does Sanna "once again" leave? Why are the passions at home safer?
7. What are the strengths of this poem? Consider descriptive language and voice.
8. Compare the themes of desire and of longing in this poem with works by Marvell and by Silko.

■■ JOURNAL ENTRIES ■■

1. Create a short dialogue between the two personae.
2. Freewrite about the poem.

■■■ IDEAS FOR WRITING ■■■

1. Discuss love as unattainable, and refer to Kristeva and to Plato. Take a position on this issue.
2. Connect the Rilke quotation to themes of the poem.

For My Lover, Returning to His Wife

Anne Sexton

*The poet characterizes illicit and married love and makes
distinctions between the nature of the lover and of the wife.*

She is all there.
She was melted carefully down for you

and cast up from your childhood,
cast up from your one hundred favorite aggies.[1]

5   She has always been there, my darling.
She is, in fact, exquisite.
Fireworks in the dull middle of February
and as real as a cast-iron pot.

Let's face it, I have been momentary.
10 A luxury. A bright red sloop in the harbor.
My hair rising like smoke from the car window.
Littleneck clams out of season.

She is more than that. She is your have to have,
has grown you your practical your tropical growth.
15 This is not an experiment. She is all harmony.
She sees to oars and oarlocks for the dinghy,

has placed wild flowers at the window at breakfast,
sat by the potter's wheel at midday,
set forth three children under the moon,
20 three cherubs drawn by Michelangelo,

done this with her legs spread out
in the terrible months in the chapel.
If you glance up, the children are there
like delicate balloons resting on the ceiling.

25 She has also carried each one down the hall
after supper, their heads privately bent,
two legs protesting, person to person,
her face flushed with a song and their little sleep.

---

[1] Marbles that resemble agates.

I give you back your heart.
30 I give you permission—

for the fuse inside her, throbbing
angrily in the dirt, for the bitch in her
and the burying of her wound—
for the burying of her small red wound alive—

35 for the pale flickering flare under her ribs,
for the drunken sailor who waits in her left pulse,
for the mother's knee, for the stockings,
for the garter belt, for the call—

the curious call
40 when you will burrow in arms and breasts
and tug at the orange ribbon in her hair
and answer the call, the curious call.

She is so naked and singular.
She is the sum of yourself and your dream.
45 Climb her like a monument, step after step.
She is solid.

As for me, I am a watercolor.
I wash off.

■ EXPLORATIONS OF THE TEXT ■

1. Characterize the voice of the speaker in the poem.
2. What does the speaker think about the lover's/husband's attitude toward his wife? How does the speaker view herself? the wife?
3. Interpret the list of things that she gives him "permission" for: "the fuse inside her," "the bitch in her," "the burying of her small red wound," "the pale flickering flare," "the drunken sailor," "the mother's knee." What does each of these images signify?
4. What is "the curious call"?
5. Why does the speaker compare the wife to a "monument"? Why is the speaker a "watercolor"?
6. Why will the lover return to his wife and leave the speaker?

■■ JOURNAL ENTRIES ■■

1. Contrast the states of illicit and married love.
2. Contrast two relationships or lovers. Use two different sets of metaphors, as Sexton does.

■■■ IDEAS FOR WRITING ■■■

1. Compare visions of illicit love in "Love Must Not Be Forgotten," "The Dead," and "For My Lover, Returning to His Wife."
2. Explicate the shifts in tone in this poem. How do they relate to the development of voice, character, and theme?

Women

May Swenson

May Swenson (1919–1989) was born in 1919 in Logan, Utah. After she graduated from Utah State University and worked as a reporter in Salt Lake City, she moved to New York City, was an editor for New Directions from 1959–1966, and wrote poetry until her death.

Swenson produced ten volumes of work, including Another Animal *(1954),* A Cage of Spines *(1958),* To Mix With Time *(1963),* Half Sun Half Sleep *(1967),* Iconographs *(1970),* New and Selected Things Taking Place *(1978), and* In Other Words: New Poems *(1987).*

What has impressed critics about Swenson's work is its verbal inventiveness: its brilliant, lively, and original imagery. She has the power to make the reader see the world in fresh, new ways. Swenson is able "to make . . . her reader see clearly what he has merely looked at before."

"Women" is from her 1970 volume, Iconographs, *in which she experimented with* concrete *poetry: poems whose typographical, iconographic forms match the content and develop the themes of the work. The form of the poem certainly reveals truths about women's role in North American society and also creates dramatic momentum.*

Women   Or they
    should be   should be
        pedestals   little horses
            moving   those wooden
5   pedestals   sweet
            moving   oldfashioned
            to the   painted
                motions   rocking
                of men   horses

10   the gladdest things in the toyroom

            The   feelingly
            pegs   and then
            of their   unfeelingly
            ears   To be
15   so familiar   joyfully
            and dear   ridden
            to the trusting   rockingly
        fists   ridden until
    To be chafed   the restored

20 egos dismount and the legs stride away

    Immobile   willing
        sweetlipped   to be set
            sturdy   into motion
            and smiling   Women
25   women   should be
                should always   pedestals
                be waiting   to men

■ EXPLORATIONS OF THE TEXT ■

1. What is the speaker's point of view and tone? Isolate particular words that create the tone.
2. What are the central metaphors of the poem? What do they suggest about women's relations to men?
3. How do the repetition and alliteration add to meaning? What effects do they create?
4. How does the form of the poem affect the message? How effective is her technique?
5. Compare the view of women in this poem with de Beauvoir's view of woman as "Other" or with the portrayal of woman's place in society in "The Yellow Wallpaper."

■■ **JOURNAL ENTRIES** ■■

1. Write a poem about men or women in which the form illustrates the statement or character trait that you wish to present.
2. Is the poem a call for action? Why?

■■■ **IDEAS FOR WRITING** ■■■

1. What is the meaning of the symbolism of the rocking horse in this poem and in "The Rocking Horse Winner"?
2. Construct the political argument of this poem. Do you agree or disagree?
3. Discuss the theme of entrapment in this work and in one other work in this chapter.

Lot's Wife

Anna Akhmatova   Translated from the Russian by D. M. Thomas

Anna Akhmatova (1889–1966), considered one of the twentieth century's greatest lyric and political poets, was born in Odessa and spent her childhood in St. Petersburg. In 1910, she married Nikolai Gumilev, a poet. Gumilev was killed by the Bolsheviks in 1921; and, although the couple had been divorced since 1918, Akhmatova and her family were persecuted by the Communists for the next thirty years.

None of her poetry appeared in print in Russia between 1923 and 1940. A collected edition of her work was suppressed in 1945. After Stalin's death, her poetry was finally published; she began visiting friends in the West and received a D. Litt. from Oxford University in 1965.

Akhmatova's first book of poems was Evening, *published in 1910. Successive volumes include* Rosary, White Flock, Plaintain, Anno Domini, The Seventh Book, Northern Elegies, *and* Poem Without a Hero. *Her great political work, "Requiem," published in 1957, protests the injustices of the Stalinist reign of terror by presenting one woman's endless waiting outside a Leningrad prison to hear news of her son.*

Akhmatova's work has been praised for its clarity and beauty of image and of phrasing and for its sharp, evocative, and luminous detail.

"Lot's Wife" exhibits Akhmatova's sure control of her craft and her profound sense of the unbearable sadness and loss at the heart of existence.

And the just man trailed God's messenger,
His huge, light shape devoured the black hill.
But uneasiness shadowed his wife and spoke to her:
'It's not too late, you can look back still[1]

5 At the red towers of Sodom,[2] the place that bore you,
The square in which you sang, the spinning-shed,
At the empty windows of that upper storey
Where children blessed your happy marriage-bed.'

Her eyes that were still turning when a bolt
10 Of pain shot through them, were instantly blind;
Her body turned into transparent salt,
And her swift legs were rooted to the ground.

Who mourns one woman in a holocaust?
Surely her death has no significance?
15 Yet in my heart she never will be lost,
She who gave up her life to steal one glance.

■ **EXPLORATIONS OF THE TEXT** ■

1. Review the story of Sodom and Gomorrah in Genesis 19. Who is the "just man"? "God's messenger"?
2. Explore the significance of the line, "His huge, light shape devoured the black hill." Whose "shape" is it?
3. In Akhmatova's poem, why does Lot's wife look back? What does her glance reveal about women's values and concerns?
4. Why is "uneasiness" personified? What does it signify?
5. What is the significance of the speaker's questions in the last stanza? Why will Lot's wife "never . . . be lost" in the speaker's "heart"?
6. In what ways has Akhmatova changed the story? Why?
7. Why have women always been pillars of salt? What does the salt symbolize?
8. Why is Lot's wife never named? What does this detail suggest about the view of woman's position?

[1] Lot was the nephew of Abraham. His wife was transformed into a pillar of salt for looking back during their flight from Sodom (Genesis 13–19.)
[2] An ancient city destroyed by God because of its wickedness (Genesis 18–19).

■■ JOURNAL ENTRIES ■■

1. Defend the choices of Lot and of his wife. You may write in monologue form.
2. Contrast the characterizations of the wives in Akhmatova's poem and in Sexton's "For My Lover, Returning to His Wife."

■■■ IDEAS FOR WRITING ■■■

1. In *Slaughterhouse Five,* Kurt Vonnegut reflects that it is both necessary and terrifying to look back. Examine the poem in the context of this assertion by Vonnegut. Why is it necessary to look back? Why is it so terrifying?

The Love Song of J. Alfred Prufrock

T. S. Eliot

T. S. (Thomas Stearns) Eliot (1888–1965) was born in St. Louis. He graduated from Harvard University and moved in 1915 to England. For the rest of his life, he lived in London. Eliot published his first poems when he was a student, wrote "The Love Song of J. Alfred Prufrock" when he was twenty-two, and continued to produce masterpieces including The Wasteland *(1922), which depicts the spiritual breakdown of post-World War I society, and* The Four Quarters *(1943), the great autobiographical, meditative poems of his later years. He also wrote influential essays on poetry, gathered in* The Sacred Wood *(1920), and plays,* Murder in the Cathedral *(1935) and* The Cocktail Party *(1950). He was awarded the Nobel Prize for Literature in 1948.*

Eliot's poetry is noted for its evocative imagery, its range of form and style, and its allusions to myth, to legend, and to works from many different traditions.

In this poem, J. Alfred Prufrock is a representative of modern man: paralyzed, unable to act, and yearning for fulfillment.

> *S'io credessi che mia risposta fosse*
> *A persona che mai tornasse al mondo,*
> *Questa fiamma staria senza piu scosse.*
> *Ma perciocche giammai di questo fondo*

Non torno vivo alcun, s'i'odo il vero,
Senza tema d'infamia ti rispondo.[1]

Let us go then, you and I,
When the evening is spread out against the sky
Like a patient etherized upon a table;
Let us go, through certain half-deserted streets,
5 The muttering retreats
Of restless nights in one-night cheap hotels
And sawdust restaurants with oyster-shells:
Streets that follow like a tedious argument
Of insidious intent
10 To lead you to an overwhelming question . . .
Oh, do not ask, "What is it?"
Let us go and make our visit.

In the room the women come and go
Talking of Michelangelo.

15 The yellow fog that rubs its back upon the window-panes,
The yellow smoke that rubs its muzzle on the window-panes
Licked its tongue into the corners of the evening,
Lingered upon the pools that stand in drains,
Let fall upon its back the soot that falls from chimneys,
20 Slipped by the terrace, made a sudden leap,
And seeing that it was a soft October night,
Curled once about the house, and fell asleep.

And indeed there will be time
For the yellow smoke that slides along the street,
25 Rubbing its back upon the window-panes;
There will be time, there will be time
To prepare a face to meet the faces that you meet;
There will be time to murder and create,
And time for all the works and days[2] of hands
30 That lift and drop a question on your plate;
Time for you and time for me,
And time yet for a hundred indecisions,
And for a hundred visions and revisions,
Before the taking of a toast and tea.

---

[1] The epigraph from Dante's *Inferno,* spoken by Guido da Montefeltro, "If I thought that my
reply were to someone who could ever return to the world, this flame would shake no more.
But since no one has ever returned alive from this place, if what I hear is true, without fear
of infamy I answer you," suggests Prufrock's "damnation" and psychological torment.
[2] Reference to a poem by Hesiod, an eighth-century Greek writer.

35 In the room the women come and go
Talking of Michelangelo.

And indeed there will be time
To wonder, "Do I dare?" and, "Do I dare?"
Time to turn back and descend the stair,
40 With a bald spot in the middle of my hair—
(They will say: "How his hair is growing thin!")
My morning coat, my collar mounting firmly to the chin,
My necktie rich and modest, but asserted by a simple pin—
(They will say: "But how his arms and legs are thin!")
45 Do I dare
Disturb the universe?
In a minute there is time
For decisions and revisions which a minute will reverse.

For I have known them all already, known them all:
50 Have known the evenings, mornings, afternoons,
I have measured out my life with coffee spoons;
I know the voices dying with a dying fall[3]
Beneath the music from a farther room.
So how should I presume?

55 And I have known the eyes already, known them all—
The eyes that fix you in a formulated phrase,
And when I am formulated, sprawling on a pin,
When I am pinned and wriggling on the wall,
Then how should I begin
60 To spit out all the butt-ends of my days and ways?
And how should I presume?

And I have known the arms already, known them all—
Arms that are braceleted and white and bare
(But in the lamplight, downed with light brown hair!)
65 Is it perfume from a dress
That makes me so digress?
Arms that lie along a table, or wrap about a shawl.
And should I then presume?
And how should I begin? . . .

70 Shall I say, I have gone at dusk through narrow streets
And watched the smoke that rises from the pipes
Of lonely men in shirt-sleeves, leaning out of windows? . . .

---

[3] Allusion to Orsino's speech in Shakespeare's *Twelfth Night* (I, i), "That strain again! It had a dying fall."

I should have been a pair of ragged claws
Scuttling across the floors of silent seas.

75 And the afternoon, the evening, sleeps so peacefully!
Smoothed by long fingers,
Asleep . . . tired . . . or it malingers,
Stretched on the floor, here beside you and me.
Should I, after tea and cakes and ices,
80 Have the strength to force the moment to its crisis?
But though I have wept and fasted, wept and prayed,
Though I have seen my head (grown slightly bald) brought in upon a
    platter,[4]
I am no prophet—and here's no great matter;
I have seen the moment of my greatness flicker,
85 And I have seen the eternal Footman[5] hold my coat, and snicker,
And in short, I was afraid.

And would it have been worth it, after all,
After the cups, the marmalade, the tea,
Among the porcelain, among some talk of you and me,
90 Would it have been worth while,
To have bitten off the matter with a smile,
To have squeezed the universe into a ball
To roll it toward some overwhelming question,
To say: "I am Lazarus,[6] come from the dead,
95 Come back to tell you all, I shall tell you all"—
If one, settling a pillow by her head,
    Should say: "That is not what I meant at all.

    That is not it, at all."

And would it have been worth while, after all
100 Would it have been worth while,
After the sunsets and the dooryards and the sprinkled streets,
After the novels, after the teacups, after the skirts that trail along the
    floor—
And this, and so much more?—
It is impossible to say just what I mean!
105 But as if a magic lantern threw the nerves in patterns on a screen:
Would it have been worth while
If one, settling a pillow or throwing off a shawl,

---

[4] Reference to John the Baptist, who was beheaded by King Herod (Matthew 14:3–11).
[5] Figure of death or fate.
[6] Lazarus was raised from the dead by Jesus (John 11:1–44).

And turning toward the window, should say:
    "That is not it at all,
110   That is not what I meant, at all."

         . . .

No! I am not Prince Hamlet, nor was meant to be;
Am an attendant lord, one that will do
To swell a progress,[7] start a scene or two,
Advise the prince; no doubt, an easy tool,
115 Deferential, glad to be of use,
Politic, cautious, and meticulous;
Full of high sentence,[8] but a bit obtuse;
At times, indeed, almost ridiculous—
Almost, at times, the Fool.[9]

120 I grow old . . . I grow old . . .
I shall wear the bottoms of my trousers rolled.

Shall I part my hair behind? Do I dare to eat a peach?
I shall wear white flannel trousers, and walk upon the beach.
I have heard the mermaids singing, each to each.

125 I do not think that they will sing to me.

I have seen them riding seaward on the waves
Combing the white hair of the waves blown back
When the wind blows the water white and black.

We have lingered in the chambers of the sea
130 By sea-girls wreathed with seaweed red and brown
Till human voices wake us, and we drown.

■ EXPLORATIONS OF THE TEXT ■

1. Identify the "you" and "I." What are the possibilities?
2. What atmosphere do the opening simile of the evening and the personification of "the yellow smoke" and "yellow fog" create?
3. What is the state of mind of the persona, the "I" of the poem, in the first six stanzas? Why is he so concerned with "time"?
4. Why does he ask, "Do I dare/Disturb the universe?" Which details about his appearance (stanza 6) reveal his view of himself?

---

[7] A royal journey (Elizabethan English).
[8] Ideals, sentiments.
[9] Reference to the stock figure of a Fool, appearing in many dramas (e.g., Shakespeare's *King Lear*).

5. What is the significance of the refrain, "In the room the women come and go/Talking of Michelangelo."?
6. How do the concerns change in the next five stanzas? Whom and what has he "known"? Explore his state of mind.
7. Explain the meaning and impact of the following lines: "I should have been a pair of ragged claws/Scuttling across the floors of silent seas."
8. What is his "crisis" in the last nine stanzas? How do the allusions to John the Baptist, Lazarus, and Hamlet enlarge the scope of his conflict?
9. In the last stanza, what is the significance of the sea imagery and of the mermaids?
10. Conceive of Prufrock's crisis as a journey. Does Prufrock's state of mind change as the journey progresses?
11. Explore Eliot's use of figurative language (personification, simile, metaphor) and irony. What is the impact of these techniques?
12. Examine Eliot's use of repetition and parallelism. What impact do these devices have?
13. Compare Prufrock, Emiko (*And the Soul Shall Dance*), and Minnie Wright (*Trifles*).

■■ JOURNAL ENTRIES ■■

1. Explain your reactions to a simile or metaphor and its role in developing a portrait of Prufrock.
2. How does the epigraph from Dante's *Inferno* elucidate themes? Explore the allusions to Hamlet, Lazarus, and John the Baptist.
3. Write a monologue for Prufrock five years after this "love song." What is his future?

■■■ IDEAS FOR WRITING ■■■

1. Create a character analysis of Prufrock. Focus on his appearance, his questions, and his actions.
2. Will Prufrock ever find love? Construct an argumentative response to this question.
3. Do the literary allusions add to or detract from this poem? Do they confuse and intimidate a reader, or do they add depth to Eliot's vision?
4. Is this a "love song"? Why? Why not?
5. Prufrock is considered a modern antihero. Analyze his character in this context.

Poems for Further Reading

Upon Julia's Clothes
Robert Herrick (1591–1674)

Whenas in silks my Julia goes,
Then, then, methinks, how sweetly flows
That liquefaction of her clothes.

Next, when I cast mine eyes, and see
5 That brave vibration, each way free,
O, how that glittering taketh me!

The Willing Mistress
Aphra Behn (1640–1689)

Amyntas led me to a grove,
    Where all the trees did shade us;
The sun itself, though it had strove,
    It could not have betrayed us.[1]
5 The place secured from human eyes
    No other fear allows
But when the winds that gently rise
    Do kiss the yielding boughs.

Down there we sat upon the moss,
10 And did begin to play
A thousand amorous tricks,[2] to pass
    The heat of all the day.
Many kisses did he give
    And I returned the same,
15 Which made me willing to receive
    That which I dare not name.

---

[1] Exposed us.
[2] Games.

His charming eyes no aid required
  To tell their softening tale;
On her that was already fired,[3]
20 'Twas easy to prevail.
He did but kiss and clasp me round,
  Whilst those his thoughts expressed:
And laid me gently on the ground;
  Ah who can guess the rest?

The Flea

John Donne (1572–1631)

Mark but this flea, and mark in this,
How little that which thou deny'st me is;
Me it sucked first, and now sucks thee,
And in this flea, our two bloods mingled be;
5 Confess it, this cannot be said
A sin, or shame, or loss of maidenhead,
  Yet this enjoys before it woo,
  And pampered swells with one blood made of two,
  And this, alas, is more than we would do.

10 Oh stay, three lives in one flea spare,
Where we almost, nay more than married are.
This flea is you and I, and this
Our marriage bed, and marriage temple is;
Though parents grudge, and you, we are met,
15 And cloistered in these living walls of jet.
  Though use make you apt to kill me,
  Let not to this, self murder added be,
  And sacrilege, three sins in killing three.

Cruel and sudden, hast thou since
20 Purpled thy nail, in blood of innocence?
In what could this flea guilty be,
Except in that drop which it sucked from thee?

---

[3] Impassioned.

She Walks in Beauty
George Gordon, Lord Byron (1788–1824)

She walks in beauty, like the night
    Of cloudless climes and starry skies;
And all that's best of dark and bright
    Meet in her aspect and her eyes:
5 Thus mellow'd to that tender light
    Which heaven to gaudy day denies.

One shade the more, one ray the less,
    Had half impaired the nameless grace
Which waves in every raven tress,
10   Or softly lightens o'er her face;
Where thoughts serenely sweet express
    How pure, how dear their dwelling-place.

And on that cheek, and o'er that brow,
    So soft, so calm, yet eloquent,
15 The smiles that win, the tints that glow,
    But tell of days in goodness spent,
A mind at peace with all below,
    A heart whose love is innocent!

La Belle Dame sans Merci[1]
John Keats (1795–1821)

O what can ail thee, knight-at-arms,
    Alone and palely loitering?
The sedge[2] has withered from the lake,
    And no birds sing.

5 O what can ail thee, knight-at-arms,
    So haggard and so woe-begone?
The squirrel's granary is full,
    And the harvest's done.

[1] The title taken from a medieval poem means "The Beautiful Lady Without Mercy."
[2] Grasslike or marshlike vegetation growing in wet places.

I see a lily on thy brow,
10   With anguish moist and fever dew,
And on thy cheeks a fading rose
    Fast withereth too.

I met a lady in the meads,[3]
    Full beautiful—a faery's child,
15 Her hair was long, her foot was light,
    And her eyes were wild.

I made a garland for her head,
    And bracelets too, and fragrant zone;[4]
She looked at me as she did love,
20   And made sweet moan.

I set her on my pacing steed,
    And nothing else saw all day long,
For sidelong would she bend, and sing
    A faery's song.

25 She found me roots of relish sweet,
    And honey wild, and manna dew,
And sure in language strange she said,
    "I love thee true."

She took me to her elfin grot,
30   And there she wept, and sighed full sore,
And there I shut her wild wild eyes
    With kisses four.

And there she lullèd me asleep,
    And there I dreamed—Ah! woe betide!
35 The latest[5] dream I ever dreamed
    On the cold hill side.

I saw pale kings and princes too,
    Pale warriors, death-pale were they all;
They cried—"La Belle Dame sans Merci
40 "Hath thee in thrall!"

---

[3] Meadows.
[4] Belt.
[5] Last.

I saw their starved lips in the gloam,[6]
    With horrid warning gapèd wide,
And I awoke and found me here,
    On the cold hill's side.

45 And this is why I soujourn here,
    Alone and palely loitering,
Though the sedge has withered from the lake,
    And no birds sing.

How Do I Love Thee?

Elizabeth Barrett Browning (1806–1861)

How do I love thee? Let me count the ways.
I love thee to the depth and breadth and height
My soul can reach, when feeling out of sight
For the ends of Being and ideal Grace.
5 I love thee to the level of everyday's
Most quiet need, by sun and candle-light.
I love thee freely, as men strive for Right;
I love thee purely, as they turn from Praise.
I love thee with the passion put to use
10 In my old griefs, and with my childhood's faith.
I love thee with a love I seemed to lose
With my lost saints,—I love thee with the breath,
Smiles, tears, of all my life!—and, if God choose,
I shall but love thee better after death.

Annabel Lee

Edgar Allan Poe (1809–1849)

It was many and many a year ago,
    In a kingdom by the sea
That a maiden there lived whom you may know
    By the name of ANNABEL LEE;
5 And this maiden she lived with no other thought
    Than to love and be loved by me.

---

[6] Twilight.

I was a child and *she* was a child,
    In this kingdom by the sea,
But we loved with a love that was more than love—
10   I and my Annabel Lee—
With a love that the winged seraphs of heaven
    Coveted her and me.

And this was the reason that, long ago,
    In this kingdom by the sea,
15 A wind blew out of a cloud, chilling
    My beautiful Annabel Lee;
So that her highborn kinsmen came
    And bore her away from me,

To shut her up in a sepulchre
20   In this kingdom by the sea.

The angels, not half so happy in heaven,
    Went envying her and me—
Yes!—that was the reason (as all men know,
    In this kingdom by the sea)
25 That the wind came out of the cloud by night,
    Chilling and killing my Annabel Lee.

But our love it was stronger by far than the love
    Of those who were older than we—
    Of many far wiser than we—
30 And neither the angels in heaven above,
    Nor the demons down under the sea,
Can ever dissever my soul from the soul
    Of the beautiful Annabel Lee:

For the moon never beams, without bringing me dreams
35   Of the beautiful Annabel Lee;
And the stars never rise, but I feel the bright eyes
    Of the beautiful Annabel Lee:
And so, all the night-tide, I lie down by the side
Of my darling—my darling—my life and my bride,
40   In the sepulchre there by the sea—
    In her tomb by the sounding sea.

My Last Duchess

Robert Browning (1812–1889)

FERRARA

That's my last Duchess painted on the wall,
Looking as if she were alive. I call
That piece a wonder, now: Frà Pandolf's[1] hands
Worked busily a day, and there she stands.
5 Will't please you sit and look at her? I said
"Frà Pandolf" by design, for never read
Strangers like you that pictured countenance,
The depth and passion of its earnest glance,
But to myself they turned (since none puts by
10 The curtain I have drawn for you, but I)
And seemed as they would ask me, if they durst,
How such a glance came there; so, not the first
Are you to turn and ask thus. Sir, 'twas not
Her husband's presence only, called that spot
15 Of joy into the Duchess' cheek: perhaps
Frà Pandolf chanced to say "Her mantle laps
"Over my lady's wrist too much," or "Paint
"Must never hope to reproduce the faint
"Half-flush that dies along her throat": such stuff
20 Was courtesy, she thought, and cause enough
For calling up that spot of joy. She had
A heart—how shall I say?—too soon made glad,
Too easily impressed; she liked whate'er
She looked on, and her looks went everywhere.
25 Sir, 'twas all one! My favor at her breast,
The dropping of the daylight in the West,
the bough of cherries some officious fool
Broke in the orchard for her, the white mule
She rode with round the terrace—all and each
30 Would draw from her alike the approving speech,
Or blush, at least. She thanked men—good! but thanked
Somehow—I know not how—as if she ranked
My gift of a nine-hundred-years-old name
With anybody's gift. Who'd stoop to blame
35 This sort of trifling? Even had you skill
In speech—which I have not—to make your will
Quite clear to such an one, and say, "Just this

---

[1] Fra Pandolf and Claus of Innsbruck (last line) are imaginary artists.

"Or that in you disgusts me; here you miss,
"Or there exceed the mark"—and if she let
40 Herself be lessoned so, nor plainly set
Her wits to yours, forsooth, and made excuse,
—E'en then would be some stooping; and I choose
Never to stoop. Oh sir, she smiled, no doubt,
Whene'er I passed her; but who passed without
45 Much the same smile? This grew; I gave commands;
Then all smiles stopped together. There she stands
As if alive. Will't please you rise? We'll meet
The company below, then. I repeat,
The Count your master's known munificence
50 Is ample warrant that no just pretense
Of mine for dowry will be disallowed;
Though his fair daughter's self, as I avowed
At starting, is my object. Nay, we'll go
Together down, sir. Notice Neptune, though,
55 Taming a sea-horse, thought a rarity,
Which Claus of Innsbruck cast in bronze for me!

Trifles

Susan Glaspell

*Born in Davenport, Iowa, Susan Glaspell (1882–1948) graduated
from Drake University in 1899 and worked for the Des Moines* Daily
News. *Her short stories appeared in widely circulated magazines. In
1911, she moved to Greenwich Village, married George Cook in 1913,
and founded the Provincetown Players with her husband in 1915 on
Cape Cod, Massachusetts. Eugene O'Neill, Edna St. Vincent Millay,
John Reed, and Michael Gold became leading playwrights for this
group and for the Playwrights' Theater which Glaspell also helped to
create in New York City. She wrote more than twenty plays, numerous short stories, and novels. In 1930, her drama,* Alison's House,
*won the Pulitzer Prize. A fictionalized version of Emily Dickinson's
life, the play focused on psychological explorations of character.*

Glaspell's most famous work is Trifles *(1916), a one-act play
that she later transformed into a short story, "A Jury of Her Peers."
She based the play on a trial that she covered as a reporter in Iowa:
". . . I never forgot going to a kitchen of the woman who had been
locked up in town."* Trifles *concerns a murder and the different conclusions about motive made by men and women who examine the
scene of the crime.*

The Characters

County Attorney	Hale
Mrs. Peters	Mrs. Hale
Sheriff	

*Scene: The kitchen in the now abandoned farmhouse of John Wright, a
gloomy kitchen, and left without having been put in order—unwashed
pans under the sink, a loaf of bread outside the bread-box, a dish-towel
on the table—other signs of incompleted work. At the rear the outer
door opens and the Sheriff comes in followed by the County Attorney
and Hale. The Sheriff and Hale are men in middle life, the County Attorney is a young man; all are much bundled up and go at once to the
stove. They are followed by two women—the Sheriff's wife first; she is a
slight wiry woman, a thin nervous face. Mrs. Hale is larger and would
ordinarily be called more comfortable looking, but she is disturbed now*

and looks fearfully about as she enters. The women have come in slowly, and stand close together near the door.

County Attorney: *(rubbing his hands)* This feels good. Come up to the fire, ladies.

Mrs. Peters: *(after taking a step forward)* I'm not—cold.

Sheriff: *(unbuttoning his overcoat and stepping away from the stove as if to mark the beginning of official business)* Now, Mr. Hale, before we move things about, you explain to Mr. Henderson just what you saw when you came here yesterday morning.

County Attorney: By the way, has anything been moved? Are things just as you left them yesterday?

5 Sheriff: *(looking about)* It's just the same. When it dropped below zero last night I thought I'd better send Frank out this morning to make a fire for us—no use getting pneumonia with a big case on, but I told him not to touch anything except the stove—and you know Frank.

County Attorney: Somebody should have been left here yesterday.

Sheriff: Oh—yesterday. When I had to send Frank to Morris Center for that man who went crazy—I want you to know I had my hands full yesterday. I knew you could get back from Omaha by today and as long as I went over everything here myself—

County Attorney: Well, Mr. Hale, tell just what happened when you came here yesterday morning.

Hale: Harry and I had started to town with a load of potatoes. We came along the road from my place and as I got here I said, "I'm going to see if I can't get John Wright to go in with me on a party telephone." I spoke to Wright about it once before and he put me off, saying folks talked too much anyway, and all he asked was peace and quiet—I guess you know about how much he talked himself; but I thought maybe if I went to the house and talked about it before his wife, though I said to Harry that I didn't know as what his wife wanted made much difference to John—

10 County Attorney: Let's talk about that later, Mr. Hale. I do want to talk about that, but tell now just what happened when you got to the house.

Hale: I didn't hear or see anything; I knocked at the door, and still it was all quiet inside. I knew they must be up, it was past eight o'clock. So I knocked again, and I thought I heard somebody say, "Come in." I wasn't sure, I'm not sure yet, but I opened the door—this door *(indicating the door by which the two women are still standing)* and there in that rocker—*(pointing to it)* sat Mrs. Wright.

They all look at the rocker.

County Attorney: What—was she doing?

Hale: She was rockin' back and forth. She had her apron in her hand and was kind of—pleating it.

County Attorney: And how did she—look?

15 Hale: Well, she looked queer.

County Attorney: How do you mean—queer?

Hale: Well, as if she didn't know what she was going to do next. And kind of done up.

County Attorney: How did she seem to feel about your coming?

Hale: Why, I don't think she minded—one way or other. She didn't pay much attention. I said, "How do, Mrs. Wright, it's cold, ain't it?" And she said, "Is it?"—and went on kind of pleating at her apron. Well, I was surprised; she didn't ask me to come up to the stove, or to set down, but just sat there, not even looking at me, so I said, "I want to see John." And then she—laughed. I guess you would call it a laugh. I thought of Harry and the team outside, so I said a little sharp: "Can't I see John?" "No," she says, kind o' dull like. "Ain't he home?" says I. "Yes," says she, "he's home." "Then why can't I see him?" I asked her, out of patience. "'Cause he's dead," says she. "*Dead?*" says I. She just nodded her head, not getting a bit excited, but rockin' back and forth. "Why—where is he?" says I, not knowing what to say. She just pointed upstairs—like that *(Himself pointing to the room above.)*. I got up, with the idea of going up there. I walked from there to here—then I says, "Why, what did he die of?" "He died of a rope round his neck," says she, and just went on pleatin' at her apron. Well, I went out and called Harry. I thought I might—need help. We went upstairs and there he was lying—

20 County Attorney: I think I'd rather have you go into that upstairs, where you can point it all out. Just go on now with the rest of the story.

Hale: Well, my first thought was to get that rope off. It looked . . . *(Stops, his face twitches.)* . . . but Harry, he went up to him, and he said, No, he's dead all right, and we'd better not touch anything. So we went back down stairs. She was still sitting that same way. "Has anybody been notified?" I asked. "No," says she, unconcerned. "Who did this, Mrs. Wright?" said Harry. He said it business-like—and she stopped pleatin' of her apron. "I don't know," she says. "You don't *know?*" says Harry. "No," says she. "Weren't you sleepin' in the bed with him?" says Harry. "Yes," says she, "but I was on the inside." "Somebody slipped a rope round his neck and strangled him and you didn't wake up?" says Harry. "I didn't wake up," she said after him. We must 'a looked as if we didn't see how that could be, for after a minute she said, "I sleep sound." Harry was going to ask her more questions but I said maybe we ought to let her tell her story first to the coroner, or the sheriff, so Harry went fast as he could to Rivers' place, where there's a telephone.

County Attorney: And what did Mrs. Wright do when she knew that you had gone for the coroner?

Hale: She moved from that chair to this one over here *(Pointing to a small chair in the corner.)* and just sat there with her hands held together and looking down. I got a feeling that I ought to make some conversation, so I said I had come in to see if John wanted to put in a telephone, and at that she started to laugh, and then she stopped and looked at me—scared. *(The County Attorney, who has had his notebook out, makes a note.)* I dunno, maybe it wasn't scared. I wouldn't like to say it was. Soon Harry got back, and then Dr. Lloyd came, and you, Mr. Peters, and so I guess that's all I know that you don't.

County Attorney: *(looking around)* I guess we'll go upstairs first—and then out to the barn and around there. *(To the Sheriff.)* You're convinced that there was nothing important here—nothing that would point to any motive.

25 Sheriff: Nothing here but kitchen things.

The County Attorney, after again looking around the kitchen, opens the door of a cupboard closet. He gets up on a chair and looks on a shelf. Pulls his hand away, sticky.

County Attorney: Here's a nice mess.

The women draw nearer.

Mrs. Peters: *(to the other woman)* Oh, her fruit; it did freeze. *(To the County Attorney.)* She worried about that when it turned so cold. She said the fire'd go out and her jars would break.

Sheriff: Well, can you beat the women! Held for murder and worryin' about her preserves.

County Attorney: I guess before we're through she may have something more serious than preserves to worry about.

30 Hale: Well, women are used to worrying over trifles.

The two women move a little closer together.

County Attorney: *(with the gallantry of a young politician)* And yet, for all their worries, what would we do without the ladies? *(The women do not unbend. He goes to the sink, takes a dipperful of water from the pail and pouring it into a basin, washes his hands. Starts to wipe them on the roller-towel, turns it for a cleaner place.)* Dirty towels! *(Kicks his foot against the pans under the sink.)* Not much of a housekeeper, would you say, ladies?

Mrs. Hale: *(stiffly)* There's a great deal of work to be done on a farm.

County Attorney: To be sure. And yet *(With a little bow to her)* I know there are some Dickson county farmhouses which do not have such roller towels.

He gives it a pull to expose its full length again.

Mrs. Hale: Those towels get dirty awful quick. Men's hands aren't always as clean as they might be.

35 County Attorney: Ah, loyal to your sex, I see. But you and Mrs. Wright were neighbors. I suppose you were friends, too.

Mrs. Hale: *(shaking her head)* I've not seen much of her of late years. I've not been in this house—it's more than a year.

County Attorney: And why was that? You didn't like her?

Mrs. Hale: I liked her all well enough. Farmers' wives have their hands full, Mr. Henderson. And then—

County Attorney: Yes—?

40 **Mrs. Hale:** *(looking about)* It never seemed a very cheerful place.

County Attorney: No—it's not cheerful. I shouldn't say she had the home-making instinct.

Mrs. Hale: Well, I don't know as Wright had, either.

County Attorney: You mean that they didn't get on very well?

Mrs. Hale: No, I don't mean anything. But I don't think a place'd be any cheerfuller for John Wright's being in it.

45 County Attorney: I'd like to talk more of that a little later. I want to get the lay of things upstairs now.

He goes to the left, where three steps lead to a stair door.

Sheriff: I suppose anything Mrs. Peters does'll be all right. She was to take in some clothes for her, you know, and a few little things. We left in such a hurry yesterday.

County Attorney: Yes, but I would like to see what you take, Mrs. Peters, and keep an eye out for anything that might be of use to us.

Mrs. Peters: Yes, Mr. Henderson.

The women listen to the men's steps on the stairs, then look about the kitchen.

Mrs. Hale: I'd hate to have men coming into my kitchen, snooping around and criticising.

She arranges the pans under sink which the County Attorney had shoved out of place.

50 **Mrs. Peters:** Of course it's no more than their duty.

Mrs. Hale: Duty's all right, but I guess that deputy sheriff that came out to make the fire might have got a little of this on. *(Gives the roller towel a pull.)* Wish I'd thought of that sooner. Seems mean to talk about her for not having things slicked up when she had to come away in such a hurry.

Mrs. Peters: *(who has gone to a small table in the left rear corner of the room, and lifted one end of a towel that covers a pan)* She had bread set.

Stands still.

Mrs. Hale: *(eyes fixed on a loaf of bread beside the breadbox, which is on a low shelf at the other side of the room. Moves slowly toward it.)* She was going to put this in there. *(Picks up loaf, then abruptly drops it. In a manner of returning to familiar things.)* It's a shame about her fruit. I wonder if it's all gone. *(Gets up on the chair and looks.)* I think there's some here that's all right, Mrs. Peters. Yes—here; *(Holding it toward the window)* this is cherries, too. *(Looking again.)* I declare I believe that's the only one. *(Gets down, bottle in her hand. Goes to the sink and wipes it off on the outside.)* She'll feel awful bad after all her hard work in the hot weather. I remember the afternoon I put up my cherries last summer.

She puts the bottle on the big kitchen table, center of the room. With a sigh, is about to sit down in the rocking-chair. Before she is seated realizes what chair it is; with a slow look at it, steps back. The chair which she has touched rocks back and forth.

Mrs. Peters: Well, I must get those things from the front room closet. *(She goes to the door at the right, but after looking into the other room, steps back.)* You coming with me, Mrs. Hale? You could help me carry them.

They go in the other room; reappear, Mrs. Peters carrying a dress and skirt, Mrs. Hale following with a pair of shoes.

55 Mrs. Peters: My, it's cold in there.

She puts the clothes on the big table, and hurries to the stove.

Mrs. Hale: *(examining her skirt)* Wright was close. I think maybe that's why she kept so much to herself. She didn't even belong to the Ladies Aid. I suppose she felt she couldn't do her part, and then you don't enjoy things when you feel shabby. She used to wear pretty clothes and be lively, when she was Minnie Foster, one of the town girls singing in the choir. But that—oh, that was thirty years ago. This all you was to take in?

Mrs. Peters: She said she wanted an apron. Funny thing to want, for there isn't much to get you dirty in jail, goodness knows. But I suppose just to make her feel more natural. She said they was in the top drawer in this cupboard. Yes, here. And then her little shawl that always hung behind the door. *(Opens stair door and looks.)* Yes, here it is.

Quickly shuts door leading upstairs.

Mrs. Hale: *(abruptly moving toward her)* Mrs. Peters?

Mrs. Peters: Yes, Mrs. Hale?

60 Mrs. Hale: Do you think she did it?

Mrs. Peters: *(in a frightened voice)* Oh, I don't know.

Mrs. Hale: Well, I don't think she did. Asking for an apron and her little shawl. Worrying about her fruit.

Mrs. Peters: *(starts to speak, glances up, where footsteps are heard in the room above. In a low voice.)* Mr. Peters says it looks bad for her. Mr. Henderson is awful sarcastic in a speech and he'll make fun of her sayin' she didn't wake up.

Mrs. Hale: Well, I guess John Wright didn't wake when they was slipping that rope under his neck.

65 Mrs. Peters: No, it's strange. It must have been done awful crafty and still. They say it was such a—funny way to kill a man, rigging it all up like that.

Mrs. Hale: That's just what Mr. Hale said. There was a gun in the house. He says that's what he can't understand.

Mrs. Peters: Mr. Henderson said coming out that what was needed for the case was a motive; something to show anger, or—sudden feeling.

Mrs. Hale: *(who is standing by the table)* Well, I don't see any signs of anger around here. *(She puts her hand on the dish towel which lies on the table, stands looking down at table, one half of which is clean, the other half messy.)* It's wiped to here. *(Makes a move as if to finish work, then turns and looks at loaf of bread outside the breadbox. Drops towel. In that voice of coming back to familiar things.)* Wonder how they are finding things upstairs. I hope she had it a little more red-up up there. You know, it seems kind of *sneaking.* Locking her up in town and then coming out here and trying to get her own house to turn against her!

Mrs. Peters: But Mrs. Hale, the law is the law.

70 **Mrs. Hale:** I s'pose 'tis. *(Unbuttoning her coat.)* Better loosen up your things, Mrs. Peters. You won't feel them when you go out.

Mrs. Peters takes off her fur tippet, goes to hang it on hook at back of room, stands looking at the under part of the small corner table.

Mrs. Peters: She was piecing a quilt.

She brings the large sewing basket and they look at the bright pieces.

Mrs. Hale: It's log cabin pattern. Pretty, isn't it? I wonder if she was goin' to quilt it or just knot it?

Footsteps have been heard coming down the stairs. The Sheriff enters followed by Hale and the County Attorney.

Sheriff: They wonder if she was going to quilt it or just knot it!

The men laugh; the women look abashed.

County Attorney: *(rubbing his hands over the stove)* Frank's fire didn't do much up there, did it? Well, let's go out to the barn and get that cleared up.

The men go outside.

75 **Mrs. Hale:** *(resentfully)* I don't know as there's anything so strange, our takin' up our time with little things while we're waiting for them to get the evidence. *(She sits down at the big table smoothing out a block with decision.)* I don't see as it's anything to laugh about.

Mrs. Peters: *(apologetically)* Of course they've got awful important things on their minds.

Pulls up a chair and joins Mrs. Hale at the table.

Mrs. Hale: *(examining another block)* Mrs. Peters, look at this one. Here, this is the one she was working on, and look at the sewing! All the rest of it has been so nice and even. And look at this! It's all over the place! Why, it looks as if she didn't know what she was about!

After she has said this they look at each other, then start to glance back at the door. After an instant Mrs. Hale has pulled at a knot and ripped the sewing.

Mrs. Peters: Oh, what are you doing, Mrs. Hale?

Mrs. Hale: *(mildly)* Just pulling out a stitch or two that's not sewed very good. *(Threading a needle.)* Bad sewing always made me fidgety.

80 **Mrs. Peters:** *(nervously)* I don't think we ought to touch things.

Mrs. Hale: I'll just finish up this end. *(Suddenly stopping and leaning forward.)* Mrs. Peters?

Mrs. Peters: Yes, Mrs. Hale?

Mrs. Hale: What do you suppose she was so nervous about?

Mrs. Peters: Oh—I don't know. I don't know as she was nervous. I sometimes sew awful queer when I'm just tired. *(Mrs. Hale starts to say something, looks at Mrs. Peters, then goes on sewing.)* Well, I must get these things wrapped up. They may be through sooner than we think. *(Putting apron and other things together.)* I wonder where I can find a piece of paper, and string.

85 **Mrs. Hale:** In that cupboard, maybe.

Mrs. Peters: *(looking in cupboard)* Why, here's a bird-cage. *(Holds it up.)* Did she have a bird, Mrs. Hale?

Mrs. Hale: Why, I don't know whether she did or not—I've not been here for so long. There was a man around last year selling canaries cheap, but I don't know as she took one; maybe she did. She used to sing real pretty herself.

Mrs. Peters: *(glancing around)* Seems funny to think of a bird here. But she must have had one, or why would she have a cage? I wonder what happened to it.

Mrs. Hale: I s'pose maybe the cat got it.

90 **Mrs. Peters:** No, she didn't have a cat. She's got that feeling some people have about cats—being afraid of them. My cat got in her room and she was real upset and asked me to take it out.

Mrs. Hale: My sister Bessie was like that. Queer, ain't it?

Mrs. Peters: *(examining the cage)* Why, look at this door. It's broke. One hinge is pulled apart.

Mrs. Hale: *(looking too)* Looks as if someone must have been rough with it.

Mrs. Peters: Why, yes.

She brings the cage forward and puts it on the table.

95 **Mrs. Hale:** I wish if they're going to find any evidence they'd be about it. I don't like this place.

Mrs. Peters: But I'm awful glad you came with me, Mrs. Hale. It would be lonesome for me sitting here alone.

Mrs. Hale: It would, wouldn't it? *(Dropping her sewing.)* But I tell you what I do wish, Mrs. Peters. I wish I had come over sometimes when *she* was here. I—*(Looking around the room)*—wish I had.

Mrs. Peters: But of course you were awful busy, Mrs. Hale—your house and your children.

Mrs. Hale: I could've come. I stayed away because it weren't cheerful—and that's why I ought to have come. I—I've never liked this place. Maybe because it's down in a hollow and you don't see the road. I dunno what it is but it's a lonesome place and always was. I wish I had come over to see Minnie Foster sometimes. I can see now—

Shakes her head.

100 **Mrs. Peters:** Well, you mustn't reproach yourself, Mrs. Hale. Somehow we just don't see how it is with other folks until—something comes up.

Mrs. Hale: Not having children makes less work—but it makes a quiet house, and Wright out to work all day, and no company when he did come in. Did you know John Wright, Mrs. Peters?

Mrs. Peters: Not to know him; I've seen him in town. They say he was a good man.

Mrs. Hale: Yes—good; he didn't drink, and kept his word as well as most, I guess, and paid his debts. But he was a hard man, Mrs. Peters. Just to pass the time of day with him—*(Shivers.)* Like a raw wind that gets to the bone. *(Pauses, her eye falling on the cage.)* I should think she would 'a wanted a bird. But what do you suppose went with it?

Mrs. Peters: I don't know, unless it got sick and died.

She reaches over and swings the broken door, swings it again. Both women watch it.

105 **Mrs. Hale:** You weren't raised round here, were you? *(Mrs. Peters shakes her head.)* You didn't know—her?

Mrs. Peters: Not till they brought her yesterday.

Mrs. Hale: She—come to think of it, she was kind of like a bird herself—real sweet and pretty, but kind of timid and—fluttery. How—she—did—change. *(Silence; then as if struck by a happy thought and relieved to get back to everyday things.)* Tell you what, Mrs. Peters, why don't you take the quilt in with you? It might take up her mind.

Mrs. Peters: Why, I think that's a real nice idea, Mrs. Hale. There couldn't possibly be any objection to it, could there? Now, just what would I take? I wonder if her patches are in here—and her things.

They look in the sewing basket.

Mrs. Hale: Here's some red. I expect this has got sewing things in it. *(Brings out a fancy box.)* What a pretty box. Looks like something somebody would give you. Maybe her scissors are in here. *(Opens box. Suddenly puts her hand to her nose.)* Why—*(Mrs. Peters bends nearer, then turns her face away.)* There's something wrapped up in this piece of silk.

110 **Mrs. Peters:** Why, this isn't her scissors.

Mrs. Hale: *(lifting the silk)* Oh, Mrs. Peters—it's—

Mrs. Peters bends closer.

Mrs. Peters: It's the bird.

Mrs. Hale: *(jumping up)* But, Mrs. Peters—look at it! Its neck! Look at its neck! It's all—other side *to*.

Mrs. Peters: Somebody—wrung—its—neck.

Their eyes meet. A look of growing comprehension, of horror. Steps are heard outside. Mrs. Hale slips box under quilt pieces, and sinks into her chair. Enter Sheriff and County Attorney. Mrs. Peters rises.

115 County Attorney: *(as one turning from serious things to little pleasantries)* Well, ladies, have you decided whether she was going to quilt it or knot it?
Mrs. Peters: We think she was going to—knot it.
County Attorney: Well, that's interesting, I'm sure. *(Seeing the bird-cage.)* Has the bird flown?
Mrs. Hale: *(putting more quilt pieces over the box)* We think the—cat got it.
County Attorney: *(preoccupied)* Is there a cat?

Mrs. Hale glances in a quick covert way at Mrs. Peters.

120 Mrs. Peters: Well, not *now.* They're superstitious, you know. They leave.
County Attorney: *(to Sheriff Peters, continuing an interrupted conversation)* No sign at all of anyone having come from the outside. Their own rope. Now let's go up again and go over it piece by piece. *(They start upstairs.)* It would have to have been someone who knew just the—

Mrs. Peters sits down. The two women sit there not looking at one another, but as if peering into something and at the same time holding back. When they talk now it is in the manner of feeling their way over strange ground, as if afraid of what they are saying, but as if they can not help saying it.

Mrs. Hale: She liked the bird. She was going to bury it in that pretty box.
Mrs. Peters: *(in a whisper)* When I was a girl—my kitten—there was a boy took a hatchet, and before my eyes—and before I could get there—*(Covers her face an instant)* If they hadn't held me back I would have—*(Catches herself, looks upstairs where steps are heard, falters weakly)*—hurt him.
Mrs. Hale: *(with a slow look around her)* I wonder how it would seem never to have had any children around. *(Pause.)* No, Wright wouldn't like the bird—a thing that sang. She used to sing. He killed that, too.
125 Mrs. Peters: *(moving uneasily)* We don't know who killed the bird.
Mrs. Hale: I knew John Wright.
Mrs. Peters: It was an awful thing was done in this house that night, Mrs. Hale. Killing a man while he slept, slipping a rope around his neck that choked the life out of him.
Mrs. Hale: His neck. Choked the life out of him.

Her hand goes out and rests on the bird-cage.

Mrs. Peters: *(with rising voice)* We don't know who killed him. We don't know.
130 Mrs. Hale: *(her own feeling not interrupted)* If there'd been years and years of nothing, then a bird to sing to you, it would be awful—still, after the bird was still.

Mrs. Peters: *(something within her speaking)* I know what stillness is. When we homesteaded in Dakota, and my first baby died—after he was two years old, and me with no other then—

Mrs. Hale: *(moving)* How soon do you suppose they'll be through, looking for the evidence?

Mrs. Peters: I know what stillness is. *(Pulling herself back.)* The law has got to punish crime, Mrs. Hale.

Mrs. Hale: *(not as if answering that)* I wish you'd seen Minnie Foster when she wore a white dress with blue ribbons and stood up there in the choir and sang. *(A look around the room.)* Oh, I *wish* I'd come over here once in a while! That was a crime! That was a crime! Who's going to punish that?

135 **Mrs. Peters:** *(looking upstairs)* We mustn't—take on.

Mrs. Hale: I might have known she needed help! I know how things can be—for women. I tell you, it's queer, Mrs. Peters. We live close together and we live far apart. We all go through the same things—it's all just a different kind of the same thing. *(Brushes her eyes, noticing the bottle of fruit, reaches out for it.)* If I was you I wouldn't tell her her fruit was gone. Tell her it *ain't*. Tell her it's all right. Take this in to prove it to her. She—she may never know whether it was broke or not.

Mrs. Peters: *(takes the bottle, looks about for something to wrap it in; takes petticoat from the clothes brought from the other room, very nervously begins winding this around the bottle. In a false voice)* My, it's a good thing the men couldn't hear us. Wouldn't they just laugh! Getting all stirred up over a little thing like a—dead canary. As if that could have anything to do with—with—wouldn't they *laugh!*

The men are heard coming down stairs.

Mrs. Hale: *(under her breath)* Maybe they would—maybe they wouldn't.

County Attorney: No, Peters, it's all perfectly clear except a reason for doing it. But you know juries when it comes to women. If there was some definite thing. Something to show—something to make a story about—a thing that would connect up with this strange way of doing it—

The women's eyes meet for an instant. Enter Hale from outer door.

140 **Hale:** Well, I've got the team around. Pretty cold out there.

County Attorney: I'm going to stay here a while by myself. *(To the Sheriff.)* You can send Frank out for me, can't you? I want to go over everything. I'm not satisfied that we can't do better.

Sheriff: Do you want to see what Mrs. Peters is going to take in?

The County Attorney goes to the table, picks up the apron, laughs.

County Attorney: Oh, I guess they're not very dangerous things the ladies have picked out. *(Moves a few things about, disturbing the quilt pieces which cover the box. Steps back.)* No, Mrs. Peters doesn't need supervising. For that matter, a sheriff's wife is married to the law. Ever think of it that way, Mrs. Peters?

Mrs. Peters: Not—just that way.

145 **Sheriff:** *(chuckling)* Married to the law. *(Moves toward the other room.)* I just want you to come in here a minute, George. We ought to take a look at these windows.

County Attorney: *(scoffingly)* Oh, windows!

Sheriff: We'll be right out, Mr. Hale.

Hale goes outside. The Sheriff follows the County Attorney into the other room. Then Mrs. Hale rises, hands tight together, looking intensely at Mrs. Peters, whose eyes make a slow turn, finally meeting Mrs. Hale's. A moment Mrs. Hale holds her, then her own eyes point the way to where the box is concealed. Suddenly Mrs. Peters throws back quilt pieces and tries to put the box in the bag she is wearing. It is too big. She opens box, starts to take bird out, cannot touch it, goes to pieces, stands there helpless. Sound of a knob turning in the other room. Mrs. Hale snatches the box and puts it in the pocket of her big coat. Enter County Attorney and Sheriff.

County Attorney: *(facetiously)* Well, Henry, at least we found out that she was not going to quilt it. She was going to—what is it you call it, ladies?

Mrs. Hale: (her hand against her pocket) We call it—knot it, Mr. Henderson.

CURTAIN

■ EXPLORATIONS OF THE TEXT ■

1. Characterize Mrs. Hale and Mrs. Peters at the beginning of the play. How do they differ?
2. What clues lead the women to conclude that Minnie Wright killed her husband?
3. How do the men differ from the women? from each other?
4. Discuss the symbolism of the broken cage and the dead canary.
5. What do the men discover? Why do they conclude "Nothing here but kitchen things"?
6. Why do the men and women find different clues about the murder? What does Glaspell imply about the ways in which men and women were conditioned to view the world?
7. Do Mrs. Hale and Mrs. Peters change? Why? How? What makes them sympathize with Minnie Wright?
8. Characterize Minnie Wright and her husband. Describe their relationship. Why is Minnie Wright absent from the play?
9. Interpret the ending and the title. With what "crime" should Minnie Wright be charged?
10. Compare the marriage of the Wrights with those in other works in this chapter.
11. Compare Glaspell's critique of gender roles and of women's place in society with treatments of these issues by Gilman and Chopin.

■■ JOURNAL ENTRIES ■■

1. Write a journal entry in Minnie Wright's voice.
2. Are Mrs. Hale and Mrs. Peters correct when they withhold evidence concerning John Wright's murder?
3. What is the symbolism of the cage?

■■■ IDEAS FOR WRITING ■■■

1. Susan Glaspell claimed that the idea for the play came from a story which she covered as a reporter. Construct your version of her article.
2. What are the strengths and weaknesses of *Trifles?* Consider conflict, characters, setting, theme, symbol, irony, emotion, and/or general effect.
3. After the play was produced, Glaspell wrote a short story, "A Jury of Her Peers," about this subject. Read the story, and decide which version is better. Defend your choice.

NONFICTION

The Sexes
from **The Symposium**

Plato
Translated by Walter Hamilton

Plato (428–347 B.C.) was born in Athens and studied with Socrates. After the latter's execution for heresy in 399 B.C., Plato left Athens for a number of years but returned to found the Academy, often considered the first university. Plato taught philosophy and mathematics there until his death. One of the world's great philosophers, Plato wrote many treatises in the form of dialogues among Socrates and other figures in which the philosopher and his circle debate central, metaphysical questions.

In "The Sexes," an excerpt from Plato's The Symposium, *the dialogue concerns the true nature of love. Through the person of Aristophanes, Plato presents his vision of the relation of the sexes and of the reasons for the need to love.*

1 'Well, Eryximachus,' began Aristophanes,[1] 'it is quite true that I intend to take a different line from you and Pausanias. Men seem to me to be utterly insensible of the power of Love; otherwise he would have had the largest temples and altars and the largest sacrifices. As it is, he has none of these things, though he deserves them most of all. For of all the gods he is the most friendly to man, and his helper and physician in those diseases whose cure constitutes the greatest happiness of the human race. I shall therefore try to initiate you into the secret of his power, and you in turn shall teach others.

'First of all, you must learn the constitution of man and the modifications which it has undergone, for originally it was different from what it is now. In the first place there were three sexes, not, as with us, two, male and female; the third partook of the nature of both the others and has vanished, though its name survives. The hermaphrodite was a distinct sex in form as well as in name, with the characteristics of both male and female, but now the name alone remains, and that solely as a term of abuse. Secondly, each human being was a rounded whole, with double back and flanks forming a

---

[1] Aristophanes (448?–385? B.C.), Athenian comic playwright. Eryximachus, Pausanias (following), and Agathon and Socrates (later) are other participants at the banquet, where love is the topic of discussion.

complete circle; it has four hands and an equal number of legs, and two identically similar faces upon a circular neck, with one head common to both the faces, which were turned in opposite directions. It had four ears and two organs of generation and everything else to correspond. These people could walk upright like us in either direction, backwards or forwards, but when they wanted to run quickly they used all their eight limbs, and turned rapidly over and over in a circle, like tumblers who perform a cart-wheel and return to an upright position. The reason for the existence of three sexes and for their being of such a nature is that originally the male sprang from the sun and the female from the earth, while the sex which was both male and female came from the moon, which partakes of the nature of both sun and earth. Their circular shape and their hoop-like method of progression were both due to the fact that they were like their parents. Their strength and vigour made them very formidable, and their pride was overweening; they attacked the gods, and Homer's story of Ephialtes and Otus attempting to climb up to heaven and set upon the gods is related also of these beings.[2]

'So Zeus and the other gods debated what was to be done with them. For a long time they were at a loss, unable to bring themselves either to kill them by lightning, as they had the giants, and extinguish the race—thus depriving themselves for ever of the honours and sacrifice due from humanity—or to let them go on in their insolence. At last, after much painful thought, Zeus had an idea. "I think," he said, "that I have found a way by which we can allow the human race to continue to exist and also put an end to their wickedness by making them weaker. I will cut each of them in two; in this way they will be weaker, and at the same time more profitable to us by being more numerous. They shall walk upright upon two legs. If there is any sign of wantonness in them after that, and they will not keep quiet, I will bisect them again, and they shall hop on one leg." With these words he cut the members of the human race in half, just like fruit which is to be dried and preserved, or like eggs which are cut with a hair. As he bisected each, he bade Apollo turn round the face and the half-neck attached to it towards the cut side, so that the victim, having the evidence of bisection before his eyes, might behave better in the future. He also bade him heal the wounds. So Apollo turned round the faces, and gathering together the skin, like a purse with drawstrings, on to what is now called the belly, he tied it tightly in the middle of the belly round a single aperture which men call the navel. He smoothed out the other wrinkles, which were numerous, and moulded the chest with a tool like those which cobblers use to smooth wrinkles in the leather on their last. But he left a few on the belly itself round the navel, to remind man of the state from which he had fallen.

'Man's original body having been thus cut in two, each half yearned for the half from which it had been severed. When they met they threw their arms round one another and embraced, in their longing to grow together again, and they perished of hunger and general neglect of their concerns, because they

---

[2] Giants Ephialtes and Otus tried to climb to heaven by piling mountain upon mountain.

would not do anything apart. When one member of a pair died and the other was left, the latter sought after and embraced another partner, which might be the half either of a female whole (what is now called a woman) or a male. So they went on perishing till Zeus took pity on them, and hit upon a second plan. He moved their reproductive organs to the front: hitherto they had been placed on the outer side of their bodies, and the processes of begetting and birth had been carried on not by the physical union of the sexes, but by emission on to the ground, as is the case with grasshoppers. By moving their genitals to the front, as they are now, Zeus made it possible for reproduction to take place by the intercourse of the male with the female. His object in making this change was twofold; if male coupled with female, children might be begotten and the race thus continued, but if male coupled with male, at any rate the desire for intercourse would be satisfied, and men set free from it to turn to other activities and to attend to the rest of the business of life. It is from this distant epoch, then, that we may date the innate love which human beings feel for one another, the love which restores us to our ancient state by attempting to weld two beings into one and to heal the wounds which humanity suffered.

5   'Each of us then is the mere broken tally of a man, the result of a bisection which has reduced us to a condition like that of flat fish, and each of us is perpetually in search of his corresponding tally. Those men who are halves of a being of the common sex, which was called, as I told you, hermaphrodite, are lovers of women, and most adulterers come from this class, as also do women who are mad about men and sexually promiscuous. Women who are halves of a female whole direct their affections towards women and pay little attention to men; Lesbians belong to this category. But those who are halves of a male whole pursue males, and being slices, so to speak, of the male, love men throughout their boyhood, and take pleasure in physical contact with men. Such boys and lads are the best of their generation, because they are the most manly. Some people say that they are shameless, but they are wrong. It is not shamelessness which inspires their behaviour, but high spirit and manliness and virility, which lead them to welcome the society of their own kind. A striking proof of this is that such boys alone, when they reach maturity, engage in public life. When they grow to be men, they become lovers of boys, and it requires the compulsion of convention to overcome their natural disinclination to marriage and procreation; they are quite content to live with one another unwed. In a word, such persons are devoted to lovers in boyhood and themselves lovers of boys in manhood, because they always cleave to what is akin to themselves.

'Whenever the lover of boys—or any other person for that matter—has the good fortune to encounter his own actual other half, affection and kinship and love combined inspire in him an emotion which is quite overwhelming, and such a pair practically refuse ever to be separated even for a moment. It is people like these who form lifelong partnerships, although they would find it difficult to say what they hope to gain from one another's society. No one can suppose that it is mere physical enjoyment which causes the one to take such intense delight in the company of the other. It is clear that the soul of each has some other longing which it cannot express, but can only surmise and obscurely hint at. Suppose Hephaestus with his tools were to visit them as they lie together, and stand over them and ask: "What is it, mortals, that you hope to gain from one another?" Suppose too that when they could not answer he repeated his question in these terms: "Is the object of your desire to be always together as much as possible, and never to be separated from one another day or night? If that is what you want, I am ready to melt and weld you together, so that, instead of two, you shall be one flesh; as long as you live you shall live a common life, and when you die, you shall suffer a common death, and be still one, not two, even in the next world. Would such a fate as this content you, and satisfy your longings?" We know what their answer would be; no one would refuse the offer; it would be plain that this is what everybody wants, and everybody would regard it as the precise expression of the desire which he had long felt but had been unable to formulate, that he should melt into his beloved, and that henceforth they should be one being instead of two. The reason is that this was our primitive condition when we were wholes, and love is simply the name of the desire and pursuit of the whole. Originally, as I say, we were whole beings, before our wickedness caused us to be split by Zeus, as the Arcadians have been split apart by the Spartans.[3] We have reason to fear that if we do not behave ourselves in the sight of heaven, we may be split in two again, like dice which are bisected for tallies, and go about like the people represented in profile on tombstones, sawn in two vertically down the line of our noses. That is why we ought to exhort everyone to conduct himself reverently towards the gods; we shall thus escape a worse fate, and even win the blessing which Love has in his power to bestow, if we take him for our guide and captain. Let no man set himself in opposition to Love—which is the same thing as incurring the hatred of the gods—for if we are his friends and make our peace with him, we shall succeed, as few at present succeed, in finding the person to love who in the strictest sense belongs to us. I know that Eryximachus is anxious to make fun of my speech, but he is not to suppose that in saying this I am pointing at Pausanias and Agathon. They may, no doubt, belong to this class, for they are both unquestionably halves of male wholes, but I am speaking of men and women in general when I say that the way to happiness for our race lies in fulfilling the behests of Love, and in each finding for himself the mate who properly belongs to him; in a word, in returning to our original condition. If that condition was the best, it follows that it is best for us to come as near to it as our present circumstances allow; and the way to do that is to find a sympathetic and congenial object for our affections.

'If we are to praise the god who confers this benefit upon us, it is to Love that our praises should be addressed. It is Love who is the author of our well-being in this present life, by leading us towards what is akin to us, and it is Love who gives us a sure hope that, if we conduct ourselves well in the sight

---

[3] The conquering Spartans forced the residents of the Arcadian city of Mantinea to live in four separate villages.

of heaven, he will hereafter make us blessed and happy by restoring us to our former state and healing our wounds.

'There is my speech about Love, Eryximachus, and you will see that it is of quite a different type from yours. Remember my request, and don't make fun of it, but let us hear what each of the others has to say. I should have said "each of the other two," for only Agathon and Socrates are left.'

■ EXPLORATIONS OF THE TEXT ■

1. Explore the descriptions of the "three sexes," particularly of the "third" sex. How do you react to this description?
2. Describe this myth of the "fall." Compare it to the Biblical creation story and to the fall of Adam and Eve.
3. What is the concept of the "bisection"? How does Aristophanes explain homosexuality and heterosexuality?
4. How does the myth account for love?
5. What will happen if human beings set themselves "in opposition to Love"?
6. According to Aristophanes, what is "the way to happiness" for the race? Why?
7. What are Aristophanes' point of view and tone? Find key words and phrases that reveal his perspective.

■■ JOURNAL ENTRIES ■■

1. Create a myth or a fable that provides an explanation for one of the following: a) Why people fall in love; b) The nature of love or relationships; c) The nature of gender roles.
2. Take issue with one point in this treatise. Construct a counterargument.

■■■ IDEAS FOR WRITING ■■■

1. Agree or disagree with Aristophanes that happiness lies in "fulfilling the behests of love" and in finding the proper mate.
2. Are we only "half" selves, yearning for completion through our mates or through our love relationships?
3. Compare Aristophanes' (Plato's) views of love with the view in one of the love poems in this chapter.
4. Write in the persona of a character in one of the works in this chapter, and respond to Aristophanes' idea of love.

No Name Woman

Maxine Hong Kingston

Maxine Hong Kingston (1940–   ) was born in Stockton, California, to parents who immigrated from China to the United States. Her father, a teacher and scholar in China, immigrated first, working first as a manager of a gambling house. He then owned a laundry to support his wife who remained in China. For fifteen years, he sent money to Kingston's mother who, in the difficult times of the 1920s and 1930s in China, studied medicine and midwifery and then joined her husband in the United States in 1940. Kingston's parents' first two children died in China; Kingston was her parents' first American-born daughter. Her childhood was haunted by her parents' memories of China and her family's fear of the Caucasian world—the world outside Chinese culture. After graduating from the University of California, Kingston moved to Hawaii, taught in secondary schools, colleges, and the University of Hawaii. She now writes full-time.

Published in 1976, The Woman Warrior: Memoirs of a Girlhood Among Ghosts, *part autobiography, fiction, story, myth, and legend, won the National Book Critics Circle Award. It depicts Kingston's Chinese-American girlhood and her groping toward self-awareness and identity.* China Men, *her second autobiographical volume, depicts the world of her silent father and grandfather and their dreams of finding gold. According to Anne Tyler in* The New Republic, *Kingston's memoirs "are fiction at its best—novels, fairy tales, epic poems."*

In "No Name Woman," the first section of The Woman Warrior, *simultaneous messages of the power and powerlessness of women in Chinese society converge. Women are entrapped in their social roles but seek and gain liberation through words, language, and talk-stories.*

1   "You must not tell anyone," my mother said, "what I am about to tell you. In China your father had a sister who killed herself. She jumped into the family well. We say that your father has all brothers because it is as if she had never been born.

"In 1924 just a few days after our village celebrated seventeen hurry-up weddings—to make sure that every young man who went 'out on the road' would responsibly come home—your father and his brothers and your grandfather and his brothers and your aunt's new husband sailed for America, the Gold Mountain. It was your grandfather's last trip. Those lucky enough to get contracts waved good-bye from the decks. They fed and guarded the stowaways and helped them off in Cuba, New York, Bali, Hawaii. "We'll meet in California next year," they said. All of them sent money home.

"I remember looking at your aunt one day when she and I were dressing; I had not noticed before that she had such a protruding melon of a stomach. But I did not think, 'She's pregnant,' until she began to look like other pregnant women, her shirt pulling and the white tops of her black pants showing. She could not have been pregnant, you see, because her husband had been gone for years. No one said anything. We did not discuss it. In early summer she was ready to have the child, long after the time when it could have been possible.

"The village had also been counting. On the night the baby was to be born the villagers raided our house. Some were crying. Like a great saw, teeth strung with lights, files of people walked zigzag across our land, tearing the rice. Their lanterns doubled in the disturbed black water, which drained away through the broken bunds. As the villagers closed in, we could see that some of them, probably men and women we knew well, wore white masks. The people with long hair hung it over their faces. Women with short hair made it stand up on end. Some had tied white bands around their foreheads, arms, and legs.

5 "At first they threw mud and rocks at the house. Then they threw eggs and began slaughtering our stock. We could hear the animals scream their deaths—the roosters, the pigs, a last great roar from the ox. Familiar wild heads flared in our night windows; the villagers encircled us. Some of the faces stopped to peer at us, their eyes rushing like searchlights. The hands flattened against the panes, framed heads, and left red prints.

"The villagers broke in the front and the back doors at the same time, even though we had not locked the doors against them. Their knives dripped with the blood of our animals. They smeared blood on the doors and walls. One woman swung a chicken, whose throat she had slit, splattering blood in red arcs about her. We stood together in the middle of our house, in the family hall with the pictures and tables of the ancestors around us, and looked straight ahead.

"At that time the house had only two wings. When the men came back, we would build two more to enclose our courtyard and a third one to begin a second courtyard. The villagers pushed through both wings, even your grandparents' rooms, to find your aunt's, which was also mine until the men returned. From this room a new wing for one of the younger families would grow. They ripped up her clothes and shoes and broke her combs, grinding them underfoot. They tore her work from the loom. They scattered the cooking fire and rolled the new weaving in it. We could hear them in the kitchen breaking our bowls and banging the pots. They overturned the great waist-high earthenware jugs; duck eggs, pickled fruits, vegetables burst out and mixed in acrid torrents. The old woman from the next field swept a broom through the air and loosed the spirits-of-the-broom over our heads. 'Pig.' 'Ghost.' 'Pig,' they sobbed and scolded while they ruined our house.

"When they left, they took sugar and oranges to bless themselves. They cut pieces from the dead animals. Some of them took bowls that were not broken and clothes that were not torn. Afterward we swept up the rice and sewed it back up into sacks. But the smells from the spilled preserves lasted. Your aunt gave birth in the pigsty that night. The next morning when I went for the water, I found her and the baby plugging up the family well.

"Don't let your father know that I told you. He denies her. Now that you have started to menstruate, what happened to her could happen to you. Don't humiliate us. You wouldn't like to be forgotten as if you had never been born. The villagers are watchful."

10   Whenever she had to warn us about life, my mother told stories that ran like this one, a story to grow up on. She tested our strength to establish realities. Those in the emigrant generations who could not reassert brute survival died young and far from home. Those of us in the first American generations have had to figure out how the invisible world the emigrants built around our childhoods fit in solid America.

The emigrants confused the gods by diverting their curses, misleading them with crooked streets and false names. They must try to confuse their offspring as well, who, I suppose, threaten them in similar ways—always trying to get things straight, always trying to name the unspeakable. The Chinese I know hide their names; sojourners take new names when their lives change and guard their real names with silence.

Chinese-Americans, when you try to understand what things in you are Chinese, how do you separate what is peculiar to childhood, to poverty, insanities, one family, your mother who marked your growing with stories, from what is Chinese? What is Chinese tradition and what is the movies?

If I want to learn what clothes my aunt wore, whether flashy or ordinary, I would have to begin, "Remember Father's drowned-in-the-well sister?" I cannot ask that. My mother has told me once and for all the useful parts. She will add nothing unless powered by Necessity, a riverbank that guides her life. She plants vegetable gardens rather than lawns; she carries the odd-shaped tomatoes home from the fields and eats food left for the gods.

Whenever we did frivolous things, we used up energy; we flew high kites. We children came up off the ground over the melting cones our parents brought home from work and the American movie on New Year's Day—*Oh, You Beautiful Doll* with Betty Grable one year, and *She Wore a Yellow Ribbon* with John Wayne another year. After the one carnival ride each, we paid in guilt; our tired father counted his change on the dark walk home.

15   Adultery is extravagance. Could people who hatch their own chicks and eat the embryos and the heads for delicacies and boil the feet in vinegar for party food, leaving only the gravel, eating even the gizzard lining—could such people engender a prodigal aunt? To be a woman, to have a daughter in starvation time was a waste enough. My aunt could not have been the lone romantic who gave up everything for sex. Women in the old China did not choose. Some man had commanded her to lie with him and be his secret evil. I wonder whether he masked himself when he joined the raid on her family.

Perhaps she encountered him in the fields or on the mountain where the daughters-in-law collected fuel. Or perhaps he first noticed her in the marketplace. He was not a stranger because the village housed no strangers. She had to have dealings with him other than sex. Perhaps he worked an adjoining field, or he sold her the cloth for the dress she sewed and wore. His demand must have surprised, then terrified her. She obeyed him; she always did as she was told.

When the family found a young man in the next village to be her husband, she stood tractably beside the best rooster, his proxy, and promised before they met that she would be his forever. She was lucky that he was her age and she would be the first wife, an advantage secure now. The night she first saw him, he had sex with her. Then he left for America. She had almost forgotten what he looked like. When she tried to envision him, she only saw the black and white face in the group photograph the men had had taken before leaving.

The other man was not, after all, much different from her husband. They both gave orders: she followed. "If you tell your family, I'll beat you. I'll kill you. Be here again next week." No one talked sex, ever. And she might have separated the rapes from the rest of living if only she did not have to buy her oil from him or gather wood in the same forest. I want her fear to have lasted just as long as rape lasted so that the fear could have been contained. No drawn-out fear. But women at sex hazarded birth and hence lifetimes. The fear did not stop but permeated everywhere. She told the man, "I think I'm pregnant." He organized the raid against her.

On nights when my mother and father talked about their life back home, sometimes they mentioned an "outcast table" whose business they still seemed to be settling, their voices tight. In a commensal tradition,[1] where food is precious, the powerful older people made wrongdoers eat alone. Instead of letting them start separate new lives like the Japanese, who could become samurais and geishas, the Chinese family, faces averted but eyes glowering sideways, hung on to the offenders and fed them leftovers. My aunt must have lived in the same house as my parents and eaten at an outcast table. My mother spoke about the raid as if she had seen it, when she and my aunt, a daughter-in-law to a different household, should not have been living together at all. Daughters-in-law lived with their husbands' parents, not their own; a synonym for marriage in Chinese is "taking a daughter-in-law." Her husband's parents could have sold her, mortgaged her, stoned her. But they had sent her back to her own mother and father, a mysterious act hinting at disgraces not told me. Perhaps they had thrown her out to deflect the avengers.

20   She was the only daughter; her four brothers went with her father, husband, and uncles "out on the road" and for some years became western men. When the goods were divided among the family, three of the brothers took land, and the youngest, my father, chose an education. After my grandparents gave their daughter away to her husband's family, they had dispensed all the adventure and all the property. They expected her alone to keep the traditional ways, which her brothers, now among the barbarians, could fumble without detection. The heavy, deep-rooted women were to maintain the past

---

[1] A tradition which values communal meals—people's sharing of meals.

against the flood, safe for returning. But the rare urge west had fixed upon our family, and so my aunt crossed boundaries not delineated in space.

The work of preservation demands that the feelings playing about in one's guts not be turned into action. Just watch their passing like cherry blossoms. But perhaps my aunt, my forerunner, caught in a slow life, let dreams grow and fade and after some months or years went toward what persisted. Fear at the enormities of the forbidden kept her desires delicate, wire and bone. She looked at a man because she liked the way the hair was tucked behind his ears, or she liked the question-mark line of a long torso curving at the shoulder and straight at the hip. For warm eyes or a soft voice or a slow walk—that's all—a few hairs, a line, a brightness, a sound, a pace, she gave up family. She offered us up for a charm that vanished with tiredness, a pigtail that didn't toss when the wind died. Why, the wrong lighting could erase the dearest thing about him.

It could very well have been, however, that my aunt did not take subtle enjoyment of her friend, but, a wild woman, kept rollicking company. Imagining her free with sex doesn't fit, though. I don't know any women like that, or men either. Unless I see her life branching into mine, she gives me no ancestral help.

To sustain her being in love, she often worked at herself in the mirror, guessing at the colors and shapes that would interest him, changing them frequently in order to hit on the right combination. She wanted him to look back.

On a farm near the sea, a woman who tended her appearance reaped a reputation for eccentricity. All the married women blunt-cut their hair in flaps about their ears or pulled it back in tight buns. No nonsense. Neither style blew easily into heart-catching tangles. And at their weddings they displayed themselves in their long hair for the last time. "It brushed the backs of my knees," my mother tells me. "It was braided, and even so, it brushed the backs of my knees."

25   At the mirror my aunt combed individuality into her bob. A bun could have been contrived to escape into black streamers blowing in the wind or in quiet wisps about her face, but only the older women in our picture album wear buns. She brushed her hair back from her forehead, tucking the flaps behind her ears. She looped a piece of thread, knotted into a circle between her index fingers and thumbs, and ran the double strand across her forehead. When she closed her fingers as if she were making a pair of shadow geese bite, the string twisted together catching the little hairs. Then she pulled the thread away from her skin, ripping the hairs out neatly, her eyes watering from the needles of pain. Opening her fingers, she cleaned the thread, then rolled it along her hairline and the tops of her eyebrows. My mother did the same to me and my sisters and herself. I used to believe that the expression "caught by the short hairs" meant a captive held with a depilatory string. It especially hurt at the temples, but my mother said we were lucky we didn't have to have our feet bound when we were seven. Sisters used to sit on their beds and cry together, she said, as their mothers or their slaves removed the bandages for a few minutes each night and let the blood gush back into their

veins. I hope that the man my aunt loved appreciated a smooth brow, that he wasn't just a tits-and-ass man.

Once my aunt found a freckle on her chin, at a spot that the almanac said predestined her for unhappiness. She dug it out with a hot needle and washed the wound with peroxide.

More attention to her looks than these pullings of hairs and pickings at spots would have caused gossip among the villagers. They owned work clothes and good clothes, and they wore good clothes for feasting the new seasons. But since a woman combing her hair hexes beginnings, my aunt rarely found an occasion to look her best. Women looked like great sea snails—the corded wood, babies, and laundry they carried were the whorls on their backs. The Chinese did not admire a bent back: goddesses and warriors stood straight. Still there must have been a marvelous freeing of beauty when a worker laid down her burden and stretched and arched.

Such commonplace loveliness, however, was not enough for my aunt. She dreamed of a lover for the fifteen days of New Year's, the time for families to exchange visits, money, and food. She plied her secret comb. And sure enough she cursed the year, the family, the village, and herself.

Even as her hair lured her imminent lover, many other men looked at her. Uncles, cousins, nephews, brothers would have looked, too, had they been home between journeys. Perhaps they had already been restraining their curiosity, and they left, fearful that their glances, like a field of nesting birds, might be startled and caught. Poverty hurt, and that was their first reason for leaving. But another, final reason for leaving the crowded house was the never-said.

30   She may have been unusually beloved, the precious only daughter, spoiled and mirror gazing because of the affection the family lavished on her. When her husband left, they welcomed the chance to take her back from the in-laws; she could live like the little daughter for just a while longer. There are stories that my grandfather was different from other people, "crazy ever since the little Jap bayoneted him in the head." He used to put his naked penis on the dinner table, laughing. And one day he brought home a baby girl, wrapped up inside his brown western-style greatcoat. He had traded one of his sons, probably my father, the youngest, for her. My grandmother made him trade back. When he finally got a daughter of his own, he doted on her. They must have all loved her, except perhaps my father, the only brother who never went back to China, having once been traded for a girl.

Brothers and sisters, newly men and women, had to efface their sexual color and present plain miens.[2] Disturbing hair and eyes, a smile like no other threatened the ideal of five generations living under one roof. To focus blurs, people shouted face to face and yelled from room to room. The immigrants I know have loud voices, unmodulated to American tones even after years away from the village where they called their friendships out across the fields. I have not been able to stop my mother's screams in public libraries

[2] Looks.

or over telephones. Walking erect (knees straight, toes pointed forward, not pigeon-toed, which is Chinese-feminine) and speaking in an inaudible voice, I have tried to turn myself American-feminine. Chinese communication was loud, public. Only sick people had to whisper. But at the dinner table, where the family members came nearest one another, no one could talk, not the outcasts nor any eaters. Every word that falls from the mouth is a coin lost. Silently they gave and accepted food with both hands. A preoccupied child who took his bowl with one hand got a sideways glare. A complete moment of total attention is due everyone alike. Children and lovers have no singularity here, but my aunt used a secret voice, a separate attentiveness.

She kept the man's name to herself throughout her labor and dying; she did not accuse him that he be punished with her. To save her inseminator's name she gave silent birth.

He may have been somebody in her own household, but intercourse with a man outside the family would have been no less abhorrent. All the village were kinsmen, and the titles shouted in loud country voices never let kinship be forgotten. Any man within visiting distance would have been neutralized as a lover—"brother," "younger brother," "older brother"—one hundred and fifteen relationship titles. Parents researched birth charts probably not so much to assure good fortune as to circumvent incest in a population that has but one hundred surnames. Everybody has eight million relatives. How useless then sexual mannerisms, how dangerous.

As if it came from an atavism[3] deeper than fear, I used to add "brother" silently to boys' names. It hexed the boys, who would or would not ask me to dance, and made them less scary and as familiar and deserving of benevolence as girls.

35 But, of course, I hexed myself also—no dates. I should have stood up, both arms waving, and shouted out across libraries, "Hey, you! Love me back." I had no idea, though, how to make attraction selective, how to control its direction and magnitude. If I made myself American-pretty so that the five or six Chinese boys in the class fell in love with me, everyone else—the Caucasian, Negro, and Japanese boys—would too. Sisterliness, dignified and honorable, made much more sense.

Attraction eludes control so stubbornly that whole societies designed to organize relationships among people cannot keep order, not even when they bind people to one another from childhood and raise them together. Among the very poor and the wealthy, brothers married their adopted sisters, like doves. Our family allowed some romance, paying adult brides' prices and providing dowries so that their sons and daughters could marry strangers. Marriage promises to turn strangers into friendly relatives—a nation of siblings.

In the village structure, spirits shimmered among the live creatures, balanced and held in equilibrium by time and land. But one human being flaring up into violence could open up a black hole, a maelstrom that pulled in the sky. The frightened villagers, who depended on one another to maintain the real,

---

[3] Reversion to a primitive or an earlier type (or ancestral form).

went to my aunt to show her a personal, physical representation of the break she had made in the "roundness." Misallying couples snapped off the future, which was to be embodied in true offspring. The villagers punished her for acting as if she could have a private life, secret and apart from them.

If my aunt had betrayed the family at a time of large grain yields and peace, when many boys were born, and wings were being built on many houses, perhaps she might have escaped such severe punishment. But the men—hungry, greedy, tired of planting in dry soil, cuckolded—had had to leave the village in order to send food-money home. There were ghost plagues, bandit plagues, wars with the Japanese, floods. My Chinese brother and sister had died of an unknown sickness. Adultery, perhaps only a mistake during good times, became a crime when the village needed food.

The round moon cakes and round doorways, the round tables of graduated size that fit one roundness inside another, round windows and rice bowls—these talismen had lost their power to warn this family of the law: a family must be whole, faithfully keeping the descent line by having sons to feed the old and the dead, who in turn look after the family. The villagers came to show my aunt and her lover-in-hiding a broken house. The villagers were speeding up the circling of events because she was too shortsighted to see that her infidelity had already harmed the village, that waves of consequences would return unpredictably, sometimes in disguise, as now, to hurt her. This roundness had to be made coin-sized so that she would see its circumference: punish her at the birth of her baby. Awaken her to the inexorable. People who refused fatalism because they could invent small resources insisted on culpability. Deny accidents and wrest fault from the stars.

40   After the villagers left, their lanterns now scattering in various directions toward home, the family broke their silence and cursed her. "Aiaa, we're going to die. Death is coming. Death is coming. Look what you've done. You've killed us. Ghost! Dead ghost! You've never been born." She ran out into the fields, far enough from the house so that she could no longer hear their voices, and pressed herself against the earth, her own land no more. When she felt the birth coming, she thought that she had been hurt. Her body seized together. "They've hurt me too much," she thought. "This is gall, and it will kill me." Her forehead and knees against the earth, her body convulsed and then released her onto her back. The black well of sky and stars went out and out and out forever; her body and her complexity seemed to disappear. She was one of the stars, a bright dot in blackness, without home, without a companion, in eternal cold and silence. An agoraphobia rose in her, speeding higher and higher, bigger and bigger; she would not be able to contain it; there would be no end to fear.

Flayed, unprotected against space, she felt pain return, focusing her body. This pain chilled her—a cold, steady kind of surface pain. Inside, spasmodically, the other pain, the pain of the child, heated her. For hours she lay on the ground, alternately body and space. Sometimes a vision of normal comfort obliterated reality: she saw the family in the evening gambling at the dinner table, the young people massaging their elders' backs. She saw them congratulating one another, high joy on the mornings the rice shoots came up. When these pictures burst, the stars drew yet further apart. Black space opened.

She got to her feet to fight better and remembered that old-fashioned women gave birth in their pigsties to fool the jealous, pain-dealing gods, who do not snatch piglets. Before the next spasms could stop her, she ran to the pigsty, each step a rushing out into emptiness. She climbed over the fence and knelt in the dirt. It was good to have a fence enclosing her, a tribal person alone.

Laboring, this woman who had carried her child as a foreign growth that sickened her every day, expelled it at last. She reached down to touch the hot, wet, moving mass, surely smaller than anything human, and could feel that it was human after all—fingers, toes, nails, nose. She pulled it up on to her belly, and it lay curled there, butt in the air, feet precisely tucked one under the other. She opened her loose shirt and buttoned the child inside. After resting, it squirmed and thrashed and she pushed it up to her breast. It turned its head this way and that until it found her nipple. There, it made little snuffling noises. She clenched her teeth at its preciousness, lovely as a young calf, a piglet, a little dog.

She may have gone to the pigsty as a last act of responsibility: she would protect this child as she had protected its father. It would look after her soul, leaving supplies on her grave. But how would this tiny child without family find her grave when there would be no marker for her anywhere, neither in the earth nor the family hall? No one would give her a family hall name. She had taken the child with her into the wastes. At its birth the two of them had felt the same raw pain of separation, a wound that only the family pressing tight could close. A child with no descent line would not soften her life but only trail after her, ghostlike, begging her to give it purpose. At dawn the villagers on their way to the fields would stand around the fence and look.

45   Full of milk, the little ghost slept. When it awoke, she hardened her breasts against the milk that crying loosens. Toward morning she picked up the baby and walked to the well.

Carrying the baby to the well shows loving. Otherwise abandon it. Turn its face into the mud. Mothers who love their children take them along. It was probably a girl; there is some hope of forgiveness for boys.

"Don't tell anyone you had an aunt. Your father does not want to hear her name. She has never been born." I have believed that sex was unspeakable and words so strong and fathers so frail that "aunt" would do my father mysterious harm. I have thought that my family, having settled among immigrants who had also been their neighbors in the ancestral land, needed to clean their name, and a wrong word would incite the kinspeople even here. But there is more to this silence: they want me to participate in her punishment. And I have.

In the twenty years since I heard this story I have not asked for details nor said my aunt's name; I do not know it. People who can comfort the dead can also chase after them to hurt them further—a reverse ancestor worship. The real punishment was not the raid swiftly inflicted by the villagers, but the family's deliberately forgetting her. Her betrayal so maddened them, they saw to it that she would suffer forever, even after death. Always hungry, always needing, she would have to beg food from other ghosts, snatch and steal it from those whose living descendants give them gifts. She would have to fight the ghosts massed at crossroads for the buns a few thoughtful citizens leave to decoy her away from village and home so that the ancestral spirits could feast unharassed. At peace, they could act like gods, not ghosts, their descent lines providing them with paper suits and dresses, spirit money, paper houses, paper automobiles, chicken, meat, and rice into eternity— essences delivered up in smoke and flames, steam and incense rising from each rice bowl. In an attempt to make the Chinese care for people outside the family, Chairman Mao[4] encourages us now to give our paper replicas to the spirits of outstanding soldiers and workers, no matter whose ancestors they may be. My aunt remains forever hungry. Goods are not distributed evenly among the dead.

My aunt haunts me—her ghost drawn to me because now, after fifty years of neglect, I alone devote pages of paper to her, though not origamied[5] into houses and clothes. I do not think she always means me well. I am telling on her, and she was a spite suicide, drowning herself in the drinking water. The Chinese are always very frightened of the drowned one, whose weeping ghost, wet hair hanging and skin bloated, waits silently by the water to pull down a substitute.

■ EXPLORATIONS OF THE TEXT ■

1. Why does the mother tell her story about the narrator's aunt? Why is the aunt considered to have "never been born"?
2. What are the conditions—social, cultural, economic, and personal—that drive the aunt to another man?
3. Why do the villagers storm and raid the house? What do the actions in the scene suggest about the villagers and their values?
4. What is the purpose of storytelling for these first-generation Chinese-American women? What additional motives for the mother's narrative emerge?
5. Why do Chinese "guard their real names with silence"? Why do they want to confuse the gods?
6. Explain: "Adultery is extravagance." Relate the statement to Chinese values and philosophy of life.
7. How does the daughter reinterpret the story of her aunt?

---

[4] Chinese Communist leader (1893–1976).
[5] Origami, the Japanese art of decorative paper folding.

8. How does the daughter view her aunt as her precursor? Look at details of hair and appearance.
9. Why is the aunt's pregnancy so threatening to the society?
10. Why does the aunt give birth in a pigsty? Why does she drown herself and her baby in the well?
11. What are the attitudes toward sexuality, love, marriage, and women's roles in China at the time of this story?
12. Compare the aunt with Emiko in *And the Soul Shall Dance*.

■■ JOURNAL ENTRIES ■■

1. Explore the theme of silence in "No Name Woman."
2. Explain the imagery of the ghost and of the "No Name Woman." Why does she have no name?

■■■ IDEAS FOR WRITING ■■■

1. Consider the title. What are views of language and of identity in this work? What do words mean to the daughter?
2. Write a short scene for a play in which the aunt, Minnie Wright, and Emiko talk with each other. Write monologues and/or dialogue for each character.
3. Examine the theme of initiation in "No Name Woman" and in *And The Soul Shall Dance*.

Woman as Other

Simone de Beauvoir

*Simone de Beauvoir (1908–1986) had a strict middle class, Parisian, Catholic upbringing and traced the seeds of her feminism to her repugnance to that restricted social world. She studied philosophy at the Sorbonne, where she met Jean-Paul Sartre and began her career as a writer and as an existential philosopher. She also began a relationship with Sartre that endured for fifty years until his death in 1980. A prolific writer, a leftist, an intellectual, and an iconoclast, she authored philosophical essays and memoirs, chronicling her personal, political, and intellectual development—*Memoirs of a Dutiful Daughter *(1959),* Prime of Life *(1962), and* Force of Circumstance *(1965)—and several novels, including* The Mandarins *(1954), which won the Prix Goncourt in 1954.*

The Second Sex (1949; English translation, 1953), is one of the most important works of twentieth-century feminism. De Beauvoir analyzes and criticizes the historical and cultural reasons for treating women as "the second sex."

1   What is a woman?
To state the question is, to me, to suggest, at once, a preliminary answer. The fact that I ask it is in itself significant. A man would never get the notion of writing a book on the peculiar situation of the human male. But if I wish to define myself, I must first of all say: "I am a woman"; on this truth must be based all further discussion. A man never begins by presenting himself as an individual of a certain sex; it goes without saying that he is a man. The terms *masculine* and *feminine* are used symmetrically only as a matter of form, as on legal papers. In actuality the relation of the two sexes is not quite like that of two electrical poles, for man represents both the positive and the neutral, as is indicated by the common use of *man* to designate human beings in general; whereas woman represents only the negative, defined by limiting criteria, without reciprocity. In the midst of an abstract discussion it is vexing to hear a man say: "You think thus and so because you are a woman"; but I know that my only defense is to reply: "I think thus and so because it is true," thereby removing my subjective self from the argument. It would be out of the question to reply: "And you think the contrary because you are a man," for it is understood that the fact of being a man is no peculiarity. A man is in the right in being a man; it is the woman who is in the wrong. It amounts to this: just as for the ancients there was an absolute vertical with reference to which the oblique was defined, so there is an absolute human type, the masculine. Woman has ovaries, a uterus; these peculiarities imprison her in her subjectivity, circumscribe her within the limits of her own nature. It is often said that she thinks with her glands. Man superbly ignores the fact that his anatomy also includes glands, such as the testicles, and that they secrete hormones. He thinks of his body as a direct and normal connection with the world, which he believes he apprehends objectively, whereas he regards the body of woman as a hindrance, a prison, weighed down by everything peculiar to it. "The female is a female by virtue of a certain *lack* of qualities," said Aristotle;[1] "we should regard the female nature as afflicted with a natural defectiveness." And St. Thomas[2] for his part pronounced women to be an "imperfect man," an "incidental" being. This is symbolized in Genesis where Eve is depicted as made from what Bossuet[3] called "a supernumerary bone" of Adam.

---

[1] Greek philosopher (384–322 B.C.).
[2] Saint Thomas Aquinas, ecclesiastical writer and philosopher (1224?-1225–1274).
[3] Jacques Bossuet, French bishop, defended the rights of the French church against papal authority. His literary works include *Funeral Panegyrics* and *Four Great Personages* (1627–1704).

Thus humanity is male and man defines woman not in herself but as relative to him; she is not regarded as an autonomous being. Michelet[4] writes: "Woman, the relative being. . . ." And Benda[5] is most positive in his *Rapport d'Uriel:* "The body of man makes sense in itself quite apart from that of woman, whereas the latter seems wanting in significance by itself. . . . Man can think of himself without woman. She cannot think of herself without man." And she is simply what man decrees; thus she is called "the sex," by which is meant that she appears essentially to the male as a sexual being. For him she is sex—absolute sex, no less. She is defined and differentiated with reference to man and not he with reference to her; she is the incidental, the inessential as opposed to the essential. He is the Subject, he is the Absolute—she is the Other.

The category of the *Other* is as primordial as consciousness itself. In the most primitive societies, in the most ancient mythologies, one finds the expression of a duality—that of the Self and the Other. This duality was not originally attached to the division of the sexes; it was not dependent upon any empirical facts. It is revealed in such works as that of Granet[6] on Chinese thought and those of Dumézil[7] on the East Indies and Rome. The feminine element was at first no more involved in such pairs as Varuna-Mitra, Uranus-Zeus, Sun-Moon, and Day-Night[8] than it was in the contrasts between Good and Evil, lucky and unlucky auspices, right and left, God and Lucifer. Otherness is a fundamental category of human thought.

5   Thus it is that no group ever sets itself up as the One without at once setting up the Other over against itself. If three travelers chance to occupy the same compartment, that is enough to make vaguely hostile "others" out of all the rest of the passengers on the train. In small-town eyes all persons not belonging to the village are "strangers" and suspect; to the native of a country all who inhabit other countries are "foreigners"; Jews are "different" for the anti-Semite, Negroes are "inferior" for American racists, aborigines are "natives" for colonists, proletarians are the "lower class" for the privileged.

Lévi-Strauss,[9] at the end of a profound work on the various forms of primitive societies, reaches the following conclusion: "Passage from the state of Nature to the state of Culture is marked by man's ability to view biological relations as a series of contrasts; duality, alternation, opposition, and symmetry, whether under definite or vague forms, constitute not so much phenomena to be explained as fundamental and immediately given data of social reality." These phenomena would be incomprehensible if in fact human society were simply a *Mitsein* or fellowship based on solidarity and friendliness. Things become clear,

---

[4] French historian (1798–1874).

[5] Julian Benda, French novelist and philosopher (1867–1956).

[6] Francois Marius Granet, French painter, watercolorist (1775–1849).

[7] Expert on mythology.

[8] Varuna—Vedic god of skies and sea; Mitra—Vedic god of moon; Uranus—god/father of the Titans in Greek mythology; Zeus—king of the gods in Greek mythology; oppositions.

[9] Claude Lévi-Strauss, French anthropologist (1908–   ).

on the contrary, if, following Hegel,[10] we find in consciousness itself a fundamental hostility toward every other consciousness; the subject can be posed only in being opposed—he sets himself up as the essential, as opposed to the other, the inessential, the object.

But the other consciousness, the other ego, sets up a reciprocal claim. The native traveling abroad is shocked to find himself in turn regarded as a "stranger" by the natives of neighboring countries. As a matter of fact, wars, festivals, trading, treaties, and contests among tribes, nations, and classes tend to deprive the concept *Other* of its absolute sense and to make manifest its relativity; willy-nilly, individuals and groups are forced to realize the reciprocity of their relations. How is it, then, that this reciprocity has not been recognized between the sexes, that one of the contrasting terms is set up as the sole essential, denying any relativity in regard to its correlative and defining the latter as pure otherness? Why is it that women do not dispute male sovereignty? No subject will readily volunteer to become the object, the inessential; it is not the Other who, in defining himself as the Other, establishes the One. The Other is posed as such by the One in defining himself as the One. But if the Other is not to regain the status of being the One, he must be submissive enough to accept this alien point of view. Whence comes this submission in the case of woman?

There are, to be sure, other cases in which a certain category has been able to dominate another completely for a time. Very often this privilege depends upon inequality of numbers—the majority imposes its rule upon the minority or persecutes it. But women are not a minority, like the American Negroes or the Jews; there are as many women as men on earth. Again, the two groups concerned have often been originally independent; they may have been formerly unaware of each other's existence, or perhaps they recognized each other's autonomy. But a historical event has resulted in the subjugation of the weaker by the stronger. The scattering of the Jews, the introduction of slavery into America, the conquests of imperialism are examples in point. In these cases the oppressed retained at least the memory of former days; they possessed in common a past, a tradition, sometimes a religion or a culture.

The parallel drawn by Bebel[11] between women and the proletariat is valid in that neither ever formed a minority or a separate collective unit of mankind. And instead of a single historical event it is in both cases a historical development that explains their status as a class and accounts for the membership of *particular individuals* in that class. But proletarians have not always existed, whereas there have always been women. They are women in virtue of their anatomy and physiology. Throughout history they have always been subordinated to men, and hence their dependency is not the result of a historical event or a social change—it was not something that *occurred*. The reason why otherness in this case seems to be an absolute is in part that it lacks the contingent or incidental nature of historical facts. A condition brought about at a certain

---

[10] Georg Wilhelm Friedrich Hegel, German philosopher who developed the theory of dialectic (1770–1831).

[11] August Bebel, German Social Democrat leader and writer (1840–1913).

time can be abolished at some other time, as the Negroes of Haiti[12] and others have proved; but it might seem that a natural condition is beyond the possibility of change. In truth, however, the nature of things is no more immutably given, once for all, than is historical reality. If woman seems to be the inessential which never becomes the essential, it is because she herself fails to bring about this change. Proletarians say "We"; Negroes also. Regarding themselves as subjects, they transform the bourgeois, the whites, into "others." But women do not say "We," except at some congress of feminists or similar formal demonstration; men say "women," and women use the same word in referring to themselves. They do not authentically assume a subjective attitude. The proletarians have accomplished the revolution in Russia, the Negroes in Haiti, the Indochinese are battling for it in Indochina;[13] but the women's effort has never been anything more than a symbolic agitation. They have gained only what men have been willing to grant; they have taken nothing, they have only received.

10   The reason for this is that women lack concrete means for organizing themselves into a unit which can stand face to face with the correlative unit. They have no past, no history, no religion of their own; and they have no such solidarity of work and interest as that of the proletariat. They are not even promiscuously herded together in the way that creates community feeling among the American Negroes, the ghetto Jews, the workers of Saint-Denis,[14] or the factory hands of Renault.[15] They live dispersed among the males, attached through residence, housework, economic condition, and social standing to certain men—fathers or husbands—more firmly than they are to other women. If they belong to the bourgeoisie, they feel solidarity with men of that class, not with proletarian women; if they are white, their allegiance is to white men, not to Negro women. The proletariat can propose to massacre the ruling class, and a sufficiently fanatical Jew or Negro might dream of getting sole possession of the atomic bomb and making humanity wholly Jewish or black; but woman cannot even dream of exterminating the males. The bond that unites her to her oppressors is not comparable to any other. The division of the sexes is a biological fact, not an event in human history. Male and female stand opposed within a primordial *Mitsein,* and woman has not broken it. The couple is a fundamental unity with its two halves riveted together, and the cleavage of society along the line of sex is impossible. Here is to be found the basic trait of woman: she is the Other in a totality of which the two components are necessary to one another.

---

[12] Country of the West Indies.

[13] Peninsula of Southeast Asia comprised of Vietnam, Laos, Cambodia, Thailand, Burma, and the Malay Peninsula; name given to group of former French colonies.

[14] City in north central France, near Paris.

[15] French car manufacturer.

One could suppose that this reciprocity might have facilitated the liberation of woman. When Hercules sat at the feet of Omphale[16] and helped with her spinning, his desire for her held him captive; but why did she fail to gain a lasting power? To revenge herself on Jason, Medea[17] killed their children: and this grim legend would seem to suggest that she might have obtained a formidable influence over him through his love for his offspring. In *Lysistrata* Aristophanes[18] gaily depicts a band of women who joined forces to gain social ends through the sexual needs of their men; but this is only a play. In the legend of the Sabine women,[19] the latter soon abandoned their plan of remaining sterile to punish their ravishers. In truth woman has not been socially emancipated through man's need—sexual desire and the desire for offspring—which makes the male dependent for satisfaction upon the female.

Master and slave, also, are united by a reciprocal need, in this case economic, which does not liberate the slave. In the relation of master to slave the master does not make a point of the need that he has for the other; he has in his grasp the power of satisfying this need through his own action; whereas the slave, in his dependent condition, his hope and fear, is quite conscious of the need he has for his master. Even if the need is at bottom equally urgent for both, it always works in favor of the oppressor and against the oppressed. That is why the liberation of the working class, for example, has been slow.

Now, woman has always been man's dependent, if not his slave; the two sexes have never shared the world in equality. And even today woman is heavily handicapped, though her situation is beginning to change. Almost nowhere is her legal status the same as man's, and frequently it is much to her disadvantage. Even when her rights are legally recognized in the abstract, longstanding custom prevents their full expression in the mores. In the economic sphere men and women can almost be said to make up two castes; other things being equal, the former hold the better jobs, get higher wages, and have more opportunity for success than their new competitors. In industry and politics men have a great many more positions and they monopolize the most important posts. In addition to all this, they enjoy a traditional prestige that the education of children tends in every way to support, for the present enshrines the past—and in the past all history has been made by men. At the present time, when women are beginning to take part in the affairs of the world, it is still a world that belongs to men—they have no doubt of it at all and women have scarcely any. To decline to be the Other, to refuse to be a party to the deal—this would be for women to renounce all the advantages conferred upon them by

---

[16] Hercules—hero of Greek mythology, known for his strength; as a punishment, Zeus condemned Hercules to serve as a slave to Queen Omphale who required him to dress as a woman and to do women's chores.

[17] Jason—Thessalian hero who journeyed with the Argonauts in search of the Golden Fleece. Medea—a magician or sorceress who aided Jason and later murdered their two children when he betrayed her.

[18] Aristophanes—Athenian dramatist (448–380? B.C.). Lysistrata, a comedy by Aristophanes, features a rebellion by women who protest war by denying their husbands sexual favors.

[19] Allusion to the abduction of the Sabine women by the Romans (c. 290 B.C.).

their alliance with the superior caste. Man-the-sovereign will provide woman-the-liege with material protection and will undertake the moral justification of her existence; thus she can evade at once both economic risk and the meta-physical risk of a liberty in which ends and aims must be contrived without assistance. Indeed, along with the ethical urge of each individual to affirm his subjective existence, there is also the temptation to forgo liberty and become a thing. This is an inauspicious road, for he who takes it—passive, lost, ruined—becomes henceforth the creature of another's will, frustrated in his transcendence and deprived of every value. But it is an easy road; on it one avoids the strain involved in undertaking an authentic existence. When man makes of woman the *Other,* he may, then, expect her to manifest deep-seated tendencies toward complicity. Thus, woman may fail to lay claim to the status of subject because she lacks definite resources, because she feels the necessary bond that ties her to man regardless of reciprocity, and because she is often very well pleased with her role as the *Other.*

■   **EXPLORATIONS OF THE TEXT**   ■

1. Why does de Beauvoir begin with a question? with the need for definition?
2. Do you agree with her assessment that "man represents both the positive and the neutral . . . whereas woman represents only the negative"?
3. What does de Beauvoir mean when she states that woman is "imprison[ed] in her subjectivity" and that "she thinks with her glands"?
4. State in your own words her concept of "the Other." Agree or disagree with her position.
5. Why does de Beauvoir include references to the ideas of "reciprocity" and of "duality"? to master-slave relations?
6. How has woman's sexuality led historically to her position as "Other"? Why have women failed to break out of this position?
7. Outline de Beauvoir's argument. Does she argue through definition, causal analysis, or comparison? Does she argue inductively or deductively? Who is her audience?
8. Why does she include references to Haiti and Indochina, to Jews and African-Americans? Why does she include references to Hercules, Jason and Medea, Lysistrata, and the Sabine Women? Are the allusions effective?
9. De Beauvoir wrote *The Second Sex* in 1949. Do her ideas still apply to contemporary society? What aspects of women's status have changed?

■■ JOURNAL ENTRIES ■■

1. Define the "Other."
2. Do you agree with de Beauvoir's characterization of woman as "Other"?
3. What do you see as a current issue for men and women in North American society?

■■■ IDEAS FOR WRITING ■■■

1. Compare de Beauvoir's view of the woman as "Other" with the role of women in a work in this chapter.
2. Conceive of an alternative relationship for men and women. What do you see as ideal?
3. Compare de Beauvoir's argument with Plato's assessment in "The Sexes." How would de Beauvoir respond to Plato?

Student Essay: Critical Analysis

Yellow Woman

Kevin Duffy

In this essay by Kevin Duffy, a student at the State University of New York at New Paltz, the narrative frame of the writing itself becomes the critical analysis of the story. A creative response, Duffy's version approaches Yellow Woman's experience as fantasy.

I woke to the sound of the alarm clock; the radio was playing "Wild Flower," by The Cult, a song I hadn't heard in a while, so I smiled. When I realized I was sleeping with some blonde-haired girl, I tried to recount the events of the night before. I remember being really drunk, dancing to a band playing a David Bowie song, or was it The Doors? I still couldn't remember what her face looked like, never mind her name or how we ended up in my bed. Soon she started to wake, and she crawled up my body and gave me a warm, wet kiss on the lips. "Your breath reeks of alcohol," I wondered when she had smelled my breath any different. In a round-about way, so as not to seem obvious about how we met, I questioned her concerning the night before. As she talked, I began to remember some things myself. I was glad I did not drive, and I was glad I used a condom. After a few minutes I said, "I have to get up and interview my friend for my essay." "What do you have to interview her about?" she inquired as her green eyes flashed. I liked that so I kissed her. "About a story in my English book." "Interview me," her voice quivered with excitement as if we were going to play a game.

I wrote down questions as she read. After twenty odd minutes, she turned and said, "O.K." She looked a little different, no longer child-like and free, a little puzzled.

Interviewer (Me): Did you like the story?

Girl: Yeah, it was different, kinda cool.

Me: Why do you think the narrator (Yellow Woman) left home?

Girl: She was confused; she wanted to find herself. I think she must have been saying to herself, "Is that all life's about?" She just needed a break from reality for a while, a little fantasy.

Me: So do you think it was all a fantasy? Do you think she just dreamed up Silva?

Girl: Yeah, I think she just woke up the next day and imagined the whole thing. The combination of her needing a break from her family for a while and the folk stories her grandfather had told her.

Me: How do you feel about her husband and family?

Girl: Typical, I suppose, the way that she imagined her husband going to the Reservation Police and the way that her family was getting ready to eat. Maybe they were a little care-free; no one seemed exactly terrified.

Me: What kind of man do you think Yellow Woman's Grandfather was, and how does he compare with yours?

Girl: He seems like a gentle man; he likes to tell stories and enjoys the simple things in life. Similar to mine, just that mine's alive, and I get to enjoy his stories still.

She smiled for a second as she pondered this statement, then looked puzzled again. "Do you do this often? I mean, do you bring girls home?" "Hardly," I laughed. "Do you have a girlfriend?" I stuttered and stammered as I rose to my feet, "Kinda sorta," I replied with a half laugh, hoping she would not think too badly of me. As I walked to the bathroom, I read her thoughts, "Creep, Adulterer, Liar and Cheater." I stood in the bathroom, held my head up, and felt guilty. Would my girlfriend find out? Who else knew? Would anyone tell her? Then I began to feel badly for the girl. Would she see my girlfriend's picture on my nightstand? I put it all out of my mind and left the bathroom headed for my room. I heard a car start; I looked in my room, and the girl was gone. I wish I had inquired about her name.

Student Essay: Explication and
Character Analysis

The Jilting of Granny Weatherall
Leigh Grimm

Leigh Grimm graduated as a journalism major from the State University of New York at New Paltz. She recently received a national award for her work and plans to pursue a career as a journalist. She wrote this essay in response to an assignment to compose a character analysis of Granny Weatherall in Freshman Composition.

In "The Jilting of Granny Weatherall" by Katherine Anne Porter, Granny Weatherall, almost eighty years old, lies in a bed in her daughter's house dying. Granny is not consumed by thoughts of her imminent death but of thoughts of the people in her past. There is the sense that her relationships and people in her life have somehow failed her.

When she thinks about how neat and orderly she always kept her house, unlike her daughter Cornelia, Granny remembers a box of old letters in her attic from the two men in her life, George and John. She plans to do something with those letters the next day so that her children do not find them after she is gone. She is afraid that they will read the letters and know what she was like before she was their mother. These letters are the key to why she drifts into the past.

Granny Weatherall drifts off into the past where she can remember her children when they needed her. She would love to be able to go back and do things over again. She remembers her children coming home out of the chilly night air to get warm. She loved the children huddling around her until the house was all lit up. But once the lights were on, they would leave her because they were no longer afraid of the dark. They had no need to cling to her then just as they have no need to cling to her now. Granny Weatherall repeats in her head, "Never, never, never more." All that she has ever wanted was to be needed by her children, and it makes her sad to know that they do not need her anymore. She is happier to think about the way things used to be before her children betray her by growing up.

All through her life she was a strong and independent woman. She became strong when her husband John died leaving her with a house to run and children to support and nurture. She fenced in one hundred acres of land, cooked dozens of meals, made clothes for her family and kept the garden flourishing year after year.

In one of her trips to the past, she wonders if John would recognize her after all she has endured. Having to be strong and independent changed her. She says everything changed her from, "Riding country roads in the winter when women had their babies" to "sitting up nights with sick horses and sick negroes and sick children and hardly ever losing one." John also betrayed her by leaving her.

But her children and her husband are not the only ones to betray her. Before she met and married John, she was jilted by another lover. In her wedding gown Granny was left standing at the altar by George. She remembers the cake that never got eaten and the sorrow and embarrassment that she felt. In her head, she still tries to hide the scars of that day. She begins to act like a teenage girl as she asks her children to find George and to tell him that she has forgotten all about him. She wants him to know that she married a man she loved and had beautiful children with him. But the pain of that day forms a shadow that follows her to her death bed. The final jilting is that the pain of that day does not desert her; she never reaches an acceptance of her past—a reconciliation of her own past. She does not find peace and contentment—fulfillment even at the end of her life.

As the moment of death approaches "her body [is] now only a deeper mass of shadow in an endless darkness. . . ." She asks for God to give her a sign. "For the second time there [is] no sign. Again no bridegroom and the priest in the house. She [can] not remember any other sorrow because this grief [wipes] them all away."

By continually drifting into the past, Granny Weatherall shows dissatisfaction with her life. Every relationship comes to some kind of stasis that she found to be difficult and imprisoning. On her death bed she feels that she has missed something all of her life. What she has missed is life itself.

WRITING ASSIGNMENTS

1. a. What is platonic or ideal love? Write a definition.
   b. Define your ideal lover.
   c. Discuss platonic or ideal love in Donne, in Shakespeare's "Let Me Not to the Marriage of True Minds," in Senghor, in Snyder, and/or in Rosenberg.
2. a. What is romantic love? Why do people fall in love? Respond in a journal entry.
   b. Explore the vision of romantic love in several works in this chapter.
   c. Compare three views of romantic love and marriage in this chapter.
3. Discuss sexuality in Silko, Snyder, Paz, Senghor, and/or Chekhov.
4. a. What are the major problems in love relationships? Write a journal entry.
   b. Analyze the essay by Kristeva. What obstacles does she enumerate?
   c. Write an essay on obstacles in love relationships. Use three works in this chapter to support your points. Refer to Kristeva and to your journal entry.
5. Explicate "Let Me Not to the Marriage of True Minds Admit Impediments." Concentrate on persona, figurative language, and sonnet form.
6. a. In a journal entry, explore your conceptions of young love, married love, and love in old age.
   b. Categorize kinds of love. Refer to works which represent different states of love.
7. Have any of these works changed your attitude about love? Which ones? Why? Why not?
8. Write about the end of love, the acceptance of loss. Refer to Kristeva, Akhmatova, Hemingway, Porter, Joyce, and/or Sexton.
9. a. Trace the phases of a relationship which you have experienced or observed.
   b. Trace the phases of the love relationship in one of the texts in this chapter.
   c. Compare your relationship with the view of love in one of the works in the text.
10. a. Interview three people from the same cultural background. Ask about gender roles, socialization, and responsibilities.
    b. Write an essay on roles of men and women in that culture. Have gender roles changed in that culture in the twentieth century?
    c. Write an analysis of gender roles in three works in this chapter. You may choose works in other chapters if you wish.
11. a. Interview men about women; women about men. Ask about conceptions of the opposite sex, relationships, and social roles. Summarize your interviews.
    b. Analyze the results of the interviews. What misconceptions do men have about women? Women about men?

    c. "Men and women are doomed never to understand one another." Develop an argument in response to this quotation.

12. a. Freewrite about ways in which men and women might perceive conflict differently.

    b. Choose one experience, and write a monologue for each person involved in the incident.

    c. Based on a work in this chapter, write an essay about how a man and a woman develop different views of a conflict. How does the conflict resolve itself?

13. a. Have you ever felt like an "Other"? Write about this experience in your journal.

    b. In your own words, define "Other." Use your journal entry as a basis for your definition.

    c. Analyze the experience of the woman as "Other" in three works in this chapter.

14. Compare two dramatic monologues. How do voice, tone, and theme develop the personae?

15. What is most important in the development of characters in three works in this chapter? (Choose one genre, and refer to the checklists in Chapters 9–12.)

16. Analyze images of the sea in Arnold, Eliot, and Paz.

17. Examine the conflicts and characters in *Trifles* and in *And the Soul Shall Dance*. How does symbolism help to create character and theme?

18. In three works in this chapter, discuss how landscape functions in the development of character, conflict, and theme.

19. "Men are conditioned to fear a full expression of intimacy." Do you agree or disagree? Which works in this chapter support your views?

20. a. Interview another person who has read one of the works in this chapter. Ask questions about speaker, conflict, theme, language, and other literary elements. Summarize your interview.

    b. Write an essay about your interview. Examine the student essay in this chapter as a possible model for this assignment.

21. Analyze views of romantic love in works in the Thematic Preview.

WAR AND INJUSTICE

There is a cyclone fence between
ourselves and the slaughter and behind it
we hover in a calm, protected world like
netted fish, exactly like netted fish.
It is either the beginning or the end
of the world, and the choice is ourselves
or nothing.

Carolyn Forché "Ourselves or Nothing"

For people who have "hover[ed] in a calm, protected world," questions of war and injustice now become urgent. No longer may people assume that they will remain untouched by "the slaughter." The Thematic Preview examines ways in which people are touched by "the slaughter"; the works consider forms of oppression and protest. Luisa Valenzuela's "I'm Your Horse in the Night" depicts the conflicts of a woman caught up in the nightmare of a militaristic regime in Argentina. Wendy Rose's "Three Thousand Dollar Death Song" portrays the devaluation and destruction of the Native-American way of life. Sophocles' *Oedipus Rex* and Nelson Mandela's "I Am Prepared to Die" explore moral responses to injustice.

As individuals, human beings may begin to respond by claiming their identities and their rights. W. H. Auden's "Unknown Citizen," who does everything expected of him, possesses only the identity which the state has molded for him. Emily Dickinson's narrator in "I'm Nobody! Who are you?" prizes her privacy and prefers to be "nobody," but Eduardo Galeano's "Nobodies" are the forgotten, the poor whose lives do not matter; even their deaths do not matter.

How, then, does one begin? In *Oedipus Rex*, Sophocles suggested an answer two thousand years ago. The individual, he contended, has an obligation to uncover the source of injustice. Oedipus, King of Thebes, attempts to find the cause of the plague in his state. His quest ends in tragedy. In his statement to the court, Nelson Mandela explains his actions against the policy of apartheid in South Africa for which he is "prepared to die." Soyinka's speaker in "Telephone Conversation" protests with insolence and with humor against discrimination by a prospective landlady.

781

In the United States, "the beginning" requires awareness. In this case, the awareness emerges from the lives of three female slaves who eventually claimed their freedom. Sojourner Truth connects women's rights with slavery in her famous speech, "Ain't I a Woman?" Harriet Jacobs describes the unbearable sexual exploitation that she and other women suffered in *Incidents in the Life of a Slave Girl.* Susan Griffin thinks of Harriet Tubman who escaped and worked for the underground railroad that led many slaves to freedom. Griffin's persona likes to think of Harriet Tubman as a model when she contemplates the plight of children who are hungry in the United States today.

African-Americans still struggle against discrimination. In "Harlem" Langston Hughes warns about the consequences of living with "a dream deferred." Etheridge Knight describes the loss of Hardrock's spirit after the latter's visit to the hospital for the criminally insane, a spirit unbroken by the rigors of prison life. School desegregation and the famous case, Brown vs. The Board of Education, are the subjects of Gwendolyn Brooks' "The Chicago Defender Sends a Man to Little Rock." Yet the dream of an ideal, of freedom, and of a true America persists. Hughes' "Let America Be America Again" presents an eloquent plea for the dream.

In some critiques of life in the United States, desire for change, for hope, and for love of country appear. Allen Ginsberg's speaker in "America" completes his catalogue of political indictments with the promise that he is "putting [his] queer shoulder to the wheel." Gary Soto's "History" portrays an eccentric and wonderful grandmother who silently attacks the system.

In some of these works, characters respond to injustice with action, with violence, and with activism. Wendy Rose suggests in her "Death Song" that those who have violated the bones of Native-Americans and who value them only at "three thousand dollars" should begin to fear retribution. Gloria Anzaldúa describes the flaying of a horse by a group of adolescents, "gringos" who believe that they have the right to own and violate anything they choose. The "horse" returns to haunt their dreams and to change their sleep forever. In "For Anna Mae Aquash Whose Spirit Is Present Here and in the Dappled Stars," Joy Harjo memorializes a Native-American activist who was murdered in South Dakota. The speaker in the poem invokes "the righteous anger of the wind." Here images of beauty and of destruction exist side by side. Harjo's work symbolizes a general view of North America: a desire for change and an appreciation of its beauty.

War represents the ultimate form of injustice. Henry Ward Beecher once said, "It is not merely cruelty that leads men to love war, it is excitement." The soldiers in the writing in this chapter, however, do not seem to love war. Lao-tzu cautions that triumph or victory be treated as a funeral. In Wilfred Owen's "Dulce et Decorum Est," the speaker describes the terrible deaths of men in World War I. Owen indicts weapons of war in "Arms and the Boy." Tim O'Brien suggests that men became soldiers during the Vietnam War in order not to embarrass themselves, their families, and their country. They bear physical and emotional burdens in "The Things They Carried." Shusako Endō's narrator remembers the weeping of the young men who received their red papers summoning them to battle in "The War Generation," a story—an elegy—about Japan in World War II.

Parents who send their sons and daughters to war do not love the cruelty of war either; they do not find vicarious excitement in their children's service. They shield themselves from the horrors of war through rationalization and denial. In Luigi Pirandello's "War," the husband and wife mourn the prospect of saying farewell to their son who has been assigned to the front lines. The patriotic "fat man" in this story finally faces his own grief.

Only Cynthia Ozick in "The Shawl" identifies some of those who love war and find cruelty exciting; she identifies the Nazis who have created the final solution, who can toss a child into an electrified fence as if she were a puppet. The tragic suffering of Rosa and the children, Stella and Magda, demonstrates the horror of the Holocaust and the truth in Beecher's claim that cruelty leads men to love war.

In Argentina and El Salvador, governments reigned in which men loved cruelty and encouraged terror, disappearance, and death. Luisa Valenzuela creates a vivid picture of the vicious torture of an Argentinean woman in "I'm Your Horse in the Night," a woman whose courage and spirit sustain her dream of love. In "The Memory of Elena," Carolyn Forché's narrator and her friend commemorate the deaths of "those who remained/in Buenos Aires." Forché's Salvadoran colonel finds excitement by flaunting his disregard of "the rights of anyone," by throwing severed human ears on the floor to shock his North American visitors. Marjorie Agosin's account of the mothers of the Plaza de Mayo provides a model for collective protest against the government in Argentina in the late 1970s. Paulo Freire offers a pedagogical model for individual and collective "authentic liberation."

Perhaps, Forché is right about Americans "hover[ing] in a calm, protected world." If so, let this time be the beginning of the just world and the end of the unjust world. Let it be the beginning of a world in which truth is valued, one in which

> All things human take time,
> time which the damned never seem to have, time for life
> to repair at least the worst of its wounds;
> it took time to wake, time for horror
> to incite revolt, time for the recovery
> of lucidity and will.
>
> Carolyn Forché
> "Ourselves or Nothing"

Let this time be the beginning of the recovery. Indeed, the works in this chapter attest to the power of art to engender renewal.

THEMATIC PREVIEW: COMBINING THE GENRES

I'm Your Horse in the Night

Luisa Valenzuela

Valenzuela portrays the horrors of the political situation in Argentina through a female speaker who loses her freedom because of her love for a guerilla leader whom she knows only as Beto. Valenzuela left Argentina after the death of Perón in 1974 to escape the military dictatorship that ruled until 1983. During the period before she fled, she wrote, "Buenos Aires belonged then to violence and to state terrorism, and I could only sit in cafes and brood. Till I decided a book of short stories could be written in a month at those same cafe tables, overhearing scraps of scared conversations, seeping in the general paranoia. Strange Things Happen Here *(1979) was born, and with it a new political awareness. And action."*

Valenzuela discovered that writing short stories provided her with an important form of protest.

1   The doorbell rang: three short rings and one long one. That was the signal, and I got up, annoyed and a little frightened; it could be them, and then again, maybe not; at these ungodly hours of the night it could be a trap. I opened the door expecting anything except him, face to face, at last.

He came in quickly and locked the door behind him before embracing me. So much in character, so cautious, first and foremost checking his— our—rear guard. Then he took me in his arms without saying a word, not even holding me too tight but letting all the emotions of our new encounter overflow, telling me so much by merely holding me in his arms and kissing me slowly. I think he never had much faith in words, and there he was, as silent as ever, sending me messages in the form of caresses.

We finally stepped back to look at one another from head to foot, not eye to eye, out of focus. And I was able to say Hello showing scarcely any surprise despite all those months when I had no idea where he could have been, and I was able to say

I thought you were fighting up north
I thought you'd been caught
I thought you were in hiding
I thought you'd been tortured and killed
I thought you were theorizing about the revolution in another country

Just one of many ways to tell him I'd been thinking of him, I hadn't stopped thinking of him or felt as if I'd been betrayed. And there he was, always so goddamn cautious, so much the master of his actions.

5 "Quiet, Chiquita.[1] You're much better off not knowing what I've been up to."

Then he pulled out his treasures, potential clues that at the time eluded me: a bottle of cachaça[2] and a Gal Costa[3] record. What had he been up to in Brazil? What was he planning to do next? What had brought him back, risking his life, knowing they were after him? Then I stopped asking myself questions (quiet, Chiquita, he'd say). Come here, Chiquita, he was saying, and I chose to let myself sink into the joy of having him back again, trying not to worry. What would happen to us tomorrow, and the days that followed?

Cachaça's a good drink. It goes down and up and down all the right tracks, and then stops to warm up the corners that need it most. Gal Coasta's voice is hot, she envelops us in its sound and half-dancing, half-floating, we reach the bed. We lie down and keep on staring deep into each other's eyes, continue caressing each other without allowing ourselves to give in to the pure senses just yet. We continue recognizing, rediscovering each other.

Beto, I say, looking at him. I know that isn't his real name, but it's the only one I can call him out loud. He replies:

"We'll make it someday, Chiquita. But let's not talk now."

10 It's better that way. Better if he doesn't start talking about how we'll make it someday and ruin the wonder of what we're about to attain right now, the two of us, all alone.

"A noite eu so teu cavalo," Gal Costa suddenly sings from the record player.

"I'm your horse in the night," I translate slowly. And so as to bind him in a spell and stop him from thinking about other things:

"It's a saint's song, like in the *macumba*.[4] Someone who's in a trance says she's the horse of the spirit who's riding her, she's his mount."

"Chiquita, you're always getting carried away with esoteric meanings and witchcraft. You know perfectly well that she isn't talking about spirits. If you're my horse in the night it's because I ride you, like this, see? . . . Like this . . . That's all."

15 It was so long, so deep and so insistent, so charged with affection that we ended up exhausted. I fell asleep with him still on top of me.

I'm your horse in the night.

The goddamn phone pulled me out in waves from a deep well. Making an enormous effort to wake up, I walked over to the receiver, thinking it could be Beto, sure who was no longer by my side, sure, following his inveterate habit of

---

[1] Small one, little one (female).
[2] An alcoholic beverage.
[3] Chanteuse.
[4] A polytheistic religion of African origin, practiced mainly by Brazilian blacks in urban areas. A religion involving spirits.

running away while I'm asleep without a word about where he's gone. To protect me, he says.

From the other end of the line, a voice I thought belonged to Andrés—
the one we call Andrés—began to tell me:

"They found Beto dead, floating down the river near the other bank. It
looks as if they threw him alive out of a chopper. He's all bloated and decom-
posed after six days in the water, but I'm almost sure it's him."

20   "No, it can't be Beto," I shouted carelessly. Suddenly the voice no longer
sounded like Andrés: it felt foreign, impersonal.

"You think so?"

"Who is this?" Only then did I think to ask. But that very moment they
hung up.

Ten, fifteen minutes? How long must I have stayed there staring at the
phone like an idiot until the police arrived? I didn't expect them. But, then
again, how could I not? Their hands feeling me, their voices insulting and
threatening, the house searched, turned inside out. But I already knew. So
what did I care if they broke every breakable object and tore apart my dresser?

They wouldn't find a thing. My only real possession was a dream and they
can't deprive me of my dreams just like that. My dream the night before, when
Beto was there with me and we loved each other. I'd dreamed it, dreamed every
bit of it, I was deeply convinced that I'd dreamed it all in the richest detail, even
in full color. And dreams are none of the cops' business.

25   They want reality, tangible facts, the kind I couldn't even begin to give them.

Where is he, you saw him, he was here with you, where did he go? Speak up,
or you'll be sorry. Let's hear you sing, bitch, we know he came to see you, where
is he, where is he holed up? He's in the city, come on, spill it, we know he came
to get you.

I haven't heard a word from him in months. He abandoned me, I haven't
heard from him in months. He ran away, went underground. What do I know,
he ran off with someone else, he's in another country. What do I know, he
abandoned me, I hate him, I know nothing.

(Go ahead, burn me with your cigarettes, kick me all you wish, threaten,
go ahead, stick a mouse in me so it'll eat my insides out, pull my nails out, do
as you please. Would I make something up for that? Would I tell you he was
here when a thousand years ago he left me forever?)

I'm not about to tell them my dreams. Why should they care? I haven't
seen that so-called Beto in more than six months, and I loved him. The man
simply vanished. I only run into him in my dreams, and they're bad dreams
that often become nightmares.

30 Beto, you know now, if it's true that they killed you, or wherever you may be,
Beto, I'm your horse in the night and you can inhabit me whenever you wish,
even if I'm behind bars. Beto, now that I'm in jail I know that I dreamed you
that night; it was just a dream. And if by some wild chance there's a Gal Costa
record and a half-empty bottle of cachaça in my house, I hope they'll forgive
me: I will them out of existence.

■ EXPLORATIONS OF THE TEXT ■

1. Describe the situation and the occasion presented in the opening four paragraphs. Why does Beto prefer not to talk?
2. Form a portrait of Beto from the narrator's statements about him. Consider also the objects he brings with him, his dialogue, and his actions.
3. Describe the relationship between the narrator and Beto. What is the nature of their sexual relationship?
4. Discuss the meanings of the title, "I'm Your Horse in the Night."
5. Why do the police arrest the narrator? How is she able to resist their methods?
6. Explain the narrator's "dream." Why does she decide that the encounter was a dream?
7. Why does she say "And if by some wild chance there's a Gal Costa record and a half-empty bottle of cachaça in my house. I hope they'll forgive me: I will them out of existence"?
8. Examine Valenzuela's narrative technique. Why does she write so many short paragraphs?
9. Compare the political vision in this story to the views in Forché's poems and Agosin's essay.

■■ JOURNAL ENTRIES ■■

1. Write about the narrator's dream. Gloss and annotate the text. As an alternative, write a double-entry notebook concerning this story.
2. Ask several people to read this story. Interview them about their responses. How many believe that the narrator fantasized the encounter with Beto?

■■■ IDEAS FOR WRITING ■■■

1. Is this a story about dream or reality? Both? Does it matter? Incorporate Journal Entry 2 into your essay.
2. Evaluate this story. Consider character, theme, conflict, form, symbol, and/or other elements of fiction. (See Chapter 9.)
3. Compare this story with Forché's "The Colonel." What do you conclude?

Three Thousand Dollar Death Song

Wendy Rose

Born in Oakland, California, Wendy Rose (1948–   ) earned her B.A. degree in 1976 and her M.A. degree in 1978 from the University of California at Berkeley. A Hopi/Miwok, a major figure in recording and expressing Native-American culture, she has taught Native-American studies at Berkeley and is a member of many anthropological organizations. Her poetry includes Hopi Roadrunner Dancing *(1973),* Academic Squaw *(1977),* Builder Kachina: A Home-Going Cycle *(1979),* Lost Copper *(1980),* What Happened When the Hopi Hit New York *(1981), and* The Halfbreed Chronicles and Other Poems *(1985). She also has written historical works including* Long Division: A Tribal History *(1976) and* Aboriginal Tattooing in California *(1979). She has contributed to anthologies and periodicals, sometimes using the pseudonym Chiron Khanshendel.*

Rose said to the writers of Contemporary Authors, *"The usual practice in bookstores upon receiving books of poems by American Indians is to classify them as 'Native Americana' rather than as poetry; the poets are seen as literate fossils more than as living, working artists . . . The deferential treatment accorded to Indians in artistic and academic settings is just as destructive, ultimately, as out-and-out racism."*

In the title of this poem, Rose refers to a museum invoice from 1975 which reads "Nineteen American Indian skeletons from Nevada . . . valued at $3000. . . ." Her song analyzes the payments made to Native Americans for "a universe of stolen things." The speaker claims that "it's official how our bones are valued."

*"Nineteen American Indian skeletons from Nevada . . .
valued at $3000 . . ."—Museum invoice, 1975*

Is it in cold hard cash? the kind
that dusts the insides of men's pockets
lying silver-polished surface along the cloth.
Or in bills? papering the wallets of they
5 who thread the night with dark words. Or
checks? paper promises weighing the same
as words spoken once on the other side
of the grown grass and dammed rivers
of history. However it goes, it goes.
10 Through my body it goes
assessing each nerve, running its edges
along my arteries, planning ahead

for whose hands will rip me
into pieces of dusty red paper,
15 whose hands will smooth or smatter me
into traces of rubble. Invoiced now,
it's official how our bones are valued
that stretch out pointing to sunrise
or are flexed into one last foetal bend,
20 that are removed and tossed about,
catalogued, numbered with black ink
on newly-white foreheads.
As we were formed to the white soldier's voice,
so we explode under white students' hands.
25 Death is a long trail of days
in our fleshless prison.

From this distant point we watch our bones
auctioned with our careful beadwork,
our quilled medicine bundles, even the bridles
30 of our shot-down horses. You: who have
priced us, you who have removed us: at what cost?
What price the pits where our bones share
a single bit of memory, how one century
turns our dead into specimens, our history
35 into dust, our survivors into clowns.
Our memory might be catching, you know;
picture the mortars, the arrowheads, the labrets[1]
shaking off their labels like bears
suddenly awake to find the seasons have ended
40 while they slept. Watch them touch each other,
measure reality, march out the museum door!
Watch as they lift their faces
and smell about for us; watch our bones rise
to meet them and mount the horses once again!
45 The cost, then, will be paid
for our sweetgrass-smelling having-been
in clam shell beads and steatite,[2]
dentalia and woodpecker scalp, turquoise
and copper, blood and oil, coal
50 and uranium, children, a universe
of stolen things.

---

[1] Ornaments worn in perforations of the lips.
[2] Talc of grayish green or brown color; soapstone.

■   EXPLORATIONS OF THE TEXT   ■

1. Explain the title and the invoice.
2. Why does the speaker ask questions about "cash," "bills," and "checks"? Is her method of questioning effective?
3. Identify the antecedent of "it" in lines 8 to 15.
4. What happens to the bones (lines 15–25)? Interpret the symbolism of colors. Look at the verbs.
5. What is the meaning of the following lines: "Death is a long trail of days/in our fleshless prison"?
6. What is the impact of the idea that the dead might awaken and might "march out the museum door!"? What is the threat that others will "meet them and mount the horses once again"?
7. This poem is divided into two **stanzas**. What does this structure achieve?

■■   JOURNAL ENTRIES   ■■

1. Respond to the museum invoice.
2. Discuss the title. Does it have a double meaning?
3. Freewrite about the images of money in this poem.

■■■   IDEAS FOR WRITING   ■■■

1. Examine all of the imagery concerning money. Use Journal Entry 3 as a beginning.
2. Compare and contrast this poem with Griffin's "I Like to Think of Harriet Tubman."
3. Write an essay on genocide. Refer to this poem, to Ozick's "The Shawl," to Mandela's "I Am Prepared to Die," or to other works in this chapter.

Oedipus Rex

Sophocles

With Aeschylus and Euripedes, Sophocles (496–406 B.C.) is one of the three great Greek tragic dramatists. He served as a collector of tribute and as a general as well as a playwright. His first play in 468 won the prize over Aeschylus. By 450 he had written at least twenty-four plays and had initiated significant changes in the form of tragedy. Sophocles won more victories in the play competitions than any other writer. Although he wrote more than one hundred dramas, only seven complete plays survive. In his Poetics, *Aristotle praised Sophocles above other dramatists and used* Oedipus Rex *as a model for a definition of tragedy. One year before his death, one of his relatives attempted to have Sophocles declared mentally incompetent. At his trial Sophocles handed* Oedipus at Colonus, *one of his greatest plays, to the judge as his only defense. Of course, he was acquitted.*

Oedipus Rex is a remarkable psychological study; Oedipus must solve the mystery, but to do so he must search inside himself.

Characters

Oedipus, King of Thebes, supposed son of Polybos and Meropê, King and Queen of
    Corinth
Iokastê, wife of Oedipus and widow of the late King Laïos
Kreon, brother of Iokastê, a prince of Thebes
Teiresias, a blind seer who serves Apollo
Priest
Messenger, from Corinth
Shepherd, former servant of Laïos
Second Messenger, from the palace
Chorus of Theban Elders
Choragos, leader of the Chorus
Antigone and Ismene, young daughters of Oedipus and Iokastê. They appear in the
    Éxodos but do not speak.
Suppliants, Guards, Servants

The Scene. Before the palace of Oedipus, King of Thebes. A central door and two lateral doors open onto a platform which runs the length of the façade. On the platform, right and left, are altars; and three steps lead down into the orchêstra, or chorus-ground. At the beginning of the action these steps are crowded by suppliants who have brought branches and chaplets of olive leaves and who sit in various attitudes of despair. Oedipus enters.

Prologue

Oedipus: My children, generations of the living
    In the line of Kadmos,[1] nursed at his ancient hearth:
    Why have you strewn yourselves before these altars

---

[1] **Kadmos:** founder of Thebes.

In supplication, with your boughs and garlands?
5   The breath of incense rises from the city
With a sound of prayer and lamentation.
                             Children,
I would not have you speak through messengers,
And therefore I have come myself to hear you—
I, Oedipus, who bear the famous name.
10   *(To a Priest)* You, there, since you are eldest in the company,
Speak for them all, tell me what preys upon you,
Whether you come in dread, or crave some blessing:
Tell me, and never doubt that I will help you
In every way I can; I should be heartless
15   Were I not moved to find you suppliant here.
  Priest: Great Oedipus, O powerful king of Thebes!
You see how all the ages of our people
Cling to your altar steps: here are boys
Who can barely stand alone, and here are priests
20   By weight of age, as I am a priest of God,
And young men chosen from those yet unmarried;
As for the others, all that multitude,
They wait with olive chaplets in the squares,
At the two shrines of Pallas, and where Apollo
Speaks in the glowing embers.
25   Your own eyes
Must tell you: Thebes is tossed on a murdering sea
And can not lift her head from the death surge.
A rust consumes the buds and fruits of the earth;
The herds are sick; children die unborn,
30   And labor is vain. The god of plague and pyre
Raids like detestable lightning through the city,
And all the house of Kadmos is laid waste,
All emptied, and all darkened: Death alone
Battens upon the misery of Thebes.

35   You are not one of the immortal gods, we know;
Yet we have come to you to make our prayer
As to the man surest in mortal ways
And wisest in the ways of God. You saved us
From the Sphinx, that flinty singer, and the tribute
40   We paid to her so long; yet you were never
Better informed than we, nor could we teach you:
A god's touch, it seems, enabled you to help us.

Therefore, O mighty power, we turn to you:
Find us our safety, find us a remedy,
45   Whether by counsel of the gods or of men.

A king of wisdom tested in the past
Can act in a time of troubles, and act well.
Noblest of men, restore
Life to your city! Think how all men call you
50   Liberator for your boldness long ago;
Ah, when your years of kingship are remembered,
Let them not say *We rose, but later fell*—
Keep the State from going down in the storm!
Once, years ago, with happy augury,
55   You brought us fortune; be the same again!
No man questions your power to rule the land:
But rule over men, not over a dead city!
Ships are only hulls, high walls are nothing,
When no life moves in the empty passageways.
60 Oedipus: Poor children! You may be sure I know
All that you longed for in your coming here.
I know that you are deathly sick; and yet,
Sick as you are, not one is as sick as I.
Each of you suffers in himself alone
65   His anguish, not another's; but my spirit
Groans for the city, for myself, for you.

I was not sleeping, you are not waking me.
No, I have been in tears for a long while
And in my restless thought walked many ways.
70   In all my search I found one remedy,
And I have adopted it: I have sent Kreon,
Son of Menoikeus, brother of the queen,
To Delphi, Apollo's place of revelation,
To learn there, if he can,
75   What act or pledge of mine may save the city.
I have counted the days, and now, this very day,
I am troubled, for he has overstayed his time.
What is he doing? He has been gone too long.
Yet whenever he comes back, I should do ill
80   Not to take any action the god orders.
Priest: It is a timely promise. At this instant
They tell me Kreon is here.
Oedipus: O Lord Apollo!
May his news be fair as his face is radiant!
Priest: Good news, I gather! he is crowned with bay,
The chaplet is thick with berries.
85 Oedipus: We shall soon know;
He is near enough to hear us now. *(Enter Kreon.)* O prince:
Brother: son of Menoikeus:
What answer do you bring us from the god?

Kreon: A strong one. I can tell you, great afflictions
90   Will turn out well, if they are taken well.
Oedipus: What was the oracle? These vague words
          Leave me still hanging between hope and fear.
Kreon: Is it your pleasure to hear me with all these
          Gathered around us? I am prepared to speak,
          But should we not go in?
95 **Oedipus:**   Speak to them all,
          It is for them I suffer, more than for myself.
Kreon: Then I will tell you what I heard at Delphi.
          In plain words
          The god commands us to expel from the land of Thebes
100   An old defilement we are sheltering.
          It is a deathly thing, beyond cure;
          We must not let it feed upon us longer.
Oedipus: What defilement? How shall we rid ourselves of it?
Kreon: By exile or death, blood for blood. It was
105   Murder that brought the plague-wind on the city.
Oedipus: Murder of whom? Surely the god has named him?
Kreon: My lord: Laïos once ruled this land,
          Before you came to govern us.
Oedipus: I know;
          I learned of him from others; I never saw him.
110 **Kreon:** He was murdered; and Apollo commands us now
          To take revenge upon whoever killed him.
Oedipus: Upon whom? Where are they? Where shall we find a clue
          To solve that crime, after so many years?
Kreon: Here in this land, he said. Search reveals
115   Things that escape an inattentive man.
Oedipus: Tell me: Was Laïos murdered in his house,
          Or in the fields, or in some foreign country?
Kreon: He said he planned to make a pilgrimage.
          He did not come home again.
Oedipus: And was there no one,
120   No witness, no companion, to tell what happened?
Kreon: They were all killed but one, and he got away
          So frightened that he could remember one thing only.
Oedipus: What was that one thing? One may be the key
          To everything, if we resolve to use it.
125 **Kreon:** He said that a band of highwaymen attacked them,
          Outnumbered them, and overwhelmed the king.
Oedipus: Strange, that a highwayman should be so daring—
          Unless some faction here bribed him to do it.
Kreon: We thought of that. But after Laïos' death
130   New troubles arose and we had no avenger.
Oedipus: What troubles could prevent your hunting down the killers?

Kreon: The riddling Sphinx's song
     Made us deaf to all mysteries but her own.
Oedipus: Then once more I must bring what is dark to light.
135   It is most fitting that Apollo shows,
     As you do, this compunction for the dead.
     You shall see how I stand by you, as I should,
     Avenging this country and the god as well,
     And not as though it were for some distant friend,
140   But for my own sake, to be rid of evil.
     Whoever killed King Laïos might—who knows?—
     Lay violent hands even on me—and soon.
     I act for the murdered king in my own interest.

     Come, then, my children: leave the altar steps,
     Lift up your olive boughs!
145   One of you go
     And summon the people of Kadmos to gather here.
     I will do all that I can; you may tell them that. *(Exit a Page.)*
     So, with the help of God,
     We shall be saved—or else indeed we are lost.
150 Priest: Let us rise, children. It was for this we came,
     And now the king has promised it.
     Phoibos[2] has sent us an oracle; may he descend
     Himself to save us and drive out the plague. *(Exeunt Oedipus and Kreon
          into the palace by the central door. The Priest and the Suppliants
          disperse right and left. After a short pause the Chorus enters the
          orchêstra.)*

Parados[3]

Strophe 1

Chorus: What is God singing in his profound
155   Delphi of gold and shadow?
     What oracle for Thebes, the sunwhipped city?
     Fear unjoints me, the roots of my heart tremble.

---

[2] **Phoibos:** Apollo, god of light and truth.   [3] **Párodos:** The song or ode chanted by the
chorus on their entry. It is accompanied by dancing and music played on a flute. The chorus,
in this play, represents elders of the city of Thebes. They remain on stage (on a level lower
than the principal actors) for the remainder of the play. The choral odes and dances serve to
separate one scene from another (there was no curtain in Greek theater) as well as to
comment on the action, reinforce the emotion, and interpret the situation. The chorus also
performs dance movements during certain portions of the scenes themselves. *Strophe* and
antistrophe are terms denoting the movement and counter-movement of the chorus from one
side of their playing area to the other. When the chorus participates in dialogue with the
other characters, their lines are spoken by the Choragos, their leader.

Now I remember, O Healer, your power, and wonder:
Will you send doom like a sudden cloud, or weave it
160   Like nightfall of the past?
Speak to me, tell me, O
Child of golden Hope, immortal Voice.

Antistrophe 1

Let me pray to Athenê, the immortal daughter of Zeus,
And to Artemis her sister
165   Who keeps her famous throne in the market ring,
And to Apollo, archer from distant heaven—
O gods, descend! Like three streams leap against
The fires of our grief, the fires of darkness;
Be swift to bring us rest!
170   As in the old time from the brilliant house
Of air you stepped to save us, come again!

Strophe 2

Now our afflictions have no end,
Now all our stricken host lies down
And no man fights off death with his mind;
175   The noble plowland bears no grain,
And groaning mothers can not bear—
See, how our lives like birds take wing,
Like sparks that fly when a fire soars,
To the shore of the god of evening.

Antistrophe 2

180   The plague burns on, it is pitiless,
Though pallid children laden with death
Lie unwept in the stony ways,
And old gray women by every path
Flock to the strand about the altars
185   There to strike their breasts and cry
Worship of Phoibos in wailing prayers:
Be kind, God's golden child!

Strophe 3

There are no swords in this attack by fire,
No shields, but we are ringed with cries.
190   Send the besieger plunging from our homes
Into the vast sea-room of the Atlantic
Or into the waves that foam eastward of Thrace—
For the day ravages what the night spares—
Destroy our enemy, lord of the thunder!
195   Let him be riven by lightning from heaven!

Antistrophe 3

Phoibos Apollo, stretch the sun's bowstring,
That golden cord, until it sing for us,
Flashing arrows in heaven!
　　　　　　　　　　　Artemis, Huntress,
Race with flaring lights upon our mountains!
200　O scarlet god,[4] O golden-banded brow,
O Theban Bacchos in a storm of Maenads, *(Enter Oedipus, center.)*
Whirl upon Death, that all the Undying hate!
Come with blinding torches, come in joy!

Scene 1

Oedipus: Is this your prayer? It may be answered. Come,
205　Listen to me, act as the crisis demands,
And you shall have relief from all these evils.

Until now I was a stranger to this tale,
As I had been a stranger to the crime.
Could I track down the murderer without a clue?
210　But now, friends,
As one who became a citizen after the murder,
I make this proclamation to all Thebans:
If any man knows by whose hand Laïos, son of Labdakos,
Met his death, I direct that man to tell me everything,
215　No matter what he fears for having so long withheld it.
Let it stand as promised that no further trouble
Will come to him, but he may leave the land in safety.
Moreover: If anyone knows the murderer to be foreign,
Let him not keep silent: he shall have his reward from me.
220　However, if he does conceal it; if any man
Fearing for his friend or for himself disobeys this edict,
Hear what I propose to do:

I solemnly forbid the people of this country,
Where power and throne are mine, ever to receive that man
225　Or speak to him, no matter who he is, or let him
Join in sacrifice, lustration, or in prayer.
I decree that he be driven from every house,
Being, as he is, corruption itself to us: the Delphic
Voice of Apollo has pronounced this revelation.
230　Thus I associate myself with the oracle
And take the side of the murdered king.

---

[4] **scarlet god:** Bacchos, god of wine and revelry. The Maenads were his female attendants.

As for the criminal, I pray to God—
Whether it be a lurking thief, or one of a number—
I pray that that man's life be consumed in evil and wretchedness.
235   And as for me, this curse applies no less
If it should turn out that the culprit is my guest here,
Sharing my hearth.
                                    You have heard the penalty.
I lay it on you now to attend to this
For my sake, for Apollo's, for the sick
240   Sterile city that heaven has abandoned.
Suppose the oracle had given you no command:
Should this defilement go uncleansed for ever?
You should have found the murderer: your king,
A noble king, had been destroyed!
                                                    Now I,
245   Having the power that he held before me,
Having his bed, begetting children there
Upon his wife, as he would have, had he lived—
Their son would have been my children's brother,
If Laïos had had luck in fatherhood!
250   (And now his bad fortune has struck him down)—
I say I take the son's part, just as though
I were his son, to press the fight for him
And see it won! I'll find the hand that brought
Death to Labdakos' and Polydoros' child,
255   Heir of Kadmos' and Agenor's line.[5]
And as for those who fail me,
May the gods deny them the fruit of the earth,
Fruit of the womb, and may they rot utterly!
Let them be wretched as we are wretched, and worse!

260   For you, for loyal Thebans, and for all
Who find my actions right, I pray the favor
Of justice, and of all the immortal gods.
Choragos: Since I am under oath, my lord, I swear
I did not do the murder, I can not name
265   The murderer. Phoibos ordained the search;
Why did he not say who the culprit was?
Oedipus: An honest question. But no man in the world
Can make the gods do more than the gods will.
Choragos: There is an alternative, I think—
Oedipus: Tell me.

---

[5]**Labdakos, Polydoros, Kadmos, and Agenor:** father, grandfather, great-grandfather, and great-great-grandfather of Laïos.

270   Any or all, you must not fail to tell me.
    Choragos: A lord clairvoyant to the lord Apollo,
        As we all know, is the skilled Teiresias.
        One might learn much about this from him, Oedipus.
    Oedipus: I am not wasting time:
275   Kreon spoke of this, and I have sent for him—
        Twice, in fact; it is strange that he is not here.
    Choragos: The other matter—that old report—seems useless.
    Oedipus: What was that? I am interested in all reports.
    Choragos: The king was said to have been killed by highwaymen.
280 **Oedipus:** I know. But we have no witnesses to that.
    Choragos: If the killer can feel a particle of dread,
        Your curse will bring him out of hiding!
    Oedipus: No.
        The man who dared that act will fear no curse.
        (Enter the blind seer Teiresias, led by a Page.)
    Choragos: But there is one man who may detect the criminal.
285   This is Teiresias, this is the holy prophet
        In whom, alone of all men, truth was born.
    Oedipus: Teiresias: seer: student of mysteries,
        Of all that's taught and all that no man tells,
        Secrets of Heaven and secrets of the earth:
290   Blind though you are, you know the city lies
        Sick with plague; and from this plague, my lord,
        We find that you alone can guard or save us.

        Possibly you did not hear the messengers?
        Apollo, when we sent to him,
295   Sent us back word that this great pestilence
        Would lift, but only if we established clearly
        The identity of those who murdered Laïos.
        They must be killed or exiled.
                       Can you use
        Birdflight[6] or any art of divination
300   To purify yourself, and Thebes, and me
        From this contagion? We are in your hands.
        There is no fairer duty
        Than that of helping others in distress.
    Teiresias: How dreadful knowledge of the truth can be
305   When there's no help in truth! I knew this well,
        But did not act on it: else I should not have come.
    Oedipus: What is troubling you? Why are your eyes so cold?

---

[6] **Birdflight:** Prophets predicted the future or divined the unknown by observing the flight of birds.

Teiresias: Let me go home. Bear your own fate, and I'll
    Bear mine. It is better so: trust what I say.
310 Oedipus: What you say is ungracious and unhelpful
    To your native country. Do not refuse to speak.
Teiresias: When it comes to speech, your own is neither temperate
    Nor opportune. I wish to be more prudent.
Oedipus: In God's name, we all beg you—
Teiresias: You are all ignorant.
315   No; I will never tell you what I know.
    Now it is my misery; then, it would be yours.
Oedipus: What! You do know something, and will not tell us?
    You would betray us all and wreck the State?
Teiresias: I do not intend to torture myself, or you.
320   Why persist in asking? You will not persuade me.
Oedipus: What a wicked old man you are! You'd try a stone's
    Patience! Out with it! Have you no feeling at all?
Teiresias: You call me unfeeling. If you could only see
    The nature of your own feelings . . .
Oedipus: Why,
325   Who would not feel as I do? Who could endure
    Your arrogance toward the city?
Teiresias: What does it matter?
    Whether I speak or not, it is bound to come.
Oedipus: Then, if "it" is bound to come, you are bound to tell me.
Teiresias: No, I will not go on. Rage as you please.
Oedipus: Rage? Why not!
330   And I'll tell you what I think:
    You planned it, you had it done, you all but
    Killed him with your own hands: if you had eyes,
    I'd say the crime was yours, and yours alone.
Teiresias: So? I charge you, then,
335   Abide by the proclamation you have made:
    From this day forth
    Never speak again to these men or to me;
    You yourself are the pollution of this country.
Oedipus: You dare say that! Can you possibly think you have
340   Some way of going free, after such insolence?
Teiresias: I have gone free. It is the truth sustains me.
Oedipus: Who taught you shamelessness? It was not your craft.
Teiresias: You did. You made me speak. I did not want to.
Oedipus: Speak what? Let me hear it again more clearly.
345 Teiresias: Was it not clear before? Are you tempting me?
Oedipus: I did not understand it. Say it again.
Teiresias: I say that you are the murderer whom you seek.
Oedipus: Now twice you have spat out infamy. You'll pay for it!
Teiresias: Would you care for more? Do you wish to be really angry?

350 Oedipus: Say what you will. Whatever you say is worthless.
    Teiresias: I say you live in hideous shame with those
        Most dear to you. You can not see the evil.
    Oedipus: Can you go on babbling like this for ever?
    Teiresias: I can, if there is power in truth.
    Oedipus: There is:
355   But not for you, not for you,
        You sightless, witless, senseless, mad old man!
    Teiresias: You are the madman. There is no one here
        Who will not curse you soon, as you curse me.
    Oedipus: You child of total night! I would not touch you;
360   Neither would any man who sees the sun.
    Teiresias: True: it is not from you my fate will come.
        That lies within Apollo's competence,
        As it is his concern.
    Oedipus: Tell me, who made
        These fine discoveries? Kreon? or someone else?
365 Teiresias: Kreon is no threat. You weave your own doom.
    Oedipus: Wealth, power, craft of statemanship!
            Kingly position, everywhere admired!
            What savage envy is stored up against these,
            If Kreon, whom I trusted, Kreon my friend,
370   For this great office which the city once
            Put in my hands unsought—if for this power
            Kreon desires in secret to destroy me!

            He has bought this decrepit fortune-teller, this
            Collecter of dirty pennies, this prophet fraud—
            Why, he is no more clairvoyant than I am!
375   Tell us:
            Has your mystic mummery ever approached the truth?
            When that hellcat the Sphinx was performing here,
            What help were you to these people?
            Her magic was not for the first man who came along:
380   It demanded a real exorcist. Your birds—
            What good were they? or the gods, for the matter of that?
            But I came by,
            Oedipus, the simple man, who knows nothing—
            I thought it out for myself, no birds helped me!
385   And this is the man you think you can destroy,
            That you may be close to Kreon when he's king!
            Well, you and your friend Kreon, it seems to me,
            Will suffer most. If you were not an old man,
            You would have paid already for your plot.
390 Choragos: We can not see that his words or yours
            Have been spoken except in anger, Oedipus,

And of anger we have no need. How to accomplish
The god's will best: that is what most concerns us.
Teiresias: You are a king. But where argument's concerned
395   I am your man, as much a king as you.
I am not your servant, but Apollo's.
I have no need of Kreon or Kreon's name.

Listen to me. You mock my blindness, do you?
But I say that you, with both your eyes, are blind:
400   You can not see the wretchedness of your life,
Nor in whose house you live, no, nor with whom.
Who are your father and mother? Can you tell me?
You do not even know the blind wrongs
That you have done them, on earth and in the world below.
405   But the double lash of your parents' curse will whip you
Out of this land some day, with only night
Upon your precious eyes.
Your cries then—where will they not be heard?
What fastness of Kithairon[7] will not echo them?
410   And that bridal-descant of yours—you'll know it then,
The song they sang when you came here to Thebes
And found your misguided berthing.
All this, and more, that you can not guess at now,
Will bring you to yourself among your children.

415   Be angry, then. Curse Kreon. Curse my words.
I tell you, no man that walks upon the earth
Shall be rooted out more horribly than you.
Oedipus: Am I to bear this from him?—Damnation
Take you! Out of this place! Out of my sight!
420 Teiresias: I would not have come at all if you had not asked me.
Oedipus: Could I have told that you'd talk nonsense, that
You'd come here to make a fool of yourself, and of me?
Teiresias: A fool? Your parents thought me sane enough.
Oedipus: My parents again!—Wait: who were my parents?
425 Teiresias: This day will give you a father, and break your heart.
Oedipus: Your infantile riddles! Your damned abracadabra!
Teiresias: You were a great man once at solving riddles.
Oedipus: Mock me with that if you like; you will find it true.
Teiresias: It was true enough. It brought about your ruin.
430 Oedipus: But if it saved this town?
Teiresias *(To the Page):*   Boy, give me your hand.
Oedipus: Yes, boy; lead him away.

---

[7] **Kithairon:** the mountain where Oedipus was taken to be exposed as an infant.

—While you are here
We can do nothing. Go; leave us in peace.
Teiresias: I will go when I have said what I have to say.
How can you hurt me? And I tell you again:
435 The man you have been looking for all this time,
The damned man, the murderer of Laïos,
That man is in Thebes. To your mind he is foreign-born,
But it will soon be shown that he is a Theban,
A revelation that will fail to please.
A blind man,
440 Who has his eyes now; a penniless man, who is rich now;
And he will go tapping the strange earth with his staff.
To the children with whom he lives now he will be
Brother and father—the very same; to her
Who bore him, son and husband—the very same
445 Who came to his father's bed, wet with his father's blood.
Enough. Go think that over.
If later you find error in what I have said,
You may say that I have no skill in prophecy.

(Exit Teiresias, led by his Page. Oedipus goes into the palace.)

Ode 1

Strophe 1

Chorus: The Delphic stone of prophecies
450 Remembers ancient regicide
And a still bloody hand.
That killer's hour of flight has come.
He must be stronger than riderless
Coursers of untiring wind,
455 For the son[8] of Zeus armed with his father's thunder
Leaps in lightning after him;
And the Furies hold his track, the sad Furies.

Antistrophe 1

Holy Parnassos[9] peak of snow
Flashes and blinds that secret man,
460 That all shall hunt him down:
Though he may roam the forest shade
Like a bull gone wild from pasture
To rage through glooms of stone.
Doom comes down on him; flight will not avail him;
465 For the world's heart calls him desolate,
And the immortal voices follow, for ever follow.

---

[8] **son:** Apollo.   [9] **Parnassos:** mountain sacred to Apollo.

Strophe 2

But now a wilder thing is heard
From the old man skilled at hearing Fate in the wing-beat of a bird.
Bewildered as a blown bird, my soul hovers and can not find
470   Foothold in this debate, or any reason or rest of mind.
But no man ever brought—none can bring
Proof of strife between Thebes' royal house,
Labdakos' line, and the son of Polybos;
And never until now has any man brought word
475   Of Laïos' dark death staining Oedipus the King.

Antistrophe 2

Divine Zeus and Apollo hold
Perfect intelligence alone of all tales ever told;
And well though this diviner works, he works in his own night;
No man can judge that rough unknown or trust in second sight,
480   For wisdom changes hands among the wise.
Shall I believe my great lord criminal
At a raging word that a blind old man let fall?
I saw him, when the carrion woman[10] faced him of old,
Prove his heroic mind. These evil words are lies.

Scene 2

485 **Kreon:** Men of Thebes:
I am told that heavy accusations
Have been brought against me by King Oedipus.

I am not the kind of man to bear this tamely.

If in these present difficulties
490   He holds me accountable for any harm to him
Through anything I have said or done—why, then,
I do not value life in this dishonor.
It is not as though this rumor touched upon
Some private indiscretion. The matter is grave.
495   The fact is that I am being called disloyal
To the State, to my fellow citizens, to my friends.
Choragos: He may have spoken in anger, not from his mind.
Kreon: But did you not hear him say I was the one
Who seduced the old prophet into lying?
500 **Choragos:** The thing was said; I do not know how seriously.
Kreon: But you were watching him! Were his eyes steady?

---

[10] **woman:** the Sphinx.

Did he look like a man in his right mind?
Choragos: I do not know.
     I can not judge the behavior of great men.
     But here is the king himself. *(Enter Oedipus.)*
Oedipus: So you dared come back.
505   Why? How brazen of you to come to my house,
     You murderer!
                  Do you think I do not know
     That you plotted to kill me, plotted to steal my throne?
     Tell me, in God's name: am I coward, a fool,
     That you should dream you could accomplish this?
510   A fool who could not see your slippery game?
     A coward, not to fight back when I saw it?
     You are the fool, Kreon, are you not? hoping
     Without support or friends to get a throne?
     Thrones may be won or bought: you could do neither.
515 **Kreon:** Now listen to me. You have talked; let me talk, too.
     You can not judge unless you know the facts.
Oedipus: You speak well: there is one fact; but I find it hard
     To learn from the deadliest enemy I have.
Kreon: That above all I must dispute with you.
520 **Oedipus:** That above all I will not hear you deny.
Kreon: If you think there is anything good in being stubborn
     Against all reason, then I say you are wrong.
Oedipus: If you think a man can sin against his own kind
     And not be punished for it, I say you are mad.
525 **Kreon:** I agree. But tell me: what have I done to you?
Oedipus: You advised me to send for that wizard, did you not?
Kreon: I did. I should do it again.
Oedipus: Very well. Now tell me:
     How long has it been since Laïos—
Kreon: What of Laïos?
Oedipus: Since he vanished in that onset by the road?
Kreon: It was long ago, a long time.
530 **Oedipus:**   And this prophet,
     Was he practicing here then?
Kreon: He was; and with honor, as now.
Oedipus: Did he speak of me at that time?
Kreon: He never did,
     At least, not when I was present.
Oedipus: But . . . the enquiry?
     I suppose you held one?
Kreon: We did, but we learned nothing.
535 **Oedipus:** Why did the prophet not speak against me then?
Kreon: I do not know; and I am the kind of man
     Who holds his tongue when he has no facts to go on.

Oedipus: There's one fact that you know, and you could tell it.

Kreon: What fact is that? If I know it, you shall have it.

540 Oedipus: If he were not involved with you, he could not say
    That it was I who murdered Laïos.

Kreon: If he says that, you are the one that knows it!—
    But now it is my turn to question you.

Oedipus: Put your questions. I am no murderer.

Kreon: First, then: You married my sister?

545 Oedipus: I married your sister.

Kreon: And you rule the kingdom equally with her?

Oedipus: Everything that she wants she has from me.

Kreon: And I am the third, equal to both of you?

Oedipus: That is why I call you a bad friend.

550 Kreon: No. Reason it out, as I have done.
    Think of this first: Would any sane man prefer
    Power, with all a king's anxieties,
    To that same power and the grace of sleep?
    Certainly not I.

555   I have never longed for the king's power—only his rights.
    Would any wise man differ from me in this?
    As matters stand, I have my way in everything
    With your consent, and no responsibilities.
    If I were king, I should be a slave to policy.

560   How could I desire a scepter more
    Than what is now mine—untroubled influence?
    No, I have not gone mad; I need no honors,
    Except those with the perquisites I have now.
    I am welcome everywhere; every man salutes me,

565   And those who want your favor seek my ear,
    Since I know how to manage what they ask.
    Should I exchange this ease for that anxiety?
    Besides, no sober mind is treasonable.
    I hate anarchy

570   And never would deal with any man who likes it.
    Test what I have said. Go to the priestess
    At Delphi, ask if I quoted her correctly.
    And as for this other thing: if I am found
    Guilty of treason with Teiresias,

575   Then sentence me to death. You have my word
    It is a sentence I should cast my vote for—
    But not without evidence!
                      You do wrong
    When you take good men for bad, bad men for good.
    A true friend thrown aside—why, life itself
    Is not more precious!

580   In time you will know this well:

For time, and time alone, will show the just man,
Though scoundrels are discovered in a day.
Choragos: This is well said, and a prudent man would ponder it.
Judgments too quickly formed are dangerous.
585 Oedipus: But is he not quick in his duplicity?
And shall I not be quick to parry him?
Would you have me stand still, hold my peace, and let
This man win everything, through my inaction?
Kreon: And you want—what is it, then? To banish me?
590 Oedipus: No, not exile. It is your death I want,
So that all the world may see what treason means.
Kreon: You will persist, then? You will not believe me?
Oedipus: How can I believe you?
Kreon: Then you are a fool.
Oedipus: To save myself?
Kreon: In justice, think of me.
Oedipus: You are evil incarnate.
595 Kreon: But suppose that you are wrong?
Oedipus: Still I must rule.
Kreon: But not if you rule badly.
Oedipus: O city, city!
Kreon: It is my city, too!
Choragos: Now, my lords, be still. I see the queen,
Iokastê, coming from her palace chambers;
600   And it is time she came, for the sake of you both.
This dreadful quarrel can be resolved through her. *(Enter Iokastê.)*
Iokastê: Poor foolish men, what wicked din is this?
With Thebes sick to death, is it not shameful
That you should rake some private quarrel up?
(To Oedipus) Come into the house.
605   —And you, Kreon, go now:
Let us have no more of this tumult over nothing.
Kreon: Nothing? No, sister: what your husband plans for me
Is one of two great evils: exile or death.
Oedipus: He is right.
                    Why, woman I have caught him squarely
Plotting against my life.
610 Kreon: No! Let me die
Accurst if ever I have wished you harm!
Iokastê: Ah, believe it, Oedipus!
In the name of the gods, respect this oath of his
For my sake, for the sake of these people here!

Strophe 1

Choragos: Open your mind to her, my lord. Be ruled by her, I
615   beg you!

Oedipus: What would you have me do?

Choragos: Respect Kreon's word. He has never spoken like a fool,
    And now he has sworn an oath.

Oedipus: You know what you ask?

Choragos: I do.

Oedipus: Speak on, then.

Choragos: A friend so sworn should not be baited so,
620   In blind malice, and without final proof.

Oedipus: You are aware, I hope, that what you say
    Means death for me, or exile at the least.

Strophe 2

Choragos: No, I swear by Helios, first in heaven!
                May I die friendless and accurst,
625   The worst of deaths, if ever I meant that!
                It is the withering fields
            That hurt my sick heart:
                Must we bear all these ills,
            And now your bad blood as well?

630 Oedipus: Then let him go. And let me die, if I must,
            Or be driven by him in shame from the land of Thebes.
        It is your unhappiness, and not his talk,
        That touches me.
                    As for him—
        Wherever he goes, hatred will follow him.

635 Kreon: Ugly in yielding, as you were ugly in rage!
        Natures like yours chiefly torment themselves.

Oedipus: Can you not go? Can you not leave me?

Kreon: I can.
        You do not know me; but the city knows me,
        And in its eyes I am just, if not in yours. *(Exit Kreon.)*

Antistrophe 1

Choragos: Lady Iokastê, did you not ask the King to go to his
640   chambers?

Iokastê: First tell me what has happened.

Choragos: There was suspicion without evidence; yet it rankled
        As even false charges will.

Iokastê: On both sides?

Choragos: On both.

Iokastê: But what was said?

Choragos: Oh let it rest, let it be done with!
645   Have we not suffered enough?

Oedipus: You see to what your decency has brought you:
        You have made difficulties where my heart saw none.

Antistrophe 2

Choragos: Oedipus, it is not once only I have told you—
        You must know I should count myself unwise
650   To the point of madness, should I now forsake you—
          You, under whose hand,
            In the storm of another time,
          Our dear land sailed out free.
           But now stand fast at the helm!
655 **Iokastê:** In God's name, Oedipus, inform your wife as well:
      Why are you so set in this hard anger?
Oedipus: I will tell you, for none of these men deserves
      My confidence as you do. It is Kreon's work,
      His treachery, his plotting against me.
660 **Iokastê:** Go on, if you can make this clear to me.
Oedipus: He charges me with the murder of Laïos.
Iokastê: Has he some knowledge? Or does he speak from hearsay?
Oedipus: He would not commit himself to such a charge,
      But he has brought in that damnable soothsayer
      To tell his story.
665 **Iokastê:**   Set your mind at rest.
      If it is a question of soothsayers, I tell you
      That you will find no man whose craft gives knowledge
      Of the unknowable.
           Here is my proof:
      An oracle was reported to Laïos once
670   (I will not say from Phoibos himself, but from
      His appointed ministers, at any rate)
      That his doom would be death at the hands of his own son—
      His son, born of his flesh and of mine!

      Now, you remember the story: Laïos was killed
675   By marauding strangers where three highways meet;
      But his child had not been three days in this world
      Before the king had pierced the baby's ankles
      And left him to die on a lonely mountainside.

      Thus, Apollo never caused that child
680   To kill his father, and it was not Laïos' fate
      To die at the hands of his son, as he had feared.
      This is what prophets and prophecies are worth!
      Have no dread of them.
           It is God himself
      Who can show us what he wills, in his own way.
685 **Oedipus:** How strange a shadowy memory crossed my mind,
      Just now while you were speaking; it chilled my heart.
Iokastê: What do you mean? What memory do you speak of?

Oedipus: If I understand you, Laïos was killed
 At a place where three roads meet.
Iokastê: So it was said;
 We have no later story.
690 Oedipus: Where did it happen?
Iokastê: Phokis, it is called: at a place where the Theban Way
 Divides into the roads toward Delphi and Daulia.
Oedipus: When?
Iokastê: We had the news not long before you came
 And proved the right to your succession here.
695 Oedipus: Ah, what net has God been weaving for me?
Iokastê: Oedipus! Why does this trouble you?
Oedipus: Do not ask me yet.
 First, tell me how Laïos looked, and tell me
 How old he was.
Iokastê: He was tall, his hair just touched
 With white; his form was not unlike your own.
700 Oedipus: I think that I myself may be accurst
 By my own ignorant edict.
Iokastê: You speak strangely.
 It makes me tremble to look at you, my king.
Oedipus: I am not sure that the blind man can not see.
 But I should know better if you were to tell me—
705 Iokastê: Anything—though I dread to hear you ask it.
Oedipus: Was the king lightly escorted, or did he ride
 With a large company, as a ruler should?
Iokastê: There were five men with him in all: one was a herald;
 And a single chariot, which he was driving.
Oedipus: Alas, that makes it plain enough!
710   But who—
 Who told you how it happened?
Iokastê: A household servant,
 The only one to escape.
Oedipus: And is he still
 A servant of ours?
Iokastê: No; for when he came back at last
 And found you enthroned in the place of the dead king,
715 He came to me, touched my hand with his, and begged
  That I would send him away to the frontier district
  Where only the shepherds go—
  As far away from the city as I could send him.
 I granted his prayer; for although the man was a slave,
720 He had earned more than this favor at my hands.
Oedipus: Can he be called back quickly?
Iokastê: Easily.
 But why?

Oedipus: I have taken too much upon myself
    Without enquiry; therefore I wish to consult him.
Iokastê: Then he shall come.
                        But am I not one also
    To whom you might confide these fears of yours?
Oedipus: That is your right; it will not be denied you,
        Now least of all; for I have reached a pitch
        Of wild foreboding. Is there anyone
        To whom I should sooner speak?

730   Polybos of Corinth is my father.
        My mother is a Dorian: Meropê.
        I grew up chief among the men of Corinth
        Until a strange thing happened—
        Not worth my passion, it may be, but strange.
735   At a feast, a drunken man maundering in his cups
        Cries out that I am not my father's son!

        I contained myself that night, though I felt anger
        And a sinking heart. The next day I visited
        My father and mother, and questioned them. They stormed,
740   Calling it all the slanderous rant of a fool;
        And this relieved me. Yet the suspicion
        Remained always aching in my mind;
        I knew there was talk; I could not rest;
        And finally, saying nothing to my parents,
745   I went to the shrine at Delphi.

        The god dismissed my question without reply;
        He spoke of other things.
                       Some were clear,
        Full of wretchedness, dreadful, unbearable:
        As, that I should lie with my own mother, breed
750   Children from whom all men would turn their eyes;
        And that I should be my father's murderer.

        I heard all this, and fled. And from that day
        Corinth to me was only in the stars
        Descending in that quarter of the sky,
755   As I wandered farther and farther on my way
        To a land where I should never see the evil
        Sung by the oracle. And I came to this country
        Where, so you say, King Laïos was killed.

        I will tell you all that happened there, my lady.

760   There were three highways
        Coming together at a place I passed;

And there a herald came towards me, and a chariot
Drawn by horses, with a man such as you describe
Seated in it. The groom leading the horses
765   Forced me off the road at his lord's command;
But as this charioteer lurched over towards me
I struck him in my rage. The old man saw me
And brought his double goad down upon my head
As I came abreast.
                                        He was paid back, and more!
770   Swinging my club in this right hand I knocked him
Out of his car, and he rolled on the ground.
                                                        I killed him.

I killed them all.
Now if that stranger and Laïos were—kin,
Where is a man more miserable than I?
775   More hated by the gods? Citizen and alien alike
Must never shelter me or speak to me—
I must be shunned by all.
                                        And I myself
Pronounced this malediction upon myself!

Think of it: I have touched you with these hands,
780   These hands that killed your husband. What defilement!

Am I all evil, then? It must be so,
Since I must flee from Thebes, yet never again
See my own countrymen, my own country,
For fear of joining my mother in marriage
And killing Polybos, my father.
785   Ah,
If I was created so, born to this fate,
Who could deny the savagery of God?

O holy majesty of heavenly powers!
May I never see that day! Never!
790   Rather let me vanish from the race of men
Than know the abomination destined me!
Choragos: We too, my lord, have felt dismay at this.
        But there is hope: you have yet to hear the shepherd.
Oedipus: Indeed, I fear no other hope is left me.
Iokastê: What do you hope from him when he comes?
795 Oedipus: This much:
        If his account of the murder tallies with yours,
        Then I am cleared.
Iokastê: What was it that I said
        Of such importance?

Oedipus: Why, "marauders," you said,
    Killed the king, according to this man's story.
800   If he maintains that still, if there were several,
      Clearly the guilt is not mine: I was alone.
    But if he says one man, singlehanded, did it,
    Then the evidence all points to me.
Iokastê: You may be sure that he said there were several;
805   And can he call back that story now? He can not.
    The whole city heard it as plainly as I.
    But suppose he alters some detail of it:
    He can not ever show that Laïos' death
    Fulfilled the oracle: for Apollo said
810   My child was doomed to kill him; and my child—
    Poor baby!—it was my child that died first.

    No. From now on, where oracles are concerned,
    I would not waste a second thought on any.
Oedipus: You may be right.
                  But come: let someone go
815   For the shepherd at once. This matter must be settled.
Iokastê: I will send for him.
    I would not wish to cross you in anything,
    And surely not in this.—Let us go in. *(Exeunt into the palace.)*

Ode 2

Strophe 1

Chorus: Let me be reverent in the ways of right,
820   Lowly the paths I journey on;
    Let all my words and actions keep
    The laws of the pure universe
    From highest Heaven handed down.
    For Heaven is their bright nurse,
825   Those generations of the realms of light;
    Ah, never of mortal kind were they begot,
    Nor are they slaves of memory, lost in sleep:
    Their Father is greater than Time, and ages not.

Antistrophe 1

    The tyrant is a child of Pride
830   Who drinks from his great sickening cup
    Recklessness and vanity,
    Until from his high crest headlong
    He plummets to the dust of hope.
    That strong man is not strong.

835   But let no fair ambition be denied;
      May God protect the wrestler for the State
      In government, in comely policy,
      Who will fear God, and on His ordinance wait.

      Strophe 2

      Haughtiness and the high hand of disdain
840   Tempt and outrage God's holy law;
      And any mortal who dares hold
      No immortal Power in awe
      Will be caught up in a net of pain:
      The price for which his levity is sold.
845   Let each man take due earnings, then,
      And keep his hands from holy things,
      And from blasphemy stand apart—
      Else the crackling blast of heaven
      Blows on his head, and on his desperate heart.
850   Though fools will honor impious men,
      In their cities no tragic poet sings.

      Antistrophe 2

      Shall we lose faith in Delphi's obscurities,
      We who have heard the world's core
      Discredited, and the sacred wood
855   Of Zeus at Elis praised no more?
      The deeds and the strange prophecies
      Must make a pattern yet to be understood.
      Zeus, if indeed you are lord of all,
      Throned in light over night and day,
860   Mirror this in your endless mind:
      Our masters call the oracle
      Words on the wind, and the Delphic vision blind!
      Their hearts no longer know Apollo,
      And reverence for the gods has died away.

Scene 3

Enter Iokastê.

865 Iokastê: Princes of Thebes, it has occurred to me
      To visit the altars of the gods, bearing
      These branches as a suppliant, and this incense.
      Our king is not himself: his noble soul
      Is overwrought with fantasies of dread,
870   Else he would consider
      The new prophecies in the light of the old.

He will listen to any voice that speaks disaster,
And my advice goes for nothing. *(She approaches the altar, right.)*
                To you, then, Apollo,
Lycéan lord, since you are nearest, I turn in prayer.

875   Receive these offerings, and grant us deliverance
From defilement. Our hearts are heavy with fear
When we see our leader distracted, as helpless sailors
Are terrified by the confusion of their helmsman. *(Enter Messenger.)*

Messenger: Friends, no doubt you can direct me:
880   Where shall I find the house of Oedipus,
Or, better still, where is the king himself?

Choragos: It is this very place, stranger; he is inside.
This is his wife and mother of his children.

Messenger: I wish her happiness in a happy house,
885   Blest in all the fulfillment of her marriage.

Iokastê: I wish as much for you: your courtesy
Deserves a like good fortune. But now, tell me:
Why have you come? What have you to say to us?

Messenger: Good news, my lady, for your house and your husband.

Iokastê: What news? Who sent you here?

890 **Messenger:**   I am from Corinth.
The news I bring ought to mean joy for you,
Though it may be you will find some grief in it.

Iokastê: What is it? How can it touch us in both ways?

Messenger: The word is that the people of the Isthmus
895   Intend to call Oedipus to be their king.

Iokastê: But old King Polybos—is he not reigning still?

Messenger: No. Death holds him in his sepulchre.

Iokastê: What are you saying? Polybos is dead?

Messenger: If I am not telling the truth, may I die myself.

Iokastê *(to a Maidservant):* Go in, go quickly; tell this to
900   your master.
O riddlers of God's will, where are you now!
This was the man whom Oedipus, long ago,
Feared so, fled so, in dread of destroying him—
But it was another fate by which he died. *(Enter Oedipus, center.)*

905 **Oedipus:** Dearest Iokastê, why have you sent for me?

Iokastê: Listen to what this man says, and then tell me
What has become of the solemn prophecies.

Oedipus: Who is this man? What is his news for me?

Iokastê: He has come from Corinth to announce your father's death!

910 **Oedipus:** Is it true, stranger? Tell me in your own words.

Messenger: I can not say it more clearly: the king is dead.

Oedipus: Was it by treason? Or by an attack of illness?

Messenger: A little thing brings old men to their rest.

Oedipus: It was sickness, then?

Messenger: Yes, and his many years.
915 Oedipus: Ah!
         Why should a man respect the Pythian hearth,[11] or
         Give heed to the birds that jangle above his head?
         They prophesied that I should kill Polybos,
         Kill my own father; but he is dead and buried,
920   And I am here—I never touched him, never,
         Unless he died of grief for my departure,
         And thus, in a sense, through me. No. Polybos
         Has packed the oracles off with him underground.
         They are empty words.
Iokastê: Had I not told you so?
925 Oedipus: You had; it was my faint heart that betrayed me.
    Iokastê: From now on never think of those things again.
    Oedipus: And yet—must I not fear my mother's bed?
    Iokastê: Why should anyone in this world be afraid,
         Since Fate rules us and nothing can be foreseen?
930   A man should live only for the present day.

         Have no more fear of sleeping with your mother:
         How many men, in dreams, have lain with their mothers!
         No reasonable man is troubled by such things.
    Oedipus: That is true; only—
935   If only my mother were not still alive!
         But she is alive. I can not help my dread.
    Iokastê: Yet this news of your father's death is wonderful.
    Oedipus: Wonderful. But I fear the living woman.
    Messenger: Tell me, who is this woman that you fear?
940 Oedipus: It is Meropê, man; the wife of King Polybos.
    Messenger: Meropê? Why should you be afraid of her?
    Oedipus: An oracle of the gods, a dreadful saying.
    Messenger: Can you tell me about it or are you sworn to silence?
    Oedipus: I can tell you, and I will.
945   Apollo said through his prophet that I was the man
         Who should marry his own mother, shed his father's blood
         With his own hands. And so, for all these years
         I have kept clear of Corinth, and no harm has come—
         Though it would have been sweet to see my parents again.
950 Messenger: And is this the fear that drove you out of Corinth?
    Oedipus: Would you have me kill my father?
    Messenger: As for that
         You must be reassured by the news I gave you.
    Oedipus: If you could reassure me, I would reward you.

---

[11] **Pythian hearth:** Delphi.

Messenger: I had that in mind, I will confess: I thought
955   I could count on you when you returned to Corinth.
Oedipus: No: I will never go near my parents again.
Messenger: Ah, son, you still do not know what you are doing—
Oedipus: What do you mean? In the name of God tell me!
Messenger: —If these are your reasons for not going home.
960 Oedipus: I tell you, I fear the oracle may come true.
Messenger: And guilt may come upon you through your parents?
Oedipus: That is the dread that is always in my heart.
Messenger: Can you not see that all your fears are groundless?
Oedipus: Groundless? Am I not my parents' son?
Messenger: Polybos was not your father.
965 Oedipus: Not my father?
Messenger: No more your father than the man speaking to you.
Oedipus: But you are nothing to me!
Messenger: Neither was he.
Oedipus: Then why did he call me son?
Messenger: I will tell you:
        Long ago he had you from my hands, as a gift.
970 Oedipus: Then how could he love me so, if I was not his?
Messenger: He had no children, and his heart turned to you.
Oedipus: What of you? Did you buy me? Did you find me by chance?
Messenger: I came upon you in the woody vales of Kithairon.
Oedipus: And what were you doing there?
Messenger: Tending my flocks.
Oedipus: A wandering shepherd?
975 Messenger: But your savior, son, that day.
Oedipus: From what did you save me?
Messenger: Your ankles should tell you that.
Oedipus: Ah, stranger, why do you speak of that childhood pain?
Messenger: I pulled the skewer that pinned your feet together.
Oedipus: I have had the mark as long as I can remember.
980 Messenger: That was why you were given the name you bear.
Oedipus: God! Was it my father or my mother who did it?
        Tell me!
Messenger: I do not know. The man who gave you to me
        Can tell you better than I.
Oedipus: It was not you that found me, but another?
985 Messenger: It was another shepherd gave you to me.
Oedipus: Who was he? Can you tell me who he was?
Messenger: I think he was said to be one of Laïos' people.
Oedipus: You mean the Laïos who was king here years ago?
Messenger: Yes; King Laïos; and the man was one of his herdsmen.
Oedipus: Is he still alive? Can I see him?
990 Messenger: These men here

Know best about such things.
Oedipus: Does anyone here
Know this shepherd that he is talking about?
Have you seen him in the fields, or in the town?
If you have, tell me. It is time things were made plain.
995 Choragos: I think the man he means is that same shepherd
You have already asked to see. Iokastê perhaps
Could tell you something.
Oedipus: Do you know anything
About him, Lady? Is he the man we have summoned?
Is that the man this shepherd means?
Iokastê: Why think of him?
1000   Forget this herdsman. Forget it all.
This talk is a waste of time.
Oedipus: How can you say that,
When the clues to my true birth are in my hands?
Iokastê: For God's love, let us have no more questioning!
Is your life nothing to you?
1005   My own is pain enough for me to bear.
Oedipus: You need not worry. Suppose my mother a slave,
And born of slaves: no baseness can touch you.
Iokastê: Listen to me, I beg you: do not do this thing!
Oedipus: I will not listen; the truth must be made known.
Iokastê: Everything that I say is for your own good!
1010 Oedipus: My own good
Snaps my patience, then; I want none of it.
Iokastê: You are fatally wrong! May you never learn who you are!
Oedipus: Go, one of you, and bring the shepherd here.
Let us leave this woman to brag of her royal name.
1015 Iokastê: Ah, miserable!
That is the only word I have for you now.
That is the only word I can ever have. *(Exit into the palace.)*
Choragos: Why has she left us, Oedipus? Why has she gone
In such a passion of sorrow? I fear this silence:
Something dreadful may come of it.
1020 Oedipus: Let it come!
However base my birth, I must know about it.
The Queen, like a woman, is perhaps ashamed
To think of my low origin. But I
Am a child of Luck; I can not be dishonored.
1025   Luck is my mother; the passing months, my brothers,
Have seen me rich and poor.
                                        If this is so,
How could I wish that I were someone else?
How could I not be glad to know my birth?

Ode 3

Strophe

Chorus: If ever the coming time were known
1030   To my heart's pondering,
        Kithairon, now by Heaven I see the torches
        At the festival of the next full moon,
        And see the dance, and hear the choir sing
        A grace to your gentle shade:
1035   Mountain where Oedipus was found,
        O mountain guard of a noble race!
        May the god[12] who heals us lend his aid,
        And let that glory come to pass
        For our king's cradling-ground.

Antistrophe

1040   Of the nymphs that flower beyond the years,
        Who bore you,[13] royal child,
        To Pan of the hills or the timberline Apollo,
        Cold in delight where the upland clears,
        Or Hermês for whom Kyllenê's heights are piled?
1045   Or flushed as evening cloud,
        Great Dionysos, roamer of mountains,
        He—was it he who found you there,
        And caught you up in his own proud
        Arms from the sweet god-ravisher
1050   Who laughed by the Muses' fountains?

Scene 4

Oedipus: Sirs: though I do not know the man,
        I think I see him coming, this shepherd we want:
        He is old, like our friend here, and the men
        Bringing him seem to be servants of my house.
1055   But you can tell, if you have ever seen him.
        (Enter Shepherd escorted by Servants.)
Choragos: I know him, he was Laïos' man. You can trust him.
Oedipus: Tell me first, you from Corinth: is this the shepherd
        We were discussing?
Messenger: This is the very man.

---

[12] **god:** Apollo.   [13] **Who bore you:** The chorus is suggesting that perhaps Oedipus is the son of one of the immortal nymphs and of a god—Pan, Apollo, Hermes, or Dionysos. The "sweet god-ravisher" (line 1049) is the presumed mother.

Oedipus *(to Shepherd):* Come here. No, look at me. You must answer
1060   Everything I ask.—You belonged to Laïos?

Shepherd: Yes: born his slave, brought up in his house.

Oedipus: Tell me: what kind of work did you do for him?

Shepherd: I was a shepherd of his, most of my life.

Oedipus: Where mainly did you go for pasturage?

1065 **Shepherd:** Sometimes Kithairon, sometimes the hills near-by.

Oedipus: Do you remember ever seeing this man out there?

Shepherd: What would he be doing there? This man?

Oedipus: This man standing here. Have you ever seen him before?

Shepherd: No. At least, not to my recollection.

1070 **Messenger:** And that is not strange, my lord. But I'll refresh
    His memory: he must remember when we two
    Spent three whole seasons together, March to September,
    On Kithairon or thereabouts. He had two flocks;
    I had one. Each autumn I'd drive mine home
1075   And he would go back with his to Laïos' sheepfold.—
    Is this not true, just as I have described it?

Shepherd: True, yes; but it was all so long ago.

Messenger: Well, then: do you remember, back in those days,
    That you gave me a baby boy to bring up as my own?

1080 **Shepherd:** What if I did? What are you trying to say?

Messenger: King Oedipus was once that little child.

Shepherd: Damn you, hold your tongue!

Oedipus: No more of that!
    It is your tongue needs watching, not this man's.

Shepherd: My king, my master, what is it I have done wrong?

1085 **Oedipus:** You have not answered his question about the boy.

Shepherd: He does not know . . . He is only making trouble . . .

Oedipus: Come, speak plainly, or it will go hard with you.

Shepherd: In God's name, do not torture an old man!

Oedipus: Come here, one of you; bind his arms behind him.

1090 **Shepherd:** Unhappy king! What more do you wish to learn?

Oedipus: Did you give this man the child he speaks of?

Shepherd: I did.
    And I would to God I had died that very day.

Oedipus: You will die now unless you speak the truth.

Shepherd: Yet if I speak the truth, I am worse than dead.

1095 **Oedipus** *(to Attendant):* He intends to draw it out, apparently—

Shepherd: No! I have told you already that I gave him the boy.

Oedipus: Where did you get him? From your house? From somewhere else?

Shepherd: Not from mine, no. A man gave him to me.

Oedipus: Is that man here? Whose house did he belong to?

1100 **Shepherd:** For God's love, my king, do not ask me any more!

Oedipus: You are a dead man if I have to ask you again.

Shepherd: Then . . . Then the child was from the palace of Laïos.

Oedipus: A slave child? or a child of his own line?
Shepherd: Ah, I am on the brink of dreadful speech!
1105 Oedipus: And I of dreadful hearing. Yet I must hear.
Shepherd: If you must be told, then . . .
                              They said it was Laïos' child;
        But it is your wife who can tell you about that.
Oedipus: My wife—Did she give it to you?
Shepherd: My lord, she did.
Oedipus: Do you know why?
Shepherd: I was told to get rid of it.
Oedipus: Oh heartless mother!
1110 Shepherd: But in dread of prophecies . . .
Oedipus: Tell me.
Shepherd: It was said that the boy would kill his own father.
Oedipus: Then why did you give him over to this old man?
Shepherd: I pitied the baby, my king.
        And I thought that this man would take him far away
        To his own country.
1115   He saved him—but for what a fate!
        For if you are what this man says you are,
        No man living is more wretched than Oedipus.
Oedipus: Ah God!
        It was true!
                All the prophecies!
                        —Now,
1120   O Light, may I look on you for the last time!
        I, Oedipus,
        Oedipus, damned in his birth, in his marriage damned,
        Damned in the blood he shed with his own hand!
        (He rushes into the palace.)

Ode 4

Strophe 1

Chorus: Alas for the seed of men.
1125   What measure shall I give these generations
        That breathe on the void and are void
        And exist and do not exist?
        Who bears more weight of joy
        Than mass of sunlight shifting in images,
1130   Or who shall make his thought stay on
        That down time drifts away?
        Your splendor is all fallen.
        O naked brow of wrath and tears,
        O change of Oedipus!

1135   I who saw your days call no man blest—
Your great days like ghósts góne.

Antistrophe 1

That mind was a strong bow.
Deep, how deep you drew it then, hard archer,
At a dim fearful range,
1140   And brought dear glory down!
You overcame the stranger[14] —
The virgin with her hooking lion claws—
And though death sang, stood like a tower
To make pale Thebes take heart.
1145   Fortress against our sorrow!
True king, giver of laws,
Majestic Oedipus!
No prince in Thebes had ever such renown,
No prince won such grace of power.

Strophe 2

1150   And now of all men ever known
Most pitiful is this man's story:
His fortunes are most changed; his state
Fallen to a low slave's
Ground under bitter fate.
1155   O Oedipus, most royal one!
The great door[15] that expelled you to the light
Gave at night—ah, gave night to your glory:
As to the father, to the fathering son.
All understood too late.
1160   How could that queen whom Laïos won,
The garden that he harrowed at his height,
Be silent when that act was done?

Antistrophe 2

But all eyes fail before time's eye,
All actions come to justice there.
1165   Though never willed, though far down the deep past,
Your bed, your dread sirings,
Are brought to book at last.
Child by Laïos doomed to die,
Then doomed to lose that fortunate little death,
1170   Would God you never took breath in this air
That with my wailing lips I take to cry:

---

[14] **stranger:** the Sphinx.   [15] **door:** Iokastê's womb.

For I weep the world's outcast.
I was blind, and now I can tell why:
Asleep, for you had given ease of breath
1175   To Thebes, while the false years went by.

Exodos[16]

Enter, from the palace, Second Messenger.

Second Messenger: Elders of Thebes, most honored in this land,
    What horrors are yours to see and hear, what weight
    Of sorrow to be endured, if, true to your birth,
    You venerate the line of Labdakos!
1180   I think neither Istros nor Phasis, those great rivers,
    Could purify this place of all the evil
    It shelters now, or soon must bring to light—
    Evil not done unconsciously, but willed.

    The greatest griefs are those we cause ourselves.
1185 Choragos: Surely, friend, we have grief enough already;
    What new sorrow do you mean?
Second Messenger: The queen is dead.
Choragos: O miserable queen! But at whose hand?
Second Messenger: Her own.
    The full horror of what happened you can not know,
    For you did not see it; but I, who did, will tell you
1190   As clearly as I can how she met her death.

    When she had left us,
    In passionate silence, passing through the court,
    She ran to her apartment in the house,
    Her hair clutched by the fingers of both hands.
1195   She closed the doors behind her; then, by that bed
    Where long ago the fatal son was conceived—
    That son who should bring about his father's death—
    We heard her call upon Laïos, dead so many years,
    And heard her wail for the double fruit of her marriage,
1200   A husband by her husband, children by her child.

    Exactly how she died I do not know:
    For Oedipus burst in moaning and would not let us
    Keep vigil to the end: it was by him
    As he stormed about the room that our eyes were caught.
1205   From one to another of us he went, begging a sword,

---

[16] final scene.

Hunting the wife who was not his wife, the mother
Whose womb had carried his own children and himself.
I do not know: it was none of us aided him,
But surely one of the gods was in control!
1210   For with a dreadful cry
He hurled his weight, as though wrenched out of himself,
At the twin doors: the bolts gave, and he rushed in.
And there we saw her hanging, her body swaying
From the cruel cord she had noosed about her neck.
1215   A great sob broke from him, heartbreaking to hear,
As he loosed the rope and lowered her to the ground.

I would blot out from my mind what happened next!
For the king ripped from her gown the golden brooches
That were her ornament, and raised them, and plunged them down
1220   Straight into his own eyeballs, crying, "No more,
No more shall you look on the misery about me,
The horrors of my own doing! Too long you have known
The faces of those whom I should never have seen,
Too long been blind to those for whom I was searching!
1225   From this hour, go in darkness!" And as he spoke,
He struck at his eyes—not once, but many times;
And the blood spattered his beard,
Bursting from his ruined sockets like red hail.

So from the unhappiness of two this evil has sprung,
1230   A curse on the man and woman alike. The old
Happiness of the house of Labdakos
Was happiness enough: where is it today?
It is all wailing and ruin, disgrace, death—all
The misery of mankind that has a name—
1235   And it is wholly and for ever theirs.
Choragos: Is he in agony still? Is there no rest for him?
Second Messenger: He is calling for someone to open the doors wide
So that all the children of Kadmos may look upon
His father's murderer, his mother's—no,
I can not say it!
1240   And then he will leave Thebes,
Self-exiled, in order that the curse
Which he himself pronounced may depart from the house.
He is weak, and there is none to lead him,
So terrible is his suffering.
                             But you will see:
1245   Look, the doors are opening; in a moment
You will see a thing that would crush a heart of stone.
(The central door is opened; Oedipus, blinded, is led in.)

Choragos: Dreadful indeed for men to see.
    Never have my own eyes
    Looked on a sight so full of fear.

1250   Oedipus!
    What madness came upon you, what daemon
    Leaped on your life with heavier
    Punishment than a mortal man can bear?
    No: I can not even
1255   Look at you, poor ruined one.
    And I would speak, question, ponder,
    If I were able. No.
    You make me shudder.
Oedipus: God. God.
1260   Is there a sorrow greater?
    Where shall I find harbor in this world?
    My voice is hurled far on a dark wind.
    What has God done to me?
Choragos: Too terrible to think of, or to see.

Strophe 1

1265 Oedipus: O cloud of night,
    Never to be turned away: night coming on,
    I can not tell how: night like a shroud!
    My fair winds brought me here.
                                    O God. Again
    The pain of the spikes where I had sight,
1270   The flooding pain
    Of memory, never to be gouged out.
Choragos: This is not strange.
    You suffer it all twice over, remorse in pain,
    Pain in remorse.

Antistrophe 1

1275 Oedipus: Ah dear friend
    Are you faithful even yet, you alone?
    Are you still standing near me, will you stay here,
    Patient, to care for the blind?
                                    The blind man!
    Yet even blind I know who it is attends me,
1280   By the voice's tone—
    Though my new darkness hide the comforter.
Choragos: Oh fearful act!
    What god was it drove you to rake black
    Night across your eyes?

Strophe 2

1285 Oedipus: Apollo. Apollo. Dear
Children, the god was Apollo.
He brought my sick, sick fate upon me.
But the blinding hand was my own!
How could I bear to see
1290   When all my sight was horror everywhere?
Choragos: Everywhere; that is true.
Oedipus: And now what is left?
Images? Love? A greeting even,
Sweet to the senses? Is there anything?
1295   Ah, no, friends: lead me away.
Lead me away from Thebes.
                        Lead the great wreck
And hell of Oedipus, whom the gods hate.
Choragos: Your misery, you are not blind to that.
Would God you had never found it out!

Antistrophe 2

1300 Oedipus: Death take the man who unbound
My feet on that hillside
And delivered me from death to life! What life?
If only I had died,
This weight of monstrous doom
1305   Could not have dragged me and my darlings down.
Choragos: I would have wished the same.
Oedipus: Oh never to have come here
With my father's blood upon me! Never
To have been the man they call his mother's husband!
1310   Oh accurst! Oh child of evil,
To have entered that wretched bed—
                        the selfsame one!
More primal than sin itself, this fell to me.
Choragos: I do not know what words to offer you.
You were better dead than alive and blind.
1315 Oedipus: Do not counsel me any more. This punishment
That I have laid upon myself is just.
If I had eyes,
I do not know how I could bear the sight
Of my father, when I came to the house of Death,
1320   Or my mother: for I have sinned against them both
So vilely that I could not make my peace
By strangling my own life.
                  Or do you think my children,
Born as they were born, would be sweet to my eyes?

Ah never, never! Nor this town with its high walls,
Nor the holy images of the gods.

1325
                    For I,
Thrice miserable!—Oedipus, noblest of all the line
Of Kadmos, have condemned myself to enjoy
These things no more, by my own malediction
Expelling that man whom the gods declared

1330
To be a defilement in the house of Laïos.
After exposing the rankness of my own guilt,
How could I look men frankly in the eyes?
No, I swear it,
If I could have stifled my hearing at its source,

1335
I would have done it and made all this body
A tight cell of misery, blank to light and sound:
So I should have been safe in my dark mind
Beyond external evil.
                    Ah Kithairon!
Why did you shelter me? When I was cast upon you,

1340
Why did I not die? Then I should never
Have shown the world my execrable birth.

Ah Polybos! Corinth, city that I believed
The ancient seat of my ancestors: how fair
I seemed, your child! And all the while this evil
Was cancerous within me!

1345
                    For I am sick
In my own being, sick in my origin.

O three roads, dark ravine, woodland and way
Where three roads met: you, drinking my father's blood,
My own blood, spilled by my own hand: can you remember

1350
The unspeakable things I did there, and the things
I went on from there to do?
                            O marriage, marriage!
The act that engendered me, and again the act
Performed by the son in the same bed—
                                    Ah, the net
Of incest, mingling fathers, brothers, sons,

1355
With brides, wives, mothers: the last evil
That can be known by men: no tongue can say
How evil!
            No. For the love of God, conceal me
Somewhere far from Thebes; or kill me; or hurl me
Into the sea, away from men's eyes for ever.

1360
Come, lead me. You need not fear to touch me.
Of all men, I alone can bear this guilt. *(Enter Kreon.)*

Choragos: Kreon is here now. As to what you ask,
   He may decide the course to take. He only
   Is left to protect the city in your place.
1365 Oedipus: Alas, how can I speak to him? What right have I
   To beg his courtesy whom I have deeply wronged?
Kreon: I have not come to mock you, Oedipus,
   Or to reproach you, either.
         (To Attendants) —You, standing there:
   If you have lost all respect for man's dignity,
1370 At least respect the flame of Lord Helios:
   Do not allow this pollution to show itself
   Openly here, an affront to the earth
   And Heaven's rain and the light of day. No, take him
   Into the house as quickly as you can.
1375 For it is proper
   That only the close kindred see his grief.
Oedipus: I pray you in God's name, since your courtesy
   Ignores my dark expectation, visiting
   With mercy this man of all men most execrable:
1380 Give me what I ask—for your good, not for mine.
Kreon: And what is it that you turn to me begging for?
Oedipus: Drive me out of this country as quickly as may be
   To a place where no human voice can ever greet me.
Kreon: I should have done that before now—only,
1385 God's will had not been wholly revealed to me.
Oedipus: But his command is plain: the parricide
   Must be destroyed. I am that evil man.
Kreon: That is the sense of it, yes; but as things are,
   We had best discover clearly what is to be done.
1390 Oedipus: You would learn more about a man like me?
Kreon: You are ready now to listen to the god.
Oedipus: I will listen. But it is to you
   That I must turn for help. I beg you, hear me.

   The woman in there—
1395 Give her whatever funeral you think proper:
   She is your sister.
        —But let me go, Kreon!
   Let me purge my father's Thebes of the pollution
   Of my living here, and go out to the wild hills,
   To Kithairon, that has won such fame with me,
1400 The tomb my mother and father appointed for me,
   And let me die there, as they willed I should.
   And yet I know
   Death will not ever come to me through sickness
   Or in any natural way: I have been preserved
1405 For some unthinkable fate. But let that be.

As for my sons, you need not care for them.
They are men, they will find some way to live.
But my poor daughters, who have shared my table,
Who never before have been parted from their father—
1410 Take care of them, Kreon; do this for me.

And will you let me touch them with my hands
A last time, and let us weep together?
Be kind, my lord,
Great prince, be kind!
                    Could I but touch them,
They would be mine again, as when I had my eyes.
1415 *(Enter Antigone and Ismene, attended.)*
Ah, God!
Is it my dearest children I hear weeping?
Has Kreon pitied me and sent my daughters?
Kreon: Yes, Oedipus: I knew that they were dear to you
1420 In the old days, and know you must love them still.
Oedipus: May God bless you for this—and be a friendlier
Guardian to you than he has been to me!

Children, where are you?
Come quickly to my hands: they are your brother's—
1425 Hands that have brought your father's once clear eyes
To this way of seeing—
                    Ah dearest ones,
I had neither sight nor knowledge then, your father
By the woman who was the source of his own life!
And I weep for you—having no strength to see you—,
1430 I weep for you when I think of the bitterness
That men will visit upon you all your lives.
What homes, what festivals can you attend
Without being forced to depart again in tears?
And when you come to marriageable age,
1435 Where is the man, my daughters, who would dare
Risk the bane that lies on all my children?
Is there any evil wanting? Your father killed
His father; sowed the womb of her who bore him;
Engendered you at the fount of his own existence!
That is what they will say of you.
1440   Then, whom
Can you ever marry? There are no bridegrooms for you,
And your lives must wither away in sterile dreaming.

O Kreon, son of Menoikeus!
You are the only father my daughters have,

1445   Since we, their parents, are both of us gone for ever.
They are your own blood: you will not let them
Fall into beggary and loneliness;
You will keep them from the miseries that are mine!
Take pity on them; see, they are only children,
1450   Friendless except for you. Promise me this,
Great prince, and give me your hand in token of it.
(Kreon clasps his right hand.)
Children:
I could say much, if you could understand me,
But as it is, I have only this prayer for you:
1455   Live where you can, be as happy as you can—
Happier, please God, than God has made your father.

Kreon: Enough. You have wept enough. Now go within.

Oedipus: I must; but it is hard.

Kreon: Time eases all things.

Oedipus: You know my mind, then?

Kreon: Say what you desire.

Oedipus: Send me from Thebes!

1460 **Kreon:**   God grant that I may!

Oedipus: But since God hates me . . .

Kreon: No, he will grant your wish.

Oedipus: You promise?

Kreon: I can not speak beyond my knowledge.

Oedipus: Then lead me in.

Kreon: Come now, and leave your children.

Oedipus: No! Do not take them from me!

Kreon: Think no longer
1465   That you are in command here, but rather think
How, when you were, you served your own destruction. *(Exeunt into the house all but the Chorus; the Choragos chants directly to the audience.)*

Choragos: Men of Thebes: look upon Oedipus.

This is the king who solved the famous riddle
And towered up, most powerful of men.
1470   No mortal eyes but looked on him with envy,
Yet in the end ruin swept over him.

Let every man in mankind's frailty
Consider his last day; and let none
Presume on his good fortune until he find
1475   Life, at his death, a memory without pain.

■ EXPLORATIONS OF THE TEXT ■

1. Discuss the character of Oedipus. Why is he so impetuous? Why does he not believe Teiresias?
2. Discuss the situation in the play. Why was Oedipus left to die as an infant? Why was he not told about his origins?
3. Discuss the character of Iokastê. Why does she not see the truth?
4. What function does the chorus perform?
5. Discuss Teiresias and Kreon at length.
6. Discuss the nature of prophecy and fate in this tragedy. Does Oedipus have a tragic flaw? (See **hamartia** in the Glossary.) Does fate or character create this tragedy?
7. By the end of the play, what does Oedipus learn about himself, about the gods, about truth?
8. Why is Oedipus' tragedy both personal and political?
9. How does this drama resemble a mystery? Discuss **dramatic irony**. What other devices create suspense?
10. In what ways is it significant that Oedipus blinds himself?

■■ JOURNAL ENTRIES ■■

1. Since seeing and insight are so valuable, why do human beings resist them?
2. Find one example of **dramatic irony** in *Oedipus Rex,* and discuss its function and effectiveness.

■■■ IDEAS FOR WRITING ■■■

1. Explore images of darkness and light in *Oedipus Rex.*
2. Is Oedipus a victim or the agent of his own downfall?
3. How is *Oedipus Rex* a political play?

I Am Prepared to Die

Nelson Mandela

Born in South Africa, the son of a tribal chief, Nelson Mandela (1918–   ) is a political organizer and leader of the African National Congress. He has devoted his life to the struggle against apartheid, the government system that excluded his country's black majority from the rights of citizenship. He began his political work after earning a law degree from the University of South Africa in 1942. He urged nonviolent methods of protest such as boycotts, general strikes, and demonstrations; but when the government responded repressively to the general strike of May 1961, he reluctantly founded a guerilla movement. He was sentenced to prison in 1964 for sabotage and treason. He continued to be influential from his cell through messages to his visitors and through his writing.

His works include No Easy Walk to Freedom *(1965),* Nelson Mandela Speaks *(1970), and* The Struggle Is My Life *(1978). Both during his incarceration and since his release from prison in 1992, he has consistently been viewed as the foremost hope for a peaceful resolution to the conflict in South Africa. He won the Nobel Peace Prize in 1993, and in 1994 he became the first democratically elected President of South Africa.*

Nelson Mandela, on trial on four charges of sabotage against the government of South Africa, delivered this statement in his own defense in Pretoria Supreme Court, April 20, 1964. With Walter Sisuli, Goran Mbeki, Raymond Mhlaba, Elias Motsoaledi, Andrew Mlangeni, Ahmed Kathrada, and Denis Goldberg, he was convicted and sentenced to life imprisonment despite the eloquence of his plea.

1 **I** am the First Accused.

2 I hold a Bachelor's Degree in Arts and practised as an attorney in Johannesburg for a number of years in partnership with Oliver Tambo. I am a convicted prisoner serving five years for leaving the country without a permit and for inciting people to go on strike at the end of May 1961.

3 At the outset, I want to say that the suggestion made by the State in its opening that the struggle in South Africa is under the influence of foreigners or communists is wholly incorrect. I have done whatever I did, both as an individual and as a leader of my people, because of my experience in South Africa and my own proudly felt African background, and not because of what any outsider might have said.

4 In my youth in the Transkei I listened to the elders of my tribe telling stories of the old days. Amongst the tales they related to me were those of wars fought by our ancestors in defence of the fatherland. The names of Dingane and Bambata, Hintsa and Makana, Squngthi and Dalasile, Moshoeshoe and Sekhukhuni, were praised as the glory of the entire African nation. I hoped then that life might offer me the opportunity to serve my people and make my own humble contribution to their freedom struggle. This is what has motivated me in all that I have done in relation to the charges made against me in this case.

5 Having said this, I must deal immediately and at some length with the question of violence. Some of the things so far told to the Court are true and

some are untrue. I do not, however, deny that I planned sabotage. I did not plan it in a spirit of recklessness, nor because I have any love of violence. I planned it as a result of a calm and sober assessment of the political situation that had arisen after many years of tyranny, exploitation, and oppression of my people by the Whites.

6   I admit immediately that I was one of the persons who helped to form Umkhonto we Sizwe, and that I played a prominent role in its affairs until I was arrested in August 1962.

7   In the statement which I am about to make I shall correct certain false impressions which have been created by State witnesses. Amongst other things, I will demonstrate that certain of the acts referred to in the evidence were not and could not have been committed by Umkhonto. I will also deal with the relationship between the African National Congress and Umkhonto, and with the part which I personally have played in the affairs of both organizations. I shall deal also with the part played by the Communist Party. In order to explain these matters properly, I will have to explain what Umkhonto set out to achieve; what methods it prescribed for the achievement of these objects, and why these methods were chosen. I will also have to explain how I became involved in the activities of these organizations.

8   I deny that Umkhonto was responsible for a number of acts which clearly fell outside the policy of the organization, and which have been charged in the indictment against us. I do not know what justification there was for these acts, but to demonstrate that they could not have been authorized by Umkhonto, I want to refer briefly to the roots and policy of the organization.

9   I have already mentioned that I was one of the persons who helped to form Umkhonto. I, and the others who started the organization, did so for two reasons. Firstly, we believed that as a result of Government policy, violence by the African people had become inevitable, and that unless responsible leadership was given to canalize and control the feelings of our people, there would be outbreaks of terrorism which would produce an intensity of bitterness and hostility between the various races of this country which is not produced even by war. Secondly, we felt that without violence there would be no way open to the African people to succeed in their struggle against the principle of white supremacy. All lawful modes of expressing opposition to this principle had been closed by legislation, and we were placed in a position in which we had either to accept a permanent state of inferiority, or to defy the Government. We chose to defy the law. We first broke the law in a way which avoided any recourse to violence; when this form was legislated against, and then the Government resorted to a show of force to crush opposition to its policies, only then did we decide to answer violence with violence.

10   But the violence which we chose to adopt was not terrorism. We who formed Umkhonto were all members of the African National Congress, and had behind us the ANC tradition of non-violence and negotiation as a means of solving political disputes. We believe that South Africa belongs to all the people who live in it, and not to one group, be it black or white. We did not want an interracial war, and tried to avoid it to the last minute. If the Court

is in doubt about this, it will be seen that the whole history of our organization bears out what I have said, and what I will subsequently say, when I describe the tactics which Umkhonto decided to adopt. I want, therefore, to say something about the African National Congress.

11   The African National Congress was formed in 1912 to defend the rights of the African people which had been seriously curtailed by the South Africa Act, and which were then being threatened by the Native Land Act. For thirty-seven years—that is until 1949—it adhered strictly to a constitutional struggle. It put forward demands and resolutions; it sent delegations to the Government in the belief that African grievances could be settled through peaceful discussion and that Africans could advance gradually to full political rights. But White Governments remained unmoved, and the rights of Africans became less instead of becoming greater. In the words of my leader, Chief Lutuli, who became President of the ANC in 1952, and who was later awarded the Nobel Peace Prize:

> *Who will deny that thirty years of my life have been spent knocking in vain, patiently, moderately, and modestly at a closed and barred door? What have been the fruits of moderation? The past thirty years have seen the greatest number of laws restricting our rights and progress, until today we have reached a stage where we have almost no rights at all.*

12   Even after 1949, the ANC remained determined to avoid violence. At this time, however, there was a change from the strictly constitutional means of protest which had been employed in the past. The change was embodied in a decision which was taken to protest against apartheid legislation by peaceful, but unlawful, demonstrations against certain laws. Pursuant to this policy the ANC launched the Defiance Campaign, in which I was placed in charge of volunteers. This campaign was based on the principles of passive resistance. More than 8,500 people defied apartheid laws and went to jail. Yet there was not a single instance of violence in the course of this campaign on the part of any defier. I and nineteen colleagues were convicted for the role which we played in organizing the campaign, but our sentences were suspended mainly because the Judge found that discipline and non-violence had been stressed throughout. This was the time when the volunteer section of the ANC was established, and when the word 'Amadelakufa'[1] was first used: this was the time when the volunteers were asked to take a pledge to uphold certain principles. Evidence dealing with volunteers and their pledges has been introduced into this case, but completely out of context. The volunteers were not, and are not, the soldiers of a black army pledged to fight a civil war against the whites. They were, and are, dedicated workers who are prepared to lead campaigns initiated by the ANC to distribute leaflets, to organize strikes, or do whatever the particular campaign required. They are called volunteers

---

[1] People who will make sacrifices.

because they volunteer to face the penalties of imprisonment and whipping which are now prescribed by the legislature for such acts.

13   During the Defiance Campaign, the Public Safety Act and the Criminal Law Amendment Act were passed. These Statutes provided harsher penalties for offences committed by way of protests against laws. Despite this, the protests continued and the ANC adhered to its policy of non-violence. In 1956, 156 leading members of the Congress Alliance, including myself, were arrested on a charge of high treason and charges under the Suppression of Communism Act. The non-violent policy of the ANC was put in issue by the State, but when the Court gave judgement some five years later, it found that the ANC did not have a policy of violence. We were acquitted on all counts, which included a count that the ANC sought to set up a communist state in place of the existing regime. The Government has always sought to label all its opponents as communists. This allegation has been repeated in the present case, but as I will show, the ANC is not, and never has been, a communist organization.

14   In 1960 there was the shooting at Sharpeville,[2] which resulted in the proclamation of a state of emergency and the declaration of the ANC as an unlawful organization. My colleagues and I, after careful consideration, decided that we would not obey this decree. The African people were not part of the Government and did not make the laws by which they were governed. We believed in the words of the Universal Declaration of Human Rights, that 'the will of the people shall be the basis of authority of the Government', and for us to accept the banning was equivalent to accepting the silencing of the Africans for all time. The ANC refused to dissolve, but instead went underground. We believed it was our duty to preserve this organization which had been built up with almost fifty years of unremitting toil. I have no doubt that no self-respecting White political organization would disband itself if declared illegal by a government in which it had no say.

15   In 1960 the Government held a referendum which led to the establishment of the Republic. Africans, who constituted approximately 70 per cent of the population of South Africa, were not entitled to vote, and were not even consulted about the proposed constitutional change. All of us were apprehensive of our future under the proposed White Republic, and a resolution was taken to hold an All-In African Conference to call for a National Convention, and to organize mass demonstrations on the eve of the unwanted Republic, if the Government failed to call the Convention. The conference was attended by Africans of various political persuasions. I was the Secretary of the conference and undertook to be responsible for organizing the national stay-at-home which was subsequently called to coincide with the declaration of the Republic. As all strikes by Africans are illegal, the person organizing such a strike must avoid arrest. I was chosen to be this person, and consequently I had to leave my home and family and my practice and go into hiding to avoid arrest.

---

[2] Site of conflict between South African police and demonstraters who were protesting South Africa's pass laws in which sixty-nine people were killed and 178 were wounded.

16   The stay-at-home, in accordance with ANC policy, was to be a peaceful demonstration. Careful instructions were given to organizers and members to avoid any recourse to violence. The Government's answer was to introduce new and harsher laws, to mobilize its armed forces, and to send Saracens[3], armed vehicles, and soldiers into the townships in a massive show of force designed to intimidate the people. This was an indication that the Government had decided to rule by force alone, and this decision was a milestone on the road to Umkhonto.

17   Some of this may appear irrelevant to this trial. In fact, I believe none of it is irrelevant because it will, I hope, enable the Court to appreciate the attitude eventually adopted by the various persons and bodies concerned in the National Liberation Movement. When I went to jail in 1962, the dominant idea was that loss of life should be avoided. I now know that this was still so in 1963.

18   I must return to June 1961. What were we, the leaders of our people, to do? Were we to give in to the show of force and the implied threat against future action, or were we to fight it and, if so, how?

19   We had no doubt that we had to continue the fight. Anything else would have been abject surrender. Our problem was not whether to fight, but was how to continue the fight. We of the ANC had always stood for a non-racial democracy, and we shrank from any action which might drive the races further apart than they already were. But the hard facts were that fifty years of non-violence had brought the African people nothing but more and more repressive legislation, and fewer and fewer rights. It may not be easy for this Court to understand, but it is a fact that for a long time the people had been talking of violence—of the day when they would fight the White man and win back their country—and we, the leaders of the ANC, had nevertheless always prevailed upon them to avoid violence and to pursue peaceful methods. When some of us discussed this in May and June of 1961, it could not be denied that our policy to achieve a non-racial State by non-violence had achieved nothing, and that our followers were beginning to lose confidence in this policy and were developing disturbing ideas of terrorism.

20   It must not be forgotten that by this time violence had, in fact, become a feature of the South African political scene. There had been violence in 1957 when the women of Zeerust were ordered to carry passes; there was violence in 1958 with the enforcement of cattle culling in Sekhukhuniland; there was violence in 1959 when the people of Cato Manor protested against pass raids; there was violence in 1960 when the Government attempted to impose Bantu Authorities in Pondoland. Thirty-nine Africans died in these disturbances. In 1961 there had been riots in Warmbaths, and all this time the Transkei had been a seething mass of unrest. Each disturbance pointed clearly to the inevitable growth among Africans of the belief that violence was the only way out—it showed that a Government which uses force to maintain its rule teaches the oppressed to use force to oppose it. Already small groups had

---

[3] British-made military troop carriers.

arisen in the urban areas and were spontaneously making plans for violent forms of political struggle. There now arose a danger that these groups would adopt terrorism against Africans, as well as Whites, if not properly directed. Particularly disturbing was the type of violence engendered in places such as Zeerust, Sekhukhuniland, and Pondoland amonsgt Africans. It was increasingly taking the form, not of struggle against the Government—though this is what prompted it—but of civil strife amongst themselves, conducted in such a way that it could not hope to achieve anything other than a loss of life and bitterness.

21   At the beginning of June 1961, after a long and anxious assessment of the South African situation, I, and some colleagues, came to the conclusion that as violence in this country was inevitable, it would be unrealistic and wrong for African leaders to continue preaching peace and non-violence at a time when the Government met our peaceful demands with force.

22   This conclusion was not easily arrived at. It was only when all else had failed, when all channels of peaceful protest had been barred to us, that the decision was made to embark on violent forms of political struggle, and to form Umkhonto we Sizwe. We did so not because we desired such a course, but solely because the Government had left us with no other choice. In the Manifesto of Umkhonto published on 16 December 1961, which is Exhibit AD, we said:

> *The time comes in the life of any nation when there remain only two choices—submit or fight. That time has now come to South Africa. We shall not submit and we have no choice but to hit back by all means in our power in defence of our people, our future, and our freedom.*

23   This was our feeling in June of 1961 when we decided to press for a change in the policy of the National Liberation Movement. I can only say that I felt morally obliged to do what I did.

24   We who had taken this decision started to consult leaders of various organizations, including the ANC. I will not say whom we spoke to, or what they said, but I wish to deal with the role of the African National Congress in this phase of the struggle, and with the policy and objectives of Umkhonto we Sizwe.

25   As far as the ANC was concerned, it formed a clear view which can be summarized as follows:

   a. It was a mass political organization with a political function to fulfil. Its members had joined on the express policy of non-violence.
   b. Because of all this, it could not and would not undertake violence. This must be stressed. One cannot turn such a body into the small, closely knit organization required for sabotage. Nor would this be politically correct, because it would result in members ceasing to carry out this essential activity: political propaganda and

organization. Nor was it permissible to change the whole nature of the organization.

c.   On the other hand, in view of this situation I have described, the ANC was prepared to depart from its fifty-year-old policy of non-violence to this extent that it would no longer disapprove of properly controlled violence. Hence members who undertook such activity would not be subject to disciplinary action by the ANC.

26   I say 'properly controlled violence' because I made it clear that if I formed the organization I would at all times subject it to the political guidance of the ANC and would not undertake any different form of activity from that contemplated without the consent of the ANC. And I shall now tell the Court how that form of violence came to be determined.

27   As a result of this decision, Umkhonto was formed in November 1961. When we took this decision, and subsequently formulated our plans, the ANC heritage of non-violence and racial harmony was very much with us. We felt that the country was drifting towards a civil war in which Blacks and Whites would fight each other. We viewed the situation with alarm. Civil war could mean the destruction of what the ANC stood for; with civil war, racial peace would be more difficult than ever to achieve. We already have examples in South African history of the results of war. It has taken more than fifty years for the scars of the South African War to disappear. How much longer would it take to eradicate the scars of inter-racial civil war, which could not be fought without a great loss of life on both sides?

28   The avoidance of civil war had dominated our thinking for many years, but when we decided to adopt violence as part of our policy, we realized that we might one day have to face the prospect of such a war. This had to be taken into account in formulating our plans. We required a plan which was flexible and which permitted us to act in accordance with the needs of the times; above all, the plan had to be one which recognized civil war as the last resort, and left the decision on this question to the future. We did not want to be committed to civil war, but we wanted to be ready if it became inevitable.

29   Four forms of violence were possible. There is sabotage, there is guerrilla warfare, there is terrorism, and there is open revolution. We chose to adopt the first method and to exhaust it before taking any other decision.

30   In the light of our political background the choice was a logical one. Sabotage did not involve loss of life, and it offered the best hope for future race relations. Bitterness would be kept to a minimum and, if the policy bore fruit, democratic government could become a reality. This is what we felt at the time, and this is what we said in our Manifesto (Exhibit AD):

We of Umkhonto We Sizwe have always sought to achieve liberation without bloodshed and civil clash. We hope, even at this late hour, that our first actions will awaken everyone to a realization of the disastrous situation to which the Nationalist policy is leading. We hope that we will bring the Government and its supporters to their senses before it is too late, so that both the Government and its policies can be changed before matters reach the desperate stage of civil war.

31   The initial plan was based on a careful analysis of the political and economic situation of our country. We believed that South Africa depended to a large extent on foreign capital and foreign trade. We felt that planned destruction of power plants, and interference with rail and telephone communications, would tend to scare away capital from the country, make it more difficult for goods from the industrial areas to reach the seaports on schedule, and would in the long run be a heavy drain on the economic life of the country, thus compelling the voters of the country to reconsider their position.

32   Attacks on the economic life lines of the country were to be linked with sabotage on Government buildings and other symbols of apartheid. These attacks would serve as a source of inspiration to our people. In addition, they would provide an outlet for those people who were urging the adoption of violent methods and would enable us to give concrete proof to our followers that we had adopted a stronger line and were fighting back against Government violence.

33   In addition, if mass action were successfully organized, and mass reprisals taken, we felt that sympathy for our cause would be roused in other countries, and that greater pressure would be brought to bear on the South African Government.

34   This then was the plan. Umkhonto was to perform sabotage, and strict instructions were given to its members right from the start, that on no account were they to injure or kill people in planning or carrying out operations. These instructions have been referred to in the evidence of 'Mr. X' and 'Mr. Z'.[4]

35   The affairs of the Umkhonto were controlled and directed by a National High Command, which had powers of co-option and which could, and did, appoint Regional Commands. The High Command was the body which determined tactics and targets and was in charge of training and finance. Under the High Command there were Regional Commands which were responsible for the direction of the local sabotage groups. Within the framework of the policy laid down by the National High Command, the Regional Commands had authority to select the targets to be attacked. They had no authority to go beyond the prescribed framework and thus had no authority to embark upon acts which endangered life, or which did not fit into the overall plan of sabotage. For instance, Umkhonto members were forbidden ever to go armed into operation. Incidentally, the terms High Command and Regional Command were an importation from the Jewish national underground organization Irgun Zvai Leumi, which operated in Israel between 1944 and 1948.

---

[4] Witnesses for the prosecution whose names were withheld for their protection.

36   Umkhonto had its first operation on 16 December 1961, when Government buildings in Johannesburg, Port Elizabeth and Durban were attacked. The selection of targets is proof of the policy to which I have referred. Had we intended to attack life we would have selected targets where people congregated and not empty buildings and power stations. The sabotage which was committed before 16 December 1961 was the work of isolated groups and had no connection whatever with Umkhonto. In fact, some of these and a number of later acts were claimed by other organizations.

37   The Manifesto of Umkhonto was issued on the day that operations commenced. The response to our actions and Manifesto among the white population was characteristically violent. The Government threatened to take strong action, and called upon its supporters to stand firm and to ignore the demands of the Africans. The Whites failed to respond by suggesting change; they responded to our call by suggesting the laager.

38   In contrast, the response of the Africans was one of encouragement. Suddenly there was hope again. Things were happening. People in the townships became eager for political news. A great deal of enthusiasm was generated by the initial successes, and people began to speculate on how soon freedom would be obtained.

39   But we in Umkhonto weighed up the white response with anxiety. The lines were being drawn. The whites and blacks were moving into separate camps, and the prospects of avoiding a civil war were made less. The white newspapers carried reports that sabotage would be punished by death. If this was so, how could we continue to keep Africans away from terrorism?

40   Already scores of Africans had died as a result of racial friction. In 1920 when the famous leader, Masabala, was held in Port Elizabeth jail, twenty-four of a group of Africans who had gathered to demand his release were killed by the police and white civilians. In 1921, more than one hundred Africans died in the Bulhoek affair. In 1924 over two hundred Africans were killed when the Administrator of South-West Africa led a force against a group which had rebelled against the imposition of dog tax. On 1 May 1950, eighteen Africans died as a result of police shootings during the strike. On 21 March 1960, sixty-nine unarmed Africans died at Sharpeville.

41   How many more Sharpevilles would there be in the history of our country? And how many more Sharpevilles could the country stand without violence and terror becoming the order of the day? And what would happen to our people when that stage was reached? In the long run we felt certain we must succeed, but at what cost to ourselves and the rest of the country? And if this happened, how could black and white ever live together again in peace and harmony? These were the problems that faced us, and these were our decisions.

42   Experience convinced us that rebellion would offer the Government limitless opportunities for the indiscriminate slaughter of our people. But it was precisely because the soil of South Africa is already drenched with

the blood of innocent Africans that we felt it our duty to make preparations as a long-term undertaking to use force in order to defend ourselves against force. If war were inevitable, we wanted the fight to be conducted on terms most favourable to our people. The fight which held out prospects best for us and the least risk of life to both sides was guerrilla warfare. We decided, therefore, in our preparations for the future, to make provision for the possibility of guerrilla warfare.

43   All whites undergo compulsory military training, but no such training was given to Africans. It was in our view essential to build up a nucleus of trained men who would be able to provide the leadership which would be required if guerrilla warfare started. We had to prepare for such a situation before it became too late to make proper preparations. It was also necessary to build up a nucleus of men trained in civil administration and other professions, so that Africans would be equipped to participate in the government of this country as soon as they were allowed to do so.

44   At this stage it was decided that I should attend the Conference of the Pan-African Freedom Movement for Central, East, and Southern Africa, which was to be held early in 1962 in Addis Ababa, and, because of our need for preparation, it was also decided that, after the conference, I would undertake a tour of the African States with a view to obtaining facilities for the training of soldiers, and that I would also solicit scholarships for the higher education of matriculated Africans. Training in both fields would be necessary, even if changes came about by peaceful means. Administrators would be necessary who would be willing and able to administer a non-racial State and so would men be necessary to control the army and police force of such a State.

45   It was on this note that I left South Africa to proceed to Addis Ababa as a delegate of the ANC. My tour was a success. Wherever I went I met sympathy for our cause and promises of help. All Africa was united against the stand of White South Africa, and even in London I was received with great sympathy by political leaders, such as Mr. Gaitskell and Mr. Grimond. In Africa I was promised support by such men as Julius Nyerere, now President of Tanganyika; Mr. Kawawa, then Prime Minister of Tanganyika; Emperor Haile Selassie of Ethiopia; General Abboud, President of the Sudan; Habib Bourguiba, President of Tunisia; Ben Bella, now President of Algeria; Modibo Keita, President of Mali; Leopold Senghor, President of Senegal; Sékou Touré, President of Guinea; President Tubman of Liberia; and Milton Obote, Prime Minister of Uganda. It was Ben Bella who invited me to visit Oujda, the Headquarters of the Algerian Army of National Liberation, the visit which is described in my diary, one of the Exhibits.

46   I started to make a study of the art of war and revolution and, whilst abroad, underwent a course in military training. If there was to be guerrilla warfare, I wanted to be able to stand and fight with my people and to share the hazards of war with them. Notes of lectures which I received in Algeria are contained in Exhibit 16, produced in evidence.

Summaries of books on guerrilla warfare and military strategy have also been produced. I have already admitted that these documents are in my writing, and I acknowledge that I made these studies to equip myself for the role which I might have to play if the struggle drifted into guerrilla warfare. I approach this question as every African Nationalist should do. I was completely objective. The Court will see that I attempted to examine all types of authority on the subject—from the East and from the West, going back to the classic work of Clausewitz,[5] and covering such a variety as Mao Tse Tung[6] and Che Guevara[7] on the one hand, and the writings on the Anglo-Boer War on the other. Of course, these notes are merely summaries of the books I read and do not contain my personal views.

47   I also made arrangements for our recruits to undergo military training. But here it was impossible to organize any scheme without the co-operation of the ANC offices in Africa. I consequently obtained the permission of the ANC in South Africa to do this. To this extent then there was a departure from the original decision of the ANC, but it applied outside South Africa only. The first batch of recruits actually arrived in Tanganyika when I was passing through that country on my way back to South Africa.

48   I returned to South Africa and reported to my colleagues on the results of my trip. On my return I found that there had been little alteration in the political scene save that the threat of a death penalty for sabotage had now become a fact. The attitude of my colleagues in Umkhonto was much the same as it had been before I left. They were feeling their way cautiously and felt that it would be a long time before the possibilities of sabotage were exhausted. In fact, the view was expressed by some that the training of recruits was premature. This is recorded by me in the document which is Exhibit R.14. After a full discussion, however, it was decided to go ahead with the plans for military training because of the fact that it would take many years to build up a sufficient nucleus of trained soldiers to start a guerrilla campaign, and whatever happened the training would be of value.

49   I wish to turn now to certain general allegations made in this case by the State. . . .

50   [One] of the allegations made by the State is that the aims and objects of the ANC and the Communist Party are the same. I wish to deal with this and with my own political position, because I must assume that the State may try to argue from certain Exhibits that I tried to introduce Marxism into the ANC. The allegation as to the ANC is false. This is an old allegation which was disproved at the Treason Trial and which has again reared its head. But since the allegation has been made again, I shall deal with it as well as with the relationship between the ANC and the Communist Party and Umkhonto and that party.

51   The ideological creed of the ANC is, and always has been, the creed of African Nationalism. It is not the concept of African Nationalism expressed

---

[5] Prussian general and military strategist.
[6] Leader of the Chinese Communist Revolution (1893–1976).
[7] Latin American revolutionary leader (1928–1967).

in the cry, 'Drive the White man into the sea'. The African Nationalism for which the ANC stands is the concept of freedom and fulfilment for the African people in their own land. The most important political document ever adopted by the ANC is the 'Freedom Charter'. It is by no means a blueprint for a socialist state. It calls for redistribution, but not nationalization, of land; it provides for nationalization of mines, banks, and monopoly industry, because big monopolies are owned by one race only, and without such nationalization racial domination would be perpetuated despite the spread of political power. It would be a hollow gesture to repeal the Gold Law prohibitions against Africans when all gold mines are owned by European companies. In this respect the ANC's policy corresponds with the old policy of the present Nationalist Party which, for many years, had as part of its programme the nationalization of the gold mines which, at that time, were controlled by foreign capital. Under the Freedom Charter, nationalization would take place in an economy based on private enterprise. The realization of the Freedom Charter would open up fresh fields for a prosperous African population of all classes, including the middle class. The ANC has never at any period of its history advocated a revolutionary change in the economic structure of the country, nor has it, to the best of my recollection, ever condemned capitalist society.

52   As far as the Communist Party is concerned, and if I understand its policy correctly, it stands for the establishment of a State based on the principles of Marxism. Although it is prepared to work for the Freedom Charter, as a short-term solution to the problems created by white supremacy, it regards the Freedom Charter as the beginning, and not the end, of its programme.

53   The ANC, unlike the Communist Party, admitted Africans only as members. Its chief goal was, and is, for the African people to win unity and full political rights. The Communist Party's main aim, on the other hand, was to remove the capitalists and to replace them with a working-class government. The Communist Party sought to emphasize class distinctions whilst the ANC seeks to harmonize them. This is a vital distinction.

54   It is true that there has often been close co-operation between the ANC and the Communist Party. But co-operation is merely proof of a common goal—in this case the removal of white supremacy—and is not proof of a complete community of interests.

55   The history of the world is full of similar examples. Perhaps the most striking illustration is to be found in the co-operation between Great Britain, the United States of America, and the Soviet Union in the fight against Hitler. Nobody but Hitler would have dared to suggest that such co-operation turned Churchill or Roosevelt into communists or communist tools, or that Britain and America were working to bring about a communist world.

56   Another instance of such co-operation is to be found precisely in Umkhonto. Shortly after Umkhonto was constituted, I was informed by some of its members that the Communist Party would support Umkhonto, and this then occurred. At a later stage the support was made openly.

57   I believe that communists have always played an active role in the fight by colonial countries for their freedom, because the short-term objects of communism would always correspond with the long-term objects of freedom movements. Thus communists have played an important role in the freedom struggles fought in countries such as Malaya, Algeria, and Indonesia, yet none of these States today are communist countries. Similarly in the underground resistance movements which sprung up in Europe during the last World War, communists played an important role. Even General Chiang Kai-Shek,[8] today one of the bitterest enemies of communism, fought together with the communists against the ruling class in the struggle which led to his assumption of power in China in the 1930s.

58   This pattern of co-operation between communists and non-communists has been repeated in the National Liberation Movement of South Africa. Prior to the banning of the Communist Party, joint campaigns involving the Communist Party and the Congress movements were accepted practice. African communists could, and did, become members of the ANC, and some served on the National, Provincial, and local committees. Amongst those who served on the National Executive are Albert Nzula, a former Secretary of the Communist Party; Moses Kotane, another former Secretary; and J. B. Marks, a former member of the Central Committee.

59   I joined the ANC in 1944, and in my younger days I held the view that the policy of admitting communists to the ANC, and the close co-operation which existed at times on specific issues between the ANC and the Communist Party, would lead to a watering down of the concept of African Nationalism. At that stage I was a member of the African National Congress Youth League, and was one of a group which moved for the expulsion of communists from the ANC. This proposal was heavily defeated. Amongst those who voted against the proposal were some of the most conservative sections of African political opinion. They defended the policy on the ground that from its inception the ANC was formed and built up, not as a political party with one school of political thought, but as a Parliament of the African people, accommodating people of various political convictions, all united by the common goal of national liberation. I was eventually won over to this point of view and I have upheld it ever since.

60   It is perhaps difficult for white South Africans, with an ingrained prejudice against communism, to understand why experienced African politicians so readily accept communists as their friends. But to us the reason is obvious. Theoretical differences amongst those fighting against oppression is a luxury we cannot afford at this stage. What is more, for many decades communists were the only political group in South Africa who were prepared to treat Africans as human beings and

---

[8] Chinese general and President of the Chinese Republic of Taiwan (1887–1975).

their equals; who were prepared to eat with us; talk with us, live with us, and work with us. They were the only political group which was prepared to work with the Africans for the attainment of political rights and a stake in society. Because of this, there are many Africans who, today, tend to equate freedom with communism. They are supported in this belief by a legislature which brands all exponents of democratic government and African freedom as communists and bans many of them (who are not communists) under the Suppression of Communism Act. Although I have never been a member of the Communist Party, I myself have been named under that pernicious Act because of the role I played in the Defiance Campaign. I have also been banned and imprisoned under that Act.

61   It is not only in internal politics that we count communists as amongst those who support our cause. In the international field, communist countries have always come to our aid. In the United Nations and other Councils of the world the communist *bloc* has supported the Afro-Asian struggle against colonialism and often seems to be more sympathetic to our plight than some of the Western powers. Although there is a universal condemnation of apartheid, the communist *bloc* speaks out against it with a louder voice than most of the white world. In these circumstances, it would take a brash young politician, such as I was in 1949, to proclaim that the Communists are our enemies.

62   I turn now to my own position. I have denied that I am a communist, and I think that in the circumstances I am obliged to state exactly what my political beliefs are.

63   I have always regarded myself, in the first place, as an African patriot. After all, I was born in Umtata, forty-six years ago. My guardian was my cousin, who was the acting paramount chief of Tembuland, and I am related both to the present paramount chief of Tembuland, Sabata Dalindyebo, and to Kaizer Matanzima, the Chief Minister of the Transkei.

64   Today I am attracted by the idea of a classless society, an attraction which springs in part from Marxist reading and, in part, from my admiration of the structure and organization of early African societies in this country. The land, then the main means of production, belonged to the tribe. There were no rich or poor and there was no exploitation.

65   It is true, as I have already stated, that I have been influenced by Marxist thought. But this is also true of many of the leaders of the new independent States. Such widely different persons as Gandhi, Nehru, Nkrumah, and Nasser all acknowledge this fact. We all accept the need for some form of socialism to enable our people to catch up with the advanced countries of this world and to overcome their legacy of extreme poverty. But this does not mean we are Marxists.

66   Indeed, for my own part, I believe that it is open to debate whether the Communist Party has any specific role to play at this particular stage of our political struggle. The basic task at the present moment is the removal of race discrimination and the attainment of democratic rights on the basis of the Freedom Charter. In so far as that Party furthers this task, I

welcome its assistance. I realize that it is one of the means by which people of all races can be drawn into our struggle.

67 From my reading of Marxist literature and from conversations with Marxists, I have gained the impression that communists regard the parliamentary system of the West as undemocratic and reactionary. But, on the contrary, I am an admirer of such a system.

68 The Magna Charta, the Petition of Rights, and the Bill of Rights are documents which are held in veneration by democrats throughout the world.

69 I have great respect for British political institutions, and for the country's system of justice. I regard the British Parliament as the most democratic institution in the world, and the independence and impartiality of its judiciary never fail to arouse my admiration.

70 The American Congress, that country's doctrine of separation of powers, as well as the independence of its judiciary, arouses in me similar sentiments.

71 I have been influenced in my thinking by both West and East. All this has led me to feel that in my search for a political formula, I should be absolutely impartial and objective. I should tie myself to no particular system of society other than of socialism. I must leave myself free to borrow the best from the West and from the East. . . .

72 There are certain Exhibits which suggest that we received financial support from abroad, and I wish to deal with this question.

73 Our political struggle has always been financed from internal sources—from funds raised by our own people and by our own supporters. Whenever we had a special campaign or an important political case—for example, the Treason Trial—we received financial assistance from sympathetic individuals and organizations in the Western countries. We had never felt it necessary to go beyond these sources.

74 But when in 1961 the Umkhonto was formed, and a new phase of struggle introduced, we realized that these events would make a heavy call on our slender resources, and that the scale of our activities would be hampered by the lack of funds. One of my instructions, as I went abroad in January 1962, was to raise funds from the African states.

75 I must add that, whilst abroad, I had discussions with leaders of political movements in Africa and discovered that almost every single one of them, in areas which had still not attained independence, had received all forms of assistance from the socialist countries, as well as from the West, including that of financial support. I also discovered that some well-known African states, all of them non-communists, and even anti-communists, had received similar assistance.

76 On my return to the Republic, I made a strong recommendation to the ANC that we should not confine ourselves to Africa and the Western countries, but that we should also send a mission to the socialist countries to raise the funds which we so urgently needed.

77 I have been told that after I was convicted such a mission was sent, but I am not prepared to name any countries to which it went, nor am I

at liberty to disclose the names of the organizations and countries which gave us support or promised to do so.

78 As I understand the State case, and in particular the evidence of 'Mr. X', the suggestion is that Umkhonto was the inspiration of the Communist Party which sought by playing upon imaginary grievances to enrol the African people into an army which ostensibly was to fight for African freedom, but in reality was fighting for a communist state. Nothing could be further from the truth. In fact the suggestion is preposterous. Umkhonto was formed by Africans to further their struggle for freedom in their own land. Communists and others supported the movement, and we only wish that more sections of the community would join us.

79 Our fight is against real, and not imaginary, hardships or, to use the language of the State Prosecutor, 'so-called hardships'. Basically, we fight against two features which are the hallmarks of African life in South Africa and which are entrenched by legislation which we seek to have repealed. These features are poverty and lack of human dignity, and we do not need communists or so-called 'agitators' to teach us about these things.

80 South Africa is the richest country in Africa, and could be one of the richest countries in the world. But it is a land of extremes and remarkable contrasts. The whites enjoy what may well be the highest standard of living in the world, whilst Africans live in poverty and misery. Forty per cent of the Africans live in hopelessly overcrowded and, in some cases, drought-stricken Reserves, where soil erosion and the over-working of the soil makes it impossible for them to live properly off the land. Thirty per cent are labourers, labour tenants, and squatters on white farms and work and live under conditions similar to those of the serfs of the Middle Ages. The other 30 per cent live in towns where they have developed economic and social habits which bring them closer in many respects to white standards. Yet most Africans, even in this group, are impoverished by low incomes and high cost of living.

81 The highest-paid and the most prosperous section of urban African life is in Johannesburg. Yet their actual position is desperate. The latest figures were given on 25 March 1964 by Mr. Carr, Manager of the Johannesburg Non-European Affairs Department. The poverty datum line for the average African family in Johannesburg (according to Mr. Carr's department) is R42.84 per month. He showed that the average monthly wage is R32.24 and that 46 per cent of all African families in Johannesburg do not earn enough to keep them going.

82 Poverty goes hand in hand with malnutrition and disease. The incidence of malnutrition and deficiency diseases is very high amongst Africans. Tuberculosis, pellagra, kwashiorkor, gastro-enteritis, and scurvy bring death and destruction of health. The incidence of infant mortality is one of the highest in the world. According to the Medical Officer of Health for Pretoria, tuberculosis kills forty people a day (almost all Africans), and in 1961 there were 58,491 new cases reported. These diseases not only destroy the vital organs of the body, but they result in retarded mental conditions and lack of initiative, and reduce

powers of concentration. The secondary results of such conditions affect the whole community and the standard of work performed by African labourers.

83   The complaint of Africans, however, is not only that they are poor and the whites are rich, but that the laws which are made by the whites are designed to preserve this situation. There are two ways to break out of poverty. The first is by formal education, and the second is by the worker acquiring a greater skill at his work and thus higher wages. As far as Africans are concerned, both these avenues of advancement are deliberately curtailed by legislation.

84   The present Government has always sought to hamper Africans in their search for education. One of their early acts, after coming into power, was to stop subsidies for African school feeding. Many African children who attended schools depended on this supplement to their diet. This was a cruel act.

85   There is compulsory education for all white children at virtually no cost to their parents, be they rich or poor. Similar facilities are not provided for the African children, though there are some who receive such assistance. African children, however, generally have to pay more for their schooling than whites. According to figures quoted by the South African Institute of Race Relations in its 1963 journal, approximately 40 per cent of African children in the age group between seven to fourteen do not attend school. For those who do attend school, the standards are vastly different from those afforded to white children. In 1960–61 the *per capita* Government spending on African students at State-aided schools was estimated at R12.46. In the same years, the *per capita* spending on white children in the Cape Province (which are the only figures available to me) was R144.57. Although there are no figures available to me, it can be stated, without doubt, that the white children on whom R144.57 per head was being spent all came from wealthier homes than African children on whom R12.46 per head was being spent.

86   The quality of education is also different. According to the Bantu Educational Journal, only 5,660 African children in the whole of South Africa passed their Junior Certificate in 1962, and in that year only 362 passed matric.[9] This is presumably consistent with the policy of Bantu education about which the present Prime Minister said, during the debate on the Bantu Education Bill in 1953:

> *When I have control of Native education I will reform it so that Natives will be taught from childhood to realize that equality with Europeans is not for them . . . . People who believe in equality are not desirable teachers for Natives. When my Department controls Native education it will know for what class of higher education a*

---

[9] Junior Certificate examination taken by white South Africans when they are fifteen; matriculation occurs two years later.

Native is fitted, and whether he will have a chance in life to use his knowledge.

87   The other main obstacle to the economic advancement of the African is the industrial colour-bar under which all the better jobs of industry are reserved for Whites only. Moreover, Africans who do obtain employment in the unskilled and semi-skilled occupations which are open to them are not allowed to form trade unions which have recognition under the Industrial Conciliation Act. This means that strikes of African workers are illegal, and that they are denied the right of collective bargaining which is permitted to the better-paid White workers. The discrimination in the policy of successive South African Governments towards African workers is demonstrated by the so-called 'civilized labour policy' under which sheltered, unskilled Government jobs are found for those white workers who cannot make the grade in industry, at wages which far exceed the earnings of the average African employee in industry.

88   The Government often answers its critics by saying that Africans in South Africa are economically better off than the inhabitants of the other countries in Africa. I do not know whether this statement is true and doubt whether any comparison can be made without having regard to the cost-of-living index in such countries. But even if it is true, as far as the African people are concerned it is irrelevant. Our complaint is not that we are poor by comparison with people in other countries, but that we are poor by comparison with the white people in our own country, and that we are prevented by legislation from altering this imbalance.

89   The lack of human dignity experienced by Africans is the direct result of the policy of white supremacy. White supremacy implies black inferiority. Legislation designed to preserve white supremacy entrenches this notion. Menial tasks in South Africa are invariably performed by Africans. When anything has to be carried or cleaned the white man will look around for an African to do it for him, whether the African is employed by him or not. Because of this sort of attitude, whites tend to regard Africans as a separate breed. They do not look upon them as people with families of their own; they do not realize that they have emotions—that they fall in love like white people do; that they want to be with their wives and children like white people want to be with theirs; that they want to earn enough money to support their families properly, to feed and clothe them and send them to school. And what 'house-boy' or 'garden-boy' or labourer can ever hope to do this?

90   Pass laws, which to the Africans are among the most hated bits of legislation in South Africa, render any African liable to police surveillance at any time. I doubt whether there is a single African male in South Africa who has not at some stage had a brush with the police over his pass. Hundreds and thousands of Africans are thrown into jail each year under pass laws. Even worse than this is the fact that pass laws keep husband and wife apart and lead to the breakdown of family life.

91   Poverty and the breakdown of family life have secondary effects. Children wander about the streets of the townships because they have no schools to go to, or no money to enable them to go to school, or no parents at home to see that they go to school, because both parents (if there be two) have to work to keep the family alive. This leads to a breakdown in moral standards, to an alarming rise in illegitimacy, and to growing violence which erupts not only politically, but everywhere. Life in the townships is dangerous. There is not a day that goes by without somebody being stabbed or assaulted. And violence is carried out of the townships in the white living areas. People are afraid to walk alone in the streets after dark. Housebreakings and robberies are increasing, despite the fact that the death sentence can now be imposed for such offences. Death sentences cannot cure the festering sore.

92   Africans want to be paid a living wage. Africans want to perform work which they are capable of doing, and not work which the Government declares them to be capable of. Africans want to be allowed to live where they obtain work, and not be endorsed out of an area because they were not born there. Africans want to be allowed to own land in places where they work, and not to be obliged to live in rented houses which they can never call their own. Africans want to be part of the general population, and not confined to living in their own ghettoes. African men want to have their wives and children to live with them where they work, and not be forced into an unnatural existence in men's hostels. African women want to be with their menfolk and not be left permanently widowed in the Reserves. Africans want to be allowed out after eleven o'clock at night and not to be confined to their rooms like little children. Africans want to be allowed to travel in their own country and to seek work where they want to and not where the Labour Bureau tells them to. Africans want a just share in the whole of South Africa; they want security and a stake in society.

93   Above all, we want equal political rights, because without them our disabilities will be permanent. I know this sounds revolutionary to the whites in this country, because the majority of voters will be Africans. This makes the white man fear democracy.

94   But this fear cannot be allowed to stand in the way of the only solution which will guarantee racial harmony and freedom for all. It is not true that the enfranchisement of all will result in racial domination. Political division, based on colour, is entirely artificial and, when it disappears, so will the domination of one colour group by another. The ANC has spent half a century fighting against racialism. When it triumphs it will not change that policy.

95   This then is what the ANC is fighting. Their struggle is a truly national one. It is a struggle of the African people, inspired by their own suffering and their own experience. It is a struggle for the right to live.

96   During my lifetime I have dedicated myself to this struggle of the African people. I have fought against white domination, and I have fought against black domination. I have cherished the ideal of a democratic and free society in which all persons live together in harmony and with equal opportunities. It is an ideal which I hope to live for and to achieve. But if needs be, it is an ideal for which I am prepared to die.

■ EXPLORATIONS OF THE TEXT ■

1. Discuss the situation, the point of view, the occasion, the purpose, and the context of this statement.
2. What was Nelson Mandela's role in the African National Conference? Why was he jailed for his role in the "stay-at-home"?
3. What does Mandela mean by "properly controlled violence"? Why did the ANC decide to depart from its policy of nonviolence?
4. Explore the reasons for the organization of Umkhonto. What are the four possible forms of violence?
5. Why did Mandela go to Addis Ababa? What were the consequences of his travels and of his military training?
6. What is Mandela's position on Communism? Why does he think Marxism has taken hold in Africa?
7. What evidence does Mandela give concerning the fight against poverty and lack of human dignity? Be specific about his grievances. Why is he "prepared to die"?
8. Evaluate Mandela's statement as argument. Compare and/or contrast it with Martin Luther King's "Letter from the Birmingham Jail" in Chapter 12.

■■ JOURNAL ENTRIES ■■

1. Gloss and annotate the text, and write an end note.
2. Outline Mandela's statement.
3. Freewrite about a section of the text that provokes a strong response.

■■■ IDEAS FOR WRITING ■■■

1. Analyze Mandela's statement. Use Journal Entry 1 or 2 as a beginning.
2. Compare King's letter in Chapter 12 and Mandela's statement as models of argument.
3. Agree or disagree with Mandela, with the ANC, and/or with the Umkhonto. Suggest a solution.
4. Write about the forms of and responses to injustice in the works by Valenzuela, by Rose, by Sophocles, and by Mandela.
5. Create a dialogue about injustice among the characters presented in the works by Valenzuela, Rose, Sophocles, and Mandela.

FICTION

War

Luigi Pirandello

Born in Sicily, Luigi Pirandello (1867–1936) earned his doctorate in philology, the study of language, from Bonn University. An Italian playwright, novelist, short story writer, essayist, and poet, he created "grotesco," the expressionist theatre form that deals with the psychological realities which lie beneath social appearances. Supported as a writer by a stipend from his father, he and his family found their way of life overturned when the sulfur mines were devastated by floods and his father's income was lost. It is possible that his wife's mental breakdown following this crisis was the seed of Pirandello's interest in psychological themes. Eventually, Mussolini patronized Pirandello, who joined the Fascist party in 1924. He won the Nobel Prize in Literature in 1934.

Pirandello is considered to be one of the greatest short story writers of the twentieth century and among the greatest modern playwrights. He wrote more than forty plays which include It Is So! (If You Think So) *(1917),* Six Characters In Search of an Author *(1921),* Henry IV *(1922),* Naked *(1922),* The Life I Gave You *(1924), and* Each in His Own Way *(1924). A prevalent theme in his dramas is the interplay between illusion and reality.*

In this story, Pirandello presents a journey on a night express train during wartime. Parents discuss their sorrow and apprehension about sending their sons to the front to fight.

1 The passengers who had left Rome by the night express had had to stop until dawn at the small station of Fabriano in order to continue their journey by the small old-fashioned local joining the main line with Sulmona.

At dawn, in a stuffy and smoky second-class carriage in which five people had already spent the night, a bulky woman in deep mourning was hoisted in—almost like a shapeless bundle. Behind her, puffing and moaning, followed her husband—a tiny man, thin and weakly, his face death-white, his eyes small and bright and looking shy and uneasy.

Having at last taken a seat he politely thanked the passengers who had helped his wife and who had made room for her; then he turned round to the woman trying to pull down the collar of her coat, and politely inquired:

"Are you all right, dear?"

5 The wife, instead of answering, pulled up her collar again to her eyes, so as to hide her face.

"Nasty world," muttered the husband with a sad smile.

And he felt it his duty to explain to his traveling companions that the poor woman was to be pitied, for the war was taking away from her her only son, a boy of twenty to whom both had devoted their entire life, even breaking up their home at Sulmona to follow him to Rome, where he had to go as a student, then allowing him to volunteer for war with an assurance, however, that at least for six months he would not be sent to the front and now, all of a sudden, receiving a wire saying that he was due to leave in three days' time and asking them to go and see him off.

The woman under the big coat was twisting and wriggling, at times growling like a wild animal, feeling certain that all those explanations would not have aroused even a shadow of sympathy from those people who—most likely—were in the same plight as herself. One of them, who had been listening with particular attention, said:

"You should thank God that your son is only leaving now for the front. Mine has been sent there the first day of the war. He has already come back twice wounded and been sent back again to the front."

"What about me? I have two sons and three nephews at the front," said another passenger.

"Maybe, but in our case it is our *only* son," ventured the husband.

"What difference can it make? You may spoil your only son with excessive attentions, but you cannot love him more than you would all your other children if you had any. Paternal love is not like bread that can be broken into pieces and split amongst the children in equal shares. A father gives *all* his love to each one of his children without discrimination, whether it be one or ten, and if I am suffering now for my two sons, I am not suffering half for each of them but double . . ."

"True . . . true . . ." sighed the embarrassed husband, "but suppose (of course we all hope it will never be your case) a father has two sons at the front and he loses one of them, there is still one left to console him . . . while . . ."

"Yes," answered the other, getting cross, "a son left to console him but also a son left for whom he must survive, while in the case of the father of an only son if the son dies the father can die too and put an end to his distress. Which of the two positions is the worse? Don't you see how my case would be worse than yours?"

"Nonsense," interrupted another traveler, a fat, red-faced man with blood-shot eyes of the palest gray.

He was panting. From his bulging eyes seemed to spurt inner violence of an uncontrolled vitality which his weakened body could hardly contain.

"Nonsense," he repeated, trying to cover his mouth with his hand so as to hide the two missing front teeth. "Nonsense. Do we give life to our children for our own benefit?"

The other travelers stared at him in distress. The one who had had his son at the front since the first day of the war sighed: "You are right. Our children do not belong to us, they belong to the Country. . . ."

"Bosh," retorted the fat traveler. "Do we think of the Country when we give life to our children? Our sons are born because . . . well, because they must be born and when they come to life they take our own life with them. This is the truth. We belong to them but they never belong to us. And when they reach twenty they are exactly what we were at their age. We too had a father and mother, but there were so many other things as well . . . girls, cigarettes, illusions, new ties . . . and the Country, of course, whose call we would have answered—when we were twenty—even if father and mother had said no. Now at our age, the love of our Country is still great, of course, but stronger than it is the love for our children. Is there any one of us here who wouldn't gladly take his son's place at the front if he could?"

20   There was a silence all round, everybody nodding as to approve.

"Why then," continued the fat man, "shouldn't we consider the feelings of our children when they are twenty? Isn't it natural that at their age they should consider the love for their Country (I am speaking of decent boys, of course) even greater than the love for us? Isn't it natural that it should be so, as after all they must look upon us as upon old boys who cannot move any more and must stay at home? If Country exists, if Country is a natural necessity, like bread, of which each of us must eat in order not to die of hunger, somebody must go to defend it. And our sons go, when they are twenty, and they don't want tears, because if they die, they die inflamed and happy (I am speaking, of course, of decent boys). Now, if one dies young and happy, without having the ugly sides of life, the boredom of it, the pettiness, the bitterness of disillusion . . . what more can we ask for him? Everyone should stop crying; everyone should laugh, as I do . . . or at least thank God—as I do—because my son, before dying, sent me a message saying that he was dying satisfied at having ended his life in the best way he could have wished. That is why, as you see, I do not even wear mourning. . . ."

He shook his light fawn coat as to show it; his livid lip over his missing teeth was trembling, his eyes were watery and motionless, and soon after he ended with a shrill laugh which might well have been a sob.

"Quite so . . . quite so . . ." agreed the others.

The woman who, bundled in a corner under her coat, had been sitting and listening had—for the last three months—tried to find in the words of her husband and her friends something to console her in her deep sorrow, something that might show her how a mother should resign herself to send her son not even to death but to a probably dangerous life. Yet not a word had she found amongst the many which had been said . . . and her grief had been greater in seeing that nobody—as she thought—could share her feelings.

25   But now the words of the traveler amazed and almost stunned her. She suddenly realized that it wasn't the others who were wrong and could not understand her but herself who could not rise up to the same height of those fathers and mothers willing to resign themselves, without crying, not only to the departure of their sons but even to their death.

She lifted her head, she bent over from her corner trying to listen with great attention to the details which the fat man was giving to his companions about the way his son had fallen as a hero, for his King and his Country, happy and without regrets. It seemed to her that she had stumbled into a world she had never dreamt of, a world so far unknown to her and she was so pleased to hear everyone joining in congratulating that brave father who could so stoically speak of his child's death.

Then suddenly, just as if she had heard nothing of what had been said and almost as if waking up from a dream, she turned to the old man, asking him:

"Then . . . is your son really dead?"

Everybody stared at her. The old man, too, turned to look at her, fixing his great, bulging, horribly watery light gray eyes, deep in her face. For some little time he tried to answer, but words failed him. He looked and looked at her, almost as if only then—at that silly, incongruous question—he had suddenly realized at last that his son was really dead—gone for ever—for ever. His face contracted, became horribly distorted, then he snatched in haste a handkerchief from his pocket and, to the amazement of everyone, broke into harrowing, heart-rending, uncontrollable sobs.

■ EXPLORATIONS OF THE TEXT ■

1. Discuss the function and effectiveness of the night train as a setting for the story.
2. Describe each of the passengers. What do their physical and emotional traits reveal about their attitudes toward war?
3. Analyze the conversation between the "husband" and the father with two sons. What do you conclude?
4. Why is "the fat man's" speech about love of country so compelling and persuasive? How does his appearance at the end of his speech foreshadow the conclusion of the story?
5. The grieving mother begins to feel "amazed" and "stunned." What is the source of her question: "Then . . . is your son really dead?"
6. What happens to the fat man? What is the meaning of his insight?
7. Consider the economy of Pirandello's style. What do you learn about the value of concise and terse writing?
8. Compare the themes of this story with those in works by O'Brien, Ozick, and Endō.

■■ JOURNAL ENTRIES ■■

1. What reasons compel "decent" young people to go to war? Would you go to war?
2. Why does "the fat man" rationalize his son's death? Write about the nature of grief.
3. Assume that you are about to become a soldier. Write an entry about your position on war.

■■■ IDEAS FOR WRITING ■■■

1. Explore the concept of the train journey. What does Pirandello accomplish with this setting?
2. Compare Hemingway's and Pirandello's styles. Use your journal entry as a beginning.
3. Analyze the character of "the fat man."
4. Do young people feel more patriotic and bellicose than older people?

The Shawl

Cynthia Ozick

Cynthia Ozick (1928–   ) was born in New York City. The anti-Semitism that she experienced as a child and her extensive reading of Jewish philosophy and history are often evident in her work, which includes the novels, Trust *(1966) and* The Cannibal Galaxy *(1983); a novella,* The Messiah of Stockholm *(1987); and the volumes of short fiction,* The Pagan Rabbi and Other Stories *(1971) and* Bloodshed and Three Novellas *(1976). Several of Ozick's short stories have been chosen for* The Best American Short Stories *(1976), notably "The Shawl," and its companion piece, the novella, "Rosa." Her work also won first prize in the annual O'Henry Prize Stories collection in 1975, 1981, and 1984.*

"The Shawl" was originally published in The New Yorker. *The story describes in horrifying detail the suffering of Rosa and the children, Stella and Magda, during the Holocaust.*

1 Stella, cold, cold, the coldness of hell. How they walked on the roads together, Rosa with Magda curled up between sore breasts, Magda wound up in the shawl. Sometimes Stella carried Magda. But she was jealous of Magda. A thin girl of fourteen, too small, with thin breasts of her own, Stella wanted to be wrapped in a shawl, hidden away, asleep, rocked by the march, a baby, a round infant in arms. Magda took Rosa's nipple, and Rosa never stopped walking, a walking cradle. There was not enough milk; sometimes Magda sucked air; then she screamed. Stella was ravenous. Her knees were tumors on sticks, her elbows chicken bones.

Rosa did not feel hunger; she felt light, not like someone walking but like someone in a faint, in trance, arrested in a fit, someone who is already a floating angel, alert and seeing everything, but in the air, not there, not touching the road. As if teetering on the tips of her fingernails. She looked into Magda's face through a gap in the shawl: a squirrel in a nest, safe, no one could reach her inside the little house of the shawl's windings. The face, very round, a pocket mirror of a face: but it was not Rosa's bleak complexion, dark like cholera, it was another kind of face altogether, eyes blue as air, smooth feathers of hair nearly as yellow as the Star sewn into Rosa's coat. You could think she was one of *their* babies.

Rosa, floating, dreamed of giving Magda away in one of the villages. She could leave the line for a minute and push Magda into the hands of any woman on the side of the road. But if she moved out of line they might shoot. And even if she fled the line for half a second and pushed the shawl-bundle at a stranger, would the woman take it? She might be surprised, or afraid; she might drop the shawl, and Magda would fall out and strike her head and die. The little round head. Such a good child, she gave up screaming, and sucked now only for the taste of the drying nipple itself. The neat grip of the tiny gums. One mite of a tooth tip sticking up in the bottom gum, how shining, an elfin tombstone of white marble, gleaming there. Without complaining, Magda relinquished Rosa's teats, first the left, then the right; both were cracked, not a sniff of milk. The duct crevice extinct, a dead volcano, blind eye, chill hole, so Magda took the corner of the shawl and milked it instead. She sucked and sucked, flooding the threads with wetness. The shawl's good flavor, milk of linen.

It was a magic shawl, it could nourish an infant for three days and three nights. Magda did not die, she stayed alive, although very quiet. A peculiar smell, of cinnamon and almonds, lifted out of her mouth. She held her eyes open every moment, forgetting how to blink or nap, and Rosa and sometimes Stella studied their blueness. On the road they raised one burden of a leg after another and studied Magda's face. "Aryan," Stella said, in a voice grown as thin as a string; and Rosa thought how Stella gazed at Magda like a young cannibal. And the time that Stella said "Aryan," it sounded to Rosa as if Stella had really said, "Let us devour her."

5   But Magda lived to walk. She lived that long, but she did not walk very well, partly because she was only fifteen months old, and partly because the spindles of her legs could not hold up her fat belly. It was fat with air, full and round. Rosa gave almost all her food to Magda, Stella gave nothing; Stella was ravenous, a growing child herself, but not growing much. Stella did not menstruate. Rosa did not menstruate. Rosa was ravenous, but also not; she learned from Magda how to drink the taste of a finger in one's mouth. They were in a place without pity, all pity was annihilated in Rosa, she looked at Stella's bones without pity. She was sure that Stella was waiting for Magda to die so she could put her teeth into the little thighs.

Rosa knew Magda was going to die very soon; she should have been dead already, but she had been buried away deep inside the magic shawl, mistaken there for the shivering mound of Rosa's breasts; Rosa clung to the shawl as if it covered only herself. No one took it away from her. Magda was mute. She never cried. Rosa hid her in the barracks, under the shawl, but she knew that one day someone would inform; or one day someone, not even Stella, would steal Magda to eat her. When Magda began to walk Rosa knew that Magda was going to die very soon, something would happen. She was afraid to fall asleep; she slept with the weight of her thigh on Magda's body; she was afraid she would smother Magda under her thigh. The weight of Rosa was becoming less and less, Rosa and Stella were slowly turning into air.

Magda was quiet, but her eyes were horribly alive, like blue tigers. She watched. Sometimes she laughed — it seemed a laugh, but how could it be? Magda had never seen anyone laugh. Still, Magda laughed at her shawl when the wind blew its corners, the bad wind with pieces of black in it, that made Stella's and Rosa's eyes tear. Magda's eyes were always clear and tearless. She watched like a tiger. She guarded her shawl. No one could touch it; only Rosa could touch it. Stella was not allowed. The shawl was Magda's own baby, her pet, her little sister. She tangled herself up in it and sucked on one of the corners when she wanted to be very still.

Then Stella took the shawl away and made Magda die.

Afterward Stella said: "I was cold."

10   And afterward she was always cold, always. The cold went into her heart: Rosa saw that Stella's heart was cold. Magda flopped onward with her little pencil legs scribbling this way and that, in search of the shawl; the pencils faltered at the barracks opening, where the light began. Rosa saw and pursued. But already Magda was in the square outside the barracks, in the jolly light. It was the roll-call arena. Every morning Rosa had to conceal Magda under the shawl against a wall of the barracks and go out and stand in the arena with Stella and hundreds of others, sometimes for hours, and Magda, deserted, was quiet under the shawl, sucking on her corner. Every day Magda was silent, and so she did not die. Rosa saw that today Magda was going to die, and at the same time a fearful joy ran in Rosa's two palms, her fingers were on fire, she was astonished, febrile: Magda, in the sunlight, swaying on her pencil legs, was howling. Ever since the drying up of Rosa's nipples, ever since Magda's last scream on the road, Magda had been devoid of any syllable; Magda was a mute. Rosa believed that something had gone wrong with her vocal cords, with her windpipe, with the cave of her larynx; Magda was defective, without a voice; perhaps she was deaf; there might be something amiss with her intelligence; Magda was dumb. Even the laugh that came when the ash-stippled wind made a clown out of Magda's shawl was only the air-blown showing of her teeth. Even when the lice, head lice and body lice, crazed her so that she became as wild as one of the big rats that plundered the barracks at daybreak looking for carrion, she rubbed and scratched and kicked and bit and rolled without a whimper. But now Magda's mouth was spilling a long viscous rope of clamor.

"Maaaa —"

It was the first noise Magda had ever sent out from her throat since the drying up of Rosa's nipples.

"Maaaa . . . aaa!"

Again! Magda was wavering in the perilous sunlight of the arena, scribbling on such pitiful little bent shins. Rosa saw. She saw that Magda was grieving the loss of her shawl, she saw that Magda was going to die. A tide of commands hammered in Rosa's nipples: Fetch, get, bring! But she did not know which to go after first, Magda or the shawl. If she jumped out into the arena to snatch Magda up, the howling would not stop, because Magda would still not have the shawl; but if she ran back into the barracks to find the shawl, and if she found it, and if she came after Magda holding it and shaking it, then she would get Magda back, Magda would put the shawl in her mouth and turn dumb again.

15   Rosa entered the dark. It was easy to discover the shawl. Stella was heaped under it, asleep in her thin bones. Rosa tore the shawl free and flew—she could fly, she was only air—into the arena. The sunheat murmured of another life, of butterflies in summer. The light was placid, mellow. On the other side of the steel fence, far away, there were green meadows speckled with dandelions and deep-colored violets; beyond them, even farther, innocent tiger lilies, tall, lifting their orange bonnets. In the barracks they spoke of "flowers," of "rain": excrement, thick turd-braids, and the slow stinking maroon waterfall that slunk down from the upper bunks, the stink mixed with a bitter fatty floating smoke that greased Rosa's skin. She stood for an instant at the margin of the arena. Sometimes the electricity inside the fence would seem to hum; even Stella said it was only an imagining, but Rosa heard real sounds in the wire: grainy sad voices. The farther she was from the fence, the more clearly the voices crowded at her. The lamenting voices strummed so convincingly, so passionately, it was impossible to suspect them of being phantoms. The voices told her to hold up the shawl, high; the voices told her to shake it, to whip with it, to unfurl it like a flag. Rosa lifted, shook, whipped, unfurled. Far off, very far, Magda leaned across her air-fed belly, reaching out with the rods of her arms. She was high up, elevated, riding someone's shoulder. But the shoulder that carried Magda was not coming toward Rosa and the shawl, it was drifting away, the speck of Magda was moving more and more into the smoky distance. Above the shoulder a helmet glinted. A light tapped the helmet and sparkled it into a goblet. Below the helmet a black body like a domino and a pair of black boots hurled themselves in the direction of the electrified fence. The electric voices began to chatter wildly. "Maamaa, maaamaaa," they all hummed together. How far Magda was from Rosa now, across the whole square, past a dozen barracks, all the way on the other side! She was no bigger than a moth.

All at once Magda was swimming through the air. The whole of Magda traveled through loftiness. She looked like a butterfly touching a silver vine. And the moment Magda's feathered round head and her pencil legs and balloonish belly and zigzag arms splashed against the fence, the steel voices went mad in their growling, urging Rosa to run and run to the spot where Magda had fallen from her flight against the electrified fence; but of course Rosa did not obey them. She only stood, because if she ran they would shoot, and if she tried to pick up the sticks of Magda's body they would shoot, and if she let the wolf's screech ascending now through the ladder of her skeleton break out, they would shoot; so she took Magda's shawl and filled her own mouth with it, stuffed it in and stuffed it in, until she was swallowing up the wolf's screech and tasting the cinnamon and almond depth of Magda's saliva; and Rosa drank Magda's shawl until it dried.   [1980]

■ **EXPLORATIONS OF THE TEXT** ■

1. Describe the agony of Rosa, Stella, and Magda as they walk to the camp. What is the attitude of each toward the shawl?
2. Why does Magda's existence remain secret?
3. Explore Stella's relationships with Rosa and with Magda.
4. Examine the agony of Magda's first cry. Consider the language which describes Magda's death. What are the major images?
5. Explain the ending: "Rosa drank Magda's shawl until it dried." Has Ozick chosen the right response for Rosa? Why? Why not?
6. Why does the speaker begin her description of Magda's death only to interrupt it with a fantasy of saving her?
7. How does Stella "make" Magda die? Why is Stella's heart "cold"?
8. Compare the fates of the central characters in works by O'Brien, Endō, Pirandello, and Valenzuela.

■■ **JOURNAL ENTRIES** ■■

1. Discuss the symbolism of the shawl.
2. React to Stella's character.
3. Is Stella to be blamed for Magda's death?

■■■ **IDEAS FOR WRITING** ■■■

1. Evaluate the descriptive language in this story. Does it enhance and create meaning?
2. Discuss "The Shawl's" portrayal of the inhumanity and cruelty of the concentration camps during the Holocaust. Is it powerful?
3. Analyze Rosa's or Stella's character.

The War Generation

Shusaku Endō

Born in Tokyo, Japan, Shusaku Endō (1923–   ) spent his early child-hood in Manchuria before returning to Japan to live with his mother in the home of a Roman Catholic aunt after his parents separated. He received a B.A. degree from Keio University in Tokyo and studied French literature at Lyon University in France. A playwright, novel-ist, and short story writer, Endō has frequently written about the clash between Eastern and Western morals and philosophy.

Endō's works, translated into English, include the novels, The Sea and Poison *(1958),* Volcano *(1959),* Silence *(1966) and* Samurai *(1980); and the volume of eleven short stories that combines two Japanese collections,* Stained Glass Elegies *(1979). He has won many awards. In "The War Generation," Endō explores both contemporary Japanese society and Tokyo during World War II. Konishi, who drinks too much sake every night after work, believes that his generation has lived continuously with death since the war. Van C. Gessel describes Endō's theme in the introduction to* Stained Glass Elegies, *"His [Endō's] concern is with the realities that confront the war generation—the group with perhaps the greatest sense of personal and national loss in the history of Japanese civilization."*

1   Outside it was raining, and the restaurant was crowded. A steaming pot on a white charcoal brazier in front of them, office workers and various other customers blew on their onions and *kiritanpo*[1] before eating them. A young woman dressed in a dark blue kimono with white splashes went from table to table setting down bottles of *sake.*[2]

'Are these seats taken?' a businessman with a young woman in tow asked Konishi.

'No.' With this *sake* cup still at his lips, Konishi shook his head sourly. In truth he had wanted this table all to himself.

'Shall we have the fish broth?'

5   'Anything. I'm starving.'

She took a cigarette from her brown handbag and began to smoke. Looking at her, Konishi thought of his wife and daughters waiting for him at home. This woman would be about the same age as his oldest girl, but she brought the cigarette to her lips like a habitual smoker. It was a distressing sight.

'Don't you think they're charging a little too much for the year-end party this time?'

'What can we do? We have to go.'

Listening without interest to the whispered conversation between these two, Konishi concluded that they must work in the same section at some company. Their talk shifted from the cost of the year-end party to backbiting against their co-workers.

10   He consumed a good deal of time slowly drinking down his second bottle of *sake*. At home, his wife and daughters had probably already started dinner. He often stopped off for a few drinks on his way home from work, so his family would wait until seven o'clock and then go ahead and eat without him. Konishi felt more comfortable having them do that than making them wait for him.

As intoxication began to settle in, Konishi thought about the funeral of one of his fellow workers that he had attended the previous day. Mimura had

---

[1] A kind of stew, pounded into a mortar and served with chicken.
[2] A kind of alcoholic beverage, made of rice and served warm.

been Personnel Director at the company, and was the same age as Konishi—fifty-two. He had heard that Mimura's blood pressure was a little high, but when the two of them had been tested together a year before in the company examination room, Konishi's blood pressure had been 150, Mimura's around 160. They had talked about how, by taking medicine, the pressure could be held below 200, and so there was nothing to worry about. But Mimura had died suddenly of a heart attack.

A photograph of Mimura, smiling and wearing a golfing hat, had been placed above the Buddhist memorial tablet surrounded by chrysanthemums. To one side sat the drooping figures of Mimura's wife, dressed in mourning kimono, and his son, wearing his high-school uniform. As he pressed his hands together reverently and gazed at Mimura's photograph, Konishi thought that this would be happening to him too before very long. Death, which had until now seemed still some distance away, had suddenly closed in on him with a whirr. In fact, two other funerals he had attended this year were for men in their fifties; he had to be on his guard.

'On my guard . . . ?' he muttered to himself. The woman who was sharing his table was putting fish and onions from the broth into a bowl for her date. The man, puffing on a cigarette, watched her as though he expected such treatment. Doubtless they had already slept together.

I must be on my guard. . . . But what was he supposed to do at this point? He was by no means satisfied with his job, but he had no intention of leaving. Eventually he would become an executive. Thereby he would avoid mandatory retirement. These days he had to feel very grateful for the position he was in. In his youth he had never imagined that his declining years would take their present shape. When he entered the Department of Law, he had planned to become a government official. Those plans had been aborted when he was taken out of school and sent off to war.

15 But Konishi had not been the only one that had happened to. All around him in those days were people who had had to change the direction of their lives because of the war. It was a matter of course for Konishi's generation.

He finished off his second bottle, and while he was debating whether to order a third, the glass door of the restaurant opened with a clatter. In the artificial light the rain looked like needles. A tall, thin woman in a black raincoat, around fifty or so, came into the restaurant.

Her nose was as pronounced as a foreigner's. Flecks of silver streaked her hair, like a foreigner's. Droplets of rain glimmered on her black raincoat. She asked the kimono-clad hostess a brief question and disappeared into a room at the back.

Still holding the empty *sake* bottle in his hand, Konishi let out an unintentional gasp. The man at the next table gave him a peculiar look.

None of the other customers in the restaurant knew who the woman was. But Konishi recognized the middle-aged woman as the violinist Ono Mari.

20 There was not a single clear sky over Tokyo in the days just before Konishi went into the army. Each day was leadenly overcast.

Though he knew it couldn't be the case, he wondered if the ashen skies over Tokyo had something to do with the city being as dark as his own feelings at the time. He had been at the university, and his boarding-house was located at Shinano-machi. Even the main road from there to Shinjuku was always deserted, every store had its glass doors tightly shut and displayed signs reading 'Closed'. Outside the shops, sandbags, buckets and fire blankets had been stacked in preparation for air raids. But there were no signs of human life.

Every day the sky looked as though it had been stuffed full of tattered cotton swabs. He could remember hearing sounds like faint explosions echoing constantly from the sky.

There was no longer anything resembling classes at the university. Instead, students like Konishi were sent to the F. Heavy Industries factory in Kawasaki, where they assembled airplane parts.

On the wintry mornings, factory workers and students dressed in work clothes and gaiters and carrying knapsacks over their shoulders lined up in single file on the square in front of Kawasaki Station. Buffeted by the cold wind, they waited and waited for their bus to come. Inside Konishi's knapsack he had some soya beans wrapped in paper, the only food that would help in some small way to stave off his hunger throughout the entire day.

25   Towards the end of 1944, the factory suffered a shortage of raw materials, and many machines ground to a halt. Even so, Konishi and the other grease-covered students had to stand in front of their drill presses all day long. Supervisors continued to make their rounds, marking down the names of any students whose work was slack. Those whose names were logged were not given any of the watery porridge that was brought around each day at three o'clock. Diluted as it was, the ravenous students coveted the porridge.

They were starved for more than just food. They likewise craved books. They yearned for heated rooms. They were hungry for human conversation, and for love. And so during the noon break, as they lined up in groups of five or six with their backs to the sunlit concrete wall, they discussed food and books. Then with sighs of longing they talked about certain members of the women's volunteer corps, who worked in a separate building. Dressed in their work pantaloons and wearing headbands, these women sorted the various machine parts. Throughout the factory hung posters that read: 'Advance to Attu Island!'[3]

As that year drew to a close, however, one after another of the young men who basked in that noonday sun received their draft notices printed on red paper. Each morning at the factory it was easy to tell from the looks on people's faces just who had received their orders. They would try to force a smile, but the dark, heavy circles under their eyes betrayed them.

'It's come,' the latest recipient would announce to everyone in a low voice, as though he were confessing some dark secret.

'When do you leave?'

30   'In two weeks.'

---

[3] Island southwest of Alaska, the most western of the Aleutians.

Of course, no one mouthed empty phrases like 'Congratulations' or 'Give it your best!' Sooner or later the same piece of paper would be coming their way. They all stared at the tall factory chimney. Again today the smoke from the chimney swirled straight up into the sombre sky. The scene was unchanged from yesterday or the day before. It seemed as though it would stay that way for eternity.

'When is this war going to end?' No one knew. They felt as though it would linger on and on for ever.

Whenever a new recruit left Tokyo, everyone assembled at Shinjuku or Tokyo Station to see him off. The students formed a circle on the crowded platform and sang their school song in an angry roar. They howled and leaped about, less interested in seeing off their friend than in masking the anxiety and fear that lurked in their own hearts. As the train carrying their comrade vanished from sight, looks of bleak emptiness appeared on the faces of those who had been so boisterous just a few moments before.

1945 came, and still Konishi had not received his induction notice. Around that time the enemy air raids gradually intensified. The previous November the Nakashima Aircraft Plant in Musashino had been bombed, and enemy planes appeared fifteen times the following month. Strangely, F. Factory in Kawasaki was untouched. Often the trains packed with exhausted workers at the end of the day would come to a stop with a groan. Sometimes there appeared to be an attack over the downtown area; from the train windows they could see the sky in that direction glowing a dark red. The train service was often suspended, and Konishi would have to crouch for a long while on a connecting platform at Tokyo Station, staring at the reddened sky, realizing with a start that death was all that lay before them.

35   On 28 February his good friend Inami received his draft notice, and the feeling that his own turn was coming soon struck Konishi with greater force than ever before. The night Inami's orders came, four or five of them gathered in his room for a farewell party. They drank rationed liquor and some watered-down medicinal alcohol they had stolen from the factory. Later that night, the landlord and the owner of an electrical shop who represented the local veterans' association came in and clumsily began to chant some Chinese poetry. 'Do your best! Work for your country.' They spouted callous words of encouragement. Inami, his face sallow, sat up straight in the student uniform he had not put on for some time.

That night he and Konishi slept in his room under the same blanket. Inami turned over, and Konishi could hear him weeping softly. He listened in silence for a while, then whispered, 'I'll be getting drafted too, before long.'

'Uh-huh,' Inami nodded. He turned so that Konishi could see the profile of his face. 'If you want anything of mine, you can have it.'

'I don't want any books. My red slip will be coming before I could finish reading any of them.'

'Probably. In that case, would you go to a concert in my place? I had to fight to get the ticket. I wanted to go to just one concert before the army got me.' He slipped out of bed in his worn-out underwear and rifled through his desk drawer

until he found a brown-coloured ticket. Inami was engrossed in music: he had
his own record collection, and even had a phonograph in his room.

40   'Whose concert?'

'Ono Mari on the violin. You've heard of her, haven't you—Ono Mari?
They say she's a young genius.'

'I've heard the name a lot.'

In the dim light from the lamp swathed in a black cloth, Konishi looked at
the brown ticket. On the coarse paper had been printed the words: 'Ono Mari
Solo Violin Concert, March 10.' It hardly seemed possible that a concert could
be held in Tokyo now that death was everywhere.

'Are you sure I can have this?'

45   'Please go. In my place.'

Inami set out from Shinjuku Station the following morning. The usual
clusters of students had gathered in circles on the platform to sing. Inami
seemed thinner and shorter than the other students who were boarding the
trains. He blinked his eyes behind glasses that kept sliding down his nose,
and bowed his head repeatedly to his friends.

On the night of 9 March, a large formation of B-29s attacked Tokyo. The hour
was approximately 12 a.m.

There was a strong northerly wind that night. A heavy snow had fallen in
Tokyo two or three days earlier, and a thick layer of black ice still remained
along the sides of the streets. Around six o'clock, Mari finished rehearsing for
the following day's performance at the home of her accompanist, a White Russian named Sapholo, who lived nearby. She returned home, but because of the
wind that had stirred up around noon, the long hair that was her trademark
kept blowing across her face, and she had to stop many times along the way.

At the age of fourteen, she had left all the older violinists in the dust and
taken first place in a music competition sponsored by the Mainichi Newspaper Corporation. Thereafter she attracted many fans. As a young child she
had been in poor health, and the rowdy children at elementary school had
made fun of her. Unable to endure the atmosphere, she had pleaded with her
parents not to make her continue in school; they had agreed to let her pursue
her violin and other essential studies at home. Perhaps that was why she was
fawned upon there.

50   That evening, as she warmed her legs under the *kotatsu*[4] and ate the
potato pie and unsweetened black tea her mother had prepared for her,
she discussed with her parents the possibility of going to Manchuria.[5] The
Musicians' Patriotic Society had proposed a series of concerts in Manchuria,
and if possible she wanted her mother to go with her. Her father, wearing a

---

[4] Heated charcoal, wrapped in cloth or blankets to preserve warmth and often covered with a
box. Used only in winter, the *kotatsu* can be placed in a central location at dinner so that
everyone seated for the meal can enjoy the comfort of the heat.

[5] A region in Northeast China, including Heilongjiang, Tilin, and Liaoning provinces and part
of Inner Mongolia.

frayed dressing-gown, agreed that they should go for about half a year, treating it as a kind of evacuation; there would be no air raids in Manchuria, and they would probably not have to contend with food shortages.

'This war should be over within half a year anyway.' Her artist father, who had studied in France as a young man, hated the military. He took an active part in air-raid drills and went to pay his respects to departing soldiers, but at the dinner table he often shared his grim outlook on the war situation with his wife and daughter.

Mari eventually grew tired and put her hand to her mouth to yawn. The radio had been playing a song called 'Look, a Parachute!', but suddenly it was interrupted by a shrill buzzer, and the announcer began to read a report from the Eastern Military Command.

'Enemy planes have been sighted over the ocean south of the city. They are approaching the mainland.' The announcer repeated the words three times.

'It's all right,' Mari's mother said. 'They're probably just reconnaissance planes.'

55   'Why don't we just go to bed instead of putting out the lights,' her father replied, extinguishing the coals in the *kotatsu*. 'I'm not about to do everything the army wants us to do.'

Mari fell asleep in her upstairs room. She had placed her violin case, air-raid hood and knapsack by her pillow, ready for an emergency, and had then dropped off to sleep as swiftly as a shower of falling pebbles. Soon in her dreams the orchestra members began to tune their instruments. The reverberations from the instruments were jumbled and confused, and somehow refused to modulate together as they usually did. Someone was beating on the kettledrum.

'Wake up! Mari, wake up!'

Someone was shouting at her bedside. She opened her eyes and dimly saw her father standing there wearing a metal helmet. Her ears still rang with the discordant strains of the orchestra.

'We've got to get away. It's an air raid! The flames are coming closer to us!'

60   For some reason her father's voice seemed to come from far away. She felt no sense of urgency at the words 'air raid.' Like a marionette she did as she was instructed and stumbled out of bed. It was then that she realized the noises in her ears were not those of an orchestra tuning up, but the crackling of fires somewhere nearby.

They joined her mother at the foot of the stairs and started for the air-raid shelter in the garden. As they hurried along, they looked up and saw that the sky over Honjo and Fukagawa was a flaming red. There was a popping sound like roasting beans, and they could hear the shouting, clamouring voices of many people. When they reached the shelter, their noses were stung by the smells of straw and damp earth.

'We can't stay here. We've got to run!' her father shouted. To her mother, who was carrying a rucksack and her purse, he called, 'Leave that. You don't need it.' Carrying just one rucksack on his back, he hurried the two women out through the gate. From the neighbouring Yoshimura house came clattering noises of others preparing to flee; on a road nearby a child cried, 'Ma-a-ama!'

The main street was already a maelstrom of people. The sky behind them was a sombre red. In the torrent were a man pulling his belongings along in a bicycle trailer, a young man carrying bedding in a hand-cart and a woman with a blanket wrapped around her body. All of them streamed towards the west, as though drawn by some phantom power. Time and again Mari's father shouted, 'Stay together!' Mari realized that the only thing she was carrying was her violin case. Another explosion shook the sky. The white bodies of the B-29s, their arms outstretched, appeared in the searchlights. The anti-aircraft guns opened fire, but the B-29s continued to soar calmly overhead. The wind still blew fiercely. From the distance echoed a succession of thunderous noises, as though a pile-driver were pounding the ground.

At his Shinano-machi boarding-house, Konishi was unable to get to sleep until about 2 a.m., thanks to the searchlights that glanced off his window and the explosion of anti-aircraft guns in the distance. The next morning he learned from the Imperial Headquarters bulletin that part of the city had been indiscriminately bombed by a hundred and thirty B-29s. The information bureau of the Headquarters and the newspapers reported without comment that fifty of the enemy planes had been damaged and fifteen shot down. But that day as he set out for the factory on the sporadically paralysed train line, Konishi saw that nearly all of the downtown sector had been consumed by fire in the previous night's raid. At the plant, workers gathered in small groups here and there, talking in subdued voices. Many of the labourers they were used to seeing had not shown up for work. From the student work-force, Taguchi, Ueno and Fujimoto were absent. A supervisor appeared and roared at the group, 'Get back to work!'

65   The ticket he had received from Inami was still carefully tucked into his train pass holder, but as he worked, Konishi began to have doubts that the concert would be held under the present circumstances. Besides, even if he tried to go to the concert, and there was another air raid like the one the night before, he would not be able to get back to his boarding-house. He decided it would be better not to go. When he reached that conclusion, though, he could hear Inami's plaintive voice echoing in his ears: 'I had to fight to get the ticket. Please go in my place.' He began to feel that wasting the brown ticket would be akin to betraying his friend. Without even asking, Konishi knew full well what sort of trials Inami was now enduring in the army.

At five o'clock the long, heavy siren announcing the end of the working day blared out. Still uncertain whether or not to go to the concert, Konishi crowded into the bus for Kawasaki Station with the other workers, then transferred to the equally packed train. Those who had found seats and those who dangled from the straps all had their eyes closed, and their faces looked as if they belonged to overworked beasts of burden.

It was pitch black at the deserted Yūraku-chō Station when Konishi got off the train and started walking towards Hibiya Public Hall. Along the way he took some of the paper-wrapped soya beans from his knapsack and chewed them. At the end of the day's labours his legs felt heavy and his stomach empty. When the dark hall at last came into view, he had to sit down on a rock in the park and rest for a while. Then he stood up and walked to the steps of the hall, where about fifty people had gathered by the entrance. Each of them wore gaiters and work pants and carried a knapsack on his shoulders.

As it was nearly six o'clock and the doors still hadn't been opened, someone asked his neighbour in the queue, 'Is there going to be a concert or not?' Word of mouth had it that the fires caused by the previous night's air raid had driven both Mari and her accompanist Sapholo from their homes; their whereabouts were unknown, and the hall was presently attempting to contact them. Still no one made a move to leave; they all stood patiently at the entrance.

Two men with stern faces, dressed in patriotic uniforms, appeared and bellowed, 'Hmph, what are you doing listening to enemy music in times like these? Go home, all of you!' The group lowered their eyes and said nothing. The men shrugged their shoulders and disappeared.

70 Before long a timid, middle-aged employee came out of the hall and announced apologetically, 'We have not been able to make contact. The concert is cancelled. I'm very sorry.'

No one protested. With shadows of resignation flickering on their backs, they silently began to disperse. Feeling somehow relieved, Konishi started to follow them out of the park. Just then a man at the front of the procession called, 'She's here!'

Everyone stopped walking. A weary, long-haired girl dressed in men's trousers and carrying a violin case was walking towards the hall with a look of pain on her face. It was Ono Mari.

'There's going to be a concert!' The shout passed from one person to the next like the baton in a relay race. The music enthusiasts turned on their heels like a flock of ducks and went back to the hall.

It was a peculiar concert, the sort not likely to have been seen before or since. The audience filled only half of Hibiya Public Hall, so the patrons dressed in their working clothes picked out seats to their liking and waited eagerly for Ono Mari to make her appearance.

75 Soon Mari came out onto the dusty stage, clutching her violin and bow in one hand. She had not had time to adjust her make-up, and the pained expression lingered as she stood in the centre of the stage. Exhaustion was etched into her face, and the renowned long hair and the wide, almost European eyes seemed agonizingly incongruous with the tattered men's trousers she was wearing. But no one laughed.

'We were burned out of our house,' she apologized, the violin and bow dangling from her hands. 'The trains couldn't go any further than Yotsuya . . . I walked here from Yotsuya. I had to come . . . knowing this might be my last concert.'

She bit her lip, and the audience knew she was choking down her emotions. There was not even a suggestion of applause. Everyone remained silent, pondering what she had just said.

At that moment, Konishi thought, 'This just might be the last concert I'll ever hear.'

Mari shook her head vigorously to get the hair out of her face, tucked the violin under her chin, leaned forward, bent her slender wrist sharply, and adjusted her bow.

80   From beneath that wrist the strains of Fauré's *Elegy* [6] began to pour out. Not a single cough came from the audience. The tired, begrimed patrons closed their eyes and listened to the music, absorbed in their own private thoughts and individual griefs. The dark, low melody pierced the hearts of each one. As he followed the music, Konishi thought about the dying city of Tokyo. He thought of the scorched, reddish sky he had seen from the station platform. He thought of the drafted workers and students waiting in the chill winter wind for a bus to pick them up at Kawasaki Station. He remembered the thin face of Inami, the tear-stained face he had buried in his bedcovers the night before his induction. Perhaps the air-raid sirens would whine again tonight, and many more people would die. Tomorrow morning Konishi, the other members of the audience and Ono Mari might be reduced to charred grey corpses. Even if he did not die today, before long he would be carted off to the battlefield. When that happened, only the strains of this melody would remain to reach the ears of those who survived.

When she finished the *Elegy*, Mari played Fauré's *Après un réve,* then performed the Saint-Saëns 'Rondo Capriccioso'[7] and Beethoven's 'Romance'. No one even considered the possibility that at any moment the alarms might sound, that the sky might be filled with a deafening roar, and that bombs might start to fall with a screeching howl.

Something sticky brushed against his head. A spider had woven its web in the *yatsude* plants in front of his house. Konishi clicked his tongue and opened the glass door.

From the parlour he could hear music playing on the television. As a man in his fifties, he could not begin to comprehend the electric guitar music that so delighted his daughters. It sounded to him like nothing more than someone banging noisily on metal buckets.

He was balancing himself with one hand on the shoe cabinet and removing his shoes when his wife came out of the parlour. 'Welcome home,' she said, and a moment later his second daughter, a high-school girl, appeared and begrudgingly repeated the greeting.

85   'Clean up the entranceway. How many times do I have to tell you?'

His wife and daughter said nothing. With a sour expression he washed his hands in the bathroom and then gargled, making a sound exactly like a duck. When he had changed his clothes he went into the parlour. The two daughters who had been watching television got abruptly to their feet, looked at him coldly, and muttering, 'We've got homework to do,' headed for their rooms. Konishi cast a disappointed glance after them.

Konishi's wife chattered as she filled his rice bowl, 'Remember I told you that the owner of the Azusa-ya was complaining of stiff shoulders?' The

---

[6] François-Félix Fauré, French composer (1843–1924).
[7] Charles Camille Saint-Saëns, French composer (1835–1921).

Azusa-ya was a grocery store by the bus stop. 'He's gone into hospital. His wife says he's got some kind of growth in his chest. It looks like cancer.'

The shop-owner was not much older than Konishi. Once again he felt death closing in on him with a whirring sound. He remembered the funeral of Mimura, his co-worker who had died of a heart attack. No, death was not closing in on them. Since their schooldays, death had always lived alongside the members of his generation. That smouldering red sky he had seen from the platform at Tokyo Station. The buzz of enemy planes that constantly filled the clogged grey skies. Inami had died of an illness on the battlefield in Korea. Other friends had been killed in the South Seas or on islands in the Pacific. Somewhere within, he felt as though the postwar period was just an extension of life that he had been granted.

'Toshiko wants to go on a vacation to Guam with some of her friends.' Glumly he continued to eat while his wife went on talking. Her face was fleshy around the eyelids and chin. It occurred to him that when he had seen Ono Mari in the restaurant tonight, her hair was streaked with flecks of silver.

90   'I saw Ono Mari today,' he said, almost to himself.

'Who's she?' His wife smothered a yawn.

■ EXPLORATIONS OF THE TEXT ■

1. Describe the occasion and the setting. What do you learn about Konishi in the restaurant?
2. Why does Endō emphasize sky imagery?
3. Discuss Konishi's experience in the factory during the war. Why are the young men so unhappy when the red paper arrives?
4. Analyze the section on Ono Mari and her family. Why is this section in the narrative?
5. Why is Konishi so moved by Ono Mari's appearance in the restaurant many years later? What is the significance of her "hair streaked with flecks of silver"?
6. Examine Konishi's relationships at home. What accounts for his estrangement from his wife and daughters?
7. What are the ironies of the end of the story?
8. Compare the view of the brutality of war in this story with the treatment of the same theme in Pirandello's "War" and in O'Brien's "The Things They Carried."

■■ JOURNAL ENTRIES ■■

1. List your preconceptions of the Japanese during World War II. Does this story change your views in any way?
2. React to Konishi's character. What does he fear?

■■■ IDEAS FOR WRITING ■■■

1. Characterize Konishi. How does he represent and symbolize the "war generation"?
2. What does the story reveal about life in Japan during World War II? Use Journal Entry 1 as a beginning.
3. What is Ono Mari's role in the story?
4. Compare the attitudes about war and about being a soldier in Endō's story, in Owen's "Dulce et Decorum Est," in O'Brien's "The Things They Carried," and/or in Pirandello's "War."
5. Discuss Endō's use of imagery, tone, and point of view.

The Things They Carried

Tim O'Brien

Born in Austin, Minnesota, Tim O'Brien (1946–   ) earned a B.A. degree from Macalester College and pursued graduate study at Harvard University. Ultimately attaining the rank of sergeant, he served in the U.S. Army in Vietnam. Much of his writing reflects his experiences during the Vietnam conflict and, through skillfully woven fact and fiction, brilliantly communicates the madness and horror of war.

O'Brien's works include the volume of autobiographical anecdotes, If I Die in a Combat Zone, Box Me Up and Ship Me Home *(1973); and the novels,* Northern Lights *(1974),* Going After Cacciato *(1978), for which he won the National Book Award. He is a frequent contributor to magazines and literary journals.*

In this story, from the volume, The Things They Carried *(1990), Tim O'Brien characterizes soldiers in Vietnam by the things they carry. The real burdens represent the "emotional baggage of men who might die. Grief, terror, love, longing—these were intangibles, but the intangibles had their own mass and specific gravity, they had tangible weight."*

1 First Lieutenant Jimmy Cross carried letters from a girl named Martha, a junior at Mount Sebastian College in New Jersey. They were not love letters, but Lieutenant Cross was hoping, so he kept them folded in plastic at the bottom of his rucksack. In the late afternoon, after a day's march, he would dig his foxhole, wash his hands under a canteen, unwrap the letters, hold them with the tips of his fingers, and spend the last hour of light pretending. He would imagine romantic camping trips into the White Mountains in New Hampshire. He would sometimes taste the envelope flaps,

knowing her tongue had been there. More than anything, he wanted Martha to love him as he loved her, but the letters were mostly chatty, elusive on the matter of love. She was a virgin, he was almost sure. She was an English major at Mount Sebastian, and she wrote beautifully about her professors and roommates and midterm exams, about her respect for Chaucer[1] and her great affection for Virginia Woolf.[2] She often quoted lines of poetry; she never mentioned the war, except to say, Jimmy, take care of yourself. The letters weighed ten ounces. They were signed "Love, Martha," but Lieutenant Cross understood that "Love" was only a way of signing and did not mean what he sometimes pretended it meant. At dusk, he would carefully return the letters to his rucksack. Slowly, a bit distracted, he would get up and move among his men, checking the perimeter, then at full dark he would return to his hole and watch the night and wonder if Martha was a virgin.

The things they carried were largely determined by necessity. Among the necessities or near necessities were P-38 can openers, pocket knives, heat tabs, wrist watches, dog tags, mosquito repellent, chewing gum, candy, cigarettes, salt tablets, packets of Kool-Aid, lighters, matches, sewing kits, Military Payment Certificates, C rations, and two or three canteens of water. Together, these items weighed between fifteen and twenty pounds, depending upon a man's habits or rate of metabolism. Henry Dobbins, who was a big man, carried extra rations; he was especially fond of canned peaches in heavy syrup over pound cake. Dave Jensen, who practiced field hygiene, carried a toothbrush, dental floss, and several hotel-size bars of soap he'd stolen on R&R in Sydney, Australia. Ted Lavender, who was scared, carried tranquilizers until he was shot in the head outside the village of Than Khe in mid-April. By necessity, and because it was SOP,[3] they all carried steel helmets that weighed five pounds including the liner and camouflage cover. They carried the standard fatigue jackets and trousers. Very few carried underwear. On their feet they carried jungle boots—2.1 pounds—and Dave Jensen carried three pairs of socks and a can of Dr. Scholl's foot powder as a precaution against trench foot. Until he was shot, Ted Lavender carried six or seven ounces of premium dope, which for him was a necessity. Mitchell Sanders, the RTO,[4] carried condoms. Norman Bowker carried a diary. Rat Kiley carried comic books. Kiowa, a devout Baptist, carried an illustrated New Testament that had been presented to him by his father, who taught Sunday school in Oklahoma City, Oklahoma. As a hedge against bad times, however, Kiowa also carried his grandmother's distrust of the white man, his grandfather's old hunting hatchet. Necessity dictated. Because the land was mined and booby-trapped, it was SOP for each man to carry a steel-centered, nylon-covered flak jacket, which weighed 6.7 pounds, but which on hot days seemed much

---

[1] Geoffrey Chaucer, English poet, author of *The Canterbury Tales* (1342–1400).
[2] British novelist (1882–1941).
[3] Standard operating procedure.
[4] Radio telephone operator.

heavier. Because you could die so quickly, each man carried at least one large compress bandage, usually in the helmet band for easy access. Because the nights were cold, and because the monsoons were wet, each carried a green plastic poncho that could be used as a raincoat or ground sheet or makeshift tent. With its quilted liner, the poncho weighed almost two pounds, but it was worth every ounce. In April, for instance, when Ted Lavender was shot, they used his poncho to wrap him up, then to carry him across the paddy, then to lift him into the chopper that took him away.

They were called legs or grunts.

To carry something was to "hump" it, as when Lieutenant Jimmy Cross humped his love for Martha up the hills and through the swamps. In its intransitive form, "to hump" meant "to walk," or "to march," but it implied burdens far beyond the intransitive.

5   Almost everyone humped photographs. In his wallet, Lieutenant Cross carried two photographs of Martha. The first was a Kodachrome snapshot signed "Love," though he knew better. She stood against a brick wall. Her eyes were gray and neutral, her lips slightly open as she stared straight-on at the camera. At night, sometimes, Lieutenant Cross wondered who had taken the picture, because he knew she had boyfriends, because he loved her so much, and because he could see the shadow of the picture taker spreading out against the brick wall. The second photograph had been clipped from the 1968 Mount Sebastian yearbook. It was an action shot—women's volleyball—and Martha was bent horizontal to the floor, reaching, the palms of her hands in sharp focus, the tongue taut, the expression frank and competitive. There was no visible sweat. She wore white gym shorts. Her legs, he thought, were almost certainly the legs of a virgin, dry and without hair, the left knee cocked and carrying her entire weight, which was just over one hundred pounds. Lieutenant Cross remembered touching that left knee. A dark theater, he remembered, and the movie was *Bonnie and Clyde,* and Martha wore a tweed skirt, and during the final scene, when he touched her knee, she turned and looked at him in a sad, sober way that made him pull his hand back, but he would always remember the feel of the tweed skirt and the knee beneath it and the sound of the gunfire that killed Bonnie and Clyde, how embarrassing it was, how slow and oppressive. He remembered kissing her good night at the dorm door. Right then, he thought, he should've done something brave. He should've carried her up the stairs to her room and tied her to the bed and touched that left knee all night long. He should've risked it. Whenever he looked at the photographs, he thought of new things he should've done.

What they carried was partly a function of rank, partly of field specialty.

As a first lieutenant and platoon leader, Jimmy Cross carried a compass, maps, code books, binoculars, and a .45-caliber pistol that weighed 2.9 pounds fully loaded. He carried a strobe light and the responsibility for the lives of his men.

As an RTO, Mitchell Sanders carried the PRC-25 radio, a killer, twenty-six pounds with its battery.

As a medic, Rat Kiley carried a canvas satchel filled with morphine and plasma and malaria tablets and surgical tape and comic books and all the things a medic must carry, including M&M's for especially bad wounds, for a total weight of nearly twenty pounds.

10   As a big man, therefore a machine gunner, Henry Dobbins carried the M-60, which weighed twenty-three pounds unloaded, but which was almost always loaded. In addition, Dobbins carried between ten and fifteen pounds of ammunition draped in belts across his chest and shoulders.

As PFCs or Spec 4s, most of them were common grunts and carried the standard M-16 gas-operated assault rifle. The weapon weighed 7.5 pounds unloaded, 8.2 pounds with its full twenty-round magazine. Depending on numerous factors, such as topography and psychology, the riflemen carried anywhere from twelve to twenty magazines, usually in cloth bandoliers, adding on another 8.4 pounds at minimum, fourteen pounds at maximum. When it was available, they also carried M-16 maintenance gear—rods and steel brushes and swabs and tubes of LSA oil—all of which weighed about a pound. Among the grunts, some carried the M-79 grenade launcher, 5.9 pounds unloaded, a reasonably light weapon except for the ammunition, which was heavy. A single round weighed ten ounces. The typical load was twenty-five rounds. But Ted Lavender, who was scared, carried thirty-four rounds when he was shot and killed outside Than Khe, and he went down under an exceptional burden, more than twenty pounds of ammunition, plus the flak jacket and helmet and rations and water and toilet paper and tranquilizers and all the rest, plus the unweighed fear. He was dead weight. There was no twitching or flopping. Kiowa, who saw it happen, said it was like watching a rock fall, or a big sandbag or something—just boom, then down—not like the movies where the dead guy rolls around and does fancy spins and goes ass over teakettle—not like that, Kiowa said, the poor bastard just flat-fuck fell. Boom. Down. Nothing else. It was a bright morning in mid-April. Lieutenant Cross felt the pain. He blamed himself. They stripped off Lavenders' canteens and ammo, all the heavy things, and Rat Kiley said the obvious, the guy's dead, and Mitchell Sanders used his radio to report one U.S. KIA[5] and to request a chopper. Then they wrapped Lavender in his poncho. They carried him out to a dry paddy, established security, and sat smoking the dead man's dope until the chopper came. Lieutenant Cross kept to himself. He pictured Martha's smooth young face, thinking he loved her more than anything, more than his men, and now Ted Lavender was dead because he loved her so much and could not stop thinking about her. When the dust-off arrived, they carried Lavender aboard. Afterward they burned Than Khe. They marched until dusk, then dug their holes, and that night Kiowa kept explaining how you had to be there, how fast it was, how the poor guy just dropped like so much concrete. Boom-down, he said. Like cement.

---

[5] Killed in action.

In addition to the three standard weapons—the M-60, M-16, and M-79—they carried whatever presented itself, or whatever seemed appropriate as a means of killing or staying alive. They carried catch-as-catch-can. At various times, in various situations, they carried M-14s and CAR-15s and Swedish Ks and grease guns and captured AK-47s and Chi-Coms and RPGs and Simonov carbines and black-market Uzis and .38-caliber Smith & Wesson handguns and 66 mm LAWs and shotguns and silencers and blackjacks and bayonets and C-4 plastic explosives.[6] Lee Strunk carried a slingshot; a weapon of last resort, he called it. Mitchell Sanders carried brass knuckles. Kiowa carried his grandfather's feathered hatchet. Every third or fourth man carried a Claymore antipersonnel mine—3.5 pounds with its firing device. They all carried fragmentation grenades—fourteen ounces each. They all carried at least one M-18 colored smoke grenade—twenty-four ounces. Some carried CS or tear-gas grenades. Some carried white-phosphorus grenades. They carried all they could bear, and then some, including a silent awe for the terrible power of the things they carried.

In the first week of April, before Lavender died, Lieutenant Jimmy Cross received a good-luck charm from Martha. It was a simple pebble, an ounce at most. Smooth to the touch, it was a milky-white color with flecks of orange and violet, oval-shaped, like a miniature egg. In the accompanying letter, Martha wrote that she had found the pebble on the Jersey shoreline, precisely where the land touched water at high tide, where things came together but also separated. It was this separate-but-together quality, she wrote, that had inspired her to pick up the pebble and to carry it in her breast pocket for several days, where it seemed weightless, and then to send it through the mail, by air, as a token of her truest feelings for him. Lieutenant Cross found this romantic. But he wondered what her truest feelings were, exactly, and what she meant by separate-but-together. He wondered how the tides and waves had come into play on that afternoon along the Jersey shoreline when Martha saw the pebble and bent down to rescue it from geology. He imagined bare feet. Martha was a poet, with the poet's sensibilities, and her feet would be brown and bare, the toenails unpainted, the eyes chilly and somber like the ocean in March, and though it was painful, he wondered who had been with her that afternoon. He imagined a pair of shadows moving along the strip of sand where things came together but also separated. It was phantom jealousy, he knew, but he couldn't help himself. He loved her so much. On the march, through the hot days of early April, he carried the pebble in his mouth, turning it with his tongue, tasting sea salts and moisture. His mind wandered. He had difficulty keeping his attention on the war. On occasion he would yell at his men to spread out the column, to keep their eyes open, but then he would slip away into daydreams, just pretending, walking barefoot along the Jersey shore, with Martha, carrying nothing. He would feel himself rising. Sun and waves and gentle winds, all love and lightness.

---

[6] Weaponry.

What they carried varied by mission.

15   When a mission took them to the mountains, they carried mosquito netting, machetes, canvas tarps, and extra bug juice.

If a mission seemed especially hazardous, or if it involved a place they knew to be bad, they carried everything they could. In certain heavily mined AOs,[7] where the land was dense with Toe Poppers and Bouncing Betties, they took turns humping a twenty-eight pound mine detector. With its headphones and big sensing plate, the equipment was a stress on the lower back and shoulders, awkward to handle, often useless because of the shrapnel in the earth, but they carried it anyway, partly for safety, partly for the illusion of safety.

On ambush, or other night missions, they carried peculiar little odds and ends. Kiowa always took along his New Testament and a pair of moccasins for silence. Dave Jensen carried night-sight vitamins high in carotin. Lee Strunk carried his slingshot; ammo, he claimed, would never be a problem. Rat Kiley carried brandy and M&M's. Until he was shot, Ted Lavender carried the starlight scope, which weighed 6.3 pounds with its aluminum carrying case. Henry Dobbins carried his girlfriend's pantyhose wrapped around his neck as a comforter. They all carried ghosts. When dark came, they would move out single file across the meadows and paddies to their ambush coordinates, where they would quietly set up the Claymores and lie down and spend the night waiting.

Other missions were more complicated and required special equipment. In mid-April, it was their mission to search out and destroy the elaborate tunnel complexes in the Than Khe area south of Chu Lai. To blow the tunnels, they carried one-pound blocks of pentrite high explosives, four blocks to a man, sixty-eight pounds in all. They carried wiring, detonators, and battery-powered clackers. Dave Jensen carried earplugs. Most often, before blowing the tunnels, they were ordered by higher command to search them, which was considered bad news, but by and large they just shrugged and carried out orders. Because he was a big man, Henry Dobbins was excused from tunnel duty. The others would draw numbers. Before Lavender died there were seventeen men in the platoon, and whoever drew the number seventeen would strip off his gear and crawl in head first with a flashlight and Lieutenant Cross's .45-caliber pistol. The rest of them would fan out as security. They would sit down or kneel, not facing the hole, listening to the ground beneath them, imagining cobwebs and ghosts, whatever was down there— the tunnel walls squeezing in—how the flashlight seemed impossibly heavy in the hand and how it was tunnel vision in the very strictest sense, compression in all ways, even time, and how you had to wiggle in—ass and elbows—a swallowed-up feeling—and how you found yourself worrying about odd things—will your flashlight go dead? Do rats carry rabies? If you screamed, how far would the sound carry? Would your buddies hear it? Would they have

---

[7] Areas of operation.

the courage to drag you out? In some respects, though not many, the waiting was worse than the tunnel itself. Imagination was a killer.

On April 16, when Lee Strunk drew the number seventeen, he laughed and muttered something and went down quickly. The morning was hot and very still. Not good, Kiowa said. He looked at the tunnel opening, then out across a dry paddy toward the village of Than Khe. Nothing moved. No clouds or birds or people. As they waited, the men smoked and drank Kool-Aid, not talking much, feeling sympathy for Lee Strunk but also feeling the luck of the draw. You win some, you lose some, said Mitchell Sanders, and sometimes you settle for a rain check. It was a tired line and no one laughed.

20   Henry Dobbins ate a tropical chocolate bar. Ted Lavender popped a tranquilizer and went off to pee.

After five minutes, Lieutenant Jimmy Cross moved to the tunnel, leaned down, and examined the darkness. Trouble, he thought—a cave-in maybe. And then suddenly, without willing it, he was thinking about Martha. The stresses and fractures, the quick collapse, the two of them buried alive under all that weight. Dense, crushing love. Kneeling, watching the hole, he tried to concentrate on Lee Strunk and the war, all the dangers, but his love was too much for him, he felt paralyzed, he wanted to sleep inside her lungs and breathe her blood and be smothered. He wanted her to be a virgin and not a virgin, all at once. He wanted to know her. Intimate secrets—why poetry? Why so sad? Why the grayness in her eyes? Why so alone? Not lonely, just alone—riding her bike across campus or sitting off by herself in the cafeteria. Even dancing, she danced alone—and it was the aloneness that filled him with love. He remembered telling her that one evening. How she nodded and looked away. And how, later, when he kissed her, she received the kiss without returning it, her eyes wide open, not afraid, not a virgin's eyes, just flat and uninvolved.

Lieutenant Cross gazed at the tunnel. But he was not there. He was buried with Martha under the white sand at the Jersey shore. They were pressed together, and the pebble in his mouth was her tongue. He was smiling. Vaguely, he was aware of how quiet the day was, the sullen paddies, yet he could not bring himself to worry about matters of security. He was beyond that. He was just a kid at war, in love. He was twenty-two years old. He couldn't help it.

A few moments later Lee Strunk crawled out of the tunnel. He came up grinning, filthy but alive. Lieutenant Cross nodded and closed his eyes while the others clapped Strunk on the back and made jokes about rising from the dead.

Worms, Rat Kiley said. Right out of the grave. Fuckin' zombie.

25   The men laughed. They all felt great relief.

Spook City, said Mitchell Sanders.

Lee Strunk made a funny ghost sound, a kind of moaning, yet very happy, and right then, when Strunk made that high happy moaning sound, when he went *Ahhooooo,* right then Ted Lavender was shot in the head on his way back from peeing. He lay with his mouth open. The teeth were broken. There was a swollen black bruise under his left eye. The cheekbone was gone. Oh shit, Rat Kiley said, the guy's dead. The guy's dead, he kept saying, which seemed profound—the guy's dead. I mean really.

The things they carried were determined to some extent by superstition. Lieutenant Cross carried his good-luck pebble. Dave Jensen carried a rabbit's foot. Norman Bowker, otherwise a very gentle person, carried a thumb that had been presented to him as a gift by Mitchell Sanders. The thumb was dark brown, rubbery to the touch, and weighed four ounces at most. It had been cut from a VC[8] corpse, a boy of fifteen or sixteen. They'd found him at the bottom of an irrigation ditch, badly burned, flies in his mouth and eyes. The boy wore black shorts and sandals. At the time of his death he had been carrying a pouch of rice, a rifle, and three magazines of ammunition.

You want my opinion, Mitchell Sanders said, there's a definite moral here.

30   He put his hand on the dead boy's wrist. He was quiet for a time, as if counting a pulse, then he patted the stomach, almost affectionately, and used Kiowa's hunting hatchet to remove the thumb.

Henry Dobbins asked what the moral was.

Moral?

You know. *Moral.*

Sanders wrapped the thumb in toilet paper and handed it across to Norman Bowker. There was no blood. Smiling, he kicked the boy's head, watched the flies scatter, and said, It's like with that old TV show—Paladin. Have gun, will travel.

35   Henry Dobbins thought about it.

Yeah, well, he finally said. I don't see no moral.

There it *is,* man.

Fuck off.

They carried USO[9] stationery and pencils and pens. They carried Sterno, safety pins, trip flares, signal flares, spools of wire, razor blades, chewing tobacco, liberated joss sticks and statuettes of the smiling Buddha, candles, grease pencils, *The Stars and Stripes,* fingernail clippers, Psy Ops[10] leaflets, bush hats, bolos, and much more. Twice a week, when the resupply choppers came in, they carried hot chow in green Mermite cans and large canvas bags filled with iced beer and soda pop. They carried plastic water containers, each with a two-gallon capacity. Mitchell Sanders carried a set of starched tiger fatigues for special occasions. Henry Dobbins carried Black Flag insecticide. Dave Jensen carried empty sandbags that could be filled at night for added protection. Lee Strunk carried tanning lotion. Some things they carried in common. Taking turns, they carried the big PRC-77 scrambler radio, which weighed thirty pounds with its battery. They shared the weight of memory.

---

[8] Vietcong; North Vietnamese soldier.
[9] United Service Organization.
[10] Psychological operations.

They took up what others could no longer bear. Often, they carried each other, the wounded or weak. They carried infections. They carried chess sets, basketballs, Vietnamese-English dictionaries, insignia of rank, Bronze Stars and Purple Hearts, plastic cards imprinted with the Code of Conduct. They carried diseases, among them malaria and dysentery. They carried lice and ringworm and leeches and paddy algae and various rots and molds. They carried the land itself—Vietnam, the place, the soil—a powdery orange-red dust that covered their boots and fatigues and faces. They carried the sky. The whole atmosphere, they carried it, the humidity, the monsoons, the stink of fungus and decay, all of it, they carried gravity. They moved like mules. By daylight they took sniper fire, at night they were mortared, but it was not battle, it was just the endless march, village to village, without purpose, nothing won or lost. They marched for the sake of the march. They plodded along slowly, dumbly, leaning forward against the heat, unthinking, all blood and bone, simple grunts, soldiering with their legs, toiling up the hills and down into the paddies and across the rivers and up again and down, just humping, one step and then the next and then another, but no volition, no will, because it was automatic, it was anatomy, and the war was entirely a matter of posture and carriage, the hump was everything, a kind of inertia, a kind of emptiness, a dullness of desire and intellect and conscience and hope and human sensibility. Their principles were in their feet. Their calculations were biological. They had no sense of strategy or mission. They searched the villages without knowing what to look for, not caring, kicking over jars of rice, frisking children and old men, blowing tunnels, sometimes setting fires and sometimes not, then forming up and moving on to the next village, then other villages, where it would always be the same. They carried their own lives. The pressures were enormous. In the heat of early afternoon, they would remove their helmets and flak jackets, walking bare, which was dangerous but which helped ease the strain. They would often discard things along the route of march. Purely for comfort, they would throw away rations, blow their Claymores[11] and grenades, no matter, because by nightfall the re-supply choppers would arrive with more of the same, then a day or two later still more, fresh watermelons and crates of ammunition and sunglasses and woolen sweaters—the resources were stunning—sparklers for the Fourth of July, colored eggs for Easter. It was the great American war chest—the fruits of science, the smokestacks, the canneries, the arsenals at Hartford, the Minnesota forests, the machine shops, the vast fields of corn and wheat—they carried like freight trains; they carried it on their backs and shoulders—and for all the ambiguities of Vietnam, all the mysteries and unknowns, there was at least the single abiding certainty that they would never be at a loss for things to carry.

40 After the chopper took Lavender away, Lieutenant Jimmy Cross led his men into the village of Than Khe. They burned everything. They shot chickens and dogs,

---

[11] Mine.

they trashed the village well, they called in artillery and watched the wreckage, then they marched for several hours through the hot afternoon, and then at dusk, while Kiowa explained how Lavender died, Lieutenant Cross found himself trembling.

He tried not to cry. With his entrenching tool, which weighed five pounds, he began digging a hole in the earth.

He felt shame. He hated himself. He had loved Martha more than his men, and as a consequence Lavender was now dead, and this was something he would have to carry like a stone in his stomach for the rest of the war.

All he could do was dig. He used his entrenching tool like an ax, slashing, feeling both love and hate, and then later, when it was full dark, he sat at the bottom of his foxhole and wept. It went on for a long while. In part, he was grieving for Ted Lavender, but mostly it was for Martha, and for himself, because she belonged to another world, which was not quite real, and because she was a junior at Mount Sebastian College in New Jersey, a poet and a virgin and uninvolved, and because he realized she did not love him and never would.

Like cement, Kiowa whispered in the dark. I swear to God — boom-down. Not a word.

45   I've heard this, said Norman Bowker.

A pisser, you know? Still zipping himself up. Zapped while zipping.

All right, fine. That's enough.

Yeah, but you had to see it, the guy just —

I *heard,* man. Cement. So why not shut the fuck *up?*

50   Kiowa shook his head sadly and glanced over at the hole where Lieutenant Jimmy Cross sat watching the night. The air was thick and wet. A warm, dense fog had settled over the paddies and there was the stillness that precedes rain.

After a time Kiowa sighed.

One thing for sure, he said. The Lieutenant's in some deep hurt. I mean that crying jag—the way he was carrying on—it wasn't fake or anything, it was real heavy-duty hurt. The man cares.

Sure, Norman Bowker said.

Say what you want, the man does care.

55   We all got problems.

Not Lavender.

57   No, I guess not, Bowker said. Do me a favor, though.

Shut up?

That's a smart Indian. Shut up.

60   Shrugging, Kiowa pulled off his boots. He wanted to say more, just to lighten up his sleep, but instead he opened his New Testament and arranged it beneath his head as a pillow. The fog made things seem hollow and unattached. He tried not to think about Ted Lavender, but then he was thinking how fast it was, no drama, down and dead, and how it was hard to feel anything except surprise. It seemed un-Christian. He wished he could find

some great sadness, or even anger, but the emotion wasn't there and he couldn't make it happen. Mostly he felt pleased to be alive. He liked the smell of the New Testament under his cheek, the leather and ink and paper and glue, whatever the chemicals were. He liked hearing the sounds of night. Even his fatigue, it felt fine, the stiff muscles and the prickly awareness of his own body, a floating feeling. He enjoyed not being dead. Lying there, Kiowa admired Lieutenant Jimmy Cross's capacity for grief. He wanted to share the man's pain, he wanted to care as Jimmy Cross cared. And yet when he closed his eyes, all he could think was Boom-down, and all he could feel was the pleasure of having his boots off and the fog curling in around him and the damp soil and the Bible smells and the plush comfort of night.

After a moment Norman Bowker sat up in the dark.

What the hell, he said. You want to talk, *talk*. Tell it to me.

Forget it.

No, man, go on. One thing I hate, it's a silent Indian.

65 For the most part they carried themselves with poise, a kind of dignity. Now and then, however, there were times of panic, when they squealed or wanted to squeal but couldn't, when they twitched and made moaning sounds and covered their heads and said Dear Jesus and flopped around on the earth and fired their weapons blindly and cringed and sobbed and begged for the noise to stop and went wild and made stupid promises to themselves and to God and to their mothers and fathers, hoping not to die. In different ways, it happened to all of them. Afterward, when the firing ended, they would blink and peek up. They would touch their bodies, feeling shame, then quickly hiding it. They would force themselves to stand. As if in slow motion, frame by frame, the world would take on the old logic—absolute silence, then the wind, then sunlight, then voices. It was the burden of being alive. Awkwardly, the men would reassemble themselves, first in private, then in groups, becoming soldiers again. They would repair the leaks in their eyes. They would check for casualties, call in dust-offs, light cigarettes, try to smile, clear their throats and spit and begin cleaning their weapons. After a time someone would shake his head and say, No lie, I almost shit my pants, and someone else would laugh, which meant it was bad, yes, but the guy had obviously not shit his pants, it wasn't that bad, and in any case nobody would ever do such a thing and then go ahead and talk about it. They would squint into the dense, oppressive sunlight. For a few moments, perhaps, they would fall silent, lighting a joint and tracking its passage from man to man, inhaling, holding in the humiliation. Scary stuff, one of them might say. But then someone else would grin or flick his eyebrows and say, Roger-dodger, almost cut me a new asshole, *almost*.

There were numerous such poses. Some carried themselves with a sort of wistful resignation, others with pride or stiff soldierly discipline or good humor or macho zeal. They were afraid of dying but they were even more afraid to show it.

They found jokes to tell.

They used a hard vocabulary to contain the terrible softness. *Greased,* they'd say. *Offed, lit up, zapped while zipping.* It wasn't cruelty, just stage presence. They were actors and the war came at them in 3-D. When someone died, it wasn't quite dying, because in a curious way it seemed scripted, and because they had their lines mostly memorized, irony mixed with tragedy, and because they called it by other names, as if to encyst and destroy the reality of death itself. They kicked corpses. They cut off thumbs. They talked grunt lingo. They told stories about Ted Lavender's supply of tranquilizers, how the poor guy didn't feel a thing, how incredibly tranquil he was.

There's a moral here, said Mitchell Sanders.

70   They were waiting for Lavender's chopper, smoking the dead man's dope.

The moral's pretty obvious, Sanders said, and winked. Stay away from drugs. No joke, they'll ruin your day every time.

Cute, said Henry Dobbins.

Mind-blower, get it? Talk about wiggy—nothing left, just blood and brains.

They made themselves laugh.

75   There it is, they'd say, over and over, as if the repetition itself were an act of poise, a balance between crazy and almost crazy, knowing without going. There it is, which meant be cool, let it ride, because oh yeah, man, you can't change what can't be changed, there it is, there it absolutely and positively and fucking well *is.*

They were tough.

They carried all the emotional baggage of men who might die. Grief, terror, love, longing—these were intangibles, but the intangibles had their own mass and specific gravity, they had tangible weight. They carried shameful memories. They carried the common secret of cowardice barely restrained, the instinct to run or freeze or hide, and in many respects this was the heaviest burden of all, for it could never be put down, it required perfect balance and perfect posture. They carried their reputations. They carried the soldier's greatest fear, which was the fear of blushing. Men killed, and died, because they were embarrassed not to. It was what had brought them to the war in the first place, nothing positive, no dreams of glory or honor, just to avoid the blush of dishonor. They died so as not to die of embarrassment. They crawled into tunnels and walked point and advanced under fire. Each morning, despite the unknowns, they made their legs move. They endured. They kept humping. They did not submit to the obvious alternative, which was simply to close the eyes and fall. So easy, really. Go limp and tumble to the ground and let the muscles unwind and not speak and not budge until your buddies picked you up and lifted you into the chopper that would roar and dip its nose and carry you off to the world. A mere matter of falling, yet no one ever fell. It was not courage, exactly; the object was not valor. Rather, they were too frightened to be cowards.

By and large they carried these things inside, maintaining the masks of composure. They sneered at sick call. They spoke bitterly about guys who had found release by shooting off their own toes or fingers. Pussies, they'd say. Candyasses. It was fierce, mocking talk, with only a trace of envy or awe, but even so, the image played itself out behind their eyes.

They imagined the muzzle against flesh. They imagined the quick, sweet pain, then the evacuation to Japan, then a hospital with warm beds and cute geisha nurses.

80   They dreamed of freedom birds.

At night, on guard, staring into the dark, they were carried away by jumbo jets. They felt the rush of takeoff. *Gone!* they yelled. And then velocity, wings and engines, a smiling stewardess—but it was more than a plane, it was a real bird, a big sleek silver bird with feathers and talons and high screeching. They were flying. The weights fell off, there was nothing to bear. They laughed and held on tight, feeling the cold slap of wind and altitude, soaring, thinking *It's over, I'm gone!*—they were naked, they were light and free—it was all lightness, bright and fast and buoyant, light as light, a helium buzz in the brain, a giddy bubbling in the lungs as they were taken up over the clouds and the war, beyond duty, beyond gravity and mortification and global entanglements—*Sin loi!*[12] they yelled, *I'm sorry, motherfuckers, but I'm out of it, I'm goofed, I'm on a space cruise, I'm gone!*—and it was a restful, disencumbered sensation, just riding the light waves, sailing that big silver freedom bird over the mountains and oceans, over America, over the farms and great sleeping cities and cemeteries and highways and the golden arches of McDonald's. It was flight, a kind of fleeing, a kind of falling, falling higher and higher, spinning off the edge of the earth and beyond the sun and through the vast, silent vacuum where there were no burdens and where everything weighed exactly nothing. *Gone!* they screamed, *I'm sorry but I'm gone!* And so at night, not quite dreaming, they gave themselves over to lightness, they were carried, they were purely borne.

On the morning after Ted Lavender died, First Lieutenant Jimmy Cross crouched at the bottom of his foxhole and burned Martha's letters. Then he burned the two photographs. There was a steady rain falling, which made it difficult, but he used heat tabs and Sterno to build a small fire, screening it with his body, holding the photographs over the tight blue flame with the tips of his fingers.

He realized it was only a gesture. Stupid, he thought. Sentimental, too, but mostly just stupid.

Lavender was dead. You couldn't burn the blame.

85   Besides, the letters were in his head. And even now, without photographs, Lieutenant Cross could see Martha playing volleyball in her white gym shorts and yellow T-shirt. He could see her moving in the rain.

When the fire died out, Lieutenant Cross pulled his poncho over his shoulders and ate breakfast from a can.

There was no great mystery, he decided.

In those burned letters Martha had never mentioned the war, except to say, Jimmy, take care of yourself. She wasn't involved. She signed the letters "Love," but it wasn't love, and all the fine lines and technicalities did not matter.

---

[12] Sorry about that.

The morning came up wet and blurry. Everything seemed part of everything else, the fog and Martha and the deepening rain.

90   It was a war, after all.

Half smiling, Lieutenant Jimmy Cross took out his maps. He shook his head hard, as if to clear it, then bent forward and began planning the day's march. In ten minutes, or maybe twenty, he would rouse the men and they would pack up and head west, where the maps showed the country to be green and inviting. They would do what they had always done. The rain might add some weight, but otherwise it would be one more day layered upon all the other days.

He was realistic about it. There was that new hardness in his stomach.

No more fantasies, he told himself.

Henceforth, when he thought about Martha, it would be only to think that she belonged elsewhere. He would shut down the daydreams. This was not Mount Sebastian, it was another world, where there were no pretty poems or midterm exams, a place where men died because of carelessness and gross stupidity. Kiowa was right. Boom-down, and you were dead, never partly dead.

95   Briefly, in the rain, Lieutenant Cross saw Martha's gray eyes gazing back at him.

He understood.

It was very sad, he thought. The things men carried inside. The things men did or felt they had to do.

He almost nodded at her, but didn't.

Instead he went back to his maps. He was now determined to perform his duties firmly and without negligence. It wouldn't help Lavender, he knew that, but from this point on he would comport himself as a soldier. He would dispose of his good-luck pebble. Swallow it, maybe, or use Lee Strunk's slingshot, or just drop it along the trail. On the march he would impose strict field discipline. He would be careful to send out flank security, to prevent straggling or bunching up, to keep his troops moving at the proper pace and at the proper interval. He would insist on clean weapons. He would confiscate the remainder of Lavender's dope. Later in the day, perhaps, he would call the men together and speak to them plainly. He would accept the blame for what had happened to Ted Lavender. He would be a man about it. He would look them in the eyes, keeping his chin level, and he would issue the new SOPs in a calm, impersonal tone of voice, an officer's voice, leaving no room for argument or discussion. Commencing immediately, he'd tell them, they would no longer abandon equipment along the route of march. They would police up their acts. They would get their shit together, and keep it together, and maintain it neatly and in good working order.

100   He would not tolerate laxity. He would show strength, distancing himself.

Among the men there would be grumbling, of course, and maybe worse, because their days would seem longer and their loads heavier, but Lieutenant Cross reminded himself that his obligation was not to be loved but to lead. He would dispense with love; it was not now a factor. And if anyone quarreled or complained, he would simply tighten his lips and arrange his shoulders in the correct command posture. He might give a curt little nod. Or he might not. He might just shrug and say Carry on, then they would saddle up and form into a column and move out toward the villages of Than Khe.

■ EXPLORATIONS OF THE TEXT ■

1. List the "things" carried by each man. What determines "the things they carried"? Characterize each person.
2. What are the heavy intangible weights carried by these men?
3. Discuss Ted Lavender's death. Why does Lieutenant Cross believe that he is responsible?
4. Evaluate the responses of each character to Lavender's death. What do you conclude?
5. Why does Mitchell Sanders declare "There's a moral here"? Is there a moral? How do you know?
6. The story begins with Lieutenant Cross's fantasies about Martha. How do these fantasies change? Why?
7. What is innovative about this story? Consider characterization, narrative structure, and style.
8. What is the attitude toward war in this story? Compare it to the stances of Ozick and of Endō.

■■ JOURNAL ENTRIES ■■

1. Write a reader response to one of the characters. Discuss the "things" he carried, and theorize about his hopes, demons, and values.
2. Are fantasies destructive, an avoidance of reality, or a method for bearing the unbearable?

■■■ IDEAS FOR WRITING ■■■

1. "Soldiers are dreamers." Apply this statement to "The Things They Carried." Is dreaming a vital element in the story?
2. Respond to the suggestion that soldiers come to war not out of dreams of glory or honor but out of fear of dishonor.
3. Evaluate this story. What are its major strengths? Use the fiction checklist in Chapter 9 for guidance in your evaluation.
4. Create a dialogue in which one of the characters in O'Brien's story responds to "the fat man" in Pirandello's "War."

POETRY

The Unknown Citizen

W. H. Auden

Considered one of the finest poets of the twentieth century, W. H. Auden (1907–1973) also gained recognition as a critic, an essayist, a dramatist, an editor, and a translator. He was born in the industrial countryside of York, England, and received a scholarship to Oxford University where he studied science and engineering, and eventually changed his field of study to English. Many references to industry, technology, and science appear in his poetry, reflecting these early interests. In 1946, he became a citizen of the United States, where he taught at many prestigious colleges, including Swarthmore, the University of Michigan, Bryn Mawr, Bennington, and Barnard.

Auden wrote introductions to many collections of verse and translated a number of works. His own works of poetry and drama include Poems *(1928),* Some Poems *(1940),* City Without Walls and Many Other Poems *(1969); and the plays,* The Dance of Death *(1934) and* No More Peace! A Thoughtful Comedy *(1936). His many awards include the King's Gold Medal for poetry in 1937 and the Pulitzer Prize in poetry in 1948 for his collection,* The Age of Anxiety.

In this poem, Auden satirizes the trends in modern society that encourage people to lose their identities in order to conform to social norms. The citizen honored by the state receives a "Marble Monument" because he was "one against whom there was no official complaint."

(To JS/07/M/378
This Marble Monument
Is Erected by the State)

He was found by the Bureau of Statistics to be
One against whom there was no official complaint,
And all the reports on his conduct agree
That, in the modern sense of an old-fashioned word, he was a saint,
5 For in everything he did he served the Greater Community.
Except for the War till the day he retired
He worked in a factory and never got fired,
But satisfied his employers, Fudge Motors Inc.
Yet he wasn't a scab or odd in his views,

10 For his Union reports that he paid his dues,
(Our report on his Union shows it was sound)
And our Social Psychology workers found
That he was popular with his mates and liked a drink.
The Press are convinced that he bought a paper every day
15 And that his reactions to advertisements were normal in every way.
Policies taken out in his name prove that he was fully insured,
And his Health-card shows he was once in hospital but left it cured.
Both Producers Research and High-Grade Living declare
He was fully sensible to the advantages of the Installment Plan
20 And had everything necessary to the Modern Man,
A phonograph, a radio, a car and a frigidaire.
Our researchers into Public Opinion are content
That he held the proper opinions for the time of year;
When there was peace, he was for peace; when there was war, he went.
25 He was married and added five children to the population,
Which our Eugenist[1] says was the right number for a parent of his
     generation,
And our teachers report that he never interfered with their education.
Was he free? Was he happy? The question is absurd:
Had anything been wrong, we should certainly have heard.

■ EXPLORATIONS OF THE TEXT ■

1. Identify the **allusion** in the title. Why is it ironic? What is the occasion?
2. Why is the citizen called a "saint" in "the modern sense" of this word? What is "the modern sense" of the word?
3. How does he serve "the Greater Community"? Describe his work and his relationship to his union.
4. In lines 18 to 21, "the unknown citizen" is depicted as a perfect consumer. How? Why?
5. What is the importance of the following line: "And our teachers report that he never interfered with their education"?
6. With all the sources of information on the citizen, "Was he free? Was he happy?" Does it matter? Why was he "unknown"?
7. What critique of modern culture does Auden offer? Is his analysis still relevant?

---

[1]A scientist who studies ways to improve species, especially the human species, through careful selection of offspring by genetic means.

■■ JOURNAL ENTRIES ■■

1. Make a list of ways in which you are a conformist or a nonconformist.
2. Agree or disagree with Auden's arguments.
3. Discuss the **irony** in the closing.

■■■ IDEAS FOR WRITING ■■■

1. Characterize a contemporary unknown citizen.
2. Compare and contrast this poem with Dickinson's "I'm Nobody! Who are you?" and with Ginsberg's "America."

Quelling War

Lao-Tzu

Lao-tzu lived during the sixth century B.C. in the ancient state of Ch'u in China. One of the main legends about Lao-tzu describes how he fled the deteriorating Chou dynasty and came to the Hsien-ku pass, where the guardian of the pass persuaded him to record his philosophy. The Tao-te-Ching, *the major document of Taoism, was the result.*

The Tao-te-Ching, *however, may not be the work of a single person; some of its sayings may date from the time of Confucius, but others are certainly later; and the book as a whole may possibly date from 300 B.C. Although the name Lao-tzu may represent a type of sage and not a specific person, the work attributed to him has continued to be respected in China and throughout the world.*

The Tao-te-Ching *is a collection of eighty-one poems or segments which present an eloquent expression of withdrawal from action, the way to virtue. The poem, "Quelling War," describes an attitude toward arms and toward war which suggests that "people had better shun them."*

1. Even victorious arms are unblest among tools, and people had better shun them. Therefore he who has Reason does not rely on them.
2. The superior man when residing at home honors the left. When using arms, he honors the right.
3. Arms are unblest among tools and not the superior man's tools. Only when it is unavoidable he uses them. Peace and quietude he holdeth high.

4. He conquers but rejoices not. Rejoicing at a conquest means to enjoy the slaughter of men. He who enjoys the slaughter of men will most assuredly not obtain his will in the empire.

■ EXPLORATIONS OF THE TEXT ■

1. Why should the person "who has Reason" not rely on arms?
2. What is the difference between "left" and "right" in section 2?
3. Why does Lao-tzu say that one may use arms "when it is unavoidable"? Why does he honor "peace and quietude"?
4. Why should the victor not "rejoice"? Why is taking pleasure in "the slaughter of men" wrong, according to Lao-tzu?
5. Compare this poem with Owen's "Arms and the Boy" and "Dulce et Decorum Est" and O'Brien's "The Things They Carried."

■■ JOURNAL ENTRIES ■■

1. Respond to the following quotation from the *Tao-te-Ching:*
   To quicken but not to own, to make but not to claim.
   To raise but not to rule, this is called profound virtue.
2. Explore themes of "Quelling War."

■■■ IDEAS FOR WRITING ■■■

1. Agree or disagree with the following statements: "Arms are unblest among tools and not the superior man's tools. Only when it is unavoidable he uses them."
2. Compare this work with "Arms and the Boy" by Owen.

Dulce et Decorum Est

Wilfred Owen

Born in Shropshire, England, Wilfred Owen (1893–1918) attended the University of London and later worked as a tutor in France. In 1915, he joined the British Army and served in a rifle corps during World War I. After seven months, he was injured and sent to a war hospital in Scotland where he met another patient, poet Siegfried Sassoon, who encouraged him to write. After recovering from his injury, Owen returned to the battlefield in France and was awarded the Military Cross for gallantry under fire. He was killed while leading

*troops across the Sambre Canal just a week before the Armistice.
His work was collected and published by Sassoon in a volume titled*
Poems *(1920). The influence of Owen's work is evident in the poetry of
W. H. Auden and Stephen Spender.*

*Owen invented para-rhyme, which is achieved by matching the
first and last letters of words. His poetry also emphasizes assonance,
the repetition of similar vowel sounds in several words, and alliteration, the repetition of initial consonant sounds.*

*The title of Owen's poem contains part of a quotation from the
Roman poet Horace. Translated, it means "It is sweet and fitting to die
for one's country." The speaker's attitude toward war, "the old lie," is
both negative and ironic. His poems do not convey rage against war as
much as they express pity.*

Bent double, like old beggars under sacks,
Knock-kneed, coughing like hags, we cursed through sludge,
Till on the haunting flares we turned our backs
And towards our distant rest began to trudge.
5 Men marched asleep. Many had lost their boots
But limped on, blood-shod. All went lame; all blind;
Drunk with fatigue; deaf even to the hoots
Of tired, outstripped Five-Nines[1] that dropped behind.

Gas! Gas! Quick, boys!—An ecstasy of fumbling,
10 Fitting the clumsy helmets just in time;
But someone still was yelling out and stumbling
And flound'ring like a man in fire or lime . . .
Dim, through the misty panes and thick green light,
As under a green sea, I saw him drowning.

15 In all my dreams, before my helpless sight,
He plunges at me, guttering, choking, drowning.

If in some smothering dreams you too could pace
Behind the wagon that we flung him in,
And watch the white eyes writhing in his face,
20 His hanging face, like a devil's sick of sin;
If you could hear, at every jolt, the blood
Come gargling from the froth-corrupted lungs,
Obscene as cancer, bitter as the cud
Of vile, incurable sores on innocent tongues,—
25 My friend, you would not tell with such high zest
To children ardent for some desperate glory,
The old Lie: Dulce et decorum est
Pro patria mori.

---

[1] Gas shells.

■ EXPLORATIONS OF THE TEXT ■

1. Discuss the **similes** in lines 1 and 2. What images of the young soldiers does Owen present?
2. Find the words with negative **connotations** in stanza 1. Why are the men "lame," "blind," "drunk with fatigue," and "deaf"?
3. Why does Owen shift to the **first person** in the second verse? What effect does this highly personal testimony achieve?
4. Whom does the narrator address as "you" in stanza 4? What is his purpose? Who is the audience?
5. Give a synopsis of the narrative in this poem. What is the attitude of the speaker? Describe the tone.
6. Discuss figures of speech, rhyme scheme and sound. How do they contribute to the effectiveness of this work?
7. Compare "Dulce et Decorum Est" to "The Things They Carried."

■■ JOURNAL ENTRIES ■■

1. Identify and react to the similes in this poem.
2. Respond to the vision of war in stanza 4 or the attitude toward war in stanza 2.

■■■ IDEAS FOR WRITING ■■■

1. Write an essay that takes a position on Horace's quotation. Refer to works in the chapter to support your points.
2. Explicate this poem. Concentrate on point of view, tone, and imagery. (Look at the analysis of Owen's "Arms and the Boy" in Chapter 10 as a model.)
3. Does this poem persuade you that "war is Hell"? Why or why not?

Arms and the Boy

Wilfred Owen

*In this poem, Owen creates a narrative in which a boy is encouraged
by soldiers to examine a bayonet and rifle.*

> Let the boy try along this bayonet-blade
> How cold steel is, and keen with hunger of blood;
> Blue with all malice, like a madman's flash;
> And thinly drawn with famishing for flesh.
>
> 5 Lend him to stroke these blind, blunt bullet-heads
> Which long to nuzzle in the hearts of lads,
> Or give him cartridges of fine zinc teeth,
> Sharp with the sharpness of grief and death.
>
> For his teeth seem for laughing round an apple
> 10 There lurk no claws behind his fingers supple;
> And God will grow no talons at his heels,
> Nor antlers through the thickness of his curls.

■ EXPLORATIONS OF THE TEXT ■

1. Why does the persona wish to "let the boy try" the bayonet in the first
   stanza?
2. Examine the personification of the bullets, of the blade. What is the
   effect of their longing "to nuzzle in the hearts of lads"?
3. What is the effect of the repetition of "sharp" in line four of the second
   stanza? What is the impact of the sounds of the words? How does
   alliteration function here?
4. Why is it important that the boy has "no claws"? Why will
   "God . . . grow no talons at his heels,/Nor antlers" on his head?
5. Characterize the speaker and his attitudes. Imagine the occasion and
   the context. Are they intended to be specific or general?
6. Compare Owen's themes concerning war with those of Pirandello,
   Endō, O'Brien, and/or Agosín.

■■ JOURNAL ENTRIES ■■

1. What is the speaker's attitude toward weapons? Do you agree?
2. Write a response to the persona in the voice of one of the other
   soldiers.

■■■   **IDEAS FOR WRITING**   ■■■

1. Evaluate the explication of this poem in Chapter 10.
2. Write an argumentative essay on children and/or adolescents and weapons.
3. Write a description of a weapon of war. Like Owen, reveal your attitude toward the weapon through detail and **figurative language**.

Let America Be America Again

Langston Hughes

Born in Joplin, Missouri, Langston Hughes (1902–1967) wrote more than twenty books—poetry, fiction, drama, and nonfiction—and became the best-known African-American writer of his generation. He spent most of his childhood with his grandmother in Lawrence, Kansas. When she died, Hughes was thirteen; and he lived with his mother in Lincoln, Illinois. A year later, they moved to Cleveland where Hughes began writing poetry. His first poem, "The Negro Speaks of Rivers," was published in The Crisis *after he finished high school and before he entered Columbia. After he left college, he became a seaman. He threw his books "as far as he could out to sea" and decided to be a writer. In 1924, he went to Rotterdam and then lived in Paris for a while.*

Returning to the United States, he worked at many jobs. As a busboy at the Wardman Park Hotel in Washington, D.C., Hughes met Vachel Lindsay, the poet, who admired Hughes' work. Within the next year, he became a member of a group of artists and writers now known as the Harlem Renaissance. In 1926, Hughes published his first book of poems, The Weary Blues. *During the 1930s, he traveled to Russia and Spain where he served as a correspondent during the Civil War. In 1961, he became a member of the National Academy of Arts and Letters.*

His works include Shakespeare in Harlem *(1942),* Jim Crow's Last Stand *(1943),* Lament for Dark Peoples *(1944),* One Way Ticket *(1949),* Montage of a Dream Deferred *(1951),* Selected Poems *(1959),* Ask Your Mamma *(1961), and* The Panther and the Lash *(1967).*

In this poem, Hughes presents a dream of America as a land of the free and as a nightmare vision for the poor—the refugees, the Native-Americans, the African-Americans, the Irish, the Poles. The poem's form and rhythms reveal Hughes' interest in African-American music—jazz, blues, gospel.

Let America be America again.
Let it be the dream it used to be.
Let it be the pioneer on the plain
Seeking a home where he himself is free.

5   (America never was America to me.)

Let America be the dream the dreamers dreamed —
Let it be that great strong land of love
Where never kings connive nor tyrants scheme
That any man be crushed by one above.

10 (It never was America to me.)

O, let my land be a land where Liberty
Is crowned with no false patriotic wreath,
But opportunity is real, and life is free,
Equality is in the air we breathe.

15 (There's never been equality for me,
Nor freedom in this "homeland of the free.")

Say who are you that mumbles in the dark?
And who are you that draws your veil across the stars?

I am the poor white, fooled and pushed apart,
20 I am the red man driven from the land.
I am the refugee clutching the hope I seek —
But finding only the same old stupid plan

Of dog eat dog, of mighty crush the weak.
I am the Negro, "problem" to you all.
25 I am the people, humble, hungry, mean —
Hungry yet today despite the dream.
Beaten yet today — O, Pioneers!
I am the man who never got ahead,
The poorest worker bartered through the years.
30 Yet I'm the one who dreamt our basic dream
In that Old World while still a serf of kings,
Who dreamt a dream so strong, so brave, so true,
That even yet its mighty daring sings
In every brick and stone, in every furrow turned
35 That's made America the land it has become.
O, I'm the man who sailed those early seas
In search of what I meant to be my home —
For I'm the one who left dark Ireland's shore,

And Poland's plain, and England's grassy lea,
40 And torn from Black Africa's strand I came
To build a "homeland of the free."

The free?
Who said the free? Not me?
Surely not me? The millions on relief today?
45 The millions who have nothing for our pay
For all the dreams we've dreamed
And all the songs we've sung
And all the hopes we've held
And all the flags we've hung,
50 The millions who have nothing for our pay—
Except the dream we keep alive today.

O, let America be America again—
The land that never has been yet—
And yet must be—the land where *every* man is free.
55 The land that's mine—the poor man's, Indian's, Negro's, ME—
Who made America,
Whose sweat and blood, whose faith and pain,
Whose hand at the foundry, whose plow in the rain,
Must bring back our mighty dream again.

60 O, yes,
I say it plain,
America never was America to me,
And yet I swear this oath—
America will be!

■ **EXPLORATIONS OF THE TEXT** ■

1. What does the title mean? Who is the speaker? For whom does he speak?
2. What dreams of America emerge in the first three stanzas? What is the meaning of America in the refrain?
3. Describe the transformation of the speaker which begins in line 19: "I am the poor white, fooled and pushed apart."
4. What criticisms of America does the speaker make? Compare them to Ginsberg's "America." Are the issues similar?
5. Analyze the **paradox**:
   "O let America be America again—
   The land that never has been yet—"
6. How does the speaker's attitude change in the last stanza?
7. Examine Hughes' use of **irony**. (See Chapter 11 for a discussion of irony.)

8. Consider the form of this poem—line length, repetition, stanza divisions—and compare this work with Whitman's "Out of the Cradle Endlessly Rocking" in Chapter 4.

■■ **JOURNAL ENTRIES** ■■

---

1. Write about one of Hughes' two Americas.
2. Respond to Hughes' poem in a double-entry notebook.
3. Respond to a contemporary event as if you were Hughes.

■■■ **IDEAS FOR WRITING** ■■■

---

1. Write about speaker and voice in "Let America Be America Again."
2. Agree or disagree with Hughes' analysis of America.
3. Explicate and evaluate this poem. Focus on imagery, paradox, tone, irony, and/or form.
4. Compare this poem with Ginsberg's "America."

Harlem

Langston Hughes

Hughes' poem about Harlem remains his most famous work. The speaker asks important questions about the fate of "a dream deferred."

What happens to a dream deferred?

Does it dry up
like a raisin in the sun?
Or fester like a sore—
5 And then run?
Does it stink like rotten meat?
Or crust and sugar over—
like a syrupy sweet?

Maybe it just sags
10 like a heavy load.

Or does it explode?

■   EXPLORATIONS OF THE TEXT   ■

---

1. What is the connection between the title and the opening question?
2. What possible consequences does the speaker suggest?
3. Why does Hughes create so many **similes**? Are they effective? Why does he use so many questions? Are they effective?
4. Why does the persona speak only one declarative sentence?
5. Why is the last question isolated and written in italics? What are the implications? What is the answer?
6. Examine the rhyme scheme and other formal elements in the poem. What makes "Harlem" work?
7. Compare themes in this poem to those in works by Auden, Ginsberg, and Knight.

■■   JOURNAL ENTRIES   ■■

---

1. Annotate the poem, and write an end comment.
2. Write about "a dream deferred" in your own life. Compare your experience with the lost hopes of the poem.

■■■   IDEAS FOR WRITING   ■■■

---

1. Explicate formal elements—figures of speech, sound, rhyme, and rhythm—in "Harlem." Use Journal Entry 1 as a beginning.
2. Answer the questions in the poem. Use Journal Entry 2 as a beginning.
3. Consider each of the similes and paraphrase them. Write a cause-effect analysis of the "dream deferred."

The Chicago Defender Sends a Man to Little Rock

Gwendolyn Brooks

Born in Topeka, Kansas, Gwendolyn Brooks (1917–   ) graduated from Wilson Junior College in 1936. A novelist and poet, she taught at a number of colleges and universities, including Columbia University and the University of Wisconsin. She was Distinguished Professor of the Arts at City College in New York in 1971. She is well-versed in the finer aspects of sonnet form, which she expertly blends with African-American speech patterns. In the 1960s, her poetry began to portray the condition of African-Americans and to express the rage and despair arising from it.

Brooks' many works include the novel, Maud Martha *(1953); and the volumes of poetry,* A Street in Bronzeville *(1945),* Annie Allen *(1949), which won the 1950 Pulitzer Prize in poetry,* The Bean Eaters *(1960),* In the Time of Detachment, In the Time of Cold *(1965),* In the Mecca *(1968),* To Disembark *(1981),* Black Love *(1982), and others. She was the first African-American poet to win the Pulitzer Prize, and she has received numerous other awards and honors. She is Poet Laureate of the state of Illinois.*

In 1954, the Supreme Court ordered desegregation of schools "with all deliberate speed" in a landmark decision in the case of Brown vs. The Board of Education of Little Rock, Arkansas. *Brooks' poem describes life in this setting.*

In Little Rock[1] the people bear
Babes, and comb and part their hair
And watch the want ads, put repair
To roof and latch. While wheat toast burns
5 A woman waters multiferns.

Time upholds or overturns
The many, tight, and small concerns.

In Little Rock the people sing
Sunday hymns like anything,
10 Through Sunday pomp and polishing.

And after testament and tunes,
Some soften Sunday afternoons
With lemon tea and Lorna Doones.[2]

I forecast
15 And I believe
Come Christmas Little Rock will cleave
To Christmas tree and trifle, weave,
From laugh and tinsel, texture fast.

In Little Rock is baseball; Barcarolle.[3]
20 That hotness in July . . . the uniformed figures raw and
   implacable
And not intellectual,
Batting the hotness or clawing the suffering dust.

---

[1] Little Rock, Arkansas, scene of the first Supreme Court case (Brown vs. The Board of Education) concerning desegregation of schools.
[2] Cookies.
[3] Venetian boat song with a rowing rhythm or music imitating such songs.

The Open Air Concert, on the special twilight green. . . .
When Beethoven[4] is brutal or whispers to lady-like air.
25 Blanket-sitters are solemn, as Johann[5] troubles to lean
To tell them what to mean. . . .

There is love, too, in Little Rock. Soft women softly
Opening themselves in kindness,
Or, pitying one's blindness,
30 Awaiting one's pleasure
In azure
Glory with anguished rose at the root. . . .
To wash away old semi-discomfitures.
They re-teach purple and unsullen blue.
35 The wispy soils go. And uncertain
Half-havings have they clarified to sures.

In Little Rock they know
Not answering the telephone is a way of rejecting life,
That it is our business to be bothered, is our business
40 To cherish bores or boredom, be polite
To lies and love and many-faceted fuzziness.
I scratch my head, massage the hate-I-had.
I blink across my prim and pencilled pad.
The saga I was sent for is not down.
45 Because there is a puzzle in this town.
The biggest News I do not dare
Telegraph to the Editor's chair:
"They are like people everywhere."

The angry Editor would reply
50 In hundred harryings of Why.

And true, they are hurling spittle, rock,
Garbage and fruit in Little Rock.
And I saw coiling storm a-writhe
On bright madonnas. And a scythe
55 Of men harassing brownish girls.
(The bows and barrettes in the curls
And braids declined away from joy.)

I saw a bleeding brownish boy. . . .

The lariat lynch-wish I deplored.

60 The loveliest lynchee was our Lord.

---

[4] Ludwig van Beethoven. German composer (1770–1827).
[5] Johann Sebastian Bach. German composer (1685–1750).

■ **EXPLORATIONS OF THE TEXT** ■

1. Examine the first four stanzas, and describe life in Little Rock.
2. Who is the narrator? Why is the narrator in Little Rock?
3. What is the nature of love in Little Rock? Describe the "soft women." Interpret this section carefully.
4. Why is the narrator so puzzled that the citizens of Little Rock "are like people everywhere"? What are the implications of this conclusion?
5. What has the man sent to Little Rock actually seen? What acts of harassment and violence happen there?
6. Why are the last three lines separated into stanzas? What is the effect?
7. What is traditional about the form of this poem?
8. Compare and contrast this poem with works by Hughes, Knight, and Ginsberg.
9. How does this poem illustrate Freire's arguments?

■■ **JOURNAL ENTRIES** ■■

1. Respond to the idea that the people in Little Rock who opposed desegregation "are like people everywhere."
2. Is this poem still relevant, or is it an interesting and powerful description of a singular moment in history?

■■■ **IDEAS FOR WRITING** ■■■

1. Write a brief research paper on the historical context of this poem.
2. Analyze this poem, and connect the situation to Freire's "The Banking Concept of Education."
3. What are the functions of setting in this poem?

Hard Rock Returns to Prison from the Hospital for the Criminal Insane

Etheridge Knight

In this poem, Knight characterizes Hard Rock, "the doer of things" that others only "dreamed of doing," who returns to prison from a mental hospital. After this experience, Hard Rock no longer fights the prison system. The poem focuses on the responses of others to the change in Hard Rock's behavior.

Hard Rock was "known not to take no shit
From nobody," and he had the scars to prove it:
Split purple lips, lumped ears, welts above
His yellow eyes, and one long scar that cut
5 Across his temple and plowed through a thick
Canopy of kinky hair.

The WORD was that Hard Rock wasn't a mean nigger
Anymore, that the doctors had bored a hole in his head,
Cut out part of his brain, and shot electricity
10 Through the rest. When they brought Hard Rock back,
Handcuffed and chained, he was turned loose,
Like a freshly gelded stallion, to try his new status.
And we all waited and watched, like indians at a corral,
To see if the WORD was true.

15 As we waited we wrapped ourselves in the cloak
Of his exploits: "Man, the last time, it took eight
Screws[1] to put him in the Hole." "Yeah, remember when he
Smacked the captain with his dinner tray?" "He set
The record for time in the Hole—67 straight days!"
20 "Ol Hard Rock! man, that's one crazy nigger."
And then the jewel of a myth that Hard Rock had once bit
A screw on the thumb and poisoned him with syphilitic spit.

The testing came, to see if Hard Rock was really tame.
A hillbilly called him a black son of a bitch
25 And didn't lose his teeth, a screw who knew Hard Rock
From before shook him down and barked in his face.
And Hard Rock did *nothing*. Just grinned and looked silly,
His eyes empty like knot holes in a fence.

And even after we discovered that it took Hard Rock
30 Exactly 3 minutes to tell you his first name,
We told ourselves that he had just wised up,
Was being cool; but we could not fool ourselves for long,

And we turned away, our eyes on the ground. Crushed.
He had been our Destroyer, the doer of things
35 We dreamed of doing but could not bring ourselves to do,
The fears of years, like a biting whip,
Had cut grooves too deeply across our backs.

---

[1] Guards.

■ **EXPLORATIONS OF THE TEXT** ■

1. How does the speaker describe Hard Rock in stanza 1? What does the characterization imply?
2. What is "the WORD" about Hard Rock?
3. Why do the prisoners wrap themselves "in the cloak/Of his exploits"? Are his exploits real? Does it matter?
4. What tests prove that Hard Rock has broken "like a freshly gelded stallion"?
5. Why do the inmates try to fool themselves? Why are they crushed?
6. What does the persona mean when he says, "The fears of years, like a biting whip,/Had cut grooves too deeply across our backs"?
7. What does Hard Rock symbolize? What is the speaker's attitude toward the change in Hard Rock?
8. Compare/contrast Hard Rock and Auden's "The Unknown Citizen."

■■ **JOURNAL ENTRIES** ■■

1. Characterize Hard Rock. Why is his situation so important to others?
2. Describe a person whose strengths and whose defeat have influenced your life.
3. Which lines are most powerful? Why?

■■■ **IDEAS FOR WRITING** ■■■

1. Compare this poem to Valenzuela's "I'm Your Horse in the Night."
2. What views of prison life emerge in this poem?

America

Allen Ginsberg

Allen Ginsberg (1926–   ) was born in New Jersey in 1926, his father a high school English teacher and poet and his mother a Communist who probably sparked his radical politics. After receiving a B.A. degree from Columbia University in 1948, Ginsberg went to San Francisco, where he worked on his long poem, Howl, which was published in 1956 and which distinguished him as a major "Beat" writer in the company of William Burroughs, Jack Kerouac, and Gregory Corso. During the early 1960s, he traveled extensively talking to many Far

Eastern religious teachers in his search for alternatives to drugs as a means of expanding consciousness. In the late 1960s, he received a Guggenheim fellowship and visited many North American colleges and universities, where he read his poems to students and advised them. Ginsberg teaches at City College of New York and Naropa Institute in Colorado. His work, Collected Poems *(1984), gives a view of American life over several decades and introduces the reader to hundreds of personalities of the times. Ginsberg's poetry is innovative, concrete, and reflects William Carlos Williams' instruction to him, "No ideas but in things."*

Some of Ginsberg's other poetry volumes include Empty Mirror: Early Poems *(1961),* Kaddish and Other Poems, 1958–1960 *(1961),* Reality Sandwiches *(1963),* Wichita Vortex Sutra *(1966),* Planet News: 1961–1967 *(1968),* Airplane Dreams *(1968),* The Fall of America *(1973),* Iron Horse *(1973),* Mind Breaths, Poems *(1978),* Plutonium Ode, Poems 1977–1980 *(1982). His prose works contain many interviews, lectures, letters, journals, e.g.,* Indian Journals *(1970),* As Ever: Collected Correspondence Allen Ginsberg and Neal Cassady *(1977), and* Straight Hearts Delight, Love Poems and Selected Letters 1947– 1988 *w/Peter Orlovsky (1980). His most recent works are* White Shroud Poems: 1980–85 *and* Your Reason and Blake's System *(1988).*

In "America," Ginsberg creates a **first-person** *narrator who claims that he is not in his right mind and who criticizes almost every aspect of life in the United States—he speaks of the "end . . . [of] human war," "libraries full of tears," and the "bad Russians."*

America I've given you all and now I'm nothing.
America two dollars and twentyseven cents January 17, 1956.
I can't stand my own mind.
America when will we end the human war?
5 Go fuck yourself with your atom bomb.
I don't feel good don't bother me.
I won't write my poem till I'm in my right mind.
America when will you be angelic?
When will you take off your clothes?
10 When will you look at yourself through the grave?
When will you be worthy of your million Trotskyites?[1]
America why are your libraries full of tears?
America when will you send your eggs to India?
I'm sick of your insane demands.
15 When can I go into the supermarket and buy what I need with my good looks?

---

[1] Those who believe in principles proposed by Trotsky, especially the adoption of worldwide communism through revolution.

America after all it is you and I who are perfect not the next world.
Your machinery is too much for me.
You made me want to be a saint.
There must be some other way to settle this argument.
20 Burroughs[2] is in Tangiers[3] I don't think he'll come back it's sinister.
Are you being sinister or is this some form of practical joke?
I'm trying to come to the point.
I refuse to give up my obsession.
America stop pushing I know what I'm doing.
25 America the plum blossoms are falling.
I haven't read the newspapers for months, everyday somebody goes on trial
    for murder.
America I feel sentimental about the Wobblies.[4]
America I used to be a communist when I was a kid I'm not sorry.
I smoke marijuana every chance I get.
30 I sit in my house for days on end and stare at the roses in the closet.
When I go to Chinatown I get drunk and never get laid.
My mind is made up there's going to be trouble.
You should have seen me reading Marx.[5]
My psychoanalyst thinks I'm perfectly right.
35 I won't say the Lord's Prayer.
I have mystical visions and cosmic vibrations.
America I still haven't told you what you did to Uncle Max after he came
    over from Russia.

I'm addressing you.
Are you going to let your emotional life be run by Time Magazine?
40 I'm obsessed by Time Magazine.
I read it every week.
Its cover stares at me every time I slink past the corner candystore.
I read it in the basement of the Berkeley Public Library.
It's always telling me about responsibility. Businessmen are serious.
45   Movie producers are serious. Everybody's serious but me.
It occurs to me that I am America.
I am talking to myself again.

Asia is rising against me.
I haven't got a chinaman's chance.
50 I'd better consider my national resources.
My national resources consist of two joints of marijuana millions of
    genitals

---

[2] American novelist (1914–   ).
[3] Port on the Strait of Gibralter in North Morocco.
[4] Members of the Industrial Workers of the World.
[5] Karl Marx. German philosopher and Socialist (1818–1883).

an unpublishable private literature that jetplanes 1400 miles
an hour and twentyfive-thousand mental institutions.
I say nothing about my prisons nor the millions of underprivileged who
55   live in my flowerpots under the light of five hundred suns.
I have abolished the whorehouses of France, Tangiers is the next to go.
My ambition is to be President despite the fact that I'm a Catholic.

America how can I write a holy litany in your silly mood?
I will continue like Henry Ford my strophes are as individual as his
60   automobiles more so they're all different sexes.
America I will sell you strophes $2500 apiece $500 down on your old
      strophe
America free Tom Mooney[6]
America save the Spanish Loyalists[7]
America Sacco & Vanzetti must not die[8]
65 America I am the Scottsboro boys.[9]
America when I was seven momma took me to Communist Cell meetings
      they sold us garbanzos a handful per ticket a ticket costs a nickel
      and the speeches were free everybody was angelic and sentimental
      about the workers it was all so sincere you have no idea what a
70   good thing the party was in 1835 Scott Nearing was a grand old
      man a real mensch Mother Bloor the Silk-strikers' Ewig-Weibliche[10]
      made me cry I once saw the Yiddish orator Israel Amter plain.[11]
      Everybody must have been a spy.
America you don't really want to go to war.
75 America it's them bad Russians.
Them Russians them Russians and them Chinamen. And them Russians.
The Russia wants to eat us alive. The Russia's power mad. She wants to
      take our cars from out our garages.
Her wants to grab Chicago. Her needs a Red *Reader's Digest.* Her wants
80   our auto plants in Siberia. Him big bureaucracy running our
      fillingstations.
That no good. Ugh. Him make Indians learn read. Him need big black
      niggers. Hah. Her make us all work sixteen hours a day. Help.
America this is quite serious.
America this is the impression I get from looking in the television set.
85 America is this correct?

---

[6] American Wobbly, convicted for murder in 1916 and pardoned more than twenty years later.
[7] Spaniards, Republicans, who opposed Franco's Nationalists during the Spanish Civil War
(1936–1939).
[8] Nicola Sacco (1891–1927) and Bartolemeo Vanzetti (1888–1927). American anarchists who
were executed.
[9] Nine African-American youths convicted of raping two white women; a controversial case
because of lack of evidence.
[10] Ewig-Weibliche. "Eternal feminine" in German.
[11] Nearing, Bloor, and Amter; American leftists.

I'd better get right down to the job.
It's true I don't want to join the Army or turn lathes in precision parts
   factories, I'm nearsighted and psychopathic anyway.
America I'm putting my queer shoulder to the wheel.

■ EXPLORATIONS OF THE TEXT ■

1. Describe the speaker. Focus on his character traits, tone, values, and attitudes.
2. In addressing "America" as his audience, to whom does he speak? What are his criticisms of his culture?
3. Why does he state "It occurs to me that I am America./I am talking to myself again"?
4. Analyze the section beginning: "Asia is rising against me." From whose view is the persona speaking? Is this change of point of view effective?
5. Discuss the speaker's vocation as a writer.
6. How are the historical allusions—Spanish Loyalists, Sacco and Vanzetti, Communist cell meetings—important to the poem?
7. Why does he speak in baby talk, in "Indian" dialect? When does the voice shift?
8. What impact does the humor have? Does it develop themes of the work?
9. In the last line, does the speaker change his point of view and attitude? How?
10. Compare this poem to the poems by Brooks and Hughes.

■■ JOURNAL ENTRIES ■■

1. Characterize the speaker.
2. Make a catalogue of the criticisms of America. Are they valid?
3. Write a humorous critique about some aspect of life in the United States. Begin with "America, I . . . ."

■■■ IDEAS FOR WRITING ■■■

1. Analyze the speaker in this poem. How does Ginsberg achieve this characterization? Discuss voice, tone, imagery, humor, word choice, and/or theme.
2. Compare themes of this poem with another work in this chapter.
3. Compare this poem with Whitman's "Out of the Cradle Endlessly Rocking" in Chapter 4.

History

Gary Soto

In Soto's "History," the speaker learns from his grandmother about the places where his family began.

Grandma lit the stove.
Morning sunlight
Lengthened in spears
Across the linoleum floor.
5 Wrapped in a shawl,
Her eyes small
With sleep.
She sliced papas,[1]
Pounded chiles
10 With a stone
Brought from Guadalajara.[2]
                                        After

Grandpa left for work,
She hosed down
15 The walk her sons paved
And in the shade
Of a chinaberry,
Unearthed her
Secret cigar box
20 Of bright coins
And bills, counted them
In English,
Then in Spanish,
And buried them elsewhere.
25 Later, back
From the market,
Where no one saw her,
She pulled out
Pepper and beet, spines
30 Of asparagus
From her blouse,
Tiny chocolates
From under a paisley bandana,
And smiled.

---

[1] Potatoes.
[2] Mexican city.

35 That was the '50s,
And Grandma in her '50s,
A face streaked
From cutting grapes
And boxing plums.
40 I remember her insides
Were washed of tapeworm,
Her arms swelled into knobs
Of small growths—
Her second son
45 Dropped from a ladder
And was dust.
And yet I do not know
The sorrows
That sent her praying
50 In the dark of a closet,
The tear that fell
At night
When she touched
Loose skin
55 Of belly and breasts.
I do not know why
Her face shines
Or what goes beyond this shine,
Only the stories
60 That pulled her
From Taxco[3] to San Joaquin,
Delano to Westside,[4]
The places
In which we all begin.

■ **EXPLORATIONS OF THE TEXT** ■

1. What impression of Grandma emerges in stanza 1? Which details are most important? How does the setting function?
2. How does the portrayal of the grandmother change in stanza 2? Examine the tone, and discuss the attitudes of the speaker.
3. What are the difficulties of the 1950s? Why is the description of Grandma more poignant? What are her "sorrows"?
4. What does the narrator mean by "The places/In which we all begin"?
5. Analyze the character of the speaker. What does his grandmother mean to him?

---

[3] Mexican city.
[4] Cities in California.

6. Define history. How does Soto alter the traditional meaning of history?
7. Compare the speaker in this work with the personae in other poems in this chapter.

■■ **JOURNAL ENTRIES** ■■

1. Respond to the grandmother's shoplifting. How does it affect your attitude toward her?
2. Create a vision of your cultural history through a portrait of a relative.

■■■ **IDEAS FOR WRITING** ■■■

1. Analyze Soto's definition of personal and of Mexican-American history.
2. Characterize Grandma.

---

horse

Gloria Anzaldúa

Gloria Evangelina Anzaldúa is a Chicana, *feminist, a poet, and a fiction writer. Born and raised on the border between Mexico and Texas where her father was a sharecropper for Rio Farms Incorporated, Anzaldúa writes in* Borderlands: La Frontera—The New Mestiza *(1987) of the difficulties experienced by anyone caught between cultures, an alien everywhere "Because [she], a Mestiza,/continually walk[s] out of one culture/and into another,/because [she is] in all cultures at the same time. . . ." She has worked in the migrant farmers movement; and she has taught at the University of Texas at Austin, San Francisco State University, and Vermont College of Norwich University. Her first book,* This Bridge Called My Back: Writings by Radical Women of Color, *co-edited by Cherríe Moraga, won the 1986 Before Columbus Foundation American Book Award.*

In "horse," Anzaldúa describes an unspeakable act of cruelty committed by adolescents who torture a horse in Hargill, Texas. The work reflects the tensions between the Mexicans and the gringos.

(para la gente de Hargill, Texas)[1]

Great horse running in the fields
come thundering toward
the outstretched hands
nostrils flaring at the corn
5 only it was knives in the hidden hands
can a horse smell tempered steel?

Anoche[2] some kids cut up a horse
it was night and the *pueblo*[3] slept
the Mexicans mutter among themselves:
10 they hobbled the two front legs
the two hind legs, kids aged sixteen
but they're *gringos*[4]
and the sheriff won't do a thing
he'd just say boys will be boys
15 just following their instincts.

But it's the mind that kills
the animal the *mexicanos* murmur
killing it would have been a mercy
black horse running in the dark
20 came thundering toward
the outstretched hands
nostrils flaring at the smell
only it was knives in the hidden hands
did it pray all night for morning?

25 It was the owner came running
30-30 in his hand
put the *caballo*[5] out of its pain
the Chicanos shake their heads
turn away some rich father
30 fished out his wallet
held out the folds of green
as if green could staunch red

pools dripping from the ribbons
on the horse's flanks
35 could cast up testicles

---

[1] For the people of Hargill, Texas.
[2] Last night.
[3] Village.
[4] Whites.
[5] Horse.

grow back the ears on the horse's head
no ears of corn but sheaths
hiding blades of steel
earth drinking blood sun rusting it
40 in that small Texas town
the *mexicanos* shuffle their feet
shut their faces stare at the ground.

Dead horse neighing in the night
come thundering toward the open faces
45 hooves iron-shod hurling lightning

only it is red red in the moonlight
in their sleep the *gringos* cry out
the *mexicanos* mumble if you're Mexican
you are born old.

■ EXPLORATIONS OF THE TEXT ■

1. Examine the image of the horse in stanza 1. What is the effect of "the outstretched hands"? of the "knives"? What is the meaning of the corn?
2. Does the story of the boys who cut the horse have symbolic meaning?
3. Explain: "It's the mind that kills."
4. Why does the speaker repeat the image of the horse and the hands with the corn and the knives? Is the repetition effective?
5. Why do the Mexicanos "shuffle their feet/shut their faces stare at the ground" and "mumble"?
6. Examine the **paradox** in the next-to-last stanza. How can the dead horse still thunder "toward the open faces"?
7. Why do the gringos "cry"?
8. How do the last two lines convey themes of the work?
9. Discuss symbolism, imagery, and language in this poem. Is the use of Spanish words and phrases effective?
10. Compare the themes of oppression and bigotry in this poem with similar ideas in "Harlem" or "The Chicago Defender Sends a Man to Little Rock."

■■ JOURNAL ENTRIES ■■

1. Gloss and annotate the poem, and write an end comment. See the example in Chapter 2.
2. React to the situations of the Mexicans and Chicanos. Why are they "born old"?

■■■   **IDEAS FOR WRITING**   ■■■

1. What does the story symbolize about the attitudes of the gringos toward other people, animals, land, things? Do you agree?
2. Compare the endings of this poem and the endings of works by Griffin, Rose, and Harjo. Discuss the reversals, the anger, and the desire for change and for retribution.

For Anna Mae Aquash Whose Spirit Is Present Here and in the Dappled Stars

Joy Harjo

Joy Harjo (1951–   ) was born in Tulsa, Oklahoma. Harjo has taught writing at Arizona State University in Tempe and at the Institute of American Indian Arts in Santa Fe, New Mexico. Her volumes of poetry include The Last Song *(1975),* What Moon Drove Me to This *(1980), and* She Has Some Horses *(1983).*

Anna Mae Aquash was a young Micmac Indian activist who was mysteriously murdered in 1976 on the Pine Ridge Reservation in South Dakota. In this poem, Harjo's speaker mourns the death of Aquash.

For we remember the story and must tell it again so we may all live

Beneath a sky blurred with mist and wind,
                          I am amazed as I watch the violet
heads of crocuses erupt from the stiff earth
                          after dying for a season,
5   as I have watched my own dark head
                          appear each morning after entering
the next world
                          to come back to this one,
                          amazed.
10 It is the way in the natural world to understand the place
                          the ghost dancers[1] named
after the heart breaking destruction.

---

[1] Dancers who performed the Ghost Dance, a group dance begun by late nineteenth-century Native-Americans to promote the return of the dead and the restoration of the spiritual life of the tribe.

Anna Mae,
everything and nothing changes
15 You are the shimmering young woman
who found her voice
when you were warned to be silent, or have your body cut away
from you like an elegant weed.
You are the one whose spirit is present in the dappled stars.
20 (They prance and lope like colored horses who stay with us
through the streets of these steely cities. And I have seen them
nuzzling the frozen bodies of tattered drunks
on the corner.)
This morning when the last star is dimming
25 and the buses grind toward
the middle of the city, I know it is ten years since they buried
you the second time in Lakota, a language that could
free you.
I heard about it in Oklahoma, or New Mexico
30 how the wind howled and pulled everything down
in a righteous anger.
(It was the women who told me) and we understood wordlessly
the ripe meaning of your murder.
As I understand ten years later after the slow changing
35 of the seasons
that we have just begun to touch
the dazzling whirlwind of our anger,
we have just begun to perceive the amazed world the ghost
dancers entered
40 crazily, beautifully.

■ **EXPLORATIONS OF THE TEXT** ■

---

1. Describe the setting and season. What is the attitude of the speaker?
   Explain the following lines: "as I have watched my own dark
   head/appear each morning after entering/the next world/to come back
   to this one,/amazed."
2. What is the place "the ghost dancers named"? How can it be
   understood?
3. How is Anna Mae invoked and described? Consider the star imagery
   and the extension of the **metaphor**.
4. What does the speaker mean when she says "I know it is ten years
   since they buried/you the second time in Lakota, a language that
   could/free you"?
5. Examine the last five lines. What is "the dazzling whirlwind" of anger?
   What is "the amazed world the ghost/dancers entered"?

6. Discuss the images of beauty and of destruction in this poem. How do they reveal theme?
7. Compare the political message of this poem to the ideas in Hughes's "Let America Be America Again" and Ginsberg's "America."

■■ JOURNAL ENTRIES ■■

1. Imitate this poem, and write to someone who has died for a political cause.
2. Write a double-entry journal on this poem.
3. Freewrite about the line: "everything and nothing changes."

■■■ IDEAS FOR WRITING ■■■

1. Characterize the speaker and Anna Mae.
2. Analyze the imagery in this poem.

I Like to Think of Harriet Tubman

Susan Griffin

Born in California, Susan Griffin (1943–) graduated from San Francisco State University in 1965. Continuing to live in California, she has worked as a waitress, teacher, house painter, and switchboard operator. Her collection, Made from this Earth: An Anthology of Writings, *appeared in 1982. Her second major collection of poems,* Unremembered Country *was published by Copper Canyon Press in 1987, and* A Chorus Of Stones: The Private Life of War *which deals with the psychological effects of war and violence appeared in 1992.*

Griffin always has been feminist in her writing, exploring the issue of the oppression of women. Her work has a positive thrust, affirming woman's potential and energy. Adrienne Rich has said that her poetry reflects "female anger as power, female presence as transforming force."

In this poem, Griffin refers to Harriet Tubman (c. 1820–1913) who was an escaped slave and a leader in the Underground Railroad, a network that aided slaves in their flight to freedom. She describes details from Tubman's life. The narrator draws strength from the example of Harriet Tubman when she considers such a contemporary issues as hungry children in the United States.

I like to think of Harriet Tubman.[1]
Harriet Tubman who carried a revolver,
who had a scar on her head from a rock thrown
by a slave-master (because she
5 talked back), and who
had a ransom on her head
of thousands of dollars and who
was never caught, and who
had no use for the law
10 when the law was wrong,
who defied the law. I like
to think of her.
I like to think of her especially
when I think of the problem of
15 feeding children.

The legal answer
to the problem of feeding children
is ten free lunches every month,
being equal, in the child's real life,
20 to eating lunch every other day.
Monday but not Tuesday.
I like to think of the President
eating lunch Monday, but not
Tuesday.
25 And when I think of the President
and the law, and the problem of
feeding children, I like to
think of Harriet Tubman
and her revolver.

30 And then sometimes
I think of the President
and other men,
men who practice the law,
who revere the law,
35 who make the law,
who enforce the law,
who live behind
and operate through
and feed themselves
40 at the expense of

---

[1] African-American escaped slave and abolitionist; leader of the Underground Railroad that arranged safe passage for slaves who sought freedom (c. 1820–1930).

starving children
because of the law.

Men who sit in paneled offices
and think about vacations
45 and tell women
whose care it is
to feed children
not to be hysterical
not to be hysterical as in the word
50 hysterikos, the greek for
womb suffering,
not to suffer in their
wombs,
not to care,
55 not to bother the men
because they want to think
of other things
and do not want
to take the women seriously.
60 I want them
to take women seriously.

I want them to think about Harriet Tubman,
and remember,
remember she was beat by a white man
65 and she lived
and she lived to redress her grievances,
and she lived in swamps
and wore the clothes of a man
bringing hundreds of fugitives from
70 slavery, and was never caught,
and led an army,
and won a battle,
and defied the laws
because the laws were wrong, I want men
75 to take us seriously.
I am tired wanting them to think
about right and wrong.
I want them to fear.
I want them to feel fear now
80 as I have felt suffering in the womb, and
I want them
to know
that there is always a time
there is always a time to make right

85 what is wrong,
    there is always a time
    for retribution
    and that time
    is beginning.

■ EXPLORATIONS OF THE TEXT ■

1. Why does the speaker "like to think of Harriet Tubman"? What details of Tubman's life are important to her?
2. What is the speaker's attitude toward the "law"? What is the tone of the second and third stanzas?
3. What is the role of women? Why does the persona want men "to take the women seriously"?
4. Explain: "I want them to think about Harriet Tubman." Why does the speaker want men "to fear"?
5. At the end, what does the speaker mean by "retribution"?
6. Examine the use of repetition as a rhetorical device in the poem. Is it effective?
7. Compare this poem to "horse," "Three Thousand Dollar Death Song," or "For Anna Mae Aquash . . . ."

■■ JOURNAL ENTRIES ■■

1. React to the portrait of Harriet Tubman, or react to the speaker's voice.
2. Is the time of retribution beginning?

■■■ IDEAS FOR WRITING ■■■

1. Compare Griffin's poem to Rose's "Three Thousand Dollar Death Song." Focus on persona and themes.
2. Write about a law which you consider to be unjust.
3. What does Griffin believe about the role of women? Is she redefining gender roles?

Telephone Conversation

Wole Soyinka

Born in Isara, Nigeria, Wole Soyinka (1934–) was immersed during his childhood in two cultures. Ake, his village, was comprised largely of members of the Yoruba tribe; and his grandfather taught him about the Yoruba gods. His father, however, was headmaster of a British-run school; and his mother was a Christian convert. He attended the University of Ibadan and received a B.A. degree with honors from the University of Leeds in England. During the 1960s, he opposed Nigeria's civil war and the government's repressive responses to the Ibo people who desired to form an independent nation, Biafra. In 1967, he was arrested and, though never formally charged with any crime, imprisoned for more than two years. Although he was refused any writing materials, Soyinka made his own ink and wrote on toilet paper. His poetry, which was smuggled out of prison, was an inspiration to his supporters. After he was released from prison when the Biafrans were defeated in 1969, he left Nigeria until a change of power took place in 1975.

Considered by many critics to be Africa's best writer, Soyinka has published drama, poetry, novels, and nonfiction. His plays meld traditional Yoruban folk drama with European dramatic form. Among his other works are the novels, The Interpreters *(1965) and* Season of Anomy *(1973); and nonfiction volumes,* The Man Died: Prison Notes of Wole Soyinka *(1972) and* Ake: The Years of Childhood *(1981). Among his many awards is the 1986 Nobel Prize in Literature for* The Interpreters. *Soyinka's writing reflects contemporary Africa's political upheaval and efforts to blend traditional culture with technological advances.*

In this poem, Soyinka describes a telephone inquiry about renting lodging. The prospective tenant confesses that he is African. The landlady asks, "ARE YOU LIGHT/OR VERY DARK?" The answer to this incredible query is humorous, but ultimately angry.

    The price seemed reasonable, location
    Indifferent. The landlady swore she lived
    Off premises. Nothing remained
    But self-confession. 'Madam,' I warned,
5   'I hate a wasted journey—I am African.'
    Silence. Silenced transmission of
    Pressurized good-breeding. Voice, when it came,
    Lipstick coated, long gold-rolled
    Cigarette-holder pipped. Caught I was, foully.

10 'HOW DARK?' . . . I had not misheard . . . 'ARE YOU LIGHT
OR VERY DARK?' Button B. Button A. Stench
Of rancid breath of public hide-and-speak.
Red booth. Red pillar-box. Red double-tiered
Omnibus squelching tar. It *was* real! Shamed
15 By ill-mannered silence, surrender
Pushed dumbfoundment to beg simplification.
Considerate she was, varying the emphasis—
'ARE YOU DARK? OR VERY LIGHT?' Revelation came.
'You mean—like plain or milk chocolate?'
20 Her assent was clinical, crushing in its light
Impersonality. Rapidly, wave-length adjusted,
I chose. 'West African sepia'—and as afterthought,
'Down in my passport.' Silence for spectroscopic
Flight of fancy, till truthfulness clanged her accent
25 Hard on the mouthpiece. 'WHAT'S THAT?' conceding
'DON'T KNOW WHAT THAT IS.' 'Like brunette.'
'THAT'S DARK, ISN'T IT?' 'Not altogether.
Facially, I am brunette, but madam, you should see
The rest of me. Palm of my hand, soles of my feet
30 Are a peroxide blonde. Friction, caused—
Foolishly madam—by sitting down, has turned
My bottom raven black—One moment madam!'—sensing
Her receiver rearing on the thunderclap
About my ears—'Madam,' I pleaded, 'wouldn't you rather
35 See for yourself?'

■ EXPLORATIONS OF THE TEXT ■

1. In the opening lines, why is the tone reportial? What happens when
   the persona confesses that he is African?
2. Is the speaker surprised by the question? Where does this situation
   happen? Examine details in lines 11 to 14.
3. Characterize the persona. What does he intend when he describes his
   skin as "West African sepia"?
4. Characterize the landlady.
5. Examine the speaker's final description of his skin (beginning in line 28).
   What is the meaning of the narrator's last question?
6. What does Soyinka accomplish with humor? Compare this poem with
   the humor in the speech by Sojourner Truth or in Griffin's poem about
   Harriet Tubman.

■■ Journal Entries ■■

---

1. Create a telephone conversation about renting a room or apartment. Like Soyinka, create a speaker who cannot succeed in his or her quest because of bigotry.
2. Respond to the closing lines of the poem.

■■■ Ideas for Writing ■■■

---

1. Analyze the character of the speaker or of the landlady.
2. Discuss humor as a political response. Refer to this poem and to other works which you have read.

The Colonel

Carolyn Forché

Born in Detroit, Michigan, Carolyn Forché (1950–   ) began writing poetry at age nine. She earned her B.A. degree from Michigan State University and her M.F.A. degree from Bowling Green State University. She has been a visiting lecturer in poetry or a visiting writer at a number of colleges. She lived in El Salvador from 1978 to 1980, working as a journalist and human rights' activist.

Her publications include the volumes of poetry, Gathering the Tribes *(1976), which won the Yale University Younger Poets Award, and* The Country Between Us *(1981), which was named the Lamont Selection of the Academy of American Poets. She is associated with Amnesty International and has translated the works of Salvadoran poets. A recipient of fellowships from the National Endowment for the Arts and from the Guggenheim Foundation, she also has lived in South Africa and currently resides in Paris. She has edited an anthology of poetry of witness:* Against Forgetting *(1993).*

Reviewer and poet Katha Pollitt comments in the Nation, *"Forché's poems have the immediacy of war correspondence, postcards from the volcano of twentieth-century barbarism." "The Colonel," which follows, arose from Forché's encounter with a Salvadoran colonel who belittled her concern for human rights when he dumped a sack of human ears at her feet and said, "Something for your poetry, no?" "The Colonel," a prose poem, appeared in a series of pieces on El Salvador in* The Country Between Us.

1   What you have heard is true. I was in his house. His wife carried a tray of coffee and sugar. His daughter filed her nails, his son went out for the night. There were daily papers, pet dogs, a pistol on the cushion beside him. The moon swung bare on its black cord over the house. On the television was a cop show. It was in English. Broken bottles were embedded in the walls around the house to scoop the kneecaps from a man's legs or cut his hands to lace. On the windows there were gratings like those in liquor stores. We had dinner, rack of lamb, good wine, a gold bell was on the table for calling the maid. The maid brought green mangoes, salt, a type of bread. I was asked how I enjoyed the country. There was a brief commercial in Spanish. His wife took everything away. There was some talk then of how difficult it had become to govern. The parrot said hello on the terrace. The colonel told it to shut up, and pushed himself from the table. My friend said to me with his eyes: say nothing. The colonel returned with a sack used to bring groceries home. He spilled many human ears on the table. They were like dried peach halves. There is no other way to say this. He took one of them in his hands, shook it in our faces, dropped it into a water glass. It came alive there. I am tired of fooling around he said. As for the rights of anyone, tell your people they can go fuck themselves. He swept the ears to the floor with his arm and held the last of his wine in the air. Something for your poetry, no? he said. Some of the ears on the floor caught this scrap of his voice. Some of the ears on the floor were pressed to the ground.

■ EXPLORATIONS OF THE TEXT ■

1. Discuss the details of the Colonel's home, family, and dinner. Explain the first statement.
2. Look at the first half of the poem. Do any images **foreshadow** the events of the conclusion?
3. Where does the mood of the poem shift?
4. Why has the Colonel collected human ears "like dried peach halves" in a sack? Why does he drop one in a glass of water? Why does he sweep the ears to the floor?
5. What does the Colonel mean when he says "I am tired of fooling around . . . As for the rights of anyone, tell your people they can go fuck themselves"?
6. Does the Colonel believe that the ears might serve as images for poetry, or is he being ironic?
7. Explain the ending. How can the disconnected ears be "pressed to the ground"?
8. Discuss the form of this prose poem. Why does the narrator speak in simple, declarative sentences?
9. Compare this poem with Agosín's essay and with Valenzuela's story. Focus on speaker and voice.

■■   JOURNAL ENTRIES   ■■

1. Freewrite about the Colonel's sack of dried human ears.
2. Write a political prose poem which shifts its tone and subject. Use "The Colonel" as a model.
3. React to the color imagery in the poem.

■■■   IDEAS FOR WRITING   ■■■

1. Discuss the issue of human rights in Forché's poems.
2. Why do soldiers collect such bizarre trophies of war? Use Journal Entry 1 as a beginning.
3. Compare this poem to O'Brien's "The Things They Carried." Focus on the images of tokens of war and "the things they carried."
4. Characterize the Colonel.

The Memory of Elena

Carolyn Forché

In this poem, as the narrator contemplates Elena's love for her dead husband, she begins to transform every object into reminders of the fragility of life, of the terror of dictatorship.

> We spend our morning
> in the flower stalls counting
> the dark tongues of bells
> that hang from ropes waiting
> 5 for the silence of an hour.
> We find a table, ask for *paella*, [1]
> cold soup and wine, where a calm
> light trembles years behind us.
>
> In Buenos Aires[2] only three
> 10 years ago, it was the last time his hand
> slipped into her dress, with pearls
> cooling her throat and bells like
> these, chipping at the night—

---

[1] A Spanish dish made with rice, saffron, chicken, sausage, and seafood.
[2] A city in Argentina.

As she talks, the hollow
15 clopping of a horse, the sound
of bones touched together.
The *paella* comes, a bed of rice
and *camarones,*[3] fingers and shells,
the lips of those whose lips
20 have been removed, mussels
the soft blue of a leg socket.

This is not *paella,* this is what
has become of those who remained
in Buenos Aires. This is the ring
25 of a rifle report on the stones,
her hand over her mouth,
her husband falling against her.

These are the flowers we bought
this morning, the dahlias tossed
30 on his grave and bells
waiting with their tongues cut out
for this particular silence.

■ EXPLORATIONS OF THE TEXT ■

1. Examine the first stanza. What happens? Which words have negative **connotations** and **foreshadow** the ending?
2. Describe the relationship of Elena and her husband. What does the sensuality of the marriage contribute to the meaning of the poem?
3. Explain the transformation of the images in stanza 3. Examine the "clopping of a horse" and the personification of the food into horrible examples of torture.
4. Why does the speaker become so direct in the fourth verse? What happened to Elena's husband? Why is it presented so simply?
5. Analyze the flowers and the bells in the last verse. Look again at the opening. How has the imagery changed or expanded?
6. Discuss the title, the form of the poem, and the themes. Does the title contain multiple meanings?
7. Compare the themes of political violence in this poem with similar ideas in "The Colonel" and in works by Valenzuela and Agosin.

---

[3] Shrimp or prawns.

■■ JOURNAL ENTRIES ■■

1. React to one of the images in the poem: silence, tongues, bells, flowers, or food.
2. Gloss and annotate the poem, and write an end comment.

■■■ IDEAS FOR WRITING ■■■

1. Explicate this poem. Focus on tone, imagery, and formal elements. Use your annotation as a beginning.
2. Begin a paper on the two poems by Forché with this quotation by Margaret Atwood: "Here is a poetry of courage and passion, which manages to be tender and achingly sensual and what is often called 'political' at the same time."
3. Write about Elena and about those people in Central and South America who mourn the "disappeared." Refer to Agosin's essay.

I'm Nobody! Who are you?

Emily Dickinson

Emily Dickinson (1830–1886) was born in Amherst, Massachusetts. She spent almost her entire life under her father's roof in obscure, self-imposed isolation, yet her mind was well-travelled and cultivated. Her poems are uniformly short—usually four-line stanzas—and written in a terse, aphoristic style. While she personally rejected Calvinism, her poetry is worldly and rich with biblical imagery, ponderings about death, and the pervasive spirit of nature. Not until 1955 were her complete poems published—sixty-nine years after her death.

In this brief poem, Dickinson captures the lack of identity felt by a speaker who prefers such privacy to being "Somebody."

I'm Nobody! Who are you?
Are you—Nobody—Too?
Then there's a pair of us?
Don't tell! they'd advertise—you know!

5 How dreary—to be—Somebody!
How public—like a Frog—
To tell one's name—the livelong June—
To an admiring Bog!

■ EXPLORATIONS OF THE TEXT ■

1. Examine the first three lines. Why are they questions? To whom does the speaker refer as "you" and as "us"?
2. Why must the "nobodies" preserve their anonymity from advertisement or announcement?
3. What is the meaning of the simile about the "Frog." Why is it "dreary" and "public" to be "somebody"?
4. Analyze tone, punctuation, rhyme, and other formal aspects of the poem. Consider this work as typical of Emily Dickinson's poetry. What do you conclude?
5. Compare the idea of nobody in this poem with the same subject in "Nobodies" by Galeano.

■■ JOURNAL ENTRIES ■■

1. Agree or disagree with the speaker's view of fame.
2. Write a parody of this work.

■■■ IDEAS FOR WRITING ■■■

1. Compare and contrast this poem with Galeano's "Nobodies." Concentrate on **persona** and themes.
2. Discuss the necessity of the human desire for identity and for a name. Refer to works in this chapter.
3. Should identity be a public issue?

Nobodies

Eduardo Galeano

*Born in Montevideo, Uruguay, Eduardo Galeano (1940–   ) is a jour-
nalist, historian, political activist, and writer. He began his career
in journalism at the age of thirteen, becoming editor-in-chief of the
weekly newspaper,* Marcha, *when he was twenty. Later, he was imprisoned following a right-wing military coup and eventually was forced
to flee to Argentina. He remained in exile until he was permitted to
return to Uruguay in 1984.*

His many works, translated into English, include the nonfiction
Guatemala: Occupied Country *(1969); the memoir,* Days and Nights of

Love and War, *for which he received the award Premio Casa de las Americas in 1978; and the trilogy,* Memory of Fire: Genesis *(1985),* Memory of Fire: Faces and Masks *(1987), and* Memory of Fire: Century of the Wind *(1988), which received the American Book Award in 1989.* The Book of Embraces *appeared in 1992. Galeano has said, "Unable to distance myself, I take sides: I confess it and am not sorry."*

In "Nobodies," a short section from The Book of Embraces, *he describes the inescapable quality of poverty in Uruguay. He defines the nobodies as the "owners of/nothing. . . ." and "running like rabbits, dying through life. . . ." He defines them through negatives, through their lack of identity in and importance to their society.*

1 Fleas dream of buying themselves a dog, and
nobodies dream of escaping poverty: that one
magical day good luck will suddenly rain down
on them—will rain down in buckets. But good
luck doesn't rain down yesterday, today, tomorrow, or ever. Good luck doesn't even fall in a
fine drizzle, no matter how hard the nobodies
summon it, even if they prick their left hand, or
raise their right foot, or start the new year with a
change of brooms.

The nobodies: nobody's children, owners of
nothing. The nobodies: the no ones, the nobodies, running like rabbits, dying through life,
screwed every which way.

Who are not, but could be.

Who don't speak languages, but dialects.

5 Who don't have religion, but superstitions.

Who don't create art, but handicrafts.

Who don't have culture, but folklore.

Who aren't human beings, but human
resources.

Who don't have faces, but arms.

10 Who don't have names, but numbers.

Who don't appear in the history of the world,
but in the police blotter of the local paper.

The nobodies, who are not worth the bullet
that kills them.

■ EXPLORATIONS OF THE TEXT ■

1. Explore the analogy in the first sentence. What is the source of its power?
2. Examine the examples of luck which represent the dream of the "nobodies." Focus on the extended **metaphor** of the rain.

3. Who are the "nobodies"? Why does Galeano choose the plural form "nobodies"?
4. Why does Galeano describe who and what they are not? Analyze each definition.
5. Consider the repetition of clauses which begin with "who." Is this repetition effective?
6. What is the impact of the final line?
7. Compare the effectiveness of this work with your assessment of works by Dickinson, Agosin, and Hughes.

■■ JOURNAL ENTRIES ■■

1. Who are the "nobodies" in your culture?
2. Respond to one of Galeano's definitions.
3. Respond to the last line of the poem.

■■■ IDEAS FOR WRITING ■■■

1. Compare and contrast themes in works by Galeano, Dickinson, and/or Hughes.
2. Describe a specific situation in the United States which is similar to Galeano's portrait of "nobodies" in Uruguay.

Poems for Further Reading

A Description of the Morning
Jonathan Swift (1667–1745)

Now hardly here and there a hackney-coach
Appearing, showed the ruddy morn's approach.
Now Betty from her master's bed had flown,
And softly stole to discompose her own;
5 The slip-shod 'prentice from his master's door
Had pared the dirt and sprinkled round the floor.
Now Moll had whirled her mop with dext'rous airs,
Prepared to scrub the entry and the stairs.
The youth with broomy stumps began to trace
10 The kennel-edge, where wheels had worn the place.[1]
The small-coal man was heard with cadence deep,
Till drowned in shriller notes of chimney-sweep:
Duns at his lordship's gate began to meet;
And brickdust Moll had screamed through half the street.
15 The turnkey now his flock returning sees,
Duly let out a-nights to steal for fees:[2]
The watchful bailiffs take their silent stands,
And schoolboys lag with satchels in their hands.

London
William Blake (1757–1827)

I wander through each chartered[1] street,
Near where the chartered Thames does flow,
And mark in every face I meet
Marks of weakness, marks of woe.

---

[1] The youth is scavenging in the tracks of wheels in the road.
[2] The "turnkey" (the jailer) has let his incarcerated criminals out in the night to steal.
[1] Pre-empted by the State and leased by royal patent.

5 In every cry of every man,
   In every Infant's cry of fear,
In every voice, in every ban,
   The mind-forged manacles I hear.

How the Chimney-sweeper's cry
10 Every black'ning Church appalls;
And the hapless Soldier's sigh
   Runs in blood down Palace walls.

But most through midnight streets I hear
How the youthful Harlot's curse
15 Blasts the new-born Infant's tear,
   And blights with plagues the Marriage hearse.

The Slave Auction

Frances Ellen Watkins Harper (1825–1911)

The sale began—young girls were there,
   Defenceless in their wretchedness,
Whose stifled sobs of deep despair
   Revealed their anguish and distress.

5 And mothers stood with streaming eyes,
   And saw their dearest children sold;
Unheeded rose their bitter cries,
   While tyrants bartered them for gold.

And woman, with her love and truth—
10   For these in sable[1] forms may dwell—
Gaz'd on the husband of her youth,
   With anguish none may paint or tell.

And men, whose sole crime was their hue,
   The impress of their Maker's hand,
15 And frail and shrinking children, too,
   Were gathered in that mournful band.

Ye who have laid your love to rest,
   And wept above their lifeless clay,

---

[1] Black.

Know not the anguish of that breast,
20   Whose lov'd are rudely torn away.

Ye may not know how desolate
    Are bosoms rudely forced to part,
And how a dull and heavy weight
    Will press the life-drops from the heart.

The Man He Killed

Thomas Hardy (1840–1928)

"Had he and I but met
By some old ancient inn,
We should have sat us down to wet
Right many a nipperkin[1]

5   "But ranged as infantry,
And staring face to face,
I shot at him as he at me,
And killed him in his place.

"I shot him dead because—
10 Because he was my foe,
Just so: my foe of course he was;
That's clear enough; although

"He thought he'd 'list, perhaps,
Off-hand like—just as I—
15 Was out of work—had sold his traps[2]—
No other reason why.

"Yes; quaint and curious war is!
You shoot a fellow down
You'd treat if met where any bar is,
20 Or help to half-a-crown."

---

[1] Half-pint cup.
[2] Personal possessions or property.

Love's Coming

Ella Wheeler Wilcox (1850–1919)

She had looked for his coming as warriors come,
    With the clash of arms and the bugle's call;
But he came instead with a stealthy tread,
    Which she did not hear at all.

5 She had thought how his armor would blaze in the sun,
    As he rode like a prince to claim his bride:
In the sweet dim light of the falling night
    She found him at her side.

She had dreamed how the gaze of his strange, bold eye
10   Would wake her heart to a sudden glow:
She found in his face the familiar grace
    Of a friend she used to know.

She had dreamed how his coming would stir her soul,
    As the ocean is stirred by the wild storm's strife:
15 He brought her the balm of a heavenly calm,
    And a peace which crowned her life.

"Ain't I a Woman?"

Sojourner Truth

Born into slavery in 1797 in Ulster County, New York, Sojourner Truth's legal name was Isabella Van Wagener, after Issac Van Wagener who bought her and set her free just before New York State abolished slavery in 1827. In 1829, she went to New York City, where she preached in the streets. Taking the name Sojourner Truth in answer to a divine call, she left the city and began preaching and singing at camp meetings across the country. Although she never abandoned her messages of God's goodness, she added to her speeches concern for the abolition of slavery and the rights of women. Her brilliance at speech-making attracted many listeners.

In "Ain't I a Woman?" Truth argues eloquently for women's rights. In his new biography of Sojourner Truth, Carlton Mabee argues that she never spoke these words.

1   Well, children, where there is so much racket there must be something out of kilter. I think that 'twixt the negroes of the South and the women at the North, all talking about rights, the white men will be in a fix pretty soon. But what's all this here talking about?

2   That man over there says that women need to be helped into carriages, and lifted over ditches, and to have the best place everywhere. Nobody ever helps me into carriages, or over mud-puddles, or gives me any best place! And ain't I a woman? Look at me! Look at my arm! I have ploughed and planted, and gathered into barns, and no man could head me! And ain't I a woman? I could work as much and eat as much as a man—when I could get it—and bear the lash as well! And ain't I a woman? I have borne thirteen children, and seen them most all sold off to slavery, and when I cried out with my mother's grief, none but Jesus heard me! And ain't I a woman?

3   Then they talk about this thing in the head; what's this they call it? [Intellect, someone whispers.] That's it, honey. What's that got to do with women's rights or negro's rights? If my cup won't hold but a pint, and yours holds a quart, wouldn't you be mean not to let me have my little half-measure full?

4   Then that little man in black there, he says women can't have as much rights as men, 'cause Christ wasn't a woman! Where did your Christ come from? Where did your Christ come from? From God and a woman! Man had nothing to do with Him.

5   If the first woman God ever made was strong enough to turn the world upside down all alone, these women together ought to be able to turn it back, and get it right side up again! And now they is asking to do it, the men better let them.

6   Obliged to you for hearing me, and now old Sojourner ain't got nothing more to say.

■ EXPLORATIONS OF THE TEXT ■

1. What is the occasion? Why does Truth connect women's rights with racial issues in the first section of her speech?
2. Examine the vision of woman presented in paragraph 2. What is the effect of the repetition of "ain't I a woman?"
3. What is the argument about intellect?
4. Why does she include religion in her speech? What does she accomplish when she contends that "Man had nothing to do with [Jesus]"? How does she use humor?
5. Consider Truth's version of Eve, "the first woman." Is her argument logical or true?
6. What elements of persuasion does Truth use effectively? (See Chapter 12.) Are her arguments inductive, deductive, or both? (See Chapter 3.)
7. Characterize the voice of the speaker.
8. Compare this speech with Mandela's "I Am Prepared to Die."

■■ JOURNAL ENTRIES ■■

1. Respond to this speech.
2. Why was the speaker doubly vulnerable?

■■■ IDEAS FOR WRITING ■■■

1. Analyze the rhetorical structure of Sojourner Truth's speech. See checklist for nonfiction in Chapter 12.
2. Compose a contemporary version of "Ain't I a Woman?"

Incidents in the Life of a Slave Girl

Harriet Jacobs

Born a slave in Edenton, North Carolina, Harriet Lyn Jacobs (1815–1897) was orphaned as a child. Her owner/mistress taught her to read and write. When her mistress died, Jacobs became the property of a child whose father, "Dr. Flint," subjected Jacobs to continuous sexual harassment which she resisted. As a teenager, however, she had two children fathered by another white man. She escaped and was sheltered by her grandmother, a freed slave, for many years. During this period, the father of her children bought them from "Flint" and sent them to live with Jacobs' grandmother. However, they were never "freed."

In 1842, still attempting to claim her children, Jacobs escaped North. In New York City, while working as a nurse to the daughter of Nathaniel Willis, Jacobs secretly wrote a book about her life. In 1849, Harriet Jacobs moved to Rochester, New York, where she established an anti-slavery reading room. Eventually, she returned to New York City, and she and her children were purchased and freed by Willis. With encouragement from Amy Post, feminist and abolitionist, and with assistance from William C. Nell, African-American abolitionist and writer, Jacobs published a narrative of her life under the pseudonym Linda Brent.

During the Civil War, Jacobs nursed black soldiers in Washington, D.C.; and she later returned to the South where she and her daughter represented New York Quakers.

In her book, Harriet Jacobs presents a thesis concerning the sexual exploitation of female slaves by white men. Jacobs describes her life at "Dr. Flint's," her seven years of hiding in the garret of her grandmother's shed, and her preparations for flight to the North.

CHILDHOOD

1   I was born a slave; but I never knew it till six years of happy childhood had passed away. My father was a carpenter, and considered so intelligent and skilful in his trade, that, when buildings out of the common line were to be erected, he was sent for from long distances, to be head workman. On condition of paying his mistress two hundred dollars a year, and supporting himself, he was allowed to work at his trade, and manage his own affairs. His strongest wish was to purchase his children; but, though he several times offered his hard earnings for that purpose, he never succeeded. In complexion my parents were a light shade of brownish yellow, and were termed mulattoes. They lived together in a comfortable home; and, though we were all slaves, I was so fondly shielded that I never dreamed I was a piece of merchandise, trusted to them for

safe keeping, and liable to be demanded of them at any moment. I had one brother, William, who was two years younger than myself—a bright, affectionate child. I had also a great treasure in my maternal grandmother, who was a remarkable woman in many respects. She was the daughter of a planter in South Carolina, who, at his death, left her mother and his three children free, with money to go to St. Augustine;[1] where they had relatives. It was during the Revolutionary War; and they were captured on their passage, carried back, and sold to different purchasers. Such was the story my grandmother used to tell me; but I do not remember all the particulars. She was a little girl when she was captured and sold to the keeper of a large hotel. I have often heard her tell how hard she fared during childhood. But as she grew older she evinced so much intelligence, and was so faithful, that her master and mistress could not help seeing it was for their interest to take care of such a valuable piece of property. She became an indispensable personage in the household, officiating in all capacities, from cook and wet nurse to seamstress. She was much praised for her cooking; and her nice crackers became so famous in the neighborhood that many people were desirous of obtaining them. In consequence of numerous requests of this kind, she asked permission of her mistress to bake crackers at night, after all the household work was done; and she obtained leave to do it, provided she would clothe herself and her children from the profits. Upon these terms, after working hard all day for her mistress, she began her midnight bakings, assisted by her two oldest children. The business proved profitable; and each year she laid by a little, which was saved for a fund to purchase her children. Her master died, and the property was divided among his heirs. The widow had her dower in the hotel, which she continued to keep open. My grandmother remained in her service as a slave; but her children were divided among her master's children. As she had five, Benjamin, the youngest one, was sold, in order that each heir might have an equal portion of dollars and cents. There was so little difference in our ages that he seemed more like my brother than my uncle. He was a bright, handsome lad, nearly white; for he inherited the complexion my grandmother had derived from Anglo-Saxon ancestors. Though only ten years old, seven hundred and twenty dollars were paid for him. His sale was a terrible blow to my grandmother; but she was naturally hopeful, and she went to work with renewed energy, trusting in time to be able to purchase some of her children. She had laid up three hundred dollars, which her mistress one day begged as a loan, promising to pay her soon. The reader probably knows that no promise or writing given to a slave is legally binding; for, according to Southern laws, a slave, *being* property, can *hold* no property. When my grandmother lent her hard earnings to her mistress, she trusted solely to her honor. The honor of a slaveholder to a slave!

To this good grandmother I was indebted for many comforts. My brother Willie and I often received portions of the crackers, cakes, and preserves, she

---

[1] City in Florida.

made to sell; and after we ceased to be children we were indebted to her for many more important services.

Such were the unusually fortunate circumstances of my early childhood. When I was six years old, my mother died; and then, for the first time, I learned, by the talk around me, that I was a slave. My mother's mistress was the daughter of my grandmother's mistress. She was the foster sister of my mother; they were both nourished at my grandmother's breast. In fact, my mother had been weaned at three months old, that the babe of the mistress might obtain sufficient food. They played together as children; and, when they became women, my mother was a most faithful servant to her whiter foster sister. On her death-bed her mistress promised that her children should never suffer for any thing; and during her lifetime she kept her word. They all spoke kindly of my dead mother, who had been a slave merely in name, but in nature was noble and womanly. I grieved for her, and my young mind was troubled with the thought who would now take care of me and my little brother. I was told that my home was now to be with her mistress; and I found it a happy one. No toilsome or disagreeable duties were imposed upon me. My mistress was so kind to me that I was always glad to do her bidding, and proud to labor for her as much as my young years would permit. I would sit by her side for hours, sewing diligently, with a heart as free from care as that of any free-born white child. When she thought I was tired, she would send me out to run and jump; and away I bounded, to gather berries or flowers to decorate her room. Those were happy days—too happy to last. The slave child had no thought for the morrow; but there came that blight, which too surely waits on every human being born to be a chattel.

When I was nearly twelve years old, my kind mistress sickened and died. As I saw the cheek grow pale and the eye more glassy, how earnestly I prayed in my heart that she might live! I loved her; for she had been almost like a mother to me. My prayers were not answered. She died, and they buried her in the little churchyard, where, day after day, my tears fell upon her grave.

5   I was sent to spend a week with my grandmother. I was now old enough to begin to think of the future; and again and again I asked myself what they would do with me. I felt sure I should never find another mistress so kind as the one who was gone. She had promised my dying mother that her children should never suffer for any thing; and when I remembered that, and recalled her many proofs of attachment to me, I could not help having some hopes that she had left me free. My friends were almost certain it would be so. They thought she would be sure to do it, on account of my mother's love and faithful service. But, alas! we all know that the memory of a faithful slave does not avail much to save her children from the auction block.

After a brief period of suspense, the will of my mistress was read, and we learned that she had bequeathed me to her sister's daughter, a child of five years old. So vanished our hopes. My mistress had taught me the precepts of God's Word: "Thou shalt love thy neighbor as thyself." "Whatsoever ye would that men should do unto you, do ye even so unto them." But I was her slave, and I suppose she did not recognize me as her neighbor. I would give much to blot out from my memory that one great wrong. As a child, I loved my mistress; and, looking back on the happy days I spent with her, I try to think with less bitterness of this act of injustice. While I was with her, she taught me to read and spell; and for this privilege, which so rarely falls to the lot of a slave, I bless her memory.

She possessed but few slaves; and at her death those were all distributed among her relatives. Five of them were my grandmother's children, and had shared the same milk that nourished her mother's children. Notwithstanding my grandmother's long and faithful service to her owners, not one of her children escaped the auction block. These God-breathing machines are no more, in the sight of their masters, than the cotton they plant, or the horses they tend.

THE NEW MASTER AND MISTRESS

Dr. Flint, a physician in the neighborhood, had married the sister of my mistress, and I was now the property of their little daughter. It was not without murmuring that I prepared for my new home; and what added to my unhappiness, was the fact that my brother William was purchased by the same family. My father, by his nature, as well as by the habit of transacting business as a skilful mechanic, had more of the feelings of a freeman than is common among slaves. My brother was a spirited boy; and being brought up under such influences, he early detested the name of master and mistress. One day, when his father and his mistress both happened to call him at the same time, he hesitated between the two; being perplexed to know which had the strongest claim upon his obedience. He finally concluded to go to his mistress. When my father reproved him for it, he said, "You both called me, and I didn't know which I ought to go to first."

"You are *my* child," replied our father, "and when I call you, you should come immediately, if you have to pass through fire and water."

10   Poor Willie! He was now to learn his first lesson of obedience to a master. Grandmother tried to cheer us with hopeful words, and they found an echo in the credulous hearts of youth.

When we entered our new home we encountered cold looks, cold words, and cold treatment. We were glad when the night came. On my narrow bed I moaned and wept, I felt so desolate and alone.

I had been there nearly a year, when a dear little friend of mine was buried. I heard her mother sob, as the clods fell on the coffin of her only child, and I turned away from the grave, feeling thankful that I still had something left to love. I met my grandmother, who said, "Come with me, Linda;" and from her tone I knew that something sad had happened. She led me apart from the people, and then said, "My child, your father is dead." Dead! How could I believe it? He had died so suddenly I had not even heard that he was sick. I went home with my grandmother. My heart rebelled against God, who had taken from me mother, father, mistress, and friend. The good grandmother tried to comfort me. "Who knows the ways of God?" said she. "Perhaps they have been kindly taken from the evil days to come." Years afterwards I often thought of this. She promised to be a mother to her grandchildren, so far as she might be permitted to do so; and strengthened by her love, I returned to my master's. I thought I should be allowed to go to my father's house the next morning; but I was ordered to go for flowers, that my mistress's house might be decorated for an evening party. I spent the day gathering flowers and weaving them into festoons,[2] while the dead body of my father was lying within a mile of me. What cared my owners for that? he was merely a piece of property. Moreover, they thought he had spoiled his children, by teaching them to feel that they were human beings. This was blasphemous doctrine for a slave to teach; presumptuous in him, and dangerous to the masters.

The next day I followed his remains to a humble grave beside that of my dear mother. There were those who knew my father's worth, and respected his memory.

My home now seemed more dreary than ever. The laugh of the little slave children sounded harsh and cruel. It was selfish to feel so about the joy of others. My brother moved about with a very grave face. I tried to comfort him, by saying, "Take courage, Willie; brighter days will come by and by."

15   "You don't know any thing about it, Linda," he replied. "We shall have to stay here all our days; we shall never be free."

I argued that we were growing older and stronger, and that perhaps we might, before long, be allowed to hire our own time, and then we could earn money to buy our freedom. William declared this was much easier to say than to do; moreover, he did not intend to *buy* his freedom. We held daily controversies upon this subject.

Little attention was paid to the slaves' meals in Dr. Flint's house. If they could catch a bit of food while it was going, well and good. I gave myself no trouble on that score, for on my various errands I passed my grandmother's house, where there was always something to spare for me. I was frequently threatened with punishment if I stopped there; and my grandmother, to avoid detaining me, often stood at the gate with something for my breakfast or dinner. I was indebted to *her* for all my comforts, spiritual or temporal. It was *her* labor that supplied my scanty wardrobe. I have a vivid recollection of the linsey-woolsey[3] dress given me every winter by Mrs. Flint. How I hated it! It was one of the badges of slavery.

While my grandmother was thus helping to support me from her hard earnings, the three hundred dollars she had lent her mistress were never repaid. When her mistress died, her son-in-law, Dr. Flint, was appointed executor. When grandmother applied to him for payment, he said the estate was insolvent, and the law prohibited payment. It did not, however, prohibit him

---

[2] A decorative chain or strip hanging between two points.
[3] A coarse sturdy fabric of wool and linen or cotton.

from retaining the silver candelabra, which had been purchased with that money. I presume they will be handed down in the family, from generation to generation.

My grandmother's mistress had always promised her that, at her death, she should be free; and it was said that in her will she made good the promise. But when the estate was settled, Dr. Flint told the faithful old servant that, under existing circumstances, it was necessary she should be sold.

20   On the appointed day, the customary advertisement was posted up, proclaiming that there would be a "public sale of negroes, horses, &c." Dr. Flint called to tell my grandmother that he was unwilling to wound her feelings by putting her up at auction, and that he would prefer to dispose of her at private sale. My grandmother saw through his hypocrisy; she understood very well that he was ashamed of the job. She was a very spirited woman, and if he was base enough to sell her, when her mistress intended she should be free, she was determined the public should know it. She had for a long time supplied many families with crackers and preserves; consequently, "Aunt Marthy," as she was called, was generally known, and every body who knew her respected her intelligence and good character. Her long and faithful service in the family was also well known, and the intention of her mistress to leave her free. When the day of sale came, she took her place among the chattels, and at the first call she sprang upon the auction-block. Many voices called out, "Shame! Shame! Who is going to sell *you,* aunt Marthy? Don't stand there! That is no place for *you.*" Without saying a word, she quietly awaited her fate. No one bid for her. At last, a feeble voice said, "Fifty dollars." It came from a maiden lady, seventy years old, the sister of my grandmother's deceased mistress. She had lived forty years under the same roof with my grandmother; she knew how faithfully she had served her owners, and how cruelly she had been defrauded of her rights; and she resolved to protect her. The auctioneer waited for a higher bid; but her wishes were respected; no one bid above her. She could neither read nor write; and when the bill of sale was made out, she signed it with a cross. But what consequence was that, when she had a big heart overflowing with human kindness? She gave the old servant her freedom.

At that time, my grandmother was just fifty years old. Laborious years had passed since then; and now my brother and I were slaves to the man who had defrauded her of her money, and tried to defraud her of her freedom. One of my mother's sisters, called Aunt Nancy, was also a slave in his family. She was a kind, good aunt to me; and supplied the place of both housekeeper and waiting maid to her mistress. She was, in fact, at the beginning and end of every thing.

Mrs. Flint, like many southern women, was totally deficient in energy. She had not strength to superintend her household affairs; but her nerves were so strong, that she could sit in her easy chair and see a woman whipped, till the blood trickled from every stroke of the lash. She was a member of the church; but partaking of the Lord's supper did not seem to put her in a Christian frame of mind. If dinner was not served at the exact time on that particular Sunday, she would station herself in the kitchen, and wait till it was dished, and then spit in all the kettles and pans that had been used for cooking. She did this to prevent the cook and her children from eking out their meagre fare with the remains of the gravy and other scrapings. The slaves could get nothing to eat except what she chose to give them. Provisions were weighed out by the pound and ounce, three times a day. I can assure you she gave them no chance to eat wheat bread from her flour barrel. She knew how many biscuits a quart of flour would make, and exactly what size they ought to be.

Dr. Flint was an epicure.[4] The cook never sent a dinner to his table without fear and trembling; for if there happened to be a dish not to his liking, he would either order her to be whipped, or compel her to eat every mouthful of it in his presence. The poor, hungry creature might not have objected to eating it; but she did object to having her master cram it down her throat till she choked.

They had a pet dog, that was a nuisance in the house. The cook was ordered to make some Indian mush[5] for him. He refused to eat, and when his head was held over it, the froth flowed from his mouth into the basin. He died a few minutes after. When Dr. Flint came in, he said the mush had not been well cooked, and that was the reason the animal would not eat it. He sent for the cook, and compelled her to eat it. He thought that the woman's stomach was stronger than the dog's; but her sufferings afterwards proved that he was mistaken. The poor woman endured many cruelties from her master and mistress; sometimes she was locked up, away from her nursing baby, for a whole day and night.

25   When I had been in the family a few weeks, one of the plantation slaves was brought to town, by order of his master. It was near night when he arrived, and Dr. Flint ordered him to be taken to the work house, and tied up to the joist, so that his feet would just escape the ground. In that situation he was to wait till the doctor had taken his tea. I shall never forget that night. Never before, in my life, had I heard hundreds of blows fall, in succession, on a human being. His piteous groans, and his "O, pray don't, massa," rang in my ear for months afterwards. There were many conjectures as to the cause of this terrible punishment. Some said master accused him of stealing corn; others said the slave had quarrelled with his wife, in presence of the overseer, and had accused his master of being the father of her child. They were both black, and the child was very fair.

I went into the work house next morning, and saw the cowhide still wet with blood, and the boards all covered with gore. The poor man lived, and continued to quarrel with his wife. A few months afterwards Dr. Flint handed them both over to a slavetrader. The guilty man put their value into his pocket, and had the satisfaction of knowing that they were out of sight and hearing. When the mother was delivered into the trader's hands, she said, "You *promised* to treat me well." To which he replied, "You have let your tongue run too far;

---

[4] A person devoted to sensual pleasure.
[5] Corn meal pudding.

damn you!" She had forgotten that it was a crime for a slave to tell who was the father of her child.

From others than the master persecution also comes in such cases. I once saw a young slave girl dying soon after the birth of a child nearly white. In her agony she cried out, "O Lord, come and take me!" Her mistress stood by, and mocked at her like an incarnate fiend. "You suffer, do you?" she exclaimed. "I am glad of it. You deserve it all, and more too."

The girl's mother said, "The baby is dead, thank God; and I hope my poor child will soon be in heaven, too."

"Heaven!" retorted the mistress. "There is no such place for the like of her and her bastard."

30   The poor mother turned away, sobbing. Her dying daughter called her, feebly, and as she bent over her, I heard her say, "Don't grieve so, mother; God knows all about it; and HE will have mercy upon me."

Her sufferings, afterwards, became so intense, that her mistress felt unable to stay; but when she left the room, the scornful smile was still on her lips. Seven children called her mother. The poor black woman had but the one child, whose eyes she saw closing in death, while she thanked God for taking her away from the greater bitterness of life.

THE LOOPHOLE OF RETREAT
(LINDA BRENT ESCAPES)

A small shed had been added to my grandmother's house years ago. Some boards were laid across the joists at the top, and between these boards and the roof was a very small garret, never occupied by any thing but rats and mice. It was a pent roof, covered with nothing but shingles, according to the southern custom for such buildings. The garret was only nine feet long and seven wide. The highest part was three feet high, and sloped down abruptly to the loose board floor. There was no admission for either light or air. My uncle Phillip, who was a carpenter, had very skilfully made a concealed trap-door, which communicated with the storeroom. He had been doing this while I was waiting in the swamp. The storeroom opened upon a piazza. To this hole I was conveyed as soon as I entered the house. The air was stifling; the darkness total. A bed had been spread on the floor. I could sleep quite comfortably on one side; but the slope was so sudden that I could not turn on the other without hitting the roof. The rats and mice ran over my bed; but I was weary, and I slept such sleep as the wretched may, when a tempest has passed over them. Morning came. I knew it only by the noises I heard; for in my small den day and night were all the same. I suffered for air even more than for light. But I was not comfortless. I heard the voices of my children. There was joy and there was sadness in the sound. It made my tears flow. How I longed to speak to them! I was eager to look on their faces; but there was no hole, no crack, through which I could peep. This continued darkness was oppressive. It seemed horrible to sit or lie in a cramped position day after day, without one gleam of light. Yet I would have chosen this, rather than my lot as a slave, though white people considered it an easy one; and it was so compared with the fate of others. I was never cruelly over-worked; I was never lacerated with the whip from head to foot; I was never so beaten and bruised that I could not turn from one side to the other; I never had my heel-strings cut to prevent my running away; I was never chained to a log and forced to drag it about, while I toiled in the fields from morning till night; I was never branded with hot iron, or torn by bloodhounds. On the contrary, I had always been kindly treated, and tenderly cared for, until I came into the hands of Dr. Flint. I had never wished for freedom till then. But though my life in slavery was comparatively devoid of hardships, God pity the woman who is compelled to lead such a life! My food was passed up to me through the trap-door my uncle had contrived; and my grandmother, my uncle Phillip, and aunt Nancy would seize such opportunities as they could, to mount up there and chat with me at the opening. But of course this was not safe in the daytime. It must all be done in darkness. It was impossible for me to move in an erect position, but I crawled about my den for exercise. One day I hit my head against something, and found it was a gimlet. My uncle had left it sticking there when he made the trap-door. I was as rejoiced as Robinson Crusoe could have been at finding such a treasure. It put a lucky thought into my head. I said to myself, "Now I will have some light. Now I will see my children." I did not dare to begin my work during the daytime, for fear of attracting attention. But I groped round; and having found the side next the street, where I could frequently see my children, I stuck the gimlet in and waited for evening. I bored three rows of holes, one above another; then I bored out the interstices between. I thus succeeded in making one hole about an inch long and an inch broad. I sat by it till late into the night, to enjoy the little whiff of air that floated in. In the morning I watched for my children. The first person I saw in the street was Dr. Flint. I had a shuddering, superstitious feeling that it was a bad omen. Several familiar faces passed by. At last I heard the merry laugh of children, and presently two sweet little faces were looking up at me, as though they knew I was there, and were con-scious of the joy they imparted. How I longed to *tell* them I was there!

My condition was now a little improved. But for weeks I was tormented by hundreds of little red insects, fine as a needle's point, that pierced through my skin, and produced an intolerable burning. The good grandmother gave me herb teas and cooling medicines, and finally I got rid of them. The heat of my den was intense, for nothing but thin shingles protected me from the scorching summer's sun. But I had my consolations. Through my peeping-hole I could watch the children, and when they were near enough, I could hear their talk. Aunt Nancy brought me all the news she could hear at Dr. Flint's. From her I learned that the doctor had written to New York to a col-ored woman, who had been born and raised in our neighborhood, and had breathed his contaminating atmosphere. He offered her a reward if she could find out any thing about me. I know not what was the nature of her reply; but he soon after started for New York in haste, saying to his family that he had business of importance to transact. I peeped at him as he passed on his way to the steamboat. It was a satisfaction to have miles of land and water between us, even for a little while; and it was a still greater satisfaction to know that he believed me to be in the Free States. My little den seemed less dreary than it had done. He returned, as he did from his former journey to New York, without obtaining any satisfactory information. When he passed our house next morning, Benny[6] was standing at the gate. He had heard them say that he had gone to find me, and he called out, "Dr. Flint, did you bring my mother home? I want to see her." The doctor stamped his foot at him in a rage, and exclaimed, "Get out of the way, you little damned rascal! If you don't, I'll cut off your head."

Benny ran terrified into the house, saying, "You can't put me in jail again. I don't belong to you now." It was well that the wind carried the words away from the doctor's ear. I told my grandmother of it, when we had our next conference at the trap-door; and begged her not to allow the children to be impertinent to the irascible old man.

35   Autumn came, with a pleasant abatement of heat. My eyes had become accustomed to the dim light, and by holding my book or work in a certain position near the aperture I contrived to read and sew. That was a great relief to the tedious monotony of my life. But when winter came, the cold penetrated through the thin shingle roof, and I was dreadfully chilled. The winters there are not so long, or so severe, as in northern latitudes; but the houses are not built to shelter from cold, and my little den was peculiarly comfortless. The kind grandmother brought me bed-clothes and warm drinks. Often I was obliged to lie in bed all day to keep comfortable; but with all my precautions, my shoulders and feet were frostbitten. O, those long, gloomy days, with no object for my eye to rest upon, and no thoughts to occupy my mind, except the dreary past and the uncertain future! I was thankful when there came a day sufficiently mild for me to wrap myself up and sit at the loophole to watch the passers by. Southerners have the habit of stopping and talking in the streets, and I heard many conversations not intended to meet my ears. I heard slave-hunters planning how to catch some poor fugitive. Several times I heard allusions to Dr. Flint, myself, and the history of my children, who, perhaps, were playing near the gate. One would say, "I wouldn't move my little finger to catch her, as old Flint's property." Another would say, "I'll catch *any* nigger for the reward. A man ought to have what belongs to him, if he *is* a damned brute." The opinion was often expressed that I was in the Free States. Very rarely did any one suggest that I might be in the vicinity. Had the least suspicion rested on my grandmother's house, it would have been burned to the ground. But it was the last place they thought of. Yet there was no place, where slavery existed, that could have afforded me so good a place of concealment.

Dr. Flint and his family repeatedly tried to coax and bribe my children to tell something they had heard said about me. One day the doctor took them

---

[6] Brent's son.

into a shop, and offered them some bright little silver pieces and gay handkerchiefs if they would tell where their mother was. Ellen[7] shrank away from him, and would not speak; but Benny spoke up, and said, "Dr. Flint, I don't know where my mother is. I guess she's in New York; and when you go there again, I wish you'd ask her to come home, for I want to see her; but if you put her in jail, or tell her you'll cut her head off, I'll tell her to go right back."

PREPARATIONS FOR ESCAPE

I hardly expect that the reader will credit me, when I affirm that I lived in that little dismal hole, almost deprived of light and air, and with no space to move my limbs, for nearly seven years. But it is a fact; and to me a sad one, even now; for my body still suffers from the effects of that long imprisonment, to say nothing of my soul. Members of my family, now living in New York and Boston, can testify to the truth of what I say.

Countless were the nights that I sat late at the little loophole scarcely large enough to give me a glimpse of one twinkling star. There, I heard the patrols and slave-hunters conferring together about the capture of runaways, well knowing how rejoiced they would be to catch me.

Season after season, year after year, I peeped at my children's faces, and heard their sweet voices, with a heart yearning all the while to say, "Your mother is here." Sometimes it appeared to me as if ages had rolled away since I entered upon that gloomy, monotonous existence. At times, I was stupefied and listless; at other times I became very impatient to know when these dark years would end, and I should again be allowed to feel the sunshine, and breathe the pure air.

40 After Ellen left us, this feeling increased. Mr. Sands had agreed that Benny might go to the north whenever his uncle Phillip could go with him; and I was anxious to be there also, to watch over my children, and protect them so far as I was able. Moreover, I was likely to be drowned out of my den, if I remained much longer; for the slight roof was getting badly out of repair, and uncle Phillip was afraid to remove the shingles, lest some one should get a glimpse of me. When storms occurred in the night, they spread mats and bits of carpet, which in the morning appeared to have been laid out to dry; but to cover the roof in the daytime might have attracted attention. Consequently, my clothes and bedding were often drenched; a process by which the pains and aches in my cramped and stiffened limbs were greatly increased. I revolved various plans of escape in my mind, which I sometimes imparted to my grandmother, when she came to whisper with me at the trap-door. The kind-hearted old woman had an intense sympathy for runaways. She had known too much of the cruelties inflicted on those who were captured. Her memory always flew back at once to the sufferings of her bright and handsome son, Benjamin, the youngest and dearest of her flock. So, whenever I alluded to the subject, she

---

[7] Brent's daughter.

would groan out, "O, don't think of it, child. You'll break my heart." I had no good old aunt Nancy now to encourage me; but my brother William and my children were continually beckoning me to the north.

And now I must go back a few months in my story. I have stated that the first of January was the time for selling slaves, or leasing them out to new masters. If time were counted by heart-throbs, the poor slaves might reckon years of suffering during that festival so joyous to the free. On the New Year's day preceding my aunt's death, one of my friends, named Fanny, was to be sold at auction, to pay her master's debts. My thoughts were with her during all the day, and at night I anxiously inquired what had been her fate. I was told that she had been sold to one master, and her four little girls to another master, far distant; that she had escaped from her purchaser, and was not to be found. Her mother was the old Aggie I have spoken of. She lived in a small tenement belonging to my grandmother, and built on the same lot with her own house. Her dwelling was searched and watched, and that brought the patrols so near me that I was obliged to keep very close in my den. The hunters were somehow eluded; and not long afterwards Benny accidentally caught sight of Fanny in her mother's hut. He told his grandmother, who charged him never to speak of it, explaining to him the frightful consequences; and he never betrayed the trust. Aggie little dreamed that my grandmother knew where her daughter was concealed, and that the stooping form of her old neighbor was bending under a similar burden of anxiety and fear; but these dangerous secrets deepened the sympathy between the two old persecuted mothers.

My friend Fanny and I remained many weeks hidden within call of each other; but she was unconscious of the fact. I longed to have her share my den, which seemed a more secure retreat than her own; but I had brought so much trouble on my grandmother, that it seemed wrong to ask her to incur greater risks. My restlessness increased. I had lived too long in bodily pain and anguish of spirit. Always I was in dread that by some accident, or some contrivance, slavery would succeed in snatching my children from me. This thought drove me nearly frantic, and I determined to steer for the North Star at all hazards. At this crisis, Providence opened an unexpected way for me to escape. My friend Peter came one evening, and asked to speak with me. "Your day has come, Linda," said he. "I have found a chance for you to go to the Free States. You have a fortnight to decide." The news seemed too good to be true; but Peter explained his arrangements, and told me all that was necessary was for me to say I would go. I was going to answer him with a joyful yes, when the thought of Benny came to my mind. I told him the temptation was exceedingly strong, but I was terribly afraid of Dr. Flint's alleged power over my child, and that I could not go and leave him behind. Peter remonstrated earnestly. He said such a good chance might never occur again; that Benny was free, and could be sent to me; and that for the sake of my children's welfare I ought not to hesitate a moment. I told him I would consult with uncle Phillip. My uncle rejoiced in the plan, and bade me go by all means. He promised, if his life was spared, that he would either bring or send my son to me as soon as I reached a place of safety. I resolved to go, but thought nothing had better be said to my grandmother till very near the time of departure. But my uncle thought she would feel it more keenly if I left her so suddenly. "I will reason with her," said he, "and convince her how necessary it is, not only for your sake, but for hers also. You cannot be blind to the fact that she is sinking under her burdens." I was not blind to it. I knew that my concealment was an ever-present source of anxiety, and that the older she grew the more nervously fearful she was of discovery. My uncle talked with her, and finally succeeded in persuading her that it was absolutely necessary for me to seize the chance so unexpectedly offered.

The anticipation of being a free woman proved almost too much for my weak frame. The excitement stimulated me, and at the same time bewildered me. I made busy preparations for my journey, and for my son to follow me. I resolved to have an interview with him before I went, that I might give him cautions and advice, and tell him how anxiously I should be waiting for him at the north. Grandmother stole up to me as often as possible to whisper words of counsel. She insisted upon my writing to Dr. Flint, as soon as I arrived in the Free States, and asking him to sell me to her. She said she would sacrifice her house, and all she had in the world, for the sake of having me safe with my children in any part of the world. If she could only live to know *that* she could die in peace. I promised the dear old faithful friend that I would write to her as soon as I arrived, and put the letter in a safe way to reach her; but in my own mind I resolved that not another cent of her hard earnings should be spent to pay rapacious slaveholders for what they called their property. And even if I had not been unwilling to buy what I had already a right to possess, common humanity would have prevented me from accepting the generous offer, at the expense of turning my aged relative out of house and home, when she was trembling on the brink of the grave.

I was to escape in a vessel; but I forbear to mention any further particulars. I was in readiness, but the vessel was unexpectedly detained several days. Meantime, news came to town of a most horrible murder committed on a fugitive slave, named James. Charity, the mother of this unfortunate young man, had been an old acquaintance of ours. I have told the shocking particulars of his death, in my description of some of the neighboring slaveholders. My grandmother, always nervously sensitive about runaways, was terribly frightened. She felt sure that a similar fate awaited me, if I did not desist from my enterprise. She sobbed, and groaned, and entreated me not to go. Her excessive fear was somewhat contagious, and my heart was not proof against her extreme agony. I was grievously disappointed, but I promised to relinquish my project.

45   When my friend Peter was apprised of this, he was both disappointed and vexed. He said, that judging from our past experience, it would be a long time before I had such another chance to throw away. I told him it need not be thrown away; that I had a friend concealed near by, who would be glad enough to take the place that had been provided for me. I told him about poor

Fanny, and the kind-hearted, noble fellow, who never turned his back upon any body in distress, white or black, expressed his readiness to help her. Aggie was much surprised when she found that we knew her secret. She was rejoiced to hear of such a chance for Fanny, and arrangements were made for her to go on board the vessel the next night. They both supposed that I had long been at the north, therefore my name was not mentioned in the transaction. Fanny was carried on board at the appointed time, and stowed away in a very small cabin. This accommodation had been purchased at a price that would pay for a voyage to England. But when one proposes to go to fine old England, they stop to calculate whether they can afford the cost of the pleasure; while in making a bargain to escape from slavery, the trembling victim is ready to say, "Take all I have, only don't betray me!"

The next morning I peeped through my loophole, and saw that it was dark and cloudy. At night I received news that the wind was ahead, and the vessel had not sailed. I was exceedingly anxious about Fanny, and Peter too, who was running a tremendous risk at my instigation. Next day the wind and weather remained the same. Poor Fanny had been half dead with fright when they carried her on board, and I could readily imagine how she must be suffering now. Grandmother came often to my den, to say how thankful she was I did not go. On the third morning she rapped for me to come down to the storeroom. The poor old sufferer was breaking down under her weight of trouble. She was easily flurried now. I found her in a nervous, excited state, but I was not aware that she had forgotten to lock the door behind her, as usual. She was exceedingly worried about the detention of the vessel. She was afraid all would be discovered, and then Fanny, and Peter, and I, would all be tortured to death, and Phillip would be utterly ruined, and her house would be torn down. Poor Peter! If he should die such a horrible death as the poor slave James had lately done, and all for his kindness in trying to help me, how dreadful it would be for us all! Alas, the thought was familiar to me, and had sent many a sharp pang through my heart. I tried to suppress my own anxiety, and speak soothingly to her. She brought in some allusion to aunt Nancy, the dear daughter she had recently buried, and then she lost all control of herself. As she stood there, trembling and sobbing, a voice from the piazza called out, "Whar is you, aunt Marthy?" Grandmother was startled, and in her agitation opened the door, without thinking of me. In stepped Jenny, the mischievous housemaid, who had tried to enter my room, when I was concealed in the house of my white benefactress. "I's bin huntin ebery whar for you, aunt Marthy," said she. "My missis wants you to send her some crackers." I had slunk down behind a barrel, which entirely screened me, but I imagined that Jenny was looking directly at the spot, and my heart beat violently. My grandmother immediately thought what she had done, and went out quickly with Jenny to count the crackers locking the door after her. She returned to me, in a few minutes, the perfect picture of despair. "Poor child!" she exclaimed, "my carelessness has ruined you. The boat ain't gone yet. Get ready immediately, and go with Fanny. I ain't got another word to say against it now; for there's no telling what may happen this day."

Uncle Phillip was sent for, and he agreed with his mother in thinking that Jenny would inform Dr. Flint in less than twenty-four hours. He advised getting me on board the boat, if possible; if not, I had better keep very still in my den, where they could not find me without tearing the house down. He said it would not do for him to move in the matter, because suspicion would be immediately excited; but he promised to communicate with Peter. I felt reluctant to apply to him again, having implicated him too much already; but there seemed to be no alternative. Vexed as Peter had been by my indecision, he was true to his generous nature, and said at once that he would do his best to help me, trusting I should show myself a stronger woman this time.

He immediately proceeded to the wharf, and found that the wind had shifted, and the vessel was slowly beating down stream. On some pretext of urgent necessity, he offered two boatmen a dollar apiece to catch up with her. He was of lighter complexion than the boatmen he hired, and when the captain saw them coming so rapidly, he thought officers were pursuing his vessel in search of the runaway slave he had on board. They hoisted sails, but the boat gained upon them, and the indefatigable Peter sprang on board.

The captain at once recognized him. Peter asked him to go below, to speak about a bad bill he had given him. When he told his errand, the captain replied, "Why, the woman's here already; and I've put her where you or the devil would have a tough job to find her."

50   "But it is another woman I want to bring," said Peter. "*She* is in great distress, too, and you shall be paid any thing within reason, if you'll stop and take her."

"What's her name?" inquired the captain.

"Linda," he replied.

"That's the name of the woman already here," rejoined the captain. "By George! I believe you mean to betray me."

"O!" exclaimed Peter, "God knows I wouldn't harm a hair of your head. I am too grateful to you. But there really *is* another woman in great danger. Do have the humanity to stop and take her!"

55   After a while they came to an understanding. Fanny, not dreaming I was any where about in that region, had assumed my name, though she called herself Johnson. "Linda is a common name," said Peter, "and the woman I want to bring is Linda Brent."

The captain agreed to wait at a certain place till evening, being handsomely paid for his detention.

Of course, the day was an anxious one for us all. But we concluded that if Jenny had seen me, she would be too wise to let her mistress know of it; and that she probably would not get a chance to see Dr. Flint's family till evening, for I knew very well what were the rules in that household. I afterwards believed that she did not see me; for nothing ever came of it, and she was one of those base characters that would have jumped to betray a suffering fellow being for the sake of thirty pieces of silver.

I made all my arrangements to go on board as soon as it was dusk. The intervening time I resolved to spend with my son. I had not spoken to him for seven years, though I had been under the same roof, and seen him every day, when I was well enough to sit at the loophole. I did not dare to venture beyond the storeroom; so they brought him there, and locked us up together, in a place concealed from the piazza door. It was an agitating interview for both of us. After we had talked and wept together for a little while, he said, "Mother, I'm glad you're going away. I wish I could go with you. I knew you was here; and I have been *so* afraid they would come and catch you!"

I was greatly surprised, and asked him how he had found it out.

60   He replied, "I was standing under the eaves, one day, before Ellen went away, and I heard somebody cough up over the wood shed. I don't know what made me think it was you, but I did think so. I missed Ellen, the night before she went away; and grandmother brought her back into the room in the night; and I thought maybe she'd been to see *you,* before she went, for I heard grandmother whisper to her, 'Now go to sleep; and remember never to tell.'"

I asked him if he ever mentioned his suspicions to his sister. He said he never did; but after he heard the cough, if he saw her playing with other children on that side of the house, he always tried to coax her round to the other side, for fear they would hear me cough, too. He said he had kept a close lookout for Dr. Flint, and if he saw him speak to a constable, or a patrol, he always told grandmother. I now recollected that I had seen him manifest uneasiness, when people were on that side of the house, and I had at the time been puzzled to conjecture a motive for his actions. Such prudence may seem extraordinary in a boy of twelve years, but slaves, being surrounded by mysteries, deceptions, and dangers, early learn to be suspicious and watchful, and prematurely cautious and cunning. He had never asked a question of grandmother, or uncle Phillip, and I had often heard him chime in with other children, when they spoke of my being at the north.

I told him I was now really going to the Free States, and if he was a good, honest boy, and a loving child to his dear old grandmother, the Lord would bless him, and bring him to me, and we and Ellen would live together. He began to tell me that grandmother had not eaten any thing all day. While he was speaking, the door was unlocked, and she came in with a small bag of money, which she wanted me to take. I begged her to keep a part of it, at least, to pay for Benny's being sent to the north; but she insisted, while her tears were falling fast, that I should take the whole. "You may be sick among strangers," she said, "and they would send you to the poorhouse to die." Ah, that good grandmother!

For the last time I went up to my nook. Its desolate appearance no longer chilled me, for the light of hope had risen in my soul. Yet, even with the blessed prospect of freedom before me, I felt very sad at leaving forever that old homestead, where I had been sheltered so long by the dear old grandmother; where I had dreamed my first young dream of love; and where, after that had faded away, my children came to twine themselves so closely round my desolate heart. As the hour approached for me to leave, I again descended to the storeroom. My grandmother and Benny were there. She took me by the hand, and said, "Linda, let us pray." We knelt down together, with my child pressed to my heart, and my other arm round the faithful, loving old friend I was about to leave forever. On no other occasion has it ever been my lot to listen to so fervent a supplication for mercy and protection. It thrilled through my heart, and inspired me with trust in God.

Peter was waiting for me in the street. I was soon by his side, faint in body, but strong of purpose. I did not look back upon the old place, though I felt that I should never see it again.

■ EXPLORATIONS OF THE TEXT ■

1. Describe life in Dr. Flint's home. Explore the treatment of slaves.
2. Characterize the grandmother, Aunt Marthy. What is the importance of the candelabra?
3. Consider the beating of the field slave. What does Jacobs indicate about the cause of the arguments between the man and woman?
4. Characterize Mrs. Flint. What is the position of the jealous mistress? What does Jacobs think of Southern women?
5. Describe the years in the garret. Explain the following quotation: "My body still suffers from the effects of the long imprisonment, to say nothing of my soul."
6. What are the preparations for escape? What aspects of the flight are most memorable?
7. Characterize the narrator. Is she strong? What evidence suggests an answer to the previous question?
8. Determine the point of view, purpose, and audience for this narrative.
9. Compare speakers in this work with those in Sojourner Truth's speech and in Griffin's poem.

■■ JOURNAL ENTRIES ■■

1. Write an entry in the voice of Dr. Flint, of the grandmother, of Mrs. Flint, or of the narrator.
2. Why does sexual exploitation become the central issue of this work?

■■■ IDEAS FOR WRITING ■■■

1. Characterize the narrator, Linda Brent.
2. Write about the portraits of slave owners in these excerpts of Jacobs' narrative.

The Banking Concept of Education

Paulo Freire

Born in Recife, Brazil, Paulo Freire (1921–   ) is an educator and author. He has taught at Harvard University and at the Catholic University of São Paulo in Brazil. He has served as general coordinator of Brazil's National Plan of Adult Literacy and as a consultant to the UNESCO Institute of Research and Training in Agrarian Reform. Much of his work has been centered on his method of teaching illiterate peasants to read. Among his many writings are Pedagogy of the Oppressed *(1970),* Education for Critical Consciousness *(1973),* Education: The Practice of Freedom *(1976), and* Christian Ideology and Adult Education in Latin America *(1982).*

Ann Berthoff, in her foreword to Literacy: Reading the Word and the World, *a dialogue between Freire and Donaldo Macedo, cites Freire as claiming, "The act of learning to read and write has to start from a very comprehensive understanding of the act of reading the world, something which human beings do before reading the words."*

Paulo Freire describes the "banking" concept of education in The Pedagogy of the Oppressed *where he suggests that teachers deposit knowledge and students passively accept the deposits as "receptacles." He contrasts this kind of learning with "problem-posing education."*

A careful analysis of the teacher-student relationship at any level, inside or outside the school, reveals its fundamentally *narrative* character. This relationship involves a narrating Subject (the teacher) and patient, listening objects (the students). The contents, whether values or empirical dimensions of reality, tend in the process of being narrated to become lifeless and petrified. Education is suffering from narration sickness.

The teacher talks about reality as if it were motionless, static, compartmentalized, and predictable. Or else he expounds on a topic completely alien to the existential experience of the students. His task is to "fill" the students with the contents of his narration—contents which are detached from reality, disconnected from the totality that engendered them and could give them significance. Words are emptied of their concreteness and become a hollow, alienated, and alienating verbosity.

The outstanding characteristic of this narrative education, then, is the sonority of words, not their transforming power. "Four times four is sixteen; the capital of Pará is Belém." The student records, memorizes, and repeats these phrases without perceiving what four times four really means, or realizing the true significance of "capital" in the affirmation "the capital of Pará is Belém," that is, what Belém means for Pará and what Pará means for Brazil.

Narration (with the teacher as narrator) leads the students to memorize mechanically the narrated content. Worse yet, it turns them into "containers," into "receptacles" to be "filled" by the teacher. The more completely he fills the receptacles, the better a teacher he is. The more meekly the receptacles permit themselves to be filled, the better students they are.

5   Education thus becomes an act of depositing, in which the students are the depositories and the teacher is the depositor. Instead of communicating, the teacher issues communiqués and makes deposits which the students patiently receive, memorize, and repeat. This is the "banking" concept of education, in which the scope of action allowed to the students extends only as far as receiving, filing, and storing the deposits. They do, it is true, have the opportunity to become collectors or cataloguers of the things they store. But in the last analysis, it is men themselves who are filed away through the lack of creativity, transformation, and knowledge in this (at best) misguided system. For apart from inquiry, apart from the praxis, men cannot be truly human. Knowledge emerges only through invention and reinvention, through the restless, impatient, continuing, hopeful inquiry men pursue in the world, with the world, and with each other.

In the banking concept of education, knowledge is a gift bestowed by those who consider themselves knowledgeable upon those whom they consider to know nothing. Projecting an absolute ignorance onto others, a characteristic of the ideology of oppression, negates education and knowledge as processes of inquiry. The teacher presents himself to his students as their necessary opposite; by considering their ignorance absolute, he justifies his own existence. The students, alienated like the slave in the Hegelian dialectic, accept their ignorance as justifying the teacher's existence—but, unlike the slave, they never discover that they educate the teacher.

The *raison d'être* of libertarian education, on the other hand, lies in its drive towards reconciliation. Education must begin with the solution of the teacher-student contradiction, by reconciling the poles of the contradiction so that both are simultaneously teachers *and* students.

This solution is not (nor can it be) found in the banking concept. On the contrary, banking education maintains and even stimulates the contradiction through the following attitudes and practices, which mirror oppressive society as a whole:

a. the teacher teaches and the students are taught;
b. the teacher knows everything and the students know nothing;
c. the teacher thinks and the students are thought about;
d. the teacher talks and the students listen—meekly;
e. the teacher disciplines and the students are disciplined;
f. the teacher chooses and enforces his choice, and the students comply;
g. the teacher acts and the students have the illusion of acting through the action of the teacher;
h. the teacher chooses the program content, and the students (who were not consulted) adapt to it;

i. the teacher confuses the authority of knowledge with his own professional authority, which he sets in opposition to the freedom of the students;

j. the teacher is the Subject of the learning process, while the pupils are mere objects.

It is not surprising that the banking concept of education regards men as adaptable, manageable beings. The more students work at storing the deposits entrusted to them, the less they develop the critical consciousness which would result from their intervention in the world as transformers of that world. The more completely they accept the passive role imposed on them, the more they tend simply to adapt to the world as it is and to the fragmented view of reality deposited in them.

10   The capability of banking education to minimize or annul the students' creative power and to stimulate their credulity serves the interests of the oppressors, who care neither to have the world revealed nor to see it transformed. The oppressors use their "humanitarianism" to preserve a profitable situation. Thus they react almost instinctively against any experiment in education which stimulates the critical faculties and is not content with a partial view of reality but always seeks out the ties which link one point to another and one problem to another.

Indeed, the interests of the oppressors lie in "changing the consciousness of the oppressed, not the situation which oppresses them";[1] for the more the oppressed can be led to adapt to that situation, the more easily they can be dominated. To achieve this end, the oppressors use the banking concept of education in conjunction with a paternalistic social action apparatus, within which the oppressed receive the euphemistic title of "welfare recipients." They are treated as individual cases, as marginal men who deviate from the general configuration of a "good, organized, and just" society. The oppressed are regarded as the pathology of the healthy society, which must therefore adjust these "incompetent and lazy" folk to its own patterns by changing their mentality. These marginals need to be "integrated," "incorporated" into the healthy society that they have "foreseen."

The truth is, however, that the oppressed are not "marginals," are not men living "outside" society. They have always been "inside"—inside the structure which made them "beings for others." The solution is not to "integrate" them into the structure of oppression, but to transform that structure so that they can become "beings for themselves." Such transformation, of course, would undermine the oppressors' purposes; hence their utilization of the banking concept of education to avoid the threat of student *conscientização*.[2]

---

[1] Simone de Beauvoir, *La Pensée de Droite, Aujourd'hui* (Paris); ST, *El Pensamiento politico de la Derecha* (Buenos Aires, 1963), p. 34.

[2] According to Freire's translator, "The term *conscientização* refers to learning to perceive social, political, and economic contradictions, and to take action against the oppressive elements of reality."

The banking approach to adult education, for example, will never propose to students that they critically consider reality. It will deal instead with such vital questions as whether Roger gave green grass to the goat, and insist upon the importance of learning that, on the contrary, Roger gave green grass to the rabbit. The "humanism" of the banking approach masks the effort to turn men into automatons—the very negation of their ontological vocation to be more fully human.

Those who use the banking approach, knowingly or unknowingly (for there are innumerable well-intentioned bank-clerk teachers who do not realize that they are serving only to dehumanize), fail to perceive that the deposits themselves contain contradictions about reality. But, sooner or later, these contradictions may lead formerly passive students to turn against their domestication and the attempt to domesticate reality. They may discover through existential experience that their present way of life is irreconcilable with their vocation to become fully human. They may perceive through their relations with reality that reality is really a *process,* undergoing constant transformation. If men are searchers and their ontological vocation is humanization, sooner or later they may perceive the contradiction in which banking education seeks to maintain them, and then engage themselves in the struggle for their liberation.

15   But the humanist, revolutionary educator cannot wait for this possibility to materialize. From the outset, his efforts must coincide with those of the students to engage in critical thinking and the quest for mutual humanization. His efforts must be imbued with a profound trust in men and their creative power. To achieve this, he must be a partner of the students in his relations with them.

The banking concept does not admit to such partnership—and necessarily so. To resolve the teacher-student contradiction, to exchange the role of depositor, prescriber, domesticator, for the role of student among students would be to undermine the power of oppression and serve the cause of liberation.

Implicit in the banking concept is the assumption of a dichotomy between man and the world: man is merely *in* the world, not *with* the world or with others; man is spectator, not re-creator. In this view, man is not a conscious being (*corpo consciente*); he is rather the possessor of *a* consciousness: an empty "mind" passively open to the reception of deposits of reality from the world outside. For example, my desk, my books, my coffee cup, all the objects before me—as bits of the world which surrounds me—would be "inside" me, exactly as I am inside my study right now. This view makes no distinction between being accessible to consciousness and entering consciousness. The distinction, however, is essential: the objects which surround me are simply accessible to my consciousness, not located within it. I am aware of them, but they are not inside me.

It follows logically from the banking notion of consciousness that the educator's role is to regulate the way the world "enters into" the student. His task is to organize a process which already occurs spontaneously, to "fill" the students by making deposits of information which he considers to constitute true knowledge.[3] And since men "receive" the world as passive entities, education should make them more passive still, and adapt them to the world. The educated man is the adapted man, because he is better "fit" for the world. Translated into practice, this concept is well suited to the purposes of the oppressors, whose tranquility rests on how well men fit the world the oppressors have created, and how little they question it.

The more completely the majority adapt to the purposes which the dominant minority prescribe for them (thereby depriving them of the right to their own purposes), the more easily the minority can continue to prescribe. The theory and practice of banking education serve this end quite efficiently. Verbalistic lessons, reading requirements,[4] the methods for evaluating "knowledge," the distance between the teacher and the taught, the criteria for promotion: everything in this ready-to-wear approach serves to obviate thinking.

20   The bank-clerk educator does not realize that there is no true security in his hypertrophied role, that one must seek to live *with* others in solidarity. One cannot impose oneself, nor even merely co-exist with one's students. Solidarity requires true communication, and the concept by which such an educator is guided fears and proscribes communication.

Yet only through communication can human life hold meaning. The teacher's thinking is authenticated only by the authenticity of the students' thinking. The teacher cannot think for his students, nor can he impose his thought on them. Authentic thinking, thinking that is concerned about *reality,* does not take place in ivory tower isolation, but only in communication. If it is true that thought has meaning only when generated by action upon the world, the subordination of students to teachers becomes impossible.

Because banking education begins with a false understanding of men as objects, it cannot promote the development of what Fromm calls "biophily," but instead produces its opposite: "necrophily."

> While life is characterized by growth in a structured, functional manner, the necrophilous person loves all that does not grow, all that is mechanical. The necrophilous person is driven by the desire to transform the organic into the inorganic, to approach life mechanically, as if all living persons were things. . . . Memory, rather than experience; having, rather than being, is what counts. The necrophilous person can relate to an object—a flower or a person—only if he possesses it; hence a threat to his possession is a threat to himself; if he

---

[3] This concept corresponds to what Sartre calls the "digestive" or "nutritive" concept of education, in which knowledge is "fed" by the teacher to the students to "fill them out." See Jean-Paul Sartre, "Une idée fundamentale de la phénomenologie de Husserl L'intentionalité," *Situations I* (Paris, 1947).

[4] For example, some professors specify in their reading lists that a book should be read from pages 10 to 15—and do this to "help" their students!

> *loses possession he loses contact with the world. . . . He loves control, and in the act of controlling he kills life.* [5]

23   Oppression—overwhelming control—is necrophilic; it is nourished by love of death, not life. The banking concept of education, which serves the interests of oppression, is also necrophilic. Based on a mechanistic, static, naturalistic, spatialized view of consciousness, it transforms students into receiving objects. It attempts to control thinking and action, leads men to adjust to the world, and inhibits their creative power.

24   When their efforts to act responsibly are frustrated, when they find themselves unable to use their faculties, men suffer. "The suffering due to impotence is rooted in the very fact that the human equilibrium has been disturbed."[6] But the inability to act which causes men's anguish also causes them to reject their impotence, by attempting

> *. . . to restore [their] capacity to act. But can [they], and how? One way is to submit to and identify with a person or group having power. By this symbolic participation in another person's life, [men have] the illusion of acting, when in reality [they] only submit to and become part of those who act.* [7]

25   Populist manifestations perhaps best exemplify this type of behavior by the oppressed, who, by identifying with charismatic leaders, come to feel that they themselves are active and effective. The rebellion they express as they emerge in the historical process is motivated by that desire to act effectively. The dominant elites consider the remedy to be more domination and repression, carried out in the name of freedom, order, and social peace (that is, the peace of the elites). Thus they can condemn—logically, from their point of view—"the violence of a strike by workers and [can] call upon the state in the same breath to use violence in putting down the strike."[8]

26   Education as the exercise of domination stimulates the credulity of students, with the ideological intent (often not perceived by educators) of indoctrinating them to adapt to the world of oppression. This accusation is not made in the naïve hope that the dominant elites will thereby simply abandon the practice. Its objective is to call the attention of true humanists to the fact that they cannot use banking educational methods in the pursuit of liberation, for they would only negate that very pursuit. Nor may a revolutionary society inherit these methods from an oppressor society. The revolutionary society which practices banking education is either misguided or mistrusting of men. In either event, it is threatened by the specter of reaction.

---

[5] Eric Fromm, *The Heart of Man* (New York, 1966), p. 41.
[6] *Ibid.*, p. 31.
[7] *Ibid.*
[8] Reinhold Niebuhr, *Moral Man and Immoral Society* (New York, 1960), p. 130.

Unfortunately, those who espouse the cause of liberation are themselves surrounded and influenced by the climate which generates the banking concept, and often do not perceive its true significance or its dehumanizing power. Paradoxically, then, they utilize this same instrument of alienation in what they consider an effort to liberate. Indeed, some "revolutionaries" brand as "innocents," "dreamers," or even "reactionaries" those who would challenge this educational practice. But one does not liberate men by alienating them. Authentic liberation—the process of humanization—is not another deposit to be made in men. Liberation is a praxis: the action and reflection of men upon their world in order to transform it. Those truly committed to the cause of liberation can accept neither the mechanistic concept of consciousness as an empty vessel to be filled, nor the use of banking methods of domination (propaganda, slogans—deposits) in the name of the liberation.

Those truly committed to liberation must reject the banking concept in its entirety, adopting instead a concept of men as conscious beings, and consciousness as consciousness intent upon the world. They must abandon the educational goal of deposit-making and replace it with the posing of the problems of men in their relations with the world. "Problem-posing" education, responding to the essence of consciousness—*intentionality*—rejects communiqués and embodies communications. It epitomizes the special characteristic of consciousness: being *conscious of,* not only as intent on objects but as turned in upon itself in a Jasperian "split"—consciousness as consciousness *of* consciousness.

Liberating education consists in acts of cognition, not transferrals of information. It is a learning situation in which the cognizable object (far from being the end of the cognitive act) intermediates the cognitive actors—teacher on the one hand and students on the other. Accordingly, the practice of problem-posing education entails at the outset that the teacher-student contradiction be resolved. Dialogical relations—indispensable to the capacity of cognitive actors to cooperate in perceiving the same cognizable object—are otherwise impossible.

30   Indeed, problem-posing education, which breaks with the vertical patterns characteristic of banking education, can fulfill its function as the practice of freedom only if it can overcome the above contradiction. Through dialogue, the teacher-of-the-students and the students-of-the-teacher cease to exist and a new term emerges: teacher-students with students-teacher. The teacher is no longer merely the-one-who-teaches, but one who is himself taught in dialogue with the students, who in turn while being taught also teach. They become jointly responsible for a process in which all grow. In this process, arguments based on "authority" are no longer valid; in order to function, authority must be *on the side of* freedom, not *against* it. Here, no one teaches another, nor is anyone self-taught. Men teach each other, mediated by the world, by the cognizable objects which in banking education are "owned" by the teacher.

The banking concept (with its tendency to dichotomize everything) distinguishes two stages in the action of the educator. During the first he cognizes a cognizable object while he prepares his lessons in his study or his laboratory; during the second, he expounds to his students about that object. The students are not called upon to know, but to memorize the contents narrated by the teacher. Nor do the students practice any act of cognition, since the object towards which that act should be directed is the property of the teacher rather than a medium evoking the critical reflection of both teacher and students. Hence in the name of the "preservation of culture and knowledge" we have a system which achieves neither true knowledge nor true culture.

The problem-posing method does not dichotomize the activity of the teacher-student: he is not "cognitive" at one point and "narrative" at another. He is always "cognitive," whether preparing a project or engaging in dialogue with the students. He does not regard cognizable objects as his private property, but as the object of reflection by himself and the students. In this way, the problem-posing educator constantly re-forms his reflections in the reflection of the students. The students—no longer docile listeners—are now critical co-investigators in dialogue with the teacher. The teacher presents the material to the students for their consideration, and re-considers his earlier considerations as the students express their own. The role of the problem-solving educator is to create, together with the students, the conditions under which knowledge at the level of the *doxa* is superseded by true knowledge, at the level of the *logos*.

Whereas banking education anesthetizes and inhibits creative power, problem-posing education involves a constant unveiling of reality. The former attempts to maintain the *submersion* of consciousness; the latter strives for the *emergence* of consciousness and *critical intervention* in reality.

Students, as they are increasingly posed with problems relating to themselves in the world and with the world, will feel increasingly challenged and obliged to respond to that challenge. Because they apprehend the challenge as interrelated to other problems within a total context, not as a theoretical question, the resulting comprehension tends to be increasingly critical and thus constantly less alienated. Their response to the challenge evokes new challenges, followed by new understandings; and gradually the students come to regard themselves as committed.

35   Education as the practice of freedom—as opposed to education as the practice of domination—denies that man is abstract, isolated, independent, and unattached to the world; it also denies that the world exists as a reality apart from men. Authentic reflection considers neither abstract man nor the world without men, but men in their relations with the world. In these relations consciousness and world are simultaneous: consciousness neither precedes the world nor follows it.

La conscience et le monde sont donnés d'un même coup: extérieur par essence à la conscience, le monde est, par essence relatif à elle. [9]

---

[9] Sartre, *op cit.*, p. 32. [The passage is obscure but could be read as "Consciousness and the world are given at one and the same time: the exterior world as it enters consciousness is relative to our ways of seeing and understanding that world." Editors' note.]

In one of our culture circles in Chile, the group was discussing . . . the anthropological concept of culture. In the midst of the discussion, a peasant who by banking standards was completely ignorant said: "Now I see that without man there is no world." When the educator responded: "Let's say, for the sake of argument, that all the men on earth were to die, but that the earth itself remained, together with trees, birds, animals, rivers, seas, the stars . . . wouldn't all this be a world?"

"Oh, no," the peasant replied emphatically. "There would be no one to say: 'This is a world.'"

The peasant wished to express the idea that there would be lacking the consciousness of the world which necessarily implies the world of consciousness. *I* cannot exist without a *not-I*. In turn, the *not-I* depends on that existence. The world which brings consciousness into existence becomes the world of that consciousness. Hence, the previously cited affirmation of Sartre: *"La conscience et le monde sont donnés d'un même coup."*

As men, simultaneously reflecting on themselves and on the world, increase the scope of their perception, they begin to direct their observations towards previously inconspicuous phenomena:

> *In perception properly so-called, as an explicit awareness* [Gewahren], *I am turned towards the object, to the paper, for instance. I apprehend it as being this here and now. The apprehension is a singling out, every object having a background in experience. Around and about the paper lie books, pencils, ink-well, and so forth, and these in a certain sense are also "perceived," perceptually there, in the "field of intuition"; but whilst I was turned towards the paper there was no turning in their direction, nor any apprehending of them, not even in a secondary sense. They appeared and yet were not singled out, were not posited on their own account. Every perception of a thing has such a zone of background intuitions or background awareness, if "intuiting" already includes the state of being turned towards, and this also is a "conscious experience," or more briefly a "consciousness of" all indeed that in point of fact lies in the co-perceived objective background.* [10]

40 That which had existed objectively but had not been perceived in its deeper implications (if indeed it was perceived at all) begins to "stand out," assuming the character of a problem and therefore of challenge. Thus, men begin to single out elements from their "background awarenesses" and to reflect upon them. These elements are now objects of men's consideration, and, as such, objects of their action and cognition.

In problem-posing education, men develop their power to perceive critically *the way they exist* in the world *with which* and *in which* they find

---

[10] Edmund Husserl, *Ideas—General Introduction to Pure Phenomenology* (London, 1969), pp. 105–106.

themselves; they come to see the world not as a static reality, but as a reality in process, in transformation. Although the dialectical relations of men with the world exist independently of how these relations are perceived (or whether or not they are perceived at all), it is also true that the form of action men adopt is to a large extent a function of how they perceive themselves in the world. Hence, the teacher-students and the students-teacher reflect simultaneously on themselves and the world without dichotomizing this reflection from action, and thus establish an authentic form of thought and action.

Once again, the two educational concepts and practices under analysis come into conflict. Banking education (for obvious reasons) attempts, by mythicizing reality, to conceal certain facts which explain the way men exist in the world; problem-posing education sets itself the task of demythologizing. Banking education resists dialogue; problem-posing education regards dialogue as indispensable to the act of cognition which unveils reality. Banking education treats students as objects of assistance; problem-posing education makes them critical thinkers. Banking education inhibits creativity and domesticates (although it cannot completely destroy) the *intentionality* of consciousness by isolating consciousness from the world, thereby denying men their ontological and historical vocation of becoming more fully human. Problem-posing education bases itself on creativity and stimulates true reflection and action upon reality, thereby responding to the vocation of men as beings who are authentic only when engaged in inquiry and creative transformation. In sum: banking theory and practice, as immobilizing and fixating forces, fail to acknowledge men as historical beings; problem-posing theory and practice take man's historicity as their starting point.

Problem-posing education affirms men as beings in the process of *becoming*—as unfinished, uncompleted beings in and with a likewise unfinished reality. Indeed, in contrast to other animals who are unfinished, but not historical, men know themselves to be unfinished; they are aware of their incompletion. In this incompletion and this awareness lie the very roots of education as an exclusively human manifestation. The unfinished character of men and the transformational character of reality necessitate that education be an ongoing activity.

Education is thus constantly remade in the praxis. In order to *be*, it must *become*. Its "duration" (in the Bergsonian meaning of the word) is found in the interplay of the opposites *permanence* and *change*. The banking method emphasizes permanence and becomes reactionary; problem-posing education—which accepts neither a "well-be-haved" present nor a predetermined future—roots itself in the dynamic present and becomes revolutionary.

45   Problem-posing education is revolutionary futurity. Hence it is prophetic (and, as such, hopeful). Hence, it corresponds to the historical nature of man. Hence, it affirms men as beings who transcend themselves, who move forward and look ahead, for whom immobility represents a fatal threat, for whom looking at the past must only be a means of understanding more clearly what and who they are so that they can more wisely build a future.

Hence, it identifies with the movement which engages men as beings aware of their incompletion—an historical movement which has its point of departure, its Subjects and its objective.

The point of departure of the movement lies in men themselves. But since men do not exist apart from the world, apart from reality, the movement must begin with the men-world relationship. Accordingly, the point of departure must always be with men in the "here and now," which constitutes the situation within which they are submerged, from which they emerge, and in which they intervene. Only by starting from this situation—which determines their perception of it—can they begin to move. To do this authentically they must perceive their state not as fated and unalterable, but merely as limiting—and therefore challenging.

Whereas the banking method directly or indirectly reinforces men's fatalistic perception of their situation, the problem-posing method presents this very situation to them as a problem. As the situation becomes the object of their cognition, the naïve or magical perception which produced their fatalism gives way to perception which is able to perceive itself even as it perceives reality, and can thus be critically objective about that reality.

A deepened consciousness of their situation leads men to apprehend that situation as an historical reality susceptible of transformation. Resignation gives way to the drive for transformation and inquiry, over which men feel themselves to be in control. If men, as historical beings necessarily engaged with other men in a movement of inquiry, did not control that movement, it would be (and is) a violation of men's humanity. Any situation in which some men prevent others from engaging in the process of inquiry is one of violence. The means used are not important; to alienate men from their own decision-making is to change them into objects.

This movement of inquiry must be directed towards humanization— man's historical vocation. The pursuit of full humanity, however, cannot be carried out in isolation or individualism, but only in fellowship and solidarity; therefore it cannot unfold in the antagonistic relations between oppressors and oppressed. No one can be authentically human while he prevents others from being so. Attempting *to be more* human, individualistically, leads to *having more,* egotistically: a form of dehumanization. Not that it is not fundamental *to have* in order *to be* human. Precisely because it *is* necessary, some men's *having* must not be allowed to constitute an obstacle to others' *having,* must not consolidate the power of the former to crush the latter.

50 Problem-posing education, as a humanist and liberating praxis, posits as fundamental that men subjected to domination must fight for their emancipation. To that end, it enables teachers and students to become Subjects of the educational process by overcoming authoritarianism and an alienating intellectualism; it also enables men to overcome their false perception of reality. The world—no longer something to be described with deceptive words—becomes the object of that transforming action by men which results in their humanization.

Problem-posing education does not and cannot serve the interests of the oppressor. No oppressive order could permit the oppressed to begin to question: Why? While only a revolutionary society can carry out this education in systematic terms, the revolutionary leaders need not take full power before they can employ the method. In the revolutionary process, the leaders cannot utilize the banking method as an interim measure, justified on grounds of expediency, with the intention of *later* behaving in a genuinely revolutionary fashion. They must be revolutionary—that is to say, dialogical—from the outset.

■ EXPLORATIONS OF THE TEXT ■

1. What is the subject-object relationship of teachers and students?
2. What does Freire mean when he writes the following: "Education is suffering from narration sickness"? Examine the argument that students are "receptacles" which the teacher fills.
3. Define the banking concept of education. Why is it characteristic of an "ideology of oppression"?
4. What does Freire believe to be necessary for learning? Annotate the principles in which he believes.
5. How does the "humanism" of the banking approach "mask the effort to turn men into automatons"?
6. What is the role of critical or authentic thinking? Analyze the statement: "Man is spectator; not re-creator."
7. What is the concept of "necrophilia education"? Explain education "as the exercise of domination."
8. Analyze the idea of liberation as a "praxis." Why does Freire believe that "one does not liberate men by alienating them"?
9. Discuss "problem-posing" education. How do humans learn to view the world "as a reality in process, in transformation." What is "consciousness of consciousness"?
10. Discuss the idea that banking education mythologizes reality and that "problem-posing" education demythologizes reality.
11. Why must "problem-posing" education be revolutionary "from the outset"? Why is it so threatening?

■■ **JOURNAL ENTRIES** ■■

1. Create a specific example of problem-posing education or a specific example of banking education.
2. Pose a problem that challenges you.
3. Analyze your academic experience in one or more classes. How does it compare to Freire's model?

■■■ **IDEAS FOR WRITING** ■■■

1. Write about a personal experience of banking or liberating education. Apply Freire's argument and language to your analysis.
2. Design a writing assignment from the problem you posed in Journal Entry 2. Fulfill your own assignment.
3. Agree or disagree with one of Freire's arguments.
4. Describe an ideal learning situation. What would characterize the relationship of students and teachers?
5. What would improve education in the United States?

A Visit to the Mothers of the Plaza de Mayo

Marjorie Agosin   Translated by Cola Framzen and Janice Molloy

Born in Bethesda, Maryland, Marjorie Agosin (1955–   ) grew up in Chile, where her Jewish grandparents settled after they fled from Russia. A writer and professor of Spanish at Wellesley College, she has studied in Argentina as a Fulbright scholar. Among her writings are the volumes of poetry, Witches and Other Things *(1985) and* Zones of Pain *(1988), and nonfiction,* Pablo Neruda *(1986),* Women of Smoke *(1989),* Bonfires *(1990), and* Mothers of Plaza de Mayo. *She has said: "To write is to dare to be vulnerable."*

The Mothers of the Plaza de Mayo, many of whom suffered torture and even death, began their silent vigil to demand information about their relatives who had disappeared and punishment for those who had participated in political crimes in Argentina.

1   Sunday in the Plaza de Mayo. August. It is almost the end of winter in South America, and the first buds are starting to swell, a sign of the spring we have all been waiting for, one that might bring an answer to one of the most overwhelming and emotional questions of the Argentinean people: the fate of those who disappeared during the evil years of the dirty war, la guerra sucia.[1]

2   A limpid sun lights up the Plaza de Mayo this Sunday. Young fathers and their children are feeding the pigeons. Everything looks prosperous. The women of the capital are wearing elegant leather suits this season; the children are well-dressed. All these signs of well-being give the eerie sensation that nothing unusual has happened in this plaza. The appearance of normality is deceiving, for this spot where I sit, caressed by the benign sun of early spring, is the same place that has become a major symbol of protest, witness, and denunciation of the crimes committed by the military Juntas of Argentina.

3   To make a brief recapitulation of recent historical events, the armed forces of Argentina took power on March 16, 1976. They dissolved all political parties; labour unions and all universities were put under government control. Public statements of the Junta declared these measures were taken "to restore order and peace to the country." Similar measures were taken in Chile in 1973 by the Pinochet dictatorship. In both countries, in addition to the official, announced measures, another level of measures was instituted: a subterranean rule began to take shape that used undeclared and unavowed methods of terror, repression, suspicion, torture, disappearance and murder to put down opposition. At first, the victims were known opponents, such as labour union members, university activists, or journalists. Later, the choice of victims was what one can only describe as random. As the crimes increased, so did the need to keep the subterranean war hidden, and the attempts to hide all traces of the horrendous actions became more outrageous. The military embarked on a kind of final solution with their policy of "disappearing" citizens in greater and greater numbers.

4   As unbelievable as it may seem to us now, what began as a clandestine operation became, with time, routine and bureaucratic. The squads of terror settled down to using teams of men dressed in civilian clothes and driving black Falcons without license plates, who entered homes or places of work at will, in broad daylight or at night, to seize and drag off people who for one reason or another were thought to be suspicious, or who were just unlucky enough to be in that place at that time. Sometimes totally innocent individuals were taken, including children and even babies. Most of those seized went on to endure clandestine prisons, torture, disappearance and, in many cases, death. The open kidnappings sowed an atmosphere of fear and terror throughout the entire population.

---

[1] The *dirty war* designates the epoch beginning before the overthrow of the dictator Juan Perón in 1975 until the restoration of democracy and the election of Raúl Alfonsín as President in 1984.

5   Now the country is left to relive this painful era, to uncover what was so assiduously covered up. Where are those who disappeared without trace? What happened to the children snatched along with their parents? What happened to the babies that women carried in their arms as they went to prison? What became of the babies born to imprisoned women? We have begun to know answers to some of these questions, but not to all of them, and justice requires an answer to all questions. Mothers, grandmothers and wives of the disappeared have been forced by tragic necessity to rescue their lost ones from the oblivion intended by the Juntas, to inquire into the destiny of the estimated 9,000 people who disappeared between 1973 and the return to democracy in 1984.

6   The years from 1973 to 1975, saw many disappearances as well as a series of disruptive activities carried out by urban guerrillas. The actions of both sides created such a climate of mistrust and tension in the country that, for some time, people did not know who was responsible for the kidnappings and killings. Later, it became known that paramilitary groups of the extreme right, operating under the clear protection of the military of the democratically elected Peróns, were responsible for the disappearances. It was not the urban guerrillas as the military tried to pretend.[2]

7   The political situation in Argentina has always been an anomaly; it is a prosperous country with many natural resources, yet has always been politically unstable. To recapitulate briefly and to shed some light on this situation, in 1930, the Argentinean armed forces overthrew the democratically elected government of Hipólito Irigoyen of the Radical Civic Union Party. Since then, the military has overthrown five other legally elected governments, and has ruled Argentina for a longer period than all of the democratic governments together.

8   Juan Perón was a colonel who participated in the coupo d'etat that overthrew President Ramon Carillo. He used his position as the head of the National Labour Department to take control of the developing trade unions, which he corrupted and used as a tool for his own personal gains. Perón became president for the first time in 1946 and was overthrown in 1955. In 1973 Perón, who had by then become a cult figure in Argentina, returned to power. Even though Perón was chosen to be president, there were many fascists in the armed forces, and they were instrumental in the creation of the paramilitary groups even before the coup. After he died in 1974, Isabel, his second wife, became president, but on March 24, 1976 the military took power and the dirty war began. They dismissed the congress and obsessively

---

[2] It is estimated that half of the total number of disappearances, involving approximately 5000 persons, occurred in 1976 during the first year of military rule. In 1979, another 35 percent disappeared and in 1978, 15 percent disappeared. Information obtained from the following study: Eduardo Duhalde. *El estado terroísta argentino* ("The Argentinean Terrorist State"). Madrid: Argos Vergara, 1983.

took on the mission of ridding the country of what they referred to as subversive thought of any kind.[3]

9   You may be asking yourself, who were these people who disappeared? The answer is anybody at all who might possibly have been perceived as opposing the regime. One did not have to act openly against the dictatorship to be a candidate for a disappearance. One could just think one's own private thoughts and still be found guilty. Statistics show that 30 percent of the disappeared were workers, 21 percent were students, and 10 percent were professionals. The rest included anyone who happened to be caught in the net, including teenagers, housewives, and even babies, as we said earlier.

10   The world, especially a silenced and silent Argentina, has been shaken to learn, from the testimony of survivors and by subsequent excavations of unmarked graves, that the disappeared were tortured and finally killed. Many were thrown into the Rio de la Plata or into the sea from helicopters. Some of the recovered bodies showed death by drowning, that is, that the people were still alive when they were thrown out. Certain groups were subjected to especially sadistic treatment, for instance women and Jews. For the treatment of Jews in captivity, see Jacobo Timmerman's testimony in *Prisoner Without a Name, Cell Without a Number*. Women were not arrested particularly because they were women, but *because* they were women, they were subjected to rape and other violations in addition to torture in the clandestine prisons. It has been determined that a quarter of the disappeared were women, and of those, 10 percent were pregnant at the time of their arrest.

11   The state of limbo in which the families of the disappeared found themselves caused them to begin a quest to find their loved ones, even if only their bones.[4] In 1975, the mothers and wives of the disappeared started on a tortuous trek of searching which eventually led them to a period of reflection. When they went to police stations or jails to ask about the whereabouts of their children they were often told: "It's your own fault, Señora, for raising a subversive." Or they would say: "Your son is in the underground and is outside the country."

12   There are many groups of women in Latin America that have developed in authoritarian regimes. For example, in Chile a group of women formed the Asociación de Detenidos-Desaparecidos (Association of the Detained-Disappeared) in order to find their loved ones. This association was founded in 1975, and carries out a variety of protest activities, including night vigils and political marches. A similar group developed in Guatemala in 1979 called Grupo de Ayuda Mutual (Mutual Aid Group). This group consisted of about thirty women who carried out activities similar to those of the association in Chile.

---

[3] For further information, see: Ronald Dworkin. "Report from Hell," *The New York Times Book Review*, Volume XXXIII, Number 12:11–14.

[4] For a detailed account of the treatment of political prisoners, including testimony of survivors, see: Ernesto Sábato, editor. National Commission of the Rights of People (CONADEP). *Nunca Más* ("Never Again"). Buenos Aires: Eudena, 1984.

The groups vary in size; they usually have between 30 and 50 members. These women's groups are almost always formed by mothers, housewives who have been forced to leave their private spheres and go into the streets to find their loved ones.

13   Because there still exists in Argentine society the legacy of Spanish culture that treats *mothers* with a certain respect and even veneration, these mothers were treated by police and police officials with superficial politeness, but were never given a straight answer to their questions. With the guidance of leaders such as Perez Esquivel, the Argentinean human rights activist who was awarded the Nobel Peace Prize in 1981, the Mothers began to request concrete actions, such as asking for a writ of habeas corpus to be issued in specific cases. They still received no response to their requests.

14   The women then asked themselves, What could they do? What power did they actually possess? Who might make an impact in the face of such indifference? Who might have the information they sought? The group now known as the Mothers of the Plaza de Mayo was born in 1977 from this examination of the possibilities available to them. In the beginning, it was not a formal organization but simply a group of women who decided to join together to protest. Their protests took place then as now in this same plaza where children are playing and feeding the pigeons.

15   The Plaza de Mayo was a strategic location for a public demonstration. Here, Argentinean independence was proclaimed in 1810. Here, Juan Perón gave his populist speeches. In fact, the Plaza de Mayo is not only the heart of Buenos Aires, it is the heart of the country. The buildings that surround it include the old Cabildo, the Town Hall; the Presidential Palace called the Casa Rosada ("Pink House") because of its pink stone; and a number of other important government buildings and churches.

16   In the centre of the plaza, there is an obelisk that celebrates the 400th anniversary of the city's founding. On a cool April day at five o'clock in the afternoon, a few women appear in the plaza and start circling the obelisk. Each one wears a white kerchief on her head with the names of her disappeared ones embroidered around the edge, together with the date of their disappearance. The women march in absolute silence. The demonstrators, the mothers of the Plaza de Mayo, are mainly working and middle-class women, because these groups were most affected by the repression. There are some upper-class women, but they constitute a minority.

17   This civic and cooperative action on the part of a handful of women without any political power, for the most part traditional housewives who had never taken part in any public action before, was the *only public protest* made for a long time against the traffickers of death in Argentina. They were the *only ones* to stand up in favor of life. In his book, *The Madwomen of the Plaza de Mayo,* Jean Pierre Bousquet expressed the significance of this first demonstration: "When on a Thursday of April of 1977 at five o'clock in the afternoon, fourteen women, between 40 and 70 years of age, defied the ban on public gatherings promulgated by the all-powerful Military Junta and marched in the

Plaza de Mayo to make known their pain and their resolve not to accept having their questions go unanswered, the generals lost their first battle."[5]

18   The demonstrations every Thursday in the plaza are now an event, a tradition and a symbol that the Argentinean people refuse to submit to fascism, but the example was started and carried on for years by a handful of women. In the beginning, soldiers would appear and simply ask them to disperse. However, as time went on and as the demonstrations grew in size and began to have a public impact, the Junta began to make reprisals. In 1978, they kidnapped the group's first leader, Azuzena Villaflor de Vicenti, together with eleven other members of the group. At about the same time, they also kidnapped two French nuns who they later gave the sadistic name of "The Flying Nuns" because they were thrown into the sea from a helicopter after being tortured. Doña Azuzena suffered terrible tortures and martyrdom. The location of her remains is still unknown. The others kidnapped with her were finally released after an international outcry, organized mostly by the United Nations.

19   Regardless of this violent action against nuns, the clergy in Argentina has not been involved in protest as it has been in the case of Chile; on the contrary, the clergy has been so quiet that it has been accused of collaborating with the military. Likewise, liberation theology is not an issue for the Mothers.

20   At the beginning, very few women gathered; the initial number was, to be exact, thirteen. Then, other women followed, and from 1976 to the present there have usually been between 50 and 60 women marching. The same mothers march, but as the years went by and people stopped being so afraid, there were more and more people joining them. Now, people may not necessarily be mothers, but are sympathetic to the cause. The plaza activity is an outward and physical demonstration of the many things that go on in these people's lives. For example, they have weekly meetings and create new strategies of protest. These strategies vary from seeking public support in other nations to organizing national protest involving other human rights organizations. I believe the mothers have become the heroines of Argentinean society, for people realize that they were the only ones who dared to speak in a silent society. Yet they are in a difficult position with regard to President Alfonsín, because the mothers, as the voice of conscience, want all of the people responsible for the murders to be tried. Alfonsín has said that he will only try those who gave the orders.[6]

21   What is important to remember is that the Mothers of the Plaza de Mayo have a tremendous historical importance. Even if they did not contribute

---

[5] Jean Pierre Bousquet. *Las Locas de la Plaza de Mayo*. Buenos Aires: El Cid, 1982, p. 43.

[6] As of this writing in April of 1986, the nine military officers who governed Argentina through three successive Juntas have been tried in a civilian court and sentenced. The leader of the three-man junta, Videla, received a life sentence, as did Admiral Massera. Ex-president Viola received a 17-year sentence, and ex-president Galtieri was absolved. There is bitterness at this verdict, because, for the most part, the Mothers cannot accept a compromise for the guilty ones. This is a point of contention between the Mothers and the Alfonsín regime.

directly to the fall of the military, they serve as an example to other non-violent groups in Latin America.

22   It was not until 1979 that the group of women became cohesive enough to organize themselves officially into the Mothers of the Plaza de Mayo. They collected the twenty names necessary to satisfy the legal requirement to form an association at the risk of their lives. They found a location where they could meet and elect their leaders by secret ballot. The leaders have so far been women who are truly fearless, who refuse to be terrorized, and who inspire confidence in others, women such as the present leader, Hebe de Bonafini.

23   The Mothers began to have an international impact. Some travelled to Europe in 1979 and asked for and were granted an audience with the Pope. However, they really became known world-wide in 1978 when the World Cup Soccer competition was held in Buenos Aires, and the city was filled with journalists from all over the world. The demonstrations in the plaza were photographed and appeared in the newspapers, magazines and on the television screens of the five continents. The Mothers realized then that visibility and publicity were powerful weapons of protest. Though they had no political contacts and no previous experience in political affairs, they showed real shrewdness in planning and continuing their actions. They became more and more effective, in spite of censorship, in spite of silence, in spite of ostracism. Sometimes even members of their own families refused to have anything to do with these women because they were afraid. Many people were afraid to associate with families of the disappeared. It was considered dangerous, and undoubtedly was.

24   Just as the World Cup brought the cause of the Mothers to the world, a larger public began to be aware of the Argentinean atrocities and the stories of the disappeared through the Argentine movie, *The Official Story,* which tells of a typical middle-class family, unaware of the brutalities. The mother soon begins to suspect that her adopted daughter could be the child of someone who had been kidnapped and murdered. The rest of the movie involves this woman's increasing awareness of the atrocities that took place in her beloved country, and the impact that this knowledge has on her relationship with her husband and child.

25   The Mothers of the Plaza de Mayo are still visible and extremely active, even after the military was pressured to return to the barracks in 1984. The size of the demonstrations has increased with the return to democracy, even though there have been no disappearances since Alfonsín took office. The reason for this increase is that the Mothers have involved other groups in their public protest. When the Mothers are not in the Plaza, they are still attending other gatherings, always fighting, learning, reflecting. They have learned to channel their anxiety and grief into constructive paths, and to invent new political strategies. These women are priestesses — they have come to symbolize the collective conscience of the country.

26   Nobody can pretend not to see them. Here they are in the bright afternoon light with their white kerchiefs and with the photographs of the disappeared hanging from ribbons around their tired necks. They are willing to

use women's true and ineffable recourse in their battle: the body itself as a weapon, exposed, subjected to hunger strikes, to long marches, to all sorts of abuse, at times given over to torture. Students, workers and intellectuals have begun to join them in their demonstrations. On August 2, 1985, more than 80,000 persons joined a march convened by the Mothers, and wound through the centre of Buenos Aires, shouting their slogan: "Justice and punishment for the guilty."

27   Through the years, the Mothers have learned by necessity to be wary, patient and persistent, and that is the prevailing attitude even now that the much discredited military has been ousted and the popular, democratically elected Alfonsín is president. As one of Alfonsín's first official acts, he appointed a Commission, headed by the writer Ernesto Sábato, to inquire into the fate of the disappeared. The Commission's results are documented in the report called *Nunca Más* (Never Again) (CONADEP, 1984). The first trial has been held, in a civilian court, of the nine major leaders of the three Juntas; the prosecutor has asked for life sentences for some and shorter sentences for others. Some might think the Mothers should be satisfied. But few of them to date have learned the fate of their own children and grandchildren. The original search goes on; their original aims remain the same, that *all* the guilty be brought to justice. They are still asking for "Life for the disappeared and punishment for the guilty." For this reason, the demonstrations of the Mothers of the Plaza de Mayo continue, even though the kidnapping, torture, killing, and imprisonment of innocent Argentineans has stopped under Alfonsín.

28   In the early years, the Mothers were called the "Madwomen of the Plaza de Mayo," an attempt by the generals and their cohorts to dismiss them and their claims, using the age-old technique of a male-dominated society by calling women regarded as "out of their place" crazy. As mothers, they were treated with certain deference; nevertheless, their attempts to locate their loved ones were seen as being insane actions, which diminished their importance in the eyes of the military. A few centuries ago no doubt they would have been denounced as witches. But these witches, or Madwomen, have survived, have stayed united in spite of all adversities and all divisive methods used against them, including infiltration, kidnapping, torture and murder of some of their members. One cannot detect in them any political discrepancies, nor any desires for power for power's sake. They are determined and courageous; they are witnesses who dared to speak the dreadful truth about the military government. I would like to insist once again that, for years, they acted alone. Not even the Catholic Church, as an institution, supported them, although individual clergy members did. They defied the traditional, patriarchal society as well as the military Junta when they went out into the street and became public figures, and showed themselves ready to accept all the risks implicit in such rebellious activity.

29   By their public actions, they have become important and influential in Latin American politics. They have learned to use old political techniques in new and dramatic ways. For instance, their silent and passive marches speak louder and more eloquently than any oration could.

30   At the present time, the Argentinean people find themselves staggered by the testimony of survivors being given in the courtrooms. And the Madwomen are now regarded as heroines because they defied the silence. They, themselves, see their work to be the same as ever — to continue to fight until the last criminal is brought to justice.

31   As I sit sobered by these thoughts, a woman approaches me. She tells me her parents were exterminated in Auschwitz and that her son, 30 years old, disappeared from the University of Buenos Aires. It does not help her that there is now democracy in Argentina. She is still afraid; she will always be afraid. She begs me not to use her name. How can one comprehend such misfortune? How can it be that this woman has now been a victim of two holocausts?

32   The House of the Mothers is located in Hipólito Irigoyen Street and was donated by the government of Holland. Other governments who might have helped them, such as the United States government, remained silent and offered no aid. When I visited the house, there was tremendous activity. The Mothers bustle about, putting up posters, organizing meetings, receiving visitors. Said one Mother, "Here, there is much pain but much love." The walls are covered with photographs of the disappeared. I notice that most are young, attractive, brimming with good health; there are many young women among them. I cannot help asking myself again, "How can a civilized society descend to such a barbarous level?"

33   It is Thursday. We are all on our way to the plaza. I find myself walking beside Hebe Bonafini, President of the Mothers; she makes me feel tall and strong. I can think of nothing to say to her but we smile at one another. The women gather around the obelisk, greeting one another, embracing and kissing friends. I think of their sleepless nights. They arrange themselves for another march in favour of life, in defiance of death. They tell me that, while they are marching in the plaza, they feel very close to their children. They feel their children are by their sides. And the truth is, in the plaza where forgetting is not allowed, memory recovers its meaning. Cruelty of human beings to other human beings is judged. The devastation of the young, the workers, the students, the young pregnant women and the grandmothers is remembered, denounced, mourned, judged.

34   The activities of the Mothers have not changed since democratization in the sense that they continue to go to marches and there still is no answer for the disappearances of their children. The biggest change in the Mothers' group is the attempt to incorporate other human rights organizations in their plight and to pressure for more immediate answers.

35   Another Thursday in August in Buenos Aires. A conspiring sun caresses our skin. The plaza is full of life and movement: couples holding hands, old people enjoying the sun, children and pigeons. The Mothers arrive, immaculate, serene and disturbing in their white kerchiefs with the embroidered names and dates. Slowly, their healing aura spreads and creates a blue space in this plaza that is now theirs, that now has to belong to them. They form their sacred circle. Earlier, the world watched and supported them, but silent, fearful Argentina averted its eyes. Now the country joins them and

weeps with them, because the Mothers fight not only for their own children but for all children. They are marching to win all rights due a free people, to make any violation of those rights unacceptable. The Mothers have a close acquaintance with death but they are completely committed to life.[7]

I wish to express special appreciation to Nora Feminia, to whom I also dedicate this work. She helped me get to know the Mothers and very generously shared her own work with me concerning women and politics in Argentina.

■ **EXPLORATIONS OF THE TEXT** ■

---

1. Consider the contrasts between the descriptions of the spring and of the past events. Why does Agosin use a narrative frame for this essay?
2. Summarize the historical events presented in paragraphs 3–10. How does this context contribute to an understanding of the actions of the Mothers?
3. Describe the development of resistance to the terror. Why were the Mothers alone? Why did they persist even when some of them were tortured, imprisoned, and murdered?
4. Why did they choose the Plaza de Mayo?
5. Explain the quotation by Jean Pierre Bousquet from *The Madwomen of the Plaza de Mayo.* Does this analysis of the significance of their actions seem accurate?
6. Trace the growth of the organization of the Mothers. Why did they continue to protest after the election of President Alfonsín?
7. What was the importance of the World Cup Soccer competition in Buenos Aires in 1978? Who supported the Mothers? In what manner?
8. Analyze the symbolic language in the following quotation: "Slowly, their healing aura spreads and creates a blue space in this plaza that is now theirs, that now has to belong to them. They form their sacred circle."
9. Construct an outline of this essay. Does the author simply explain, or does she persuade?
10. Compare and contrast this essay with Valenzuela's story and with Forché's poems. Does Agosin's essay illuminate these other works?

---

[7] There are various books concerning the Mothers; for example, see the following books of poetry:

Juan Gelman. *La Junta Luz.* Buenos Aires: Editorial Tierra Firme, 1985.

Vicente Zito Lema. *Mater.* Buenos Aires: Editorial Tierra Firme, 1985.

Also see:

John Simpson and Jana Bennett. *The Disappeared and the Mothers of the Plaza de Mayo.* New York: St. Martin's Press, 1985.

■■ JOURNAL ENTRIES ■■

1. Respond to the "Mothers of the Plaza de Mayo."
2. What is the most powerful part of this story?

■■■ IDEAS FOR WRITING ■■■

1. Summarize Agosin's essay.
2. Make connections between Luisa Valenzuela's "I'm Your Horse in the Night" and "A Visit to the Mothers of the Plaza de Mayo."
3. Analyze the structure of Agosin's "A Visit to the Mothers of the Plaza de Mayo."
4. Analyze Agosin's essay as an example of persuasion.

Student Essay: Argument

Realizations of the Quest for Vision: A Political Interpretation

Carl Ponesse

Born in Newburgh, New York, Carl Ponesse (1967–   ) majors in Sociology at the State University of New York at New Paltz. His essay presents an argument about the political implications of the quest for vision in three works: N. Scott Momaday's "A Vision Beyond Time and Place," Raymond Carver's "Cathedral," and Sophocles' "Oedipus Rex." Clearly Ponesse favors Momaday's portrait of Old Man Cheney and the spiritual and natural paths that Cheney follows. Ponesse submitted this essay as a mid-term examination.

Socrates believed that "the unexamined life is not worth living." He did not caution that the examination might lead both to vision and to suffering, both to truth and to tragedy, both to transcendence and to despair. In works by Momaday, Carver, and Sophocles the characters realize their quests for vision: each takes a different path; each reaches a different destination; each experiences a different insight; each discovers that personal vision depends upon cultural and political conditions. I would like to argue that each of these writers presents an individual quest that does or could change the body politic.

In "A Vision Beyond Time and Place," N. Scott Momaday describes old man Cheney and his folkways, which can be explained as spirituality tightly integrated with nature. This Native-American view is contrasted with western culture. In his attempt to capture the integration between Native-American society and nature, Momaday speaks of a "testament to the realization of a quest for vision."

This quest is basic to all human beings—the desire to learn, to experience, to come to an understanding of themselves and their origins. This search is determined by society, by the perception of what environment teaches and of what human beings will strive to obtain and to support.

To Momaday, Cheney achieved self-actualization. He was a "man who saw very deeply into the distance . . . one whose vision extended far beyond physical boundaries." The author explains that this vision begins with a reverence for nature, with being overcome at witnessing a sunrise. "Wonder is a principal part of such a vision," explains Momaday. Nature is a universal entity that binds all living things; to experience the wonder of a sunrise is to experience the marvel of human life. The author ties creation to nature, to that which is not seen with the naked eye, to that which has to be seen with the soul. So when the author says, "When old man Cheney looked into the sunrise he saw as far into himself," he realizes that the Native-American values are worthwhile and that the values have been lost in the westernization of our culture.

Momaday's differentiation among cultures starts with thoughtful descriptions of Native-American characteristics. "This native vision, this gift of seeing truly, with wonder and delight, into the natural world, is informed by a certain attitude of reference and self-respect." To take Momaday one step further and to critique the westernization of a people, look at what America now believes. In the late 1800s, when the Indians were being pushed to the reaches of the west coast, something enormous was taking hold in existing cities of the United States—The Industrial Revolution. America has since been defined by it and is responsible for its feeding, a feeding that has eaten crucial natural resources. Nature is no longer revered and nurtured. Nature has suffered a damaging, gluttonous transformation because of man's economic diet.

This change has produced a more scientifically advanced society in which wonder and imagination have been replaced by an addiction to electronic media. One work which shows how people's thoughts are dominated by electronic media is "Cathedral." In this story by Raymond Carver, the main character is identified by secular society. He is tied to his television for entertainment, to marijuana and to alcohol for a heightened state of mind, and to his ignorance for security. He does not even realize his need for a quest for vision, though it is there, as indicated by his use of drugs to gain altered states. These activities do not make him a worthless character. Carver gives him some positive traits—honesty, humor, and a likability that stems from portraying this man, this couch potato, as a universal citizen. For example, when discussing Robert, the narrator assumes a comical, contemporary Archie Bunker attitude: "A blind man in my house was not something I looked forward to."

This character supports the argument concerning electronic media which dominate thought. Here the quest for vision is replaced by television. According to the narrator, "every night I smoked dope and stayed up as long as I could." Television sets, shows, and cinema are mentioned in more than fifteen paragraphs throughout the story. This repetition gives the appearance that this man's nights are totally dominated by the television. In the opening paragraph, he admits, "My idea of blindness came from the movies."

Later this character learns not only that the blind are intuitive, but also that there are totally new ways of experiencing ideas and thought. Robert, the blind man, is able to encourage his host to open his imagination by closing his eyes and seeing with other senses. As the two men draw a cathedral, the narrator is overwhelmed by this sensation. The incident breaks his passivity, his need to be entertained by the television, and frees his imagination. This transcendent moment arouses hope that the main character will embark on a quest for an even greater understanding of himself. "But I didn't feel like I was inside anything." As Momaday describes Cheney's vision, "It is a matter of extrasensory as well as sensory perception." Here the main character and Robert achieve this union. The ending implies that everyone can achieve such union and that our society must change so that individuals can attain their potential.

The quest for vision in "Oedipus Rex" explores another aspect of understanding—truth. In this drama, the spirituality is already formed by society. There is direct interaction among the gods and the characters. What becomes vital in this story is the search for truth that will lead to an understanding of the main character. As king of Thebes, Oedipus is given the duty by the gods to discover the truth about the murder of the previous ruler, Laius. Intertwined with this knowledge is the uncovering of unnatural behavior—incest and patricide. Although it is unknown by Oedipus, his life becomes the vehicle by which the gods enlighten the citizenry.

Oedipus' quest for vision is centered wholly on rescuing the city from the throes of deterioration. Through this task, Oedipus turns inward. He is indicted by the seer, Teiresias, who expatiates, "You blame my temper but you do not see your own that lives within you; it is me you chide." This accusation against Oedipus by the seer—one whose vision is not of sight but of knowledge—illuminates one of the major flaws in the character of Oedipus: he is quick to anger; he has a hot temper. For Oedipus, the quest now becomes one of further understanding himself and his place in the world.

Oedipus has the ability to find the truth. He searches for clues and for witnesses until the realization is one which is unmistakable and insufferable. His quest ends with his knowledge that he has murdered his father and married his mother, crimes which lead to his taking of his eyesight. This punishment seems instinctive. He cannot bear to see the truth; he must punish himself as he vowed; his knowledge is too burdensome. For Oedipus, his insight is linked to the god's prophecy, and, therefore, it becomes a lesson to himself and to society.

Others might contend that N. Scott Momaday simply describes and honors the Native-American view of life. Instead, he demonstrates its value for the entire culture, even though he fears that no one in the United States will hear the message. Carver's narrator experiences transcendence through his meeting with the blind man, Robert. One might interpret the story in this individual manner. Why, then, does Carver criticize the media, bigotry, self-absorption and failure to grasp our own lives, if he does not intend a larger critique and change? Sophocles can be and is interpreted as the tragedy of a great man who discovers his own blindness to the truth, a man who runs, not walks, to fulfill his destiny. However, Oedipus also is a king; and his tragedy causes the suffering of his people. His downfall teaches them a painful lesson. It is imperative to view each of these works as eloquent statements about personal and political change. Any exclusion of the political argument diminishes the achievements of these works.

In three genres—essay, fiction, and drama, the writers create characters and themes that seem intensely personal. Old man Cheney, Carver's narrator, and Oedipus all experience revelation. They find truth. However, the themes do not focus simply on one character; they focus on social critique and ultimately on political change. "The personal is the political."

WRITING ASSIGNMENTS

1. a. Write a list of positive and negative aspects of life in the United States.
   b. Write an essay on the criticisms of the United States by Ginsberg, Hughes, Brooks, and Knight. Do these writers express hope?
2. What is the relationship between identity and politics?
3. a. Write a list of themes about war.
   b. Write about one of the themes. Refer to three works in this chapter.
4. a. Interview several students about education. Ask them about Freire's banking concept and problem-solving concept of education.
   b. Summarize your findings.
   c. Write an essay on education in the United States. Refer to your interviews and to Freire.
5. a. Make double-entry notebooks on Forché's poems.
   b. Summarize Valenzuela's "I'm Your Horse in the Night."
   c. Outline Agosin's essay.
   d. Write a paper on political issues in Central and South America. Refer to Forché, to Valenzuela, and to Agosin. Consider the student essay in this chapter as a model.
6. Compare a work about the Second World War to one about the Vietnam War, e.g., "The War Generation," "The Things They Carried."
7. a. Annotate the works by Endō, Owens, and O'Brien. Concentrate on the soldiers' attitudes concerning war.
   b. Write an essay about the attitudes of soldiers toward war in the works which you have annotated.
8. a. Discuss Mandela's statement on oppression in South Africa.
   b. Write a research paper on Mandela or about a contemporary issue in South Africa.
9. a. Write about law and justice. When is law just? When is it not?
   b. Is it ever right to disobey the law?
   c. Discuss the disobedience of Mandela, Sojourner Truth, or Harriet Tubman.
10. a. Define cultural history. Refer to Soto's "History."
    b. Write about your cultural history.
    c. Compare "Three Thousand Dollar Death Song," "horse," and "History."
11. a. Gloss and annotate a political protest poem in this chapter. How effectively does the poet convey his/her political message?
    b. Analyze the poem that you have glossed and annotated. How does it achieve its impact? Focus, for example, on tone, imagery, symbolism, word choice, and/or form.
12. Write about parents whose children are endangered by war. Refer to the works by Pirandello and Ozick.
13. a. Write about the horse symbolism in works by Valenzuela, Anzaldúa, Knight, and Harjo.

    b. Write about a specific instance of political terrorism. Create a symbol to represent the terror or the hope.

    c. Compare Latino/Latina visions of the United States. Refer to Soto, Cisneros, Hijuelos, and Cruz in Chapter 4, and/or to Anzaldúa in this chapter.

14. a. Write about the anger and dreams of retribution in the poems by Rose, Anzaldúa, Griffin, and Harjo.

    b. Is anger necessary for social change? Refer to three works in this chapter.

15. Write about the strength of the human spirit and the enduring dream of freedom and equality. Refer to works by Hughes, Mandela, Griffin, Forché, Ginsberg, and/or Agosin.

16. a. Write an essay on the statement that "Soldiers are dreamers." Refer to the works by O'Brien, Endō, and/or Valenzuela.

17. Create an antiwar argument. Use examples from works in this chapter to prove your points.

18. a. Make a list of political injustices presented in works in this chapter.

    b. Write on one writer's presentation of this issue.

    c. Support a point of view that counters the presentation of one of the works in this chapter.

19. Contrast the characters of three rebels presented in this chapter.

20. Write a research paper on one of the following topics:

    a. The history of Argentina from 1976–1983.

    b. Evita or Juan Perón.

    c. Nelson Mandela.

    d. Tim O'Brien and the Vietnam War.

    e. A conflict between a minority group and the police.

    f. The use of chemical weapons in World War I or in another conflict.

    g. Ginsberg and the "Beat" generation.

    h. Taoism.

    i. Some aspect of women's suffrage.

    j. Some aspect of slavery in the United States, e.g., the Underground Railroad.

    k. The present status of the Mothers of May.

21. Analyze Sophocles' *Oedipus Rex* as a political tragedy. How does personal suffering become or cause public suffering?

22. Write about the forms of and responses to injustice in the works by Valenzuela, Rose, Sophocles, and Mandela in the Thematic Preview.

THE GLOBAL VILLAGE

"What rough beast, its hour come round at last,
Slouches towards Bethlehem to be born?"

W. B. Yeats
"The Second Coming"

We who live in the last decade of this century know more about the millennium than William Butler Yeats divined when he imagined a disastrous future—a violent and tumultuous future—symbolized by a monstrous beast. What can we discover in the present world that Yeats could not or did not predict? What will define the next century or the next two thousand years? We can observe with certainty that all people and nations on earth exist in dynamic tensions and in flux. We can admit that Yeats was, to some degree, prophetic. Unlike Yeats, we also can speak of hope and freedom and concede that the projection of visions of the future has become more complex than anyone might have expected.

From a myriad of pressing contemporary issues, we choose to focus on Africa as an example of present tensions in a postcolonial world and of the emergence of new voices and concerns in diverse places. The conflicts between traditional and "western" values emerge in Chinua Achebe's "Dead Men's Path" in which the villagers seek to preserve the way to the past and to the sacred burial ground. Their habit of walking on a forbidden road creates a problem for the school teacher who wishes to modernize his culture. In Bessie Head's "The Green Tree," this struggle between cultures leads the unnamed male narrator to madness. The violence of oppression in Africa has created generations of exiles whose views, forged in anger and in remembrance, present incessant longing for the homeland. Jofre Rocha and Mbella Sonne Dipoko have written poignant poems concerning both the efforts for freedom and revolution and the desire to return.

In the Thematic Preview, several of the works portray the system of apartheid in South Africa and the tragic consequences for all of the people who live there. In Nadine Gordimer's "Something for the Time Being," racial differences arise in personal, social, political, and economic circumstances. Athol Fugard's *"Master Harold"* . . . *and the Boys* demonstrates the depth of the ideas and practice of racial separation in the best of people. In Derek

Walcott's "A Far Cry from Africa," the speaker describes the polarity between his love of the English language and his love of his African heritage, a polarity that results in a divided self. Martin Luther King, Jr. presents hope for reconciliation of these tensions in the United States in his speech "I Have a Dream."

In the voice of Rigoberta Menchú, we discover a different tradition, a different struggle for liberation, and a different point of view. In her autobiography, Menchú describes and affirms the traditions and values of her people. She also depicts the resistance of the Indian people in Guatemala against forces intent on committing genocide. Unlike King, she believes that only organized, active rebellion can save her people.

Another imperative of living with knowledge of global conflicts becomes insistent exploration and prediction of the future. We know that actions create consequences. What is the nature of the future that we have made? Some visions present utopian or perfect worlds. King's philosophy leads to such a possibility. Some visions present dystopias, predictions of disaster, like Yeats' warning in "The Second Coming." Kurt Vonnegut's "Harrison Bergeron" describes a world in which enforced conformity leads to the destruction of individuality. Mary Gordon's "Imagination of Disaster" portrays the ultimate catastrophe, a nuclear holocaust and its aftermath. In "Stone Olives," Judith Johnson contends that our past could be our future, that we have caused and witnessed many forms of destruction against children. The poem issues an eloquent plea for remembrance and for change.

Despite all divisiveness and violence, we find hope for the future in the works of many writers. Both Rainer Maria Rilke and Muriel Rukeyser demonstrate their belief in the continuous process of transformation as hope for the future. Rabindranath Tagore engulfs us in the joy and harmony in each life and in the desire to connect with both others and divinity. In Yevgeny Yevtushenko's poem, the speaker discovers unity in diversity. Seami's Nō play, *Atsumori,* shows us redemption and salvation.

Along with the quest for spiritual meaning, humankind has searched for and continues to construct metaphysical systems in order to explain ultimate reality. Two significant and contrasting views were created by Plato in the fifth century B.C. and by Albert Camus in the twentieth century. In "The Allegory of the Cave" from Plato's *The Republic,* the philosopher distinguishes between a world of shadows and his concept of the real world in order to teach people that which is both beautiful and good. Camus, writing from an existential perspective, claims that humans, inhabiting an absurd and meaningless world, remain capable of acts of insight and of will which become redemptive.

Writers also invent myths for human interdependence and community. Adrienne Rich rejects the old "book of myths" in "Diving into the Wreck." As the speaker plunges into the sea to find the sunken ship, "the wreck," she envisions a new world of androgyny, a world in which differences between women and men may be resolved. In Gabriel García Márquez's "The Handsomest Drowned Man in the World," the villagers, through the ceremony of

burial, affirm community and the possibility of love through human connection.

   We complete this anthology with dreams of renewal. Anna Lee Walters
describes a life force, a spirit, that will rejuvenate. "Black Elk's Great Vision"
depicts a vivid dream of rebirth. Still, we balance these versions of rebirth
with a cautionary view. Edward Said demands that the reader remember that
each of us lives in a state of exile, a state which Gloria Anzaldúa names the
"borderlands." Her poem demonstrates that we exist without borders at
"crossroads" in a global village. Perhaps, this place at the "crossroads" offers
us the greatest challenge and the greatest possibilities.

THEMATIC PREVIEW: COMBINING THE GENRES

Something for the Time Being

Nadine Gordimer

Nadine Gordimer (1923–   ) was born in Johannesburg to Jewish emigrants from London. Her first novel, The Lying Days *(1953), is a semi-autobiographical narrative of a young South African woman. Her other novels include* Burger's Daughter *(1979),* July's People *(1981),* A Sport of Nature *(1987), and* My Son's Story *(1991). Her short stories are collected in* Six Feet of the Country *(1956),* Selected Stories *(1975), and* Jump, and Other Stories *(1991). Gordimer was awarded the Nobel Prize for Literature in 1991.*

In this story, Gordimer explores the political beliefs and actions of two couples, one white and one black, in South Africa. All of these characters approach tensions created by apartheid in different manners, even though each attempts to oppose the system.

1   He thought of it as discussing things with her, but the truth was that she did not help him out at all. She said nothing, while she ran her hand up the ridge of bone behind the rim of her child-sized yellow-brown ear, and raked her fingers tenderly into her hairline along the back of her neck as if feeling out some symptom in herself. Yet her listening was very demanding; when he stopped at the end of a supposition or a suggestion, her silence made the stop inconclusive. He had to take up again what he had said, carry it—where?

"Ve vant to give you a tsance, but you von't let us," he mimicked; and made a loud glottal click, half-angry, resentfully amused. He knew it wasn't because Kalzin Brothers were Jews that he had lost his job at last, but just because he had lost it, Mr. Solly's accent suddenly presented to him the irresistibly vulnerable. He had come out of prison nine days before, after spending three months as an awaiting-trial prisoner in a political case that had just been quashed—he was one of those who would not accept bail. He had been in prison three or four times since 1952; his wife Ella and the Kalzin Brothers were used to it. Until now, his employers had always given him his job back when he came out. They were importers of china and glass and he was head packer in a team of black men who ran the dispatch department. "Well, what the hell, I'll get something else," he said. "Hey?"

She stopped the self-absorbed examination of the surface of her skin for a slow moment and shrugged, looking at him.

He smiled.

5   Her gaze loosened hold like hands falling away from grasp. The ends of her nails pressed at small imperfections in the skin of her neck. He drank his tea and tore off pieces of bread to dip in it; then he noticed the tin of sardines she had opened and sopped up the pale matrix of oil in which ragged flecks of silver were suspended. She offered him more tea, without speaking.

They lived in one room of a decent, three-roomed house belonging to someone else; it was better for her that way, since he was often likely to have to be away for long stretches. She worked in a factory that made knitted socks; there was no one at home to look after their one child, a girl, and the child lived with a grandmother in a dusty, peaceful village a day's train-journey from the city.

He said, dismissing it as of no importance, "I wonder what chance they meant? You can imagine. I don't suppose they were going to give me an office with my name on it." He spoke as if she would appreciate the joke. She had known when she married him that he was a political man; she had been proud of him because he didn't merely want something for himself, like the other young men she knew, but everything, and for *the people.* It had excited her, under his influence, to change her awareness of herself as a young black girl to awareness of herself as belonging to the people. She knew that everything wasn't like something—a handout, a wangled privilege, a trinket you could hold. She would never get something from him.

Her hand went on searching over her skin as if it must come soon, come anxiously, to the flaw, the sickness, the evidence of what was wrong with her; for on this Saturday afternoon all these things that she knew had deserted her. She had lost her wits. All that she could understand was the one room, the child growing up far away in the mud house, and the fact that you couldn't keep a job if you kept being away from work for weeks at a time.

"I think I'd better look up Flora Donaldson," he said. Flora Donaldson was a white woman who had set up an office to help political prisoners. "Sooner the better. Perhaps she'll dig up something for me by Monday. It's the beginning of the month."

10   He got on all right with those people. Ella had met Flora Donaldson once; she was a pretty white woman who looked just like any white woman who would automatically send a black face round to the back door, but she didn't seem to know that she was white and you were black.

He pulled the curtain that hung across one corner of the room and took out his suit. It was a thin suit, of the kind associated with holiday-makers in American clothing advertisements, and when he was dressed in it, with a sharp-brimmed grey hat tilted slightly back on his small head, he looked a wiry, boyish figure, rather like one of those boy-men who sing and shake before a microphone, and whose clothes admirers try to touch as a talisman.

He kissed her good-bye, obliging her to put down, the lowering of a defense, the piece of sewing she held. She had cleared away the dishes from the table and set up the sewing-machine, and he saw that the shapes of cut material that lay on the table were the parts of a small girl's dress.

She spoke suddenly. "And when the next lot gets tired of you?"

"When that lot gets tired of me, I'll get another job again, that's all."

15   She nodded, very slowly, and her hand crept back to her neck.

"Who was that?" Madge Chadders asked.

Her husband had been out into the hall to answer the telephone.

"Flora Donaldson. I wish you'd explain to these people exactly what sort of factory I've got. It's so embarrassing. She's trying to find a job for some chap, he's a skilled packer. There's no skilled packing done in my workshop, no skilled jobs at all done by black men. What on earth can I offer the fellow? She says he's desperate and anything will do."

Madge had the broken pieces of a bowl on a newspaper spread on the Persian carpet. "Mind the glue, darling! There, just next to your foot. Well, anything is better than nothing. I suppose it's someone who was in the Soganiland sedition case. Three months awaiting trial taken out of their lives, and now they're chucked back to fend for themselves."

20   William Chadders had not had any black friends or mixed with coloured people on any but master-servant terms until he married Madge, but his views on the immorality and absurdity of the colour bar were sound; sounder, she often felt, than her own, for they were backed by the impersonal authority of a familiarity with the views of great thinkers, saints and philosophers, with history, political economy, sociology and anthropology. She knew only what she felt. And she always did something, at once, to express what she felt. She never measured the smallness of her personal protest against the establishment she opposed; she marched with Flora and eight hundred black women in a demonstration against African women being forced to carry passes; outside the university where she had once been a student, she stood between sandwich-boards bearing messages of mourning because a Bill had been passed closing the university, for the future, to all but white students; she had living in the house for three months a young African who wanted to write and hadn't the peace or space to get on with it in a location. She did not stop to consider the varying degree of usefulness of the things she did, and if others pointed this out to her and suggested that she might make up her mind to throw her weight on the side either of politics or philanthropy, she was not resentful but answered candidly that there was so little it was possible to do that she simply took any and every chance to get off her chest her disgust at the colour bar. When she had married William Chadders, her friends had thought that her protestant activities would stop; they underestimated not only Madge, but also William, who, although he was a wealthy businessman, subscribed to the view of absolute personal freedom as strictly as any bohemian. Besides he was not fool enough to want to change in any way the person who had enchanted him just as she was.

She reacted upon him, rather than he upon her; she, of course, would not hesitate to go ahead and change anybody. (But why not? she would have said, astonished. If it's to the good?) The attitude she sought to change would occur to her as something of independent existence, she would not see it as a cell in the organism of personality, whose whole structure would have to regroup itself round the change. She had the boldness of being unaware of these consequences.

William did not carry a banner in the streets, of course; he worked up there, among his first principles and historical precedents and economic necessities, but now they were translated from theory to practice of an anonymous, large-scale and behind-the-scenes sort—he was the brains and part of the money in a scheme to get Africans some economic power besides consumer power, through the setting up of an all-African trust company and investment corporation. A number of Madge's political friends, both white and black (like her activities, her friends were mixed, some political, some do-gooders), thought this was putting the middle-class cart before the proletarian horse, but most of the African leaders welcomed the attempt as an essential backing to popular movements on other levels—something to count on outside the unpredictability of mobs. Sometimes it amused Madge to think that William, making a point at a meeting in a boardroom, fifteen floors above life in the streets, might achieve in five minutes something of more value than she did in all her days of turning her hand to anything—from sorting old clothes to roneoing[1] a manifesto or driving people during a bus boycott. Yet this did not knock the meaning out of her own life, for her; she knew that she had to see, touch and talk to people in order to care about them, that's all there was to it.

Before she and her husband dressed to go out that evening she finished sticking together the broken Chinese bowl and showed it to him with satisfaction. To her, it was whole again. But it was one of a set, that had belonged together, and whose unity had illustrated certain philosophical concepts. William had bought them long ago, in London; for him, the whole set was damaged for ever.

He said nothing to her, but he was thinking of the bowls when she said to him as they drove off, "Will you see that chap, on Monday, yourself?"

25   He changed gear deliberately, attempting to follow her out of his preoccupation. But she said, "The man Flora's sending. What was his name?"

He opened his hand on the steering wheel, indicating that the name escaped him.

"See him yourself?"

"I'll have to leave it to the works manager to find something for him to do," he said.

"Yes, I know. But see him yourself, too?"

30   Her anxious voice made him feel very fond of her. He turned and smiled at her suspiciously. "Why?"

She was embarrassed at his indulgent manner. She said, frank and wheedling, "Just to show him. You know. That you know about him and it's not much of a job."

"All right," he said. "I'll see him myself."

---

[1] A kind of duplicating.

He met her in town straight from the office on Monday and they went to the opening of an exhibition of paintings and on to dinner and to see a play, with friends. He had not been home at all, until they returned after midnight. It was a summer night and they sat for a few minutes on their terrace, where it was still mild with the warmth of the day's sun coming from the walls in the darkness, and drank lime juice and water to quench the thirst that wine and the stuffy theatre had given them. Madge made gasps and groans of pleasure at the release from the pressures of company and noise. Then she lay quiet for a while, her voice lifting now and then in fragments of unrelated comment on the evening—the occasional chirp of a bird that has already put its head under its wing for the night.

By the time they went in, they were free of the evening. Her black dress, her ear-rings and her bracelets felt like fancy-dress; she shed the character and sat on the bedroom carpet, and, passing her, he said, "Oh—that chap of Flora's came today, but I don't think he'll last. I explained to him that I didn't have the sort of job he was looking for."

35   "Well, that's all right, then," she said enquiringly. "What more could you do?"

"Yes," he said, deprecating. "But I could see he didn't like the idea much. It's a cleaner's job; nothing for him. He's an intelligent chap. I didn't like having to offer it to him."

She was moving about her dressing table, piling out upon it the contents of her handbag. "Then I'm sure he'll understand. It'll give him something for the time being, anyway, darling. You can't help it if you don't need the sort of work he does."

"Huh, he won't last. I could see that. He accepted it, but only with his head. He'll get fed up. Probably won't turn up tomorrow. I had to speak to him about his Congress[2] button, too. The works manager came to me."

"What about his Congress button?" she said.

40   He was unbuttoning his shirt and his eyes were on the unread evening paper that lay folded on the bed. "He was wearing one," he said inattentively.

"I know, but what did you have to speak to him about it for?"

"He was wearing it in the workshop all day."

"Well, what about it?" She was sitting at her dressing-table, legs spread, as if she had sat heavily and suddenly. She was not looking at him, but at her own face.

He gave the paper a push and drew his pyjamas from under the pillow. Vulnerable and naked, he said authoritatively, "You can't wear a button like that among the men in the workshop."

45   "Good heavens," she said, almost in relief, laughing, backing away from the edge of tension, chivvying him out of a piece of stuffiness. "And why can't you?"

"You can't have someone clearly representing a political organization like Congress."

---

[2] African National Congress, South African anti-apartheid organization.

"But he's not there *representing* anything, he's there as a workman?" Her mouth was still twitching with something between amusement and nerves.

"Exactly."

"Then why can't he wear a button that signifies his allegiance to an organization in his private life outside the workshop? There's no rule about not wearing tie-pins or club buttons or anything, in the workshop, is there?"

50   "No, there isn't, but that's not quite the same thing."

"My dear William," she said, "it is exactly the same. It's nothing to do with the works manager whether the man wears a Rotary button,[3] or an Elvis Presley button, or an African National Congress button. It's damn all his business."

"No, Madge, I'm sorry," William said, patient, "but it's not the same. I can give the man a job because I feel sympathetic towards the struggle he's in, but I can't put him in the workshop as a Congress man. I mean that wouldn't be fair to Fowler. That I can't do to Fowler." He was smiling as he went towards the bathroom, but his profile, as he turned into the doorway, was incisive.

She sat on at her dressing-table, pulling a comb through her hair, dragging it down through knots. Then she rested her face on her palms, caught sight of herself and became aware, against her fingers, of the curving shelf of bone, like the lip of a strong shell, under each eye. Everyone has his own intimations of mortality. For her, the feel of the bone beneath the face, in any living creature, brought her the message of the skull. Once hollowed out of this, outside the world, too. For what it's worth. It's worth a lot, the world, she affirmed, as she always did, life rising at once in her as a fish opens its jaws to a fly. It's worth a lot; and she sighed and got up with the sigh.

She went into the bathroom and sat down on the edge of the bath. He was lying there in the water, his chin relaxed on his chest, and he smiled at her. She said, "You mean you don't want Fowler to know."

55   "Oh," he said, seeing where they were again. "What is it I don't want Fowler to know?"

"You don't want your partner to know that you slip black men with political ideas into your workshop. Cheeky kaffir agitators. Specially a man who's been in jail for getting people to defy the government!—What was his name; you never said?"

"Daniel something. I don't know. Mongoma or Ngoma. Something like that."

A line like a cut appeared between her eyebrows. "Why can't you remember his name?" Then she went on at once, "You don't want Fowler to know what you think, do you? That's it? You want to pretend you're like him, you don't mind the native in his place. You want to pretend that to please Fowler. You don't want Fowler to think you're cracked or Communist or whatever it is that good-natured, kind, jolly rich people like old Fowler think about people like us."

"I couldn't have less interest in what Fowler thinks outside our boardroom. And inside it, he never thinks about anything but how to sell more earth-moving gear."

---

[3] A civic organization.

60   "I don't mind the native in his place. You want him to think you go along with all that." She spoke aloud, but she seemed to be telling herself rather than him.

"Fowler and I run a factory. Our only common interest is the efficient running of that factory. Our *only* one. The factory depends on a stable, satisfied black labour-force, and that we've got. Right, you and I know that the whole black wage standard is too low, right, we know that they haven't a legal union to speak for them, right, we know that the conditions they live under make it impossible for them really to be stable. All that. But the fact is, so far as accepted standards go in this crazy country, they're a stable, satisfied labour-force with better working conditions than most. So long as I'm a partner in a business that lives by them, I can't officially admit an element that represents dissatisfaction with their lot."

"A green badge with a map of Africa on it," she said.

"If you make up your mind not to understand, you don't, and there it is," he said indulgently.

"You give him a job but you make him hide his Congress button."

65   He began to soap himself. She wanted everything to stop while she inquired into things, she could not go on while a remark was unexplained or a problem unsettled, but he represented a principle she subscribed to but found so hard to follow, that life must go on, trivially, commonplace, the trailing hem of the only power worth clinging to. She smoothed the film of her nightgown over the shape of her knees, over and over, and presently she said, in exactly the flat tone of statement that she had used before, the flat tone that was the height of belligerence in her, "He can say and do what he likes, he can call for strikes and boycotts and anything he likes, outside the factory, but he mustn't wear his Congress button at work."

He was standing up, washing his body that was full of scars; she knew them all, from the place on his left breast where a piece of shrapnel had gone in, all the way back to the place under his arm where he had torn himself on barbed wire as a child. "Yes, of course, anything he likes."

"Anything except his self-respect," she grumbled to herself. "Pretend, pretend. Pretend he doesn't belong to a political organization. Pretend he doesn't want to be a man. Pretend he hasn't been to prison for what he believes." Suddenly she spoke to her husband: "You'll let him have anything except the one thing worth giving."

They stood in uncomfortable proximity to each other, in the smallness of the bathroom. They were at once aware of each other as people who live in intimacy are only when hostility returns each to the confines of himself. He felt himself naked before her, where he had stepped out onto the towelling mat, and he took a towel and slowly covered himself, pushing the free end in round his waist. She felt herself an intrusion and, in silence, went out.

Her hands were tingling as if she were coming round from a faint. She walked up and down the bedroom floor like someone waiting to be summoned, called to account. I'll forget about it, she kept thinking, very fast, I'll forget about it again. Take a sip of water. Read another chapter. Don't call a halt. Let things flow, cover up, go on.

70   But when he came into the room with his wet hair combed and his stranger's face, and he said, "You're angry," it came from her lips, a black bird in the room, before she could understand what she had released—"I'm not angry. I'm beginning to get to know you."

Ella Mngoma knew he was going to a meeting that evening and didn't expect him home early. She put the paraffin lamp on the table so that she could see to finish the child's dress. It was done, buttons and all, by the time he came in at half past ten.

"Well, now we'll see what happens. I've got them to accept, *in principle,* that in future we won't take bail. You should have seen Ben Tsolo's face when I said that we lent the government our money interest-free when we paid bail. That really hit him. That was language he understood." He laughed, and did not seem to want to sit down, the heat of the meeting still upon him. "*In principle.* Yes, it's easy to accept in principle. We'll see."

She pumped the primus[4] and set a pot of stew to warm up for him. "Ah, that's nice." He saw the dress. "Finished already?" And she nodded vociferously in pleasure; but at once she noticed his forefinger run lightly along the braid round the neck, and the traces of failure that were always at the bottom of her cup tasted on her tongue again. Probably he was not even aware of it, or perhaps his instinct for what was true—the plumb line, the coin with the right ring—led him absently to it, but the fact was that she had botched the neck.

She had an almost Oriental delicacy about not badgering him and she waited until he had washed and sat down to eat before she asked, "How did the job go?"

75   "Oh that," he said. "It went." He was eating quickly, moving his tongue strongly round his mouth to marshal the bits of meat that escaped his teeth. She was sitting with him, feeling, in spite of herself, the rest of satisfaction in her evening's work. "Didn't you get it?"

"It got *me.* But I got loose again, all right."

She watched his face to see what he meant. "They don't want you to come back tomorrow?"

He shook his head, no, no, no, to stem the irritation of her suppositions. He finished his mouthful and said, "Everything very nice. Boss takes me into his office, apologizes for the pay, he knows it's not the sort of job I should have and so forth. So I go off and clean up in the assembly shop. Then at lunchtime he calls me into the office again: they don't want me to wear my A.N.C. badge at work. Flora Donaldson's sympathetic white man, who's going to do me the great favour of paying me three pounds a week." He laughed. "Well, there you are."

She kept on looking at him. Her eyes widened and her mouth tightened; she was trying to prime herself to speak, or was trying not to cry. The idea of tears exasperated him and he held her with a firm, almost belligerently inquiring gaze. Her hand went up round the back of her neck under

---

[4] Portable stove which requires oil as fuel.

her collar, anxiously exploratory. "Don't do that!" he said. "You're like a monkey catching lice."

80   She took her hand down swiftly and broke into trembling, like a sweat. She began to breathe hysterically. "You couldn't put it in your pocket, for the day," she said wildly, grimacing at the bitterness of malice towards him.

He jumped up from the table. "Christ! I knew you'd say it! I've been waiting for you to say it. You've been wanting to say it for five years. Well, now it's out. Out with it. Spit it out!" She began to scream softly as if he were hitting her. The impulse to cruelty left him and he sat down before his dirty plate, where the battered spoon lay among bits of gristle and potato-eyes. Presently he spoke. "You come out and you think there's everybody waiting for you. The truth is, there isn't anybody. You think straight in prison because you've got nothing to lose. Nobody thinks straight, outside. They don't want to hear you. What are you all going to do with me, Ella? Send me back to prison as quickly as possible? Perhaps I'll get a banishment order next time. That'd do. That's what you've got for me. I must keep myself busy with that kind of thing."

He went over to her and said, in a kindly voice, kneading her shoulder with spread fingers, "Don't cry. Don't cry. You're just like any other woman."

■ EXPLORATIONS OF THE TEXT ■

1. Characterize Daniel and Ella Mngoma. Analyze their relationship. What does the ANC mean to both of them?
2. Characterize Madge and William Chadders. Analyze their relationship. Examine their political activities.
3. What is the political situation?
4. What does William's discussion about the ANC button and about the workers reveal?
5. What is the significance of the child's dress which Ella makes?
6. What is the meaning of the last line, "You're just like any other woman." Is she?
7. What do the houses represent?
8. Interpret the title. Why does the story first focus on the Chadders?
9. Compare themes of this story with Fugard's play and with Mandela's statement in Chapter 7.

■■ JOURNAL ENTRIES ■■

1. Explore Daniel's experiences in prison and their effect on his life.
2. Why does the story reveal so much more about the Chadders than about the Mngomas?

■■■ IDEAS FOR WRITING ■■■

1. Summarize each character's position. Who is right? Is anyone right?
2. Analyze themes of "Something for the Time Being."
3. Compare this story and *"Master Harold" . . . and the Boys.* How do point of view, narrative structure, characterization, and conflict develop theme?
4. Examine the function of setting in the story.
5. Analyze the body imagery in the story. How does it advance theme?
6. Does this story suggest hope for reconciliation of racial tensions in South Africa? Refer to King's "I Have a Dream."

A Far Cry from Africa

Derek Walcott

The first Caribbean writer to win the Nobel Prize for Literature (1992), Derek Walcott was born in 1930 on the island of St. Lucia. He wrote his first book in 1948 when his mother gave him two hundred dollars to have Twenty-Five Poems *published. His books of poetry include* Sea Grapes *(1976),* Selected Poetry *(1981),* Midsummer *(1984),* Collected Poems 1948–1984 *(1986),* The Arkansas Testament *(1987), and the epic-scale* Omeros *(1990). Walcott's poetry celebrates the diversity of modern English, Creole patois, pidgin, and slang. Walcott can claim, "I had a sound colonial education./I have Dutch, nigger and English in me,/and either I'm nobody or I'm a nation."*

In this poem, Walcott's persona describes his divided loyalties between Africa and "the English tongue."

> A wind is ruffling the tawny pelt
> Of Africa. Kikuyu,[1] quick as flies,
> Batten upon the bloodstreams of the veldt.[2]
> Corpses are scattered through a paradise.
> 5 Only the worm, colonel of carrion, cries:
> 'Waste no compassion on these separate dead!'
> Statistics justify and scholars seize
> The salients of colonial policy.
> What is that to the white child hacked in bed?
> 10 To savages, expendable as Jews?

---

[1] African tribe who conducted an eight-year fight against British colonial settlers. They were known as Mau Mau.

[2] Grassland in southern Africa with sparsely growing trees and shrubs.

Threshed out by beaters,[3] the long rushes break
In a white dust of ibises whose cries
Have wheeled since civilization's dawn
From the parched river or beast-teeming plain.
15 The violence of beast on beast is read
As natural law, but upright man
Seeks his divinity by inflicting pain.
Delirious as these worried beasts, his wars
Dance to the tightened carcass of a drum,
20 While he calls courage still that native dread
Of the white peace contracted by the dead.

Again brutish necessity wipes its hands
Upon the napkins of a dirty cause, again
A waste of our compassion, as with Spain,[4]
25 The gorilla wrestles with the superman.

I who am poisoned with the blood of both,
Where shall I turn, divided to the vein?
I who have cursed
The drunken officer of British rule, how choose
30 Between this Africa and the English tongue I love?
Betray them both, or give back what they give?
How can I face such slaughter and be cool?
How can I turn from Africa and live?

■ **EXPLORATIONS OF THE TEXT** ■

1. What are the double meanings of the title?
2. Analyze the depiction and **personification** of Africa in stanza 1.
   Examine the questions in lines 9–10. Why does the speaker allude to
   the Jews?
3. Explain the image of the ibises. How does this scene function?
4. How does the violence of "beast on beast" contrast with that of
   "upright man"?
5. Why does the speaker mention "a dirty cause"? Interpret the reference
   to Spain.
6. Explain: "The gorilla wrestles with the superman."
7. Examine the divided loyalties of the speaker. Will he choose?
8. Compare the view of Africa in this poem to that of *"Master Harold"*
   . . . and the Boys.

---

[3] People hired by game hunters to beat the bush in order to chase wild animals.
[4] Allusion to the Spanish Civil War (1936–1939).

---

1. Describe a conflict, "divided to the vein," which represents your background.
2. Characterize the speaker. Respond to him. Is he "a far cry from Africa"?
3. Explicate a powerful image in the poem.
4. Relate the title of the poem to the effects of "colonial policy."

■■■   IDEAS FOR WRITING   ■■■

1. Explicate this poem. Focus on persona, imagery, and formal elements.
2. What are themes of this poem?
3. Create a prose version of the poem. What is lost? What is gained?
4. Explore the image of Africa in this poem and in another work in this chapter.
5. Compare this poem with W. B. Yeats' "The Second Coming."

"Master Harold" . . . and the Boys

Athol Fugard

Born in South Africa, Athol Fugard (1932–   ) has spent most of his life in Port Elizabeth. His 1961 production of The Blood Knot *was considered shocking because he and the African actor, Zakes Mokae, played two half-brothers, one light enough to pass for white. For the first time in South Africa, black and white actors shared the stage. Other works include* Boesman and Lena *(1969),* A Lesson from Aloes *(1978),* "Master Harold" . . . and the Boys *(1982), and* The Road to Mecca *(1984). In addition to his many award-winning dramas, Fugard has written screenplays, including* Gandhi *(1982) and* The Killing Fields *(1984). Fugard, his wife, and daughter live in Port Elizabeth where he reports that the government is starting "to relax itself in terms of the theater." He adds sadly, "But that doesn't dictate that the society is changing rapidly."*

In his Notebooks 1960–1977, *Athol Fugard describes the relationship between himself and Sam on which he based* "Master Harold" . . . and the Boys. *Fugard poignantly recalls that Sam was his best friend during his boyhood.* "Master Harold" . . . and the Boys *was first produced at the Yale Repertory Theatre. Zakes Mokae, who stars in all of Fugard's plays, played Sam.*

The St. George's Park Tea Room on a wet and windy Port Elizabeth[1] afternoon.

Tables and chairs have been cleared and are stacked on one side except for one which stands apart with a single chair. On this table a knife, fork, spoon and side plate in anticipation of a simple meal, together with a pile of comic books.

Other elements: a serving counter with a few stale cakes under glass and a not very impressive display of sweets, cigarettes and cool drinks, etc.; a few cardboard advertising handouts—Cadbury's Chocolate, Coca-Cola—and a blackboard on which an untrained hand has chalked up the prices of Tea, Coffee, Scones, Milkshakes—all flavors—and Cool Drinks; a few sad ferns in pots; a telephone; an old-style jukebox.

There is an entrance on one side and an exit into a kitchen on the other.

Leaning on the solitary table, his head cupped in one hand as he pages through one of the comic books, is Sam. A black man in his mid-forties. He wears the white coat of a waiter. Behind him on his knees, mopping down the floor with a bucket of water and a rag, is Willie. Also black and about the same age as Sam. He has his sleeves and trousers rolled up.

The year: 1950

Willie: *(Singing as he works.)*
"She was scandalizin' my name,
She took my money
She called me honey
But she was scandalizin' my name.
Called it love but was playin' a game . . ."

He gets up and moves the bucket. Stands thinking for a moment, then, raising his arms to hold an imaginary partner, he launches into an intricate ballroom dance step. Although a mildly comic figure, he reveals a reasonable degree of accomplishment.

Hey, Sam.

Sam, absorbed in the comic book, does not respond.

Hey, Boet Sam!

Sam looks up.

I'm getting it. The quickstep. Look now and tell me. *(He repeats the step.)* Well?
Sam: *(Encouragingly.)* Show me again.
Willie: Okay, count for me.
Sam: Ready?

---

[1] Southeastern South African city on the Indian Ocean.

5 **Willie:** Ready.

Sam: Five, six, seven, eight . . . *(Willie starts to dance.)* A-n-d one two three four . . . and one two three four. . . . *(Ad libbing as Willie dances.)* Your shoulders, Willie . . . your shoulders! Don't look down! Look happy, Willie! Relax, Willie!

Willie: *(Desperate but still dancing.)* I am relax.

Sam: No, you're not.

Willie: *(He falters.)* Ag no man, Sam! Mustn't talk. You make me make mistakes.

10 **Sam:** But you're too stiff.

Willie: Yesterday I'm not straight . . . today I'm too stiff!

Sam: Well, you are. You asked me and I'm telling you.

Willie: Where?

Sam: Everywhere. Try to glide through it.

15 **Willie:** Glide?

Sam: Ja, make it smooth. And give it more style. It must look like you're enjoying yourself.

Willie: *(Emphatically.)* I wasn't.

Sam: Exactly.

Willie: How can I enjoy myself? Not straight, too stiff and now it's also glide, give it more style, make it smooth. . . . Haai! Is hard to remember all those things, Boet Sam.

20 **Sam:** That's your trouble. You're trying too hard.

Willie: I try hard because it *is* hard.

Sam: But don't let me see it. The secret is to make it look easy. Ballroom must look happy, Willie, not like hard work. It must . . . Ja! . . . it must look like romance.

Willie: Now another one! What's romance?

Sam: Love story with happy ending. A handsome man in tails, and in his arms, smiling at him, a beautiful lady in evening dress!

25 **Willie:** Fred Astaire, Ginger Rogers.[2]

Sam: You got it. Tapdance or ballroom, it's the same. Romance. In two weeks' time when the judges look at you and Hilda, they must see a man and a woman who are dancing their way to a happy ending. What I saw was you holding her like you were frightened she was going to run away.

Willie: Ja! Because that is what she wants to do! I got no romance left for Hilda anymore, Boet Sam.

Sam: Then pretend. When you put your arms around Hilda, imagine she is Ginger Rogers.

Willie: With no teeth? You try.

30 **Sam:** Well, just remember, there's only two weeks left.

Willie: I know, I know! *(To the jukebox.)* I do it better with music. You got sixpence for Sarah Vaughan?[3]

---

[2] North American dancers and movie stars.

[3] Jazz singer.

Sam: That's a slow foxtrot. You're practicing the quickstep.

Willie: I'll practice slow foxtrot.

Sam: *(Shaking his head.)* It's your turn to put money in the jukebox.

35 **Willie:** I only got bus fare to go home. *(He returns disconsolately to his work.)* Love story and happy ending! She's doing it all right, Boet Sam, but is not me she's giving happy endings. Fuckin' whore! Three nights now she doesn't come practice. I wind up gramophone, I get record ready and I sit and wait. What happens? Nothing. Ten o'clock I start dancing with my pillow. You try and practice romance by yourself, Boet Sam. Struesgod, she doesn't come tonight I take back my dress and ballroom shoes and I find me new partner. Size twenty-six. Shoes size seven. And now she's also making trouble for me with the baby again. Reports me to Child Wellfed, that I'm not giving her money. She lies! Every week I am giving her money for milk. And how do I know is my baby? Only his hair looks like me. She's fucking around all the time I turn my back. Hilda Samuels is a bitch! *(Pause.)* Hey, Sam!

Sam: Ja.

Willie: You listening?

Sam: Ja.

Willie: So what you say?

40 **Sam:** About Hilda?

Willie: Ja.

Sam: When did you last give her a hiding?

Willie: *(Reluctantly.)* Sunday night.

Sam: And today is Thursday.

45 **Willie:** *(He knows what's coming.)* Okay.

Sam: Hiding on Sunday night, then Monday, Tuesday and Wednesday she doesn't come to practice . . . and you are asking me why?

Willie: I said okay, Boet Sam!

Sam: You hit her too much. One day she's going to leave you for good.

Willie: So? She makes me the hell-in too much.

50 **Sam:** *(Emphasizing his point.)* *Too* much and *too* hard. You had the same trouble with Eunice.

Willie: Because she also make the hell-in, Boet Sam. She never got the steps right. Even the waltz.

Sam: Beating her up every time she makes a mistake in the waltz? *(Shaking his head.)* No, Willie! That takes the pleasure out of ballroom dancing.

Willie: Hilda is not too bad with the waltz, Boet Sam. Is the quickstep where the trouble starts.

Sam: *(Teasing him gently.)* How's your pillow with the quickstep?

55 **Willie:** *(Ignoring the tease.)* Good! And why? Because it got no legs. That's her trouble. She can't move them quick enough, Boet Sam. I start the record and before halfway Count Basie[4] is already winning. Only time we catch up with him is when gramophone runs down.

---

[4] United States jazz musician, composer, and bandleader (1904–1984).

Sam laughs.

Haaikona, Boet Sam, is not funny.

Sam: *(Snapping his fingers.)* I got it! Give her a handicap.

Willie: What's that?

Sam: Give her a ten-second start and then let Count Basie go. Then I put my money on her. Hot favorite in the Ballroom Stakes: Hilda Samuels ridden by Willie Malopo.

Willie: *(Turning away.)* I'm not talking to you no more.

60 Sam: *(Relenting.)* Sorry, Willie . . .

Willie: It's finish between us.

Sam: Okay, okay . . . I'll stop.

Willie: You can also fuck off.

Sam: Willie, listen! I want to help you!

65 Willie: No more jokes?

Sam: I promise.

Willie: Okay. Help me.

Sam: *(His turn to hold an imaginary partner.)* Look and learn. Feet together. Back straight. Body relaxed. Right hand placed gently in the small of her back and wait for the music. Don't start worrying about making mistakes or the judges or the other competitors. It's just you, Hilda and the music, and you're going to have a good time. What Count Basie do you play?

Willie: "You the cream in my coffee, you the salt in my stew."

70 Sam: Right. Give it to me in strict tempo.

Willie: Ready?

Sam: Ready.

Willie: A-n-d . . . *(Singing.)*

"You the cream in my coffee.

You the salt in my stew.

You will always be my
    necessity.

I'd be lost without
    you. . . ." *(etc.)*

Sam launches into the quickstep. He is obviously a much more accomplished dancer than Willie. Hally enters. A seventeen-year-old white boy. Wet raincoat and school case. He stops and watches Sam. The demonstration comes to an end with a flourish. Applause from Hally and Willie.

Hally: Bravo! No question about it. First place goes to Mr. Sam Semela.

75 Willie: *(In total agreement.)* You was gliding with style, Boet Sam.

Hally: *(Cheerfully.)* How's it, chaps?

Sam: Okay, Hally.

Willie: *(Springing to attention like a soldier and saluting.)* At your service, Master Harold!

Hally: Not long to the big event, hey!

80   Sam: Two weeks.
     Hally: You nervous?
     Sam: No.
     Hally: Think you stand a chance?
     Sam: Let's just say I'm ready to go out there and dance.
85   Hally: It looked like it. What about you, Willie?

> *Willie groans.*

What's the matter?
     Sam: He's got leg trouble.
     Hally: *(Innocently.)* Oh, sorry to hear that, Willie.
     Willie: Boet Sam! You promised. *(Willie returns to his work.)*

> *Hally deposits his school case and takes off his raincoat. His clothes are*
> *a little neglected and untidy: black blazer with school badge, gray flan-*
> *nel trousers in need of an ironing, khaki shirt and tie, black shoes. Sam*
> *has fetched a towel for Hally to dry his hair.*

     Hally: God, what a lousy bloody day. It's coming down cats and dogs out
        there. Bad for business, chaps . . . *(Conspiratorial whisper.)* . . . but
        it also means we're in for a nice quiet afternoon.
90   Sam: You can speak loud, Your Mom's not here.
     Hally: Out shopping?
     Sam: No. The hospital.
     Hally: But it's Thursday. There's no visiting on Thursday afternoons. Is my
        Dad okay?
     Sam: Sounds like it. In fact, I think he's going home.
95   Hally: *(Stopped short by Sam's remark.)* What do you mean?
     Sam: The hospital phoned.
     Hally: To say what?
     Sam: I don't know. I just heard your Mom talking.
     Hally: So what makes you say he's going home?
100 Sam: It sounded as if they were telling her to come and fetch him.

> *Hally thinks about what Sam has said for a few seconds.*

     Hally: When did she leave?
     Sam: About an hour ago. She said she would phone you. Want to eat?

> *Hally doesn't respond.*

Hally, want your lunch?
     Hally: I suppose so. *(His mood has changed.)* What's on the menu? . . . as
        if I don't know.
     Sam: Soup, followed by meat pie and gravy.
105 Hally: Today's?
     Sam: No.
     Hally: And the soup?
     Sam: Nourishing pea soup.

Hally: Just the soup. *(The pile of comic books on the table.)* And these?

110 **Sam:** For your Dad. Mr. Kempston brought them.

Hally: You haven't been reading them, have you?

Sam: Just looking.

Hally: *(Examining the comics.) Jungle Jim . . . Batman and Robin . . . Tarzan*[5] *. . .* God, what rubbish! Mental pollution. Take them away.

Sam exits waltzing into the kitchen. Hally turns to Willie.

Hally: Did you hear my Mom talking on the telephone, Willie?

115 **Willie:** No, Master Hally. I was at the back.

Hally: And she didn't say anything to you before she left?

Willie: She said I must clean the floors.

Hally: I mean about my Dad.

Willie: She didn't say nothing to me about him, Master Hally.

120 **Hally:** *(With conviction.)* No! It can't be. They said he needed at least another three weeks of treatment. Sam's definitely made a mistake. *(Rummages through his school case, finds a book and settles down at the table to read.)* So, Willie!

Willie: Yes, Master Hally! Schooling okay today?

Hally: Yes, okay. . . . *(He thinks about it.)* . . . No, not really. Ag, what's the difference? I don't care. And Sam says you've got problems.

Willie: Big problems.

Hally: Which leg is sore?

Willie groans.

Both legs.

125 **Willie:** There is nothing wrong with my legs. Sam is just making jokes.

Hally: So then you *will* be in the competition.

Willie: Only if I can find me a partner.

Hally: But what about Hilda?

Sam: *(Returning with a bowl of soup.)* She's the one who's got trouble with her legs.

130 **Hally:** What sort of trouble, Willie?

Sam: From the way he describes it, I think the lady has gone a bit lame.

Hally: Good God! Have you taken her to see a doctor?

Sam: I think a vet would be better.

Hally: What do you mean?

135 **Sam:** What do you call it again when a racehorse goes very fast?

Hally: Gallop?

Sam: That's it!

Willie: Boet Sam!

Hally: "A gallop down the homestretch to the winning post." But what's that got to do with Hilda?

140 **Sam:** Count Basie always gets there first.

---

[5] Comic book characters.

Willie lets fly with his slop rag. It misses Sam and hits Hally.

Hally: *(Furious.)* For Christ's sake, Willie! What the hell do you think you're doing!

Willie: Sorry, Master Hally, but it's him. . . .

Hally: Act your bloody age! *(Hurls the rag back at Willie.)* Cut out the nonsense now and get on with your work. And you too, Sam. Stop fooling around.

Sam moves away.

No. Hang on. I haven't finished! Tell me exactly what my Mom said.

Sam: I have. "When Hally comes, tell him I've gone to the hospital and I'll phone him."

145 Hally: She didn't say anything about taking my Dad home?

Sam: No. It's just that when she was talking on the phone . . .

Hally: *(Interrupting him.)* No, Sam. They can't be discharging him. She would have said so if they were. In any case, we saw him last night and he wasn't in good shape at all. Staff nurse even said there was talk about taking more X-rays. And now suddenly today he's better? If anything, it sounds more like a bad turn to me . . . which I sincerely hope it isn't. Hang on . . . how long ago did you say she left?

Sam: Just before two . . . *(His wrist watch.)* . . . hour and a half.

Hally: I know how to settle it. *(Behind the counter to the telephone. Talking as he dials.)* Let's give her ten minutes to get to the hospital, ten minutes to load him up, another ten, at the most, to get home and another ten to get him inside. Forty minutes. They should have been home for at least half an hour already. *(Pause—he waits with the receiver to his ear.)* No reply, chaps. And you know why? Because she's at his bedside in hospital helping him pull through a bad turn. You definitely heard wrong.

150 Sam: Okay.

As far as Hally is concerned, the matter is settled. He returns to his table, sits down and divides his attention between the book and his soup. Sam is at his school case and picks up a textbook Modern Graded Mathematics for Standards Nine and Ten. Opens it at random and laughs at something he sees.

Who is this supposed to be?

Hally: Old fart-face Prentice.

Sam: Teacher?

Hally: Thinks he is. And believe me, that is not a bad likeness.

Sam: Has he seen it?

155 Hally: Yes.

Sam: What did he say?

Hally: Tried to be clever, as usual. Said I was no Leonardo da Vinci[6] and that bad art had to be punished. So, six of the best, and his are bloody good.

---

[6] Renaissance artist, creator, for example, of the Mona Lisa (1452–1519).

Sam: On your bum?

Hally: Where else? The days when I got them on my hands are gone forever, Sam.

160 Sam: With your trousers down!

Hally: No. He's not quite that barbaric.

Sam: That's the way they do it in jail.

Hally: *(Flicker of morbid interest.)* Really?

Sam: Ja. When the magistrate sentences you to "strokes with a light cane."

165 Hally: Go on.

Sam: They make you lie down on a bench. One policeman pulls down your trousers and holds your ankles, another one pulls your shirt over your head and holds your arms . . .

Hally: Thank you! That's enough.

Sam: . . . and the one that gives you the strokes talks to you gently and for a long time between each one. *(He laughs.)*

Hally: I've heard enough, Sam! Jesus! It's a bloody awful world when you come to think of it. People can be real bastards.

170 Sam: That's the way it is, Hally.

Hally: It doesn't *have* to be that way. There is something called progress, you know. We don't exactly burn people at the stake anymore.

Sam: Like Joan of Arc.[7]

Hally: Correct. If she was captured today, she'd be given a fair trial.

Sam: And then the death sentence.

175 Hally: *(A world-weary sigh.)* I know, I know! I oscillate between hope and despair for this world as well, Sam. But things will change, you wait and see. One day somebody is going to get up and give history a kick up the backside and get it going again.

Sam: Like who?

Hally: *(After thought.)* They're called social reformers. Every age, Sam, has got its social reformer. My history book is full of them.

Sam: So where's ours?

Hally: Good question. And I hate to say it, but the answer is: I don't know. Maybe he hasn't even been born yet. Or is still only a babe in arms at his mother's breast. God, what a thought.

180 Sam: So we just go on waiting.

Hally: Ja, looks like it. *(Back to his soup and the book.)*

Sam: *(Reading from the textbook.)* "Introduction: In some mathematical problems only the magnitude . . ." *(He mispronounces the word "magnitude.")*

Hally: *(Correcting him without looking up.)* Magnitude.

Sam: What's it mean?

185 Hally: How big it is. The size of the thing.

Sam: *(Reading.)* ". . . a magnitude of the quantities is of importance. In other problems we need to know whether these quantities are negative

---

[7] French military leader and heroine, later canonized by the Catholic church (1412–1431).

or positive. For example, whether there is a debit or credit bank
balance . . ."

Hally: Whether you're broke or not.

Sam: ". . . whether the temperature is above or below Zero . . ."

Hally: Naught degrees. Cheerful state of affairs! No cash and you're freezing
to death. Mathematics won't get you out of that one.

190 Sam: All these quantities are called . . . *(Spelling the word.)* . . . s-c-a-l
. . .

Hally: Scalars.

Sam: Scalars! *(Shaking his head with a laugh.)* You understand all that?

Hally: *(Turning a page.)* No. And I don't intend to try.

Sam: So what happens when the exams come?

195 Hally: Failing a maths exam isn't the end of the world, Sam. How many times
have I told you that examination results don't measure intelligence?

Sam: I would say about as many times as you've failed one of them.

Hally: *(Mirthlessly.)* Ha, ha, ha.

Sam: *(Simultaneously.)* Ha, ha, ha.

Hally: Just remember Winston Churchill[8] didn't do particularly well at
school.

200 Sam: You've also told me that one many times.

Hally: Well, it just so happens to be the truth.

Sam: *(Enjoying the word.)* Magnitude! Magnitude! Show me how to use it.

Hally: *(After thought.)* An intrepid social reformer will not be daunted by the
magnitude of the task he has undertaken.

Sam: *(Impressed.)* Couple of jaw-breakers in there!

205 Hally: I gave you three for the price of one. Intrepid, daunted and magnitude.
I did that once in an exam. Put five of the words I had to explain in one
sentence. It was half a page long.

Sam: Well, I'll put my money on you in the English exam.

Hally: Piece of cake. Eighty percent without even trying.

Sam: *(Another textbook from Hally's case.)* And history?

Hally: So-so. I'll scrape through. In the fifties if I'm lucky.

210 Sam: You didn't do too badly last year.

Hally: Because we had World War One. That at least had some action. You try
to find that in the South African Parliamentary system.

Sam: (Reading from the history textbook.) "Napoleon[9] and the principle of
equality." Hey! This sounds interesting. "After concluding peace with
Britain in 1802, Napoleon used a brief period of calm to in-sti-tute . . ."

Hally: Introduce.

Sam: ". . . many reforms. Napoleon regarded all people as equal before the
law and wanted them to have equal opportunities for advancement. All

---

[8] Prime Minister of England during World War II (1940–1945) and recipient of the Nobel Prize
in 1953 (1874–1965).

[9] French general who declared himself emperor of France from 1804–1814 (1769–1821).

ves-ti-ges of the feu-dal system with its oppression of the poor were abolished. Vestiges, feudal system and abolished." I'm all right on oppression.

215 Hally: I'm thinking. He swept away . . . abolished . . . the last remains
. . . vestiges . . . of the bad old days . . . feudal system.

Sam: Ha! There's the social reformer we're waiting for. He sounds like a man
of some magnitude.

Hally: I'm not so sure about that. It's a damn good title for a book, though.
A man of magnitude!

Sam: He sounds pretty big to me, Hally.

Hally: Don't confuse historical significance with greatness. But maybe I'm being a bit prejudiced. Have a look in there and you'll see he's two chapters
long. And hell! . . . has he only got dates, Sam, all of which you've got to
remember! This campaign and that campaign, and then, because of all the
fighting, the next thing is we get Peace Treaties all over the place. And
what's the end of the story? Battle of Waterloo,[10] which he loses. Wasn't
worth it. No, I don't know about him as a man of magnitude.

220 Sam: Then who would you say was?

Hally: To answer that, we need a definition of greatness, and I suppose that
would be somebody who . . . somebody who benefited all mankind.

Sam: Right. But like who?

Hally: *(He speaks with total conviction.)* Charles Darwin.[11] Remember him?
That big book from the library. *The Origin of the Species.*

Sam: Him?

225 Hally: Yes. For his Theory of Evolution.

Sam: You didn't finish it.

Hally: I ran out of time. I didn't finish it because my two weeks was up. But
I'm going to take it out again after I've digested what I read. It's safe. I've
hidden it away in the Theology section. Nobody ever goes in there. And
anyway who are you to talk? You hardly even looked at it.

Sam: I tried. I looked at the chapters in the beginning and I saw one called
"The Struggle for an Existence." Ah ha, I thought. At last! But what did
I get? Something called the mistletoe which needs the apple tree and
there's too many seeds and all are going to die except one . . . ! No,
Hally.

Hally: *(Intellectually outraged.)* What do you mean, No! The poor man had
to start somewhere. For God's sake, Sam, he revolutionized science. Now
we know.

230 Sam: What?

Hally: Where we come from and what it all means.

Sam: And that's a benefit to mankind? Anyway, I still don't believe it.

Hally: God, you're impossible. I showed it to you in black and white.

Sam: Doesn't mean I got to believe it.

---

[10] Town in Belgium, site of major battle in which Napoleon was defeated in 1815.

[11] Nineteenth century British scientist and naturalist who developed the theory of evolution.

235 **Hally:** It's the likes of you that kept the Inquisition in business. It's called bigotry. Anyway, that's my man of magnitude. Charles Darwin! Who's yours?

Sam: *(Without hesitation.)* Abraham Lincoln.

Hally: I might have guessed as much. Don't get sentimental, Sam. You've never been a slave, you know. And anyway we freed your ancestors here in South Africa long before the Americans. But if you want to thank somebody on their behalf, do it to Mr. William Wilberforce.[12] Come on. Try again. I want a real genius. *(Now enjoying him-self, and so is Sam. Hally goes behind the counter and helps himself to a chocolate.)*

Sam: William Shakespeare.[13]

Hally: *(No enthusiasm.)* Oh. So you're also one of them, are you? You're basing that opinion on only one play, you know. You've only read my *Julius Caesar* and even I don't understand half of what they're talking about. They should do what they did with the old Bible: bring the language up to date.

240 **Sam:** That's all you've got. It's also the only one *you've* read.

Hally: I know. I admit it. That's why I suggest we reserve our judgment until we've checked up on a few others. I've got a feeling, though, that by the end of this year one is going to be enough for me, and I can give you the names of twenty-nine other chaps in the Standard Nine class of the Port Elizabeth Technical College who feel the same. But if you want him, you can have him. My turn now. (Pacing.) This is a damned good exercise, you know! It started off looking like a simple question and here it's got us really probing into the intellectual heritage of our civilization.

Sam: So who is it going to be?

Hally: My next man . . . and he gets the title on two scores: social reform and literary genius . . . is Leo Nikolaevich Tolstoy.[14]

Sam: That Russian.

245 **Hally:** Correct. Remember the picture of him I showed you?

Sam: With the long beard.

Hally: *(Trying to look like Tolstoy.)* And those burning, visionary eyes. My God, the face of a social prophet if ever I saw one! And remember my words when I showed it to you? Here's a *man*, Sam!

Sam: Those were words, Hally.

Hally: Not many intellectuals are prepared to shovel manure with the peasants and then go home and write a "little book" called *War and Peace.* Incidentally, Sam, he was somebody else who, to quote, ". . . did not distinguish himself scholastically."

250 **Sam:** Meaning?

Hally: He was also no good at school.

Sam: Like you and Winston Churchill.

---

[12] English abolitionist (1759–1833).

[13] English poet and dramatist (1564–1616). See Chapter 4.

[14] Russian novelist, author of *Anna Karenina* and *War and Peace* (1828–1910).

Hally: *(Mirthlessly.)* Ha, ha, ha.

Sam: *(Simultaneously.)* Ha, ha, ha.

255 Hally: Don't get clever, Sam. That man freed his serfs of his own free will.

Sam: No argument. He was a somebody, all right. I accept him.

Hally: I'm sure Count Tolstoy will be very pleased to hear that. Your turn. Shoot. *(Another chocolate from behind the counter.)* I'm waiting, Sam.

Sam: I've got him.

Hally: Good. Submit your candidate for examination.

260 Sam: Jesus.

Hally: *(Stopped dead in his tracks.)* Who?

Sam: Jesus Christ.

Hally: Oh, come on, Sam!

Sam: The Messiah.

265 Hally: Ja, but still . . . No, Sam. Don't let's get started on religion. We'll just spend the whole afternoon arguing again. Suppose I turn around and say Mohammed?

Sam: All right.

Hally: You can't have them both on the same list!

Sam: Why not? You like Mohammed, I like Jesus.

Hally: I *don't* like Mohammed. I never have. I was merely being hypothetical. As far as I'm concerned, the Koran is as bad as the Bible. No. Religion is out! I'm not going to waste my time again arguing with you about the existence of God. You know perfectly well I'm an atheist . . . and I've got homework to do.

270 Sam: Okay, I take him back.

Hally: You've got time for one more name.

Sam: *(After thought.)* I've got one I know we'll agree on. A simple straightforward great Man of Magnitude . . . and no arguments. And *he* really *did* benefit all mankind.

Hally: I wonder. After your last contribution I'm beginning to doubt whether anything in the way of an intellectual agreement is possible between the two of us. Who is he?

Sam: Guess.

275 Hally: Socrates?[15] Alexandre Dumas?[16] Karl Marx?[17] Dostoevsky?[18] Nietzsche?[19]

Sam shakes his head after each name.

Give me a clue.

Sam: The letter P is important . . .

---

[15] Greek philosopher (A.D.? 470–399).

[16] Nineteenth-century French novelist (1824–1895).

[17] Nineteenth-century German political philosopher and economist whose thought provided the basis of the socialist state.

[18] Nineteenth-century Russian novelist, author of *Crime and Punishment* and *The Brothers Karamazov* (1821–1881).

[19] German philosopher (1844–1900).

Hally: Plato!

Sam: . . . and his name begins with an F.

Hally: I've got it. Freud and Psychology.[20]

280 Sam: No. I didn't understand him.

Hally: That makes two of us.

Sam: Think of mouldy apricot jam.

Hally: *(After a delighted laugh.)* Penicillin and Sir Alexander Fleming![21] And the title of the book: *The Microbe Hunters. (Delighted.)* Splendid, Sam! Splendid. For once we are in total agreement. The major breakthrough in medical science in the Twentieth Century. If it wasn't for him, we might have lost the Second World War. It's deeply gratifying, Sam, to know that I haven't been wasting my time in talking to you. *(Strutting around proudly.)* Tolstoy may have educated his peasants, but I've educated you.

Sam: Standard Four to Standard Nine.

285 Hally: Have we been at it as long as that?

Sam: Yep. And my first lesson was geography.

Hally: *(Intrigued.)* Really? I don't remember.

Sam: My room there at the back of the old Jubilee Boarding House. I had just started working for your Mom. Little boy in short trousers walks in one afternoon and asks me seriously: "Sam, do you want to see South Africa?" Hey man! Sure I wanted to see South Africa!

Hally: Was that me?

290 Sam: . . . So the next thing I'm looking at a map you had just done for homework. It was your first one and you were very proud of yourself.

Hally: Go on.

Sam: Then came my first lesson. "Repeat after me, Sam: Gold in the Transvaal, mealies in the Free State, sugar in Natal and grapes in the Cape." I still know it!

Hally: Well, I'll be buggered. So that's how it all started.

Sam: And your next map was one with all the rivers and the mountains they came from. The Orange, the Vaal, the Limpopo, the Zambezi[22] . . .

295 Hally: You've got a phenomenal memory!

Sam: You should be grateful. That is why you started passing your exams. You tried to be better than me.

They laugh together. Willie is attracted by the laughter and joins them.

Hally: The old Jubilee Boarding House. Sixteen rooms with board and lodging, rent in advance and one week's notice. I haven't thought about it for donkey's years . . . and I don't think that's an accident. God, was I glad when we sold it and moved out. Those years are not remembered as the happiest ones of an unhappy childhood.

---

[20] Founder of modern psychology; physician and psychiatrist (1856–1939).

[21] Physician and scientist who with Sir Howard Florey discovered penicillin in 1929 (1881–1955).

[22] Rivers in South Africa.

Willie: *(Knocking on the table and trying to imitate a woman's voice.)* "Hally, are you there?"

Hally: Who's that supposed to be?

300 Willie: "What you doing in there, Hally? Come out at once!"

Hally: *(To Sam.)* What's he talking about?

Sam: Don't you remember?

Willie: "Sam, Willie . . . is he in there with you boys?"

Sam: Hiding away in our room when your mother was looking for you.

305 Hally: *(Another good laugh.)* Of course! I used to crawl and hide under your bed! But finish the story, Willie. Then what used to happen? You chaps would give the game away by telling her I was in there with you. So much for friendship.

Sam: We couldn't lie to her. She knew.

Hally: Which meant I got another rowing for hanging around the "servants' quarters." I think I spent more time in there with you chaps than anywhere else in that dump. And do you blame me? Nothing but bloody misery wherever you went. Somebody was always complaining about the food, or my mother was having a fight with Micky Nash because she'd caught her with a petty officer in her room. Maud Meiring was another one. Remember those two? They were prostitutes, you know. Soldiers and sailors from the troopships. Bottom fell out of the business when the war ended. God, the flotsam and jetsam that life washed up on our shores! No joking, if it wasn't for your room, I would have been the first certified ten-year-old in medical history. Ja, the memories are coming back now. Walking home from school and thinking: "What can I do this afternoon?" Try out a few ideas, but sooner or later I'd end up in there with you fellows. I bet you I could still find my way to your room with my eyes closed. *(He does exactly that.)* Down the corridor . . . telephone on the right, which my Mom keeps locked because sombody is using it on the sly and not paying . . . past the kitchen and unappetizing cooking smells . . . around the corner into the backyard, hold my breath again because there are more smells coming when I pass your lavatory, then into that little passageway, first door on the right and into your room. How's that?

Sam: Good. But, as usual, you forgot to knock.

Hally: Like that time I barged in and caught you and Cynthia . . . at it. Remember? God, was I embarrassed! I didn't know what was going on at first.

310 Sam: Ja, that taught you a lesson.

Hally: And about a lot more than knocking on doors, I'll have you know, and I don't mean geography either. Hell, Sam, couldn't you have waited until it was dark?

Sam: No.

Hally: Was it that urgent?

Sam: Yes, and if you don't believe me, wait until your time comes.

315 Hally: No, thank you. I am not interested in girls. *(Back to his memories . . . Using a few chairs he recreates the room as he lists the items.)* A

gray little room with a cold cement floor. Your bed against that wall . . . and I now know why the mattress sags so much! . . . Willie's bed . . . it's propped up on bricks because one leg is broken . . . that wobbly little table with the washbasin and jug of water . . . Yes! . . . stuck to the wall above it are some pin-up pictures from magazines. Joe Louis . . .

Willie: Brown Bomber. World Title *(Boxing pose.)* Three rounds and knock-out.[23]

Hally: Against who?

Sam: Max Schmeling.

Hally: Correct. I can also remember Fred Astaire and Ginger Rogers, and Rita Hayworth in a bathing costume which always made me hot and bothered when I looked at it. Under Willie's bed is an old suitcase with all his clothes in a mess, which is why I never hide there. Your things are neat and tidy in a trunk next to your bed, and on it there is a picture of you and Cynthia in your ballroom clothes, your first silver cup for third place in a competition and an old radio which doesn't work anymore. Have I left out anything?

320 Sam: No.

Hally: Right, so much for the stage directions. Now the characters. *(Sam and Willie move to their appropriate positions in the bedroom.)* Willie is in bed, under his blankets with his clothes on, complaining nonstop about something, but we can't make out a word of what he's saying because he's got his head under the blankets as well. You're on your bed trimming your toenails with a knife—not a very edifying sight—and as for me . . . What am I doing?

Sam: You're sitting on the floor giving Willie a lecture about being a good loser while you get the checker board and pieces ready for a game. Then you go to Willie's bed, pull off the blankets and make him play with you first because you know you're going to win, and that gives you the second game with me.

Hally: And you certainly were a bad loser, Willie!

Willie: Haai!

325 Hally: Wasn't he, Sam? And so slow! A game with you almost took the whole afternoon. Thank God I gave up trying to teach you how to play chess.

Willie: You and Sam cheated.

Hally: I never saw Sam cheat, and mine were mostly the mistakes of youth.

Willie: Then how is it you two was always winning?

Hally: Have you ever considered the possibility, Willie, that it was because we were better than you?

330 Willie: Every time better?

Hally: Not every time. There were occasions when we deliberately let you win a game so that you would stop sulking and go on playing with us. Sam used to wink at me when you weren't looking to show me it was time to let you win.

---

[23] Nickname of United States prizefighter Joseph Louis who won the heavyweight boxing championship in 1938 against German Max Schmeling (1914–1981).

Willie: So then you two didn't play fair.

Hally: It was for your benefit, Mr. Malopo, which is more than being fair. It was an act of self-sacrifice. *(To Sam.)* But you know what my best memory is, don't you?

Sam: No.

335 **Hally:** Come on, guess. If your memory is so good, you must remember it as well.

Sam: We got up to a lot of tricks in there, Hally.

Hally: This one was special, Sam.

Sam: I'm listening.

Hally: It started off looking like another of those useless nothing-to-do afternoons. I'd already been down to Main Street looking for adventure, but nothing had happened. I didn't feel like climbing trees in the Donkin Park or pretending I was a private eye and following a stranger . . . so as usual: See what's cooking in Sam's room. This time it was you on the floor. You had two thin pieces of wood and you were smoothing them down with a knife. It didn't look particularly interesting, but when I asked you what you were doing, you just said, "Wait and see, Hally. Wait . . . and see" . . . in that secret sort of way of yours, so I knew there was a surprise coming. You teased me, you bugger, by being deliberately slow and not answering my questions!

Sam laughs.

And whistling while you worked away! God, it was infuriating! I could have brained you! It was only when you tied them together in a cross and put that down on the brown paper that I realized what you were doing. "Sam is making a kite?" And when I asked you and you said "Yes . . . !" *(Shaking his head with disbelief.)* The sheer audacity of it took my breath away. I mean, seriously, what the hell does a black man know about flying a kite? I'll be honest with you, Sam, I had no hopes for it. If you think I was excited and happy, you got another guess coming. In fact, I was shit-scared that we were going to make fools of ourselves. When we left the boarding house to go up onto the hill, I was praying quietly that there wouldn't be any other kids around to laugh at us.

340 **Sam:** *(Enjoying the memory as much as Hally.)* Ja, I could see that.

Hally: I made it obvious, did I?

Sam: Ja. You refused to carry it.

Hally: Do you blame me? Can you remember what the poor thing looked like? Tomato-box wood and brown paper! Flour and water for glue! Two of my mother's old stockings for a tail, and then all those bits and pieces of string you made me tie together so that we could fly it! Hell, no, that was now only asking for a miracle to happen.

Sam: Then the big argument when I told you to hold the string and run with it when I let go.

345 **Hally:** I was prepared to run, all right, but straight back to the boarding house.

Sam: *(Knowing what's coming.)* So what happened?

Hally: Come on, Sam, you remember as well as I do.

Sam: I want to hear it from you.

Hally pauses. He wants to be as accurate as possible.

Hally: You went a little distance from me down the hill, you held it up ready to let it go. . . . "This is it," I thought. "Like everything else in my life, here comes another fiasco." Then you shouted, "Go, Hally!" and I started to run. *(Another pause.)* I don't know how to describe it, Sam. Ja! The miracle happened! I was running, waiting for it to crash to the ground, but instead suddenly there was something alive behind me at the end of the string, tugging at it as if it wanted to be free. I looked back . . . *(Shakes his head.)* . . . I still can't believe my eyes. It was flying! Looping around and trying to climb even higher into the sky. You shouted to me to let it have more string. I did, until there was none left and I was just holding that piece of wood we had tied it to. You came up and joined me. You were laughing.

350 Sam: So were you. And shouting, "It works, Sam! We've done it!"

Hally: And we had! I was so proud of us! It was the most splendid thing I had ever seen. I wished there were hundreds of kids around to watch us. The part that scared me, though, was when you showed me how to make it dive down to the ground and then just when it was on the point of crashing, swoop up again!

Sam: You didn't want to try yourself.

Hally: Of course not! I would have been suicidal if anything had happened to it. Watching you do it made me nervous enough. I was quite happy just to see it up there with its tail fluttering behind it. You left me after that, didn't you? You explained how to get it down, we tied it to the bench so that I could sit and watch it, and you went away. I wanted you to stay, you know. I was a little scared of having to look after it by myself.

Sam: *(Quietly.)* I had work to do, Hally.

355 Hally: It was sort of sad bringing it down, Sam. And it looked sad again when it was lying there on the ground. Like something that had lost its soul. Just tomato-box wood, brown paper and two of my mother's old stockings! But, hell, I'll never forget that first moment when I saw it up there. I had a stiff neck the next day from looking up so much.

Sam laughs. Hally turns to him with a question he never thought of asking before.

Why did you make that kite, Sam?

Sam: *(Evenly.)* I can't remember.

Hally: Truly?

Sam: Too long ago, Hally.

Hally: Ja, I suppose it was. It's time for another one, you know.

360 Sam: Why do you say that?

Hally: Because it feels like that. Wouldn't be a good day to fly it, though.

Sam: No. You can't fly kites on rainy days.

Hally: *(He studies Sam. Their memories have made him conscious of the man's presence in his life.)* How old are you, Sam?

Sam: Two score and five.

365 **Hally:** Strange, isn't it?

Sam: What?

Hally: Me and you.

Sam: What's strange about it?

Hally: Little white boy in short trousers and a black man old enough to be his father flying a kite. It's not every day you see that.

370 **Sam:** But why strange? Because the one is white and the other black?

Hally: I don't know. Would have been just as strange, I suppose, if it had been me and my Dad . . . cripple man and a little boy! Nope! There's no chance of me flying a kite without it being strange. *(Simple statement of fact—no self-pity.)* There's a nice little short story there. "The Kite-Flyers." But we'd have to find a twist in the ending.

Sam: Twist?

Hally: Yes. Something unexpected. The way it ended with us was too straightforward . . . me on the bench and you going back to work. There's no drama in that.

Willie: And me?

375 **Hally:** You?

Willie: Yes me.

Hally: You want to get into the story as well, do you? I got it! Change the title: "Afternoons in Sam's Room" . . . expand it and tell all the stories. It's on its way to being a novel. Our days in the old Jubilee. Sad in a way that they're over. I almost wish we were still in that little room.

Sam: We're still together.

Hally: That's true. It's just that life felt the right size in there . . . not too big and not too small. Wasn't so hard to work up a bit of courage. It's got so bloody complicated since then.

The telephone rings. Sam answers it.

380 **Sam:** St. George's Park Tea Room . . . Hello, Madam . . . Yes, Madam, he's here . . . Hally, it's your mother.

Hally: Where is she phoning from?

Sam: Sounds like the hospital. It's a public telephone.

Hally: *(Relieved.)* You see! I told you. *(The telephone.)* Hello, Mom . . . Yes . . . Yes no fine. Everything's under control here. How's things with poor old Dad? . . . Has he had a bad turn? . . . What? . . . Oh, God! . . . Yes, Sam told me, but I was sure he'd made a mistake. But what's this all about, Mom? He didn't look at all good last night. How can he get better so quickly? . . . Then very obviously you must say no. Be firm with him. You're the boss. . . . You know what it's going to be like if he comes home. . . . Well, then, don't blame me when I fail my exams at the end of the year. . . . Yes! How am I expected to be fresh for school when I spend half the night massaging his gammy leg? . . . So am I! . . . So tell him a white lie. Say Dr. Colley wants more X-rays of his stump. Or bribe him. We'll sneak in double tots of brandy in future. . . . What? . . . Order him to get back into bed at once! If he's going to behave like a child, treat him like one. . . . All right, Mom! I was just trying to . . . I'm sorry. . . . I said I'm sorry. . . . Quick, give me your number. I'll phone you back. *(He hangs up and waits a few seconds.)* Here we go again! *(He dials.)* I'm sorry, Mom. . . . Okay . . . But now listen to me carefully. All it needs is for you to put your foot down. Don't take no for an answer. . . . Did you hear me? And whatever you do, don't discuss it with him. . . . Because I'm frightened you'll give in to him. . . . Yes, Sam gave me lunch. . . . I ate all of it! . . . No, Mom not a soul. It's still raining here. . . . Right, I'll tell them. I'll just do some homework and then lock up. . . . But remember now, Mom. Don't listen to anything he says. And phone me back and let me know what happens. . . . Okay. Bye, Mom. *(He hangs up. The men are staring at him.)* My Mom says that when you're finished with the floors you must do the windows. *(Pause.)* Don't misunderstand me, chaps. All I want is for him to get better. And if he was, I'd be the first person to say: "Bring him home." But he's not, and we can't give him the medical care and attention he needs at home. That's what hospitals are there for. *(Brusquely.)* So don't just stand there! Get on with it!

Sam clears Hally's table.

You heard right. My Dad wants to go home.

Sam: Is he better?

385 **Hally:** *(Sharply.)* No! How the hell can he be better when last night he was groaning with pain? This is not an age of miracles!

Sam: Then he should stay in hospital.

Hally: *(Seething with irritation and frustration.)* Tell me something I don't know, Sam. What the hell do you think I was saying to my Mom? All I can say is fuck-it-all.

Sam: I'm sure he'll listen to your Mom.

Hally: You don't know what she's up against. He's already packed his shaving kit and pajamas and is sitting on his bed with his crutches, dressed and ready to go. I know him when he gets in that mood. If she tries to reason with him, we've had it. She's no match for him when it comes to a battle of words. He'll tie her up in knots. *(Trying to hide his true feelings.)*

390 **Sam:** I suppose it gets lonely for him in there.

Hally: With all the patients and nurses around? Regular visits from the Salvation Army? Balls! It's ten times worse for him at home. I'm at school and my mother is here in the business all day.

Sam: He's at least got you at night.

Hally: *(Before he can stop himself.)* And we've got him! Please! I don't want to talk about it anymore. *(Unpacks his school case, slamming down* *books on the table.)* Life is just a plain bloody mess, that's all. And people are fools.

Sam: Come on, Hally.

395 **Hally:** Yes, they are! They bloody well deserve what they get.

Sam: Then don't complain.

Hally: Don't try to be clever, Sam. It doesn't suit you. Anybody who thinks there's nothing wrong with this world needs to have his head examined. Just when things are going along all right, without fail someone or something will come along and spoil everything. Somebody should write that down as a fundamental law of the Universe. The principle of perpetual disappointment. If there is a God who created this world, he should scrap it and try again.

Sam: All right, Hally, all right. What you got for homework?

Hally: Bullshit, as usual. *(Opens an exercise book and reads.)* "Write five hundred words describing an annual event of cultural or historical significance."

400 **Sam:** That should be easy enough for you.

Hally: And also plain bloody boring. You know what he wants, don't you? One of their useless old ceremonies. The commemoration of the landing of the 1820 Settlers,[24] or if it's going to be culture, Carols by Candlelight every Christmas.

Sam: It's an impressive sight. Make a good description, Hally. All those candles glowing in the dark and the people singing hymns.

Hally: And it's called religious hysteria. *(Intense irritation.)* Please, Sam! Just leave me alone and let me get on with it. I'm not in the mood for games this afternoon. And remember my Mom's orders . . . you're to help Willie with the windows. Come on now, I don't want any more nonsense in here.

Sam: Okay, Hally, okay.

Hally settles down to his homework; determined preparations . . . pen, ruler, exercise book, dictionary, another cake . . . all of which will lead to nothing.

(Sam waltzes over to Willie and starts to replace tables and chairs. He practices a ballroom step while doing so. Willie watches. When Sam is finished, Willie tries.) Good! But just a little bit quicker on the turn and only move in to her after she's crossed over. What about this one?

Another step. When Sam is finished, Willie again has a go.

Much better. See what happens when you just relax and enjoy yourself? Remember that in two weeks' time and you'll be all right.

405 **Willie:** But I haven't got partner, Boet Sam.

Sam: Maybe Hilda will turn up tonight.

---

[24] In 1819–1820, the British government paid Britons who moved to South Africa 100 acres of land per family.

Willie: No, Boet Sam. *(Reluctantly.)* I gave her a good hiding.

Sam: You mean a bad one.

Willie: Good bad one.

410 **Sam:** Then you mustn't complain either. Now you pay the price for losing your temper.

Willie: I also pay two pounds ten shilling entrance fee.

Sam: They'll refund you if you withdraw now.

Willie: *(Appalled.)* You mean, don't dance?

Sam: Yes.

415 **Willie:** No! I wait too long and I practice too hard. If I find me new partner, you think I can be ready in two weeks? I ask Madam for my leave now and we practice every day.

Sam: Quickstep non-stop for two weeks. World record, Willie, but you'll be mad at the end.

Willie: No jokes, Boet Sam.

Sam: I'm not joking.

Willie: So then what?

420 **Sam:** Find Hilda. Say you're sorry and promise you won't beat her again.

Willie: No.

Sam: Then withdraw. Try again next year.

Willie: No.

Sam: Then I give up.

425 **Willie:** Haaikona, Boet Sam, you can't.

Sam: What do you mean, I can't? I'm telling you: I give up.

Willie: *(Adamant.)* No! *(Accusingly.)* It was you who start me ballroom dancing.

Sam: So?

Willie: Before that I use to be happy. And is you and Miriam who bring me to Hilda and say here's partner for you.

430 **Sam:** What are you saying, Willie?

Willie: You!

Sam: But me what? To blame?

Willie: Yes.

Sam: Willie . . . ? *(Bursts into laughter.)*

435 **Willie:** And now all you do is make jokes at me. You wait. When Miriam leaves you is my turn to laugh. Ha! Ha! Ha!

Sam: *(He can't take Willie seriously any longer.)* She can leave me tonight! I know what to do. *(Bowing before an imaginary partner.)* May I have the pleasure? *(He dances and sings.)*

"Just a fellow with his pillow . . .

Dancin' like a willow . . .

In an autumn breeze . . ."

Willie: There you go again!

Sam goes on dancing and singing.

Boet Sam!

Sam: There's the answer to your problem! Judges' announcement in two weeks' time: "Ladies and gentlemen, the winner in the open section . . . Mr. Willie Malopo and his pillow!"

This is too much for a now really angry Willie. He goes for Sam, but the latter is too quick for him and puts Hally's table between the two of them.

Hally: *(Exploding.)* For Christ's sake, you two!

440 Willie: *(Still trying to get at Sam.)* I donner you, Sam! Struesgod!

Sam: *(Still laughing.)* Sorry, Willie . . . Sorry . . .

Hally: Sam! Willie! *(Grabs his ruler and gives Willie a vicious whack on the bum.)* How the hell am I supposed to concentrate with the two of you behaving like bloody children!

Willie: Hit him too!

Hally: Shut up, Willie.

445 Willie: He started jokes again.

Hally: Get back to your work. You too, Sam. *(His ruler.)* Do you want another one, Willie?

Sam and Willie return to their work. Hally uses the opportunity to escape from his unsuccessful attempt at homework. He struts around like a little despot, ruler in hand, giving vent to his anger and frustration.

Suppose a customer had walked in then? Or the Park Superintendent. And seen the two of you behaving like a pair of hooligans. That would have been the end of my mother's license, you know. And your jobs! Well, this is the end of it. From now on there will be no more of your ballroom nonsense in here. This is a business establishment, not a bloody New Brighton dancing school. I've been far too lenient with the two of you. *(Behind the counter for a green cool drink and a dollop of ice cream. He keeps up his tirade as he prepares it.)* But what really makes me bitter is that I allow you chaps a little freedom in here when business is bad and what do you do with it? The foxtrot![25] Specially you, Sam. There's more to life than trotting around a dance floor and I thought at least you knew it.

Sam: It's a harmless pleasure, Hally. It doesn't hurt anybody.

Hally: It's also a rather simple one, you know.

Sam: You reckon so? Have you ever tried?

450 Hally: Of course not.

Sam: Why don't you? Now.

Hally: What do you mean? Me dance?

Sam: Yes. I'll show you a simple step—the waltz—then you try it.

Hally: What will that prove?

455 Sam: That it might not be as easy as you think.

Hally: I didn't say it was easy. I said it was simple—like in simple-minded, meaning mentally retarded. You can't exactly say it challenges the intellect.

---

[25] A dance characterized by slow, quick steps.

Sam: It does other things.

Hally: Such as?

Sam: Make people happy.

460 Hally: *(The glass in his hand.)* So do American cream sodas with ice cream. For God's sake, Sam, you're not asking me to take ballroom dancing serious, are you?

Sam: Yes.

Hally: *(Sigh of defeat.)* Oh, well, so much for trying to give you a decent education. I've obviously achieved nothing.

Sam: You still haven't told me what's wrong with admiring something that's beautiful and then trying to do it yourself.

Hally: Nothing. But we happen to be talking about a foxtrot, not a thing of beauty.

465 Sam: But that is just what I'm saying. If you were to see two champions doing, two masters of the art . . . !

Hally: Oh, God, I give up. So now it's also art!

Sam: Ja.

Hally: There's a limit, Sam. Don't confuse art and entertainment.

Sam: So then what is art?

470 Hally: You want a definition?

Sam: Ja.

Hally: *(He realizes he has got to be careful. He gives the matter a lot of thought before answering.)* Philosophers have been trying to do that for centuries. What is Art? What is Life? But basically I suppose it's . . . the giving of meaning to matter.

Sam: Nothing to do with beautiful?

Hally: It goes beyond that. It's the giving of form to the formless.

475 Sam: Ja, well, maybe it's not art, then. But I still say it's beautiful.

Hally: I'm sure the word you mean to use is entertaining.

Sam: *(Adamant.)* No. Beautiful. And if you want proof, come along to the Centenary Hall in New Brighton in two weeks' time.

The mention of the Centenary Hall draws Willie over to them.

Hally: What for? I've seen the two of you prancing around in here often enough.

Sam: *(He laughs.)* This isn't the real thing, Hally. We're just playing around in here.

480 Hally: So? I can use my imagination.

Sam: And what do you get?

Hally: A lot of people dancing around and having a so-called good time.

Sam: That all?

Hally: Well, basically it is that, surely.

485 Sam: No, it isn't. Your imagination hasn't helped you at all. There's a lot more to it than that. We're getting ready for the championships, Hally, not just another dance. There's going to be a lot of people, all right, and they're going to have a good time, but they'll only be spectators, sitting

around and watching. It's just the competitors out there on the dance floor. Party decorations and fancy lights all around the walls! The ladies in beautiful evening dresses!

Hally: My mother's got one of those, Sam, and quite frankly, it's an embarrassment every time she wears it.

Sam: *(Undeterred.)* Your imagination left out the excitement.

Hally scoffs.

Oh, yes. The finalists are not going to be out there just to have a good time. One of those couples will be the 1950 Eastern Province Champions. And your imagination left out the music.

Willie: Mr. Elijah Gladman Guzana and his Orchestral Jazzonions.

Sam: The sound of the big band, Hally. Trombone, trumpet, tenor and alto sax. And then, finally, your imagination also left out the climax of the evening when the dancing is finished, the judges have stopped whispering among themselves and the Master of Ceremonies collects their scorecards and goes up onto the stage to announce the winners.

490 Hally: All right. So you make it sound like a bit of a do. It's an occasion. Satisfied?

Sam: *(Victory.)* So you admit that!

Hally: Emotionally yes, intellectually no.

Sam: Well, I don't know what you mean by that, all I'm telling you is that it is going to be *the* event of the year in New Brighton. It's been sold out for two weeks already. There's only standing room left. We've got competitors coming from Kingwilliamstown, East London, Port Alfred.

Hally starts pacing thoughtfully.

Hally: Tell me a bit more.

495 Sam: I thought you weren't interested . . . intellectually.

Hally: *(Mysteriously.)* I've got my reasons.

Sam: What do you want to know?

Hally: It takes place every year?

Sam: Yes. But only every third year in New Brighton. It's East London's turn to have the championships next year.

500 Hally: Which, I suppose, makes it an even more significant event.

Sam: Ah ha! We're getting somewhere. Our "'occasion" is now a "significant event."

Hally: I wonder.

Sam: What?

Hally: I wonder if I would get away with it.

505 Sam: But what?

Hally: *(To the table and his exercise book.)* "Write five hundred words describing an annual event of cultural or historical significance." Would I be stretching poetic license a little too far if I called your ballroom championships a cultural event?

Sam: You mean . . . ?

Hally: You think we could get five hundred words out of it, Sam?

Sam: Victor Sylvester has written a whole book on ballroom dancing.

510 **Willie:** You going to write about it, Master Hally?

Hally: Yes, gentlemen, that is precisely what I am considering doing. Old Doc Bromely—he's my English teacher—is going to argue with me, of course. He doesn't like natives. But I'll point out to him that in strict anthropological terms the culture of a primitive black society includes its dancing and singing. To put my thesis in a nutshell: The war-dance has been replaced by the waltz. But it still amounts to the same thing: the release of primitive emotions through movement. Shall we give it a go?

Sam: I'm ready.

Willie: Me also.

Hally: Ha! This will teach the old bugger a lesson. *(Decision taken.)* Right. Let's get ourselves organized. *(This means another cake on the table. He sits.)* I think you've given me enough general atmosphere, Sam, but to build the tension and suspense I need facts. *(Pencil poised.)*

515 **Willie:** Give him facts, Boet Sam.

Hally: What you called the climax . . . how many finalists?

Sam: Six couples.

Hally: *(Making notes.)* Go on. Give me the picture.

Sam: Spectators seated right around the hall. *(Willie becomes a spectator.)*

520 **Hally:** . . . and it's a full house.

Sam: At one end, on the stage, Gladman and his Orchestral Jazzonions. At the other end is a long table with the three judges. The six finalists go onto the dance floor and take up their positions. When they are ready and the spectators have settled down, the Master of Ceremonies goes to the microphone. To start with, he makes some jokes to get the people laughing . . .

Hally: Good touch! *(As he writes.)* ". . . creating a relaxed atmosphere which will change to one of tension and drama as the climax is approached."

Sam: *(Onto a chair to act out the M.C.)* "Ladies and gentlemen, we come now to the great moment you have all been waiting for this evening. . . . The finals of the 1950 Eastern Province Open Ballroom Dancing Championships. But first let me introduce the finalists! Mr. and Mrs. Welcome Tchabalala from Kingwilliamstown . . ."

Willie: *(He applauds after every name.)* Is when the people clap their hands and whistle and make a lot of noise, Master Hally.

525 **Sam:** Mr. Mulligan Njikelane and Miss Nomhle Nkonyeni of Grahamstown; Mr. and Mrs. Norman Nchinga from Port Alfred; Mr. Fats Bokolane and Miss Dina Plaatjies from East London; Mr. Sipho Dugu and Mrs. Mable Magada from Peddie; and from New Brighton our very own Mr. Willie Malopo and Miss Hilda Samuels.

Willie can't believe his ears. He abandons his role as spectator and scrambles into position as a finalist.

Willie: Relaxed and ready to romance!

Sam: The applause dies down. When everybody is silent, Gladman lifts up his sax, nods at the Orchestral Jazzonions . . .

Willie: Play the jukebox please, Boet Sam!

Sam: I also only got bus fare, Willie.

530 Hally: Hold it, everybody. *(Heads for the cash register behind the counter.)* How much is in the till, Sam?

Sam: Three shillings. Hally . . . your Mom counted it before she left.

Hally hesitates.

Hally: Sorry, Willie. You know how she carried on the last time I did it. We'll just have to pool our combined imaginations and hope for the best. *(Returns to the table.)* Back to work. How are the points scored, Sam?

Sam: Maximum of ten points each for individual style, deportment, rhythm and general appearance.

Willie: Must I start?

535 Hally: Hold it for a second, Willie. And penalties?

Sam: For what?

Hally: For doing something wrong. Say you stumble or bump into somebody . . . do they take off any points?

Sam: *(Aghast.)* Hally . . . !

Hally: When you're dancing. If you and your partner collide into another couple.

Hally can get no further. Sam has collapsed with laughter. He explains to Willie.

540 Sam: If me and Miriam bump into you and Hilda . . .

Willie joins him in another good laugh.

Hally, Hally . . . !

Hally: *(Perplexed.)* Why? What did I say?

Sam: There's no collisions out there, Hally. Nobody trips or stumbles or bumps into anybody else. That's what that moment is all about. To be one of those finalists on that dance floor is like . . . like being in a dream about a world in which accidents don't happen.

Hally: *(Genuinely moved by Sam's image.)* Jesus, Sam! That's beautiful!

Willie: *(Can endure waiting no longer.)* I'm starting! *(Willie dances while Sam talks.)*

545 Sam: Of course it is. That's what I've been trying to say to you all afternoon. And it's beautiful because that is what we want life to be like. But instead, like you said, Hally, we're bumping into each other all the time. Look at the three of us this afternoon: I've bumped into Willie, the two of us have bumped into you, you've bumped into your mother, she bumping into your Dad. . . . None of us knows the steps and there's no music playing. And it doesn't stop with us. The whole world is doing it all the time. Open a newspaper and what do you read? America has bumped into Russia, England is bumping into India, rich man bumps into poor man. Those are big collisions, Hally. They make for a lot of bruises. People get hurt in all that bumping, and we're sick and tired of it now. It's been going on for too long. Are we never going to get it right? . . . Learn to

dance life like champions instead of always being just a bunch of beginners at it?

Hally: *(Deep and sincere admiration of the man.)* You've got a vision, Sam!

Sam: Not just me. What I'm saying to you is that everybody's got it. That's why there's only standing room left for the Centenary Hall in two weeks' time. For as long as the music lasts, we are going to see six couples get it right, the way we want life to be.

Hally: But is that the best we can do, Sam . . . watch six finalists dreaming about the way it should be?

Sam: I don't know. But it starts with that. Without the dream we won't know what we're going for. And anyway I reckon there are a few people who have got past just dreaming about it and are trying for something real. Remember that thing we read once in the paper about the Mahatma Gandhi?[26] Going without food to stop those riots in India?

550 Hally: You're right. He certainly was trying to teach people to get the steps right.

Sam: And the Pope.

Hally: Yes, he's another one. Our old General Smuts as well, you know. He's also out there dancing. You know, Sam, when you come to think of it, that's what the United Nations boils down to . . . a dancing school for politicians!

Sam: And let's hope they learn.

Hally: *(A little surge of hope.)* You're right. We mustn't despair. Maybe there's some hope for mankind after all. Keep it up, Willie. *(Back to his table with determination.)* This is a lot bigger than I thought. So what have we got? Yes, our title: "A World Without Collisions."

555 Sam: That sounds good! "A World Without Collisions."

Hally: Subtitle: "Global Politics on the Dance Floor." No. A bit too heavy, hey? What about "Ballroom Dancing as a Political Vision"?

The telephone rings. Sam answers it.

Sam: St. George's Park Tea Room . . . Yes, Madam . . . Hally, it's your Mom.

Hally: *(Back to reality.)* Oh, God, yes! I'd forgotten all about that. Shit! Remember my words, Sam? Just when you're enjoying yourself, someone or something will come along and wreck everything.

Sam: You haven't heard what she's got to say yet.

560 Hally: Public telephone?

Sam: No.

Hally: Does she sound happy or unhappy?

Sam: I couldn't tell. *(Pause.)* She's waiting, Hally.

Hally: (To the telephone.) Hello, Mom . . . No, everything is okay here. Just doing my homework. . . . What's your news? . . . You've what?

---

[26] Indian religious leader and philosopher who developed the idea of satyagraha, passive resistance (1869–1948).

. . . (Pause. He takes the receiver away from his ear for a few seconds. In the course of Hally's telephone conversation, Sam and Willie discretely position the stacked tables and chairs. Hally places the receiver back to his ear.) Yes, I'm still here. Oh, well, I give up now. Why did you do it, Mom? . . . Well, I just hope you know what you've let us in for. . . . *(Loudly.)* I said I hope you know what you've let us in for! It's the end of the peace and quiet we've been having. *(Softly.)* Where is he? *(Normal voice.)* He can't hear us from in there. But for God's sake, Mom, what happened? I told you to be firm with him. . . . Then you and the nurses should have held him down, taken his crutches away. . . . I know only too well he's my father! . . . I'm not being disrespectful, but I'm sick and tired of emptying stinking chamberpots full of phlegm and piss. . . . Yes, I do! When you're not there, he asks *me* to do it. . . . If you really want to know the truth, that's why I've got no appetite for my food. . . . Yes! There's a lot of things you don't know about. For your information, I still haven't got that science textbook I need. And you know why? He borrowed the money you gave me for it. . . . Because I didn't want to start another fight between you two. . . . He says that every time. . . . All right, Mom! *(Viciously.)* Then just remember to start hiding your bag away again, because he'll be at your purse before long for money for booze. And when he's well enough to come down here, you better keep an eye on the till as well, because that is also going to develop a leak. . . . Then don't complain to me when he starts his old tricks. . . . Yes, you do. I get it from you on one side and from him on the other, and it makes life hell for me. I'm not going to be the peacemaker anymore. I'm warning you now: when the two of you start fighting again, I'm leaving home. . . . Mom, if you start crying, I'm going to put down the receiver. . . . Okay . . . *(Lowering his voice to a vicious whisper.)* Okay, Mom. I heard you. *(Desperate.)* No. . . . Because I don't want to. I'll see him when I get home! Mom! . . . *(Pause. When he speaks again, his tone changes completely. It is not simply pretense. We sense a genuine emotional conflict.)* Welcome home, chum! . . . What's that? . . . Don't be silly, Dad. You being home is just about the best news in the world. . . . I bet you are. Bloody depressing there with everybody going on about their ailments, hey! . . . How you feeling? . . . Good . . . Here as well, pal. Coming down cats and dogs. . . . That's right. Just the day for a kip and a toss in your old Uncle Ned. . . . Everything's just hunky-dory on my side, Dad. . . . Well, to start with, there's a nice pile of comics for you on the counter. . . . Yes, old Kemple brought them in. *Batman and Robin, Submariner* . . . just your cup of tea . . . I will. . . . Yes, we'll spin a few yarns tonight. . . . Okay, chum, see you in a little while. . . . No, I promise. I'll come straight home. . . . *(Pause—his mother comes back on the phone.)* Mom? Okay. I'll lock up now. . . . What? . . . Oh, the brandy . . . Yes, I'll remember! . . . I'll put it in my suitcase now, for God's sake. I know well enough what will happen if he doesn't get

it. . . . *(Places a bottle of brandy on the counter.)* I was kind to him, Mom. I didn't say anything nasty! . . . All right. Bye. *(End of telephone conversation. A desolate Hally doesn't move. A strained silence.)*

565 **Sam:** *(Quietly.)* That sounded like a bad bump, Hally.

Hally: *(Having a hard time controlling his emotions. He speaks carefully.)* Mind your own business, Sam.

Sam: Sorry. I wasn't trying to interfere. Shall we carry on? Hally? *(He indicates the exercise book. No response from Hally.)*

Willie: *(Also trying.)* Tell him about when they give out the cups, Boet Sam.

Sam: Ja! That's another big moment. The presentation of the cups after the winners have been announced. You've got to put that in.

Still no response from Hally.

570 **Willie:** A big silver one, Master Hally, called floating trophy for the champions.

Sam: We always invite some big-shot personality to hand them over. Guest of honor this year is going to be His Holiness Bishop Jabulani of the All African Free Zionist Church.

Hally gets up abruptly, goes to his table and tears up the page he was writing on.

Hally: So much for a bloody world without collisions.

Sam: Too bad. It was on its way to being a good composition.

Hally: Let's stop bullshitting ourselves, Sam.

575 **Sam:** Have we been doing that?

Hally: Yes! That's what all our talk about a decent world has been . . . just so much bullshit.

Sam: We did say it was still only a dream.

Hally: And a bloody useless one at that. Life's a fuck-up and it's never going to change.

Sam: Ja, maybe that's true.

580 **Hally:** There's no maybe about it. It's a blunt and brutal fact. All we've done this afternoon is waste our time.

Sam: Not if we'd got your homework done.

Hally: I don't give a shit about my homework, so, for Christ's sake, just shut up about it. *(Slamming books viciously into his school case.)* Hurry up now and finish your work. I want to lock up and get out of here. *(Pause.)* And then go where? Home-sweet-fucking-home. Jesus, I hate that word.

Hally goes to the counter to put the brandy bottle and comics in his school case. After a moment's hesitation, he smashes the bottle of brandy. He abandons all further attempts to hide his feelings. Sam and Willie work away as unobtrusively as possible.

Do you want to know what is really wrong with your lovely little dream, Sam? It's not just that we are all bad dancers. That does happen to be perfectly true, but there's more to it than just that. You left out the cripples.

Sam: Hally!

Hally: *(Now totally reckless.)* Ja! Can't leave them out, Sam. That's why we always end up on our backsides on the dance floor. They're also out there dancing . . . like a bunch of broken spiders trying to do the quickstep! *(An ugly attempt at laughter.)* When you come to think of it, it's a bloody comical sight. I mean, it's bad enough on two legs . . . but one and a pair of crutches! Hell, no, Sam. That's guaranteed to turn that dance floor into a shambles. Why you shaking your head? Picture it, man. For once this afternoon let's use our imaginations sensibly.

585 Sam: Be careful, Hally.

Hally: Of what? The truth? I seem to be the only one around here who is prepared to face it. We've had the pretty dream, it's time now to wake up and have a good long look at the way things really are. Nobody knows the steps, there's no music, the cripples are also out there tripping up everybody and trying to get into the act, and it's all called the All-Comers-How-to-Make-a-Fuckup-of-Life Championships. *(Another ugly laugh.)* Hang on, Sam! The best bit is still coming. Do you know what the winner's trophy is? A beautiful big chamber-pot with roses on the side, and it's full to the brim with piss. And guess who I think is going to be this year's winner.

Sam: *(Almost shouting.)* Stop now!

Hally: *(Suddenly appalled by how far he has gone.)* Why?

Sam: Hally? It's your father you're talking about.

590 Hally: So?

Sam: Do you know what you've been saying?

Hally can't answer. He is rigid with shame. Sam speaks to him sternly.

No, Hally, you mustn't do it. Take back those words and ask for forgiveness! It's a terrible sin for a son to mock his father with jokes like that. You'll be punished if you carry on. Your father is your father, even if he is a . . . cripple man.

Willie: Yes, Master Hally. Is true what Sam say.

Sam: I understand how you are feeling, Hally, but even so . . .

Hally: No, you don't!

595 Sam: I think I do.

Hally: And I'm telling you you don't. Nobody does. *(Speaking carefully as his shame turns to rage at Sam.)* It's your turn to be careful, Sam. Very careful! You're treading on dangerous ground. Leave me and my father alone.

Sam: I'm not the one who's been saying things about him.

Hally: What goes on between me and my Dad is none of your business!

Sam: Then don't tell me about it. If that's all you've got to say about him, I don't want to hear.

For a moment Hally is at loss for a response.

600 Hally: Just get on with your bloody work and shut up.

Sam: Swearing at me won't help you.

Hally: Yes, it does! Mind your own fucking business and shut up!

Sam: Okay. If that's the way you want it, I'll stop trying.

He turns away. This infuriates Hally even more.

Hally: Good. Because what you've been trying to do is meddle in something you know nothing about. All that concerns you in here, Sam, is to try and do what you get paid for—keep the place clean and serve the customers. In plain words, just get on with your job. My mother is right. She's always warning me about allowing you to get too familiar. Well, this time you've gone too far. It's going to stop right now.

No response from Sam.

You're only a servant in here, and don't forget it.

Still no response. Hally is trying hard to get one.

And as far as my father is concerned, all you need to remember is that he is your boss.

605 Sam: *(Needled at last.)* No, he isn't. I get paid by your mother.

Hally: Don't argue with me, Sam!

Sam: Then don't say he's my boss.

Hally: He's a white man and that's good enough for you.

Sam: I'll try to forget you said that.

610 Hally: Don't! Because you won't be doing me a favor if you do. I'm telling you to remember it.

A pause. Sam pulls himself together and makes one last effort.

Sam: Hally, Hally . . . ! Come on now. Let's stop before it's too late. You're right. We *are* on dangerous ground. If we're not careful, somebody is going to get hurt.

Hally: It won't be me.

Sam: Don't be so sure.

Hally: I don't know what you're talking about, Sam.

615 Sam: Yes, you do.

Hally: *(Furious.)* Jesus, I wish you would stop trying to tell me what I do and what I don't know.

Sam gives up. He turns to Willie.

Sam: Let's finish up.

Hally: Don't turn your back on me! I haven't finished talking.

He grabs Sam by the arm and tries to make him turn around. Sam reacts with a flash of anger.

Sam: Don't do that, Hally! *(Facing the boy.)* All right, I'm listening. Well? What do you want to say to me?

620 Hally: *(Pause as Hally looks for something to say.)* To begin with, why don't you also start calling me Master Harold, like Willie.

Sam: Do you mean that?

Hally: Why the hell do you think I said it?

Sam: And if I don't.

Hally: You might just lose your job.

625 Sam: *(Quietly and very carefully.)* If you make me say it once, I'll never call you anything else again.

Hally: So? *(The boy confronts the man.)* Is that meant to be a threat?

Sam: Just telling you what will happen if you make me do that. You must decide what it means to you.

Hally: Well, I have. It's good news. Because that is exactly what Master Harold wants from now on. Think of it as a little lesson in respect, Sam, that's long overdue, and I hope you remember it as well as you do your geography. I can tell you now that somebody who will be glad to hear I've finally given it to you will be my Dad. Yes! He agrees with my Mom. He's always going on about it as well. "You must teach the boys to show you more respect, my son."

Sam: So now you can stop complaining about going home. Everybody is going to be happy tonight.

630 Hally: That's perfectly correct. You see, you mustn't get the wrong idea about me and my Dad, Sam. We also have our good times together. Some bloody good laughs. He's got a marvelous sense of humor. Want to know what our favorite joke is? He gives out a big groan, you see, and says: "It's not fair, is it, Hally?" Then I have to ask: "What, chum?" And then he says: "A nigger's arse" . . . and we both have a good laugh.

The men stare at him with disbelief.

What's the matter, Willie? Don't you catch the joke? You always were a bit slow on the uptake. It's what is called a pun. You see, fair means both light in color and to be just and decent. *(He turns to Sam.)* I thought *you* would catch it, Sam.

Sam: Oh ja, I catch it all right.

Hally: But it doesn't appeal to your sense of humor.

Sam: Do you really laugh?

Hally: Of course.

635 Sam: To please him? Make him feel good?

Hally: No, for heaven's sake! I laugh because I think it's a bloody good joke.

Sam: You're really trying hard to be ugly, aren't you? And why drag poor old Willie into it? He's done nothing to you except show you the respect you want so badly. That's also not being fair, you know . . . and *I* mean just or decent.

Willie: It's all right, Sam. Leave it now.

Sam: It's me you're after. You should just have said "Sam's arse" . . . because that's the one you're trying to kick. Anyway, how do you know it's not fair? You've never seen it. Do you want to? *(He drops his trousers and underpants and presents his backside for Hally's inspection.)* Have a good look. A real Basuto[27] arse . . . which is about as nigger as they can

---

[27] A person from Basutoland, South Africa.

come. Satisfied? *(Trousers up.)* Now you can make your Dad even happier when you go home tonight. Tell him I showed you my arse and he is quite right. It's not fair. And if it will give him an even better laugh next time, I'll also let *him* have a look. Come, Willie, let's finish up and go.

Sam and Willie start to tidy up the tea room. Hally doesn't move. He waits for a moment when Sam passes him.

640 **Hally:** *(Quietly.)* Sam . . .

Sam stops and looks expectantly at the boy. Hally spits in his face. A long and heartfelt groan from Willie. For a few seconds Sam doesn't move.

Sam: *(Taking out a handkerchief and wiping his face.)* It's all right, Willie.

To Hally.

Ja, well, you've done it . . . Master Harold. Yes, I'll start calling you that from now on. It won't be difficult anymore. You've hurt yourself, Master Harold. I saw it coming. I warned you, but you wouldn't listen. You've just hurt yourself *bad.* And you're a coward, Master Harold. The face you should be spitting in is your father's . . . but you used mine, because you think you're safe inside your fair skin . . . and this time I don't mean just or decent. *(Pause, then moving violently towards Hally.)* Should I hit him, Willie?
Willie: *(Stopping Sam.)* No, Boet Sam.
Sam: *(Violently.)* Why not?
Willie: It won't help, Boet Sam.
645 **Sam:** I don't want to help! I want to hurt him.
Willie: You also hurt yourself.
Sam: And if he had done it to you, Willie?
Willie: Me? Spit at me like I was a dog? *(A thought that had not occurred to him before. He looks at Hally.)* Ja. Then I want to hit him. I want to hit him hard!

A dangerous few seconds as the men stand staring at the boy. Willie turns away, shaking his head.

But maybe all I do is go cry at the back. He's little boy, Boet Sam. Little *white* boy. Long trousers now, but he's still little boy.
Sam: *(His violence ebbing away into defeat as quickly as it flooded.)* You're right. So go on, then: groan again, Willie. You do it better than me. *(To Hally.)* You don't know all of what you've just done . . . Master Harold. It's not just that you've made me feel dirtier than I've ever been in my life . . . I mean, how do I wash off yours and your father's filth? . . . I've also failed. A long time ago I promised myself I was going to try and do something, but you've just shown me . . . Master Harold . . . that I've failed. *(Pause.)* I've also got a memory of a little white boy when he was still wearing short trousers and a black man, but they're not flying a kite. It was the old Jubilee days, after dinner one night. I was in

my room. You came in and just stood against the wall, looking down at the ground, and only after I'd asked you what you wanted, what was wrong, I don't know how many times, did you speak and even then so softly I almost didn't hear you. "Sam, please help me to go and fetch my Dad." Remember? He was dead drunk on the floor of the Central Hotel Bar. They'd phoned for your Mom, but you were the only one at home. And do you remember how we did it? You went in first by yourself to ask permission for me to go into the bar. Then I loaded him onto my back like a baby and carried him back to the boarding house with you following behind carrying his crutches. *(Shaking his head as he remembers.)* A crowded Main Street with all the people watching a little white boy following his drunk father on a nigger's back! I felt for that little boy . . . Master Harold. I felt for him. After that we still had to clean him up, remember? He'd messed in his trousers, so we had to clean him up and get him into bed.

650 **Hally:** *(Great pain.)* I love him, Sam.

Sam: I know you do. That's why I tried to stop you from saying these things about him. It would have been so simple if you could have just despised him for being a weak man. But he's your father. You love him and you're ashamed of him. You're ashamed of so much! . . . And now that's going to include yourself. That was the promise I made to myself: to try and stop that happening. *(Pause.)* After we got him to bed you came back with me to my room and sat in a corner and carried on just looking down at the ground. And for days after that! You hadn't done anything wrong, but you went around as if you owed the world an apology for being alive. I didn't like seeing that! That's not the way a boy grows up to be a man! . . . But the one person who should have been teaching you what that means was the cause of your shame. If you really want to know, that's why I made you that kite. I wanted you to look up, be proud of something, of yourself . . . *(Bitter smile at the memory.)* . . . and you certainly were that when I left you with it up there on the hill. Oh, ja . . . something else! . . . If you ever do write it as a short story, there *was* a twist in our ending. I couldn't sit down there and stay with you. It was a "Whites Only" bench. You were too young, too excited to notice then. But not anymore. If you're not careful . . . Master Harold . . . you're going to be sitting up there by yourself for a long time to come, and there won't be a kite in the sky. *(Sam has got nothing more to say. He exits into the kitchen, taking off his waiter's jacket.)*

Willie: Is bad. Is all all bad in here now.

Hally: *(Books into his school case, raincoat on.)* Willie . . . *(It is difficult to speak.)* Will you lock up for me and look after the keys?

Willie: Okay.

Sam returns. Hally goes behind the counter and collects the few coins in the cash register. As he starts to leave . . .

655 **Sam:** Don't forget the comic books.

Hally returns to the counter and puts them in his case. He starts to leave again.

Sam: *(To the retreating back of the boy.)* Stop . . . Hally . . .

Hally stops, but doesn't turn to face him.

Hally . . . I've got no right to tell you what being a man means if I don't behave like one myself, and I'm not doing so well at that this afternoon. Should we try again, Hally?

Hally: Try what?

Sam: Fly another kite, I suppose. It worked once, and this time I need it as much as you do.

Hally: It's still raining, Sam. You can't fly kites on rainy days, remember.

660 Sam: So what do we do? Hope for better weather tomorrow?

Hally: *(Helpless gesture.)* I don't know. I don't know anything anymore.

Sam: You sure of that, Hally? Because it would be pretty hopeless if that was true. It would mean nothing has been learnt in here this afternoon, and there was a hell of a lot of teaching going on . . . one way or the other. But anyway, I don't believe you. I reckon there's one thing you know. You don't *have* to sit up there by yourself. You know what that bench means now, and you can leave it any time you choose. All you've got to do is stand up and walk away from it.

Hally leaves. Willie goes up quietly to Sam.

Willie: Is okay, Boet Sam. You see. Is . . . *(He can't find any better words.)* . . . is going to be okay tomorrow. *(Changing his tone.)* Hey, Boet Sam! *(He is trying hard.)* You right. I think about it and you right. Tonight I find Hilda and say sorry. And make promise I won't beat her no more. You hear me, Boet Sam?

Sam: I hear you, Willie.

665 Willie: And when we practice I relax and romance with her from beginning to end. Non-stop! You watch! Two weeks' time: "First prize for promising newcomers: Mr. Willie Malopo and Miss Hilda Samuels." *(Sudden impulse.)* To hell with it! I walk home. *(He goes to the jukebox, puts in a coin and selects a record. The machine comes to life in the gray twilight, blushing its way through a spectrum of soft, romantic colors.)* How did you say it, Boet Sam? Let's dream. *(Willie sways with the music and gestures for Sam to dance.)*

Sarah Vaughan sings.

> "Little man you're crying,
> I know why you're blue,
> Someone took your kiddy car away;
> Better go to sleep now,
> Little man you've had a busy day." *(etc. etc.)*
>   You lead. I follow.

The men dance together.

"Johnny won your marbles,
Tell you what we'll do;
Dad will get you new ones
right away;
Better go to sleep now,
Little man you've had a
busy day."

■ **EXPLORATIONS OF THE TEXT** ■

1. Describe the characters in the initial scene. What does the dancing symbolize? What is the nature of the relationship between Sam and Willie before Hally enters?
2. Describe Hally. How does his relationship with his father affect him? Analyze his attitudes toward Willie and Sam.
3. To what extent are the relationships in this play determined by South African history, culture, economics, and politics?
4. Why is Hally so pessimistic? Explain: "It's a bloody awful world when you come to think of it. People can be real bastards."
5. Explore the discussion of history, "magnitude," and social reformers. What does it reveal about Hally? about Sam?
6. What does the kite symbolize? How does Hally describe the event? Why does Sam not give a true answer to Hally's question, "Why did you make that kite, Sam?"
7. Why does Hally long to be in the Jubilee again? Why did life "[feel] the right size in there"?
8. What can be inferred from the first telephone conversation? What is Hally's attitude toward his father's returning home from the hospital? How does it affect his attitude about life?
9. Why does Sam believe that ballroom dancing is an art? Why does Hally choose to write about the contest? Is the scene **ironic**?
10. Consider the line: "There's no collisions out there, Hally." What are the big collisions?
11. What does dreaming represent to Sam?
12. Why does Hally not finish his composition on "A World Without Collisions"?
13. Examine the second telephone conversation. Why does Hally say, "Life's a fuck-up and it's never going to change"?
14. Why do "the cripples" trip everyone else? Why does Sam warn Hally to be careful about mocking his father? Why does Hally warn Sam?
15. Why does Hally insult Sam and Willie? Why does Hally insist on being called "Master Harold"?
16. Why does Hally spit in Sam's face? Why does Sam retort, "The face you should be spitting in is your father's"?

17. Discuss the incident in the Central Hotel Bar.
18. Why did Sam build the kite? Why did he want Hally or "Master Harold" not to be ashamed?
19. Will Hally leave "the bench" now that he knows what it means?
20. Discuss the relationships of the characters at the end of the play. Look carefully at the title and the punctuation in the title.
21. Fugard wrote in his notebook about a moment in his childhood that led him to spit in Sam's face. After this action, Fugard stated that he was "overwhelmed" with "shame." Consider this personal revelation in relation to the play and to works by Walcott, by King, and by Gordimer.

■■ Journal Entries ■■

1. Write an entry in the voice of Hally, Sam, or Willie.
2. Respond to the final incident.
3. What is Willie's function in the play?

■■■ Ideas for Writing ■■■

1. Describe Sam as a spiritual father or as a mentor.
2. Discuss power and powerlessness in the play. Refer to Gordimer and to Mandela in Chapter 7.
3. Write a character analysis of Sam or Hally.
4. Analyze the structure of the play. Why are there no scenes or acts?

I Have a Dream

Martin Luther King, Jr.

Martin Luther King, Jr. (1929–1968) was born in Atlanta, Georgia. He entered the ministry as had his father and grandfather and received his doctorate in theology from Boston University in 1955.

In 1954, King became pastor of the Dexter Avenue Baptist Church in Montgomery, Alabama and came to public attention a year later as the leader of a small group of civil rights workers who boycotted the Montgomery transit system after the arrest of Rosa Parks for violation of the city's segregation law. In 1956, the buses were desegregated.

As the founder and director of the Southern Christian Leadership Conference, King actively lectured for the cause of civil rights throughout the United States and abroad, where he consulted with religious leaders and heads of state. At this time, he became convinced that Mohandas Gandhi's policy of nonviolent resistance was the best way for oppressed groups to achieve freedom and equality.

He worked unceasingly for civil rights and was arrested fourteen times for his participation in nonviolent protests and sit-ins. In August 1963, King joined other civil rights leaders to organize a March on Washington, an interracial demonstration of more than 200,000 people gathered at the Lincoln Memorial, to demand equality for all citizens. King was a prolific and fluent writer. Some of his most important books are Stride Through Freedom: The Montgomery Story *(1958),* Why We Can't Wait *(1964), and* Where Do We Go From Here: Chaos or Community? *(1967).*

With the passage of the Civil Rights Act of 1964, King's work for human rights and dignity was recognized throughout the world; in that same year, he was awarded the Nobel Peace Prize for his contributions to racial harmony and for his advocacy of nonviolent response to aggression. He was assassinated in Memphis, Tennessee, in 1968.

King delivered his famous "I Have a Dream" speech at the Lincoln Memorial during the March on Washington. On this occasion, he articulated his dream of equality for all people in passionate, eloquent, and unforgettable terms.

1 I am happy to join with you today in what will go down in history as the greatest demonstration for freedom in the history of our nation.

Five score years ago, a great American, in whose symbolic shadow we stand today, signed the Emancipation Proclamation. This momentous decree came as a great beacon light of hope to millions of Negro slaves who had been seared in the flames of withering injustice. It came as a joyous daybreak to end the long night of their captivity.

But one hundred years later, the Negro still is not free; one hundred years later, the life of the Negro is still sadly crippled by the manacles of segregation and the chains of discrimination; one hundred years later, the Negro lives on a lonely island of poverty in the midst of a vast ocean of material prosperity; one hundred years later, the Negro is still languished in the corners of American society and finds himself in exile in his own land.

So we've come here today to dramatize a shameful condition. In a sense we've come to our nation's capital to cash a check. When the architects of our republic wrote the magnificent words of the Constitution and the Declaration of Independence, they were signing a promissory note to which every American was to fall heir. This note was the promise that all men, yes, black men as well as white men, would be guaranteed the unalienable rights of life, liberty, and the pursuit of happiness.

5 It is obvious today that America has defaulted on this promissory note in so far as her citizens of color are concerned. Instead of honoring this sacred

obligation, America has given the Negro people a bad check, a check which has come back marked "insufficient funds." But we refuse to believe that the bank of justice is bankrupt. We refuse to believe that there are insufficient funds in the great vaults of opportunity of this nation. And so we've come to cash this check, a check that will give us upon demand the riches of freedom and the security of justice.

We have also come to this hallowed spot to remind America of the fierce urgency of now. This is no time to engage in the luxury of cooling off or to take the tranquilizing drug of gradualism. Now is the time to make real the promises of democracy; now is the time to rise from the dark and desolate valley of segregation to the sunlit path of racial justice; now is the time to lift our nation from the quicksands of racial injustice to the solid rock of brotherhood; now is the time to make justice a reality for all of God's children. It would be fatal for the nation to overlook the urgency of the moment. This sweltering summer of the Negro's legitimate discontent will not pass until there is an invigorating autumn of freedom and equality.

Nineteen sixty-three is not an end, but a beginning. And those who hope that the Negro needed to blow off steam and will now be content, will have a rude awakening if the nation returns to business as usual. There will be neither rest nor tranquility in America until the Negro is granted his citizenship rights. The whirlwinds of revolt will continue to shake the foundations of our nation until the bright day of justice emerges.

But there is something that I must say to my people, who stand on the worn threshold which leads into the palace of justice. In the process of gaining our rightful place, we must not be guilty of wrongful deeds. Let us not seek to satisfy our thirst for freedom by drinking from the cup of bitterness and hatred. We must forever conduct our struggle on the high plain of dignity and discipline. We must not allow our creative protests to degenerate into physical violence. Again and again we must rise to the majestic heights of meeting physical force with soul force. The marvelous new militancy, which has engulfed the Negro community, must not lead us to a distrust of all white people. For many of our white brothers, as evidenced by their presence here today, have come to realize that their destiny is tied up with our destiny. And they have come to realize that their freedom is inextricably bound to our freedom. We cannot walk alone. And as we walk, we must make the pledge that we shall always march ahead. We cannot turn back.

There are those who are asking the devotees of Civil Rights, "When will you be satisfied?" We can never be satisfied as long as the Negro is the victim of the unspeakable horrors of police brutality; we can never be satisfied as long as our bodies, heavy with the fatigue of travel, cannot gain lodging in the motels of the highways and the hotels of the cities; we cannot be satisfied as long as the Negro's basic mobility is from a smaller ghetto to a larger one; we can never be satisfied as long as our children are stripped of their selfhood and robbed of their dignity by signs saying "For Whites Only"; we cannot be satisfied as long as the Negro in Mississippi cannot vote and a Negro in New York believes he has nothing for which to vote. No! No, we are not satisfied, and we will not be satisfied until "justice rolls down like waters and right-eousness like a mighty stream."

10   I am not unmindful that some of you have come here out of great trials and tribulations. Some of you have come fresh from narrow jail cells. Some of you have come from areas where your quest for freedom left you battered by the storms of persecution and staggered by the winds of police brutality. You have been the veterans of creative suffering. Continue to work with the faith that unearned suffering is redemptive. Go back to Mississippi. Go back to Alabama. Go back to South Carolina. Go back to Georgia. Go back to Louisiana. Go back to the slums and ghettos of our Northern cities, knowing that somehow this situation can and will be changed. Let us not wallow in the valley of despair.

I say to you today, my friends, so even though we face the difficulties of today and tomorrow, I still have a dream. It is a dream deeply rooted in the American dream. I have a dream that one day this nation will rise up and live out the true meaning of its creed, "We hold these truths to be self-evident, that all men are created equal." I have a dream that one day on the red hills of Georgia, sons of former slaves and the sons of former slave owners will be able to sit down together at the table of brotherhood. I have a dream that one day even the state of Mississippi, a state sweltering with the heat of injustice, sweltering with the heat of oppression, will be transformed into an oasis of freedom and justice. I have a dream that my four little children will one day live in a nation where they will not be judged by the color of their skin, but by the content of their character.

12   I HAVE A DREAM TODAY!

I have a dream that one day down in Alabama—with its vicious racists, with its Governor having his lips dripping with the words of interposition and nullification—one day right there in Alabama, little black boys and black girls will be able to join hands with little white boys and white girls as sisters and brothers.

I HAVE A DREAM TODAY!

15   I have a dream that one day every valley shall be exalted, and every hill and mountain shall be made low. The rough places will be plain and the crooked places will be made straight, "and the glory of the Lord shall be re-vealed, and all flesh shall see it together."

This is our hope. This is the faith that I go back to the South with. With this faith we will be able to hew out of the mountain of despair a stone of hope. With this faith we will be able to transform the jangling discords of our nation into a beautiful symphony of brother-hood. With this faith we will be able to work together, to pray together, to struggle together, to go to jail to-gether, to stand up for freedom together, knowing that we will be free one day. And this will be the day. This will be the day when all of God's children will be able to sing with new meaning, "My country 'tis of thee, sweet land of liberty, of thee I sing. Land where my father died, land of the pilgrim's pride, from every mountainside, let freedom ring." And if America is to be a great nation, this must become true.

So let freedom ring from the prodigious hilltops of New Hampshire; let freedom ring from the mighty mountains of New York; let freedom ring from the heightening Alleghenies of Pennsylvania; let freedom ring from the snow-capped Rockies of Colorado; let freedom ring from the curvaceous slopes of California. But not only that. Let freedom ring from Stone Mountain of Georgia; let freedom ring from Lookout Mountain of Tennessee; let freedom ring from every hill and mole hill of Mississippi. "From every mountainside, let freedom ring." And when this happens, and when we allow freedom to ring, when we let it ring from every village and every hamlet, from every state and every city, we will be able to speed up that day when all of God's children, black men and white men, Jews and Gentiles, Protestants and Catholics, will be able to join hands and sing in the words of the old Negro spiritual: "Free at last. Free at last. Thank God Almighty, we are free at last."

■ EXPLORATIONS OF THE TEXT ■

1. What are the occasion and the situation? Why does King allude to Lincoln and to the Emancipation Proclamation?
2. Explain the images of the "promissory note" and the "check."
3. What is the "fierce urgency of now"? Why is 1963 "not an end, but a beginning"? Why does King mention "whirlwinds of revolt"?
4. Why does King argue that "physical force" must be met with "soul force"? Why does he ask that "the new militancy" include whites? Who is his audience?
5. Analyze paragraphs 11 to 15. What is the nature of King's "dream"? How does it relate to the American dream?
6. How does paragraph 15 differ from King's other statements about his dream?
7. Is the closing effective? Why does King quote "My country 'tis of thee" and the spiritual?
8. Analyze rhetorical elements in the speech (imagery, allusion, repetition, parallelism, tone).
9. Compare this speech to King's "Letter from the Birmingham Jail" (Chapter 12) and to Mandela's "I Am Prepared to Die" (Chapter 8).

■■ JOURNAL ENTRIES ■■

1. Write a response to this speech or a double-entry journal about it.
2. Gloss and annotate the sections concerning the dream.

■■■ IDEAS FOR WRITING ■■■

1. Argue in support or in disagreement with King's position.
2. What changes in civil rights have happened since 1963? Has King's dream come true?
3. Compare this speech with another work in this chapter, such as "Black Elk's Great Vision" or Anzaldúa's "To live in the Borderlands means you."
4. Construct a dream for the millennium.
5. Consider: "The ability to conceive the position of another creates the possibility for harmony." Discuss this ideal of harmony in King's speech, Fugard's play, Gordimer's story, and Walcott's poem.
6. Violence is necessary for social change. Agree or disagree.
7. If you have seen news film of King's speech, write about the differences between the spoken and written word.

FICTION

Harrison Bergeron

Kurt Vonnegut, Jr.

Born in Indianapolis, Indiana, Kurt Vonnegut, Jr. (1922–) enlisted in the army in World War II and was captured by the Germans in 1944. He survived the fire bombing of Dresden in which more civilians perished than in the atomic bomb explosions in both Hiroshima and Nagasaki. He and his fellow prisoners were given the task of searching for corpses in the aftermath of the destruction. This experience was the source of one of his novels, Slaughterhouse Five, *published in 1969. His other novels include* The Sirens of Titan *(1959),* Cat's Cradle *(1963),* God Bless You, Mr. Rosewater *(1965),* Breakfast of Champions *(1973),* Slapstick *(1976),* Jailbird *(1979),* Dead-Eye Dick *(1982),* Galapagos *(1985),* Bluebeard *(1987), and* Hocus Pocus *(1990). His short stories are collected in* Canary in a Cathouse *(1961) and* Welcome to the Monkey House *(1968).*

In "Harrison Bergeron," Vonnegut creates a nightmarish view of a North American world in 2081—a world in which total equality leads to complete conformity. Being average is enforced as the highest good.

1 The year was 2081, and everybody was finally equal. They weren't only equal before God and the law. They were equal every which way. Nobody was smarter than anybody else. Nobody was better looking than anybody else. Nobody was stronger or quicker than anybody else. All this equality was due to the 211th, 212th, and 213th Amendments to the Constitution, and to the unceasing vigilance of agents of the United States Handicapper General.

Some things about living still weren't quite right, though. April, for instance, still drove people crazy by not being springtime. And it was in that clammy month that the H-G men took George and Hazel Bergeron's fourteen-year-old son, Harrison, away.

It was tragic, all right, but George and Hazel couldn't think about it very hard. Hazel had a perfectly average intelligence, which meant she couldn't think about anything except in short bursts. And George, while his intelligence was way above normal, had a little mental handicap radio in his ear. He was required by law to wear it at all times. It was tuned to a government transmitter. Every twenty seconds or so, the transmitter would send out some sharp noise to keep people like George from taking unfair advantage of their brains.

George and Hazel were watching television. There were tears on Hazel's cheeks, but she'd forgotten for the moment what they were about.

5   On the television screen were ballerinas.

A buzzer sounded in George's head. His thoughts fled in panic, like bandits from a burglar alarm.

"That was a real pretty dance, that dance they just did," said Hazel.

"Huh?" said George.

"That dance—it was nice," said Hazel.

10   "Yup," said George. He tried to think a little about the ballerinas. They weren't really very good—no better than anybody else would have been, anyway. They were burdened with sashweights and bags of birdshot, and their faces were masked, so that no one, seeing a free and graceful gesture or a pretty face, would feel like something the cat drug in. George was toying with the vague notion that maybe dancers shouldn't be handicapped. But he didn't get very far with it before another noise in his ear radio scattered his thoughts.

George winced. So did two out of the eight ballerinas.

Hazel saw him wince. Having no mental handicap herself, she had to ask George what the latest sound had been.

"Sounded like somebody hitting a milk bottle with a ball peen hammer," said George.

"I'd think it would be real interesting, hearing all the different sounds," said Hazel, a little envious. "All the things they think up."

15   "Um," said George.

"Only, if I was Handicapper General, you know what I would do?" said Hazel. Hazel, as a matter of fact, bore a strong resemblance to the Handicapper General, a woman named Diana Moon Glampers. "If I was Diana Moon Glampers," said Hazel, "I'd have chimes on Sunday—just chimes. Kind of in honor of religion."

"I could think, if it was just chimes," said George.

"Well—maybe make 'em real loud," said Hazel. "I think I'd make a good Handicapper General."

"Good as anybody else," said George.

20   "Who knows better'n I do what normal is?" said Hazel.

"Right," said George. He began to think glimmeringly about his abnormal son who was now in jail, about Harrison, but a twenty-one-gun salute in his head stopped that.

"Boy!" said Hazel, "that was a doozy, wasn't it?"

It was such a doozy that George was white and trembling, and tears stood on the rims of his red eyes. Two of the eight ballerinas had collapsed to the studio floor, were holding their temples.

"All of a sudden you look so tired," said Hazel. "Why don't you stretch out on the sofa, so's you can rest your handicap bag on the pillows, honeybunch." She was referring to the forty-seven pounds of birdshot in a canvas bag, which was padlocked around George's neck. "Go on and rest the bag for a little while," she said. "I don't care if you're not equal to me for a while."

25   George weighed the bag with his hands. "I don't mind it," he said. "I don't notice it any more. It's just a part of me."

"You been so tired lately—kind of wore out," said Hazel. "If there was just some way we could make a little hole in the bottom of the bag, and just take out a few of them lead balls. Just a few."

"Two years in prison and two thousand dollars fine for every ball I took out," said George. "I don't call that a bargain."

"If you could just take a few out when you came home from work," said Hazel. "I mean—you don't compete with anybody around here. You just set around."

"If I tried to get away with it," said George, "then other people'd get away with it—and pretty soon we'd be right back to the dark ages again, with everybody competing against everybody else. You wouldn't like that, would you?"

30   "I'd hate it," said Hazel.

"There you are," said George. "The minute people start cheating on laws, what do you think happens to society?"

If Hazel hadn't been able to come up with an answer to this question, George couldn't have supplied one. A siren was going off in his head.

"Reckon it'd fall all apart," said Hazel.

"What would?" said George blankly.

35   "Society," said Hazel uncertainly. "Wasn't that what you just said?"

"Who knows?" said George.

The television program was suddenly interrupted for a news bulletin. It wasn't clear at first as to what the bulletin was about, since the announcer, like all announcers, had a serious speech impediment. For about half a minute, and in a state of high excitement, the announcer tried to say, "Ladies and gentlemen—"

He finally gave up, handed the bulletin to a ballerina to read.

"That's all right—" Hazel said of the announcer, "he tried. That's the big thing. He tried to do the best he could with what God gave him. He should get a nice raise for trying so hard."

40   "Ladies and gentlemen—" said the ballerina, reading the bulletin. She must have been extraordinarily beautiful, because the mask she wore was hideous. And it was easy to see that she was the strongest and most graceful of all the dancers, for her handicap bags were as big as those worn by two-hundred-pound men.

And she had to apologize at once for her voice, which was a very unfair voice for a woman to use. Her voice was a warm, luminous, timeless melody. "Excuse me—" she said, and she began again, making her voice absolutely uncompetitive.

"Harrison Bergeron, age fourteen," she said in a grackle squawk, "has just escaped from jail, where he was held on suspicion of plotting to overthrow the government. He is a genius and an athlete, is under-handicapped, and should be regarded as extremely dangerous."

A police photograph of Harrison Bergeron was flashed on the screen upside down, then sideways, upside down again, then right side up. The picture showed the full length of Harrison against a background calibrated in feet and inches. He was exactly seven feet tall.

The rest of Harrison's appearance was Halloween and hardware. Nobody had ever borne heavier handicaps. He had outgrown hindrances faster than the H-G men could think them up. Instead of a little ear radio for a mental handicap, he wore a tremendous pair of earphones, and spectacles with thick wavy lenses. The spectacles were intended to make him not only half blind, but to give him whanging headaches besides.

45 Scrap metal was hung all over him. Ordinarily, there was a certain symmetry, a military neatness to the handicaps issued to strong people, but Harrison looked like a walking junkyard. In the race of life, Harrison carried three hundred pounds.

And to offset his good looks, the H-G men required that he wear at all times a red rubber ball for a nose, keep his eyebrows shaved off, and cover his even white teeth with black caps at snaggle-tooth random.

"If you see this boy," said the ballerina, "do not—I repeat, do not—try to reason with him."

There was the shriek of a door being torn from its hinges.

Screams and barking cries of consternation came from the television set. The photograph of Harrison Bergeron on the screen jumped again and again, as though dancing to the tune of an earthquake.

50 George Bergeron correctly identified the earthquake, and well he might have—for many was the time his own home had danced to the same crashing tune. "My God—" said George, "that must be Harrison!"

The realization was blasted from his mind instantly by the sound of an automobile collision in his head.

When George could open his eyes again, the photograph of Harrison was gone. A living, breathing Harrison filled the screen.

Clanking, clownish, and huge, Harrison stood in the center of the studio. The knob of the uprooted studio door was still in his hand. Ballerinas, technicians, musicians, and announcers cowered on their knees before him, expecting to die.

"I am the Emperor!" cried Harrison. "Do you hear? I am the Emperor! Everybody must do what I say at once!" He stamped his foot and the studio shook.

55 "Even as I stand here—" he bellowed, "crippled, hobbled, sickened—I am a greater ruler than any man who ever lived! Now watch me become what I *can* become!"

Harrison tore the straps of his handicap harness like wet tissue paper, tore straps guaranteed to support five thousand pounds.

Harrison's scrap-iron handicaps crashed to the floor.

Harrison thrust his thumbs under the bar of the padlock that secured his head harness. The bar snapped like celery. Harrison smashed his headphones and spectacles against the wall.

He flung away his rubber-ball nose, revealed a man that would have awed Thor, the god of thunder.

60   "I shall now select my Empress!" he said, looking down on the cowering people. "Let the first woman who dares rise to her feet claim her mate and her throne!"

    A moment passed, and then a ballerina arose, swaying like a willow.

    Harrison plucked the mental handicap from her ear, snapped off her physical handicaps with marvelous delicacy. Last of all, he removed her mask.

    She was blindingly beautiful.

    "Now—" said Harrison, taking her hand, "shall we show the people the meaning of the word dance? Music!" he commanded.

65   The musicians scrambled back into their chairs, and Harrison stripped them of their handicaps, too. "Play your best," he told them, "and I'll make you barons and dukes and earls."

    The music began. It was normal at first—cheap, silly, false. But Harrison snatched two musicians from their chairs, waved them like batons as he sang the music as he wanted it played. He slammed them back into their chairs.

    The music began again and was much improved.

    Harrison and his Empress merely listened to the music for a while— listened gravely, as though synchronizing their heartbeats with it.

    They shifted their weights to their toes.

70   Harrison placed his big hands on the girl's tiny waist, letting her sense the weightlessness that would soon be hers.

    And then, in an explosion of joy and grace, into the air they sprang!

    Not only were the laws of the land abandoned, but the law of gravity and the laws of motion as well.

    They reeled, whirled, swiveled, flounced, capered, gamboled, and spun.

    They leaped like deer on the moon.

75   The studio ceiling was thirty feet high, but each leap brought the dancers nearer to it.

    It became their obvious intention to kiss the ceiling.

    They kissed it.

    And then, neutralizing gravity with love and pure will, they remained suspended in air inches below the ceiling, and they kissed each other for a long, long time.

    It was then that Diana Moon Glampers, the Handicapper General, came into the studio with a double-barreled ten-gauge shotgun. She fired twice, and the Emperor and the Empress were dead before they hit the floor.

80   Diana Moon Glampers loaded the gun again. She aimed it at the musicians and told them they had ten seconds to get their handicaps back on.

    It was then that the Bergerons' television tube burned out.

    Hazel turned to comment about the blackout to George. But George had gone out into the kitchen for a can of beer.

    George came back in with the beer, paused while a handicap signal shook him up. And then he sat down again. "You been crying?" he said to Hazel.

    "Yup," she said.

85   "What about?" he said.

    "I forget," she said. "Something real sad on television."

"What was it?" he said.

"It's all kind of mixed up in my mind," said Hazel.

"Forget sad things," said George.

90 "I always do," said Hazel.

"That's my girl," said George. He winced. There was the sound of a riveting gun in his head.

"Gee—I could tell that one was a doozy," said Hazel.

"You can say that again," said George.

"Gee—" said Hazel, "I could tell that one was a doozy."

■ EXPLORATIONS OF THE TEXT ■

---

1. React to the first paragraph. What associations does the concept of "equality" evoke?
2. Why do people in the story have "handicaps"?
3. Contrast Hazel and George. Why does George's "mental handicap radio" make noise?
4. Analyze Harrison's appearance, character, behavior, and rebellion. Why is he depicted as a fourteen-year-old? Why is Harrison dangerous?
5. Explain the conclusion of the story. Is it **ironic**?
6. Evaluate the **satire** and humor in the story.
7. Why does Vonnegut create a series of short paragraphs to depict Harrison's and the ballerina's dance? What is the effect of this technique?
8. Discuss the world of 2081. What are its collective values? In what ways does Vonnegut criticize North American society and its values?

■■ JOURNAL ENTRIES ■■

---

1. React to Vonnegut's vision of equality.
2. Begin a journal entry: "It was 2081 and. . . ." Freewrite. (Imagine that you are a character in a place. Begin writing.)
3. Write a monologue in Diana Glampers' or in Harrison's voice.

■■■ IDEAS FOR WRITING ■■■

---

1. What critique of North American society is presented?
2. Compare this story's view of individuality with the view of identity in "To live in the Borderlands means you."
3. What is lost in this society?

The Imagination of Disaster

Mary Gordon

*Born on Long Island, Mary Gordon (1950–   ) has written four nov-
els:* Final Payments *(1978),* The Company of Women *(1980),* Men
and Angels *(1985), and* The Other Side *(1989). Her collection of
short stories,* Temporary Shelter *(1987), and her volume of nonfiction,* Dead Girls and Bad Boys and Other Essays *(1991), were published by Viking Press. Her most recent work, a series of novellas,*
The Rest of Life, *appeared in 1993. Winner of the Kafka Prize for
fiction, she currently holds the McIntosh Chair as Professor of English at Barnard College.*

*In her writing she probes the Irish Catholic world of her child-
hood in Queens and attributes her gift for language both to her father who was a great storyteller and to her mother who taught her
to listen to the words of women. "My subject as a writer has far more
to do with family happiness than with the music of the spheres. I
don't know what the nature of the universe is, but I have a good ear.
What it hears best are daily rhythms, for that is what I value, what
I wish to preserve. My father would have thought this a stubborn
predilection for the minor. My mother knows better." In Gordon's
work the reader discovers a rare combination of voice, of the power
of observation, and of moral imagination.*

*In this story, the speaker contemplates the "unimaginable": the
aftermath of a nuclear holocaust and its effects upon her and her
family.*

1   I am aware of my own inadequacies, of course, but if this happens, no one
will be adequate: to be adequate requires a prior act of the imagination,
and this is impossible. We are armed; they are armed; someone will take the
terrible, the unimaginable, vengeful step. And so we think in images of all
that we have known to be the worst. We think of cold, of heat, of heaviness.
But that is not it; that does not begin to be it. A mother thinks: how will I
carry my children, what will I feed them? But this is not it, this is not it.
There will be no place to carry them, food itself will be dangerous. We cannot
prepare ourselves; we have known nothing of the kind.

But some days I think: I should prepare, I should do only what is difficult. I think: I will teach myself to use a gun. I hide behind the curtain, and
when the mailman comes I try to imagine his right temple in the gunsight as
he goes down the sidewalk. How sure one must be to pull the trigger, even to
kill for one's own children, for their food, their water, perhaps even poison.
The imagination is of no use.

The imagination is of no use. When I run two miles a day, I make myself
run faster, farther, make myself feel nauseated, make myself go on despite my

burning ribs. In case this one day will be a helpful memory, a useful sensation. Of endurance and of pain. My daughter comes and asks my help in making clay animals. On days like this, I want to say: no, no clay animals, we'll dig, we'll practise digging, once your father was a soldier, he will teach you to use a gun. But of course I cannot do this; I cannot pervert her life so that she will be ready for the disaster. There is no readiness; there is no death in life.

* * *

My baby son is crying. Will it be harder for males or females? Will they capture boy children to wander in roving gangs? Will my son, asleep now in his crib, wander the abashed landscape, killing other boys for garbage? Will my daughter root among the grain stalks, glistening with danger, for the one kernel of safe nourishment? Ought I to train them for capitulation? I croon to him; I rock him, watch the gold sun strike a maple, turn it golder. My daughter comes into the room, still in her long nightgown. Half an hour ago, I left her to dress herself. She hasn't succeeded; she's used the time to play with my lipstick. It is all over her face, her hands, her arms. Inside her belly is another tiny belly, empty. Will she have the chance to fill herself with a child, as I have filled myself with her and with her brother? On days like this I worry: if she can't dress herself in half an hour, if she cannot obey me in an instant, like the crack of a whip, will she perish? She can charm anyone. Will there be a place for charm after the disaster? What will be its face?

5   When the babysitter comes, I get into my car. She can make my daughter obey in an instant; she can put my son to sleep without rocking him, or feeding him, or patting him in his crib. On days like this I think I should leave them to her and never come back, for I will probably not survive and with her they will have a greater chance of surviving.

To calm myself I read poetry. When it comes, will the words of "To His Coy Mistress"[1] comfort me, distract me as I wait to hear the news of the death of everything? I want to memorize long poems in case we must spend months in hiding underground. I will memorize "Lycidas,"[2] although I don't like Milton. I will memorize it because of what Virginia Woolf[3] said: "Milton is a comfort because he is nothing like our life." At that moment, when we are waiting for the news of utter death, what we will need is something that is nothing like our life.

* * *

I come home, and begin making dinner. I have purposely bought a tough cut of meat; I will simmer it for hours. As if that were an experience that would be helpful; as if that were the nature of it: afterwards only tough cuts of meat. I pretend I am cooking on a paraffin stove in a basement. But I cannot

---

[1] Poem by Andrew Marvell. See Chapter 6.
[2] Poem by John Milton, English poet (1608–1684).
[3] English novelist and essayist (1882–1941).

restrain myself from using herbs; my own weakness makes me weep. When it comes, there will be no herbs, or spices, no beautiful vegetables like the vegetables that sit on my table in a wooden bowl: an eggplant, yellow squash, tomatoes, a red pepper and some leeks. The solid innocence of my vegetables! When it comes, there will be no innocence. When it comes, there will be no safety. Even the roots hidden deep in the earth of forests will be the food of danger. There will be nothing whose history will be dear. I could weep for my furniture. The earth will be abashed; the furniture will stand out, balked and shameful in the ruin of everything that was our lives.

We have invited friends to dinner. My friend and I talk about our children. I think of her after the disaster; I try to imagine how she will look. I see her standing with a knife; her legs are knotted and blue veins stick out of them like bruised grapes. She is wearing a filthy shirt; her front teeth are missing; her thick black hair is falling out. I will have to kill her to keep her from entering our shelter. If she enters it she will kill us with her knife or the broken glass in her pocket. Kill us for the food we hide which may, even as we take it in, be killing us. Kill us for the life of her own children.

We are sitting on the floor. I want to turn to my friend and say: I do not want to have to kill you. But they have not had my imagination of disaster, and there can be no death in the midst of life. We talk about the autumn; this year we'll walk more in the country, we agree. We kiss our friends good night. Good night, good night, we say, we love you. Good night, I think, I pray I do not have to kill you for my children's food.

$$* \quad * \quad *$$

10 My husband puts on red pajamas. I do not speak of my imagination of disaster. He takes my nightgown off and I see us embracing in the full-length mirror. We are, for now, human, beautiful. We go to bed. He swims above me, digging in. I climb and meet him, strike and fall away. Because we have done this, two more of us breathe in the next room, bathed and perfect as arithmetic.

I think: Perhaps I should kill us all now and save us from the degradation of disaster. Perhaps I should kill us while we are whole and dignified and full of our sane beauty. I do not want to be one of the survivors; I am willing to die with my civilization. I have said to my husband: Let us put aside some pills, so that when the disaster strikes we may lie down together, holding each other's hands and die before the whole earth is abashed. But no, he says, I will not let you do that, we must fight. Someone will survive, he says, why not us? Why not our children?

Because the earth will be abashed, I tell him. Because our furniture will stand out shamed among the glistening poisoned objects. Because we cannot imagine it; because imagination is inadequate; because for this disaster, there is no imagination.

But because of this I may be wrong. We live with death, the stone in the belly, the terror on the road alone. People have lived with it always. But we live knowing not only that we will die, that we may suffer, but that all that we hold dear will finish; that there will be no more familiar. That the death we fear we cannot even imagine, it will not be the distinguished thing, it will not be the face of dream, or even nightmare. For we cannot dream the poisoned earth abashed, empty of all we know.

■ EXPLORATIONS OF THE TEXT ■

1. Explain the many references to "when it comes."
2. Why is no one able to be "adequate"? Why is the "imagination . . . of no use"?
3. Discuss: "when we are waiting for the news of utter death, what we will need is something that is nothing like our life."
4. How does the narrator try to prepare for the disaster? Do some of her thoughts about preparation seem foolish? cruel?
5. "I shall have to kill her to keep her from entering our shelter." Would you kill a friend to preserve your own life? your children's lives?
6. Explore the conclusion: "The death we fear we cannot even imagine."
7. The word "imagination" appears frequently. Does the word always have the same meaning?
8. Gordon describes the earth as "abashed" several times. How can the earth be "abashed"?
9. Why will the furniture in her house be "balked and shameful" and "shamed among the glistening poisoned objects"?
10. Contrast this dystopian vision with Vonnegut's story. What is the "unimaginable" in each vision?

■■ JOURNAL ENTRIES ■■

1. Imagine your response to this "disaster."
2. What would you do to preserve your life? your children's lives?
3. Do you agree: "We live with death, the stone in the belly, the terror on the road alone"?

■■■ IDEAS FOR WRITING ■■■

1. Discuss the oppositions of life and death in this story. How does imagery create this tension?
2. Analyze the character of the narrator. Concentrate on point of view and tone.
3. Imagine the "unimaginable." Write a descriptive essay. Use Journal Entry 1 as a beginning.

The Green Tree

Bessie Head

Bessie Amelia Emery Head (1937–1986) was born in South Africa in a mental hospital, where her white mother had been committed because of an interracial relationship. Her mother spent the rest of her life in the hospital, and Head was placed in foster care.

At the age of thirteen, she was sent to a mission orphanage. After being educated as a primary teacher, Head taught for four years. She also worked as a journalist at Drum Publications for two years in Johannesburg. In 1963, Head moved to Botswana, where she spent the rest of her life. She lived for fifteen years in a refugee community located in Bamangwato Development Farm in Botswana, and where she was granted citizenship in 1979. Head told an interviewer that she found peace of mind there, "In South Africa, all my life I lived in shattered little bits. All those shattered bits began to grow together here."

Her first novel, When Rain Clouds Gather *(1969), was followed by* Maru *(1971) and* A Question of Power *(1973). She also wrote* The Collector of Treasures and Other Botswana Village Tales *(1977),* Serowe; Village of the Rain Wind *(1981), and* A Bewitched Crossroad: An African Saga *(1984). She was working on an autobiography at the time of her death from hepatitis.*

In "The Green Tree," the speaker meditates on the future of his small village, which he sees invaded by strangers. In surprising ways, the narrator connects these changes and his village's fate with a "green tree" and an imagined woman, a "deceitful stranger."

1   This small hill of my village in Africa abounds with the song of birds. The birds are small and brown and seem bound up in the thick profusion of dark brown branches. The green leaves of the trees are so minute that the eye can hardly see them. Everything that is green in my country is minute and cramped for my country is semi-desert.

2   From this hill you may think the village below a fertile valley. It is shrouded and hidden in tall greenery. But that greenery is unproductive, contained and drawn into itself, concerned alone with its silent fight for survival. We call it the green tree. It came here as a stranger and quickly adapted itself to the hardness of our life. It needs no water in the earth but draws into itself the moisture of the air for its life. We use it as a hedge. It also protects us from the sandstorms that blow across our desolate and barren land.

3   If you tell my people that there are countries with hills and hills of green grass where no cattle graze, they will not believe you. Our cattle graze on parched grass that is paper-dry. Our goats eat the torn shreds of windscattered papers and thrust their mouths into the thorn bushes to nibble at the

packed clusters of leaves that look like pin-points of stars farflung in the heavens. That is our life. Everything is jealously guarded. Nothing is ever given out. All strength and energy must be contained for the fight to survive tomorrow and tomorrow and tomorrow.

4 Many strangers traverse our land these days. They are fugitives from the south fleeing political oppression. They look on our lives with horror and quickly make means to pass on to the paradises of the north. Those who are pressed by circumstances and forced to tarry a while, grumble and complain endlessly. It is just good for them that we are inbred with habits of courtesy, hospitality and kindness. It is good that they do not know the passion we feel for this parched earth. We tolerate strangers because the things we love cannot be touched by them. The powdery dust of the earth, the heat, the cattle with their slow, proud walk—all this has fashioned our way of life. Our women with their tall thin hard bodies can drive a man to the depths of passion. All this is ours. Few are they, strangers, who like the green tree are quickly able to adapt themselves to our way of life. They are to be most feared for the adaptation is merely on the surface, like a mask, while underneath they are new and as strange as ever. They cause a ripple on the smooth pond of life that cannot be stopped from spreading from one thing to another.

5 None can be more sure of this than I. For thirty-eight years of my life I have lived in full control of myself. Now, I am full of conflict due to unaccustomed feelings that have taken possession of me. I am weakened and confused and no longer recognise myself as the man I once was. I am at one moment enraged to the point of blind destruction and the next overcome by a terrifying and utterly foreign feeling of tenderness.

6 With women a man must be direct, blunt, and brutal. If not, he soon finds that he loses his pride and becomes dependent on her. It is not necessary to control the passions but it is necessary to be in full control of the heart.

7 This strange obsession crept in on my life unawares. I do not know where I first saw her. I have not even spoken to her but now my eyes seek her out in every corner of the village and I am persued by a thousand devils of restlessness if I do not see her. Deceitful stranger, she has put on the mask of adaptability and assumed our ways and manners but to her, the woman, all gates are closed. It is just as well that she fears me. Sometimes I could destroy her with the thunderbolt of violence that is within me and I see the shock and terror reflected in her eyes. Then, when I am not able to control the feelings that obsess me, it is I in turn who tremble at her sharp darting look of gloating power and indifference. It is I who stand unmanned, drained of strength and will and my rage and hatred at the loss of my pride and independence drive me beyond the bounds of sanity.

8 Everything I have wanted I have had through force, cunning or calculation. Now, I lie awake at night, craving something I fear to possess. Just as our cattle would go insane at the unaccustomed sight of a hill covered with

greenery; so do I live in fear of the body of a woman that has been transplanted by upheaval and uncertain conditions into harsh and barren soil. Sometimes I feel it beneath me: cool, like the depths of night when the moon brings the pale light of heaven to earth and makes the dust shimmer like gold. Then my hands reach out to crush the life out of the thing that torments me.

■ **EXPLORATIONS OF THE TEXT** ■

1. What do the symbolic dimensions of setting reveal about the villagers' way of life?
2. Interpret the symbolism of "the green tree."
3. From where and from what do the villagers flee? How does the narrator view these outsiders?
4. How do the point of view, tone, and mood shift in paragraphs 4 and 5?
5. Characterize the point of view and voice of the narrator. Is the narrator reliable?
6. Examine the narrator's attitude toward women. Analyze paragraph 6. Why is it a separate paragraph?
7. Explain the narrator's "strange obsession," his inner torment, and his conflicting views of the unnamed woman.
8. Consider the concluding paragraph of the story. Why do his "hands reach out to crush the life out of the thing that torments [him]"?
9. How is the story an allegory about the development of modern Africa? Concentrate on the narrator, the symbolism of "the green tree," the woman, and the plot.
10. Contrast this vision of Africa with Gordimer's "Something for the Time Being."

■■ **JOURNAL ENTRIES** ■■

1. Create a portrait of the narrator. Imagine his age, appearance, gestures, and actions.
2. Write a journal entry in the voice of the narrator.
3. Continue the story.
4. Discuss a theme of this story.

■■■ IDEAS FOR WRITING ■■■

---

1. Analyze the point of view of the story. Is the narrator reliable? How does he change?
2. Discuss the story as allegory. Explain the symbolism of the figure of the woman and of the image of the green tree.
3. Why do you think the author, a woman, created a male narrator with violent feelings about women?
4. Write a character analysis of the portrait of the narrator. Refer to Journal Entry 1.

Dead Men's Path

Chinua Achebe

"Your personal god fights for you." These words translate the name of Chinua Achebe, born Albert Chinualumogo Achebe (1930–   ) in the village of Ogidi, Nigeria. In writing about the clash between cultures and the quest for independence, Achebe has celebrated the spirit of Africa by writing essays, children's books, poetry, short stories, and five novels. His volumes include the novels Things Fall Apart *(1958),* No Longer At Ease *(1960),* Arrow of God *(1964),* A Man of the People *(1966), and* Anthills of the Savannah *(1988). His collections of poetry are* Beware, Soul Brother and Other Poems *(1971) and* Christmas in Biafra and Other Poems *(1973).*

"Dead Men's Path" vivifies the tensions between the traditional and the modern in contemporary Africa, as a schoolmaster and villagers come into conflict over a footpath on school property that leads to the village's ceremonial burial grounds.

1   Michael Obi's hopes were fulfilled much earlier than he had expected. He was appointed headmaster of Ndume Central School in January 1949. It had always been an unprogressive school, so the Mission authorities decided to send a young and energetic man to run it. Obi accepted this responsibility with enthusiasm. He had many wonderful ideas and this was an opportunity to put them into practice. He had had sound secondary school education which designated him a "pivotal teacher" in the official records and set him apart from the other headmasters in the mission field. He was outspoken in his condemnation of the narrow views of these older and often less-educated ones.

"We shall make a good job of it, shan't we?" he asked his young wife when they first heard the joyful news of his promotion.

"We shall do our best," she replied. "We shall have such beautiful gardens and everything will be just *modern* and delightful . . ." In their two years of married life she had become completely infected by his passion for "modern methods" and his denigration of "these old and superannuated people in the teaching field who would be better employed as traders in the Onitsha market." She began to see herself already as the admired wife of the young headmaster, the queen of the school.

The wives of the other teachers would envy her position. She would set the fashion in everything . . . Then, suddenly, it occurred to her that there might not be other wives. Wavering between hope and fear, she asked her husband, looking anxiously at him.

5   "All our colleagues are young and unmarried," he said with enthusiasm which for once she did not share. "Which is a good thing," he continued.

"Why?"

"Why? They will give all their time and energy to the school."

Nancy was downcast. For a few minutes she became sceptical about the new school; but it was only for a few minutes. Her little personal misfortune could not blind her to her husband's happy prospects. She looked at him as he sat folded up in a chair. He was stoop-shouldered and looked frail. But he sometimes surprised people with sudden bursts of physical energy. In his present posture, however, all his bodily strength seemed to have retired behind his deep-set eyes, giving them an extraordinary power of penetration. He was only twenty-six, but looked thirty or more. On the whole, he was not unhandsome.

"A penny for your thoughts, Mike," said Nancy after a while, imitating the woman's magazine she read.

10   "I was thinking what a grand opportunity we've got at last to show these people how a school should be run."

Ndume School was backward in *every* sense of the word. Mr. Obi put his whole life into the work, and his wife hers too. He had two aims. A high standard of teaching was insisted upon, and the school compound was to be turned into a place of beauty. Nancy's dream-gardens came to life with the coming of the rains, and blossomed. Beautiful hibiscus[1] and allamanda[2] hedges in brilliant red and yellow marked out the carefully tended school compound from the rank neighbourhood bushes.

One evening as Obi was admiring his work he was scandalized to see an old woman from the village hobble right across the compound, through a marigold flower-bed and the hedges. On going up there he found faint signs of an almost disused path from the village across the school compound to the bush on the other side.

---

[1] Tropical plants or shrubs with large colored flowers.
[2] A tropical vine having yellow flowers.

"It amazes me," said Obi to one of his teachers who had been three years in the school, "that you people allowed the villagers to make use of this footpath. It is simply incredible." He shook his head.

"The path," said the teacher apologetically, "appears to be very important to them. Although it is hardly used, it connects the village shrine with the place of burial."

15   "And what has that got to do with the school?" asked the headmaster.

"Well, I don't know," replied the other with a shrug of the shoulders. "But I remember there was a big row some time ago when we attempted to close it."

"That was some time ago. But it will not be used now," said Obi as he walked away. "What will the Government Education Officer think of this when he comes to inspect the school next week? The villagers might, for all I know, decide to use the schoolroom for a pagan ritual during the inspection."

Heavy sticks were planted closely across the path at the two places where it entered and left the school premises. These were further strengthened with barbed wire.

Three days later the village priest of *Ani* called on the headmaster. He was an old man and walked with a slight stoop. He carried a stout walking-stick which he usually tapped on the floor, by way of emphasis, each time he made a new point in his argument.

20   "I have heard," he said after the usual exchange of cordialities, "that our ancestral footpath has recently been closed . . ."

"Yes," replied Mr. Obi. "We cannot allow people to make a highway of our school compound."

"Look here, my son," said the priest bringing down his walking-stick, "this path was here before you were born and before your father was born. The whole life of this village depends on it. Our dead relatives depart by it and our ancestors visit us by it. But most important, it is the path of children coming in to be born . . ."

Mr. Obi listened with a satisfied smile on his face.

"The whole purpose of our school," he said finally, "is to eradicate just such beliefs as that. Dead men do not require footpaths. The whole idea is just fantastic. Our duty is to teach your children to laugh at such ideas."

25   "What you say may be true," replied the priest, "but we follow the practices of our fathers. If you reopen the path we shall have nothing to quarrel about. What I always say is: let the hawk perch and let the eagle perch." He rose to go.

"I am sorry," said the young headmaster. "But the school compound cannot be a thoroughfare. It is against our regulations. I would suggest your constructing another path, skirting our premises. We can even get our boys to help in building it. I don't suppose the ancestors will find the little detour too burdensome."

"I have no more words to say," said the old priest, already outside.

Two days later a young woman in the village died in childbed. A diviner was immediately consulted and he prescribed heavy sacrifices to propitiate ancestors insulted by the fence.

Obi woke up next morning among the ruins of his work. The beautiful hedges were torn up not just near the path but right round the school, the flowers trampled to death and one of the school buildings pulled down . . . That day, the white Supervisor came to inspect the school and wrote a nasty report on the state of the premises but more seriously about the "tribal-war situation developing between the school and the village, arising in part from the misguided zeal of the new headmaster."

■ **EXPLORATIONS OF THE TEXT** ■

1. Characterize the schoolmaster and his wife. Discuss their attitudes toward their placement at the Ndume School.
2. Why do the villagers use the footpath? What is its symbolic significance?
3. Why does the headmaster oppose the villagers' use of the path? What are the implications of this conflict?
4. Explain the **irony** in the closing paragraph.
5. Compare Achebe's view of the tensions in African culture with those expressed in Head's "The Green Tree."

■■ **JOURNAL ENTRIES** ■■

1. Write a reaction to the schoolmaster or to his wife.
2. Write a reaction to the title.

■■■ **IDEAS FOR WRITING** ■■■

1. Analyze the portrayal of the headmaster. Examine physical description, gestures, and actions.
2. Discuss the symbolism of the school compound: "Nancy's dream-gardens," "the barbed wire," and the path.
3. Explore the collision of belief systems presented in this story.
4. What is the role of ancestors?

The Handsomest Drowned Man in the World

Gabriel García Márquez Translated by Gregory Rabassa

Gabriel García Márquez (1928–), born in the coastal village of Aracataca, Colombia, was the oldest of twelve children and was raised by his maternal grandparents. After studying at the University of Colombia at Bogota and the University of Cartagena, he travelled throughout South America, the United States, and Europe as a reporter and began writing short stories. Although he has lived in Mexico City for the past thirty years, he returns frequently to his native Colombia, the setting for most of his novels. His fiction has been translated into more than twenty languages, and English translations include Leaf Storm and Other Stories *(1972),* No One Writes to the Colonel and Other Stories *(1962),* The Autumn of the Patriarch *(1976),* Chronicle of a Death Foretold *(1983),* Love in the Time of Cholera *(1987),* The General in His Labyrinth *(1991), and several collections of short stories. His most famous work is* One Hundred Years of Solitude *(1972). García Márquez was awarded the Nobel Prize for literature in 1982.*

In this remarkable tale, an enormous, drowned man, covered with mud and vegetation, is washed ashore near a village high on a cliff. The fantastic, huge corpse of this stranger changes the people and the place forever.

1　The first children who saw the dark and slinky bulge approaching through the sea let themselves think it was an empty ship. Then they saw it had no flags or masts and they thought it was a whale. But when it washed up on the beach, they removed the clumps of seaweed, the jellyfish tentacles, and the remains of fish and flotsam, and only then did they see that it was a drowned man.

2　They had been playing with him all afternoon, burying him in the sand and digging him up again, when someone chanced to see them and spread the alarm in the village. The men who carried him to the nearest house noticed that he weighed more than any dead man they had ever known, almost as much as a horse, and they said to each other that maybe he'd been floating too long and the water had got into his bones. When they laid him on the floor they said he'd been taller than all other men because there was barely enough room for him in the house, but they thought that maybe the ability to keep on growing after death was part of the nature of certain drowned men. He had the smell of the sea about him and only his shape gave one to suppose that it was the corpse of a human being, because the skin was covered with a crust of mud and scales.

3   They did not even have to clean off his face to know that the dead man was a stranger. The village was made up of only twenty-odd wooden houses that had stone courtyards with no flowers and which were spread about on the end of a desertlike cape. There was so little land that mothers always went about with the fear that the wind would carry off their children and the few dead that the years had caused among them had to be thrown off the cliffs. But the sea was calm and bountiful and all the men fit into seven boats. So when they found the drowned man they simply had to look at one another to see that they were all there.

4   That night they did not go out to work at sea. While the men went to find out if anyone was missing in neighboring villages, the women stayed behind to care for the drowned man. They took the mud off with grass swabs, they removed the underwater stones entangled in his hair, and they scraped the crust off with tools used for scaling fish. As they were doing that they noticed that the vegetation on him came from faraway oceans and deep water and that his clothes were in tatters, as if he had sailed through labyrinths of coral. They noticed too that he bore his death with pride, for he did not have the lonely look of other drowned men who came out of the sea or that haggard, needy look of men who drowned in rivers. But only when they finished cleaning him off did they become aware of the kind of man he was and it left them breathless. Not only was he the tallest, strongest, most virile, and best built man they had ever seen, but even though they were looking at him there was no room for him in their imagination.

5   They could not find a bed in the village large enough to lay him on nor was there a table solid enough to use for his wake. The tallest men's holiday pants would not fit him, nor the fattest ones' Sunday shirts, nor the shoes of the one with the biggest feet. Fascinated by his huge size and his beauty, the women then decided to make him some pants from a large piece of sail and a shirt from some bridal Brabant[1] linen so that he could continue through his death with dignity. As they sewed, sitting in a circle and gazing at the corpse between stitches, it seemed to them that the wind had never been so steady nor the sea so restless as on that night and they supposed that the change had something to do with the dead man. They thought that if that magnificent man had lived in the village, his house would have had the widest doors, and highest ceiling, and the strongest floor; his bedstead would have been made from a midship frame held together by iron bolts, and his wife would have been the happiest woman. They thought that he would have had so much authority that he could have drawn fish out of the sea simply by calling their names and that he would have put so much work into his land that springs would have burst forth from among the rocks so that he would have been able to plant flowers on the cliffs. They secretly compared him to their own men, thinking that for all their lives theirs were incapable of doing what he could do in one night, and they ended up dismissing them deep in their

---

[1] Former region of Western Europe including the current Brabant province of Netherlands and Brabant and Antwerp regions of Belgium.

hearts as the weakest, meanest, and most useless creatures on earth. They were wandering through that maze of fantasy when the oldest woman, who as the oldest had looked upon the drowned man with more compassion than passion, sighed:

6   "He has the face of someone called Esteban."

7   It was true. Most of them had only to take another look at him to see that he could not have any other name. The more stubborn among them, who were the youngest, still lived for a few hours with the illusion that when they put his clothes on and he lay among the flowers in patent leather shoes his name might be Lautaro. But it was a vain illusion. There had not been enough canvas, the poorly cut and worse sewn pants were too tight, and the hidden strength of his heart popped the buttons on his shirt. After midnight the whistling of the wind died down and the sea fell into its Wednesday drowsiness. The silence put an end to any last doubts: he was Esteban. The women who had dressed him, who had combed his hair, had cut his nails and shaved him were unable to hold back a shudder of pity when they had to resign themselves to his being dragged along the ground. It was then that they understood how unhappy he must have been with that huge body since it bothered him even after death. They could see him in life, condemned to going through doors sideways cracking his head on crossbeams, remaining on his feet during visits, not knowing what to do with his soft pink, sealion hands while the lady of the house looked for her most resistant chair and begged him, frightened to death, sit here, Esteban, please, and he, leaning against the wall, smiling, don't bother, ma'am, I'm fine where I am, his heels raw and his back roasted from having done the same thing so many times whenever he paid a visit, don't bother, ma'am, I'm fine where I am to avoid the embarrassment of breaking up the chair, and never knowing perhaps that the one who said don't go, Esteban, at least wait till the coffee's ready, were the ones who later on would whisper the big boob finally left, how nice, the handsome fool has gone. That was what the women were thinking beside the body a little before dawn. Later, when they covered his face with a handkerchief so that the light would not bother him, he looked so forever dead, so defenseless, so much like their men that the first furrows of tears opened in their hearts. It was one of the younger ones who began the weeping. The others, coming to, went from sighs to wails, and the more they sobbed the more they felt like weeping, because the drowned man was becoming all the more Esteban for them, and so they wept so much, for he was the most destitute, most peaceful, and most obliging man on earth, poor Esteban. So when the men returned with the news that the drowned man was not from the neighboring villages either, the women felt an opening of jubilation in the midst of their tears.

8   "Praise the Lord," they sighed, "he's ours!"

9   The men thought the fuss was only womanish frivolity. Fatigued because of the difficult nighttime inquiries, all they wanted was to get rid of the bother of the newcomer once and for all before the sun grew strong on that arid, windless day. They improvised a litter with the remains of foremasts and gaffs, tying

it together with rigging so that it would bear the weight of the body until they reached the cliffs. They wanted to tie the anchor from a cargo ship to him so that he would sink easily into the deepest waves, where the fish are blind and divers die of nostalgia, and bad currents would not bring him back to shore, as had happened with other bodies. But the more they hurried, the more the women thought of ways to waste time. They walked about like startled hens, pecking with the sea charms on their breasts, some interfering on one side to put a scapular of the good wind on the drowned man, some on the other side to put a wrist compass on him, and after a great deal of *get away from there, woman, stay out of the way, look, you almost made me fall on top of the dead man,* the men began to feel mistrust in their livers and started grumbling about why so many main-altar decorations for a stranger, because no matter how many nails and holywater jars he had on him, the sharks would chew him all the same, but the women kept on piling on their junk relics, running back and forth, stumbling, while they released in sighs what they did not in tears, so that the men finally exploded with *since when has there ever been such a fuss over a drifting corpse, a drowned nobody, a piece of cold Wednesday meat.* One of the women, mortified by so much lack of care, then removed the handkerchief from the dead man's face and the men were left breathless too.

10   He was Esteban. It was not necessary to repeat it for them to recognize him. If they had been told Sir Walter Raleigh,[2] even they might have been impressed with his gringo accent, the macaw on his shoulder, his cannibal-killing blunderbuss, but there could be only one Esteban in the world and there he was, stretched out like a sperm whale, shoeless, wearing the pants of an undersized child, and with those stony nails that had to be cut with a knife. They had only to take the handkerchief off his face to see that he was ashamed, that it was not his fault that he was so big or so heavy or so handsome, and if he had known that this was going to happen, he would have looked for a more discreet place to drown in; seriously, I even would have tied the anchor off a galleon around my neck and staggered off a cliff like someone who doesn't like things in order not to be upsetting people now with this Wednesday dead body, as you people say, in order not to be bothering anyone with this filthy piece of cold meat that doesn't have anything to do with me. There was so much truth in his manner that even the most mistrustful men, the ones who felt the bitterness of endless nights at sea fearing that their women would tire of dreaming about them and begin to dream of drowned men, even they and others who were harder still shuddered in the marrow of their bones at Esteban's sincerity.

11   That was how they came to hold the most splendid funeral they could conceive of for an abandoned drowned man. Some women who had gone to get flowers in the neighboring villages returned with other women who could not believe what they had been told, and those women went back for more flowers when they saw the dead man, and they brought more and more until there were so many flowers and so many people that it was hard to walk about. At the

---

[2] English navigator, courtier, and historian (1554–1618).

final moment it pained them to return him to the waters as an orphan and they chose a father and mother from among the best people, and aunts and uncles and cousins, so that through him all the inhabitants of the village became kinsmen. Some sailors who heard the weeping from a distance went off course, and people heard of one who had himself tied to the mainmast, remembering ancient fables about sirens. While they fought for the privilege of carrying him on their shoulders along the steep escarpment by the cliffs, men and women became aware for the first time of the desolation of their streets, the dryness of their courtyards, the narrowness of their dreams as they faced the splendor and beauty of their drowned man. They let him go without an anchor so that he could come back if he wished and whenever he wished, and they all held their breath for the fraction of centuries the body took to fall into the abyss. They did not need to look to one another to realize that they were no longer all present, that they would never be. But they also knew that everything would be different from then on, that their houses would have wider doors, higher ceilings, and stronger floors so that Esteban's memory could go everywhere without bumping into beams and so that no one in the future would dare whisper the big boob finally died, too bad, the handsome fool has finally died, because they were going to paint their house fronts gay colors to make Esteban's memory eternal and they were going to break their backs digging for springs among the stones and planting flowers on the cliffs so that in future years at dawn the passengers on great liners would awaken, suffocated by the smell of gardens on the high seas, and the captain would have to come down from the bridge in his dress uniform, with his astrolabe,[3] his pole star, and his row of war medals and, pointing to the promontory of roses on the horizon, he would say in fourteen languages, look there, where the wind is so peaceful now that it's gone to sleep beneath the beds, over there, where the sun's so bright that the sunflowers don't know which way to turn, yes, over there, that's Esteban's village.

■ EXPLORATIONS OF THE TEXT ■

1. Why does García Márquez subtitle the story "A Tale for Children"? What expectations does the subtitle create in the reader?
2. Why do the children play with the body? What is their attitude toward death?
3. What is the meaning of the symbolism of the vegetation and mud on the drowned man's body?
4. What are the consequences of the women's comparisons to their own men? What is the importance of identifying him as Esteban?
5. Examine the imaginary conversation about his size. How does he become "the big boob" and "the handsome fool"? Why do the villagers feel "jubilation" when Esteban becomes their drowned man?

---

[3] An instrument used to observe and calculate the positions of stars and planets before the invention of the sextant.

6. Explore the men's attitudes, the funeral, and the behavior of the women. How does Esteban win the people with his sincerity?
7. Describe the ritual of the "most splendid funeral." How does the experience with the drowned man transform the people and the village?
8. Compare the transformation of the people in this story with the change in the narrator in Wright's "A Blessing."

■■ JOURNAL ENTRIES ■■

1. Write a story which imitates both the style and theme of "The Handsomest Drowned Man in the World."
2. Gloss and annotate the story. Consider the use of **hyperbole**.
3. React to the idea of Esteban as "the stranger" who is taken into the community.

■■■ IDEAS FOR WRITING ■■■

1. Analyze the transformation of the people and their village.
2. Discuss the symbolism of the drowned man.
3. How do the settings (village and sea) elucidate theme?
4. Look for elements of fairy tales in this story. How are they effective?
5. Contrast García Márquez's view of death with the attitude of Thomas in "Do Not Go Gentle . . . ."
6. Compare the idea of community in García Márquez, King, and Achebe.
7. Argue: Without imagination, people live constricted, static lives.

POETRY

The Second Coming

William Butler Yeats

William Butler Yeats (1865–1939), born in Dublin, Ireland, is considered one of the twentieth century's most important and controversial poets. He was the leader of the Irish Renaissance, and in 1904, he helped found the Abbey Theater. In 1922, he was elected to a six-year term as senator after the Irish Free State was formed. Yeats's writing displays an imaginative, skillful blend of Eastern and Western cultures and ancient and modern thought. Despite this impressive eclecticism, Yeats always remains an Irish poet, longing for an Ireland free of British dominance. His first volume of poems, The Wandering of Oisin and Other Poems *(1889) includes a long, mystical narrative poem based on Irish legend.*

Among Yeats' prose works are Fairy and Folk Tales of the Irish Peasantry *(1888),* The Celtic Twilight *(1893), and* Autobiographies *(1926). His poetical works include* The Green Helmet *(1910),* The Wild Swans at Coole *(1917),* The Tower *(1928),* The Winding Stair *(1929), and* The Collected Poems *(1933). Yeats was awarded the Nobel Prize for Literature in 1923.*

"The Second Coming" alludes both to the Beast of the Apocalypse (Revelation 13:1) and the Second Coming (Matthew 24) in the New Testament.[1] *Yeats believed that history moved in cycles of two thousand years, and he explained his theory by the visual symbol of the gyre, or cone. Here a single gyre opens to its widest point, the moment when the age will become violent and a new cycle will begin.*

> Turning and turning in the widening gyre
> The falcon cannot hear the falconer;
> Things fall apart; the center cannot hold;
> Mere anarchy is loosed upon the world,
> 5 The blood-dimmed tide is loosed, and everywhere
> The ceremony of innocence is drowned;
> The best lack all conviction, while the worst
> Are full of passionate intensity.

---

[1] Allusion to Jesus' prediction of his second coming. Written in 1919, the poem refers to the Black and Tan War in Ireland when British soldiers were sent to quell the republicans.

Surely some revelation is at hand.
10 Surely the Second Coming is at hand.
The Second Coming! Hardly are those words out
When a vast image out of *Spiritus Mundi*[2]
Troubles my sight: somewhere in sands of the desert
A shape with lion body and the head of a man,[3]
15 A gaze blank and pitiless as the sun,
Is moving its slow thighs, while all about it
Reel shadows of the indignant desert birds.
The darkness drops again; but now I know
That twenty centuries[4] of stony sleep
20 Were vexed to nightmare[5] by a rocking cradle,
And what rough beast, its hour come round at last,
Slouches towards Bethlehem[6] to be born?

■ EXPLORATIONS OF THE TEXT ■

1. What do the symbols of the "gyre," "the falcon," and "the falconer" suggest about the speaker's view of the state of the world?
2. Why do "Things fall apart"? Why is it that "the centre cannot hold"?
3. Explore the significance of the images of the Egyptian sphinx, the "blank and pitiless" gaze, and the "shadows of the indignant desert birds."
4. Why does Yeats choose the word "reel" in line 17? What is the effect of this word choice?
5. What is the speaker's view of the millennium? of the Apocalypse? What will be "born"?
6. Examine the rhyme scheme of the poem. Why do you think Yeats rhymes only certain lines?
7. Discuss the meaning and **irony** of the title and of the ending.
8. Contrast Yeats' vision with Black Elk's "Great Vision."

■■ JOURNAL ENTRIES ■■

1. React to the view of the future expressed in the poem.
2. Do you agree with Yeats' view of the decline of civilization?

[2] The author's term for divine inspiration or for a place from which images are received, never invented.
[3] The Egyptian sphinx.
[4] Reference to twenty centuries of Christianity.
[5] Implication that Christianity created its opposite.
[6] Birthplace of Jesus.

■■■ IDEAS FOR WRITING ■■■

1. Does Yeats' vision seem relevant today? What world events may be evoked by references in the poem?
2. Contrast Yeats' view of the future with the ideas in two other works in this chapter.

Stone Olives

Judith Emlyn Johnson

Judith Emlyn Johnson (1936–) is Professor of English at the State University of New York at Albany. In 1992, her latest book of poems was published as The Ice Lizard. *Recipient of many awards, she served as President of the Poetry Society of America, 1975–1978. Johnson says, "Before poetry was anything else, it was a physical act: the act of making sounds in the throat." About fiction she says there was, ". . . the current of concentration uniting the story teller with his or her listeners around the campfire or in the workplace, when the hands moved and the minds moved, and the dancer and the dance were one moving creature." She believes that her work "must keep the dynamism of these beginnings." Johnson's poetry also contains strong political messages.*

In "Stone Olives," the speaker mourns the death of a student on Pam Am Flight 103, a plane destroyed by a terrorist bomb over Lockerbee, Scotland, in December 1988.

(in memoriam Melina Hudson, of Albany, Pan Am Flight 103, December 1988)

Tulip-flowered wind, night-smelling sea,
long swell of desert sands, and the roar of tractors
crawling up from the Hudson,[1] from under water
into Albany's Washington Park:[2] what is that ploughing?

5   It is the sound
        of olive trees.
First one, then two, then the whole grove, they drop
        their small, hard fruits,
and their tears are gathered up,

---

[1] A major river in New York.
[2] Reference to a park where Melina Hudson enjoyed leisure time with her friends, among them the poet's daughter.

10   packed into baskets, then carried
        to the earth-floored rooms.
                        Some go into jars.
        Some have their centers plucked out
        to be filled with slivered almonds or roasted
15   red peppers. Some go to the press
                where they're crushed. From their pulp
                        oozes the purest gold,
                to be strained into jars and sold.
        Little dead ones, they sing, *blink blink,*
20   as they fall, *little dead ones, blink blink*
        la muerte, ay, los niños, ay, la muerte. [3]
Take my hand, come down, dance with me, take my hand.

Tulip-fluttered wind, night-swelling sea:
in the smell of desert sands, before we were born,
25 the tractors ploughed back time from under Mount Sinai[4]
    into Washington Park. There, carved stone
    Moses[5] watches his wise God stand hard by
    as the father prepares to spill on the quickening sand
    his son. No olive trees whisper here. Does Abraham[6]
30 see that no scapegoat waits at hand? His son
            and his son's sons and daughters,
    sucked down, will sweeten that sand, no matter how many
    small, innocent, wordless furs squeak out their lives.
    What is dying now, even as we speak, to save us?

35   It is the stand
            of apple trees behind the barbed wire.
            First one, then two, then the whole grove, the sun
                    flattens them. Gravid, they droop,
                    ripen, and men lean ladders,
40   and their treasures are gathered, packed,
                    into baskets, then ferried out
                    from the earth-walled rooms.
                        Some are rendered down,
                    some peeled of their skins, grated
45   with almonds, and mixed to haroseth that makes sweet
            the bitter herbs. Some have their teeth plucked out
            for the fillings. Some go to the press.

---

[3] "Death, oh, the children, oh, death" (from the Spanish).
[4] Mountain of NE Egypt on the Sinai Peninsula.
[5] Hebrew prophet who led the Israelites out of Egyptian slavery. He delivered to them the
    commandments of their God's covenant at Mt. Sinai.
[6] Allusion to patriarch of the Jews regarded as the founder of the Hebrew people through his
    son Isaac. This passage refers to God's commanding Abraham to sacrifice Isaac.

From their pulped flesh oozes the purest gold,
sweeter, oh Lord their God, than the fruit of the vine
50   to be filtered through cheesecloth and sold.
Little dead ones, they sing, *shalom,* [7]
as they drop, *little dead ones, shalom*
ich sterbe hier, [8] *nicht versteh,* [9] *je crêve,* [10] *nou verbeshti,* [11] *mamaye.* [12]
Take my hand, come down, dance with me, take my hand.

55 Tulip-sequined wind, night-shimmying sea,
long bloom of desert sands, and the roar of the spring
festival onto the grass: tell me the mother,
before our history sprouted, should have thrown
herself under the blades to save her child. Yes, tell me
60 the father should have given to God the Father
his own life, not his son's. Tell me, if all,
man, woman, child, had thrown their lives away
rather than take that dumb, furred sacrifice
still squeaking its lives out under our knives
65 would all our history have borne different fruits?
We planted no orchard here next to City Hall[13]
but the walls still shake. What are we ploughing under
when we do that prime time shimmy?

It is the sands
70   of the pyramids.
One grain, then two, then whole stones, they melt.
Their sharp, unlanded granules
drill from their homeless camps the far away dam.
The wind lifts them, gathers them in, and they ride
75   the red tide's maternal breast
from their hulled earth rooms to their ghost of a promised land.
Stones fall, whole shoulders drop
from the Sphinx[14] who was raised
by forced labor. Eyes run
80   from their heads. Scalps, halves of scalps rain down.
Melina, who once danced
at proms far from Beirut,[15] laughed with my daughter

---

[7] Hebrew for "peace."
[8] "I'm dying here." (German).
[9] "I don't understand" (German).
[10] "I'm collapsing"; "I'm being slaughtered"; "I'm dying like a dog." (French)
[11] "Shut up"; "don't talk"; literally "no more words." (Roumanian).
[12] "Mommy." (Roumanian).
[13] In Albany, New York.
[14] Egyptian statue in the form of a lion, having a man's head.
[15] Capital city of Lebanon.

years after Hiroshima[16] broke into flower, told
her beads in a church the Gulag[17] never touched,
85   now pours down through our air
her young hands full with the seventeen pressed years
        that are all she can hold
        of spring: will the Dead Sea[18]
grow fat with these fragments? Our mouths are being stuffed
90 with our sons and daughters, our centers plucked out
        with tongs. From our poor,
        pressed through heat, through cold
over vents and gratings, flow simples, poultices, tinctures
        to be forced into jars and sold.
95 *Little dead ones,* they sing, *ushh, ushh,*
as they drop, *little dead ones, ushh, ushh.*
d d d kkkkk d d d kkkkk aaaaaaah heart
Take my hand, come down, dance with me, take my hand.

Tulip-grinning wind, night-crying sea,
100 long shudder of desert sands, and the drowned tractors
bubbling up from our bodies, cut from our tongues
deep into Washington Park where Moses holds
his law in his hands: they told me God Himself
gave His Son's life to stop it as Abraham
105 gave Isaac. But what if each father
should give himself? What if we all stand up,
we, who are old enough to have held our lives,
and empty out, not our children, but ourselves?
        Why do I hear no such ploughing?

110   Instead, I hear the bend
        beyond the asteroids bleed.
First one, then two, then whole planets they fall
        and their milk will be pressed out,
their hulled tears, neither water or salt, hold elements
115   we can neither measure nor read
        their red shift to name. They carry
no life we know as life in their milled earths.
        Their centaurs[19] are long gone
        replaced by an airless patience,
120   their languages hot ores,
        or frozen metals.

---

[16] City in Japan. In this case, an allusion to the United States dropping an atomic bomb
    during World War II, an action which destroyed the city and ended the war in the Pacific.
[17] Network of labor camps in the former U.S.S.R.
[18] Salt lake on the boundary between Israel and Jordan.
[19] Creature fabled to be half man and half horse.

Of their forgiveness nothing remains, not even Aztec
> gold to be ferried away
to the galaxies and sold. We know what their silence says.
125 *Little dead ones,* they sing as they shimmy, *aaah nnnnn,*
as they drop, *little dead ones, aaah nnnnnnnn*
eiaa mohsrden, aiee, eiaa khilsderin, aiee, eiaaaa mohsdenn
nnnnhh *aaaaaqaaaaahhhhh.*[20]
Take my hand, come down, dance with me, take my hand.

■ EXPLORATIONS OF THE TEXT ■

1. What worlds converge in stanza 1? What does the "ploughing" signify?
2. How does the symbolism of the "olive trees" change throughout the poem. With what are the olives connected?
3. With whom does the speaker identify at the end of stanza 2?
4. Explain the references to Abraham and Isaac. (See Genesis 22.)
5. Analyze the following: "What is dying now, even as we speak, to save us?"
6. What historical allusions are suggested in stanzas 3, 4, and 6?
7. What does the speaker present as the alternative to the sacrifice of "our children"?
8. In the last stanza, why does Johnson enlarge her vision to include the "fall" of the "planets"? What poetic device is used?
9. Discuss the contrasting images of "gold," pressed blood and flesh, and the pressed pulp of fruit.
10. What is the significance of the repetition and variation of the lines: "Tulip-flowered wind, night-smelling sea,/long swell of desert sands"?
11. What is the significance of the repetition of "Little dead ones" and "Take my hand, come down, dance with me, take my hand"?
12. Who is the speaker? What is the speaker's role in the poem?
13. Why does Johnson include lines in different languages?
14. Compare the speaker's view of global issues with Gordon's. What futures do these writers imagine?

■■ JOURNAL ENTRIES ■■

1. Read this poem aloud, and react to it.
2. Paraphrase the message of each stanza. How does the argument progress?
3. React to the visions of the past, of the present, and of the future. Do you agree with those visions?

---

[20] Invented language intended to convey the cries of the children; equivalent to "ay, los ninos," or "Ick sterbe hier."

■■■ IDEAS FOR WRITING ■■■

1. Analyze the symbolism of the "stone olives."
2. Discuss the theme of sacrifice.
3. Who is the speaker? What is the speaker's role?
4. What is the connection of past and future?

Gitanjali: Songs I and II

Rabindranath Tagore

Born in Calcutta, India, Rabindranath Tagore (1861–1941) was the oldest of seven sons of a wealthy Brahmin writer, scholar, mystic, and religious reformer. Tagore had a mystical experience in 1883 which led him to a conception of god as intimate, a wellspring of inspiration that greatly influenced his work. He penned nearly sixty volumes of verse, more than forty plays, fourteen novels, two hundred short stories, and thousands of songs, in addition to numerous essays, journals, and religious and philosophical tracts. In 1913, shortly after he wrote Gitanjali *(1910, "Song Offerings"), a collection of serenely mystical poems inspired by the deaths of his father, wife, two daughters, and youngest son, Tagore became the first Indian writer to win the Nobel Prize for Literature; he also was knighted.*

In these two poems from Tagore's Gitanjali *or Songs, the speaker acknowledges a realization of the endless self and a sense of joy that "melts into one sweet harmony."*

I

Thou hast made me endless, such is thy pleasure. This frail vessel thou emptiest again and again, and fillest it ever with fresh life.

This little flute of a reed thou hast carried over hills and dales, and has breathed through it melodies eternally new.

At the immortal touch of thy hands my little heart loses its limits in joy, and gives birth to utterance ineffable.

Thy infinite gifts come to me only on these very small hands of mine. Ages pass, and still thou pourest, and still there is room to fill.

II

When thou commandest me to sing, it seems that my heart would break with pride; and I look to thy face, and tears come to my eyes.

All that is harsh and dissonant in my life melts into one sweet harmony—and my adoration spreads wings like a glad bird on its flight across the sea.

I know thou takest pleasure in my singing. I know that only as a singer I come before thy presence.

■ EXPLORATIONS OF THE TEXT ■

I

1. What does the speaker experience? Examine the images of the "vessel," the "flute," and the "heart."
2. What does the speaker mean when he describes "utterance ineffable"?
3. Interpret the last line. Explain the **paradox**.
4. Compare this view of the world with Black Elk's vision.

II

1. What is the commandment "to sing"?
2. Why does "all that is harsh and dissonant" melt? Describe the speaker's version of harmony.
3. Explain the bird **simile**.
4. Why can the speaker come into the presence of divinity only as a singer? What does the joy of "singing" suggest?
5. Compare Tagore's and Rilke's views of spirit and divinity.

■■ JOURNAL ENTRIES ■■

1. Describe the voice in these lyrics.
2. Create your own version of a third song in this sequence. Consider speaker, tone, imagery, and theme.
3. What is the source of joy in these works?

■■■ IDEAS FOR WRITING ■■■

1. Write about the concept of divinity in these poems.
2. Characterize the speaker.
3. How does Tagore's poetry differ from other poets?

Sonnet 1

Rainer Maria Rilke

Born in Czechoslovakia, Rainer Maria Rilke (1875–1926) went to military school as a child and attended university in his native Prague and in Berlin and in Munich. His earliest published works in the 1890s were primarily love poems. The work that first gained him recognition as a poet was The Book of Images *(1902). Rilke wrote only intermittently and then in great prolific bursts which he believed were periods of grace when the poems were "dictated" to him. Rilke composed* The Sonnets to Orpheus *in 1923 while he lived alone in a tower in Switzerland, but they were not published until eight years after his death from blood poisoning. The Sonnets are considered by some to be the greatest poems in German literature, and others insist that Rilke's ten* Duino Elegies *(1923) deserve this honor. His poems appeared in a posthumous collection,* Later Poems *(English trans. 1934).*

Rilke's "Sonnet 1" from Sonnets to Orpheus *concerns transcendence and the power of the sound of the music of the ancient Greek musician Orpheus to call forth the animals. All of the sonnets portray amazing transformations.*

> There arose a tree. Oh, pure transcension!
> Oh, Orpheus sings[1]! Oh, tall tree in the ear!
> And all was still. But even in this suspension
> new beginnings, signs, and changes were.
>
> 5 Animals from the silence, from the clear
> now opened wood came forth from nest and den;
> and it so came to pass that not from fear
> or craftiness were they so quiet then,

---

[1] According to Greek mythology, Orpheus was the son of Oeagrus, a river god, and one of the Muses (Polyhymnia, Clio, or Calliope). Born in Thrace, Orpheus may have been king of some Thracian tribes and was famous as a great singer, musician, and poet. In some legends, he supposedly invented the lyre. Because of the magic of his songs, all of nature responded to his music. Wild animals followed him, trees and plants leaned in his direction, and he tamed the souls of the wildest men.

The most famous exploit of Orpheus concerns his descent into the underworld to save his wife, Eurydice, who died when a serpent bit her. Inconsolable, he charmed monsters guarding the gates of hell and the gods of the dead in order to rescue her. For a brief moment, even the damned were relieved of pain by his music. The underworld deities, Hades and Persephone, agreed to allow Eurydice to return to earth with one stipulation: that Orpheus, followed by Eurydice, leave and that he not look back at her. When he could not resist temptation, he turned around, and she disappeared—lost to him forever.

but to be listening. Howling, cry, roar
10 seemed little to their hearts. Where scarce a
humble
hut for such reception was before,

a hiding-place of the obscurest yearning,
with entrance shaft whose underpinnings tremble,
15 you made for the beasts temples in the hearing.

■ EXPLORATIONS OF THE TEXT ■

1. What is the "transcension" in the first **quatrain**? What does the tree symbolize? What is the "tall tree in the ear"?
2. Why do the animals come forth? Why is the silence significant?
3. Explicate: "Howling, cry, roar/seemed little to their hearts."
4. Explain the last line. Who is "you"? Interpret "temples in the hearing."
5. What has Orpheus accomplished?
6. Explore the form of the poem as a version of the **Petrarchan sonnet**, with two **quatrains** (an **octave**) and two **tercets** (a **sestet**). What other formal elements are noteworthy?
7. Compare the tone of this sonnet to the tone in Rich's "Diving into the Wreck" and in Tagore's lyrics.

■■ JOURNAL ENTRIES ■■

1. Gloss, annotate, and comment on this sonnet.
2. Create a scene in which music or art transforms animals and/or people.
3. Write about the **paradoxes** in the poem.
4. Freewrite about silence in this sonnet.

■■■ IDEAS FOR WRITING ■■■

1. Write about the figure of Orpheus. What are his powers?
2. Explicate and evaluate this sonnet. Use Journal Entry 1 as a beginning. Focus on imagery and form. (See Chapter 10.)
3. Explore the theme of transformation in this poem, in "Diving into the Wreck," and in "My Name Is 'I am Living.'"

Sonnet 29

This sonnet, the last from Sonnets to Orpheus, *discusses transformation as exploration and the attainment of wisdom. The most difficult experience teaches the greatest lesson. The Orphic poet takes the confusion of the senses and creates art.*

Still friend of many distances, feel yet
how your breathing is augmenting space.
From the beamwork of gloomy belfries let
yourself ring. What devours you will increase

5 more strongly from this food. Explore and win
knowledge of transformation through and
     through.
What experience was the worst for you?
Is drinking bitter, you must turn to wine.

10 Be the magic power of this immense
midnight at the crossroads of your senses,
be the purport of their strange meeting.
     Though

earth itself forgot your very name,
15 say unto the tranquil earth: I flow.
To the fleeting water speak: I am.

■ **EXPLORATIONS OF THE TEXT** ■

1. Who is the "friend"?
2. How does the poet "win" "transformation"? What is the value of the "worst" "experience"?
3. Why does the speaker mean: "Be the magic power of this immense/midnight at the crossroads of your senses"?
4. Interpret the last three lines. What is the meaning of the declarations "I flow" and "I am"?
5. Compare the form of this sonnet with Sonnet 1.

■■ **JOURNAL ENTRIES** ■■

1. Does a person or poet learn from bitter experiences?
2. Respond to the sonnet.
3. Discuss transformation in Rilke's sonnets.

■■■ **IDEAS FOR WRITING** ■■■

---

1. Analyze the form of the poem. Is it effective?
2. Write a **parody** of this sonnet. Analyze your parody. Focus on point of view, tone, imagery, and form.
3. Can the poet or his or her art change the world?

Diving into the Wreck

Adrienne Rich

Born in Baltimore, Maryland, Adrienne Rich (1929–   ) is one of America's finest poets and most influential feminists. She is also an essayist and teacher, holding the position of Professor of English and Feminist Studies at Stanford University. Her works include the collections of poetry, A Change of World *(1951), selected by W. H. Auden for the Yale Younger Poets Award,* Snapshots of a Daughter-in-Law *(1963),* The Will to Change *(1971),* The Dream of a Common Language *(1978),* A Wild Patience Has Taken Me This Far *(1981),* Your Native Land, Your Life *(1986),* Facts of a Doorframe *(1984), and* An Atlas of the Difficult World *(1991), as well as* On Lies, Secrets, and Silence—Selected Prose 1966–1978 *(1979). Awards include the National Book Award for* Diving into the Wreck *in 1974.*

The speaker in the poem describes a symbolic journey, "diving into the wreck," a process of submergence that leads to illumination: "to see the damage that was done/and the treasures that prevail."

> First having read the book of myths,
> and loaded the camera,
> and checked the edge of the knife-blade,
> I put on
> 5 the body-armor of black rubber
> the absurd flippers
> the grave and awkward mask.
> I am having to do this
> not like Cousteau[1] with his
> 10 assiduous team
> aboard the sun-flooded schooner
> but here alone.

---

[1] French underwater explorer and film maker (1910–   ).

There is a ladder.
The ladder is always there
15 hanging innocently
close to the side of the schooner.
We know what it is for,
we who have used it.
Otherwise
20 it's a piece of maritime floss
some sundry equipment.

I go down.
Rung after rung and still
the oxygen immerses me
25 the blue light
the clear atoms
of our human air.
I go down.
My flippers cripple me,
30 I crawl like an insect down the ladder
and there is no one
to tell me when the ocean
will begin.

First the air is blue and then
35 it is bluer and then green and then
black I am blacking out and yet
my mask is powerful
it pumps my blood with power
the sea is another story
40 the sea is not a question of power
I have to learn alone
to turn my body without force
in the deep element.

And now: it is easy to forget
45 what I came for
among so many who have always
lived here
swaying their crenellated[2] fans
between the reefs
50 and besides
you breathe differently down here.

---

[2] Having notched or scalloped projections.

I came to explore the wreck.
The words are purposes.
The words are maps.
55 I came to see the damage that was done
and the treasures that prevail.
I stroke the beam of my lamp
slowly along the flank
of something more permanent
60 than fish or weed

the thing I came for:
the wreck and not the story of the wreck
the thing itself and not the myth

the drowned face always staring
65 toward the sun
the evidence of damage
worn by salt and sway into this threadbare beauty
the ribs of the disaster
curving their assertion
70 among the tentative haunters.

This is the place.
And I am here, the mermaid whose dark hair
streams black, the merman in his armored body
We circle silently
75 about the wreck
we dive into the hold.
I am she: I am he

whose drowned face sleeps with open eyes
whose breasts still bear the stress
80 whose silver, copper, vermeil[3] cargo lies
obscurely inside barrels
half-wedged and left to rot
we are the half-destroyed instruments
that once held to a course
85 the water-eaten log
the fouled compass

We are, I am, you are
by cowardice or courage
the one who find our way

---

[3] Metal that is gilded.

90 back to this scene
   carrying a knife, a camera
   a book of myths
   in which
   our names do not appear.

■ EXPLORATIONS OF THE TEXT ■

1. Trace and paraphrase the stages of this journey. What is your reaction to the metaphor of diving? Why does Rich choose the metaphor of "diving into the wreck"?
2. Why does the speaker switch from "I" to "we" to "you"?
3. What does the "book of myths" represent?
4. Why does the speaker refer to Cousteau in line 9?
5. Explore the water imagery. What do the "sea" and "the deep element" symbolize (stanzas 3, 4, 5)?
6. Explain stanza 6. What does "the wreck" signify? Why are the words "purposes" and "maps"? What are "the damage" and "the treasures"?
7. Interpret: "the wreck and not the story of the wreck/the thing itself and not the myth" (lines 62–63).
8. Why is the speaker "the mermaid"? Why is she androgynous ("I am she: I am he")? With whom does she merge?
9. Examine the symbolism of the "cargo" and the drowned remnants of the captain's quarters: "instruments," "log," and "compass."
10. Consider the conclusion of the poem. What revelation does the speaker experience? Is the ending hopeful? pessimistic?

■■ JOURNAL ENTRIES ■■

1. Write about a time in your life when you searched "the wreck." What "damage" and "treasures" did you discover?
2. Write about a person who guided you when your own "instruments" became "half-destroyed."
3. Write a double-entry notebook for this poem.

■■■ IDEAS FOR WRITING ■■■

1. Explore the symbolism of "diving into the wreck." Interpret the images and the symbolism of each stage of the journey.
2. What new mythology for men and for women emerges in the poem?
3. Create an alternative mythology for the relation of men and of women.
4. In an essay, "When We Dead Awaken: Writing as Re-Vision," Rich asserts that "re-vision—the act of looking back, of seeing with fresh eyes . . . —is for women more than a chapter in cultural history; it is an act of survival." Is this poem a model of the process of "re-vision"? Argue.

This Place in the Ways

Muriel Rukeyser

Muriel Rukeyser (1913–1980) was born in New York City where she lived for most of her life. She attended Vassar College where, with Elizabeth Bishop and Mary McCarthy, she founded a literary magazine. Through the thirties and forties, Rukeyser's work reflected her feelings about social problems in the United States and about the atrocities committed under the Nazi regime before and during World War II. She produced The Soul and Body of John Brown *(1940),* Wake Island *(1942),* Beast in View *(1944), and* The Green Wave *(1948). Her later work includes* Body of Waking *(1958),* The Speed of Darkness *(1968),* Breaking Open *(1973), and* The Gates *(1976).*

Rukeyser wrote "This Place in the Ways" in 1951 as an expression of new hope for world peace after the horrors of World War II. Her message seems equally appropriate today.

> Having come to this place
> I set out once again
> On the dark and marvelous way
> From where I began:
> 5 Belief in the love of the world,
> Woman, spirit, and man.
>
> Having failed in all things
> I enter a new age
> Seeing the old ways as toys,
> 10 The houses of a stage

Painted and long forgot;
And I find love and rage.

Rage for the world as it is
But for what it may be
15 More love now than last year.
And always less self-pity
Since I know in a clearer light
The strength of the mystery.

And at this place in the ways
20 I wait for song,
My poem-hand still, on the paper,
All night long.
Poems in throat and hand, asleep,
And my storm beating strong!

■ EXPLORATIONS OF THE TEXT ■

1. What does "this place in the ways" (line 19) represent? What does "the new age" (line 7) signify?
2. What is "the dark and marvelous way"? In what does the speaker want to believe?
3. Why does the speaker "find love and rage" in regarding "the old ways"? How is the past depicted?
4. What does "the strength of the mystery" signify?
5. Why does the speaker "wait for song"? What does the "storm beating strong" suggest?
6. What metaphor guides the poem?
7. What hope for the future does the poem convey? What is the speaker's approach to facing the future?
8. "Place in the ways," "new age," "mystery," "storm": what is the effect of such deliberately vague word choices?
9. Compare Rukeyser's view of the future with Black Elk's vision and with the speaker's ideas in "My Name is 'I am Living.'"

■■ JOURNAL ENTRIES ■■

1. Define "this place in the ways" or "the mystery."
2. What is your way of dealing with the unknown, with change?
3. Summarize and react to the philosophy of life expressed in the poem.

■■■ **IDEAS FOR WRITING** ■■■

---

1. Is Rukeyser's vision affirmative? Why or why not?
2. Compare Rukeyser's view of the future with "I Have a Dream," "Black Elk Speaks," and/or Tagore's songs.

Poem of Return

Jofre Rocha

Born in Angola, Jofre Rocha (1941–   ) was a member of the M.P.L.A., the Popular Movement for the Liberation of Angola, and he was imprisoned a number of times. After Angola achieved independence from Portugal in 1975, he became Minister of External Trade. A poet, his lyrics in translation appear in Poems From Angola *(1979).*

In "Poem of Return," Rocha creates a speaker who longs to return "from the land of exile and silence" to commemorate the lives, experiences, and rebellion of his people.

When I return from the land of exile and silence,
do not bring me flowers.

Bring me rather all the dews,
tears of dawns which witnessed dramas.
5 Bring me the immense hunger for love
and the plaint of tumid sexes in star-studded night.
Bring me the long night of sleeplessness
with mothers mourning, their arms bereft of sons.

When I return from the land of exile and silence,
10 no, do not bring me flowers . . .

Bring me only, just this
the last wish of heroes fallen at day-break
with a wingless stone in hand
and a thread of anger snaking from their eyes.

■ EXPLORATIONS OF THE TEXT ■

1. What initial impressions of the speaker do you gain from the first two lines?
2. What do "dews," "tears of dawn," "hunger for love," and "the long night of sleeplessness" represent? What poetic device is used in this and the closing stanza?
3. How does the speaker view the heroes? Why must they be remembered? What do lines 13–14 suggest about the heroes?
4. Contrast "silence" and memory. What is the function of memory?
5. Why does the speaker reject "flowers"? Why does he repeat the refrain and add "no" (lines 9–10)?
6. Contrast this speaker's sense of exile and desire for return with Dipoko's "Exile."

■■ JOURNAL ENTRIES ■■

1. React to the mood and tone of the poem.
2. With what does the speaker desire to unite?

■■■ IDEAS FOR WRITING ■■■

1. How does Rocha envision his country and its struggle for independence?

Exile

Mbella Sonne Dipoko

Mbella Sonne Dipoko (1936–   ) was born in Cameroon and grew up in Western Cameroon and in Nigeria. He worked as a news reporter for the Nigerian Broadcasting Corporation from 1958 to 1960 in France. There he briefly studied law at Paris University, but he primarily has devoted his time to painting and to poetry. His published works include the novels, A Few Nights and Days *(1966) and* Because of Women *(1969); the volume of poems,* Black and White in Love *(1972); and the play,* Overseas *(1968). He now lives in Paris.*

"Exile," like many of Dipoko's poems, has both a revolutionary and a mystical stance.

In silence
The overloaded canoe leaves our shores

But who are these soldiers in camouflage,
These clouds going to rain in foreign lands?

5 The night is losing its treasures
The future seems a myth
Warped on a loom worked by lazy hands.

But perhaps all is not without some good for us
As from the door of a shack a thousand miles away
10 The scaly hand of a child takes in greeting
The long and skinny fingers of the rain.

■ EXPLORATIONS OF THE TEXT ■

1. What does the "overloaded canoe" signify? Who are "these soldiers in camouflage"? To what does Dipoko refer?
2. Why is the night "losing its treasures"? Why is the future "a myth"? Explain the metaphor of weaving.
3. What do the images of the last two lines suggest? What is the **irony** in the closing?
4. How does the speaker in "exile" view the future of his country?

■■ JOURNAL ENTRIES ■■

1. Paraphrase the speaker's view of the future.

■■■ IDEAS FOR WRITING ■■■

1. What themes of exile emerge in this poem?
2. Compare the speaker's vision of the future with the persona's views in Rocha's poem.

To live in the Borderlands means you

Gloria Anzaldúa

In this poem, the speaker begins by reflecting on being a "mulata"[1]—Hispanic, Indian, Black, Spanish, and White. She expands her vision to conceptualize all forms of North American ethnic identity, till North America itself becomes the "Borderlands," without borders, a "crossroads" of all cultures.

To live in the Borderlands means you
    are neither *hispana india negra española*[2]
    ni[3] *gabacha,*[4] *eres mestiza,*[5] *mulata,* half-breed
    caught in the crossfire between camps
    while carrying all five races on your back
    not knowing which side to turn to, run from;

To live in the Borderlands means knowing
    that the *india* in you, betrayed for 500 years,
    is no longer speaking to you,
    that *mexicanas* call you *rajetas,*[6]
    that denying the Anglo inside you
    is as bad as having denied the Indian or Black;

Cuando vives en la frontera[7]
    people walk through you, the wind steals your voice,
    you're a *burra,*[8] *buey,*[9] scapegoat,
    forerunner of a new race,
    half and half—both woman and man, neither—
    a new gender;

To live in the Borderlands means to
    put *chile* in the borscht,
    eat whole wheat *tortillas,*
    speak Tex-Mex with a Brooklyn accent;
    be stopped by *la migra* at the border checkpoints;

---

[1] A person of mixed racial ancestry.
[2] Spanish, Indian, Black, Black Spanish woman.
[3] Neither (nor).
[4] A Chicano term for a white woman [Author's note].
[5] You are of mixed blood.
[6] Literally, "Split," that is, having betrayed your word [Author's Note].
[7] When you live in the borderlands.
[8] Donkey [Author's Note].
[9] Oxen [Author's Note].

Living in the Borderlands means you fight hard to
    resist the gold elixer beckoning from the bottle,
    the pull of the gun barrel,
    the rope crushing the hollow of your throat;

In the Borderlands
    you are the battleground
    where enemies are kin to each other;
    you are at home, a stranger,
    the border disputes have been settled
    the volley of shots have shattered the truce
    you are wounded, lost in action
    dead, fighting back;

To live in the Borderlands means
    the mill with the razor white teeth wants to shred off
    your olive-red skin, crush out the kernel, your heart
    pound you pinch you roll you out
    smelling like white bread but dead;

To survive the Borderlands
    you must live *sin fronteras* [10]
    be a crossroads.

■   **EXPLORATIONS OF THE TEXT**   ■

---

1. Who is "you"? How does the speaker characterize "you"?
2. In the Borderlands, "people walk through you, the wind steals your voice"—why?
3. How does the speaker extend her vision beyond the "mestiza"? Whom does her vision include? What are the other borders?
4. Analyze stanzas 5–8. To what specific historical contexts does Anzaldúa refer in stanzas 5 and 6?
5. Explain the symbolism of "the mill" in stanza 7. What is the central metaphor?
6. Examine the speaker's conclusion. What **paradox** is apparent?
7. Analyze the impact of the Spanish words. What do they add to the poem's effect?
8. Compare views of language, heritage, and naming in this poem with those in Walcott's "A Far Cry from Africa," Rich's "Diving into the Wreck," or Menchú's essay.

---

[10] Without borders [Author's Note].

▪▪ JOURNAL ENTRIES ▪▪

1. React to this poem. How do you respond to the violent images?
2. Choose one stanza, and write a reader response. Do you agree with the persona's views?
3. Analyze the poem's structure as if it were an expository essay. What modes of development does Anzaldúa employ?

▪▪▪ IDEAS FOR WRITING ▪▪▪

1. Compare processes of awakening and revelation in this poem and in "Diving into the Wreck."
2. How does Anzaldúa envision/re-envision North American ethnic identity? Do you agree?
3. Paraphrase and analyze the political argument of this poem.
4. Compare the clash of traditions in this poem with the conflicts in *"Master Harold"* . . . *and the Boys,* "Dead Men's Path," and/or "The Green Tree."
5. Contrast Anzaldúa's view of "living in the borderlands" with Tagore's view of a limitless world.

My Name Is "I Am Living"

Anna Lee Walters

A member of the Pawnee and Otoe-Missouria tribes of Oklahoma, Anna Lee Walters (1946–) is a technical writer, an author of text-books, and a poet. Her volumes of poetry include The Man to Send Rain Clouds *(1974),* Warriors of the Rainbow *(1975), and* The Third Woman *(1978). She is director of the Navajo Community College Press, which publishes books about Native Americans, past and present.*

In this poem the speaker acknowledges her union with all living things and presents concrete images of birth and of renewal.

My name is "I am living."
My home is all directions and is everlasting.
Instructed and carried to you by the wind,
I have felt the feathers in pale clouds and bowed before the Sun
5 who watches me from a blanket of faded blue.

In a gentle whirlwind I was shaken,
made to see on earth in many ways,
And when in awe my mouth fell open,
I tasted a fine red clay.
10 Its flavor has remained after uncounted days.
This gave me cause to drink from a crystal stream
that only I have seen.
So I listened to all its flowing wisdom
and learned from it a Song—
15 This song the wind and I
have since sung together.
Unknowing, I was encircled by its water and cleansed.
Naked and damp, I was embraced and dried
by the warmth of your presence.
20 Dressed forever in the scent of dry cedar,
I am purified and free.
And I will not allow you to ignore me.
I have brought to you a gift.
It is all I have but it is yours.
25 You may reach out and enfold it.
It is only the strength in the caress of a gentle breeze,
But it will carry you to meet the eagle in the sky.
My name is "I am living." I am here.
My name is "I am living." I am here.

■ EXPLORATIONS OF THE TEXT ■

1. Who is the "I" in the poem? Characterize the voice of the speaker. Is she real? mythic?
2. Explain: "My home is all directions and is everlasting."
3. Why is the speaker "purified and free"?
4. Who is the "you"? What does the speaker give to the "you"?
5. What is the symbolism of "the eagle in the sky"?
6. Why does line 29 repeat line 28 in the closing refrain?
7. Discuss the poem's chanting rhythm.
8. Contrast the theme of this poem with "Diving into the Wreck," "The Second Coming," or "Stone Olives."

■■ JOURNAL ENTRIES ■■

1. Characterize the speaker. Whom does the speaker address? What is the speaker's purpose?
2. Write a reader-response journal entry for this poem.
3. Write your own poem or chant. You may begin with "I am living. . . ."

■■■ IDEAS FOR WRITING ■■■

---

1. Analyze this poem as a chant, not as a written expression. Examine the role of the speaker and the presentation of the message. You may use Journal Entry 1 as a beginning.
2. Explain the imagery in this poem.
3. Compare the speaker and themes in this poem with those in Johnson's "Stone Olives."

I Would Like

Yevgeny Yevtushenko

Born in Siberia, Yevgeny Aleksandrovich Yevtushenko (1933–) is well-known in the West for risking his freedom to seek the release of Russian dissidents. His Collected Poems: 1952–1990 *appeared in English translation in 1991. Among his many other volumes are* Yevtushenko: Poems *(1962),* The Poetry of Yevgeny Yevtushenko *(1967),* Stolen Apples *(1971),* Yevtushenko's Reader *(1972),* From Desire to Desire *(1976),* A Dove in Santiago: A Novella in Verse *(1982), and* Almost at the End *(1987). In his introduction to the* Collected Poems, *Albert C. Todd characterizes Yevtushenko and his poetry: "The raw edge of the blade of experience and the rough texture of life itself are honestly reflected and preserved in his unpolished and uninhibited directness."*

"I Would Like" is both an exuberant vision of life and of the future and a close look at human suffering.

1 I would like
          to be born
               in every country,
have a passport
5   for them all
to throw
        all foreign offices
              into panic,
be every fish
10   in every ocean
and every dog
          in the streets of the world.
I don't want to bow down
          before any idols

15 or play at being
                    a Russian Orthodox[1] church hippie,
    but I would like to plunge
                          deep into Lake Baikal[2]
    and surface snorting
20   somewhere,
                        why not in the Mississippi?
    In my damned beloved universe
                          I would like
    to be a lonely weed,
25   but not a delicate Narcissus[3]
    kissing his own mug
                    in the mirror.
    I would like to be
                    any of God's creatures
30 right down to the last mangy hyena—
    but never a tyrant
                    or even the cat of a tyrant.
    I would like to be
                    reincarnated as a man
35   in any image:
    a victim of prison tortures,
    a homeless child in the slums of Hong Kong,
    a living skeleton in Bangladesh,[4]
    a holy beggar in Tibet,[5]
40 a black in Cape Town,[6]
    but never
                    in the image of Rambo.[7]
    The only people whom I hate
                    are the hypocrites—
45 pickled hyenas
                    in heavy syrup.
    I would like to lie
                    under the knives of all the surgeons in the world,
    be hunchbacked, blind,

---

[1] Russian orthodox Christianity, traditional religion of majority of eastern Slavs.
[2] Lake in Eastern Siberia; one of deepest lakes in the world.
[3] A figure from Greek mythology who gazed into a stream and fell in love with his own
   shadow.
[4] Reference to famine in Bangladesh, a republic in South Asia, on the Bay of Bengal between
   India and Burma.
[5] A country in South Asia.
[6] City in South Africa.
[7] Reference to a series of movies starring Sylvester Stallone as a military hero—Rambo—from
   the Vietnam War.

50   suffer all kinds of diseases,
                          wounds and scars,
be a victim of war,
           or a sweeper of cigarette butts,
just so a filthy microbe of superiority
55   doesn't creep inside.
I would not like to be in the elite,
nor, of course,
         in the cowardly herd,
nor be a guard dog of that herd,
60 nor a shepherd,
           sheltered by that herd.
And I would like happiness,
              but not at the expense of the unhappy,
and I would like freedom,
65   but not at the expense of the unfree.
I would like to love
           all the women in the world,
and I would like to be a woman, too—
              just once . . .
70 Men have been diminished
           by Mother Nature.
Why couldn't we give motherhood
             to men?
If an innocent child
75   stirred
            below his heart,
man would probably
         not be so cruel.
I would like to be man's daily bread—
80 say,
     a cup of rice
          for a Vietnamese woman in mourning,
cheap wine
       in a Neapolitan workers' trattoria,[8]
85 or a tiny tube of cheese
         in orbit round the moon.
Let them eat me,
         let them drink me,
only let my death
90   be of some use.
I would like to belong to all times,
             shock all history so much

---

[8] Cafe.

that it would be amazed
                what a smart aleck I was.
95 I would like to bring Nefertiti[9]
                   to Pushkin[10] in a troika.
I would like to increase
               the space of a moment
                       a hundredfold,
100 so that in the same moment
                I could drink vodka with fishermen in Siberia
and sit together with Homer,[11]
               Dante,[12]
                  Shakespeare,[13]
105   and Tolstoy,
drinking anything,
            except, of course,
                Coca-Cola,
—dance to the tom-toms in the Congo,
110 —strike at Renault,[14]
—chase a ball with Brazilian boys
               at Copacabana Beach.[15]
I would like to know every language,
               like the secret waters under the earth,
115 and do all kinds of work at once.
              I would make sure
that one Yevtushenko was merely a poet,
              the second—an underground fighter
                   somewhere,
120 I couldn't say where
           for security reasons,
the third—a student at Berkeley,
            the fourth—a jolly Georgian[16] drinker,
and the fifth—
125   maybe a teacher of Eskimo children in Alaska,
the sixth—
        a young president,
          somewhere, say, modestly speaking, in Sierra Leone,[17]

---

[9] Ancient Egyptian queen (fourth century B.C.E.) known for her beauty.
[10] Nineteenth-century Russian poet (1799–1837).
[11] Ancient Greek epic poet who wrote *The Iliad* (ninth to eighth century B.C.E.?).
[12] Medieval Italian poet who wrote *The Inferno* (1265–1321).
[13] Renaissance dramatist and poet. See Chapter 4.
[14] French car manufacturer.
[15] Famous beach in Rio de Janeiro, Brazil.
[16] Georgia, one of the newly formed republics in what was the Soviet Union.
[17] Country in Africa.

the seventh—
130   would still be shaking a rattle in his stroller,
and the tenth . . .
                          the hundredth . . .
                                    the millionth . . .
For me it's not enough to be myself,
135   let me be everyone!
Every creature
               usually has a double,
but God was stingy
                    with the carbon paper,
140 and in his Paradise Publishing Corporation
                               made a unique copy of me.
But I shall muddle up
               all God's cards—
                          I shall confound God!
145 I shall be in a thousand copies to the end of my days,
so that the earth buzzes with me,
                          and computers go berserk
in the world census of me.
I would like to fight on all your barricades,
150   humanity,
dying each night
               like an exhausted moon,
and resurrecting each morning
                          like a newborn sun,
155 with an immortal soft spot—fontanel—
                          on my head.
And when I die,
               a smart-aleck Siberian François Villon,[18]
do not lay me in the earth
160   of France
                          or Italy,
but in our Russian, Siberian earth,
                          on a still-green hill,
where I first felt
165   that I was
               everyone.

---

[18] French poet (1431–1462?).

■ **EXPLORATIONS OF THE TEXT** ■

---

1. Why does the speaker wish "to be born/in every country"? Why does he desire to be a "fish" or a "dog"?
2. Why does he call the world his "damned beloved universe"? Why does he enumerate those who suffer?
3. Who does he not wish to be? Why?
4. Explain the historical, geographical, religious, and political allusions.
5. What are the ten incarnations of Yevtushenko? Describe the speaker's sense of humor. Find examples of **hyperbole.**
6. Explain the speaker's view of his identity at the end of the poem. Begin with line 66. Analyze the images and themes.
7. How does this poem remind you of works by Whitman and Giovanni (Chapter 4), and Ginsberg (Chapter 7)? How does the poem connect to lyrics by Tagore, Rilke, and Walters in this chapter?

■■ **JOURNAL ENTRIES** ■■

---

1. Write a poem with the same title. Imitate Yevtushenko's style.
2. Choose and react to the best or the worst lines in the poem.
3. Respond to "I Would Like."

■■■ **IDEAS FOR WRITING** ■■■

---

1. Discuss the themes of this poem, (such as unity in diversity or the expansiveness of self).
2. Compare this poem's imagery, form, and themes to those in Giovanni's "Ego Tripping." How do they differ?
3. Analyze the character of the speaker in the poem.

Poems for Further Reading

My Heart Leaps Up When I Behold

William Wordsworth (1770–1850)

> My heart leaps up when I behold
> A rainbow in the sky:
> So was it when my life began;
> So is it now I am a man;
> 5 So be it when I shall grow old,
> Or let me die!
> The Child is father of the Man;
> And I could wish my days to be
> Bound each to each by natural piety.

Kubla Khan: or, a Vision in a Dream[1]

Samuel Taylor Coleridge (1772–1834)

> In Xanadu[2] did Kubla Khan[3]
> A stately pleasure-dome decree:
> Where Alph, the sacred river, ran
> Through caverns measureless to man
> 5 Down to a sunless sea.
> So twice five miles of fertile ground
> With walls and towers were girdled round:
> And here were gardens bright with sinuous rills
> Where blossomed many an incense-bearing tree;
> 10 And there were forests ancient as the hills,
> Enfolding sunny spots of greenery.

---

[1] The poem resulted from a dream induced by Opium. Since he was interrupted, Coleridge remembered only a fragment.
[2] Summer capitol of Kubla Khan.
[3] Kubla Khan (1216–1294), grandson of Genghis Khan, and founder of the Mongol Empire in China.

But oh! that deep romantic chasm which slanted
Down the green hill athwart a cedarn cover!⁴
A savage place! as holy and enchanted
15 As e'er beneath a waning moon was haunted
By woman wailing for her demon-lover!
And from this chasm, with ceaseless turmoil seething,
As if this earth in fast thick pants were breathing,
A mighty fountain momently was forced,
20 Amid whose swift half-intermitted burst
Huge fragments vaulted like rebounding hail,
Or chaffy grain beneath the thresher's flail:
And 'mid these dancing rocks at once and ever
It flung up momently the sacred river.
25 Five miles meandering with a mazy motion
Through wood and dale the sacred river ran,
Then reached the caverns measureless to man,
And sank in tumult to a lifeless ocean:
And 'mid this tumult Kubla heard from far
30 Ancestral voices prophesying war!

The shadow of the dome of pleasure
Floated midway on the waves;
Where was heard the mingled measure
From the fountain and the caves.
35 It was a miracle of rare device,
A sunny pleasure-dome with caves of ice!

A damsel with a dulcimer
In a vision once I saw;
It was an Abyssinian⁵ maid,
40 And on her dulcimer she played,
Singing of Mount Abora.⁶
Could I revive within me
Her symphony and song,
To such a deep delight 'twould win me,
45 That with music loud and long,
I would build that dome in air,
That sunny dome! those caves of ice!
And all who heard should see them there,
And all should cry, Beware! Beware!

---

⁴ Spanning a grove of cedars.
⁵ Ethiopian.
⁶ Mount Abora in Abyssinia, referred to by Milton, *Paradise Lost* 4:28.

50 His flashing eyes, his floating hair!
    Weave a circle round him thrice,
    And close your eyes with holy dread,
    For he on honey-dew hath fed,
    And drunk the milk of Paradise.

Ode on a Grecian Urn

John Keats (1795–1821)

I

    Thou still unravished bride of quietness,
      Thou foster child of silence and slow time,
    Sylvan[1] historian, who canst thus express
      A flowery tale more sweetly than our rhyme:
5 What leaf-fringed legend haunts about thy shape
      Of deities or mortals, or of both,
        In Tempe[2] or the dales of Arcady?[3]
      What men or gods are these? What maidens loath?
    What mad pursuit? What struggle to escape?
10   What pipes and timbrels? What wild ecstasy?

II

    Heard melodies are sweet, but those unheard
      Are sweeter; therefore, ye soft pipes, play on;
    Not to the sensual ear, but, more endeared,
      Pipe to the spirit ditties of no tone:
15 Fair youth, beneath the trees, thou canst not leave
      Thy song, nor ever can those trees be bare;
        Bold Lover, never, never canst thou kiss,
    Though winning near the goal—yet, do not grieve;
        She cannot fade, though thou hast not thy bliss,
20   Forever wilt thou love, and she be fair!

---

[1] Referring to woods or forest.
[2] Valley in Greece.
[3] Valleys of Arcadia, symbolic of pastoral life and beauty.

III

Ah, happy, happy boughs! that cannot shed
    Your leaves, nor ever bid the Spring adieu;
And, happy melodist, unwearièd,
    Forever piping songs forever new;
25 More happy love! more happy, happy love!
    Forever warm and still to be enjoyed,
        Forever panting, and forever young;
All breathing human passion far above,
    That leaves a heart high-sorrowful and cloyed,
30   A burning forehead, and a parching tongue.

IV

Who are these coming to the sacrifice?
    To what green altar, O mysterious priest,
Lead'st thou that heifer lowing at the skies,
    And all her silken flanks with garlands dressed?
35 What little town by river or sea shore,
    Or mountain-built with peaceful citadel,
        Is emptied of this folk, this pious morn?
And, little town, thy streets forevermore
    Will silent be; and not a soul to tell
40   Why thou art desolate, can e'er return.

V

O Attic[4] shape! Fair attitude! with brede[5]
    Of marble men and maidens overwrought,[6]
With forest branches and the trodden weed;
    Thou, silent form, dost tease us out of thought
45 As doth eternity: Cold Pastoral![7]
    When old age shall this generation waste,
    Thou shalt remain, in midst of other woe
    Than ours, a friend to man, to whom thou say'st,
"Beauty is truth, truth beauty,—that is all
50   Ye know on earth, and all ye need to know."

---

[4] Referring to Athens or Athenians.
[5] Braid.
[6] Elaborate; highly decorated.
[7] An idealized vision of country or rural life.

The Haunted Palace

Edgar Allan Poe (1809–1849)

I

In the greenest of our valleys,
    By good angels tenanted,
Once a fair and stately palace—
    Radiant palace—reared its head.
5 In the monarch Thought's dominion—
    It stood there!
Never seraph spread a pinion
    Over fabric half so fair.

II

Banners yellow, glorious, golden,
    On its roof did float and flow;
(This—all this—was in the olden
    Time long ago)
And every gentle air that dallied,
    In that sweet day,
Along the ramparts plumed and pallid,
    A winged odor went away.

III

Wanderers in that happy valley
    Through two luminous windows saw
Spirits moving musically
    To a lute's well-tunèd law,
Round about a throne, where sitting
    (Porphyrogene!)[1]
In state his glory well befitting,
    The ruler of the realm was seen.

---

[1] Born to purple, in royal demeanor.

IV

25 And all with pearl and ruby glowing
    Was the fair palace door,
Through which came flowing, flowing, flowing
    And sparkling evermore,
A troop of Echoes whose sweet duty
30   Was but to sing,
In voices of surpassing beauty,
    The wit and wisdom of their king.

V

But evil things, in robes of sorrow,
    Assailed the monarch's high estate;
35 (Ah, let us mourn, for never morrow
    Shall dawn upon him, desolate!)
And, round about his home, the glory
    That blushed and bloomed
Is but a dim-remembered story
40   Of the old time entombed.

VI

And travelers now within that valley,
    Through the red-litten windows see
Vast forms that move fantastically
    To a discordant melody;
45 While, like a rapid ghastly river,
    Through the pale door,
A hideous throng rush out forever,
    And laugh—but smile no more.

Facing West from California's Shores
Walt Whitman (1819–1892)

Facing west from California's shores,
Inquiring, tireless, seeking what is yet unfound,
I, a child, very old, over waves, towards the house of maternity,
    the land of migrations, look afar,
Look off the shores of my Western sea, the circle almost circled;
5 For starting westward from Hindustan, from the vales of Kashmere,
From Asia, from the north, from the God, the sage, and the
      hero,
From the south, from the flowery peninsulas and the spice islands,
Long having wander'd since, round the earth having wander'd,
Now I face home again, very pleas'd and joyous,
10 (But where is what I started for so long ago?
And why is it yet unfound?)

Uphill
Christina Rossetti (1830–1894)

Does the road wind uphill all the way?
    Yes, to the very end.
Will the day's journey take the whole long day?
    From morn to night, my friend.

5 But is there for the night a resting place?
    A roof for when the slow dark hours begin.
May not the darkness hide it from my face?
    You cannot miss that inn.

10 Shall I meet other wayfarers at night?
    Those who have gone before.
Then must I knock, or call when just in sight?
    They will not keep you standing at that door.

Shall I find comfort, travel-sore and weak?
15   Of labor you shall find the sum.
Will there be beds for me and all who seek?
    Yea, beds for all who come.

The New Colossus
Emma Lazarus (1849–1887)

Not like the brazen giant of Greek fame,[1]
With conquering limbs astride from land to land;
Here at our sea-washed, sunset gates shall stand
A mighty woman with a torch, whose flame
5 Is the imprisoned lightning, and her name
Mother of Exiles. From her beacon-hand
Glows world-wide welcome; her mild eyes command
The air-bridged harbor that twin cities frame.
"Keep, ancient lands, your storied pomp!" cries she
10 With silent lips. "Give me your tired, your poor,
Your huddled masses yearning to breathe free,
The wretched refuse of your teeming shore.
Send these, the homeless, tempest-tost to me,
I lift my lamp beside the golden door!"

Sailing to Byzantium[1]
William Butler Yeats (1865–1939)

I

That is no country[2] for old men. The young
In one another's arms, birds in the trees
—Those dying generations—at their song,
The salmon-falls, the mackerel-crowded seas,
5 Fish, flesh, or fowl, commend all summer long
Whatever is begotten, born, and dies.
Caught in that sensual music all neglect
Monuments of unageing intellect.

---

[1] Reference to the huge statue of Helios at Rhodes. The Colossus of Rhodes, one of the Seven Wonders of the World.

[1] Capitol of the Byzantine Empire; revered by Yeats as a place where artistry reached its apex. Now called Istanbul, "Byzantium was the center of European civilization and the source of its spiritual philosophy, so I symbolize the search for spiritual life by a journey to that city." (Yeats, B.B.C., 1931)

[2] Ireland

II

An aged man is but a paltry thing,
10 A tattered coat upon a stick, unless
Soul clap its hands and sing, and louder sing
For every tatter in its mortal dress,
Nor is there singing school but studying
Monuments of its own magnificence;
15 And therefore I have sailed the seas and come
To the holy city of Byzantium.

III

O sages standing in God's holy fire
As in the gold mosaic of a wall,
Come from the holy fire, perne in a gyre[3]
20 And be the singing-masters of my soul.
Consume my heart away; sick with desire
And fastened to a dying animal
It knows not what it is; and gather me
Into the artifice of eternity.

IV

25 Once out of nature I shall never take
My bodily form from any natural thing,
But such a form as Grecian goldsmiths make
Of hammered gold and gold enamelling[4]
To keep a drowsy Emperor awake;
30 Or set upon a golden bough to sing
To lords and ladies of Byzantium
Of what is past, or passing, or to come.

---

[3] Whirl in spirals. The gyre or cone represented cycles of history and the fate of the individual.
The speaker asks the sages in the mosaic to take him from the ordinary world and to the
eternal world of art.
[4] Yeats read that the emperor's palace contained a tree of gold and silver and artificial birds
that could sing.

Desert Places

Robert Frost (1874–1963)

Snow falling and night falling fast, oh, fast
In a field I looked into going past,
And the ground almost covered smooth in snow,
But a few weeds and stubble showing last.

5 The woods around it have it—it is theirs.
All animals are smothered in their lairs.
I am too absent-spirited to count;
The loneliness includes me unawares.

And lonely as it is that loneliness
10 Will be more lonely ere it will be less—
A blanker whiteness of benighted snow
With no expression, nothing to express.

They cannot scare me with their empty spaces
Between stars—on stars where no human race is.
15 I have it in me so much nearer home
To scare myself with my own desert places.

The Waking

Theodore Roethke (1908–1963)

I wake to sleep, and take my waking slow.
I feel my fate in what I cannot fear.
I learn by going where I have to go.

We think by feeling. What is there to know?
5 I hear my being dance from ear to ear.
I wake to sleep, and take my waking slow.
Of those so close beside me, which are you?
God bless the Ground! I shall walk softly there,
And learn by going where I have to go.

10 Light takes the Tree; but who can tell us how?
The lowly worm climbs up a winding stair;
I wake to sleep, and take my waking slow.

Great Nature has another thing to do
To you and me; so take the lively air,
15 And, lovely, learn by going where to go.

This shaking keeps me steady. I should know.
What falls away is always. And is near.
I wake to sleep, and take my waking slow.
I learn by going where I have to go.

Do Not Go Gentle into That Good Night

Dylan Thomas (1914–1953)

Do not go gentle into that good night,
Old age should burn and rave at close of day;
Rage, rage against the dying of the light.

Though wise men at their end know dark is right,
5 Because their words had forked no lightning they
Do not go gentle into that good night.

Good men, the last wave by, crying how bright
Their frail deeds might have danced in a green bay,
Rage, rage against the dying of the light.

10 Wild men who caught and sang the sun in flight,
And learn, too late, they grieved it on its way,
Do not go gentle into that good night.

Grave men, near death, who see with blinding sight
Blind eyes could blaze like meteors and be gay,
15 Rage, rage against the dying of the light.

And you, my father, there on the sad height,
Curse, bless, me now with your fierce tears, I pray.
Do not go gentle into that good night.
Rage, rage against the dying of the light.

A Blessing

James Wright (1927–1980)

Just off the highway to Rochester, Minnesota,
Twilight bounds softly forth on the grass.
And the eyes of those two Indian ponies
Darken with kindness.
5 They have come gladly out of the willows
To welcome my friend and me.
We step over the barbed wire into the pasture
Where they have been grazing all day, alone.
They ripple tensely, they can hardly contain their happiness
10 That we have come.
They bow shyly as wet swans. They love each other.
There is no loneliness like theirs.
At home once more,
They begin munching the young tufts of spring in the darkness.
15 I would like to hold the slenderer one in my arms.
For she has walked over to me
And nuzzled my left hand.
She is black and white,
Her mane falls wild on her forehead,
20 And the light breeze moves me to caress her long ear
That is delicate as the skin over a girl's wrist.
Suddenly I realize
That if I stepped out of my body I would break
Into blossom.

Far Inland

Anonymous Eskimo Woman

Far inland
go my sad thoughts.
It is too much
never to leave this bench.
5 I want to wander
far inland.

I remember
hunting animals,
the good food.
10 It is too much
never to leave this bench.
I want to wander
far inland.

I hunted
15 like men. I carried
weapons, shot reindeer,
bull, cow, and calf,
killed them with my arrows
one evening
20 when almost winter
twilight fell
far inland.

I remember
how I struggled
25 inland
under the dropping sky
of snow.
The earth is white
far inland.

Atsumori

Seami Motokiyo

Seami Motokiyo (1363/64–1443), often called simply Seami or Zeami, spent his early years in training for the theater. He became one of the favorites of the powerful Shogun, Ashikaga Yoshimitsu, and under his patronage, he developed the Nō drama into its highest form. Trained in Zen Buddhist philosophy, Seami strove in his plays to show his audience the path to perfect peace through serene meditation on beauty.

Nō plays have fascinated many twentieth-century poets and dramatists. Characterized by a minimal script, which becomes elaborate through conventions of acting, dancing, chanting, and singing, the Nō play features both poetry and prose. The focus is not on the action, but on the effects of the action on the characters or their ghosts. Much of the complexity of the poetic language is lost in translation, but the contemporary reader can achieve a sense of its power to convey aesthetic beauty and religious consolation.

Atsumori, Seami's prototypical Nō play, is based on the twelfth-century wars between the Taira and Minamoto clans. In 1183, the Minamotos attacked the Taira and completely defeated them. Atsumori, the nephew of Kiyomori, the chief of the Tairas, was killed by Kumagai, who appears as the priest in the drama. Atsumori becomes the ghost or spirit who returns as a young reaper.

Persons

The Priest Rensei (formerly the warrior Kumagai).
A Young Reaper, who turns out to be the ghost of Atsumori.
His Companion.
Chorus.

Priest:
    Life is a lying dream, he only wakes
    Who casts the World aside.
I am Kumagai no Naozane, a man of the country of Musashi. I have left my home and call myself the priest Rensei; this I have done because of my grief at the death of Atsumori, who fell in battle by my hand. Hence it comes that I am dressed in priestly guise.

And now I am going down to Ichi-no-Tani[1] to pray for the salvation of Atsumori's soul.

(He walks slowly across the stage, singing a song descriptive of his journey.)

I have come so fast that here I am already at Ichi-no-Tani, in the country of Tsu.

Truly the past returns to my mind as though it were a thing of to-day.

But listen! I hear the sound of a flute coming from a knoll of rising ground. I will wait here till the flute-player passes, and ask him to tell me the story of this place.

Reapers *(together)*:

> To the music of the reaper's flute
> No song is sung
> But the sighing of wind in the fields.

Young Reaper:

> They that were reaping,
> Reaping on that hill,
> Walk now through the fields
> Homeward, for it is dusk.

Reapers *(together)*:

> Short is the way that leads
> From the sea of Suma back to my home.[2]
> This little journey, up to the hill
> And down to the shore again, and up to the hill,—
> This is my life, and the sum of hateful tasks.
> If one should ask me
> I too would answer
> That on the shore of Suma
> I live in sadness.
> Yet if any guessed my name,
> Then might I too have friends.
> But now from my deep misery
> Even those that were dearest
> Are grown estranged. Here must I dwell abandoned
> To one thought's anguish:
> That I must dwell here.

5 **Priest:**

> Hey, you reapers! I have a question to ask you.

Young Reaper:

> Is it to us you are speaking? What do you wish to know?

---

[1] Means "First Valley."
[2] A reference to the distance from his home in Kyōto. Suma is five kilometers west of Kobi on the coast.

Priest:

    Was it one of you who was playing on the flute just now?

Young Reaper:

    Yes, it was we who were playing.

Priest:

    It was a pleasant sound, and all the pleasanter because one does not look for such music from men of your condition.

10 Young Reaper:

    Unlooked for from men of our condition, you say!

    Have you not read:

    "Do not envy what is above you

    Nor despise what is below you"?

    Moreover the songs of woodmen and the flute-playing
        of herdsmen,

    Flute-playing even of reapers and songs of wood-
        fellers.

    Through poets' verses are known to all the world.

    Wonder not to hear among us

    The sound of a bamboo-flute.

Priest:

    You are right. Indeed it is as you have told me.

    Songs of woodmen and flute-playing of herdsmen . . .

Reaper:

    Flute-playing of reapers . . .

Priest:

    Songs of wood-fellers . . .

Reapers:

    Guide us on our passage through this sad world.

15 Priest:

    Song . . .

Reaper:

    And dance . . .

Priest:

    And the flute . . .

Reaper:

    And music of many instruments . . .

Chorus:

    These are the pastimes that each chooses to his
        taste.

    Of floating bamboo-wood

    Many are the famous flutes that have been
        made;

    Little-Branch and Cicada-Cage,

    And as for the reaper's flute,

    Its name is Green-leaf;

    On the shore of Sumiyoshi

The Corean flute they play.
And here on the shore of Suma
On Stick of the Salt-kilns
The fishers blow their tune.[3]

20 **Priest:**

How strange it is! The other reapers have all gone home, but you alone stay loitering here. How is that?

Reaper:

How is it, you ask? I am seeking for a prayer in the voice of the evening waves. Perhaps *you* will pray the Ten Prayers for me?

Priest:

I can easily pray the Ten Prayers for you, if you will tell me who you are.

Reaper:

To tell you the truth—I am one of the family of Lord Atsumori.

Priest:

One of Atsumori's family? How glad I am!
Then the priest joined his hands *(he kneels down)* and prayed—

> Namu Amidabu.

> Praise to Amida Buddha![4]
> "If I attain to Buddhahood,
> In the whole world and its ten spheres
> Of all that dwell here none shall call on my
> > name
> And be rejected or cast aside."

25 **Chorus:**

> "Oh, reject me not!
> One cry suffices for salvation,
> Yet day and night
> Your prayers will rise for me.
> Happy am I, for though you know not my name,
> Yet for my soul's deliverance
> At dawn and dusk henceforward I know that
> > you will pray."

So he spoke. Then vanished and was seen no more.

(Here follows the Interlude between the two Acts, in which a recitation concerning Atsumori's death takes place. These interludes are subject to variation and are not considered part of the literary text of the play.)

Priest:

Since this is so, I will perform all night the rites of prayer for the dead, and calling upon Amida's name will pray again for the salvation of Atsumori.

(The ghost of Atsumori appears, dressed as a young warrior.)

---

[3] Different kinds of flutes, made of various materials often determined by the occupation of the player.
[4] Reference to a timeless, ideal Buddha named Amida, "Lord of Boundless Light."

Atsumori:

>Would you know who I am
>That like the watchmen at Suma Pass
>Have wakened at the cry of sea-birds roaming
>Upon Awaji shore?
>Listen, Rensei. I am Atsumori.

Priest:

How strange! All this while I have never stopped beating my gong and performing the rites of the Law. I cannot for a moment have dozed, yet I thought that Atsumori was standing before me. Surely it was a dream.

Atsumori:

Why need it be a dream? It is to clear the karma of my waking life that I am come here in visible form before you.

30 Priest:

Is it not written that one prayer will wipe away ten thousand sins? Ceaselessly I have performed the ritual of the Holy Name that clears all sin away. After such prayers, what evil can be left? Though you should be sunk in sin as deep . . .

Atsumori:

>As the sea by a rocky shore,
>Yet should I be salved by prayer.

Priest:

>And that my prayers should save you . . .

Atsumori:

>This too must spring
>From kindness of a former life.[5]

Priest:

>Once enemies . . .

35 Atsumori:

>But now . . .

Priest:

>In truth may we be named . . .

Atsumori:

>Friends in Buddha's Law.

Chorus:

There is a saying, "Put away from you a wicked friend; summon to your side a virtuous enemy." For you it was said, and you have proven it true.

And now come tell with us the tale of your confession, while the night is still dark.

Chorus:

>He[6] bids the flowers of Spring
>Mount the tree-top that men may raise their eyes
>And walk on upward paths;

---

[5] Atsumori must have done Kumagai some kindness in a former incarnation. This action would account for Kumagai's remorse.
[6] Buddha.

He bids the moon in autumn waves be drowned
In token that he visits laggard men
And leads them out from valleys of despair.

40 **Atsumori:**

Now the clan of Taira, building wall to wall,
Spread over the earth like the leafy branches of a
    great tree:

Chorus:

Yet their prosperity lasted but for a day;
It was like the flower of the convolvulus.
There was none to tell them[7]
That glory flashes like sparks from flint-stone,
And after,—darkness.
Oh wretched, the life of men!

Atsumori:

When they were on high they afflicted the humble;
When they were rich they were reckless in pride.
And so for twenty years and more
They ruled this land.
But truly a generation passes like the space of a dream.
The leaves of the autumn of Juyei[8]
Were tossed by the four winds;
Scattered, scattered (like leaves too) floated their
    ships.
And they, asleep on the heaving sea, not even in
    dreams
Went back to home.
Caged birds longing for the clouds,—
Wild geese were they rather, whose ranks are broken
As they fly to southward on their doubtful journey.
So days and months went by; Spring came again
And for a little while
Here dwelt they on the shore of Suma
At the first valley.[9]
From the mountain behind us the winds blew down
Till the fields grew wintry again.
Our ships lay by the shore, where night and day
The sea-gulls cried and salt waves washed on our
    sleeves.
We slept with fishers in their huts
On pillows of sand.
We knew none but the people of Suma.
And when among the pine-trees

---

[7] The translator has omitted a line, the force of which depends upon a play of words.
[8] The Taira evacuated the capital in the second year of Juyei, 1188.
[9] Ichi-no-Tani.

The evening smoke was rising,
Brushwood, as they called it,[10]
Brushwood we gathered
And spread for carpet.
Sorrowful we lived
On the wild shore of Suma,
Till the clan Taira and all its princes
Were but villagers of Suma.

Atsumori:

But on the night of the sixth day of the second month
My father Tsunemori gathered us together.
"To-morrow," he said, "we shall fight our last fight.
To-night is all that is left us."
We sang songs together, and danced.

Priest:

Yes, I remember; we in our siege-camp
Heard the sound of music
Echoing from your tents that night;
There was the music of a flute . . .

45 Atsumori:

The bamboo-flute! I wore it when I died.

Priest:

We heard the singing . . .

Atsumori:

Songs and ballads . . .

Priest:

Many voices

Atsumori:

Singing to one measure.

(Atsumori dances.)

First comes the Royal Boat.

50 Chorus:

The whole clan has put its boats to sea.
He[11] will not be left behind;
He runs to the shore.
But the Royal Boat and the soldiers' boats
Have sailed far away.

Atsumori:

What can he do?
He spurs his horse into the waves.
He is full of perplexity.
And then

---

[10] The name of such a humble thing was unfamiliar to the Taira lords.

[11] Atsumori. This passage is mimed throughout [Translator's Note].

Chorus:
> He looks behind him and sees
> That Kumagai pursues him;
> He cannot escape.
> Then Atsumori turns his horse
> Knee-deep in the lashing waves,
> And draws his sword.
> Twice, three times he strikes; then, still saddled,
> In close fight they twine; roll headlong together
> Among the surf of the shore.
> So Atsumori fell and was slain, but now the Wheel
>> of Fate
> Has turned and brought him back.

(Atsumori rises from the ground and advances towards the Priest with uplifted sword.)

> "There is my enemy," he cries, and would strike,
> But the other is grown gentle
> And calling on Buddha's name
> Has obtained salvation for his foe;
> So that they shall be re-born together
> On one lotus-seat.
> "No, Rensei is not my enemy.
> Pray for me again, oh pray for me again."

■ **EXPLORATIONS OF THE TEXT** ■

1. Examine the first couplet, a convention in Nō drama. Discuss the **paradoxes.**
2. Characterize Kumagai. What is the tone of his first speech?
3. How does the chorus of the Reapers function? Why are they sad? For whom do they speak?
4. What is the role of "music of many instruments"? Look at the brief catalogue of flutes.
5. Why does the Priest pray for the salvation of Atsumori? What happens when the ghost identifies himself?
6. What are themes of the play? Why has the Taira clan suffered?
7. Examine the death of Atsumori. Why does Atsumori describe himself in the third person?
8. Analyze the conclusion. How is rebirth achieved?
9. Compare character, conflict, structure, and theme in this play with those in *"Master Harold"* . . . *and the Boys, Ghosts, Oedipus Rex,* or *Hamlet.*

■■ JOURNAL ENTRIES ■■

1. Write about the appearance of the ghost.
2. React to the description of Atsumori's death.
3. Write a double-entry notebook for this play.

■■■ IDEAS FOR WRITING ■■■

1. Compare the appearances of ghosts in *Atsumori* and in *Hamlet*. Use Journal Entry 1 as a beginning.
2. Write a brief documented essay on some aspect of Nō drama or on Seami.
3. Discuss the themes of forgiveness and salvation in *Atsumori*.
4. Analyze the symbolism of the flute and the music imagery in the play. Refer to your double-entry notebook.

ESSAYS

Reflections on Exile

Edward Said

Edward Said (1935–) was born in Jerusalem. He is currently Pro-
fessor of English and Comparative Literature at Columbia Univer-
sity. In 1966, he published a critical biography, Joseph Conrad and
the Fiction of Autobiography. *Other works include* Orientalism
(1979), The Question of Palestine *(1979),* The World, the Text and
the Critic *(1983), and* Culture and Imperialism *(1993).*

In this essay, Said defines exile as a state in the contemporary
world as close to tragedy as possible. From the condition of exile
emerges a "decentered" life which necessitates contrapuntal vision,
a vision that shifts and never settles into comfort or rootedness,
never settles into predictability or complacency.

1   Exile is strangely compelling to think about but terrible to experience. It is
the unhealable rift forced between a human being and a native place, between the self and its true home: its essential sadness can never be surmounted. And while it is true that literature and history contain heroic,
romantic, glorious, even triumphant episodes in an exile's life, these are no
more than efforts meant to overcome the crippling sorrow of estrangement.
The achievements of exile are permanently undermined by the loss of something left behind for ever.

2   But if true exile is a condition of terminal loss, why has it been transformed
so easily into a potent, even enriching, motif of modern culture? We have become accustomed to thinking of the modern period itself as spiritually orphaned and alienated, the age of anxiety and estrangement. Nietzsche taught us
to feel uncomfortable with tradition, and Freud to regard domestic intimacy as
the polite face painted on patricidal and incestuous rage. Modern Western culture is in large part the work of exiles, émigrés, refugees. In the United States,
academic, intellectual and aesthetic thought is what it is today because of
refugees from fascism, communism and other regimes given to the oppression
and expulsion of dissidents. The critic George Steiner has even proposed the
perceptive thesis that a whole genre of twentieth-century Western literature is
"extraterritorial," a literature by and about exiles, symbolizing the age of the
refugee. Thus Steiner suggests

It seems proper that those who create art in a civilization of quasi-barbarism, which has made so many homeless, should themselves be poets unhoused and wanderers across language. Eccentric, aloof, nostalgic, deliberately untimely . . .

3   In other ages, exiles had similar cross-cultural and transnational visions, suffered the same frustrations and miseries, performed the same elucidating and critical tasks—brilliantly affirmed, for instance, in E.H. Carr's classic study of the nineteenth-century Russian intellectuals clustered around Herzen, *The Romantic Exiles.* But the difference between earlier exiles and those of our own time is, it bears stressing, scale: our age—with its modern warfare, imperialism and the quasi-theological ambitions of totalitarian rulers—is indeed the age of the refugee, the displaced person, mass immigration.

4   Against this large, impersonal setting, exile cannot be made to serve notions of humanism. On the twentieth-century scale, exile is neither aesthetically nor humanistically comprehensible: at most the literature about exile objectifies an anguish and a predicament most people rarely experience at first hand; but to think of the exile informing this literature as beneficially humanistic is to banalize its mutilations, the losses it inflicts on those who suffer them, the muteness with which it responds to any attempt to understand it as "good for us." Is it not true that the views of exile in literature and, moreover, in religion obscure what is truly horrendous: that exile is irremediably secular and unbearably historical; that it is produced by human beings for other human beings; and that, like death but without death's ultimate mercy, it has torn millions of people from the nourishment of tradition, family and geography?

* * *

5   To see a poet in exile—as opposed to reading the poetry of exile—is to see exile's antinomies embodied and endured with a unique intensity. Several years ago I spent some time with Faiz Ahmad Faiz, the greatest of contemporary Urdu[1] poets. He was exiled from his native Pakistan[2] by Zia's military regime, and found a welcome of sorts in strife-torn Beirut.[3] Naturally his closest friends were Palestinian, but I sensed that, although there was an affinity of spirit between them, nothing quite matched—language, poetic convention, or life-history. Only once, when Eqbal Ahmad, a Pakistani friend and a fellow-exile, came to Beirut, did Faiz seem to overcome his sense of constant estrangement. The three of us sat in a dingy Beirut restaurant late one night, while Faiz recited poems. After a time, he and Eqbal stopped translating his verses for my benefit, but as the night wore on it did not matter. What I watched required no translation: it was an

---

[1] Official language of Pakistan; language used by Muslims in India.
[2] Country in Southern Asia.
[3] City and port of Lebanon.

enactment of a homecoming expressed through defiance and loss, as if to say, "Zia, we are here." Of course Zia was the one who was really at home and who would not hear their exultant voices.

6   Rashid Hussein was a Palestinian. He translated Bialik, one of the great modern Hebrew poets, into Arabic, and Hussein's eloquence established him in the post-1948 period as an orator and nationalist without peer. He first worked as a Hebrew language journalist in Tel Aviv, and succeeded in establishing a dialogue between Jewish and Arab writers, even as he espoused the cause of Nasserism[4] and Arab nationalism. In time, he could no longer endure the pressure, and he left for New York. He married a Jewish woman, and began working in the PLO office at the United Nations, but regularly outraged his superiors with unconventional ideas and utopian rhetoric. In 1972 he left for the Arab world, but a few months later he was back in the United States: he had felt out of place in Syria and Lebanon, unhappy in Cairo. New York sheltered him anew, but so did endless bouts of drinking and idleness. His life was in ruins, but he remained the most hospitable of men. He died after a night of heavy drinking when, smoking in bed, his cigarette started a fire that spread to a small library of audio cassettes, consisting mostly of poets reading their verse. The fumes from the tapes asphyxiated him. His body was repatriated for burial in Musmus, the small village in Israel where his family still resided.

7   These and so many other exiled poets and writers lend dignity to a condition legislated to deny dignity—to deny an identity to people. From them, it is apparent that, to concentrate on exile as a contemporary political punishment, you must therefore map territories of experience beyond those mapped by the literature of exile itself. You must first set aside Joyce and Nabokov[5] and think instead of the uncountable masses for whom UN agencies have been created. You must think of the refugee-peasants with no prospect of ever returning home, armed only with a ration card and an agency number. Paris may be a capital famous for cosmopolitan exiles, but it is also a city where unknown men and women have spent years of miserable loneliness: Vietnamese, Algerians, Cambodians, Lebanese, Senegalese, Peruvians. You must think also of Cairo, Beirut, Madagascar, Bangkok, Mexico City. As you move further from the Atlantic world, the awful forlorn waste increases: the hopelessly large numbers, the compounded misery of "undocumented" people suddenly lost, without a tellable history. To reflect on exiled Muslims from India, or Haitians in America, or Bikinians in Oceania, or Palestinians throughout the Arab world means that you must leave the modest refuge provided by subjectivity and resort instead to the abstractions of mass politics. Negotiations, wars of national liberation, people bundled out of their homes and prodded, bussed or

---

[4] Gamal Nasser, president of Egypt (1956–1970) (1918–1970).
[5] James Joyce, twentieth century English novelist (1882–1941). See Chapter 6. Vladimir Nabokov, Russian novelist and poet who spent most of his life in the United States (1899–1977).

walked to enclaves in other regions: what do these experiences add up to? Are they not manifestly and almost by design irrecoverable?

* * *

8 We come to nationalism and its essential association with exile. Nationalism is an assertion of belonging in and to a place, a people, a heritage. It affirms the home created by a community of language, culture and customs; and, by so doing, it fends off exile, fights to prevent its ravages. Indeed, the interplay between nationalism and exile is like Hegel's[6] dialectic of servant and master, opposites informing and constituting each other. All nationalisms in their early stages develop from a condition of estrangement. The struggles to win American independence, to unify Germany or Italy, to liberate Algeria were those of national groups separated—exiled—from what was construed to be their rightful way of life. Triumphant, achieved nationalism then justifies, retrospectively as well as prospectively, a history selectively strung together in a narrative form: thus all nationalisms have their founding fathers, their basic, quasi-religious texts, their rhetoric of belonging, their historical and geographical landmarks, their official enemies and heroes. This collective ethos forms what Pierre Bourdieu, the French sociologist, calls the *habitus,* the coherent amalgam of practices linking habit with inhabitance. In time, successful nationalisms consign truth exclusively to themselves and relegate falsehood and inferiority to outsiders (as in the rhetoric of capitalist versus communist, or the European versus the Asiatic).

9 And just beyond the frontier between "us" and the "outsiders" is the perilous territory of not-belonging: this is to where in a primitive time peoples were banished, and where in the modern era immense aggregates of humanity loiter as refugees and displaced persons.

10 Nationalisms are about groups, but in a very acute sense exile is a solitude experienced outside the group: the deprivations felt at not being with others in the communal habitation. How, then, does one surmount the loneliness of exile without falling into the encompassing and thumping language of national pride, collective sentiments, group passions? What is there worth saving and holding on to between the extremes of exile on the one hand, and the often bloody-minded affirmations of nationalism on the other? Do nationalism and exile have any intrinsic attributes? Are they simply two conflicting varieties of paranoia?

11 These are questions that cannot ever be fully answered because each assumes that exile and nationalism can be discussed neutrally, without reference to each other. They cannot be. Because both terms include everything from the most collective of collective sentiments to the most private of private emotions, there is hardly language adequate for both. But there is certainly nothing about nationalism's public and all-inclusive ambitions that touches the core of the exile's predicament.

---

[6] German philosopher (1770–1831).

12   Because exile, unlike nationalism, is fundamentally a discontinuous state of being. Exiles are cut off from their roots, their land, their past. They generally do not have armies or states, although they are often in search of them. Exiles feel, therefore, an urgent need to reconstitute their broken lives, usually by choosing to see themselves as part of a triumphant ideology or a restored people. The crucial thing is that a state of exile free from this triumphant ideology—designed to reassemble an exile's broken history into a new whole—is virtually unbearable, and virtually impossible in today's world. Look at the fate of the Jews, the Palestinians and the Armenians.

*   *   *

13 Noubar is a solitary Armenian, and a friend. His parents had to leave Eastern Turkey in 1915, after their families were massacred: his maternal grandfather was beheaded. Noubar's mother and father went to Aleppo,[7] then to Cairo. In the middle-sixties, life in Egypt became difficult for non-Egyptians, and his parents, along with four children, were taken to Beirut by an international relief organization. In Beirut, they lived briefly in a pension and then were bundled into two rooms of a little house outside the city. In Lebanon, they had no money and they waited: eight months later, a relief agency got them a flight to Glasgow.[8] And then to Gander.[9] And then to New York. They rode by Greyhound bus from New York to Seattle: Seattle was the city designated by the agency for their American residence. When I asked: "Seattle?," Noubar smiled resignedly, as if to say better Seattle than Armenia—which he never knew, or Turkey where so many were slaughtered, or Lebanon where he and his family would certainly have risked their lives. Exile is sometimes better than staying behind or not getting out: but only sometimes.

14   Because *nothing* is secure. Exile is a jealous state. What you achieve is precisely what you have no wish to share, and it is in the drawing of lines around you and your compatriots that the least attractive aspects of being in exile emerge: an exaggerated sense of group solidarity, and a passionate hostility to outsiders, even those who may in fact be in the same predicament as you. What could be more intransigent than the conflict between Zionist Jews and Arab Palestinians? Palestinians feel that they have been turned into exiles by the proverbial people of exile, the Jews. But the Palestinians also know that their own sense of national identity has been nourished in the exile milieu, where everyone not a blood-brother or sister is an enemy, where every sympathizer is an agent of some unfriendly power, and where the slightest deviation from the accepted group line is an act of the rankest treachery and disloyalty.

15   Perhaps this is the most extraordinary of exile's fates: to have been exiled by exiles: to relive the actual process of up-rooting at the hands of exiles. All Palestinians during the summer of 1982 asked themselves what inarticulate

---

[7] City of northwest Syria near the Turkish border.
[8] City in Scotland.
[9] Town in northeast Newfoundland.

urge drove Israel, having displaced Palestinians in 1948, to expel them continuously from their refugee homes and camps in Lebanon. It is as if the reconstructed Jewish collective experience, as represented by Israel and modern Zionism,[10] could not tolerate another story of dispossession and loss to exist alongside it—an intolerance constantly reinforced by the Israeli hostility to the nationalism of the Palestinians, who for forty-six years have been painfully reassembling a national identity in exile.

16   This need to reassemble an identity out of the refractions and discontinuities of exile is found in the earlier poems of Mahmud Darwish, whose considerable work amounts to an epic effort to transform the lyrics of loss into the indefinitely postponed drama of return. Thus he depicts his sense of homelessness in the form of a list of unfinished and incomplete things:

> But I am the exile.
> Seal me with your eyes.
> Take me wherever you are—
> Take me whatever you are.
> Restore to me the color of face
> And the warmth of body
> The light of heart and eye,
> The salt of bread and rhythm,
> The taste of earth . . . the Motherland.
> Shield me with your eyes.
> Take me as a relic from the mansion of sorrow.
> Take me as a verse from my tragedy;
> Take me as a toy, a brick from the house
> So that our children will remember to return.

17   The pathos of exile is in the loss of contact with the solidity and the satisfaction of earth: homecoming is out of the question.

18   Joseph Conrad's[11] tale "Amy Foster" is perhaps the most uncompromising representation of exile ever written. Conrad thought of himself as an exile from Poland, and nearly all his work (as well as his life) carries the unmistakable mark of the sensitive émigré's obsession with his own fate and with his hopeless attempts to make satisfying contact with new surroundings. "Amy Foster" is in a sense confined to the problems of exile, perhaps so confined that it is not one of Conrad's best-known stories. This, for example, is the description of the agony of its central character, Yanko Goorall, an Eastern European peasant who, en route to America, is shipwrecked off the British coast:

> *It is indeed hard upon a man to find himself a lost stranger helpless, incomprehensible, and of a mysterious origin, in some obscure corner of the earth. Yet amongst all the adventurers shipwrecked in all*

---

[10] International movement for the establishment and continued support of the State of Israel.
[11] Novelist, born in the Ukraine of Polish parents, who wrote primarily in English (1857–1924).

*the wild parts of the world, there is not one, it seems to me, that ever
had to suffer a fate so simply tragic as the man I am speaking of, the
most innocent of adventurers cast out by the sea. . . .*

19   Yanko has left home because the pressures were too great for him to go
on living there. America lures him with its promise, though England is where
he ends up. He endures in England, where he cannot speak the language and
is feared and misunderstood. Only Amy Foster, a plodding, unattractive peasant girl, tries to communicate with him. They marry, have a child, but when
Yanko falls ill, Amy, afraid and alienated, refuses to nurse him; snatching
their child, she leaves. The desertion hastens Yanko's miserable death, which
like the deaths of several Conradian heroes is depicted as the result of a combination of crushing isolation and the world's indifference. Yanko's fate is described as "the supreme disaster of loneliness and despair."

20   Yanko's predicament is affecting: a foreigner perpetually haunted and
alone in an uncomprehending society. But Conrad's own exile causes him to
exaggerate the differences between Yanko and Amy. Yanko is dashing, light and
bright-eyed, whereas Amy is heavy, dull, bovine; when he dies, it is as if her
earlier kindness to him was a snare to lure and then trap him fatally. Yanko's
death is romantic: the world is coarse, unappreciative; no one understands
him, not even Amy, the one person close to him. Conrad took this neurotic exile's fear and created an aesthetic principle out of it. No one can understand or
communicate in Conrad's world, but paradoxically this radical limitation on
the possibilities of language doesn't inhibit elaborate efforts to communicate.
All of Conrad's stories are about lonely people who talk a great deal (for indeed
who of the great modernists was more voluble and "adjectival" than Conrad
himself?) and whose attempts to *impress* others compound, rather than reduce, the original sense of isolation. Each Conradian exile fears, and is condemned endlessly to imagine, the spectacle of a solitary death illuminated, so
to speak, by unresponsive, uncommunicating eyes.

21   Exiles look at non-exiles with resentment. *They* belong in their surroundings, you feel, whereas an exile is always out of place. What is it like to
be born in a place, to stay and live there, to know that you are of it, more or
less for ever?

* * *

22 Although it is true that anyone prevented from returning home is an exile,
some distinctions can be made between exiles, refugees, expatriates and émigrés. Exile originated in the age-old practice of banishment. Once banished,
the exile lives an anomalous and miserable life, with the stigma of being an
outsider. Refugees, on the other hand, are a creation of the twentieth-century
state. The word "refugee" has become a political one, suggesting large
herds of innocents and bewildered people requiring urgent international
assistance, whereas "exile" carries with it, I think, a touch of solitude and
spirituality.

23   Expatriates voluntarily live in an alien country, usually for personal or social reasons. Hemingway and Fitzgerald[12] were not forced to live in France. Expatriates may share in the solitude and estrangement of exile, but they do not suffer under its rigid proscriptions. Émigrés enjoy an ambiguous status. Technically, an émigré is anyone who emigrates to a new country. Choice in the matter is certainly a possibility. Colonial officials, missionaries, technical experts, mercenaries and military advisers on loan may in a sense live in exile, but they have not been banished. White settlers in Africa, parts of Asia and Australia may once have been exiles, but as pioneers and nation-builders the label "exile" dropped away from them.

24   Much of the exile's life is taken up with compensating for disorienting loss by creating a new world to rule. It is not surprising that so many exiles seem to be novelists, chess players, political activists, and intellectuals. Each of these occupations requires a minimal investment in objects and places a great premium on mobility and skill. The exile's new world, logically enough, is unnatural and its unreality resembles fiction. Georg Lukács, in *Theory of the Novel,* argued with compelling force that the novel, a literary form created out of the unreality of ambition and fantasy, is *the* form of "transcendental homelessness." Classical epics, Lukács wrote, emanate from settled cultures in which values are clear, identities stable, life unchanging. The European novel is grounded in precisely the opposite experience, that of a changing society in which an itinerant and disinherited middle-class hero or heroine seeks to construct a new world that somewhat resembles an old one left behind for ever. In the epic there is no *other* world, only the finality of *this* one. Odysseus returns to Ithaca after years of wandering; Achilles will die because he cannot escape his fate.[13] The novel, however, exists because other worlds *may* exist, alternatives for bourgeois speculators, wanderers, exiles.

25   No matter how well they may do, exiles are always eccentrics who *feel* their difference (even as they frequently exploit it) as a kind of orphanhood. Anyone who is really homeless regards the habit of seeing estrangement in everything modern as an affectation, a display of modish attitudes. Clutching difference like a weapon to be used with stiffened will, the exile jealously insists on his or her right to refuse to belong.

26   This usually translates into an intransigence that is not easily ignored. Wilfulness, exaggeration, overstatement: these are characteristic styles of being an exile, methods for compelling the world to accept your vision—which you make more unacceptable because you are in fact unwilling to have it accepted. It is yours, after all. Composure and serenity are the last things associated with the work of exiles. Artists in exile are decidedly unpleasant, and their stubbornness insinuates itself into even their exalted works. Dante's[14] vision in *The Divine Comedy* is tremendously powerful in its universality and

---

[12] Ernest Hemingway, North American novelist and fiction writer (1899–1961). See Chapter 6. Francis Scott Key Fitzgerald, North American fiction writer and novelist (1896–1940).

[13] Allusion to the odyssey and the Iliad of Homer; Greek epic poet (ninth–eighth centuries B.C.E.).

[14] Dante Alighieri, Italian poet (1265–1321).

detail, but even the beatific peace achieved in the *Paradiso* bears traces of the vindictiveness and severity of judgment embodied in the *Inferno*. Who but an exile like Dante, banished from Florence, would use eternity as a place for settling old scores?

27   James Joyce *chose* to be in exile: to give force to his artistic vocation. In an uncannily effective way—as Richard Ellmann has shown in his biography—Joyce picked a quarrel with Ireland and kept it alive so as to sustain the strictest opposition to what was familiar. Ellmann says that "whenever his relations with his native land were in danger of improving, [Joyce] was to find a new incident to solidify his intransigence and to reaffirm the rightness of his voluntary absence." Joyce's fiction concerns what in a letter he once described as the state of being "alone and friendless." And although it is rare to pick banishment as a way of life, Joyce perfectly understood its trials.

*   *   *

28 But Joyce's success as an exile stresses the question lodged at its very heart: is exile so extreme and private that any instrumental use of it is ultimately a trivialization? How is it that the literature of exile has taken its place as a *topos* of human experience alongside the literature of adventure, education or discovery? Is this the *same* exile that quite literally kills Yanko Goorall and has bred the expensive, often dehumanizing relationship between twentieth-century exile and nationalism? Or is it some more benign variety?

29   Much of the contemporary interest in exile can be traced to the somewhat pallid notion that non-exiles can share in the benefits of exile as a redemptive motif. There is, admittedly, a certain plausibility and truth to this idea. Like medieval itinerant scholars or learned Greek slaves in the Roman Empire, exiles—the exceptional ones among them—do leaven their environments. And naturally "we" concentrate on that enlightening aspect of "their" presence among us, not on their misery or their demands. But looked at from the bleak political perspective of modern mass dislocations, individual exiles force us to recognize the tragic fate of homelessness in a necessarily heartless world.

30   A generation ago, Simone Weil[15] posed the dilemma of exile as concisely as it has ever been expressed. "To be rooted," she said, "is perhaps the most important and least recognized need of the human soul." Yet Weil also saw that most remedies for uprootedness in this era of world wars, deportations and mass exterminations are almost as dangerous as what they purportedly remedy. Of these, the state—or, more accurately, statism—is one of the most insidious, since worship of the state tends to supplant all other human bonds.

31   Weil exposes us anew to that whole complex of pressures and constraints that lie at the center of the exile's predicament, which, as I have suggested, is as close as we come in the modern era to tragedy. There is the sheer fact of isolation and displacement, which produces the kind of narcissistic masochism that resists all efforts at amelioration, acculturation and community. At this extreme

---

[15] French mathematician and philosopher who became an exile in England during World War II.

the exile can make a fetish of exile, a practice that distances him or her from all connections and commitments. To live as if everything around you were temporary and perhaps trivial is to fall prey to petulant cynicism as well as to querulous lovelessness. More common is the pressure on the exile to join—parties, national movements, the state. The exile is offered a new set of affiliations and develops new loyalties. But there is also a loss—of critical perspective, of intellectual reserve, of moral courage.

32   It must also be recognized that the defensive nationalism of exiles often fosters self-awareness as much as it does the less attractive forms of self-assertion. Such reconstitutive projects as assembling a nation out of exile (and this is true in this century for Jews and Palestinians) involve constructing a national history, reviving an ancient language, founding national institutions like libraries and universities. And these, while they sometimes promote strident ethnocentrism, also give rise to investigations of self that inevitably go far beyond such simple and positive facts as "ethnicity." For example, there is the self-consciousness of an individual trying to understand why the histories of the Palestinians and the Jews have certain patterns to them, why in spite of oppression and the threat of extinction a particular ethos remains alive in exile.

33   Necessarily, then, I speak of exile not as a privilege, but as an *alternative* to the mass institutions that dominate modern life. Exile is not, after all, a matter of choice: you are born into it, or it happens to you. But, provided that the exile refuses to sit on the sidelines nursing a wound, there are things to be learned: he or she must cultivate a scrupulous (not indulgent or sulky) subjectivity.

34   Perhaps the most rigorous example of such subjectivity is to be found in the writing of Theodor Adorno, the German-Jewish philosopher and critic. Adorno's masterwork, *Minima Moralia,* is an autobiography written while in exile; it is subtitled *Reflexionen aus dem beschädigten Leben (Reflections from a Mutilated Life).* Ruthlessly opposed to what he called the "administered" world, Adorno saw all life as pressed into ready-made forms, prefabricated "homes." He argued that everything that one says or thinks, as well as every object one possesses, is ultimately a mere commodity. Language is jargon, objects are for sale. To refuse this state of affairs is the exile's intellectual mission.

35   Adorno's reflections are informed by the belief that the only home truly available now, though fragile and vulnerable, is in writing. Elsewhere, "the house is past. The bombings of European cities, as well as the labor and concentration camps, merely precede as executors, with what the immanent development of technology had long decided was to be the fate of houses. These are now good only to be thrown away like old food cans." In short, Adorno says with a grave irony, "it is part of morality not to be at home in one's home."

36   To follow Adorno is to stand away from "home" in order to look at it with the exile's detachment. For there is considerable merit in the practice of noting the discrepancies between various concepts and ideas and what they actually produce. We take home and language for granted; they become nature, and their underlying assumptions recede into dogma and orthodoxy.

37   The exile knows that in a secular and contingent world, homes are always provisional. Borders and barriers, which enclose us within the safety of famil-

iar territory, can also become prisons, and are often defended beyond reason or necessity. Exiles cross borders, break barriers of thought and experience.

38   Hugo of St. Victor, a twelfth-century monk from Saxony, wrote these hauntingly beautiful lines:

> It is, therefore, a source of great virtue for the practiced mind to learn, bit by bit, first to change about invisible and transitory things, so that afterwards it may be able to leave them behind altogether. The man who finds his homeland sweet is still a tender beginner; he to whom every soil is as his native one is already strong; but he is perfect to whom the entire world is as a foreign land. The tender soul has fixed his love on one spot in the world; the strong man has extended his love to all places; the perfect man has extinguished his.

39 Erich Auerbach, the great twentieth-century literary scholar who spent the war years as an exile in Turkey, has cited this passage as a model for anyone wishing to transcend national or provincial limits. Only by embracing this attitude can a historian begin to grasp human experience and its written records in their diversity and particularity; otherwise he or she will remain committed more to the exclusions and reactions of prejudice than to the freedom that accompanies knowledge. But note that Hugo twice makes it clear that the "strong" or "perfect" man achieves independence and detachment by *working through* attachments, not by rejecting them. Exile is predicated on the existence of, love for, and bond with, one's native place; what is true of all exile is not that home and love of home are lost, but that loss is inherent in the very existence of both.

40   Regard experiences as if they were about to disappear. What is it that anchors them in reality? What would you save of them? What would you give up? Only someone who has achieved independence and detachment, someone whose homeland is "sweet" but whose circumstances makes it impossible to recapture that sweetness, can answer those questions. (Such a person would also find it impossible to derive satisfaction from substitutes furnished by illusion or dogma.)

41   This may seem like a prescription for an unrelieved grimness of outlook and, with it, a permanently sullen disapproval of all enthusiasm or buoyancy of spirit. Not necessarily. While it perhaps seems peculiar to speak of the pleasures of exile, there are some positive things to be said for a few of its conditions. Seeing "the entire world as a foreign land" makes possible originality of vision. Most people are principally aware of one culture, one setting, one home; exiles are aware of at least two, and this plurality of vision gives rise to an awareness of simultaneous dimensions, an awareness that—to borrow a phrase from music—is *contrapuntal*.

42   For an exile, habits of life, expression or activity in the new environment inevitably occur against the memory of these things in another environment. Thus both the new and the old environments are vivid, actual, occurring together contrapuntally. There is a unique pleasure in this sort of

apprehension, especially if the exile is conscious of other contrapuntal jux-tapositions that diminish orthodox judgment and elevate appreciative sym-pathy. There is also a particular sense of achievement in acting as if one were at home wherever one happens to be.

43   This remains risky, however: the habit of dissimulation is both wearying and nerveracking. Exile is never the state of being satisfied, placid, or secure. Exile, in the words of Wallace Stevens,[16] is "a mind of winter" in which the pathos of summer and autumn as much as the potential of spring are nearby but unobtainable. Perhaps this is another way of saying that a life of exile moves according to a different calendar, and is less seasonal and settled than life at home. Exile is life led outside habitual order. It is nomadic, decentered, contrapuntal; but no sooner does one get accustomed to it than its unsettling force erupts anew.

■ EXPLORATIONS OF THE TEXT ■

1. How does Said define exile? (See paragraph 1.)
2. Is "Modern Western culture . . . the work of exiles"? Why is this century different from the nineteenth century?
3. Why does Said find exile to be "horrendous"? Consider the examples of Faiz and Hussein.
4. Why does reflection on exile require consideration of "mass politics"?
5. What is the "interplay between nationalism and exile"? Examine both terms. Consider Noubar and his family.
6. Interpret Darwish's poem and Said's analysis of Conrad's "Amy Foster." How do these works extend the meaning of "exile"?
7. Consider: "To be rooted in perhaps the most important and least recognized need of the human soul." Is uprootedness "as close as we come in the modern era to tragedy"?
8. Explore the state of exile as a way "to transcend national or provincial limits," as a "contrapuntal" stance, as a "mind of winter."
9. Compare this essay with Dipoko's and Rocha's poems.

■■ JOURNAL ENTRIES ■■

1. Define exile.
2. Describe an exiled person whom you know.
3. Summarize Said's essay.
4. Respond to one of Said's arguments or examples.

---

[16] American poet (1879–1955).

■■■ IDEAS FOR WRITING ■■■

1. Evaluate this essay. Examine purpose, audience, organization, arguments, examples, details, language, and effect.
2. Explore themes of exile and return. Refer to Said, to Dipoko, and to Rocha.
3. Agree or disagree with Said's essay. Begin with Journal Entry 4.
4. Create a story of exile.

Conflict with the Landowners and the Creation of the CUC

Rigoberta Menchú

Rigoberta Menchú (1959/60–   ) is a Mayan Indian from Northwest Guatemala. Like most Indians of Central and South America, she virtually had no childhood. Instead, she worked as a migrant worker in the fields alongside her parents. Her father, Vicente, headman of their village, was one of the early organizers of an agrarian trade union (CUC) called the United Peasant Committee. Before Rigoberta Menchú was twenty, her brother and both of her parents had been brutally killed because of their activities on behalf of their peasant communities. As she herself became increasingly active in the cause for which her father and mother had worked, Menchú went into exile in Mexico. From there she went to Paris, where she met Elisabeth Burgos-Debray, who recorded Menchú's life history. The latter spoke her story into a tape recorder, which Burgos-Debray faithfully transcribed and then edited into the autobiography, I, Rigoberta Menchú. *Menchú won the Nobel Peace Prize in 1992.*

In this selection from her autobiography, Menchú recounts her growing activism and involvement in the struggle for the rights of her people.

'Gather in your grain and seeds and collect the young shoots, because times of drought and hunger are approaching. Sharpen your weapons because it will not be long before enemies, hidden behind mountains and hills, will espy with greed the expanse and richness of these lands.'

—Popol Vuh

1   This was the first time my father went to prison. My brother said, 'We don't know what to do for him because the lawyers say Papá will be in jail for eighteen years. We need money to get educated people to help us.' In Guatemala this is what happens with the poor, especially Indians, because they can't speak Spanish. The Indian can't speak up for what he wants. When they put my father in jail, the landowners gave large amounts of money to the judge there. The judge in El Quiché, that is. There are several levels of authority. First, there is the Military Commissioner. He sometimes lives in the villages or is based in the town, and he tries to impose his own law. Then there is what we call the Mayor who represents the authorities which administer justice when they say someone has broken the law. Next come the Governors who govern the whole region, each province. And finally, there are the Deputies—God knows who they are! To get to see the Military Commissioner, you first have to give him a *mordida,* that's what we call a bribe in Guatemala. To see the Mayor, you have to get witnesses, sign papers and then give him a *mordida* so he will support your case. To see the Governor you need not only witnesses from the village, and money, but also lawyers or other intermediaries to talk for you. The Governor is a *ladino*[1] and doesn't understand the language of the people. He'll only believe something if a lawyer or educated person says it. He won't accept anything from an Indian. The Mayor is a *ladino* too. But he's a *ladino* who's come from our people. The Military Commissioner is also a *ladino* although this varies a bit, because in some places the commissioners are Indians who have done military service and lived in the barracks. There comes a time when they return to their village, brutalized men, criminals.

2   My father fought for twenty-two years, waging a heroic struggle against the landowners who wanted to take our land and our neighbours' land. After many years of hard work, when our small bit of land began yielding harvests and our people had a large area under cultivation, the big landowners appeared: the Brols. It's said there that they were even more renowned criminals than the Martinez and Garcia families, who owned a *finca*[2] there before the Brols arrived. The Brols were a large family, a whole gang of brothers. Five of them lived on a *finca* they had taken over by forcibly throwing the Indians of the region off their land. That was what happened to us. We lived in a small village. We cultivated maize, beans, potatoes and all sorts of vegetables. Then the Garcias arrived and started measuring the land in our village. They brought inspectors, engineers and Heaven knows who else; people they said were from the Government. In Guatemala if it's to do with the Government, there's no way we can defend ourselves. So they came and started measuring our land. My father went round collecting signatures in the village, and they held meetings. Then he went to the capital, to the INTA, Institute

---

[1] Any Guatemalan—whatever his economic position—who rejects, either individually or through his cultural heritage, Indian values of Mayan origin. It also implies mixed blood [Author's Note].

[2] Plantation, estate [Author's Note].

Nacional de Transformación Agraria de Guatemala: Guatemalan National Institute for Agrarian Transformation. But the landowners and the Government had made a deal to take the peasants' land away from them. When my father went to protest about the way the landowners were forcing us off our land, the people in the INTA asked the landowners for money to be allowed to go on measuring. On the other hand, they gave the peasants a piece of paper which, according to them, said they didn't have to leave their land. It was a double-sided game. They called my father in. Papá used to be . . . well, I don't mean foolish exactly because it's the thieves who steal our land who are foolish. . . . Well, they asked my father to sign a paper but he didn't know what it said because he'd never learned to read or write. In fact, the paper said that the peasants confirmed, once again, that they would leave their land. This gave the landowners power, since he, the community's representative, had signed the paper. My father went back again to protest, this time through some lawyers. The INTA people and the lawyers started getting fat off us. Many lawyers wanted to help us and offered us different sorts of help. They said we were doing the right thing. The peasants trusted them but realized afterwards that they made them pay through the nose, even for a simple signature. My father dedicated himself entirely to our community's problems. The INTA told my father: 'You must get engineers to measure the land and then you'll be the owners of the land you live on. Don't worry, grow what you want. Don't worry, go ahead and clear the undergrowth because the land is yours.' With this encouragement, my father went home and called meetings in the village.

3   We were very happy and went on working until the landowners arrived with their engineers again. Our little bit of land has probably been measured something like twenty times, if I'm not mistaken. Engineers after engineers. What I can't forgive, and this is something which has contributed to my hate for these people, is that they said they came to help us. My father, mother, all the community, were very distressed. They were *ladinos*. They couldn't eat our food, our *tortillas* with salt. If we didn't feed them well they would probably favour the landowners. So we treated them very well, out of fear. We gave them our best, our fattest animals. We'd kill chickens for them to eat. Our community, which never bought so much as a bottle of oil, had to buy them rice, oil, eggs, chickens, meat. We had to buy coffee and sugar, because they couldn't eat *panela*. [3] Our community never ate these things. We all had to go to town. The village got together, gave in their ten *centavos* [4] and with this collection we bought what was needed. Earning ten *centavos* is hard for us, it's earned by a lot of sweat. It was worse when the inspectors stayed a whole week. When they left, the village breathed a sigh of relief and we were much poorer. *We* didn't eat meat. *They* did. They got their information with no difficulty. They went to the further points of our land and, of course, needed someone to go with them. But our people have no time to spare. It was my

---

[3] Unrefined sugar. Brown sugar [Author's Note].
[4] Monetary unit. A hundred centavos = 1 quetzal [Author's Note].

father who gave up his time because he loved the community, even if it meant we often had nothing to eat at home. My mother felt responsible for looking after these men. She saw how in need our neighbours were. So my mother stayed at home and said to us, 'You children go and work because I have to attend to these men.' My parents attended to them because, as leaders of the community, it was their responsibility—they were the most important people in the village. They looked after them very well. My mother even made them small *tortillas*[5] because they couldn't eat our large ones. She had to make ones to suit them. So neither of my parents could work while those men were there. Our neighbours contributed what they could, but they didn't have very much. We couldn't speak Spanish. My father spoke a little, just enough to understand the inspectors. The INTA used to send for him. They sometimes made him go to Quetzaltenango, Huehuetenango,[6] El Quiché[7] or to the capital just to sign a piece of paper. You can imagine the cost of those journeys in food and transport. And on top of all this, we had to pay the lawyers who shuffle the papers.

4   The Government says the land belongs to the nation. It owns the land and gives it to us to cultivate. But when we've cleared and cultivated the land, that's when the landowners appear. However, the landowners don't just appear on their own—they have connections with the different authorities that allow them to manoeuvre like that. Because of this, we faced the Martinez family, the Garcias, and then the Brols arrived. This meant we could either stay and work as *peónes*[8] or leave our land. There was no other solution. So my father travelled all over the place seeking advice. We didn't realize then that going to the Government authorities was the same as going to the landowners. They are the same. My father was tireless in his efforts to seek help. He went to other sectors, like the workers' unions. He asked them to help because we were already being thrown off our land.

5   The first time they threw us out of our homes was, if I remember rightly, in 1967. They turned us out of our houses, and out of the village. The Garcias' henchmen set to work with ferocity. They were Indians too, soldiers of the *finca*. First they went into the houses without permission and got all the people out. Then they went in and threw out all our things. I remember that my mother had her silver necklaces, precious keepsakes from my grandmother, but we never saw them again after that. They stole them all. They threw out our cooking utensils, our earthenware cooking pots. We don't use those sort of . . . special utensils, we have our own earthenware pots. They hurled them into the air, and, Oh God! they hit the ground and broke into pieces. All our plates, cups, pots. They threw them out and they all broke. That was the vengeance of the landowner on the peasants because we wouldn't give up our land. All the maize cobs they found in the *tapanco*, they threw away.

---

[5] Maize pancake which is the main food of the Central American people [Author's Note].
[6] Province, and provincial capital. Centre of the Mam people [Author's Note].
[7] Province of El Quiché.
[8] Laborers.

Afterwards all the peasants had to work together to collect them up. We did it together and put them in another place. I remember it was pouring with rain, and we had nothing to protect ourselves from the rain. It took us two days to make a roughly built hut out of leaves. We only had those nylon sheets the peasants use to cover themselves in the rain. The first night we spent in the fields with streams of water running along the ground. It wasn't raining then but the ground was sodden.

6   Those few days confirmed my hatred for those people. I saw why we said that *ladinos* were thieves, criminals and liars. It was as our parents had told us. We could see that they were doing the same to us. They killed our animals. They killed many of our dogs. To us, killing an animal is like killing a person. We care for all the things of the natural world very much and killing our dogs wounded us very deeply. We spent more than forty days in the fields. Then the community held a meeting and said, 'If they throw us out again, we will die of hunger.' We had no utensils for cooking our *tortillas,* and no grinding stones. They'd been thrown away into the undergrowth. We organized ourselves, all of us, and said 'Let's collect our things together.' We went looking for any of our things that were still more or less all right. My father said, 'If they kill us they kill us, but we'll go back to our houses.' Our people looked on my father as their own father, and so we went back to our houses. There was another village quite near ours and they helped us. People brought cooking pots and plates so that we could cook our maize and eat. So we went back to our houses. And the landowners came back again for what they called 'collective negotiations.' They told us we should resign ourselves to working as *peónes* because the land belonged to them. We could stay in our houses, but the land was not ours. If we didn't agree, they would throw us off again. But my father said: 'We were the first families to come and cultivate this land and nobody can deceive us into thinking that this land is theirs. If they want to be the owners of more land, let them go and cultivate the mountains. There is more land but it is not land where things grow.' Who knows, perhaps if the community had been alone, we would have become *peónes* and our land would now be part of a big *finca.* But my father would have none of it. He said, 'Even if they kill us, we will do it.' Of course, in those days we didn't have enough political clarity to unite with others and protest about our land. What we did we did as an individual community. So we went back to our homes and did not accept the landowners' deal. They left us alone for a month or two. Then there was another raid. All our things were broken for a second time, all the things our neighbours in the other village had given us. We couldn't stand what they were doing to us any longer and decided to go to the *finca,* abandoning our land. But we couldn't live in the *finca* all the time. What were we going to do? What would happen to us if we went to the *finca?* That's when we united and said: 'We won't go!'

7   We love our land very much. Since those people tried to take our land away, we have grieved very much. My grandfather used to cry bitterly and say: 'In the past, no one person owned the land. The land belonged to everyone. There were no boundaries.' We were sadder still when we saw our animals

going hungry because of us. If our animals went near our crops, they were killed by the Garcías' henchmen who were guarding them. (I remember, that the wickedest landowner was Honorio García. The other was Angel Martínez.) My grandfather said, 'If they kill our animals, we must kill them.' That was the idea that came to my grandfather. We spent about fifteen days away from our house after the second raid and our elders advised us to burn them and leave. But where to? We didn't know whether it was better to go to the *finca* or agree to be labourers on the landowner's estate. We couldn't decide. We discussed it with all our neighbours. Among the whole community. During all this time we couldn't celebrate our culture; none of our ceremonies. That's when my father took his stand. He said, 'If they kill me for trying to defend the land that belongs to us, well, they'll have to kill me.' The idea of life without a father, or that Papá would be shot by those guards, was terrible for us. Sometimes my mother was very distressed and begged my father not to put his life in danger with those guards.

8   My father went on travelling. He was hardly ever at home now. He didn't pay us much attention, or talk to us like he used to. He'd arrive, call a meeting of the community, talk to them and then sometimes leave the next day. We began to lose contact with him. When the landowners saw my father working so hard to save our land, they started threatening him. So he said, 'The best guardians, the best protection a man has are his animals. Our dogs must learn to defend us.' We had some good dogs, they were very fierce. We spent time teaching the dogs to bite those men when they came to our houses—sometimes in the middle of the night.

9   Our life was now such that we couldn't go down to the *finca* because if we did our houses probably wouldn't be there when we got back. The community decided to eat plants or whatever they could find in the fields rather than go down to the *finca*. Or part of a family would go and the other part would stay and watch over the house. We became much more united. When the landowners came we'd unite so that they either had to throw us all off, kill us all or leave us alone. We began teaching the children to keep watch and tell us when the landowners were coming. We lived for quite a while like this—with all this tension. I kept on going down to the *finca* with my brothers and sisters. My mother always stayed in the house. Or my father was there. My father never went down to the *fincas* because the landowners would take advantage of this and go into the village. Then they started trying other things. We had maize and beans but we had to carry all our produce down from the village to the town which was a long way away. So the landowners set up a temporary market, a place to sell produce and tried to isolate us from the town even more, so that they could take over our land more easily.

10   Then the INTA came and told us that the problem was solved. They said: 'We're going to give you a title to the land for you to sign and the land will be yours. No-one will bother you on your land. You can sow your crops, clear the undergrowth and go further into the mountains. This proposal comes from the Government.' We signed it. I remember even the children signed it. We

can't sign with a pen or a pencil. We signed it in ink with our fingerprints on the paper. My father insisted they read the paper out even though we didn't understand it all. We did understand some. But they didn't want to read it. The INTA inspectors said we could rely on the paper, it was the title to the land. So we signed it.

11   They left us alone for two and a half years, I think it was, to let us calm down. Our people went on working. We hardly ever went down to the *finca* now so that we could cultivate more land. We tried to clear large areas of the undergrowth, into the mountains. We had a dream, a real dream. In five or eight years our land would yield its fruit. Two and a half years went by when we saw the engineers on our land again, shouting, measuring, with the landowners' guards. Now, not only the Martínez' and the Garcias, but the Brols were all measuring part of our land. This time the problem was more complicated because they brought with them the document we had signed, which said we had agreed to stay on the land and live off its produce for two years only; that when the two years were up, we had another place to go to and would leave the land. This wasn't true. We didn't know what it was we had signed. My father said, 'This is unjust, because we were deceived.'

12   This is how my father started getting more deeply involved with the unions. I remember my father asked some unions in the FASGUA, Federación Autónoma Sindical de Guatemala—Guatemalan Federation of Independent Unions, to help us because they were unions for workers, for labourers, and we were peasants—agricultural labourers. The unions helped us a lot. They said they would denounce the fact that we were being thrown off our land. My father was continually going to see the unions, the INTA, the lawyers. It nearly drove him mad. He told us, 'My children, you must get to know the places I go to because otherwise, if they kill me the community will lose its land.' Very well. One of my older brothers began to travel with my father and began learning Spanish. The community had to contribute to my father's fares. He very often had no money at all and my mother had to sell our animals to pay for his trips. But at least we didn't leave our land. My mother thought about us more and more because, of course, they were growing up. They wondered how much their children would suffer afterwards. The whole community wondered.

13   When my father started going to the unions and getting their support, the landowners offered a great deal of money to the judge who dealt with land claims, and my father was arrested. They accused him of 'compromizing the sovereignty of the state.' He was endangering the 'sovereignty and the well-being of the Guatemalans'! They put him in prison. I remember that I'd been working as a maid for a year. I'd saved a little money to take home as a surprise for my family, especially my mother. I'd saved it so that my mother wouldn't have to go to the *finca* for a couple of months. My brother told me: 'They're asking for money. We don't know what to do.' I decided to leave my job and go back to the *finca*. From the money I'd saved and my brothers' wages in the *finca,* we had to pay for witnesses, lawyers, documents, secretaries. There were so many things we had to pay for to be able to get to see the

authorities. Since we didn't speak Spanish, we had to find an intermediary to translate my mother's statements. The lawyer was a *ladino* and didn't understand our language, so we had to get an intermediary to interpret for him. From the beginning the landowners paid the interpreter not to say what we said. The interpreter 'sold himself' to the landowners and, instead of our statements, he said something else. They played so many tricks on us. The result was that our lawyer had nothing to do because, according to the interpreter, we ourselves acknowledged that the land belonged to those landowners. They had paid us to cultivate the land. That wasn't true. We were very afraid that they would send my father to the state prison. As long as he was in the local prison, his case wasn't so serious, but once he got to the state prison, the one in El Quiché, we'd have no way of preventing him from having to carry out the sentence he'd been given. If he went to the criminals' prison, as the authorities in Quetzaltenango said, it meant he would be in jail for eighteen years or more.

14   We had enormous trouble getting my father out of prison. My mother had to go and work as a maid in Santa Cruz del Quiché, and the rest of us . . . in the *finca*. All our earnings went towards paying lawyers, intermediaries, everything we needed for my father's case. I remember that the year my father was in prison, I didn't get home even once. I didn't stop working. My brother went up to the *Altiplano* once a month to give my mother the money. She and the community worked for my father. For a whole year, we went back again and again to the law courts. The whole community helped get my father out. The landowners thought that my father was the King, the village Chief, and that if they defeated the Chief, they could defeat the whole community. But they soon realized that it wasn't like that. My father carried out the wishes of the community. He didn't make the laws. The most distressing thing for us was not being able to speak. That was when I told myself: 'I must learn to speak Spanish, so that we don't need intermediaries.' They asked the village for 19,000 *quetzals* [9] to buy the land. The Government asked for it through the INTA. They were just making fun of us, like saying peasants aren't worth a shit. They knew that peasants couldn't even dream of 19,000 *quetzals*. We had barely ten *centavos*. Saying 19,000 was like saying, 'Get off that land quick.' So my father came out of prison. He came out with such courage and such joy.

15   I remember when I left my maid's job, I said: 'Before I go and work in the *finca*, I'm going to visit my father in prison.' I went to the Santa Cruz prison. I'd never been in this prison in Santa Cruz del Quiché before. My father was there with the other prisoners. They were hitting each other, biting each other, and most of them were mad. He was there among all these people. Some of them had fleas. They ate with their hands and were constantly fighting. You could see blood on all their faces. I said: 'How can he be made to live here? If he's here for eighteen years, he'll go mad too.' I thought this was an

---

[9] Guatemalan money. Divided into a hundred units of one centavo [Author's Note].

enormous punishment, a cruel punishment to give my father. I said: 'I'll do everything I can to get him out, even if it means my mother has to suffer as a maid and all her work goes to pay for lawyers.' We were all willing to do it. I worked willingly, so did my brothers and sisters, waiting to hear about my father's case, to hear that he wouldn't have to go to the state prison. 'What could it possibly be like there,' I said, 'if the local prison is already Hell?' My father, humble as he was, found a friend in prison. He was a man who'd been in prison for thirty years, I think. I don't know what he'd done. He did all his own things in prison, made his own food and everything. He was in charge of the prisoners' work. They made bags, typical *morrales,* [10] baskets, all sorts of things, and this man paid them for their work. My father made friends with him and started eating well. He ate what his friend ate. He did his work, making *morrales* and other things, and he was paid for it. So from inside prison my father was helping us with money to pay to get him out. They made my father make an endless stream of statements. Every five days they took him before the judge and asked him the same things to see if he'd changed his mind or changed the statement justifying his case. That is to say, the judges had no valid justification, so they were looking for something to appease the landowners. The landowners arrived with more and more money to pressurize the judges into 'selling' my father and keeping him in prison like a criminal. We were very unhappy because we didn't see our mother or our father as we were working all the time in the *finca.*

16   In the end, we managed to get him out. Papá was in prison for a year and two months. His enemies were furious when he came out. He came out so happy and determined to fight. He said: 'Our ancestors were never cowardly. And prison doesn't eat people. Prison is a punishment for the poor, but it doesn't eat people. I must go home and go on fighting.' He didn't rest for a minute. That's how he maintained his contacts with the unions and gained their support.

17   We were very sad each time he said goodbye and went away. He said: 'Children, look after yourselves because if I don't come back, you have to continue my work. I don't do it alone: you are all part of it too. We'll never give the landowners satisfaction. I am very hopeful. We must go on fighting.' My father was away travelling for three months after he got out of prison. Then they kidnapped him and we said, 'They'll have finished him off.' In those days, they were criminals, but a different sort. The landowners' henchmen kidnapped my father near our house on the path going to town. One of my brothers was with him as we hardly ever let him go alone after they'd threatened so often to kill him. We were worried. So even if it meant less work, it was better for the community if someone went with him. He always went with a neighbour or one of his children. My brother escaped and immediately mobilized the whole village. They couldn't take him very far because we cut off the paths right away. We used weapons, our everyday weapons, for the first time. The people took machetes, sticks, hoes and stones to fight the guards.

---

[10] Game bags; sacks.

They would have beaten or killed any of them, they were so angry. Around midday we found my father. He'd been tortured and abandoned. There was no sign of the torturers but we knew they were the landowners' guards. My father was on the ground. They had torn off the hair on his head on one side. His skin was cut all over and they'd broken so many of his bones that he couldn't walk, lift himself or move a single finger. He looked as if he was dying. It was almost unbearable for us. The community made him one of those chairs the people use for carrying their wounded and we took him down to the town. He was almost cold. He was almost dead when we arrived at the Health Centre but they wouldn't attend to him there because the landowners had got there before us and paid them not to look after my father. They'd given the doctors money so none of them would see my father. All the doctors were *ladinos*. So my mother had to call an ambulance from Santa Cruz del Quiché which took him to a hospital called San Juan de Dios in El Quiché. He arrived there half dead. They gave him serum and said he'd have to stay there for about nine months for some of the very badly damaged parts of his body to heal. They'd broken many of his bones and he was an old man so they wouldn't mend quickly. More bitterness for my mother. She had to go to El Quiché and look after my father. She worked there to pay for his medicine and some special care.

18   My brothers and sisters decided not to go down to the *finca* now. They said: 'From now on we'll stay here, even if we starve to death because we have to cultivate our land. We'll try and grow enough crops to live on and not go to the *finca*.' My mother used to come once every fifteen days perhaps. She'd stay a day and then go back. We had a little sister and we looked after her so that my mother didn't have to take her with her. Some neighbours had a little goat which gave milk. We gave her goat's milk because we didn't have any cows. My little sister was about one and a half then.

19   Later on we received another threat. A message came saying that they were going to kidnap my father from the hospital. The community was frightened and said it would be better for him to come home and be looked after where they couldn't kidnap him. We told my mother straight away. One of my brothers went to El Quiché to warn her about the message we'd received. With the help of the priests and nuns, who gave us money, we put my father in a secret place where the landowners couldn't find him. He was in the hospital of San Juan de Dios for six months and in the other place for another five months. After that he came home but he was in so much pain that he was never his old self again. He couldn't carry things; he couldn't walk very well and it was a big effort for him to walk to the town. At night he couldn't sleep because his bones ached and all the parts where he'd been beaten hurt him.

20   He returned home with a greater hate for his enemies. If before they'd been enemies of the community, now they were even more the enemies of my father. We hated all those people. We weren't only angry with the landowners, but with all the *ladinos*. To us, all the *ladinos* in that region were evil. In the hospital my father had talked to many people and found that we had many

things in common with the Indians in other areas. This gave us a different view; another way of seeing things. After this my father went on working with the help of the unions. When he couldn't go to the capital, the unions looked after his affairs there. Whatever my father was organizing was done by one of the unions helping us.

21   Then in 1977, my father was put in prison again. They wouldn't leave us in peace. After my father came out of hospital and returned home, they kept on threatening him because they knew as long as the community was united they couldn't send their engineers to the villages. We would use machetes or stones. So they went on threatening my father and said they were going to catch him on the road again and kill him. But my father said: 'They are cowards, they just talk, they never do it.' But it worried us a lot because it would be very difficult for us if they did. That was when my father started advising us not to put our trust in him alone but in the whole community. 'I'm your father now,' he said, 'but afterwards the community will be your father.' He went on travelling and refused to keep quiet. He went on doing his work. It was in 1977 that they arrested him again and sent him to prison.

22   I was learning some Spanish at the time with the priests and nuns. I used to travel too. The priests helped me to go to the capital and stay with the nuns in a convent for a few days. When my father came out of hospital, I started travelling with him too, to get to know the circles he moved in. We were already thinking about my father's death. They could kill him any minute, so we needed to know where it was he went. I began accompanying him all the time. The community, the priests and some friends of my father helped us. Some Europeans were helping us too. They sent us a lot of money. They were people who had worked for a time teaching the peasants how to farm. But the way they plant isn't the way we do it. Indians reject the chemical fertilizers they tried to teach us about. They weren't really welcomed so they left, but they were very good friends of my father and helped us. They knew the problems of our village. They went back to their country but they still love Guatemala and help my father. We saved the money we received for my father's trips, all our trips, so that the village wouldn't have to contribute. At that time the INTA was asking for 45 *quetzals* a month for papers and expenses. They never gave us a receipt. Who knows where all that money has gone!

23   When my father was arrested the second time, they considered him a political prisoner. The case against him was much worse this time. Now that he was a political prisoner, he was sentenced to life imprisonment. He was a communist, a subversive, they said. The same Military Commissioners as the first time came and got him from our house with clubs and took him to prison. They beat him and tied him up. He was a political prisoner. This was much worse for him. But by now the community was more aware of all these things. They had their own means of self-defense against the landowners. My brothers now spoke a bit of Spanish and my mother had also learned something from all the suffering, all the knocks, all the responsibility she'd had. We also had the support of the priests, the nuns, the unions and our community. It wasn't just my father now, it was a whole people behind him. My father was well-known and well-loved in

many places so there was a big protest against my father's arrest. The unions especially pressed for his release. They still wanted witnesses, lawyers and all those things of course, but my father was soon out of prison. They started threatening him again even before he was out. They said if he continued his work, he would be assassinated and this time if they couldn't kill him they'd kill one of his children. This was his death sentence from the authorities. Of course, the authorities didn't exactly say that *they* would kill him, but they said the landowners would take care of it.

24   He was in prison for fifteen days. Then he came home. He was very proud and very happy because in prison he'd met another prisoner who really *was* a political prisoner. He was someone who defended the peasants and he told my father the peasants should unite and form a Peasants' League to reclaim their lands. He said it wasn't our problem alone: our enemies weren't the landowners but the whole system. This man saw things more clearly than my father. So my father came back very proudly and said, 'We must fight the rich because they have become rich with our land, our crops.' That was when my father started to join up with other peasants and discussed the creation of the CUC with them. A lot of peasants had been discussing the Committee but nothing concrete had been done, so my father joined the CUC and helped them understand things more clearly. My father didn't have to be told how to organize. Many peasants had been thinking of how they would form the CUC, so, in fact, the peasants had already shown they were unhappy with their situation. My father was in clandestinity from 1977 onwards, that is, he was in hiding. He left our house so he wouldn't involve us. He left his family and went to work with the peasants in other regions. He came back now and again but had to come via the mountains because if he passed through the town the landowners would know he was at home.

25   It was very sad for us that he couldn't live with us at home. He came at night and left at night. Or he spent several days at home but didn't go out. Our community suffered a great deal because they loved him as if he were their own father. Everything in our life is like a film. Constant suffering. We began thinking, with the help of other friends, other *compañeros,*[11] that our enemies were not only the landowners who lived near us, and above all not just the landowners who forced us to work and paid us little. It was not only now we were being killed; they had been killing us since we were children, through malnutrition, hunger, poverty. We started thinking about the roots of the problem and came to the conclusion that everything stemmed from the ownership of land. The best land was not in our hands. It belonged to the big landowners. Every time they see that we have new land, they try to throw us off it or steal it from us in other ways.

---

[11] Companions, comrades, partners, mates.

■ EXPLORATIONS OF THE TEXT ■

1. What do you learn about the legal system in Guatemala?
2. Why were the families ejected from their houses and lands in 1967 by the Garcías?
3. Why does Menchú's father take "his stand"? Why do the people become united?
4. What finally happens to her father?
5. Why do Menchú and all her family hate *ladinos?*
6. Why does Menchú learn Spanish? How is language equated with power and powerlessness?
7. What larger causes does Menchú's father realize are connected with their struggle?
8. What system of protest does Menchú seem to advocate? Compare her form of protest with the views of King and Mandela.

■■ JOURNAL ENTRIES ■■

1. React to the situation of the Indians described in this excerpt. Choose one particular passage.
2. Create a Bill of Rights or Declaration of Independence for Menchú's people.
3. What system of government would Menchú advocate?
4. Discuss the Indians' vision of community.

■■■ IDEAS FOR WRITING ■■■

1. Write a character analysis of Menchú's father.
2. Describe Menchú.
3. What view of life for the Indians emerges in this excerpt?
4. Contrast Menchú's vision and mode of protest with Mandela's (Chapter 7) and King's (Chapter 8).

Black Elk's Great Vision

John Neihardt

Born in Illinois, John G. Neihardt (1881–1973) was raised in Kansas and Nebraska. He worked with the Office of Indian Affairs and became a friend of the Sioux warrior and holy man, Black Elk. Unlike many people at that time who looked on Native-Americans as savages, Neihardt tried to understand the perspectives of both the native Plains tribes and the settlers. Neihardt was a prolific writer, but his best-known work is Black Elk Speaks, *the life story of his Sioux friend.*

In this selection from Black Elk Speaks, *the medicine man recounts a vision of the future that came to him in a dream.*

1 I entered the village, riding, with the four horse troops behind me—the blacks, the whites, the sorrels, and the buckskins; and the place was filled with moaning and with mourning for the dead. The wind was blowing from the south like fever, and when I looked around I saw that in nearly every tepee the women and the children and the men lay dying with the dead.

So I rode around the circle of the village, looking in upon the sick and dead, and I felt like crying as I rode. But when I looked behind me, all the women and the children and the men were getting up and coming forth with happy faces.

And a Voice said: "Behold, they have given you the center of the nation's hoop to make it live."

So I rode to the center of the village, with the horse troops in their quarters round about me, and there the people gathered. And the Voice said: "Give them now the flowering stick that they may flourish, and the sacred pipe that they may know the power that is peace, and the wing of the white giant that they may have endurance and face all winds with courage."

5 So I took the bright red stick and at the center of the nation's hoop I thrust it in the earth. As it touched the earth it leaped mightily in my hand and was a waga chun, the rustling tree,[1] very tall and full of leafy branches and of all birds singing. And beneath it all the animals were mingling with the people like relatives and making happy cries. The women raised their tremolo of joy, and the men shouted all together: "Here we shall raise our children and be as little chickens under the mother sheo's[2] wing."

Then I heard the white wind blowing gently through the tree and singing there, and from the east the sacred pipe came flying on its eagle wings, and stopped before me there beneath the tree, spreading deep peace around it.

---

[1] The cottonwood [Author's Note].
[2] Prairie hen [Author's Note].

Then the daybreak star was rising, and a Voice said: "It shall be a relative to them; and who shall see it, shall see much more, for thence comes wisdom; and those who do not see it shall be dark." And all the people raised their faces to the east, and the star's light fell upon them, and all the dogs barked loudly and the horses whinnied.

Then when the many little voices ceased, the great Voice said: "Behold the circle of the nation's hoop, for it is holy, being endless, and thus all powers shall be one power in the people without end. Now they shall break camp and go forth upon the red road, and your Grandfathers shall walk with them." So the people broke camp and took the good road with the white wing on their faces, and the order of their going was like this:

First, the black horse riders with the cup of water; and the white horse riders with the white wing and the sacred herb; and the sorrel riders with the holy pipe; and the buckskins with the flowering stick. And after these the little children and the youths and maidens followed in a band.

10 Second, came the tribe's four chieftains, and their band was all young men and women.

Third, the nation's four advisers leading men and women neither young nor old.

Fourth, the old men hobbling with their canes and looking to the earth.

Fifth, old women hobbling with their canes and looking to the earth.

Sixth, myself all alone upon the bay with the bow and arrows that the First Grandfather gave me. But I was not the last; for when I looked behind me there were ghosts of people like a trailing fog as far as I could see—grandfathers of grandfathers and grandmothers of grandmothers without number. And over these a great Voice—the Voice that was the South—lived, and I could feel it silent.

15 And as we went the Voice behind me said: "Behold a good nation walking in a sacred manner in a good land!"

Then I looked up and saw that there were four ascents ahead, and these were generations I should know. Now we were on the first ascent, and all the land was green. And as the long line climbed, all the old men and women raised their hands, palms forward, to the far sky yonder and began to croon a song together, and the sky ahead was filled with clouds of baby faces.

When we came to the end of the first ascent we camped in the sacred circle as before, and in the center stood the holy tree, and still the land about us was all green.

Then we started on the second ascent, marching as before, and still the land was green, but it was getting steeper. And as I looked ahead, the people changed into elks and bison and all four-footed beings and even into fowls, all walking in a sacred manner on the good red road together. And I myself was a spotted eagle soaring over them. But just before we stopped to camp at the end of that ascent, all the marching animals grew restless and afraid that they were not what they had been, and began sending forth voices of trouble, calling to their chiefs. And when they camped at the end of that ascent, I looked down and saw that leaves were falling from the holy tree.

And the Voice said: "Behold your nation, and remember what your Six Grandfathers gave you, for thenceforth your people walk in difficulties."

20 Then the people broke camp again, and saw the black road before them towards where the sun goes down and black clouds coming yonder; and they did not want to go but could not stay. And as they walked the third ascent, all the animals and fowls that were the people ran here and there, for each one seemed to have his own little vision that he followed and his own rules; and all over the universe I could hear the winds at war like wild beasts fighting.[3]

And when we reached the summit of the third ascent and camped, the nation's hoop was broken like a ring of smoke that spreads and scatters and the holy tree seemed dying and all its birds were gone. And when I looked ahead I saw that the fourth ascent would be terrible.

Then when the people were getting ready to begin the fourth ascent, the Voice spoke like some one weeping, and it said: "Look there upon your nation." And when I looked down, the people were all changed back to human, and they were thin, their faces sharp, for they were starving. Their ponies were only hide and bones, and the holy tree was gone.

And as I looked and wept, I saw that there stood on the north side of the starving camp a sacred man who was painted red all over his body, and he held a spear as he walked into the center of the people, and there he lay down and rolled. And when he got up, it was a fat bison standing there, and where the bison stood a sacred herb sprang up right where the tree had been in the center of the nation's hoop. The herb grew and bore four blossoms on a single stem while I was looking—a blue,[4] a white, a scarlet, and a yellow—and the bright rays of these flashed to the heavens.

I know now what this meant, that the bison were the gift of a good spirit and were our strength, but we should lose them, and from the same good spirit we must find another strength. For the people all seemed better when the herb had grown and bloomed, and the horses raised their tails and neighed and pranced around, and I could see a light breeze going from the north among the people like a ghost; and suddenly the flowering tree was there again at the center of the nation's hoop where the four-rayed herb had blossomed.

25 I was still the spotted eagle floating, and I could see that I was already in the fourth ascent and the people were camping yonder at the top of the third long rise. It was dark and terrible about me, for all the winds of the world were fighting. It was like rapid gun-fire and like whirling smoke, and like women and children wailing and like horses screaming all over the world.

---

[3] At this point Black Elk remarked, "I think we are near that place now, and I am afraid something very bad is going to happen all over the world." He cannot read and knows nothing of world affairs [Author's Note].

[4] Blue as well as black may be used to represent the power of the west [Author's Note].

I could see my people yonder running about, setting the smoke-flap poles and fastening down their tepees against the wind, for the storm cloud was coming on them very fast and black, and there were frightened swallows without number fleeing before the cloud.

Then a song of power came to me and I sang it there in the midst of that terrible place where I was. It went like this:

> A good nation I will make live.
> This the nation above has said.
> They have given me the power to make over.

And when I had sung this, a Voice said: "To the four quarters you shall run for help, and nothing shall be strong before you. Behold him!"

Now I was on my bay horse again, because the horse is of the earth, and it was there my power would be used. And as I obeyed the Voice and looked, there was a horse all skin and bones yonder in the west, a faded brownish black. And a Voice there said: "Take this and make him over; and it was the four-rayed herb that I was holding in my hand. So I rode above the poor horse in a circle, and as I did this I could hear the people yonder calling for spirit power, "A-hey! a-hey! a-hey! a-hey!" Then the poor horse neighed and rolled and got up, and he was a big, shiny, black stallion with dapples all over him and his mane about him like a cloud. He was the chief of all the horses; and when he snorted, it was a flash of lightening and his eyes were like the sunset star. He dashed to the west and neighed, and the west was filled with a dust of hoofs, and horses without number, shiny black, came plunging from the dust. Then he dashed toward the north and neighed, and to the east and to the south, and the dust clouds answered, giving forth their plunging horses without number—whites and sorrels and buckskins, fat, shiny, rejoicing in their fleetness and their strength. It was beautiful, but it was also terrible.

Then they all stopped short, rearing, and were standing in a great hoop about their black chief at the center, and were still. And as they stood, four virgins, more beautiful than women of the earth can be, came through the circle, dressed in scarlet, one from each of the four quarters, and stood about the great black stallion in their places; and one held the wooden cup of water, and one the white wing, and one the pipe, and one the nation's hoop. All the universe was silent, listening; and then the great black stallion raised his voice and sang. The song he sang was this:

> "My horses, prancing they are coming.
> My horses, neighing they are coming;
> Prancing, they are coming.
> All over the universe they come.
> They will dance; may you behold them.
>
> >   (4 times)
>
> A horse nation, they will dance. May you behold them."
>
> >   (4 times)

His voice was not loud, but it went all over the universe and filled it. There was nothing that did not hear, and it was more beautiful than anything can be. It was so beautiful that nothing anywhere could keep from dancing. The virgins danced, and all the circled horses. The leaves on the trees, the grasses on the hills and in the valleys, the waters in the creeks and in the rivers and the lakes, the four-legged and the two-legged and the wings of the air—all danced together to the music of the stallion's song.

30 And when I looked down upon my people yonder, the cloud passed over, blessing them with friendly rain, and stood in the east with a flaming rainbow over it.

Then all the horses went singing back to their places beyond the summit of the fourth ascent, and all things sang along with them as they walked.

And a Voice said: "All over the universe they have finished a day of happiness." And looking down, I saw that the whole wide circle of the day was beautiful and green, with all fruits growing and all things kind and happy.

Then a Voice said: "Behold this day, for it is yours to make. Now you shall stand upon the center of the earth to see, for there they are taking you."

I was still on my bay horse, and once more I felt the riders of the west, the north, the east, the south, behind me in formation, as before, and we were going east. I looked ahead and saw the mountains there with rocks and forests on them, and from the mountains flashed all colors upward to the heavens. Then I was standing on the highest mountain of them all, and round about beneath me was the whole hoop of the world.[5] And while I stood there I saw more than I can tell and I understood more than I saw; for I was seeing in a sacred manner the shapes of all things in the spirit, and the shape of all shapes as they must live together like one being. And I saw that the sacred hoop of my people was one of many hoops that made one circle, wide as daylight and as starlight, and in the center grew one mighty flowering tree to shelter all the children of one mother and one father. And I saw that it was holy.

35 Then as I stood there, two men were coming from the east, head first like arrows flying, and between them rose the daybreak star. They came and gave a herb to me and said: "With this on earth you shall undertake anything and do it." It was the day-break-star herb, the herb of understanding, and they told me to drop it on the earth. I saw it falling far, and when it struck the earth it rooted and grew and flowered, four blossoms on one stem, a blue, a white, a scarlet, and a yellow; and the rays from these streamed upward to the heavens so that all creatures saw it and in no place was there darkness.

Then the Voice said: "Your Six Grandfathers—now you shall go back to them."

I had not noticed how I was dressed, until now, and I saw that I was painted red all over, and my joints were painted black, with white stripes

---

[5] Black Elk said the mountain he stood upon in his vision was Harney Peak in the Black Hills. "But anywhere is the center of the world," he added.

between the joints. My bay had lightning stripes all over him, and his mane was cloud. And when I breathed, my breath was lightning.

Now two men were leading me, head first like arrows slanting upward—the two that brought me from the earth. And as I followed on the bay, they turned into four flocks of geese that flew in circles, one above each quarter, sending forth a sacred voice as they flew: Br-r-r-p, br-r-r-p, br-r-r-p, br-r-r-p!

Then I saw ahead the rainbow flaming above the tepee of the Six Grandfathers, built and roofed with cloud and sewed with thongs of lightning; and underneath it were all the wings of the air and under them the animals and men. All these were rejoicing, and thunder was like happy laughter.

40   As I rode in through the rainbow door, there were cheering voices from all over the universe, and I saw the Six Grandfathers sitting in a row, with their arms held toward me and their hands, palms out; and behind them in the cloud were faces thronging, without number, of the people yet to be.

"He has triumphed!" cried the six together, making thunder. And as I passed before them, each gave again the gift that he had given me before—the cup of water and the bow and arrows, the power to make live and to destroy; the white wing of cleansing and the healing herb; the sacred pipe; the flowering stick. And each one spoke in turn from west to south, explaining what he gave as he had done before, and as each one spoke he melted down into the earth and rose again; and as each did this, I felt nearer to the earth.

Then the oldest of them all said: "Grandson, all over the universe you have seen. Now you shall go back with power to the place from whence you came, and it shall happen yonder that hundreds shall be sacred, hundreds shall be flames! Behold!"

I looked below and saw my people there, and all were well and happy except one, and he was lying like the dead—and that one was myself. Then the oldest Grandfather sang, and his song was like this:

> "There is someone lying on earth in a sacred manner.
> There is someone—on earth he lies.
> In a sacred manner I have made him to walk."

Now the tepee, built and roofed with cloud, began to sway back and forth as in a wind, and the flaming rainbow door was growing dimmer. I could hear voices of all kinds crying from outside: "Eagle Wing Stretches is coming forth! Behold him!"

45   When I went through the door, the face of the day of earth was appearing with the daybreak star upon its forehead; and the sun leaped up and looked upon me, and I was going forth alone.

And as I walked alone, I heard the sun singing as it arose, and it sang like this:

> "With visible face I am appearing.
> In a sacred manner I appear.
> For the greening earth a pleasantness I make.

The center of the nation's hoop I have made pleasant.
With visible face, behold me!
The four-leggeds and two-leggeds, I have made them to walk;
The wings of the air, I have made them to fly.
With visible face I appear.
My day, I have made it holy."

When the singing stopped, I was feeling lost and very lonely. Then a Voice above me said: "Look back!" It was a spotted eagle that was hovering over and spoke. I looked, and where the flaming rainbow tepee, built and roofed with cloud, had been, I saw only the tall rock mountain at the center of the world.

I was all alone on a broad plain now with my feet upon the earth, alone but for the spotted eagle guarding me. I could see my people's village far ahead, and I walked very fast, for I was homesick now. Then I saw my own tepee, and inside I saw my mother and my father, bending over a sick boy that was myself. And as I entered the tepee, some one was saying: "The boy is coming to; you had better give him some water."

Then I was sitting up; and I was sad because my mother and my father didn't seem to know I had been so far away.

■ EXPLORATIONS OF THE TEXT ■

1. Establish the context for the vision. What has happened to the Indian people?
2. What do "the flowering stick," "pipe," and "nation's hoop" signify? What does the "Voice" represent?
3. Analyze the images and the stages of the ascent. Discuss particularly the "fourth ascent," the "sacred man," "horse," "black stallion," the "four virgins," "a flaming rainbow."
4. Explain Black Elk's final vision on the mountaintop when he sees the "whole hoop of the world." What spirit and forces does he witness?
5. Who are the Six Grandfathers? What gifts do they bring Black Elk?
6. What is Black Elk's role in relation to his people?
7. Analyze the symbolism of the "spotted eagle."
8. How is this vision a story of rebirth? How is Black Elk a prophet?
9. What does the vision convey about the Native-American view of the world? What image of the future is presented?
10. Compare this dream of the future with the ideas in Walters' poem.

■■ JOURNAL ENTRIES ■■

---

1. React to one aspect of Black Elk's vision.
2. Create a dream of the future.
3. Recount a dream or nightmare about the future or about *your* future.

■■■ IDEAS FOR WRITING ■■■

---

1. Explore the imagery in Black Elk's vision.
2. Compare Black Elk's vision with King's "I Have a Dream," Gordon's "The Imagination of Disaster," or Yeats' "The Second Coming."
3. Compare Black Elk's dream of the future with the views of Plato and Camus.

The Allegory of the Cave

Plato

Translated by Benjamin Jowett

The "Allegory of the Cave" appears in Plato's Republic. *In this dialogue, Plato, through the persona of Socrates, explains the dual forces at work in the universe: the insubstantial world "of shadows" (that is, of physical appearances, appetites, change and flux) and the world of ideas (that is, of the light, the good, and the permanent). Plato contends that the true aim of a civilization is to promote justice, and that to do so enlightened leaders must embrace a knowledge of the good.*

1   And now, I[1] said, let me show in a figure how far our nature is enlightened or unenlightened:[2]—Behold! human beings housed in an underground cave, which has a long entrance open towards the light and as wide as the interior of the cave; here they have been from their childhood, and have their legs and necks chained, so that they cannot move and can only see before them, being prevented by the chains from turning round their heads. Above and behind them a fire is blazing at a distance, and between the fire and the

---

[1] From *The Republic,* Book 7. Socrates speaks to Glaucon.
[2] In the original Greek, the words for enlightened and unenlightened are "paideia" and "apaideusia." The former, depending on context, also may be understood as "education," "culture," or "knowledge." [Translator's note]

prisoners there is a raised way; and you will see, if you look, a low wall built along the way, like the screen which marionette players have in front of them, over which they show the puppets.

I see.

And do you see, I said, men passing along the wall carrying all sorts of vessels, and statues and figures of animals made of wood and stone and various materials, which appear over the wall? While carrying their burdens, some of them, as you would expect, are talking, others silent.

You have shown me a strange image, and they are strange prisoners.

5   Like ourselves, I replied; for in the first place do you think they have seen anything of themselves, and of one another, except the shadows which the fire throws on the opposite wall of the cave?

How could they do so, he asked, if throughout their lives they were never allowed to move their heads?

And of the objects which are being carried in like manner they would only see the shadows?

Yes, he said.

And if they were able to converse with one another, would they not suppose that the things they saw were the real things?

10   Very true.

And suppose further that the prison had an echo which came from the other side, would they not be sure to fancy when one of the passers-by spoke that the voice which they heard came from the passing shadow?

No question, he replied.

To them, I said, the truth would be literally nothing but the shadows of the images.

That is certain.

15   And now look again, and see in what manner they would be released from their bonds, and cured of their error, whether the process would naturally be as follows. At first, when any of them is liberated and compelled suddenly to stand up and turn his neck round and walk and look towards the light, he will suffer sharp pains; the glare will distress him, and he will be unable to see the realities of which in his former state he had seen the shadows; and then conceive someone saying to him that what he saw before was an illusion, but that now, when he is approaching nearer to being and his eye is turned towards more real existence, he has a clearer vision,—what will be his reply? And you may further imagine that his instructor is pointing to the objects as they pass and requiring him to name them,—will he not be perplexed? Will he not fancy that the shadows which he formerly saw are truer than the objects which are now shown to him?

Far truer.

And if he is compelled to look straight at the light, will he not have a pain in his eyes which will make him turn away to take refuge in the objects of vision which he can see, and which he will conceive to be in reality clearer than the things which are now being shown to him?

True, he said.

And suppose once more, that he is reluctantly dragged up that steep and rugged ascent, and held fast until he is forced into the presence of the sun himself, is he not likely to be pained and irritated? When he approaches the light his eyes will be dazzled, and he will not be able to see anything at all of what are now called realities.

20   Not all in a moment, he said.

He will require to grow accustomed to the sight of the upper world. And first he will see the shadows best, next the reflections of men and other objects in the water, and then the objects themselves; and, when he turned to the heavenly bodies and the heaven itself, he would find it easier to gaze upon the light of the moon and the stars at night than to see the sun or the light of the sun by day?

Certainly.

Last of all he will be able to see the sun, not turning aside to the illusory reflections of him in the water, but gazing directly at him in his own proper place, and contemplating him as he is.

Certainly.

25   He will then proceed to argue that this is he who gives the seasons and the years, and is the guardian of all that is in the visible world, and in a certain way the cause of all things which he and his fellows have been accustomed to behold?

Clearly, he said, he would arrive at this conclusion after what he had seen.

And when he remembered his old habitation, and the wisdom of the cave and his fellow-prisoners, do you not suppose that he would felicitate himself on the change, and pity them?

Certainly, he would.

And if they were in the habit of conferring honours among themselves on those who were quickest to observe the passing shadows and to remark which of them went before and which followed after and which were together, and who were best able from these observations to divine the future do you think that he would be eager for such honours and glories, or envy those who attained honour and sovereignty among those men? Would he not say with Homer,[3]

"Better to be a serf, labouring for a landless master,"

and to endure anything, rather than think as they do and live after their manner?

30   Yes, he said, I think that he would consent to suffer anything rather than live in this miserable manner.

Imagine once more, I said, such a one coming down suddenly out of the sunlight, and being replaced in his old seat; would he not be certain to have his eyes full of darkness?

To be sure, he said.

---

[3] Greek epic poet (c. 9th–8th centuries B.C.).

And if there were a contest, and he had to compete in measuring the shadows with the prisoners who had never moved out of the cave, while his sight was still weak, and before his eyes had become steady (and the time which would be needed to acquire this new habit of sight might be very considerable), would he not make himself ridiculous? Men would say of him that he had returned from the place above with his eyes ruined; and that it was better not even to think of ascending; and if anyone tried to loose another and lead him up to the light, let them only catch the offender, and they would put him to death.

No question, he said.

35   This entire allegory, I said, you may now append, dear Glaucon, to the previous argument; the prison-house is the world of sight, the light of the fire is the power of the sun, and you will not misapprehend me if you interpret the journey upwards to be the ascent of the soul into the intellectual world according to my surmise, which, at your desire, I have expressed—whether rightly or wrongly God knows. But, whether true or false, my opinion is that in the world of knowledge the Idea of good appears last of all, and is seen only with an effort; although, when seen, it is inferred to be the universal author of all things beautiful and right, parent of light and of the lord of light in the visible world, and the immediate and supreme source of reason and truth in the intellectual; and that this is the power upon which he who would act rationally either in public or private life must have his eye fixed.

I agree, he said, as far as I am able to understand you.

Moreover, I said, you must agree once more, and not wonder that those who attain to this vision are unwilling to take any part in human affairs; for their souls are ever hastening into the upper world where they desire to dwell; which desire of theirs is very natural, if our allegory may be trusted.

Yes, very natural.

Then, I said, the business of us who are the founders of the State will be to compel the best minds to attain that knowledge which we have already shown to be the greatest of all, namely, the vision of the good; they must make the ascent which we have described; but when they have ascended and seen enough we must now allow them to do as they do now.

40   What do you mean?

They are permitted to remain in the upper world, refusing to descend again among the prisoners in the cave, and partake of their labours and honours, whether they are worth having or not.

But is not this unjust? he said; ought we to give them a worse life, when they might have a better?

You have again forgotten, my friend, I said, the intention of our law, which does not aim at making any one class in the State happy above the rest; it seeks rather to spread happiness over the whole State, and to hold the citizens together by persuasion and necessity, making each share with others any benefit which he can confer upon the State; and the law aims at producing such citizens, not that they may be left to please themselves, but that they may serve in binding the State together.

True, he said, I had forgotten.

45   Observe, Glaucon, that we shall do no wrong to our philosophers but rather make a just demand, when we oblige them to have a care and providence of others; we shall explain to them that in other States, men of their class are not obliged to share in the toils of politics; and this is reasonable, for they grow up spontaneously, against the will of the governments in their several States; and things which grow up of themselves, and are indebted to no one for their nurture, cannot fairly be expected to pay dues for a culture which they have never received. But we have brought you into the world to be rulers of the hive, kings of yourselves and of the other citizens, and have educated you far better and more perfectly than they have been educated, and you are better able to share in the double duty. Wherefore each of you, when his turn comes, must go down to rejoin his companions, and acquire with them the habit of seeing things in the dark. As you acquire that habit, you will see ten thousand times better than the inhabitants of the cave, and you will know what the several images are and what they represent, because you have seen the beautiful and just and good in their truth. And thus our State, which is also yours, will be a reality and not a dream only, and will be administered in a spirit unlike that of other States, in which men fight with one another about shadows only and are distracted in the struggle for power, which in their eyes is a great good. Whereas the truth is that the State in which those who are to govern have least ambition to do so is always the best and most quietly governed, and the State in which they are most eager, the worst.

Quite true, he replied.

And will our pupils, when they hear this, refuse to take their turn at the toils of State, when they are allowed to spend the greater part of their time with one another in the heavenly light?

Impossible, he answered; for they are just men, and the commands which we impose upon them are just. But there can be no doubt that every one of them will take office as a stern necessity, contrary to the spirit of our present rulers of State.

Yes, my friend, I said; and there lies the point. You must contrive for your future rulers another and a better life than that of a ruler, and then you may have a well-ordered State; for only in the State which offers this, will they rule who are truly rich, not in gold, but in virtue and wisdom, which are the true blessings of life. Whereas if men who are destitute and starved of such personal goods go to the administration of public affairs, thinking to enrich themselves at the public expense, order there can never be; for they will be fighting about office, and the civil and domestic broils which thus arise will be the ruin of the rulers themselves and of the whole State.

50   Most true, he replied.

And the only life which looks down upon the life of political ambition is that of true philosophy. Do you know of any other?

Indeed, I do not, he said.

And those who govern should not "make love to their employment?" For, if they do there will be rival lovers, and they will fight.

No question.

55   Whom, then, will you compel to become guardians of the State? Surely those who excel in judgement of the means by which a State is administered, and who at the same time have other honours and another and a better life than that of politics?

None but these, he replied.

■ EXPLORATIONS OF THE TEXT ■

1. Describe or sketch the scene in the cave. Where are the "prisoners," "fire," and "screen"? What do the elements of the allegory represent?
2. What does the "light" signify? Why is it difficult for the prisoners to adjust to the "light"?
3. Describe the stages of illumination presented by Socrates.
4. According to Socrates, how can the "uneducated" and the unenlightened become enlightened?
5. What is the role of the "best minds" of the State? Who are the true rulers? What is the goal of the State? Do you agree to Plato's views?
6. Plato creates a dialogue that is supposed to instruct. Does it? What are the effects of this technique?

■■ JOURNAL ENTRIES ■■

1. Agree or disagree: "The state in which rulers are most reluctant to govern is always the best . . . and the State in which they are most eager, the worst."
2. Does learning something or changing one's mind cause pain? Cite an incident or experience from your own life.
3. Provide your own examples and descriptions of Plato's distinction between the worlds of "shadows" and "light."

■■■ IDEAS FOR WRITING ■■■

1. Connect Plato's concept of conversion with another experience of awakening, of knowledge, or of faith (for instance, Carver's "Cathedral" in Chapter 4).
2. Argue for or against Plato's view of the ideal ruler and the nature of politics.
3. Explore the definitions of the word "see" or "light" in this essay. How do they advance Plato's argument?
4. Write an allegory or a fable to explain an abstraction (death, love, faith).

The Myth of Sisyphus

Albert Camus

Albert Camus (1913–1960) was born in Algeria, at that time a colony of France. While studying philosophy at the University of Algiers, he organized and directed a small theater company and became involved in various political causes. He was active in the French Resistance in World War II, during which time he also wrote The Stranger, *a novel, and* The Myth of Sisyphus, *a philosophical essay, both important works in existential thought and literature of the absurd. Other of Camus' major works are the novel,* The Stranger *(1946),* The Plague *(1948), the short story collection,* Exile and the Kingdom *(1958), and the play collection,* Caligula and Three Other Plays *(1958). Camus' work earned him the Nobel Prize for Literature in 1957.*

"The Myth of Sisyphus," excerpted from the volume of the same name, articulates people's places and destinies in an absurd world. In Greek mythology, Sisyphus, punished by the gods for disobedience, is forced to roll a boulder up a hill, only to watch it tumble down the slope to its original location, and eternally to begin again.

1   The gods had condemned Sisyphus to ceaselessly rolling a rock to the top of a mountain, whence the stone would fall back of its own weight. They had thought with some reason that there is no more dreadful punishment than futile and hopeless labor.

2   If one believes Homer,[1] Sisyphus was the wisest and most prudent of mortals. According to another tradition, however, he was disposed to practice the profession of highwayman. I see no contradiction in this. Opinions differ as to the reasons why he became the futile laborer of the underworld. To begin with, he is accused of a certain levity in regard to the gods. He stole their secrets. Ægina,[2] the daughter of Æsopus, was carried off by Jupiter. The father was shocked by that disappearance and complained to Sisyphus. He, who knew of the abduction, offered to tell about it on condition that Æsopus would give water to the citadel of Corinth. To the celestial thunderbolts he preferred the benediction of water. He was punished for this in the underworld. Homer tells us also that Sisyphus had put Death in chains. Pluto[3] could not endure the sight of his deserted, silent empire. He dispatched the god of war, who liberated Death from the hands of her conqueror.

3   It is said also that Sisyphus, being near to death, rashly wanted to test his wife's love. He ordered her to cast his unburied body into the middle of the public square. Sisyphus woke up in the underworld. And there, annoyed by

---

[1] Greek epic poet (c. 9th to 8th centuries B.C.) who wrote about Sisyphus in *The Iliad.*
[2] A story from Greek mythology.
[3] Greek god of the underworld.

an obedience so contrary to human love, he obtained from Pluto permission to return to earth in order to chastise his wife. But when he had seen again the face of this world, enjoyed water and sun, warm stones and the sea, he no longer wanted to go back to the infernal darkness. Recalls, signs of anger, warnings were of no avail. Many years more he lived facing the curve of the gulf, the sparkling sea, and the smiles of earth. A decree of the gods was necessary. Mercury[4] came and seized the impudent man by the collar and, snatching him from his joys, led him forcibly back to the underworld, where his rock was ready for him.

4   You have already grasped that Sisyphus is the absurd hero. He *is*, as much through his passions as through his torture. His scorn of the gods, his hatred of death, and his passion for life won him that unspeakable penalty in which the whole being is exerted toward accomplishing nothing. This is the price that must be paid for the passions of this earth. Nothing is told us about Sisyphus in the underworld. Myths are made for the imagination to breathe life into them. As for this myth, one sees merely the whole effort of a body straining to raise the huge stone, to roll it and push it up a slope a hundred times over; one sees the face screwed up, the cheek tight against the stone, the shoulder bracing the clay-covered mass, the foot wedging it, the fresh start with arms outstretched, the wholly human security of two earth-clotted hands. At the very end of his long effort measured by skyless space and time without depth, the purpose is achieved. Then Sisyphus watches the stone rush down in a few moments toward that lower world whence he will have to push it up again toward the summit. He goes back down to the plain.

5   It is during that return, that pause, that Sisyphus interests me. A face that toils so close to stones is already stone itself! I see that man going back down with a heavy yet measured step toward the torment of which he will never know the end. That hour like a breathing space which returns as surely as his suffering, that is the hour of consciousness. At each of those moments when he leaves the heights and gradually sinks toward the lairs of the gods, he is superior to his fate. He is stronger than his rock.

6   If this myth is tragic, that is because its hero is conscious. Where would his torture be, indeed, if at every step the hope of succeeding upheld him? The workman of today works every day in his life at the same tasks, and this fate is no less absurd. But it is tragic only at the rare moments when it becomes conscious. Sisyphus, proletarian of the gods, powerless and rebellious, knows the whole extent of his wretched condition: it is what he thinks of during his descent. The lucidity that was to constitute his torture at the same time crowns his victory. There is no fate that cannot be surmounted by scorn.

7   If the descent is thus sometimes performed in sorrow, it can also take place in joy. This word is not too much. Again I fancy Sisyphus returning toward his rock, and the sorrow was in the beginning. When the images of earth cling too tightly to memory, when the call of happiness becomes too insistent, it happens that melancholy rises in man's heart: this is the rock's victory, this

---

[4] Roman god; messenger to the other gods.

is the rock itself. The boundless grief is too heavy to bear. These are our nights of Gethsemane.[5] But crushing truths perish from being acknowledged. Thus, Oedipus[6] at the outset obeys fate without knowing it. But from the moment he knows, his tragedy begins. Yet at the same moment, blind and desperate, he realizes that the only bond linking him to the world is the cool hand of a girl. Then a tremendous remark rings out: "Despite so many ordeals, my advanced age and the nobility of my soul make me conclude that all is well." Sophocles' Oedipus, like Dostoevsky's Kirilov,[7] thus gives the recipe for the absurd victory. Ancient wisdom confirms modern heroism.

8   One does not discover the absurd without being tempted to write a manual of happiness. "What! by such narrow ways—?" There is but one world, however. Happiness and the absurd are two sons of the same earth. They are inseparable. It would be a mistake to say that happiness necessarily springs from the absurd discovery. It happens as well that the feeling of the absurd springs from happiness. "I conclude that all is well," says Oedipus, and that remark is sacred. It echoes in the wild and limited universe of man. It teaches that all is not, has not been, exhausted. It drives out of this world a god who had come into it with dissatisfaction and a preference for futile sufferings. It makes a fate a human matter, which must be settled among men.

9   All Sisyphus' silent joy is contained therein. His fate belongs to him. His rock is his thing. Likewise, the absurd man, when he contemplates his torment, silences all the idols. In the universe suddenly restored to its silence, the myriad wondering little voices of the earth rise up. Unconscious, secret calls, invitations from all the faces, they are the necessary reverse and price of victory. There is no sun without shadow, and it is essential to know the night. The absurd man say yes and his effort will henceforth be unceasing. If there is a personal fate, there is no higher destiny, or at least there is but one which he concludes is inevitable and despicable. For the rest, he knows himself to be the master of his days. At that subtle moment when man glances backward over his life, Sisyphus returning toward his rock, in that slight pivoting he contemplates that series of unrelated actions which becomes his fate, created by him, combined under his memory's eye and soon sealed by his death. Thus, convinced of the wholly human origin of all that is human, a blind man eager to see who knows that the night has no end, he is still on the go. The rock is still rolling.

10   I leave Sisyphus at the foot of the mountain! One always finds one's burden again. But Sisyphus teaches the higher fidelity that negates the gods and raises rocks. He too concludes that all is well. This universe henceforth without a master seems to him neither sterile nor futile. Each atom of that stone, each mineral flake of that night-filled mountain, in itself forms a world. The struggle itself toward the heights is enough to fill a man's heart. One must imagine Sisyphus happy.

---

[5] Garden outside Jerusalem. A reference to Jesus' discussion with his disciples the night before his crucifixion.
[6] See Chapter 7.
[7] Character who kills himself in Dostoevsky's novel, *The Possessed* (1871).

■ EXPLORATIONS OF THE TEXT ■

1. Why does Camus include two different versions of Sisyphus's fate? What common thread connects them? What does Sisyphus represent to Camus?
2. Explain: "When he leaves the heights and gradually sinks toward the lairs of the gods, he is superior to his fate."
3. What does Camus mean by consciousness? Why does the "tragic" occur at the point of being "conscious"?
4. What does Camus mean by the "absurd"? Why is Sisyphus "the absurd hero"? What is the "absurd" man's fate?
5. This excerpt is part of Camus's longer essay considered by critics to be a meditation on suicide. What arguments does Camus offer to oppose suicide?
6. Characterize the voice of the persona in the essay and his approach to the audience.
7. Compare Camus' and Plato's views of enlightenment.

■■ JOURNAL ENTRIES ■■

1. Create contemporary parallels for each aspect of the allegory (Sisyphus, his meaningless labor, his act of defiance, the gods).
2. Do you agree with Camus' view of the absurd universe? his vision of people's fates in such a world?

■■■ IDEAS FOR WRITING ■■■

1. How does Camus' define tragedy?
2. Compare Camus' presentation of Oedipus's fate with that in Sophocles" drama in Chapter 7.
3. Write an essay discussing Camus' concept of the absurd.
4. Do you agree with Camus' statement: "The absurd man says yes, and his effort will henceforth be unceasing. If there is a personal fate, there is no higher destiny?"

Student Essay: Critical Thematic Analysis

About "Heritage"

Yvette Ho

Eighteen-year-old Yvette Ho hails from Queens, New York, where she has ample access to Manhattan's sociocultural milieu. In this essay, Ho compares her Chinese-American background with the view discussed in Linda Hogan's "Heritage."

In the poem "Heritage," Linda Hogan expresses the confusion that results from having a diversified ancestry and the obligation she feels toward preserving it. The rich culture of her father's Native-American "red" blood, however, could never quite mix with her mother's American "pale-skinned" culture, and she resents this conflict that led her to view her "whiteness [as] a shame." Pressured by the beliefs and rituals taught to her by her ancestors, she feels a resentment toward them because of "learning the secrets/of never having a home."

I am both Chinese and American and can identify with the speaker's mixed beliefs and confusion of identity as the result of her dual "heritage." I was born and raised here in the United States by traditional Chinese parents and have experienced the difficulties in differentiating which Chinese customs should be kept and which American ones should be adopted. The Chinese, one of thousands of foreign cultures to emigrate here, feel obligated, like Hogan, to defend and preserve our race and customs. At the same time, they must adapt to the diverse, yet racist society of America.

I consider my heritage to be Chinese-American—not solely Chinese due to my rearing here, and not completely American since through my blood runs thousands of years of my Chinese ancestry. My parents raised me to believe in myself and to take advantage of the opportunities here since my ancestors were never provided with such opportunities and most back in Communist China never will be. But, I was also told never forget who I am; I am Chinese and proud of my heritage. I will always have Chinese physicalities and view things through the mind of a Chinese person regardless of whatever changes occur in the universe—my identity will follow me to my death.

My parents have taught me to respect others and, in turn, respect will be reciprocated. The Chinese are taught to honor their superiors, whether they be leaders or parents, and not to question authority, as honor is a principal belief in most Asian cultures. "Do what you are supposed to do," "Your teachers are always right," "Education is the key to your future," they would repeat in their broken English. I respected and followed these requests, but as I got older, I began to question their validity.

I realized that my parents' experiences were very different from my own. They no longer live in a Communist country fearing the government's authority. It was then that, like Hogan, I began to differentiate the positive and negative aspects of my heritage, and I understood that my beliefs opposed the beliefs my parents imposed on me.

The Chinese, for the most part, are relatively passive individuals. We are taught to avoid hassles whenever possible, and to laugh and smile whenever we deem it necessary to divert attention away from troublesome situations. The passivity has led to racism and stereotypes that will never be broken, stereotypes that are immediately mentally retrieved when one sees a Chinese person, or for that matter any Asian person. This stereotype is a scar, not unlike Linda Hogan's "brown stain/that covered her white shirt." It stands out often overcoming rational thought and is nearly impossible to be rid of it.

Most adults believe that the only way to acquire knowledge is through the teachings of our educators. This example is only one of the negative aspects of my heritage. We do not have to follow what our "superiors" have taught us. Our authority figures here are not necessarily doing what is best for the people, so it is up to us to question these figures and retain knowledge that we find appropriate to believe. This trait was not passed on to me, but *will* be passed on to my children who shall be raised with ideas of equality and self-belief. My parents will continue to believe their views that reinforce the "slitty-eyed, unquestioning" stereotype. For this reason, they feel that I have forgotten my culture, that I have been "Americanized." My refusal to accept stereotypes has created a naive image of me within them. "Don't be so stupid. You know how those White people are. Be careful," they ignorantly state. They stubbornly hold on to their beliefs—another negative aspect of many of the Chinese. They are headstrong, somewhat racist individuals. Being the victims of oppression by Koreans and the English in history, they continue to hold the "grudges" of the past. These racist ideas are reflected in the language. Within the Chinese language exist colloquialisms for nationalities other than the Chinese, labelling them "ghosts"—as threatening, evil spirits. These slang words are widely accepted and commonly used. The ignorance and rigid ways of the Chinese prevent them from exploring the diversity of the United States, the beauty of the different interacting cultures and not just the hate and corruption.

There are many negative aspects of the typical Chinese person, but despite these beliefs, there is a rich history that should never be forgotten. This history is the positive trait that I *will* pass on to my children—the thousands of years of tradition, culture, and language, the oppression my ancestors and family overcame to obtain freedom, providing for me the different opportunities and freedoms I have here in America. My children will be taught to recognize these ancestors, their past and their history, and not to forget where they are originally from or who their ancestors were. Their cultural history will show them their true heritage. From there on, their identity will be based on their experiences, education, and decisions.

Despite Linda Hogan's childhood confusion about her dual "heritage," she was able to attain her identity. Now an avid author and educator supporting the Native-American movement, she differentiates between the negative and positive aspects of her heritage and retains certain beliefs she chooses to pass on to others. Her grandfather's "silence" and grandmother's "tobacco" will remain a part of her. Her Native-American heritage will forever exist in those images as her dual cultures unify.

Heritage

Linda Hogan

From my mother, the antique mirror
where I watch my face take on her lines.
She left me the smell of baking bread
to warm fine hairs in my nostrils,
5 she left the large white breasts that weigh down
my body.

From my father I take his brown eyes,
the plague of locusts that leveled our crops,
they flew in formation like buzzards.

10 From my uncle the whittled wood
that rattles like bones
and is white
and smells like all our old houses
that are no longer there. He was the man
15 who sang old chants to me, the words
my father was told not to remember.

From my grandfather who never spoke
I learned to fear silence.
I learned to kill a snake
20 when you're begging for rain.

And grandmother, blue-eyed woman
whose skin was brown,
she used snuff.[1]

---

[1] Finely ground tobacco that can be drawn up through the nose and inhaled.

When her coffee can full of black saliva
25 spilled on me
it was like the brown cloud of grasshoppers
that leveled her fields.
It was the brown stain
that covered my white shirt,
30 my whiteness a shame.
That sweet black liquid like the food
she chewed up and spit into my father's mouth
when he was an infant.
It was the brown earth of Oklahoma
35 stained with oil.
She said tobacco would purge your body of poisons.
It has more medicine than stones and knives
against your enemies.

That tobacco is the dark night that covers me.
40 She said it is wise to eat the flesh of deer
so you will be swift and travel over many miles.
She told me how our tribe has always followed a stick
that pointed west
that pointed east.

45 From my family I have learned the secrets
of never having a home.

WRITING ASSIGNMENTS

1. Compare the view of the future in "The Imagination of Disaster," "Harrison Bergeron," "Black Elk's Great Vision," and "The Handsomest Drowned Man in the World."
2. Compare views of obedience and conformity suggested in Vonnegut's "Harrison Bergeron" and in Griffin's "I Like to Think of Harriet Tubman" (Chapter 7).
3. Examine the views of global and environmental issues presented in the following: "Stone Olives" and "My Name Is 'I Am Living.'"
4. a. What were your preconceptions of Africa before you read the works in this chapter? What did you know about Africa?
   b. Explore conceptions of Africa presented in the Thematic Preview section.
   c. Compare your original ideas with your observations after the reading.
   d. In several works about Africa, trace one theme, such as apartheid, sense of exile, or the tension between the traditional and the modern.
5. a. What does Anzaldúa mean by "borderland"?
   b. Describe a "borderland" in which you live.
   c. Compare your "borderland" with a work in this chapter that presents a borderland.
   d. Compare Anzaldúa's view of "the borderland" with Menchú's view of ethnicity in Guatemala.
6. Discuss the concept of exile presented in three works in this chapter.
7. a. Explain the concept of renewal in one work in this chapter.
   b. The possibility and impossibility of renewal and rebirth in a global world are recurring themes in this chapter. Compare and contrast three visions of renewal.
   c. Which works present the most convincing and/or believable visions?
8. Explicate "Diving into the Wreck" or one of Rilke's sonnets. Focus on point of view, imagery, figurative language, and form. (See Chapter 10.)
9. a. Explore the water or natural imagery in three works in this chapter.
   b. Explain kite imagery in *"Master Harold"* . . . *and the Boys* and in "A Christmas Memory" (in Chapter 5).
10. Compare the points of view of three speakers in three poems. How does point of view relate to tone, imagery, and theme?
11. a. What new myths of the future emerge in "Diving into the Wreck" and "The Second Coming"?
    b. Create your own myth or allegory for a view of the future.
12. Contrast "Black Elk's Great Vision" with selections from Menchú's "Conflict with the Landowners." Contrast the voices of the speakers,

their messages, and their styles. (Both of these works began as oral histories and interviews.)

13. a. Ask several people to envision the world in the year 2095. What do they fear about the future, and what do they wish for the future?
    b. Analyze your results. What patterns do you perceive?
    c. Use one interview as the basis for an essay.
    d. Compare one of your interviewer's views of the future with a work in this chapter.

14. Create a science fiction short story. Develop a view of a utopian or dystopian society.

15. As Martin Luther King does, conceive of a "dream" for society in which there is harmony among people of different cultural or ethnic backgrounds.

16. Choose one of the following topics as the basis for research: apartheid, Nelson Mandela, world hunger, world drought, ecological issues (the destruction of the Brazilian rain forest, acid rain, oil spills), nuclear holocaust—nuclear winter, Hiroshima and Nagasaki, genetic engineering, African nations, tensions between traditional (tribal) beliefs and Christianity in African culture (or a writer's treatment of this theme: Achebe, Head, Soyinka), a contemporary African novelist or poet, Buddhism, Nō drama, or Utopian literature, existentialism.

17. Write a character analysis of Hally or Sam from *"Master Harold" . . . and the Boys.* (Refer to the model in Chapter 11.)

18. Compare two works which present hopeful views of the future.

19. a. Evaluate your favorite work in this chapter. Argue for its inclusion in the next edition of this text. Write a letter to the authors.
    b. Evaluate your favorite work in this book. Assume that your audience is the publisher of this anthology.
    c. Select one work from *Legacies* that has changed your views. Explain your reaction to it. How did it change your perspective?

20. Write an argument, agreeing or disagreeing with Yeats' "The Second Coming." You may refer to other works in this chapter.

21. a. Summarize Said's arguments in "Reflections on Exile."
    b. Agree or disagree with Said's contention that exile is the nature of the human condition in the global village.
    c. Posit an alternative to Said's view of the human condition in the global village.
    d. Compare Said's views with the speaker's ideas in Anzaldúa's poem.
    e. Evaluate Said's essay. (Refer to Chapter 12.)

22. Create comments for several characters from works in this chapter about the following: "the secrets/of never having a home" (Linda Hogan, "Heritage").

23. Discuss the ideal versus the reality of harmony among people of different races and/or cultures in the works in this chapter's Thematic Preview. You also may refer to "The Handsomest Drowned Man in the World."
24. Compare the views of Plato, Camus, and Black Elk on the cosmos and on human beings and their destinies.

Part Three

Reading and Writing

About the Genres

FICTION

Fiction is the imagined creation of character and action for the purpose of conveying a vision of life. Like forms of nonfictional narration (storytelling), fiction depends on a recording of a sequence of events (as in historical rendering) and on an organization of incident and action (as in reporting). Fiction also requires a colorful, vivid depiction of characters and action (as in oral storytelling).

Fundamental to short fiction are a concentration on characters and the changes in characters brought about by events. Discussing the components of plot in *Aspects of the Novel*, E. M. Forster, differentiates between an account of incidents and plot. He states that "The king died, and then the queen died" does not form a story line for fiction; however, the following presents the kernel of a tale, "The king died, and the queen died of grief." In the second version, the fiction emerges from the effect of the husband's death on the wife; a vision of mourning and loss is implied.

FORMS OF NARRATIVE

The earliest forms of narrative stories are the **myths** that ancient people conceived to explain their worlds—natural phenomena, human behavior, beliefs, and values—and to satisfy their need for transcendent experiences and meanings. Creation myths appear in the Old Testament, in Norse legends, and in Native-American tribal lore. Greek and Roman myths of gods and goddesses and the creation of the world are written in such works as Thesiod's *Theogeny* and Ovid's *Metamorphoses*. The *Vedas,* the sacred Sanskrit texts of the Hindus, explore the origins of the gods of India.

Many myths explain facts of life, death, and immortality. "Coyote and the Shadow People," a Nez Percé myth, for example, relates the story of Coyote, who longs for his wife's return from the dead. The Death Spirit permits Coyote's wife to live in the world as a shadow for a three-day trial, but, because Coyote touches his wife's shadow, he loses the opportunity to regain his wife permanently. In "Summer Water and Shirley" (Chapter 5), Durango Mendoza intertwines Native-American myth and legend in the story of a brother's devotion to his sister.

Some stories, called **parables**, provide moral instruction or convey moral, religious, or spiritual truths. Consider the story of the prodigal son in the New Testament, a story in which the younger son squanders his share of his father's wealth in riotous living, while his older brother stays and works with the father. The prodigal son endures hard times and returns to his father to ask for mercy, and the father joyously welcomes him and celebrates his homecoming. When the elder son protests, the father replies, "Be glad: for this thy brother was dead and is alive again and was lost and is found." This tale teaches the need for charity, compassion, and forgiveness. In the Zen parable, "Temper," the Zen master asks questions about those qualities of self, contrary to righteous and ethical behavior and to the religious life; and his student must meditate to discover an answer.

> *A Zen student came to Bankei and complained: "Master, I have an ungovernable temper. How can I cure it?"*
>
> *"You have something very strange," replied Bankei. "Let me see what you have."*
>
> *"Just now I cannot show it to you," replied the other.*
>
> *"When can you show it to me?" asked Bankei.*
>
> *"It arises unexpectedly," replied the student.*
>
> *"Then," concluded Bankei, "it must not be your own true nature. If it were, you could show it to me at any time. When you were born you did not have it, and your parents did not give it to you. Think that over."*

Luisa Valenzuela in "The Verb to Kill" (Chapter 4) creates a short story in parabolic language to suggest the effects of violence on children who live under a militaristic regime.

A **fable**, another kind of moralizing story, commonly features animals or inanimate objects endowed with human qualities. Their experiences and behavior teach a lesson, stated explicitly at the conclusion of the tale. Some of the oldest fables may be traced to Aesop, a sixth-century Roman. In his story, "The Tortoise and the Hare," for instance, the hare, conceited and overly confident, falls asleep during a race while the slower tortoise plods ahead and wins. The moral of the tale is "slow but steady wins the race." In "My Life with the Wave," Octavio Paz, working out of the tradition of the fable, creates a male character who falls in love with a wave, a female lover (Chapter 6). The lesson of the story concerns the power and consequences of romantic love.

Every culture also has its epics—stories of the exploits of heroes and mythical creatures—and folk tales that provide entertainment and present moral truths. Like myths, **epic poems** were passed from generation to generation as strictly oral entertainment before being written down and read as literature. *The Iliad and The Odyssey,* the oldest known Western epics, recount the exploits of the warriors of the Trojan War and the wanderings of the Greek hero Odysseus after the war. The *Mahabharata,* a monumental Hindu epic, depicts the strife of two Indian royal families and the spiritual development of the Indian hero, Krishna.

Each culture enjoys folk tales. The fairy tales we learned as children from Hans Christian Andersen or from the Brothers Grimm were actually Danish and German stories. *Cinderella,* for example, has many incarnations as a French folk tale transcribed by Perrault; as a German story recorded by the Brothers Grimm; as Algonquin Indian and Chinese tales. Although each version transmits different cultural values, fairy tales around the world convey recurring and familiar motifs: they portray the struggle between parents and children, between innocence and corruption, between good and evil, and between life and death. Short story writers often draw on folk and fairy tales in the development of character, plot, and theme. Gabriel Garciá Márquez deliberately titles "The Handsomest Drowned Man in the World" (Chapter 8) a "Tale for Children" to highlight its fairy tale elements.

Other forms of narrative emerged in the Middle Ages and the Renaissance. The epic, the tale of the hero, became transformed into romances in which knights fought battles for the love of their ladies. Sometimes the quest for romance also became a quest for spiritual salvation, as in many of the stories of King Arthur, his knights of the Round Table, and their search for the Holy Grail, as in the poem, *Sir Gawain and the Green Knight.*

The word **novella** came into existence to describe the short tales of Boccacio written in the fourteenth century. Now the term signifies a work of fiction, longer than and more expansive than a short story, but less complex than a novel. They were stories of love, designed as courtly entertainment. Boccacio's *The Decameron* is a collection of one hundred short stories told by ten residents of Florence who attempted to escape the plague. James Joyce's "The Dead" (Chapter 6) is an example of a modern novella.

Lady Murasaki of Japan wrote the first **novel**, *The Tale of Genji,* in 1022. The novel emerged as a form of fictional prose narrative in the seventeenth century in England with the advent of a middle class that had both the leisure and a level of literacy to read and to support magazines. The first English protonovels were Aphra Behn's *Oroonoko* (1688) and Daniel Defoe's *Robinson Crusoe* (1719), a tale of a man abandoned on an island. The reading public and the demand for novels grew in the eighteenth century. The nineteenth century, however, became the great age of the British novel. The fullest representation of a story line, the novel captures a moment in time, a moment in a culture. This form incorporates the breadth and depth created by development of many characters, plots, subplots, and themes.

The invention of the modern **short story** is often attributed to Edgar Allen Poe. His most famous works include "The Masque of the Red Death," "The Pit and the Pendulum," and "The Telltale Heart." Poe suggested that a reader should be able complete a story in a single sitting. In the nineteenth century, the tradition of the American short story began with the publication of works by Poe, Nathaniel Hawthorne, Herman Melville, Mary Wilkins Freeman, Sarah Orne Jewett, and Kate Chopin. See, for example, Jewett's "A White Heron" (Chapter 4).

A single concentrated story line, a single plot that involves a conflict or crisis that leads to a climax and to a resolution, and a limited number of characters distinguish the short story. Another usual feature of the genre is that it, like poetry, is compressed so that all elements may develop character, plot, and theme.

The modern short story was influenced by James Joyce's conception that a central character should be involved in a conflict or momentary experience that leads to discovery or to an awakening—in Joyce's term—an epiphany. However, contemporary short stories portray characters caught in experiences that may not lead to a climax, resolution, or realization. The stories conclude without the characters undergoing any change or gaining any great insight. The characters—in stasis—remain in a cycle of sterility. According to its creators, this form of development mirrors the absurdity and lack of meaning in the modern world.

In the following short story by Clarice Lispector, a contemporary Portuguese fiction writer, many forms of narrative converge. Her short story intertwines narrative, parable, fable, and fairy tale. Like many fiction writers today, Lispector, aware of the history of the genre, mixes narrative techniques to create a new form of the short story.

The Dead Man in the Sea at Urca

I was at the apartment of Doña Lourdes, my seamstress, trying on a new dress designed by Olly—and Doña Lourdes said: "A man drowned in the sea, look at the firemen." I looked and only saw the sea, which must have been very salty; blue sea, white houses. And the dead man?

The dead man pickled in brine. I don't want to die! I screamed to myself, silent within my dress. The dress is yellow and blue. And I? Dying of heat, not dying of a blue sea.

I'll tell you a secret: my dress is beautiful, and I don't want to die. On Friday the dress will be at home, and on Saturday I'll wear it. Without death, just blue sea. Do yellow clouds exist? Golden ones do. I have no story. Does the dead man? He does: he went to take a swim in the sea at Urca, the fool, and he died—who told him to go? I'm careful when I bathe in the sea, I'm no fool, and I only go to Urca to try on a new dress. And three blouses. S. went with me. She is most particular at a fitting. And the dead man? Particularly dead?

I'll tell you a story: once upon a time there was a young fellow who liked to swim in the sea. So, one Wednesday morning he went to Urca. I don't go to Urca, to the rocks of Urca, because it's full of rats. But the young man didn't pay attention to the rats. Nor did the rats pay any attention to him. Urca's cluster of white houses. That he noticed. And then there was a woman trying on a dress, who arrived too late: The young man was already dead. Briny. Were there piranhas in the sea? I pretend not to understand. I don't, in fact, understand death. A boy, dead?

Dead like the fool he was. One should only go to Urca to try on a gay dress. The woman, who is me, only wants gaiety. But I bow down before death. That will come, will come, will come. When? Ah, that's just it, it can come at any moment. But I, who was trying on a dress in the heat of the morning, asked God for a sign. And I felt something so intense, an overwhelming scent of roses. So, I had my proof, in two tests: of God and of my dress.

One should only die a natural death, never in an accident, never drowned in the sea. I beg protection for my own, who are many. And the protection, I am sure, will come.

But what of the young man? And his story? He might have been a student. I will never know. I simply stood staring out at the sea and the cluster of houses. Doña Lourdes, imperturbable, asked if she should take it in at the waist a bit more. I said yes, a waistline is there to be seen tight. But I was in shock. In shock in my beautiful new dress.

The work begins with traditional story elements: a setting, an apartment, two characters—Doña Lourdes and the speaker—a plot line and motivation (the speaker hears of a death of a man from Doña Lourdes and reacts with sadness to the tragedy). A conflict also arises between Doña Lourdes and the speaker (Doña Lourdes prefers to ignore the reality of death whereas the speaker cannot be immune). The story develops as the narrator imagines the circumstances of the man's drowning and experiences certain revelations, "I bow down before death," and "One should only die a natural death, never in an accident, never drowned in the sea."

The work becomes a parable of the young man who represents the irrational, unpredictable, natural forces defeating human beings. "The Dead Man in the Sea at Urca," also becomes a fable warning the reader of the dangers of becoming immune to the facts of life and death—the consequences of being unmoved by another's suffering. In this lesson about indifference, the characters seem to signify human attitudes toward death and tragedy. The moral of the tale clearly urges people to remain human: one must not allow oneself to be isolated, to deny others' suffering. One must have the empathy and moral imagination to care about people and to respond.

In the tale, after she imagines the story of the drowned sailor, the speaker appears to be in shock. Is she in shock because she recognizes her own privileged, untouched position? Is she in shock because Doña Lourdes' "imperturbable" posture surprises her? Is she in shock because life is unfair, tragic, and cruel? Is she in shock because she is helpless to save "the drowned man?" After all, she arrives "too late." The story ends with these questions. It leaves the reader puzzled and does not resolve the plot or the character's crisis. This fable concludes with possible questions rather than with obvious lessons. One of the intriguing features of the modern short story is its open-endedness, a quality that simulates the complexity and fragility of contemporary life.

The story also reminds the reader of a fairy tale, though evil, not good, prevails in the end. The innocent young woman who will wear the blue dress must face the irrationality and the certainty of death. The "damsel" is not discovered by a prince, does not fall in love and live happily ever after; she learns about a dead man "pickled in brine" and realizes that she does not "want to die!" She cannot do anything about death, but "bow down before" it and comprehend that it "will come, will come, will come . . . at any moment." The fact of death, of evil, prevails over good, over the innocent perspective of the young woman, who must come to a more complex understanding of life. Thus, this deceptively simple story becomes a complex, multilayered parable, fable, and fairy tale about the inescapable nature of death.

ELEMENTS OF FICTION

Point of View

Many elements of fiction—**point of view, setting, plot, characters, conflict, symbolism,** and **theme**—combine to create a work. We use these elements when we create even a simple, informal narrative, as when we recount a tragedy reported in the news or describe the previous night's party. Read this ghost story:

> *I woke up in the middle of the night because I thought someone was watching me. When I awakened, a girl, dressed in a white nightgown, stood at the foot of my bed. She had long, yellow hair and large, luminous eyes, staring at me. I was petrified. I freaked. I closed my eyes. She was still there. I pulled the pillow over my head. When I lifted the pillow, she had disappeared. Only later, much later, did I tell my husband this story. He told me that he had shared the same experience. Later, much later, I learned that a little girl had died in our house in Kentucky, in the house where we experienced those nightmares.*

Many elements of fiction are prevalent in this short tale, including a certain **point of view**, a narrative perspective. The choice of narrative perspective shapes the direction of the tale and is intertwined with plot, character, and theme. In this case, the story presents a first-person, singular point of view—"I." Writers create a sense of immediacy and personal involvement with first-person narrators.

An alternative to the first-person point of view is third-person narrative. To recognize the third-person point of view, look for the use of "he," "she," and "they." In third-person, the narrative perspective presents the characters and action and tells the tale from a certain distance. Recast the ghost story into third-person, using *she* and *her* in place of *I* and *me*. Such a change may result in a loss of intimacy, immediacy, and urgency.

There are several forms of third-person narration. An omniscient narrator assumes the vantage point of knowing everything in his or her characters' minds. Readers gain insights into the consciousness of all characters in the story. A narrator with limited knowledge discloses information about one or several, but not all, of the narrative points of view. In detached or dramatic narrative point of view, the speaker describes the characters and actions with no insight into characters' feelings. If the ghost story appeared in third-person, the narrator could develop his or her perspective, or possibly the husband's, or even the ghost's point of view. The story would progress differently. Consider this excerpt from Joyce Carol Oates' "Where Are You Going, Where Have You Been?" (Chapter 4):

> Her name was Connie. She was fifteen and she had a quick nervous giggling habit of craning her neck to glance into mirrors, or checking other people's faces to make sure her own was all right. Her mother, who noticed everything and knew everything and who hadn't much reason any longer to look at her own face, always scolded Connie about it. "Stop gawking at yourself, who are you? You think you're so pretty?" she would say. Connie would raise her eyebrows at these familiar complaints and look right through her mother, into a shadowy vision of herself as she was right at that moment: she knew she was pretty and that was everything. Her mother had been pretty once too, if you could believe those old snapshots in the album, but now her looks were gone and that was why she was always after Connie.

Oates creates a limited third-person narrative perspective to depict her main character's struggles in adolescence. The reader gains insight into Connie's feelings about her appearance and about her disdainful attitudes toward her mother, but does not learn anything about Connie from the mother's point of view.

We also may characterize a narrator as participant or as nonparticipant. A participant narrator is a presence within the story who creates and engages in the action. A nonparticipant narrator observes the action. In the ghost story, a participant first-person narrator tells her own tale. Imagine this first-person narrator as a nonparticipant in the action, a woman who recounts a tale she heard from her friend. The story would have a different dramatic impact.

A participant narrator also may be trustworthy or untrustworthy. We consider a narrator trustworthy when we accept his or her view of the situation, when we think it is credible or, perhaps, represents the position of the author. In a story with an untrustworthy narrator, we question the narrative's stance and ask if it is credible, biased, or even, perhaps, delusional or hysterical. We question the validity of the point of view and realize that a distinction exists between the narrative and authorial point of view. In the ghost story, the narrator is trustworthy because her responses seem skeptical and because she qualifies her discussion. We accept her version of the truth. Imagine an untrustworthy narrator, extremely overwrought, talking to the ghost—we would not believe her version.

Setting

Setting is the location, time, place, and/or environment in which the story takes place. In the ghost story, the location is the bedroom of a house, the time is night and the present; and the environment is a middle class household in the 1980s in Kentucky. The setting creates a particular mood, sense of place, and context. The ghost story would have little impact if the event occurred in broad daylight, in a city, and in a less scientific and skeptical age.

Plot

A **plot** presents the sequence of events in a story. In a short story the sequence of events is concentrated and does not necessarily represent actual time. Events in daily life, perhaps having taken place over a period of time, or events that appear random or fragmentary are often shaped, developed, and given cohesive form. For example, routine trips to work on the bus may become the basis for a central episode in a story, or a chance encounter with an old friend may be transformed into the central action of a tale. In the case of the ghost story, the sighting may represent many nights of uneasy feelings or partial glimpses.

Since a short story is so compressed, usually the sequence of events narrows to a single moment, a series of moments, or action that reveals a larger truth of character and life. The sequence builds to a **climax**, a high point of action. In an adventure or horror short story, the climax may be an apex of suspense; in a short story focused on character, the climactic point may be a moment of discovery, awakening, or revelation. For example, in the ghost story, the most important event is not the appearance of the spirit, but the discovery that a child had died in the house, and, indeed, that the apparition could be a real ghost; in short, the narrator begins to recognize the possibility of supernatural occurrences.

Short story writers also manipulate the sequence of events in a story; they may not present the events in chronological (time) order. For example, the story may begin in the middle of the action or at the end of the sequence, and then the narrator may *flashback*—move back in time—to the beginning of the action. The ghost story, for instance, could have begun with the sighting of the ghost and then could have returned to the beginning of the night's sleep. Flashback techniques add dramatic impact and meaning to the unfolding events since the reader already knows what will transpire; the technique also may shift the focus from the plot to character development since attention moves away from the rendering of the action. *Flash forward* is another method of manipulating time in which the narrator relates the beginning of the tale, then moves quickly to the ending, and then returns to the beginning of the story. This technique adds dramatic impact and irony (double meanings) to each stage of the action since the reader is aware of the contribution of each moment to the unfolding of the action. In a rendering of the ghost story, the narrator could have quickly moved to the sighting, then returned to see partial, mysterious glimpses of the face, hair, clothes, and eyes of a figure—these glimpses would have dramatic impact for a reader. Short stories also may unfold through associations and may move backward and forward in time.

Conflict

Conflict is the tension between two forces; the exposition of a problem; an internal battle between two forces, psychic or external. Major conflicts in fiction arise between people and nature, between people and their environments, among people, or within a person. In the ghost story, the conflict, an internal struggle, centers on whether the narrator believes that she has seen a ghost. The plot of the short story concentrates on and develops such a conflict until it is resolved after a moment of crisis. In conventional short stories, the climax prompts the resolution through a moment of reckoning, recognition, awakening, or discovery. However, many contemporary short stories do not present resolutions of conflict. Again in the ghost story, no answers exist to test the validity of the reported sighting of the apparition. The story leaves questions open. The story ends in an ambivalent, mysterious way.

Character

The short story primarily concentrates on the presentation of **characters**: the people in the story and their conflicts. In the ghost story, the characters are the first-person narrator, the apparition, and the husband. The conflict concerns the tension within the narrator between believing and negating the presence of the little girl. We learn about characters through action, dialogue, and physical appearance. Their personalities evolve through events and through interaction with others.

In fiction, E. M. Forster has distinguished between **round** and **flat** characters. Round characters are multidimensional, capable of growth and change. Flat characters, according to Forster, are one-dimensional and often stereotypical. The effective short story concentrates on presenting at least one round character in conflict with others. Because of the length and complicated texture of a short story, the writer of this genre cannot develop as many characters in depth as can writers of such longer forms as the novella or novel. In a further draft of the ghost story, the narrator could become the round character and the ghost of the little girl, the flat, one-dimensional character.

Language

The **language** in a short story is compressed. Each word is well-chosen and contributes to the impact of the whole. Sharp, vivid sensory details involve the reader in the world of the narrator, in setting, in characters, in the unfolding drama of the plot. In addition, short story writers often choose elements of poetic diction: images, figurative language, symbolism, allusion, and irony to create their worlds (see Chapter 2).

Short story writers also work with the **denotations** (dictionary definitions) and **connotations** (associations) of words to create effect. Because the form is concentrated, each word must have impact and add to the presentation of theme (messages of the work). Think of the word, "Briny," in Lispector's story as it describes the dead man literally as salted or preserved in salt. The connotations, which may include pickled, shrivelled, deformed, and lifeless, lead readers to form a picture of a human corpse, desiccated, dead, grotesque, less than human.

Another element of language is the texture of the prose: the sounds and the rhythms of the language. Storytelling, originally oral entertainment, does exist as "music." Think of paragraph three of Lispector's work. The short staccato sentences and questions reflect the narrator's tension. The repetition of the "s" and the "d" sounds evoke feelings of sharpness and of harshness, appropriate to the confrontation with death. They "thud" like the inescapable face of death.

In addition, aspects of style that create the rhythm of language are repetition and parallelism (repeated and balanced wording). In paragraph two of "The Dead Man in the Sea at Urca," the repeated form of "dying" and the contrast of the balanced phrases—"dying" and "not dying"—add dramatic impact to the sentence and momentum to the entire piece.

For stories to be powerful, writers also avoid **clichés** (hackneyed or overused expressions and figures of speech). Clichés detract from impact because they belong to everyday conversational speech, not to the heightened language of fiction; and, therefore, they are jarring and destructive to the mood. They also do not add descriptive detail or image because they cannot evoke word pictures since their meanings are predictable and often taken for granted. In Lispector's story, imagine that she describes the dead man as "dead as a door nail" instead of "briny." The former phrase would have detracted from the vision of the drowned man.

Tone

Tone, the sense of the narrator, emerges from the connotations, the inferences, of every word. Tone also conveys the attitude of the narrator toward his or her subject, for example, characters and events in the work. Apparent from the first word, tone colors every detail of the work—dialogue, imagery, symbol, and setting. In the ghost story, the tone shifts from fear to puzzlement to mystery as the narrator learns about the death of the child.

Symbolism

A **symbol** is a person, place, object, thing, name, title, aspect of setting that suggests something beyond itself and has a range of meanings. Since a short story, like poetry, is compressed, all aspects of the story—title, setting, characters' names, appearance, dialogue, and events of the plot—may contain symbolic meanings and create the theme. For example, even in the informal telling of the ghost story, the girl's yellow hair and white dress suggest her innocence; the head under the pillow, the denial of truth. In Lispector's work, the dead man symbolizes the irrationality of death; the blue dress, the conventions of daily life that mask the reality.

Theme

The **theme** of the short story is the message presented by the work. No story has a single central idea; there may be several themes. As he or she is crafting the story, the writer may be conscious of several themes of the work and may shape it with these ideas in mind. In addition, readers may discover other messages from careful analyses of the text. In Lispector's work, one theme concerns the omnipresence of death, another the human drive to negate that reality; another message evolves from the young woman's preoccupation with the untimeliness of the "young fellow['s]" death. The story also conveys a vision of an absurd world in which seemingly random events—"accident[s]"—occur and have no meaning.

All aspects of an effective short story may create themes: point of view, setting, plot, character, conflict, tone, and symbolism. In Lispector's story, one theme centers on the impossibility of escaping death: We must "bow down before death." The point of view—first person—gives the reader the thoughts of the woman who struggles with the realization that tragic "accident[s]" do occur. The setting also develops this theme. The seamstress's apartment indicates the narrator's upper class status as does the "new dress designed by Olly." These details highlight the social class of the main character and imply that even the wealthy are not invulnerable. The sea, chaotic, unpredictable, mysterious, and uncontrollable, suggests the world outside the civilized order. The tension and conflict in the plot center on the narrator's—the main character's—awareness and anxiety concerning her own fate. For if a "young fellow" can swim in the sea at Urca and drown, she too could die. The "imperturbable" Doña Lourdes serves as a character who opposes the stance of the narrator; she is unmoved by the death and refuses to acknowledge this reality. The tone of the story, restrained yet evocative, reinforces the character portrayal and theme. The spare style suits this depiction of life, yet the colorful, vivid details of the "blue sea," "white houses," "yellow and blue" dress, and the "scent of roses" and the woman's reflections and questions ("Were there piranhas in the sea? . . . I don't, in fact, understand death. A boy, dead?") highlight the tensions between life and death apparent in the work. Finally, the symbolic contrasts between the dead man and the "blue and yellow" dress suggest the chaotic force of death and the conventions of daily life that shield us from this irrational force. These polarities reach a climax in the woman's plea, "I beg protection for my own, who are many." In this statement, she voices human fears of fragility and vulnerability. This short story becomes a tightly developed and structured exploration of facing the reality of death.

THE READING/WRITING PROCESS: FICTION

In addition to critical reading responses, we recommend a process for understanding fiction. First, read the story; and involve yourself on the level of point of view and plot. Ask yourself who is telling the story, and explore your reactions to the narrative point of view? Is the narrator part of the story? Is the narrator objective about the events? Is the narrator trustworthy? As you read, remember the main events and follow the sequence of action. Who are the main characters? With whom do you sympathize? Locate the problems and conflicts. As you read, notice the shifts in conflict and the development of crisis. At the story's conclusion, ask yourself if the conflicts are resolved. Ask if any of the characters have changed. How have they developed? Ask if your sympathies and involvement with certain characters have shifted. What messages have you discovered in the text? Explore the emotional impact of the work. Ask how you felt after finishing the story. In a second or third reading, analyze the function of point of view, setting, tone, symbolism, word choice, detail, imagery, and figurative language used by the writer in building the story. Throughout your reading, explore your own reactions and associations with the story. Assess your reactions to the themes of the narrative.

CHECKLIST FOR READING SHORT FICTION

1. What point of view is apparent? First person? Third person? Omniscient? Limited? Detached? What is the impact of this choice of narrative perspective? participant or nonparticipant narrative point of view?

2. What is the setting of the story? Time? Place? Environment? What moods are created by the setting in the story? What social, cultural, historical contexts are established by setting?

3. What are the key events of the plot? Does the plot build to a climax? What are the conflicts in the story? Are the conflicts resolved? Is there a moment of awakening or discovery?

4. Who are the main characters? Are they round? flat? With whom do you relate? sympathize? How are they related to each other? What is the role of minor characters?

5. What is the tone of the story? What can you tell about the tone from the opening? Why? From key descriptions and details?

6. Characterize word choice. Is there vivid detail? Figurative language? Irony?

7. What are the symbolic details (title, names, setting, gesture, objects, events)? How does symbolism create theme?

8. What are the themes of the work? Do all elements of the story contribute to the theme?

Student Portfolio:
Response to Kate Chopin's "The Story of an Hour"

The Story of an Hour

Kate Chopin

1 Knowing that Mrs. Mallard was afflicted with a heart trouble, great care was taken to break to her as gently as possible the news of her husband's death.

It was her sister Josephine who told her, in broken sentences; veiled hints that revealed in half concealing. Her husband's friend Richards was there, too, near her. It was he who had been in the newspaper office when intelligence of the railroad disaster was received, with Brently Mallard's name leading the list of "killed." He had only taken the time to assure himself of its truth by a second telegram, and had hastened to forestall any less careful, less tender friend in bearing the sad message.

She did not hear the story as many women have heard the same, with a paralyzed inability to accept its significance. She wept at once, with sudden, wild abandonment, in her sister's arms. When the storm of grief had spent itself she went away to her room alone. She would have no one follow her.

There stood, facing the open window, a comfortable, roomy armchair. Into this she sank, pressed down by a physical exhaustion that haunted her body and seemed to reach into her soul.

5 She could see in the open square before her house the tops of trees that were all aquiver with the new spring life. The delicious breath of rain was in the air. In the street below a peddler was crying his wares. The notes of a distant song which some one was singing reached her faintly, and countless sparrows were twittering in the eaves.

There were patches of blue sky showing here and here through the clouds that had met and piled one above the other in the west facing her window.

She sat with her head thrown back upon the cushion of the chair, quite motionless, except when a sob came up into her throat and shook her, as a child who had cried itself to sleep continues to sob in its dreams.

She was young, with a fair, calm face, whose lines bespoke repression and even a certain strength. But now there was a dull stare in her eyes, whose gaze was fixed away off yonder on one of those patches of blue sky. It was not a glance of reflection, but rather indicated a suspension of intelligent thought.

There was something coming to her and she was waiting for it, fearfully. What was it? She did not know; it was too subtle and elusive to name. But she felt it, creeping out of the sky, reaching toward her through the sounds, the scents, the color that filled the air.

10   Now her bosom rose and fell tumultuously. She was beginning to recognize this thing that was approaching to possess her, and she was striving to beat it back with her will—as powerless as her two white slender hands would have been.

When she abandoned herself a little whispered word escaped her slightly parted lips. She said it over and over under her breath: "free, free, free!" The vacant stare and the look of terror that had followed it went from her eyes. They stayed keen and bright. Her pulses beat fast, and the cursing blood warmed and relaxed every inch of her body.

She did not stop to ask if it were or were not a monstrous joy that held her. A clear and exalted perception enabled her to dismiss the suggestion as trivial.

She knew that she would weep again when she saw the kind, tender hands folded in death; the face that had never looked save with love upon her, fixed and gray and dead. But she saw beyond that bitter moment a long procession of years to come that would belong to her absolutely. And she opened and spread her arms out to them in welcome.

There would be no one to live for her during those coming years; she would live for herself. There would be no powerful will bending hers in that blind persistence with which men and women believe they have a right to impose a private will upon a fellow-creature. A kind intention or a cruel intention made the act seem no less a crime as she looked upon it in that brief moment of illumination.

15   And yet she had loved him—sometimes. Often she had not. What did it matter! What could love, the unsolved mystery, count for in face of this possession of self-assertion which she suddenly recognized as the strongest impulse of her being!

"Free! Body and soul free!" she kept whispering.

Josephine was kneeling before the closed door with her lips to the keyhole, imploring for admission. "Louise, open the door! I beg; open the door—you will make yourself ill. What are you doing, Louise? For heaven's sake open the door."

"Go away. I am not making myself ill." No; she was drinking in a very elixir of life through that open window.

Her fancy was running riot along those days ahead of her. Spring days, and summer days, and all sorts of days that would be her own. She breathed a quick prayer that life might be long. It was only yesterday she had thought with a shudder that life might be long.

20   She arose at length and opened the door to her sister's importunities. There was a feverish triumph in her eyes, and she carried herself unwittingly like a goddess of Victory. She clasped her sister's waist, and together they descended the stairs. Richards stood waiting for them at the bottom.

Someone was opening the front door with a latchkey. It was Brently Mallard who entered, a little travel-stained, composedly carrying his grip-sack and umbrella. He had been far from the scene of the accident, and did not even know there had been one. He stood amazed at Josephine's piercing cry; at Richards' quick motion to screen him from the view of his wife.

But Richards was too late.

When the doctors came they said she had died of heart disease—of joy that kills.

*   *   *

The following works present a student's reaction responses to Kate Chopin's "The Story of an Hour." To demonstrate the process of constructing a response essay to a work, we include Maria Taylor's initial journal entry and three drafts of her essay.

The thesis of the essay evolved from Taylor's freewrite (composed in her journal), designed to spur personal connections with the work. Students in the class were asked to write a monologue in the voice of Mrs. Mallard. After the completion of her assignment, Taylor discovered that she empathized with Mrs. Mallard and shared her feelings of imprisonment. Taylor's position is voiced in the lines: "I want to be free to be for me, only me." She begins with Mrs. Mallard's exclamations ("'free, free, free. . . . '") and moves to her own: "I never really felt free," and "It was the only house I knew as woman." She shifts from speaking in Mrs. Mallard's voice to her own ideas and experiences. The discovery gained from the freewrite became the kernel of the first draft of the reaction essay. In this version, she expresses her yearning.

A collage writer, Taylor jumps from association to association: household duties, her relationship with her husband, the memories of his goodness and his abuse, her need for "balance," her panic, eating disorder, and fear. In her next two drafts, she more freely articulates her connections with Mrs. Mallard, organizes her thoughts, and treats her responses in a systematic manner and arranges them in stages that follow Mrs. Mallard's process of discovering her desire to be free. She also includes the quotations from the work that spark her insights.

Journal Entry

Freewrite: A Monologue Spoken by Mrs. Mallard

By Maria Taylor

I've said it over and over under my breath, "I want to be free, free, free." I want to be free to be for me, only me. To be no-one's mother, daughter, wife. I want to be free to come and go as I please, when I please, how I please. The words "free, free, free" speak to my longing soul.

I never really felt free. I went from Dad's household to my husband's control. The transition was easy for me; it was a role I always wanted. It was expected of me. It was the only role I knew as woman.

As a female, I was to be wife, mother, daughter, depending on 'man' in all roles. I never realized then, in playing out my role I was always depending on a man for my well being. If I needed nurturing, I went to him. If I needed money, I went to him.

Note following reading of the story:

I could see so clearly the truth in the quotation "free." I see the dichotomy in her.

Taylor's First Draft

I want to enjoy a relationship based on equality. Do I sound selfish? Well—it may be—but maybe it's my time, huh? I don't want to cook, clean, do laundry, shop, have to be home, say when I'll be home, where I'll be etc., be questioned about anything—anymore. I want to be free, and yet, I want to be connected. I suppose that would be with and to him. He is my husband, and he has been a good one. He is the father of my four incredible children, and he has been a good father. But there are the horrendous memories of his drinking and emotional and psychological abuse, all of which he denies to this day. He's demeaning of me and my role as woman, wife, person. I want out. I feel selfish and wrong and guilty, but I cannot continue to be a wife anymore. I want a balance in my life. No, this isn't even true. I want it all to be for me now. I know I cannot fulfill my roles anymore because my own health is beginning to fail. I have "panic attacks" regularly, and they are the most painful, terrorizing feelings I have ever experienced. I cannot control my food intake, anymore. Food has become my friend, lover, consoler, comforter. All things except what it truly is—I feel my own life has been fused to others for so long, and in that fusion, I've become lost. I am so frightened. I wonder how I can go on and on and what is left for me? Would I have been better off never knowing him or any man and just be for me?
Conclusion?
Is there ever a relationship between man and woman that is based on true equality and true freedom? Isn't love supposed to give these gifts? Will I, like Mrs. Mallard, have to die before I am truly free?

In the next draft, Taylor creates paragraphs to explore each topic.

Taylor's Second Draft

It's almost too difficult to write to express on paper, but I know this story. I have in many ways lived it.

I suppose you would have to be married for a while to understand Mrs. Mallard. I have been married for thirty-one years, so I understand her. (We can only really understand someone when we have walked in her shoes.)

I like Chopin's Mrs. Mallard's wish to be free. Free to be, for me—only me, no-one else. Free to sleep and eat, come and go—do, not do, whatever I want, when I want, for a while.

And yet am I afraid of this? Yes, for I have never lived for myself, lived by myself. I have never taken care of myself financially. I always took care of others and was taken care of financially by others.

I went from Dad's home living under his jurisdiction to my husband's home living under his jurisdiction. This sounds so cynical; doesn't it? But this is how I feel and how it was.

I never felt "free." Their control was always so subtle and elusive, but I knew it was there like Mr. Mallard and that I had to walk within the lines of their boundaries. If not, I would be abandoned, emotionally, physically and financially. Then how would I exist? I was programmed to believe I could not live without them.

And yet I love him. I believe I do anyway. But I so want to be free. I want to be like Mrs. Mallard looking out the window. I want to continue to love him, but I do not want to live within the confines of what he believes that love should be.

In the final draft, Taylor develops substantial responses and connection to the work.

Taylor's Final Draft
"Free, Free, Free": Chopin's "The Story of an Hour"

1 Under her breath, Mrs. Mallard says, "free, free, free!" Over and over again. I have said the same words over and over again under my breath. I want to be free. Free to be for me, only me, to be no one's daughter, wife or mother. I do not want to be caregiver, support, keeper. I want to live only for myself. I want to be free to come and go as I please, when I please, how I please.

2 The adjectives, "free, free, free," speak to my longing soul. And yet I am afraid. Yes, for I have never lived for myself, lived by myself. I have never taken care of myself

financially. In many ways, I am like Mrs. Mallard's sobbing child. I always took care of others and was taken care of financially by others. I took care of both my parents when they were ill. Then I became a wife and mother. Emotionally, all of my energies were out there, caring for others all my life, leaving very little energy for nurturing myself. Consequently, I feel uncomfortable and I question whether or not I can be free. At fifty-one, this is a sorry commentary. Like Mrs. Mallard, I have never lived for myself.

3   I went from Dad's house, living under his jurisdiction, to my husband's home, living under his jurisdiction. Coming from a patriarchal home and environment, I thought that this simply was the way that it was for all women. I thought that the "powerful will bending [mine] in that blind persistence with which men and women believe they have a right to impose a private will upon a fellow-creature" was to be expected and the way it should be.

4   I never felt free. Their control was always so subtle and elusive, but I knew it was there and that I had to walk within the lines of their boundaries. If not, I would be abandoned, emotionally, physically and financially. Then how would I exist, survive? I was programmed to believe I could not live without them. As a result, I felt as if I danced around this big bear that lived in the center of the living room for most of my life. I do not want to dance anymore. Like Mrs. Mallard, who said "she would live for herself," I too wish for autonomy.

5   I want to continue a relationship with him, but I do not want to live within the confines of what he believes that love should be. I want to feel "spring days, and summer days. . . . that would be [my] own."

6   My husband is a domineering man. He often treats me in a way that suffocates me. His constant questions, his lack of trust, his knee jerk anger oppress and fatigue me. I understand his fear, that he will lose me, that he doesn't understand me any more, and I empathize with him. But I no longer can claim this shattering as my own. When I do, I become shattered myself. I love my husband, and yet I want to be free.

7   I want to enjoy a relationship based on equality and freedom. Can a relationship between a man and a woman be based on these things? Is it possible? Is it possible with my relationship with him? Has he snatched that away from me too? Would I have been happier never knowing my love or any man and just be, for me? Will I like Mrs. Mallard have to die before I feel free, before I feel that "monstrous joy"—the "joy that kills?"

In the introduction to this last draft, Taylor states her thesis, the yearning "to be free" that she shares with Mrs. Mallard. In the middle paragraphs, she explains the origins of that desire, tracing her need for autonomy to her family background (paragraph 2), and to her marriage, an extension of that "patriarchal home and environment" (paragraph 3). She next presents (in paragraphs 5 and 6) her desire for autonomy; finally, she articulates her dilemma: the conflict between her love and loyalty to her husband and her need to find a "relationship based on equality and freedom." Her conclusion contains her pessimistic assessment: "Will I like Mrs. Mallard have to die before I feel free, before I feel that 'Monstrous joy'—the 'joy that kills'?" She builds the essay to its dramatic conclusion.

Taylor also strives to include more quotations from the story so that the progression in her thinking mirrors, in some ways, the logic and progression of the plot of "Story of An Hour." She begins, citing Mrs. Mallard's wish to be "free, free, free," which appears midway in Chopin's story. In the description of her relationship to her husband, she includes Mrs. Mallard's realization that after her husband's death, there will be no "powerful will bending [her]" into submission. By following the pattern of Mrs. Mallard's recognition, Taylor makes their situations analogous and strengthens the comparison of her situation with the character's plight. They both came to similar despairing assessments of the possibility of "true equality" in the relation of men and women. Chopin's character dies . . . death is her only release. Taylor despairs of the possibility of finding relationships based on a "true balance" between the sexes.

Taylor's connections with "The Story of an Hour" are made explicit: her understanding of Mrs. Mallard's imprisonment caused by her social role; Mrs. Mallard's inability to change her circumstances; the protagonist's inhibited desire for freedom and her ambivalent feelings toward her husband; her desire for release from a marriage that denies her autonomy.

POETRY

When asked to define poetry, a student responded, "Poems make words dance." This brief reply stimulates many provocative ideas and images concerning a difficult question. The excellent answer implies that poems are metaphorical, paradoxical, and dynamic. In poetry the images do not work if they do not inspire sudden connection and insight. The words must "dance," or they cannot create effective and astonishing meanings. This definition also suggests the necessity of rhythm, beat, and accent. If the work lacks these intrinsic qualities, it is not poetry.

What else does this definition signify? It indicates that poems create themes, character, and contexts through compressed language, through figures of speech, through economy of form, and through sound. If academic definitions always require appropriate language, then the student's answer insists upon such words. If academic definitions insist upon rhythm or meter, then the student's answer alludes to rhythm through the word "dance." If academic definitions require that poetry elicit feelings and imagination, the student's answer implies that poetry creates these responses in the reader or the listener.

The word "make," above all, connotes *art* and insists that words have the power of the visual to imitate, signify, please, mean, and construct new realities and truths. In ancient cultures, chants and religious rituals were poetry; epics and dramas were poetry. We appreciate the enduring value of the genre as an accessible source of wisdom and pleasure, a significant form of enrichment and of redemption, and an expression of the deepest experiences and truths of human existence.

KINDS OF POETRY

In general, every poem falls into one of three broad categories: **narrative poetry** tells a story, **lyric poetry** gives a brief account of the person's feelings, ideas, or moods, and **dramatic poetry** presents monologues and soliloquies.

Narrative Poetry

Any poem that spins a tale may be defined as a *narrative* work. In Gwendolyn Brooks' "The Chicago Defender Sends a Man to Little Rock" (Chapter 7), the speaker catalogues the daily actions of citizens who bear children, celebrate holidays, play baseball, attend concerts, and love each other. The persona wants to report that "they are like people everywhere." Another story, however, exists in Little Rock; people are "hurling spittle, rocks, garbage, and fruit." The speaker must recount this conflict. Why? The Supreme Court had ordered desegregation of the schools in an historic decision in the case of Brown vs. The Board of Education, a case never directly mentioned in Brooks' narrative. Because of its political context, "The Chicago Defender Sends a Man to Little Rock" may be called a *protest poem.*

Other forms of narrative poetry include the epic and the ballad. **Epics**, written in many eras and in many cultures, derive from oral tradition and describe the adventures and accomplishments of great heroes. The story assumes grand proportions and often includes supernatural beings and their actions that create monumental consequences. The language of epics is formal and figurative, and almost all epics share similar conventions. *The Iliad* and *Odyssey* by Homer (Greek), *The Epic of Gilgamesh* (Babylonian), *Sundiata* (Mali), and *Beowulf* (Anglo-Saxon) represent works in this tradition.

African epics, for example, were first told by griots, ancient singers who preserved cultural histories by memorizing them. The famous epic, *Sundiata,* originated in Mali in West Africa in the thirteenth century. Sundiata, the son of Sogolon, a hunchback princess, and Maghan, "the handsome," fulfilled the prophecy that the twelve kingdoms of Mali would be united into a single empire reaching from the Atlantic to Timbuktu. A mixture of history and legend, *Sundiata* presents a brilliant vision of a medieval African empire. A brief excerpt of a prose translation of the poem follows:

> Listen, then, sons of Mali, children of the black
> people,
> Listen to my Lord, for I am going to tell you of
> Sundiata, the father of the Bright Country, of the Savanna
> land, the ancestor of those who draw the bow, the Master
> of a hundred vanquished kinds.
> I am going to talk of Sundiata, Manding Diaia, Lion
> of Mali, Sogolon Djata, Son of Sogolon, Nare Maghan Djata,
> son of Maghan, Sogo Sogo Simbon Salaba, hero of many names.
> I am going to tell you of Sundiata, he whose exploits
> will astonish men for a long time. He was great among
> kings; he was peerless among men; he was beloved of God
> because he was the last of the great conquerors.

Note the formal, elevated language, the promise of great adventures, the recounting of history, the great stature of the heroic figures, and the celebration of victory. These conventions in *Sundiata* appear in most epics.

Ballads, another form of narrative poetry, also derive from oral tradition since originally they were songs. Literary ballads include most features of the oral form: repetition and refrain—phrases or lines reappearing at certain places in the poem. Ballads alternate lines of eight and six syllables, with rhymes in the second and fourth lines. Not every ballad must be written in the standard stanzaic pattern. Not every ballad contains a refrain. The Beatles, for example, wrote a humorous song about "Rocky Raccoon" that mimics "Frankie and Johnny"; both are ballads. More serious works tell stories of young women such as Thomas Hardy's "The Ruined Maid."

Lyric Poetry

Lyrics are short and subjective; in these poems, the speakers describe their thoughts or feelings. The original definition of the lyric meant a song accompanied by a lyre. This category includes the following forms:

1. An **elegy** mourns the death of a particular person, or sometimes, the inexorable fate of humans, their mortality. Ben Jonson's "On My First Son" presents a father's grief, a sorrow so deep that it renders his identity as a poet meaningless (see Chapter 5).

2. A **meditation** centers on a particular object as a method for consideration of metaphysical ideas. (see "Dover Beach" by Mathew Arnold in Chapter 6.)

3. An **ode**, a song of praise, is long, serious, and formal in all of its aspects. It always has a complex stanzaic pattern. Keats' "Ode on a Grecian Urn" is an example of this form (see Chapter 8).

4. A **pastoral** celebrates the idyllic nature of country life. James Wright's "A Blessing" represents a modern version of the pastoral (see Chapter 8).

Matsuo Bashō, a Japanese poet who lived in the seventeenth century, wrote haiku, unrhymed three-line poems with seventeen syllables. Haiku also may be considered lyrical in nature:

On New Year's Day

Spring that no man
has seen—plum-bloom on the back
of the mirror
("Hito nō mina haru ya kagami-nō ura-nō ume")

Notice that Bashō has compressed a strong image into three lines. The meaning depends on sudden insight and a connection between nature and human activity. At first glance, the poem seems to celebrate the beauty of spring with a single image—a plum blossom. The title, "On New Year's Day," however, implies that spring might be a memory, an expectation, or a state of mind, especially since the image appears on the "back" of a mirror and "no man/has seen" it.

Dramatic Poetry

In **dramatic poetry**, the speaker becomes an actor. In his **monologue**, "My Last Duchess" (see Chapter 6), for example, Robert Browning creates a speaker who treats his wife as an object of art. Through this technique, the persona often reveals qualities or facts about himself or herself which he or she does not intend to expose. Browning's Duke does not perceive his crass and pompous attitudes; he does not see his cruelty, but the reader does.

Other forms of dramatic poems include epistolary monologues—letters written as poems. In the most familiar example of this kind of work, Ezra Pound's "The River Merchant's Wife: A Letter," loosely translated from a poem in Chinese written by Rihaku (also known as Li Po), the speaker has loved her husband deeply since childhood. The young Chinese wife waits patiently for his return and expresses her loneliness and longing in the letter. Admired as a model of dignity and of marital love, this eighth century poem by Li Po presents great autobiographical detail in highly controlled and terse language.

Although readers wish to designate strict categories for poems, some works defy such classification. Contemporary poetry often combines narrative and lyric modes; poets often extend the limits of traditional forms; and in their experiments, they create new language and images; they step into the borderland between narration and lyric, a place where new voices may sing and be heard.

ELEMENTS OF POETRY

Voice

Poems, like fiction, present speakers who tell about events, experiences, emotions, or ideas. The poet remains separate from the persona or speaker, although in some works little distance exists between the two. In all cases, however, the reader should assume that poet and speaker have distinct identities. Often the poet creates a voice exceedingly different from him or herself. The speaker may even be anonymous.

One of the best methods of interpreting poetry is to define the voice, to discover as much as possible about its quality, mood, and concerns. In "Danaë," a voice poem based on Greek myth, the poet alludes to the imprisonment of the virgin, Danaë, by her father, a crime that he committed to circumvent the fulfillment of a prophecy which predicted the death of Acrisius at the hands of his grandson. Zeus, however, seduced Danaë in a shower of gold; and from this magical union, Perseus was born. Eventually the curse was fulfilled. Listen to the voice of Danaë. Consider the poem, and answer the following questions:

1. Who is the speaker?
2. What is the point of view?

3. What is the situation of the speaker?
4. How is the story told?
5. What details and words characterize the speaker?
6. To whom does the speaker talk? Who is the audience?

Danaë

to be born to a curse
is all of history
that dark will
is all I knew
5 in the dark cavern
I lived
I saw just the
immediate edge of my body
the dark shadings and contours
10 of that shell
and you live in it
as if it were light
as if it gave you light
then one day
15 a rain came
a gold rain
a sheen of rain
a cool yellow breeze
a shimmer of gold
20 a sift of gold all over my skin
a wash of yellow light
and in this way
he came
my child
25 came as rain fell
came as silently
to life
came to me
a rinse of yellow gold
30 that boy child
my words
my history
my unsaid self
a blessing
35 too fragile
to be dreamt

The poet retells the story of Danaë with a first person point of view and adds some new details to the ancient Greek myth. The persona expresses her sadness and loneliness as she considers her body as something to "live in." Subject to "the dark will," she exists in shadow "as if it were light." She seems concerned about the body, its history; and she feels resignation. She does not speak in anger, but she acknowledges indirectly that men and gods have power over her body. Yet the men are completely absent from the speaker's story.

The poet devotes half of the poem to the gold rain that impregnates Danaë and gives her a son. The repetition of "rain," "gold," "yellow," and "light" introduces a sense of quiet joy into the poem. These details about the conception of the child allow the speaker to claim herself, her history, and her child through words. In this connection between language and the body, the poet transforms Danaë into a contemporary woman.

Tone

The **tone** of a poem establishes the mood of the piece, the changing emotions of the speaker, or the attitude of the persona toward the subject. The poem may be sad, angry, shocking, nostalgic, or humorous. In "Daddy" by Sylvia Plath, the speaker begins with a mildly angry tone as she announces her rejection of her father, but the voice quickly becomes sad as she admits, "you died before I had time" (Chapter 5). In the monologue, the young woman, the persona, calls her father a god, a Nazi, and the devil. At the end, she attempts to exorcise him through a darkly humorous allusion to Dracula in vampire movies:

> There's a stake in your fat black heart
> And the villagers never liked you.
> They are dancing and stamping on you.
> They always knew it was you.
> 5 Daddy, daddy, you bastard, I'm through.

Here the speaker refers to the only method that kills a vampire: a stake in the heart. She indicates that the villagers in Transylvania always knew that the vampire really was Count Dracula who lived in the eerie castle above the town. As a final shock, the speaker calls "Daddy" a "bastard" and declares wildly that she is "through." Some critics find the tone too exaggerated and do not believe that the ending convinces; others praise the poem for its devastating truth about the impact of the death of a parent and about the overwhelming anger of the betrayed and bereaved child.

Theme

Poems can explore any **theme**, any central idea. The poet can write about the terror of war, the ecstasy of love or religion, the mysteries or certainties of life or ideas. A poem may protest injustice, define itself, or mourn the death of a particular person. Many of these themes recur frequently. In every culture, poets write about time, death, love, and art. They celebrate achievements and laugh at and satirize human error and folly.

In order to determine the theme of a poem, look at images, voice, symbols, form, and sound. Combined, these aspects create the conceptions central to meaning. Because poetry is allusive and highly compressed, however, many interpretations become possible. Each reader may discover a different theme; but most of the time, a poem, rich in language and content, leads to certain agreements about thematic intent.

Chasing Fire Engines

The women in my family
always chase fire engines,
sirens wailing in their ears,
long funnels down and in,
5 a throb in their arms—
the urge to touch men,
the big hoses, eyes on the stream
arching toward smoke.
I was born with arson
10 in my heart, the desire
to light fires, to set
aflame every hand
that brushes my wrist,
to incinerate.

15 Now I dream of a stranger,
incendiary fingers on my breast.
I rise toward shadow,
light a match to identify
the face, to reach
20 the tender place;
and I smell ashes,
push the hand aside,
heat cooling
as I wake, women
25 in my family running
after fire engines, watching
men dowse flames,
water arching and arching:
the spray, the spray.

30 Then you turn to me in sleep,
move your leg over mine,
easy in your skin,
and I slide under you,

old luminations surround us,
35 the longing for arson
rising in my throat,
a moan subsides
as I chase the engines.
Fires, burning everywhere,
40 light the pillow where
your head circles mine.

In "Chasing Fire Engines," the persona speaks of natural curiosity and obsessions about sexuality; she feels the "heat cooling" and fantasizes about strangers; finally, she embraces her lover, familiar fires circling their heads on the pillow. Traditional themes about love and loss are deflated, but they remain relevant. The themes in this work center on the highly sexual nature of men and women, represented by the fire, the hoses, the spray. The heat cools in relationships, but every person eventually discovers that familiarity and "old luminations" in love remain more important than initial and easy incendiary impulses.

Setting

Every poem presents a persona and a theme or themes; every poem takes place in a **setting**—the place, location, or atmosphere. Consider the various places in "Chasing Fire Engines." At first, the persona remembers the world of her childhood, a time when all of the men in the family served in the volunteer fire department and when the women and children hurried to watch the men in action. Of necessity, the town must have been small— perhaps, a village located in the South or Midwest. The setting also becomes a dream where a stranger touches the speaker, and the place seems shadowy and dark. As the third setting, the speaker alludes to a bed where she and her lover sleep; and, as they awaken, fire circles their heads on a pillow. Through an examination of setting, you can discover new aspects of meaning in every poem. By carefully describing locations in "Chasing Fire Engines," for example, you learn that the shifts in settings create important complications in the poem, complications that enrich its texture and significance.

Imagery

Everyone's first experience with reality begins with an **image**—a message from the world that comes to consciousness through the senses. It may enter through the eye as shape and shade; it may enter the nose as odor; it may enter the ear as sound; it may tingle the tongue as taste; it may caress the skin as touch. Every strong memory exists as an image or as a series or composite of images. Every dream emerges as vivid, often surreal, imagery. Poets and scientists confirm the inextricable relationship between ideas and images. Einstein arrived at his theory of relativity by picturing a man traveling on a wave of light. Goethe complained that he no sooner had an idea before "it [turned] into an image."

Certainly poetry cannot exist without **imagery**. Those things that appear as physical sensation are called **concrete images**; those which represent ideas may be **abstract images**. Consider this short poem by Margaret Atwood:

You Fit Into Me

you fit into me
like a hook into an eye.

a fish hook
an open eye

The first two lines create the picture of the fitting together of the two parts of a familiar household fastener to connote a couple's embracing, caressing, or making love. The next two images twist the meaning—the hook becomes a fish hook penetrating a literal, not a metaphorical, eye—and shock the reader with deliberate announcement of pain. The relationship is an agonizing, not a loving, one.

Economy and brevity represent the advantages of images in poetry. They suggest; they enable readers to imagine experiences or sensations. They provide emotional connotations that color responses and evoke feelings in readers. William Carlos Williams' poem, "The Red Wheelbarrow," represents the compressed nature of poetry:

so much depends
upon

a red wheel
barrow

5 glazed with rain
water

beside the white
chickens.

What does the picture suggest? For a moment, the wet wheelbarrow beside the white chickens composes the world in a particular order, one that ascribes harmony and beauty to an ordinary scene. Through the first two lines Williams takes his representation of a bucolic scene and transforms it into a vision of the pleasures and purposes of perception. Williams suggests that the ability to perceive the relationship of images gives meaning to life. This poem exemplifies the tenets of the Imagist movement of the early twentieth century. Ezra Pound, who created such poetry, stated, "In a poem of this sort, one is trying to record the precise instant when a thing outward and objective transforms itself, or darts into a thing inward and subjective."

Poems often present highly complicated series of images that are woven through the entire work, strands that become a fabric of meaning. In this extension of imagery lies much of the pleasure of poetic form. In Walt Whitman's "When I Heard the Learn'd Astronomer," the speaker sits in a classroom and listens to a lecture. The first six lines of the poem introduce the astronomer and extend the images associated with him: "proofs," "figures," "charts and diagrams." The speaker, "sick" from the aridity of technical explanations, glides outside to enjoy the "mystical" experience of looking at the stars. The final lines emphasize and elaborate images of freedom in the natural world.

> When I heard the learn'd astronomer,
> When the proofs, the figures, were 'ranged in columns
>   before me,
> When I was shown the charts and diagrams, to add,
> 5   divide and measure them,
> When I sitting heard the astronomer where he lectured
>   with much applause in the lecture-room,
> How soon unaccountable I became tired and sick
> Till rising and gliding out I wander'd off by myself,
> 10 In the mystical moist night-air, and from time to time,
> Look'd up in perfect silence at the stars.

Note the passivity of the persona who listens, who "heard," and who "was shown," as the astronomer teaches in a "lecture-room." The speaker must perform calculations—"add/divide and measure"—in order to understand the "columns" placed before him. The proliferation and repetition ("when") of images denigrate the concrete, scientific atmosphere of the academy. The beautiful, abstract, active quality of the imagery that evokes the natural world, the world of "mystical moist night-air" and "stars," creates a "perfect" and silent contrast to the confinement of the lecture and the lecture-room. Whitman demonstrates the value of human experience and his view of the dangers of science by weaving images of a boring, sickening astronomy lecture and active perception of a starry night as threads through his work.

Figures of Speech

Figures of speech, expressions that suggest more than their literal meanings, present implied or direct comparisons which give readers the experience of an abstraction or of an emotion. Some figures are **metaphor, simile, personification, synecdoche, metonymy,** and **hyperbole.** In this famous section from Keats' "Endymion," the first line contains a metaphor:

> A thing of beauty is a joy for ever.
> Its loveliness increases; it will never
> Pass into nothingness; but still will keep
> A bower quiet for us, and a sleep
> 5 Full of sweet dreams, and health, and quiet breathing.

> Therefore, on the morrow, are we wreathing
> A flowery band to bind us to the earth,
> Spite of despondence, of the inhuman death
> Of noble natures, of the gloomy days,
> 10 Of all the unhealthy and o'er-darkened ways
> Made for our searching; yes, in spite of all,
> Some shape of beauty moves away the pall
> From our dark spirits.

Metaphor and Simile

The **metaphor** equates "A thing of beauty" with eternal joy and expresses Keats' belief that beauty transcends time, space, and matter, that beauty redeems the darkness in human life. A metaphor pictures a thing or an idea, "thing of beauty," and juxtaposes it with something different, "a joy forever," and implies an analogy between them. Look at the passage, and notice the additional comparisons that Keats creates. The "thing of beauty" becomes a "flowery band" and "some shape" that "moves away the pall." In fact, Keats extends the metaphor of beauty beyond the first line and elaborates the idea with numerous images. **Extended metaphors**, sometimes called conceits, often appear in poetry and serve to complicate its form and meaning, to create depth. In "The Love Song of J. Alfred Prufrock," T. S. Eliot describes the fog as a cat in stanzas two and three (Chapter 6). This extraordinary extended metaphor presents the fog in such a catlike manner that the comparison becomes obvious—even though Eliot never mentions the word *cat*.

Similes make a direct comparison of one thing to another; usually the words "like" or "as" serve to create connections. Keats, for example, could have written the first line of the passage from "Endymion" as a simile, "A thing of beauty is [like] a joy for ever." Think of William Wordsworth's "I Wandered Lonely *as* a Cloud." In this title, Wordsworth's speaker convinces the reader of his loneliness through a concrete object, a cloud. Its solitary movement in the sky suddenly illuminates the emotional state of the persona.

Personification, Synecdoche, Metonymy, and Hyperbole

These figures of speech appear frequently in poetry:

> **Personification** is the attribution of human traits to objects, ideas, or creatures. In Keats' "Endymion" beauty possesses human powers to "keep" and to "move." Keats endows beautiful things with noble human qualities which can negate the dark nature of life.
>
> **Synecdoche**, sometimes considered a special type of metonymy, is a figure of speech in which part of a thing is used to represent the whole. References to a monarch as the crown and to sailors as hands provide familiar samples of this technique.
>
> **Metonymy** is a figure of speech in which a single name of a person, place, or thing stands for a more complex situation or experience

with which the name is associated. Washington sometimes represents all branches of the government of the United States.

Hyperbole or **exaggeration** is overstatement of the situation, idea, person in order to shock, to create humor, to command attention. In Nikki Giovanni's "Ego Tripping," the entire poem becomes an exercise in hyperbole (Chapter 4). The speaker makes wild claims that she "gives oil to the Arab World," that her son is Hannibal, that she "cannot be comprehended."

Symbol, Myth, Allusion

Symbol

A **symbol** is an object or event that represents something else or that has meaning beyond itself. Everyday objects become symbols when a red cross signifies an international relief organization, when a ram's horns symbolize a football team, or when a swastika stands as a Nazi emblem.

In many cultures, poetic symbols have conventional meanings: cherry blossoms, jade, birds, and roses all have well-established significance in Japanese, Chinese, or English poetry. Many contemporary poets, however, create private symbols that readers may interpret from a close reading of the work. This development can make symbols more difficult to discover and to comprehend. Adrienne Rich's "Diving into the Wreck" presents a complex system of symbols that can be read simply as a dive to a sunken ship for treasure and as a personal search through the wreckage of a life (Chapter 8). In the end, however, the poet shifts from the first person singular "I" to plural and multiple points of view:

> We are, I am, you are
> by cowardice or courage
> the one who finds our way
> back to this scene
> 5 carrying a knife, a camera
> a book of myths
> in which our names do not appear

The "we" who dive into the wreck become an androgynous "one who finds our way/back" to a place where "a book of myths" denies existence through the absence of names. Rich seems to proclaim that none can have identity if the "book of myths" is not replaced by the recognition of personhood and autonomy for women as well as for men, for the oppressed as well as for the oppressors, by a merging, in fact, of these categories.

Myth

A **myth** is similar to a symbol, but it includes a story which stands for something else. In many cultures and traditions, myths explain the inexplicable and the mysterious; they preserve history, culture, customs; they describe the actions of supernatural beings. Some of these beings symbolize natural forces—

fertility, harvest, the sea. Some of them represent abstract qualities—love, wisdom, cunning, evil. A **mythology**, a system or collection of myths, represents the beliefs of a culture or a particular group; these myths often originated in religious belief and ritual. Among the mythologies most commonly found in poetry are Greek, Roman, Germanic, Native-American, and Egyptian.

In Audre Lorde's "From the House of Yemanjá," the reference to the great African mother from whose breasts all rivers flow augments the power of the mother of the speaker of the poem (Chapter 5). In one legend, Lorde notes that Yemanjá's husband insulted her long breasts. She escaped with her pots, and he followed her and beat her. Rivers flowed from her breasts, and all of the other Yoruban gods were born from her body. Therefore, when the speaker claims twice that her "mother had two faces and a broken pot," she implies that her mother is Yemanjá or, at least, resembles her. When she claims that her mother's breasts are "huge exciting anchors/in the midnight storm," she also suggests that Yemanjá represents her good mother. The myth enlarges and complicates the meaning of the poem.

ALLUSION

An **allusion** refers to a well-known literary work, person, event, or place. Whether it is implicit or explicit, the allusion enlarges the world of the poem. In "Sailing to Byzantium," for example, Yeats refers to the city where the beauty and culture of the Byzantine Empire reached its height in the fifth and sixth centuries (Chapter 8). Judith Johnson writes about Abraham and Isaac and the divine command that Abraham sacrifice his son in her poem, "Stone Olives" (Chapter 8). She also alludes to the terrorists who killed the passengers on Pan Am Flight 103, the plane which exploded near Lockerbee, Scotland, in December 1988. In particular, the speaker mourns the death of Melina Hudson of Albany, New York:

> Melina, who once danced
> at proms far from Beirut, laughed with my daughter
> years after Hiroshima broke into flower, told
> her beads in a church the Gulag never touched
> 5   now pours down through our air.

Johnson traces the senseless deaths of children in Beirut, Lebanon, in the atomic bomb blast in Hiroshima, in the Russian Gulag camps as she pictures the fragments of Melina's body raining to the ground. In "Stone Olives," the persona suggests that fathers allow and cause the sacrifice of children.

STRUCTURE

Stanzas

Historically poems originated as oral expression. Poets accompanied their songs with instruments, or they performed with choral or instrumental groups. The first aspect of the poem in any analysis of sound should be the visual picture of lines arranged on a page. The lines of a poem may be divided into separate groups or units called **stanzas** which function like paragraphs in fiction and in essays. Some questions to pose about stanzaic patterns include: How are the poetic groups or stanzas divided? Where do they begin and end? How does the punctuation provide cues for reading? The strong marks of punctuation—periods, semicolons, dashes, question marks, colons, exclamation points—require longer pauses than a comma. Examine Gwendolyn Brooks' poem:

We Real Cool
The Pool Players
Seven at the Golden Shovel

We real cool. We
Left school. We

Lurk late. We
Strike straight. We

Sing sin. We
Thin gin. We

Jazz June. We
Die soon.

The short sentences, each three words long, require a fast pace and regular beat. The two line stanzas, called **couplets**, are open because each line and each couplet ends with "we." A line of poetry that ends without punctuation or pause is known as a run-on line, also as **enjambment**. The internal periods command pauses, and the repetitions and positions of the pronoun "we" also demand emphasis. Read the poem as eight short sentences, and then read it according to stanzaic and line arrangements. What is the connection between sound and meaning?

Rhyme and Sound

Rhyme, the repetition of sounds usually at the ends of lines in regular patterns, represents a traditional technique which pleases the ear and which enhances the effects of images and symbols. In Brooks' poem, each line rhymes because all except the last line end with the same word. In each couplet, Brooks has used internal rhyme: cool, school; late, straight; sin, gin; June, soon. If these rhymes were **end rhymes**, the **rhyme scheme** would read aa, bb, cc, dd. To determine the scheme of any rhymed poem, simply assign letters of the alphabet to each new rhyming sound, and begin with *a*.

Another good example of rhyme is Shakespeare's "Shall I Compare Thee to a Summer's Day?" (See page 541.) Its form, called a **Shakespearean** or

Elizabethan sonnet, divides the traditional fourteen lines into three four-line verses or quatrains and a final couplet. The rhyme scheme reads abab, cdcd, efef, gg. Sonnets also may take **Petrarchan** form, named for the famous Italian poet, Petrarch. In this kind of sonnet, the poet writes two **quatrains**, called the **octave** (eight lines), and two **tercets**, three-line verses, called the **sestet** (six lines). The theme shifts radically at the ninth line in Petrarchan sonnets; this turn is known as the volta. The rhyme scheme in the octave usually reads abba abba. The sestet may rhyme in a number of ways: cdecde, cdccdc, cdedce. Another technique for rhyming in free verse or formal poetry includes slant or half rhyme, one in which words almost rhyme.

The sounds of the words contribute to the meaning of the poem. The repetition of the initial sounds of accented consonant syllables at close intervals, called **alliteration**, may create effects that enlarge, reinforce, or contradict the ideas and mood of the poem. In Brooks' work, for example, the alliteration begins with the identification of the speakers as *p*ool *p*layers, and she continues this pattern in *l*urk *l*ate, in *str*ike *str*aight, in *s*ing *s*in, in *j*azz *J*une. This frequent use of alliteration in such a short poem heightens the sense of jazz and music. Brooks also employs **assonance**, the repetition of vowel sounds of stressed syllables or important words at close intervals: *coo*l *schoo*l. Notice that this poem relies heavily on sound for meaning. Notice that the long, sighing vowel in d*ie* in the last line stands alone, a jarring conclusion.

Rhythm

One of the indispensable elements distinguishing poetry is **rhythm**. Like song or dance, no poem can exist without a beat that augments its meaning and beauty or contradicts and conflicts with its themes and images to create tension. Poets choose rhythms from four basic categories: *traditional meters, strong stress rhythms, syllabic counts,* and *free verse*.

Meter

Meter is a rhythmic pattern of stressed (/) and unstressed (∪) syllables in a poem. Each unit, called a *foot*, has either two or three syllables. The most common feet in poetry follow:

Foot	Designation	Example
iamb or iambic	(∪/)	delight
trochee or trochaic	(/∪)	coral
spondee or spondaic	(//)	ho hum
pyrrhus or pyrrhic	(∪∪)	advantage of
anapest or anapestic	(∪∪/)	in a flash
dactyl or dactylic	(/∪∪)	night coming

Line lengths can be measured in number of feet.

Line Length	Number of Feet
monometer	one foot
dimeter	two feet

trimeter	three feet
tetrameter	four feet
pentameter	five feet
hexameter	six feet
heptameter	seven feet
octometer	eight feet

Scansion

In order to discover the meter of a poem, each line is scanned for accented and unaccented syllables. This process, called **scansion**, enables you to examine the effects of rhythm in the work. Look at this scansion of Shakespeare's parody of the conceits in the sonnet tradition. Note that each syllable is marked to indicate stressed or unstressed pronunciations.

```
 ⌣ ⁄ ⌣   ⁄  ⌣ ⁄ ⌣   ⁄  ⌣ ⁄
My mistress' eyes, are nothing like the Sun;
 ⁄ ⌣ ⌣ ⁄  ⌣ ⁄   ⌣ ⁄  ⌣  ⁄
Coral is far more red, than her lips' red:
 ⌣ ⁄ ⌣  ⁄  ⌣ ⁄ ⌣   ⁄   ⌣ ⁄
If snow be white, why then her breasts are dun;
 ⌣ ⁄  ⌣ ⁄   ⌣ ⁄ ⌣  ⌣ ⌣ ⁄
If hairs be wires, black wires grow on her head.
 ⌣ ⁄  ⌣ ⁄ ⌣ ⁄  ⌣  ⁄ ⌣ ⁄
I have seen Roses damasked, red and white,
 ⌣ ⁄  ⌣ ⁄ ⌣ ⁄ ⁄ ⌣ ⌣   ⁄
But no such Roses see I in her cheeks;
 ⌣ ⁄  ⌣ ⁄ ⌣  ⁄ ⌣  ⁄ ⌣ ⁄
And in some perfumes is there more delight
 ⌣ ⁄ ⌣  ⁄  ⌣  ⁄ ⌣ ⁄  ⌣  ⁄
Than in the breath that from my Mistress reeks.
 ⌣ ⁄ ⌣ ⁄  ⌣  ⁄  ⌣ ⁄ ⌣  ⁄
I love to hear her speak, yet well I know
 ⌣  ⁄ ⌣ ⁄ ⌣ ⁄  ⌣  ⁄ ⌣  ⁄
That music hath a far more pleasing sound:
 ⌣ ⁄  ⌣ ⁄ ⌣ ⁄ ⌣ ⁄  ⌣ ⁄
I grant I never saw a goddess go,
 ⁄ ⌣ ⌣   ⁄  ⌣ ⁄   ⁄ ⌣ ⌣  ⁄
My Mistress, when she walks treads on the ground.
 ⌣ ⁄ ⌣ ⁄ ⌣ ⌣ ⌣ ⁄  ⌣ ⁄ ⌣ ⁄
And yet, by heaven, I think my love as rare
 ⌣ ⁄ ⌣ ⁄ ⌣ ⁄  ⌣  ⁄  ⌣ ⁄
As any she belied with false compare.
```

With very little variation, this poem's meter is iambic pentameter (five iambic feet), the most frequent and natural rhythm in English. Line two contains a trochee (córăl), as does line six (Í iň). Such variety prevents boredom, a singsong quality, and commands attention. In this sonnet, Shakespeare makes little attempt to provide alternate rhythm. The boring regularity suits the purposes of his parody.

Strong Stress Meter

Early Anglo-Saxon and Germanic rhythms featured only strong stresses or **accents**, each line containing four stressed syllables. *Beowulf* and some

Middle English poetry exemplify accentual meter. Strong stress rhythms still appear in such children's rhymes as "Hickory Dickory Dock." Gerard Manley Hopkins, an English poet, developed sprung rhythm, a variant of accentual meter, in the nineteenth century. In his poems, each line begins with a stressed syllable that may be followed by one, two, or three unaccented syllables or that may stand alone.

Syllabic Rhythm

Poetry also may receive its beat from patterns of **counted syllables**, a method that disregards accentual feet. In this mode, the poet chooses any combination of syllables and repeats the pattern. In Sylvia Plath's "Metaphors," she writes a riddle in nine lines, each containing nine syllables:

```
1   2 3  4 5   6    7 8  9
I'm a riddle in nine syllables

1   2 3 4   5 6 7  8   9
An elephant, a ponderous house
```

This clever poem catalogues metaphors about pregnancy. Japanese haiku also represents a form in which syllabic count is fixed and traditional: five syllables; seven; five syllables. Remember Bashō's lyric, "On New Year's Day."

Free Verse

More than eighty years ago, Ezra Pound theorized about composing "in the sequence of the metrical phrase, not in the sequence of a metronome. . . ." Pound noted that some poets had abandoned traditional meters and explored natural rhythms, and he advocated **free verse** as an exciting alternative to traditional meters. Pound was not the first poet to recognize the value of this approach, but his description certainly provides an apt definition.

Free verse has no strict meter or line length. Traditional feet appear but in natural order. Such rising feet as iambs and anapests may occur together; such falling feet as trochees and dactyls may occur together. One of the most famous examples of free verse is Walt Whitman's great poem of love and death, "Out of the Cradle Endlessly Rocking" (Chapter 4). Read the first few lines without any attempt at analysis; follow the surge of the sea.

> Out of the cradle endlessly rocking,
> Out of the mocking-bird's throat, the musical shuttle,
> Out of the Ninth-month midnight,
> Over the sterile sands and the fields beyond, where the child
> 5   leaving his bed wander'd alone, bareheaded, barefoot,
> Down from the shower'd halo, ...

The repetition of such adverbial phrases as "Out of" (known as anaphora) and Biblical rhythm characterize this poem.

Needless to say, poets change and combine all of these categories. Every culture's poetic tradition recognizes rhythm as essential to the enjoyment and meaning of poetry because rhythm remains central to all natural movement: the beating of the heart, the rocking of the cradle, the swaying of the sea.

THE READING/WRITING PROCESS: POETRY

A poem requires more than one reading. Several examinations of the text may be necessary simply to understand the general idea of the piece. Any work of art worth attention—a Verdi opera, a Rembrandt painting, Lady Murasaki's *The Tale of Genji*—becomes more exciting and more valuable after careful examination.

The second task in understanding poetry should become the constant use of a dictionary. The multiple meanings of words in each poem result from the compression which characterizes this form. Any dictionary will suffice, but the *Oxford English Dictionary* presents the most comprehensive history of the meanings of words in English. A reader also should have access to other reference books on world mythology and to religious texts.

Listen to the sounds of poetry. Since poems originated in song and in oral tradition, the meaning resides in the sounds as well as in the words. Read poems aloud, and begin with your favorites. In your interpretation, be animated. Muriel Rukeyser once stated that fear of poetry is a fear of emotion. The feelings and meaning already exist in a poem; they will express themselves. In any attempt to render the work as an oral interpretation, find the patterns of rhythm, grammar, and punctuation. Try not to swallow the last lines or important words.

The central purpose of the poem becomes the next question. The speaker in "Daddy" feels angry and concludes: "Daddy, you bastard, I'm through." Victimized like the Jews in Nazi concentration camps, she transforms her father from God into a devil and later into a vampire. The purpose of the poem appears to reside in the speaker's desire to resolve her feelings about her father's death.

Ask, then, about the achievement of purpose. How is it achieved? Find the answer by describing the organization of ideas in the poem. In Plath's soliloquy, she begins with fairy tale; then she describes Daddy as "a bag full of God." Her speaker relates his roots, his language, to German history; and she contends that every woman wants a brutal father and that her speaker marries a "man in black with a Meinkampf look" (like Hitler) in order to recover her father. Finally, both men are symbolically killed, and Daddy becomes the villain in a Dracula movie. The purpose is achieved. Readers find the poem powerful; not everyone likes it or believes that the speaker has resolved her losses.

When reading a poem, give it what Shakespeare called "passionate attention." Consider voice, tone, theme, setting, imagery, figures of speech, symbols, sounds, and rhythm. These elements of poetry will reveal the richness of meaning and evoke responses and evaluation.

CHECKLIST FOR WRITING ABOUT POETRY

1. What is the category for the poem? Is it lyrical, narrative, or dramatic?

2. Who is the speaker? What is the point of view? What is the speaker's attitude toward the subject? What details, images, and uses of language give information about the persona?

3. What is the tone, and does it change? Why?

4. What are the significant figures of speech? How do they function?

5. Describe the setting.

6. Which senses do the images evoke? Does the poem have one image or a series of images? Are the images related? Is there a pattern? What concepts do the images represent? How do the images support the theme? How effective is the use of imagery?

7. What is the central symbol? Are the symbols universal or private? How does symbolism function in the poem?

8. Does the poem refer to mythological figures? Does the poet change the myth?

9. Are there any allusions? What are the specific historical events, names, and/or literary references in the poem? How do the allusions work? Are they effective?

10. What sounds are important? Does the poem contain alliteration or assonance? How does the poet arrange the lines?

11. What is the rhythm of the poem? How does rhythm function?

12. Does the poem have a conventional form? Is the poem a sonnet, villanelle, or sestina? Is the poem an open form?

13. Is the poem effective? What is best about this work? What are its flaws? What is the final evaluation of this work?

Student Portfolio:
Response to Wilfred Owen's "Arms and the Boy"

Ursula Lebris' work presents a model of an explication of Wilfred Owen's "Arms and the Boy" and evolves from a gloss of the text, from notes, from freewriting, and from several drafts. An explication offers a careful analysis of a poem. The methodology requires an examination of the work to gain knowledge of each of its aspects and parts, and it attempts to determine the relation of all of the elements in the poem to the meaning of the whole. Note that the first draft of "Let the Boy Try" is articulate and structured, but that it is seriously underdeveloped and lacking in precision. The final draft overcomes these deficiencies and demonstrates outstanding mastery of this poem.

Title refers to weapons, but also to physical arms, protection.

Lebris' Gloss of Wilfred Owen's
"Arms and the Boy"

Why?
(imperative)   *allusion?*
Arms and the
Boy

Is the speaker cruel?

Let the boy try along this bayonet-blade   *alliteration*
How cold steel is, and keen with hunger of blood;   *(effect?)*
Blue with all malice, like a madman's flash;   *Tone serious*
And thinly drawn with famishing for flesh.   *? or ironic?*

Why? (Again imperatives)

Lend him to stroke these blind, blunt bullet-heads
Which long to nuzzle in the hearts of lads,
Or give him cartridges of fine zinc teeth,
Sharp with the sharpness of grief and death.

repetition — good!

For his teeth seem for laughing round an apple.   *Why animal*
There lurk no claws behind his fingers supple;   *imagery?*
And God will grow no talons at his heels,
Nor antlers through the thickness of his curls.   *Consonants*
                                                      used throughout
Can't or won't?   *poem. (effect?)*
Does speaker believe in God?

Notes

bayonet - a weapon attached to the muzzle of a rifle

keen - eager and sharp

malice - intention to injure others

thinly drawn - a sword is "drawn" in order to fight; the
    shape of the bayonet is like a thin line; also can mean
    drawn in (i.e., with hunger)

famishing - suffering extreme hunger

zinc - bluish white metallic element

talons - claws, esp. of a bird of prey

antlers - the horns of a stag or deer

Personification - the bayonet is starving to death
    ("famishing for flesh") and capable of emotion ("blue
    with all malice."). The bullets "long to nuzzle" and
    the cartridges feel "grief and death." The poem is
    divided into three quatrains; the first two discuss
    human weapons; the third introduces "natural"
    (animal) weapons. I don't think the poem uses a
    particular meter, but in the first two quatrains each
    line ends with a heavily stressed syllable. I really
    hear this when I read the poem aloud. The emphasis
    (e.g., on "blade" and "blood") makes the weapons seem
    more threatening.

Alliteration - the hard "b" sounds are like explosions and the "sh" sounds are like the hiss of bullets through the air.

What about consonance (half-rhyme)? The words seem to rhyme at first but there is a jarring effect. Is this significant?

Simile - "like a madman's flash." This is weird. Is a flash kind of fit? I suppose like a flash of anger (malice). Why *blue?* Metal can look bluish. Ok. Also the blue flash of gunfire.

Metaphor - "blind, blunt bullet-heads." They are blunt but they are not literally *blind.* The bullets are made to seem vulnerable like newly-born animals, but all they want to do is kill young "lads." They do not see their targets; they are not meant to see.

Freewrite

I remember years ago taking my father's gun out of its case, even though I was forbidden to touch it. I wanted to see what all the fuss was about. So I can understand why a young boy would want to test the sharpness of a blade or play with bullets and cartridges. But I don't understand why the speaker in the poem wants him to. I feel frustrated by the poem overall. I like the way the weapons are described as being alive because it makes them seem even more threatening. But allowing a kid to play with things which intend to kill him is pretty sadistic. I suppose it's the final verse which really throws me. Ok, the boy's teeth are innocent compared to the "grief and death" of the cartridge teeth, but why does the poet then go on to talk about claws and talons and antlers? Maybe the claw is meant to represent the trigger of a gun. "And God will grow no talons at his heels"—is it that God can protect the boy, but won't? Why "talons"? I suppose that unlike animals the boy has no natural defenses. So "give him cartridges of fine zinc teeth" so that he can protect himself. But I think the poet is implying that to fight is to go against God—human beings are not naturally equipped for battle ("Thou shalt not kill"). Anyway the poem is deliberately shocking because Owen wants to show how vulnerable the young boy is. Let him touch these weapons, and maybe he will realize how sick war is before it is too late.

Essay: First Draft: "Let the Boy Try"

At first "Arms and the Boy" may seem to be a cruel, even sadistic, poem, for in the first two stanzas a young boy is encouraged to play with potentially lethal weapons. However, in the final stanza the poet's compassion for the young lives lost in World War I is revealed. Although the poem is only twelve lines long, Owen makes the reader vividly aware of the vulnerability of youth by using several techniques to emphasize the horror of war.

The technique of personification is perhaps the most important. The bayonet is not only some starving animal "famishing for flesh." This simile likens the blue flash of gunfire to the indiscriminate malice of a madman. The bullets are also personified but in a different way. Far from being evil madmen, they are like the new-born young of some animal which "long to nuzzle in the hearts of lads." This perverse image is intended to shock: Owen wants the reader to realize how sick and unnatural war is.

The disturbing images of the first two quatrains are intensified through alliteration. The repetition of consonants in "blade," "blood," "blind," and "blunt" creates a hard, explosive effect like that of gunfire, while the "s," "f," and "sh" sounds suggest the hiss of blades or bullets through the air. These sounds, along with the strongly stressed syllables at the end of each line, give the poem a threatening tone, as though the speaker is talking through clenched teeth. The use of half-rhyme combines certain key images in the reader's mind while giving a jarring effect that adds to the tension in these first two quatrains.

The sinister effects created by personification, alliteration, and meter disappear in the final quatrain. The boy's youthful innocence is shown in the comparison between his laughing teeth and the "grief and death" of the cartridge teeth and by references to "his fingers supple" and "the thickness of his curls." These images emphasize how vulnerable he is. The boy has no natural defenses, and since "God will grow no talons at his heels" perhaps it is necessary to "give him cartridges of fine zinc teeth" so that he may survive. However, this is no answer because the weapons intended to protect him are bent on his destruction.

The figurative language and the several possible readings of the final quatrain make "Arms and the Boy" a somewhat difficult poem. But despite this the reader cannot help but share the poet's compassion for the young victims of armed conflict. And there is a more hopeful interpretation—

perhaps if the boy experiences the 'grief and death' of the weapons now, he will decide against becoming part of the horror and insanity that is war.

Lebris' Final Draft: "Let the Boy Try"

1   "Arms and the Boy" is a short lyric poem of great power, comprising three quatrains and employing the rhyme scheme AABB CCDD EEFF. The alliteration used throughout is an important feature, as it creates a tension appropriate to the subject matter. At first "Arms and the Boy" may seem to be a cruel, even sadistic, poem, for in the initial two stanzas, the speaker encourages another to give potentially lethal weapons to a young boy. The final stanza, however, reveals the deep compassion felt for the young lives lost on the battlefield. As an officer in the First World War, Wilfred Owen witnessed firsthand the atrocities inflicted by men upon other men. Although the poem is only twelve lines long, he succeeds in making the reader vividly aware of the vulnerability of youth and of the horror and perversity of war.

2   It is significant that the poem begins with an imperative statement: "Let the boy try along this bayonet-blade/ How cold steel is, and keen with hunger of blood." The note of challenge introduced here quickly becomes one of menace as the description of the bayonet shifts rapidly from the literal "cold steel" to the figurative "keen with hunger of blood." This personification of the weaponry is one of the most important devices used in the poem, as it transforms them from inanimate objects into evil personalities with conscious intentions. The bayonet, "keen" in the sense of both eager *and* sharp, is not only like a starving animal but also "Blue with all malice, like a madman's flash." This startling simile takes the blue flash of gunfire and likens it to the indiscriminate malice of a psychopath, a telling indication of how Owen himself had come to view military action. Note that "blue" also suggests the hue of cold steel and the pallor of death.

3   The second quatrain continues the menacing tone with another imperative statement: "Led him to stroke these blind, blunt bullet-heads/Which long to nuzzle in the hearts of lads." Again personification is used, but this time in a slightly different way. Far from being like evil madmen, the bullets are described as being like the new-born young of some animal. Paradoxically, it is they who seem vulnerable rather than the young boy who is being allowed to play with them. The use of the casual, inoffensive "lads" here is also

significant; it strikes an even more chilling note into the metaphor. The sexual connotations of "stroke" and "nuzzle," in conjunction with the phallic symbolism of the bayonet and the bullets, create a very unsettling undercurrent in an already disturbing poem. That instruments of death should be described in sexual, hence creative, terms does, however, highlight the poem's main theme—that war is something perverse and unnatural.

4   The second quatrain concludes with the third imperative statement: "Or give him cartridges of fine zinc teeth,/Sharp with the sharpness of grief and death." There is an important progression here in the level of involvement implied: the boy was initially allowed to touch the bayonet, was then lent bullets, and is now *given* cartridges. Although it is never made clear whom the speaker in the poem is addressing, there is a note of accusation here which implicates a far wider group of people than just a few soldiers on sentry duty. That the boy should be encouraged to play with weapons which actively seek to harm him is the key paradox in the poem, and it is this action which gives the final quatrain its power.

5   The sinister mood of the first two quatrains is intensified through a variety of poetic devices. The alliteration in "blood," "blade," "blind," and "blunt" creates a hard, exploding effect like that of gunfire, while the softer "s," "f," and "sh" sounds suggest the hiss of blades or bullets through the air. These sounds, along with the strongly stressed syllables at the end of each line, further contribute to the threatening tone, as though the speaker is talking through clenched teeth. Although the poem does not employ any fixed metrical pattern, the groups of unstressed syllables followed by several stressed syllables ("Blue with all malice, like a madman's flash") seem to mimic the stabbing motion of a bayonet. Certain key images are combined in the reader's mind through consonance ("blade"/"blood"), while the jarring effect of the half-rhyme adds an appropriate air of tension to the first eight lines.

6   In the final quatrain, however, the tone changes, and the sinister effects created by personification, alliteration, and meter disappear. Consonance is still used, but weak rhyme replaces the strong, heavily stressed rhyme of the first two quatrains, giving the last four lines a much more gentle mood. The boy's youthful innocence is shown in the comparison between his teeth "laughing round an apple" and the "grief and death" of the cartridge teeth. It is at this point that the disturbing images of the first two quatrains are justified, and the apparent sadism of the

speaker is now revealed as compassion. The poet emphasizes the boy's vulnerability through references to "his finger supple" and "the thickness of his curls," while his complete lack of aggression is expressed through a series of negative statements ("no claws," "no talons," "nor antlers"). The boy, unlike animals, has no natural defenses, and since "God will grow no talons at his heels," perhaps it is necessary to "give him cartridges of fine zinc teeth" so that he may survive. But the meaning of the poem cannot be quite as straightforward as this, because the implication is that for any human being to fight, whether boy or man, is to go against God. The poem's power comes from its tragic irony—that the weapons meant to protect the boy are intent only on his destruction.

7   The several possible readings of the final quatrain, along with the figurative language used throughout, make "Arms and the Boy" a somewhat difficult poem. It is also a shocking poem, and intentionally so, for Owen seems to have had in mind an audience of complacent armchair patriots. The poem's message is, of course, not limited to his contemporaries of the First World War but is, regrettably, still very relevant today. The knowledge that Owen himself was killed on the front lines at the age of twenty-five adds another dimension to the poem, but even without this fact, the reader cannot help but feel sadness and anger at the young lives which were, and still are, wasted on the battlefield. But there is a more hopeful interpretation—perhaps if the boy experiences the "grief and death" of weaponry secondhand, he will decide against becoming involved in the horror and insanity that is war.

* * *

The gloss and notes identify and explore the grammar, figurative language, sounds, and meaning of Owen's poem. The writer focuses on the formal elements of "Arms and the Boy" and on the connection between form and meaning. The journal entry describes a personal experience of touching a weapon and reveals the writer's attitudes toward violence, toward the poem, and toward war. In the journal the initial ideas for the essay are formulated.

The first draft contains an excellent introduction. The explication analyzes personification and alliteration in the first two stanzas or quatrains. The third paragraph discusses the meaning of the last verse, and the conclusion is excellent.

In the final version of "Let the Boy Try," the writer enlarges the vision of the poem and announces her view in the introduction which seems slightly cluttered with the rhyme scheme and with a comment concerning alliteration. Although the paper is well-organized, the introduction fails to focus exclusively on the writer's plan. The beginning, however, engages the reader's interest and expresses the major ideas. The paragraphs on the three quatrains are brilliantly conceived and brilliantly illustrated. The careful reading of imagery, significant figures of speech, grammatical constructions (imperative statements), sounds, tone, speaker, and theme result in an exemplary performance. The introduction of biographical details about Wilfred Owen emphasizes the dramatic conclusion about the "insanity that is war."

DRAMA

In *As You Like It,* Shakespeare claims that "all the world's a stage." His declaration captures the deep connection between dramatic literature and life; and, by extension, Shakespeare captures the human fascination with all of the imaginative arts. Every person views his or her experience as dramatic; each views the world as a setting for personal and public actions and ideas, for triumphs and crises, for the ordinary and the sublime. Plays and other forms of literature, therefore, are not simply imitations of life; they represent much more. They order, concentrate, and elevate acts of interpretation that may be crucial to daily life.

Theater existed in human cultures long before recorded history. Societies developed dramatic rituals with characters, costumes, makeup, masks, settings, and special effects to inspire, educate, entertain, initiate, worship the gods, and control the environment. Music became the universal accompaniment. In the rain dance of the Dieri in Australia, for instance, a lodge was constructed; and then, at the end of the ritual, it was destroyed by dancers who knocked it down with their heads. This ceremony signified the elimination of clouds so that rain could fall. In the drama of the Great Serpent held to celebrate the March moon, the Hopis burned fires in the kivas (ceremonial chambers) which they built; a prop person smothered the blazes to produce smoke curtains at certain intervals to facilitate changes in scenes and actors. They also devised sets with painted backdrops containing holes through which symbols of dancing serpents appeared. These performances exemplify the complexity of the drama before the practice of writing scripts. Some early comedies appeared as animal impersonations. For entertainment, one society in the Philippines created a comic play in which a searcher for honey experienced many outrageous indignations. Religious expression was central to many of these productions, but secular concerns also provided subject matter and impetus for public spectacles. Except for written scripts, the elements of modern drama—setting, character, action, plot—existed in prototype in these ceremonies.

The oldest evidences of scripts for drama are the fifty-five Pyramid Texts (3000 B.C.) of Egypt. Written on the walls of tombs and pyramids, they contain stage directions and lines for different characters. The major theme of these dramas was resurrection; and scholars estimate that more than four thousand texts once existed, developed, perhaps, from rituals celebrating the return of spring. The Egyptians also performed Coronation Festival plays that hailed the crowning of a new monarch.

FORMS OF DRAMA:
A GLOBAL PERSPECTIVE

European Dramatic Forms

Much of the theater, as it exists today, originated in Greece. Performances to honor gods or to commemorate rites of spring developed into formal productions. The most famous playwrights, Aeschylus (525–426 B.C.), Sophocles (496–406 B.C.), and Euripedes (c.480–406 B.C.) composed plays for the annual Dionysian Festivals. Presented to a selection group and later evaluated by judges, the plays—three tragedies and one comedy by each playwright—were performed in a semicircular theater.

Tragedy is a form of drama about fortunes and misfortunes, about disaster. Broadly defined, tragedy refers to dramatic representations of serious and significant actions that result in disaster for the protagonist or main character. In classical plays, these disasters happened to human beings with high position and great power such as Oedipus, Agamemnon, and Antigone. These characters possessed noble qualities and high passion. In tragedy, these attributes could not, however, save them from self-destruction or from fate.

Aristotle's classic theory in the *Poetics* (fourth century B.C.) describes tragedy as "the imitation of an action that is serious and also, as having magnitude, complete in itself," written in dramatic form and in poetic language. The tragic drama features "incidents arousing pity and fear, wherewith to accomplish the catharsis of such emotion." This **catharsis**, or purging of emotion, implies that the play will leave the audience or reader with feelings of relief or even exaltation. According to Aristotle, the play focuses on a **tragic hero** who has higher than ordinary moral values. This hero suffers a change or reversal of fortune, caused by his or her **tragic flaw, hamartia**, an "error in judgment." One common expression of hamartia in Greek drama is **hubris** or excessive pride.

Greek **comedy** first appeared in fertility rites and in the worship of Dionysus. From the time of Aristophanes (c.448–c.380 B.C.), the greatest Greek comic playwright, the form has been associated primarily with drama. Aristophanes wrote a variety of comedies combining lyrics, dance, satire, social comment, fantasy, and buffoonery. He attempted to reveal truth by exposing political deceit and pretense in such plays as *Lysistrata, The Wasps,* and *The Peace.* His more philosophical works include *The Clouds, The Frogs,* and *The Birds.* Aristotle distinguished comedy from tragedy by suggesting that it features ordinary people in amusing, everyday situations. It derives from the word **komos** or revel.

Few of the early tragedies or comedies still exist, but those that have survived convey the beauty and wisdom, the bawdy humor, the awe and wonder of classical Greece. They establish without a doubt the incredible influence of the Greek theater on world drama during the past two thousand years.

Fifteen years after the death of Aristophanes, scenic entertainments to appease the gods began in Rome (364 B.C.). Like Greek theater, Roman drama also originated in ritual ceremonies and secular entertainment. The most famous Roman dramatist was Seneca (3 B.C.–A.D. 65), although his tragedies may never have been performed in public.

During the Roman Empire, comedy employed two kinds of subjects: one derived from Greek dramas and the other concerned Roman materials. Seventy works from the Roman-based comedies are recorded, but the two best known Roman dramatists who wrote comedies depended on Greek plays. They are Maccius Plautus and Publius Terentius Afer, known as Terence. Plautus created the form known as **tragicomedy** by referring to the unconventional mixture of kings and servants in his play *Amphitrus,* as *tragico-comedia.* Choosing elements of both comedy and tragedy, the playwright attempted to balance a conflict of vision. The extant plays of both Plautus and Terence greatly influenced Elizabethan theater and, in turn, modern theater. Mime and pantomime, which developed as elaborate performances separate from dramas, also represent an original contribution of the Romans to the art.

The theatre did not die with the fall of Rome. Until the twelfth century, it survived in public entertainment and in religious performances, in particular, in cycles and in noncyclical plays. In England, Elizabethan drama developed from religious plays performed at medieval festivals during the twelfth and thirteenth centuries. These **mystery plays,** as they were called, presented Biblical stories—Noah and the ark, Jonah and the whale, the passion of Jesus—in town squares or in churches. As the dramas grew in popularity, platforms, called **pageants,** were wheeled from city to city; and the plays often expanded into a series that was enacted over a period of several days.

The **miracle play,** another dramatic genre related to the mystery play, presented saints' lives and miracles. It often centered on the divine acts of the Virgin Mary. A famous cycle of forty-two plays, the *Miracles de Notre Dame,* is extant in France. Other European examples are the German *Marienklage* (*The Complaint of Mary*), and the Dutch *Mariken Van Nieumaghen* (*Mary of Nieumaghen*). In England where the cult of the Virgin Mary did not flourish, most miracle plays dramatized the lives of saints.

During the fourteenth and fifteenth centuries, **morality plays** allegorized Christian values. Characters symbolized Christian virtues and vices. The most famous play, *Everyman* (1500), presented positive and negative human qualities in a single representative figure whose conflicts mirrored all life processes.

In the sixteenth century, Greek and Roman drama began to influence English theater. Secular plays became popular as interest in religious dramatizations waned. At first the new plays, based on classic Greek models, focused on murder and revenge. Roman dramatists, Seneca and Menander, also influenced the writers of these plays. Professional actors performed plays in courtyards and later in theaters. Audiences were composed of both educated and illiterate spectators.

From the defeat of the Spanish Armada in 1588 until 1642 when all theaters were closed during the Civil War, the English theater reached its highest development through the genius of such playwrights as Christopher

Marlowe, Ben Jonson, Thomas Kyd, Thomas Dekker, John Webster, and William Shakespeare. In *Tamburlaine* and *Dr. Faustus,* Marlowe (1564–1593) invented blank verse, or unrhymed iambic pentameter, a rhythm that became the dominant meter of Elizabethan drama.

The greatest genius of the reigns of Queen Elizabeth I and James I was William Shakespeare. A writer of comedies, tragedies, and histories, Shakespeare was the best of many astonishingly fine dramatists. A member of the Lord Chamberlain's company (1594), he joined a group that constructed the Globe Theater (1599), a most successful structure, small enough to fit into the orchestra area of the Greek Theater of Dionysius. At most, the Globe could have accommodated two thousand people.

The stage was a platform that projected into the audience. In the rear was an area with a curtain for intimate scenes; above was a balcony. There was a trap door for such purposes as the gravedigger scene in *Hamlet,* and ghosts descended on ropes from an overhead canopy. The theater had no painted sets, and props were minimal. As in Greek drama, all actors were male. Elizabethan theaters were designed like courtyards. Six hundred "groundlings" sat or stood in the open yards. More privileged spectators occupied tiers of covered balconies.

In *Hamlet,* the prince lectures the actors who perform the play-within-the-play and defines the purpose of drama: "to hold, as 'twere, the mirror up to nature." This blossoming of dramas in England focused on imitation of reality. At the same time, the performances of plays in the open theaters created a wonderful and wild public life—real entertainment.

The excitement of the Renaissance renewed interest in drama in Italy, France, and Germany; and audiences enjoyed many kinds of theater. No great dramatic literature emerged during the Renaissance in these countries. However, innovations in theater architecture influenced the development and form of modern drama: horseshoe seating, the **proscenium arch** (a frame enclosing the stage area behind which the front curtain hangs), painted sets, indoor lighting, and spectacular costumes.

In Spain, Lope de Vega and Calderón wrote spectacular plays, the most famous in Spanish literature. More than two thousand actors are listed in public records, and public playhouses in Spain developed in the same patterns as English theaters. They accommodated the same kind of enthusiastic audiences. Complete professionalization of theater and establishment of repertory groups represent significant accomplishments during this period.

In the seventeenth century, French theater was greatly influenced by Greek and Roman drama. During this time, the most significant drama was written by Molière, Racine, and Corneille. The actors developed revolutionary performing styles, and the first national European theater, the Comèdie Francaise, began.

During the Restoration in England (after 1688), the great achievement became the comedy of manners—hard, brilliant, accomplished. The major playwrights were George Etherege, William Wycherley, and William Congreve. In the eighteenth century in England, theater did not occupy a primary place. Oliver Goldsmith and Richard Brinsley Sheridan are notable exceptions. The art of acting, however, reached new heights; the best performer was the legendary David Garrick. This period also produced the **picture frame stage** and very large theaters.

On the European continent, Voltaire and Diderot in France and Goethe and Lessing in Germany wrote memorable and classic works. Dramatic theory and criticism received great attention. Many great actors emerged, and the number of theaters increased. Spectacular effects appeared in stage design. All of these developments received more attention in the nineteenth and twentieth centuries.

Asian Dramatic Forms

Drama flourished in India, China, and Japan at the same time as the emergence of formal theatre in Europe. In India, for example, the *Natyashastra,* treatise on drama, (c.200 B.C.–A.D. 200) declares that Brahma created theater by combining speech, music, mimetic art, and *rasa,* sentiment, from the four *Vedas* (c.1500 B.C.), the sacred writings of the Hindus. Drama became the fifth *Veda.* Other versions of the origins of Indian plays suggest that Vedic rituals, combined with dialogues, evolved into theater. Some posit that the two major epics, the *Ramayana* and the *Mahabharata,* were central to the development of drama—these works provided stories for plays and recitations throughout Southeast Asia. Mime and puppet shows are possible secular origins of theater. From these sources, modern Sanskrit drama emerged and existed as the only kind of formal dramatic literature for one thousand years between the decline of Roman drama and the development of dramatic traditions in China in the eighth century and in the Middle Ages in the West.

With elaborate aesthetics esthetics, the major tenet of Indian drama is **rasa** (sentiment) and its evocation in the audience; such evocation creates artistic pleasure and serenity. The plays always culminate in reconciliation. The Indian view of life dictates the rejection of conflict as central to drama. Sanskrit theater reached its greatest expression in the work of Kalidasa (c.200 B.C.–A.D. 500) who wrote *Shakuntala* and other works. *Mrichchhakatika (The Toy Cart),* whose authorship remains hotly debated, is as well-known and as brilliant as *Shakuntala.*

Chinese theater originated in rituals and shamanistic dances, in the court performances and jesters of the Zhou dynasty (1027–256 B.C.) and the Qin dynasty (221–206 B.C.). Many kinds of skits and shows, combat sketches like the *Witch of Liaodong* (A.D. 260), dance plays, and other performances represented forms of mimetic entertainment. None, however, resulted in formal drama.

The first form of theater appeared in the eighth century. The **canjunxi** or adjutant plays were slapstick comedies, duos between butt and knave. During the Sông and Jin dynasties, two kinds of drama arose; the Sông **zaju** (variety play) and the Jin **yuanben** (court texts). The first mature drama with extended conflicts and full development was the Yuan *zaju* (variety play) which blossomed during the reign of Kubla Khan (1261–1294) in Beijing.

In the sixteenth and seventeenth centuries, Liang Chenyu, Shen Jing, and Tang Xianzu added music and acting to **chuanqi** (marvel presentation). Ji Tianxiang and Li Xingfu wrote the earliest dramas translated into western languages. At the center of traditional Chinese theater was and is song; speech, dance, costumes, and makeup remained secondary in importance. Even today, Beijing opera represents the quintessential Chinese theatrical performance.

Like most drama, Japanese plays began in religious ceremonies. Its origins are unknown, but legend suggests that the first production was a dance by a goddess, Heavenly Alarming Female, to entertain the gods and to coax the sun goddess out of the cave in which she had hidden. From this myth and others, sacred rituals and highly stylized performances called **kagura** developed. **Bugaku**, a dance form from Tibet or India, came to Japan from China and from Korea. Still popular today, bugaku reached its peak in the Heian period (794–1192). Another form of entertainment, **sarugaku**, featured acrobatics, magic, songs, dances, juggling, and eventually comic skits.

In 1368, a famous performer of sarugaku, Kannami (1333–1384) combined his presentation with narrative dance and created **Nō** drama. As conceived by Kannami and by his son, Seami, the greatest genius of Nō drama, the form blends dances, music, and speech into a highly ceremonious and subtle play. In Nō the unspoken and the unseen are far more significant than the actual visual and auditory experiences. Through their discipline and inner strength, the great actors of Nō could remain motionless and draw the audience into spiritual knowledge. Nō, therefore, requires study by members of the audience. Because of its relationship to Zen, Nō was protected and patronized by the warriors in Japan for many centuries.

Most Nō plays have two parts: a priest (the *waki*) arrives at a place and encounters a man (the *shite* or chief actor) who tells the story. In the second part, the *shite* appears in his true identity, usually as a ghost, and performs a dance that describes the significant moral of his life. The *waki* often attains the release of the soul of the *shite*. **Kyōgen** are short comic skits performed between the two parts. See, for example, Seami's *Atsumori* in Chapter 8.

Kabuki theater, derived from popular entertainments, was formalized by Okuni in the seventeenth century. It was a combination of dance, narrative elements, and comedy. The greatest Kabuki playwright, Chikamatsu Monzaemon (1653–1725) wrote plays about young men who, through their own mistakes or through the plots of enemies, suffered destruction and often committed suicide. Kabuki continued to develop and to become more sophisticated, longer, and more complex. Finally, Sanjuro VII (1791–1859) studied Nō and performed the first Kabuki drama which emulated the original Nō. This play, Namiki Gohei III's *The Subscription List,* remains one of the masterpieces of Kabuki.

Both Nō and Kabuki enjoy popularity in contemporary Japan, and public theater thrives through innovative productions of modern plays. The center of Asian theater remains the skill of the artists, and as drama historian V. Roberts claims, ". . . in the timeless atmosphere of Asia, this art has reached a great refinement."

Arabic Dramatic Forms

From earliest times, Arabic cultures had an oral tradition based on the odes of early Arabia concerning battles and hunting and celebrating patriotism. Professionals, called **sawis**, recited them aloud. **Hakawatis** told of the deeds of Muhammad and of those who followed him. Theater in the Arabic-speaking countries developed later than the other forms of literature. It began in the latter half of the nineteenth century and derived from European drama and was not an extension of Arab or Islamic oral tradition or folklore.

African Dramatic Forms

In African cultures, drama originated in secular festivals, religious cere-monies, and rituals. Families enjoyed storytelling, riddles, songs, and dance dramas around their fires at night. These rich oral traditions have survived colonization and continue to inspire contemporary dramatists. For instance, **praise songs** (eulogies) have become comic devices in Kola Ogunmola's Yoruban opera *The Palmwine Drunkard* (1963) and in Wole Soyinka's *Kongi's Harvest*.

Even though plays were written by students in such academies as the French William Ponty School (Dakar, 1913) and even though classic dramas by Shakespeare and Molière frequently were produced in the late nineteenth and early twentieth centuries, the oral traditions of Africa strongly influenced per-formances of European drama. In almost every country in West Africa, univer-sities fostered the development of theater. In almost every country, African and European plays were transformed by elements of folk tale, drama, and song—the result of the preservation of cherished African roots. For example, in Nige-ria, the Traveling Theater's *The Taming of the Shrew* opened with songs and with the actors engaging the audience in a discussion of the difficulties be-tween men and women, a technique that forced the audience to understand the conflicts in Shakespeare and that changed the play through the introduc-tion of African dramatic conventions.

African drama can be defined both by its history of early European pro-ductions and by a history of plays of African writers whose work emerged in the twentieth century, the best training and works developing in the last fifty years. In Nigeria, the Arts Theatre Group, founded by Geoffrey Axwor-thy and Martin Banham in Ibadan (1958), presented European classics. Ax-worthy also participated in the University Dramatic Society where he directed Soyinka's first play, *The Swamp Dwellers* (1959). By 1962, the Uni-versity School of Drama, founded by the Rockefeller Foundation and di-rected by Axworthy, was created. The students, anxious to reach the people, initiated their famous theater on wheels. Wole Soyinka, now considered to be the most famous African playwright, became Director of the School of Drama in 1967.

In Ghana, where theater also has flourished in the twentieth century, the School of Music and Drama at Accra opened in 1962, directed by J. W. K.

Nketia, a musicologist. Playwrights Efua Sutherland, Felix Morisseau-Leroy, a Haitian, and Joe de Graft developed the theater with an emphasis on play-writing, on traveling troups, and on rural projects. At the University of Legon, generations of young dramatists were educated and encouraged. Among them was Christiana Ama Ata Aidoo who wrote *Dilemma of a Ghost* (1965) and *Anowa* (1970), a play about a young woman who refuses to marry the man chosen by her parents.

In South Africa, records exist of performances of *The Barber of Seville* and of *The Marriage of Figaro* in 1781. The first theater opened in 1801, but schools did not produce plays in indigenous languages (Zulu and Sotho) until the 1920s. The first published African play was G. B. Singo's *Debeza Baboons* (1925). Herbert J. Dhlomo wrote *The Girl Who Killed To Save* (1935), the first African drama written in English. Athol Fugard, a white African, has created numerous plays concerning racial conflict, but many South African dramatists were forced into exile, for example, Ezekiel Mphahlele, Bob Leshoai, and Lewis Nkosi. The most original and exciting theater in South Africa has remained subversive and scarcely legal. Today, as apartheid finally falls, perhaps, theater can be expected to flourish.

Central and South American Dramatic Forms

In Latin America, missionaries and explorers discovered sites for theaters with seats surrounding flat performance areas. Their searches for written scripts failed, however, because the Incan "quipu" (patterns of colored and knotted strings), the Mayan hieroglyphs, and the Aztec pictographs were not used to write or to preserve scripts. The native cultures of Latin America created dramatic ceremonies and performances for religious rites and for enjoyment, but they valued them as oral traditions. The subject matter from these early dramas, however, became the bases for plays written after conquest and colonization.

The first drama in Spanish intended for Christian entertainment for the Duke of Alba between 1491 and 1500, served as a model for *Ollantay* (1781). This drama, once considered to be an Incan play, recounts the story of a man who loves the daughter of the Emperor, Pachacutec in 1468. The play, in the original Quechua version and with Spanish translations copied by Padre Antonio Valdés, still survives. Like all other written plays which missionaries or others reported as indigenous drama, *Ollantay* appears to contain many European conventions. No one can claim to have discovered Latin American plays.

The first European-style drama, *Los pastores* (*The Shepherds*), was performed in Mexico by friars in 1519. Translated into many indigenous languages, *The Shepherds* became popular throughout Mexico and in the Southwestern United States where it still is seen by audiences in small villages during the holiday season. Plays, composed by priests for instruction and for religious warnings, appeared throughout Latin America. For example, minutes of the councils of Mexico record payment to actors—usually soldiers—for performances and for memorizing dialogue, for example, *Elanto de la gula* (*Play of the Glutton,* 1535).

Copies of secular plays began to arrive in each of the Spanish colonies during the sixteenth and seventeenth centuries because of the success of such outstanding dramatists as Lope de Vega, Calderón, Augustín Moreto, and Tirso de Molina. These dramas, performed for official entertainment in large cities, also found their way into the vernacular, the scripts supplemented by Central or South American conventions of dance, song, or poetry. When Philip II closed the Madrid theater in 1578, companies sailed to South America, especially to Lima, Peru, known for its interest in drama.

From the sixteenth to the nineteenth centuries every nation produced plays by writers born in the Americas; most of the playwrights, however, had Spanish parents, even though they often wrote in native languages about stories and themes important to the people. In Argentina, citizens watched a creole play set in Brazil, written by Juan Manuel Macial in the 1780s. In *Love of the Peasant Girl* (*El amor de la estanciera*), the father disapproves of the marriage of his daughter to a native gaucho. Fernando Calderón of Guadalahara, Mexico, wrote such romantic plays as *The Tourney* (1838), in which a mysterious English knight fights an evil baron.

Among Uruguayan playwrights the most famous include Father Martínez who wrote *The Most Astonishing Loyalty and Buenos Aires Avenged* in 1806. Francisco Xavier de Acha whose most well-known drama was *The Fusion* (1851), and Alejandro Magariños Cervantes (1825–1895) who wrote the historical play *Love and Fatherland* (*Amor y patria*, 1856). During this period, a blend of native and Spanish, English, French, and Portuguese elements enriched Latin American drama.

In the twentieth century, therefore, the same patterns exist: plays written in the European tradition, as a blend of cultures, and as expressions of the indigenous people. Mexico, for example, has experienced a renaissance in theater; and the contributors to this success include a number of women: Luisa Josefina Hernández (*The Deaf-Mutes,* 1953) and Maruxa Vilalta (*Tonight, Together,* 1970 and *The Story of "Him,"* 1964). In Argentina, many of the playwrights whose works appeared between 1950 and 1970 achieved international reputations, for example, Andrés Lizárraga, Osvaldo Dragún, and Griselda Gambaro. Political themes became central to these writers. The outstanding composer in Paraguay's native theater was Julio Correa (1890–1950). Contemporary drama in Mexico, Central and South America thrives in every country. Especially in Colombia, significant national theater developed through Enrique Buenaventura's Teatro Experimental de Cali and the Grupo La Candelaria directed by playwright Santiago García. In Guatemala, the Teatro National directed by Andrés Morris and TESP have fostered such plays about political turmoil and the fate of the Mayans as *El Guarezama* (1966) and *A Man's Work* (1967). After the overthrow of Somoza, Nicaraguan theater flourishes as collective ventures in urban ghettos and attempts both to educate and to entertain. The richness and variety of twentieth-century Latin American drama arise from political and social change and from determination to preserve and honor indigenous cultures.

NINETEENTH- AND TWENTIETH-CENTURY DRAMA

In Europe and in North America, three major movements in drama have developed in the last century: realism, Theater of the Absurd, Symbolist Drama.

At the end of the nineteenth century, writers began to create realistic dramas that presented accurate versions of the world and of human nature, of ordinary people leading ordinary lives. In dramatic literature, realism avoided all that was visionary and unbelievable. These dramatists chose serious, often tragic themes and well-developed characters who did not possess special status. They reacted against the spirit of Romanticism in England and in Europe which emphasized the emotions and imagination above reason and intellect. They also reacted against melodrama, plays which depend on spectacle, action, and extravagant emotional appeal.

Realism, as it is defined and recognized today, is primarily the invention of Henrik Ibsen, a nineteenth century Norwegian playwright. This dramatic movement corresponded to great cultural upheavals—the Napoleonic Wars, the Industrial Revolution, the rise of the middle class. People longed for critical analysis of social institutions.

In Russia, Anton Chekhov, Leo Tolstoy, and Maxim Gorki wrote realistic plays and fiction. In France, Emile Zola and Guy de Maupassant provided analysis of a movement which they called naturalism. The bases for this theory were Charles Darwin's idea of the survival of the fittest and Karl Marx's contention that economic conditions shape human life.

Ibsen influenced George Bernard Shaw, August Strindberg, and, subsequently, an entire generation of famous dramatists. Ibsen's work deeply affected Stanislavsky's teaching of method acting. Many North American playwrights—Eugene O'Neill, Arthur Miller, and Tennessee Williams—adopted fundamental tenets of realism.

Theater of the Absurd

The notion that life is absurd is not new, but it has acquired more specific meaning in the last century. Philosophers have defined the purposeless role of humans in a purposeless universe as absurd—mathematically, a surd is that which cannot be expressed in finite terms of ordinary numbers or quantities. It is in this mathematical sense that the philosophy of the absurd has been defined. (See Camus' "The Myth of Sisyphus" in Chapter 8.). The theatrical phrase was coined by Martin Esslin who wrote *The Theatre of the Absurd* in 1961. Scholars trace the lineage of this form from Roman mime plays to the comic techniques of Medieval and Renaissance drama, especially commedia dell' arte, comedy originating in the Italian Renaissance which featured improvisation, stock characters, and masks. Finally, Esslin cites the influence of August Strindberg and of Bertolt Brecht.

In the 1950s, this concept was expressed in a number of plays that focus on characters struggling with existential angst, anxiety, and anguish. The human condition is presented as essentially meaningless. The plays have no formal logic and lack conventional structure. The following dramatists and works represent this tradition: Samuel Beckett, *Waiting for Godot, Endgame;* Jean Genet, *Les Negres* (The Blacks), *Le Balcon* (The Balcony); Eugene Ionesco, *La Leçon* (The Lesson), *La Cantatrice Chauve* (The Bald Soprano), *Rhinoceros;* Harold Pinter, *The Birthday Party, The Homecoming;* Edward Albee, *The Zoo Story* and *The Sandbox.*

Symbolist Drama

With the advent of **realism**, twentieth century theater relinquished many traditional sources of dramatic tension—poetic language, symbols, illusions like the ghost in *Hamlet.* Like symbols in poetry and fiction, the actions and characters in symbolist drama refer to eternal ideas, abstract concepts. In such a play, a woman might encounter an abandoned child. The situation would not be presented as criticism of a particular society. Instead, the event might indicate the woman's discovery of her real and autonomous self; it might mean that humans are always abandoned in life.

Most plays contain symbols, but most dramatists do not intend that all action be interpreted as symbolic. **Symbolist dramas**, however, may feature many traditional poetic symbols, allegorical names, and they employ dreamlike atmospheres. This mode traces its roots to Kabuki theater, to Nō plays, to morality plays, and to the folk dramas of William Butler Yeats and of John Millington Synge. (See *Riders to the Sea* in Chapter 5.) Contemporary Chinese-American playwright, David Henry Hwang, has written such symbolist dramas as *The Sound of a Voice* and *M Butterfly.*

Film and Television

An important twentieth century development that influences public interest in theater is the moving image—film. The advent of moving pictures and of television has changed the viewing habits of human beings forever. As laser disc technology becomes available for computers and interactive television becomes more sophisticated, a revolution will occur, a revolution that will make knowledge and images of all kinds immediately available. What will these innovations mean to writers and readers, to public and commercial theaters? Hopefully, they will mean a multiplicity of choices for everyone. They will mean a heightening of imaginative power, of creativity, and of artistic vision for every society—a positive transformation.

Film shares many characteristics with literature: setting, character, conflict, dialogue, images, symbolism, and theme. The image adds new dimensions to language on screen; in drama, the work retains a more powerful position. Films, like drama, require conventions. For example, movies generally have music in the background—a score that helps to determine tone or mood.

One advantage of film is the capacity to change settings and locations. Since movies are shot in small scenes and out of sequence, the screenwriter can defy all of the dramatic unities. A film can span centuries and continents.

Special effects and computers can create new worlds that stage sets can only suggest.

Like fiction writers, screenwriters have enormous freedom with point of view. Cameras can determine viewer response by the angle of the shot. A close-up can create the illusion of intimacy just as a first-person narrator in a novel may achieve the same effect. A long shot provides distance, objectivity, and a sweeping view. A zoom can accomplish both purposes. A wide-angle shot of helicopters in the air with Richard Wagner's "Ride of the Valkyries" playing in the background in Francis Ford Coppola's *Apocalypse Now* gives the viewer an idea of the idiocy of war and of the powerful exhilaration of battle before it subsides inescapably into horror. A close-up of Martin Sheen's face as he witnesses his friend's severed head renders the terror personal and human.

Television shares many techniques with film; the great difference, of course, is the size of the screen. Because the viewing area is confined, television employs more close-up shots. Programs are shaped by segments and by commercials, and series require twenty-six episodes each season. These constraints determine character, theme, conflict, and quality.

With the expansion of cable and pay per view television, specialty networks—news, music, science fiction, cartoons, movie, sports—make the possibilities endless. At the same time, Bruce Springsteen still sings that he has "fifty-seven channels and nothing to watch." Surely, more exciting productions will come from artists in the future as they explore the full potential of television.

ELEMENTS OF DRAMA

Character

Imagined people stand at the center of almost all of the forms of literature. Anyone who appears in a work is called a **character**, a term chosen carefully for its meaning—those innate faculties which give a person identity and which distinguish him or her from others. Plays present a special framework for characters because the genre differs from fiction and from poetry since most dramas function without narration and narrators.

The *major* characters tend to be round, dynamic, and well-developed whereas *minor* characters remain flat, static, and slightly developed. Often a character appears in order to illuminate, double, or contradict a main character—a foil. Because they are easily recognized types, some characters are known as **stereotypes** or **stock** characters. In commedia dell' arte, for example, the harlequin always plays the same part—always acts in a predictable manner. All of the characters in this kind of drama are stereotypes by definition. This comfortable recognition allows the playwright to create characters easily.

The personae in most plays, however, grow and change; the development of the characters leads to important knowledge concerning the meaning of the drama. For example, at the end of *Oedipus Rex,* Oedipus recognizes his responsibility for the tragedy which has ruined both his life and the city of Thebes. Characterization, then, represents the most important element in drama. Through the personae, the playwright creates everything else.

Soliloquy, Monologue, Dialogue

A character's language reveals his or her feelings, values, situation, and/or beliefs. In a **soliloquy**—a long speech by one character, the speaker communicates special information to the audience. Think of Hamlet's famous words on suicide, "To be or not to be." Through this eloquent aside, the audience learns of the pain which Hamlet experiences as he contemplates his duty to exact revenge for his father's death, a pain which makes life unbearable. Hamlet resents his situation, his mother, his uncle; he feels increasingly angry, desperate, sad, and suicidal. Indeed, he cannot decide on an adequate response to the unreasonable demands of life (Chapter 4). Unlike a soliloquy, a **monologue** may be addressed to other characters as well as to the audience. It serves the same function; it permits an extended discussion of information, attitudes, or ideas by one character.

Most words in a play, however, are spoken between two characters. This exchange, called **dialogue**, demonstrates agreements, conflicts, relationships, differing or similar beliefs and motives between personae. Dialogue becomes the main element in the play for the development of character, plot, and theme. Consider the following lines from Synge's *Riders to the Sea* (Chapter 5), in which Synge writes about the power of family ties and about the power of the sea. The mother, Maurya, fears that her son, Michael, is dead; and she awaits news of his being washed ashore after buying wood to build a coffin for his burial. She entreats Bartley, her remaining son, not to leave the island. Examine the language:

> **Bartley** *(beginning to work with the rope):* I've no halter the way I can ride down on the mare, and I must go now quickly. This is the one boat going for two weeks or beyond it, and the fair will be a good fair for horses I heard them saying below.
>
> **Maurya:** It's a hard thing they'll be saying below if the body is washed up and there's no man in it[1] to make the coffin, and I after giving a big price for the finest white boards you'd find in Connemara.
>
> **Bartley:** How would it be washed up, and we after looking[2] each day for nine days, and a strong wind blowing a while back from the west and south?
>
> **Maurya:** If it isn't found itself,[3] that wind is raising the sea, and there was a star up against the moon, and it rising in the night. If it was a

---

[1] i.e., the house.
[2] when we have been looking.
[3] even if it isn't found.

hundred horses, or a thousand horses you had itself, what is the price of a thousand horses against a son where there is one son only?

The poetry of Maurya's language, the persuasive quality of her description of the landscape and of the horses, and the value that she places on her love for and need of her sons make the difference. Bartley leaves wishing "the Blessing of God" on his family. Ironically, the audience knows at the moment of Bartley's departure that he, too, will ride to the sea and drown. Synge's use of accent, dialect, ungrammatical constructions, figurative language, and poetic style are examples of effective use of dialogue to create meaning.

Action

Every character, played by an actor, not only speaks, but also acts and reacts to others and to events. A character may portray motivation through action. In *"Master Harold"* . . . *and the Boys,* Hally's action of spitting on Sam reveals his motive. Sam is African, but Sam represents Hally's spiritual father. Hally's action, in many ways, is unexplicable and unforgivable. His motives, however arise from a lifetime of subtle bigotry and personal frustration.

The audience also can learn about characters when they refuse to act according to normal expectations. Mrs. Hale and Mrs. Peters do not reveal their knowledge about the Wright murder to the sheriff. They realize that Mrs. Wright was motivated to commit such violence by actions which the men would consider *Trifles* (Chapter 6). In this play, Susan Glaspell artfully portrays character through *in*action.

Much of the interaction in drama becomes quite complicated. Hamlet kills Polonius by mistake; Ophelia kills herself because she erroneously believes that Hamlet does not love her; Laertes agrees to kill Hamlet with a foil dipped in poison because he thinks that Hamlet has deliberately caused the deaths of his father and sister. All of these actions involve misunderstandings, and they represent only a small proportion of the intricate events in the play. Such complexity in relationships among characters deepens the texture and meaning of drama.

Plot

The **plot** in a dramatic or narrative work is the structure of its actions, ordered to achieve emotional and aesthetic effects. This definition becomes complicated by the relationship between plot and character. The actions, both verbal and physical, are performed by characters; they provide the vehicle through which characters reveal their moral and personal traits. Plot is more, much more, than the "story" of a play which is a simple synopsis of the temporal events. Only when the story becomes related to discussions of relationships and organization of actions in order to produce meaning does it become part of the definition of plot.

Numerous patterns for plots exist; each depends on the mode of drama and its purposes. Is it tragedy? Comedy? Romance? Satire? Ritual? Melodrama?

Whatever the genre, all plots share certain elements in traditional forms of dramatic literature.

In any play, the interest centers on the **protagonist**, the hero or heroine. Usually this character struggles against an opponent or enemy, the character designated as the **antagonist**. The relation between them becomes the **conflict**. Many, but not all, plays contain one or more conflicts. In Shakespeare's *Hamlet,* the prince is the protagonist, and King Claudius, the antagonist. As Hamlet seeks revenge for his father's murder, a conflict between them escalates and complicates until both men die. Often the protagonist struggles in conflict with fate or circumstance; often the conflict resides within the main character.

Sometimes a character concocts a scheme which entraps another person, one who is naive, trusting, and vulnerable. This scheme is called **intrigue**. Rosencrantz and Guildenstern agree to assist Claudius in his plans against Hamlet; this intrigue fails. Many comedies also depend upon this device.

As the audience or reader begins to follow and to sympathize with characters, the plot builds **suspense** about its events and resolutions. If the action contradicts readers' expectations, the result becomes **surprise**. The relationship of suspense and surprise provides the essential dynamism in a play and must be predicated on the effectiveness of motive and of previous action.

A traditional plot has what Aristotle called **unity of action**, by which he meant that every part or event becomes necessary and integral to the whole and that the loss of any part destroys the whole. Aristotle considered *Oedipus Rex* as a perfect example of unity of action in plot. The slow unravelling of Oedipus as the murderer of Laius, as the scourge of Thebes, incident by incident, clue by clue, exemplifies this quality (Chapter 7).

Other plays include **double plots**, as in Elizabethan drama. Such plays involve a second story that becomes fascinating on its own merits and that enlarges understanding of the main plot. Such a **subplot** exists in *Hamlet* in the relationship between Hamlet and Ophelia. Plays may have multiple subplots.

In this traditional definition of plot, a sequence of events provides a *beginning* which establishes the situation and introduces characters, a *middle* which complicates the actions and develops character and an *end* which completes the action. The beginning of Hamlet captures attention with the appearance of the ghost and an exposition which implies that "something is rotten in the state of Denmark." The middle reveals Claudius as murderer, Hamlet as a pretended madman with a plan "to capture the conscience of a king." At this moment, the conflict reaches its highest point of tension for the protagonist, a point called the **apex**. By the end, Claudius has plotted the death of Hamlet; Ophelia has committed suicide; Hamlet has killed Polonius; Gertrude has swallowed poison; Laertes has killed Hamlet. Only Horatio remains to mourn the death of his "sweet prince" and to welcome Fortinbras.

In *Technique of the Drama* (1863), Gustav Freytag described plot in a configuration known as **Freytag's Pyramid**. According to this schema, a plot begins with rising action. In *Hamlet* this complication includes the appearance of the ghost; it includes the conflict between Claudius and Hamlet and events which eventually lead to Hamlet's success in achieving control. This rising action reaches a **climax** or **apex** for the hero. In *Hamlet* it becomes the proof of Claudius' crime through the play-within-the-play. Then comes the crisis where Hamlet fails to kill Claudius because the latter is praying. Then the **falling action** leads to the ascendance of Claudius until a **catastrophe** happens, as in the deaths of the main characters. This catastrophe may also be called the **denouement**, for not all plays end in tragic circumstances. Contemporary dramas often deliberately defy expectations of conventional plots, and some attempt to eliminate plot entirely.

Setting

In drama, **setting** differs greatly from other forms of literature because of the imperative for performance. In stage directions and in dialogue, the dramatist describes the place and time for the play. A designer creates stage sets which suggest the background for each scene. Shakespeare, for example, places Hamlet in Denmark; yet the stage can only be transformed into semblances of rooms in a castle, a graveyard, or a ship. The audience or reader must imagine the drowning of Ophelia and the battle won by Fortinbras. Still, the stage adds a dimension to drama which other forms of literature lack—visual and auditory images, live action, and spatial and temporal realities.

Props, scenery, costumes, and lights can change as the play progresses; but the setting on stage remains both limited and central to all productions. For instance, the set for *Riders to the Sea* should indicate the poverty of the modest cottage. One entrance must lead to the external world, to the sea which gives each family work and which claims each family's sons. Setting in drama may reveal economic status, geographic location, time period, and personal taste. Unlike fiction writers and poets, the playwright does not describe place in great detail, and he or she leaves much more to the imagination or to the stage.

Symbolism

In dramatic literature, **symbols** often are not subtle. They appear on stage as visual reminders of their central place in the meaning of the play. In Yamauchi's *And The Soul Shall Dance* (Chapter 6), one of the symbols takes the form of a song about a caged bird. In the lyrics to this popular Japanese song, separated lovers express their loneliness. The woman describes herself as a "caged bird, unable to leave" in the third stanza. This bird represents Emiko who is lost in the past, who is lost in exile, who is lost in the desert, and who is finally lost in madness. She, like the bird, is "unable to leave."

Irony

Dramatic irony appears in a play or in fiction when a situation or action becomes apparent to the audience but remains unknown to a character or to characters. Consequently, the persona acts in ignorance and often inappropriately.

The Greek tragedians, whose conflicts and stories were already known to their audiences, based their works on a constant use of this technique. In Sophocles's *Oedipus Rex* the irony is **tragic** since the king searches for a murderer whose deeds have caused the plague in Thebes. The audience knows that Oedipus will find himself guilty of the crimes which he decries.

Other kinds of irony:

- **Verbal irony** is a statement in which the meaning is different from the message which is expressed. Jonathan Swift's "A Modest Proposal" for eating children as a solution to the problem caused by the potato famine in Ireland depends greatly on this device.
- **Structural irony** which sustains double meaning throughout the work. In drama, this technique requires a naive protagonist; in fiction an unreliable narrator often serves this purpose.

Theme

The **themes** of a play are not its subjects, but rather its central idea or ideas. One theme of *Oedipus Rex* concerns the protagonist's search for vision and for truth. Oedipus reluctantly discovers the secrets of his identity and the meaning of his past actions. Knowledge of his personal guilt forces him into exile. The unbearable consequences of his pride result in patricide, suicide, and blindness—the fulfillment of a hideous destiny. Because Oedipus solves the riddle of the Sphinx, he saves Thebes and becomes king. Because he unknowingly murders his father, he then brings a new plague upon the city. Therefore, another theme in this drama focuses on the political importance of the personal tragedy of the king. His errors not only ruin him and his family, but they also destabilize the state. Like Shakespeare's *Hamlet,* the fall of the hero creates a political tragedy. Surely Sophocles intended these two intertwined thematic threads; surely these related themes contribute to the play's greatness.

THE READING/WRITING PROCESS: DRAMA

Begin with impressions about a play. Feelings often provide guidelines to intellectual analysis and responses. Reread the drama, and examine its parts—character, plot, theme—to determine their relationship to the whole. Grasping the wholeness in a drama depends on looking carefully at all of its elements. Consider characters and their development; consider the conflicts and their complications and possible resolutions. Consider how themes emerge. Evaluate how well the play comes together.

Take notes, and be careful to pay close attention to stage directions, prologues, epilogues, and important quotations. Determine the play's meaning, and assess its ability to force a reader or audience to face matters of enduring value.

CHECKLIST FOR WRITING ABOUT DRAMA

1. Does the play have a **narrator**? How does this character function? Is he or she reliable?

2. Are the main characters fully developed? How do they change? What actions or words demonstrate such change? How do minor characters function in the play? What do you learn about characters from the dialogue of others? Is the character sympathetic? How would an audience react? What different interpretations of these characters are possible?

3. What is the central conflict? How is it resolved? Are there subplots? Which acts or scenes represent the **rising action**? Identify the **climax**. Is there suspense? Which acts or scenes represent the falling action? How do the **subplots** get resolved?

4. How does the **dialogue** contribute to the **plot**? How do characters advance the plot or plots? How does **setting** function in relation to plot? Does offstage action contribute to the development of conflict? How?

5. Does the play contain **irony**? What kinds of irony are present? Is the irony effective?

6. Are there symbols that suggest the theme?

7. What information about production is included in the stage directions? What information does the play give about costume, set, lighting, sound effects?

8. What are central themes? What are other significant issues? How do characters and conflicts illuminate themes?

9. Discuss conflict, character, language, theme in relation to the total effect of the play. Does it work? What does it mean?

10. What is the best feature of the play? What is the weakest feature of the play? What is the final evaluation?

Student Portfolio:
Response to Yamauchi's *And the Soul Shall Dance*

The assignment for this essay, analysis of one or more characters in Yamauchi's play, required a number of writing responses and a series of drafts. Jane Jamiokowski's paper on *And The Soul Shall Dance* analyzes two characters who represent two generations of Japanese immigrants in Southern California in the 1930s. (See Chapter 6.) The writer contends that Yamauchi has captured a truth about the experience of these characters, "caught between worlds." The development of this analysis progresses in several steps: (1) brainstorming,

(2) notes, (3) informal outline, and (4) essay. Jamiokowski wrote journal responses and versions of the essay as well as the work published here.

Jamiokowski's brainstorming lists reveal her talent for organizing ideas. She immediately begins to focus on two characters to represent the Issei and the Nisei. Her exhaustive notes confirm her penchant for close reading and enable her to find details and references. Her outline, reminiscent of her brainstorming lists, offers a thesis, topics and subtopics about Emiko and Masako, and a conclusion about the difficulties of living in one culture and longing for another and about surviving such conflicts. Note that the essay contains a clear introduction and thesis statement, extensive development of character analysis, specific details and quotations from the play to support the main points, good transitions, and an excellent conclusion.

Jamiokowski's Brainstorming

Two characters in *And The Soul Shall Dance*.
Two generations of Japanese Americans.

Emiko lives in the past:

1. She longs to return to Japan because of her true love, because of her artistic life, because of freedom.
2. She drinks too much. She and Oka brew liquor and hide it in the desert. The song, "And The Soul Shall Dance" refers in each stanza to green wine which enables the parted lovers to dream.
3. Hana says that Emiko cannot get over the good times in Japan, that she doesn't know how to bend.

Emiko's present is unbearable:

1. Oka is abusive; he beats her. He blames her for his first wife's death. He calls her a second hand woman. He prefers Kiyoko who obediently assimilates, cooks, wears American clothing. (The relationship is incestuous in some ways.)
2. She is the "caged bird" of the popular song. She has no way to return, no money, no friends, no exit. Oka takes her money.
3. When the money is gone and when she cannot sell the kimonos, her hope dies.

Masako is a spirited, intelligent child:

1. Hana often mentions that Masako does not obey. She is not a typical Japanese child. She burns the bathhouse at the beginning. She does not respond to Kiyoko. She tells Oka that "everyone has a soul."
2. She is an excellent student. She eventually becomes friends with Kiyoko, and she teaches her English.
3. She is quite aware of Emiko's situation. She reports that she witnessed Oka beating Emiko. She speaks to Emiko and watches her sad dance at the end. These painful experiences provide an initiation into the adult world.

Masako is a second generation Japanese child who does not wish to return to Japan.

1. She asks about the plight of Japanese Americans. "How come they don't write books about us?"
2. She says that she does not want to return to Japan. She is the *only* character who does not have this dream.
3. However, she does not try to imitate Americans. Her hair remains straight and smooth. She maintains her Japanese identity in a new country and understands the complexities of her situation.

Note: Emiko represents the destruction of the immigrant who longs to return to the homeland. Masako represents the new generation who learns from the pain of those who are caught between cultures. Emiko is the extreme; all of the other Issei characters also dream of return. They will not return. Masako will triumph.

Jamiokowski's Notes

Act I

Scene 1:

June, Imperial Valley, Southern California.
Masako is eleven, Nisei, second generation.
She accidentally burns the bathhouse.
Hana, the mother, is angry, indicates that Masako often needs to be reminded.

The Japanese Americans are poor, lease land, dream of making money to "go home and live like a king."

Oka, the neighbor, asks Masako to be his daughter's friend when she arrives from Japan, mentions that his second marriage was arranged by proxy.

Hana declares that Emiko, his wife, is strange.

They will take Victrola in order to curtail conversation when they use Oka's bathhouse.

Scene 2:

Stage directions indicate that Emiko is 30 (Oka, 45).

Oka has not told Emiko that Murata and family have been invited to bathe.

Emiko does not fetch glasses, sits alone, does not look at records. Stage directions indicate her silence and lack of response.

When she hears "Kazo No Tori," "The Caged Bird," a popular song on the Victrola, she cries.

Masako is concerned about her; others dismiss the fears.

"She drifts into a dance."

Masako plays "The Soul Shall Dance," and Emiko dances, translates the lyrics about drinking the green wine. Sad, Emiko speaks of returning to Japan.

Oka says Emiko has no soul; Masako disagrees. Oka slaps Emiko; she has "large purple welt on her face."

Emiko speaks of her song, then classes in the city, of almost being a certified artiste. City allowed her freedom.

Masako asks Hana if Emiko is "kitchigai," crazy. Hana replies that Emiko can't get over Japan, can't "bend."

Hana and Murata would return to Japan—not Masako.

Hana mentions the drinking of Oka and Emiko.

Emiko has black eye; Masako saw Oka hit her.

Scene 3:

Argument between Oka and Emiko. He says "Nothing more disgusting than a drunk woman," calls her "a second hand woman." She says she is true to one man, not Oka. She thinks he waits for her; Oka thinks not—she has been in the U.S. for ten years. He knocks her off the bench, but eventually admits that she did not want her sister, Shizui, his first wife, to die and that he is too old for

her. He reiterates that he did not ask for her, but will
try to be kinder.

Emiko makes speech about exile and keeping the dream
alive—otherwise she would die.

Act II

Scene 1:

Mid-September
They discuss arrival of Kiyoko.
Masako asks why no one writes books about Japanese
Americans. Her mother says "Because we're nobodies."
Masako is not interested in Kiyoko, and her mother is
annoyed.
Oka spent money from the sale of horse on Kiyoko, is
proud. Describes discrimination in restaurant.
Masako and Emiko have conversation outside. She is
uninvited by Oka. Tells Masako about love.
Masako has abortive conversation with Kiyoko, gives
up.

Scene 2:

November—Thunder and lightning
Masako mentions that Kiyoko has no friends at school
and follows her around.
They worry about crops. Hana says that she would be in
Japan if praying were the answer. Murata more
conciliatory.
Kiyoko arrives in storm and says she wants to die. Oka
and Emiko drinking and fighting. Says Emiko hates her.
Hana replies that Emiko hates the U.S. and wants to go
home. She discusses responsibilities and children and
concludes "Eventually everything passes." She lectures
Oka when he arrives, especially about Kiyoko. Tells
Kiyoko to make the best of it.

Scene 3:

The girls practice words. Kiyoko tells Masako that she
cannot pronounce Japanese; they laugh.
Hana and Murata—"We'll be back in Japan in two years."

Scene 4:

Spring
Kiyoko is dressed up, curly hair. Masako says that she is not allowed to have permanent.
Oka makes incestuous comments.
Japanese cannot own land, must lease, move every few years.
Emiko discovers that Oka has taken her "going home money" for Kiyoko.
He tells her to "swim to Japan."
In stage directions, she cries alone, begins touching herself, reminding herself of lover's hands.

Scene 5:

Same day
Masako bangs wind chime—a gift from Kiyoko.
Emiko tries to sell them two beautiful kimonos, but Hana admits that they cannot afford them.
Masako is disappointed; Emiko is devastated.
Hana strokes her hair—"straight, nice."
Murata enters, sees mother and child, speaks fondly of Masako becoming a woman.

Scene 6:

Desert
Emiko sings "And The Soul Shall Dance."
Masako crouches under a shrub.
Emiko wears kimono, carries sage branch, dances, laughs, acts out fantasy. She is in another world, has been pushed over the edge. Emiko leaves and the image of her face is on Masako's mind.
The words of the songs indicate that the dream is scattered; the lovers are apart and drink the green wine alone. "And The Soul Shall Dance." Emiko is the caged bird. Masako will fly free.

Jamiokowski's Outline

I.   Introduction

    A. Play shows Japanese-American culture in 1930s.

    B. Japanese songs symbolize Emiko's plight—first generation.

    C. Masako represents second generation.

    D. Thesis statement.

II. Emiko

    A. She lives in the past because of lover.

    B. She longs for Japan because of freedom and because of education.

    C. Liquor is green wine of the soul.

    D. Present is unbearable because of Oka.

    E. She has no way to leave, becomes mad.

III. Transition—Emiko represents the plight of the first generation.

IV. Masako

    A. She is intelligent, spirited, slightly disobedient.

    B. She is not typical Japanese, but she does not choose American customs. Kiyoko as foil, as friend.

    C. She is sensitive to Emiko's plight.

    D. Her strength comes from the love of her parents.

    E. Her strength comes from the blend of cultures.

    F. Her bearing witness to destruction is initiation.

V. Conclusion

    A. First generation lives in struggle.

    B. There is hope for second generation, e.g., Masako.

    C. The play presents universal experience for all immigrants caught between two cultures, two worlds.

Jamiokowski's Final Essay
Yamauchi's *And The Soul Shall Dance:*
Two Characters, Two Generations, Two Dreams

1 Wakako Yamauchi's *And The Soul Shall Dance* creates an authentic view of Japanese-American culture in the 1930s through character, dialogue, setting, stage directions, and symbolism. Two Japanese songs, one written by Yamauchi and one a popular piece, symbolize the dreams and difficulties of the first generation of Japanese-Americans, the Issei. These lyrics especially elucidate the situation of

Emiko, a thirty year old woman married to an abusive husband. With every breath, she longs for her homeland and for her lost lover. Only one character, Masako, represents the second generation, the Nisei. Masako remains the only person in the play who does not dream of returning to Japan, who is not an exile. In her characterizations of Emiko and Masako, Yamauchi reveals the struggle of immigrants caught between two worlds.

2   Her marriage to Oka arranged by proxy, Emiko has lived in the Imperial Valley for ten years. She does not really dwell in Southern California, however; she lives in the past. Like Gretta in "The Dead" and like Granny Weatherall, Emiko's true life ended when she parted from her first love in Japan, when she became what Oka calls "a second hand woman." She insists that her lover waits for her; Oka replies that the man probably has married someone else. She tells Masako that love keeps one alive; she cries over the separated lovers in the song "And The Soul Shall Dance." The lyrics imply that dreams and green wine sustain the lovers whose souls then dance.

3   Emiko also longs for the city where her aunt allowed her freedom, where she attended classes, where she sang, where she almost became "a certified artiste." Oka recalls that she was favored by her family because of her beauty, that her father planned to marry her to a wealthy man. Kiyoko vaguely remembers her constant happiness and laughter. Clearly, Emiko's past in Japan brings her fond memories; she enjoyed passion, freedom, and education.

4   In order to maintain this illusion, Emiko drinks too much. Her liquor is not the exquisite green wine of the song, and it does not make her soul dance. It is, instead, illegal brew which she and Oka hide in the desert. Oka declares that there exists "nothing more disgusting than a drunken woman. . . ." She drinks and dances; she touches her body as if her hands belong to her lover, but her soul does not dance.

5   Her efforts to sustain her dream of "the good times in Japan" prevent any possibility of connection with others. Hana declares that Emiko does not know how to bend and implies that she will not survive in the United States.

6   What causes Emiko's failure to embrace Oka, Kiyoko, and life in the desert? What causes her to live in stasis, in the past? Her present situation truly is unbearable. Oka beats her, shoves her off benches, blackens her eye, and blames her for the death of her sister, Shizui, his first wife. He calls her names and taunts her as a fallen woman. Finally,

he replaces her with his own daughter on whom he spends his money and for whom he sells his horse.

7 Emiko has become the "caged bird" of the popular song, "Kazo No Tori" (I, 2) which Masako plays on the Victrola:

> (She)
> > Your voice calling me
> > I have not forgotten, but
> > To leave, to be able to leave
> > No choice for the caged bird. (II, 6)

Emiko has no choice; she lives in an arranged marriage; she is not "able to leave." The symbol of the bird in the cage emphasizes her situation which becomes worse when Oka steals her "going home money" for Kiyoko's dresses, permanent, and magazines. The final blow is struck when Hana cannot afford to buy her last two beautiful kimonos for Masako. Emiko then slips into her fantasy world forever. Earlier she had proclaimed: "Because I must keep the dream alive . . . the dream is all I live for. I am only in exile now. If I let you make me believe this is all there is, the dream would die. I would die." (I, 3) And so, in the end, she dies into madness.

8 Like Emiko, the first generation adult Japanese-Americans, the Issei, continue to dream of returning to their homeland. Murata believes that his family will be in Japan within two years. He believes that it is "Everybody's dream. Make money, go home and live like a king" (I, 1). In the United States, the Japanese do not make money. Only one man, Yagata, has earned extra money. The Japanese cannot own land; they must lease their farms and move every few years. They must take their lunches on trips or suffer discrimination in restaurants. They do not appear in books because, as Hana says, they are "nobodies." She tells her daughter, Masako, not to dream; a dream "makes it harder." (II, 1)

9 Masako, however, is a second generation Japanese-American, a Nisei. She is intelligent, a good student, an inquisitive child who questions her parents and who draws her own conclusions. She is careless, slightly and consistently disobedient, and beloved by her parents. She burns the bathhouse by accident (I, 1); she reports Oka's abuse of Emiko; she befriends Kiyoko only on her own terms. She dislikes Kiyoko's willingness to adopt American customs and dress. Kiyoko becomes her friend only when she proves herself superior in the pronunciation of

Japanese, only when she states her equality. Then Masako is willing to laugh and to accept Kiyoko.

10   Masako is sensitive to Emiko's plight. Only she notices her wounds, her exclusion from family gatherings; only she talks to Emiko about the meaning of love, about music, about secrets. Masako chastises Oka when he claims that Emiko possesses no soul. "Everyone has a soul," Masako declares.

11   Although Masako understands that Japanese-Americans suffer discrimination, she does not wish to live in Japan. What gives her such conviction? Why does she not wish she were dead as Kiyoko does? Her parents, caught in poverty, caught in the desert where crops must always be reseeded after the rain, love her. They allow her not to be a typical Japanese child, but they honor and preserve their own rituals and customs. Her mother praises her straight, black hair, and her father celebrates her approaching womanhood as she runs to turn off the irrigation system:

> Hana: She's growing up.
> Murata: Must be that time of the month.
> Hana: Oh, Papa, she's too young for that yet.
> Murata: (Genially as they enter the house) Got to start some
>   time. Looks like I'll be outnumbered soon. I'm
>   outnumbered already. (II, 5)

Masako becomes the beneficiary of the strengths of both cultures even in such difficult circumstances. She watches the destruction of Emiko; she watches the transformation of Kiyoko; she watches the cruel and incestuous behavior of Oka. These sad events end in the final dance of Emiko which only Masako witnesses. Emiko slips away into a fantastic and permanent world of madness, and Masako passes through these initiations into womanhood. For Masako, the dream lives. Her soul will dance.

12   Yamauchi has shown the painful conditions of Japanese immigrants in the United States in a particular time and place. She has suggested some ways in which the two cultures might blend through the child, Masako. For everyone who has been or is caught between two worlds, Yamauchi has captured a significant human truth.

Jamiokowski's final essay analyzes the characterization of Emiko and Masako through personal traits, relationships, symbols, and theme. She adds details and long quotations from the text to develop the characterization of Masako. She introduces two generations of Japanese-Americans and suggests that Emiko, who symbolizes the first immigrants, cannot survive and that

Masako, who represents the Nisei or second group, witnesses the pain and will thrive because of "the blend of cultures." First she proves her theory about these characters through a thorough analysis of Emiko's tragic life. The details of her longing, her terrible marriage, her alcoholism, and her madness clearly establish Jamiokowski's idea that the first generation may never embrace life in the United States. She does not develop the interpretation of the second character, Masako, as extensively. She constructs a persuasive case, but she might expand her idea that Masako becomes a survivor because of her parents, because of their love. The theme of initiation also deserves more attention. The essay, in any case, is a fine model—extraordinarily clear, persuasive, well-written, and detailed.

NONFICTION

When we think of nonfiction prose, we envision objective writing designed to convey information: newswriting or scientific and business communications. Nonfiction also may be creative, evocative essays replete with a sense of voice and power. Imaginative reaction, passionate commitment, and the urgency of personal perspective play a role in some kinds of nonfiction. Many forms have features of fiction, poetry, and drama: vivid, descriptive detail, narrative example, metaphoric language, and dialogue.

In nonfiction, we may be drawn into the world of the writing just as we are in fiction, in poetry, or in drama. However, we become involved in different ways. We read to absorb, to react, perhaps to be moved and enlightened by facts, arguments, issues, and ideas. As Susan Sontag suggests, "an essay could be as much an event, a transforming event, as a novel or a poem."

FORMS OF NONFICTION

Speech

As major civilizations and communal life flourished, public discourse evolved. The **speech**, oral communication designed to be delivered to an audience, became a popular form of public communication in Greek times, particularly during the fifth century B.C., the age of Pericles, at the height of Athenian democracy. In his treatise, *The Rhetoric*, Aristotle (384–322 B.C.), a Greek philosopher, categorized the three kinds of speeches prevalent in his society: orations delivered in the law courts, in the political arena, at ceremonial occasions. Many examples of these declamations, of course, did not survive because they were not transcribed. One famous speech is Pericles' funeral oration for the Athenian dead (430 B.C.), which appears in Thucydides' *History of the Peloponnesian Wars*. Among other arguments, Pericles praises the Athenian democratic "system of government" as a "model to others." Many famous Greek orators and teachers developed the form of the speech between the fifth and fourth centuries, including Isocrates and Demosthenes whose political works are notable examples. Roman rhetoric was patterned after Greek models. Cicero (106–43 B.C.), a Roman statesman, politician, and rhetorician, excelled at oratory and published his own speeches which still serve as exemplars of classical argument. (See Chapter 3.) Examples of speeches in *Legacies* include Sojourner Truth's "Ain't I a Woman" (Chapter 7), Nelson Mandela's "I Am Prepared to Die" (Chapter 7), and Martin Luther King's "I Have a Dream" (Chapter 8), delivered at the March on Washington, August 1963.

Philosophical Treatise

Another human imperative has been to speculate on the state of the world and on human nature. One of the earliest forms of nonfiction has been the **philosophical treatise**, an extended formal meditation on a philosophical, religious, or political subject. Such treatises convey the central ideas, beliefs, and values of many Western and Eastern societies. Interestingly, at approximately the same time (*circa* 600 B.C.), Pythagoras wrote about mathematics in ancient Greece, Confucius was a teacher in China, and Hindu sages created the *Upanishads,* the central documents of Hindu thought in India.

Plato (428–347 B.C.), one of the foremost Greek philosophers, wrote tracts on such subjects as the nature of love, "The Symposium" (Chapter 6) and the ideal state, *The Republic* (Chapter 8). The wisdom of Confucius (551–479(?) B.C.), a Chinese scholar and teacher, instructed people to live a good life in harmony with others. Confucius suggests, for example, that a ruler must "govern by virtue. . . .": "Govern the people by virtue . . . and the people . . . will be reformed of themselves." Another Chinese philosopher, known as Lao-tzu (575–485(?) B.C.), assumes a different religious stance: withdrawal from the world, meditation, mysticism, and the cultivation of silence as the way of the spirit. Lao-tzu is considered responsible for the *Tao te Ching,* the opening line of which states, "The way that can be spoken of is not the way. . . ."

Examples of political, philosophical, and or religious treatises abound in world history. Think of the documents of the American or the French revolution; the Communist Manifesto; Chairman Mao's sayings; the sacred texts of world religions. The poem of Lao-tzu (Chapter 7) and the reflections of Albert Camus (Chapter 8) also exemplify this form of nonfiction.

Autobiography

One structured type of personal writing is **autobiography**, defined as writing about one's life. Autobiography became prevalent with the rise of Christianity as people had the urge to document their spiritual conversions. One of the earliest stories of such a conversion, St. Augustine's *Confessions,* written between A.D. 397 and 400, describes the author's childhood, his conversion to Christianity at thirty-two, and his transformation from sinner to Christian.

The desires to fashion a story of one's life, to create from memories—from inchoate reminiscences—an ordered vision of one's past, and to seek personal meaning from one's past are deep needs in human beings. The autobiographical impulse has taken hold of writers throughout the ages as diverse as Machiavelli, Helen Keller, and Maya Angelou. Autobiography becomes a particularly powerful means of expression for those groups who feel disenfranchised because this form of writing defines and asserts selfhood in response to the lack of recognition of ethnic identity. Alice Walker has written many autobiographical essays which explore her stance as an African-American woman, for example, "In Search of our Mothers' Gardens" (Chapter 5). One particularly North American form of autobiography is the **slave narrative**, a story which portrays the slave's efforts to secure release from bondage and to gain freedom. Read Harriet Jacobs' autobiography, *Incidents in the Life of a Slave Girl* in Chapter 7.

Memoir

As eras of conquest and travel progressed during the Middle Ages and the Renaissance, another autobiographical form emerged. **Memoir** presents the remembrances of a public figure and the events of an historical era. Perhaps, one of the earliest examples of such a document is Julius Caesar's record of his military campaigns in Gaul 102–44 B.C. Other examples of memoir include Marco Polo's travels in China and India (*The Travels of Marco Polo,* 1293), Leo Africanus's account of Africa written when he was taken captive and held as a slave by pirates (1526), and Babur's (Zahir Ud-Din Mohammed's) recounting of his battles in India (1526). Contemporary memoirists include Winston Churchill and Richard Nixon. Rigoberta Menchú's autobiography, *I, Rigoberta Menchú* (Chapter 8), may be considered part-memoir since Menchú attempts to document an historical reality: her Indian people's political resistance against the oppressive government in Guatemala.

Journal

The **journal**, another form of personal writing, concerns the self exclusively, and the presumed audience is the author. Some of the earliest examples include the lists of Sei Shonogan—a form of a diary kept by a woman in the court of the emperor in tenth-century Japan. Titles from Shonogan's diary reveal, "Things that Make One's Heart Beat Faster"; "Things that Arouse a Fond Memory of the Past"; "Hateful Things"; "Depressing Things."

As journals developed, many types emerged: travel diaries, diaries of spiritual life, journals kept during the settlement of the frontier by the pioneers in North America, and diaries kept by women during the Civil War. Throughout literary history, numerous artists and writers were inveterate journal keepers: Leonardo da Vinci wrote and drew in sketchbooks; Henry David Thoreau composed more than 60,000 pages of journals; Anaïs Nin had at least sixteen volumes of journals.

Letter writing represents another form of personal expression; often in letter writing, the assumption of a public as well as a private audience exists. Benjamin Franklin composed letters to his son; F. Scott Fitzgerald communicated by letter with his daughter, Scottie. Martin Luther King's "Letter from Birmingham Jail" presents a complex political argument that suggests the fusion of both the public and the private self and the impossibility of separating these selves in the response to political oppression.

Essay

During the Renaissance, with its emphasis on individual will and consciousness, the **essay** developed, a form of prose that presented a person's
reflections and ideas on a specific topic. The essay (derived from the French
verb assayer—meaning to try, to attempt) presents a concise, prose discussion of a limited topic and of limited length, designed for a general audience. Although the origin of the essay can be traced to ancient Rome—to
Seneca and to Plutarch who wrote works with such titles as "On Envy and
Hate," "On the Control of Anger," and "On Having Many Friends,"—Francis
Bacon, the English scientist and philosopher (1561–1628), often receives
credit for inventing the modern form of the genre. He wrote volumes of essays on subjects as varied as the relation of parents and children, death,
truth, adversity, anger, revenge, atheism, suspicion, and cunning. During
the 1600s and 1700s, many writers experimented with this form, including
Blaise Pascal who produced his *Pensées* (Thoughts, 1670), a collection of
his thoughts; Montaigne who penned his *Essais* (1580), his meditations;
and in England in the 1700s Joseph Addison and Richard Steele who wrote
essays for their literary journal, *The Spectator*. The essay flourished in
the hands of such eighteenth-century British writers as Jonathan Swift,
Samuel Johnson, and William Hazlitt and such nineteenth-century North
American writers as Henry David Thoreau and Ralph Waldo Emerson who
wrote "Civil Disobedience" and "The American Scholar," respectively. Essay
writing reached its apex in Britain and in North America in the eighteenth
and nineteenth centuries.

Kinds of Essays

EXPOSITION

Exposition, the main form of nonfiction, explains or conveys information to
a particular audience. Exposition may have a range of approaches—objective,
subjective, factual, or reflective. An expository essay may describe, explain,
give examples, compare, define, analyze, or demonstrate cause-effect. Lewis
Thomas's essay, "The Medusa and the Snail" (in Chapter 4), takes the example
of the symbiosis between the Medusa jellyfish and the snail and transforms it
into a frightening analogy to explore growth of identity. His examination
prompts us to evaluate our own concepts of selfhood.

Expository essays may fall into two classes: *formal* and *informal* writing. In a formal expository essay, the writing may be organized with an introduction, middle paragraphs, and conclusion. The essay is carefully and
tightly developed: a thesis and subtopics exist; the writer orders ideas into
supporting paragraphs with clear topic sentences and supporting evidence;
a direct and logical progression of points moves toward the conclusion.
The point of view and tone may be more objective and less personal. "The
Medusa and the Snail" (Chapter 4) represents a superb example of a tightly
and formally organized essay. The informal essay may be organized by

associations and may utilize techniques of fiction (personal, symbolic detail, dialogue, narrative excerpts) and of poetry (imagery, figurative language, repetition). Witness Maxine Hong Kingston's mix of description, reminiscence, narration, character sketch, and reflection in "No Name Woman" (Chapter 6).

ARGUMENTATION

In **argumentation**, one of the primary forms of nonfiction prose, the writer presents a personal opinion with the intention of convincing an audience about his or her point of view, constructs reasons for that position, and develops supporting evidence. Informal and formal modes of structuring argument exist. Informal argument may take the form of persuasive writing in which emotional appeals, detail, narrative and personal examples provide the proof designed to convince a reader. For instance, if a writer composed an essay for a local paper to convince the audience that eighteen-year-olds' drunk driving poses a serious threat to others, he or she refers to the experience of witnessing a violent and fatal accident caused by an eighteen-year-old. Or the writer may recount a tale about his or her child or another teenager in order to persuade readers. The intent is to convince an audience of the validity of the position or to persuade people to take some action.

In formal argument, the writer also will develop an argumentative thesis (a position) and reason with his or her audience in mind. However, the position and the thesis will be more objectively stated; the reasons supported with proofs, data, statistics, examples. One option is to shape an argument in classic, Aristotelian style (see Chapter 3). Nelson Mandela's "I Am Prepared to Die" (Chapter 7) is an excellent example of a formally structured, complex argumentative essay.

At the heart of argumentative writing remains a solid statement of thesis (position), development of reasons and supporting evidence, and sound, logical reasoning. Compare Marjorie Agosin's exploratory, allusive, lyrical, personal political argument against oppression in "A Visit to the Mothers of the Plaza De Mayo" (Chapter 7) with Simone de Beauvoir's logically structured presentation of women's position as "object" in "Woman as Other" (Chapter 6).

ELEMENTS OF NONFICTION

All forms of nonfiction share some similarities. A writer thinks of the audience, of the occasion for writing, of the reasons for the writing; he or she then shapes the writing with audience in mind. The writer becomes aware of purposes, intentions and overall goals and chooses relevant details, examples, facts, and reasons. Furthermore, he or she considers **point of view**, voice, the attitude and relationship to material and to audience, and thinks about the relationship between point of view and the persona in the work. This relationship provides readers with a sense of the writer as the character, the person behind the writing. Is the person honest? Does the voice sound real? truthful? distant? impassioned? angry? The persona and point of view of the writer influence the slant of the piece, the main idea, the thesis, the organization, the details, and the word choice. Rhetoricians label this consciousness of audience, occasion, purpose, goals, intent, and point of view the *rhetorical situation*.

Tone involves the feeling, mood, and attitude that readers infer from the content of the essay. In Truman Capote's essay, "A Christmas Memory" (Chapter 5), part of the tone emanates from his sadness caused by remembrance of loneliness in childhood; another aspect becomes his nostalgia about the times with his cousin which lessened his sense of isolation.

The crux of effective nonfiction prose, detail and specific example, makes the piece come alive. The power of nonfiction rests in the interplay of the general and of the specific, of the abstract and of the concrete. Return to the drunk driving example. Just saying eighteen-year-olds should not drive when they are drunk will not convince a reader. An example of a car accident or a statistic regarding the number of eighteen-year-olds involved in drunk-driving accidents and the consequence for others—death, injury of passengers—is much more persuasive.

A college freshman, Jody Levy, wrote the following paragraph. The sensory details, including "as a calm river, soon interrupted by rapids," intensify the description of a commonplace object.

Incense

I watched a stick of incense burn. It was a pale brown colored stick of musk incense, with a red hot tip that slowly smoldered downward. A stream of smoke rose from it, and moved with the wind. It was relaxing to watch the dreamy mist. It was calm and controlled, mesmerizing and hypnotic. The smoke ascended straight towards the ceiling, and, then broke its flow; it spurt, swirled, waved, and curled. It started as a calm river, soon interrupted by rapids. Ashes fell, and, crumbled on the tissue underneath, creating a pile of dirt. Dead and used. I let out a deep breath, and, the smoke scrambled. More ashes formed on the top as the red dot moved down. The ashes bent, and then broke, but they did not fall. They hung like a dead leaf on a tree. I followed the smoke with my eyes—thin, thick, straight, smooth, wavy, curly, spiral, fast, slow, short, long,—always moving and changing—floating lines and forms. A continuous flow of greyish, whitish, bluish smoke. Beautiful, like silk thread . . . As the stick became shorter, the room smelled nicer; the smoke spiraled off with its musk scent. I liked the smell. The scent obscured the smell of my roommate's fat and odorous boyfriend. My roommate walked in; she hates the smell of incense. And the smoke rose in circles, like a horn shouting out scent. Two lines streamed from the stick, sometimes synchronized, cooperating to make forms. Other times, they crossed and waved in opposition, independently creating their own design, and then coming together again. The smoke formed a tunnel, and, then a spiral shell. . . . The incense neared its end, and spurted its last breaths of smoke that slowly floated away and disappeared; but they wafted somewhere in the air. For hours after the final stream of smoke was gone. The red glow faded and left the stick, solitary and lifeless, with a head of ashes. It died and left a lasting memory.

In this piece, the reader senses the persona of the observer: her awe as the stick of incense assumes a life of its own as a "river," as "dirt," as "a dead leaf," then as smoke "like silk thread." The details—color, shape, texture, and smell—of the concrete comparisons and figurative language give this vision of incense its "lasting" place in our minds.

The **organization** of an essay remains crucial. The introduction attracts readers and involves them in the world of the writing and the main idea (the thesis); the middle paragraphs compel through their treatment of evidence (the interplay of generalization and specifics; details and example); and the conclusion reinforces the thesis and leaves the reader, with a view to contemplate, feeling enriched, enlivened, convinced, and intellectually aware.

Word choice and *style* are crucial in nonfiction. The writer selects words as carefully as a novelist, poet, or dramatist. He or she plays with words: ironic, witty, comic, lyrical; evocative word play and figurative language become crucial to nonfiction. Inexact or diffuse wording leads readers astray; and the work loses its impact. In "Incense" Jody Levy occasionally undermines vivid descriptions by the use of vague words and clichés. For example, after describing the "smoke" as "silk thread," Levy then depicts the room which "smelled nicer." The "nicer" smell, vague, not at all suggestive of any odor, causes the piece to lose some of its power. The work also loses impact at the end because "lasting memory" is a cliché, a hackneyed means of stating the effect of a moment. Levy easily could have omitted the last sentence.

The total effect of a piece of nonfiction prose is its message: the total meaning of a work. As parts of a short story, drama, poem, build themes, so parts of a nonfiction essay build the message or thesis.

Examine this excerpt from John Haines' "Moments and Journeys," a selection which comprises a mini-essay within a longer meditation.

1   When life is simplified, its essence becomes clearer, and we know our lives as part of some ancient human activity in a time measured not by clocks and calendars but by the turning of a great wheel, the positions of which are not wage-hours, nor days and weeks, but immense stations called Spring, Summer, Autumn, and Winter. I suppose it will seem too obvious to say that this sense of things will be far less apparent to people closed off in the routine of a modern city. I think many people must now and then be aware of such moments as I have described, but do not remember them, or attach no special significance to them. They are images that pass quickly from view because there is no place for them in our lives. We are swept along by events we cannot link together in a significant pattern, like a flood of

refugees pushed on by the news of a remote disaster. The rush of conflicting impressions keeps away stillness, and it is in stillness that the images arise, as they will, fluently and naturally, when there is nothing to prevent them.

2   There is the dream journey and the actual life. The two seem to touch now and then, and perhaps when men lived less complicated and distracted lives the two were not separate at all, but continually one thing. I have read somewhere that this was once true for the Yuma Indians who lived along the Colorado River. They dreamed at will, and moved without effort from waking into dreaming life; life and dream were bound together. And in this must be a kind of radiance, a very old and deep assurance that life has continuity and meaning, that things are somehow in place. It is the journey resolved into one endless present.

3   And the material is all around us. I retain strong images from treks with my stepchildren: of a night seven years ago when we camped on a mountaintop, a night lighted by snow patches and sparks from a windy fire going out. Sleeping on the frozen ground, we heard the sound of an owl from the cold, bare oak trees above us. And there was a summer evening I spent with a small class of schoolchildren near Painted Rock in central California. We had come to learn about Indians. The voices of the children carried over the burned fields under the red glare of that sky, and the rock gave back heat in the dusk like an immense oven. There are ships and trains that pull away, planes that fly into the night; or the single figure of a man crossing an otherwise empty lot. If such moments are not as easily come by, as clear and as resonant as they once were in the wilderness, it may be because they are not so clearly linked to the life that surrounds them and of which they are part. They are present nonetheless, available to imagination, and of the same character.

4   One December day a few years ago, while on vacation in California, I went with my daughter and a friend to a place called Pool Rock. We drove for a long time over a mountain road, through meadows touched by the first green of the winter rains, and saw few fences or other signs of people. Leaving our car in a small campground at the end of the road, we hiked four miles up a series of canyons and narrow gorges. We lost our way several times but always found it again. A large covey of quail flew up from the chaparral on a slope above us; the tracks of deer and bobcat showed now and then in the sand under our feet. An extraordinary number of coyote droppings scattered along the trail attracted our attention. I poked one of them with a stick, saw that it contained much rabbit fur and bits of bone. There were patches of ice in the streambed, and a few leaves still yellow on the sycamores.

5   We came to the rock in mid-afternoon, a great sandstone pile rising out of the foothills like a sanctuary or a shrine to which one

comes yearly on a pilgrimage. There are places that take on symbolic value to an individual or a tribe, "soul-resting places," a friend of mine has called them. Pool Rock has become that to me, symbolic of that hidden, original life we have done so much to destroy.

6   We spent an hour or two exploring the rock, a wind- and rain-scoured honeycomb stained yellow and rose by a mineral in the sand. Here groups of Chumash Indians used to come, in that time of year when water could be found in the canyons. They may have come to gather certain foods in season, or to take part in magic rites whose origin and significance are no longer understood. In a small cave at the base of the rock, the stylized figures of headless reptiles, insects, and strange birdmen are painted on the smoke-blackened walls and ceiling. These and some bear paw impressions gouged in the rock, and a few rock mortars used for grinding seeds, are all that is left of a once-flourishing people.

7   We climbed to the summit of the rock, using the worn footholds made long ago by the Chumash. We drank water from the pool that gave the rock its name, and ate our lunch, sitting quietly in the cool sunlight. And then the wind came up, whipping our lunchbag over the edge of the rock; a storm was moving in from the coast. We left the rock by the way we had come, and hiked down the gorge in the windy, leaf-blown twilight. In the dark, just before the rain, we came to the campground, laughing, speaking of the things we had seen, and strangely happy.

From the first paragraph, we have a sense of the writer's rhetorical situation (purpose, occasion, conceived audience, and point of view). Haines suggests that people, "closed off in the routine of a modern city," do not lead "simplified lives" and, thereby, lose contact with those moments in life when images and essential truths of existence are revealed. He wants to impress upon readers that enslavement to "clocks" and "calendars"—to the hubbub of daily living—"keeps away stillness," periods of reflection when life's "essence becomes clearer." We feel the meditative urgency of his voice, expressed in such repetitive and parallel phrases as "part of some ancient human activity in a time measured not by clocks but by the turning of a great wheel. . . ." We feel his appeal not to neglect such opportunities in the image of people as a "flood of refugees," "swept along by events . . . [that] cannot [be] [linked] together," "pushed on by the news of a remote disaster." We feel the passion of his injunction: Embrace "stillness." By the end of this first paragraph, we conceive his point of view, his persona. We feel the tone behind the words—contemplative, insightful, open to life, to image, and to experience: to the possibilities of the marvelous and profound in the experience of daily living. We wonder where the piece is going. We ask: How will the persona evolve? How will the argument develop? We may ask if he will share such moments of "stillness" because he seems a credible witness, a trustworthy narrative presence, whose opening promises insight.

Haines has established his thesis—his central idea: People are not in touch with those moments of "stillness" that will enrich their lives. Next Haines develops his argument and supports his thesis with subtopics and evidence. He treats the "dream journey and the actual life" of the Yuma Indians to suggest that the spiritual and the actual, the miraculous and the ordinary, can be fused in people's lives. Then he provides evidence with events from his own life; three narratives of "treks" in the wilderness with children. The selection moves tightly from point to point.

At the heart of the writing are the specific details and examples of these hiking trips, the vital, textured scenes of people in the wilderness. Such evocative images as the "night lighted by snow patches," "the sound of an owl," the peaceful and idyllic feeling of the "voices of the children [which] carried over the burned fields under the red glare of the sky" suggest reverence for what Haines in a different section of this essay calls "things on this earth," the values of life spent in contact with nature, and the enrichments of such a way of living.

The selection concludes with the longer narrative of the writer's hike with his daughter and a friend to Pool Rock. The sensory details of the journey—a "large covey of quail," "the tracks of deer and bobcat," for example, the "wind- and rain-scoured honeycomb stained yellow and rose" rock involve an audience and prepare readers for the moment of awakening and awe. The writer and his companions discover "the stylized figures of headless reptiles, insects, and . . . birdmen . . . painted on the smoke-blackened walls and ceilings," the symbolic reminders of a "once-flourishing people," and of a sacred way of life for a people who lived in harmony with and revered the natural world. This scene reminds the readers of what people have lost by straying from such a connection with the sacred, natural world. When we read the closing, like the writer and his companions, we "[drink] water from the pool that gave the rock its name . . ." are nourished, and perhaps "[come]" to the end of the work "laughing, speaking of the things we [have] seen, and strangely happy." We have entered into a moment of "stillness."

When we finish reading, perhaps, we are convinced by the writer's argument that "the rush of conflicting impressions keeps away stillness" and that we must cultivate in ourselves the ability that the speaker has exhibited: to wrest from the chaos of our lives such transfiguring moments. In this essay, as surely as in a short story, we are drawn into a world, live with a character, and undergo a "transforming" experience, in Susan Sontag's terms, that reveals truths of existence and leads us to understand our worlds in new ways.

THE READING/WRITING RESPONSE: NONFICTION

When you read nonfiction prose, a checklist of questions will help you analyze the text.

CHECKLIST OF QUESTIONS FOR NONFICTION PROSE

1. What form of nonfiction prose am I reading: speech, treatise, autobiography, memoir, journal, essay?
2. Is it exposition or argument?
3. What is the rhetorical situation (purpose, occasion, audience)?
4. What is the writer's point of view? persona?
5. What is the writer's tone?
6. How do I, as a reader, respond to the point of view and tone?
7. What is the thesis? supporting points?
8. What are significant details? examples?
9. How is the essay organized? formally? informally?
10. What do I notice about style, word choice?
11. What have I learned from reading this work?

Student Portfolio:
Response to King's "Letter from Birmingham Jail"*

The portfolio presents a model that demonstrates the stages in the process of writing an evaluation essay. Because King's work is so complex, Jack Ferguson created both a gloss and outline of the essay to make sure that he grasped the structure of the argument. He next wrote a double-entry notebook. Finally, he composed first and final drafts of his essay. In the final draft, the writer tightened the introduction, clarified King's use of appeals, and analyzed his style.

Ferguson's Gloss

> *My Dear Fellow Clergymen:*
> While confined here in the Birmingham city jail,
> I came across your recent statement calling my
> present activities "unwise and untimely." Seldom do
> I pause to answer criticism of my work and ideas. If I

---

* This response to a published statement by eight fellow clergymen from Alabama (Bishop C. C. J. Carpenter, Bishop Joseph A. Durick, Rabbi Hilton L. Grafman, Bishop Paul Hardin, Bishop Holan B. Harmon, the Reverend George M. Murray, the Reverend Edward V. Ramage and the Reverend Earl Stallings) was composed under somewhat constricting circumstances. Begun on the margins of the newspaper in which the statement appeared while I was in jail, the letter was continued on scraps of writing paper supplied by a friendly Negro trusty, and concluded on a pad my attorneys were eventually permitted to leave me. Although the text remains in substance unaltered, I have indulged in the author's prerogative of polishing it for publication. [King's note]

sought to answer all the criticisms that cross my desk, my secretaries would have little time for anything other than such correspondence in the course of the day, and I would have no time for constructive work. But since I feel that you are men of genuine good will and that your criticisms are sincerely set forth, I want to try to answer your statement in what I hope will be patient and reasonable terms.

King adopts a non-confrontational "Rogerian" stance.

Appeal to character— King wants to appear trust-worthy.

opposing argument #1

Refutation a)

I think I should indicate why I am here in Birmingham, since you have been influenced by the view which argues against "outsiders coming in." I have the honor of serving as president of the Southern Christian Leadership Conference, an organization operating in every southern state, with headquarters in Atlanta, Georgia. We have some eighty-five affiliated organizations across the South, and one of them is the Alabama Christian Movement for Human Rights. Frequently we share staff, educational, and financial resources with our affiliates. Several months ago the affiliate here in Birmingham asked us to be on call to engage in a nonviolent direct-action program if such were deemed necessary. We readily consented, and when the hour came we lived up to our promise. So I, along with several members of my staff, am here because I was invited here. I am here because I have organizational ties here.

Appeal to character— establishes credibility.

b)

But more basically, I am in Birmingham because injustice is here. Just as the prophets of the eighth century B.C. left their villages and carried their "thus saith the Lord" far beyond the boundaries of their home towns, and just as the Apostle Paul left his village of Tarsus and carried the gospel of Jesus Christ to the far corners of the Greco-Roman world, so am I compelled to carry the gospel of freedom beyond my own home town. Like Paul, I must constantly respond to the Macedonian call for aid.

Biblical allusions indicate his audience.

c)

Moreover, I am cognizant of the interrelatedness of all communities and states. I cannot sit idly by in Atlanta and not be concerned about what happens in Birmingham. Injustice anywhere is a threat to justice everywhere. We are caught in an inescapable network of mutuality, tied in a single garment of destiny. Whatever affects one directly, affects all indirectly. Never again can we afford to live with the narrow, provincial "outside agitator" idea. Anyone who lives inside the United States can never be considered an outsider anywhere within its bounds.

opposing argument #2

You deplore the demonstrations taking place in Birmingham. But your statement, I am sorry to say, fails to express a similar concern for the conditions that brought about the demonstrations. I am sure that none of you would want to rest content with the superficial kind of social analysis that deals merely with effects and does not grapple with underlying causes. It is unfortunate that demonstrations are taking place in Birmingham, but it is even more unfortunate that the city's white power structure left the Negro community with no alternative.

Rogerian approach to opponents.

Refutation

a)

In any nonviolent campaign there are four basic steps: collection of the facts to determine whether injustices exist; negotiation; self-purification; and direct action. We have gone through all these steps in Birmingham. There can be no gainsaying the fact that racial injustice engulfs this community. Birmingham is probably the most thoroughly segregated city in the United States. Its ugly record of brutality is widely known. Negros have experienced grossly unjust treatment in the courts. There have been more unsolved bombings of Negro homes and churches in Birmingham than in any other city in the nation. These are the hard, brutal facts of the case. On the basis of these conditions, Negro leaders sought to negotiate with the city fathers. But the latter consistently refused to engage in good-faith negotiation.

Evidence— but maybe this could have been more specific.

b)

Then, last September, came the opportunity to talk with leaders of Birmingham's economic community. In the course of the negotiations, certain promises were made by the merchants—for example, to remove the stores' humiliating racial signs. On the basis of these promises, the Reverend Fred Shuttlesworth and the leaders of the Alabama Christian Movement for Human Rights agreed to a moratorium on all demonstrations. As the weeks and months went by, we realized that we were the victims of a broken promise. A few signs, briefly removed, returned; the others remained.

c)

As in so many past experiences, our hopes had been blasted, and the shadow of deep disappointment settled upon us. We had no alternative except to prepare for direct action, whereby we would present our very bodies as a means of laying our case before the conscience of the local and the national community. Mindful of the difficulties involved, we decided to undertake a process of self-purification. We began a series of workshops on nonviolence, and we repeatedly asked ourselves: "Are you able to accept blows without retaliating?" "Are you able to endure the ordeal of jail?" We decided to schedule our direct-action program for the Easter season, realizing that except for Christmas, this is the main shopping period of the year. Knowing that a strong economic-withdrawal program would be the by-product of direct action, we felt that this would be the best time to bring pressure to bear on the merchants for the needed change.

Then it occurred to us that Birmingham's mayoral election was coming up in March, and we speedily decided to postpone action until after election day. When we discovered that the Commissioner of Public Safety, Eugene "Bull" Connor, had piled up enough votes to be in the run-off, we decided again to postpone action until the day after the run-off so that the demonstrations could not be used to cloud the issues. Like many others, we wanted to see Mr. Connor defeated, and to this end we endured postponement after postponement. Having aided in this community need, we felt that our direct-action program could be delayed no longer.

Appeal to character.

d) You may well ask, "Why direct action? Why sit-ins, marches, and so forth? Isn't negotiation a better path?" You are quite right in calling for negotiation. Indeed, this is the very purpose of direct action. Nonviolent direct action seeks to create such a crisis and foster such a tension that a community which has constantly refused to negotiate is forced to confront the issue. It seeks so to dramatize the issue that it can no longer be ignored. My citing the creation of tension as part of the work of the nonviolent-resister may sound rather shocking. But I must confess that I am not afraid of the word "tension." I have earnestly opposed violent tension, but there is a type of constructive, nonviolent tension which is necessary for growth. Just as Socrates felt that it was necessary to create a tension

Appeal to reason.

Interesting!

in the mind so that individuals could rise from the bondage of myths and half-truths to the unfettered realm of creative analysis and objective appraisal, so must we see the need for nonviolent gadflies to create the kind of tension in society that will help men rise from the dark depths of prejudice and racism to the majestic heights of understanding and brotherhood.

King seeks to establish common ground.

The purpose of our direct-action program is to create a situation so crisis-packed that it will inevitably open the door to negotiation. I therefore concur with you in your call for negotiation. Too long has our beloved Southland been bogged down in a tragic effort to live in monologue rather than dialogue.

"Our" implies unity.

One of the basic points in your statement is that the action that I and my associates have taken in Birmingham is untimely. Some have asked: "Why didn't you give the new city administration time to act?" The only answer that I can give to this query is that the new Birmingham administration must be prodded about as much as the outgoing one, before it will act. We are sadly mistaken if we feel that the election of Albert Boutwell as mayor will bring the millennium to Birmingham. While Mr. Boutwell is a much more gentle person than Mr. Connor, they are both segregationists, dedicated to maintenance of the status quo. I have hoped that Mr. Boutwell will be reasonable enough to see the futility of massive resistance to desegregation. But he will not see this without pressure from devotees of civil rights. My friends, I must say to you that we have not made a single gain in civil rights without determined legal and nonviolent pressure. Lamentably, it is an historical fact that privileged groups seldom give up their privileges voluntarily. Individuals may see the moral light and voluntarily give up their unjust posture; but, as Reinhold Niebuhr has reminded us, groups tend to be more immoral than individuals.

opposing argument #3

Refutation

Appeal to reason.

Uses outside authority to support his argument.

We know through painful experience that freedom is never voluntarily given by the oppressor; it must be demanded by the oppressed. Frankly, I have yet to engage in a direct-action campaign that was "well timed" in the view of those who have not suffered unduly from the disease of segregation. For years now I have heard the word "Wait!" It rings in

the ear of every Negro with piercing familiarity. This
"Wait" has almost always meant "Never." We must
come to see, with one of our distinguished jurists,
that "justice too long delayed is justice denied."

We have waited for more than 340 years for our
constitutional and God-given rights. The nations of
Asia and Africa are moving with jetlike speed toward
gaining political independence, but we still creep at
horse-and-buggy pace toward gaining a cup of coffee
at a lunch counter. Perhaps it is easy for those who
have never felt the stinging darts of segregation to
say, "Wait." But when you have seen vicious mobs
lynch your mothers and fathers at will and drown
your sisters and brothers at whim; when you have
seen hate-filled policemen curse, kick, and even kill
your black brothers and sisters; when you see the
vast majority of your twenty million Negro brothers
smothering in an airtight cage of poverty in the
midst of an affluent society; when you suddenly find
your tongue twisted and your speech stammering as
you seek to explain to your six-year-old daughter why
she can't go to the public amusement park that has
just been advertised on television, and see tears
welling up in her eyes when she is told that Funtown
is closed to colored children, and see ominous
clouds of inferiority beginning to form in her little
mental sky, and see her beginning to distort her
personality by developing an unconscious bitterness
toward white people; when you have to concoct an
answer for a five-year-old son who is asking,
"Daddy, why do white people treat colored people so
mean?"; when you take a cross-country drive and
find it necessary to sleep night after night in the
uncomfortable corners of your automobile because
no motel will accept you; when you are humiliated
day in and day out by nagging signs reading "white"
and "colored"; when your first name becomes
"nigger," your middle name becomes "boy" (however
old you are) and your last name becomes "John," and
your wife and mother are never given the respected
title "Mrs."; when you are harried by day and
haunted by night by the fact that you are a Negro,
living constantly at tiptoe stance, never quite
knowing what to expect next, and are plagued
with inner fears and outer resentments; when you
are forever fighting a degenerating sense of

[Handwritten annotations in margin:]

good contrast

Appeal to emotion.

parallelism and repetition

Personal examples— very persuasive

"nobodiness"—then you will understand why we find it difficult to wait. There comes a time when the cup of endurance runs over, and men are no longer willing to be plunged into the abyss of despair. I hope, <u>sirs,</u> you can understand our legitimate and unavoidable impatience.

"Sirs" indicates respect — King does not want to alienate his audience.

You express a great deal of anxiety over our willingness to break laws. <u>This is certainly a legitimate concern.</u> Since we so ⟨diligently⟩ urge people to obey the Supreme Court's decision of 1954 outlawing segregation in the public schools, at first glance it may seem rather paradoxical for us consciously to break laws. One may well ask: "How can you advocate breaking some laws and obeying others?" The answer lies in the fact that there are two types of laws: just and unjust. I would be the first to advocate obeying just laws. One has not only a legal but a moral responsibility to obey just laws. Conversely, one has a moral responsibility to disobey unjust laws. <u>I would agree with St. Augustine that "an unjust law is no law at all."</u>

opposing argument #4

Refutation

Appeal to reason.

Now, what is the difference between the two? How does one determine whether a law is just or unjust? A law is a man-made code that squares with the moral law or the law of God. An unjust law is a code that is out of harmony with the moral law. To put it in the terms of St. Thomas Aquinas: An unjust law is a human law that is not rooted in eternal law and natural law. Any law that uplifts human personality is just. Any law that degrades human personality is unjust. All segregation statutes are unjust because segregation distorts the soul and damages the personality. It gives the segregator a false sense of superiority and the segregated a false sense of inferiority. <u>Segregation, to use the terminology of the Jewish philosopher Martin Buber, substitutes an "I-it" relationship for an "I-thou" relationship and ends up relegating persons to the status of things.</u> Hence segregation is not only politically, economically, and sociologically unsound, it is morally wrong and sinful. Paul Tillich has said that sin is separation. Is not segregation an existential expression of man's tragic separation, his awful estrangement, his terrible sinfulness? Thus it is that I can urge men to obey the 1954 decision of the Supreme Court, for it is morally right; and I can

Again King refers to a respected authority to support his argument.

urge them to disobey segregation ordinances, for they are morally wrong.

Let us consider a more concrete example of just and unjust laws. An unjust law is a code that a numerical or power majority group compels a minority group to obey but does not make binding on itself. This is difference made legal. By the same token, a just law is a code that a majority compels a minority to follow and that it is willing to follow itself. This is sameness made legal.

Let me give another explanation. A law is unjust if it is inflicted on a minority that, as a result of being denied the right to vote, had no part in enacting or devising the law. Who can say that the legislature of Alabama which set up that state's segregation laws was democratically elected? Throughout Alabama all sorts of devious methods are used to prevent Negroes from becoming registered voters, and there are some counties in which, even though Negroes constitute a majority of the population, not a single Negro is registered. Can any law enacted under such circumstances be considered democratically structured?

Again I think his evidence could be more specific —what methods?

Sometimes a law is just on its face and unjust in its application. For instance, I have been arrested on a charge of parading without a permit. Now, there is nothing wrong in having an ordinance which requires a permit for a parade. But such an ordinance becomes unjust when it is used to maintain segregation and to deny citizens the First-Amendment privilege of peaceful assembly and protest.

I hope you are able to see the distinction I am trying to point out. In no sense do I advocate evading or defying the law, as would the rabid segregationist. That would lead to anarchy. One who breaks an unjust law must do so openly, lovingly, and with a willingness to accept the penalty. I submit that an individual who breaks a law that conscience tells him is unjust, and who willingly accepts the penalty of imprisonment in order to arouse the conscience of the community over its injustice, is in reality expressing the highest respect for law.

Of course, there is nothing new about this kind of civil disobedience. It was evidenced sublimely in the refusal of Shadrach, Meshach, and Abednego to

These biblical allusions create a common ground between King and his audience.

obey the laws of Nebuchadnezzar, on the ground that a higher moral law was at stake. It was practiced superbly by the early Christians, who were willing to face hungry lions and the excruciating pain of chopping blocks rather than submit to certain unjust laws of the Roman empire. To a degree, academic freedom is a reality today because Socrates practiced civil disobedience. In our own nation, the Boston Tea Party represented a massive act of civil disobedience.

Wasn't Thoreau a big influence on M.L. King?

We should never forget that everything Adolph Hitler did in Germany was "legal" and everything the Hungarian fighters did in Hungary was "illegal." It was "illegal" to aid and comfort a Jew in Hitler's Germany. Even so, I am sure that, had I lived in Germany at the time, I would have aided and comforted my Jewish brothers. If today I lived in a Communist country where certain principles dear to the Christian faith are suppressed, I would openly advocate disobeying that country's antireligious laws.

This is a pretty challenging parallel to draw.

I must make two honest confessions to you, my Christian and Jewish brothers. First, I must confess that over the past few years I have been gravely disappointed with the white moderate. I have almost reached the regrettable conclusion that the Negro's great stumbling block in his stride toward freedom is not the White Citizen's Counciler or the Ku Klux Klanner, but the white moderate who is more devoted to "order" than to justice; who prefers a negative peace which is the absence of tension to a positive peace which is the presence of justice; who constantly says, "I agree with you in the goal you seek, but I cannot agree with your methods of direct action"; who paternalistically believes he can set the timetable for another man's freedom; who lives by a mythical concept of time and who constantly advises the Negro to wait for a "more convenient season." Shallow understanding from people of good will is more frustrating than absolute misunderstanding from people of ill will. Lukewarm acceptance is much more bewildering than outright rejection.

parallelism

I had hoped that the white moderate would understand that law and order exist for the purpose of establishing justice and that when they fail in this purpose they become the dangerously structured dams that block the flow of social progress. I had

strong metaphor

hoped that the white moderate would understand that the present tension in the South is a necessary phase of the transition from an obnoxious negative peace, in which the Negro passively accepted his unjust plight, to a substantive and positive peace, in which all men will respect the dignity and worth of human personality. Actually, we who engage in nonviolent direct action are not the creators of tension. We merely bring to the surface the hidden tension that is already alive. We bring it out in the open, where it can be seen and dealt with. Like a boil that can never be cured so long as it is covered up but must be opened with all its ugliness to the natural medicines of air and light, injustice must be exposed, with all the tension its exposure creates, to the light of human conscience and the air of national opinion, before it can be cured.

This is a great analogy—racism is something that festers beneath the surface.

Opposing argument #5

In your statement you assert that our actions, even though peaceful, must be condemned because they precipitate violence. But is this a logical assertion? Isn't this like condemning a robbed man because his possession of money precipitated the evil act of robbery? Isn't this like condemning Socrates because his unswerving commitment to truth and his philosophical inquiries precipitated the act by the misguided populace in which they made him drink hemlock? Isn't this like condemning Jesus because his unique God-consciousness and never-ceasing devotion to God's will precipitated the evil act of crucifixion? We must come to see that, as the federal courts have consistently affirmed, it is wrong to urge an individual to cease his efforts to gain his basic constitutional rights because the quest may precipitate violence. Society must protect the robbed and punish the robber.

False analogy maybe?

Isn't this a little weak? He uses rhetorical questions instead of specific evidence.

I had hoped that the white moderate would reject the myth concerning time in relation to the struggle for freedom. I have just received a letter from a white brother in Texas. He writes: "All Christians know that the colored people will receive equal rights eventually, but it is possible that you are in too great a religious hurry. It has taken Christianity almost two thousand years to accomplish what it has. The teachings of Christ take time to come to earth." Such an attitude stems from a tragic misconception of time, from the strangely irrational notion that there is something in the very flow of time that will inevitably cure all ills. <u>Actually, time itself is neutral; it can be used either destructively or constructively.</u> More and more I feel that the people of ill will have used time much more effectively than have the people of good will. <u>We will have to repent in this generation not merely for the hateful words and actions of the bad people, but for the appalling silence of the good people.</u> Human progress never rolls in on wheels of inevitability; it comes through the tireless efforts of men willing to be co-workers with God, and without this hard work, time itself becomes an ally of the forces of social stagnation. We must use time creatively, in the knowledge that the time is always ripe to do right. Now is the time to make real the promise of democracy and transform our pending national elegy into a creative psalm of brotherhood. Now is the time to lift our national policy from the quicksand of racial injustice to the solid rock of human dignity.

Opposing argument #6

Refutation

You speak of our activity in Birmingham as extreme. At first I was rather disappointed that fellow clergymen would see my nonviolent efforts as those of an extremist. I began thinking about the fact that I stand in the middle of two opposing forces in the Negro community. One is a force of complacency, made up in part of Negroes who, as a result of long years of oppression, are so drained of self-respect and a sense of "somebodiness" that they have adjusted to segregation; and in part of a few middle-class Negroes who, because of a degree of academic and economic security and because in some ways they profit by segregation, have become insensitive to the problems of the masses. The other force is one of bitterness and hatred, and it comes perilously close to advocating violence. It is expressed in the various black nationalist groups that are springing up across the nation, the largest and best-known being Elijah Muhammad's Muslim movement. Nourished by the Negro's frustration over the continued existence of racial discrimination, this movement is made up of people who have lost faith in America, who have absolutely repudiated Christianity, and who have concluded that the white man is an incorrigible "devil."

I have tried to stand between these two forces, saying that we need (emulate) neither the "do-nothingism" of the complacent nor the hatred and despair of the black nationalist. <u>For there is the more excellent way of love and nonviolent protest.</u> I am grateful to God that, through the influence of the Negro church, the way of nonviolence became an integral part of our struggle.

He constantly reminds his audience of this.

If this philosophy had not emerged, by now many streets of the South would, I am convinced, be flowing with blood. And I am further convinced that if our white brothers dismiss as "rabble-rousers" and "outside agitators" those of us who employ nonviolent direct action, and if they refuse to support our nonviolent efforts, millions of Negroes will, out of frustration and despair, seek (solace) and security in black-nationalist (ideologies)—a development that would inevitably lead to a frightening racial nightmare.

Oppressed people cannot remain oppressed forever. The yearning for freedom eventually manifests itself, and that is what has happened to the American Negro. Something within has reminded him of his birthright of freedom, and something without has reminded him that it can be gained. Consciously or unconsciously, he has been caught up by the Zeitgeist, and with his black brothers of Africa and his brown and yellow brothers of Asia, South America, and the Caribbean, the United States Negro is moving with a sense of great urgency toward the promised land of racial justice. If one recognizes this vital urge that has engulfed the Negro community, one should readily understand why public demonstrations are taking place. The Negro has many pent-up resentments and (latent) frustrations, and <u>he</u> must release them. So let <u>him</u> march; let <u>him</u> make prayer pilgrimages to the city hall; let <u>him</u> go on freedom rides—and try to understand why he must do so. <u>If his repressed emotions are not released in nonviolent ways, they will seek expression through violence; this is not a threat but a fact of history.</u> So I have not said to my people, "Get rid of your discontent." Rather, I have tried to say that this normal and healthy discontent can be channeled into the creative outlet of nonviolent

Rhetorical questions create strong tone.

Again parallelism is used for emotional emphasis.

King wants to connect Christian tradition with American history.

direct action. And now this approach is being termed extremist.

But though I was initially disappointed at being categorized as an extremist, as I continued to think about the matter I gradually gained a measure of satisfaction from the label. Was not Jesus an extremist for love: "Love your enemies, bless them that curse you, do good to them that hate you, and pray for them which despitefully use you, and persecute you." Was not Amos an extremist for justice: "Let justice roll down like waters and righteousness like an everflowing stream." Was not Paul an extremist for the Christian gospel: "I bear in my body the marks of the Lord Jesus." Was not Martin Luther an extremist: "Here I stand; I cannot do otherwise, so help me God." And John Bunyan: "I will stay in jail to the end of my days before I make a butchery of my conscience." And Abraham Lincoln: "This nation cannot survive half slave and half free." And Thomas Jefferson: "We hold these truths to be self-evident, that all men are created equal. . . ." So the question is not whether we will be extremists, but what kind of extremists we will be. Will we be extremists for hate or for love? Will we be extremists for the preservation of injustice or for the extension of justice? In that dramatic scene on Calvary's hill three men were crucified. We must never forget that all three were crucified for the same crime—the crime of extremism. Two were extremists for immorality, and thus fell below their environment. The other, Jesus Christ, was an extremist for love, truth, and goodness, and thereby rose above his environment. Perhaps the South, the nation, and the world are in dire need of creative extremists.   ✓

I had hoped that the white moderate would see this need. Perhaps I was too optimistic; perhaps I expected too much. I suppose I should have realized that few members of the oppressor race can understand the deep groans and passionate yearnings of the oppressed race, and still fewer have the vision to see that injustice must be rooted out by strong, persistent, and determined action. I am thankful, however, that some of our white brothers in the South have grasped the meaning of this social revolution and committed themselves to it. They are still all too few in quantity, but they are big in quality. Some—such as Ralph McGill, Lillian Smith, Harry Golden, James McBridge Dabbs, Ann Braden, and Sarah Patton Boyle—have written about our struggle in eloquent and prophetic terms. Others have marched with us down nameless streets of the South. They have languished in filthy, roach-infested jails, suffering the abuse and brutality of policemen who view them as "dirty nigger-lovers." Unlike so many of their moderate brothers and sisters, they have recognized the urgency of the moment and sensed the need for powerful "action" antidotes to combat the disease of segregation.

Let me take note of my other major disappointment. I have been so greatly disappointed with the white church and its leadership. Of course, there are some notable exceptions. I am not unmindful of the fact that each of you has taken some significant stands on this issue. I commend you, Reverend Stallings, for your Christian stand on this past Sunday, in welcoming Negroes to your worship service on a nonsegregational basis. I commend the Catholic leaders of this state for integrating Spring Hill College several years ago.

But despite these notable exceptions, I must honestly reiterate that I have been disappointed with the church. I do not say this as one of those negative critics who can always find something wrong with the church. I say this as a minister of the gospel, who loves the church; who was nurtured in its bosom; who has been sustained by its spiritual blessings and who will remain true to it as long as the cord of life shall lengthen.

When I was suddenly catapulted into the leadership of the bus protest in Montgomery, Alabama, a few years ago, I felt we would be supported by the white church. I felt that the white ministers, priests, and rabbis of the South would be among our strongest allies. Instead, some have been outright opponents, refusing to understand the freedom movement and misrepresenting its leaders; all too many others have been more cautious than courageous and have remained silent behind the anesthetizing security of stained-glass windows.

In spite of my shattered dreams, I came to Birmingham with the hope that the white religious leadership of this community would see the justice of our cause and, with deep moral concern, would serve as the channel through which our just grievances could reach the power structure. I had hoped that each of you would understand. But again I have been disappointed.

I have heard numerous southern religious leaders (admonish) their worshipers to comply with a desegregation decision because it is the law, but I have longed to hear white ministers declare: "Follow this decree because integration is morally right and because the Negro is your brother." In the midst of blatant injustices inflicted upon the Negro, I have watched white churchmen stand on the sideline and mouth pious irrelevancies and (sanctimonious) trivialities. In the midst of a mighty struggle to rid our nation of racial and economic injustice, I have heard many ministers say: "Those are social issues, with which the gospel has no real concern." And I have watched many churches commit themselves to a completely otherworldly religion which makes a strange, un-Biblical distinction between body and soul, between the sacred and the secular.

I have traveled the length and breadth of Alabama, Mississippi, and all the other southern states. On sweltering summer days and crisp autumn mornings I have looked at the South's beautiful churches with their lofty spires pointing heavenward. I have beheld the impressive outlines of her massive religious-education buildings. Over and over I have found myself asking: "What kind of people worship here? Who is their God? Where were their voices when the lips of Governor Barnett dripped with words of (interposition) and nullification? Where were they when Governor Wallace gave a clarion call for defiance and hatred? Where were their voices of support when bruised and weary Negro men and women decided to rise from the dark dungeons of complacency to the bright hills of creative protest?"

Again, series of questions creates strong tone.

Opposition

Yes, these questions are still in my mind. In deep disappointment I have wept over the (laxity) of the church. But be assured that my tears have been tears of love. There can be no deep disappointment where there is not deep love. Yes, I love the church. How could I do otherwise? I am in the rather unique position of being the son, the grandson, and the great-grandson of preachers. Yes, I see the church as the body of Christ. But, oh! <u>How we have blemished and scarred that body through social neglect and through fear of being nonconformists.</u>

There was a time when the church was very powerful—in the time when the early Christians rejoiced at being deemed worthy to suffer for what they believed. In those days the church was not merely a thermometer that recorded the ideas and principles of popular opinion; it was a thermostat that transformed the mores of society. Whenever the early Christians entered a town, the people in power became disturbed and immediately sought to convict the Christians for being "disturbers of the peace" and "outside agitators." But the Christians pressed on, in the conviction that they were "a colony of heaven," called to obey God rather than man. Small in number, they were big in commitment. They were too God-intoxicated to be "astronomically intimidated." By their effort and example they brought an end to such ancient evils as infanticide and gladiatorial contests.

<u>Things are different now.</u> So often the <u>contemporary church is a weak, ineffectual voice with an uncertain sound. So often it is an archdefender of the status quo. Far from being disturbed by the presence of the church, the power structure of the average community is consoled by the church's silent—and often even vocal—sanction of things as they are.</u>

But the judgment of God is upon the church as never before. If today's church does not recapture the sacrificial spirit of the early church, it will lose its authenticity, forfeit the loyalty of millions, and be dismissed as an irrelevant social club with no meaning for the twentieth century. <u>Every day I meet young people whose disappointment with the church has turned into outright disgust.</u>

Perhaps I have once again been too optimistic. Is organized religion too inextricably bound to the status quo to save our nation and the world? Perhaps I must turn my faith to the inner spiritual church, the church within the church, as the true ekklesia and the hope of the world. But again I am thankful to God that some noble souls from the ranks of organized religion have broken loose from the

[margin note:] Note use of 'we' here — King wants to create an impression of unity, rather than one of alienation.

paralyzing chains of conformity and joined us as active partners in the struggle for freedom. They have left their secure congregations and walked the streets of Albany, Georgia, with us. They have gone down the highways of the South on tortuous rides for freedom. Yes, they have gone to jail with us. Some have been dismissed from their churches, have lost the support of their bishops and fellow ministers. But they have acted in the faith that right defeated is stronger than evil triumphant. Their witness has been the spiritual salt that has preserved the true meaning of the gospel in these troubled times. They have carved a tunnel of hope through the dark mountain of disappointment.

I hope the church as a whole will meet the challenge of this decisive hour. But even if the church does not come to the aid of justice, I have no despair about the future. I have no fear about the outcome of our struggle in Birmingham, even if our motives are at present misunderstood. We will reach the goal of freedom in Birmingham and all over the nation, because the goal of America is freedom. Abused and scorned though we may be, our destiny is tied up with America's destiny. Before the pilgrims landed at Plymouth we were here. Before the pen of Jefferson etched the majestic words of the Declaration of Independence across the pages of history, we were here. For more than two centuries our forebears labored in this country without wages; they made cotton king; they built the homes of their masters while suffering gross injustice and shameful humiliation—and yet out of a bottomless vitality they continued to thrive and develop. If the inexpressible cruelties of slavery could not stop us, the opposition we now face will surely fail. We will win our freedom because the sacred heritage of our nation and the eternal will of God are embodied in our echoing demands.

This is an important aspect of his argument—the fate of the black Americans is linked with the fate of the nation as a whole.

*

Before closing I feel impelled to mention one other point in your statement that has troubled me profoundly. You warmly commended the Birmingham police force for keeping "order" and "preventing violence." I doubt that you would have so warmly commended the police force if you had seen its dogs sinking their teeth into unarmed, nonviolent Negroes. I doubt that you would so

more parallelism

quickly commend the policemen <u>if you were to</u>
<u>observe</u> their ugly and inhumane treatment of
Negroes here in the city jail; <u>if you were to watch</u>
them push and curse old Negro women and young
Negro girls; if you were to see them slap and kick old
Negro men and young boys; <u>if you were to observe</u>
<u>them,</u> as they did on two occasions, refuse to give us
food because we wanted to sing our grace together. I
cannot join you in your praise of the Birmingham
police department.

emotional language

    <u>It is true that the police have exercised a degree</u>
<u>of discipline in handling the demonstrators.</u> In this
sense they have conducted themselves rather
"nonviolently" in public. But for what purpose? To
preserve the evil system of segregation. Over the
past few years I have consistently preached that
nonviolence demands that the means we use must be
as pure as the ends we seek. I have tried to make
clear that it is wrong to use immoral means to attain
moral ends. But now I must affirm that it is just as
wrong, or perhaps even more so, to use moral means
to preserve immoral ends. Perhaps Mr. Connor and
his policemen have been rather nonviolent in public,
as was Chief Pritchett in Albany, Georgia, but they
have used the moral means of nonviolence to
maintain the immoral end of racial injustice. <u>As T. S.</u>
<u>Eliot has said, "The last temptation is the greatest</u>
<u>treason: To do the right deed for the wrong reason."</u>

Concedes opposing point of view but immediately modifies it.

    I wish you had commended the Negro sit-inners
and demonstrators of Birmingham for their sublime
courage, their willingness to suffer, and their
amazing discipline in the midst of great provocation.
One day the South will recognize its real heroes.
<u>They will be</u> the James Merediths, with the noble
sense of purpose that enables them to face jeering
and hostile mobs, and with the agonizing loneliness
that characterizes the life of the pioneer. <u>They will</u>
be old, oppressed, battered Negro women,
symbolized in a seventy-two-year-old woman in
Montgomery, Alabama, who rose up with a sense of
dignity and with her people decided not to ride
segregated buses, and who responded with
ungrammatical profundity to one who inquired
about her weariness: "My feets is tired, but my soul
is at rest." <u>They will be</u> the young high school and
college students, the young ministers of the gospel

and a host of their elders, courageously and nonviolently sitting in at lunch counters and willingly going to jail for conscience' sake. <u>One day the South will know that when these disinherited children of God sat down at lunch counters, they were in reality standing up for what is best in the American dream and for the most sacred values in our Judaeo-Christian heritage, thereby bringing our nation back to those great wells of democracy which were dug deep by the founding fathers in their formulation of the Constitution and the Declaration of Independence.</u>

Never before have I written so long a letter. I'm afraid it is much too long to take your precious time. I can assure you that it would have been much shorter if I had been writing from a comfortable desk, but what else can one do when he is alone in a narrow jail cell, other than write long letters, think long thoughts, and pray long prayers?

appeal to emotion

appeal to character

If I have said anything in this letter that overstates the truth and indicates an unreasonable impatience, I beg you to forgive me. If I have said anything that understates the truth and indicates my having a patience that allows me to settle for anything less than brotherhood, I beg God to forgive me.

King addresses his audience directly to establish personal tone.

I hope this letter finds you strong in the faith. I also hope that circumstances will soon make it possible for me to meet each of you, not as an integrationist or a civil-rights leader but as a fellow clergyman and a Christian brother. Let us all hope that <u>the dark clouds of racial prejudice</u> will soon pass away and the <u>deep fog of misunderstanding</u> will be lifted from our <u>fear-drenched communities</u>, and in some not too distant tomorrow the <u>radiant stars</u> of love and brotherhood will shine over our great nation with all their scintillating beauty.

Figurative language here—to stir his readers' imaginations by reminding his audience of their common national identity.

Yours for the cause of Peace and Brotherhood,
MARTIN LUTHER KING, JR.

Ferguson's Outline of Argument

This letter was written by King as a direct answer to the criticisms made by eight clergymen that his involvement in the Birmingham demonstrations was "unwise and untimely." For the most part, the essay consists of a point-by-point refutation of his opponents' arguments.

POINT 1: As an "outsider," King has not right to be in Birmingham.
Refutation:
(a) As president of the Southern Christina Leadership Conference, King was invited by the Birmingham affiliate to take part in the demonstrations.
(b) As a Christian, King cannot ignore injustice, but must respond to any "call for aid" no matter where it comes from.
(c) The term "outside agitator" is dated and narrow-minded. "Injustice anywhere is a threat to justice everywhere."

POINT 2: The demonstrations in Birmingham were deplorable and cannot be justified.
Refutation:
(a) The Negro community had no choice. Birmingham is one of the most segregated cities in the country.
(b) Previous attempts at negotiation had failed.
(c) Self-purification workshops were held to ensure that the demonstrations were peaceful.
(d) Direct action is the only way to force a complacent system to face the issue.

POINT 3: The new Boutwell administration should have been given time to act.
Refutation:
The new administration is also segregationist and will not act without direct pressure from the Negro community.

POINT 4: The civil rights movement is hypocritical in its willingness to break certain laws while upholding others.
Refutation:
Only just laws should be obeyed.

POINT 5: Direct action leads to violence.
Refutation:
It is illogical to condemn peaceful protestors for precipitating violence. The fault lies with those who seek to disrupt the demonstrations. Those seeking their

constitutional rights should be protected from violence by law.

POINT 6: King's activity in Birmingham has been extreme.
Refutation:
King does, in fact, occupy a moderate position between the two extremes of violence and passivity. Without this moderate position, the streets of the South would be "flowing with blood."

King then expresses his disappointment with both the white moderate and the white church. He criticizes the church in particular for its lack of moral initiative, its lack of strong leadership, and its failure to support the civil rights movement.

King's last main point is that it is the demonstrators who should be commended for their self-control, not the police. He calls for the recognition of the "real heroes" of the civil rights movement, such as the "James Merediths."

The essay concludes on a uplifting note as King expresses his hope that "the dark clouds of racial prejudice will soon pass away . . . and in some not too distant tomorrow the radiant stars of love and brotherhood will shine over our great nation with all their scintillating beauty."

Excerpt from Ferguson's Double-Entry Notebook

Quotes and Summaries

"I doubt you would have so warmly commended the police force if you had seen its dogs sinking their teeth into unarmed, nonviolent Negroes."

Reactions

King really knows how to use language to involve the reader emotionally. His reasonable tone allows him to do this without losing his reader's trust. So rather than just saying 'dogs attacking Negroes' he says "dogs *sinking* their teeth into *unarmed, nonviolent* Negroes." He's making an appeal to emotion here and uses parallelism to increase the effect ("if you were to watch," "if you were to see" etc.). His use of the word "Negro" makes me kind

Quotes and Summaries	Reactions
	of uncomfortable. It seems so dated now. At first it makes it seem as though a lot has changed since King wrote this essay. But how much is different? really? We hardly live in an equitable society. Maybe that's why "Negro" bothers me so much. We've made the terminology "politically correct" but the injustices remain.
King concedes that the police officers may have appeared restrained in public, but argued that their behavior is still indefensible. No actions can be considered moral if they are used for immoral purposes.	King doesn't want to antagonize his audience, so he sometimes concedes the opposing point of view. Here he quickly turns the point around so that his own argument doesn't lose any ground. Nonviolent law enforcement cannot be commended if it is used to enforce unjust laws. It's important that King addresses this point because otherwise he might seem to be avoiding the issue. I mean, ignoring evidence in favor of the police would make him look biased. Instead, he makes this possible weakness into one of his strengths.
As T. S. Eliot has said, "The last temptation is the greatest treason: To do the right deed for the wrong reason."	King does this a lot—brings in some respected individual to support his argument. It shows that he is writing for a literate audience, and also that King himself is well-educated (appeal to character again).

Quotes and Summaries

Reactions

King suggests that his fellow clergymen commend the demonstrators for their self-control, not the police.

I admire King for his forthright criticisms of the white church. He's not afraid to say what he really thinks, despite his non-confrontational approach. I wonder how these clergymen reacted to the letter. I imagine it made them pretty uncomfortable. I hope so.

"One day the South will recognize its real heroes."

I've come to realize through studying this essay that there is a reason for everything King does. Here I think he is deliberately bringing the focus back to ordinary people after a lot of fairly abstract discussion. The "My feets is tired but my soul is at rest" quote suddenly makes it all real. You can feel the struggle and frustration. Again King uses parallelism for emphasis.

One day the South will know that when these disinherited children of God sat down at lunch counters, they were in reality standing up for what is best in the American dream and for the most sacred values in our Judaeo-Christian heritage, thereby bringing our nation back to those great wells of democracy which were dug deep by the founding fathers in their formulations of the Constitution and the Declaration of Independence.

I've quoted this whole passage because I think it's one of the most important in the whole essay. It gives the civil rights movement an historical context—this is not just about one town in the South; it's about American and Christian traditions. This prevents people from seeing the protest movement as "outside agitation." In referring to the Constitution etc. King is playing on his audience's patriotic feelings and trying to stir their emotions. I think this is a legitimate tactic. He's not distorting anything—the

Quotes and Summaries	Reactions

Reactions: American dream is meant to be about freedom and equality for all. But he is being quite clever here—these patriotic references ensure that no one can accuse him of being "unAmerican."

I like the opposition between "sat down" and "standing up."

"Let us all hope that the dark clouds of racial prejudice will soon pass away and the deep fog of misunderstanding will be lifted from our fear-drenched communities, and in some not too distant tomorrow the radiant stars of love and brotherhood will shine over our great nation with all their scintillating beauty."

King really likes long sentences. The repetition of "hope" is important—King wants to lift the tone of the essay and end on a positive note. He wants to involve the reader emotionally so he uses a lot of figurative language. The "dark clouds" and "deep fog" are contrasted with the "radiant stars." (Religious imagery here? Dark vs light etc.) The reference to "our great nation" reminds the audience again of common national identity. These final sentences are uplifting and inspiring, but they rather depress me, too. We are still waiting for those "radiant stars of love and brotherhood" to shine. Has King's "not too distant tomorrow" come much closer in the past thirty years, or not?

Ferguson's First Draft

"Letter from Birmingham Jail" is a powerful, persuasive essay which argues for the necessity of direct, nonviolent action to end racial segregation in the city of Birmingham in 1963. King wrote it while in solitary confinement, in response to the published criticisms of eight white clergymen, but its scope goes far beyond that of a personal letter. In the course of the essay's pages, King demonstrates the most important aspects of argument, such as the use of appeals to character, emotion, and reason, logical structure and development, and the effective refutation of the opposition. Through reading "Letter from Birmingham Jail" I have a greater appreciation of persuasive writing and also of Martin Luther King himself.

King begins by establishing his own credibility—as the president of the Southern Christian Leadership Conference, he has a great deal of experience in the civil rights movement. This is part of the appeal to character which King maintains all the way through the essay. Aware that his audience is not sympathetic to his position, King also seeks to establish common ground between them by emphasizing their mutual involvement in the church. Himself a preacher, King draws attention to his thoroughly respectable background, "I am in the rather unique position of being the son, the grandson, and the great-grandson of preachers." By making a great many Biblical allusions, King hopes to win the trust of his opponents and so lead them towards his way of thinking. For the same reason, he presents their point of view in a calm and reasonable manner, "It is true that the police have exercised a degree of discipline in handling the demonstrators. In this sense, they have conducted themselves nonviolently in public. But for what purpose? To preserve the vile system of segregation." By fairly presenting the opposing point of view, which King does through the essay, he shows that he is unbiased and objective and, therefore, trustworthy.

The reasonable tone and the strong appeal to character allow King to manipulate his audience emotionally without losing his own credibility. He does this through the skillful use of such devices as vivid detail, metaphorical language, parallelism, and repetition. For instance, in response to the criticism that the campaign was "untimely," King creates a sharp metaphorical contrast to emphasize the natural impatience of the African American community,

> "We have waited more than 340 years for our constitutional and God-given rights. The nations of Africa and Asia are moving with jetlike speed toward gaining political independence, but we still creep at horse and buggy pace toward gaining a cup of coffee at a lunch counter."

King builds on this point by using a great deal of vivid detail, as in "when you have seen hate-filled policemen

> curse, kick, and even kill your Negro brothers and sisters; when you see the vast majority of your Negro brothers smothering in an airtight cage of poverty in the midst of an affluent society . . ."

This appeal to emotion is further strengthened through parallelism and repetition as King lists examples of his own personal humiliations. The reader cannot help but feel shocked and disgusted by these many injustices and must agree with King's final comment, "I hope, sirs, you can understand our legitimate and unavoidable impatience."

King also makes constant appeals to reason when refuting the opposing point of view, most notably when answering the criticism that the movement was too ready to break the law. While King agrees that this is "certainly a legitimate concern," he points out that "there are two types of law—just and unjust." In an extended appeal to reason, King argues that "An unjust law is a code that a numerical or power majority group compels a minority group to obey but does not make binding on itself." He then illustrates this by referring to the segregation laws of Alabama and further supports his argument by bringing in the opinions of respected individuals such as Paul Tillich and Martin Buber. King deliberately and methodically makes the distinction between just and unjust laws, and again draws on the Bible to remind his audience of the common ground between them.

In his powerful and moving conclusion, King expresses his hope that "the dark clouds of racial prejudice will soon pass away." A great deal may have changed in the thirty years since King wrote "Letter from Birmingham Jail," but we are still waiting for "the radiant stars of love and brotherhood" to shine over "our great nation." Racism is still a "hidden tension" in our society, and we desperately need "creative extremists" such as Martin Luther King to bring it to the surface and cure it. The value of this essay is not just that it demonstrates the most important features of persuasive writing, but that it reminds us that racism is something that affects us all in our common identity as American citizens. As King said of himself and his followers, "our destiny is tied up with America's destiny."

An Analysis of "Letter from Birmingham Jail"

Ferguson's Final Draft

1 "Letter from Birmingham Jail" was written by Martin Luther King in 1963 while he was being held in solitary confinement for daring to lead a protest march against the city's segregationist policies. It is a direct response to the statement published by eight white clergymen criticizing King's direct action campaign, but its scope goes far beyond that of a personal letter. Rather than being simply a justification of his own actions, King's carefully constructed and eloquently worded argument is a justification of the civil rights movement itself. In his lengthy essay, King systematically addresses each of his opponents' points, refutes them in turn, and concludes with a series of his own criticisms of white moderates and church leaders. "Letter from Birmingham Jail" is a remarkable piece of persuasive writing which demonstrates both the principal features of argument and those individual aspects of King's style which made him such a powerful preacher and political activist.

2 Perhaps, the essay's greatest strength is King's non-confrontational or Rogerian approach to the argument. To avoid antagonizing an unsympathetic audience, King must appear to be a reasonable, well-informed individual whose views on this sensitive issue can be trusted. This is done very effectively in a number of ways. For instance, at the start of the essay he establishes his own credibility by describing his involvement in the Southern Christian Leadership Conference. As the president of this respected organization, it can be assumed that he has a great deal of experience in the civil rights movement. Furthermore, King constantly emphasizes his own involvement in the Church, pointing out that he is "the son, the grandson, and the great-grandson of preachers." He also compares himself with famous Christian figures, "Like Paul, I must constantly respond to the Macedonian call for aid." These somewhat obscure Biblical allusions not only show that King is thoroughly familiar with the Scriptures, but also establish a common ground between two adversaries who have little else in common but the Church. To further lessen any sense of conflict King refers to his fellow clergymen as "my friends" and "my Christian and Jewish brothers" and calls them "men of genuine good faith." Finally, King presents the opposing point of view in a calm and reasonable manner,

often conceding its validity before presenting his own case: "It is true that the police have exercised a degree of discipline in handling the demonstrators. In this sense they have conducted themselves "nonviolently" in public. But for what purpose? To preserve the vile system of segregation." By fairly addressing the opposition, King shows that he is unbiased and capable of viewing the situation objectively. Therefore, when he attacks the white church for its lack of leadership and moral initiative, his criticisms carry real weight.

3   This strong appeal to character is maintained throughout and allows King to play on his audience's emotions without losing his own credibility. He proceeds through the constant use of metaphorical language, vivid detail, parallelism, and repetition, all of which combine to create his own unique style. For instance, in response to the criticism that the direct action campaign was "untimely" King stresses the natural impatience of his people:

> We have waited more than 340 years for our constitutional and God-given rights. The nations of Africa and Asia are moving with jetlike speed toward gaining political independence, but we still creep at horse and buggy pace toward gaining a cup of coffee at a lunch counter.

The contrast of these metaphors causes the reader to feel the frustration and humiliation of segregation. King builds on this by combining further metaphor with vivid detail, as in "when you have seen hate-filled policemen curse, kick, and even kill your Negro brothers and sisters; when you see the vast majority of your Negro brothers smothering in an airtight cage of poverty in the midst of an affluent society . . ." This appeal to emotion is given even more impact through the skillful parallelism and repetition of "when you have seen . . . when you see . . . when you suddenly find . . . when you have to concoct . . ." The effect on the reader of this catalog of social injustice is one of shock and disgust, so that even the most conservative individual would have to concur with King's final comment, "I hope, sirs, you can understand our legitimate and unavoidable impatience." It is noteworthy that, despite the emotional intensity of this long passage, King never loses his self-control. With the simple insertion of "sirs" he maintains the modest and respectful tone which characterizes the whole essay.

4   While the appeals to character and emotion are arguably the most memorable aspects of the essay, King also makes constant appeals to reason in his defense of the direct action campaign in Birmingham. One of the best examples of his use of logic is his refutation of one of the most damaging criticisms of the movement—its "willingness to break laws." King concedes that this is "certainly a legitimate concern" but points out that "there are two types of law: just and unjust." In an extended appeal to reason, King argues that "An unjust law is a code that a numerical or power majority group compels a minority group to obey but does not make binding on itself." He then illustrates this general statement with a specific example:

> "Who can say that the legislature of Alabama which set up that state's segregation laws was democratically elected? Throughout Alabama all sorts of devious methods are used to prevent Negroes from becoming registered voters, and there are even some counties in which, even though Negroes constitute a majority of the population, not a single Negro is registered."

Perhaps King could have given more detailed evidence here, by describing the "devious methods" used and identifying the counties in question. He does, however, refer repeatedly to respected intellectuals such as Paul Tillich and Martin Buber to support his points, and it must be remembered that his essay was composed in a jail cell where there were no reference books.

5   In his powerful and moving conclusion, King expresses his hope that "the dark clouds of racial prejudice will soon pass away." The highly figurative language in this final paragraph creates another strong appeal to emotion, but this time the effect is one of promise and elation rather than shock and disgust. Throughout the letter, King has made references to the American Dream, the Constitution, and symbolic figures such as Thomas Jefferson and Abraham Lincoln, and this is continued in "our great nation." These references not only stir positive, patriotic feelings in his audience but also create a feeling of a shared national identity. For me, the value of this essay is not just in its tone, its skillful use of appeals, or its powerful language, but in its reminder that racism is something which affects us all in our common cultural identity. As King said of himself and of his followers, "our destiny is tied up with America's destiny." This is something none of us should forget. A great deal may have changed in the thirty

years since King wrote "Letter from Birmingham Jail," but we are still waiting for "the radiant stars of love and brotherhood" to shine. Racism is still a "hidden tension" in our society and more than ever we need "creative extremists" such as Martin Luther King to bring it to the surface and to cure it.

In the final draft, the writer moves from a diffuse focus on imagery to a concentration on the three forms of appeal and the stylistic devices that create the appeals and that make them persuasive.

Part Four

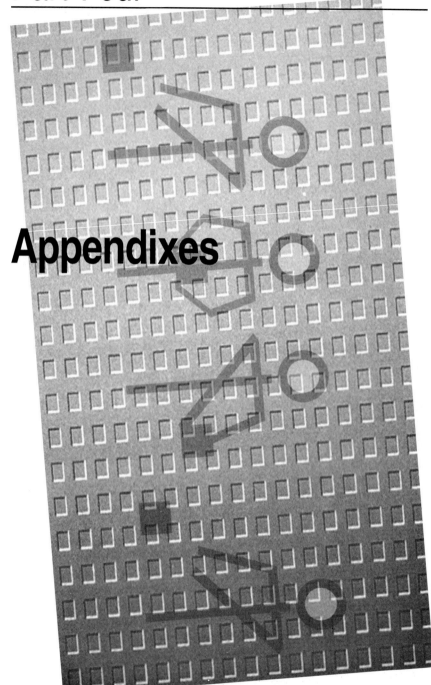

Appendixes

RESEARCH CASEBOOK:
D. H. LAWRENCE
"THE ROCKING-HORSE WINNER"

This casebook presents source materials, all of which provide significant information about D. H. Lawrence's "The Rocking-Horse Winner," which appears in the Thematic Preview in Chapter 5. Each of the articles contains information and interpretations of the short story; each offers the reader opportunities to expand his or her comprehension of the work. The letter from Lawrence represents a **primary source** about the writer's life. The varying views of critics, **secondary sources**, explore psychological, feminist, social, political, and stylistic aspects of "The Rocking-Horse Winner" and of Lawrence's fiction in general. These divergent perspectives will enrich your understanding of the story.

1. Correspondence: Letter from D. H. Lawrence to Rachel Annand Taylor
   Trilling, Diana, ed. *The Selected Letters of D. H. Lawrence.* New York: Farrar, Straus, and Giroux, 1958. 6–8.
2. Source Material
   Meyers, Jeffrey. *D. H. Lawrence: A Biography.* New York: Knopf, 1990. 120–123.
3. Source Material
   Nehls, Edward, ed. *D. H. Lawrence: A Composite Biography.* Volume 3, *1925–1930.* Madison: University of Wisconsin Press, 1959. 43–44.
4. Interpretation of Biographical Material
   Davies, Rosemary Reeves. "Lawrence, Lady Cynthia Asquith, and 'The Rocking-Horse Winner.'" *Studies in Short Fiction* 20 (1983): 121–126.
5. Sexual Motifs
   Snodgrass, W. D. "A Rocking Horse: The Symbol, The Pattern, The Way to Live." *The Hudson Review,* XI (Summer 1958): 191–200.

6. Style: Ironic and Fabular
    Padhi, Bibhu. *D. H. Lawrence: Modes of Fictional Style.* Troy: Whitson Publishing, 1989. 49–52.
7. Treatment of Women
    Pullin, Faith. "Lawrence's Treatment of Women in *Sons and Lovers." Lawrence and Women.* Ed. Anne Smith. London: Vision Press, 1978. 49–50.
8. Marxist Interpretation
    Watkins, Daniel P. "Labor and Religion in D. H. Lawrence's 'The Rocking-Horse Winner.'" *Studies in Short Fiction* 24 (1987): 295–301.

Correspondence

Letter from D. H. Lawrence to Rachel Annand Taylor

Lynn Croft Eastwood Notts, 3 Dec. 1910.

Dear Mrs. Taylor,
I did not know where you were. I am glad you wrote to me.

I have been at home now ten days. My mother is very near the end. Today I have been to Leicester. I did not get home till half past nine. Then I ran upstairs. Oh she was very bad. The pains had been again.

"Oh my dear" I said, "is it the pains?"

"Not pain now—oh the weariness" she moaned, so that I could hardly hear her. I wish she could die tonight.

My sister and I do all the nursing. My sister is only 22. I sit upstairs hours and hours till I wonder if ever it were true that I was at London. I seem to have died since, & that is an old life, dreamy.

I will tell you. My mother was a clever, ironical, delicately moulded woman of good, old burgher descent. She married below her. My father was dark, ruddy, with a fine laugh. He is a coal miner. He was one of the sanguine temperament, warm & hearty, but unstable: he lacked principle, as my mother would have said. He deceived her & lied to her. She despised him—he drank.

Their marriage life has been one carnal, bloody fight. I was born hating my father: as early as ever I can remember. I shivered with horror when he touched me. He was very bad before I was born.

This has been a kind of bond between me and my mother. We have loved each other, almost with a husband & wife love, as well as filial & maternal. We knew each other by instinct. She said to my aunt—about me:

"But it has been different with him. He has seemed to be part of me."—And that is the real case. We have been like one, so sensitive to each other that we never needed words. It has been rather terrible & has made me, in some respects, abnormal.

I think this peculiar fusion of soul (don't think me high-falutin) never comes twice in a life-time—it doesn't seem natural. When it comes it seems to distribute one's consciousness far abroad from oneself, & one understands! I think no one has got 'Understanding' except through love. Now my mother is nearly dead, and I don't quite know how I am.

I have been to Leicester today, I have met a girl who has always been warm for me—like a sunny happy day—and I've gone & asked her to marry me: in the train, quite unpremeditated, between Rothley & Quorn—she lives at Quorn. When I think of her I feel happy with a sort of warm radiation—she is big & dark and handsome. There were five other people in the carriage. Then when I think of my mother: if you've ever put your hand round the bowl of a champagne glass and squeezed it & wondered how near it is to crushing-in & the wine all going through your fingers—that's how my heart feels—like the champagne glass. There is no hostility between the warm happiness & the crush of misery: but one is concentrated in my chest, & one is diffuse—a suffusion, vague.

Muriel is the girl I have broken with. She loves me to madness, & demands the soul of me. I have been cruel to her, & wronged her, but I did not know.

Nobody can have the soul of me. My mother has had it, & nobody can have it again. Nobody can come into my very self again, and breathe me like an atmosphere. Don't say I am hasty this time—I know. Louie—whom I wish I could marry the day after the funeral—she would never demand to drink me up & have me. She loves me—but it is a fine, warm, healthy, natural love—not like Jane Eyre, who is Muriel, but like—say Rhoda Fleming or a commoner Anna Karénin. She will never plunge her hands through my blood & feel for my soul, & make me set my teeth & shiver & fight away. Ugh—I have done well—& cruelly—tonight.

I look at my father—he is like a cinder. It is very terrible, mismarriage.

They sent me yesterday one copy of the Peacock for my mother. She just looked at it. It will not be out till spring.

I will tell you next time about that meeting when I gave a paper on you. It was *most* exciting. I worked my audience up to red heat—& I laughed.

Are you any better?—you don't say so. Tell me you are getting strong, & then you & I will not re-act so alarmingly—at least, you on me.

Goodnight,
D. H. Lawrence.

Source Material

From: D. H. Lawrence: A Biography

Jeffrey Meyers

Lawrence was drawn to lovely, lonely, titled and tragic ladies with artistic temperaments. These women accepted him as a didactic prophet and spiritual adviser who analyzed, interpreted and re-created their lives in his art.

In July 1913, while Lawrence and Frieda were on a seaside holiday at Broadstairs in Kent, Edward Marsh introduced them to Lady Cynthia Asquith, a "radiant *quattrocento* beauty" with perfect features and "heavy gold hair falling to her knees." Lawrence portrayed Cynthia as Lady Daphne in "The Ladybird," describing her elegance and refinement as well as the subtlety of her skin and hair: "Her face was lovely, fair, with a soft exotic white complexion and delicate pink cheeks. Her hair was soft and heavy, of a lovely pallid gold colour, ash-blond. Her hair, her complexion were so perfectly cared for."

Cynthia, the daughter of the eleventh Earl of Wemyss, was born in a great country house in Wiltshire in 1887. She was educated at Cheltenham Ladies' College, presented at court, painted by John Singer Sargent and by Augustus John. In 1910 she had married Herbert Asquith, a barrister and the second son of the prime minister, who had been president of the Oxford Union and had once nourished political ambitions. They had two sons: John, born in 1911, and Michael, born in 1914. Herbert had practiced law unsuccessfully, then spent four years on active service in France and Flanders. He was badly shell-shocked in the war, found it difficult to live up to his father's name, tried to be a poet and man of letters, and worked for Hutchinson publishers. Unlike her sisters, Cynthia married a man with no money and received only a small dowry. Surrounded by the rich, she was always short of cash. During the war, when she had to live on Herbert's subaltern's pay, she became secretary, companion and confidante to the playwright Sir James Barrie. She worked for Barrie for twenty years and was left a considerable legacy when he died, in 1937.

Cynthia, an extremely sympathetic woman, was a lively though not mischievous gossip. She loved cultivating intimate but not sexual friendships with men as different as the literary critic Desmond MacCarthy and the distinguished New Zealand general, Bernard Freyberg.

According to her son Michael, Lawrence was a bit naive about the extent of her political power, for she was more a social chameleon or a "long swaying water-weed" than a kingmaker. She did not have much influence on the prime minister and, in any case, would have been reluctant to use it.

Michael was critical, even resentful, of the glamorous yet elusive figure who, like many women of her class, neglected her children and was not a good mother. He felt she was too ambitious for her sons, made them part of

her own aura and vanity, and forced them to follow the difficult and sometimes impossible plans she had made for them. Her love seemed conditional
on their success; and Michael, always in and out of favor, resented having to
play courtier. Her elder son, John, who was thought to be brain damaged by
a forceps at birth but was actually an undiagnosed autistic, she considered
a blemish. John was always disobedient and subject to violent outbursts;
and they did not know enough about his illness at that time to be able to
help him.

Class differences—with Cynthia as with Frieda—made the friendship interesting on both sides. Lawrence was attracted to sympathetic upper-class
women, Cynthia was drawn to Lawrence's literary genius, to his utter absorp-
tion in the task of the moment and to the extraordinary vitality of the man
she called "half-faun, half-prophet." Illness was one common factor that
drew them together (as it did Lawrence, Mansfield and Gertler), for in March
1913 (only four months before she met Lawrence) Cynthia had been diagnosed as tubercular. She spent three months in a sanatorium on the river Dee
in Scotland and had just been released, apparently cured but still not free of
suspicion.

An entry in Cynthia's diaries suggests the numerous reasons for her attraction to Lawrence. Unlike many of his friends—most notably Kot, Morrell,
Russell and Brett—she liked Frieda, got along well with her and did not
arouse her jealousy. She found Lawrence intellectually alive, mentally stimulating and personally acute, and compared being with him to the Christian
festival that celebrates the descent of the Holy Ghost on the apostles:

> I find them the most intoxicating company in the world. I never hoped to
> have such mental pleasure with anyone. It is so wonderful to be such a
> perfect à trois. I am so fond of her. She has spontaneousness and warm
> cleverness, and such adoration and understanding of him. He interests
> and attracts me quite enormously. His talk is so extraordinarily real and
> living—such humour and yet so much of the fierceness and resentment
> which my acquiescent nature loves and covets. He is a Pentecost to one,
> and has the gift of intimacy and such perceptiveness that he introduces
> one to oneself. I have never known such an X-ray psychologist.

Lawrence sometimes chided Cynthia for her superficiality and materialism.
She was sufficiently perceptive to realize that "she had a detachment, a dislike of reality, a fatal lack of self-knowledge," and hoped to acquire new insight from her friend.

Always interested in and sympathetic to children, Lawrence was positively riveted by the freakishness of her son John. Throughout the war
Lawrence tried to advise Cynthia (who had doubtless sought his help) about
how to deal with the remote and deeply troubled child. He perceived the boy's
resentment of her selfish demands (later articulated by Michael), believed
John had been repressed, warped and even possessed by an evil spirit that also
existed within his parents. (That Lawrence could state and Cynthia accept

this cruel criticism says a good deal about the strength of their friendship.) He tried to encourage her and (using a mechanical metaphor) offered to look after, help and perhaps even cure the boy:

> Your own soul is deficient, so it fights for the love of the child. . . . Put yourself aside with regard to him. You have no right to his love. Care only for his good and well-being: make *no* demands on him. . . .
>
> He is a direct outcome of repression and falsification of the living spirit, in many generations of the Charterises [Cynthia's family] and Asquiths. He is possessed by an evil spirit that *you* have kept safely inside yourself, cynic and unbelieving. . . . John will come out all right. If ever there is an opportunity, I will help with him. . . . Perhaps, if we felt it might be any good, Frieda and I might have him with us for a time. I'm certain there is nothing primarily wrong—only something locked in the running.

Lawrence's famous story "The Rocking-Horse Winner" (1926) was inspired by the desperate unhappiness in the Asquith family: by the parents' remoteness from each other (because of the war and its aftermath) as well as from the children, by Cynthia's obsession with money, by John's autistic frenzy and by the impossible demands she made on him. It portrays upper-class financial anxiety and social pretension, modern man's mad mechanical gallop for wealth and material goods, and the destruction of a family that chooses money above affection.

The opening paragraph, which echoes a fairy tale, describes the situation: "There was a woman who was beautiful, who started with all the advantages, yet she had no luck. . . . Everybody else said of her: 'She is such a good mother. She adores her children.' Only she herself, and her children themselves, knew it was not so. They read it in each other's eyes." The woman's anxiety and dissatisfaction are sexual as well as financial, and these two problems are linked. The wife seems sexually frigid. The anonymous and absent husband has no substance or significance and cannot give her what she wants. The parents' unhappiness encourages the boy's Oedipal urge to replace his father in his mother's affections. Despite her coldness and hard heart, the mother has ambivalent feelings about her children: she resents them and also has suppressed affection for them.

Paul's frantic riding on a toy horse becomes a substitute for maternal love—as money is for sexual love—and he makes a Faustian bargain with evil powers for forbidden knowledge. The extreme tension is gradually built up by the whispering house, estrangement of the children, financial troubles, anxiety about betting and Paul's frenzy on the toy horse. The rocking horse stands for real horses and actual races as well as for childish intuition and the instinctual rather than rational approach to experience. It also represents a self-induced, demonic and prophetic mania (analogous to John's illness) and the sexual act—or a child's imitation of the act—which goes and gets nowhere. Sex for Lawrence is the link between man and unknown powers.

And Paul's orgasmic release enables him to divine and declare the winner of the race. Driven by his devouring mother, and by his desire to win her favor and redeem her love, Paul restores the family fortune by sacrificing his own wretched life. "The Rocking-Horse Winner" is a brilliant example of how Lawrence, imagining the consequences of Cynthia's limitations, could transform his perception of a friend's life into fiction.

Source Material

From *D. H. Lawrence: A Composite Biography*

Earl H. Brewster

After leaving Ceylon [1922] we eventually returned to our old haunts, Torre dei Quattro Venti, Capri, where we remained during the next four years. In March, 1926, we were again preparing to go East. During this interval the Lawrences had travelled much—to New Mexico, Old Mexico, to Europe, back to America, and now they had returned again recently to Europe.

On the eve of our departure for India everything at Quattro Venti was being packed, when Lawrence had appeared, asking if it would be inconvenient to put him up. He was keener than ever about our getting a lugger and all of us going to the East by way of it; he recalled someone who had purchased an old freighter and when finally arriving in China had sold the boat at a profit. The lugger was postponed; but Lawrence promised to join us in India in the autumn if we advised it.

Out on the terrace of Quattro Venti, sitting in the spring sunshine, we were talking about the curse of money. He related his story of "The Rocking-Horse Winner," bringing money, but the little boy's death. The tale was told of a woman's inheriting a fortune, whereupon she bought herself a close collar of pearls; soon afterward a bee stung her on the throat, which swelled before the collar could be removed, choking her to death. Someone else recounted that a poor farmer inherited forest land which he sold for ten thousand dollars. When he was told it should have brought twenty thousand, he was so chagrined that he hanged himself on one of the trees. There seemed no end of such tales. Lawrence decided at once to write a volume of them under the title of *Tales of the Four Winds* from which the proceeds should be divided equally among us, that the curse of the riches should be shared by us all. We might invest them in a lugger.

Interpretation of Biographical Material

Lawrence, Lady Cynthia Asquith, and "The Rocking-Horse Winner"

Rosemary Reeves Davies

D. H. Lawrence's habit of making identifiable use of his friends and acquaintances in his novels and short stories has been well documented, as has his lack of concern for the possible distress such portraits might cause. Lady Ottoline Morrell and Philip Heseltine were outraged by their appearance in *Women in Love* as Hermione and Halliday, and although Lawrence tried to assure his friend Mark Gertler that he was not the model for the rat-like Loerke in the same novel, it is generally agreed that he was. John Middleton Murry, despite his admiration for Lawrence, was never able to forgive him for the group of short stories in which Murry is made to look ridiculous, and Compton Mackenzie was annoyed at finding himself the protagonist in "The Man Who Loved Islands." "England, My England," with its satiric portraits of Percy Lucas and the Meynell family, was published shortly before Lucas' death in France, and has been called Lawrence's "cruelest story *à clef*."[1] To these and other stories can be added another based upon a real-life situation, "The Rocking-Horse Winner."

This story was first published in the fall of 1926 in a collection called *The Ghost Book* assembled by Lawrence's longtime friend, Lady Cynthia Asquith. As I hope to show, the story was probably suggested by the tragic illness of Lady Cynthia's oldest son John and by the Asquith marriage itself.[2] Although it is unlikely that Lady Cynthia recognized herself in the character Hester, or connected her son's tragedy—at its height almost ten years before the story was written—with Paul, biographical materials demonstrate that Lawrence found in the Asquith household the ingredients for his story on destructive materialism.[3]

That Lawrence used these materials as he did is surprising because it is generally agreed that Lady Cynthia occupied a rather special place in his life. His biographer, Harry T. Moore, remarks that "Lawrence felt a respectful affection, if not love for her," and her *Diaries* show that she held the novelist in considerable esteem.[4] In her memoir, written many years after Lawrence's death,

---

[1] Harry T. Moore, *The Priest of Love* (New York: Farrar, Straus and Giroux, 1974), p. 10.

[2] Although I did not see his book until after my article was written, another scholar mentions Lady Cynthia and her son in connection with this story, but does not develop the parallel (Paul Delaney, *D. H. Lawrence's Nightmare* [New York: Basic Books, Inc., 1978], p.).

[3] For a refutation of the claim that Lawrence's story grew out of his visits to the household of Sir Charles Brooke, see my article "'The Rocking-Horse Winner' Again: A Correction," *Studies in Short Fiction*, 18 (Summer, 1981), 320–22.

[4] *The Priest of Love*, p. 222. George A Panichas has also written about the relationship between Lawrence and Lady Cynthia and confirms the love and respect between them. He suggests that the Asquiths represented for Lawrence the kindness and decency of the aristocratic England that was destroyed by the Great War ("The End of the Lamplight," *Modern Age*, XIV: 1 [1970], 65–74).

she speaks very warmly of him, stressing his electric aliveness and gentleness.[5] In other stories in which she is the model for the heroine, she is treated with tact and affection. An early sketch, "The Thimble," was intended as a "word-picture" of her, and was sent to her for her criticism. She was uneasy about its probable contents; having read *The Rainbow* in manuscript, she feared a "minute 'belly' analysis" of herself. But she was pleased by the story and found it "extremely well-written. . . . I think some of his character hints are damnably good."[6] Two later stories, *The Ladybird* and "Glad Ghosts," are also considered to contain heroines modeled on Lady Cynthia, both attractive figures.[7]

Not only is Lady Cynthia pleasantly presented, but most stories in which she was the model for the heroine do not end unhappily. In "The Thimble" the couple is re-born, and becomes capable of growing into full maturity and love as a result.[8] In *The Ladybird,* Lady Daphne, unfulfilled by her adoring husband, reaches unity of being through her love affair with Count Dionys. In "Glad Ghosts" Carlotta's husband, stimulated by the advice of a Lawrence-like house guest, suddenly gains insight into the importance of the body. His marriage is revitalized, his bad luck overcome, and Carlotta gives birth to a charming blond boy "like a little crocus" nine months later. (Lawrence had nicknamed Lady Cynthia's son "Jonquil.") Rather ambiguously, the guest is visited at night by a feminine ghost, and he is uncertain in the morning whether it was a ghost or a living woman.[9] It has been suggested that Lawrence decided against sending this story to Lady Cynthia because of the implications of its conclusion, and after considering it, submitted "The Rocking-Horse Winner" instead.[10]

Biographical materials will show the striking similarities between the Asquith family and the family in the story. Lady Cynthia, like Carlotta and Hester, was visited by very bad luck indeed in her firstborn son. In his infancy he seemed normal, and his charm and sweet temper delighted everyone.

---

[5] *Remember and Be Glad* (New York: Charles Scribner's Sons, 1952), pp. 133–50.

[6] *Diaries: 1915–1918,* ed. E. M. Horsley (New York: Alfred A. Knopf, 1969), pp. 94–95. Subsequent citations will be made in the text.

[7] Some doubts have been cast on her contribution to *The Ladybird.* George H. Ford reports that Lady Cynthia had told him in 1956 that she was not the model for Lady Daphne (*Double Measure* [New York: Holt, Rinehart and Winston, 1965], p. 231). However, an editorial note in her *Diaries* states that this story contains recognizable portraits of both her and her mother (p. 510). Additional evidence is found in the elaborate description of the country house in the story; it closely resembles Lady Cynthia's family home, Stanway House (*Diaries,* p. xiv).

[8] "The Thimble" is not included in *The Complete Short Stories,* but is reprinted in *Phoenix II,* ed. Warren Roberts and Harry T. Moore (New York: Penguin Books, 1978), pp. 53–63.

[9] Some evidence that Lawrence had the same person in mind when he created both Carlotta and Hester is contained in the stories themselves. Carlotta marries into a family known to be unlucky, and promises to have "luck for two." But her three children die, and she and her husband become "the living dead." Similarly, Hester "had no luck" and her love "turned to dust." Carlotta, in evening dress as her guest arrives, has "something glittering on a dull green dress." Hester enters her son's room after the party in "a dress of pale green and crystal."

[10] Moore, *The Priest of Love,* p. 415.

Lawrence in letters written in 1913 inquired about "the fat and smiling John," and asked, "How is the jonquil with the golden smile."[11] But by the time the boy was four years old, it had become obvious that something was seriously wrong with him. The editor of the *Diaries* labels his condition autism, a disorder still not well understood (p. xviii). And the Lawrences' close association with the Asquiths began just as the mother's fears were beginning to crystalize.

The Lawrences visited Lady Cynthia in Brighton in May 1915, and John had tea with them. She reports in her diary that "the Lawrences were riveted by the freakishness of John, about whom they showed extraordinary interest and sympathy . . . he was in a wild, monkey mood—very challenging, just doing things for the sake of being told not to—impishly defiant and still his peculiar, indescribable detachment" (*Diaries,* p. 18). The next day Lawrence and Lady Cynthia strolled to the cliffs overlooking Brighton and discussed John's condition for several hours. The mother, who elsewhere expresses her admiration for Lawrence's deep insight into character, received a long and depressing analysis. She was upset to learn that her friend believed she was responsible for her son's condition, that the boy was reacting to her scepticism and cynicism, to her lack of positive belief that made her appear, on the surface, charmingly tolerant and kind (*Diaries,* pp. 19–20). Later he told her that her spirit was "hard and stoical," a judgment which she rejected, but which is parallel to Hester who "knew that at the center of her heart was a hard little place that could not feel love . . . "(*Diaries,* p. 22).

A few days later Lawrence wrote a long letter about John in which he argued that she and her husband lacked a living belief in anything, that the world in which she lived had stunted her soul, and she had not resisted. "Your own soul knew . . . that it was itself bound in like a tree that grows under a low roof and can never break through, and which must be deformed, unfulfilled. Herbert Asquith must have known the same thing, in his soul." John had been born from the womb and loins of unbelief, distorted from his conception: ". . . the soul of John acts from your soul, even from the start: because he knows that you are Unbelief, and he reacts from your affirmation of belief always with hostility."[12] He cautions her against trying to force her son's love: "That you fight is only a sign that you are wanting in yourself. The child knows that. Your own soul is deficient, so it fights for the love of the child" (*Letters,* I, 341–42).

A recent article on "The Rocking-Horse Winner" reaches conclusions on the story itself that are very similar to Lawrence's analysis. Commenting on the wildness of Paul's obsession, Charles Koban says, "It is as if an alien spirit inhabited and drove him . . . and the spirit is of course the spirit of the

---

[11] *The Collected Letters of D. H. Lawrence,* ed. Harry T. Moore (New York: The Viking Press, 1962), I, 220, 233. Subsequent citations will be made in the text.

[12] The idea expressed here is comparable to lines in "Glad Ghosts," in which the husband, speaking of his three dead children, says, "And the children, it is well they are dead. They were born of our will and our disembodiment."

mother, the spirit of greed." It is Paul's "mystical openness to her that leaves him vulnerable to the terrible forces she unleashes in her own household."[13] It must be made clear that there is little to suggest that Lady Cynthia or her husband were as obsessed with money and material things as the couple in the story. But from Lawrence's perspective, the Asquiths could not avoid obsessive concern for possessions, given their chosen style of life. Lady Cynthia describes Lawrence strolling about their living room after tea, and suddenly noticing a small Louis XV table. After he stared at it for a moment, "'Come away!' he shrilled out, looking at me as if I stood in immediate deadly peril. 'Come away. Free yourself at once, or before you know where you are, your furniture will be on top instead of under you.' This admonition gave me a nightmare in which I was trampled to death by the legs of my own tables and chairs."[14] A harmless antique table became an instant symbol of the money-lie. Despite Lawrence's fondness for this couple, the link between possessions and the failure of human relationships seems clearly established.

Another letter concerned with Herbert Asquith also prefigures the story, as Lawrence tries to persuade Lady Cynthia not to push her husband into the money-making trap. The Asquiths were not rich, and lack of money was a constant concern. That Lawrence was well aware of this is shown in "The Thimble" where the heroine, left alone when her husband goes to war, cannot maintain the family town house, and takes a small flat which she furnishes with second-hand furniture bought from friends. Lady Cynthia herself spent the war years "cuckooing," that is, living with friends and family to avoid the expense of her own establishment. She worked for some years as a secretary for Sir James Barrie, wrote and published books, and like Hester, once received a summons for debt, a "wretched fourteen-shillings bill" (*Diaries*, p. 433). Like the couple in the story, the Asquiths were poor relations compared to the social set to which they belonged by birth. Lawrence, who was tortured by the money-hunger he saw everywhere, urged his friend to realize the connection between money-lust and war:

> It doesn't matter whether you *need* money or not. You *do* need it. But the fact that you would ask him to work, put his soul into getting it, makes him love better war and pure destruction. The thing is painfully irrational. How can a man be so developed to be able to devote himself to making money, and at the same time keep himself in utter antagonism to the whole system of money . . . . (*Letters*, I, 359)

The defeated, inarticulate husband in "The Rocking-Horse Winner," who goes "into town to some office," is foreshadowed here and in other letters. In one written in 1915, when the Lawrences were planning to leave England, he

---

[13] Charles Koban, "Allegory and the Death of the Heart in 'The Rocking-Horse Winner,'" *Studies in Short Fiction*, 15 (Fall 1978), 394–95.

[14] *Remember and Be Glad*, pp. 145–46. The incident is also reported in Herbert Asquith's memoir (*Moments of Memory* [New York: Charles Scribner's Sons, 1938], p. 190).

urged Lady Cynthia to consider leaving also. It was her duty, he felt, to remove her children from "this slow flux of destruction," and to seek a truer
existence: "Your husband should have left this decomposing life. There was
nowhere to go. Perhaps now he is beaten. Perhaps now the true living is defeated in him. But it is not defeated in you . . . . So don't give John to this
decline and fall. Give him to the *future* . . ." (*Letters,* I, 382).

The Lawrences did not leave England, however, until 1919, and during
these years Lady Cynthia records her growing distress at her son's condition.
She speaks of his "eerie Puck faces," of his sitting "silent and absorbed in his
own thoughts" at a lively family tea party, and of the "strange completeness
about him as he is. . . ." After a dedicated governess managed to teach him to
read and write, the mother comments sadly that his performance "gives you
the impression of a *tour de force* like a performing animal." Her growing inability to believe that the boy would ever be normal was becoming strong just
as the Lawrences again entered her orbit. In April 1917 Lawrence visited her,
and again insisted that the boy's condition was spiritual, not psychological. His
mother had submitted to an unreal existence, "the result being that John is
quite off the plane I have violated myself in order to remain on" (*Diaries,*
p. 294). Almost a year later, Lawrence again discussed John, still certain that he
could be helped by "proper psychic influence," and offered to take him for a
time to see if association with him and Frieda would help (*Letters,* I, 537).

And finally Lady Cynthia lost her capacity to love her son, although she
struggled not to do so. In a diary entry two days after the Lawrences had
come to tea, she speaks of "the John tragedy," which blackened her life for
her. It was a nightmare for her to be in the same room with him, and she was
violently reproached by his governess for her apparent callousness. Her
growing horror of the boy increased, no doubt because his affliction grew
steadily more disturbing as he grew older, and in her diary she speaks of a
visit to him as "an ordeal behind me." Since the Lawrences were seeing Lady
Cynthia during this time period, it is quite likely that he at least was aware of
the mother who could not love her son, and of the strong guilt feelings she
experienced in consequence.

It is to be regretted that the editor of the *Diaries* felt it necessary to
remove much of the material concerning John, since some of the omitted
passages might have provided additional links with the story. But the descriptions of him that remain suggest Paul's behavior in the story: his wildness, his self-absorption, his uncanny faces, his non-human quality, and the
sense of his isolation from other members of the household. And it is a matter of common knowledge that a behavior trait among children afflicted
with autism is a forward-backward rocking motion of their bodies. It is
likely that John would have had a rocking horse, and that he would have
used it long after he outgrew it, given his condition. But about these possible, even probable, clues we can only speculate.

A small but significant hint in the story itself suggests that Lawrence had
the Asquiths in mind, particularly since the phrasing seems to be a minor slip of
the pen. Hester "was at a big party in town, when one of her rushes of anxiety

about her boy, her first-born, gripped her heart until she could hardly speak." Not only does the sudden rush of concern describe what Lady Cynthia unquestionably must have experienced on many occasions, but the stipulation "first-born" is interesting. Earlier in the story we are told that Paul has an *elder* sister. Lawrence seems to have deliberately rearranged the ages and sexes of the children—Lady Cynthia had in fact three children, all boys—but unconsciously returned, as he wrote of the mother's anguish, to the original model for his character.

It would seem that in the Asquiths and in their eldest son Lawrence found ample background material for his story. Lady Cynthia was personally a charming and lovable woman, quite unlike the cold and selfish Hester. And yet Lawrence believed that basic deficiencies in her character had worked against her son's health and happiness. Her marriage had begun as a love match, opposed by her father because neither family could provide an adequate income for the couple. But Lawrence implied his belief that her relationship with her husband could not be satisfactory both in his direct comments in his letters and in the fact that he arranges a better marital relationship, a rebirth, for the heroines in three of his Asquith-inspired stories. The Asquith's social position, well-connected but comparatively poor, parallels the one described in "The Rocking-Horse Winner." And concerning what was apparently his last visit to her in October 1925, a visit during which she probably asked him to write something for her anthology, he reported laconically to a friend, "Went to Cynthia Asquith's—more sense of failure" (*Letters*, II, 863). It was this sense of failure in her life, as well as in the lives of other friends and acquaintances whom Lawrence visited during his brief stay in England, that produced the bitterness and discouragement of "The Rocking-Horse Winner."

Sexual Motifs

A Rocking-Horse: The Symbol, the Pattern, the Way to Live

W. D. Snodgrass

"Daddy! Daddy!" he cried to his father. "Daddy, look what they are doing! Daddy, they're beating the poor little horse!"

—*Crime and Punishment*

The Rocking-Horse Winner" seems the perfect story by the least meticulous of serious writers. It has been anthologized, analyzed by New Critics and force-fed to innumerable undergraduates. J. Arther Rank has filmed it. Yet no one has seriously investigated the story's chief structural feature, the symbolic extensions of the rocking-horse itself, and I feel that in ignoring several meaning-areas of this story we ignore some of Lawrence's most stimulating thought.

Though the reach of the symbol is overwhelming, in some sense the story is "about" its literal, narrative level: the life of the family that chooses money instead of some more stable value, that takes money as its nexus of affection. The first fault apparently lay with the mother. The story opens:

> There was a woman who was beautiful, who started with all the advantages, yet she had no luck. She married for love, and the love turned to dust. She had bonny children, yet she felt they had been thrust upon her, and she could not love them . . . at the center of her heart was a hard little place that could not feel love, not for anybody.

We never learn much more about her problems, about *why* her love turned to dust. But the rhyming verb *thrust* is shrewdly chosen and placed; knowing Lawrence, we may well guess that Hester's dissatisfaction is, at least in large part, sexual. We needn't say that the sexual factor is the sole or even primary cause of her frigidity, but it is usually a major expression and index of it, and becomes casual. Lawrence wrote in an amazing letter to John Middleton Murry:

> A woman unsatisfied must have luxuries. But a woman who loves a man would sleep on a board. . . . You've tried to satisfy Katherine with what you could earn for her, give her: and she will only be satisfied with what you *are.*

There could scarcely be a more apt description of Hester's situation. As for her husband, we cannot even guess what he *is;* he gives too few clues. Failing to supply the luxuries that both he and his wife demand; he has withdrawn, ceased to exist. The one thing he could always give—himself, the person he is—seems part of a discarded currency.

The mother, the father, finally the boy—each in turn has withdrawn his vital emotions and affections from commitment in and to the family. Withdrawing, they have denied their own needs, the one thing that could be "known" and "sure." They have, instead, committed their lives to an external, money, and so to "luck," since all externals are finally beyond control and cannot be really known. Thus, it is Paul's attempt to bring an external into his control by knowledge which destroys him. It is a failure of definition.

The father's withdrawal, of course, leaves a gap which encourages Paul in a natural Oedipal urge to replace him. And money becomes the medium of that replacement. So the money in the story must be taken literally, but is also a symbolic substitute for love and affection (since it has that meaning to the characters themselves), and ultimately for sperm. We know that money is not, to Paul, a good in itself—it is only a way to win his mother's affection, "compel her attention," show her that *he* is lucky though is father is not. That money has no real use for Hester either becomes only too clear in that crucial scene where Paul sends her the birthday present of five thousand pounds hoping to alleviate her problems, relax the household, and so release her affections. His present only makes her colder, harder, more luxurious, and:

> . . . the voices in the house, behind the sprays of mimosa and almond blossom, and from under the piles of iridescent cushions, simply trilled and screamed in a sort of ecstasy: "There *must* be more money! Oh-h-h; there *must* be more money. Oh, now, now-w! Now-w-w—there must be more money;—more than ever!"

The mother and father have driven themselves to provide the mother with what she, actually, needs least. And she has squandered it, one would guess, precisely to show her scorn for it and for the husband who provides it. Money as a symbolic substitute has only sharpened the craving it was meant to satisfy; the family has set up a vicious circle which will finally close upon Paul.

As several critics have noted, the story resembles many well-known fairy tales or magical stories in which the hero bargains with evil powers for personal advantages or forbidden knowledge. These bargains are always "rigged" so that the hero, after his apparent triumphs, will lose in the end—this being, in itself, the standard "moral." Gordon and Tate sum up their interpretation: "the boy, Paul, has invoked strange gods and pays the penalty with his death." Robert Gorham Davis goes on to point out that many witches supposedly rode hobby-horses of one sort or another (*e.g.,* the witch's broom) to rock themselves into a magical and prophetic trance. When he rides, Paul's eyes glare blue and strange, he will speak to no one, his sisters fear him. He stares into the horse's wooden face: "Its red mouth was slightly open, its big eye was wide and glassy-bright." More and more engrossed in his doom as the story progresses, he becomes "wild-eyed and strange . . . his big blue eyes blazing with a sort of madness." We hear again and again of the uncanny blaze of his eyes until finally, at his collapse, they are "like blue stones." Clearly enough, he is held in some self-induced prophetic frenzy, a line of meaning carefully developed by the story. When Paul first asserts to his mother that he is "lucky," he claims that God told him so. This seems pure invention, yet may well be a kind of *hubris,* considering the conversation that had just passed with his mother:

> "Nobody ever knows why one person is lucky and another unlucky."
> "Don't they? Nobody at all? Does nobody know?"
> "Perhaps God. But He never tells."

Whether Paul really believes that God told him so, he certainly does become lucky. And others come to believe that superhuman powers are involved. Bassett thinks of "Master Paul" as a seer and takes an explicitly worshipful tone towards him. He grows "serious as a church" and twice tells Uncle Oscar in a "secret, religious voice. . . . 'It's as if he had it from heaven.'" These hints of occultism culminate in Uncle Oscar's benediction:

"My God, Hester, you're eighty-odd thousand to the good, and a poor devil of a son to the bad. But poor devil, poor devil, he's best gone out of a life where he rides his rocking-horse to find a winner."

So, in some sense, Paul *is* demonic, yet a poor devil; though he has compacted with evil, his intentions were good and he has destroyed only himself. At first metaphorically, in the end literally, he has committed suicide. But that may be, finally, the essence of evil.

It is clear, then, that the story is talking about some sort of religious perversion. But *what* sort? Who are the strange gods: how does Paul serve them and receive their information? We must return here, I think, to the problem of knowledge and intellection. Paul is destroyed, we have said, by his desire to "know." It is not only that he has chosen wrong ways of knowing or wrong things to know. The evil is that he *has* chosen to know, to live by intellection. Lawrence wrote, in a letter to Ernest Collings:

> My great religion is a belief in the blood, the flesh, as being wiser than the intellect. We can go wrong in our minds. But what our blood feels and believes and says, is always true. *The intellect is only a bit and bridle.* What do I care about knowledge. . . . I conceive a man's body as a kind of flame . . . and the intellect is just the light that is shed on to the things around. . . . A flame isn't a flame because it lights up two, or twenty objects on a table. It's a flame because it is itself. And we have forgotten ourselves. . . . The real way of living is to answer to one's wants. Not "I want to light up with my intelligence as many things as possible" but ". . . I want that liberty, I want that woman, I want that pound of peaches, I want to go to sleep, I want to go to the pub and have a good time, I want to look a beastly swell today, I want to kiss that girl, I want to insult that man."

(I have italicized the bit and bridle metaphor to underscore an immediate relationship to the rocking-horse of the story.)

Not one member of this family really knows his wants. Like most idealists, they have ignored the most important part of the command *Know thyself,* and so cannot deal with their most important problem, their own needs. To know one's needs is really to know one's own limits, hence one's definition. Lawrence's notion of living by "feeling" or "blood" (as opposed to "knowledge," "mind" or "personality") may be most easily understood, perhaps, as living according to what you *are,* not what you think you should be made over into; knowing yourself, not external standards. Thus, what Lawrence calls "feeling" could well be glossed as "knowing one's wants." Paul's family, lacking true knowledge of themselves, have turned their light, their intellect, outward, hoping to control the external world. The mother, refusing to clarify what her emotions really *are,* hopes to control herself and her world by acting "gentle and anxious for her children." She tries to be or act what she thinks she should be, not taking adequate notice of what she is or needs. She acts from precepts about motherhood, not from recognition of her own will, self-respect for her own motherhood. Thus, the apparent contradiction between Hester's coldness, the "hard . . . center of her heart," and, on the other hand, "all her tormented motherhood flooding upon her" when Paul collapses near the end of the story. Some deep source of affection has apparently lain hidden (and so tormented) in her, all along; it was her business to find and release it sooner. Similarly, Paul has a need for affection which he does not, and perhaps cannot, understand or manage: Like his mother, he is trying to cover this lack of self-knowledge with knowledge about the external world, which he hopes will bring him a fortune, and so affection.

Paul is, so, a symbol of civilized man, whipping himself on in a nervous endless "mechanical gallop," an "arrested prance," in chase of something which will destroy him if he ever catches it, and which he never really wanted anyway. He is the scientist, teacher, theorist, who must always know about the outside world so that he can manipulate it to what he believes is his advantage. Paradoxically, such knowledge comes to him only in isolation, in withdrawal from the physical world, so that his intellect may operate upon it unimpeded. And such control of the world as he can gain is useless because he has lost the knowledge of what he wants, what he is.

This, then, is another aspect of the general problem treated by the story. A still more specific form of withdrawal and domination is suggested by the names of the horses on which Paul bets. Those names—like the names of the characters—are a terrible temptation to ingenuity. One should certainly be wary of them. Yet two of them seem related to each other and strongly suggest another area into which the story's basic pattern extends. Paul's first winner, Singhalese, and his last, Malabar, have names which refer to British colonial regions of India. (A third name, Mirza, suggests "Mirzapur"—still another colonial region. But that is surely stretching things.) India is obviously one of the focal points of the modern disease of colonial empire; for years Malabar and Singhalese were winners for British stockholders and for the British people in general. The British, like any colonial power or large government or corporation, have gambled upon and tried to control peoples and materials which they never see and with which they never have any vital physical contacts. (Lawrence's essay "Men must Work and Women as Well" is significant here.) They have lived by the work of others, one of the chief evils of which is that their own physical energies have no outlet and are turned into dissatisfactions and pseudo-needs which must be filled with more and more luxuries. And so long as they "knew," placed their bets right, they were rich, were able to afford more and more dissatisfactions. A similar process destroyed Spain: a similar process destroyed Paul.

Though these last several areas of discussion are only tenuously present, most readers would agree, I think, that the rocking-horse reaches symbolically toward such meanings: into family economy and relations, into the occult, into the modern intellectual spirit, into the financial and imperial manipulations of the modern State. But surely the sexual area is more basic to the story—is, indeed, the basic area in which begins the pattern of living which the rocking-horse symbolizes. It is precisely this area of the story and its interpretation which has been ignored, perhaps intentionally, by other commentators. Oddly enough, Lawrence himself has left an almost complete gloss of this aspect of the story in his amazing, infuriating, and brilliant article, "Pornography and Obscenity." There, Lawrence defines pornography not as art which stimulates sexual desire, but rather as art which contrives to make sex ugly (if only by excluding it) and so leads the observer away from sexual intercourse and toward masturbation. He continues:

> When the grey ones wail that the young man and young woman went and had sexual intercourse, they are bewailing the fact that the young man and the young woman didn't go separately and masturbate. Sex must go somewhere, especially in young people. So, in our glorious civilisation, it goes in masturbation. And the mass of our popular literature, the bulk of our popular amusements just exists to provoke masturbation. . . . The moral guardians who are prepared to censor all open and plain portrayal of sex must now be made to give their only justification: We prefer that the people shall masturbate.

Even a brief reading of the essay should convince one that Paul's mysterious ecstasy is not only religious, but sexual and onanistic. That is Paul's "secret of secrets." Just as the riding of a horse is an obvious symbol for the sex act, and *"riding"* was once the common sexual verb, so the rocking-horse stands for the child's imitation of the sex act, for the riding which goes nowhere.

We note in the passage quoted above that Lawrence thinks of masturbation chiefly as a substitute for some sort of intercourse. Similarly in the story:

> "Surely, you're too big for a rocking-horse!" his mother remonstrated.
> "Well, you see, mother, till I can have a *real* horse, I like to have some sort of animal about," had been his quaint answer.

This is one of several doctrinal points where the reader will likely disagree with Lawrence. Nonetheless, the idea was prevalent at the time of writing and is common enough today that most men probably still think of masturbation chiefly as a sex substitute. And like the money substitute mentioned before, it can only famish the craving it is thought to ease. So we find another area in which the characters of the story don't know what they need; another and narrower vicious circle.

The tightening of that circle, the destruction of Paul, is carefully defined; here, one feels both agreement with Lawrence's thought and a strong admiration for his delineation of the process:

> . . . He went off by himself, vaguely, in a childish way, seeking for the clue to "luck." Absorbed, taking no heed of other people, he went about with a sort of stealth, seeking inwardly for luck.

Stealth becomes more and more a part of Paul. We hear again and again of his secret, his "secret within a secret," we hear his talk with Uncle Oscar:

> "I shouldn't like mother to know I was lucky," said the boy.
> "Why not, son?"
> "She'd stop me."
> "I don't think she would."
> "Oh!"—and the boy writhed in an odd way—"I *don't* want her to know, uncle."

We may quote here a passage from "Pornography and Obscenity":

> Masturbation is the one thoroughly secret act of the human being, more secret even than excrementation.

Naturally, any act accompanied by such stealth is damaging to the personality and to its view of itself. It involves an explicit denial of the self, a refusal to affirm the self and its acts (an imaginative suicide) and consequently a partial divorce from reality. But this is only part of that same general process of isolation. In the essay, Lawrence says:

> Most of the responses are dead, most of the awareness is dead, nearly all the constructive activity is dead, and all that remains is a sort of a shell, a half empty creature fatally self-preoccupied and incapable of either giving or taking. . . . And this is masturbation's result. Enclosed within the vicious circle of the self, with no vital contacts outside, the self becomes emptier and emptier, till it is almost a nullus, a nothingness.

And this is the process dramatized by the story. Paul draws back from this family, bit by bit, until he becomes strange and fearful to his sisters and will speak to no one, has grown beyond the nurse and has no real contact with his parents. Even Uncle Oscar feels uncomfortable around him. Finally he has moved his rocking-horse away from the family and taken it with him "to his own bedroom at the top of the house."

Lawrence believes that man's isolation is an unavoidable part of his definition as a human being—yet he needs all the contact he can possibly find. In his essay on Poe, Lawrence writes:

> Love is the mysterious vital attraction which draws things together, closer, closer together. For this reason sex is the actual crisis of love. For in sex the two blood-systems, in the male and female, concentrate and come into contact, the merest film intervening. Yet if the intervening film breaks down, it is death. . . .
>
> In sensual love, it is the two blood-systems, the man's and the woman's, which sweep up into pure contact, and almost *fuse*. Almost mingle. Never quite. There is always the finest imaginable wall between the two blood waves, through which pass unknown vibrations, forces, but through which the blood itself must never break, or it means bleeding.

Sex, then, is man's closest link to other human beings and to the "unknown," his surest link into humanity, and it is this that Paul and his family have foresworn in their wilful isolation. And this isolation is more than physical. Again in "Pornography and Obscenity," we find:

> The great danger of masturbation lies in its merely exhaustive nature. In sexual intercourse, there is a give and take. A new stimulus enters as the native stimulus departs. Something quite new is added as the old surcharge is removed. And this is so in all sexual intercourse where two creatures are concerned, even in the homosexual intercourse. But in masturbation there is nothing but loss. There is no reciprocity. There is merely the spending away of a certain force, and no return. The body remains, in a sense, a corpse, after the act of self-abuse.

To what extent Lawrence thinks this reciprocity, this give and take, to be physical, I am not sure; I *am* sure it could easily be exaggerated. Lawrence makes a sharp distinction between the physical and the material. At any rate, it seems to me that the most important aspect of this sexual give-and-take is certainly emotional and psychological and that the stimulus which enters in sexual intercourse lies in coming to terms with an actual sexual partner who is real and in no wise "ideal." Thus, such a partner will afford both unexpectable pleasures and very real difficulties which must be recognized and overcome. But in masturbation these problems can be avoided. Most psychologists would agree that the most damaging thing about masturbation is that it is almost always accompanied by fantasy about intercourse with some "ideal" partner. Thus, one is led away from reality with its difficulties and unpredictable joys, into the self and its repetitive fantasies. This may seem rather far from the story, but I suggest that this explains the namelessness of the rocking-horse. (It also, of course, suggests shame and is valuable in manipulating the plot.) The real partner has a name which is always the same and stands for a certain configuration of personality with its quirks and glories; the fantasy partner, having no personality, has no name of his or her own but is given the name of such "real" partners as one might wish from week to week.

These, then, are the gods which Paul has invoked. This sexual problem gives, also, a startling range of irony to the religious texture of the story. The "secret within a secret . . . that which had no name" comes to be not only the shame of Paul's masturbation, but also a vicious and astounding parody of the "word within a word"—that which cannot be named. It should be clear from the material already quoted, and even more so from a reading of "Pornography and Obscenity," that it is popular religion—Christian idealism—that Lawrence is attacking, for it supports the "purity lie" and leaves masturbation as the only sexual expression, even at times openly condoning it. The strange gods are the familiar ones; the occult heresy is popular Christian piety.

It is not clear, however, how Paul receives knowledge from his onanistic gods. Lawrence himself does not pretend to know *how* this comes about, he only knows that it does exist:

The only positive effect of masturbation is that it seems to release a certain mental energy, in some people. But it is mental energy which manifests itself always in the same way, in a vicious circle of analysis and impotent criticism, or else a vicious circle of false and easy sympathy, sentimentalities. This sentimentalism and the niggling analysis, often self-analysis, of most of our modern literature, is a sign of self-abuse.

This momentary release of energy is, I take it, equivalent to finding the name of the "winner" in the story. Thus the two great meaning-streams of the story, intellection and masturbation, relate. Masturbation stands as the primary area: the withdrawal and stealth, the intellectual participation in the physical, the need to know and magically control the external, the driving of the self into a rigid, "mechanical gallop," the displacement of motive, the whole rejection of self, all begins here. And the pattern, once established, spreads, gradually infecting all the areas of life, familial, economic, political, religious. Here, again, the reader may feel a doctrinal disagreement, suspecting that masturbation is more symptomatic than causal. Such disagreement scarcely touches the story, however, whose business is not to diagnose or cure, but to create a vision of life, which it does with both scope and courage.

I want to quote finally, one more passage from the essay "Pornography and Obscenity" to round off the argument and tie up some loose ends, and also simply because of its value, its sincerity. It is a kind of summation of the story's meaning and opens with a sentence roughly equivalent to Uncle Oscar's judgment: "he's best gone out of a life where he rides a rocking-horse to find a winner":

> If my life is merely to go on in a vicious circle of self-enclosure, masturbating self-consciousness, it is worth nothing to me. If my individual life is to be enclosed within the huge corrupt lie of society today, purity and the dirty little secret, then it is worth not much to me. Freedom is a very great reality. But it means, above all things, freedom from lies. It is, first, freedom from myself; from the lie of my all-importance, even to myself; it is freedom from the self-conscious masturbating thing I am, self-enclosed. And second, freedom from the vast lie of the social world, the lie of purity and the dirty little secret. All the other monstrous lies lurk under the cloak of this one primary lie. The monstrous lie of money lurks under the cloak of purity. Kill the purity-lie and the money-lie will be defenseless.
>
> We have to be sufficiently conscious, and self-conscious, to know our own limits and to be aware of the greater urge within us and beyond us. Then we cease to be primarily interested in ourselves. Then we learn to leave ourselves alone, in all the affective centres: not to force our feelings in any way, and never to force our sex. Then we make the great onslaught on the outside lie, the inside lie being settled. And that is freedom and the fight for freedom.

Style: Ironic and Fabular

From *D. H. Lawrence: Modes of Fictional Style*

Bibhu Padhi

IV

Lawrence wrote at least three stories which combine the ironic and the fabular modes of fictional style. The are "The Rocking-Horse Winner," *The Princess,* and *The Man Who Loved Islands.* In each of these stories there are also two "voices," representing the two modes. There is a readily recognized voice which the reader is normally disposed to accept as trustworthy; but there is also a less explicit voice that seems to contradict the validity and worth of what the other offers. The result is, in the language of Wayne C. Booth, "an inescapable ironic invitation" (*Irony,* 61). In Lawrence's stories, however, there is no distinction between a "false" voice and a "correct" voice that Booth proposes, with the "correct voice . . . repudiating all or most of what the ostensible speaker has said" (Booth, *Irony,* 62). Rather, one voice is implicit in the other; and while the implicit voice is all the while turning away from the other, it is nonetheless relying on the explicit voice in order to be clearly and correctly heard. An examination of the three stories will show the importance of these two "voices" and of the two modes they represent, for Lawrence the artist.

In "The Rocking-Horse Winner," the world of material profit invades the world of fantasy. The "house" in the story is haunted by the ghost of money, whispering repeatedly the terrible command, "There must be more money." The repetition creates a trance-like state into which all the inmates of the house finally throw themselves. Material values expand to highly abstract, almost demoniacal proportions, so that at certain points in the story it becomes difficult to distinguish the evil aspect of the theme from the "innocent" method that Lawrence employs to bring the evil into the folds of his fiction.

The story is a kind of inverted fairy tale, with its head on the earth. The essential ingredients of a fairy tale are all present here: the saviour-prince with this flying horse (Paul), the maiden in distress (Paul's mother), and the difficult voyages through immensely active obstacles (Paul on his rocking-horse, anxiously predicting the winning horses). But this fairy tale does not introduce the reader into a world where everything seems possible and possessible; it rather introduces him into the depressing experience of an empty success. Love and heroism, so very essential to the ethos of the fairy tale world, have been ironically replaced by money, even as the innocence and simplicity of the child-hero has been corroded by his desire for a power over bookmakers. The child faces the dangerously real adult villains of a very real world.

Paul's mother thinks that she has not been "lucky," although she does not know how to define "luck." Consequently, she does not know the way out of the anxiety which conditions her everyday behaviour and which, at times, brings her to the point of despair. The whole story is in fact a comment on— and against—the extreme involvement of the nerves from which the twentieth century man suffers and which drives him from sober reflection toward dogmatic self-assertion. Paul's family, "lacking true knowledge of themselves, have turned light, their intellect, outward, hoping to control the external world. Appropriately, Paul's relationship with his horses lacks the vitality of an intimate physical contact with another living creature and turns out to be merely a means of acquiring an advantage over other gamblers. Appropriate also is his not being given a horse to ride with the vital breath within it, but one that cannot take him anywhere. It is not the smoothly flying horse of the fairy tale, but an artefact that can only bring to its rider parapsychic intimations of the outcome of horse races.

The story concentrates on the problem of repression and release on various levels—sexual, economic, emotional, and religious. Its irony, as W. D. Snodgrass points out, evolves out of an intersuggestion of these several levels, the masturbatic satisfaction in riding the horse, for instance, being implied in the identification of the moment of autoerotic pleasure with an almost revelatory encounter with the nameless "secret within a secret" (*LAH,* 93). Similarly, Paul's long discussions of the horse races with his gardener and his uncle, are burdened with a heavy, solemn accent, as though they were "speaking of religious matters" (*LAH,* 85).

The process of getting "luckier" than before is seen as one that makes everything look less and less real. Paul's luck has its basis in his isolation from his immediate surroundings, his gradual drifting away from the socially real, so that his final bit of luck cannot be anything less than a meningitic fever from which he never recovers. Luck has eventually gone into his head: it is no longer outside his body as it is outside his mother's. He asserts that he is lucky, but we know that to be lucky, to be a master of luck, is also to be a servant of it. The little "master" is really the unintended victim of his own commands.

In a sense, Paul's sickness is fortunate. It brings him and his mother their highest luck, by releasing both from body-induced suffering. We hear the words of Paul's uncle with which the story ends: "Poor devil, poor devil, he's best gone out of a life where he rides his rocking-horse to find a winner." To possess luck is to move outside of one's ordinary self, to deny one's identity in a suicidal way: the recognition of this truth is the basis of the ironic mode in the story. The journey outward in order to "get there" is also a journey inward, so that "getting there" amounts to looking into that blank space into which one has reduced oneself in one's passion to be "lucky."

The rocking-horse, as a symbol, expands in the course of the story, by adding to itself new meanings, though, for the discerning reader, its significance remains relatively clear throughout. This significance is felt and recognized not only through a multiplication of meanings within a single symbol, but also through a "voice" that repudiates all that the narrative ostensibly tells. It is a voice that makes all that the story seems to say—beginning with its opening sentence, "There was a woman who was beautiful"—suspect. The voice is rarely heard in any distinct manner, but the sober, detached, matter-of-fact tone somehow seems to struggle against the nervous, unsteady pace of the other voice. It comes up victorious from time to time and warns the interpreting reader against accepting anything at its face value. We may consider, for example, its announcement of Paul's series of failures: "The Grand National had gone by: he had not 'known,' and had lost a hundred pounds. Summer was at hand. He was in agony for the Lincoln. But even for the Lincoln he didn't 'know,' and he lost fifty pounds" (*LAH,* 92). These moments of pure objectivity that the voice creates, provide the reader the stable ground from which he is able to look in the hazier directions that the story suggests and to evaluate the true nature of the case.

Treatment of Women

Lawrence's Treatment of Women in *Sons and Lovers*
Faith Pullin

> It is not of love that we are fulfilled, but of love in such intimate equipoise with hate that the transcendence takes place.

Lawrence is a ruthless user of women; in *Sons and Lovers,* the mother, Miriam and Clara are all manipulated in Paul's painful effort at self-identification, the effort to become himself. In many respects, Lawrence never emerged from the infantile state in which other people are merely instruments. This leads him to make confusing and contradictory demands on his characters, as well as on the women with whom he interacted in his real life. Paul Morel is a curiously passive figure. The other children make lives for themselves outside the home, especially William, who, until his death, is *the* lover and of whom Paul is jealous. But Paul, at the age of fourteen, when he is expected to go out into the world and make his living, has no higher aim than the regressive one of living with his mother:

> His ambition, as far as this world's gear went, was quietly to earn his thirty or thirty-five shillings a week somewhere near home, and then, when his father died, have a cottage with his mother, paint and go out as he liked, and live happily ever after.

This wish-fulfilment is actually expressed by Lawrence himself in a letter to Ernest Collings (17 January 1913) when he said

> It is hopeless for me to try to do anything without I have a woman at the back of me . . . I daren't sit in the world without a woman behind me.

Lawrence is an extremely egotistical writer. In his portraits of women, he is usually defining some aspect of himself, rather than attempting the creation of the other sex. Many critics have argued that Lawrence (whether homosexual or bisexual in fact himself) was the true androgynous artist and therefore attuned to the inner experience of both sexes. My purpose here is to emphasize the point that Lawrence's main object was always to examine the male psyche and to use his women characters to that end. Indeed, even when a character like Ursula in *The Rainbow* is given a female name, she is merely a vehicle from the Lawrentian autobiography. When Ursula reappears, in *Women in Love,* she is a much lesser figure, since Lawrence, in Birkin, is able to present himself as a man. Lawrence's women are allowed their liberty only in so far as they will always, finally, acknowledge him the master. Lawrence remained deeply bound to his early Eastwood life, in that his later relations with women were determined by his privileged mother's boy status and his taking over many feminine characteristics (*becoming* his mother). Lawrence's later longing for a tender male friendship comes from the nurturing companionship between his father and his father's male friends at the pit: a community life, from which the women were rigorously excluded. Morel's ineffectual attempts to control his wife and to dominate her, by physical means if necessary, were later mirrored in Lawrence's struggles with Frieda. However much these difficulties are the result of cultural conditioning, in that working class patriarchy insists on the pre-eminence of the male (husbands in *Sons and Lovers* are called masters), they are equally the result of Lawrence's own personal psychic conflicts. Clever dodges such as presenting a female critique of his overbearing views, wrapped up in a fake abstract system, through the mouths of women characters (as in *Women in Love*) do not succeed in masking the fact that Lawrence must always have the last word. Lawrence was not really interested in his woman characters, or only for as long as they supported and encouraged the male. Lawrence isn't concerned with women as themselves, but only as examples; he has a marked tendency to undervalue individuality in women (clever women he distrusted and hated). Mrs. Morel is much more of a stereotype than her husband. Indeed, it's clear that to Lawrence, Morel himself is a more compelling figure and the one on whom he was to base the positive values of his later life. As a child Lawrence himself was unable to appreciate his father's qualities, since this would have been seen as treachery by his mother (on whom he depended for emotional security and self-esteem). May Holbrook, Jessie Chambers' elder sister, noted at the time that Lawrence was afraid to reveal any similarities between himself and his father or any understanding or liking for him:

> Next time Bert was at our tea table, I offered him the cream.
> "You know Bert doesn't take cream," remarked Mother. But I pressed it on him till he said:
> "I don't like it, I like the taste of the tea." And I informed my family, "Those are the very words his father used when I passed him the cream jug!"

> Bert reddened. "Yes, he doesn't take it." And I followed up: "Fancy you inheriting his taste!" For I couldn't forget the waves of hate that came from him as he humped himself up.

On another occasion, there is an argument about some mushrooms. It turns out that Lawrence wanted them for his father's tea:

> "Well!" I cried in sheer surprise, "and you hating him as you hate him! You don't hate him as you pretend you do, or you'd never make trouble with your friends to take their mushrooms for him!"
>
> "I have to hate him for Mother's sake," he replied. "But I can take mushrooms home when I find them, and they'll be for his tea because he loves wild things you find."

It's because Lawrence is afraid that he is like his father that he presents Paul as a male version of Mrs. Morel. He even looks like her:

> Paul was now fourteen, and was looking for work. He was a rather small and rather finely-made boy, with dark brown hair and light blue eyes.
>
> (p. 112)

There is a great deal of class antagonism here. Paul, through his mother, is determined that he will not be a common labourer. Upward social mobility demands that he take on the characteristics of Mrs. Morel's lower middle class status. The children refuse to speak in dialect and they read books. In real life, this worked against both Lawrence and his mother since Lawrence rose a little too high and found that his mother was not pleased when he put *The White Peacock* into her dying hands. She would have preferred him to have written a romance.

Paul and his father are unable to talk to each other, since the father has been cast as the enemy. The only time when contact is possible is when Morel works about the house. Then the children can come to terms with him: "they united with him in the work, in the actual doing of something, when he was his real self again." Significantly, Morel is the storyteller, the creator. He comes into his own when he tells the children tales of the pit ("Morel had a warm way of telling a story. He made one feel Taffy's cunning"). Morel, too, is the dancer of the family, whereas Mrs. Morel is unable to dance, even if her Puritan principles would let her:

> "You don't dance yourself, do you missis?", asked her nearest neighbour, in October, when there was great talk . . .
>
> "No—I never had the least inclination to", Mrs. Morel replied.
>
> "Fancy! An' how funny as you should ha' married your Mester. You know he's quite a famous one for dancing."
>
> (p. 22)

What emerges from all this (and Lawrence himself realized it later) is that the true love in *Sons and Lovers* is between Paul and his father. His deepest adolescent desire is to be a painter, a creator and celebrator of life, like his father. His mother, on the other hand, thinks in terms of material advancement. She wishes to impose herself on the world through her sons (William was like her knight who wore *her* favour in the battle), she is not interested in the thing itself—only in the recognition that achievement will bring (p. 113).

All through his life, Lawrence found it hard to resist the temptation of blaming women. For coming too close and impinging on his divine selfhood or for being too detached and daring to have a life of their own.

Marxist Interpretation

Labor and Religion in D. H. Lawrence's "The Rocking-Horse Winner"

Daniel P. Watkins

It is a commonplace that D. H. Lawrence's "The Rocking-Horse Winner" is a story about the devastating effects that money can have on a family, and, further, that Lawrence's specific objections in the story are not to money abstractly conceived, but to money as it is understood and valued by capitalist culture. This is one of Lawrence's most savage and compact critiques of what he elsewhere calls "the god-damn bourgeoisie" and of individuals who, despite their natural or potential goodness, "swallow the culture bait" and hence become victims to the world they (wrongly) believe holds the key to human happiness.[1] The most interesting and in many ways the best analysis of the story along these lines appeared nearly thirty years ago, when W. D. Snodgrass offered a virtually exhaustive interpretation of the role of money in the story, going so far as identifying the names of the various horses young Paul bets on as British colonies in India, and showing the way other images reflect important aspects of capitalist culture.[2] This essay, indeed, establishes convincingly Lawrence's awareness of the intrusion of capitalism into every aspect of contemporary life.

Despite the excellent groundbreaking work of Snodgrass, however, critics have not explored the full implications of his thesis for "The Rocking-Horse Winner," and in fact significant portions of the socioeconomic dimension of

---

[1] These quotations are from Lawrence's poems "Red-Herring" and "Don'ts," respectively.
Quotations from "The Rocking-Horse Winner" are taken from *The Complete Short Stories of D. H. Lawrence,* III (London: William Heinemann Ltd., 1955), and page numbers are cited in the text.

[2] W. D. Snodgrass, "A Rocking-Horse: The Symbol, the Pattern, the Way to Live," *The Hudson Review,* 11 (1958), 191–200.

the story have remained (at best) only partially explained, thus leaving obscured the full scope and power of Lawrence's vision. In the present essay, I want to build upon the thesis of Snodgrass in an attempt to elaborate certain ideas that his argument points to but leaves undeveloped and to clarify others that, I believe, he does not satisfactorily explain. Specifically, like Snodgrass, I want to consider the story as a symbolic formulation of social life in the grip of capitalism; but unlike him I wish to begin with a very brief sketch of how capitalist society works, using this sketch as the basis for a discussion of two of its constituent elements that are emphasized in Lawrence's story, namely labor and religion. While my thesis could be extended to include various other issues in the story, ranging from sexuality to alienation, Snodgrass has discussed these fully and persuasively, and thus I omit them here, assuming that my particular arguments could be placed alongside his discussion of these matters.

My understanding of capitalism generally, and of its role in "The Rocking-Horse Winner" particularly, is heavily indebted to a recent book by Robert L. Heilbroner, entitled *The Nature and Logic of Capitalism,* and can be summarized briefly. The key to Heilbroner's definition of capitalism is his assertion that *"Capital is . . . not a material thing but a process that uses material things as moments in its continuously dynamic existence.* It is, moreover, a social process, not a physical one." This means that isolated data cannot be gathered to explain it: capitalism is not "business," or "money," or "labor." While money, for instance, may be one "measure" of capital, only "money-in-use"—that is, only money that functions in a specific way within the dominant social formations of culture, strengthening and extending the prevailing structures of authority—can become capital itself. As a social process, in other words, capitalism pervades and constitutes culture—it is not imposed upon culture from without—and is manifested as "behavior-shaping institutions and relationships."[3] In terms of the story itself, this means that the various images and details that Lawrence sets down as key ingredients of Paul's world point to the workings of capital even while they appear to have autonomous status, or appear to be important (say) only in psychological terms. The desire for money that pervades the home, the withdrawal of the child into his private fantasy world, the naming of winning horses after British colonies: all of the concerts that Snodgrass traces tell us something about the power relations governing the world that young Paul and the other characters inhabit.

One of the key components of capitalism is labor, but, again, not labor abstractly conceived. Labor under capitalism is defined in terms of two principal matters. First, it yields profits in the form of money that can be invested to produce more profits.[4] For this to happen—and this is the second point—

---

[3] Robert L. Heilbroner, *The Nature and Logic of Capitalism* (New York: Norton, 1985), pp. 19, 36–37. I am relying on Heilbroner rather than on Marx for my discussion of capitalism because Heilbroner's account is compact, lucid, and perhaps more immediately accessible to the general reader.

[4] This is a crude but (in my opinion) accurate reduction of the matter, and it is taken from Marx's diagrammatic explanation of profit in *Capital* as M — > C — > M, where M = money and C = commodity.

exploitation is necessary. As Heilbroner says, "The essential meaning of exploitation is that a surplus is seized from the working population for the benefit of a superior class. Such a seizure will be exploitative even if the surplus yields social benefits at large, in addition to the power or prestige for which it was originally brought into being, as in the case of Roman roads, Christian churches, or the factories of capitalism."[5] Lawrence is very careful to present labor in these terms, and particularly to dramatize the connection between labor and profit, though (as we shall see) he does not follow a simple and absolute division in the story between labor and capital. His understanding of this issue is evident not only in the way he introduces money at the beginning of the story as a major and obsessive issue, but also, more strikingly, in his depiction of the way money is gained, how it changes hands, and what the exchange means for the world that his characters inhabit.

The class nature of labor under capital is presented symbolically in the story in terms of the adult and non-adult worlds. That is, social reality is controlled by parents whose primary concern is to bring in money sufficient to "the social position which they (have) to keep up" (790). While they have a small income, and while "The father went in to town to some office" (790), they never are really seen to work actively and productively. Rather, they set a tone of need in their world that generates intense and pervasive anxiety, which then is passed down to their children, who interiorize the values and attitudes of the adult world and set about (as best they can) to satisfy the demands of that world. Even when money is produced, however, the demands of the adult world are never fully met, but, quite the reverse, intensify further, so that more labor is necessary. In this context, work is not a means of meeting basic human needs, but rather only a way of producing greater sums of money, and thus it is clearly socially unproductive. Seen from this perspective, it is not important that the parents are not capitalists in the crudest sense (that is, they are not drawn as investors of money); what is important is that they both set the tone (economic scarcity) and determine the values (consumerism) of the world they inhabit, and in addition expropriate the wealth that others produce for their own private consumption.

Young Paul exemplifies vividly the sort of work that arises under capital. Simply put, he is a laborer for his mother, to whom he gives all of his money, only to find that the more he gives the more she needs. It is true, of course, that as a handicapper he invests money, betting on a profitable return on his investment, and that in this sense he is a sort of capitalist; indeed, it is his betting that is the literal sign of the economic relations controlling the world of the story. But at the same time his character is made to carry a much larger symbolic significance, for what he is investing, in real terms, is himself, selling his skills to generate wealth that he is not free to possess, but that is necessary to the maintenance of existing social relations. As his mother touches the money he earns, she uses it not to satisfy family needs—it has

---

[5] Heilbroner, *The Nature and Logic of Capitalism*, p. 74

little or no *use* value—but to extend her social position and social power, and the process of extension of course is never ending, requiring ever greater sums of money: "There were certain new furnishings, and Paul had a tutor. He was *really* going to Eton, his father's school, in the following autumn. There were flowers in the winter, and a blossoming of the luxury Paul's mother had been used to. And yet the voices in the house, behind the sprays of mimosa and almond-blossom, and from under the piles of iridescent cushions, simply trilled and screamed in a sort of ecstasy: 'There *must* be more money!'" (800). This passage clearly focuses the priority of money over commodity and the relentlessness with which the power associated with money controls even the most personal dimension of life.

The work itself that Paul performs cannot, under such conditions, be personally satisfying, and this is shown powerfully by the sort of work he does. The rocking horse is a brilliant symbol of non-productive labor, for even while it moves it remains stationary: even while Paul is magically (humanly) creative, producing untold wealth for this mother, he does not advance in the least, and in fact becomes increasingly isolated and fearful that even the abilities he now possesses will be taken from him. The labor, which drives him to "a sort of madness," that consumes him to an ever greater degree, leaves him nothing for himself, driving him down a terrible path to emotional and then physical distress. He is never satisfied with what he produces because it in no way relieves the pressure that his world places on him, and thus his anxiety and alienation grow to the point of destroying any sense of real personal worth and removing him literally from all meaningful social exchange, as when he takes his rocking horse to his bedroom and rides alone late into the night trying to find the key to wealth.

As Lawrence presents it, the situation Paul finds himself in is not created and maintained directly or even mainly by physical means; ideological constraints shape it in significant ways. That is, prevailing and quite specific social structures appear to him to constitute reality itself; they allow no vision of life as anything other than what it is under capital. Paul's motives and actions are, expectedly, shaped to a very large extent by this fact. One main way this absolute assumption about the nature of personal and social life is held in place is through religion, which not only absorbs the contradictions of Paul's world into an ideal of spiritual purity, but more importantly endorses existing codes that determine the human possibilities and limitations within this world. This is seen both through the passing yet carefully manipulated references to religion and through the symbolic presentation of religion as a pervasive and sanctifying presence.

The position I wish to advance here regarding religion challenges Snodgrass's provoking (but in my opinion incorrect) argument about the occultish nature of the religious issues in the story, and it is grounded upon our acknowledgment and understanding of the story's allegorical dimension. Relying upon the devices of allegory, Lawrence sets in place a definite set of religious interests that illustrate the role of Christianity under capitalism. Indeed, he locates the trinity at the very center of the story's thematic interests, suggesting both its power within capitalism and the extent to which it must be held accountable for what happens to human life under capitalism. The presence of Christianity in the story is set forth most readily, of course, in the depiction of the young Paul as a Christ figure: not only is he referred to repeatedly as "son," but he also possesses a seemingly magical power that comes from heaven. (Other features that we will discuss momentarily associate him even more clearly with Christ.) The symbolic dimension of Paul's characterization becomes even more apparent when it is placed in the context of the descriptions of Bassett and Uncle Oscar, who are presented as participants in the serious money-making scheme to which Paul is committed. Not only is Bassett a permanent presence in the garden, storing there Paul's winnings; he is also described (as Snodgrass has noted) in religious terms and he speaks of Paul's betting in the most reverent voice: "'Master Paul comes and asks me, so I can't do more than tell him, sir,' said Bassett, his face terribly serious, as if he were speaking of religious matters" (794). Or again when he explains to the doubting Oscar how Paul knows which horse will win, he says: "it's as if he had it from heaven, sir" (797). Uncle Oscar, in his turn, is presented as a sort of father figure, evidenced not only in the fact that he is the only male adult consistently present in the story, but more importantly in the way he expresses his relationship to Paul in paternal terms: "All right, son! We'll manage it without her knowing" (798). "I leave it to you, son" (799). "Let it alone, son! Don't you bother about it!" (800).

If we approach the religious issue in this way, the occultish elements that Snodgrass notes disappear and religion comes to be seen as orthodox religion, and it is socially pervasive, explaining and justifying the activities of its adherents. That the betting scheme is held in secret does not at all call orthodoxy into doubt, but rather makes an important point about Christianity, namely that it is essentially the acceptable religion within an entirely privatized culture, and as such reflects and sanctions private pursuit to the exclusion of all else. Moreover, it is firmly committed to a money ethic that becomes the basis for all human value and the key to all human exchange. As Paul tells Uncle Oscar at the moment the trinity emerges as an actual and discernible presence in the story, "'If you'd like to be a partner, uncle, with Bassett and me, we could be partners. Only, you'd have to promise, honor bright, uncle, not to let it go beyond us three'" (796). This is Lawrence's Christianity fully exposed; it is a creed with a firm and confident code of honor, but its honor is understood solely in terms of the private pursuit of wealth and is measured in terms of the private nature generally of human action. This value scheme explains clearly the secrecy that is seen everywhere in the story: in Paul's "secret within a secret" (801); in the decision of Paul, Bassett, and Oscar to withhold information from the mother; in the mother's response to the money that falls her way, as if from heaven; in the mother's secret work "in the studio of a friend" (799), and more.

Even while Lawrence carefully places Christianity at the center of the story as a religion of money, he subtly employs a rhetorical strategy that points up its impurity and ultimately its viciousness. This is seen in several minor touches, beginning with the description of Bassett. While he is "serious as a church" when talking about money, and spends much of his time cultivating the garden under his care, at the same time Bassett is not untouched by the world; in fact he is clearly scarred: "Bassett, the young gardener, who had been wounded in the left foot in the war and got his present job through Oscar Cresswell, whose batman he had been, was a perfect blade of the 'turf'" (794). Likewise, despite Oscar's language and his confident paternal nature that would seem to suggest his innocence and integrity, he is not a real father; he only plays the role, assuming authority, for instance, to sign the agreement that allows Paul's mother to touch all of the money he wins.

The most telling example of the true nature of Lawrence's trinity, however, is of course Paul himself, who willingly sacrifices himself to save the world into which he was born. His death gives his family the financial independence that it has sought all along, but the creed that has made this independence possible, even while it appears holy and pure, is in fact emphatically devilish. As Uncle Oscar tells his sister after Paul's death: "My God, Hester, you're eighty-odd thousand to the good and a poor devil of a son to the bad. But, poor devil, he's best gone out of a life where he rides his rocking horse to find a winner" (804). Again, these references are not a sign of the occultish nature of Paul's religion, but quite the reverse a sign of the truly demonic quality of a Christianity that willingly and even insistently sacrifices human life in the pursuit of personal excellence and advancement.

And this brings the story around once again to its human dimension and specifically to Lawrence's vision of the connection between religion and labor. While Paul is portrayed on one level as a symbol of Christianity, as one who gives his life so that others may have a better life, he is shown at the same time in human terms as a worker who is exploited to the point of death, even while those who exploit him (his mother, for example) are entirely oblivious to the harm they are doing him: the religious creed does not allow them—as it does not allow Paul—to see this human dimension, because to see this would be to call into question the world view, the monetary underpinnings of religion, the values that constitute reality for them.

While it is possible to show that Lawrence's politics are essentially reactionary and that his art grows out of this reactionary stance,[6] at the same time the art itself, in its very resistance to bourgeois culture, constitutes a powerful critique of the problems of modern culture. That is, his best works, as "The Rocking-Horse Winner" attests, are not simply blind responses to a personally unappealing situation; they both register the workings of bourgeois life and offer an active critical perspective that can be used as the basis for elaborating the various levels of material and ideological control that modern culture exercises over people. Like Carlyle before him, Lawrence can be charged with often failing to offer a tenable argument about what needs to be done to assure human betterment, but his actual critique of what is wrong with society is extensive, compelling, and in its best moments potentially liberating.

---

[6] See, for instance, John R. Harrison, *The Reactionaries* (London: Victor Gollancz Ltd., 1967), pp. 163–92.

THE RESEARCH PROCESS AND MLA DOCUMENTATION

The reason for doing research is to attain information that will enlarge your understanding and analysis of a subject or topic. In your research, you may conceive of yourself as a detective, posing problems, deciphering the mysteries in the text or texts that need to be solved. You begin with clues, the words on a page; the clues reveal patterns. You discard false leads, red herrings, and develop a vision of a work or topic—your interpretation—expanded by information that you have gained from reading sources other than the work itself (if your subject concerns one particular text). The technical term in the research process for the work itself is the primary source. Other primary or original sources include autobiography, letters, journals, documents, and manuscripts. After you examine primary documents, then you study secondary sources that give you commentary about the topic. These materials may be biographical, historical, or critical.

An instructor may assign a specific subject for the research paper, for example, the role of the ghost or the play within the play in *Hamlet*. Other instructors may offer you the opportunity to determine the topic. If no particular assignment is given, you may want to concentrate on one of these areas:

- The biography of the author.
- The relationship between the writer's life and works.
- The artistic influences upon the writer.
- Analysis of the process of the writer through examination of drafts.
- Features of a particular work, characteristic of the genre, e.g., point of view and symbolism in a short story, imagery and tone in a poem, character and conflict in a play.
- The social, historical, and political contexts of a work.
- A particular critical approach, e.g., a formalist analysis of Keats "Ode on a Grecian Urn"; a feminist reading of "The Yellow Wallpaper."

These key topic areas may be posed as beginning questions for research:

- What biographical facts do I need to know about the writer that will help me understand the topic?
- What are the connections between the life and works?
- How did the writer develop his or her work? What can I learn by examining successive drafts of a work or by reading about the writer's artistic techniques?
- What features of the genre do I want to explore? Refer to the checklists for the evaluation of short fiction, poetry, drama, and nonfiction in Chapters 9 through 12.
- What themes seem most important?
- How did the historical, social, political, and cultural realities of the time influence the writer?
- How are the intellectual movements of the writer's time evident in his or her work?
- How will my reading of criticism enlarge my vision of the topic?
- What aspects of the subject do I find most puzzling?
- What interpretations of the topic do I find most debatable?
- What schools of thought will enlarge my understanding and provide new intellectual contexts and directions for further analysis?

Any one of these questions may provide a starting point.

THE RESEARCH PROCESS

For the sake of discussion, assume that you have chosen a particular work that interests or intrigues you. Before you begin your research project, you need to develop an understanding of the work. Perhaps you have discussed it in class. Perhaps you have talked about the reading in collaborative learning groups or with friends. Perhaps you have determined your own topic and have selected and studied a work not assigned or discussed in the course. After you analyze the text, you are ready to begin your research. Some suggested stages of the process follow. As you become more comfortable with the process, you may adapt or modify these stages to fit your needs.

Begin with a full exploration of the work. Engage in forms of reader response; annotate the text, brainstorm, freewrite, compose a double-entry notebook, and write several journal entries. Determine your interpretation, analyze your interpretation, and identify questions that remain. Discover the most puzzling areas concerning the topic. Then formulate a list of research questions. Check the most interesting queries. Have potential directions for research before you go to the library.

Next you explore other primary and secondary sources that will provide you with further information about the work. In the library, you may want to consult a general encyclopedia for information on the writer and his or her work. Often the encyclopedia will have a signed entry by an expert and additional bibliographic sources. You may assume that the author of the encyclopedia entry is a reliable expert on the topic as are the other writers of cited secondary references. You now have a beginning point for research. After you complete this overview of a writer's life and works, you may choose a specialized biographical source, including the *Dictionary of National Biography, Dictionary of American Biography, Contemporary Authors* (for contemporary writers), *Twentieth-Century Authors,* the *Oxford Companion to American Literature,* and the *Oxford Companion to English Literature.* These works are found in the Reference Room of your library. These biographical reference books will give you a more comprehensive view of the writer and his or her work and additional sources for research.

After you gather information about a writer's life and works, you may narrow your focus to a single research area. At this point, you also will consult the card catalog, the computerized catalog, or computer indices of information to discover and gain additional secondary sources concerning biography and criticism. In many cases, collections of essays on the author and substantial critical treatments of the writer's life and works exist. You then survey and skim your materials with a slant or idea in mind. Before writing in order to determine a focus, review biographical and critical materials so that you do not take too many preliminary notes.

As you consult sources, you write bibliographic entries. Each source may appear on a separate card, or you may devise some other system. The entry should contain the following information for a book: Author, Title, Publication Information (Place Published, Publisher, Date), and Library of Congress reference number so that you can find the book again without searching for it in the catalog. A bibliographic entry for a journal should contain the following: Author, Title of the Article, Journal, Publication Source, Volume, Year, Date, and Page. Include a brief evaluation of the source.

Book

Bundtzen, Lynda K.	PS
Plath's Incarnations: A Woman and the Creative Process	3566 .L27 Z588
Ann Arbor: University of Michigan Press, 1983	1983
Good evidence and analysis of theme of transcendence.	

Journal

Pollitt, Katha	PMLA Bibliography

"A Note of Triumph"
Nation.

16 January 1982: 52–55.

Excellent review of *Collected Poems* by Plath

Both biographical and critical treatments of the author and collections of essays may provide additional reference materials. You also may want to consult such general indices as *The Reader's Guide to Periodical Literature* (for information on current writers), *The New York Times Index,* and *The Book Review Digest* as well as computerized general subject indices for information in periodicals, magazines, journals, and newspapers and for reviews of current authors. The reference room also contains specialized bibliographies. For example, there are several bibliographies of women's studies materials. A standard bibliography for information on literature is the *Modern Language Association International Bibliography of Books and Articles on Modern Language and Literature.* This bibliography indexes the major scholarship in the discipline and lists entries for authors according to field of literature, nationality, and time period. For example, Ernest Hemingway's name would appear in the section, Twentieth Century American Literature.

After you have decided on a research question and after you have narrowed your focus and established a preliminary direction for research, isolate the materials that you plan to study. At this point, you have an initial list of "works consulted" and a working bibliography of those books and articles from which you genuinely intend to gather information. Your instructor may want to check your bibliography and to offer further directions for research. As you shape your bibliography, examine your sources of information. You want to be aware of the publication date of your secondary sources so that you do not rely on outdated materials or interpretations of works.

Now, the notetaking phase of the research process begins. Before you start taking notes, however, keep your research questions and possible subtopics or subheadings for analysis on a separate sheet of paper so that they are foremost in your mind. You also may draft a potential thesis and determine a tentative purpose and audience for your essay. The purposes of research essays about literature are informative, argumentative, or evaluative; that is, the writer explains an interpretation, argues a point of view, or evaluates the effectiveness of a work or a writer's use of a particular technique. You may assume that your audience is your instructor and a community of knowledgeable peers. Having a beginning idea of questions, of topics, of thesis, of purpose, and of audience will direct your thinking and notetaking and will help you to assess the information from your sources. As you take notes, be aware that you may change your approach, thesis, topics, purpose, and audience.

Read and review your secondary sources carefully. Some people prefer to take notes on index cards; others use sheets of paper; others take minimal notes on cards or paper and create a system of notes that refers to xeroxed information. You may put notes in the margins of duplicated information. In addition, you may wish to enter data into a computer. Whatever method you use, as you take notes, you engage in a combination of summarizing, paraphrasing, and quoting. When you summarize, you compress the central idea and main points in a work. When you paraphrase, you "translate" a passage from a work into your own words. Paraphrasing keeps the length, spirit, tone, logic, and ideas of the original passage, but the wording is different. When you quote, you are recording the author's statement exactly. Be certain not to include any words from the original work within your summary or paraphrase without using quotation marks. Any material from a source in the words of the author *must* be quoted. For this reason, take notes meticulously. Summarize, paraphrase, and quote accurately on the front of a note card or page. Then write your reaction and comments on the back of the card or paper or xerox so that you have carefully documented and differentiated between your words and the language in the source, between your view and the critic's interpretations.

Each note also should contain an abbreviated annotation for source and page and a heading so that you may arrange your notes into categories of discussion and reshuffle them as your thesis and topics evolve.

PRINCIPLES OF DOCUMENTATION

You need to follow principles of documentation in your research process. Documentation indicates the sources of your information to a reader and demonstrates that you have absorbed and synthesized the materials from your secondary sources. Information that you should document in the text of your research paper includes the following:

- Facts that are not common knowledge (that could not be verified in several sources).
- Paraphrased information from a source (information from a source that you have put into your own words).
- Quoted material.
- Other people's views—even when they are paraphrased, not quoted—interviews, and other sources of information.

All of the above forms of information must be documented. If you do not document thoroughly or if you inadequately paraphrase the source, you will be plagiarizing. **Plagiarism** is the taking of someone else's ideas or words and representing them as your own. This act, which constitutes academic "theft," is a serious matter.

Once you have refined your research question, decided upon a focus for your research, a preliminary approach, thesis, and subtopics, and conducted research, you are ready to revise your thesis, to create an outline, and to draft your essay. The final stage in the research process is actually composing the essay. During this phase, you may repeat the acts of the writing process although you already have done considerable prewriting and planning: brainstorming, shaping, drafting, revising, and writing several versions of your paper. In this research-writing process, however, you must document carefully from all your sources.

For students, another issue in the research process becomes the value of their own opinions and thinking. During the drafting of a research essay, you focus on an original thesis and idea. Your thesis emerges from your thinking, reading, and research. The exploration, evaluation, and synthesis of evidence from sources also emanate from your own thinking. When you piece together your opinions, analysis, and information from primary and secondary sources, you may discover that you may experience the satisfaction of exploring and validating your thesis and of sharing your findings with others.

FORM OF MLA DOCUMENTATION—CITATION WITHIN THE TEXT

All sources must be cited; that is, you must give the reader information about the material to which you refer. The accepted method of documenting information in research is MLA citation form that requires three steps: (1) use parenthetical references within your research essay; (2) include a "Works Cited" page that contains an alphabetized list of all of the primary and secondary sources that you have used in the development of your essay; and (3) include explanatory endnotes, if necessary.

The parenthetical reference involves two parts: an indication of author and of page. If the author's name is mentioned in the discussion, then you only need to indicate page number. If the author has written two books and if the title of the book is not given, then you should include an abbreviated title in the citation.

The common forms of parenthetical citation for papers about literature appear in the following examples. Examine these manuscript and punctuation forms—the conventions for citations:

1. Discussion (author and page)
   (Alexander 200)
2. Discussion—author already mentioned
   (79).
3. Two Works by Same Author whose name is mentioned
   ("Hope" 265) (*Ariel* 54).
4. Paraphrased and Summarized Material—author not mentioned
   (Alexander 302)

5. Direct Quotation—author mentioned

   Kroll states that "it is uncertain how seriously the speaker will entertain the theme of purity, and its related theme of transcendence" (178).

   Note: Citation appears after quotation mark and before final punctuation.

6. Indented quotation—more than two lines of poetry and four lines of prose:

   This poem is about two kinds of fire—
   the fires of hell, which merely
   agonize, and the fires of hell which
   purify. During the poem, the first
   suffers into the second. (Newman 62)

If you interpret only one literary work, you may indicate the paragraphs or pages of a short story, the lines of a poem, or the acts and scenes of a drama in a citation rather than the author and title since they previously have appeared in the introduction to the essay.

"WORKS CITED" PAGE

The "Works Cited" page also has a specific format, a particular pattern for each form of reference, dictated by the conventions of the MLA documentation system. The following are the most common bibliographic forms for the "Works Cited" page. Consult the handbook used in your Freshman Composition Program for further information.

Common Forms of Bibliographic Entries for the "Works Cited" Page

For a Book

Gilligan, Carol. *In a Different Voice:*
     Psychological Theory and Women's Development.
     Cambridge; Harvard University Press, 1982.

Kincaid, Jamaica. *Annie John.* New York: Farrar,
     Straus, Giroux, 1985.

Morrison, Toni. *Beloved.* New York: Knopf, 1987.
   The citation is double-spaced, the author's name is placed at the margin, and the second line indented (5 spaces). There are periods between parts of the entry. The citation includes author's name, the title of the work and publication information—place published, publisher, and date.

For a Book with Two Authors

Flynn, Elizabeth A. and Patrocino Schweickart, eds.
Gender and Reading: Essays on Readers, Texts and
Contexts. Baltimore: John Hopkins Press, 1986.

When there are two authors, the second author's name is presented first name and then last name.

For an Author with Two Works

Rich, Adrienne. An Atlas of a Difficult World: Poems
1988-1991. New York: W.W. Norton, 1991.

- - -. On Lies, Secrets and Silence: Selected Prose
1966-1978. New York: W.W. Norton, 1979.

Note the alphabetical order of books for the author and three hyphens with a period to indicate the repeated name.

For Three or More Authors

Belenky, Mary Field, et al. Women's Ways of Knowing:
The Development of Self, Voice, and Mind. New
York: Basic Books, 1986.

Notice the use of "et al." to indicate the additional authors.

Translation

Wolf, Christa. The Quest for Christa T. Trans.
Christopher Middletown. New York: Farrar,
Straus, and Giroux, 1970.

Note that the translator's name appears after title and before publication information.

A Work Within an Anthology of Works

Mukherjee, Bharati. "Courtly Vision." Sudden
Fiction International: Sixty Short-Short
Stories. Eds. Robert Shapard and James Thomas.
New York: W.W. Norton, 1989. 215-219.

The author's name and work appear before the title of the anthology which follows. The names of the authors of the anthology are acknowledged, with the abbreviation indicating that they are the editors. Finally, the publication information is given.

Additional Entries for Works in an Anthology

Bogarad, Carley and Jan Zlotnik Schmidt, eds.
Legacies. Fort Worth: Harcourt Brace, 1995.

Shakespeare, William. *Hamlet.* Bogarad and Schmidt,
eds. 162-274.

Keats, John. "Ode on a Grecian Urn." Bogarad and
Schmidt, eds. 1089-1090.

If you cite more than one selection from the same anthology, list
the anthology as a separate entry with all publication information.
If you use more than one work from the same anthology, also list
each selection. Give the author's name and title of the selection,
but mention only the name(s) of the editor(s) of the anthology and
the page numbers.

Other Examples of a Short Story, Poem, or Play in an Edited Anthology

Borowski, Tadeusz. "Silence." *Literature: Reading,
Reacting, Writing.* Eds. Laurie G. Kirzner and
Stephen R. Mandell. Fort Worth: Harcourt Brace,
1993. 315-316.

Note the indication of page numbers.

Kumin, Maxine. "The Envelope." *Tangled Vines: A
Collection of Mother and Daughter Poems.* Ed. Lyn
Lifshin. New York: Harcourt, Brace, Jovanovich,
1992. 143.

Childress, Alice. *Wedding Band. 9 Plays by Black
Women.* Ed. Margaret B. Wilkerson. New York: New
American Library, 1986. 69-133.

Note that titles of short stories, poems, and essays require quotation marks and that titles of plays are underlined or italicized. As a
general rule, complete works are underlined, and shorter works appear in quotation marks.

Work in Several Volumes

Eagleton, T. Allston. *A History of the New York
Stage.* 3 vols. New York: Prentice Hall, 1987.

Note the indication of volumes.

One Work in a Several Volume Work

Eagleton, T. Allston. *A History of the New York
    Stage.* New York: Prentice Hall, 1987. Vol. 2.

Note the indication of the particular volume cited in the essay at
the end of the note.

An Edited Anthology Cited as a Whole Work, Not as a Single Citation of a Particular Selection

Halpern, Daniel, ed. *The American Poetry Anthology.*
    New York: Avon, 1975.

Note the indication that Halpern is the editor.

An Article in a Critical Anthology

Volpe, Edmond L. "The Wasteland of Nathanael West."
    *Nathanael West: A Collection of Critical
    Essays.* Ed. Jay Martin. Englewood Cliffs, NJ:
    Prentice Hall, 1971. 91-101.

An Article or Selection in a Weekly Magazine for General Audiences, Paginated Anew in Each Issue

Barthelme, Frederick. "Law of Averages." *The New
    Yorker,* 5 October 1987: 36-39.

Notice the format for presentation of articles: Author, Title of Work,
Name of Magazine, Date, a colon, and then pages.

An Article in an Academic Journal Paginated Continuously Throughout the Volume Year

Wilentz, Gay. "Toward a Diaspora Literature: Black
    Women Writers from Africa, the Caribbean and the
    United States." *College English* 54 (1992):
    385-445.

Note the addition of volume number after the title of the journal
and the placement of year within parentheses.

An Article in a Journal That Comes Out Once a Month, That Is Paginated Anew Each Month, and That Has a Volume and Issue Number

Muscatine, Charles. "Faculty Responsibility for the
    Curriculum." *Academe* 71.5 (1985): 18-21.

Notice that 71 is the volume number and that 5 is the issue number.

An Encyclopedia

Blotner, Joseph L. "James Joyce." *The Webster Family Encyclopedia*, 1984 ed.

You do not need to include publication information for well-known reference sources.

An Article in a Newspaper

Sontag, Deborah. "Making 'Refugee Experience' Less Daunting." *New York Times* 27 September 1992: Sec.1:1,35.

Interview

Dove, Rita. "An Interview with Helen Vendler." The National Humanities Center, January 16, 1989.

Bogarad, Carley. "Sylvia Plath's and Ted Hughes' Poetry." Talk given at State University of New York College at New Paltz. New Paltz, October 24, 1990.

ENDNOTES

When you use parenthetical citation form, you may create endnotes to include explanatory information that is not necessary to the text. This information may be additional sources, added biographical data, or an opposing critical view. Endnotes are numbered, follow in numerical order in the essay, and are indicated by a number in superscript above the line.[1] The "Endnote" page, labeled "Notes," is doubled-spaced, appears after the last page of your paper, and is your last numbered page. The "Works Cited" page is the last page of your research essay.

Here is an example of an endnote designed to provide additional bibliographic information:

Text of Essay: In recent years, there have been many attempts to define women's separate ways of knowing and developing moral consciousness.[1]

Notes

[1] See, for example, Belenky et al. and Gilligan.

Here is an endnote designed to provide a differing critical view:

Text of Essay: *House on Mango Street* is considered by many critics to be Cisneros' best work. This first, auto-biographical work brought her critical acclaim.[1]

Notes

[1] Although *House on Mango Street* brought Cisneros acclaim, I would contend that *Woman Hollering Creek* is a more complex and subtle work.

AN EXAMPLE OF THE RESEARCH PROCESS— MLA DOCUMENTATION

This case study presents the research and writing process of a student, Kevin Stoffel. It includes a journal entry, an outline, and the final version of the essay with annotations by the editors. The assignment for the research paper offered the option of literary analysis, and Stoffel immediately chose to write about Sylvia Plath. The instructor required eight typewritten pages and a variety of sources. The paper was due in six weeks. In order to assure success, the instructor established deadlines for parts of the work. She encouraged her students to conduct research and writing according to the processes described in this chapter. Stoffel created a work schedule, chose and defined a topic, thought about the rhetorical situation, took notes, kept a journal, and made careful copies of sources to avoid plagiarism. When he submitted his complete portfolio, it contained far more work than the instructor had assigned. In the folder, he placed copies of original drafts of Plath's poems, an essay on "Lady Lazarus," several handwritten versions of the paper, many articles on the topic, note cards, and copious written notes and summaries of articles and of books, and his final research project.

In many ways, Kevin Stoffel began his college composition research project in high school when he watched a segment of the PBS series on American poets, *Voices and Visions*. The program on Sylvia Plath sparked his interest in her poetry and impelled him to purchase, to read, and to memorize *Ariel,* her most famous single volume. In the first conference with his composition professor, he discussed his desire to write about Plath; and he presented a number of ideas in order to choose an original thesis for his research paper. Possible ideas included Plath's marriage and her poetry; *The Bell Jar;* Plath's suicide; her obsession with death. As he prepared his bibliography, read primary and secondary sources, and took notes, he received critiques and suggestions from other students in the class.

His instructor then encouraged him to consult with a member of the English Department faculty whose research focused on Plath; and she, in turn, called Ruth Mortimer, curator of the Rare Book Room of the Neilson Library at Smith College which owns the manuscripts of sixty-six of the lyrics known as the "Ariel Poems" by Sylvia Plath. At this point, Stoffel's term paper became an adventure. He drove to Smith College, a long journey, and worked extensively in the Sylvia Plath Collection.

He began with three research questions:

1. What is the relation between Plath's life and her poems?
2. Is the poetry totally personal, depressing, and suicidal?
3. What is the connection between death and transformation?

These questions led him to a thematic consideration of several poems in *Ariel,* and he began to focus on the theme of transcendence in Plath's draft versions. His research in the original manuscripts clarified some of his questions and suggested a new problem: What do the draft versions reveal about themes of the works? He wanted to answer these questions, and he wanted to explore Plath's revisions.

During his visit to Smith, he copied by hand all drafts of "Lady Lazarus," "Stings," "Edge," "Fever 103°," and "Ariel" since the Plath estate permitted no duplication of manuscripts. He also wrote all significant emendations in pencil (no pens permitted) in the margins and between the lines of his battered copy of *Ariel.* In the following journal entry, he records his responses to his encounter with the original drafts of these poems:

> *I have just returned from Smith College where I worked in the Sylvia Plath Collection. For such a long time, I have admired Plath's poems, and I can hardly believe that the facsimiles of the manuscript lay in my hands, that I touched her books, that I scrutinized her list of submissions. I am in awe of Plath's poetic powers, and I feel exhilarated, happy, great.*
>
> *In high school, I became fascinated by her poems when I watched the Plath segment of PBS' Voices and Visions on American poets. I began reading her books over and over, and eventually my interest resulted in a paper on "Daddy" that my teacher really liked. He encouraged me to continue my research. When I took the Regents examination in English, Plath's poem "Mirror" appeared in a major question. My passion for Plath paid off in a truly unexpected moment.*
>
> *Now after studying the manuscripts of "Lady Lazarus," "Edge," "Ariel," and "Fever 103°" closely, I believe that my idea about her search for transcendence holds validity and that the drafts have exciting new information in them, information that seems, at first glance, to support my thesis. I feel certain that I can write an original paper because no one has published any materials from these*

*drafts and all important scholars seem to have divided opinions on
the question of transcendence.*

After a number of drafts of his essay, Stoffel submitted a version to the
class and to his professor. In order to assist him with his revisions, they asked
these questions about his tentative paper:

Do you want to include the texts of the poems so that readers may
  refer to them?

Where is your thesis?

What is the connection between the biographical details and your
  paper?

How does the theme of transcendence connect to the draft versions of
  the poems?

What is the organizing principle (the thesis) of the paper? of the
  paragraphs?

How does "Edge" become transcendent?

Why does the analysis of "Edge" focus on the drafts and *not* on the
  theme?

Who is your audience?

They praised Stoffel's intention and passion for his subject, his command of
the research process, and his enormous portfolio. Everyone expressed a sense
of enrichment and excitement which he or she attributed to Stoffel's conception of himself as a scholar.

Stoffel then reorganized and revised his essay according to the suggestions given by his instructor and his peers. On the basis of their critiques, he
clarified his thesis and decided to limit his interpretations to "Fever 103°"
and to "Ariel." He realized that he could not complete his ambitious project
successfully unless he concentrated more fully on his two best examples. He
eliminated "Lady Lazarus" because of the length of the poem and because of
the number of draft versions. Since he believed that the analysis of the
manuscripts of "Edge" in his rough draft included new material about Plath's
attitude toward the dead children in the poem, he reluctantly chose to omit
that section. A careful reading of his first essay, however, convinced him that
he had lost the thematic emphasis in his interpretation of "Edge" and that his
description of the drafts lacked specificity. He concluded that his paper
changed focus at that point and that the analysis was not necessary for the
final revision of his paper.

His instructor asked him to review MLA notation form since his draft
contained inaccurate citations and to revise his "Works Cited" list to include
his primary sources, *Ariel* and the Sylvia Plath Collection at Smith College.
She requested that he include copies of the poems with his essay. His outline

and final research paper which follow offer clarity of organization, a revised thesis, and expanded interpretations of the theme of transcendence in "Fever 103°" and "Ariel." Notice the inclusion of secondary sources and of interesting examples from the manuscripts of the drafts. The citations, the Notes, and the "Works Cited" list now are correct, and they provide models for MLA documentation. Kevin Stoffel selected an extremely difficult topic, and he received high praise for his original project. His paper represents an excellent example of the value of research and of writing.

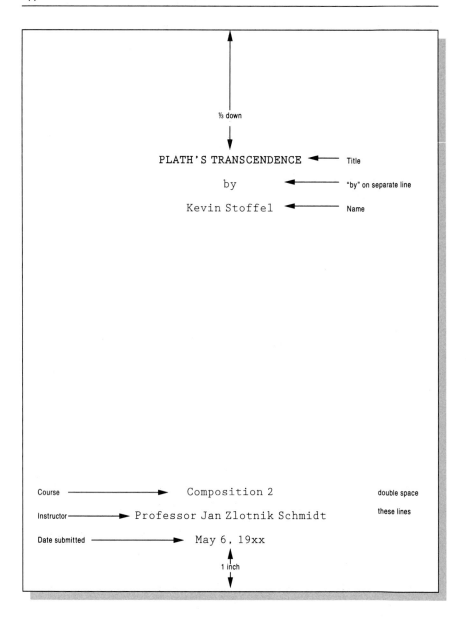

½ inch

Stoffel i

Name, number. (Number appears in lower case Roman numerals)

OUTLINE

Center the word "Outline." Place one inch from top of page. Double space outline.

I. Introduction
    A. Critics interpret Plath's poems as
    autobiography.
    B. Theme of transcendence is central to
    Plath's poems, and draft versions reveal
    Plath's movement away from autobiography
    toward universal experience of transcendence.
    C. "Fever 103°" and "Ariel" are two versions of
    transcendence and prove hypothesis about
    revisions.

Thesis statement

Stoffel writes a topic outline.

II. Autobiography in "Fever 103°" and in "Ariel":
    A. "Fever 103°" versions show omission of
    materials on Ted Hughes in order to focus on
    transformation.
    B. "Ariel" recounts a real event on a runaway
    horse, but experience becomes transcendent.

Divide major sections with Roman numerals.

Each part in a major section of the outline should be numbered A, B, C, etc.

Strive for parallel constructions.

III. Interpretation of "Fever 103°"
    A. Plath's statement on two kinds of fire.
    B. Purity defined by opposite images of hell,
    sexual sin.
    C. Universal death from radiation (Hiroshima)
    caused by adultery.
    D. Purgation by retching.

All verbs should be in the present tense.

Stoffel ii

    E. Transformations:
      1. lantern.
      2. camellia.
      3. acetylene virgin.
    F. Draft versions.

IV. Transition
    A. Use of sexual imagery in "Fever 103°"—it is
    the sin.
    B. Use of sexual imagery as metaphor for
    ecstatic transformation in "Ariel."

V. Interpretation of "Ariel"
    A. The ride on the horse:
      1. sexual imagery
      2. out-of-control
      3. the hooks
    B. "Something else hauls me through air"—the
    beginning of merging, of transformation.
    C. White Godiva:
      1. She "unpeels"
      2. "Dead hands, dead stringencies."
    D. Arrow and dew—evaporated into the
    sun/annihilation:
      1. Creative energy.
      2. Unification with sun.
    E. Draft versions.

VI. Conclusion
    A. Summary of thesis and proofs.
    B. Quote from Katha Pollitt.

ARIEL

Sylvia Plath

Stasis in darkness.
Then the substanceless blue
Pour of tor and distances.

God's lioness,
How one we grow,
Pivot of heels and knees!—The furrow

Splits and passes, sister to
The brown arc
Of the neck I cannot catch,

Nigger-eye
Berries cast dark
Hooks—

Black sweet blood mouthfuls,
Shadows,
Something else

Hauls me through air—
Thighs, hair;
Flakes from my heels.

Stoffel iv

White
Godiva, I unpeel—
Dead hands, dead stringencies

And now I
Foam to wheat, a glitter of seas.
The child's cry

Melts in the wall,
And I
Am the arrow,

The dew that flies
Suicidal, at one with the drive
Into the red

Eye, the cauldron of morning.

27 October 1962

FEVER 103°

Sylvia Plath

Pure? What does it mean?
The tongues of hell
Are dull, dull as the triple

Tongues of dull, fat Cerberus
Who wheezes at the gate. Incapable
Of licking clean

Stoffel v

The aguey tendon, the sin, the sin.
The tinder cries.
The indelible smell

Of a snuffed candle!
Love, Love, the low smokes roll
From me like Isadora's scarves, I'm in a fright

One scarf will catch and anchor in the wheel
Such yellow sullen smokes
Make their own element. They will not rise,

But trundle round the globe
Choking the aged and the meek,
The weak

Hothouse baby in its crib,
The ghastly orchid
Hanging its hanging garden in the air,

Devilish leopard!
Radiation turned it white
And killed it in an hour.

Greasing the bodies of adulterers
Like Hiroshima ash and eating in.
The sin. The sin.

Stoffel vi

Darling, all night
I have been flickering, off, on, off, on.
The sheets grow heavy as a lecher's kiss.

Three days. Three nights.
Lemon water, chicken
Water, water make me retch.

I am too pure for you or anyone.
Your body
Hurts me as the world hurts God. I am a lantern—

My head a moon
Of Japanese paper, my gold beaten skin
Infinitely delicate and infinitely expensive.

Does not my heat astound you. And my light.
All by myself I am a huge camellia
Glowing and coming and going, flush on flush.

I think I am going up,
I think I may rise—
The beads of hot metal fly, and I, love, I

Am a pure acetylene
Virgin
Attended by roses,

By kisses, by cherubim,
By whatever these pink things mean.
Not you, nor him

Not him, nor him
(My selves dissolving, old whore petticoats)—
To Paradise.

                                        20 October 1962

½ inch

1

PLATH'S TRANSCENDENCE

Sylvia Plath's suicide in 1963 casts a shadow
over her poems, a long shadow which seems to
encourage readers and critics to interpret her
work as autobiography. Her writing certainly
includes details from her life, and no one can
challenge M. L. Rosenthal's definition of her
poetry as "confessional" in *The New Poets* (79).
However, strong evidence of Plath's emphasis on
transformation and of her control of both form
and content which consistently made her poems
less personal appears in her late poetry[1] and in
the draft versions of the poems from *Ariel* in the
Sylvia Plath Collection in the Neilson Library
at Smith College.[2]

In "Fever 103°" and in "Ariel," Plath creates
two kinds of transcendent visions, and drafts of
both poems reveal her careful revisions through
handwritten and typed versions—each draft a
movement away from personal anger and outrage,
from desire for revenge, and from confession.

Both poems begin in personal suffering, and
both poems refer to events in her life. "Fever
103°" alludes to Plath's separation from her
husband, Ted Hughes, now Poet Laureate of
England, and to his affair with Assia Wevill
which ended their marriage in 1962 (Alexander
290). The poem's preoccupation with sexuality

PAGE NUMBER—Because Stoffel
uses a cover page, he typed the
number 1 in the right hand corner,
placed one half inch from the top.

TITLE—Stoffel's title is required,
and it indicates the thematic
emphasis of his paper.

INTRODUCTORY
MATERIAL—Stoffel mentions
Plath's suicide and
autobiographical interpretations as
a way of gaining the reader's
attention and of giving background
information. He attempts to show
that Plath "transcends" her
personal history.

ENDNOTES—Endnotes give
information not necessary in text.

THESIS STATEMENT

EXPLANATION OF THESIS

Stoffel 2

On every sheet, except page 1, Stoffel types his name before the number.

and with sin and its emphasis on "adulterers" may stem from Plath's experience with Hughes, but the drafts demonstrate repeated efforts to eliminate direct references to him. "Ariel" recounts a wild ride on a horse, Sam, which galloped out of control (Alexander 302), but the drafts transform the incident into "something else." Sylvia Plath begins with her own pain and despair, with the concrete details of her daily life, but she often focuses on transcendence, and she often revises autobiography into stunning and symbolic figures including the "pure acetylene/virgin" (*Ariel* 54)[3] of "Fever 103°" and the "White/Godiva" (*Ariel* 26) of "Ariel."

PARENTHETICAL REFERENCE TO SOURCE.

PARAPHRASE OF SOURCE—To avoid too many quotations, Stoffel paraphrases central events from Alexander's biography of Plath.

In a statement prepared for a BBC reading, Plath describes "Fever 103°": "This poem is about two kinds of fire—the fires of hell, which merely agonize, and the fires of heaven which purify. During the poem, the first sort suffers into the second" (Newman 62). "Fever 103°" is one of several poems by Plath in which fire serves to create a sense of purity equivalent to a type of transcendence, a movement to a higher plane. However, in the beginning of the poem, Judith Kroll suggests that "it is uncertain how seriously the speaker will entertain the theme of purity, and its related theme of transcendence" (178). The speaker inquires about the meaning of the term "pure," but she defines it through descriptions of its opposite, images

Parenthetical reference to author not named in the text. The source (author and page) is added in parentheses.
TOPIC SENTENCE
Stoffel analyzes theme in "Fever 103°."

Stoffel 3

of hell—all evil, impure images. The speaker, in
her feverish state, descends into the classical
underworld. In order for its fires to purify and
for death, rebirth, and transcendence to occur,
she must confront sexual sins, lust, and the
"full images of hell" (Bassnett 127). These
depths include Cerberus, the mythological
three-headed dog that guards the gates of Hades.
His disgusting tongues cannot ". . .clean/The
aguey tendon, the sin, the sin" (*Ariel* 53).
Nothing can clean the sin. This image blends into
the sulfurous smell of a "snuffed candle" (*Ariel*
53) and into the speaker's illness rolling from
her like the scarves of Isadora Duncan, scarves
that can choke and kill. The smokes "will not
rise" (*Ariel* 53). Instead, they reach a universal
level as they "trundle round the globe" (*Ariel*
53). This sexual circle of hell with the smell
and smoke and taste of sin engulfs the world and
seems "dull" and "sullen" (*Ariel* 53), a parody of
its Biblical and classical counterparts.

    The smoke of hell murders the old and the
young. The speaker ceases her concern for her own
plight and for the sins committed against her
which render her impure, and she moves to a
global level as the smokes choke "The weak/
Hothouse baby in its crib" (*Ariel* 53), and "The
ghastly orchid" (*Ariel* 53). The smokes transform
into radiation which kills the "Devilish
leopard" (*Ariel* 53). The nuclear fall-out from

Evidence of purifying fires in poem. Quotation within sentence. Stoffel quotes Bassnett and fits her description into his sentence.

Evidence of sexual sin, impurity.

Stoffel 4

the destruction of Hiroshima—a version of hell
on earth—greases ". . .the bodies of adulterers/
Like Hiroshima ash. . ." (*Ariel* 54). Even in this
form, the radiation becomes a punishment for
adultery and for sexual sin. Some of its victims
are not innocent like those upon whom the atomic
bomb was dropped.

Thus, the speaker, by being impure, takes on
the role of a Hiroshima radiation victim:

> Darling, all night
> I have been flickering, off,
> on, off, on,
> The sheets grow heavy as a
> lecher's kiss
>
> Three days. Three nights.
> Lemon water, chicken
> Water, water makes me retch. (*Ariel* 54)

An apt and accurate description of a feverish
state, the flickering clearly connotes
sexuality—the rhythm of the lines, the lecher.
The speaker begins to experience purgation
through retching.

After being a victim of the bombing of
Hiroshima, the speaker becomes ". . .a huge
camellia/Glowing and coming and going, flush on
flush" (*Ariel* 54). This orgasmic blossom creates

LONG QUOTATION. A quotation of more than four typewritten lines is separated from the rest of the text.

Stoffel indents ten spaces and double spaces the quotation.

The reference for the quotation is given in parentheses after the quotation. Since Stoffel uses two Plath references in his paper, he gives the name of the volume to indicate which primary source by Plath serves as the text.

Stoffel 5

its own metamorphosis, "all by [it]self" (*Ariel*
54). Then the speaker enters a state of purity.
The first fire "suffers into the second." Plath
alludes to the Ascension of Mary: "I think I am
going up,/I think I may rise" (*Ariel* 54) (Note
the sexual implications of her language.). The
speaker transforms herself into a virgin, not
because she wants this persona, but because she
still retains the "glow" and the "heat" of the
radiation. She "emerges from her suffering as an
infinitely desirable, but untouchable virgin"
(Bundtzen 199)—too hot for any man to touch or to
enjoy. All men are pushed aside as she rises. She
needs no one as she ascends to heaven, as she
overflows with purity. She turns all men away
from her "unquenchable fire" (Bundtzen 199). All
of the sins, "old whore petticoats" (*Ariel* 54),
dissolve as she ascends, through purification,
into Paradise.

This transcendence becomes a kind of
purification of the fiery "acetylene/Virgin"
(*Ariel* 54) in three draft versions of this poem
written on October 20, 1962. In the first two
drafts of this poem, Plath refers to the devilish
leopard as "you": "Oh that devilish leopard!/
Radiation turned you white/And killed you in an
hour" (Plath Collection, Smith College). Here she
reveals her anger about Hughes' affair with Assia
Wevill. However, in the third and final version,

QUOTATION FROM DRAFT
VERSIONS. Stoffel indicates the
source of the quotation from Plath
because he has used two entries
for Plath: *Ariel* and the Sylvia
Plath Collection.

Stoffel 6

she changes the "you" to "it" in order to
depersonalize the image and to move the poem from
a personal to a general level. The lover, the man,
the darling is not killed, simply left behind.

    In both poems, Plath creates sexual imagery,
but the imagery serves different purposes. In
"Fever 103°," the illness clearly serves as
metaphor for the speaker's pain, for her descent
into hell because of adultery and because of
sexual sin. "Your Body/Hurts me as the world
hurts God. . . ." (*Ariel* 54). The purgation of
illness leads to transcendence, even though the
virgin in this case rises to Paradise from "hot
beads" and from fire. She is not the image of a
Renaissance madonna. Still, she transcends her
experience of impurity and suffering; and she
reaches Paradise, the ultimate state of
blessedness. In "Ariel," however, the sexual
imagery stands for transformation of the speaker
into a bare, "White Godiva" from whom things drop
away, and the speaker's annihilation becomes a
unification of personal and artistic energy
through evaporation into the source of all human
life, the sun, ". . .the red/eye, the cauldron of
morning" (*Ariel* 27). The sexual ride and the
connotations represent "something else" which
"hauls [her] through air" (*Ariel* 26). The sexual
imagery is *not* the subject matter here as it is in
"Fever 103°." The subject matter is "something
else" (*Ariel* 26).

Movement to more general level of interpretation.

Paraphrase of third draft.

TRANSITION
Sexual imagery in both poems.

Transition to interpretation of theme in "Ariel."

Stoffel 7

"Ariel" begins in a motionless and black state—"Stasis in darkness" (Ariel 26)—as the persona describes the commencement of a ride on a horse that gallops out of control. The name, Ariel, refers to a favorite horse that Plath rode in Devonshire (Butscher 377). The name also conveys a key to the poem. It refers to Jerusalem (Isaiah 29:1-3). The derivation may be either "lioness of God," which was underlined in her dictionary and which was written at the top of the first page of the first draft of the poem (Plath Collection, Smith College), or "altar of God" (Isaiah 29:1-3). In forming a connection between the horse and the Biblical allusions, Plath also infers that the horse is an altar upon which the speaker can be consumed. The horse is the "scrobis" upon which the speaker can shed all of the "inessentials of life, thus becoming free and pure" (Kroll 181). Plath also invokes the air spirit, Ariel, from Shakespeare's *The Tempest*, the spirit who seeks only to be free.

> Paraphrase of numerous primary and secondary sources. Plath, the *Bible*, and Shakespeare represent primary sources. Kroll is a secondary source.

In the first two tercets of the poem, the speaker becomes one with the runaway horse, God's lioness. The violent ride itself merges woman and horse, female and male. In every image, the reader discovers sexual connotations: "Pivot of heels and knees!—The furrow/Splits and passes. . ." (*Ariel* 26). Yet the concrete details of the "brown arc/of the neck. . ." (*Ariel* 26) and of the "Black sweet blood

> Paraphrase of action of the poem. The horse and woman merge. The speaker becomes one with the horse.

Stoffel 8

mouthfuls" (*Ariel* 26) of the berries eventually
become "Shadows" (*Ariel* 26). The wild galloping
ends, and the speaker is "Haul[ed]. . .through
air" (Ariel 26) by "Something else" (Ariel 26)
as she transforms into a symbolic figure like
Lady Godiva as she sheds her body and her past:

> White
> Godiva, I unpeel—
> Dead hands, dead stringencies. (*Ariel* 27)

When she experiences the orgasmic "foam[ing] to
wheat" (*Ariel* 26), she transforms again. "Thus the
identity not only of the rider but also of the
horse is dissolved: the newly created self is an
'arrow'. . ." (Wagner 116). After this merging
with the landscape, "seas" of "wheat" (*Ariel* 26),
the speaker becomes one with the horse, even
though, at the beginning of the poem, she is
restrained from this unity. The berries "still
tried to catch her with their hooks" (Kroll 182).
Thus, just as "the child's cry/Melts in the wall"
(Ariel 26-27), the speaker blends with the horse
and the landscape, escapes her body and her
suffering (the "White/Godiva" (*Ariel* 26)), and
"flies" as the "arrow" and "the dew" (*Ariel*
27)—pure energy—into the sun. The flight is both
suicidal and ecstatic since the transcendence
leads to the creative source. The poem which

Stoffel 9

begins in motionless darkness ends in infinite
motion and light. The speaker enters a
"revelation of a new world. It is a transcendence
into a new world written at no one's expense but
her own. . . . 'Ariel' is Plath's most
triumphant assertion of her poetic powers. . ."
(Bundtzen 256).[4]

> Endnote acknowledges alternative
> interpretations of the ending.

How does Plath create the amazing
transformations in "Ariel"? To what degree does
she control autobiographical detail for artistic
and thematic purposes? She writes about a real
event and a real horse. She changes the name of the
horse for symbolic reasons (Sam becomes Ariel.).

> Evidence of control of personal
> materials for thematic purposes.

She invents an extended sexual metaphor for the
experience, and an examination of draft versions
reveals that she controls the erotic imagery
through revision. In the first three drafts of
"Ariel," Plath calls the horse "crude mover whom I
move/And burn to love," "oh, bright beast,"
"lover," "the plunging/Hooves" (Plath Collection,
Smith College). The fourth draft consists mainly
of versions of one tercet, the pivotal stanza
about the unpeeling Godiva. Here she presents the
same tendency to kill the lover (Hughes) that
appears in the drafts of "Fever 103°."

> Hands, hearts, dead men,
> Dead men,
> Hands, heads, peel off. (Plath
>   Collection, Smith College)

> Use of primary source. Draft
> versions of poems.

Stoffel 10

Plath attempts six different revisions of the
above stanza before she writes:

> White
> Godiva, I unpeel—
> Dead hands, dead stringencies. (Plath
>   Collection, Smith College)

Note that she eliminates the desire for revenge,
the thinly veiled details of her life. She had
written the same lines which appear in the above
stanza in the first three versions, but she had
not ordered them as a separate tercet. In the
fourth draft, she attempts numerous revisions of

Analysis of theme in draft of "Ariel."

the idea before she returns to her original
language and rearranges it as a distinct stanza.
Once again, the reader discovers that Plath
controls her personal anger in order to enhance
the effect of her poem and to attain a larger
meaning. These draft versions reveal a
tightening of the language which creates a fast
tempo and an ecstatic tone, the idea of
transcending, of changing to another form, of
merging with the sun.

Plath fully develops the theme of

CONCLUSION

transcendence in "Fever 103°" and in "Ariel."
Through revision, she crafts great poems and
often eliminates her private angers and desire
for revenge in order to create deeply human

Stoffel 11

themes. Through rising and blending images, the
ideas of rebirth and of transcendence to a higher
plane are expressed with great intensity. The
strength of her poetic vision emerges and begins
to balance the widely held conception of her
negativity. These poems—wonderfully controlled,
brilliantly worded, deeply felt, wisely
conceived—earn her an important place in
twentieth century poetry. As Katha Pollitt
writes in the *Nation*: "She was always becoming
more distinctly herself, and by the time she came
to write her last seventy or eighty poems, there
was no other voice like hers on earth" (53).

Quotation with author and source named in the text.

1 inch

Stoffel 12

NOTES

¹ See Susan R. Van Dyne's essay, "'More Terrible
Than She Ever Was': The Manuscripts of Sylvia
Plath's Bee Poems" in Wagner's Collection for
confirmation of this thesis.

² I wish to acknowledge the assistance of Ruth
Mortimer and her staff at the Rare Book Room of
Neilson Library at Smith College and to express my
gratitude for permission to quote from the
manuscripts to the library and to the Plath Estate
through Faber and Faber.

³All future references to the two poems are
taken from Sylvia Plath. <u>Ariel</u>. New York: Harper
and Row, 1973 or from draft versions in the Plath
Collection at Smith College.

⁴ Such critics as Alvarez and Rosenthal
interpret this poem pessimistically.

"Notes" appear on separate numbered page, the last numbered page of the essay. The endnotes give material that does not fit into the text.

The note begins with number in superscript and is indented five spaces for the first line. All notes are double spaced. Stoffel offers comparison with his thesis.

Stoffel acknowledges the assistance of Ruth Mortimer at Smith College and permission to quote from Plath material.

Stoffel acknowledges alternatives to his interpretations.

Stoffel 13

WORKS CITED

Alexander, Paul. *Rough Magic: A Biography of Sylvia Plath*. New York: Viking Press, 1991.

Alvarez, A., *The Savage God*. New York: Random House, 1972.

Bassnett, Susan. *Sylvia Plath*. Totowa, New Jersey: Barnes and Noble Books, 1987.

Bundtzen, Lynda K. *Plath's Incarnations: A Woman and the Creative Process*. Ann Arbor: University of Michigan Press, 1983.

Butscher, Edward. *Sylvia Plath: Method and Madness*. New York: Simon and Schuster, 1977.

Kroll, Judith. *Chapters in a Mythology: The Poetry of Sylvia Plath*. New York: Harper and Row, 1976.

Newman, Charles. *The Art of Sylvia Plath*. Bloomington: Indiana University Press, 1970.

Perloff, Marjorie. "Angst and Animism in the Poetry of Sylvia Plath." *Critical Essays on Sylvia Plath*. Ed. Linda W. Wagner. Boston: G. K. Hall and Company, 1984. 109-124.

Plath, Sylvia. *Ariel*. New York: Harper and Row, 1973.

---. Unpublished Manuscripts. Sylvia Plath Collection. Rare Book Room, Neilson Library, Smith College.

Pollitt, Katha. "A Note of Triumph." *Nation* 16 January 1982:52-55.

Rosenthal, M. L. *The New Poets*. New York: Oxford University Press, 1967.

Bibliography, named "Works Cited," appears at the end of the paper. Entries are alphabetized by author's last name, with a five space indentation after the first line of each citation. Double space entries, and double space between entries.

Entry for a book by a single author.

Essay in an edited book.

Second work by the same author. Three hyphens and a period represent the author's name. Works are listed in alphabetical order by title. Entry for an essay in a journal. Essay title is in quotation marks; the journal, date, and year appear, and page numbers are denoted without pp. designation.

CRITICAL APPROACHES TO LITERATURE

We approach literary texts with presuppositions, often undefined, about what literature is, about what it means, and about what determines its worth. Critical theories enable us to articulate assumptions and to devise methodologies for reading, for analyzing, for interpreting, for evaluating, and for writing about literary works. At present, a number of theories offer complementary and competing views of the constructed work: of language itself, of the meaning or meanings of the text, of the process of creating meaning, and of the question concerning who or what creates meaning—the work, the writer, the reader, the culture.

Some critics think of a work of literature as fixed—a thing in itself with no relationship to the author or to his or her purpose or experiences, with no relationship to the reader, or with no relationship to the culture of the writer. The work, according to such a view, is objective and, consequently, free from the subjectivity of the writer or the reader. We begin with these theories that focus on the text; then we move to critical approaches that center on the writer, the reader, or the culture.

FORMALISM

Formalist criticism considers formal elements of literature to determine meaning—organization, structure, and language. Each work must remain independent, complete in itself. Everything extrinsic to the piece becomes irrelevant. The formalist is not concerned with the state of mind of the writer, with any biographical, economic, political, or social information. The critic's interest centers on such intrinsic features as plot, character, narrative technique, language, irony, and paradox. In an effort to discover multiple meanings, the formalist critic attempts to resolve the tensions in the text in order to present a coherent, unified "close reading." This view implies that *only objective criteria* apply to literature and that such subjective elements as writer and as reader do not enter into the theory and method of formalism. This movement in English language criticism began with I. A. Richards' *Practical Criticism* (1929) in England. He theorized about his students' explications of famous poems, responses predicated on the "poem itself" since the students knew nothing about the poets.

In formalist criticism, the reader can make assumptions about the validity of interpretation and about the worth of the work of art; that is, some interpretations, based on evidence from the text, are better than others; and some works of art, based on their complexity, beauty, and depth, may be considered greater than others.

NEW CRITICISM

In the 1940s, a group of North American critics, among them Cleanth Brooks, Robert Penn Warren, and Rene Wellek, created a movement that dominated the practice of criticism in the United States for two decades and that remains influential at present. Their method, new criticism, demonstrates formal unity through examination of every element and every part of the whole in order to determine the central meaning of a text. In every act of interpretation, the critic looks for organic unity, that which arises from an analysis of the parts and is not superimposed on the individual work. In Wellek and Warren's *Theory of Literature,* Wellek claims that art is "an object of knowledge," and that "a literary work of art is in exactly the same position as a system of language." Through these statements he establishes the text as "objective" and interpretation as nonsubjective. Indeed, he concludes that "all relativism is defeated." To discover meaning in a text, the formalist reader examines the tensions and discovers the unity that resolves the tensions.

In "The Story of an Hour" by Kate Chopin (Chapter 9), the tension arises from the conflict that develops when Mrs. Mallard reacts to news of Brently Mallard's death. A formalist critic might focus on the ending where the wife, Mrs. Mallard, "afflicted with a heart trouble" dies when she discovers that her "kind, tender" husband has not perished in a train accident. In an ironic twist, Louise suffers a fatal heart attack because she is no longer "free, free, free!" Is this ending a carefully planned, unifying culmination of the tensions, or is it merely a trick—a simple surprise? To decide about the meaning of the death, a new critical approach would include an examination of images. Mrs. Mallard grieves immediately for her husband, but her emotions quickly transform into joy. "The tops of the trees" are "all aquiver with the new spring life." This imagery evokes rebirth. She is renewed by "the delicious breath of rain" and the songs of the birds.

Finally, she celebrates briefly a sense of autonomy and a determination to "live for herself." She dies of grief and of shock, not for the loss of her husband's life, but for the loss of her own emergent selfhood. Everyone assumes that her heart has broken from joy. Only the reader understands the true and ironic reason for her death. Through such an exploration, the New Critic can begin to determine the unifying principle of the ending.

STRUCTURALISM

Structuralism, like new criticism, attempts to offer objective analysis of the meaning of literature. The structuralist critic also seeks to eliminate considerations of history, economics, and politics. The theory aspires to scientific inquiry through ideas and methods borrowed from linguistics and from anthropology. Each work becomes a system, and the critic's task becomes the discovery of the laws which pertain to the interaction of elements in the system. The structuralist examines surface phenomena in order to uncover "a deep structure." For instance, the structuralist attempts to define conventions of literary forms; he or she might aspire to understand the features or elements that identify a text as a poem or drama.

Because structuralism developed from linguistics, some critics apply linguistic approaches to literature. In *Course in General Linguistics* (1915), Ferdinand de Saussure, a French linguist, called the relationship between an object and the name by which the object is designated (a sign) arbitrary. A word only makes sense within the system of an entire language, and it only signifies meaning to those who know that particular language system. Saussure further assumes that signs or words are useful when they emphasize difference: a hand and a foot are both appendages, but a hand has fingers and a foot has toes. A hand is attached to an arm; a foot is attached to a leg.

Saussure theorized about the rules that govern the complex system of signs in language. He claimed that a *semiotic* (a science of signs) principle, one that enables humans to communicate through a system of signs, exists and governs the structure of language. Literary critics who apply linguistics to texts assume that poems, fiction, and drama are part of a larger system. Any analysis of a work requires the comprehension of the system in which the work operates and of the difference between that system and other systems. Structuralism also requires readers to discover the way in which other kinds of sign systems (structures) create meaning.

"The Story of an Hour" has features that encourage the reader to define it as a narrative, as a story, not as a poem or a drama. It is self-contained; it incorporates the general laws of discourse concerning fiction. It begins with Mrs. Mallard's learning of the death of her husband. It has a middle that complicates the action—she uncharacteristically finds herself joyful because of her newly acquired freedom. The end, which has a surprising twist, also is Mrs. Mallard's end since she suffers a fatal coronary when she learns that her husband still lives. The doctors assume that she has died because of joy. The reader recognizes conventions of plot, theme, and character that appear in similar stories. The O. Henry ending, for example, began as a device in mystery stories and remains a recognizable structure in short fiction. The reader can recall other stories in which characters gain autonomy and happiness in a strange manner only to suffer a tragic reversal of fortune, a reversal both surprising and ironic. A scheme for the structure of this story might be: a character who encounters an opposing figure who reverses her good fortune. The structure of the story inverts and then repeats the scheme.

I. Initial structure
$$b - a = b - a$$
Brently − Louise = Brently
The marriage is oppressive, though Brently is kind and well-intentioned. Louise exists as a minus quantity.

II. Middle structure (Inversion of structure)
$a - b = a - b$
Louise − Brently = Louise
She is free because of Brently's reported death.

III. Final Structure   Repetition of initial structure
$b - a = b - a$
Brently − Louise = Brently
Louise dies because Brently lives, not because of "joy that kills."

The structure must be inferred from signs (words) which signify Louise's recognition of her state of mind and of her loss of self. Surface phenomena suggest that all characters (except Louise) assume another structure:

$$a + b = ab$$
$$ab - b = a$$
$$ab - a = b$$

The false or secondary system complicates the story and produces some of the ironic meanings. This structure depends on utterances (signs) from Josephine, Louise's sister, and from the doctors who signify their beliefs in an untrue state of mind for Louise and in an untrue conception of the marriage. The true structure illuminates the meaning of the story, and the false surface system creates the irony and surprise.

Structuralist criticism lost favor in the 1970s, and many new theories that borrowed from Saussure or that contradicted the objectivist approach appeared. Scholars often consider contemporary criticism as "Post Structuralism."

DECONSTRUCTION

Deconstructionist critics contend that literary works do not contain unified or stable meanings. Unlike the new critics who seek close readings to reconcile tensions in a text in order to establish the relation of the parts to the whole work, deconstructionists argue that any close examination of a text uncovers contradictions which inevitably "deconstruct" or dissolve the possibility of unity. Because they believe that language can never truly convey single, fixed messages, they postulate that language, by nature, creates endless meanings that destabilize a text and that create contradictions which cannot be reconciled.

As described by its most prominent theorist, Jacques Derrida (b. 1930), a French philosopher, language or linguistic response always reveals its opposite (A and Not-A) and, therefore, any close reading of a text uncovers basis of belief. Derrida calls this opposition *différance*, a term that contains two meanings: "to be different" and "to defer." When a reader or critic discovers "différance," he or she must resist the bias of the language in the text and uncover the contradictions which arise from the opposition. The inherent contradictions clearly cannot be reconciled, and no single meaning can be considered correct or stable.

Like structuralists and new critics, deconstructionists focus on the text. In deconstructing a work, however, the reader examines ambiguities, word play, competing meanings. The deconstructionist looks for metaphor because such an approach assumes that all language is naturally metaphorical since the word or sign which signifies an object is separate from that object, since the sign "stands" for something else, the object or idea, and is, therefore, metaphorical. Because words can only signify, they cannot serve as reality or as truth. They must always tangle and contradict; every written text contains elements which must destabilize it. The task of the critic becomes questioning which leads to the transcendence of ideological bias and to the virtual unraveling of the fabric of the text. There are no absolutes.

A deconstructionist reading of "The Story of an Hour" might focus on the ending. Does the narrator share the doctors' view? Then there exists no irony. Then there exists an indictment of Louise. Such an interpretation would posit a much more critical and shaded view of Mrs. Mallard and of her nascent and short-lived freedom than readers usually assume. What if the paradoxical statement that "she . . . died of heart disease—of joy that kills" signifies that the doctors recognize immediately that Louise experienced emotions other than joy? Joy does not usually "kill." Does the narrator ascribe such wisdom to the doctors? What does the narrator mean? What do the doctors mean? The reader immediately begins to open the text to possible readings which contradict each other and which expose certain biases in the work. In the end, Chopin's language reveals différance and enough ambiguity for a careful reader to ask questions and to uncover possible meanings which cannot be reconciled. The questions about the ending pose serious opposition to currently accepted interpretations of this story.

PSYCHOLOGICAL CRITICISM

Psychological criticism shifts the focus from the text itself both to the writer's and to the reader's roles in shaping the work. First, psychological critics attempt to demonstrate the connection between the author's life and works—between events in the author's personal life and work and forces influencing the author's personality—and the concerns, subject matter, themes of his or her art. They consider these connections central to an understanding of the work. For example, D. H. Lawrence's biographers connect his early family life, his relationships with his strong and seemingly overprotective mother and his ambivalence about his father, with the portrayal of characters in his fiction.

In Kate Chopin's "The Story of an Hour," the reader might discover many similarities between Chopin's life and her heroine's existence: Chopin represented her traditional marriage in which her role as a woman was restricted in her depiction of Mrs. Mallard's relationship to Brently. She recreated her genteel, bourgeois existence as the wife of a Creole cotton trader in her portrayal of Mrs. Mallard's domestic situation. The biographical critic might note that Chopin suppressed her own needs and desires until her husband died as does Mrs. Mallard. Chopin, consequently, chose to pursue a career as a writer to support her six children; Mrs. Mallard, however, never experiences that choice. The biographical critic might suggest that Chopin created versions of her own life again and again in her fiction.

Psychological criticism also takes another form—psychological analysis. In the late nineteenth and early twentieth centuries, psychology emerged as a science that studied forms of human behavior and the human mind. To understand this kind of criticism, one must know some general principles derived from the work of Sigmund Freud who is considered to be the father of modern psychology. Freud suggests that at the root of the make-up of human beings are irrational, sexual, aggressive, libidinal impulses or drives. These impulses exist in direct conflict with the civilizing drive: the need to fulfill duties and responsibilities within a cultural order. As people move from infancy, to adolescence, to adulthood, Freud theorizes that they learn to deny, to control, and to direct these impulses into socially acceptable forms of behavior. Freud then posits that people constantly live in a state of repression: people constantly must deny impulse and conform to the dictates of duty and conscience. These impulses, according to Freud, are driven into the unconscious where they manifest themselves symbolically in dreams. Art is a symbolic representation of the wishes of the unconscious.

In children, the main manifestation of sexual impulse emerges in unconscious desires to unite with the parent of the opposite sex. In boys, Freud labels this drive the Oedipus complex. Because of this unconscious desire, children fear the retribution of the jealous parent of the same sex. Boys fear castration by the father. This unconscious turmoil resolves as children mature and learn to direct their energies to appropriate objects of love and desire. If this conflict persists, children become paralyzed, often becoming plagued by guilt or self-inflicted punishment (masochism).

Certain terminology from Freud's theory is crucial to understanding psychological criticism. Freud envisions the human mind as composed of three forces: the id, the source of the irrational, sexual, aggressive drive; the ego, the mitigating force regulating the interaction between the id and the superego and determining behavior in one's waking life; the superego, the force of conscience and moral probity that controls the impulses of the id. Freud describes human development as a constant negotiation among these forces. He views the counterforce to the id as repression: the denial of sexual desire. And then he contends that sexual desire is sublimated: transformed and channeled in socially acceptable directions. The irrational, aggressive instinct human beings also tend to deny or to displace—project onto someone else; people see in another's behavior a mirror image of their own negative, unacceptable actions.

Today, psychological critics use the schema and terminology of Freudian psychoanalysis to understand the dynamics of a literary work. They may see the writer's unconscious mind represented in symbolic terms in the text itself as if it were a dream. They may see patterns of sublimation, transference, and projection. Or they may analyze the themes of literature and explore characters' dilemmas and development in terms of psychological behavior and problems. Other psychoanalytic critics—Jung, Lacan, Kristeva—would examine and analyze the work according to their theories of human behavior and produce different psychological interpretations.

The Freudian psychological critic would concentrate on "The Story of an Hour" as a view on the unconscious drives of its author. Mrs. Mallard, genteel wife, would represent Kate Chopin at an earlier phase in her life—submitting to her husband's "powerful will." The husband's supposed death is a projection and a transference of Kate Chopin's unconscious earlier desire to annihilate her husband as a force in her life. Mrs. Mallard's death is a projection of her own unconscious guilt at her own desire to "kill" the husband. She punishes herself through projecting her own guilt onto Mrs. Mallard. Annihilating Mrs. Mallard punishes her own alter ego.

The psychological critic also would discuss the motif of sexual repression in the story. The world of "The Story of an Hour" is one in which sexual feelings are denied. Mrs. Mallard herself is treated "gently" by those around her as if she were a child, not a grown, mature woman. Mr. Mallard is seen at the end of the story as an authority figure—devoid of sexual energy. He has his gripsack and umbrella; he carries a phallic symbol, suggestive of male dominance and patriarchal authority. Mrs. Mallard's awakening would be viewed as a sexual one. She emerges from a state of "physical exhaustion" to sense something creeping toward her, "creeping out of the sky," coming to possess her, as if she is taken over by a sexual force. Next her physical posture changes: her "vacant stare" becomes "keen and bright"; her weak pulse becomes "fast"; her "coursing blood warmed and relaxed her. . . ." Her "fancy . . . running riot," she experiences a "feverish triumph." Images of sexual arousal and orgasm abound. The story ends on an orgiastic note; she experiences a "joy that kills." The double entendres suggest climax, release, and death.

READER RESPONSE CRITICISM

Another form of psychological criticism is *reader response criticism*. In this theory, the emphasis is on the connections between the reader and the text. Reader response critics suggest that the text is not an independent entity, but that it is created in the mind of a reader. They differ in terms of how much independence they give to the text as a separate object of study. Louise Rosenblatt, for example, views the reading process as interactive, as "transactive," as an interaction between the world of the reader and the world of the text. Norman Holland envisions the reading process as a recreation based on a dynamic interaction between a reader who has a particular "identity theme," a particular personality pattern, and a text which is recreated and shaped by the demands of the reader's identity theme. Holland theorizes that identity replicates itself—in all acts of living and of reading. David Bleich, another reader response theorist, contends in his early works, *Readings and Feelings* (1975) and *Subjective Criticism* (1978), that the reader response process primarily is individual and subjective and that the interpretation of a text is based on the reader's subjective response to that text: the reader's "resymbolization" of that work. In his more current work, *The Double Perspective: Language, Literacy, and Social Relations* (1988), Bleich acknowledges the role of gender and social context in shaping the reader's "resymbolization" of a work. What finally accounts for and governs response? Are there only totally idiosyncratic, subjective individual responses to works? For reader response critics, the reading process always will be individual and personal; however, the totality of response depends on what another critic, Stanley Fish, labels "the interpretive community of readers." That is, part of the process is influenced by the intellectual community and concerns of readers. The community helps to shape the intellectual background, the approach, views, and values of the reader. Reader response critics also maintain that interpretation of a text may change depending on when a person reads the work. People read differently at different phases of their lives. Part of this process is determined by cultural context. The world of the 1990s in the United States, for example, contrasts drastically with the United States of the 1950s.

The student's essay in Chapter 9 is a reader response to "The Story of an Hour." The writer compares Mrs. Mallard's entrapment and desire for freedom with her own situation: her own marriage and yearning for autonomy. What follows is another person's reader response to "The Story of an Hour." In several freewrites, the writer reflects on the changes of her view of the story at varying stages in her life.

When I first read "The Story of an Hour," I thought about how entrapped Mrs. Mallard was and how limited her life and her options were. She seemed totally cowed by the authority figures in her life: her sister, her husband. She seemed spineless.

I tasted her single delightful moment of freedom and felt sorry for her. I truly felt pity. As a young twenty-two year old, I couldn't imagine a life without infinite possibility.

* * *

I reread the story in my thirties when I taught it in a creative writing class to a group of older, returning women students. I saw it as a story of awakenings. I saw it as a reflection of changing values. She recognized her own oppression. She realized a possibility for freedom. That opening up was vividly depicted in her looking out the window.

That view of the story very much seemed to go with the times, with the burgeoning of the women's movement in the mid 1970s, with the faith that roles for women could be, as Adrienne Rich said, "re-envision[ed]." It was all in the recognition of oppression and the opening up. Writing was an act of consciousness. Mrs. Mallard's opening up of consciousness seemed the center of the work and her death—just as the point of dawning awareness seemed tragic.

* * *

As I reread the work to teach it again in my forties, what strikes me anew is imprisonment. Roles are being redefined—but not as quickly or as easily. Women are still trapped. Women are not able to let go of traditional roles. Many women are still caught in the same bind: the struggle between duty and responsibility and self-fulfillment.

Mrs. Mallard's imprisonment and her only way out—death—seem more poignant—and even more realistic now.

As criticism moves away from concentrating on the text and toward embracing both the writer and the reader, theory also moves to suggest the place of the text within the larger social order. Sociological critics analyze the work within its social, cultural context. Treatment is given to the ways in which the text mirrors the social and cultural concerns of the age and also is defined by social and cultural influences.

FEMINIST CRITICISM

One important form of sociological criticism is *feminist theory* which views the work in terms of sexual politics, in terms of the relationships between men and women, more specifically in terms of the treatment of the power relationships between the sexes. Feminist critics focus on the dominance of the patriarchy, of male authority. They conceive the world and the word as male-centered. They theorize that throughout history, men have been in the dominant position: women in a subservient position, in the position of Simone de Beauvoir's other: a being whose identity and role are determined by her relation to man. They view language and experience as male dominated and defined. In the 1960s, feminist criticism attempted to expose the inequities and inequalities between the sexes and women's oppression and silencing by men. This exposure often took the form of analysis of the treatment of women in literary works written by men. Kate Millett's *Sexual Politics* (1969) and Mary Ellmann's *Thinking About Women* (1968) represent this line of criticism. In the 1970s, feminist criticism focused on bringing women out of silence and invisibility: on rediscovering works by women; on examining works by women; on rendering women's voices and experiences; on claiming and legitimizing women's places and roles in society; on discovering language for expression of female experience. During this time, many works by women were republished. Feminist critics are still challenging the male canon and striving to modify, to expand, and to reconfigure the canon to include the voices of women and of women's experiences. Contemporary feminist criticism moves toward new visions for both men and for women and studies gender roles to determine how these roles are shaped by psychological, social, and cultural forces. Critics have debated whether inherent biological male or female qualities exist or whether gender roles are primarily culturally determined. During the current wave of feminist criticism, issues of class, race, ethnic background, and economic situations figure prominently in the analyses of theorists.

A feminist would chart Mrs. Mallard's changes of heart. The feminist critic first would concentrate on Mrs. Mallard's ambivalent reactions to those around her. The feminist critic would notice Mrs. Mallard's submissive pose. She sank into a "roomy armchair," "pressed down by a physical exhaustion that haunted her body and seemed to reach into her soul." Next the critic would concentrate on Mrs. Mallard's dawning consciousness and focus on the images of the open window, as suggestive of awakening, of spring, and of rebirth ("the tops of trees . . . aquiver with the new spring life"; "the delicious breath of rain"; "the patches of blue sky"). The critic, however, would suggest that she still remains powerless, for her dawning sense of autonomy emerges as if an alien form has taken over her being. Not until she absorbs this recognition and makes it her own does she become "free." This recognition is expressed in her acknowledgment that she no longer has to bend her will to the "powerful will" of her husband: "There would be no one to live for her during those coming years: she would live for herself. There would be no powerful will bending hers in that blind persistence with which men and women believe they have a right to impose a private will upon a fellow-creature." The feminist critic would applaud her disavowal of her traditional role and would concentrate on her pronouncement: "'Free! Body and soul free!'" The feminist critic then would focus on Mrs. Mallard's assertion of power and autonomy and the subsequent tragedy: the loss of selfhood. The critic would view Mrs. Mallard's "weak heart" as exemplifying the destructive quality of social roles.

NEW HISTORICISM

The *new historicism* currently represents another variant of sociological criticism. The new historicist views the work within its cultural milieu and also uses historical, social, new critical, reader response, and biographical materials to view the work in its broadest contexts or frameworks. The new historicist concentrates particularly on the works of the marginalized, the disenfranchised, and brings that work to the forefront of study. This impulse to recognize the marginal as the center of study arises from the assumption that all forms of writing exemplify cultural realities. The new historicist considers popular culture, song, autobiography, letters, documents, icons of popular culture all worthy of examination to comprehend the ways in which cultural and social forces influence the writer and the ways in which language itself becomes both a product of and a force creating cultural realities.

The new historicist might look at "The Story of an Hour" as a turn of the century document that forecasts women's growing impatience with and anger at their imprisonment within social roles. The story would be viewed as an exposure of women's position as other and as oppressed person. The story also might be seen in context with *The Yellow Wallpaper* (1892) and *Trifles* (1916)—works that treat women's victimization. A new historicist might examine Chopin's biography and place this story in the context of the public reception to Chopin's later work, *The Awakening,* particularly her frank treatment of women's sexual and emotional awakenings. The novel shocked St. Louis's readers. One critic at the time, for example, called it a "vulgar story." In fact, the book so scandalized St. Louis society that Chopin was assailed by acquaintances and by critics, found herself unable to get her work published between 1899–1904, and was barely able to survive economically. She died of a stroke in 1904, and some critics have concluded that one cause of that stroke was the personal turmoil occasioned by the critics' reactions to *The Awakening* and the disastrous consequences for Chopin. Mrs. Mallard's fate then becomes an ironic foreshadowing of the author's death. Finally, a new historicist might study other social documents of the time, study women's roles, attitudes toward marriage, and liberation and perhaps examine the work of the prominent suffragists.

CONCLUSION

If one views a work, then, through the lens of many critical interpretations, the work becomes kaleidoscopic. The fear, perhaps, arises that the text will disintegrate and not bear the pressure of so many critical approaches. The work, however, is a pattern of many layers, and one may focus on one pattern or look at the text as three dimensional: as a multiple overlay of many successive meanings. In any case, the work does not necessarily become a confusing montage or double-exposed.

Moreover, not all works yield themselves to particular interpretations, and each framework for critical interpretation is not equally justified. In one class, for example, many years ago, a student's reader response to Williams' "A Red Wheelbarrow" suggested that the poem reveals the pervasive influence of a Communist threat and foreshadows the eventual takeover of Communist regimes. After all, he contended, "the red wheelbarrow," was next to the "white chickens." This impression immediately was corrected by the voices of students in the class who argued that a political interpretation of the bucolic country scene seemed implausible, based on their assumption about Williams' poetry, his motivations for writing, his artistic technique, and the relationship of that section of the poem to the themes of the work. In other words, the students, the intellectual community of readers, cited biographical, psychological, historical, and new criticism as the bases for their responses to his view. The community of readers pointed out more applicable interpretations of the poem.

Critical interpretation leads ultimately to an enriched vision of the text: a pluralistic one in which many meanings coexist. Each interpretation always must be contextualized. Each work is a particular confluence of linguistic, biographical, cultural realities—a single artifact of language that exhibits and represents these realities. This artifact, then, has the power to sensitize a reader to the forces shaping values, to the ways in which interpretations of the world are based on these systems of values, and to prompt investigations of both the texts and the world in new and expansive ways.

Glossary of Terms

abstract and concrete abstract language uses a high proportion of *abstract nouns*, which refer to concepts, qualities or general conditions ("truth," "honesty," "poverty"). Concrete language, on the other hand, uses more *concrete nouns*, which refer to things perceivable through the senses ("building," "rain," "tree"). Effective writing creates a balance between the two, in which abstract ideas are illustrated by specific detail.

act a major division in a play; each act normally comprises several scenes.

accent the vocal emphasis or stress placed upon a syllable. This is particularly noticeable in lines of poetry when it can play an important part in the overall meaning.

affective responses the emotional responses, including feeling, remembering, and associating.

allegory a story in verse or prose which can be understood on both a literal and symbolic level. In *The Pilgrim's Progress* by John Bunyan (1678), Christian, the hero, embarks on a pilgrimage which takes him through the Slough of Despond, the Valley of the Shadow of Death, etc., until finally he reaches the Celestial City. Christian represents Everyman, and his journey is an allegory of Christian salvation.

alliteration the repetition of consonant sounds for poetic effect, particularly at the beginnings of words. A famous example is Coleridge's description of the River Alph in "Kubla Khan": "Five miles meandering with a mazy motion" (Chapter 8).

allusion a reference to events, literary works, private experience, people. Allusion develops and deepens the meaning of the work, e.g., Plath's "Daddy."

antagonist the character or force opposing the protagonist (the main character) in a play.

apex the height of the action in a drama.

archetype a theme, emblem, or character which reoccurs so frequently in all literature that it is accepted as universal. One very common theme is that of the quest, in which the protagonist sets out on a journey of self-discovery.

argument one of the four basic rhetorical modes emphasized in composition courses (the other three being description, narration, and exposition). Argument seeks, through logic and reason, to convince a reader by providing factual evidence to support a certain point of view. Persuasion, which uses emotion rather than reason, is an important aspect of argument.

aside in drama, words spoken in an undertone to the audience, which are assumed to be inaudible to the other characters on the stage.

assonance the repetition of similar vowel sounds, usually close together, for poetic effect. The first line of Keats' "Ode on a Grecian Urn" contains a number of long /i/ sounds, creating a sensual, unhurried effect: "Thou *sti*ll unravished *bri*de of quietness, / Thou foster *chi*ld of *si*lence and slow *ti*me" (Chapter 8).

autobiography writing about one's life.

ballad a narrative poem, usually arranged in quatrains, which employs the rhyme scheme ABCB. There are two types. The folk ballad, a form of great antiquity, is transmitted orally amongst illiterate and semi-literate people of all cultures. It tells a dramatic story in a vivid, if impersonal, way and is invariably anonymous. A literary ballad, on the other hand, is a conscious imitation of this form by a poet well-versed in his or her literary heritage. Many of the most famous literary ballads were written during the Romantic Period, such as Coleridge's "Rime of the Ancient Mariner" and Keats' "La Belle Dame sans Merci."

blank verse a poetic form consisting of unrhymed iambic pentameter.

bugaku a Japanese dance form, originating in Tibet and India.

canjunxi Chinese slapstick comedies, duos between butt and knave.

catastrophe the tragic conclusion of action in a play.

catharsis Aristotle's term for the therapeutic sense of release supposedly felt by an audience which witnesses the tragic or terrifying on stage.

cause and effect a form of process analysis which explains the factors creating a certain situation or the consequences of a particular event. The downfall of a tragic hero can be analyzed in terms of cause and effect, as can the growth of bacteria, as can a sociological phenomenon such as rising unemployment.

character any person represented in a literary work. Characters are commonly described as being *round* (psychologically complex and convincing), *flat* (simplistic and often stereotypical) or as being *foils* (existing only to highlight certain aspects of the protagonist). It is also useful to distinguish between *dynamic* characters (those undergoing change) and *static* characters (those remaining unchanged).

chorus a group of players in Greek drama who provide a collective commentary on the action and the main characters. Although an essential part of Greek tragedy, a full chorus has rarely been used in English or American drama. Two exceptions are Milton's *Samson Agonistes* (1671) and T. S. Eliot's *Murder in the Cathedral* (1935).

chuanqi Chinese marvel presentation.

classification the process of grouping items together according to their similarities. Thus, poetry can be classified according to such categories as the sonnet, the ballad, the ode, etc.

cliché an overused, and hence ineffective, figure of speech such as "pretty as a picture" or "white as snow." Since the purpose of figurative language is to surprise the reader into a new way of seeing, writers should aim to be as original as possible.

climax the point in a narrative or play at which a crisis is reached and resolution achieved.

colloquial expressions informal words and phrases which are a normal part of everyday speech but which are inappropriate in more formal writing situations.

comedy a term usually applied to drama, although any work can have comic elements. There are many different types of comedy (high, low, romantic, satiric, etc.), but overall the genre is characterized by humor and the traditional "happy ending." In the movement from complication to resolution, individual and social problems are frequently resolved by marriage.

commedia dell' arte a sixteenth century form of drama with mimes, skits, buffoonery and with such stereotypical characters as the harlequin, the young lover.

comparison–contrast the process of analyzing and determining similarities and differences in objects, phenomena, literary works; often essays on literature compare

character, theme, style. For organization of essays, see Chapter 3.

conceit a figure of speech comparing two dissimilar things or states; an elaborate and extended metaphor. See Chapter 10.

conflict an aspect of plot which concerns the tensions between opposing forces. Conflicts exist within characters, between or among characters, between characters and such forces as nature, society, the cosmos. In *Hamlet*, the major conflict arises between Hamlet and Claudius. The conflict develops within Hamlet himself (Chapter 4).

connotation the meanings and associations evoked by a word.

counted syllables syllabic verse, a method that disregards accentual feet and creates rhythm through regularized pattern of counted syllables.

couplets in poetry, two-line stanzas.

denotation the dictionary definitions of a word.

dialect a manner of speaking peculiar to an individual, class, or region which may differ quite considerably from the standard language of the country. While perfectly acceptable within its own context, dialect should be avoided in most formal writing situations, as the writer cannot assume a knowing audience. Dialect is most frequently found in fiction or drama, where it is used to make individual characters more realistic.

dialogue the direct speech of characters in any literary context.

double plots a second story that becomes fascinating on its own merits and enlarges the meaning of the main plot.

drafting composing and concentrating on organization, development, and fluency in the early stages of the writing process.

drama any work meant to be performed on a stage by actors rather than read. Usually the work is divided into acts and scenes.

dramatic irony a situation or action which becomes apparent to the audience but remains unknown to a character or characters in a place or in fiction.

dramatic poetry the speaker becomes an actor, as in a monologue or soliloquy.

editing the stage of the writing process concerned with sharpening word choice and style to clarify meaning and to strengthen presentation of message.

elegy a poem that expresses mourning for the death of humans or of mortality.

Elizabethan or Shakespearean Sonnet divides the traditional fourteen lines of this form into three four-line verses (quatrains) and a final couplet.

empirical a generalization, founded upon experiment or experience, about a whole group, based on observation of some members of the group.

end rhymes rhymes that occur at the end of verse lines.

enjambment a line of poetry that ends without punctuation or pause, a run-on line.

epic poems poems derived from oral tradition that describes the adventures and accomplishments of great heroes, e.g., *Sundiata* (Chapter 10).

essay a concise prose discussion of a limited topic of limited length for a general audience.

evidence the use of facts, statistics, personal experiences or the opinions of respected authorities to support a writer's claims or conclusions.

explication the close reading of a text, usually involving line-by-line analysis.

exposition one of the four basic rhetorical modes emphasized in composition courses (the other three being description, narration, and argument). Intended primarily to inform, exposition can take a variety of different forms, such as classification, definition, process analysis, comparison/contrast, and cause and effect.

extended metaphors see *conceit.*

figurative language language that includes figures of speech.

figures of speech expressions which are intended to be interpreted imaginatively rather than literally and which are based on implied comparisons. Their purpose is to surprise the reader into a new way of seeing. Some of the most common are *simile, metaphor, personification, hyperbole,* and *litotes.*

first person singular point of view.

flashback although this term derived originally from the cinema, it is now applied to any scene which is inserted into a literary work in order to show an earlier event.

foreshadowing using the current action in a literary work to anticipate later events.

free verse verse with no regular meter or line length. Although at first it may appear haphazard, free verse can acquire rhythms and melodies of its own.

Freytag's Pyramid Gustav Freytag conceived of plot in drama as rising action, climax, falling action which leads to denouement. His conception took the shape of a pyramid.

generalization a broad statement, which may well be true, but which is not supported by concrete evidence. For instance, "People who smoke are susceptible to lung cancer." Student writers tend to rely too much on generalizations, and, thus, their essays frequently lack substance.

genre a literary type or class. The major classical genres are tragedy, comedy, satire, epic, and lyric.

hakawatis Arabic storytellers who related deeds of Muhammad.

hamartia a tragic error in judgment in Greek drama.

hubris excessive pride (Greek drama).

hyperbole a figure of speech which uses deliberate exaggeration, usually for comic effect.

iamb a poetic foot consisting of an unstressed syllable followed by a stressed syllable, as in "behold."

illustration the use of concrete examples to support a generalization.

imagery concrete language which appeals to the senses. An image does not have to be interpreted literally; however, many are conveyed by figurative language. (See *figures of speech.*)

inductive and deductive reasoning two different forms of thinking used on a daily basis, although not always consciously. *Inductive reasoning* uses specific examples to formulate a general truth. *Deductive reasoning,* on the other hand, takes a general truth and then seeks to demonstrate it through example.

intrigue scheme in drama in which a character entraps another person, one who is naive, trusting, vulnerable.

introduction the first section of a paper, which should get the reader's attention, state the thesis, and establish the tone and point of view. In most college writing assignments, one paragraph will be sufficient. In longer papers, the introductory material may consist of several paragraphs.

irony a complex form of humor which relies on contrast for its effect. There are two basic categories: verbal and situational. *Verbal irony* contrasts what is said with what is meant (i.e., "You really are too kind" said with great bitterness). *Dramatic irony* contrasts what is expected with what actually happens. (A man laughs at another's misfortune, unaware that the same misfortune is happening to him.)

jargon the specialized vocabulary of a particular field or trade, which the general reader is unlikely to understand.

journal a form of personal writing concerning the self. The presumed audience is the author.

kabuki seventeenth century Japanese theater; a combination of dance, narrative, and comedy.

kagura sacred Japanese rituals and highly stylized performances.

komos revel in Greek drama; derivation of the word comedy.

kyōgen comic skits performed between the two parts of Nō drama.

letter writing a form of personal writing directed at another person or persons.

literary theory/criticism a critical framework for understanding and interpreting a work of art. Read Appendix B.

litotes the opposite of *hyperbole,* this figure of speech uses understatement for humorous effect.

lyric this term can be applied broadly to any short, non-narrative poem which deals subjectively with the thoughts and feelings of a single speaker. Although written in the first person, the sentiments are not necessarily those of the poet, but may be those of an adopted *persona.*

meditation a reflection on a scene or object which moves from observation of the object to consideration of metaphysical ideas.

memoir the remembrances of a public figure and the events of an historical era; another autobiographical form.

metaphor an implied comparison which brings together two dissimilar things without the use of "like" or "as." For instance, the metaphorical equivalent of Burns' famous simile "My love's like a red, red rose" would be "My love *is* a red, red rose."

metaphoric reference See *metaphor.*

meter the pattern of stressed and unstressed syllables in lines of verse, each unit being termed a *foot.* / denotes a long or *stressed* syllable; U denotes a short or *unstressed* syllable. The most common feet in English verse are:

iamb—U /   e.g., desíre
trochee—/ U   e.g., wómen
anapaest—U U /   e.g., in a flásh
dactyl—/ U U   e.g., yésterday
spondee— / /   e.g., óutwíth

In addition, lines are named according to the number of feet they contain:

monometer—one foot
dimeter—two feet
trimeter—three feet
tetrameter—four feet
pentameter—five feet
hexameter—six feet
heptameter—seven feet
octameter—eight feet

miracle plays a dramatic genre presenting saints' lives and miracles.

monologue a sustained speech by a single character, either with or without a direct audience.

mood the atmosphere or tone of a literary work, created not only by the characters and events but also by the author's style and choice of language.

morality plays a dramatic genre which allegorized Christian values.

motif a theme or image which occurs repeatedly within a work, and which hence acquires symbolic value.

multiculturalism the increasing emphasis on race, class (and gender) in education. In recognition of the racial diversity of most schools, the traditional curriculum is being modified to encompass the achievements and experiences of all ethnic groups.

mystery plays dramas presenting Biblical stories.

myth a story involving supernatural beings which usually explains the cosmos and the mysteries of life and death, e.g., creation, harvest, death, love. See Camus' "The Myth of Sisyphus" (Chapter 8).

narration one of the four basic rhetorical modes emphasized in composition courses (the other three being description, argument, and exposition). Effective narration seeks to recreate a series of events (i.e., a "story") as vividly as possible using descriptive detail.

narrative poetry form of poetry that tells a story.

narrator person telling a story.

Nō drama classic form of Japanese theater that blends dance, music, and speech, e.g., *Atsumori* (Chapter 8).

novel an extended work of prose fiction which, although traditionally realistic, can now be highly experimental.

novella a work of fiction, longer than and more expansive than a short story, but less complex than a novel.

objective and subjective these terms are used to describe the extent of the author's involvement. *Objective* writing is primarily factual and maintains a detached, impersonal tone. *Subjective* writing, on the other hand, reveals the author's own feelings and attitudes and often seeks to involve the reader emotionally.

octave see *Petrarchan Sonnet.*

ode a formal and elaborate lyric poem which praises either a person (i.e., Tennyson's "Ode on the Death of the Duke of Wellington") or a thing (i.e., Keats' "Ode to Autumn"). The *Pindaric Ode,* named after the Greek poet Pindar, traditionally celebrates a noteworthy individual upon some public occasion. Designed to be performed by a chorus similar to that found in Greek drama, its highly formal arrangement consists of a *strophe* (chanted while moving to the left), an *antistrophe* (chanted while moving to the right), and an *epode* (chanted while standing still). Early English poets preserved this strophic arrangement by varying stanzaic form, but by the 19th century the structure had become less rigid. Wordsworth's "Ode on Intimations of Immortality" (1802–4) is one of the finest examples of the irregular Pindaric Ode.

onomatopoeia the creation and/or use of words which imitate the actual sounds they represent, i.e., "crash," "buzz," etc.

organization the way a writer chooses to develop ideas in both paragraphs and essays, according to the *purpose* and *audience.* The five main methods are: 1) *Deductive* (from general statement to specific example, 2) *Inductive* (from specific example to general statement, 3) *Climactic* (from least to most important), 4) *Chronological* (according to time sequence), 5) *Spatial* (according to physical location).

pageants the platforms used in productions of mystery, miracle, and morality plays.

parable a story with a moral, often religious, the purpose of which is instruction. See discussion of the prodigal son in Chapter 9.

paradox a statement which seems self-contradictory (even absurd) but which does, in fact, reveal something essentially true about the subject. The following example is from Congreve's *Amoret:* "Careless she is with artful care, / Affecting to seem unaffected."

paragraph a group of logically related sentences, which together develop a central idea. This idea is stated broadly in a topic sentence and illustrated with supporting detail. Paragraphs break information down into smaller units, which the reader can then assimilate more easily.

paraphrase a detailed restatement of information in words other than those of the original source.

parody the imitation of a certain author's style, tone, or attitude with the intent to ridicule. The technique is similar to that used in cartoon caricatures, in that certain features are deliberately exaggerated.

pastoral a poem celebrating the idyllic nature of country life.

persona from the Latin for "mask," this term originally referred to the false face of clay worn by actors. It now denotes the identity adopted by an author in any literary work.

personification the attribution of human qualities to inanimate things for poetic effect. The following example is from T. S. Eliot's "The Love Song of J. Alfred Prufrock": "The night is like a patient / Etherized upon a table."

Petrarchan Sonnet named for the famous Italian poet, Petrarch; contains two quatrains called the octave (eight lines) and two tercets, three-line verses, called the sestets (six lines). The theme shifts at the ninth line in Petrarchan Sonnet. This turn is called the volta.

philosophical treatise an extended formal meditation on a philosophical, religious or political subject (see Chapter 12).

picture frame stage an innovation in European drama that created the effect of framing the stage.

plagiarism the representation of another's words or ideas as though they were the writer's own. This academic "theft," whether conscious or unconscious, is a serious offense. To avoid plagiarism, all outside information must be documented.

plot the arrangement of events in a narrative or dramatic work. When two story-lines are developed in equal depth, the work is said to have a *double plot.* When one story-line dominates another, the latter is said to be a *sub-plot.*

point of view the perspective from which a story is told. Events can be narrated in the *first person* (the narrator is part of the action), or the *third person* (the narrator is outside the action). Narration in the second person is rare. An *omniscient narrator* uses the third person and is all-knowing.

praise songs eulogies in African cultures.

premises supporting statements.

prewriting the generating of ideas prior to the initial drafting of a paper. The common strategies are *freewriting* and *brainstorming.* Freewriting involves writing non-stop for a short period of time. The writer is not concerned with grammar or spelling but with the free-association of ideas. Brainstorming involves quickly listing anything and everything related to the topic. Ideas can then be grouped or sub-divided to establish what is relevant.

primary and secondary sources primary sources are original materials, whether novels, speeches, scientific reports, or government documents. Secondary sources are studies of those materials. Thus Wilfred Owen's poem "Arms and the Boy" is a primary source. A critical analysis of its themes is a secondary source (Chapter 10).

proofreading the final stage of the writing process, in which the writer rereads the finished draft carefully for grammatical, spelling, or mechanical errors.

proscenium arch a frame enclosing the stage area behind which the front curtain hangs.

protagonist the principal character in a work of drama or fiction.

purpose and audience a writer's purpose, generally speaking, can be to *entertain,* to *inform,* to *explain,* to *explore,* or to *persuade.* Often several purposes will overlap, but the writer's overall intention will be closely tied to the *audience* being addressed. This can be any individual or group, whether the self, as in a journal entry, or the general public, as in a newspaper article.

quatrains in poetry, four-line stanzas.

rasa sentiment in Indian or Hindu thought, creating artistic pleasure and serenity.

realism while all literature is clearly artificial, certain works can be said to represent life more accurately than others. Such works attend to the minutia of everyday experience and present characters and events realistically rather than romantically.

revision this stage of the writing process involves rewriting a rough draft to improve both form and content. *Purpose* and *audience* should be reconsidered, as should the overall focus and development of the paper. Material may be cut, expanded, or moved around, while the language itself should be reworked for clarity and conciseness.

rhetorical question   a question to which no answer is expected, or to which the answer is self-evident. Used primarily for stylistic effect, this device encourages an emotional response from the reader and, thus, is often used in persuasive writing. Shelley concludes his "Ode to the West Wind" with a rhetorical question: "If Winter comes, can Spring be far behind?"

rhetorical situation   purpose, audience, occasion, and point of view for the generation of a work. It is mainly a term used for analyzing nonfiction. See, for example, the speech by Sojourner Truth (Chapter 7).

rhyme   in English poetry, the repetition of the last accented vowel and all succeeding sounds following that vowel (e.g., boy–joy).

rhyme scheme   fixed pattern of rhymes characterizing a poem or its stanzas.

rhythm   in poetry or prose, the patterns of beats which establish the rise and fall of sounds; cadence. See the analysis of rhythm in Shakespeare's Sonnet, "My Mistress' Eyes Are Nothing Like the Sun" in Chapter 10 and the chanting patterns in Anna Lee Walters' "My Name Is 'I Am Living'" (Chapter 8).

rising action   the development of action leading to a climax in a drama. See *Freytag's Pyramid.*

sarugaku   Japanese entertainment featuring acrobatics, magic, songs, dance, juggling, and comic skits.

satire   literature which exposes human vice and folly and seeks to correct it through ridicule. While the irony employed in satire can be amusing, the intent is not simply to entertain but to enlighten an audience. Swift's essay "A Modest Proposal" is a classic example.

sawis   professionals who recited Arabic odes aloud.

scansion   the process of measuring poetry, of marking accented and unaccented syllables, of dividing lines into feet in order to discover the metrical pattern of the poem and to notice deviations from the pattern.

scene   a unit of continuous action in a play in which the setting remains unchanged. Groups of inter-related scenes comprise larger units of the work, known as *acts.*

sestet   six lines of poetry. See Petrarchan sonnet.

setting   the time, place, and/or environment of a literary work. See, for example, Synge's *Riders to the Sea* (Chapter 5).

sexist language   the misrepresentation or exclusion of either sex. One of the most common forms of sexist language is the use of the male pronoun "he" for an individual of undetermined gender.

Shakespearean Sonnet   see *Elizabethan Sonnet.*

shaping   the planning phase of the writing process.

short story   a fictional narrative of more limited scope than the novel which often focuses on a single incident or a particular character. It is, however, a challenging medium, as the theme must be developed and brought to a satisfactory conclusion in around thirty pages.

simile   a figure of speech which compares one thing with another using "like" or "as." See *metaphor.*

slave narrative   a form of nineteenth-century autobiography that documents the slaves' journey from bondage to freedom.

soliloquy   a dramatic convention in which a character, alone on the stage, voices his or her own private thoughts. It is generally assumed that the feelings expressed are sincere.

sonnet   a poem of fourteen lines, usually in iambic pentameter, which employs a highly formal pattern of organization. Although there are a great number of possible rhyme schemes, the two most common are the *English* and the *Italian.* The English (or Shakespearean) consists of three quatrains and a concluding couplet and employs the rhyme scheme ABAB/CDCD/EFEF/GG. The Italian (or Petrarchan) consists of an eight-line octave followed by a six-line sestet and employs the rhyme scheme ABBA/ABBA/CDC/CDC.

speech   oral communication designed to be delivered to an audience.

stanza   the basic unit of structure in a poem. Each unit consists of a group of inter-related lines arranged in a pattern which is usually, although not always, repeated throughout the poem.

stereotypes   easily recognized types of characters, e.g., the fool.

stock characters   see *stereotypes.*

structural irony   double meanings throughout a drama or a work of fiction.

subplots   secondary plot or plots in drama.

summary   a concise restatement of a longer piece of writing, containing only the essential information.

surprise   essential element of plot which contradicts audience's or reader's expectations.

suspense   element of plot which builds excitement and uncertainty about the resolution of events.

syllogism   a deductive argument in three parts which moves from a major and minor premise to a logical conclusion. For example, "Water is wet. Rain is water. Therefore, rain is wet."

symbol   an object, character, or action which stands for something more than itself. Thus, Eliot's *The Wasteland* comes to represent the spiritual sterility of a generation.

symbolist dramas   form of drama which features many traditional poetic symbols, allegorical names, and dream-like atmosphere. All of the action would be interpreted symbolically.

synonyms   words which are close enough in meaning to be interchangeable. Exact synonyms are rare, however, since all words have slightly different connotations.

syntax   the arrangement of words within a sentence and the way this arrangement can affect the meaning.

tercets   three-line stanzas.

theater of the absurd   a form of drama prevalent in the 1950s and associated with such playwrights as Pinter, Ionesco, and Beckett. Although literature has always explored the potentially comic aspects of humankind, the Theater of the Absurd reflects explicitly the 20th century philosophical view of a meaningless universe, in which there is no coherence and little dignity. The plays themselves are, therefore, intentionally "meaningless."

theme   the central idea or message in a work, which can be dealt with either directly or indirectly.

thesis statement   usually contained in the introduction, the thesis statement establishes the focus of the essay—what it is about—in one or two sentences. Experienced writers sometimes use an *implied thesis statement,* where the purpose of the essay is clear without being stated directly in a particular group of sentences. Student writers, however, should ensure that the thesis statement is identifiable at the start of each essay.

tone   created by both word choice and syntax, tone reflects the author's attitude towards the subject matter, which can be humorous, sarcastic, etc.

topic sentence   effective writing requires that each paragraph within an essay develops a particular idea. The topic sentence is a concise statement of this idea, which is then developed in the rest of the paragraph. The topic sentence focuses a paragraph in the same way that the thesis statement focuses an essay.

tragic flaw   see *hamartia.*

tragic hero   protagonist in tragedy; a person of high moral stature.

tragicomedy   a mixture of tragedy and comedy created by classic Roman dramatist, Plautus.

tragedy   a term usually applied to drama, tragedy traditionally traces the downfall of an initially noble character in a serious and elevated manner. In Greek drama, this downfall is invariably attributed to some tragic flaw in the protagonist, a device also seen frequently in Shakespearean tragedy. Modern tragedy is often said to lack the grandeur of classical tragedy, perhaps because it aims at broader social commentary and deals more with ordinary people in everyday situations.

transitional expressions   essential to effective writing, these signal connections between ideas, thus allowing fluency between sentences and paragraphs. Some common transitional expressions are: however, therefore, consequently, on the other hand.

triplets   in poetry, three-line stanzas.

unity of action   In the *Poetics,* Aristotle wrote that every part of the action in a play must be integral to the whole. Any part that is missing destroys the whole.

verbal irony   a statement in which the meaning is different from the message which is expressed.

villanelle   a poem consisting of five tercets (three-line stanzas) and a quatrain, based on two rhymes and with systematic repetitions of lines one and three of the first tercet.

voice   the individual personality of the author. Thus although a work may have many different characters and may shift in tone according to the subject matter, there will remain a distinct authorial presence beyond even a first person narrator. Student writers should recognize the importance of allowing their own voices to develop in their writing.

yuanben   Chinese court texts.

zaju   Chinese variety plays.

Literary Credits

Chinua Achebe, "Dead Men's Path," from GIRLS AT WAR AND OTHER STORIES by Chinua Achebe. Copyright © 1972, 1973 by Chinua Achebe. Used by permission of Doubleday, a division of Bantam Doubleday Dell Publishing Group, Inc.

Marjorie Agosin, "A Visit to the Mothers of the Plaza de Mayo," from *The Mothers of Plaza De Mayo: The Story of Renee Epelbaum* by Marjorie Agosin. Copyright © 1990 by Marjorie Agosin. Reprinted by permission of The Red Sea Press, Inc.

Anna Akhmatova, "Lot's Wife," From SELECTED POEMS by Anna Akhmatova. Translation copyright © 1985 by D. M. Thomas. Reprinted by permission of John Johnson, Ltd.

Gloria Anzaldúa, "horse," "To live in the Borderlands means you," from *Borderlands/La Frontera: The New Mestiza* © 1987 by Gloria Anzaldúa. Reprinted with permission from Aunt Lute Books (415) 558-8116.

Margaret Atwood, "Game After Supper," from *The Circle Game* by Margaret Atwood. Copyright © by Margaret Atwood. Reprinted by permission of Stoddart Publishing Company Limited, Don Mills, Ontario, Canada.

W. H. Auden, "The Unknown Citizen," from W. H. AUDEN: COLLECTED POEMS by W. H. Auden, edited by Edward Mendelson. Copyright © 1940 and renewed 1968 by W. H. Auden. Reprinted by permission of Random House, Inc.

James Baldwin, "Sonny's Blues," from *Going to Meet the Man* by James Baldwin. Copyright © 1957 by James Baldwin. Used by permission of The James Baldwin Estate.

Amiri Baraka, "Preface to a Twenty Volume Suicide Note," from *Preface to a Twenty Volume Suicide Note* by Amiri Baraka. Reprinted by permission of Sterling Lord Literistic, Inc. Copyright © 1961 by Amiri Baraka.

Roland Barthes, "Toys," from MYTHOLOGIES by Roland Barthes, translated by Annette Lavers. Translation copyright © 1972 by Jonathan Cape Ltd. Reprinted by permission of Hill and Wang, a division of Farrar, Straus, & Giroux, Inc.

Matsuo Bashó, "On New Year's Day," by Matsuo Bashó. Copyright © by and reprinted by permission of Penguin Books, Ltd.

Simone de Beauvoir, "Woman as Other," from THE SECOND SEX by Simone de Beauvoir, trans. by H. M. Parshley. Copyright © 1952 by Alfred A. Knopf, Inc. Reprinted by permission of Alfred A. Knopf, Inc.

T. Coraghessan Boyle, "If the River Was Whiskey," from IF THE RIVER WAS WHISKEY by T. Coraghessan Boyle. Copyright © 1989 by T. Coroghessan Boyle. Used by permission of Viking Penguin, a division of Penguin Books USA Inc.

Earl H. Brewster, Excerpt from *D. H. Lawrence: A Composite Biography*, Volume III by Earl H. Brewster, edited by Edward H. Nehls. Copyright © 1963 by University of Wisconsin Press. Reprinted by permission of University of Wisconsin Press.

Gwendolyn Brooks, "The Chicago Defender Sends a Man to Little Rock," and "We Real Cool," from *Blacks* by Gwendolyn Brooks. Copyright © 1991 by Gwendolyn Brooks. Reprinted by permission of Gwendolyn Brooks. Published by Third World Press, Chicago.

Olga Broumas, "Song For Sanna," from *Beginning with O* by Olga Broumas. Copyright © 1977 by and reprinted by permission of Yale University Press.

Albert Camus, "The Myth of Sisyphus," from THE MYTH OF THE SISYPHUS AND OTHER ESSAYS by Albert Camus, trans. by Justin O'Brien. Copyright © 1955 Alfred A. Knopf, Inc. Reprinted by permission of Alfred A. Knopf, Inc.

Truman Capote, "A Christmas Memory," from A CHRISTMAS MEMORY by Truman Capote. Copyright © 1956 by Truman Capote. Reprinted by permission of Random House, Inc.

Raymond Carver, "Cathedral," from CATHEDRAL by Raymond Carver. Copyright © 1981 by Raymond Carver. Reprinted by permission of Alfred A. Knopf, Inc.

Lorna Dee Cervantes, "Uncle's First Rabbit," reprinted from EMPLUMADA by Lorna Dee Cervantes, by permission of the University of Pittsburgh Press. Copyright © 1981 by Lorna Dee Cervantes.

Sandra Cisneros, "House of My Own," "Mango Says Goodbye," and "My Name," from THE HOUSE ON MANGO STREET by Sandra Cisneros. Copyright © 1989 by Sandra Cisneros. Published in the United States by Vintage Books, a division of Random House, Inc. New and distributed in Canada by Random House of Canada Limited, Toronto. Originally published in somewhat different form, by Arte Publico Press in 1984, and revised in 1989. Reprinted by permission of Susan Bergholz Literary Services, New York.

Victor Hernandez Cruz, "Energy," from SNAPS by Victor Hernandez Cruz. Copyright © 1968, 1969 by Victor Hernandez Cruz. Reprinted by permission of Random House, Inc.

Countee Cullen, "Incident," reprinted by permission of GRM Associates, Inc., Agents for the Estate of Ida M. Cullen. From the book COLOR by Countee Cullen. Copyright © 1925 by Harper & Brothers, copyright renewed 1953 by Ida M. Cullen.

E. E. Cummings, "My Father Moved Through Dooms of Love," by e. e. cummings. Reprinted from COMPLETE POEMS, 1913–1962, by E. E. Cummings, by permission of Liveright Publishing Corporation. Copyright © 1923, 1925, 1931, 1935, 1938, 1939, 1940, 1944, 1945, 1946, 1947, 1948, 1949, 1950, 1951, 1952, 1953, 1954, 1955, 1956, 1957, 1958, 1959, 1960, 1961, 1962 by the Trustees for the E. E. Cummings Trust. Copyright © 1961, 1963, 1968 by Marion Morehouse Cummings.

Rosemary Reeves Davies, "Lawrence, Lady Cynthia Asquith, and 'The Rocking-Horse Winner,'" by Rosemary Reeves Davies. From *Studies in Short Fiction 20* (1983): 121–126. Copyright © 1983 by Newberry College. Reprinted by permission.

Emily Dickinson, "I'm Nobody! Who are you?," and "My Life Has Stood—," reprinted by permission of the publishers and the Trustees of Amherst College from THE POEMS OF EMILY DICKINSON, Thomas H. Johnson, ed., Cambridge, Mass.: The Belknap Press of Harvard University Press, Copyright © 1951, 1955, 1979, 1983 by the President and Fellows of Harvard College.

Mbella Sonne Dipoko, "Exile," from *Because of Women* by Mbella Sonne Dipoko. Copyright © 1969 by Mbella Sonne Dipoko. Reprinted by permission of the author.

Rita Dove, "Adolescence I," "Adolescence II," and "Adolescence III," by Rita Dove. Reprinted from *The Yellow House on the Corner* by permission of Carnegie Mellon University Press and by Rita Dove.

Lonne Elder III, CEREMONIES IN DARK OLD MEN by Lonne Elder III. Copyright © 1965, 1969 by Lonne Elder III. Reprinted by permission of Farrar, Straus, & Giroux, Inc. ***Caution:*** Professional and amateurs are hereby warned

Index of Authors, Titles, and First Lines of Poetry

First lines of poetry are in italic.

Subject Index